MW01641589

1984 MEMBERSHIP DIRECTORY

p 179
Ed'D 1st
listing

of the

INDUSTRIAL RELATIONS RESEARCH ASSOCIATION

DAVID R. ZIMMERMAN
Secretary-Treasurer

MEMBERSHIP DIRECTORY 1984. Copyright © 1984 by INDUSTRIAL RELATIONS RESEARCH ASSOCIATION. Printed in the United States of America. All rights reserved. The Directory is for reference purposes only. It may not be used as a general mailing list.

Library of Congress Catalog Card Number: 50-20362
PRICE $15.00
ISBN 0-913447-26-9

INDUSTRIAL RELATIONS RESEARCH ASSOCIATION

PROCEEDINGS OF THE ANNUAL MEETING (Spring publication)
PROCEEDINGS OF THE SPRING MEETING (Fall publication)
Annual Research Volume (Membership Directory published every sixth year in lieu of the annual research volume)
IRRA NEWSLETTER (published quarterly)

Inquiries and other communications regarding membership, meetings, publications, and general affairs of the Association, as well as orders for publications, copyright requests on publications prior to 1978, and notice of address changes should be addressed to the IRRA office.

INDUSTRIAL RELATIONS RESEARCH ASSOCIATION
7226 Social Science Building, University of Wisconsin
Madison, WI 53706 U.S.A. Telephone 608/262-2762

IRRA MEMBERSHIP DIRECTORY 1984

Contents

INDUSTRIAL RELATIONS RESEARCH ASSOCIATION OFFICERS 1948-1985

PRESIDENTS

1948 Edwin E. Witte,° University of Wisconsin
1949 Sumner H. Slichter,° Harvard
1950 George W. Taylor,° University of Pennsylvania
1951 William M. Leiserson,° Johns Hopkins
1952 J. Douglas Brown, Princeton
1953 Ewan Clague, USDL
1954 Clark Kerr, University of California
1955 Lloyd G. Reynolds, Yale
1956 Richard A. Lester, Princeton
1957 Dale Yoder, University of Minnesota
1958 E. Wight Bakke,° Yale
1959 William Haber, University of Michigan
1960 John T. Dunlop, Harvard
1961 Philip Taft,° Brown University
1962 Charles A. Myers, MIT
1963 William F. Whyte, Cornell
1964 Solomon Barkin, Textile Workers of America
1965 Edwin Young, University of Wisconsin
1966 Arthur M. Ross,° University of California
1967 Neil W. Chamberlain, Columbia
1968 George P. Shultz, University of Chicago
1969 Frederick H. Harbison,° Princeton
1970 Douglass V. Brown, MIT
1971 George H. Hildebrand, USDL
1972 Benjamin Aaron, UCLA
1973 Douglas H. Soutar, American Smelting & Refining Co.
1974 Nathaniel Goldfinger,° AFL-CIO
1975 Gerald G. Somers,° University of Wisconsin
1976 Irving Bernstein, UCLA
1977 F. Ray Marshall, University of Texas
1978 Charles C. Killingsworth, Michigan State
1979 Jerome M. Rosow, Work in America Institute
1980 Jack Barbash, University of Wisconsin
1981 Rudolph A. Oswald, AFL-CIO
1982 Milton Derber, University of Illinois
1983 Jack Stieber, Michigan State
1984 Wayne L. Horvitz, Consultant, Washington, D.C.
1985 Everett M. Kassalow, University of Wisconsin

SECRETARY-TREASURERS

1948-50 William H. McPherson
1951-53 Robben W. Fleming
1954-62 Edwin Young
1963-72 David B. Johnson
1973-77 Richard U. Miller
1978- David R. Zimmerman

EDITORS

1948-50 Milton Derber
1951-56 L. Reed Tripp
1957-74 Gerald G. Somers °
1975-77 Barbara D. Dennis and James L. Stern
1978- Barbara D. Dennis

° Deceased

FOREWORD

This is the seventh Membership Directory in the IRRA series. Previous Directories were published in 1949, 1954, 1966, 1972, and 1979, and distributed to members and subscribers in lieu of the annual research volume.

Members' biographies were compiled from questionnaires returned in the fall and winter of 1983-84. Listings for active members who did not return questionnaires include only the name, address and other information taken from IRRA current mailing data.

In the geographic section, members are listed first by location (country, state/province, and city) and alphabetically within location. The entries also indicate the business or professional affiliation of members.

The occupational classification is based on the first occupation listed by members in response to the questionnaire item asking members to indicate up to three professions, in order of importance. Second and third occupations, when indicated by the member, can be found in the member's biography. It should be noted that the categories, "Consulting" and "Arbitration" exclude many members who do this work but did not indicate it was their primary occupation.

As in previous Directories, this volume includes supplementary information about the IRRA, such as Constitution and Bylaws, limited membership statistics, and local chapter organization listings. A separate listing of libraries and other institutional subscribers is also included. New to this edition is a listing of college and university industrial relations programs that have been brought to the attention of the Association.

On behalf of the Association, I want to express appreciation to several IRRA Staff and others who prepared the Directory for publication. In particular, I acknowledge with the utmost gratitude the contribution of Marion Leifer, who undertook responsibility for the overall effort, performed many of the major activities—including typing the camera-ready manuscript—herself, and supervised all the other tasks. In addition, I wish to thank Larry Leifer, whose assistance in all phases of the organization and production of the Directory was invaluable to its publication. This Directory is truly a product of the Leifer team effort. As usual, Marjorie Lamb brought important knowledge and insight about the Association—as well as cheerful and timely assistance—to all aspects of the planning and production effort. We also want to express appreciation to IRRA Editor Barbara Dennis for her important editorial help and valuable assorted "hints" on the publication of the volume. Finally, I want to thank Mike Dolan and the staff at Pantagraph Printing for their responsiveness and helpful advice in the printing of the Directory.

We trust that members will find the Directory to be of value, and we welcome comments and suggestions which will make future editions even more useful.

DAVID R. ZIMMERMAN
Secretary-Treasurer

INDUSTRIAL RELATIONS RESEARCH ASSOCIATION

CONSTITUTION

1. NAME. This Association shall be known as the Industrial Relations Research Association.
2. PURPOSE. The purposes of this Association are:
   1. the encouragement of research in all aspects of the field of labor—social, political, economic, legal, and psychological—including employer and employee organization, labor relations, personnel administration, social security, and labor legislation;
   2. the promotion of full discussion and exchange of ideas regarding the planning and conduct of research in this field;
   3. the dissemination of the significant results of such research; and
   4. the improvement of the materials and methods of instruction in the field of labor.

   The Association will take no partisan attitude on questions of policy in the field of labor, nor will it commit its members to any position on such questions.
3. MEMBERSHIP. In accordance with the Bylaws, membership shall be open to anyone interested in the purposes of the Association.

BYLAWS

I. Membership

1. Any person interested in its purposes may, upon payment of dues, become a member of this Association.
2. There shall be the following classes of members: Regular Members; Family Members (living at the same address as another member, but not receiving the publications of the Association); Junior Members (graduate and undergraduate students, limited to three consecutive years in each classification); Retired Members (who have been members for 10 years or more and who are not gainfully employed); Foreign Members (from countries other than the United States and Canada); Contributing Members. Persons who paid dues for 1948 have been designated as Charter Members of their respective classifications.
3. Every member except a Family Member is entitled to receive the publications issued by the Association during membership. Special publications may be offered to members at a discount.
4. The dues schedule may be changed at the discretion of the Executive Board in proportion to the change in relevant price and wage indexes.

II. Officers

1. The Association shall have the following elective officers: a President, a President-Elect, and fourteen elected members of the Executive Board. The terms of office of the President and the President-Elect shall be one year. The terms of office of the members elected to the Executive Board shall be three years, rotated so that four terms expire one year, five the next, and five the third. Each regular term of office shall coincide with a calendar year.
2. As early in each year as practicable, the Executive Board shall elect a Nominating Committee consisting of seven other members of the Association, one of whom shall be designated as chairman by the Executive Board. The names of the Nominating Committee shall be published with an invitation to the general membership that suggestions of nominees for the various offices be sent to the chairman of the Committee. The Committee shall be instructed to present to the Secretary-Treasurer of the Association on or before September 1 of each year a nominee for the presidency, a nominee for the office of President-Elect who will be nominated for the presidency in the ensuing year, and two or more nominees for each other elective office to be filled, the nominees being members of the Association. Selection and method of nomination shall facilitate membership on the Executive Board of individuals drawn from the several disciplines and types of research activity represented within the Association. The candidates for President and President-Elect shall be selected by an electoral college consisting of the members of the Nominating Committee and the Executive Board, with space provided on the ballot for an individual voter's alternative choice.
3. Elective officers shall be chosen through elections to be held during the last six months of the term of office of their predecessors under the rules determined by the Executive Board. Each member shall be given the opportunity to vote by mail. The results of the election shall be tabulated, certified and announced by the Secretary-Treasurer under the supervision of the Executive Board.
4. The Association shall have the following officers who shall be appointed by the Executive Board: a Secretary-Treasurer, an Editor, and a Counsel. The appointments to

each of these offices shall be for three years, which may be terminated for cause by a majority vote of all voting members of the Executive Board. The Editor shall, with the advice of the President and Executive Board, appoint an Editorial Board for each research volume.

5. The Executive Board shall consist of the President, the President-Elect, the Secretary-Treasurer, the Editor, the previous year's president, and fourteen elected members, providing that the Secretary-Treasurer and the Editor shall not be entitled to vote.
6. With the advice and consent of the Executive Board, the President may appoint a Program Committee for the annual meeting, consisting of the Editor, the previous year's president, the Secretary-Treasurer, and representatives of the several areas of interest of the Association's membership. The President shall be the chairman of this Committee.

III. Duties of Officers

1. The President of the Association shall preside at all business meetings of the Association and at all meetings of the Executive Board and the Program Committee. In case of disability, the duties shall devolve upon the President-Elect pending cessation of such disability or until expiration of the term.
2. The Secretary-Treasurer shall keep the records of the Association; receive and have the custody of the funds of the Association, subject to the rules of the Executive Board; and perform such other duties as the Executive Board may assign.
3. The Executive Board shall have the control and management of the funds of the Association. It may fill vacancies in the list of officers, and may adopt any rules or regulations for the conduct of its business not inconsistent with the Constitution or Bylaws or with rules adopted at the annual meeting. It shall act as a committee on time and place of the annual meetings and perform such other duties as the Association shall delegate to it. A quorum shall consist of seven voting members.

IV. Local Chapters

1. The Association will recognize as affiliated local chapters, by means of certificate of recognition, a local organization formed to advance the purposes of the Association, provided the bylaws of the local group are consistent with those of the Association and require the officers of the local chapter to be members of the Association, and provided further that no financial obligation of the local chapter shall be a contingent obligation of the Association. Student chapters must have a faculty advisor who must be a member of the Association.
2. Any local group desiring to affiliate with the Association will send its request for affiliation, together with a copy of its bylaws and a list of its program, to the Secretary-Treasurer, who shall present the request to the Executive Board. The Executive Board may accept or refuse the affiliation.
3. The Association will not interfere with activities of the local chapters, provided that they conform with the purposes of the Association. The affiliation of any local chapter, whose program or activities are inconsistent with the aims and purposes of the Association, may be terminated by vote of the Executive Board.
4. Each local chapter will pay an annual fee to the national IRRA with a credit to be returned to the local chapter based on the percentage of local chapter members who are also members of the national IRRA.

V. Amendments to the Constitution or Bylaws

1. Amendments that have been approved by the Executive Board may be adopted (a) by a majority of the members present at the annual business meeting of the Association or (b) by a majority of the votes cast in a mail ballot authorized by the Executive Board.
2. The Executive Board shall report to the annual business meeting any amendments proposed during the year, but not approved for adoption. Upon motion of any member present at the annual business meeting, the Executive Board may be instructed by majority vote to submit such amendment to mail ballot to the membership.

(Major amendments to the Bylaws are summarized on the following page.)

The IRRA Constitution and ByLaws were drafted and adopted by the Organizing Committee October 25, 1947 in New York City *(Proceedings of the First Annual Meeting, 1948, p. 3).*

In addition to a number of changes and amendments made during the first two years (see "Minutes of Meetings and Business Reports," *Proceedings of the First Annual Meeting, 1948,* and *Proceedings of the Second Annual Meeting, 1949*), the Constitution and ByLaws have been amended as follows:

1950 Section I, Paragraph 2: Raised Regular Member dues from $5 to $6 annually, and
Article IV, Section 1: Removed the requirement that members of all committees of the local chapter be members of the Association.
Proceedings of the Third Annual Meeting, 1950, p. 381, and *Proceedings of the Fourth Annual Meeting, 1951,* p. 280.

1952 Section II, Paragraph 1: Increased the twelve elected members of the Executive Board to fourteen elected members. *Proceedings of the Fifth Annual Meeting, 1952,* p. 245.

1960 Section II, Paragraphs 1, 2 and 5: Created the new office of President-Elect. The elected incumbent of this office would serve for one year and the ensuing year succeed to the Presidency. *Proceedings of the Thirteenth Annual Meeting, 1960,* p. 302.

1963 Section I, Paragraph 2: Raised Regular Member dues from $6 to $8 and Student Member dues from $3 to $4 annually. *Proceedings of the Sixteenth Annual Meeting, 1962,* p. 270, and the *IRRA Autumn Newsletter, 1963.*

1967 Section I, Paragraph 2: Added the category Foreign Members (from countries other than the United States and Canada) paying annual dues of $4; and changed several minor editorial anachronisms to read:
Section I, Paragraph 2, first sentence: "Persons who paid dues for 1948 have been designated as Charter Members of their respective classifications."
Section II, Paragraph 1, third sentence: "The terms of office of members elected to the Executive Board shall be three years, rotated so that four terms expire one year, five the next, and five the third."
Section II, Paragraph 4, changed the last sentence: "The Editor shall, with the advice of the President and the Executive Board appoint an Editorial Board for each research volume." *Proceedings of the Twentieth Annual Meeting, 1967,* pp. 400–401.

1968 Section I, Paragraph 2: Added the category Retired Members (who have been members for 10 years or more and who are not gainfully employed) paying annual dues of $4. *Proceedings of the Twenty-First Annual Meeting, 1968,* p. 396; and
Raised Regular Member dues from $8 to $10, and Student, Foreign and Retired Member dues from $4 to $5 annually to begin in 1970. *Proceedings of the Twenty-Second Annual Meeting, 1969,* p. 344.

1973 Raised Regular Member dues from $10 to $15, and Student, Foreign and Retired Member dues from $5 to $6 annually to begin in 1974. *Proceedings of the Twenty-Sixth Annual Meeting, 1973,* p. 285.

1975 Section IV, Paragraph 4: Required local chapter fee payments to be made to the national IRRA with a credit to be returned to the local chapter based on the percentage of local chapter members who are also members of the national.
Section I, Paragraph 2: Removed the category Life Members, retroactive to January 1, 1975.
Section I, Paragraph 2: Empowered the Executive Board to make future dues changes at its discretion in proportion to the change in relevant

wage price indexes.* *Proceedings of the Twenty-Seventh Annual Meeting, 1974*, p. 368 *and Proceedings of the Twenty-Eighth Annual Meeting, 1975*, pp. 289-290.

1976 Section II. Paragraph 3: Permitted the election of officers to be held during the last six months of the term of their predecessors. *Proceedings of the Twenty-Ninth Annual Meeting, 1976*, pp. 358-59.

---

* May 8, 1976—Dues were raised by Executive Board vote from $15 to $18 for Regular Members, and from $5 to $6 for Junior, Foreign and Retired Members annually to begin in 1977. *Proceedings of Twenty-Ninth Annual Meeting, 1976*, p. 358.

* August 29, 1978—Dues were raised by Executive Board vote from $18 to $24 for Regular Members, from $6 to $7.50 for Student, Foreign and Retired Members, and from $1 to $2 for Family Members annually to begin in 1979. *Proceedings of Thirty-First Annual Meeting, 1978*, p. 340.

* December 28, 1979—Dues were raised by Executive Board vote from $24 annually to $30 for Regular Members, and from $6 to $9 annually for Junior, Foreign and Retired Members to begin in 1981. *Proceedings of the Thirty-Second Annual Meeting, 1979*, p. 379.

* September 5, 1980—Dues were raised by Executive Board vote from $30 annually to $33 for Regular Members and the Secretary-Treasurer was instructed to "change the ratio of other membership categories to regular membership dues to more closely reflect the ratios that existed in previous years," to begin in 1982. *Proceedings of the Thirty-Third Annual Meeting, 1980*, p. 343. [1982 annual dues were set at: Regular, $33; Retired and Student, $13; Family, $4; Contributing, $100, Foreign, $33 + $4 mailing charge.]

* December 27, 1981—Dues were raised by Executive Board vote from $33 annually to "an amount approximately to the cost of living increase, but not to exceed $3." to begin in 1983. *Proceedings of the Thirty-Fourth Annual Meeting, 1981*, p. 425. [1983 annual dues were set at: Regular, $36; Retired and Student, $14; Family, $4; Contributing, $100; $4 mailing charge for members outside U.S.]

IRRA BIOGRAPHIC LIST OF MEMBERS

Biographies are compiled primarily from questionnaires returned by members. Listings for members who did not return questionnaires or who returned them after the deadline include only the name, address, and information from current IRRA mailing list.

Library and other institutional subscribers are listed in the section starting on page 317.

A

AALUND, LEE A. Legal Practice. BS 1979, JD 1983, AM 1983, LIRI-U of Ill. INT: labor law, arb/med, coll barg. ASSN: Wash State Bar Assn, Seattle-King County Bar Assn, ABA. POSITION: Assoc/Attorney at Law, Sax and MacIver, 1700 Peoples Natl Bank, 1415 Fifth Avenue, Seattle, WA 98171. 206/624-1940

AARON, BENJAMIN Academic: Law, Ind Rels; Arbitration. AB 1937, U of Mich; LLB 1940, Harvard. PUBL: Public Sector Bargaining, (co-editor w J. Stern & J. Grodin), 1979; Industrial Conflict (co-editor) w. K. W. Wedderburn), 1972; Labor Courts & Grievance Settlement in Western Europe, (editor), 1971. INT: labor law, intl comparative labor, arb/med. ASSN: Southern Calif IRRA, Intl Soc for Labor Law & Social Security, NAA, ABA. POSITION: Dir, UCLA Inst of Ind Rels, 1960-75; and (since 1960) Prof, School of Law, Univ of Calif, Los Angeles, CA 90024. 213/825-1296

ABBEY, AUGUSTUS Academic: Org Beh/Pers, Ind Rels, Bus Admin. BA 1973, U of Ghana; MBA 1976, PhD 1981 U of Ariz. PUBL: Technological Innovation: R&D Work Environment, UMI Research Press, 1982; "R&D Work Climate and Innovation in Semiconductors," Academy of Mgmt J, 1983, V 26, #2, pp 362-368. INT: org beh, personnel, coll barg. ASSN: Academy of Mgmt, IIRA, Technology Transfer Soc. POSITION: (since 1981) Asst Prof, Univ of Wis-La Crosse, Dept of Mgmt and Marketing, La Crosse, WI 54601. 608/785-8776.

ABBOTT, JAROLD GUY Academic: Org Beh/Pers. AB 1956, William Jewell Coll; PhD 1960, MIT. PUBL: "History and Theory of Performance Appraisal," Handbook of Wage and Salary Admin, Ed. by Milton Rock, McGraw Hill, 1982 (w Fred Schuster); The Supervisor As An Effective Manager, (w Thomas McElheny), American Center for Mgmt Development. "Role Congruence and Discrepancies in Self and Supervisory Performance Evaluations," (w H. John Bernardin), Academy of Mgmt, Dallas, 1983. INT: personnel, org beh, mgmt/-educ. ASSN: ASPA, Academy of Mgmt, Southern Mgmt Assn. POSITIONS: Owner, Jarold Abbot and Associates, 1960; and (since 1971, Prof of Mgmt, Florida Atlantic Univ, Boca Raton, FL 33431. 305/393-3661

ABBOUSHI, SUHEIL Academic: Ind Rels, Org Beh/Pers. POSITION: Birzeit Univ, PO Box 14, Birzeit, W Bank, Israel.

ABEL, THEODORE Bus:Pers/Ind Rels. BA 1952, U of Penn. POSITIONS: Admin Asst, 1962, Asst Dir, 1968, and, since 1969, Dir, Personnel Research, Philadelphia Electric Co, 2301 Market St, N1-2, Philadelphia, PA 19101. 215/841-4343

ABENHAIM, LUCIEN LEWYS Acad: Occupational Health, Safety Res/Admin. MD 1976, U of Paris; MSc 1980, McGill U. PUBL: "Proposals for a Prevention Policy: an Analysis of the French Report," (w W. Dab), in Effective Health Care, 1983; "An Integrated Decision-Making Algorithm for Preventative Action and Research in Occupational Health and Safety," (w W. Dab), in Effective Health Care, 1984; "Travial et sante: dialectique d'un rapport social," in Traite d'anthropologie medicale. Ed. Inst quebecois de recherche sur la culture, 1984. INT: govt labor policy, method/statis. ASSN: Amer Public Health Assn, Canadian Public Health Assn, Assn pour la sante pobluque du Quebec. POSITIONS: Res Assoc, 1979, Visiting Prof, 1981, School of Ind Rels, Univ of Montreal; and (since 1982) Chief, Special Projects Program, Inst de recherche en sante et en securite du travail du Quebec, 505 Ouest De Maisonneuve, Montreal, PQ H3A 3C2 Canada. 514/288-1551

ABERNATHY, JOHN H. Arbitration; Acad: Ind Rels. MS 1958, MS 1960, U of Ala; PhD 1969, LSU. INT: arb/med, coll barg, empl/trng programs. ASSN: AAA, SPIDR, NAA. POSITIONS: Prof, Southern Oregon State Coll, 1970; Mediator, State of Oregon, 1970; and (since 1976) Arbitrator, Western Arb Assoc, PO Box 2029, Lake Oswego, OR 97034. 503/635-9915

ABERNETHY, BYRON ROBERT Arbitration. POSITION: Arbitrator, Monterey Professional Bldg, 3102 50 St, Lubbock, TX 79413. 806/795-6316

ABERS, JACOB H. 116 Forest View Dr, San Francisco, CA 94132. 415/731-4801

ABOUD, ANTONE Academic: Univ Admin, Ind Rels; Consulting. BA 1969, Cornell U; PhD 1974, NYSSILR-Cornell. PUBL: "The Right to Strike in Public Employment," (w G. Sterrett); "Public Policy and Public Sector Strike Behavior," (w S. Schram). INT: coll/barg, govt labor policy, labor law. ASSN: Western Penna IRRA, AAA. POSITIONS: Asst Prof, SUC of Tech, Utica, NY 1979; Assoc Prof, SUC, Potsdam, NY, 1980; and, since 1982, Dir, Grad School of Ind Rels, St. Francis Coll, Loretto, PA. ADDRESS: Route 2, Box 51, Hollidaysburg, PA 16648. 814/472-7000

ABOWD, JOHN M. Academic: Econ, Ind Rels, Bus Admin. AB 1973, U of Notre Dame; AM 1975, PhD 1977, U of Chicago. PUBL: "Job Queries and the Union Status of Workers," Ind and Labor Rels Review, 1982 (w H. Farber); "Anticipated Unemployment, Temporary Layoffs and Compensating Wage Differentials," Studies in Labor Markets, 1981 (w O. Ashenfelter); "Do Minority/White Unemployment Differences Exist?" J of Bus and Econ Statis, 1984 (w M. Killingsworth). INT: labor market econ, methodology/statis. ASSN: AEA, Econometric Soc, American Statis Assn. POSITIONS: Asst Prof, Princeton U, 1977-79;Asst Prof, 1979, and, since 1982, Assoc Prof, Grad School of Bus, Univ of Chicago, 1101 E 58th St, Chicago, IL 60637. 312/962-7510.

ABRAHAM, KATHARINE G. Academic: Econ. BS 1976, Iowa State U; PhD 1982, Harvard U. PUBL: "Structural/Frictional versus Deficient Demand Unemployment," AER, Sept 1983, pp 708-724; "Length of Service and Operation of Internal Labor Market," IRRA Proceedings of 35th Annual Meeting, Dec 1982, pp 308-318 (w J. L. Medoff); "Experience Performance and Earnings," QJE, Dec 1980, pp 703-736 (w J.L. Medoff). INT: labor market econ. ASSN: AEA. POSITION: Since 1980, Asst Prof, Sloan School of Mgmt, MIT, Cambridge, MA 02139. 617/253-2661

ABRAMS, NINA DODGE Legal Practice. AMLS 1965, MBA 1970, U of Mich; JD 1976, Loyola U of Chicago. INT: arb/med, org beh. ASSN: Detroit IRRA, State Bar of Mich, Women Lawyers of Mich, SPIDR. POSITION: Librarian, IR Libr, U of Chicago, 1972-76; Attorney (self-employed), 1976; and, currently, Partner-Attorney, Schwartz, Kanuer, Meisner & Abrams, 30700 Telegraph, Suite 4470, Birmingham, MI 48010. 313/645-9000

ACOSTA, ROBERT A. Union. INT: coll barg, labor law, arb/med. ASSN: Orange County IRRA. POSITION: (since 1978) Bus Rep, Orange County District Council of Carpenters, 2011 West Chapman, #200, Orange, CA 92668. 714/987-6232

ADAMS, JOHN P., JR. Academic: Econ; Consulting. MA 1968, PhD 1972, Claremont Grad School (Calif). INT: labor market econ, methodology/statis. POSITION: Economics Dept, CPSU, San Luis Obispo, CA 93407. 805/-546-2783

ADAMS, JON S. Student. Loyola U of Chicago. ADDRESS: 6307 N Glenwood, #3, Chicago, IL 60660.

ADAMS, LEONARD PALMER Retired. ADDRESS: 1648 White Plains, Terr, North Fort Meyers, FL 33903. 813/997-2051

ADAMS, ROY JOSEPH Academic: Ind Rels. BA 1967, Penna State U; MA 1970, PhD 1973, U of Wis. PUBL: "Canada-U.S. Labour Link Under Stress," Ind Rels, 1976, 15, #3, pp 295-312; "Industrial Relations Systems in Europe and North America," (w J. Anderson & M. Gunderson), Union Mgmt Rels in Canada, Toronto, Addison,Wesley, 1982; Education and Working Canadians, (w P. M. Draper & C. Ducharme), Report of the Commission on Educational Leave and Productivity, Ottawa, Labour Canada, 1979. INT: intl comparative labor, govt labor policy, union org. ASSN: Hamilton & Dist IRRA, Canadian IRA. POSITIONS: Ind Rels Specialist, 1967, Chase Manhatten Bank, NY; Chairman, Canadian Commission on Educational Leave and Productivity, 1978, and, currently, McMaster U, (since 1973), Assoc Prof of IR, (since 1978), Hamilton, Ont L8S 1R5, Canada. 416/525-9140.

ADDINGTON, Thomas H. Bus:Pers/Ind Rels, Bus:Mgmt/Admin, Arbitration. BS, BA 1962, U of Tenn. INT: arb/med, coll barg, personnel. ASSN: Tenn Valley Pers Assoc, Natl Mgmt Assoc. POSITIONS: Supr Mgmt Services, 1976, Asst to Dir of Construction, 1977, and, since 1979, Chief Salary Policy Contract Admin, Labor Rels Staff, TVA, 200 Liberty Bldg, Knoxville, TN 37902. 615/632-2147

ADELSON, YOLANDE CHAMBERS Arbitration. BA 1950, Hampton Inst; JD 1953, Yale Law School. PUBL: "Retraining Program Upsets Test Predictions: An Experiment in Retraining Disadvantaged Employees," Pers Services, Bulletin of the Natl Retail Merchants Assoc, Sept 1965; Veterans Outreach Manual: Suggestions for an Effective Veterans Program for Colleges, Co-editor, U.S. Office of Education. INT: arb/med. ASSN: Orange County IRRA. SPIDR, AAA, Black Women Lawyers. POSITIONS: Grievance Admin and Trng Officer, Calif St Univ and Colleges, 1971-73; Dir, - Dept of Human Development, UCLA Ext, 1973-83 ADDRESS: 228 Monte Grigio Dr, Pacific Palisades, CA 90272.

ADEN, IRMA Student. UCLA, Grad School of Mgmt. ADDRESS: 6391 Chapman Ave, Garden Grove, CA 92645. 714/898-7004

ADERINTO, ADEYEMO Acad: Econ, Ind Rels. BSc 1967, U of Ife-Nigeria; MA 1973, U of Wis-Madison; PhD 1982, U of Lagos. PUBL: "Labour Mobility in Nigeria: Patterns and Implications For Balanced Development," Labour & Soc, vol 6, #2, 1981; "Internal Labour Mobility and Economic Opportunity: The Case of Urban Lagos," Manpower J, vol XVI, #4, Jan-Mar, 1981; "Regional and Social Development Problems in Nigeria," Quart J of Admin, vol XIV, #3, Apr 1980., INT: labor market econ, mgmt/educ, coll barg. ASSN: IIRA, Inst of Pers Mgmt of Nigeria, Nigerian Econ Soc. POSITIONS: Sr Res Fellow, U of Lagos, 1978; Visiting Fellow, Inst of Develop Studies, U of Sussex, England; and (since 1978) Sr Research Fellow, Human Resources Res Unit, Univ of Lagos, Lagos, Nigeria

ADKINS, ROGER L. Econ. BA 1965, Marshall U; MA 1967, Ohio U; PhD 1981, Kansas State U. INT: arb/med, coll barg, labor market econ. ASSN: WV IRRA, AEA, AEE, Comparative Econ Assn. POSITIONS: Asst Prof, Marymount Coll of Kansas, 1972-79; Asst Prof, Ind U of Penna, 1980; and, since 1981, Asst Prof Econ, Dept of Econ, Marshall Univ, Huntington, WV 25701. 304/696-6498

ADLER, SARA Arbitration; Law. BA 1961, U of Chicago; JD 1969, UCLA. INT: arb/med, emply/trng programs. ASSN: Southern Calif IRRA, AAA, SPIDR, ABA, Labor Law Section. POSITIONS: Assoc Dir Paralegal Inst, U of S Calif, 1972; Attorney, Wyman, Bautzer, Rothman, Kuchel & Silbert, 1974; and since 1978, Arbitrator, 1034 Selby Ave, Los Angeles, CA 90024. 213/474-5170

ADOMA, OSEI J. Bus: Pers/Ind Rels; Law. Pol Sci 1973, Youngstown State U; JD 1979, Cleveland Marshall Coll of Law. INT: coll barg, arb/med, labor law. ASSN: Atlanta IRRA, ASPA. POSITIONS: Pers Mgr, (Canton Oh), 1979, Pers Mgr-Corp Tech Center, 1981, and since 1982, Pers Mgr, St. Regis Corp, 840 Woodrow St SW, Atlanta, GA 30310. 404/753-4131

AGONIA, ROBERT J. Government. BA 1961, Calif Stat U, Long Beach. INT: personnel,coll barg, emply/trng programs. ASSN: Nevada IRRA. POSITIONS: Sr. Affirmative Action Officer, 1974, Ind Rels Specialist, 1979, and, since 1980, Chief, Ind Rels Branch, U.S. Dept of Energy, PO Box 14100, Las Vegas, NV 89102. 702/295-1005

AHERN, EILEEN Bus:Pers/Ind Rels, Consulting. PUBL: Federal Policy and Worker Status Since the Thirties," IRRA Research Volume, 1976 (edtited by Goldberg, Ahern, Haber & Oswald); Collective Bargaining in the Office, American Mgmt Assoc, 1950; Handbook of Pers Forms and Records, American Mgmt Assn,1949. INT: mgmt/educ, arb/med, personnel. ASSN: NY IRRA. POSITIONS: Research Assoc & Consultant, American Mgmt Assn, 1946; Mgr, Ind Rels Research, The Continental Group Inc, NY, 1962-75; and, since 1975, Retired. ADDRESS: 510 E 20th St, New York, NY 10009. 212/777-4744

AHERN, JOHN THOMAS Arbitraor-Mediator. MA 1970, SUNY. PUBL: "Public School Labor Relations for the 80's," NYS Council School Supts. INT: arb/med, coll barg, labor mgmt committees. ASSN: Long Island IRRA, SPIDR, AAA. ADDRESS: 11 Tanager Lane, Northport, NY 11768. 516/757-0020

AHERN, LAWRENCE JAMES Union. BS 1949, U of Conn. INT: union org, coll barg, govt labor policy. POSITIONS: Research and Educ Dir, 1961, Coll Barg Dir, 1969, and since 1980, Vice Pres, Intl Chemical Workers Union. ADDRESS: 814 Cliffside Dr, Akron, OH 44313. 216/867-2444

AHERN, ROBERT WILLIAM Arbitration, Consulting. BS 1960, Cornell U. INT: arb/med, org beh, coll barg. ASSN: Western NY IRRA, SPIDR. POSITION: Exec Dir, Buffalo-Erie County Labor Mgmt Council, Suite 407, One Convention Tower, Buffalo, NY 14202. 716/856-6611

AHLBURG, DENNIS ALLEN Academic: Economics. POSITION: Industrial Rels Center, Univ of Minnesota, Minneapolis, MN 55455. 612/373-4122

AHMUTY, ALICE LYNNE Government. BS 1966, U of MD; MILR 1968, Mich State U. PUBL: "Tripartite Cooperative Endeavors in Labor Relations in the U.S.;" "Railway Labor Act: Unfair Labor Practices, Representation Dispute Procedures, Problems and Issues;" "Women and Minority Employment in the Blue Collar Skilled Trades." INT: govt labor policy, labor market econ, intl comparative labor. ASSN: Wash DC IRRA, AFEE POSITIONS: Employee Rels Hearing Officer, State of Md, 1975; Consultant Labor Economist, FMCS, 1976, and, since 1978, Analyst in Labor Economics and Rels, Congressional Research Service, Library of Congress. ADDRESS: 9408 Bullring La, Columbia, MD 21045. 202/287-7575

AHRENS, DAVID Union. MS, U of Wis. INT: coll/barg, health & hosp care, labor history. ASSN: Wisconsin IRRA. POSITION: Intl Rep, 1977, Research Specialist, 1980, and since 1981, District Rep WIS Council 40, AFSCME, AFL-CIO, 5 Odana Ct, Madison, WI 53719. 608/274-9100

AKABAS. SHEILA H. Ind Social Work. BS 1951, Cornell U; MBA 1953, PhD 1970, New York U. PUBL: Work, Workers & Work Organizations, 1982, Prentice Hall (w Paul Kurzman); "Industrial Social Work: Influencing the System at the Workplace," Social Work in a Turbulant World, 1983, Natl Assn of Social Workers; "Social Service at the Workplace," (w Seth Akabas), Mgmt Review, May 1982, pp 15-20. INT: ind social work, empl/trng programs, org beh. ASSN: Council on Social Work Educ, American Orthopsychiatric Assn. POSITIONS: Research Dir: Mental Health, Amalgamated Clothing & Textile Workers, 1961; and, since 1969, Prof and Dir, Ind Soc Welfare Center, Columbia Univ, 622 W 113th St, New York, NY 10025.212/280-5173

AKARAKCIAN, ARLENE A Student. Mich State U. ADDRESS: 3021 Beau Jardin, Lansing, MI 48910. 517/394-4937

AKINS, J. REID, JR. Bus:Pers/Ind Rels. LLB 1947, Atlanta Law School. Advanced Mgmt Trng, 1970, Emory U. INT: coll barg, arb/med, personnel. ASSN: Atlanta IRRA, Personnel Roundtable. POSITIONS: Pers Unit Supr, 1962, Labor Rels Mgr, 1965, and, since 1979, Dir Labor Rels & Plant Pers, Lockheed-Georgia Co, 86 S Cobb Dr, Marietta, GA 30063. 404/424-5296

AKSELROD, LEONARD JEFFREY Government. BA 1981, SUNY-Albany; MILIR 1983, U of Ill. INT: coll barg, quality of work life, Union org admin. ASSN: New York IRRA. POSITION: (since 1984) Research Analyst, QWL Program, Mayor's Office of Municipal Labor Rels. ADDRESS: 334 W 87th St, #8B, New York, NY 10024. 212/618-8310

ALBRITON, JAMES E. Student. 1917 Lyttonsville Rd, Silver Spring, MD 20910

ALDAG, RAMON J. Acad: Org Behavior,/-Pers, Bus Admin, Consulting. BS 1966, MBA 1968, PhD 1974, Mich State U. PUBL: Task Design and Employee Motivation, (w W. P. Brief), Scott Foresman & Co, 1979; Managing Organizational Behavior, (w A. P. Brief), West Publ Co, 1981; "Measurement of Perceived Task Characteristics," (w S. H. Barr & A. P. Brief), Psych Bull, 1981, 90, pp 415-431. INT: org beh, ind psych, personnel. ASSN: Academy of Mgmt, Amer Ins for Decisions Sciences. POSITIONS: Asst Prof of Bus, 1973, Assoc Prof of Bus, 1978, and, since 1982, Prof of Bus, Univ of Wis, 1155 Observatory Dr, Madison, WI 53706. 608/263-3771

ALDEN, JOHN R. Business, Arbitration, Legal Practice. POSITION: Vice-Pres, Ind Rels, Packaging Corp of America, 1605 Orrington Ave, Evanston, IL 60204. 312/492-6948

ALDRICH, EMMETT I. Government, Bus/Mgmt/Admin, Pers/Ind Rels. AA 1976, BS 1978, George Washington U; MS 1983, U of D.C. PUBL: "Dispute Resolution in the Federal Sector: Are Strikes Necessary?" Fed Service Labor Rels Rev, v 4, #2, Spring 1982; Guide to Costing Labor Agreements: A Simplified Model," (Pamphlet), U. S. Dept of Interior, July 1983; Constitution and By-Laws of the Labor Studies Student Assn, (cont on next page)

Assn, (Pamphlet), Labor Studies Center, U of DC. ASSN: Wash DC IRRA, SFLRP, IPMA, Labor Studies Org, U of DC. POSITIONS: Pers Mgmt Spec (+ Labor Rels Spec), U. S. Dept of Transportation, 1976; Bureau Labor Rels Officer, U. S. Bureau of Mines, 1979, and, since 1983, Labor Rels Specialist, Office of the Secretary, U. S. Dept of the Interior, 4603 7th St NE, Washington DC 20017. 202/343-6754

ALDRICH, HOWARD EARL Sociology. PhD 1969, U of Mich. PUBL: Organizations and Environments, Prentice Hall, 1979; "Differentiation Within the U.S. Capitalist Class: Workforce Size and Income Differences," American Soc Rev, 46, 1981, pp 279-289; "Mintzberg Was Right! A Replication and Extension of the Nature of Managerial Work," Mgmt Science, August 1983. INT: org/beh, ind/sociology. ASSN: American Sociol Assn, Intl Sociol Assn, Southern Sociol Assn. POSITIONS: Prof of Org Behavior, NYSS-ILR, Cornell, 1969; and, (since 1982) Prof of Sociol, Univ of North Carolina, Hamilton Hall 070A, Chapel Hill, NC 27514. 919/962-5044

ALERS, BENJAMIN Municipal Hosp System. BA 1972, John Jay Coll of Criminal Justice; MSW-CSW 1976, Fordham U; MS 1982, NY Inst of Tech. INT: personnel, arb/med, ind/sociology. ASSN: Long Island IRRA, ASPA, Amer Assn of Ind Soc Workers, Hispanic Assn of Health Services Exec. POSITIONS: Labor Rels Mgr, Lumex Inc, 1979; Labor Rels Hearing Officer, Lincoln Medical & Mental Health Center, 1980; and (since 1983) Personnel Dir, Seaview Hospital and Home, New York. ADDRESS: Apt 4A, 35 N Long Beach Ave, Freeport, NY 11520. 212/390-8272

ALEXANDER, GABRIEL N. Arbitration. BA 1930, JD 1933, U of Mich. INT: arb/med, coll barg, labor law. POSITION: Arbitrator, Suite 123, 17000 W Ten Mile Rd, Southfield, MI 48075. 313/552-9301

ALEXANDER, JOAN B. Legal Practice. BS 1972, NYSSILR-Cornell; JD 1975, SUNY-Buffalo. INT: labor law, arb/med, coll barg. ASSN: Western New York IRRA, Fla State Bar Assn, Erie County Bar Assn, Women Lawyers of Western New York. POSITIONS: Attorney, Internal Revenue Service, 1975-78; Confidential Law Clerk, NYS Supreme Court Justice J. D. Mintz; and (since 1979) Attorney (self-employed), 196 Crestwood Lane, Williamsville, NY 14221. 716/688-6115

ALEXANDER, JOSEPH Economics. BS 1946, U of Okla; MA 1947, Columbia U; PhD 1956, New York U. PUBL: "Presidential Interventionism: The Crisis in Collective Bargaining," Miss Valley J of Bus and Econ, Spring 1967; "The Question of Relevance As It Applies to Economic Theory and Analytics," Community Coll Soc Science Quar, Fall 1974; "The Caribbean Initiative: An Unworkable Extension of Reagonmics," Proceedings, NA Econ and Finance Assn, 1982. INT: govt labor policy, coll barg, labor history. ASSN: AEA, Regional Science Assn, NA Econ and Finance Assn. POSITIONS: Econ Faculty, 1950, and, since 1960, Prof of Econ, Babson College, Babson Park (Wellesley) MA 02157. 617/235-1200.

ALEXANDER, KENNETH O. Econ, Ind Rels. BA 1949, Mich State U; PhD 1957, MIT. PUBL: "Market Practices and Collective Bargaining in Automotive Parts," J of Political Economy, Vol LXIX, #1, Feb 1961; "Conglomerate Mergers and Collective Bargaining," Ind and Labor Rels Review, Vol 24, #3, April 1971; "Scientists, Engineers and the Organization of Work," Amer J of Econ and Sociol, Vol 40, #1, Jan 1981. INT: coll barg, org beh, arb/med. ASSN: AEA, Assn for Soc Econ. POSITIONS: Instructor and Asst Prof, Mich State Univ, 1955; Prof and Assoc Dir, Univ of Iowa, 1964; and (since 1965) Prof, Mich Technological Univ, Houghton, MI 49931. 906/487-2801

ALICEN, BOBBIE Union. BA 1960, Antioch Coll. INT: arb/med, union org/admin, org beh. POSITION: (since 1981) Organization Specialist, Univ of Hawaii Professional Assembly, 1649 Kalakau Ave, Honolulu, HI 96826. 808/947-3917

ALLAN, PETER Acad: Org Beh, Bus Admin. BSS 1949, CCNY, MS 1950, Columbia U; PhD 1969, New York U. PUBL: Public Personnel and Administrative Behavior; "Managers At Work," Acad of Mgmt J; "Getting a Managerial Performance System Underway," Public Admin Rev. INT: personnel, org beh, mgmt educ. ASSN: Acad of Mgmt, ASPA, AEA. POSITIONS: Dir of Res, 1975, Deputy City Pers Dir, New York City Dept of Pers, 1981; and (since 1982) Prof of Mgmt, Pace Univ Grad School of Business. ADDRESS: 1482 15th St, Ft. Lee, NJ 07024. 212/488-1847

ALLARD, MICHEL Bus:Pers/Ind Rels. BIR 1973, U of Montreal. INT: coll barg, personnel, ind psychology. ASSN: Montreal IRRA. POSITION: Pers and Ind Rels Mgr, Chromasco Limited, Canal Rd, Beauharnois, Quebec J6N 1W5, Canada. 514/691-6220

ALLEN, EDWARD WILLIAM Government. INT: coll barg, arb/med, labor market econ. ASSN: San Diego IRRA, State Bar of Calif (Labor & Empl Section). POSITIONS: Mediator, 1968, Presiding Mediator/Northern Calif, 1970, and, since 1976, Supervisor, State Mediation and Conciliation, State of Calif, PO Box 603, San Francisco, CA 94101. 415/557-2426

ALLEN, ROBERT EDWARD Academic: Ind Rels; Arbitration. BS 1968, MBA 1970, PhD 1976, SUNY-Buffalo. PUBL: Contemporary Labor Relations; "Correlates of Faculty Interest in Unionization," J of Applied Psychology; "The Demise of the Hollywood Ceramics Doctrine (Again)," Employee Rels Law J. INT: arb/med, coll barg, labor law. ASSN: Rocky Mt IRRA, Academy of Mgmt, SPIDR. POSITIONS: Since 1974, Assoc Prof of Bus Admin, Dept of Bus Admin, Univ of Wyoming, Laramie, WY 82071. 307/766-6332.

ALLEN, ROGER K. Academic: Ind Rels. BS 1965, Eastern Mich U; MA 1979, U of Mich. INT: coll barg, arb/med, labor law. ASSN: Detroit Area IRRA, Natl Org on Legal Problems of Educ, Mich Public Empl Labor Rels Assn, Mich Negotiators Assn. POSITIONS: Exec Dir, Mich Educ Assn, 1970; Staff Dir Employee Rels, 1975, and, since 1983, Executive Dir Operations and Empl Rels, Board of Education, 923 E Kearsley, Flint, MI 48502. 313/762-1943

ALLEN, RUSSELL W. Union. BA 1942, Weselyan (Conn); MA 1947, U of Chicago. INT: coll barg, labor educ, govt labor policy. ASSN: ACLU, Univ and Coll Labor Educ Assn. POSITIONS: Educ Dir, Ind Union Dept, AFL-CIO, 1957; Prof, School of Labor & Ind Rels, Mich State U, 1964; and (since 1972) Deputy Dir, George Meany Center for Labor Studies. ADDRESS: 14805 Harold Rd, Silver Spring, MD 20904. 301/431-6400

ALLEN, STEVEN G. Economics. BA 1973, MA 1974, Mich State U; PhD 1978, Harvard U. PUBL: "Unionized Construction Workers Are More Productive," Quart J of Econ, 1984; "Trade Unions, Absenteeism, 2nd Exit-Voice," Ind and Labor Rels Rev, 1984; "Much Ado About Davis-Bacon: A Critical Review and New Evidence," J of Law and Econ, Oct 1983. INT: labor market econ, coll barg, govt labor policy. ASSN: AEA, Amer Econometric Soc. POSITIONS: Asst Prof of Econ and Bus, 1978, and, since 1983, Assoc Prof of Econ and Bus North Carolina State Univ, PO Box 5368, Raleigh, NC 27606. (Concurrently since 1983, Research Economist, Natl Bureau of Econ Research.) 919/737-3886

ALLEN, WILLIAM S. Student, Ind Rels. BSBA 1980, Auburn U; MSILR 1984, North Tex State. INT: mgmt/educ, personnel, labor market econ. ASSN: ASPA. POSITIONS: Compensation Analyst, 1981, Safety/Security Admin, RCA Service Co, Andros Island-Bahamas; and (since 1983) Student/Research Asst, North Tex State Univ. ADDRESS: 2411 West Hickory, #226, Denton, TX 76201. 817/565-3483

ALLER, CURTIS C. Univ Admin, Econ; Arbitration. PhD 1958, Harvard U. INT: labor market econ, emply/trng programs, coll barg. ASSN: San Francisco IRRA, AEA, WEA, AAA. POSITIONS: Assoc Manpower Admin, USDL, 1965; Prof of Econ, 1959, and, since 1982, Dean, School of Behavioral Soc Sciences, San Francisco State Univ, 1600 Holloway Ave, San Francisco, CA 94132. 415/469-2409

ALLEY, DOUGLAS M. Bus:Pers/Ind Rels. BComm 1975, U of British Columbia. INT: coll barg, arb/med, labor law. ASSN: B.C. IRRA, Ind Rels Mgmt Assn of BC. POSITION: Mgr, Labour Rels, British Columbia Packers Limited, Box 5000, Vancouver BC, V6B 4A8, Canada. 604/277-2212

ALLISON, JAMES MICHAEL Bus:Pers/Ind Rels. BS 1976, U of Tenn; MA 1972, U of Ill. INT: labor law, arb/med, coll barg. POSITIONS: Chief Negotiations Staff, TVA, 1977; and (since 1983) Labor Relations Manager, Indiana and Mich Electric Co. ADDRESS: 2530 Culpepper Ct, Fort Wayne, IN 46825. 219/425-2144

ALLMENDINGER, RAYMOND C. Government. POSITION: Commissioner Dept Labor, Suffolk County, 455 Wheeler Rd, Hauppauge, NY 11788

ALTMAN, STEVE Univ Admin, Bus Admin; Arbitration. BA 1967, UCLA; MBA 1969, DBA 1975, U of Southern Calif. PUBL: Organizational Behavior, Organizational Development, Profit Basics. INT: org beh, mgmt/educ, personnel. ASSN: ASPA, Academy of Mgmt, SPIDR. POSITIONS: Chairman, Div of Mgmt, 1972, Assoc Vice Pres, 1978, and, since 1982, Provost & Vice Pres for Academic Affairs, Florida Intl Univ, Tamiami Tr, Miami, FL 33199. 305/554-2151

ALTOMONTE, VINCENZO Student. 6346 Lawrendeau, Montreal, PQ H4E 3Y2 Canada.

ALUTTO, JOSEPH A. Acad: Univ Admin, Org Beh/Pers; Arbitration. BBA 1962, Manhatten Coll; MA 1965, U of Ill; PhD 1968, Cornell. PUBL: Theory Testing In Organizational Behavior, (w F. Dansereau & F. Yahmarind), Prentice Hall, 1984; "Absenteeism Rates as Measures of Organizational Experiments," (w Markham & Dansereau), Rev of Bus and Econ Awards, 1983; "Stress, Organizational Commitment and Turnover, (w S. Parasurandhan), Acad of Mgmt J, Winter, 1984. INT: org beh, ind psych, arb/med. ASSN: Amer Psych Assn, Acad of Mgmt, Amer Sociol Assn. POSITION: (since 1967) Dean and Prof of Org Beh, School of Mgmt, SUNY-Buffalo. ADDRESS: 655 Le Brun Rd, Amherst, NY 14226. 716/831-3533

AMANN, JOSEPH Government, Consulting. LLB 1960, American U. INT: labor law, coll barg, arb/med. ASSN: Wash DC IRRA, Federal Bar Assn, Intl Pers Mgmt Assn. POSITIONS: Attorney, NLRB, 1962, Labor Rels, Dept of Navy, 1967, and, since 1971, Labor Rels, U. S. Government Printing Office. ADDRESS: 10526 Providence Way, Fairfax, VA 22030. 202/275-2655

AMAR, JAMES C. Government. MLIR 1977, Mich State U. PUBL: "Pay Parity Between Police & Fire Fighters," J of Collective Negotiations in the Public Sector; "History of the Michigan State Fire Fighters Union," Mich Professional Fire Fighters. INT: arb/med, coll barg, labor law. ASSN: Detroit Area IRRA, SPIDR. POSITION: Exec Asst, Mich Employment Rels Commission, Detroit. ADDRESS: 123 Union, Plymouth, MI 48170. 313/256-3540

AMBA-RAO, SITA C. Academic: Org Beh/Pers, Bus Admin. BS 1965, BL 1958, Mysore U, India; MS 1961, PhD 1967, Purdue Univ. PUBL: "Human Resource Management in Small Firms: Selected Policies and Practices, and Their Implications," Univ of Wis: Wis Small Bus Forum; "Relevancy of Human Relations Training for Employee Participative Programs: Perceptions of Non-Supervisory Employees, Union Officers and Managers," in T. W. Jones & P. L. Schaffer (eds) Decision Sciences in the Public and Private Sectors, S. W. Aids, 1982; "The Managerial Mainstream and Indian Women," Indian Mgmt, 18:11, Nov 1979, pp 2-9. INT: personnel, org beh. ASSN: Acad of Mgmt, Amer Inst of Decision Sciences, ASPA. POSITIONS: Sr. Pers Officer, S. V. Space Center, Trivandrum, India, 1974; Chief Pers Mgr, Bharat Dynamics, Hyderabad, India, 1976; and (since 1978) Asst Prof of Mgmt, Div of Bus and Econ, Indiana Univ at Kokomo, 2300 S Washington St, Kokomo, IN 46902. 317/453-2000

AMES, CLAUDE DAWSON Arbitration, Legal Practice. BS 1974, U of Calif-Berkeley; JD 1977, U of Calif-Hastings. INT: arb/med, labor law, mgmt/educ. ASSN: ABA, Labor and Employ Law Section, AAA, SPIDR. POSITION: Partner, Crowell, Massengale & Ames, 629 Oakland, CA 94610. 415/654-4388

AMES, MARTIN Legal Practice; Academic: Ind Rels, Bus Admin. BS 1954, Cornell U; MBA 1958, New York U; MA 1961, U of Calif-Berkeley; JD 1969, Suffolk U-Law School. INT: labor law, arb/med, mgmt/educ. ASSN: Boston IRRA. POSITION: Attorney, Seven Fletcher St. ADDRESS: PO Box 251, Chelmsford, MA 01824 617/256-8115

AMSLER, TERRY Mediation. BA 1972, SUNY New Paltz. INT: arb/med, org beh, ind sociol. ASSN: SPIDR, Natl Criminal Justice Assn, Intl Ombudsman Inst. POSITION: Dir for Program Development, Community Board Center for Policy and Trng, 149 Ninth St, San Francisco, CA 94103. 415/552-1250

ANDERSON, ARNOLD O. Arbitration. AB 1940, UCLA; MBA 1959, U of Calif-Berkeley. INT: arb/med. ASSN: San Francisco IRRA, Natl Academy of Arbitrators, SPIDR, AAA. POSITIONS: Instructor, Union-Mgmt Rels, Univ of Calif-Berkeley, 1957-78; Civilian Pers Officer, U.S. Navy, 1945-76; Arbitrator (self employed) since 1957, 128 Diablo View Rd, Orinda, CA 94563. 415/254-3705

ANDERSON, ARVID Government. BL 1948, U of Wis. PUBL: "The Impact of the New National Labor Policy on Public Sector Bargaining," Hofstra Labor Law Forum; "Interest Arbitration in New York City," AAA Vol 37, #4, 12-1982; "Collective Bargaining and the Fiscal Crisis in New York City: Cooperation for Survival," Fordham Urban Law, Vol X, 1981-82, #3. INT: arb/med, coll barg, labor market econ. ASSN: New York and Wis IRRA, Natl Academy of Arbitrators, ABA, SPIDR. POSITIONS: Commissioner, Wis Employ Rels Commission, 1959, and (since 1967) Chairman, Office of Coll Barg, 110 Church St, 11th Fl, New York, NY 10007. 212/618-8218

ANDERSON, BERNARD E. Foundation; Academic: Econ, Ind Rels. AB 1959, Livingstone Coll, MA 1961, Mich State U; PhD 1969, U of Penna. PUBL: Youth Employment and Public Policy, Prentice Hall, 1980; "The Quest for Economic Equality," Daedulus, Spring 1981; Black Managers in American Business, McGraw Hill, 1979. INT: labor market econ, govt labor policy, emply/trng programs. ASSN: New York IRRA, AEA, NEA. POSITIONS: Prof of Industry, Wharton School, U of Penna, 1969; and (since 1979) Dir, Social Sciences Div, The Rockefeller Foundation, 1133 Avenue of the Americas, New York, NY 10036. 212/869-8500

ANDERSON, CAROLYN S. Acad: Student, Ind Rels, Sociology. MA 1979, PhD 1984, UCLA. PUBL: "Alienation and Alcohol: The Role of Work, Mastery and Community," Amer Sociol Rev, Feb 1983, 6077; Building California: The Story of the Carpenters Union, (joint author), Los Angeles: Inst of Ind Rels, UCLA, 1982. INT: ind sociol, coll barg, union org/admin. ASSN: Los Angeles IRRA, Amer Sociol Assn, Sociologist for Women in Society, AFSME. POSITION: (since 1982) Asst to Dir, Inst of Ind Rels, UCLA, 9244 Bunche Hall, Los Angeles, CA 90024. 213/825-7013

ANDERSON, CLAIRE J. Acad: Bus Admin. BA 1967, U of Md; MBA 1970, American U; PhD 1976, U of Mass. PUBL: "Role of Expectations in Professional Education," Proc of Souther Mgmt Assn, 1983; "Employment at Will: The New Threat to Corporate America," Proc, Southwest Acad of Mgmt, 1984; "The Utility of the JDI in Organizational Diagnosis," Northeast Div of Amer Inst of Decision Sciences, Proc, 1984. INT: personnel, mgmt/educ, arb/med. ASSN: Acad of Mgmt, ASPA, Amer Mgmt Assn. POSITIONS: Career Military Officer, US Air Force, 1957; Asst Prof, U of Lowell, 1974; and (since 1977) Assoc Prof, Coll of Bus Admin, Loyola Univ, 6363 St. Charles Ave, New Orleans, LA 70118. 504/865-2441

ANDERSON, DONALD A. Acad: Bus Admin. BA 1955, MA 1956, USC. INT: arb/med. ASSN: Southern Calif IRRA, NAA, SFLRP, AAA. POSITIONS: Prof of Bus, Loyola-Marymount, III, 1972-83; and (since 1972) Arbitrator. ADDRESS: 2225 Chelsea Rd, Palos Verdes Estates, CA 90274. 213/377-2590

ANDERSON, JAMES K. Government. BA 1941, Willamette U; Accredited Exec in Pers, 1977. PUBL: Democratic Values & The Right of Management, (co-author), Columbia U Press, 1963; "Personnel Management in County Government," Cornell U, 1967; Manpower for Government: A Decade's Forecast, (pamphlet w E. Ginzberg), Public Pers Assn, 1958. INT: personnel, coll barg, govt labor policy. ASSN: Amer Soc for Public Admin, Intl Pers Mgmt Assn. POSITIONS: Research Assoc, Consortium of Human Resources Project, Columbia Univ, 1949-61, and (since 1961) Personnel Officer, County of Rockland (NY), County Office Bldg, New York, NY 10956. 914/425-5200

ANDERSON, JOAN Bus:Pers/Ind Rels. BA 1983, Loyola Marymount U. INT: arb/med, org beh, personnel. ASSN: Southern Calif IRRA, ABWA, AAA, Toastmaster. POSITIONS: Office, Mgr, 1973, Pers Mgr, Devlin Pharmaceuticals, 1978, and (since 1981) Pers Mgr, P. Leiner Nutritional Products. ADDRESS: 2225 Chelsea Rd, Palos Verdes Estates, CA 90274. 213/377-2590

ANDERSON, ROGER L. Academic: Ind Rels. PhD 1984, U of Ore. PUBL: "When People and Robots Work Together;" "Implementation of Autonomous Work Groups In Unionized Settings." INT: ind sociol, labor law, personnel. ASSN: Acad of Mgmt. POSITION: (since 1982) Asst Prof, McIntire School of Commerce, Monroe Hall, Univ of Va, Charlottesville, VA 22903. 804/924-7921

ANDERSON, RUTH Arbitration, Mediation. AB 1932, Stanford U; Cert Labor Arbitrator, U of Calif-Hastings. INT: arb/med, community development, personnel. POSITIONS:Arbitrator and Mediator, 1977--, Hearing Officer, Calif Youth Authority, Amer Arb Panel, 1981--; and (since 1974) Arbitrator, (self employed) 128 Diablo View Rd, Orinda, CA 94563. 415/254-3705

ANDERSON, SAMUEL L. Bus:Pers/Ind Rels. POSITION: Manager, Ind Rels, Whitaker Cable Corp, 203 E 14th Ave, North Kansas City, MO 64116.

ANDERSON, WAYNE G. Arbitration. POSITION: Arbitrator, 119 E. Maple St., Decatur, GA 30030.

ANDIAPPAN, PALANIAPPAN Academic: Bus Admin. MLitt 1969, U of Madras; MS 1973, U of Mass; PhD 1977, U of Iowa. PUBL: "Characteristics of Female Union Officers in Canada," Relations Industrielles, 1982; "Sex Effects on Managerial Hiring Decisions," Academy of Mgmt J, 1978; Women and Work: Sex Discrimination in Employment in India and the U.S., Somaiya, Bombay, 1980. INT: Sex Discrimination in emply, intl comparative law, coll barg. ASSN: IIRA, Canadian IRA, Admin Sciences Assn of Canada. POSITIONS: Asst Prof, Univ of New Brunswick, 1977; and (since 1980) Assoc Prof, Univ of Windsor, Windsor, Ontario N9B 3P4 Canada. 519/253-4232

ANDREASSI, SCOTT J. Student. BA 1983, MA 1984, Ind U of Penna. INT: health & hosp care. ASSN: Western Penna & IUP IRRA, ASPA. POSITIONS: (since 1983) Grad Student, Ind Univ of Penna. ADDRESS: 131 Dolores Circle A-2, Indiana, PA 15701. 412/357-2645

ANDREN, MARC DAVID Student. 2791 Charter Blvd, #114, Troy, MI 48083. 313/583-3275

ANDREWS, FRYA WAGNER Org Beh/Pers, Ind Rels, Bus Admin. DBA 1981, Memphis State U. INT: personnel, arb/med, org beh. ASSN: Academy of Mgmt, Amer Mgmt Assn. POSITIONS: Asst Pers Dept Mgr, Federal Reserve Bank of St. Louis-Memphis Branch, 1971; Asst Prof, Memphis State Univ, 1981; and (since 1982) Asst Prof, Eastern Mich Univ, Mgmt Dept, Ypsilanti, MI 48197. 313/487-0348.

ANDREWS, JOEL FRANCIS Bus:Pers/Ind Rels. BS 1971, MS-IR 1981, U of Wis-Madison. INT: personnel, empl/trng programs. ASSN: ASTD, ASPA, ASSE. POSITIONS: Pers Asst, 1982, Pers Rep, 1982, Miller Brewing Co, Reidsville Container, PO Box 1170, Reidsville, NC 27320. 919/342-7224

ANDREWS, ORVILLE E. Arbitration. AB 1940, SW Mo State U. INT: arb/med. POSITIONS: Asst to Dir, NLRB, 1947; and (since 1972) Arbitrator, Self Employed, 5777 W Fork Rd, Cincinnati, OH 45247. 513/574-8146

ANDRIANI, ROBERT NICHOLAS Bus:Pers/Ind Rels, Consulting; Academic: Org Beh/Pers. BA 1976, Iona Coll; MSIR 1982, U of Ore. INT: mgmt/-educ, org beh, personnel. ASSN: Amer Soc for Trng Development. POSITION: Regional Coordinator, Trng and Exec Development, Diamond's, A Div of Dayton Hudson. ADDRESS: 1325 Barnard Dr, Las Vegas, NV 89102. 702-733-2008

ANDRIS, V. O. Bus:Pers/Ind Rels. POSITION: Administrative Personnel, Coopers & Lybrand 1800 M St. NW, Washington DC 20036

ANDRISANI, PAUL J. Academic: Ind Rels; Consulting. BS 1968, MBA, 1970, U of Del; PhD 1973, Ohio State U. PUBL: Work Attitudes and Labor Market Experience, Praeger Publishers Inc, 1978; "Internal-External Attitudes, Sense of Efficacy, and Labor Market Experience," J of Human Resources, 1981; "The Health and Economic Status of Very Early Retirees," Work and Aging, 1983. INT: labor market econ, empl/-trng programs, methodology/statis. ASSN: Philadelphia IRRA, AEA, Gerontological Soc of Amer, Academy of Mgmt. POSITIONS: Dir, Bureau of Econ and Bus Research, 1977, Assoc Prof of Ind Rels, 1977, and since 1983, Prof of Ind Rels, Temple Univ. ADDRESS: 104 Hackney Cir, Wilmington, DE. 19803. 215/787-8193

ANDSTEIN, CLIFF Union. BA 1969, Simon Fraser U; MA 1971, U of Wis. INT: coll barg, arb/med, labor law. ASSN: British Columbia IRRA, Canadian Ind Rels Assn, Pacific Group for Policy Alternatives. POSITIONS: Lecturer, Public Sector Labour Rels, U of Victoria, 1982; Asst General Secretary, 1976, and, since 1978, Dir, Coll Barg and Arbitration, B. C. Government Employees Union, 4911 Canada Way, Burnaby, BC V5G 3W3 Canada. 604/291-9611

ANGELL, H. THOMAS Legal Practice. Angell, Wolney and Lech, 2600 Cadillac Tower, Detroit, MI 48226. 313/964-0234

ANGLE, HAROLD L. Org Beh/Pers. BA 1956, UCLA; MA 1971, San Diego State Coll; PhD 1980 U of Calif-Irvine. PUBL: Labor-Management Relations & Public Agency Effectiveness, (w J. L. Perry), Pergamon Press, 1980. "The Politics of Organizational Boundary Roles in Collective Bargaining," (w J. L. Perry), Academy of Mgmt Rev, 1980, Vol 4; "Bargaining Unit Structure & Organizational Outcomes (w J. L. Perry), Inds Rels, 1981, Vol 20. INT: org beh, ind psychology, coll barg. ASSN: Academy of Mgmt, Amer Psych Assn, Soc for Ind Org Psychology. POSITIONS: Lt Colonel, U.S. Marine Corps, 1956; and (since 1980) Assoc Professor, School of Mgmt, Univ of Minn, 271 19th Ave So, Minneapolis, MN 55455. 612/376--7160

ANNABLE, JAMES E., JR. Bank Economist. AB 1965, Kenyon Coll; PhD 1971, Princeton U. PUBL: The Price of Industrial Labor, 1984; "A Theory of Downward-Rigid Wages and Cyclical Unemployment," Econ Inquiry, 1977; "An Earnings Function for High Level Manpower," Ind Labor Rels Rev, 1973. INT: labor market econ, coll barg, org behavior. ASSN: AEA, Royal Econ Soc, Natl Assn of Bus Economists. POSITIONS: Section Chief, Board of Governors, Federal Reserve, 1974; Deputy Asst Dir, Congressional Budget Office, 1978; (since 1981) Vice Pres, First Chicago Corp, 1214 N Astor St, Chicago, IL 60610.

ANNUNZIATO, FRANK Union. 1873 Chapel St, New Haven, CT 06515. 203/397-2415

ANSELL, SHERMAN DAVID Government, Econ Development. 1965 PhD, U of Wis. INT: empl/trng programs, mgmt/educ, labor market econ. ASSN: Wis IRRA, Amer Soc Mech Engrs, Robotics Intern'l of SME, Amer Solar Energy Soc. POSITION: (since 1972) Energy and Econ Development Consultant, Wis Board Voc Tech and Adult Educ, ADDRESS: 1114 Frisch Rd, Madison, WI 53711. 608/266-3316

ANTCZAK, KEN Bus:Pers/Ind Rels. BA 1976, U of Mich. INT: labor law, health and hosp care, personnel. ASSN: Detroit IRRA, Hospital Pers Admin Assn. POSITIONS: Labor Rels Rep, 1976, Workers Compensation Rep, Chrysler Corp,1980;(since 1980) Employee Rels Mgr, Hutzel Hospital, 4707 St. Antoine, Detroit, MI 48201. 313/494-7015

ANTHONY, CHER Bus:Mgmt/Admin. 7090 North Fruit, #138, Fresno, CA 93711. 209/432-6292

ANTHONY, WILLIAM PHILIP Org Beh/Pers. BBA 1965, MBA 1967, PhD 1971, Ohio State U. PUBL: Managing Your Boss, Amacom, 1984; Management: Competencies and Incompetencies, Addison-Wesley, 1981; Managing Incompetence, Amacom, 1982. INT: empl/trng programs, mgmt/-educ, org beh. ASSN: Academy of Mgmt, Southern Mgmt Assn. POSITION: Prof of Mgmt, College of Business, Florida State Univ, Tallahassee, FL 32306. 904/644-6828

APARICIO, LUIS POSITION: Director, Analisis Laboral, Pablo Bermudez 285 OF, 701 Lima 11 Peru

APPLEBAUM, LEON Econ, Univ Admin. BA 1951, Brooklyn Coll; MA 1955, PhD 1959, U of Wis-Madison. INT: coll barg, labor market econ, labor history. ASSN: AEA. POSITIONS: Assoc Prof of Labor Studies and Econ, Ohio State Univ, 1965; Prof of Econ, 1967, and, currently, Prof of Econ & Chairman, Soc Science Div, Univ of Wis-Parkside, Kenosha, WI 53141. 414/553-2377

ARANOFF, ARTHUR M. Academic: Ind Rels. POSITION: Mgmt Educ Dept IMLR, Rutgers Univ, Clifton Ave, New Brunswick, NJ 08903

AREWAH, PETER JOSEPH OMO Government. PO Box 51618, Falomo Ikoyi, Lagos State, Nigeria

ARMENTI, CARMEN Student. BAIREc 1984, McGill U. INT: coll barg, arb/med, personnel. ASSN: McGill Ind Rels Assn. POSITION: Student, McGill Univ. ADDRESS: 7658 9th Ave, Montreal, PQ H2A 3C3 Canada

ARMIGER, SUSAN S. Acad: Univ Admin. AB 1969, Beaver Coll; MA 1970, Teachers Coll-Columbia U. INT: mgmt/educ, coll barg, arb/med. POSITIONS: Assoc Dean of Coll, 1977, Assoc Dean for Pers and Labor Rels, 1981, and (since 1983) Acting Dean of External Affairs, Labor Rels & Pers, LaGuardia Community College, CUNY, 31-10 Thomson Ave, Long Island City, NY 11101. 212/626-5052

ARMITAGE, G. NELSON Union. POSITION: Organization Specialist, UHPA, 1649 Kalakaua Ave, Honolulu, HI 96826.

ARNDT, CATHERINE C. Bus:Health/Hosp Care. MM 1981, Northwestern U. INT: org beh, mgmt/educ, health & hosp care. ASSN: ASTD. POSITION: (since 1982) Senior Trng Specialist, Univ of Chicago Medical Center, Box 218, 5841 S. Maryland, Chicago, IL 60637. 312/962-1930

ARONIN, LOUIS Arbitration; Acad: Law. BA 1945, Brooklyn Coll; LLB 1960, U of Baltimore. INT: arb/med, coll barg, labor law. ASSN: Wash DC IRRA, NAA, SPIDR, ABA. POSITIONS: Exec Dir, NJ Public Empl Rels Commission, 1968; Deputy Dir, Office of Labor Mgmt Rels, U.S. Civil Service Commission, 1970; and (since 1978) Arbitrator, (self-employed) 200 N Pickett St, Alexandria, VA 22304. 703/370-4512

ARONSON, ROBERT L. Acad: Econ, Ind Rels, Mediation. PhD 1953, Princeton. POSITION: Prof of Labor Econ, School of Ind and Labor Rels, Cornell Univ, Ithaca, NY 14853. 607/257-2646

ASHE, JULIAN L. Arbitration. JC 1951, UCLA. INT: arb/med, ind psychology, intl comparative labor. ASSN: Central Calif IRRA, SPIDR, AAA. POSITIONS: Grand Lodge Rep, Intl Assn of Machinists and Aerospace Workers, 1947; Mediator, FMCS, 1962; and (since 1976) Arbitrator (self-employed) 3731 N Augusta, Fresno CA 93726. 209/226-5970

ASHENFELTER, ORLEY Economics; Consulting. BA 1964, Claremont-McKenna Coll; PhD 1970, Princeton U. PUBL: "Racial Discrimination and Trade Unionism," J of Pol Economy, May-/June, 1972; "Bargaining Theory, Trade Union and Industrial Strike Activity," Am Econ Rev, March 1969; "Models of Arbitrator Behavior: Theory and Evidence," Amer Econ Rev, 1984. INT: labor market econ, income maintenance, arb/med. ASSN: Econometric Soc, AEA, Amer Statis Assn. POSITIONS: Dir, Office of Evaluation, U.S. Dept of Labor, 1972; and (since 1973) Prof of Econ and Dir of Ind Rels Section, Princeton Univ, PO Box 248, Princeton, NJ 08544. 609/452-4040

ASHER, LESTER Legal Practice. BA 1930, JD 1932, U of Chicago. INT: labor law. ASSN: Chicago IRRA. POSITIONS: Chairman & Member, Attorney Regulations & Regulatory Comm, State of Illinois 1973; Chairman, Section of Labor and Employment Law, ABA, 1977, and, since 1951, Sr Partner, Asher, Pavalon, Gittler, Greenfield & Segall Ltd, 2 N LaSalle St, Chicago, IL 60602. 312/263-1500

ASHER, WILLIAM S. Bus:Pers/Ind Rels. B.S. 1950, NYSSILR-Cornell U. INT: coll barg, arb/med. POSITION: (since 1973) Dir, Corporate Ind Rels, Xerox Corp, PO Box 1600, Stamford, CT 06904. 203/329-8700

ASIN, CARLOS GUILLERMO Bus:Pers/Ind Rels, Bus Admin. LRI 1973, Univ of Carabobo-Venezuela. POSITION: Jefe, Dept of Entrenamiento, Y.P. F.B., Casilla 526, Cochabamba, Bolivia.

ASMONDY, ROBERT N. Union. INT: labor law, coll barg, health & hosp care. ASSN: Wis IRRA. POSITION: Bus Mgr, Local #317 IUOE, 3152 S 27th St, Milwaukee, WI 53215. 414/671-3258

ATCHISON, THOMAS JOSEPH Acad: Org Beh/Pers. PhD 1965, U of Wash. PUBL: "Comparable Worth: Issues for the 80's," in Pers Admin, John Wiley, 1984; Management Today, Harcourt Brace, 1978; "Compensation for Work," in Dubin, Work, Organization and Society, 1976. POSITION: Prof of Mgmt, Dept of Mgmt, San Diego State Univ, San Diego, CA 92115. 619/265-6845

ATLAS, CRAIG Student. BA 1980, MLIR 1981, Mich State U. Currently SUNY at Buffalo. ADDRESS: 356 Traverse Blvd, Kenmore, NY 14223. 716/875-7409

ATLESON, JAMES BENJAMIN Acad: Law; Arbitration. BA 1960, JD 1962, Ohio State U; LLM 1964, Stanford U. PUBL: Values and Assumptions in American Labor Law, U of Mass Press, 1983; Collective Bargaining in Private Employment, (co-author) BNA. INT: coll barg, labor history, labor law. ASSN: Western NY IRRA, Union Democracy Assn. POSITION: (since 1964) Prof, Faculty of Law, SUNY, O'Brien Hall, Amherst, NY 14226. 716/636-2381

AUDET, MICHEL Acad: Ind Rels; Consulting. MAIR1982, BAIR 1979, U of Laval. PUBL: Le Comite' patronal-syndical de l'industrie Canadienne des textiles: lecons de l'experience depuis, 1967, 1982; Technologie et emplor: un inventaire des strategies nationales, 1983; "La remuneration des travailleuses de l'industrie du vetement au Quebec; bilan comparatif," 1982. INT: personnel, emp/trng programs, govt labor policy. ASSN: Canadian Ind Rels Assn. POSITIONS: Consultant in Ind Rels, COGERI Inc, 1979; and (since 1982) Substitute Prof, Univ Laval, Dept of Relations Industrielles, Cite Univ, Quebec, G1K 7P4 Canada. 418/656-5940

AUER, HELGA Education. ADDRESS: Josef Moser-Gasse 1, A1170 Vienna, Austria.

AUSSIEKER, BILL Bus Admin, Ind Rels, Org Beh/Pers. BS 1968, MBA 1969, PhD 1974, U of Calif-Berkeley. INT: coll barg, labor market econ, org beh. ASSN: Central Calif IRRA, Academy of Mgmt. POSITION: Prof and Dept Head, Mgmt Dept, Calif Poly State Univ, School of Business, San Luis Obispo, CA 93407. 805/546-1301

AUSTERMILLER, CARL J. Academic: Econ, Ind Rels; Consulting. BS 1961, Kansas State U; MA 1965, Wayne State U. INT: labor market econ, arb/med, coll/barg. ASSN: Detroit IRRA, AEA, AAA. POSITIONS: Visiting Prof, Univ of Guam, 1973; and (since 1968) Chairperson, Dept of Econ, Oakland Community Coll, Farmington Hills, MI 48018. 313/471-7630

AUSTIN, DENNIS GEORGE Labor Rels, Bus:Pers/Ind Rels. BA 1972, U of Mass; JD 1975, Suffolk U Law School. INT: coll barg, labor law, arb/med. ASSN: Boston IRRA, AAA, Mass Bar Assn-Labor Law Committee. POSITIONS: Labor Rels Dir/Counsel, City of Boston 1975, Mgmt Attorney, Murphy, Lamere, Murphy-Braintree, 1981; and (since 1982) Sr. Labor Rels Specialist, Raytheon Co, 141 Spring St, Lexington, MA 02173

AUSTIN, H. MATTSON Consulting. BA 1978, MLIR 1981, Mich State U. INT: arb/med, coll barg, labor law. POSITION: President, Austin, Cullinane & Assoc Inc. 7830 Ducor Ave, Canoga Park, CA 91304. 213/876-4433

AUZENNE, GEORGE R. Acad: Univ Admin. ADDRESS: 3705 Longford Dr, Tallahassee, FL 32308. 904/599-3018

AXELROD, JONATHAN G. Legal Practice. POSITION: Bein, Axelrod & Osborn, 1200 15th St NW #505, Washington DC 20005.

AXON, GARY L. Arbitration. BA 1964, Buena Vista Coll; JD 1966, Drake U. INT: arb/med, coll barg, labor law. ASSN: Natl Academy of Arbitrators, AAA, Oregon State Bar Assn. POSITIONS: Attorney, 1966; Prof of Bus, Southern Ore State College, 1966; and (since 1975) Arbitrator, 1465 Pinecrest Terr, Ashland, OR 97520. 503/488-1573.

AYOUB, EDMUND Union. POSITION: Asst to the President, United Steelworkers of America, 5 Gateway Center, Room 910, Pittsburgh, PA 15222. 412/562-2352

AYRES, RICHARD C. Acad: Bus Admin. Route 12, Box 18, Bowling Green, KY 42101. 501/777-1229

AZAR, ELIAS R. Acad: Student, Econ, Ind Rels. BS 1981, MS 1983, Ind State U. INT: labor market econ, personnel, income maint. ASSN: AEA, Amer Assn of Bus Economists. POSITIONS: Pers Specialist, Bechtel Corp, 1975; Grad Asst (Research), 1982, and, currently, student, Indiana State Univ. ADDRESS: 1320 S 19th St, Terre Haute, IN 47803. 812/232-6311

AZVEDO, ROSS EAMES Academic: Ind Rels. BA 1964, U of Calif-Davis; MS 1966, PhD 1972, Cornell U. POSITION: Ind Rels Center, Univ of Minn, Minneapolis, MN 55455.

AZZAN, CYNTHIA CONWAY Consulting. BGS 1976, Wayne State U; MS 1982, U of Dist of Columbia. PUBL: "A New Beginning: Labor Education in the Graphic Arts Union," Labor Studies J, Winter 1983, vol 7, #3; "Adult Education: A New Threshold of the Labor Movement," Interface, Dept for Professional Empl, AFL-CIO, Summer, 1981; vol 10, #2. INT: labor education, union org/admin, empl/trng programs. ASSN: Wash DC IRRA, Univ & Coll Labor Educ Assn, To Educate the People Consortium. POSITIONS: Ext Program Coordinator, College of Lifelong Learning, Wayne State U, 1974; Program Developer/Trainer, Assoc Consultants Inc, Wash DC, 1979; and (since 1981) Consultant, 332 N Street SW, Washington DC 20024. 202/484-2380

B

BACHMAN, AL Bus:Pers/Ind Rels. BS 1970, Mich State U. INT: org beh, coll barg, arb/med. POSITIONS: Pers Mgr, Auto Specialties Mfg Co,1976; Pers Mgr, St. John's Plant, 1978, and, since 1983, Div Employee Rels Mgr, Federal Mogul, 8111 Middlebelt Rd, Romulus, MI 48174. 313/326-9550

BADELLA, MARSHA ELLEN Bus:Pers/Ind Rels, Bus:Mgmt/Admin. BS 1982, Calif State U-Hayward. INT: coll barg, arb/med, labor law. ASSN: Amer Soc for Trng and Development, ASPA, Amer Mgmt Assn. POSITIONS: Secretary, 1971, Admin Super, 1977, and, since 1983, Ind Rels Rep, Pacific Gas & Electric Co. 2680 Hilton St, Union City, CA 94587. 415/541-6274

BADERSCHNEIDER, JEAN ANN 121 Summerfield Hall, School of Bus, Univ of Kansas, Lawrence KS 66044. 913/864-3117

BAEK, GWANG-GI Student. BA 1977, Sung Kyun Kwan U, Korea; MIM 1981, AGSIM,AZ. Research Asst, & currently, Grad School, UCLA. ADDRESS: Doctoral Office, GSM,UCLA, Los Angeles, CA 90024. 213/824-5062

BAILER, LLOYD HARDING Arbitration; Acad: Ind Rels. BA 1934, MA 1936, Wayne State U; PhD 1943, U of Mich. POSITION: Arbitrator, 645 Walther Way, Los Angeles, CA 90049. 213/472-5896

BAILEY, BART Bus:Pers/Ind Rels. BSME 1966, Purdue U; MBA 1980, Northwestern U. INT: personnel, empl/trng programs, health and hosp care. ASSN: ASPA, Twin Cities Pers Assn. POSITIONS: Mgr, Compensation and Develop, Intl Harvester Co, 1977; President, Iowa Inds Hydraulics, 1980; and (since 1983) Vice Pres, Human Resources, McQuay Inc, 13600 Industrial Pk Blvd, Plymouth, MN 55440. 612/553-5014

BAILEY, THOMAS R. Economics, Ind Rels. AB 1976, Harvard U; PhD 1983, MIT. ADDRESS: 2880 Broadway, 4th Floor, New York, NY 10025. 212/280-2132

BAILEY, WILLIAM R. Government; Acad: Econ. BA 1954, Wesleyan U; MA-PhD 1966, George Washington U. PUBL: "Employer Expenditures for Private Retirement and Insurance Plans," (w A. E. Schwenk) Monthly Labor Rev, July, 1972; "Wage Rate Variation by Size of Establishment," (w A. E. Schwenk) Ind Rels, Spring, 1980; "Compensation Cost Increases," Monthly Labor Rev, June, 1983. INT: labor market econ, coll barg, empl/trng programs. ASSN: Wash DC IRRA, AEA. POSITION: Labor Economist, U.S. Bureau of Labor Statis. ADDRESS: 6613 Sandover Ct, Springfield, VA 22152. 202/523-1508

BAIN, GEORGE SAYERS Academic: Ind Rels. BA 1961, MA 1964, U of Manitoba; DPhil 1968, U of Oxford. PUBL: The Growth of White Collar Unionism, Oxford: Clarendon Press, 1970; Union Growth and the Business Cycle, Oxford:Blackwell, 1976; Profiles of Union Growth, Oxford:Blackwell, 1980. INT: union org, coll barg, arb/med. ASSN: British Univ Ind Res Assn, IIRA, Canadian Ind Rels Assn. POSITIONS: Dir, Ind Rels, Research Unit, 1974, and, since 1979, Prof of Ind Rels, School of Ind & Bus Studies, University of Warwick, Coventry CV4 7AL England. 0203/24011 ext. 2433.

BAIN TREVOR, Acad: Econ, Ind Rels; Arbitration. BA 1953, CUNY; MILR 1957, Cornell; PhD 1964, U of Calif-Berkeley. PUBLS: "German Co-Determination and Employment Adjustments in Steel and Autos," Columbia J of World Bus, Summer,1963; "CETA Prime Sponsor Organization and Performance," IRRA Proceedings, Dec 1981; "Private Sector Labor Relations in the South," Labor Law J, August, 1981. INT: labor market econ, coll barg, empl/trng programs. ASSN: Academy of Mgmt, AEA, SPIDR. POSITIONS: Visiting Assoc Prof, U of Mich, 1967; Visiting Assoc Prof, Queen's Coll, CUNY, 1969; (since 1974) Prof, Grad School of Bus, Univ of Alabama, Box J, University, AL 35486. 205/3485023

BAIRD, WILLIAM M. Acad: Econ. AB 1957, Wittenberg U; MA 1958, PhD 1968, Ohio State U. INT: coll barg, labor history, labor market econ. ASSN: AEA. POSITION: Prof of Econ, College of Wooster, Wooster, OH 44691. 216/-263-2000.

BAIRSTOW, FRANCES Acad: Ind Rels; Arbitration. BS 1920, U of Wis. PUBL: "Employment Security in Civil Aviation; "Collective Bargaining for White Collar Workers," "Inquiry Commission Report on Wider-Based Bargaining." INT: arb/med, coll barg, union org. ASSN: Natl Academy of Arbitrators, SPIDR, Canadian Ind Rels Res Inst. POSITIONS: McGill U, 1960, and, since 1970, Dir, Ind RelsCentre, McGill Univ, Montreal H3A 1G5, Canada. 514/392-3077

BAITSELL, JOHN MORTON Bus: Pers/Ind Rels. POSITION: Mgr, Corp Labor Rels, Mobil Oil Corp, 150 E 42nd St, Room 1056, New York, NY 10017. 212/883-4242

BAKER, HOWE EDWARD Student. ADDRESS: 2437 Amsterdam Rd, Villa Hills, KY 41017. 606/3314464

BAKER, JACKIE B. Bus:Pers/Ind Rels. BA 1968, U of Tex-Arlington. INT: personnel, affirmative action-EEO, empl/trng programs. ASSN: North Tex IRRA, OFCCP Liaison Gr, Plans for Progress Inc. POSITIONS: Contracting Specialist, Gen Servcs Admin, 1971, Compliance Officer, USDL,1972; (since 1981) Mgr, Affirmative Action, Rockwell Intl, PO Box 10462, Dallas, TX 75207. 214/996-7217

BAKHTIARI, PAUL Acad: Ind Rels. ADDRESS: #N-6 Meadow East, Star Route 75, Box 21, Potsdam, NY 13676. 315/265-7093

BAKKEN, GORDON M. Univ. Admin. BA 1966, MS 1967, PhD, 1970, JD 1973, U of Wis. PUBL: The Development of Law on the Rocky Mountain Frontier, 1850-1912; "The Arizona Constitutional Convention of 1910," Ariz State Law J; "Campus Common Law," J of Law and Educ. POSITIONS: Prof of History, 1969, and, since 1974, Dir of Faculty Affairs & Records, Calif State Univ, Fullerton, 800 North State College Blvd, Fullerton, CA 92634. 714/-773-2125

BALANIS, FRANK A. Acad: Ind Rels, Org Beh/Pers; Consulting. MBA 1952, Case Western Reserve U. INT: personnel, org beh, arb/med. ASSN: San Francisco IRRA, Academy of Mgmt, ASPA, ASTD. POSITIONS: Group Dir, Ind Rels, Whitaker Corp, 1978; Dir, Ind Rels, Liquid Air Inc, 1970; and Lecturer, San Francisco State U, School of Bus, 1600 Holloway Ave, San Francisco, CA 94132. 415/469-1508

BALANOFF, THOMAS Union. BA 1972, Ind U; MA-LIR 1974, U of Ill. PUBL: Fire Fighter Mortality Report; "Right to Refuse Imminently Dangerous Work." INT: coll barg, labor educ, union org. POSITIONS: Project Admin, Intl Assn of Fire Fighters, 1974; Asst Research Dir, Allied Ind Workers, 1976; and (since 1979) Dir of Technical Services, United Cement,Lime Gypsum & Allied Workers, 2500 Brickvale Rd, Elk Grove Village, IL 60007. 312/595-5171

BALDWIN, STEPHEN E. Government. BA 1962, MA 1965, PhD 1968, U of Wash. PUBL: "Occupational Wage Determination in the Boston Labor Market," (w J.E. Duggan) N England J of Bus & Econ, 1983; "Occupational Information and Vocational Education," Chapter in The Federal Role in Voc Ed, NCEP Report, #12, 1981; "Wage Levels and Labor Market Tightness," Quart Rev of Econ & Bus, 1978. INT: empl/trng programs, labor market econ, govt labor policy. ASSN: AEA, Western Econ Assn, Soc of Government Economists. POSITIONS: Asst Prof of Econ, Chico State Coll, 1970; Economist, BLS, 1971; and (since 1980) Sr Staff Economist, Natl Commission for Employment Policy, 1522 K St NW, Suite 300, Washington DC 20005. 202/7241571

BALFOUR, G. ALAN Acad: Ind Rels; Arbitration. JD 1969, U of Mich; PhD 1975, Mich State U. PUBL: Collective Bargaining in State and Local Government, BNA, 1984; "The Effectiveness of No Strike Laws for Public School Teachers;" "Chaos in Union Recognition Procedures." INT: coll barg, arb/med, labor history. ASSN: Central Florida IRRA. POSITIONS: Research Dir, Advisory Empl Rels Committee, State of Mich, 1973; Asst Prof, U of Okla, 1974; and (since 1980) Assoc Prof, U of South Florida, Coll of Bus Admin. ADDRESS: 13704 Sweetwater Cove, Lutz, FL 33549. 813/974-4155

BALK, MADELINE Legal Practice. 405 Lexington Ave, NY 10017. 212/682-5327

BALL, EDGAR L. Union. BBA 1948, U of Tex, LLB 1951, S Tex Coll of Law. POSITION: Dist 37 Dir, United Steelworkers of Amer, 10202 E Freeway Dr 104, Houston, TX 77029. 713/626-1141

BALLANTINE, JOHN WINTHROP Econ, Bus Admin, Ind Rels. PhD 1955, Harvard U. PUBL: The Human Side of Economics, Mimes, Madison, WI, 1973; "Using Labor Market Information to Evaluate Industrial Performance," J of Econ Issues, Dec 1983; "America's Small Businesses: Their Competitive Performance and Financial Structures," Beatley Coll, Waltham MA Proceedings, 1983. ASSN: AEA, Assn for Evaluating Econ, Assn for Org Econ. POSITIONS: Labor Mediator, NY State Bd of Mediation, 1949; Dir, Ind Rels, Baldwin-Ehret-Hill Inc, 1955; and (since 1963) Assoc Prof, Stevens Inst, Castle Point P.O., Hoboken, NJ 07030. 201/420-5384

BALLON, ROBERT JEAN Acad: Intl Bus, Bus Admin, Ind Rels. BA 1941, U of Louvain (Belgium); Lic in Theology 1955, Montreal; MA 1957, Catholic U. PUBL: The Japanese Employee, Tokyo: Tuttle, 1969; Foreign Investment and Japan, Tokyo:Kodansha, 1972; Financial Reporting in Japan, Tokyo: Kodansha, 1976. INT: personnel, mgmt/educ, ind sociology. ASSN: Japan Ind Rels Res Assn, Japan Mgmt Res Assn, European Found for Mgmt Develop.

POSITIONS: Socio-Econ Inst, 1970, Dir, Intl Mgmt Develop Seminars, 1981, and (since 1963) Prof, Sophia Univ, 4 Yonbancho, Chiyoda-ku, Tokyo 102, Japan.

BALOG, JULIUS JR. Government, Arbitration; Acad: Econ. AB 1960, Oberlin Coll; AM 1968, Ind U. INT: coll barg, arb/med, govt labor policy. ASSN: Wash DC IRRA, Naval Reserve Assn, Foreign Serv Impasse Dispute Panel. POSITIONS: Supervisory Ind Rels Specialist, USDL, 1974; (since 1983) Sr. Ind Rels Advisor, Labor-Mgmt Services, Office of Labor Mgmt Rels Servcs. ADDRESS: 12804 Cedarbrook Lane, Laurel, MD 20811. 202/523-6475

BAMBER. GREG J. Acad: Ind Rels, Bus Admin; Arbitration. BSc 1971, U of Manchester; PhD. PUBL: Technological Change and Industrial Relations: An International Symposium, Special Issue of Bull of Comparative Labour Rels, Vol 12, 1983, Kluwer, Holland; Managers in Unions: a Study of Union Growth and Industrial Relations in the Steel Industry, CUP Cambridge, 1984. INT: intl comparative labor, arb/med, org beh. ASSN: IIRA, British Univ Ind Rels Assn, Ind Rels Soc (Australia). POSITIONS: Ind Rels Officer, Commission on Ind Rels, London, 1971; Regional Secretary, Steel Industry Mgmt Assn, UK, 1975; and (since 1979) Dir Research/Ind Rels Lecturer, DUBS/Ind Rels Group, Univ of Durham, Durham City, DM1 3LB, England. 0385 41919

BANAS, PAUL A. Bus:Pers/Ind Rels. PhD 1964, U of Minn. POSITION: Manager, Pers Research, Ford Motor Co, Room 431, American Rd/World Hdqtr, Dearborn, MI 48121. 313/322-6490

BANCROFT, KAREN LOW Government. POSITION: Human Resource Director, Utah Transit Authority, PO Box 31810, Salt Lake City, UT 84131. 801/262-5626

BANKS, ROBERT FREDERICK Acad: Univ. Admin, Ind Rels. BA 1958, Washington & Lee U; PhD 1965, London School of Econ and Pol Sci. PUBL: Multinationals, Unions and Industrial Relations in Industrialized Countries, (w J. Stieber) NYSSILR, 1977; "British Collective Bargaining: The Challenges of the 1970's," Relations Industrielles, July 1971; "Labor Education Role in Britain," Ind Rels, Feb 1966. INT: intl comparative labor, coll barg, labor educ. ASSN: Coll and Univ Pers Assn. POSITIONS: Asst Prof, Labor and Ind Rels, 1967, Dean, James Madison Coll, 1972, and, since 1979, Asst Provost, Academic Pers Admin, Mich State Univ, East Lansing, MI 48824. 517/353-5300

BANNISTER, R SCOTT Bus:Pers/Ind Rels. BS 1970, U of Ore. INT: ind psychology, org beh, methodology/statis. POSITION: Director-Pers, Union Pacific System, 1416 Dodge St, Omaha, NB 68179. 402/271-3996

BARBASH, JACK Acad: Econ, Ind Rels. BS 1932, MS 1937, NYU. PUBL: Elements of Industrial Relations; Trade Unions and National Economic Policy; "Which Work Ethic?" INT: union org, coll barg, intl comparative labor. ASSN: Wis IRRA, Assn for Evolutionary Econ. POSITIONS: Staff Dir, US Senate Sub Committee on Labor/Labor Mgmt Rels, 1949; Res/Educ Dir, Ind Union Dept, AFL-CIO, 1955; and (since 1957) Prof of Econ, currently Bascom Prof of Economics and IR (Emeritus), Univ of Wis. ADDRESS: 1836 Keyes Avenue, Madison, WI 53711. 608/262-7977

BARBASH, JOSEPH Legal Practice. AB 1941, Rutgers U; LLB 1948, Harvard U. POSITION: (since 1950) Debevoise & Plimpton, 875 3rd Ave, New York, NY 10022. 212/909-6483

BARCLAY, LIZABETH ANN Acad: Org Beh/Pers, Ind Rels. BA 1971, Mich State U; MS 1976, Eastern Mich U; PhD 1981, Wayne State U. PUBL: "Social Learning Theory: A Framework for Discrimination Research," Academy of Mgmt Rev, 1982,7,4,587-594; "Student Attitudes Toward Faculty Strikes in Higher Educ," J of Coll Negotiations in the Public Sector, 1982, 11, 4, 373-381 (w A. Inn & H. Rosen.) INT: org beh, ind psychology, personnel. ASSN: Amer Psych Assn, Academy of Mgmt. POSITION: Asst Prof of Mgt, School of Econ and Mgt. Oakland Univ, Rochester, MI 48063. 313/377-4002

BARCZYK, CASIMIR C. Student. BS 1975, Loyola of Chicago, MUPP 1982, U of Ill. INT: org beh, personnel, health & hosp care. ASSN: LIRA, Champaign, Acad of Mgmt, Amer Health Planning Assn, Amer Hosp Assn. POSITIONS: Office Mgr, Rush-Presbyterian-St. Lukes's Medical Center, 1976, Dir of Pers and Res, Incomm Intl, 1981; and, since 1982, Grad Res Asst, U of Ill-UC, and, since 1983, Instructor, Ill State Univ. ADDRESS: 107 E White, #2, Champaign, IL 61820. 217/333-0984

BARGER, MICHAEL Bus:Pers/Ind Rels. BA 1977, Hobart Coll, NY; MS 1979, Stevens Inst of Tech. INT: coll barg, ind psych, personnel. ASSN: Houston IRRA. POSITIONS: Res Consultant, Pers Res, Metropolitan Life, 1978; Pers Specialist, 1979, and, since 1982, Pers Assoc, General Foods, Corp, 3900 Harrisburg, Houston, TX 77001. 713/228-9501

BARGMANN, JEANNE McCARRICH Union. BA 1975, U of San Francisco; MLIR Mich State U. PUBL: "Roots of Public Support for Labor Education," (w R. Peters) Labor Studies J, Fall,-1976. INT: coll barg, union, arb/med. ASSN: Coalition of Labor Union Women, Salaried Professional Women's Committee, Dept for Professional Employees, AFL-CIO, Alpha Sigma Nu. POSITIONS: Grad Asst, School of Labor & Ind Rels, Mich State U, 1975; Bus Rep, AFTRA, AFL-CIO, 1978; and (since 1979) Intl Rep, Natl Assoc of Broadcast Empl & Tech, AFL-CIO, 126 Hyde St, Suite C, San Francisco, CA 94102. 415/771-5350

BARGMANN, RUSSELL M., JR. Union. BA 1975, U of Calif-Davis; MLIR 1978, Mich State U. ADDRESS: 160 Walnut Ct, Hercules, CA 94547. 415/820-4673

BARKEY, FRED A. Acad: Bus Admin/Mgmt. 4930 Dempsey Rd, Charleston, WV 25313. 304/-768-9711

BARKIN, SOLOMON Acad: Econ; Arbitration. BS 1928, CCNY; MA 1929, Columbia. PUBL: Labor Militancy and Its Consequences, 2nd Edition, 1983, Prager Publ; Decline of the Labor Movement and What Can Be Done About It, Center for Study of Dem Inst, Santa Barbara, 1961. INT: coll barg, intl comparative labor, labor history. ASSN: Assn for Evolutionary Econ. POSITIONS: Prof of Econ, Univ of Mass; and(since 1978) Retired. ADDRESS: 49 Long Hill Rd, Leverett, MA 01054.

BARLOW, ROBERT F. Acad: Econ. Whittemore School Bus and Econ, McConnell Hall, Univ of New Hampshire, Durham, NH 03824. 603/868-7145

BARNES, ANN W. Bus:Ind Rels. BS 1976, NYSSILR, Cornell U. POSITION: Ind Rels, CBS Inc, 51 W 52nd St, New York, NY 10019. 212/975-5512

BARNES, JERRY B. Bus:Pers/Ind Rels. BS 1963, Va Polytech Inst. INT: abr/med, coll barg, labor law. ASSN: Atlanta IRRA. POSITION: (since 1979) Division Mgr, Southern Bell Tel & Tel Co, 675 W. Peachtree, 42L69, Atlanta, GA 30375. 404/529-7133

BARNES, RICHARD L. Legal Practice. BA 1962, MB 1964, U of Okla. INT: labor law, arb/-med, mgmt/educ. ASSN: ABA Okla Bar Assn, AMA. POSITIONS: Attorney, Hall, Estill, Hardwick et al, 1970; and (since 1973) Sr Member, Nichols & Wolfe Inc, 124 E 4th, Suite 400, Tulsa, OK 74103. 918/584-5182

BARNES, ROBERT DAVID Acad: Student, Ind Rels; Bus/Mgmt/Educ. BS 1979, MS 1980, WV U. INT: arb/med, mgmt/educ, personnel. ASSN: WV IRRA, Sigma Delta Chi. POSITIONS: Mgr, Better Times Weekly Publ Co; Mgmt Analyst, Concorde Corp; and, currently, Student full time on doctorate. ADDRESS: PO Box 3148, Morgantown, WV 26503. 304/594-2676

BARNES, SCOTT D. Acad: Econ. BA 1966, Ripon Coll; MACT 1969, U of Tenn. INT: coll barg, personnel, arb/med. ASSN: Central NY IRRA, NYS Econ Assn. POSITIONS: Instructor of Econ, Glenville State College, WV, 1968; and (since 1970) Prof of Bus & Soc Sci, Cayuga Community Coll, Auburn, NY 13021. 315/255-1743.

BARNHILL, HELEN Consulting. INT: mgmt/-educ, union org, org beh. ASSN: Wis IRRA, ASPA, Intl Assn of Pers Women, Amer Mgmt Assn. POSITION: (since 1973) President, Barnhill Hayes, Inc, 788 N Jefferson St, Milwaukee, WI 53202. 414/276-4554

BARNUM, DAROLD T. Econ: Bus Admin; Consulting. BBA 1966, U of Tex-Arlington; MBA 1970, PhD 1972, U of Penn. PUBL: "Influencing the Electorate: Experience with Referenda on Public Employee Bargaining," (w I. B. Helburn) Ind and Labor Rels Rev, Vol 35, #3, April, 1982,pp 330-342; "Toward Valid Measures of Public Sector Productivity: Performance Indicators in Urban Transit," (w J. Gleason) Mgmt Science, Vol 28, #4, April,1982) pp 379-386; From Private Sector to Public Sector: Labor Relations in Urban Mass Transit, Bloomington, Ind U Inst for Urban Transportation, 1983 (second printing). INT: Strategic Mgmt, coll barg, methodology/-statis. ASSN: Amer Inst for Decision Sciences, Transportation Research Board. POSITIONS: Inst/Asst Prof of Econ, SUNY-Brockport, 1971; Asst/Assoc Prof of Mgmt, Tex Tech Univ, 1973; and (since 1976) Prof of Mgmt, Ind University Northwest, 3400 Broadway, Gary, IN 46408. 219/980-6868

BAROCCI, THOMAS ANDRES Academic: Bus Admin. BS 1968, MA 1969, PhD 1972, U of Wis-Madison. POSITION: Assoc Prof, MIT, Sloan School of Mgmt E52-443B, Cambridge, MA 02139. 617/253-5227

BARONE, DALE V. Government. ADDRESS: 3880 Rodman St NW B #212, Washington DC, 20016.

BARR, KEVIN A. Bus:Pers/Ind Rels. BSILR 1981, Cornell. INT: personnel, empl/trng programs, mgmt/educ. POSITIONS: Human Resource Trainee, 1981, Mgr, External Recruiting, 1982, and, since 1983, Empl Mgr, Chase Manhatten Bank. ADDRESS: 85 Barrymore Blvd, Franklin Square, NY 11010. 212/676-4925

BARR, S. William Bus:Pers/Ind Rels. BA 1961, Long Island U; JSD 1964, Fordham U. INT: labor law, coll barg, health & hosp care. ASSN: NYC Bar Assn, NYS Bar Assn (Labor Law Committee). POSITIONS: Ind Rels/EEO Counsel, Gulf & Western Ind Inc, 1980; Dir-Labor Rels/EEO, 1983, and (since 1983), Director-Labor Rels/EEO, The Kendall Co, One Federal St, PO Box #10, Boston, MA 02101. 617/423-2000 ext 2840

BARRES, SAMUEL LAWRENCE BS 1949, MA 1951, Boston U; PhD 1967, MIT-Sloan School. INT: ind psych, org beh, personnel. ASSN: ASPA, Amer Psych Assn, Intl Assoc of Applied Psych. POSITIONS: Dir of Pers and Educ Services, Faulkner Hosp,1971, Licensed Psychologist,(independent practice), Retired. ADDRESS: 132 Sargent St, Newton, MA 02158. 617/332-8214

BARRETT, BRIAN COLIN Acad: Ind Rels; Arbitration, Consulting. BA 1962, U of Bristol-England;. MSc 1967, London School of Econ, U of London. PUBL: Industrial Relations and the Wider Society, Collier MacMillan, 1975; "Approaches to the Study of Industrial Relations," Open Univ Course Unit, 1976; "Attitudes Towards Training in the Hotel Industry," HCIMA J Sept, 1979. INT: coll barg, arb/med, intl comparative labor. ASSN: Inst of Pers Mgmt (Great Britain), Ind Law Soc (Great Britain), British Univ Ind Rels Assn. POSITIONS: (since 1981) Dir of Studies M.Sc Ind Rels, School of Mgmt, Univ of Bath, Claverton Down, Bath BA2 7A7, England. Phone: Bath 61244 Ext 690.

BARRETT, EAMONN Academic: Bus Admin. ADDRESS: 1425 Monterey Blvd, San Francisco, CA 94127 415-666-6236

BARRETT, JEROME T. Acad: Ind Rels; Consulting, Arbitration. BA 1959, Coll of St. Thomas; MA 1963, U of Minn; EdD 1983, George Washington U. PUBL: "The Psychology of Mediation," SPIDR, Occasional Paper #83-1, 1983; "Helping Labor & Mgmt See & Solve Problems," Monthly Labor Rev, Sept 1982; "FMCS Role In Age Discrimination Complaints: New Uses of Mediation," Labor Law J, Nov, 1981. INT: coll barg, arb/med, empl/trng programs. ASSN: Cincinnati IRRA, SPIDR, ASTD. POSITIONS: Chief Div Publ Empl Labor Rels, USDL, 1970; Assoc Dir Office of Mediation, FMCS, 1973; and (since 1982) Assoc Prof and Dir Ind and Labor Rels, Northern Kentucky Univ, Highland Heights, KY 41076. 606-781-6161

BARRIERE, LIONEL F. Consulting. BS 1957, Cornell U. INT: coll barg, arb/med, personnel. ADDRESS: PO Box 357, Aylmer, Quebec J9H 5E7, Canada.

BARRINGTON, KAREN Arbitration. BS/BA 1975, Lowell Tech Inst. INT: arb/med. ASSN: Conn Valley IRRA, Hartford Womens Network, SPIDR. POSITION: Regional Dir, AAA, 2 Hartford SQ W, Hartford, CT 06106. 203/278-5000

BARRON, PAUL Acad: Law; Arbitration. BA 1965, U of Pittsburgh; JD 1968, Univ of Penna. PUBL: "A Theory of Protected Employer Rights: A Revisionist Analysis of the Supreme Court's Interpretation of The National Labor Rels Act," 59 Tax Law Rev, 421, 1981. INT:

labor law, arb/med, coll barg. ASSN: AAA, ABA. POSITIONS: Asst Prof, Wharton School, U of Penna, 1970; and (since 1976) Prof, Tulane Law School, 6801 Freret St, New Orleans, LA 70118. 504/865-5989

BARROWS, DAVID WAYNE Bus: Pers/Ind Rels. BA 1963, MA 1969, U of Detroit. INT: coll barg, labor law, arb,med. ASSN: Cincinnati IRRA, ASPA. POSITIONS: Mgr, Pers/Empl Rels, Clarksville-Montgomery Cty(TN), 1979; Empl Rels Rep, 1982, and since 1983, Mgr, Empl Rels, Mead Corp, Containers Div, 5533 Fair Lane, Cinicnnati, OH 45227. 513/271-8100

BARRY, JOSEPH CLEMENT Arbitration. AB 1937, JD 1947, MA 1957, Boston Coll. INT: arb/med, labor law, intl comparative labor. ASSN: Boston IRRA, IIRA, Mass Bar Assn, AAA. POSITIONS: Senior Examiner, NLRB, 1948; (since 1980) Arbitrator (Labor Mgmt-self employed), 12 Atlantis St, West Roxbury, MA 02132. 617/325-4006

BARSOTTI, FRANK Bus/Ind Rels/Pers. POSITION: Sr. Pers Rep, Hewlett Packard, PO Box 69, Marysville, WA 98270. 206/335-2023

BARTAREAU, EARL Bus:Pers/Ind Rels. BA 1938, Culver Stockton Coll; MBA 1945, Wash U. INT: coll barg, arb/med, labor law. ASSN: Gateway IRRA, ASPA, Ind Rels Assn of Greater St. Louis, East Side Ind Rels Assn. POSITIONS: Pers Dir, Natl Rejectors Inc - (UML),1945; Ind Rels Mgr, East Alton, 1967, and, since 1967, Ind Rels Mgr, Olin Corp, Olin Works, Shamrock Rd, East Alton, IL 62024. 618/258-2945

BARTH, MICHAEL CARL Consulting. BA 1962, SUNY; MA 1964, U of Ill; PhD 1972, CUNY. PUBL: Toward An Effective Income Support System; Greenhouse Effect and Sea Level Rise; "Market Effects of a Wage Subsidy," ILRR, 1974. INT: empl/trng programs, income maint, labor market econ. ASSN: AEA. POSITIONS: Visiting Asst Prof of Econ, 1975; Dept Asst Sec, HHS, 1976; and (since 1980) Principal, ICF Inc-Wash DC. ADDRESS: 3818 Military Rd NW, Washington DC 20016. 202/862-1100

BARTON, DAVID R. Bus:Mgmt/Admin, Bus:-Pers/Ind Rels; Acad: Econ. BA 1973, U of Mich; MA 1975, MLIR 1976, Mich State U. PUBL: "The Impact of House Staff Unionization," Mich Medicine, Vol 80, #26, Sept 1981. pp. 485-486, "Arbitration and the Rights of Mentally Handicapped Workers," Monthly Labor Rev, Vol 103, #4, April, 1980, pp 41-47. INT: health & hosp care, coll barg, labor law. ASSN: Amer Mgmt Assn, Mich Hosp Pers Dir Assn, Intl Pers Mgmt Assn. POSITION: Asst to the Dir, Hurley Medical Center, ADDRESS: 1026 Prospect, Flint, MI 48503. 313/257-9000

BARTOSIC, FLORIAN Acad: Univ Admin, Law; Arbitration. BA 1948, Pontifical Coll Josephinum; BCL 1956, Coll of William and Mary; LLM 1957, Yale Law School. PUBL: "Labor Myth in the Supreme Court, 1981 Term: A Plea for Realistic and Coherent Theory," (w Minda), 30 UCLA L Rev, 271, 1982; "Union Fiduciaries, Attorneys and Conflicts of Interest," (w Minda), 15 UC Davis L Rev 227, 1981; Labor Relations Law in the Private Sector, (w Hartley), 1977. INT: labor law, arb/med, intl comparative law. ASSN: Northern Calif IRRA, AAA, SPIDR, Amer Law Inst. POSITIONS: Council, Intl Brotherhood of Teamster, 1959; Prof of Law, Wayne State Univ, 1971; and (since 1980) Dean and Prof of Law, U.C. Davis School of Law, Davis, CA 95616. 916/752-0243

BARTTER, NANCY ELLEN Student. BS 1979, Ohio State U. INT: ind sociol, govt labor policy, union org/admin. ASSN: U of Ill-LIRA. POSITIONS: Weatherization Coop Dir and Organizer, Citizen/Labor Energy Coalition, 1979; Dir, Ohio Public Interest Res Group, 1981; and (since 1983) Research Asst, ILIR-U of Ill, 504 E Armory, Champaign, IL 61820. 217/333-0984

BASIL, THOMAS ANTHONY Consulting, Arbitration; Acad: Ind Rels. BA 1962 Wheeling Coll; MA 1964, Marquette U-Milw. INT: coll barg, arb/med, personnel. ASSN: Northeastern Mich IRRA, AAA, Mich Negotiation Assn, Assn of Educational Negotiators. POSITIONS: Labor Rels Supr, Saginaw Malleable Iron, GMC, 1965; Consultant, 1969, and, since 1979, President, Luce, Basil and Collins, Inc, 1115 N Center, Saginaw, MI 48603. 517/793-6462

BASSEN, HAROLD R. Employee Benefit Plans, Arbitration. BA 1939, CCNY; LLB 1955, New York U. PUBL: "Liability of the Decision Maker," Textbook for Employee Benefit Plan Trustees, Admin, & Advisors, vol 19, Annual Proc, Intl Found of Employee Benefit Plans. INT: jointly trusteed empl benefit plans, coll-barg, arb/med. ASSN: ABA. POSITIONS: Mediator, Labor Disputes, NYC Dept of Labor, 1955; currently, Wages & Ind Rels Committee of the Bus Res Advisory Committee, BLS-USDL, and, since 1961, Lawyer, 211 E 43rd St, New York, NY 10017. 212/697-5551

BASSEN, NED H. Legal Practice, (rep mgmt). BS 1970, JD 1973, Cornell U. PUBL: "The Effect of Strikes Upon Vacations," 57 Cornell Law Rev 633, 1972. INT: labor law, arb/med, coll barg. ASSN: ABA & NY Bar Assn-Labor Law Section. POSITION: Partner, Kelley, Drye and Warren, 101 Park Ave, New York, NY 10178. 212/808-7837

BATES, CHARLES W. Bus:Pers/Ind Rels; Acad: Student, BA 1975, MLIR 1977, Mich State U; JD 1984, William Mitchell Coll of Law. INT: personnel, labor law, empl/trn programs. ASSN: ASPA, Twin Cities Pers Assn, ABA. POSITIONS: Asst Plant Pers Mgr, 1980, Pers Mgr, Marketing, 1981, and, since 1982, Pers Mgr, Consumer Foods Marketing Div, General Mills, Inc. ADDRESS: 3905 Lancaster Lane, N, Apt #325, Plymouth, MN 55441. 612/544-9882

BATES, CHRISTOPHER M. Government. BA 1976, U of the Pacific; MA Johns Hopkins U. PUBL: "Fel Pro: Portrait of a Successful Exporter," BusAmer J, June 1982. INT: labor market econ, personnel, coll barg. ASSN: Wash DC IRRA, ASPA. POSITIONS: Legislative Aide, U. S. House of Rep, Office of Rep. James Leach, 1977, Economist, USDL, 1978, and, since 1981, International Economist, U. S. Dept of Commerce-Wash DC. ADDRESS: 3907 Larchwood Rd, Falls Church, VA 22041. 202/377-1419

BAU, FREDERICK J. Government. BA 1969, Marquette U. INT: coll barg, arb/med, labor law. ASSN: Wisconsin IRRA, Natl Public Employer Labor Rels Assn, Wis Public Employer Labor Rels Assn, Municipal Empl Assn of Wis. POSITIONS: Labor Rels Analyst, Dept of Labor Rels, 1978, and, since 1980, Labor Rels Specialist, Div of Labor Rels, City of

Milwaukee, 200 E Wells St, Room 701-A, Milwaukee, WI 53202. 414/278-2356

BAUER, SCOTT C. Student. BS 1981, MS 1983,NYSSILR, Cornell U. INT: org beh, coll barg, methodology/statis. ADDRESS: 600 Warren Rd #2-2F, Ithaca, NY 14850.

BAUM, JEFFREY Bus Admin. MBA 1974, U of Chicago. INT: personnel, coll barg, arb/-med. POSITIONS: Asst Dir for Planning, NC Div of Mental Health Services, 1975; (since 1979) Lecturer, Dept of Econ and Bus, State Univ College at Oneonta. ADDRESS: 22 Church St, Oneonta, NY 13820. 607/431-3189

BAUMAN, ALVIN Government. BA 1955, New York U; MA-ILR 1957, U of Ill. INT: coll barg, govt labor policy, labor market econ. ASSN: Wash DC IRRA. POSITION: Chief, Div of Developments in Labor-Mgmt Rels, BLS-Wash DC. ADDRESS: 12508 Stable House Court, Potomac, MD 20854. 202/523-1143

BAUMAN, SUSAN J. Legal Practice. MS & JD, 1981, U of Wis-Madison. PUBL: "Limitations on Final Offer Proposals," Labor Law J, Vol 33, 1982. INT: labor law, coll barg, arb/med. ASSN: ABA, Wis Bar Assn, Wis Ind Rels Alumni Assn. POSITION: Attorney, Thomas, Parsons, Schaefer & Bauman, S.C. ADDRESS: 4809 Hillview Terr, Madison, WI 53711. 608/255-4440

BAUMANN, CHARLES A. Bus:Pers/Ind Rels. BS 1949, UW-Madison. INT: coll barg, personnel, empl/trng programs. ASSN: Wis IRRA, ASPA, Labor Policy Assn, Wis Assn of Manufacturers and Commerce. POSITIONS: Pers Mgr, Granite,IL Plant, 1969, Dir, Ind Res, Automotive Div, 1973, and, since 1981, Vice Pres, Human Resources, A. O. Smith Corp, PO Box 584, Milwaukee, WI 53201. 414/-447-3945

BAUSINGER, KENNETH E. Government. BA 1967, Penn State. INT: govt labor policy, arb/med, mgmt/educ. ASSN: Harrisburg Area IRRA, Intl Pers Mgmt Assn. POSITION: Labor Rels Rep, PA Dept of Transportation, 805 Transportation & Safety Bldg, Harrisburg, PA 17120. 717/787-8056

BAZERMAN, MAX H. Ind Rels, Org Beh/Pers, Psychology. BSE 1976, Wharton School, U of Penna; PhD 1979, Carnegie Mellon U. PUBL: Negotiations in Organizations, Sage, 1983; "The Role of Perspective Training Ability in Negotiating Under Different Forms of Arbitration," ILRR, 1983; "A Critical Look At the Rationality of Negotiator Judgement," American Behavioral Scientist, 1983. INT: org beh, coll barg, arb/med. ASSN: APA, Academy of Mgmt. POSITIONS: Asst Prof, U of Tex-Austin, 1979; Asst Prof, B.U., 1981; and (since 1983) Asst Prof, E52-562 Sloan, MIT, Cambridge, MA 02139. 617/253-3638

BEACH, DALE STUART Ind Rels, Org Beh/-Pers, Bus Admin. BS & MSILR 1952, Cornell U. PUBL: Personnel: The Management of People at Work, 4th Ed, Macmillan 1980; Managing People at Work: Readings in Personnel, 3rd Ed, Macmillan, 1980. INT: arb/med, personnel, mgmt/educ. ASSN: NY Capital Dist IRRA, Academy of Mgmt, AAA, AAUP. POSITION: (since 1954) Prof, School of Mgmt, Rennsselaer Polytech Inst. ADDRESS: 22 Caroline St, Latham, NY 12110. 518/266-6768

BEADLES, N.A. Arbitration, Consulting; Acad: Econ. PhD 1964, Harvard U. INT: arb/-med, intl comparative labor, labor law. ASSN: S.E. IRRA, AAUP, AEA, SPIDR. POSITION: Prof of Econ, Coll of Bus, Univ of Georgia, Athens, GA 30602. 404/542-1311

BEATY, JOHN R. Bus: Pers/Ind Rels. POSITION: Pers Mgr, Dresser Ind P & M Mfg Div, PO Box 1106, Dallas, TX 75221. 214/421-4101

BEATY, JOHN WILLIAM Government. POSITION: Area Administrator, LMSA, USDL, 6 South 504 Millcreek Lane, Naperville, IL 60540. 312/353-7264

BEAUDIN, BRIAN V. Prof Assn. INT: labor law, arb/med, govt labor policy. ASSN: Connecticut Valley IRRA. POSITION: (since 1981) Secretary & Dir of Mgmt Educ, Manufacturers Assn of Hartford County, 80 S Main St, West Hartford, CT 06107. 203/521-4800

BEAUMONT, PHILLIP B. Acad: Ind Rels. BEcon 1971, MEcon 1973, Monash U,Australia; PhD 1976, Glasgow U, Scotland. PUBL: Safety at Work and the Unions, HELM, London, 1983; "Third Party Conciliation and Trade Union Recognition," Relations Industrielles, #4, 1982; "Egalitarian Wage Structures and the Public Sector in Britain," J of Coll Negotiations in the Public Sector, #4, 1982. INT: coll barg, union org/admn personnel. ASSN: British Univ Ind Rels Assn. POSITIONS: Res Fellow, 1976, Lecturer, Ind Rels, 1978, and, since 1983, Sr Lecturer, Ind Rels, Dept of Social and Econ Res, Univ of Glasgow, Adam Smith Bldg, Glasgow, Scotland.

BEAUMONT, RICHARD A. Bus:Mgmt/Admin, Consulting. AB 1951, UCLA; MA 1956, U of Hawaii. INT: org beh, coll barg, intl comparative labor. POSITION: President, Organization Resources Counselors Inc, 1211 Ave of the Americas, NY. ADDRESS: PO Box 535, Sharon, CT 06069. 212/719-3400

BECKER, BRIAN Acad: Ind Rels. PhD 1977, U of Wis-Madison. PUBL: The Impact of Collective Bargaining on Hospitals, (co-author) Praeger,1979; "The Long Run Effects of Job Changes and Unemployment Among Male Teenagers," (w S. Hills), JHR 1983; "Sex Discrimination in the Promotion Process," (w C. Olson), ILRR, 1983. INT: labor market econ, coll barg, methodology/statis. POSITIONS: Asst Prof, 1977, and, since 1983, Assoc Prof, School of Mgmt, SUNY-Buffalo. ADDRESS: 33 Howard, Williamsville, NY. 14221. 716/831-3327

BECKER, JOHN P. Government. AB 1958, Brown U; MA 1971, Boston U. INT: intl comparative labor, labor history. POSITION: Labor-Attache, American Embassy Vienna, c/o Dept of State, Washington DC 20520.

BECKLES, LIONEL Bus/Mgmt. POSITION: Pers Mgr, Trinidad Home Developers, 27 Pembroke St, PO Box 544, Port of Spain, Trinidad, West Indies.

BECKMAN, DAVID L. Arbitration. ADDRESS: 517 Hurstbourne Park, Louisville, KY 40222. 502/426-5305

BEDELL, WILLARD R. Consulting. INT: coll barg, arb/med, labor market econ. ASSN: Wash DC IRRA. POSITIONS: VP, Labor Rels, Kroger Co, 1950; and (since 1977) Chairman,

Joint Labor-Mgmt Committee, Retail Food-Wash DC. ADDRESS: 1101 S. Arlington Ridge, Arlington, VA 22202. 202/331-0950

BEDIKIAN, MARY Arbitration. POSITION: American Arbitration Assn, Ford Bldg, 10th Floor, Detroit, MI 48226.

BEE, PETER A. Legal Practice. JD 1976, St. John's U, NY. INT: labor law, coll barg, govt labor policy. ASSN: Long Island IRRA, Nassau Cty Bar Assn-Labor Law Committee, NYS Public Empl Labor Rels Assn. POSITIONS: Deputy Cty Attorney, County of Nassau, 1977; and (since 1980) Partner, Bee and DeAngelis, 170 Old Country Rd, Mineola, NY 11501. 516/746-5599

BEER, RICHARD Acad: Student, Ind Rels. INT: coll barg, govt labor policy, intl comparative labor. POSITION: Student, McGill Univ. ADDRESS: 7514 Guelph, Cote St. Luc, PQ H4W 1H3 Canada.

BEGIN, JAMES P. Acad: Ind Rels, Univ Admin; Arbitration. BS 1967, MS 1965, PhD 1969, Purdue U. PUBL: The Practice of Collective Bargaining; Academics On Strike; Academic Bargaining - Origins and Growth. INT: coll barg, IR systems theory, arb/med. ASSN: New Brunswick IRRA, Natl Academy of Arbitrators, Academy of Mgmt, SPIDR. POSITION: Prof and Dir, Inst of Mgmt and Labor Rels, Rutgers Univ, Ryders Lane, New Brunswick, NJ 08903. 201/932-8851

BEGLEY, CONSTANCE Bus:Pers/Ind Rels. BS 1978, East Tenn U. INT: personnel, empl/trng programs, mgmt/educ. ASSN: Orange Cty IRRA, Los Angeles Basin Equal Opportunity League, AAUW. POSITIONS: Mgr, Empl Rels, Thomsen Equip Co, 1978, and (since 1981) Supervisor, Empl Rels, Byron Jackson Pump/Borg Warner. ADDRESS: 8992 Friesland Dr, Huntington Beach, CA 92647. 213/587-6171

BEHMAN, SARA Acad: Econ; Consulting. AB 1943, MGA 1945, U of Penna; PhD 1966, U of Calif-Berkeley. PUBL: "Interstate Differentials in Wages and Unemployment," Ind Rels, May 1978. INT: labor market econ, govt labor policy. ASSN: AEA, Amer Statis Assn. POSITIONS: Prof, Calif Polytech State U, San Luis Obispo, 1971; Deputy Dir and Chief Div of Labor Statis and Res, Calif Dept of Ind Rels, 1976; and (since 1979) Adjunct Prof and Private Consultant, St. Mary's Coll, Exec MBA Program. ADDRESS: 240 N Creek Cir, Walnut Creek, CA 94598.

BEHR, ARMIN Government. MILR 1955, Cornell U. INT: empl/trng programs, govt labor policy. ASSN: Amer Soc for Trng and Develop. POSITIONS: Dir of Contract Compliance, 1966, and since 1979, Mgmt Analyst, U.S. Dept of Energy. ADDRESS: 6310 Swords Way, Bethesda, MD 20817. 202/252-9035

BEINHAUER, MYRTLE T. PhD 1956 U of Minn. ASSN: Southwest Mich IRRA. POSITIONS: Prof of Econ, Western Mich U, 1957; Dir, Center Econ Educ, Olivet College. (Retired) ADDRESS: 918 Farrell, Kalamazoo, MI 49007.

BEITNER, ELLIOT I. Arbitration. BA, JD, 1957, Wayne State U. INT: arb/med, labor law. ASSN: Detroit IRRA, Natl Academy of Arbitrators, SPIDR, ABA. POSITIONS: Asst Prosecution Attorney, Wayne Cty, 1957-60; (since 1983) Mich Reg Chairman, NAA; (since 1961) Private Law Practice. ADDRESS: 4000 Town Center #910, Southfield, MI 48075.

BELANGER, JACQUES Acad: Ind Rels. BSc Soc (RI) 1975, MA (RI) 1978, Univ Laval. INT: union org, coll barg, ind sociol. ASSN: Canadian Ind Rels Assn, IIRA. POSITION: Research Student, Ind Rels Res, Univ of Warwick, 1978; and (since 1980) Asst Prof, Dept of Ind Rels, Univ Laval, Quebec G1K 7P4, Canada. 418/656-2722

BELCHER, A LEE Arbitration. INT: arb/med, fact-finding, labor law. ASSN: Kansas City and St. Louis IRRAs, SPIDR, AAA. NAA. POSITIONS: Asst to Pres, Univ of Missouri, 1967; and (since 1967) Arbitrator (self-employed), 2109 Valley View Rd, Columbia, MO 65201. 314/443-7162

BELCHER, DAVID W. Acad: Org Beh/Pers, Ind Rels. BBA 1939, MA 1948, PhD 1951, U of Minn. PUBL: "Pay and Performance," Compensation Rev, 1981, pp 14-20; "Pay Equity or Pay Fairness," Compensation Rev, Second Quart, 1979, pp 31-35; "Wage and Salary Administration," in Yoder & Heneman (eds) ASPA Handbook of Pers and Ind Rels, Wash DC: BNA 1979. INT: personnel, labor market econ, coll barg. ASSN: Acad of Mgmt, Amer Compensation Assn, AAUP. POSITIONS: Prof of Commerce, School of Commerce, U of Wis-Madison, 1950; Prof of Mgmt, School of Bus, Univ of Ariz, 1956, and (since 1957), Prof of Mgmt, Coll of Bus Admin, San Diego State Univ, San Diego, CA 92182. 714/265-5337

BELETZ, ELAINE F. Intl Org. ADDRESS: 1000 Conestoga Rd, #B-328, Rosemont, PA 19010.

BELITSKY, ABRAHAM HARVEY Government Research. BA 1952, U of Wis; MA 1953, Syracuse U; PhD 1960, Harvard U. PUBL: The Job Hunt, Johns Hopkins Press, 1966 (w H. L. Sheppard); Productivity and Job Security: Retraining to Adapt to Technological Change, Natl Center for Productivity and Quality of Work Life, Winter, 1977; "Metalworking Machinery in Technology and Labor in Four Industries," USDL Bull 2104, Jan 1982. INT: research in worker adjustment to tech change, empl/trng programs, labor market econ. ASSN: Wash DC IRRA. POSITION: (since 1979) Labor Economist, Bureau of Labor Statistics, USDL. ADDRESS: 7821 Morningside Dr NW, Washington DC 20012. 202/523-9311

BELL, DEBORAH E. Union. BA 1972, Harvard U. PUBL: "Unionized Women in State & Local Government," R. Milkham ed, Women in 20th Century Labor History,1984. INT: coll barg, labor market econ, union org/adm. ASSN: Coalition of Labor Union Women, Planners Network. POSITIONS: Res Assoc, Bureau of Applied Soc Res, Columbia U, 1972; City Planner, NYC Dept of City Planning, 1975; and (since 1978) Asst Dir of Res and Negotiations, Dist Council 37,AFSCME, AFL-CIO. ADDRESS: 25 Indian Rd, New York, NY 10034. 212/766-1032

BELL, JAMES F. Arbitration; Acad: Law. BA 1936, DePauw U; JD 1939, Ohio State U. INT: arb/med. ASSN: AAA, Ohio State Bar Assn, The Florida Bar. POSITIONS: Justice, Supreme Court of Ohio, 1955; General Counsel, General Telephone Co of Florida, 1971; and (since 1980) Dir/Instructor, Labor Arbitration Services, Inc, 612 Gladstone Lane, Holmes Beach, FL 33510. 813/778-2242

BELL, JEFFREY WAYNE Bus:Mgmt/Admin. 2309 Southern Oak Dr, 1033, Arlington, TX 76011. 214/790-1122

BELL, JOSEPH Legal Practice. POSITION: Kleinbard, Bell and Brecker, 1550 United Engineers Bldg, 30 S 17th St, Philadelphia, PA 19103. 215/568-2000

BELL, LYNN Consulting, market res/soc sci res, market planning. BA 1969, MA 1972, Temple U. INT: methodology/statis, ind sociol, labor market econ. ASSN: AEA, Amer Marketing Assn. POSITIONS: Sr Analyst, Dir of Wash DC Office, Contract Res Corp,1978; Consultant (self employed), 1978; and (since 1983) Research Dir, Hanlahan/Parker (Div of Maritz Inc)-Whittier. ADDRESS: 14306 Riverside Dr #206, Sherman Oaks, CA 91403. 213/947-4602

BELLA, SALVATORE JOSEPH Acad: Bus Admin; Consulting. BS in BA 1947, AM 1948, Boston U; PhD 1962, Cornell U. INT: coll barg, mgmt/educ, personnel. ASSN: Academy of Mgmt, Amer Assn of Univ Prof. POSITION: (since 1963) Jesse Jones Prof of Mgmt, Univ of Notre Dame. ADDRESS: 1029 Clermont Dr, South Bend, IN 46617. 219/239-7429

BELLACE, JANICE R. Law, Ind Rels. BA 1971, JD 1974, U of Penna; MSc (IR) London School of Econ. PUBL: The Landrum-Griffin Act: Twenty Years of Federal Protection of Union Members' Rights, 1979; "A Right of Fair Dismissal: Enforcing a Statutory Guarantee," U of Mich J of Law Reform, Vol 16, #2, Winter, 1983; "Regulating Secondary Action: The British and American Approaches," Comparative Labor Law, Vol 4, #2, Spring 1981. INT: intl comparative labor, labor law, coll barg. ASSN: Philadelphia IRRA, ABA (labor & empl law section), Amer Bus Law Assn, Intl Soc for Labor Law and Soc Legislation. POSITIONS: Legal Journalist, Income Data Services (London), 1976; Sr. Res Specialist, 1977, and, since 1979, Asst Prof of Legal Studies and Mgmt, Wharton School, U of Penna. ADDRESS: 2501 Naudain St, Philadelphia, PA 19146. 215/898-6851

BELLER, ANDREA H. Acad: Econ; Consulting. BA 1966, Case-Western Reserve U; MA PhD, 1974, Columbia U. "Trends in Occupational Segregation By Sex and Race: 1960-1981," in B. Reskin (ed), Sex Segregation in the Workplace: Trends, Explanations, Remedies Wash DC, Natl Academy Press, 1984. "Occupational Segregation by Sex, Determinants and Changes," J of Human Resources, 17 Summer, 1982, pp 371-92; "The Impact of Equal Opportunity Policy On Sex Differentials in Earnings and Occupations," Amer Econ Rev, 72 May 1982, pp 171-75. INT: labor market econ, govt labor policy, income maint. ASSN: AEA, Population Assn of Amer, Amer Home Econ Assn. POSITIONS: Res Assoc, Inst for Research on Poverty, U Wis, 1975; Res Assoc, Bunting Inst of Radcliffe Coll, 1977; and (since 1979) Asst Prof, Dept of Family and Consumer Econ, Univ of Ill, 274 Bevier Hall, 905 S Goodwin, Urbana, IL 61801. 217/333-7257

BELLINGER, WILLIAM K. Acad: Econ. BA 1972, Mich State U; MS 1975, Cornell U; ABD 1981, Northwestern U. INT: labor market econ, govt labor policy, empl/trng programs. POSITIONS: Instructor, Trinity Coll (Conn.), 1976; Instructor (Part Time), Northwestern U, 1981; and, since 1982, Instructor, Dept of Econ, Dickinson Coll, Carlisle, PA 17013. 717/-245-1381

BELLMAN, HOWARD Government. BA 1959, LLB, 1962, U of Cincinnati; LLM 1963, New York U. INT: govt labor policy, coll barg, arb/med. ASSN: Wisconsin IRRA, ABA, NAA. POSITIONS: Commissioner, Wis Empl Rels Commission, 1965; Arb-Mediator, 1976; and (since 1983) Secretary, Wis Dept of Ind, Labor and Human Rels. ADDRESS: 6621 Montclair Lane, Madison, WI 53711. 608/266-7552

BELOUS, RICHARD S. Prof Assn. ADDRESS: #605, 4141 N Henderson Rd, Arlington, VA 22203.

BEMMELS, BRIAN G. Acad: Ind Rels. BA 1978, PhD 1984, U of Minn. INT: labor market econ, coll barg, arb/med. ASSN: AEA. POSITION: Asst Prof of Ind Rels, Dept of Ind and Legal Rels, Faculty of Bus, Univ of Alberta, Edmonton, Alberta T6G 2E8, Canada. 403/432-3054

BEN-ASHER, DANIEL L. Government. AB 1968, Rutgers U; MA (IR) 1970, U of Minn. INT: labor law, govt labor policy, arb/med. ASSN: New York and New Brunswick IRRA. POSITIONS: Plant Pers Admin, Tanatex Chemical Co Div of Sybron Corp, 1970; and (since 1971) Res Assoc, NJ Office of Legislative Services. ADDRESS: 5 Whitemarsh Drive, Lawrenceville, NJ 08648. 609/984-0445

BENCA, THEODORE JOHN Government. POSITION: Employee Rels, Civil Service, 320 S Walnut, PO Box 30002, Lansing, MI 48913. 517/373-9168

BENEDETTO, FREDERICK Union. Acad: Ind Rels. INT: arb/med, coll barg, labor law. ASSN: Central New York IRRA. POSITION: (since 1968) Directing Bus Rep, Intl Assn of Machinists & Aerospace Workers, 119 Sherman St, Watertown, NY 13601. 315/782-3771

BENHAMOU, ANNIE Prof Assn. POSITION: Service AFF Intl, UIMM, 56 Ave de Wagram, 75854 Paris, France.

BENJAMIN, DALE L. Bus:Pers/Ind Rels. BA 1951, U of Idaho. INT: coll barg, labor law, arb/-med. ASSN: Southwestern Conn IRRA, Res Advisory Group-Wharton School. POSITIONS: Dir of Pers, General Telephone Co of Wis, 1965; Dir of Mgmt Placement, 1975, and (since 1976), Dir-Labor Rels, GTE Service Corp, One Stamford Forum, Stamford, CT 06904. 203/965-3154

BENJAMIN, ERNST Univ Admin. BA 1958, Ohio Wesleyan; MA 1960, PhD 1972, U of Chicago. PUBL: "Final Offer Arbitration in Michigan;" "Wayne County Charter Issues: Labor Relations Management;" "Towards A Collective Bargaining Alliance in Higher Education." INT: coll barg, union org/admn, govt labor policy. ASSN: Detroit IRRA, Amer Pol Sci Assn, AAUP. POSITIONS: Coordinator, Labor Studies, 1980, Dir, Weekend Coll Program, 1982, and, since 1983, Dean, Coll of Lifelong Learning, Wayne State Univ. ADDRESS: 34015 Oakland, Farmington, MI 48024. 313/577-4675

BENJAMIN, JESSE Government; Acad: Econ, Ind Rels. BA 1957, CCNY. PUBL: "The Employment Outlook for the College Graduate,"' June, 1983; "Underlying Economic Issues for Collective Bargaining," March 1983; "The Changing Character of Work, and Workers in the American Economy," Feb, 1983. INT: labor market econ, coll barg, empl/trng programs. ASSN: New York IRRA, AEA, Amer Statis Assn, MET Econ Assn. POSI-

TIONS: Economist, 1959, Chief, Program Res Evaluation, 1970, and since 1974, Asst Reg Comm of Labor Statistics, USDL, New York, NY. ADDRESS: 110-50 71 Rd, Forest Hills, NY 11375. 212/944-3128

BENNETT, DONALD J. Bus:Pers/Ind Rels. IR Rep, ITT Continental Baking Co, PO Box 209, Grandview, MO 64030.

BENNETT, JOSEPH C., JR. Bus:Mgmt/Admin. ADDRESS: PO Box 442, Bath, NY 14810. 607/-776-3738

BENSINGER, STEPHEN C. Government. Acad: Student (JD). BA 1980, Penna State U . INT: labor law. ASSN: Wash DC IRRA. POSITION: (since 1979) Field Examiner, NLRB, Reg 5-Resident Office. ADDRESS: 4118 Military Rd, Washington DC 20015. 202/254-5837

BENSON, FRANCES Publisher. BA 1967, Wells Coll. INT: coll barg, ind sociol, union org/admn. POSITION: Dir, ILR Press, NYSSILR, Cornell U, Ithaca, NY 14853. 607/256-3061

BENSON, PHILIP GERALD Psychology. BS 1973, MS 1978, PhD 1982, Colorado State U. PUBL: "Mixed Standard Scale Response Inconsistencies As Reliability Indices," (w Dickinson) Educ Psych Measurement, 1983; "Industrial Psychologists As Expert Witnesses: Role Conflicts In Fair Employment Litigation,"(w Thornton) Labor Law J, 1980; "Measuring Cross-Cultural Adjustment: The Problem of Criteria," Intl J of Intercultural Rels, 1978. INT: ind psych, personnel, org beh. ASSN: Amer Psych Assn, Natl Council on Measurement in Educ, Soc for Intercultural Educ, Trng and Res. POSITION: (since 1980) Asst Prof, Auburn Univ, Dept of Psych, Auburn, AL 36849. 205/826-4413

BERENBLUM, MARVIN B. Bus:Mgmt/Admin. BA 1956, Yale. INT: mgmt/educ, personnel, coll barg. ASSN: New York IRRA, Cornell ILR Alumni Assn, Mgmt Devlopment Forum, NY Pers Mgmt Assn. POSITION: Sr Vice Pres, Continental Grain Co, 277 Park Ave, New York, NY 10172. 212/826-5571

BERES, MARY-BETH Acad: Org Beh/Pers. BS 1969, Siena Heights Coll; PhD 1976, Northwestern U. PUBL: "Usefulness as a Research Criteria: Reflections of a Critical Advocate," in Producing Useful Knowledge for Organizations, R.H.Kilman et al, eds, Praeger; "The Conflict Carousel: A Contingency Approach to Conflict Management," (w S.M. Schmidt), in Conflict Management and Industrial Relations Kluwer Nijhoff Publ, 1982; "Sociocultural Influences on Organizations: An Analysis of Recent Research," (w J.D. Portwood) in The Functioning of Complex Organizations, Oelgeschlager, Bunn & Hain, 1981. INT: org beh, intl comparative organizations, mgmt/educ. ASSN: Academy of Mgmt, Amer Inst for Decision Sci, Assn for Soc Econ. POSITIONS: Mathematics Teacher, St. Ambrose High School-Detroit, 1969; Visiting Inst, NYSSILR-Cornell, 1973; and (since 1974) Assoc Prof, School of Bus Admin, Temple Univ, Philadelphia, PA 19122. 215/787-6906

BERG, IVAR ELIS Acad: Sociol, Ind Rels, Bus Admin. AB 1954, Colgate U; PhD 1959, Harvard U. PUBL: Education and Jobs: The Great Training Robbery, Praeger, 1970; Managers and Work Reform: A Limited Engagement," NY: Free Press, 1978; Industrial Sociology," Prentice Hall, 1979. INT: ind sociol, labor market econ, mgmt/educ. ASSN: Amer Sociol Assn, Amer Assoc for Advancement of Sci, Soc for Study of Psych Issues. POSITIONS: Prof of Soc and Econ, Vanderbilt U, 1975; Prof and Chairman, Dept of Sociol, U of Penna, 1979; and (since 1983) Justin Potter Prof of Amer Competitive Bus, Owen Grad School of Mgmt, Vanderbilt Univ, Nashville, TN 37203. 615/322-2673

BERGER, CHRIS J. Acad: Org Beh/Pers, Ind Rels. MS 1974, PhD 1978, U of Wis-Madison. PUBL: "Effects of Unions on Job Satisfaction;" Effects of Fringe Benefits on Pay Satisfaction;" "Utility Model for Turnover." INT: personnel, methodology/statis, org beh. ASSN: Academy of Mgmt. POSITIONS: Asst Prof, Univ of Kansas, 1976; and (since 1978) Asst Prof, Krannert School of Bus, Purdue, Univ , West Lafayette, IN 47904. 317/494-4524

BERGER, MARK Acad: Law; Arbitration. AB 1966, Columbia U; JD 1969, Yale U. PUBL: Taking the Fifth: The Supreme Court and the Privilege Against Self-Incrimination. INT: arb/med, labor law. ASSN: Kansas City IRRA, SPIDR, ABA. POSITIONS: Legal Advisor, New Haven,CT, Police Dept, 1969; and (since 1973) Prof of Law, UMKC Law School, 5100 Rockhill Road, Kansas City, MO 64110. 816/276-1651

BERGER, MARTIN Union. INT: labor history, union org/admn, labor market econ. ASSN: Central Penna IRRA. POSITION: Asst Dir, ILGWU, AFL-CIO, 2926 N 7th St, Harrisbrug, PA 17110. 717/236-7975

BERGER, RALPH S. Arbitration, Government. BS 1974, Cornell U; JD 1978, Hofstra Law. PUBL: "Training Programs For Neutrals," in Collective Bargaining by Government Workers, Baywood Publ, 1983; "The Courts and the EEOC View Sex Discrimination Against Males," ILR Forum, Mar 1974. INT: arb/med, coll barg, labor law. ASSN: New York IRRA, SPIDR, NYSBA(labor law section), AAA. POSITIONS: Attorney, NLRB, 1978; (since 1981) Trial Examiner, Office of Coll Barg and (since 1982) Arbitrator, (self-employed) 100 Remsen St, 7E, Brooklyn, NY 11201. 212/618-8211

BERGER, RICHARD B. Union, Consulting. BA 1976, New York U; MAIR 1978, U of Minn. PUBL: "Parity: An Evaluation of Recent Court and Board Decisions," (co-author) Labor Law J, March 1978. INT: coll barg, union org/admn, labor market econ. ASSN: Southwestern Conn IRRA. POSITIONS: Per Rep, New York City Health and Hosp Corp, 1978; and (since 1979) Asst Dir Res, Natl Maritime Union of America, AFL-CIO, 346 West 17 St, New York, NY 10011. 212/620-5700

BERGER, SUSAN LYNNE Acad: Library; Research/Writing. BA 1973, Fordham U; MA 1976, Rutgers U. INT: govt labor policy, labor history, library org/soc sci. POSITION: Full time writer and researcher. ADDRESS: Apt H522, 463 West St, New York, NY 10014.212/989-0232

BERGMAN, P. D. Acad: Student, Bus Admin, Org Beh/Pers. BA 1976, MBA 1983, U of Western Ontario. INT: org beh, coll barg, personnel. ASSN: Admin Sci Assn of Canada. POSITIONS: Clasroom Inst, Middlesex Cty Bd of Educ, Hyde Park Ont, 1971; (since 1983) Doctoral Candidate, Univ of Western Ontario. ADDRESS: R 1, Ilderton, Ontario N0M 2A0, Canada.

BERGMANN, RALPH H. Acad: Ind Rels. Ba 1943, Cornell U; PhD 1950, MIT. PUBL: "Automation in Developing Countries," (w W.P. Strassmann), ILO, Geneva, 1972; "Report on the Meeting for Directors of Centres for Advanced Labour Studies," Labour and Soc, July, 1977. INT: coll barg, intl comparative labor, union org/admn. ASSN: Central Calif IRRA. POSITIONS: Res Dir, United Rubber Workers, AFL-CIO, 1951; Sr Official, ILO-Geneva, 1962; and (since 1979) Prof, Calif State Univ-Fresno, Fresno, CA 93740. 209/294-2326

BERGMANN, THOMAS J. Acad: Org Beh/-Pers, Ind Rels, Compensation Admin. BA 1968, Loras Coll; MSIR 1970, Loyola U-Chicago; PhD 1976, U of Minn. "Pay Compression: Causes, Results and Possible Solutions," (w F. Hills), Compensation Rev, Vol 15, #2, 1983, pp 17-26; "Internal Labor Markets and Industrial Pay Discrimination," (w F. Hills) Compensation Rev, Vol 14, #4, 1982, pp 41-50; "Managers and Their Organizations: An Interactive Approach to Multidimensional Job Satisfaction," J of Occupational Psych, Vol 54, 1981 pp 275-288. INT: personnel, compensation admin & theory, org beh. ASSN: Academy of Mgmt, ASPA, Amer Compensation Assn. POSITION: Assoc Prof, 300 B Schneider Soc Sci Bldg, Univ of Wis-Eau Claire, Eau Claire, WI 54701 715/836-3677

BERGSTROM, ROBERT B, SR. Government. Commissioner, FMCS, 3377 Feather Ridge Rd, Toddville, IA 52341. 319/393-5307

BERKELEY, ARTHUR E. Acad: Ind Rels; Arbitration. BS JLR 1964, Cornell U; JD 1967, New York U; MS-Pers 1980, George Washington U. PUBL: "Observations on Labor Arbitration;" "Arbitration: The Process and the Participants." INT: arb/med, coll barg. ASSN: Maryland IRRA, Natl Academy of Arbitrators, SPIDR. POSITIONS: Dir of Labor Rels, Tanners Assn, 1971; Asst Prof, Essex Community Coll, 1973; and (since 1978) Asst Prof, Univ of Baltimore. ADDRESS: 7002 Pinecrest Rd, Baltimore, MD 21228. 301/625-3376

BERKELHAMER, LESTER Legal Practice. ADDRESS: Lipkowitz & Plaut, 1290 Ave of the Americas, New York, NY 10104.

BERKLEY, GAIL W. Acad: Psychology; Arbitration, Consulting. MS 1979, San Francisco State U. INT: arb/med, union org/admin, empl/-trng programs. ASSN: Calif IRRA, Calif Assn of Marriage & Family Therapists, SPIDR, AAA. POSITIONS: Special Educ, San Francisco School Dist, 1979-81; and (since 1981) Psychotherapist (self-employed), 36 S El Camino Real, Suite 304, San Mateo, CA 94401. 415/342-1315

BERKOFF, MARSHALL R. Legal Practice. BA 1959, U of Wis; LLB 1962, Harvard U. INT: coll barg, arb/med, labor law. POSITION: (since 1962) Partner, Michael, Best & Friedrich, 250 E Wisconsin Ave, Milwaukee, WI 53202. 414/271-6560

BERKOWITZ, MONROE Acad: Econ; Arbitration. PhD 1951, Columbia U. INT: income maint, labor market econ, arb/med. ASSN: AEA, Natl Academy of Arbitrators. POSITION: (since 1981) Chair, Dept of Econ, Rutgers Univ, New Brunswick, NJ 08903. 201/846-1057

BERKOWITZ, NORMAN Arbitration. BA Publ Admin 1945, Wayne State U; MA Pub Admin 1952, Mich State U. INT: arb/med, govt labor policy, personnel. ASSN: Mid-Mich IRRA. POSITIONS: Asst State Supt of Public Inst, Mich Dept of Educ, 1966; Deputy Sec of State, Mich Dept of State, 1971; and (since 1982) Arbitrator (self-employed), 1704 Wood, Lansing, MI 48912. 517/485-8738

BERMAN, MICHAEL B. Government. BA 1964, Iowa Weselyan Coll; MAT 1973, Trenton State Coll; MA 1977, Rutgers U; JD 1984, Cardozo School of Law-Teshiva U. INT: coll barg, govt labor policy, labor law. ASSN: ABA, SPIDR. POSITIONS: Asst to Chairman, NJ PERC, 1973; and (since 1983) Asst to Exec Dir, NJ Board of Mediation. ADDRESS: 20 Merlin Dr, Lakewood, NJ 08701. 201/648-2860

BERNFELD, JACK Union. Union Rep, AFSCME, 5 Odana Ct, Madison, WI 53719. 608/274-9100

BERNHEIM, JACOB L. Legal Practice. BA 1948, LLB 1949, U of Wis-Madison. INT: labor law, arb/med, coll barg.ASSN: Wis IRRA, State Bar-Wis. ABA, Federal Bar Assn. POSITION: Member, Michael, Best and Friedrich, 250 E Wisconsin Ave, Milwaukee, WI 53202. 414/271-6560

BERNIER, JEAN Acad: Ind Rels. Ma Ind Rels 1964, U Laval; PhD 1975, U of Paris. PUBL: "Le code du travail et la regie interne des syndicats, in La gestion des relations du travail au Quebec - le cadre juridique et institutionnel, McGraw-Hill, 1980, pp 213-220; "La loi sur les normes du travial: continuite, modernisation ou rupture," in Les conditions minimales de travail: un choix politique, XXXVe Congres des relations industrielles, PUL, 1980, pp 17-32; "L'extension juridique des conventions collectives au Quebec: une approche comparative," accepte pour parution dans Relations Industrielles Vol 38, 1983. INT: coll barg, intl comparative labor, arb/med. ASSN: ACRI, CAQ. POSITIONS: Prof, Dept of Ind Rels, 1968, and, since 1980, Vice-Dean, Faculty of Social Sciences, Laval Univ, Ste Foy, GIV 272, Quebec, Canada. 418/681-8383

BERNSTEIN, IRVING Acad: Ind Rels; Arbitration. BA 1937, Rochester U; MA 1938, PhD 1948, Harvard U. PUBL: The Lean Years; Turbulent Years; Arbitration of Wages. INT: labor history, govt labor policy, arb/med. ASSN: Southern Calif IRRA, Natl Academy of Arbitrators. POSITIONS: Chairman, San Francisco Wage Stabilization Bd, 1951; Member, Federal Service Impasse Panel, 1978; and (since 1948) Prof, Pol Sci Dept, Univ of Calif, Los Angeles, CA 90024. 213/825-4152

BERNSTEIN, MERTON CLAY Acad: Law; Arbitration. BA 1943, Oberlin Coll; LLB 1948, Columbia U. PUBL: Private Dispute Settlement: Material and Cases on Arbitration; The Future of Private Pensions; "Third Party Claims in Worker's Compensation: A Proposal to Do More With Less," Wash Univ Law Quart 543, 1977. INT: income maint. health & hosp care, arb/med. ASSN: Gateway IRRA, Intl Soc for Labor Law and Social Legislation, NAA, AAUP. POSITIONS: Visiting Fulbright Prof, Leiden U, The Netherlands, 1975; Principal Consultant, Natl Comm on Social Security Reform, 1981; and (since 1975) Coles Prof of Law, Washington University, St. Louis, MO 63130. 314/889-6457.

BERNSTEIN, PAUL Univ Admin. PhD 1955, U of Penna. PUBL: "The Work Ethic That Never Was," Wharton Mag. 1980; "Unraveling of Labor- Mgmt Rels in Sweden," Pers J, June 1983; 'Using Soft Approaches to Get Hard Results," Business, June 1983. INT: ind psych, org beh, labor history. ASSN: Assn for General and Liberal Studies. POSITIONS: Chairman, Dept of Soc Sci, SUNY/Plattsburgh, 1964; Dean of Liberal Arts, 1966, and, since 1976, Dean of Grad Studies, Rochester Inst of Technology, 1 Lomb Memorial Dr, Rochester, NY 14623. 716/475-6523

BERNSTEIN, SEYMOUR Health and Hosp Care. POSITION: Vice Pres, Group Health Inc, 330 W 42nd St, New York, NY 10036. 212/760-6440

BERRY, ALAN PERCIVAL Union. POSITION: Engineering Empl Assn, 18 Davenport Rd, Coventry CV5 6PX England.

BERRY, DONN J. Arbitration. PUBL: Joint Affirmative Action Plan for the Electrical Construction Industry of Greater Boston, (co-author). INT: arb/med, labor educ, mgmt/educ. ASSN: Boston IRRA,AAA. POSITIONS: Bus Mgr, L.U. 103 Intl Brotherhood of Electrical Workers, 1964; Asst Dir, Commonwealth of Mass, 1979; and (since 1983) Arbitrator of Labor Disputes (self employed), 105 Elmer Rd, South Weymouth, MA 02190. 617/337-0607

BERRY, ELAWRENCE Government. POSITION: District Director, US Government, 231 West Lafayette, #431, Detroit, MI 48226.

BERRY, JAMES H., JR. Legal Practice. POSITION: Jones, Day, Reavis & Pogue, 1 Century PZ, 3600, 2029 Century Park E, Los Angeles, CA 90067. 213/553-3939

BERRY, JOHN ELWOOD Acad: Bus Admin, Ind Rels; Arbitration. BA 1966, Mich State U; MBA 1969, Calif State U-Long Beach; MS (IR) 1973, UCLA. INT: labor law, personnel, arb/med. ASSN: SPIDR, Academy of Mgmt, AEA. POSITIONS: Pers Admins, Aerospace Corp, 1969 & 1972; Asst Prof, Calif State U-Long Beach,1969; and (since 1980) Asst Prof, Mgmt/Marketing Dept, Calif State U-Dominguez Hills. ADDRESS: 11107 S St. Andrews Pl, Los Angeles, CA 90047. 213/516-3551/3560

BERRYHILL, RONNIE D. Bus:Pers/Ind Rels. POSITION: CCSD Personnel, Rockwell, 3200 E Renner Rd, Mail Station 461-100, Richardson, TX 75081. 214/996-0521

BERS, MELVIN K. Acad: Econ. AB 1943, MA 1948, George Washington U; PhD 1954, U of Calif-Berkeley. INT: coll barg, govt labor policy, union org/admn. ASSN: AEA. POSITION: Prof of Econ, SUNY-Albany. ADDRESS: 22 Sunset Dr, Delmar NY 12054. 518/457-7917

BERTANI, CHARLES L. Union. POSITION: President, IAM & AW Lodge 15 AFL-CIO, 6640 Long Point, Houston, TX 77055. 713/686-9464

BETCHERMAN, GORDON Acad: Student, Ind Rels. BA 1973, U of Toronto; MA 1978, Carleton U. PUBL: "Diagnosing Labour Market Imbalances in Canada," Canadian Public Policy; "Reshaping Training," Policy Options; "Meeting Skill Requirements," Econ Council of Canada Res Study. INT: govt labor policy, empl/trng programs, labor market econ. ASSN: Canadian Ind Rels Assn. POSITIONS: Researcher, Econ Council of Canada, 1977; and (since 1982) PhD student, UCLA. ADDRESS: 11601 Dunstan Way #205, Los Angeles, CA 90049. 213/825-1964

BETHKE, ARTHUR LEON Acad: Ind Rels, Org Beh/Pers, Bus Admin. BA 1965, MA 1969, Central Mo State U; PhD 1972, Nebraska U. PUBL: "A Longitudinal Study of Norma Rae," Proceedings, SW Div Academy of Mgmt, March 1982; "Reducing Absenteeism with Fixed and Variable Reinforcement," Rev of Bus and Econ Res Spring, 1980. INT: coll barg, personnel, arb/med. ASSN: Academy of Mgmt, Southern Mgmt Asssn, ASPA. POSITIONS: Marketing Rep, Mobil Oil Corp, 1965; Asst Prof, U of Tenn-Martin, 1972; and (since 1974) Assoc Prof of Mgmt & Marketing, Northeast Louisiana Univ, Monroe, LA 71209. 318/342-3098

BETTER, MAURICE BERNARD Acad: Workers Educ. PhD 1973, U of Wis-Madison. PUBL: "How Workers In the Benelux Bargain Over Work Place Problems;" "Unionism Among Unskilled Workers in the South." INT: labor educ, coll barg, intl comparative labor. ASSN: IIRA, SPIDR, Univ & Coll Labor Educ Assn. POSITIONS: Asst Prof, 1978, and, since 1983, Assoc Prof, School for Workers, Library Bldg, RM 720H, Univ of Wis-Ext, Green Bay, WI 54302. 414/465-2082

BETTON, JOHN H. Student. 104 Woodway Woodland Village, Columbia, SC 29210. 803/798-6582

BETTS, ROBERT JAMES Bus:Pers/Admin, Bus:Pers/Ind Rels, Government. BS 1951, JD 1955, U of Tenn. INT: personnel, coll barg, mgmt/educ.ASSN: ABA-Labor Law Sec, Tenn Valley Pers Assn, Natl Mgmt Assn. POSITIONS: Supt Ind Rels Div, Union Carbide-Nuclear Div, 1967; Dir of Pers, 1973, and, since 1979, Asst to Dir, Property and Services, Tenn Valley Authority. ADDRESS: 6832 Northshore Dr, Knoxville, TN 37919. 615/632-3152

BHATTACHERJEE, DEBASHISH Acad: Student, Ind Rels, Econ. MA 1979, J. Nehru Univ-New Delhi; AMLIR 1982, U of Ill. INT: intl comparative labor, labor market econ, ind sociol. ASSN: AEA. POSITION: PhD Student and Teaching Asst, ILIR, U of Ill, 504 E Armory Ave, Champaign, IL 61820. 217/333-0984

BIAGI, MARCO Acad: Law, Ind Rels. Law Degree, 1973, U of Bologna,Italy. PUBL: La Dimensione Dell'Impresa Nel Diritto Del Lavoro; Cooperative E Rapporti DI Lavoro; "Labor Administration in Italy." INT: labor law, intl comparative law, union org/admn. ASSN: IIRA, Assn Italiana di Diritto Del Lavoro, Assn Italiana Di Diritto Comparato. POSITIONS: Assoc Prof, Law School,U of Ferrara, Italy,1979; Visiting Prof, Johns Hopkins Univ-Bologna Center, Bologna, 1980; and (since 1982) Assoc Prof, Facolta Dfecomomia, Univ Di Modena, Viale Giardini 41100 Modena, Italy. Home Phone: (051) 26.10.50

BIALOGORSKY, RAPHAEL Univ Admin; Bus Admin. POSITION: Deputy Dir-Gen Personnel, Tel Aviv Univ, Ramat Aviv, Tel Aviv 69978, Israel.

BICKNER, MEI LIANG Acad: Ind Rels; Arbitration. BA 1962, MBA 1964, PhD 1968, UCLA. PUBL: Women at Work, UCLA Inst of Ind Rels, 1974; "Scope of Bargaining and Participation in Decision Making," (w A. Kleingartner), Professional Workers and Coll Barg, U of Calif, 1977. INT: arb/med, coll barg, labor law. ASSN: Orange Cty IRRA, AAA, SPIDR. POSITIONS: Asst Prof, Grad School of Mgmt, U of Calif-Irvine, 1968; Assoc Prof of Ind Rels, 1974, and, since 1978, Prof of Ind Rels, Calif State University-Fullerton, Fullerton, CA 92634. 714/773-3828/2251

BIENSTOCK, HERBERT Acad: Univ Admin, Ind Rels; Consulting. BA 1945, CCNY. INT: labor market econ, empl/trng programs, coll barg. ASSN: New York IRRA, AEA, Amer Statis Assn. POSITIONS: Reg Commissioner of Labor Statistics, BLS, 1945, and (since 1980) Alumni Merit Prof, Labor and Urban Values, CUNY-Queens Coll. ADDRESS: 52-12 Oceania St, Bayside NY 11346. 212/520-7058

BIER, JOSEPH V. Bus:Pers/Ind Rels. BS 1948, Georgetown U. INT: ind rels research, personnel. ASSN: Wash DC IRRA. POSITIONS: Ind Rels Specialist, Martin Marietta, 1957, Pers Dir, Howmet Corp, MISCO Div, 1966; and (since 1948), Asst Dir Econ Res, Natl Railway Labor Conf, 1901 L St NW Suite 500, Washington DC 20036. 202/862-7223

BIERLEIN, MARCILEE A. Government. BA 1964, MA 1968, U of Kansas; MPA 1978, U of Del. PUBL: Collective Bargaining in Delaware State Government: Analysis and Recommendations, (w L. Hsu and M. Haskell). INT: empl/trng programs, govt labor policy. ASSN: Philadelphia IRRA, ASPA, Intl Assn of Pers in Emply Security. POSITIONS: Admin Asst to Council Pres, New Castle County Council, Del, 1978; Exec Asst to Del Sec'y of Labor, 1979, and since 1984, Director, Div of Employment Services, Delaware Labor Dept, PO Box 9029, Newark, DE 19711. 302/368-6810

BIES, ROBERT J. Acad: Org Beh/Pers, Bus Admin. BA 1975, MBA 1977, U of Wash; PhD 1982, Stanford U. INT: org beh, ind psych. ASSN: Acad of Mgmt, Amer Psych Assn. POSITION: (since 1982) Asst Prof of Org Beh, Kellogg Grad School of Mgmt, Northwestern Univ, 2001 Sheridan Rd, Evanston, IL 60201. 312/492-3470

BIGGICA, RUSSELL J. Bus:Pers/Ind Rels. BA 1974, Gannon U-Erie, PA; MA-IR 1983, St. Francis Coll-Loretto, PA. INT: arb/med, coll barg, govt labor policy. POSITIONS: Special Asst Intragovernmental, 1977, and, since 1978, Pers Dir, Dept Auditor General, Penna. ADDRESS: 305 Oak St, Harrisburg, PA 17109. 717/787-3192.

BIGLER, ESTA R. 380 E 18th St, Brooklyn, NY 11226.

BIGONESS, WILLIAM J. Acad: Bus Admin. BA 1969, St. Michael's Coll; MLIR 1972, PhD 1974, Mich State U. PUBL: "Effects of Mediation and Alternative Forms of Arbitration Upon Bargaining Behavior," J of App Psych, 1982,67,pp 549-554; "Labor-Management Aspects of Occupational Risk," Annual Rev of Public Health, 1982, 3, pp 201-224; "Correlates of Faculty Attitudes Toward Collective Bargaining," J of App Psych, 1978, 63, pp 228-235. INT: arb/med, coll barg, org beh. ASSN: Academy of Mgmt, Amer Psych Assn, Amer Inst for Decision Sci. POSITIONS: Asst Prof of Bus Admin, U of Maine, 1974; Asst Prof of Bus Admin, 1976, and, since 1980, Assoc Prof of Bus Admin, School of Bus Admin, Univ of North Carolina, Chapel Hill, NC 27514. 919/962-3116

BIHUN, JOHN D. Bus:Pers/Ind Rels. MSIR 1980, W Va U. INT: org beh, empl/trng programs, arb/med. POSITION: (since 1981) Pers Asst, Consolidation Coal Co. ADDRESS: 111 Brookhaven Rd, Morgantown, WV 26505. 304/-296-3461

BILLET, LEWIS M. Bus:Pers/Ind Rels, Arbitration, Union. POSITION: Labor Rels Mgr, Gulf Western Ind, 1 Gulf Western Plaza, New York, NY 10023. 212/333-4764

BINGMAN, MICHAEL B. Union. AB 1966, Washington U (St. Louis); MA 1980, Webster U. INT: union org/admn, coll barg, personnel. ASSN: Gateway IRRA, Educ Press Assn, Phi Delta Kappa-St Louis Field Chapter, NE. POSITIONS: Dir of School Community Rels, Hancock Place School Dist, 1966; Dir of Communications and Public Rels, 1973, and, since 1974, Field Rep, Missouri Natl Educ Assn, 10330 Old Olive St Rd, St. Louis, MO 63141. 314/432-2425

BIONDO, JOSEPH Government. BBA 1956, U of Pittsburgh. INT: arb/med, coll barg, labor history. ASSN: Western Penna IRRA. POSITION: Commissioner, FMCS, Pittsburgh. ADDRESS: 1197 Colgate Dr, Monroeville, PA 15146. 412/644-2992

BIRCH, JUAN Bus:Pers/Ind Rels, Government. CPA 1973, BSc-Econ 1979, U of West Indies. INT: coll barg, personnel, methodology/statis. POSITIONS: Sr. Statistician, 1976, Economist, 1979, Ministry of Labor, Kingston, Jamaica; and (since 1981) Ind Rels Officer, Jamaica Public Service Co. ADDRESS: 5 Edam Dr, Kingston 8, Jamaica, West Indies. Phone: 92-63190

BIRMINGHAM, MARY NEIL Legal Practice, Bus:Pers/Ind Rels. BS 1969, JD 1977, U of Tulsa; MA (Labor Rels) 1979, Eastern Wash U. INT: labor law, coll barg, empl/trng programs. ASSN: Inland Empire IRRA, Okla Bar Assn, AAA. POSITIONS: Research Fellow, Adjunct Asst Prof, Eastern Wash Univ, 1978, and (since 1980) Field Rep, Public School Employees of Wash, Puyallup. ADDRESS: E-205, 425 Columbia Cir Blvd, Kennewick, WA 99336. 509/735-2455, 206/848-1586

BIRNBAUM, ROBERT Acad: Higher Educ. BA 1958, U of Rochester; MA 1964, Ed D 1967, Teachers Coll, Columbia. PUBL: Creative Academic Bargaining: Managing Conflict in the Unionized College and University, Teachers Coll Press, 1980; 'Making Faculty Bargaining Work," Educ Record, Summer 1983; "The Effect of a Neutral Third Party on Faculty Perceptions of Institutional Climate and Academic Bargaining Relationships," J of Higher Educ, (in press). INT: coll barg, org beh, arb/med. ASSN: Assn for the Study of Higher Educ, Amer Assn of Univ Prof, Amer Assn for Higher Educ. POSITIONS: Vice-Chancellor, NJ Dept of Higher Educ, 1972; Chancellor, Univ of Wis-Oshkosh, 1974; and (since 1979) Prof of Higher Educ, Teachers Coll, Columbia Univ, New York, NY 10027. 212/678-3751

BISHOP, JOHN HILLMAN Acad: Econ. PhD 1974, U of Mich. PUBL: "Jobs, Cash Transfer and Marital Instability," JHR, Summer, 1980; "The General Equilibrium Impact of Alternative Antipoverty Strategies," Ind Rels Rev, Jan 1979; "Selective Employment Subsidies:

Can Okuns Law Be Repealed?" AER, May 1979. INT: labor market econ, govt labor policy, income maint. ASSN: Central Ohio IRRA, AEA, ASA, Econometric Soc. POSITIONS: Res Assoc, Inst for Research on Poverty, U of Wis, 1972, and (since 1981) Assoc Dir; Research Div, Natl Center for Research in Vocational Educ, Ohio State Univ, Columbus. ADDRESS: 960 Spring Grove Ln, Worthington, OH 43085. 614/486-3655

BISHOW, HOWARD Bus:Pers/Ind Rels. POSITION: Dir, Ind Rels, New York Times, 229 W 43rd St, New York, NY 10036. 212/556-1277

BISTLINE, WILLIAM J. Bus:Pers/Ind Rels. INT: org beh, coll barg, arb/med. ASSN: San Diego IRRA, AMA. POSITIONS: Supr-Corp Labor Rels, Rohr Industries Inc, San Diego, 1967; Dir,Ind Rels, Flexible Co-Ohio, 1976; and (since 1979) Mgr Pers/Ind Rels, Martin Marietta Aluminum, 19200 Southwestern Ave, Torrance, CA 90509. 213/618-3208

BJERKE, PAUL Bus:Pers/IndRels. BA 1981, MLIR 1982, Mich State U. INT: empl/trng programs. ASSN: Twin Cities Pers Assn. POSITION: Employment Rep, Sperry Computer Systems, St. Paul. ADDRESS: 3922 Ulysses St NE, Minneapolis, MN 55421. 612/635-6018

BJURMAN, GERALD LUDVIG Bus:Pers/Ind Rels. ADDRESS: 1321 W Birchwood Ave #209, Chicago, IL 60626. 312/764-6621

BLACKMAN, JOHN Acad: Econ, Ind Rels. AB 1930, Haverford Coll; MA 1948, PhD 1957, Harvard U. PUBL: Presidential Seizure in Labor Disputes, 1967; "Labor Legislation," in Dictionary of U.S. History, 1976. INT: coll barg, labor law, labor market econ. ASSN: Boston IRRA. POSITIONS: Assoc Prof of Econ, 1960, and, since 1978, Assoc Prof of Econ, Emeritus, Univ of Mass. ADDRESS: 29 Hickory Lane, Amherst, MA 01002.

BLAIR, LARRY M. Research Lab (non-profit). BS 1964, MA 1965, Central Mo State U; PhD 1971, Claremont Grad School. PUBL: "An Approach to Assessing the Supply of Workers to Large Construction Projects;" "The Returns to the Associate Degree for Technicians;" "Speech Styles and Employment Opportunities." INT: labor market econ, methodology/statis, empl/trng programs. ASSN: AEA, Souther Econ Assn, Intl Assn of Energy Econ. POSITIONS: Instructor, Central Missouri State U, 1965; Asst Prof of Econ, U of Utah, 1969; and (since 1974) Dir, Labor and Policy Studies Programs, Oak Ridge Assoc Univ, PO Box 117, Oak Ridge TN 37830. 615/576-3413

BLAIR, SANFORD S. Union. BA 1955 CCNY; MS 1983, NYIT. INT: coll barg, arb/med, labor law. ASSN: New York IRRA. POSITION: Dist Rep (& Exec Bd Member), United Federation of Teachers Local 2, American Fed of Teachers, AFL-CIO, New York. ADDRESS: 39-B Adler Pl. Bronx, NY 10475. 212/379-6200

BLAKE, CHARLES A. Government. BA 1958, Duquesne U. INT: govt labor policy, coll barg, personnel. POSITION: Labor Rels Officer, NOAA, US Dept of Commerce, Rockville, MD. ADDRESS: 8237 Rupert Rd S, Millersville, MD 21108. 301/443-8261

BLAKE, CHARLES H., JR. Economics. PhD 1966, U of Wis-Madison. INT: coll/barg, labor market econ, labor history. ASSN: AEA. POSITION: (since 1966) Assoc Prof, Wright State Univ, Dayton, OH 45435. 513/873-3480

BLAKE, WILLIAM E. Bus:Pers/Ind Rels. MSIR 1967, U of Wis. INT: personnel, org beh, mgmt/educ. POSITION: Mgr, Salaried Pers, Ford Motor Co Steel Div, 295 Arthur, Plymouth, MI 48170. 313/337-8075

BLAKEY, MADGE E. Government. 13970 Sagewood Dr, Poway, CA 92064.

BLALOCK, M. LYNN Bus:Pers/Ind Rels. AB 1973, MBA 1981, Georgia State U. INT: arb/med, labor law, mgmt/educ. ASSN: Atlanta IRRA, ASPA, SPIDR, NMA. POSITIONS: Project Coordinator, Medical Res Found, Inc-Atlanta, 1978; Empl Rels Mgr, Natl Smelting & Refining Co, Atlanta, 1981; and (since 1982) Equal Opportunity Programs Rep, Lockheed-Georgia Co, Marietta. ADDRESS: 1803 W Walker Ave, College Park, GA 30337. 404/424-2680

BLANDFORD, LINDA Bus:Pers/Ind Rels. BA 1976, U of Va; MA(LIR) 1977, U of Ill. INT: org/beh, labor market econ, arb/med. POSITIONS: Compensation Analyst, 1982, Supr Compensation Analyst, 1982, and, since 1983, Sr Pers Rep, Pacific Gas and Electric Co, San Francisco. ADDRESS: 3 El Toyonal Rd, Orinda, CA 94563. 415/781-4211 ext 4442

BLANK, DALE L. Government, Arbitration. MSIR 1972, Loyola U-Chicago; JD 1975, DePaul U. INT: labor law, arb/med, govt labor policy. ASSN: ABA, San Francisco Bar Assn, State Bar Assn-Labor & Empl Sec. POSITIONS: Trial Attorney, 1975, and, since 1978, Discrimination Programs Officer, USDL, 3421 25th St, San Francisco, CA 94110. 415/285-8571

BLANK, DORIS S. Union. BS 1950, MA 1954, Columbia U. INT: coll barg, arb/med, labor law. POSITIONS: Vice Pres, Central Labor Body,AFL-CIO, Westchester & Putnam Counties, and, currently, Pres, Port Chester Teachers Assn, AFT #2934, AFL-CIO, 3 Newberry PL, Rye NY 10580. 914/967-1030

BLANK, IRA LEONARD Legal Practice. BS 1972 U of Ala; MILR 1974, Cornell U; JD 1979, Washington U. PUBL: "The Settlement of the American Railway Union Strike Against the Great Northern Railway in 1894," 9 Ind and Rels Forum pp 69-97, 1973. INT: labor law, personnel, coll barg. ASSN: Bar Assn of Metro St.Louis, Mo Bar, Amer Bar Assn-Labor Law Sections. POSITIONS: Area Ind Rels Mgr, Continental Group Inc, 1974, and (since 1979) Attorney, Popkin, Stern, Heifetz, Lurie et al. ADDRESS: 50 Highgate, St. Louis, MO 63132. 314/862-0900

BLANPAIN, ROGER ROBERT Ind Rels, Law. MA 1956, Columbia U; PhD-Law 1961, K.U. Leuven, Belgium. PUBL: International Encyclopedia for Labour Relations and Labour Law (ed) Kluwer; Comparative Labour Law and Industrial Relations, Kluwer, 1982; OECD Guidelines for Multinational Enterprises and Labour Relations, Kluwer, 1982. INT: arb/med, coll barg, intl comparative labor. POSITION: Prof, Law School, K.U. Leuven, Inst for Labor Rels, Tiensestraat 41, B-3000 Leuven, Belgium. Phone: 016/23 09 71

BLASER, ANN CATHERINE Student. 2245 Shady Oaks Ct NE, Cedar Rapids, IA 52402. 319/393-7141

BLAU, FRANCINE D. Acad: Econ, Ind Rels. BS 1966, Cornell U; AM 1969, PhD 1975, Harvard U. PUBL: "The Use of Transfer Payments by Immigrants," Ind and Labor Rels Rev, Jan, 1984. pp 222-239; "Causes and Consequences of Layoffs," (w L. Kahn), Econ Inquiry, Apr 1981, pp 270-96; "Occupational Segregation by Sex: Trends and Prospects," (w W. Hendricks), J of Human Resources, Spring 1979, pp 197-210. INT: labor market econ, coll barg, income maint. ASSN: AEA, Midwest Econ Assn. POSITIONS: Asst Prof, 1973-75, Assoc Prof, 1978-83, and, since 1983, Prof of Econ and Labor & Ind Rels, Univ of Ill, 504 E Armory Ave, Champaign, IL 61820. 217/333-4842

BLAUFELD, SAMUEL S. Legal Practice. The Bank Tower, 307 Fourth Ave, Pittsburgh, PA 15223. 412/391-4305

BLAUSTEIN, SAUL J. Foundation-Research. BBS 1948, CCNY. PUBL: Unemployment Insurance Fund Insolvency & Debt in Michigan, 1982; Job and Income Security, 1981; "New Directions in Unemployment Insurance," in J of Urban Law, U of Detroit, Summer 1982. INT: income maint, labor market econ, govt labor policy. ASSN: Southwest Mich IRRA, AEA. POSITIONS: Price and Cost of Living Economist, BLS, 1951, Program Res Dir & Analyst, Unemployment Insurance Service, USDL, 1955; and (since 1967) Sr Staff Economist, W E Upjohn Inst for Empl Res, 300 S Westnedge Ave, Kalamazoo, MI 49007. 616/343-5541

BLICKSILVER, JACK Acad: Econ. BA 1948, Queens Coll NYC; MA 1953, PhD 1955, Northwestern U. PUBL: Home Service Method of Marketing Life & Health Insurance, Life Insurers Conf, 1973. INT: labor history, govt labor policy, intl comparative labor. ASSN: Atlanta IRRA, Econ History Assn, AEA, Amer Historical Assn. POSITIONS: Visiting Prof, Grad School of Bus, Harvard Univ, 1962-63; and (since 1955) Prof of Econ, Georgia State Univ, Univ Plaza, Atlanta, GA 30303. 404/658-2777

BLISS, KAREN S. Union. BA 1978, Allegheny Coll; MA 1983, George Washington U. INT: labor market econ, coll barg. ASSN: Wash DC IRRA. POSITION: Economist, Communications Workers of America, 1925 K St NW, Washington DC 20006. 202/728-2397

BLISS, RAYMOND C. Union. BA 1976, Williams Coll; MILR 1978, NYSSILR Cornell U; JD 1984, Catholic U of America. INT: labor market econ, labor law, coll barg. ASSN: Washington DC IRRA. POSITION: Research Dir, Bricklayers and Allied Craftsmen, 815 15th St NW, Washington DC 20005. 202/783-3788

BLITZSTEIN, DAVID S. Union. BA 1976, U of Penna; MS 1978, U of Mass-Amherst. INT: coll barg, labor market econ, intl comparative labor. POSITIONS: Res Asst, U of Mass, 1977; Research Assoc, United Food & Commercial Workers, 1978; and (since 1984) Research Economist, United Mineworkers of America, 900 15th St NW, Washington DC 20005. 202/842-7314

BLOCH, JOSEPH W.. ASSN: Wash DC IRRA. Retired. ADDRESS: 10400 Rodney Rd, Silver Spring, MD 20903.

BLOCH, RICHARD I. Arbitration. ADDRESS: 4335 Cathedral Ave NW, Washington DC 20016. 202/686-1140

BLOCK, JUSTIN M. Student. BS 1984, NYSS-ILR-Cornell. INT: arb/med, labor law, personnel. ASSN: Long Island IRRA, Soc for Arb & Neutral Educ-Cornell, Amer Soc for Pers Admin. ADDRESS: 777 Stewart Ave, Ithaca, NY 14850.

BLOCK, RICHARD NORMAN Acad: Ind Rels; Arbitration. BS Econ, MS Econ, U of Ill; PhD Ind Rels 1977, Cornell U. PUBL: "Union Organizing and the Allocation of Union Resources," Inds and Labor Rels Rev, Vol 34, #1, Oct 1980; "Case Processing Time and the Outcome of Representation Election," (w M. Roomkin), U of Ill Law Rev, Vol 1981, #1; The Collective Bargaining Process: Readings and Analysis, (w J. Baderschneider and J. Fossum), Bus Publ, Inc, 1983. INT: labor law, govt labor policy, coll barg. ASSN: Mid-Mich IRRA, AEA, AAA, Law and Soc Assn. POSITION: Assoc Prof and Assoc Dir, School of Labor and Ind Rels, Mich State Univ, East Lansing, MI 48824. 517/355-3284

BLOOM, DAVID ELLIOTT Acad: Econ, Ind Rels; Arbitration. BS 1976, Cornell; MA 1978, PhD 1980, Princeton U. PUBL: "Models of Arbitrator Behavior," (w O. Ashenfelter), Amer Econ Rev, 1984; "Is Arbitration Really Compatible with Bargaining?" Ind Rels; "Pay Discrimination Research and Litigation: The Use of Repression," (w M. Killingsworth), Ind Rels. INT: labor market econ, arb/med, method/statis. ASSN: AAA, AEA, Population Assn of Amer. POSITIONS: Asst Prof of Econ, Carnegie Mellon U, 1980, and (since 1982) Asst Prof of Econ, Dept of Econ, Littauer Center, Harvard Univ, Cambridge, MA 02138. 617/495-4690

BLOOM, EDWIN J., JR. Consulting; Acad: Org Beh/Pers, Bus Admin. BS 1957, Cornell U. INT: org beh, personnel, empl/trng programs. ASSN: Mass Businessman's Assn. POSITIONS: Dir, Empl Rels, Rauland Div, Zenith Radio Corp, 1970; Vice Pres Pers, Lechmere Sales Div, Dayton Hudson Corp, 1973; and (since 1977) President, Employee Rels Assoc Inc. ADDRESS: 265 Oak Hill Circle, Concord, MA 01742. 617/369-0356

BLOOM, GEORGE R. Consulting. POSITION: President, Ind Rels Assoc Inc, 2909 Waysata Blvd, Minneapolis, MN 55405. 612/374-9100

BLOOM, GORDON F. Acad: Law; Bus:Mgmt/-Admin. PhD 1946, LLB 1948, Harvard U. PUBL: Economics of Labor Relations, (9th Ed w J. R. Northrup), R. D. Irwin, 1981; Productivity in the Food Industry, MIT Press, 1972; Negro In Retail Trade, U of Penna Press, 1972. INT: labor law, labor market econ, coll barg. ASSN: Phi Beta Kappa, Amer Marketing Inst, ABA. POSITIONS: President, Marathon Realty Corp, 1969; and (since 1968) Sr Lecturer, Sloan School of Mgmt, MIT. ADDRESS: 1 Pine St, Weston, MA 02193. 617/253-6618

BLOOM, STEVEN Student. PhD Candidate, Harvard U., BS ILR 1980, Cornell U. INT: labor market econ, coll barg, personnel. ADDRESS: Dept of Economics, Harvard U, Cambridge, MA 02138.

BLOOMQUIST, CARL A. Bus:Mgmt. POSITION: VP Human Resources, Peabody Intl, 4 Landmark Sq, Stamford, CT 06901. 203/348-0000

BLOSS, BRIEN H. Bus:Pers/Ind Rels, Mgmt/-Admin. BS 1967, U of Wis-Madison. PUBL: Newsletter Editor, Calif Agricultural Personnel Mgmt Assn; "Productivity: Quality and Quantity

Control in Agriculture Harvest Operations." INT: org beh, personnel, mgmt/educ. ASSN: Calif Agric Pers Mgmt Assn, Southern Calif Builders Conference. POSITIONS: Pers Mgr, Oscar Mayer Inc, 1969, Plant Mgr, Claussen Pickle Co, Oscar Mayer Inc, 1976; and (since 1978) Human Resources Mgr-Real Estate Operations, The Irvine Co, PO Box 1, Newport Beach, CA 92660. 714/720-2503

BLUM, ALBERT A. Acad: Ind Rels, Comparative Labor; Arbitration. BS 1947, CCNY; MA 1948, PhD 1953, Columbia U. PUBL: Contemporary Developments in Comparative Ind Rels; White Collar Workers; Drafted or Deferred: Practices Past and Present. INT: intl comparative labor, labor history, arb/med. ASSN: Acad of Intl Bus, Acad of Mgmt, European Labor & Working Class History. POSITIONS: Prof, School of Labor & Ind Rels, Mich State Univ, 1960; Prof, Lyndon B. Johnson School of Public Affairs, U ofTexas, 1974; and (since 1982) George Wilson Prof of Intl Mgmt, Univ of the Pacific, Stockton, CA 95211. 209/946-2476

BLUM, PETER R. Legal Practice. ADDRESS: One Linden Place, Apt 301, Hartford, CT 06106. 203/527-8111

BLUMENGARTEN, LOUIS HIRAM Government. MA-ILR, 1967, U of Ill. INT: affirmative action, empl/trng programs, labor history. POSITION: Equal Opportunity Specialist, USDL, Office of Federal Compliance Programs, New York. ADDRESS: Apt 9G, 1740 Ocean Ave, Brooklyn, NY 11230. 212/944-3400

BLUMROSEN, ALFRED WILLIAM Acad: Law; Consulting, Legal Practice. BA 1950, JD 1953, U of Mich. PUBL: Black Employment and the Law, 1971; "Strangers in Paradise: Griggs v. Duke Power Co. and the Concept of Employment Discrimination," 71 Mich Law Rev 59, 1972; "Six Conditions for Meaningful Self Regulation," 69 Amer Bar Assn J 1264, 1983. INT: labor law, empl/trng, coll barg. ASSN: Intl Soc for Labor Law and Soc Legislation. POSITIONS: Consultant to Chair, U. S. Equal Empl Opportunity Commission, 1977-1979; Consultant Of Counsel, Kaye, Scholer, Fierman, Hays & Handler, 1979-82; and (since 1955) Prof of Law, Rutgers School of Law, Rutgers Univ, 15 Washington St, Newark, NJ 07102. 201/648-5332

BLUMROSEN, RUTH G. Acad: Law, Ind Rels; Consulting. BA 1947, JD 1953, U of Mich. PUBL: "Wage Discrimination, Job Segregation & Title VII of Civil Rights Act of 1964," 12 U of Mich J. L. Ref 397, 1979; "Analysis of Wage Discrimination in N. J. State Service," Report of N. J. Comm on Sex Discrimination in the Statutes, Trenton, 1983; "Worksharing, STC, and Affirmative Action," chapter in Short Time Compensation: A Formula for Worksharing, (edited by MaCoy and Morand), 1984. INT: EEO, labor law, arb/med. ASSN: Mich Bar Assn, U. S. Supreme Ct-Bar. POSITIONS: Consultant, EEOC (U. S.), 1979-80, Consultant, U. S. Dept of Health & Human Serv, 1981; and (since 1973) Prof, Grad School of Mgmt, Rutgers Univ. ADDRESS:Box 225B, Route 4, Sussex, NJ 07463. 201/648-5395

BLUNT, KEITH ROGER Acad: Ind Rels; Arbitration. BA 1953, MA 1954, PhD 1958, U of Iowa. INT: arb/med, personnel, mgmt/educ. ASSN: Acad of Mgmt. POSITIONS: Ind Rels Specialist, Western Electric Co, 1957; Sr Res Assoc, Planning Research Corp, 1964; and (since 1967) Prof and Chairman, Dept of Mgmt, Calif State Univ-Los Angeles. ADDRESS: 2040 El Cajonita Dr. La Habra Heights, CA 90631. 213/224-2961

BLUTH, ARLENE Acad: Student; Bus:Mgmt/-Admin. POSITION: Student-Cornell ILR. ADDRESS: 16 Patricia Dr, New York, NY 10956. 607/257-0420

BOARDMAN-FREE, RHONA Acad: Econ. BA 1978, Sarah Lawrence Coll; MA 1981, PhD 1983, U of Notre Dame. PUBL: "Collective Bargaining and Occupational Health & Safety." INT: labor market econ, coll barg, govt labor policy. ASSN: Eastern Econ Assn, AEA. POSITION: Asst Prof, Eastern Conn State Univ, Willimantic, CT 06226. 203/456-2231

BOCKOVEN, KATHERINE B. Arbitration. MBA 1982, U of R. I. PUBL: "Arbitration in the Schools," Warwick (RI) School Comm & Warwick Teachers Union, Report #161, July 1983; "Labor Arbitration in Government," City of Pawtucket and AFSCME, Local 1012, vol 13, #7, July 15, 1983; "Labor Arbitration in Government," City of East Providence & IAFF, Local 850, vol 13, #3, March 15, 1983. INT: arb/med, coll barg. ASSN: Boston IRRA, AAA (Labor Panel). POSITION: Labor Arbitrator. ADDRESS: 95 Tamarack Dr, East Greenwich, RI 02818. 401/884-1894

BODDY, DONNA C. Bus:Pers/Ind Rels, Consulting. BA 1973, U of Ill-UC. PUBL: Film: Breaking Through A Mgmt Training Program Regarding the Employment of the Handicapped, BNA Communications Inc. INT: personnel, EEO/-affirmative action, coll barg. ASSN: Women in Mgmt, Affirmative Action Assn-Chicago, Midwest Pers Mgmt Assn. POSITION: (since 1977) Pers Manager, Daily Machine Corp. ADDRESS: 8826 Butterfield Ln, Orland Park, IL 60462. 312/361-1925

BODLE, GEORGE Arbitration, Legal Prac. AB 1930, JD 1933, Stanford U. PUBL: The Developing Labor Law, BNA 1972. INT: arb/med, govt labor policy, coll barg. ASSN: Southern Calif IRRA, ABA, AAA, L. A. Cty Bar Assn. POSITIONS: Commissioner, LA Cty Econ and Efficiency Committee, 1974; Member, LA City Empl Rels Board, 1980; and (since 1979) Attorney & Arbitrator (self-employed), 344 S Rossmore Ave, Los Angeles, CA 90020. 213/938-7145

BOETTCHER, J. W. Consulting: Exec Search. BA 1941 (Econ & Law), U of Wis-Madison. INT: exec search, org beh, health & hosp care. ASSN: Wis IRRA, Ind Advisory Committee/Wis Manufacturers & Commerce. POSITIONS: Sr. V. P. for Pers, Ind Rels & Public Rels, Harnischfeger Corp, 37 yrs service, and, since 1982, Sr Vice Pres, Conley Assoc Inc, 810 Cardinal Lane, Hartland, WI 53029. 414/367-7300

BOGART, AGNES Bus:Mgmt/Admin. AB 1936, U of Chicago. PUBL: "Part Time Employment Makes Retirees a Valuable Resource," Pers Admin, June 1983; "New Personnel Management Information System Creates Single Data Base," Resource (Life Office Mgmt Assn), July 20, 1983; ASSN: New York IRRA, Ind Comm Council, Intl Assn of Bus Communicators. POSITIONS: Exec Editor, Compensation Rev, Amer Mgmt Assn, 1969-70; and (since 1972) Dir Communication Pers Policy Development Office, The Equitable Life Assurance Society of the U.S., 1285 Avenue of the Americas, New York, NY 10019. 212/554-2002.

BOGNANNO, MARIO FRANK Acad: Ind Rels; Arbitration, Consulting. BS 1962, Georgetown U; MA 1965, PhD 1969, U of Iowa. PUBL: Contemporary Collective Bargaining, (w H. Davey and D. E. Stenson), 4th ed, Prentice Hall, 1982; "Collective Bargaining in Korea," (w S. K. Kim), IRRA Proc of 34th Annual Meeting, 1982; "Union-Management Contracts in Higher Education," (w D. Estenson and E. Suntrup), Ind Rels, May 1978. INT: coll barg, arb/-med, labor market econ. ASSN: AAA, AEA, NAA. POSITION: (since 1970) Prof and Director, Ind Rels Center, Univ of Minnesota, Minneapolis, MN 55455. 612/373-3826

BOGUE, BONNIE Acad: Ind Rels, Law; Arbitration. JD 1973, U of Calif-Berkeley. PUBL: Affirmative Action vs. Seniority-Is Conflict Inevitable? Berkeley: Inst of Ind Rels, UC 1977 (second edition in progress); "Arbitration in California: the State of the Law,"50 Calif Publ Empl Rels, 2 Sept 1981; "An Anylysis of 1979-80 Strikes in California's Public Sector, 48 CPER 2, Mar 1981. INT: labor law, arb/med, coll barg. ASSN: SPIDR, ABA (labor law section), AAA. POSITIONS: Admin & Res Asst, Labor Center, U of Calif-Berkeley; 1977 to present, Arbitrator; and (since 1973) Assoc Dir of CPER Program, Inst of Ind Rels, U of Calif-Berkeley. ADDRESS: 2521 Channing Way, Berkeley, CA 94720. 415/642-0323

BOHLANDER, GEORGE W. Acad: Ind Rels, Bus Admin. PhD 1978, UCLA. PUBL: "How the Rank and File Views Local Union Administration: A Survey," Empl Rels Law J, Vol 8, #2, Autumn 1982; "Employee Protected Concerted Activity: The Non-Union Setting," Labor Law J, Vol 33, #6, June 1982; "The Legal Side of Productivity Through Employee Involvement," Natl Productivity Rev, Vol II, #4, Fall 1983. INT: labor law, arb/med, coll barg. ASSN: Ariz IRRA, Academy of Mgmt, East Valley Pers Assoc. POSITION: (since 1977) Assoc Prof of Mgmt, Arizona State Univ. ADDRESS: 2705 W Nido Avenue, Mesa AZ 85202. 602/961-2282

BOIVIN, JEAN Acad: Ind Rels. MA 1968, Laval U; PhD 1975, Cornell U. PUBL: Les relations Patronales-Syndicales au Quebec, (G. Morin ed), Chicoutimi, Que, Canada, 1982; "U. S.-Quebec Trade Union Relations,: chap 4 in The United States and Quebec, A. O. Hero Jr and M. Daneau, eds, Westview Press: Boulder, CO 1983; "Labor Relations in Quebec," chap 18 in Union-Management Rels in Canada, J. Anderson and M. Gunderson eds, Addison-Wesley Publ, Don Mills, Ont, 1982. INT: coll barg, labor history, intl comparative labor. ASSN: Canadian Ind Rels Assn. POSITION: (since 1972) Prof of Ind Rels, Dept of Ind Rels, Laval Univ. ADDRESS: 1239 Du Golf, Cap Rouge PG G0A 1K0 Canada. 418/656-3258

BOLWEG, JOEP F. Acad: Org Beh/Pers. PhD 1974, U of Wis. PUBL: Job Design and Industrial Democracy, Nyhoff, 1975; Company Statute and Workers Participation, JUA, 1981; "Personnel Policy and Organizational Change." INT: personnel, mgmt/educ, org beh. ASSN: NVA (Dutch J.R. Assn), NVP (Dutch Pers Mgmt Assn). POSITIONS: (since 1975) Organzational Consultant (self-employed) and Lecturer, J.R. Katholieke Heergangen. ADDRESS: Hengelstraat 7, 512EA Gilze, Netherlands.

BOMZER, DAVID J. Student. BS 1983, Mich State U. INT: personnel, org beh, coll barg. ASSN: U of Ill IRRA, Amer Soc of Pers Admin. POSITION: (since 1984) Grad Asst, Inst of Labor and Ind Rels, Univ of Ill. ADDRESS: 1334 Center Dr, Mount Pleasant MI 48858. 517/773-4917

BONEBRAKE, DANIEL Government. Empl Rels Officer, County of Sacramento, 700 H St, 5th Floor, Sacramento, CA 95814.

BONER, PATRICK J. Arbitration; Acad: Ind Rels. AB 1947, Penna State U. INT: arb/med, mgmt/educ, labor educ. ASSN: Northern Calif IRRA, Northern Calif Ind Rels Council, AAA. POSITIONS: BID Registrar, Santa Clara-San Benito BID Register, 1969-71; Sr. Empl Rels, Santa Clara Transit Dist, 1971-74; and (since 1974) Arbitrator (self-employed). ADDRESS: 1566 Alta Vista Dr, San Jose, CA 95125. 408/354-8578

BONGIOVANI, ANTHONY Bus:Mgmt/Admin, Bus:Pers/Ind Rels. MAM 1982, U of Phoenix. INT: health and hosp care, mgmt/educ, org beh. ASSN: Ariz IRRA, ASPA, Ariz Hosp Pers Assoc. POSITIONS: Dir of Pers, 1976, Vice Pres, and, since 1978, Vice Pres, Human Resources, St. Mary's Hosp and Health Center, 1601 W St. Mary's Rd, Tucson, AZ 85745. 602/622--5833

BONIFIELD, WILLIAM C. Univ Admin. PhD 1968, U of Minn. PUBL: "Clergy Labor Markets and Wage Determination;" "Yugoslavia's Valuable Export: Her People." INT: labor market econ, empl/trng programs, arb/med. ASSN AEA. POSITIONS: Prof of Econ, Wabash Coll, 1964; and (since 1981) Dean, Coll of Bus Admin, Butler Univ, Indianapolis, IN 46208. 317/283-9221

BOONIN, ROBERT A. Legal Practice, Bus.-Pers/Ind Rels. BS Econ 1976, Wharton U of Penna; MLIR 1980, Mich State U. INT: labor law, coll barg, arb/med. ASSN: Detroit IRRA, ABA. POSITIONS: Consultant, Labor Rels, Mich Assn School Boards, 1978; Law Student (JD expected 1985), Univ of Mich. ADDRESS: 2344 S Circle Dr, Ann Arbor, MI 48103.

BOOTH, PAUL R. Union. AFSCME AFL-CIO, Ste 1216, 201 N Wells, Chicago, IL 60606.

BORBA, PHILIP S. Regulation: Insurance. BA 1976, U of Calif-Berkeley; MS 1979, PhD 1982, Cornell U. INT: labor market econ, methodology/statis, income maint. ASSN: AEA. POSITIONS: Sr. Economic Analyst, Natl Econ Res Assoc, 1980, and (since 1982) Sr. Res Economist, Natl Council on Compensation Insurance, 1 Penn Plaza, New York, NY 10119. 212/560 1059

BORDEN, WILLIAM S. Bus:Mgmt/Admin. BA 1949, Mexico City Coll; MS 1983, Rutgers U. INT: arb/med, coll barg, personnel. POSITIONS: Dir In Flight Pers, 1976, Gen Mgr In Flight Services, 1978, and, since 1983, Staff Vice Pres, Trans World Airlines, 605 Third Ave, New York, NY 10016. 212/557-3650

BORDWELL, CHARLOTTE Arbitration. ADDRESS: 867 River Rd, Piermont NY 10968. 914/359-1396

BORNMAN, JOHN W. Bus:Mgmt/Admn. ADDRESS: 7450 NW 21st Ct, Sunrise, FL 33313. 305/393-3661

BORNSTEIN, TIM L. Law. Prof of Law and IR, U of Mass, 35 Morgan Cir, RFD 3, Amherst MA 01002.

BORUS, MICHAEL ELIOT Acad: Econ. BA 1959, Trinity Coll (Conn); MA 1960, PhD 1964, Yale U. PUBL: Tomorrow's Workers, ed & author, D.C. Heath, Lexington, MA 1983; Evaluating the Impact of Health Programs (co-author) MIT Press, 1982; Measuring the Impact of Employment-Related Social Programs, W. E. Upjohn Inst for Empl Rels, 1979. INT: empl/trng programs, labor market econ, method/statis. ASSN: New Brunswick IRRA, AEA, Soc of Government Economists. POSITIONS: Prof of Labor & Ind Rels, Mich State U, 1964; Dir, Center for Human Resources Res & Prof of Labor and Human Resources, Ohio State Univ, 1977; and (since 1983) Prof of Ind Rels and Human Resources, Rutgers Univ, PO Box 231, New Brunswick, NJ 08903. 201/932-9022

BOSANAC, PAUL A. Government. BA-Econ 1970, MS-Ind Rels, 1974, U of Wis-Madison; JD 1978, Marquette U. PUBL: "Concession Bargaining, Work Transfers and Mid-Contract Modification," Los Angeles Marine Hardware Co, Labor Law J, Feb 1973. INT: labor law, coll barg. ASSN: Wis Bar Assn, ABA. POSITION: (since 1978) Field Attorney, NLRB, Milwaukee. ADDRESS: 8921 W Orchard St., West Allis, WI 53214. 414/291-3900

BOSS, ANDREW C., SJ Acad: Ind Rels, Econ; Arbitration. INT: labor education, arb/med, coll barg. POSITIONS: Prof of Econ and Ind Rels, U of San Francisco, 1948; Chairman, Calif Manpower Commission, 1963; Retired. ADDRESS: 2130 Fulton St, San Francisco, CA 94117.

BOTAN, CARL H. Student-Speech. MA 1982, Wayne State U. PUBL: "Do Workers Trust Unions?" (w L. R. Frey) Communications Monographs, Sept 1983. INT: labor educ, org beh, union org/-admin. ASSN: Speech Communication Assn, Amer Inst of Parliamentarians. POSITION: (since 1980) Grad Asst, Wayne State Univ. ADDRESS: 84 Worcester, Detroit, MI 48203. 313/577-2943

BOTTORF, ROGER N. Student. ADDRESS: 3720 N Sheffield, #2, Chicago, IL 60613. 312/897-3017

BOUDREAU, JOHN W. Acad: Org Beh/Pers. POSITION: NYSSILR, 393 Ives Hall, Cornell Univ, Ithaca, NY 14853. 607/256-7785

BOURASSA, DAVID W. Student. BA 1981, Keene State Coll; MS IRHR 1984, Rutgers Univ. INT: personnel, labor law, mgmt/educ. POSITION: Student Intern, Markem Corp. ADDRESS: Rte 1 Laurel St, Marlborough, NH 03455. 603/352-1130

BOURDON, CLINT C. Bus:Pers/Ind Rels. ADDRESS: 108 Tanbark Lane, Williamsburg, VA 23185.

BOURDON, R. Bus:Pers/Ind Rels, Law. INT: labor law, coll barg, govt labor policy. ASSN: Barreau du Quebec. POSITIONS: Mgr, Labour Rels, Telebec Ltd, 1978; Section Mgr (Labour Rels) 1979, and, since 1982, Asst Dir Labour Rels, Bell Canada, 1050 Beaver Hall Hill, Montreal Quebec H2Z 1S4, Canada. 514/989-1392

BOURNE, RICHARD M. Acad: Bus Admin. BS 1931, Colo State U; MS 1932, U of Ill; PhD 1949, U of Nebr. INT: personnel, govt health policy, arb/med. ASSN: ASPA, SPIDR, Admin Mgmt Soc. POSITIONS: Economist, U. S. Govt Office of Price Admin, 1941, and (since 1945) Prof of Mgmt (Emeritus), Univ of Nebraska, 4818 Woodhaven Dr, Lincoln, NE 68516. 402/488-2738

BOUVIER, EMILE E., SJ Acad: Admin, Econ, Ind Rels. POSITION: Prof of Labor Rels, 2625 Portland, Apt 5, Sherbrooke, PQ J1J 1V6, Canada. 819/565-4563

BOVA, DANIEL Union. POSITION: Bus Manager, IBEW, 617 W Genessee St., Syracuse, NY 13202.

BOWEN, W. S., Bus:Mgmt/Admin. POSITION: Solar Turbines Inc, 2200 Pacific Hwy, PO Box 80966, San Diego, CA 92138.

BOWERS, MOLLIE HEATH Arbitration. BA 1967, MA 1969, U of Wis-Madison; PhD 1974, NYSSILR-Cornell. PUBL: "Grievance Mediation: Settle Now, Don't Pay Later," Federal Service Labor Rels Rev, vol 5, #2, Spring 1981, pp 25-35; Contract Administration in the Public Sector, PERL #53, Intl Pers Mgmt Assn, 1976; "Public Sector Labor Relations in 1978: A Turning Point," Municipal Yearbook, Intl City Mgmt Assn, 1978, pp 251-255. INT: arb/med, coll barg, govt labor policy. ASSN: SPIDR, SFLRP, Intl Assn of Pers Women. POSITIONS: Asst Prof, Grad School of Bus, George Washington Univ, 1980; Assoc Prof, Adjunct, Grad School of Bus, Marymount Coll, 1982, and at present, and, since 1975, Arbitrator/Mediator (self-employed), 4614 B South 36th St, Arlington, VA 22206. 703/379-4917

BOWERS, PHILLIP A. Government. POSITION: Office of Employee Relations, Hillsborough County, PO Box 1110, Tampa, FL 33601.

BOWLBY, ROGER L. Acad: Econ. BA 1950, MA 1951, Mich State U; PhD 1958, Texas U. PUBL: "Bluffing and the 'Split the Difference' Theory of Wage Bargaining," ILRR, Jan 1978; "Academic Ability and Rates of Return to Vocational Training," ILRR, April 1973; "Vocational Training and the Income Education Linkage," IR, May 1972. INT: labor law, labor history labor market econ. ASSN: AEA, Assn for Evolutionary Econ. POSITIONS: Labor Economist, USDL, 1963; Manpower Expert, ILO, Geneva, 1971; and (since 1965) Prof, Univ of Tennessee, Dept of Econ, Knoxville, TN 37996. 615/974-3303

BOWMAN, GERALD J. Bus:Pers/Ind Rels. POSITION: Vice Pres, Human Resources, Paradyne Corp, Box 2826, 8550 Ulmerton Rd, Largo, FL 33540. 813/530-2251

BOWMAN, YVONNE MARIE Bus:Labor Rels. 41-40 Union St., Apt 9N, Flushing, NY 11355. 212/908-6103

BOX, J. RICHARD Acad: Admin, Ind Rels. AB 1943, Bowling Green U; MBA 1949, U of Mich; PhD 1958, Ohio State U. PUBL: "Review of B. Schneider's Staffing Organization and D. Hall's Careers in Organizations," Acad of Mgmt Rev, Oct 1976. INT: personnel, coll barg, arb/med. POSITIONS: Instructor in Bus Admin & Econ, Bowling Green State U, 1949-52; Asst Prof of Mgmt, 1954-55, and, since 1964, Prof of Mgmt, Miami U, 307-7 Laws Hall, Oxford, OH 45056. 513/529-3181

BOYAJIAN, HAIG M. Bus:Pers/Ind Rels. BBA 1956, U of Miami; MILR 1958, Cornell. INT: method/statis. POSITION: The Grand Union Co, Hialeah. ADDRESS: 1478 NW 113th Way, Pembroke Pines, FL 33026. 305/885-2531

BOYD, ILENE RAE Bus:Mgmt/Admin. POSITION: Vice Pres, Alexander & Alexander, 600 Fisher Bldg, Detroit, MI 48202.

BOYER, GREGORY P. Bus:Mgmt/Admin. INT: coll barg. POSITION: Metropolitan Sewer Dist, 2000 Hampton Ave, St. Louis, MO 63139. 314/768-6213

BOYER, JOHN WILLIAM, JR. Bus:Pers/Ind Rels. POSITION: School of Business & Econ, Univ of Minnesota, Duluth, MN 55812.

BOYLE, EDWARD F. Bus:Mgmt/Admin, Consulting; Acad: Ind Rels. AB 1953, Dartmouth; MBA 1954, Amos Tuck School Bus Admin; MS 1976, U of Mass. POSITION: Dir IR, Archdiocese of Boston, 761 Harrison Ave, Boston, MA 02118. 617/536-9440

BOYLE, GEORGE V. Acad: Ind Rels. BA 1950, St. Peter's Coll; MA 1963, Rutgers U. PUBL: "Defining Labor Education Needs," Adult Leadership; "Goals of Unions and Universities in Labor Education," Labor Studies J; "Changing Living Patterns in Labor and Leisure," Natl Recreation & Parks Admin Conf Proc. INT: labor educ, coll barg, arb/med. ASSN: Gateway IRRA, Univ & Coll Labor Educ Assn, Natl Univ Continuing Educ Assn, Adult Educ Assn. POSITIONS: Cost Accounting, Texaco Inc, 1950; Assoc Prof, Rutgers, 1958; and (since 1968) Dir, Labor Educ Program, Univ of Missouri, 1004 Elm St, Columbia, MO 65211. 314/882-8358

BOYNTON, ROBERT EDWARD Acad: Org Beh/Pers. BBA 1956, MAIR 1962, U of Minn; PhD 1968, Stanford U. INT: mgmt/educ, personnel, arb/med. ASSN: Acad of Mgmt, Amer Soc of Public Admin. POSITION: Assoc Prof, DRMEC, Naval Post Grad School, Monterey, CA 93943. 408/646-2301

BRACKEN, WILLIAM GEORGE Consulting-Public Sector/Teachers. BBA 1974, MS, 1976, U of Wis-Madison. PUBL: "Time to Review Basics of Med-Arb Law," School Empl Rels Rev, WASB, July 1982; "Common Board Mistakes in Bargaining," Suprd, vol 15, #4, Sept 1983; "Statistical War: Measuring Inflation," Suprd, Apr 1981. INT: arb/med, coll barg, personnel. POSITION: Membership Consultant, Wis Assn of School Boards, 132 W Main St, Box 160, Winneconne, WI 54986. 414/582-4443

BRADBURN, WALTER V., JR. Bus:Mgmt/Admin. POSITION: Crown Central Petroleum, PO Box 1759, Houston, TX 77251. 713/472-2461

BRADFORD, W. S. Arbitration. BS 1931, LTI. PUBL: "Motion & Time Study;" "Job Evaluation;" "Wage Incentive Systems." POSITION: Federal Mediator, 72 Myrtle Rd, Woodstock, GA 30188. 404/926-4777

BRADLEY, G. WAYNE Acad: Ind Rels, Political Science; Consulting. BA 1966, U of Calif-Berekely; MA 1968, PhD 1969, U of Oregon. PUBL: "Review of European Industrial Democracy," Amer Pol Sci Rev, Mar, 1983; "Review of Contemporary Yugoslavia,: Amer Pol Sci Rev, Dec, 1970; Political Alienation, Chandler Press. POSITION: Dir of Labor Studies, Chairman of Political Sci, San Francisco State Univ, 1600 Holloway Ave, San Francisco, CA 94132. 415/469-1179.

BRADY, THOMAS F. Acad: IndRels; Arbitration, Consulting. BS 1958, Ind U; MBA 1971, U of Chicago. INT: ind engineering, mgmt/educ, arb/med. ASSN: Inst of Ind Engineers. POSITION: (since 1975) Assoc Prof, Purdue Univ, North Central-Westville. ADDRESS: 2811 Elbridge Way, Michigan City, IN 46360. 219/872-0527

BRAFF, JEFFREY LEWIS Legal Practice. BS 1973 NYSSILR-Cornell; JD 1978, U of Penna. INT: labor law, fair empl practices. ASSN: Philadelphia IRRA. POSITIONS: Asst Gen Labor Counsel, Consolidated Rail Corp, 1978, and (since 1982) Assoc, Wolf, Block, Schorr, Solis & Cohen, Packard Bldg, Philadelphia, PA 19102. 215/977-2120

BRAMS, STANLEY HOWARD Arbitration. INT: arb/med, coll barg, health & hosp care. ASSN: Detroit IRRA, Eng Soc of Detroit, Soc of Automotive Eng, Detroit Press Club. POSITIONS: President, 1961-1977,Chairman, Intermedia Group Inc 1977-1983; Retired. ADDRESS: 24500 Southfield Rd, Southfield, MI 48075.

BRANDON, DANIEL JOSEPH Consulting. BA 1956, St. Peters Coll; MS 1968, N. J. Inst of Tech. INT: coll barg, arb/med. ASSN: AMA, AAA. POSITIONS: Marketing Rep, Doubleday Co, 1960; Consultant, Metzler Assoc, 1969; and (since 1978), President, Cassetta Brandon & Taylor, 300 Maple Ave, South Plainfield, NJ 07080. 201/561-7805

BRANDT, GARY Union. UAW Region 2, 300 Liberty Plaza, Cleveland, OH 44131. 216/861-0580

BRANDWEIN, ETHEL BA 1944, Barnard Coll; MA 1947, Columbia U. Retired. ADDRESS: 2306 Blaine Dr, Chevy Chase, MD 20815.

BRANDWEIN, SEYMOUR Government. BA 1944 Brooklyn Coll. INT: empl/trng programs, labor market econ, govt labor policy. ASSN: Wash DC IRRA, ASPA, Evaluation Res Soc. POSITIONS: Dir of Program Evaluation, Empl & Trng Admin, USDL, 1973, and (since 1983) Visiting Scholar, Natl Academy of Sciences, Natl Research Council, Wash DC. ADDRESS: 2306 Blaine Dr, Chevy Chase, MD 20815. 202/334-2300

BRANNEN, DALTON E. Acad: Ind Rels, Univ Admin; Arbitration. BS 1969, MBA 1971, U of West Fla; PhD 1976, U of Miss. PUBL: "Why Few Arbitrators Are Selected;" "Limited Usefulness of Japanese Human Resources Management in the U.S.." INT: arb/med, personnel, mgmt/educ. ASSN: ASPA, AAA, Acad of Mgmt. POSITIONS: Ind Engineer, Westinghouse, 1971; Systems Eng, Fla Dept of Trans, 1973; and (since 1976) Dir of MBA Program & Prof of Mgmt, Univ of Southwestern Louisiana, PO Box 44212, Lafayette, LA 70504. 318/231-6215

BRANSTED, ZELDA N. Union. Sec-Treas, Colorado AFL-CIO, 360 Acoma, Room 300, Denver, CO 80233. 303/733-2401

BRAUER, WALTER C III Legal Practice. BS in Bus 1961, U of Kansas, AM 1962, U of Ill; JD 1965, U of Kansas. INT: labor law, union org/admn, coll barg. ASSN: Rocky Mt IRRA, ABA. POSITION: President and Shareholder, Brauer,Simons & Buescher P.C., 1563 Gaylord St, Denver, CO 80206. 303/333-7751

BRAUN, KURT Acad: Ind Rels, Law. JSD 1922, U of Breslau. INT: govt labor policy, intl comparative labor, labor law. ASSN: Wash DC IRRA, AEA. POSITIONS: Wash Correspondent, Fed of German Employees Assoc, Cologne, Germany, and (self-employed) Consultant. ADDRESS: 2904 Argyle Dr, Alexandria, VA 22305. 703/836-4462.

BRAUN, THOMAS MITCHELL Bus:Pers/Ind Rels. BS 1972, MS 1974, U of Wis. INT: personnel, coll barg. POSITIONS: Pers Mgr, Plant 14, Calif Canner & Growers, 1974; Mgr, Empl Rels, Schlegel Corp, Rochester NY, 1979; and (since 1981) Dist Empl Rels Mgr, Emery Air Freight Corp, 2222 Camden Ct, Oak Brook IL 60521. 312/686-6301

BRAZIER, JAMES EDWARD 1185 Palmer Lane #D, East Lansing, MI 48823.

BRECHER, CHARLES Publ Admin. BA 1965 U of Fla; PhD 1973, CUNY. PUBL: Upgrading Blue Collar and Service Workers, John Hopkins Univ Press, 1972; Where Have All the Dollars Gone? Praeger Publ; Setting Municipal Priorities 1983, NY Univ Press, 1982. INT: health & hosp care, empl/trng programs, income maint. ASSN: ASPA, Amer Pol Sci Assn. POSITIONS: Sr. Res Assoc, Columbia U, 1968; Assoc Prof, New School for Soc Res, 1977; and (since 1980) Assoc Prof, Grad School of Publc Admin, New York Univ. ADDRESS: 165 Juniper Rd, Scarsdale, NY 10583. 212/598-3246

BREDHOFF, ELLIOT Legal Practice. POSITION: Special Counsel, USA, AFL-CIO, Suite 1300, 1000 Connecticut Ave NW, Washington DC 20036. 202/833-9340

BREITENBECK, JOSEPH T. Bus:Pers/Ind Rels. BS History 1972, MA Ind Rels, 1983, Wayne State U. INT: personnel, coll barg, labor history. ASSN: Detroit IRRA, Ind Rels Assn of Detroit. POSITION: (since 1982) Sr. Pers Consultant, Maccabees Mutual Life Ins Co, Southfield. ADDRESS: 11032 Livonia, MI 48150. 313/357-4800

BREMER, CHARLES E. Union/Labor Org. BS 1965, Ohio U. INT: empl/trng, govt labor policy, health & hosp care. POSITIONS: Owner-Mgr, Private Business, 1973; Labor-Mgmt Rels Mgr, City of New York, 1976; and (since 1978) Assoc Dir, A Philip Randolph Educ Fund, 260 Park Ave S, New York NY 10010. 212/533-8000

BRENNAN, JOHN PAUL Bus:Pers/Ind Rels. 2830 Old State Rd, Schenectady, NY 12303. 518/355-0275

BRENNAN, PAUL J. Bus.Pers/Ind Rels. POSITION: Manager-IR & Pers, Federal Products Corp, 1144 Eddy St, Providence, RI 02905. 401/781-9300

BRENNER, DAVID JON Bus:Pers/Ind Rels. BBA 1971 UW-Milw. INT: personnel, succession planning, coll barg. POSITIONS: Trng Supr, B.F. Goodrich, 1978; Ind Rels Rep, 1978, and, since 1981, Human Res Planning Coordinator, Miller Brewing Co, 3939 W Highland Blvd, Milwaukee, WI 53201 414/931-4589

BRENT, ALFRED H. Arbitration, Mediation. 552 N Tilton Way, Jamesburg, NJ 08831.

BRESS, JOSEPH M. Government. POSITION: Governors Office Empl Rels, 2 Empire State Plaza, Albany, NY 12223

BRESSLER, ROBERT Arbitration. BS Econ 1949, Wharton School U of PA. INT: arb/med, coll barg, mgmt/educ. ASSN: Toledo (OH) IRRA, AAA, SPIDR, FMCS Arb Panel. POSITIONS: Pres, R. Bressler Assoc, Mgmt Consultants, 1971, and (since 1982) Arbitrator (self-employed), 4214 Carriage Drive, Sarasota, FL 33583. 813/371-2425

BRETT, JEANNE M. Acad: Org Beh/Pers. PhD 1972, U of Ill. POSITION: Prof, Org/Beh, Kellogg Grad School of Mgmt, Northwestern Univ, Evanston, IL 60201 312/492-3470

BREWER, CATHERINE HELENE Student. INT: personnel, org beh, empl/trng programs. POSITION: Student-Calif Polytechnic State Univ. ADDRESS: 200 N Santa Rosa, #304A, San Luis Obispo, CA 93401.

BREWSTER, CHRIS JOHN Bus:Pers/Ind Rels. Emp Rels: Resource Centre, 62 Hills Rd, Cambridge CB2 1LA England.

BRICKMAN, ELIZABETH Union. BA-Labor Studies 1981, Penna State U. INT: union org/-admn, labor history, labor law. POSITIONS: Intl Union Rep, 1981, and, since 1983, Field Services, Regional Coordinator, AFSCME. ADDRESS: 3904 Edmunds St NW, Washington DC 20007. 202/429-1264

BRICKNER, DALE G. Acad: Ind Rels. BA 1951, Antioch Coll; MA 1953, UCLA. Publ: "Labor and Antitrust Action," Ind & Labor Rels Rev, vol 13, #2; "A New Look at Unions Under Antitrust Action," Labor Law J, vol 11, #2; "The Status of Public Employee Bargaining," Labor Law J, vol 22, #8. INT: labor law, coll barg, arb/med. ASSN: SPIDR, Univ & Coll Labor Educ Assn. POSITIONS: Assoc Prof and Asst Dir, Labor Studies Center, Ind U, 1957; and (since 1973) Prof and Assoc Dir, School of Labor and Ind Rels, 433 S Kedzie Hall, Mich State Univ, East Lansing, MI 48824. 517/355-5070

BRIDGEWATER, BARBARA Arbitration. 2116 8th St, Suite A, Berkeley, CA 94710. 415/-845-0728

BRIGGS, STEVEN Acad: Ind Rels; Arbitration. BS-Bus Admin 1969, MS-Ind Rels 1971, Calif State-Long Beach; Phd Ind Rels 1981, UCLA. PUBL: The Municipal Grievance Process; "The Steward, The Supervisor, and The Grievance Process;" "An Empirical Investigation of Arbitrator Acceptability." INT: arb/med, coll barg, personnel. ASSN: Wis IRRA, SPIDR, AAA, Natl Academy of Arbitrators. POSITIONS: Lecturer in Ind Rels, Calif State, LongBeach, 1974; Hearing Officer, LA City Civil Serv Commission, 1979; and (since 1981) Asst Prof of Ind Rels, Coll of Bus Admin, Marquette Univ. ADDRESS: 3612 N Hackett AVE, Milwaukee, WI 53211. 414/224-7338

BRIGGS, VERNON MASON, Jr. Acad: Econ. BS 1959, U of Md; MA 1960, PhD 1965, Mich Stat U. PUBL: The Negro and Apprenticeship; The Chicano Worker; Employment, Income and Welfare in the Rural South. INT: empl/trng programs, labor market econ, govt labor policy. ASSN: AEA, Assn for Evolutionary Econ. POSITIONS: Assoc Prof of Econ, 1968, Prof of Econ, U of Texas at Austin, 1974; and (since 1978) Prof Labor Econ, NYSSILR, Cornell Univ, Ithaca, NY 14853. 607/256-4470

BRISCO, C. CHESTER Arbitration, Legal Practice. AB 1947, MBA 1953, U of Calif-Berkeley; JD 1968, U of Southern Calif. INT: arb/med, labor law, labor market econ. ASSN: Orange Cty IRRA, NAA, Calif State Bar Assn. POSITIONS: Sr. Salary Analyst, Kaiser Steel Corp, 1957; Chief Labor Rels, Ventura Div, Northrop Corp, 1960; and (since 1968) Attorney at Law, 2014 North Broadway, Santa Ana , CA 92706. 714/835-2010

BRITTON, RAYMOND L. Arbitration. ADDRESS: 6146 Olympia Dr, Houston, TX 77057. 512/828-0412

BROAS, LESLIE C. Bus:Pers/Ind Rels. INT: org beh, personnel, empl/trng programs. ASSN: Grand Rapids IRRA, Grand Rapdis Pers Assn, West Mich Chapter Intl Assn of Quality Circles, Natl Federation of Bus & Professional Women. POSITION: (since 1983) Plant Personnel Manager, Leon Plastics, 4901 Clay Ave SW, Grand Rapids, MI 616/531-7970

BROCCI, JOHN FREDERICK Bus.Pers/Ind Rels. BA-Psych 1965, Mich State U; MA Psych 1966, Central Mich U; MA Ind Rels 1967, Mich State U. INT: coll barg, ind psych, personnel. ASSN: Grand Rapids IRRA. POSITIONS: Tech Trng Admin, 1968, Labor Rels Admin, Chrysler Corp, 1976; and (since 1976) Dir Ind Rels, Sealed Power Corp, Muskegon. ADDRESS: 7095 Walker Rd, Spring Lake, MI 49456. 616/724-5447

BROCK, PATRICK E. Student. ADDRESS: 48 Dana St, Amherst, MA 01002.

BRODERICK, RENAE F. Student. BA 1973, Macalester Coll; MAIR 1978, U of Minn; PhD 1984, Cornell U. PUBL: Human Resources Planning - A Guide to Data, (w P. J. Snider) 1980; "Pay Discrimination: Legal Issues and Implications for Research, IR 1982 21,3, pp 309-317. INT: fair empl practrice Title VII, org beh, personnel. ASSN: Academy of Mgmt, APA DW. 14. POSITIONS: Org Analyst, Philip Morris U.S.A., 1979; Pers Analyst/Statis Analyst, General Motors Corp, 1981; and (since 1981) Student, Res Asst, NYSSILR-Cornell. ADDRESS: 700 Warren Rd Apt 17-1A, Ithaca, NY 14850. 607/256-6535

BRODSKY, DEBORAH M. Acad: Student, Law. BA 1978, U of Mich; MLIR 1979, Mich State Univ. INT: labor law, ind rels, arb/med. ASSN: Detroit IRRA, ABA (Labor & Empl Student Sections), State Bar of Mich, (Student Section). POSITIONS: Labor Rels Staff Asst, Jones & Laughlin, 1980; Empl Rels Specialist, Consolidated Aluminum Co, 1981; and (since 1983) Labor Law Clerk, Saks, Nunn, Kales et al, Detroit. ADDRESS: PO Box 206, Lathrup Village, MI 48076. 313/965-3464

BRODY, BERNARD Acad: Ind Rels. POSITION: Univ de Montreal, Ecole de Ind Rels, Case Postale 6128 SUCRSLA, Montreal H3C 3J7, Canada.

BRODY, DORIS PEARL Consulting. BA 1965, Brooklyn Coll; MA 1966, U of Penna; PhD 1973, NYSSILR-Cornell U. PUBL: "American Labor Education Service International Education Project: 1951-1961," Labor Studies J, Fall 1979, pp 131-147. INT: wage and salary compensation, labor history, coll barg. AD DRESS: PO Box 4014, New Haven, CT 06525.

BRODY, MATTHEW Industrial Psychology. POSITION: Chief of Psychiatry, Brooklyn Jewish Hosp, 41 Eastern Parkway, Brooklyn, NY 11238.

BROOK, RICHARD Legal Practice. BA 1964, Brooklyn Coll; LLB 1967, Columbia U. INT: labor law, coll barg, arb/med. ASSN: Long Island IRRA, ABA, NYS Bar Assn, Nassau County Bar Assn. POSITIONS: Assoc, Lorenz , Finn, Giardinos & Lambos, 1970; Partner, Delson & Gordon, 1972; and (since 1980) Richard S. Brook Esq, Garden City. ADDRESS: 46 Hampshire Rd, Great Neck, NY 11023. 516/741-8400

BROOKS, BRENDA McCHRISTON Bus:Pers/-Ind Rels. POSITION: Human Resources & Equal Opportunity, NAM, 1776 F St NW, Washington DC 20006. 202/331-3795

BROOKS, GEORGE Acad: Ind Rels. AB 1930, Yale; MA 1932, Brown U. INT: union org/admin, coll barg, labor educ. POSITION: Prof Emeritus, ILR Cornell. ADDRESS: 437 Trumbull Corners Rd, Newfield, NY 14867. 607/256-3050

BROOKSHIRE, MICHAEL LEO Acad: Ind Rels. PhD 1975, U of Tenn. PUBL: Collective Bargaining in Public Employment, D. C. Heath, 1977; "Resolving Bargaining Impasses Through Gradual Pressure Strikes," Labor Law J, 1973; "Productivity and Productivity Bargaining," in Handbook on Public Pers Admin and Labor Rels, 1983. INT: coll barg, labor law, personnel. POSITIONS: Assoc Vice Pres, U of Tenn, 1976; Vice Pres, U of Cincinnati, 1981; and (since 1983) Dir, Ind Rels Program, West Va College of Grad Studies, Institute, WV 25112. 304/768-9711

BROPHY, JACQUELINE A. Union. POSITION: Senior Staff Assoc, George Meany Center for Labor Study, 10000 New Hampshire Ave, Silver Spring, MD 20903. 315/431-6400

BROPHY, JOHN M. Acad: Org Beh/Pers Ind Rels; Fact Finding/Mediation. PhD 1947, Cornell U. INT: arb/med, mgmt/eudc, org beh. ASSN: Western New York IRRA, AAUP, Phi Delta Kappa. POSITIONS: Prof Behavioral Studies, U of Rochester, 1958-72; V. P. Academic Affairs, SUNY Coll of Tech-Utica Rome, 1972-75; Retired. ADDRESS: 530 Seneca Parkway, Rochester, NY 14613.

BROSSMAN, MARK EDWARD Legal Practice. BS 1975, Cornell U; JD 1978, LLM 1981, New York U. PUBL: Social Investing for Pensions Funds: For Love or Money, Intl Found of Empl Benefit Plans, 1982. INT: labor law, coll barg, arb/med. ASSN: New York IRRA, IIRA, ABA, Assn of the Bar of the City of New York. POSITIONS: Attorney, Morgan, Lewis & Bockius, 1983; and (since 1984) Attorney, Grutman, Miller, Greenspoon, Hendler & Levin, 505 Park Ave, New York, NY 10003. 212/888-1900

BROWN, ANDREW B. Bus.Pers/Ind Rels. BA 1979, MS 1982, Rutgers U. INT: coll barg, personnel, arb/med. ASSN: New Brunswick IRRA, ASPA. POSITIONS: Admin Analyst, City of Newark, 1981; and (since 1983) Pers Admin, Timeplex Inc, Woodcliff. ADDRESS: 69 Hamlin Rd, Edison, NJ 08817. 201/391-1111 ext 4843

BROWN, BARRY C. Arbitration. BS 1953, JD 1957, Wayne State U. PUBL: "OSHA"-State Plans," Duke U Law School: Law and Contemporary Problems, 1974; "Handicapped Rights," DePaul Law Rev, vol 27, #4, 1978; "Discrimination Claims in Arbitration," Mich State Bar J, 1984. INT: arb/med, labor law, govt labor policy. ASSN: Detroit Area IRRA, NAA, State Bar Assn (Labor Rels Law Section), Mich Empl Rels Comm (Arb Panel). POSITIONS: Dir, Mich Dept of Labor, 1969; Attorney, Sommers, Schwartz, Silver & Schwartz P.C., 1973; and (since 1974) Arbitrator, McGinty, Brown et al, P.C., 601 Abbott Rd, East Lansing, MI 48823. 517/351-0280

BROWN, CHARLES N. Bus:Pers/Ind Rels. INT: labor law, income maint, coll barg. ASSN: Houston IRRA. POSITION: Employee Rels Mgr, 1111 Shorewood Dr, Seabrook, TX 77586. 713/479-3411

BROWN, CLAIR Acad: Econ. PhD 1973, U of Md. PUBL: "Unemployment Theory and Policy, 1946-1980; Ind Rels, Spring, 1983; "Women's Economic Contribution to the Family," in R. Smith ed, The Subtle Revolution, Urban Inst, 1979; "Unemployment Insurance: A Positive Reappraisal," Ind Rels, Winter, 1979. INT: labor market econ, govt labor policy, income maint. ASSN: San Francisco IRRA, AEA. POSITION: Assoc Prof of Econ, Dept of Econ, (also Assoc Dir, Inst of Ind Rels), Univ of Calif, Berkeley, CA 94720. 415/642-0323

BROWN, DAVID HUNTER Arbitration, Legal Practice. JD 1947, U of Tex. INT: arb/-med. ASSN: Dallas IRRA, AAA, SPIDR, State Bar of Texas. POSITIONS: Judge, County Court at Law, Grayson Cty, Tex, 1947; Judge, 59th Judicial Dist, State of Tex, 1965; and (since 1966) Arbitrator, Box 370, Sherman TX, 75090. 214/893-9454

BROWN, DEBORAH A. Arbitration. BA 1970, Syracuse U. INT: arb/med, coll barg, labor law. ASSN: IRRA of Central New York. POSITIONS: Tribunal Admin, 1970, and, since 1973, Reg Dir, American Arbitration Assn, 720 State Tower Bldg, Syracuse, NY 13202. 315/472-5483

BROWN, DOUGLASS VINCENT Acad: Bus Admin. AB 1925, AM 1926, PhD 1933, Harvard U. POSITION: Prof, Emeritus, Room E52-580, Sloan School of Mgmt, MIT, Cambridge, MA 02139.

BROWN, GERALD ALTON Arbitration. POSI-TION: Arbitrator, Capitol Tower Apts 14N, 1500 7th St, Sacramento, CA 95814. 916/444-8702

BROWN, J. H. Government. POSITION: Chairman, Public Serv Staff Rels Bd, PO Box 1525, Station B, Ottawa, Ont, K1P 5V2, Canada. 613/996-2808

BROWN, JAMES DOUGLAS Univ Admin, Ind Rels. PhD, 1928, Princeton U. POSITION: Provost, Emeritus, Princeton U. ADDRESS: C-5, Meadow Lakes, Hightstown, NJ 08520.

BROWN. MARK L. Acad: Ind Rels. BA 1961, Albright Coll. ASSN: Harrisburg IRRA POSITION: Asst Prof Labor Studies, Penna State Univ. ADDRESS: 642 N 3rd St, Apt 1, Reading PA 19601. 215/375-4211

BROWN, MONTAGUE Consulting, Legal Prac; Acad: Health Admin. AB 1959, MBA 1960, U of Chicago; PhD 1971, JD 1981, U of N.C. PUBL: Hospital Management Systems; Multihospital Systems, Strategy and Planning in Health Care Management. INT: health & hosp care, org beh, mgmt/educ. ASSN: ABA, Amer Public Health Assn. POSITIONS: Assoc Prof, Grad School of Mgmt, Northwestern U, 1971; Prof, Duke Univ, 1975; and (currently) Pres, Strategic Mgmt Services Inc, Suite 308, 6803 W 64th, Shawnee Mission, KS 66202. 913/677-5157

BROWN, PATRA HELENA Student. 11830 Miami, Detroit, MI 48217. 313/388-1928

BROWN, ROBERT EDWARD Bus/Govt. POSITION: Assoc Prof, Dept of Bus & Govern, Northwest Missouri St U, Maryville, MO 64468. 816/562-1657

BROWN, SUSAN R. Arbitration. BA 1966, Antioch Coll; MA 1972, Mills Coll. PUBL: Help! A Guide to Interpreting Government Regulations for Small Employers, (pamphlet) Vermont Attorney General, 1977. INT: arb/med. ASSN: Boston IRRA, AAA, SPIDR, Vermont Labor History Assn. POSITIONS: Civil Rights Specialist, Vermont Attorney General, 1974, Hearing Officer, State of Vermont, 1979; and (since 1980), Arbitrator, Mediator, Fact-finder (Independent), 78 Lancaster Terrace, Brookline, MA 02146. 617/738-7631

BROWNE, DOLORES Union. ADDRESS: 15 Milburn Ct, Freeport, NY 11520. 516/285-6650

BRUMM. JOHN M. Acad: Ind Rels, Sociol; Union. MA 1931, Harvard. INT: labor history, health & hosp care, coll barg. ASSN: Wash DC Chapter IRRA. Retired. ADDRESS: 6103 Walhonding Rd, Bethesda, MD 20816.

BRUNING, NEALIA SUE Acad: Org Beh/Pers, Ind Rels. MA 1979, PhD 1981, U of Ala. PUBL: "Sex and Position as Predictors of Original Committment, (w R.S. Snyder) Acad of Mgmt, 1983, 26, pp 485-491; "Relationships Between EES Atts: Error Rates in Public Welfare Programs," Acad of Mgmt J, 1980, 23, pp 556-560. INT: org beh, beh aspects/ind rels activties, personnel. ASSN: Cleveland IRRA, Acad of Mgmt, Amer Psych Assn, Amer Inst for Decision Sci. POSITIONS: Program Act Coordinator, Partlow State School & Hosp, Tuscaloosa AL, 1973; Res Assoc, Mgmt Inst, Univ of Ala, 1975; and (since 1979) Asst Prof, Dept of Administrative Sci, Kent State Univ, Kent OH 44242. 216/672-2750

BRUNNHUBER, GREGORY 323 E Bell Ave, Altoona, PA 16602.

BUCCELLATO, VITO Student. BS 1984, St. Francis Coll-Brooklyn. INT: health & hosp care, personnel, ind sociology. ASSN: Long Island IRRA, Amer Public Health Assn. ADDRESS: 80 Carpenter Ave, Staten Island, NY 10314.

BUCHAN, JOHN F. Government, Arbitration, Cable TV Broadcasting. BS 1976, U of Md; MA 1979, Central Mich U. INT: mgmt/educ, personnel. ASSN: SPIDR, Soc of Federal Labor Rels Professionals, Natl Federation of Local Cable Programmers. POSITIONS: Empl Rels/Pers Specialist, Montgomery Cty (MD) School System,

1977; Arbitrator, Better Bus Bureau, Wash DC, 1981; and (since 1983) Empl/Labor Rels Specialist, ETA, USDL, Wash DC. ADDRESS: 19620 Club Lake Rd, Gaithersburg, MD 20879. 301/963-9191

BUCHEN, JOHN W. Government. BBA 1948; U of Wis. POSITION: Empl Rels, Wis Transportation Dept, PO Box 7915, Personnel, Madison, WI 53707. 608/266-7460

BUCKINGHAM, MARK H. Consulting, School Dist Rep. BS 1976, U of Illinois; MW, MPA 1979, Ohio State U. INT: arb/med, coll barg. ASSN: Central Ohio IRRA. POSITIONS: Field Rep, Dist Org, San Francisco Labor Council AFL-CIO; Labor Rels Specialist, Ohio School Boards Assoc, 1981, and, since 1983, Assoc Dir/Labor Rels, Ohio School Boards Assoc, 700 Brooksedge Blvd, Westerville, OH 43081. 614/891-6466

BUCKLEY, LOUIS F. Acad: Ind Rels. AB 1928, MA 1930, Notre Dame U. PUBL: "Economics and Guidance," in Foundations of Guidance and Counselling, ed by C.E. Smith and O. G. Mink, JB 1969; Causes of Unemployment of Unemployment Insurance Claimants," Loyola U of Chicago,1970; "Comparasion of European Unemployment Insurance Laws," in Comparative Labor Law, Vol 1, #4, Winter 1976. INT: labor market econ, govt labor policy, intl comparative labor. ASSN: Assn for Soc Econ, AEA. POSITIONS: Prof of Econ, Loyola Univ, Rome Italy, 1975-77; Lecturer in Econ, St. Ambrose Coll, Davenport, IA, 1977; and (since 1974) Prof Emeritus, Loyola Univ of Chicago. ADDRESS: 2821 E Pleasant St, Davenport, IA 52803.

BUCKNER, JEAN B. Bus:Mgmt/Admin, Pers/Ind Rels. MSIR 1973, U of Wis-Madison. INT: coll barg, arb/med, personnel. POSITIONS: E.R. Staff Specialist, Exxon Res & Engineering Co, 1973; Mgr, Career Development, 1980, and, since 1982, Manager, Labor Rels & Field Services, Mobil Oil Co (U.S. Marketing and Refining)-Valley Forge. ADDRESS: 1837 Hawthorne PL, Paoli, PA 19301. 215/644-5148

BUDD, JAMES L. Bus:Pers/Ind Rels. BA 1968, U of Del. INT: coll barg, personnel, empl/trng programs. ASSN: ASPA, U of PA-Wharton Labor Rels Council, Manufacturers Assn of Delaware Valley. POSITIONS: Supr Empl Services, I-T-E Imperial Corp, Phila, Pa, 1968; Pers Mgr, Weyerhaeuser Corp, PA, 1973; and (since 1978) V.P. Empl Rels-Mfg Group, ALCO Standard Corp, P O Box 834, Valley Forge, PA 19482. 215/296-8600

BUDLONG, CAROL A. Government. Apprentice Consultant, Calif Dept of Ind Rels, 2422 Arden Way, Suite 60, Sacramento, CA 95825. 916/920-6111

BUFORD, THOMAS G. Legal Practice. JD 1975, Golden Gate U. POSITION: Howard & Howard Attorneys, 407 Kalamazoo Bldg, Kalamazoo, MI 49007. 616/382-1483

BUJAN, RONALD JAMES Bus:Pers/Ind Rels. MSIR 1977, Loyola U of Chicago. PUBL: "A Primer on Self-Funding Health Care Benefits;" "Prescriptions for Reducing Health Care Costs;" "IR: Why Cooperation is Essential in a Changing Economy." INT: personnel, coll barg, health & hosp care. ASSN: Chicago IRRA, ASPA. POSITION: (since 1977) Director, Ind Rels, Dreis & Krump Mfg Co, 7400 S Loomis Blvd, Chicago, IL 60636. 312/874-1200

BULLARD, CHRISTOPHER KING Student; Arbitration. BA 1975, U of Penna; JD 1978, Villanova U-Law. PUBL: The Counterclaim in Litigation under Title VII: Is It a Right or Is It Retaliation?" INT: labor law, arb/med, labor history. ASSN: Penna Bar Assn, Florida Bar Assn, ABA. POSITIONS: General Attorney, EEOC, 1979; Asst Dir of Ind Rels, Amer Home Products Corp, 1980; and (since 1980) Student, Cornell U/Baruch Coll. ADDRESS: Apt 9-R, 305 East 40th St, New York, NY 10016. 212/697-5873

BULLARD, JENNIE K. Acad: Student, School Admin. BS 1966, MS 1971, Penna State Univ; PhD 1982, U of Pittsburgh; MAIR 1984, Indiana U of Penna. INT: arb/med, mgmt/educ, labor educ. ASSN: Amer Orthopsychiatric Assn. Positions: Mental Health/Retardation Admin, Centre Cty Government, 1972; Dir of Education, Hollidaysburg State Hosp, 1975; and (since 1976) Supr/Spec Educ, Pittsburgh Board of Educ. ADDRESS: Box 10, Torrance, PA 15779. 412/665-4980

BULLEN, FREDERICK H. Arbitration. BA, 1938 Cornell, 1938-40 Harvard; LLB 1957, NYU Law School. INT: arb/med, coll barg, labor law. ASSN: San Diego IRRA, NAA, AAA, ABA. POSITIONS: Vice-Chair, Natl Wage Stabilization Board, Natl Wage Stabilization Board, 1951-52; Partner, Law Firm, Kaye, Scholer, Fierman et al, New York, 1952-1977; and (since 1978) Arbitrator (self-employed) 12473 Grandee Rd, San Diego, CA 92128. 619/485-7834

BULLER, CARTER REDVERS Legal Prac. INT: labor law, arb/med, coll barg. ASSN: Philadelphia IRRA. POSITION: Partner, Montgomery, McCracken,Walker & Rhodes, 3 Parkway 20th Floor, Philadelphia, PA 19102. 215/563-0650

BULLOCK, PAUL Acad: Ind Rels. BA, 1948, MA 1949, Occidental Coll-Los Angeles. PUBL: Aspiration vs. Opportunity: 'Careers' in the Inner City, Inst of Labor & Ind Rels, U of Mich 1973; CETA at the Crossroads: Employment Policy and Politics, Inst of Ind Rels, UCLA 1981; Building California: The Story of the Carpenters' Union, (w others) Center for Labor Res and Educ, IIR, UCLA, 1982. INT: empl/trng programs, labor history, income maint. POSITIONS: Inst in Econ, Occidental Coll, Los Angeles, 1950-51; Wage Analyst, Natl Wage Stabilization Bd, Los Angeles, 1951-53; and (since 1953) Res Economist, Inst of Ind Rels, UCLA, 405 Hilgard Ave, Los Angeles, CA 90024. 213/825-3782

BULSIEWICZ, KAREN A. Legal Practice/-Mgmt. BA 1976, St. Lawrence U; JD 1981, Albany Law School. INT: labor law. ASSN: New Brunswick IRRA. NJ and NY State Bar Assn (Labor & Empl Law), ABA. POSITION: Assoc Attorney, Murray & Grarello, 25 Sycamore Ave, Little Silver NJ 07747. 201/747-2300

BUMAS, LESTER O. Acad: Econ. BEE 1950, CCNY; PhD 1967, NYU. POSITION: Assoc Prof of Econ, Polytech Inst of New York, 103-10 Queens Blvd, Forest Hills, NY 11375. 212/643-5540

BURATTO, RAYMOND JOSEPH Legal Prac, Arbitration. BA 1974, MLIR 1975, Mich State U; JD 1978, Wayne State U. INT: labor law, coll barg, arb/med. ASSN: Detroit IRRA, ABA, Mich Bar Assn. POSITIONS: Asst VP-Labor Rels, 1980, VP-Ind Rels, Interstate System,

1981; and (since 1983) Associate, Matheson, Bieneman, Parr, Schuler and Ewald, 100 W Long Lake Rd, Suite 102, Bloomfield Hills, MI 48013. 313/645-9600

BURBINE, HENRY W. Union. MED 1965, Bridgewater State; TUP, 1977, Harvard. INT: coll barg, arb/med, labor law. ASSN: Boston IRRA, Boston Labor Guild. POSITIONS: Teacher of Exceptional Children (Retarded), Town of Hanson Public Schools, 1966, and (since 1974) Consultant for Labor Rels, Mass Teachers Assn, 534 New State Hwy, Raynham, MA 02767. 617/822-5371

BURCHETT, HAROLD D. Bus:Pers/Ind Rels. Consulting. BA 1963, San Jose State. INT: coll barg, personnel, empl/trng programs. ASSN: Columbus IRRA, ASPA. POSITIONS: I. R. Regional Mgr, 1970, Gen Mgr, Labor Rels, 1973, Borden Inc, Syracuse; and (since 1976) President, Burchett & Assoc, 2850 Fisher Rd, Columbus, OH 43204. 614/276-5229

BURDETSKY, BEN Acad: Ind Rels, Bus Admin; Consulting. PhD 1968, American U. PUBL: Business and Government: We're All in It Together," The Bureaucrat, Summer 1982; "Alternative Work Patterns,: Australian Empl Work Rels J, 1982. INT: coll barg, personnel, mgmt/educ. ASSN: Wash DC IRRA, Amer Statis Assn, Intl Assn Pers in Empl Security. POSITIONS: Deputy Commissioner of Labor Statis, 1967, Deputy Asst Sec of Labor-Empl & Trng, USDL, 1973; and (since 1980) Chairman, Dept of Bus Admin, George Washington Univ. ADDRESS: 4619 N Dittmar RD, Arlington, VA 22207. 202/676-4852

BURGESON, GLENN F. Government. BS 1952, Ohio U-Athens; MA 1963, John Carroll U. PUBL: "A Comparison of Two Management Groups in a Steel Firm." INT: arb/med, coll barg, empl/trng programs. ASSN: San Francisco and Inland Empire IRRAs. POSITIONS: Labor Rels Supr, TRW Inc, 1960; Dir, Colorado Educ Assn, 1968; and (since 1974) Commissioner, FMCS, 525 Market St, 29th FL, San Francisco, CA 94501. 415/974-9860

BURGESS, BRUCE SAMPSON Union. POSITION: Regional Manager, Mass Teachers Assn, 1395 N Main St, Randolph , MA 02368. 617/961-1006

BURKE, DONALD R. Acad: Bus Admin. POSITION: Dept of Bus Admin, Villanova Univ, Villanova, PA 19085. 215/645-4336

BURKHARDT, FRANCIS XAVIER Union. POSITION: Research Director, IBPAT, 8409 Grand Haven Ave, Upper Marlboro, MD 20870. 301/627-2928

BURKI, FRED A. Union. POSITION: President, UFCW Local 881, 9865 W Roosevelt Rd, Westchester, IL 60153. 312/681-1000

BURNELL, STAN E. Union, Consulting. BA 1967, U of Iowa. INT: coll barg, arb/med, empl/trng programs. ASSN: Westrn Mich IRRA, United Staff Org, MEA, NEA. POSITIONS: Project Res Engineer Titus Res Lab, Titus Mfg Co, 1962; Teacher, Math, Cedar Rapids Community Schools, 1967; and (since 1971) Uniserv Director, Mich Educ Assn, 17232 Robbins Rd, Grand Haven, MI 49417. 616/846-2770

BURNETT, PHYLLIS D. Bus:Pers/Ind Rels, Union, Consulting. BA 1977, CUNY; MS 1981, New York Inst of Tech. INT: empl/trng programs, org beh, union org/admn. POSITION: (since 1972) Treasury Rep, Con Edison, New York. ADDRESS: 1 Lamarcus Ave, Glen Cove, NY 11542. 212/460-6644

BURNS, DEAN E. Student. INT: labor law, coll barg, labor market econ. ADDRESS: 114 Circleview Dr, Beckley, WV 25801.

BURNS, MAY C. Union. INT: coll barg, labor educ, union org/admn. ASSN: S. Nevada IRRA, Amer Bus Womens Assn. POSITION: Bus Rep/Recording Sec, Intl Brotherhood of Teamsters, Local 995, 300 Shadow Lane, Las Vegas, NV 89106. 702/385-0995

BURNS, ROBERT T. Bus:Pers/Ind Rels. BS 1959, U of Rochester. INT: union org/admn, compensation, personnel. ASSN: Amer Compensation Assn, NAM, AEA. POSITIONS: Dir, Pers Admn, Corporate, 1970, Vice Pres, Ind Rels, Bausch & Lomb Inc, 1974; and (since 1978) Vice Pres, Pers, Ohaus Scale Corp, 29 Hanover Rd, Florham Park, NJ 07932. 201/377-9000

BURNS, STEVEN R. Bus:Pers/Ind Rels. BA 1976, MAIR 1977, U of Cincinnati. INT: personnel, org planning, mgmt/educ. POSITION: Supervisor-Pers Rels, Armco Inc, Middletown Works, PO Box 600, Middleton, OH 45043. 513/425-0592

BURNS, WILLIAM L. Union. POSITION: Sr. Res Analyst, UFCW Intl Union, 1775 K Street NW, Washington DC 20006. 202/223-3111

BURROWS, SEYMOUR J. Consulting, Arbitration, Medical Interrelations. AB 1939, MBA 1953, U of Chicago. PUBL: Negotiations for Physicians, an Introduction; "Arbitration in Medical Relationships." INT: health & hosp care, arb/med. ASSN: AAA, ASPA, SPIDR. POSITIONS: Senior Assoc, John Sheridan Assoc, 1973; Assoc Dir, Amer Medical Assn, 1975; and (since 1983) Retired. ADDRESS: 3450 Lake Shore Dr, Chicago, IL 60657.

BURSTEIN, GEORGE Acad: Bus Admin, Org Beh/Pers, Health Care Mgmt. MPA 1948, NYU; MS 1949, CCNY; DPA 1977, SUNY-Albany. PUBL: "Building User Based Curriculum,: Cross Reference, Am Hosp Assoc, July/Aug 1982. INT: health & hosp care, mgmt educ, org beh. ASSN: Los Angeles IRRA, Amer Sociol Assn, Acad of Mgmt, ASPA. POSITIONS: Chief, Educ and Trng, Letchworth Development Center, 1972; Asst Prof Publ Admin, Fairleigh Dickinson Univ, 1976; and (since 1979) Assoc Prof Mgmt, Calif State Univ, 5151 State Univ Drive, Los Angeles, CA 90032. 213/224-2961

BURSTEIN, HERBERT Legal Practice. 387 Park Ave S, New York, NY 10016.

BURTON, JOHN F., JR. Acad: Ind Rels, Econ, Law. BS 1957, Cornell U; LLB 1960, PhD 1965, U of Mich. PUBL: "Compensation for Permanent Partial Disabilities," in J.D. Worrall ed, Safety and the Work Force, ILR Press 1983; "The Extent of Collective Bargaining in the Public Sector," in B. Aaron et al ed, Public Sector Bargaining, BNA/IRRA, 1979; "The Role and Consequence of Strikes by Public Employees," (w C. Krider), Yale Law J, 1970. INT: soc insurance, coll barg, labor market econ. ASSN: AEA, ABA, SPIDR. POSITIONS:

Chairman, Natl Commission on State Workmen's Compensation Laws, 1971-72; Prof, Grad School of Bus, Univ of Chicago, 1966-1978; and (since 1978) Prof, NYSSILR, Cornell Univ, 267 Ives Hall, Ithaca, NY 14853. 607/256-3249

BURTT, EVERETT JOHNSON Consulting. AB 1935, Berea Coll; MA 1937, PhD 1950, Duke Univ. PUBL: Labor in the American Economy, St. Martin's 1979; Social Perspectives in the History of Economic Theory, St. Martin's 1972; Plant Relocation and the Core City Worker, U.S. Government Printing Office, 1967. INT: labor market econ, coll barg, labor history. ASSN: Boston IRRA, AEA, Amer Soc Univ Professors. POSITIONS: Prof Econ (now Emeritus) Boston Univ, 1947-80; and (since 1980) Labor Market Consultant, 9 Mary Dyer Lane, N. Easton, MA 02356. 617/238-4766

BUSCA, MORRIS JAMES Union. BA 1969, U of Conn; MS 1979, U of Mass. INT: arb/med, labor law, coll/barg. ASSN: Conn Valley IRRA. POSITIONS: Res Analyst, Conn State Emply Assoc, 1976and (since 1979) Bus Agent, Local 531, SEIU, New Haven. ADDRESS: 3 Fir Ridge Rd, Clinton, CT 06413. 203/239-5618

BUSH, MICHAEL L. Bus:Mgmt/Admin. MAIR 1974, U of Cincinnati. INT: Empl Benefits, coll barg. POSITIONS: Mgr, Union Empl Section, Printing Industries of Southern Ohio, 1979, and (since 1982) Mgr, Welfare Plans, Mead Corp, World Headquarters, Dayton. ADDRESS: 6021 Culpepper Ct, Centerville, OH 45459. 513/222-6323

BUSH, RONALD W. Acad: Univ Admin. BS 1965, Ryder Coll; MEd 1968, St. Lawrence U. PUBL: "Technology and Human Resources," New Directions for Community Coll, Fall 1983; "Goodby With Goodwill," Assn of Governing Boards and Univ and Coll, Jan/Feb 1981; "Master Planning for Human Resources," Educ Record, Spring 1984. INT: org beh, empl/trng programs, labor market econ. ASSN: Amer Mgmt Assn, Amer Assn of Higher Educ, League for Innovation. POSITIONS: Dir of Higher Educ, Iowa state Educ Assn, 1970-72; Asst to the Pres, Middlesex Cty Community Coll, 1972-77; and (since 1978) Vice-Chancellor for Human Resources, Maricopa Community Coll, 3910 E Washington St, Phoenix, AZ 85034. 602/244--8355

BUSKIRK, PHYLLIS A. R. Econ/Non-Profit Org. AB 1951, William Smith Coll. PUBL: "The Recovery's Strength in the Kalamazoo Area: A Comparison Between 1983 and 1975," in Bus Condition in the Kalamazoo Area, pp 6-15; "Review of Local Construction Activity (for 1982) and Prospects for 1983," in Bus Conditions in the Kalamazoo Area, pp 33-36; Business Conditions in Michigan Metropolitan Areas, (w P.J. Kozlowski), W.E. Upjohn Inst, Dec 1979. INT: labor market econ, empl/trng programs, income maint. ASSN: SW Mich IRRA, Amer Statis Assn, Natl Assn of Bus Economists. POSITIONS: Res Asst, 1976, Co-editor, Bus Conditions in the Kalamazoo Area, 1979 to present, and since 1983, Sr Staff Economist, W. E. Upjohn Inst for Empl Res, 300 S Westnedge, Kalamazoo, MI 49007. 616/343-5541

BUSMAN, GLORIA BROOKS Acad: Ind Rels; Union. PUBL: Understanding Public Sector Unions; Union Representative's Guide to NLRB RC/CA Cases; "The Decertification Process-Evidence From California," (w J. Anderson & C. O'Reilly), Ind Rels, vol 21, #2. INT: labor educ, labor law, org beh. ASSN: Los Angeles IRRA, Inst of Ind Rels Assn, Calif Univ Council. POSITIONS: Rep AFL-CIO Org Committee, 1963; and (since 1976) Coordinator, Inst of Ind Rels, 9353 Bunche Hall, UCLA, Los Angeles, CA 90024. 213/825-3180

BUSSEY, ELLEN M. Arbitration; Acad: Econ, Ind Rels. PhD 1970, American U. PUBL: The Flight From Rural Poverty--How Nations Cope, DC Heath, 1973. INT: arb/med, coll barg, labor law. ASSN: Wash DC IRRA, ASPA, AEA, SPIDR. POSITION: Economist, Labor Arb, Labor, (self-employed) 6506 Old Chesterbrook Rd, Mc Lean VA, 22101. 703/734-0488

BUTLER, ARTHUR D. Acad: Econ. BA 1944, Manchester Coll; MA 1946, U of Minn; PhD 1951, U of Wis. PUBL: Labor Economics and Institutions; "Labor Force Behavior in A Full Employment Economy," "Labor Costs in the Common Market." INT: labor market econ, income maint, govt labor policy. ASSN: AEA, Amer Econometric Soc. POSITIONS: Asst Prof, 1949, Assoc Prof, 1954, and, since 1959, Prof of Econ, O'Brien Hall, SUNY-Buffalo, Amherst, NY 14260. 716/636-2121

BUTLER, GERALD L. Bus:Pers/Ind Rels. BA 1959, Seton Hall U. INT: coll barg, arb/med, personnel. ASSN: New York IRRA. POSITIONS: Dir, Empl Rels, Indian Head Corp, 1968; Mgr, Labor Rels, Chemicals Div, and, since 1979, Dir, Labor Rels, Allied Chemical Corp, PO Box 1087R, Morristown, NJ 07960. 201/455-3903

BUTLER, JAMES C. Bus:Mgmt/Admin, Bus:-Pers/Ind Rels. BA 1970, SUNY-Oneonta; MAIR 1978, St. Francis Coll. INT: coll barg, intl comparative labor, personnel. POSITIONS: Mgr Labor Rels & Benefits, Harshaw Chemical Co, Cleveland, 1978; Mgr Empl Benefits, Cordero Mining Co, Wyoming, 1980; and (since 1982) Specialist Pers Policy Div, Saudi Arabian Airlines, Box 167, Cost Center 595, Jiddah, Saudi Arabia.

BUTLER, JOHN BRUCE Consulting; Acad: Org Beh/Pers. BA 1946, Colgate U; MS 1947, Penn State U. INT: personnel, org beh. ASSN: Boston IRRA, New England Soc Pers Mgmt, ASPA, Amer Soc Trng and Development. POSITIONS: Assoc Dir,Pers, 1964-69, Dir of Pers, 1969-76, Harvard Univ; and (since 1977) Consultant (self employed). ADDRESS: 44 North St, Lexington, MA 02173. 617/862-5410

BUZBEE, ELLEN W. Arbitration. 149 Lee Rd, Scarsdale, NY 10583. 914/472-0548

BYARS, LLOYD L. Acad: Univ Admin. 4430 N Elizabeth LN NW, Atlanta, GA 30339. 404/355--6919

BYERS, JAMES F. Student. MDiv 1970, Pontifical College Josephinum; MA 1980, Ind Univ of Penna. INT: govt labor policy, labor educ, union org/admn. POSITIONS: Dir, Human Rels Commission, Diocese of Greensburg,PA, 1972; Soc Welfare Lobbyist, Penna Catholic Conference, 1982; and (since 1983) Student, IRRI-U of Wis. ADDRESS: 7120 Parkshore Ct, Middleton, WI 53562. 608/831-3388

BYNUM, THEODORE R. Union. 10330 Old Olive St Road, St. Louis, MO 63141. 314/432-2425

BYRD, BARBARA K. Student. BA 1971, Rice U; MS 1978, U of Mass. PUBL: "Discovering Working Class Culture: A Case Study in Curriculum Development," Labor Studies J, Vol 8, #1, Spring 1983, pp 18-33. INTL: labor educ, union org/admn, adult educ. ASSN: Austin IRRA, Univ & Coll Labor Educ Assn, Amer Assn Adult & Continuing Educ. POSITIONS: Coordinator, Asst Prof of Labor Studies, Indiana State Univ, 1978-1981, and (since 1982) Ins, Labor Studies, San Antonio Coll of Public Affairs, San Antonio. ADDRESS: 5703 Ave C, Austin TX 78752.

BYRNE, JEROME CAMILLUS Legal Practice. POSITION: Partner, Gibson, Dunn & Crutcher, 2029 Century PK E, 4000, Los Angeles, CA 90067. 213/652-5674

BYRNE, WILLIAM F. Legal Prac, Arbitration. BA 1967, Holy Cross Coll; MA 1974, JD 1977, W Va U. INT: arb/med. ASSN: Assn of Trial Lawyers. POSITION: (since 1977) Attorney, Stone, Gallagher and Byrne, 221 Willey St, Morgantown, WV 26505. 304/296-2571.

BYRNES, LOUISE Union. 2522A S Worchester CT, Aurora, CO 80014. 303/770-2825

C

CABE, CARL Arbitration; Acad: Ind Rels, Econ. BA 1944, MA 1946, PhD 1952, U of Ill. INT: arb/med, coll barg, labor law. ASSN: Cincinnati IRRA, AEA. POSITIONS: Asst Prof, 1952, Prof, 1958 Univ of Ky, and (since 1977) Arbitrator (self-employed). ADDRESS: 750 Shaker Dr, Suite 409, Lexington, KY 40504.606/-278-6911

CABELLY, ALAN Acad:Ind Rels, Org Beh/-Pers. BA 1972, SUNY-Stony Brook; MBA 1975, Penn State U; PhD 1980, U of Wash. PUBL: "An Empirical Test of a Behaviorial Oriented Negotiation Model in the Public Schools in the State of Washington," IRRA, 1981; "Problem Solving in Labor Negotiations," Relations Industrielles, 1981; "The Managerial Elite: The Business Schools Legacy," Exchange, 1983. INT: personnel, performance appraisal, coll barg. ASSN: Acad of Mgmt, ASPA, Pacific Northwest Pers Mgmt Assn. POSITION: Assoc Professor, Portland State Univ, PO Box 751, Portland, OR 97207. 503/229-3770, 3712

CAHN, SIDNEY L. Arbitration, Legal Prac, Mediation. 261 Madison Ave, 19th FL, New York, NY 10016. 212/902-8070

CAIN, GLEN G. Acad: Econ. BA 1955, Lake Forest Coll; MA 1957, U of Calif-Berkeley; PhD 1964, U of Chicago. PUBL: Married Women in the Labor Force; Income Maintenance and Labor Supply; "The Challenge of Segmented Labor Market Theories to Orthodox Theory," J of Econ Lit, Dec 1976. INT: labor market econ, income maint, empl/trng programs. ASSN: Wis IRRA, AEA. POSITION: Prof, Dept of Economics, Univ of Wis, Madison, WI 53706. 608/262-7897

CAIN, LEONARD F. Acad: Economics. 1026 Newton St NE, Washington DC 20017. 202/529-1634

CALLAHAN, CHARLES III Acad: Econ. Dept Bus and Econ, Northern State College, Aberdeen SD 57401.

CALLUS, RON Acad: Ind Rels, Sociology, Org Beh/Pers. BEc 1974, MEc 1978, Sydney U. "Employer Policies for the Management of a Multi-Ethnic Workforce: A Critical Examination," J of Ind Rels, Vol 21, #6, 1979; "Self Managed Research and Technological Change," in Econonmic and Ind Democracy, 1984; "Industrial Disputes Statistics: Problems & Possibilities," (w R. Morris) in Human Res Mgmt, Vol 20 #3, 1982. INT: union org/admn, contemporary IR, ind sociol. ASSN: Inst of Soc Econ, Ind Rels Soc of NSW, Australian & New Zealand Sociol Assn. POSITION: Lecturer, Univ of Sydney, Broadway, NSW, Australia 2006. Phone: 02/692 3670

CALVASINA, GERALD E. Acad: Bus Admin. BBA 1975, MBA 1978, PhD 1983, U of Miss. PUBL: "A Preliminary Analysis of Delay, Turnout, and Margin of Victory in NLRB Representation Elections: A Southern Example," Southern Mgmt Assn Proceedings, 1983; "Practical Tips for Motivation," Management Quar. INT: mgmt/educ, personnel, labor law. ASSN: Acad of Mgmt, Southern Mgmt Assn, Southeaster AIDS. POSITIONS: Field Supt, J. L. Capano, Inc, Delaware, 1975; Inst, Univ of Miss, Dept of Continuing Educ, 1979; and (since 1982) Asst Prof of Bus Admin, Univ of North Carolina at Charlotte. ADDRESS: Sharon Lakes Apts, 244 Shady Oak Trail, Charlotte, NC 28210. 704/597-4422

CAMBRIDGE, CHARLES D. Acad: Bus:Admin, Ind Rels. BA 1971, McAlester Coll; MA 1973, PhD 1981, U of Minn. PUBL: "Emerging Trends in the Industrial Relations Systems in Former Colonies in Africa: The Ratification of Industrial Labour Conventions," J of African Studies, 1984; "The Need for an Increased Minimum Wage in Kenya," Res Report: Central Org of Trade Unions of Kenya, May 1982; "Programs and Efforts to Increase the Number of Minority Engineers: an Overview," Oct 1983, Proc of the Natl Electronics Conf. INT: intl comparative labor, union org/admin, arb/med. ASSN: Northern Calif IRRA, Acad of Intl Bus, Acad of Mgmt, Assn of Caribbean Studies. POSITIONS: Labor Economist (on leave from Univ), African-American Labor Center, 1981; Advisor, (on leave from Univ), Central Org of Trade Unions of Kenya, 1981; and (since 1978), Asst Prof, Dept of Mgmt, Calif State Univ-Chico, Chico, CA 95929. 916/895-5876

CAMERANO, FRANKLIN Bus:Mgmt/Admin. BBA 1957, St. John's U; MA 1965, U of Ill; MSHA 1965, Columbia U. PUBL: "Why Community Hospitals Are Becoming More Important;" "Developing A Retirement Age Policy;" "Grievance Procedure: Heart of Collective Bargaining Agreement." INT: health & hosp care, mgmt/educ, org beh. ASSN: Amer Coll of Hosp Admn, Royal Soc of Health, Amer Hosp Assn. POSITIONS: Asst Dir, St. Vincent's Hosp & Med Center, 1968; Exec Dir, John E Runnels Hosp, 1975; and (since 1980) Sr Assoc-Exec Dir, Booth Memorial Medical Center, 56-45 Main St, Flushing NY 11355. 212/670-1021

CAMP, SIDNEY LAMAR, JR. Student. BS 1981, Georgia Inst of Tech; MLIR 1983, Mich State U. INT: arb/med, labor law, coll barg. ASSN: Atlanta IRRA, SPIDR, SFLRP, ASPA. POSITION: Research Asst (and Doctoral Cand),

Dept of IR and HR, Univ of Iowa, Iowa City, IA 52242. 319/337-4358

CAMPAGNA, ANTHONY FRANK Acad: Ind Rels, Org Beh/Pers. BS 1964, SUNY-Buffalo; MBA 1966, PhD 1971, UCLA. INT: coll barg, personnel, arb/med. ASSN: Central Ohio IRRA, Acad of Mgmt. POSITION: Assoc Prof of Mgmt and Human Res, 1775 College Rd, Ohio State Univ, Columbus, OH 43210. 614/422-5028

CAMPBELL, ARCHIE E. Acad: Bus Admin. ADDRESS: 240 Dunrovin Lane, Brighton, NY 14618.

CAMPBELL, DUNCAN COLIN Acad: Student. Ind Rels, Org Beh/Pers, . AB 1974, Bowdoin Coll; MA 1976, MBA 1981, Wharton-U of Penna. PUBL: Multinational Enterprises and the OECD Industrial Relations Guidelines, (w R. L. Rowan) U of Penna, 1983; "The Attempt fo Regulate Industrial Relations Through International Codes of Conduct," (w R. L. Rowan) Columbia J of World Bus, Fall 1983. INT: intl comparative labor, labor market econ, coll barg. ASSN: Philadelphia IRRA. POSITION: PhD Student and Inst/Dept of Mgmt, Wharton School Univ of Penna. ADDRESS: 535 Delancey St, Philadelphia, PA 19106. 215/898-5605

CAMPBELL, JOHN, JR. Acad: Economics. Savannah State Coll, Box 20392, Savannah, GA 31404.

CAMPION, DIANE LEE Union; Acad: Ind Rels. AA 1978, Dutchers Comm Coll, BS 1980, Cornell U. INT: coll barg, arb/med, union org/admin. ASSN: Coalition of Labor Union Women. POSITION: (since 1980) Labor Rels Field Rep, Civil Service Empl Assn, Fishkill. ADDRESS: 117 Haviland Rd, Poughkeepsie, NY 12601. 914/896-8180

CANNON, RICHARD S. Bus:Pers/Ind Rels. BS BA 1958, Southern Ill U. INT: personnel, mgmt/educ, labor law. ASSN: St. Louis IRRA, ASPA. POSITIONS: Sr. Labor Rels Rep, Olin Corp, 1969; Pers Dir, Metro St. Louis Sewer Dist, 1972; and (since 1975) Vice Pres, Ind Rels, Hager Hinge Company, 139 Victor St, St Louis MO 63104. 314/772-4400

CANTFIL, AUGUST F. Retired. ADDRESS: 6411 Tone Dr, Bethesda, MD 20817.

CANTOR, ARNOLD BRUCE Union. POSITION: Asst Dir, Res Dept, AFL-CIO, 9111 Alton Parkway, Silver Spring, MD 20910. 202/293-5165

CAPLES, WILLIAM G. Arbitration, Legal Prac; Acad: Ind Rels. PHB 1930, Kenyon Coll; JD 1933, Northwestern U; LLD 1969, Loyola U-Chicago. PUBL: "Public Pay Controls,"-ASPA Handbook of Personnel Rels, Vol 11. INT: arb/med, labor law, labor market econ. ASSN: Chicago IRRA, ABA, Chicago Bar Assn, AAUP. POSITIONS: Vice Pres, Inland Steel Co, 1946; Pres, Kenyon Coll, 1968; and (since 1975) of Counsel, Vedder, Price, Kaufman & Kammholz, 115 S LaSalle St, Chicago, IL 60603. 312/781-2317

CAPPELLI, PETER H. Acad: Ind Rels. POSITION: ILIR, Univ of Ill, 504 E Armory Ave, Champaign, IL 61820. 217/333-1482

CAREY, JAMES F. Bus:Ind Rels. POSITION: Employee Rels, Union Carbide Corp, PO Box 887, Niagara Falls, NY 14302. 716/278-3071

CAREY, PHILIP A., SJ Acad: Econ; Arbitration, Bus:Pers/Ind Rels. STL 1938, (Gregorian) Rome, MA Woodstock Coll of Georgetown. INT: labor educ, arb/med, labor market econ. ASSN: Roster of Natl Arbitrators, Public Empl Rels Bd (NY & NJ), AAA. POSITION: Adjunct Prof Econ Dept, Fordham Univ, 30 W 16th St, New York, NY 10011. 212/924-7900

CAREY, THOMAS F. Arbitration. ADDRESS: 646 Parkside Dr., Jericho, NY 11753. 516/433-7596

CARILLON, JAMES W. Bus:Pers/Ind Rels. Acad: Student, Org Beh/Pers. BA 1978 Marietta Coll; MA 1980, PhD 1983, U of Mich. PUBL: "The Relationship Between Union Effectiveness and the Quality of Members' Worklife," (w R. I. Sutton), J of Occupational Beh, Vol 3, 1982, pp 171-179. INT: org beh, coll barg, mgmt/-educ. ASSN: ASTD, APA, Acad of Mgmt. POSITION: Supr Trng and Development, Parke-Davis/Warner-Lambert, PO Box 1510, Rochester, MI 48063. 313/651-9081

CARLSON, CHARLES E. Univ Admin. ADDRESS: 5826 Barton Rd, Madison, WI 53711.

CARLSON, CHARLES K. Bus:Pers/Ind Rels. AB 1973, George Washington U; MBA 1973, Pace U. INT: coll barg, arb/med, empl/-trng programs. ASSN: Amer Assoc of Trng Dir. POSITIONS: Sales Mgr-NY, General Foods, 1969; V.P. Admin, Pepsi-Cola Ltd (Toronto), 1973; and (since 1977) Vice Pres Employee & Labor Rels, P&C Food Market, PO Box 4965, Syracuse, NY 13207. 315/457-9460

CARLSON, TIMOTHY ERIC Student. ADDRESS: 222 Highland Dr, Iowa City, IA 52240. 319/354-3957

CARLTON, JAMES M. Bus:Pers/Ind Rels, Consulting. AAS 1964, Syracuse U. INT: coll barg, labor educ, labor law. ASSN: Syracuse IRRA, NY State Trucking Emplyor's Assn, Employers Group of Motor Freight Carriers, Intl Foundation of Empl Benefit Funds. POSITIONS: Dir of Labor Rels, Inland Express, 1964; Owner/Consultant, NY Labor Advisory Serv, 1980, and, since 1982, Dir of Labor Rels, Red Star Express Lines, Inc, 2450 Wright Ave, Auburn, NY 13021. 315/253-2721.

CARMEL, ALAN STANLEY Acad: Ind Rels; Consulting. BA 1961, Johns Hopkins U; MA 1962, U of Penna. INT: coll barg, mgmt/educ, personnel. POSITION: (since 1965) Asst Prof, Economics Dept, Univ of Manitoba, Winnipeg, Manitoba, R3T 2N2, Canada.

CARNEVALE, CAROL M. Student. BS 1977, Cornell U; MBA 1983, U of Toledo. INT: arb/-med, coll barg, labor law. POSITIONS: Pers Supr, Owens-Corning Fiberglas Corp, 1979, and (since 1983) Grad Student/Teaching Asst, Dept of Ind Rels and Human Res, Univ of Iowa. ADDRESS: 947 A Boston Way #4, Coralville, IA 52241. 319/353-5090

CAROPRESO, ANTHONY C. Trade Assoc, Bus:Pers/Ind Rels, Bus:Mgmt/Admin. BS 1967, Siena Coll; MA 1972, SUNY-Albany. INT: coll barg, arb/med, govt labor policy. ASSN: NY Capital District IRRA. POSITIONS: Asst Managing Dir, 1969, and, since 1983, Managing Dir, Eastern Contractors Assn, Inc, 6 Airline Dr, Albany, NY 12205. 518/869-0961

CARPENTER, GEORGE E., JR. Union. POSITION: Secretary-Treas, MA Labor Council, AFL-CIO, 8 Beacon St, 3rd Floor, Boston, MA 02109. 617/227-8260

CARRIG, KENNETH J. Bus: Labor Rels. 746 East Fedora, Fresno, CA 93704. 209/226-2190

CARRIGAN, BART O. Bus:Pers/Ind Rels. 3256 Beechwood Dr, Williamston, MI 48895.

CARROLL, BRIAN Legal Practice. 382 West St Apt 1A, New York, NY 10014. 212/242-3059

CARSON, ROBERT G., JR. Arbitration. BS 1939, Clemson U; MS 1950, Ga Inst of Tech; PhD 1953, U of Mich. INT: arb/med, coll barg, mgmt/educ. ASSN: Inst of Ind Engineers, NAA, NC Soc of Engineers. POSITIONS: Head, Dept of Ind Engineering, 1955, Assoc Dean of Engineering, NC State Univ, 1957; and (since 1975) Arbitrator (self-employed). ADDRESS: 1202 Brooks Ave, Raleigh, NC 27607. 919/787-6975

CARTER, ALBERT V. Arbitration. BA 1936, U of Chattanooga. INT: arb/med. ASSN: North Texas IRRA, NAA, AAA, FMCS Panel Arb. POSITIONS: Sales Dir, 1937, Pers Dir, 1950, Great A & P Tea Co; and (since 1975) Arbitrator (self-employed), 3412 Stanford, Dallas, TX 75225. 214/369-3853

CARTER, J. N. Bus:Pers/Ind Rels. BS 1971, US Military Acad,West Point; MS CTA Tech-Atlanta. INT: coll barg, personnel, mgmt/ind rels function. ASSN: ASPA. POSITIONS: US Army Officer, 1971; Ind Rels Supr, 1980, and, since 1982, Manager, Ind Rels, Union Camp Corp, PO Box 570, Savannah, GA 31402. 912/238--7336.

CARTER, RICHARD W. Diplomat. BA 1974, LLB 1977, U of Natal, South Africa. INT: intl comparative labor, labor law, intl org. ASSN: Intl Assn Pers in Empl Security, SPIDR. POSITIONS: Legal Advisor, Cape Chamber of Industries, South Africa, 1979, and (since 1982) Counsellor:Labour, South African Embassy, 3051 Massachusetts Ave NW, Washington DC 20008. 202/232-4400

CARVALHO, DENNIS M. Bus:Pers/Ind Rels. BS 1970, U of San Francisco. MBA 1976, Ind State U; MLIR 1977, Mich State U. INT: personnel, coll barg, empl/trng programs. ASSN: Orange Cty IRRA, ASPA. POSITIONS: Sr Labor Rels Rep, 1977, Admin Labor Rels, 1979, and, since 1984, Mgr Pers, McDonnell Douglas Microelectronics Center. ADDRESS: PO Box 4039, St. Charles, MO 63302. 314/234-3422

CASEY. E. A. Union. ASSN: R. I. IRRA. POSITION: Exec Director, Rohde Island Federation of Teachers, 111 Park St, Providence, RI 02908. 401/273-9800

CASEY, EILEEN Bus:Pers/Ind Rels. POSITION: Personnel Dept, Union Labor Life Ins Co, 111 Massachusetts Ave NW, Washington DC 20001. 202/682-6637

CASEY, JOHN F. Arbitration. POSITION: John F. Casey Co LPA, 300 S 2nd St, Columbus, OH 43215. 614/221-6847

CASHMORE, PATSY J. Union. INT: govt labor policy, arb/med, coll barg. ASSN: Wisconsin IRRA, Sigma Delta Chi, Milw Press Club, Coalition of Union Women. POSITIONS: Asst News Editor, WITI-TV 6, 1968; Public Rels Mgr, Deaconess Hosp, 1973; and (since 1973) Editor, Milwaukee Labor Press, 633 S Hawley Rd, Milwaukee, WI 53214. 414/771-7070

CASSADY, PAUL A. Arbitration. BA 1935, U of Calif-Berkeley. POSITION: Labor Arbitrator, PO Box 10, Dutch Flat, CA 95714. 916/389-2632

CASSELL, FRANK H. Acad: Ind Rels. Bus:-Pers/Ind Rels, Consulting. AB 1939, Wabash Coll. PUBL: Collective Bargaining in the Public Sector, Grid, 1976; "Reflections on Management Style and Corporate Social Policy," J of Bus Ethics, March 1983; "Labor Markets and Manpower Administration," (w Juris & Roomkin), J Bus Strategy, 1984. POSITION: Prof of IR, Grad School of Mgmt, Leverone Hall, Northwestern Univ, Evanston, IL 60201. 312/492-3465

CASSETTA, RAYMOND ANTHONY Consulting. BSIE 1970, N. J. Inst of Tech; MBA 1974, Rutgers. INT: coll barg, arb/med. ASSN: New Brunswick IRRA, AIIE, AMA, AAA. POSITIONS: Consultant, Metzler Assoc, 1969; and (since 1968) Secretary/Treasurer, Cassetta Brandon & Taylor, 300 Maple Ave, South Plainfield, NJ 07080. 201/561-7805

CASSIDY, GEORGE WESLEY Acad: Econ. 1725 Loma Ave, Apt 7, Long Beach, CA 90804.

CASSIDY, WILLIAM JAMES Bus:Mgmt/Admn. BS 1927 Edinbourgh U; MS 1936, PhD 1955, U of Pittsburgh. INT: coll barg, govt labor policy, labor market econ. ASSN: Kansas City IRRA, AEA, Miss Valley Econ Assn. POSITIONS: Compliance Officer, NLRB, 1942, and, since 1964, self-employed. ADDRESS: Antiquarian Bookman, 109 E 65th St, Kansas City, MO 64113. 816/361-4271.

CASTELLANO, JOHN J. Acad: Ind Rels. BS 1958, U of New Hampshire; MBA 1965, St. Louis U; PhD 1975, SUNY-Buffalo. ADDRESS: 98 Howard St, Reading, MA 01867. 617/944-9294

CASTELLI, RONALD J. Student. 400 Gunson #10, East Lansing, MI 48823. 517/351-3794

CASTREY, BONNIE P. Government. BS 1972 Calif State U-Long Beach. PUBL: "Mediation-What It Is, What It Does," (w R. Castrey), J of Nursing Admin, Nov 1980. INT: arb/med, intl comparative labor, comparable worth. ASSN: Orange Cty, Southern Calif, San Diego IRRAs, SPIDR, IIRA, Intl Soc for Labor Law and Social Legislation. POSITIONS: Instructor, El Camino Coll-Torrance, 1971; Instructor/Coll Barg & Related, various Colleges and Univ in So. Calif, 1975-Present; and (since 1975) Commissioner, FMCS-Santa Ana. ADDRESS: 8522 Topside Cir, Huntington Beach, CA 92646. 714/836-2624

CASTREY, ROBERT T. Arbitration. PUBL: "Mediation-What It Is, What It Does," (w B. Graczyk Castrey), J of Nursing Admin, Nov 1980. INT: arb/med, empl/trng programs, intl comparative labor. ASSN: Orange Cty, Southern Calif, San Diego IRRAs, SPIDR, IIRA, AAA. POSITIONS: Chief of Ind Rels, General Dynamics Corp, 1952; Commissioner (Retired), FMCS, 1962; and (since 1981) Arbitrator. ADDRESS: 8522 Topside Cir, Huntington Beach, CA 92646. 714/963-7114

CATTANEO, R. JULIAN Acad: Org Beh/Pers. Licenciado 1972, U of Buenos Aires; Cand Phil 1980, U of Mich. PUBL: "An Analysis of Turnover Intent Among Canadian University Professors,"(w P. Andiappan), Canadian Ind Rels Assn, 20th Annual Meeting, Vancouver, 1983; "Some Leadership Attitudes of West German Expatriate Personnel," (w E. L. Miller), J of Intl Bus Studies, 13, 41-50, Spring-Summer 1982; "Influence of Expatriate Nationality and Regional Location of the Overseas Subsidiary on Participative Decision Making," Mgmt Intl Rev, 21, 31-46, 1981. INT: personnel, method/-statis, org beh. ASSN: Acad of Mgmt, Canadian Ind Rels Assn, Academy of Intl Bus. POSITIONS: Supr, Org and Pers Admin, Ford Motor, Argentina SA, 1975; Grad Asst, 1977; and (since 1980) Asst Prof, Faculty of Bus Admin, Univ of Windsor, Windsor, Ont, N9B 3P4 Canada. 519/253-4232

CAUDILL, ROY A. Union. BS 1969, Va Polytech Inst & St U; MA 1973, Hollins Coll. INT: union org/admn, coll barg, arb/med. ASSN: Wash DC IRRA. POSITION: (since 1975) Uni Serv Dir, Virginia Educ Assn. 5249 Duke St, #105, Alexandria, VA 22304. 703/370-6685

CAULER, SANDRA L. Bus:Pers/Ind Rels. BA 1972, Millersville U; MA 1981, St. Francis Coll. INT: personnel, empl/trng programs. ASSN: Harrisburg IRRA, Lancaster Cty Pers Assn, Admin Mgmt Soc, Amer Bus Women's Assn. POSITION: (since 1972) Personnel Mgr, Flexsteel Ind, Inc, Lancaster. ADDRESS: Rte 1, Indian Run Rd, Millersville, PA 17551. 717/392-4161

CAVANAUGH, VICTOR A. Legal Practice. BA 1964, Centre Coll of Ky; JD 1970, Duke U. INT: labor law, arb/med, coll barg. ASSN: Atlanta IRRA, State Bar of Va, Fla State Bar Assn. POSITION: Partner, Swift, Currie, McGhee & Hiers, 771 Spring St NW, Atlanta, GA 30379. 404/881-0844

CEDERLUND, ALBERT MERRILL Acad: Econ. POSITION: Assoc Prof of Econ & Mgmt, Univ of Lowell, 12 Kenwood St. Chelmsford, MA 01824.

CEZAIR, PERCY LUCIEN Arbitration. 36 Gordon St, Port of Spain, Trinidad.

CHACKO, THOMAS I. Acad: Org Beh/Pers. POSITION: Assoc Prof, Iowa State Univ, Ames IA 50011. 515/294-8116

CHAFFINS, GARY EDWARD Bus:Pers/Ind Rels. BS 1973, MS 1974, Wright State U. ADDRESS: 126 Clemson Dr, Oak Ridge TN 37830.

CHAISON, GARY N. Acad: Ind Rels. BBA 1965, MBA 1967, Baruch College-CUNY; PhD 1972, SUNY-Buffalo. PUBL: "Local Union Mergers: Frequency Forms and National Union Policy," J of Labor Res, 1984; "The Emerging Role of Women in National Union Governance: The Results of a Canadian Survey," Proceedings of IIRA Sixth World Congress, 1983, pp 23-24; "Union Growth and Union Mergers," Ind Rels, 1981 pp 98-108. INT: union org/admn, coll barg, intl comparative labor. ASSN: Canadian Ind Rels Assn, IIRA. POSITIONS: Asst Prof, SUNY-Buffalo, 1972; Assoc Prof, Univ of New Brunswick, 1973; and (since 1981) Assoc Prof, Clark Univ, 950 Main St, Worcester, MA 01610. 617/793-7406

CHAMBERLAIN, NEIL W. Acad: Ind Rels. AB 1937, AM 1939, Case Western Reserve U; PhD 1942, Ohio State U. PUBL: The Limits of Corporate Responsibility, Basic Books, 1978; Forces of Change in Western Europe, McGraw Hill, 1980. INT: coll barg, intl comparative labor, corp social responsibility. POSITIONS: Dir, Program in Econ Devel, Ford Foundation, 1957-61; Prof of Econ, Yale U, 1961-67; Armand G Erpf Prof Emeritus (since 1981), Grad School of Bus, Columbia Univ. Retired. ADDRESS: 49 W 24th St, New York, NY 10010. 212/691-2685

CHAMPI, PAUL L. Bus:Pers/Ind Rels. BA & MS 1980, Rutgers U. INT: labor law, coll barg, intl comparative labor. ASSN: New Brunswick IRRA. POSITION: (since 1981) Pers Admin, Johnson & Johnson, New Brunswick. ADDRESS: 100 Vanderveer Ave, Somerville, NJ 08876. 201/524-3737

CHAMPLIN, FREDERIC C., III Acad: Bus Admin, Ind Rels. BBA 1962, U of Okla; MAIR 1978, PhD 1982, U of Minn. INT: arb/med, coll barg, method/statis. ASSN: AEA. POSITIONS: Compliance Officer, USDL, 1965; Teaching/Res. Asst, U of Minn, 1977; and (since 1981) Asst Prof, Coll of Bus, Univ of Oklahoma, 307 W Brooks, Norman, OK 73069. 405/325-2651

CHANDLER, JAMES C. Government. INT: coll barg, empl/trng programs, labor history. ASSN: Houston IRRA, SPIDR. POSITIONS: Employee, Lone Star Brewery, 1950; Intl Rep,-UBFCW of America, AFL-CIO, 1954; and (since 1966) Commissioner, FMCS, Room 1110, 515 Rusk, Houston, TX 77002. 713/229-2561

CHANDLER, MARGARET K. Acad: Ind Rels. BA 1942, MA 1944, PhD 1948, U of Chicago. PUBL: Labor-Management Relations in Illini City, Vols I & II; Management Rights and Union Interests, McGraw Hill, 1964; Managing Large Systems, Harper Row, 1971. INT: arb/med, coll barg, intl comparative labor. ASSN: SPIDR. POSITIONS: Prof, Univ of Ill, 1947; and (since 1965) Prof, Grad School of Bus, 723 Uris Hall, Columbia Univ, New York, NY 10027. 212/280-4426

CHAPMAN, JACK M. Arbitration, Legal Practice. LLB 1953, U of Manitoba. INT: arb/-med, labor law, labor history. ASSN: SPIDR, AAA (Labor Panel), Canadian Bar Assn. POSITIONS: Queens Counsel, 1965, Province of Manitoba, Sr. Partner, Gallagher & Co, 1970, and, since 1981, Sr Partner, Simkin, Gallagher-Barristers & Solicitors, 6th FL, 363 Broadway, Imperial Broadway Tower, Winnipeg, Manitoba R3C 1L2, Canada. 204/944-0121

CHAREON, SIRIBHAND Acad: Law. INT: arb/med, mgmt/educ, personnel. POSITIONS: Deputy Dir General, Dept of Labor. Retired. ADDRESS: AID 493-195-1-00673, 603 Aroon Amarintara Rd, Thonburi, Thailand.

CHARNEY, ANDREW ROBERT Bus:Pers/Ind Rels. POSITION: CCSD Ind Rels Rockwell, 1401 Summit Ave, Mail Station 454-150, Plano, TX 75074. 214/424-5860

CHARONIS, VIRGINIA Government. BA 1961 CUNY. PUBL: "Wages and Hours in the Building Trades," August 1981; "Wages and Benefits of New York City Municipal Government Workers," June 1981; "Price Index of Operating Costs for Rent Stabilized Apartment Houses in New York City, June 1981. INT: labor market econ, methodology/statis, income maint. ASSN:

New York IRRA, AEA, ASA. POSITIONS: Economist, 1961, and since 1982, Chief, Branch of Price Programs (Supv Economist), USDL, BLS, Middle Atlantic Reg Office, New York. ADDRESS: 110-50 71 Rd, Forest Hills, NY 11375. 212/944-3131

CHASE, THOMAS C. Professional Assoc. BA 1967, Yale U; MA 1969, PhD 1970, U of Tex at Austin. INT: quality of work life, org beh, ind psych. ASSN: Org Development Network, Acad of Mgmt, OB Teaching Soc. POSITIONS: Asst Prof of Psych, Colgate Univ, 1971; Lecturer, W. Hemore School of Bus, UNH, 1977; and (since 1979) Conference Coordinator, Organization Development Network, R 1, Box 44A, Northwood, NH 03261. 603/942-8189

CHAUBEY, MANMOHAN D. Acad: Ind Rels. 1971, B Tech, I I T Kanpur (India); MBA 1973, U M Calcutta; PhD 1982, U of Iowa. INT: coll barg, arb/med, personnel. ASSN: Acad of Mgmt. POSITION: (since 1981) Asst Prof, Ind Rels, School of Bus and Engineering Admin, Mich Tech Univ, Houghton, MI 49931. 906/487-2771

CHEANEY, NIKKI N. Bus/Pers/Ind Rels. 7857 Nightingale Way, San Diego, CA 92123.

CHEEK, ROGER NEWBY Government; Acad: Ind Rels. BS 1969, Wayne State U; JD 1975, U of Detroit. INT: arb/med, labor law, coll barg. ASSN: Detroit Area IRRA, Intl Pers Mgmt Assn-Detroit, Mich Bar Assn (Labor Law Section). POSITIONS: Labor Rels Specialist, Labor Rels Div, City of Detroit, 1975; Part Time Instructor, Oakland Community Coll, 1983; and (since 1978) Third Deputy Chief, Detroit Police Dept, 1300 Beaubein, Room 431, Detroit, MI 48226. 313/224-4416.

CHELIUS, JAMES R. Acad: Ind Rels. BS 1965, U of Chicago; MBA 1967, U of Ill; PhD 1973, U of Chicago. PUBL: Workplace Safety and Health; "The Influence of Workers' Compensation on Safety Incentives;" "The American Experience With Occupational Safety and Health Regulation." INT: labor market econ, govt labor policy, coll barg. ASSN: AEA. POSITIONS: Economist, Natl Commission on State Workmen's Compensation Laws, 1971; Asst and Assoc Prof, Purdue Univ, 1972; and (since 1982) Assoc Prof, Inst of Mgmt and Labor Rels, Rutgers Univ, New Brunswick, NJ 08903. 201/932-9242

CHENG, LEONARD TYE-LOKE Bus:Mgmt/-Admin. BBA 1969, U of Singapore; MS 1971, U of Wis-Madison. INT: mgmt/educ, intl comparative labor, org beh. ASSN: Singapore Inst of Pers Mgmt, IIRA. POSITION: General Mgr/Dir, S.P.P. Ltd, Singapore. ADDRESS: 67 Greenleaf Dr, Singapore 1027.

CHERNICK, JACK Retired. PhD 1949, U of Minn. INT: empl/trng programs, arb/med, intl comparative labor. ASSN: New Brunswick IRRA, AEA. POSITIONS: U of Kansas, 1947-52; Professor, Rutgers Univ, 1953, now, Professor Emeritus. ADDRESS: 52 Thomas St, Metuchen NJ 08840. 201/548-0560

CHESLER, HERBERT A. Acad: Ind Rels. POSITION: Assoc Prof, Dept of Econ, Univ of Pittsburgh, Pittsburgh, PA 15260. 412/624-5709

CHESTER, HARRY L. Union. PhD 1937, U of Vienna. Retired. ADDRESS: 2327 Ferncliff, Royal Oak, MI 48073. 313/548-5794

CHESTER, ROBERT W. Government. BS 1974, Towson State U; MBA 1982, Bradley U. INT: govt labor policy, labor educ. ASSN: Soc of Federal Lab Rels Professionals. POSITIONS: Supply Specialist, Dept of Navy, 1975; Adjunct Prof of Labor Rels, Bradley U, 1983; and (since 1976) Labor/Mgmt Rels Examiner, NLRB Reg 33, 411 Hamilton Blvd, Peoria, IL 61548. 309/671-7067

CHIAPPETTA, CYNTHIA LEE Pers:Ind Rels. POSITION: Ind Rels Analyst, Coca Cola Company, PO Drawer 1734, Atlanta, GA 30301. 404/438--1044

CHIARAVALLI, ROBERT LINO Bus:Pers/Ind Rels. BA 1978, U of Mich; MILR 1981, Cornell U. INT: coll barg, arb/med, labor law. ASSN: Better Bus Bureau Natl Arb Panel, RI Committee for Progress. POSITIONS: Field Examiner, NLRB, 1979; Sr Empl Rels Admin, Bendix, 1981, and, since 1982, Sr Labor Rels Admin, Fram/A Bendix Co, East Providence. ADDRESS: 131 Larch St, Providence RI 02906. 401/434-7000 ext 424.

CHICK, MICHAEL JOHN Acad: Ind Rels, Bus Admin; Consulting. BS 1976 Robert Morris Coll; MA 1983, St. Francis Coll. INT: personnel, labor law, arb/med. ASSN: ASPA. POSITION: Pers Mgr, Penn Allegh Coal Co Inc, Tarentum. ADDRESS: 1061 Edgewood Rd, New Kensington, PA 15068. 412/362-9200

CHIESA, MARIO Arbitration, Legal Prac. BS 1970, Detroit Coll of Bus, JD 1973, Detroit Coll of Law. INT: arb/med, labor law, coll barg. ASSN: Detroit IRRA, AAA, NAA, SPIDR. POSITION: Arbitrator/Attorney, 428 N Gulley Rd, Dearborn, MI 48128. 313/277-1967

CHILDERS, KATHIE LOU Bus:Pers/Ind Rels. Quarry Hill Rd, Box 105, East Hampton, CT 06424.

CHISHOLM, LES Union. BA 1970, Fla Atlantic U; MA 1972, U of Iowa. INT: union org/admin, govt labor policy, labor law. POSITION: (since 1984) International Union Area Dir, AFSCME, 5 Odana Ct, Madison, WI 53719. 608/271-8850

CHOWN, DAVID W. Acad: Ind Rels. POSITION: M. J. Neely School of Bus, Texas Christian Univ, Ft. Worth, TX 76129.

CHRETIEN, BARBARA C. Journalism. POSITION: Assoc Editor, Publ Service Research Foundation, 8330 Old Courthouse #600, Vienna, VA 22180. 703/790-0700

CHRIST, PETER ERIC Bus:Mgmt/Admin. ASSN: Central New Jersey IRRA. POSITION: Transamerica Delaval Inc, Condenser & Filter Div, Front St, Florence, NJ 08518. 609/499-3000

CHRISTENSON, ANDREA S. Legal Practice. POSITION: Attorney, Fierman, Hayes & Handler, 1 Gracie Square Apt 7W, New York, NY 10028. 212/759-8400

CHRISTENSEN, THOMAS G. S. Legal Practice. ADDRESS: 1 Gracie Square, New York, NY 10028. 212/598-2577

CHRISTENSON, CHRISTINA Acad: Bus Admin. BA 1974, U of Ga; MBA 1978, PhD 1983, Ga State U. PUBL: Supervising, Addison Wesley, 1982. INT: intl comparative labor, health & hosp care, personnel. ASSN: Acad of Mgmt. POSITION: Asst Prof of Mgmt, Ohio

Univ, 210 Copeland Hall, Athens, OH 45701. 614/594-5161

CHRISTIAN, VIRGIL L., JR. Acad: Econ. POSITION: Dept of Econ, Univ of Kentucky, Lexington,KY 40506. 606/257-2295

CHRISTIANSON, ALICE ANN Bus:Pers/Ind Rels, Consulting. MPA 1982, U of Wis-Madison. INT: cmpl/trng programs, health & hosp care, ind sociol. ASSN: ASPA, Amer Nurses Assn. POSITIONS: Consultant, 1982, Consultant-Health Services Mgmt, The Lakewood Group, Ltd, 1982; and (since 1984) Staff Educator/Mgmt Development, Madison General Hospital. ADDRESS: 5311 Brody Dr, #201, Madison, WI 53705. 608/255-0177

CHRISTIANSON, VIRGIL J. Bus:Pers/Ind Rels. 2203 Olmstead Way, Anaheim, CA 92806.

CHRISTOVICH, LESLIE JEAN Government; Acad: Student. BA 1976, MA 1978, U of Akron, PhD 1984, U of Ill-UC. INT: govt labor policy, labor law, method/statis. ASSN: Washington DC IRRA, Evaluation Res Soc, Evaluation Network, Law & Soc Assn. POSITIONS: Student, U of Akron, 1976, Student, U of Ill, 1978; and, since 1983), Evaluator, U. S. General Accounting Office. ADDRESS: 205 3rd St NE, Washington DC 20002. 202/275-8106

CHU, PAUL B.J. Retired. ADDRESS: 11 Galaxy Ct, Belle Mead, NJ 08502.

CHYBOWSKI, ROBERT M. Union. 30203 Poplar Dr, Burlington, WI 53105.

CIGICH, ALAN J. Bus:Pers/Ind Rels. BS 1972, U of Pittsburgh; MA 1976, St. Francis Coll. INT: coll barg, org beh, personnel. ASSN: Natl Mgmt Assn, Amer Mgmt Assn, Pittsburgh Pers Assn-ASPA. POSITION: Dir of Human Resources, Rockwell Intl. ADDRESS: 42 Brushy Ridge Ct, Pittsburgh, PA 15239. 412/247-3516

CLAMP, JESSE CARL, JR. Bus:Mgmt/Admin, Consulting; Acad: Bus Admin. AB 1942, Duke U. INT: mgmt/educ, org beh. ASSN: Natl Assn Bus Econ. POSITIONS: Sr Vice Pres, Allis-Chalmers, 1963; Pres, United States Filter Corp, 1972; and (since 1983) Distinguished Lecturer in Mgmt, Coll of Bus Admin, Univ of South Carolina. ADDRESS: 3204 Barnes Spring Rd, Columbia, SC 29024.

CLARK, C. HOWARD Bus:Mgmt/Admin. POSITION: Vice Pres, Whitaker Cable, 2801 Rock Creek Parkway, North Kansas City, MO 64116.

CLARK, CHARLES E. Arbitration, Legal Prac. LLB 1948, U of Tex. PUBL: Workmen's Compensation, NACCA Law J, vols 16-21; "EEO Training for First-Line Supervisors," in Pers Mgmt: Policies and Practices, Prentis Hall, 1980; "Work Injuries and the Constitution," Wash U Law Quar, 1956. INT: arb/med, empl/trng programs, labor law. ASSN: Kansas City IRRA, Tex Bar Assn, AAA, SPIDR. POSITIONS: Sr. Compliance Officer/Counsel, Fed Contract Compliance, 1961; Regional Dir, EEO Comm, 1966; and (since 1969) Arbitrator, 6418 Washington St, Kansas City, MO 64113. 816/361-8233

CLARK, JOHN H. Government. 6812 Garner, St. Louis, MO 63139.

CLARK, PAUL L. Bus: Ind Rels. POSITION: Manager-Employee Rels, AMOCO Oil Co, PO Box 578, Yorktown, VA 23690.

CLARK, ROBERT W. Bus.Pers/Ind Rels. BA 1965, Mich State U; MBA 1974, U of Detroit. INT: coll barg, personnel, mgmt educ. ASSN: Detroit IRRA, AEA. POSITIONS: Plant Labor Rels Supr, 1971, Staff Labor Rels Analyst, 1974, and, since 1981, Labor Economist, Ford Motor Co, The American Rd, Room 393, Dearborn, MI 48121. 313/323-2888

CLARK, WAYNE B. Bus:Pers/Ind Rels, Bus:Mgmt/Admn. BS 1963, U of Wis-Stout; MS 1971, U of Wis-Madison. INT: mgmt, personnel. coll barg. ASSN: Wis Ind Rels Alumin Assn, ASPA, Accredited Exec in Pers. POSITIONS: Mgr, Eply & Community Rels, Combine Div, Allis Chalmers Corp, 1974; Dir, Empl Rels, 1977, and, since 1981, Vice-President, Human Resources, Universal Foods Corp. ADDRESS: 12112 W Holt Ave, West Allis, WI 53227. 414/271-6755

CLARKE, CAROL L. Bus:Pers/Ind Rels. POSITION: Girl Scouts of the USA, 830 Third Ave, New York, NY 10022. 212/940-7862

CLARKE, JACK Arbitration. BS 1961, JD 1971, U of New Mexico. INT: arb/med, labor law. ASSN: NAA, SPIDR, ABA (Labor Sec). POSITIONS: Assoc Prof of Law, Univ of Alabama Law School, 1971; Attorney, Henley & Clarke, 1977-81; and (since 1972) Arbitrator, ADDRESS: PO Box 3151, Tuscaloosa, AL 35404. 205/556-7651

CLARKE, JOHN DOUGLAS Acad: Bus Admin, Law. BA 1968, BEd 1970, U of Toronto; MEd 1975, Wayne State U; B Comm 1977, MBA 1980, U of Windsor; JD 1982, Detroit Coll of Law. INT: labor law, arb/med, org beh. ASSN: Detroit IRRA, ABA, State Bar of Mich. POSITIONS: Secondary School Teacher, Kent Cty (Ontario), 1970, and (since 1982) Lecturer in Bus Admin, Faculty of Bus, Univ of Windsor, Windsor, Ont N9B 3P4 Canada. 519/253-4232

CLARKE, OLIVER Government. BSc 1950, Univ Coll, London. PUBL: "The Work Ethic: an International Perspective," in J. Barbash (ed), The Work Ethic-An Analytical Rev, IRRA, 1983; "Industrial Relations in a Changing Economic Environment," in R. Blanpain (ed), Comparative Labour Law and Ind Rels, Kluwer,Deventer, 1982; "Workers' Participation in Management in Great Britain," Intl Inst of Labor Studies, Res Series, #58, Geneva, 1980. INT: intl comparative labor, govt labor policy, coll barg. ASSN: Paris IRRA, British Univ Ind Rels Assn, FrenchInd Rels Assn, British Inst of Pers. POSITIONS: Secretary, Engineering Empl London Assn, 1950; Research Fellow, London School of Econ, 1968; and (since 1970) Principal Admin, OECD, 2 rue Andre-Pascal, 75775 Paris CEDEX 16, France. Phone: 524 9168

CLARKE, PAMELA LYNN Student. ADDRESS: 8 Scotch Hill, Marcellus NY 13108. 315/673-3306

CLAYTON, ROBERT E. Bus:Ind Rels. INT: personnel, empl/trng programs. ASSN: Central Wis Pers Club, Central Wis Private Ind Council. POSITIONS: Dist Mgr, 1967, Pers Mgr, 1972, United Telephone Co of Minn; and (since 1982) Asst Vice Pres Human Resources, First

Financial S&L, 1305 Main St, Stevens Point, WI 54481. 715/346-1282

CLAYTON, SUZANNE L. Bus:Mgmt/Admin; Student (part time) Inds Rels (major). BA 1974, BA 1975, Wayne State U. ADDRESS: 44811 Tillotson Dr, Canton, MI 48187. 313/459-8132

CLEM, C. STEPHEN Union. BS 1964, Shepard Coll. INT: intl trade, coll barg, govt labor policy. POSITIONS: Res Asst, CWA, 1968; Asst Res Dir, 1969, and, since 1977, Research Dir, United Rubber Workers, 87 S High St, Akron, OH 44308. 216/376-6181

CLEMENS, JOHN P. Bus:Pers/Ind Rels. MBA 1970, Northwest Mo State U. INT: personnel, labor law, health & hosp care. ASSN: Kansas City IRRA, ASPA. POSITIONS: Pers Mgr, Quaker Oats Co, 1971; Pers Mgr, Globe Union (Johnson Controls) 1975; and (since 1977) Mgr Human Resources, St. Joseph Light & Power Co, 520 Francis St, St. Joseph, MO 64502. 816/233-8888

CLIFFORD, R. JAMES Bus:Ind Rels. POSITION: President, R.J. Clifford & Assoc, 625 Howe St, Suite 1250, Vancouver, BC V6C 2T6, Canada. 604/687-6211

CLINTON, DANIEL J. Bus:Mgmt/Admin, Bus:Pers/Ind Rels. BS, Xavier U; JD, U of Detroit. INT: arb/med, coll barg, mgmt/educ. ASSN: Detroit IRRA, State Bar of Mich. POSITION: Dir, Labor Rels/Pers, Bundy Corp, 12345 E 9 Mile Rd, Warren, MI 48090. 313/758-4511

CLINTON, J. HART Bus:Mgmt/Admin, Arbitration. AB 1926, Boston Coll; LLB & JD 1929, Harvard U. INT: arb/med, coll barg, labor law. ASSN: San Francisco IRRA, ABA, Amer Law Inst, Amer Judicature Soc. POSITIONS: Law Partner, Morrison & Foerster, 1941, and (since 1943) President, Editor and Publisher, Amphlett Printing Co, San Mateo Times, 1080 S Amphlett Blvd, San Mateo, CA 94402. 415/348-4356

CLOKE, KENNETH Arbitration, Mediation, Legal Prac. BA 1953, JD 1966, UC-Berkeley; PhD 1980, LLM 1980, UCLA. PUBL: "Mandatory Political Contributions & Union Democracy;" "Political Loyalty, Labor Democracy & the Constitution;" "Concerted Activity & the National Labor Policy." INT: arb/med, labor law, labor history. ASSN: Los Angeles IRRA, AAA, SPIDR, NAA (Law Judges). POSITIONS: Law Prof, Southwestern U School of Law, 1978; Admin Law Judge, Public Empl Rels Bd/Ag Labor Rels Bd, 1976-82; and (since 1978) Arbitrator/Mediator, 1337 Ocean Ave, Santa Monica, CA 90401. 213/451-1615

CLONEY, JOHN C. Arbitration. LLB 1952, De Paul U; MS 1964, Loyola U. INT: arb/med, coll barg, labor law. ASSN: Chicago Bar Assn, AAA. POSITIONS: Supervisor, NLRB, 1959-80; and (since 1980) Arbitrator (self-employed), 219 S. Dearborn, Suite 1412, Chicago, IL 60603. 312/782-8535

COATES, NORMAN Acad: Org Beh/Pers; Consulting. BA 1957, Sir George Williams U; MS 1959, PhD 1967, Cornell U. PUBL: "International Business Management," in J.A.F. Stoner, Management, 2nd ed, Prentice Hall, 1982, pp 586-592; "The Nature of the Australian Industrial Relations System," Proceedings, Acad of Intl Bus Asia-Pacific Hawaii, Dec 1982, pp 586-592; "A Framework for the Evaluation of Culturally-Based Differences in Multinational Corporation Performance," Proceedings, Eastern Academy of Mgmt, May 1979, pp 34-37. INT: org beh, bus policy, intl mgmt. ASSN: Acad of Mgmt, Acad of Intl Bus, IIRA. POSITIONS: Asst Prof of Ind, Wharton School-Penna, 1966; Program Specialist, Ford Foundation, NY, 1968; and (since 1971) Prof of Mgmt, Univ of Rhode Island. ADDRESS: PO Box 297, Wakefield, RI 02879. 401/792-2068

COBB, JAY JOSEPH Arbitration, Consulting. INT: arb/med, coll barg, labor law. ASSN: AAA, IIRA, ASPA. POSITIONS: Div Dir of Pers, 1969, Dir of Labor Rels, The Kendall Co (Colgate Palmolive) 1974; and (since 1983) Arbitrator/Consultant, Empl Mgmt Rels Consultant, 4150 Killion Ct, Bloomington, IN 47401. 812/876-5461

COBURN, KITTY Bus:Pers/Ind Rels. BS, Coll of William & Mary. ASSN: New York IRRA. POSITION: Asst to Vice Pres, Ind Rels & Pers, ASARCO Inc, 120 Broadway, New York, NY 10271. 212/669-1312

COCHRAN, STEVEN A. Student. 3504 Craig Ave, Cincinnati, OH 45211. 513/481-5240

COCHRAN, SUSAN TERRELL Student. 1920 Kendall Ave #2, Madison, WI 53705. 608/262-1564

COFFIN, DWIGHT Bus:Pers/Ind Rels. BA 1963, De Pauw U; MBA 1967, New York U. INT: personnel, intl comparative labor. ASSN: New York IRRA. POSITION: (since 1972) Vice Pres-Personnel, Continental Grain Co, 277 Park Avenue, New York, NY 10172. 212/207--5417

COHANE, JOHN J. Bus:Pers/Ind Rels. INT: org beh, personnel, arb/med. ASSN: Boston IRRA, ASPA. POSITIONS: Mgr,Ind Rels, Boston Gas Co, 1978, and (since 1982) Asst Vice Pres, Pers and Ind Rels, Eastern Gas and Fuel Assoc, One Beacon St, Boston, MA 02108. 617/742-8400

COHANY, HARRY P. ASSN: Wash DC IRRA: REtired. ADDRESS: 3706 Astoria Rd, Kensington MD 20895.

COHEN, CYNTHIA FRYER Acad: Ind Rels; Arbitration. BBA 1974, MBA 1975, U of Ga; PhD 1980, Ga State U. PUBL: "The Impact on Women of Proposed Changes in the Private Pension System," Ind and Labor Rels Rev, Vol 36, #2, Jan 1983, pp. 258-270; "Employee Ownership and Collective Bargaining," Bay Area Bus Rev, Vol 3, #1, 1982, pp 12-16; "The Effects of Manager's Sex and Attitudes Toward Women on the Process of Delegation," 1982 Proceedings of the Acad of Mgmt, pp 113-117. INT: arb/med, labor law, personnel. ASSN: Acad of Mgmt, Sigma Iota Epsilon, Beta Gamma Sigma. POSITIONS: Systems Engineer, Electronic Data Systems, 1975; Asst Prof, Univ of Houston at Clear Lake City, 1979; and (since 1982) Asst Prof, Dept of Mgmt, Univ of South Florida, 4202 E Fowler Ave, Tampa, FL 33620. 713/974-4155

COHEN, GEORGE H. Legal Practice. BA 1955, LLB 1957, Cornell U; LLM 1960, Georgetown U. INT: labor law, coll barg, arb/med. ASSN: Wash DC IRRA, ABA. POSITION:

(since 1969) Partner, Bredhoff and Kaiser, 1000 Connecticut Ave NW, Washington DC 20036. 202/833-9340

COHEN, MALCOLM S. Acad: Univ Admin. PhD 1967, MIT. PUBL: "New Measures of Labor Turnover," (w A. Schwartz) Mo Labor Rev Nov 1980; "Area Employment Conditions and Labor Force Participation: A Micro Study," (w Lerman & Rea), J of Pol Econ, Sept-Oct, 1971; "A Model of Work Effect and Productivity Consumption," (w E. Stafford), J of Econ Theory, Mar 1974. INT: empl/trng programs, labor market econ, labor market information. POSITIONS: Asst to Vice Pres, Planning, 1968, Res Dir, ILIR, 1972, and, since 1983, Dir, Inst of Labor and Ind Rels, Univ of Mich, 130 S 1st St, Ann Arbor, MI 48109. 313/763-3116

COHEN, MARTIN A. Acad: Ind Rels; Arbitration. MA 1941, U of Chicago. INT: arb/med, coll barg, labor law. ASSN: Chicago IRRA, NAA, SPIDR, AAA. POSITION: Assoc Prof of Econ and Mgmt, Stuart School of Bus Admin, Ill Inst of Tech, Chicago, IL. 60616. 312/567-5106

COHEN, NATHAN Arbitration. BS 1943, CCNY; JD 1950, Brooklyn Law School; LLM 1954, New York U. INT: arb/med, coll barg, labor law. ASSN: New York and Long Island IRRA, NAA, ABA, SPIDR. POSITIONS: Med/-Arb, New York State Mediation Board, 1957; Supr Mediator, NY State Publ Empl Rels Board, 1969; and (since 1957) Arbitrator, 8 Central Park Rd, Plainview, NY 11803. 516/935-1128

COHEN, SANFORD Acad: Econ. PhD 1951, Ohio State. PUBL: Labor in the United States; Labor Law; Management Preparation For Collective Bargaining. INT: govt labor policy, arb/med, labor law. ASSN: NAA, AEA, SPIDR. POSITION: (since 1966) Prof of Econ, Dept of Econ, Univ of New Mexico, Albuquerque, NM 87131. 505/277-3144

COHEN, WILBUR J. Acad: Econ; Consulting. PhB 1934, U of Wis. PUBL: Retirement Policies Under Social Security; Social Security: Problems, Policies, Programs; "Unemployment Compensation." INT: health & hosp care, income maint, labor market econ. ASSN: Austin IRRA, AEA, Amer Public Welfare Assn, Amer Public Health Assn. POSITIONS: Sec of HEW, Dept HEW, 1968-69; Prof of Public Welfare Admin, Univ of Mich, 1956; and (since 1980) Prof of Public Affairs, L.B.J. School of Public Affairs, Univ of Texas, Austin TX 78712. 512/471-7549

COHN, SAMUEL ROSS Acad: Sociology. ADDRESS: 8133 Social Science Bldg, U of Wis, Madison, WI 53706. 608/262-5983

COLE, GEORGE S. Acad: Org Beh/Pers, Bus Policy; Consulting. BA 1970, U of Del; MBA 1971, PhD 1978, Mich State U. INT: personnel, labor history, ind sociology. ASSN: Acad of Mgmt, ASPA, ASA. POSITION: Asst Prof, Bus Policy & Pers, Pennsylvania State Univ, Capitol Campus, Middletown. ADDRESS: 1416 Bradley Ave, Hummelstown, PA 17036. 717/948-6169

COLELLA, JENNIFER M. Student. Int: labor law, coll barg, arb/med. ADDRESS: 60 Wegman St, Auburn NY 13021. 315/252-5976

COLEMAN, CHARLES J. Acad: Ind Rels; Arbitration. BS 1955, St. Joseph's (Phila); MS 1957, Cornell U; MBA 1967, PhD 1971, SUNY-Buffalo. PUBL: Personnel: An Open System Approach, Winthrop Publ, 1979; "The N.J. Courts and the Decline of the Collective Negotiation System," Rutgers Law J, Dec 1983; "The Civil Service Reform Act of 1978; Its Meaning and Its Roots," Labor Law J, Apr 1980. INT: coll barg, arb med, labor law. ASSN: Philadelphia IRRA, AAUP, AAA, PERC-NJ. POSITION: Dir of Undergrad Program, Faculty of Bus Studies and (since 1971) Assoc Prof, Rutgers Univ, Camden, NJ 08102. 607/-757-6217.

COLEMAN, FRANCIS THOMAS Legal Practice. AB 1961, JD 1964, LLM 1970, Georgetown U. PUBL: The Deunionizing Handbook, Federal Publs; "Financial Disclosure under the L.M.R.D.A.: A Growing Problem for Labor Lawyers," (co-author), 67 ABA J 2/81; "Unionism in Health Care Institutions: An Overview," (co-author) ¶42, 139 Prentice Hall, Ind Rels Guide Serv, 9/82. INT: labor law, health & hosp care, arb/med. ASSN: Wash DC IRRA, ABA, Amer Soc of Hosp Attorneys, Amer Hosp Assn. POSITIONS: Attorney, Pierson, Ball & Dowd, 1978; Attorney, Venable, Baetjer, Howard & Civiletti, 1981; and (since 1983) Attorney, Boothe, Prichard & Dudley, 1000 Potomac St NW, Suite 502, Washington DC 20007. 202/333-9532

COLEMAN, GLENN Bus:Pers/Ind Rels. BA 1975, Mich State U; MSIR 1978, U of Wis-Madison. INT: coll barg, arb/med, labor law. POSITIONS: Empl Rels Analyst, Shell Oil Co, 1978; Chief Labor Rels, Metro Transit Authority, 1979; and (since 1982) Sr Labor Rels Admin, Cameron Iron Works Inc. 9719 Windsor Locks Dr, Houston, TX 77065. 713/-939-3813

COLEMAN, JAMES L. Bus:Mgmt/Admin, Consulting; Acad: Bus Admin. BA 1962, LaSalle Coll (Phila); MBA 1971 Temple U. INT: mgmt, coll barg, org beh. ASSN: ASPA. POSITION: Dir, Operations Analysis, City of Philadelphia. ADDRESS: 8 Pheasant Hill Dr, Philadelphia, PA 19115. 215/686-3490

COLEMAN, PAUL T. Government. HQ US Army 21 SUPCOM, AERCP, APO New York, NY 09325.

COLEMAN, RICHARD WILLIAM Legal Practice. POSITION: Partner, Segal, Roitman & Coleman, 11 Beacon St, Boston, MA 02108. 617/742-0208

COLINSKY, EDGAR GARRIS Bus:Pers Ind Rels. BA 1964, U of Southern Calif. INT: personnel, coll barg, arb/med. ASSN: Orange Cty IRRA, UCLA Inst of Ind Rels, Pers & Ind Rels Assn. POSITIONS: Ind Rels Mgr, Mattell, 1972; Empl Rels Dir, Tiger Air, 1979; and (since 1982) Empl Rels Dir, Burlington Northern Air Freight Inc, Newport Beach. ADDRESS: 10733 El Silbido, Fountain Valley, CA 92708. 714/752-4000

COLLINS, A. MICHAEL Union. AB 1967, Princeton U; M Phil 1972, U of Kans. PUBL: "Unions and Industrial Psychology;" Minority Income and Employment: Issues and Efforts," "Training Youth for Careers." INT: intl comparative labor, empl/mgmt programs, labor educ. ASSN: Wash DC IRRA. POSITION: Asst to Pres, Intl Union of Operating Engineers, 1125 17th St NW, Washington DC 20036. 202/429-9100

COLLINS, RONALD DOUGLAS Government, Arbitration; Acad: Ind Rels. BA 1968 1968, Occidental Coll; Cert 1974, UCLA. INT: arb/med, coll barg, govt labor policy. ASSN: Los Angles IRRA, SPIDR, Inst of Ind Rels (UCLA), Assoc of Labor Rels Agencies. POSITIONS: Arbitrator, Private Practice, 1978; Inst in Labor Rels, UCLA Ext, 1983; and (since 1972) Executive Dir, Los Angeles Empl Rels Board, 200 N Main, Room 1490, Los Angeles, CA 90012. 213/485-2066.

COLLYER, ROBERT J. Bus:Pers/Ind Rels. BS 1979, Rensselaer Polytech Inst; MS 1981, Purdue U. INT: labor law, arb/med, coll barg. ASSN: Assn of MBA Exec, Betta Gamma Sigma. POSITION: Labor Rels Rep, General Motors, Assembly Div, Wilmington. ADDRESS: 36 Woodfield Ct, Newark, DE 19713. 302/998-8831

COLOSI, MARCO L. Acad: Law, Ind Rels; Bus:Pers/Ind Rels. BA Hofstra; MS & DPA, New York Inst of Tech; APM, Pers Accredition Inst. PUBL: At Will Employment," Pers Mag, May 1984; "Divorce Union Style," Pers Advancement & Ind Rels Law J, 1982; "301 DFR", Labor Law J, 1981. INT: labor law, coll barg, arb/med. ASSN: Acad of Ind Rels, Natl Assn of Labor Councils, NYIT-Univ Chapter Advisor--Pers/Human Resources. POSITIONS: Dir of Pers & Ind Rels, Art Steel Co, 1977; Dir of Pers & Ind Rels, Celebrity Co Inc, 1978; and (since 1982) Vice Pres, Human Resources, Bronx Lebanon Hosp, 1650 Grand Concourse, Bronx, NY 10457. 212/588-7000

COLOSI, THOMAS RI Assn Exec. BS 1958 NYSSILR-Cornell U. ASSN: New York IRRA. POSITION: Vice Pres, Natl Affairs, American Arbitration Assn, 1730 Rhode Island Ave NW, Washington DC 20036. 202/296-8510

COLOSIMO, FRANK E. Bus:Pers/Ind Rels. Champion International Corp, Piedmont East, 37 Villa Rd, #402, Greenville, SC 29615. 803/297-9740

COMERFORD, JOHN K. Bus:Pers/Ind Rels, Mgmt/Admin; Acad: Org Beh/Pers. BS 1975, Mich State U; MA 1981, Wayne State U. INT: coll barg, personnel, mgmt/educ. ASSN: Ind Rels of Detroit, Wayne State M.A. in I.R. Alumni Assn, ASPA. POSITIONS: Res Analyst, Empl Assn of Detroit, 1980; Instructor, Pers Admin, Lawrence Inst of Tech, School of Mgmt, 1983; and (since 1984) Labor Rels Supervisor, Ameritch Publishing Inc, 100 E Big Beaver Rd, 14th Floor, Troy, MI 48083. 313/524-7525

COMERFORD, RICHARD D. Acad: Labor Studies and Educ, Econ, Ind Rels. BA 1969, MA 1972, U of Wis-Madison. INT: labor educ, coll barg, labor market econ. ASSN: AAA, NEA, Univ & Coll Labor Educ Assn. POSITIONS: Adjunct-Grad Human Res Mgmt Program, New School of Soc Res, NYC, 1981-present; and (since 1973) Assoc Prof & Dir, Labor Studies, Bergen Community Coll, 400 Paramus Rd, Paramus, NJ 07652. 201/447-7166

CONANT, EATON H. Acad: Ind Rels; Arbitration. BS 1956, MS 1957, & PhD 1960, U of Wis. POSITION: Prof/Dir, Ind Rels Inst, U of Oregon, 2255 Columbia St, Eugene, OR 97403. 503/344-0097

CONANT, JOHN L. Acad: Econ, Ind Rels, Consulting. MA 1978, Washington U. INT: labor market econ, personnel, coll barg. ASSN: Gateway IRRA, AEA, Midwest Bus Econ Assn, Midwest Econ Assn. POSITION: PhD Candidate, U of Tenn, and (since 1981) Asst Prof, Dept of Econ, Indiana State Univ, Terre Haute, IN 47809. 812/232-5817

CONCEPCION, DAVID A. Arbitration. BA 1959, U of Calif. PUBL: Zero Base Budgeting and the Quality of Management Program, (w L. Mancebo), a manual, U of Calif-Berkeley, 1975; Executive Compensation in Higher Education, Coll and Univ Pers Assn, res report, U of Calif-Berkeley, 1974. INT: arb/med. ASSN: San Francisco IRRA, NAA, AAA, SPIDR. POSITIONS: Dir, Mgmt Analysis, Univ of Calif-Berkeley, 1970, Assoc Dean, Hastings Coll of Law, U of Calif, 1975; and (since 1972) Arbitrator. ADDRESS: 65 Stevenson Ave, Berkeley, CA 94708. 415/849-3832

CONFER, STEPHEN H. Union. POSITION: Comm Workers of America, 1925 K St NW, Washington DC 20006. 202/785-6123

CONLAN, KATHLEEN M. Union. BA 1977, Georgetown U. INT: coll barg, govt labor policy, labor law. ASSN: Coalition of Labor Union Women. POSITION: Labor Res Advisory Committee, DOL, and (since 1983) Research Analyst, SEIU, Wash DC. ADDRESS: 11054 Saffold Way, Reston, VA 22090. 202/452-8750

CONLON, JOHN THOMAS Acad: Bus Admin; Arbitration. BBA 1949, U of Mass; MA 1951, U of Conn; PhD 1960, Mich State U. INT: arb/-med, coll barg, govt labor policy. ASSN: Boston IRRA, AAA, NAA. POSITION: (since 1958) Professor, School of Bus Admin, U of Mass, 58 Harlow Dr., Amherst, MA 01002. 413/549-0170

CONNERS, EDWARD OWEN Government. INT: arb/med, coll barg. ASSN: Mid-Mich IRRA, SPIDR. POSITIONS: Mediator, 1961, and, since 1981, Regional Mediator Supr, Mich Dept of Labor, Bureau of Empl Rels, 309 N. Washington Ave, Suite 110, Lansing, MI 48909. 517/373-3580

CONNERTY, RICHARD A. Bus.Mgmt/Admin, Consulting. BBA 1955, CCNY. INT: coll barg, personnel, org beh/mgmt educ. ASSN: Amer Mgmt Assn, ASPA, Amer Compensation Assn. POSITIONS: Dir, Labor Rels Tech Serv, Eastern Airlines, 1959; Dir, Ind Rels Div, Edison Electric Inst, New York and Wash DC until 1983. Retired. ADDRESS: 46 Greentree Ter, Lincroft, NJ 07738. 201/741-1622

CONNOLLY, WALTER B., JR. Acad: Legal. BA 1964, U of Detroit; JD 1966, U of Southern Calif. PUBL: A Practical Guide to Equal Employment Opportunity: Law, Principles and Practices, vol. 1 & 2, Law J Press, 1977, 1979; The Use of Statistics in Civil Rights Cases, 1 vol NY Law J Press Seminars, Fall, 1979; A Practical Guide to OSHA: Law, Principles and Practice, Law J Press Seminars, Sept 1982. INT: labor law, labor market econ, intl compartive labor. ASSN: Wash DC IRRA. POSITIONS: Asst Counsel, Firestone Tire & Rubber Co; private practice in Detroit and Wash DC; and (since 1983) Partner, Piper & Marbury, 888 16th St NW, Washington DC 20006. 202/785-8150

CONTE, MICHAEL R. Bus:Pers/Ind Rels. BA 1964, MBA 1969, Syracuse U. INT: personnel, labor law, empl/trng programs. ASSN: Hartford IRRA, ASPA. POSITIONS: Mgr Empl Rels Svcs,

Mgr, Pers Admin, Hamilton Standard Div, United Tech Corp; and (since 1980) Dir of Human Resources, The Superior Electric Co, 383 Middle St, Bristol CT 06010.

CONTI, ADAM J. Legal Practice. AB 1971, Georgetown U; MBA 1976, Pace U; JD 1984, Emory U. INT: labor law, arb/med, coll bar. ASSN: Soc Federal Labor Rels Professionals, ABA. POSITIONS: Supr-Labor Rels Specialist, Federal Labor Rels Authority, NY, 1979; Law Student, Emory Univ, 1981; and (since 1983) Law Clerk, Elarbee, Thompson, Trapnell, Atlanta. ADDRESS: 791 Marstevan Dr NE, Atlanta, GA 30306. 404/876-7339

CONVERSE, MARY H. Union. BA 1970, U of Mich. INT: union orgadmn, coll barg, ind sociol. ASSN: Wash DC IRRA. POSITIONS: Research Analyst, SEIU, 1972; Labor Economist, Council on Wage & Price Stability, 1979; and (since 1981) Research Coordinator, Assn of Flight Attendants, Washington. ADDRESS: 2617 N Quantico St, Arlington, VA 22207. 202/328-5436

CONWAY, JAMES E. Bus:Pers/Ind Rels. BA 1963, St. John's U-Minn; JD 1967, William Mitchell Coll; LLM 1983, Georgetown Law Center. INT: coll barg, arb/med, labor law. ASSN: Wash D IRRA. POSITIONS: Dir-Labor Rels, Northwest Airlines, 1968; Staff V.P.-Labor Rels, National Airlines, 1976; and (since 1980) V.P. & Exec Dir, Airline Intl Relations Conference, 1709 New York Ave, Washington DC 20001. 202/6264285

COOK, ALAN J. Legal Practice, Arbitration; Acad: Ind Rels. BA 1966, U of Ill; JD 1973, MSIR, 1978, Loyola U of Chicago. INT: arb/med, coll barg, labor law. ASSN: AAA, ABA, SPIDR. POSITIONS: Teacher, Chicago, 1966; Principal, St. Thomas Aquinas School, 1971; and (since 1973) Attorney. ADDRESS: Suite 1525, 77 W Washington St, Chicago, IL 60602. 312/372-8692

COOK, ALICE H. Acad: Ind Rels. PUBL: Working Women in Japan, 1981; Comparable Worth: The Problem and States' Approaches to Wage Equity, 1982; Working Mother: Problems and Programs in Nine Countries, Cornell U ILR Press, 1978 (revised). INT: govt labor policy, intl comparative law, labor market econ. ASSN: New York IRRA, IIRA, AAUP, Assn of Asian Studies. POSITIONS: Prof Emeritus, Cornell Univ. ADDRESS: 766 Elm St Ext, Ithaca, NY 14850. 607/272-2926

COOK, ARTHUR J.D. Acad: Org Beh/Personnel. 1530 E Brow Rd, Signal Mountain, TN 37377. 615/886-1242

COOK, RICHARD F. Student; Bus/Pers/Ind Rels. MLHR 1984, Ohio State U. ADDRESS: 1664 O'Toole Dr, Xenia, OH 45385. 513/376-4222

COOK, ROBERT F. Woodrow Wilson School Princeton Univ, Princeton NJ 08540.

COOK, ROY A. Acad: Bus Admin; Consulting. BBA 1971, Southwest Tex State U; MBA 1972, Sam Houston State U. PUBL: "Improving Office Management," J of Bus Educ; "The Golden Rule in Business Communications," The Balance Sheet. INT: personnel, coll barg, empl/trng programs. ASSN: Midwest Bus Admin Assn, Nebraska Econ & Bus Assn. POSITIONS: Pers Dir, Hyatt Regency/Houston, 1978; Corp Dir of Pers, Adam's Mark Hotels, 1980; and (since 1983) Instructor, Wayne State Coll, Wayne, NE 68787. 402/375-2200

COOK, WILLIAM GLEN Acad: Econ. POSITION: Assoc Prof of Econ, Dept of Econ, Marshall Univ, Huntington, WV 25701. 304/736-2242

COOK, WILLIAM R. Bus:Pers/Ind Rels. BS 1973, AM 1981, U of Ill. INT: coll barg, arb med, labor law. POSITIONS: Postal Worker, US Postal Serv, 1971; Coal Miner, Ziegler Coal Co, Murdock Ill, 1975; and (since 1980) Supr,-Pers & Ind Rels, Natl Supply Co,Well Control Systems Div. 6229 Navigation Blvd, Houston, PO Box 9163, TX 77011. 713/960-5853

COOKE, JACQUELINE R. Union. BA 1971, Tufts U; MS 1975, U of Wis. INT: labor educ, union org/admn, coll barg. ASSN: Boston IRRA. POSITIONS: Assoc Dir of Econ and General Welfare, Mass Nurses Assn, 1976; and (since 1981) New England Educ Coordinator, AFSCME, Boston. ADDRESS: 116 Harvard St, Newtonville, MA 02160. 617/367-3686

COOKE, WILLIAM N. Acad: Ind Rels, Bus Admin. PhD 1977 U of Ill. PUBL: "Determinants of the Outcomes of Union Certification Elections," Ind and Labor Rels Rev, April, 1983; "The Decline in Union Success in NLRB Representation Elections," (w. R. Seeber), Ind Rels, Winter, 1983; "Political Bias in NLRB Unfair Labor Practice Decisions," (w F. Gautschi), Ind and Labor Rev, July, 1982. INT: coll barg, govt labor policy, labor market econ. POSITIONS: Visiting Fellow, NYSSILR-Cornell U, 1980; Assoc Prof of Ind Rels, Purdue U, 1981; and (since 1983) Assoc Prof of Ind Rels, School of Bus Admin, Univ of Mich, Ann Arbor, MI 48105. 313/764-2313

COOKSEY, JOHN P. Bus:Pers/Ind Rels. POSITION: Manager, Human Resources, Amax Coal Co, PO Box 487, Booneville, IN 47601. 812/897-2870

COOLEEN, JOHN P. Bus:Pers/Ind Rels. BBA 1952, St. John's U; JD 1958, Fordham U. INT: labor law, coll barg, arb/med. POSITION: Dir, Labor Rels, The Singer Co, PO Box 10151, Stamford, CT 06904. 203/259-9793

COOLEY, MAYNARD WAYNE Bus:Pers/Ind Rels. MLIR 1980, Mich State U. INT: labor law, ind sociol, labor history. POSITION: (since 1981) Empl Rels Rep, Standard Oil Co of Calif, Chevron Res Co, Salt Lake. ADDRESS: 1013 Floret Lane, Midvale UT 84047. 801/562-5145

COOMBS, WALTER P. Academic. Social Science Dept, Calif State Polytech/Pomona, 3801 W Temple Ave, Pomona, CA 91765. 714/598-4516

COOPER, CHARLES A. Arbitration. MA 1972, Calif State U-Fresno. INT: arb/med, empl/trng programs, mgmt/educ. ASSN: SPIDR. POSITION: Reg Dir, American Arbitration Assn, 445 Bush St 5th Floor, San Francisco, CA 94108. 415/981-3901

COOPER, CHRISTINE GODSIL Acad: Law. MA 1974, U of Ill-Chicago; JD 1975, De Paul U; LLM 1976, Harvard. PUBL: "Title VII in the Academy," 16 UC Davis L Rev 975, 1983; "Reviewing T. Hanami, Labor Relations in Japan Today," 24 Harvard Intl L J 245, 1983; "Professional Nursing and the Right to Separate Representation," (w N. Brent), 58 Chicago-Kent L R 1053 1982. INT: labor law, intl comparative labor, arb/med. ASSN: ABA, SPIDR, Amer Anthropological Soc. POSITIONS: Economist, BLS, USDL, 1969; Assoc, Winston & Strawn,

1976; and (since 1978) Asst Prof of Law, Loyola Law School, 1 E. Pearson, Chicago, IL. 60611. 312/670-2948

COOPER, JERRY PHILIP Bus:Mgmt/Admin. BSBA 1980, U of Ariz. INT: mgmt/educ, arb/-med, govt labor policy. ASSN: Natl Mgmt Assn, Natl Contracts Mgmt Assn. POSITIONS: Ind Rels Rep, 1972, Sub Contract Administrator, Bechtel Corp, 1975; and (since 1977) Contracts Mgr, Washington Public Power Supply System. ADDRESS: 1703 W 12th Ave, Kennewick, WA 99336. 509/377-2501

COOPER, MARTHA R. Student. BA 1978, Princeton U; MSc 1980, London School of Econ. PUBL Business Hobbies: The Public Good and the Bottom Line, (w S. Levitan), Johns Hopkins U Press, 1984; The Search for Consensus, Paris:OECD, 1982. INT: govt labor policy, coll barg, arb/med. POSITIONS: Consultant, OECD, Paris, 1979; Res Assoc, Center for Social Policy Studies, George Wash U, 1981; and (since 1982) Student, Harvard Law School. ADDRESS: 106 Ellery St, Cambridge, MA 02138. 617/497-8321

COPAS, WILLIAM H. Union, Consulting, Arbitration. INT: coll barg, arb/med, union org/admin. POSITION: Bus Mgr, IBEW 814, AFL-CIO, 2111 W Broadway, Sedalia, MO 65301.

COPPESS, JAMES B. Legal Practice. AB 1973, U of Mich; MA 1975, Wayne State U; JD 1979, Emory U. INT: labor law, labor history, union org/admn. ASSN: Wash DC IRRA, Intl Soc for Labor Law & Soc Legislation. POSITION: (since 1977) Attorney, Adair & Goldthwaite, Suite 411, 1925 K St NW, Washington DC 20006. 202/728-2462

COPPS, JOHN ALDEN Acad: Econ. BS,MS, & PhD (1950), U of Wis-Madison. POSITION: Prof, Dept of Econ, Western Mich Univ, Kalamazoo, MI 49001. 616/383-1744

CORBETT, LAURENCE PAUL Legal Practice. AB 1943, JD 1948, Harvard. POSITION: (since 1966) Sr Partner, Corbett, Kane, Berk & Barton, Suite 500, 2200 Powell St, Oakland, CA 94608. 415/547-2434

CORBITT, LESLIE Student. 1715-4 Nemoke Tr, Haslett, MI 48840.

CORCORAN, FRANK Acad: Ind Rels. POSITION: Dept of Bus Admin, Robert Morris Coll, Narrows Run Rd, Coraopolis, PA 15108. 412/264-9300

CORDTZ, RICHARD W. Union. INT: union org/admin, coll barg. ASSN: Detroit IRRA. POSITIONS: Intl Secretary-Treasurer, SEIU, 1980, and, since 1984, President, SEIU Local 79, AFL-CIO, 2604 Fourth St, Detroit, MI 48201. 313/965-9450

CORINA, JOHN G. Acad: Ind Rels. BA 1956, MA 1958, D Phil 1960, Oxford Univ. PUBL: "Trade Unions, New Technology and Incomes Policy," Prometheus, Dec 1983; "Trade Unions and Technological Change," in The Trouble With Technology, eds. Lamberton, MacDonald, Mandeville, 1983; Labour Market Economics-A Short Survey, 1973. INT: intl comparative labor, union org/admin, labor market econ. ASSN: Fellow of Royal Econ Soc, Ind Rels Soc, Assn of Univ Teachers of Ind Rels. POSITIONS: Prof of Ind Rels, Univ of Manchester (UK), 1976-77; Fellow in Econ, Oxford U Lecturer, St. Peter's Coll, Oxford, 1965-79; and (since 1979) Prof of Ind Rels and Head of Dept of Ind Rels, Univ of Sydney. Address: 44 Downing St, Epping Sydney, NSW, Australia 2121. Phone: 692-3077

CORLEY, SUSAN Bus:Pers/Ind Rels, Bus:Mgmt-/Admin. BA 1977, MA 1982, U of Ariz; MBA 1983, U of Hawaii. INT: personnel, coll barg, intl comparative labor. ASSN: Hawaii IRRA, ASPA. POSITIONS: Pers Admin, Intl Telephone Telegraph Copr, 1979, and (since 1981) Pers Mgr, Reynolds Metal Co, 500 Crenshaw Blvd, Torrance, CA 90503. 213/320-0102

CORNFORD, D. N. Consulting, Bus:Pers/Ind Rels. AB 1957, Occidental Coll; MBA 1960, UCLA. INT: coll barg, labor law, govt labor policy. ASSN: San Francisco Bay Area IRRA. POSITIONS: Ind Rels Asst, Kaiser Steel Corp-Fontana, 1960; Mgr-Los Angeles, Western Newspapers Ind Rels Bureau, 1961; and (since 1977) Executive Dir, Hotel Employers Assoc of San Francisco, 870 Market St, #774, San Francisco, CA 94102. 415/986-5084

CORPORA, ANGELO J. Arbitration, Mediation, Bus:Pers/Ind Rels. BA 1975, Lewis U; MA 1984, Antioch U. INT: arb/med, labor law, coll barg. ASSN: Chicago IRRA, AAA, Reserve Officer Assn. POSITIONS: Asst to Pres, Bank of Elmhurst, 1977; President, AFC Group Ltd, 1980; and (since 1984) Arbitrator, 23W210 Windsor Dr, Glen Ellyn, IL 60137. 312/790-4153

CORRADINO, BARTHOLOMEW P. Bus:Pers/-Ind Rels. BA 1962, Seton Hall U; MILR 1964, Cornell. INT: coll barg, laborlaw, arb/med. POSITIONS: Asst to Pres, Seafarers Intl Union of NA, Brooklyn, 1964; Dir of Pers, Johnson & Johnson, New Brunswick, 1966; and (since 1978) CorpDir of Human Resources, Harris Graphics Corp, Melbourne. ADDRESS: 4576 Mustang Rd, Melbourne, FL 32935. 305/676-9435

CORVINO, ANTHONY J. Bus:Pers/Ind Rels. INT: coll barg, arb/med, personnel. POSITION: Vice Pres-Labor Rels, Continental Grain Co, 43rd FL, 277 Park Ave, New York, NY 10172. 212/207-5140

COTABISH, MATTHEW I. Consulting. POSITION: Consulting services, 11530 Edgewater Dr, Cleveland, OH 44102. 216/631-6690

COTE, PIERRE-MARCEL Acad: IndRels, Psychology. BA 1984, McGill U. INT: personnel, org beh, empl/trng programs. ASSN: Assn of Human Res Professional of Quebec. POSITIONS: Placement Agent, Empl & Immigration, Canada, 1983, and, currently, President, McGill IndRels Assn. ADDRESS: 10840 Peloquin, Montreal Quebec, Canada. 514/381-5402

COTLER, MIRIAN P. Acad: Econ, Health Res Admin. MS 1980, UCLA. INT: coll barg, health & hosp care, ind sociol. ASSN: APHA, Amer Soc Labor Medicine, Inst Health Serv Res. POSITION: Ins (part time) Calif State Univ North. ADDRESS: 17513 Margate St, Encino, CA 91316.

COULSON, ROBERT Arbitration. JD 1953, Harvard. PUBL: Labor Arbitration: What You Need To Know, AAA; The Termination Handbook, Free Press, 1981; Fighting Fair, Free Press, 1983. INT: arb/med. ASSN: ABA, NYS Bar, City Bar of NY. POSITION: President, American Arbitration Assn, 140 W 51st, New York, NY 10020. 212/484-4100

COUNTS, J. CURTIS Consulting, Bus:Pers/Ind-Rels, Arbitration. BA 1937, UCLA; Grad Work, 1939 USC. INT: coll barg, arb/med, personnel. ASSN: SPIDR, Intl Soc for Labor Law & Soc Security. POSITIONS: Dir, FMCS, 1969; Pres, Trucking Mgmt Inc, 1977; and (since 1980) Consultant, 3105 Haddington Dr, Los Angeles, CA 90064. 213/838-7460

COX, DAVID R. Bus:Pers/Ind Rels. BS 1965, San Jose State U. INT: coll barg, arb/med, costs/fringe benefits. ASSN: San Francisco IRRA. POSITIONS: Dir, Trust Activities, 1979, and, since 1982, Vice Pres, Northern Calif Division, Food Employers Council Inc, Drawer 1298, 3685 MT. Diablo Blvd, Lafayette, CA 94549. 415/284-9350

COYLE, JOHN B. Arbitration. Acad: Ind Rels. BS 1984, MBA 1952, U of Detroit. PUBL: "Personnel Staff Relations," Pers Admin, 1960; "Safety's Sacred Cow," Amer Machinist Mag, 1961; "Communication and Grievance Systems," Office Mgmt Mag, 1962. INT: arb/med. ASSN: Detroit IRRA, AAA, SPIDR, NAA. POSITIONS: Arbitrator, Private Prac, 1972-75; Dir of Empl Rels, Oakland U, 1975-78; and (since 1978), Arbitrator, 155 E Romeo Rd, Rochester, MI 48063. 313/652-8444

COZ, RICHARD T. Acad: Economics. Jesuit Community, Univ of Santa Clara, Santa Clara, CA 95053.

CRAFT, JAMES A. Acad: Bus Admin, Ind Rels, Org Beh/Pers. BA 1961, Claremont Men's Coll; MBA 1963, PhD 1968, U of Calif-Berkeley. PUBL: "Testing and Industrial Application," (co-author), in Goldstein and Hersen (ed) Handbook of Psychological Assessment, 1984; "The Union Image: Concept, Programs and Analysis," (co-author), J of Labor Res, Fall 1983; "Post Recession Bargaining: Mutualism or Adversarial Relations," Labor Law J, July 1983. INT: personnel, coll barg, org/admin. ASSN: Western Penna IRRA, Acad of Mgmt, Human Resources Planning Soc, ASPA. POSITIONS: Asst Prof, Krannert School, Purdue U, 1968; Manpower Analyst, USDL, Manpower Admin, 1971; and (since 1972) Prof, Grad School of Bus, Univ of Pittsburgh, Pittsburgh, PA 15260. 412/624-6280

CRAIG, ALTON W. J. Acad: Ind Rels; Consulting. B Comm 1955, St. Dunstan's U; MBA 1957, U of Western Ontario; PhD 1964, Cornell U. PUBL: The System of Industrial Relations in Canada, Scarborough, Ont, Prentice Hall, 1983; "A Framework for the Analysis of Industrial Relations Systems," in B. Barrett et al, Ind Rels and the Wider Society, London, England, Collier Macmillan, 1975; "The Collective Bargaining Process," Rels Industrielles, vol 25, #1, pp 34-45, 1970. INT: coll barg, govt health policy, personnel. ASSN: Canadian Ind Rels Assn, Admin Sci Assn of Canada, Acad of Mgmt. POSITIONS: Ind Rels Researcher, Canada Dept of Labour, 1964; Assoc Prof, 1969, and, since 1975, Prof, Faculty of Admin, Univ of Ottawa. ADDRESS: 19 Glendenning Dr, Ottawa, K2H 7Z1 Canada. 613/231-5493

CRANE, DONALD PAUL Acad: Bus Admin, Ind Rels; Arbitration. BS 1955, Cornell; MBA 1968, PhD 1969, Ga State U. PUBL: Personnel: The Management of Human Resources, Kent 1982; The Public Managers Guide, BNA 1982; "The Propensity to Manage as an Indicator of Success in Career Planning," Acad of Mgmt J, Sept 1982. INT: arb/med, coll barg, personnel. POSITIONS: Ind Rels Rep, Kennecott Copper Corp, 1957; Territory Rep, Xerox Corp 1963; and (since 1968) Prof, Dept of Mgmt, Georgia State Univ, Union Plaza, Atlanta, GA 30303. 404/658-3404

CRANE, LILI Bus:Mgmt/Admin, Pers/Ind Rels. BA 1946, Ben Franklin Coll. INT: mgmt/-educ, coll barg, personnel. ASSN: Wash DC IRRA, Amer Assn of Law Librarians. POSITIONS: Dir of Res, 1956, and, since 1983, Deputy Assoc Editor, Research and Info Services, BNA, 1231 25th St NW, Washington DC, 20037. 202/452-4525

CRANNAN, HERBERT J. Government; Acad: Ind Rels. BA 1955, St. John's U; BSCE 1966, Brooklyn Polytech Inst. INT: coll barg, personnel, mgmt/educ. ASSN: Amer Soc Civil Engineers, Intl Platform Assn, New York Acad of Sci. POSITIONS: Asst General Mgr, LR & P, 1979, and, since 1982, Asst Vice-Pres, Human Resources, New York City Transit Authority. ADDRESS: 61 Raymond Ave, Staten Island, NY 10314. 212/330-3218

CRAVANAS, V. ALEX Government; Acad: Bus Admin. BA 1976, U of Akron; JD 1979, Antioch Coll. INT: govt labor policy, labor law, mgmt/educ. ASSN: Cincinnati IRRA, Penna Bar Assn (Labor Law Section), Black Lawyer's Assn of Cincinnati. POSITIONS: Law Clerk, Div of Judges, 1978, and, since 1979, Field Attorney, NLRB, Region 9, 550 Main St, Cincinnati, OH 45202. 513/684-3653

CRAVER, CHARLES BRADFORD Acad: Law. BS 1967, MILR 1968, Cornell U; JD 1971, U of Mich. PUBL: Employment Discrimination Law, (w Smith & Clark), 1982; Labor Relations Law in the Public Sector, (w Edwards & Clark), 1979; "The Vitality of the American Labor Movement in the Twenty First Century," Ill Law Rev, 1983. INT: labor law, empl discrimination, arb/med. ASSN: Amer Law Inst, AAA, Intl Soc for Labor Law and Soc Legislation. POSITIONS: Attorney, Mamson & Foerster, San Francisco, 1972-74; and (since 1982) Prof of Law, Coll of Law, Univ of Ill, 504 E Pennsylvania Ave, Champaign, IL 61820. 217/333-0061

CRAWFORD, ANGELA C. Acad: Ind Rels. BA 1967, MS 1982, Carnegie Mellon U. ASSN: Western Penna IRRA, ASPA, Natl Assn for Female Exec. POSITIONS: Mgr, Fifth & Wood Men's, 1979, and, since 1982, Assoc Dir, Center for Labor Studies, School of Urban and Public Affairs, Carnegie Mellon Univ, Pittsburgh, PA 15213. 412/578-2177

CRAWFORD, JAMES F. Acad: Ind Rels; Consulting. PhD 1957, U of Wis-Madison. INT: coll barg, older worker issues. ASSN: Atlanta IRRA. POSITIONS: Chairman, Dept of Econ, 1962, Dir, Inst Ind Rels, GA State Univ, 1980; and (since 1982) Lecturer, Kennessee Coll. ADDRESS: 1096 Clifton Rd NE, Atlanta, GA 30307.

CREA, MARIE Bus:Pers/Ind Rels. BA 1978, St. Francis Coll; MBA 1980, Pace U. INT: personnel, empl/trng programs, labor market econ. ASSN: New York IRRA, AMBA, IAPW. POSITIONS: Interviewer/Trng Rep, Lord and Taylor, 1980; and (since 1982) Recruiter, Merrill Lynch & Co Inc, 1 Liberty Plaza, 165 Broadway, New York, NY 10080. 212/637-4656

CREEDON, GERARD T. Bus:Pers/Ind Rels. BBA 1953, CCNY. INT: coll barg, personnel, labor law. ASSN: Railroad Pers Assn, ASPA.

Railroad Ins Mgmt Assn. POSITIONS: Group Sales Rep, Metro Life Ins Co, 1957; Asst Treas, Cuyahuga Valley Railway Co, 1960; and (since 1964) Asst Sec and Dir of Insurance Relations, Monongahela Connecting Railway, 3600 Second Ave, Pittsburgh, PA 15219. 412/227-4957

CREO, ROBERT A. Arbitration, Legal Practice. BA 1974, Brandeis U; JD 1977, Washington U. PUBL: "Arbitration of Nonunion Employee Discharge Cases," ABA Barrister, Winter 1984; "Power for an Arbitrator to Compel Testimony," Persepctive, Labor Information Systems, Dec 1982 & Jan, 1983; Glossary of Legal and Labor Arbitration Terms, Community Coll of Allegheny County, Pittsburgh: 1982. INT: arb/med, labor law. ASSN: Western Penna IRRA, AAA, Federal Bar Assn (Labor Arb Committee). POSITION: FMCS-Roster of Arbitrators, and, (since 1974) Arbitrator, 220 Grant St, Pittsburgh, PA 15219. 412/281-4130

CRIPE, LAWRENCE EVERT Bus:Labor Relations. POSITION: Dir, Empl Rels, UOP Inc, Ten UOP Plaza, Des Plaines, IL 60016. 312/391-2313

CRISAFULLI, VIRGIL C. Acad: Econ & Ind Rels. AB 1938, MA 1940, PhD 1954, Ohio State U. POSITION: Emeritus Prof of Econ, Utica Coll of Syracuse U. Retired. ADDRESS: 72 Meadow St, Clinton NY 13323.

CRIST, WILLIAM DALE Academic: Econ; Union. BS 1960, MA 1962, PhD 1972, U of Nebr. PUBL: "California Public Universities-California's Piecemeal Approach to Public Sector Collective Bargaining," Mich State U, 1980; "When Collective Bargaining Comes to the California State University," Univ J, CSU Chico, 1978; "The Importance of Management and Labor Attitudes to Wage Determination, 1890-1940." INT: coll barg, labor market econ, union org/admn. ASSN: AEA. POSITION: Pres, Calif Faculty Assn, 1976 to present, and (since 1969) Prof of Econ, Calif State Coll, Stanislaus, Turlock CA 95380. 209/667-3500

CROLL, RICHARD Arbitration, Consulting. BA 1954, Adrian Coll; MA 1960, MS 1964, Eastern Mich U. INT: arb/med, coll barg, union org/-admn. ASSN: NW IRRA. POSITION: (since 1983) Arbitrator (self-employed). ADDRESS: 7316 56th Ave NE, Seattle WA 98115. 206/524-2357

CROST, PAUL Legal Practice. BA 1964, UCLA; JD 1964 U of Calif-Berkeley. INT: labor law, arb/med, govt labor policy. ASSN: Orange Cty IRRA, ABA. POSITIONS: Attorney, Brundage & Hackler, 1967, and (since 1975) Partner, Reich, Adell & Crost, 2020 W Chapman, Orange, CA 92668. 714/978-6451

CROWELL, ELIZABETH Acad: Economics. POSITION: Dept of Social Sciences, Univ of Michigan, Dearborn, MI 48128. 313/593-5305

CROWLEY, JOHN F. Union, Bus:Pers/Ind Rels. BS 1946, Marquette U. INT: labor educ, labor history, labor law. ASSN: San Francisco IRRA. POSITION: (since 1963) Secretary-Treasurer, San Francisco Labor Council, AFL-CIO, 1855 Folsom St, San Francisco, CA 94103. 415/-863-7011

CROYLE, THOMAS J. Bus:Pers/Ind Rels. BS 1974, Penna State U; MA 1978, MA 1979, St. Francis Coll. INT: personnel, labor law, mgmt/educ. ASSN: Amer Compensation Assn, ASPA. POSITIONS: Pers Dir, Kasel Manufacturing Co; Pers Supervisor, 1976, and, since 1977, Manager, Pers, Penna Mines Corp, PO Box 367, Ebensburg, PA 15931. 814/472-5140

CRUDO, FERNANDA CYNTHIA Union. POSITION: National Representative, AFTRA, AFL-CIO, 1816 Carew Tower, Cincinnati, OH 45202. 513/579-8668

CRUMPTON, ROBERT G. Union. ADDRESS: Oregon Educ Assn, 1 Plaza SW, 6900 SW Haines Rd, Tigard, OR 97223. 503/639-7651

CULL, CLEMENT PAUL Arbitration. INT: arb/med. ASSN: New York and New Brunswick IRRA. POSITION: Arbitrator. ADDRESS: 626 Linden Ave, Teaneck, NJ 07666. 201/836-5326

CULLEN, DONALD E. Acad: Ind Rels; Arbitration. BA 1947, Hobart Coll; MS 1949, PhD 1953, Cornell U. PUBL: The Bargaining Structure in Construction: Problems and Prospects (w L. Feinberg) monograph, USDL, 1980; The Labor Sector, 3rd Ed (w N. Chamberlain & D, Lewin), McGraw Hill, 1979; Two chapters in Charles Rehmus ed, The Railway Labor Act at Fifty, GPO 1977. INT: coll barg, govt labor policy, arb/med. ASSN: AAA. POSITIONS: Asst Prof, 1953, Assoc Prof, 1958, and, since 1966, Prof, NYSSILR, Cornell Univ, Ithaca, NY 14853. 607/256-3295

CULLERTON, JOHN E. Bus:Pers/Ind Rels, Governmental Affairs. Univ of Ill. INT: coll barg, govt labor policy, personnel. ASSN: Chicago IRRA. POSITION: (since 1971) Sr Vice Pres Ind Rels and Governmental Affairs, Hilton Hotels Corp, 27 E Monroe St, Chicago,IL 60603. 312/443-1500

CULLEY, JACK F. Acad: Ind Rels; Arbitration. BA 1948, Grinnell Coll; MS 1949, PhD 1952, Cornell U. INT: personnel, arb/med, mgmt/-educ. ASSN: Acad of Mgmt, SPIDR, Federal Labor Rels Professional (Rocky MT Chapter). POSITIONS: Dir of Ind Rels. A. L. Garber Co, 1952; Prof & Dir, Bureau of Labor & Mgmt, Univ of Iowa, 1955; and (since 1968) Prof, Coll of Bus, Colorado State U, Fort Collins, CO 80523. 303/491-6742

CULLINAN, MARTIN J. Union; Acad: Teacher. BA 1957 Marist Coll; MA 1963, Hunter Coll; MS 1974, St. John's U. INT: coll barg, arb/med, labor law. ASSN: Long Island IRRA. POSITION: (since 1973) Pres, Levittown United Teachers, 3017 Hempstead Turnpike, Levittown, NY 11756. 516/796-5660

CULVER, WARREN D. Union. BA 1960, Wayne State U. INT: arb/med, coll barg, empl/-trng programs. ASSN: Mid-Mich IRRA. POSITION: Director Labor Rels, Mich Educ Assn, 1216 Kendale Blvd, Box 673, East Lansing, MI 48823. 517/332-6551

CUMMINGS, LARRY L. Acad: Org Beh/Pers. AB 1959, MBA 1961, DBA 1964, Ind U. INT: org beh, ind psych, mgmt/educ. ASSN: Acad of Mgmt, Amer Psych Assn, Amer Sociol Assn. POSITIONS: Prof, Univ of Wis, 1968; and (since 1981) Kellogg Distinguished Prof of Org Beh, Northwestern Univ, Evanston, IL 60201. 312/492-3470

CUNNINGHAM, EDWARD P. Bus:Mgmt/Admin. POSITION: Employee Rels Mgr, Quaker Oats Co, PO Box 1120, Lawrence, KS 66044. 913/841-7600

CUNNINGHAM, J. DAVID Acad: News Gathering/Publishing. PhD 1983, U of Oregon. PUBL: "After a Score of Years, What's the Faculty Union Score," Community & Jr Coll J, Dec/Jan, 1983-84; "Analysis of Legislation Enabling Collective Bargaining in Public Postsecondary Education," ACBIS Special Report 17; "Institutions and Campuses with Faculty Collective Bargaining Agents," ACBIS Special Report 12. INT: labor law, arb/med, coll barg. ASSN: Wash DC IRRA, AAA, AAUP, Coll & Univ Pers Officers Assn. POSITIONS: Asst to VP for Admin & Finance, (General Admin) 1976, Asst to VP for Admin & Finance (Pers Services), U of Oregon, 1979; and (since 1983) Dir, Acad Coll Barg & Information Service (ACBIS), Labor Studies Center, Univ of the District of Columbia, 724 9th St, Suite 210, Washington DC 20001. 202/727-2903

CURETON, JOHN PORTER Bus:Pers/Ind Rels, Consulting, Bus:Mgmt/Admin. MBA 1979, U of Hartford; BA 1960, Johnson C Smith U. INT: coll barg, org beh, arb/med. ASSN: Southern Conn IRRA, ASPA, ASTD, IRS-NYC. POSITIONS Mgr. Ind Rels, Sybron Corp, 1968; Mgr Empl Rels, Heublein Co, 1975; and (since 1978) Vice Pres Ind Rels, United States Tobacco Co, Greenwich. ADDRESS: 792 Booth Hill Rd, Huntington, CT 06484. 203/661-1100

CURIA, SAMUEL Student. ADDRESS: 211 Grant Ave. Morgantown, WV 26041. 304/291-1683

CURINGTON, WILLIAM PETER Acad: Econ. BA 1970, U of Tex-Austin; MLIR 1972 Mich State U; PhD 1979, Syracuse U. PUBL: "Interaction Analysis: A Tool for Understanding Negotiations," Ind and Labor Rels Rev, April, 1983; "Income Security for the Disabled," Ind Rels, Spring 1979; "The Adequacy of Workers Compensation Payments," Res Reports of the Interdepartmental Workers Compensation Task Force. INT: labor market econ, income maint, health & hospital care. ASSN: AEA. POSITIONS: Res Asst, Health Studies Program Syracuse Univ, 1974; Asst Prof of Econ, Rochester Inst of Tech, 1978; and (since 1980) Assoc Prof, Dept of Econ, Univ of Arkansas, Fayetteville, AR 72701. 501/575-6233

CURRY, THEODORE H., II Acad: Ind Rels. MS 1974, MBA 1975, U of Kans. PUBL: "A Common Sense Approach to Employee Selection and EEO Compliance for the Smaller Employer," Pers Admin April, 1981; "The Implications of the Uniform Guidelines on Employee Selection Procedures." INT: personnel, mgmt/educ. ASSN: Detroit IRRA, ASPA, Acad of Mgmt. POSITION: (since 1981) Assoc Dir, Assoc Prof, School of Labor and Ind Rels, Mich State Univ, East Lansing, MI 48824. 517/335-9591

CURTIS, FRANCES Acad: Org Beh/Pers. W. 167 S. 6869 Oak Hill Drive, Muskego, WI 53150.

CURTIS, FRANK JUDSON, JR. Acad: Econ, Ind Rels. AB 1943, Ursinus Coll, AM 1948, PhD 1974, U of Penna. INT: labor market econ, coll barg, intl comparative labor. ASSN: West Mich and Southwestern Mich IRRAs, AEA, IIRA, Amer Acad of Pol and Soc Sci. POSITIONS: Lecturer, McGill Univ, 1955; Inst, U of Pittsburgh, 1956; and (since 1960) Prof, Dept of History, Pol Sci and Econ, Ferris State Coll, Big Rapids, MI 49307. 616/796-0461, ext 5854

CUSACK, JOHN J. Bus:Pers/Ind Rels. POSITION: Admin/Pers, North Shore Univ Hosp, 300 Community Dr, Manhasset NY 11030. 516/562--4050

CUSHMAN, BERNARD Arbitration. AB 1934, Dartmouth; JD 1939, Harvard. PUBL: "Arbitration and the Duty to Bargain," Wis Law J, Summer 1967; "Voluntary Arbitration of New Contract Terms-A Forum Search of a Dispute," Labor Law J, Dec 1965. INT: arb/-med, labor law, coll barg. ASSN: Wash DC IRRA, ABA, SPIDR, AAA. POSITIONS: Spec Asst to General Counsel, NLRB, 1967, Attorney, Bredhoff, Cushman, Gottesman & Cohen, 1969; and (since 1965) Arbitrator (self-employed). ADDRESS: 9203 Summit Rd, Silver Spring, MD 20910. 301/565-5950

CUSHMAN, EDWARD L. Acad: Univ Admin, Ind Rels; Bus:Mgmt/Admin. AB 1937, U of Mich. INT: coll barg, govt labor policy, arb/med. ASSN: Detroit IRRA, NAA, ASPA, AEA. POSITIONS: Prof of Publ Admin, Wayne State Univ, 1946; VP American Motors Corp, 1954, and (since 1966) Sr VP for Urban, Labor and Metro Studies, Exec VP Emeritus & Clarence Hilberry Univ Prof, Wayne State Univ, Detroit, MI 48202. 313/577-1886

CUTLER, S,. OLEY SJ Acad: Ind Rels, Res; Arbitration. AB 1946, MA 1948, Boston Coll; PhL 1948 Weston Coll; STL 1956, Woodstock Coll; JD 1952, Georgetown U. PUBL: Natural Law Ethics in History and Analysis, LeMoyne Coll, Aug, 1964; "Capital District Transportation Authority," Labor Arb Reports, Fall 1979; Choices in Resolving Public Sector Disputes, Prentice Hall, July 1982. INT: arb/med, coll barg, govt labor policy. ASSN: Central New York IRRA, AAA, SPIDR. POSITIONS: Asst Prof of Law, Fordham, 1959; Chairman, Ind Rels Dept, 1970, and since 1976, Adj. Assoc Prof of Ind Rels, Le Moyne Coll, Le Moyne Heights, Syracuse, NY 13214. 315/446-2882

CYPIN, JACK Acad: Econ; Government. BSS 1938, CCNY; MA 1947, Columbia U. INT: labor market econ, intl comparative labor, ind sociol. ASSN: AEA, Acad of Pol Sci, Amer Acad of Pol & Soc Sci. Retired. ADDRESS: 15 Hill Lane, Levittown, NY 11756. 516/731-4599

CZARNECKI, EDGAR R. Union. BS 1956, Marquette U; MILR 1957, Cornell; PhD 1967, Georgetown U. INT: labor educ. ASSN: Wash DC IRRA. POSITIONS: Asst Dir of Researh & Educ, IBEW, 1958; Dir, Labor Center, Univ of Iowa, 1966; and (since 1977) Asst Dir of Educ, AFL-CIO, 815 16th St NW, Washington DC 20006. 202/637-5146

CZERBINSKI, JOSEPH P. Union. 1 Randall Cir, Windsor, CT 06095. 203/749-6146

D

DABNEY, HENRIETTA L. Union. BA 1946, Queens Coll, CUNY; MBA 1977, Pace U. INT: labor market econ, coll barg, union org/admn. ASSN: New York IRRA, AEA, Amer Statis Assn. POSITIONS: Asst Dir, Econ & Genl Welfare, Amer Nurses Assn, 1961; Asst Dir of Res & Negotiations, AFSCME, 1970, and (since 1974) Assoc Dir of Res, Amalgamted Clothing and Textile Workers, New York. ADDRESS: 1 5th Ave 8K, New York, NY 10003. 212/242-0700

DADALT, ANN MORIARTY POSITION: Exec Secretary, MA Labor Rels Comm, 100 Cambridge St #1604, Boston, MA 02202. 617/727-3505

DAFFARA, JOHN C. Bus:Pers Ind Rels. BS 1973, Ill State U; AA 1971, Ill Valley Comm Coll. ADDRESS: 215 High St, Marshall, MI 49068. 616/781-9323

D'ALBA, JOEL ABBOTT Legal Practice. BA 1966, Wash U; MS 1969, Ill Inst of Tech; JD 1971, U of Ill. PUBL: "The Nature of The Duty to Bargain in Good Faith," in Portrait of a Process-Collective Negotiations in Public Employment, 1979. INT: arb/med, coll barg, health & hosp care. ASSN: Chicago IRRA, ABA (Section Labor & Empl Law). POSITIONS: Admin Asst, Mich Empl Rels Comm, 1971-73; and, currently, Attorney, Asher Pavalon et al, Two North LaSalle St, Chicago, IL 60602. 312/263-1500

DALE, CHARLES Government. BS 1966, Kent State U; MS 1970, U of Ga; MDS 1972, PhD 1978, Ga State U. PUBL: "Determinants of Enlistments: A Macroeconomic Time-Series View," (Dale et al),Armed Forces and Soc, vol 10, #2, Winter 1984, pp 192-210; "Multinomial Probit Models of Military Enlistments: A Comparison of Alternative Solution Algorithms," Proc of the Bus & Econ Statistics Section, Amer Statis Assn, Aug 1983, pp 336-340; "The Effects of the Business Cycle on the Size and Composition of the U. S. Army," (Dale et al), Atlantic Econ J, vol XI, #1, Mar 1983, pp 42-53. INT: labor market econ, govt labor policy, personnel. ASSN: Natl Economists Club, Soc of Government Economists, Operations Res Soc of Amer. POSITIONS: Financial Economist, U.S. Dept of Treasury, 1978; Intl Economist, U. S. Dept of Commerce, Intl Trade Admin, 1979; and (since 1982) Research Economist, U.S. Army Res Inst, 5001 Eisenhower Ave, Alexandria, VA 22333. 202/274-5610

DALE, LEON A. Acad: Ind Rels. BA 1946, Tulane; MA 1947, PhD 1949, U of Wis. PUBL: Marxcism and French Labor; A Bibliography of French Labor; "The Foreman as a Manager." INT: arb/med. ind psychology, mgmt/educ. ASSN: Amer Acad of Pol & Soc Sci, AAA, AEA. POSITIONS: Prof, U of Bridgeport, 1960, and (since 1969) Prof, School of Bus Mgmt, Calif State Polytech Coll, 3801 W Temple Ave, Pomona CA 91768. 714/598-0361

DALLAS, SHERMAN F. Arbitration. PhD 1955, Ind U. PUBL: Labor Relations in the Nuclear Power Industry, Nuclear Assurance Corp, 1974; "What Happened to the Darlington Case?" (w B. Schaffer), Labor Law J, Jan 1973; "Racial Bias: The Detroit Edison Case,: (w B. Schaffer), Labor Law J, Sept, 1974. INT: arb/med, coll barg. ASSN: Atlanta IRRA, NAA. POSITIONS: Regents Prof, Ga Inst of Tech, Atlanta, and, currently Arbitrator. ADDRESS: 3325 Valley Rd NW, Atlanta, GA 30305. 404/894-2609

DALY, JAMES H. Acad: Ind Rels. BSinBA 1970, Youngstown State U; MBA 1972, Akron U. INT: personnel, coll barg. ASSN: Acad of Mgmt. POSITION: (since 1972) Assoc Prof of management, Youngstown State Univ. ADDRESS: 1829 Wingate Rd, Youngstown, OH 44514. 216/742-3072

D'AMBROSIO, NORMAND Acad: Bus Admin/-Mgmt. 1029 Bou St Joseph E, Montreal, PQ H2J 1L2 Canada. 514/845-2781

DAMON, C. F., JR. Legal Practice. BA 1950, Yale; LLB 1953, U of Colo. INT: arb/med, coll barg, ind sociol. ASSN: Hawaii IRRA. POSITIONS: Dir, Labor & Ind Rels, State of Hawaii, 1962; Adjunct Prof, Univ of Hawaii Law School, 1982-84; and (since 1962) Sr Partner, Damon, Key, Char & Bocken, 810 Richards St, 10th FL, Honolulu, HI 96813. 808/531-8031

DAMRON, BOBBY JAMES Student. ADDRESS: Box 62, East Bank, WV 25067.

DANCHA, DANA RENEE Student. 301 1/2 Coleridge Ave, Altoona, PA 16602. 814/943-3933

DANIEL, MARK J. Bus:Pers/Ind Rels. PhD 1974, U of Minn. INT: labor market econ, coll barg, personnel. ASSN: Canadian Ind Rels Assn. POSITIONS: Asst Dir, Conference Board of Canada, 1979, and (since 1982) Executive Dir, Ind Rels Research, Canada Post Corp, SAC Building, Ottawa, Ont K1A 0B1 Canada. 613/998-4259

DANIELS, WILBUR Union. POSITION: Exec Vice Pres, ILGWU, 1710 Broadway, New York, NY 10019. 212/265-7000.

DANSBY, EDGAR R. Arbitration. INT: arb/med, coll barg, labor educ. ASSN: Detroit IRRA, SPIDR. POSITIONS: Intl Rep, 1960, Dir, Arbitration Services, United Auto Workers, 1976; and (since 1982) Consultant (Labor Liaison), Economic Alliance for Mich, 19311 Lauder St, Detroit MI, 48235.

DANSEREAU, ALFRED E., JR. Acad: Org Beh/Pers, Psych. PhD 1972, U of Ill. PUBL: Theory testing in Organizational Leadership Convergence: An Application of Behavior, 1984; "Within and Between Analysis to Validity," applied Psych, 1983; "Negotiations Latitude: A Within and Between Analysis," Psych Rep, 1983. INT: org beh, method/statis, ind psych. ASSN: Amer Psych Assn, NY Acad of Sci, Acad of Mgmt. POSITIONS: Res Fellow, U of Ill, 1968; Asst Prof (visiting), Baruch Coll, CUNA, 1972; and (since 1973) Assoc Prof, SUNY-Buffalo. ADDRESS: 60 Groton Dr, Apt 4, Williamsville, NY 14221.

DARCY, WILLIAM RICHARD Legal Practice. BA 1973, U of Vt; JD 1977, U of Conn. ADDRESS: PO Box 3216, Hartford, CT 06103. 203/728-6700

DASH, G. ALLEN, JR. Arbitration. ADDRESS: 323 Holmecrest Rd, Jenkintown, PA 19046. 215/884-4136

DAUGHERTY, RONALD D. Bus:Pers/Ind Rels. JD 1967, U of Okla. INT: arb/med, coll barg, labor law. ASSN: Houston IRRA, Amer Petroleum Labor Lawyers Assn, Houston Bar Assn, State Bar of Texas. POSITIONS: Labor Rels Asst, Gulf Oil Co, 1967; Labor Attorney, Bracewell & Patterson, 1970; and (since 1979) Labor Counsel, Pennzoil Co, PO Box 2967, Houston, TX 77252. 713/546-8825

DAVEY, HAROLD L. Government. AB 1951, U of Nebr; MA 1959 U of Wis. INT: intl comparative labor, govt labor policy, coll barg. POSITIONS: Foreign Service Officer, US Dept of State, 1953; Near East & So Asia Area Advisor, 1962, and since 1971, Foreign Service Coordinator, USDL, Wash DC. ADDRESS: 205 Yoakum Parkway, #1711, Alexandria, VA 22304. 202/523-6257

DAVIA, ALBERT B. Union. INT: coll barg, arb/med, health & hosp care. ASSN: Southwestern Mich IRRA. POSITION: (since 1952) Reg Rep, Allied Ind Workers of America, AFL-CIO, 611 Wheaton Ave, Kalamazoo, MI 49008. 616/342-5829

DAVID, HENRY Consulting. BA 1929 CCNY; MA 1930, PhD 1936, Columbia U; MA 1969, Cambridge U. PUBL: History of the Haymarket Affair, 1936, 1958, 1963; Manpower Policies for a Free and Democratic Society, 1965; The Final Report on the Vocational Education Study, 1981. INT: empl/trng programs, labor history, labor market econ. ASSN: AHA, Acad of Pol Sci, Amer Acad of Pol & Soc Sci. POSITIONS: Instructor, Dept of History, CCNY, 1932; Dir, Voc Ed Study, Natl Inst of Educ, 1972; and (since 1982) Consultant (self-employed). ADDRESS: 2206 Wyoming Ave NW, Washington DC 20008. 202/332-2148

DAVID, JOHN P. Acad: Ind Rels, Econ, Univ Admin. BS 1965, U of Mich; PhD 1972, WVa U. PUBL: "The 1950 UMWA Health and Retirement Fund: Its Troubled History," Essays in Ind Rels; "Practices of the UMWA Within the Bituminous Coal Industry," J of Economics; "Worker Earning in Bituminous Coal Since Mechanization," Atlantic Econ J. INT: labor educ, labor history, intl comparative labor. ASSN: West Va IRRA, AEA, Univ and Coll Labor Educ Assn Prof Council, WV Labor History Assn. POSITION: (since 1973) Prof of Econ/Labor and Chair of the Div of Soc Sci, West Va Inst of Tech. ADDRESS: PO Box 127, Kincaid, WV 25119. 304/442-3157

DAVIDSON, ASTRID Union. INT: union org/admin, labor educ, union/women. ASSN: British Columbia IRRA. POSITIONS: Res Asst, 1973, and, since 1977, Director, Women's Programs, B. C. Federation of Labour, 3110 Boundary Rd, Burnaby, BC V5M 4A2 Canada. 604/430-1421

DAVIDSON, MICHAEL EUGENE Student. ADDRESS: 4233 N Kildare, Chicago, IL 60641. 312/777-8498

DAVIDSON, NAOMI BERGER Acad: Ind Rels, Org Beh/Pers; Arbitration. BA 1962, New York U; MA 1969, Northeastern U; PhD 1981, UCLA. INT: personnel, arb/med, coll barg. ASSN: Los Angeles, IRRA, AAA. POSITIONS: Asst Prof, US Riverside, Grad School of Mgmt, 1979, and (since 1983) Assoc Prof, Calif State Univ-Northridge, Dept of Mgmt. ADDRESS: 2210 Malcolm Ave, Los Angeles, CA 90064. 213/885-2457

DAVIES, AL Bus:Pers/Ind Rels. POSITION: Vice Pres Ind Rels, Marathon Steel, PO Box 6598, Phoenix, AZ 85005. 602/252-5971

DAVILA, RAMON JOSE Student. ADDRESS: Apt 518, 633 Langdon St, Madison, WI 53703.

DAVIS, CHARLES H. Acad: Political Sci, Ind Rels. MA 1966, U of Mo-Columbia. INT: labor educ, intl comparative labor, union org/-admn. ASSN: Amer Pol Sci Assn, Labor Educ Local 189. POSITIONS: Coordinator, Labor Educ Center, SE Mass U, 1978; Asst Prof of Mgmt, Central Mo State U, 1980; and (since 1982) Asst Prof Pol Sci, Dept of Pol Sci and Philosophy, Southwest Missouri State Univ. ADDRESS: 2010 E Page St, #10, Springfield, MO 65802. 417/831-2374

DAVIS, JAMES D. Bus:Pers/Ind Rels. BA 1960, LLB 1963, West Va U. INT: coll barg, labor law, govt labor policy. ASSN: Labor Policy Assn. POSITION: Employee, 1963, and, since 1975, Dir Ind Rels, Deere & Co, John Deere Rd, Moline, IL. 61265. 309/752-4786

DAVIS, JOE C. Acad: Econ. POSITION: Dept of Economics, Trinity Univ, 715 Stadium Dr, San Antonio, TX 78284. 512/736-7226

DAVIS, JOHN R. Bus:Mgmt/Admin; Acad: Org Beh/Pers, Bus Admin. DPA 1983, U of Southern Calif. ADDRESS: 50 Jordan Pl, Palo Alto, CA 94303. 415/326-7710

DAVIS, PETER G. Government. BA 1972, Oberlin Coll; JD 1975, U of Wis-Madison. INT: labor law, arb/med, coll barg. ASSN: Wisconsin IRRA, Wis Bar Assn. POSITIONS: Arbitrator, AAA,FMCS, Iowa, 1978; Mediator, Arbitrator, Examiner, 1975, and, since 1981, General Counsel, Wis. Employment Relations Comm. ADDRESS: 216 Westmorland, Madison, WI 53705. 608/266-2993

DAWSON, JAMES LEWIS Arbitration. INT: arb/med. ASSN: Detroit IRRA, AAA, SPIDR, NAA. POSITIONS: Dir-Labor Rels, 1954, and, since 1972, Vice Pres, Emp & Public Rels, BASF-Wyandotte Corp. ADDRESS: 8127 Colony Dr, Gross Ile, MI 48138.

DAWSON, WILLIAM A. SJ Acad: Ind Rels; Arbitration. PhD 1971, U of Wis-Madison. INT: coll barg, arb/med, intlcomparative labor. ASSN: Philadelphia IRRA, ASPA. POSITION: (since 1981) Assoc Dir, Comey Inst of Ind Rels, St Joseph's Univ, 5600 City Ave, Philadelphia, PA 19131. 215/879-7656

DAY, DAVID ROBERT Acad: Org Beh/Pers, Univ Admin, Ind Rels. BS 1952, MBA 1956, Ind U; PhD 1961, Ohio State U. PUBL: "New Leader Behavior Despcription Subscales," (w O. S. Goode & R. M. Stogdill), J of Psych, 1962 Vol 54; "The Leader Behavior of Corporation Presidents," (w O. S. Goode & R. M. Stogdill), Pers Psych, Summer, 1963, Vol 6, #2; "Leader Behavior of Male and Female Supervisors: A Comparative Study," (w R.M. Stogdill), Pers Psych, Summer 1972, vol 25, #2. INT: org beh, mgmt/educ, personnel. ASSN: Acad of Mgmt, Amer Soc for Trng and Development, ASPA. POSITIONS: Prof of Org Beh, Sangamon State Univ, 1972; Dir, Mgmt Inst,

Utah State Univ, 1979; and (since 1981) Head, Mgmt Educ Programs, Univ of Ill Inst of Labor and Ind Rels, 504 E Armory, Champaign, IL 61810. 217/333-0980

DAY, VIRGIL B. Bus:Mgmt/Admin. POSITION: VP, KK & Day 47th Floor, 1 Dag Hammarskold Pl, New York, NY 10017. 212/223-1880

DAYAL, SAHIB Acad: Ind Rels, Bus Admin, Econ. MS 1968, London School of Econ, PhD 1973, Cornell U. PUBL: Industrial Relations System in India, New Dehli: Sterling Publs, 1980; "Unionized Professionals and Bargaining Priorities: An Exploratory Study of University Professors," J of Coll Negotiations in the Public Sector, Vol 13, #2, Spring 1984; "Collective Bargaining As a System of Setting Wages amd Working Conditions," Indian J of Econ, Vol LXII, #246, Jan 1982. INT: coll barg, intl comparative labor, labor market econ. ASSN: IIRA, AEA, Acad of Mgmt. POSITIONS: Sr Lecturer, School of Econ, Univ of NSW, Australia, 1974; Assoc Prof of Mgmt, 1978, and since 1983, Prof and Chairperson, Dept of Mgmt, School of Bus, Central Mich Univ, Mount Pleasant, MI 48859. 517/774-3450

DAYMONT, THOMAS N. Acad: Ind Rels. BA 1967, U of NC; MA 1974, U of Md; PhD 1978, U of Wis. PUBL: "The Health and Economic Status of Very Early Retirees," (w P. Andrisani), Aging and Work, 1983; "Why Women Earn Less Than Men: The Case of Recent College Graduates," (w P. Adrisani), IRRA Proceedings of 35th Annual Meeting, 1983; "Worker Productivity, Employement, and Aging," Stanford Univ Inst for Res on Educ Finance and Government. INT: labor markets, methodology/statis, govt labor policy. ASSN: Phliladelphia IRRA, Amer Sociol Assn, Amer Statis Assn, Gerontological Soc of Amer. POSITIONS: Sr Res Assoc, Center for Human Resource Res, Ohio State Univ, 1978, and (since 1981) Asst Prof, Ind Rels & Org Beh Dept. Temple Univ, Philadelphia, PA 19122. 215/787-8370

DE BLANDER, WILLIAM B. Acad: Bus Admin, Psychology, Student. AB 1977, Cheyney U of PA; MA 1979, MSIR, 1980, U of New Haven. INT: org beh, ind psych, coll barg. ASSN: Amer Psych Assn, Acad of Mgmt, Soc for Ind & Org Psych. POSITIONS: Instructor, Kent State Univ, Dept of Psych, 1982, and (since 1983) Lecturer (part time) Dept of Mgmt, Coll of Bus Admin, Univ of Akron. ADDRESS: 308 E College Ave, Kent OH 44240. 216/375-7037

DE MORRIS, RANDALL S. Bus:Pers/Ind Rels; Acad: Ind Rels. BA 1978, Mich State U; MAIR 1983, Wayne State U. INT: arb/med, labor law, coll barg. ASSN: Detroit IRRA, Detroit Pers Mgmt Assn, Ind Rels Assn of Detroit. POSITIONS: Pers Admin, Apex Corp, Pers Admin and, currently, Empl Manager, Aetna Industries, 24331 Sherwood, Center Line, MI 48015. 313/536-0240

DE TREAUX, WALTER HARRY, III Student. 4961 N 2nd St, Philadelphia, PA 19120. 215/457-4281

DEAN, EARL C. Student. BS 1983, U of Utah. INT: empl/trng programs, personnel, coll barg. ASSN: ASPA. ADDRESS: 848 University Village, Salt Lake City, UT 84108. 801/583-0181

DEAN, EDWIN R. Government. BA 1955, Yale U; PhD 1963, Columbia U. PUBL: Plan Implementation in Nigeria, 1962-66, Oxford Univ Press, 1972; The Supply Responses of African Farmers North-Holland, 1966; "Implicit Contracting, Union Strength and Seniority," IRRA Proc, 1983. INT: labor market econ, method/statis, govt labor policy. ASSN: AEA, Natl Economists Club, Soc of Government Economists. POSITIONS: Asst Prof of Econ, Columbia Univ, 1960; Asst Dir, Educ Finance, Natl Inst of Education, Wash DC, 1980; and (since 1983) Supervising Economist, BLS, Wash DC. ADDRESS: 207 Summers Dr, Alexandria, VA 22301. 202/523-9301

DEAN, IRWIN J., JR. Arbitration. POSITION: Arbitrator/Attorney, 100 Ross St, Pittsburgh, PA 15219.

DEANE, RICHARD GLEN Acad: Ind Rels; Bus;Pers Ind Rels. BBA 1948, MBA 1949, U of Mich. INT: coll barg, labor history, intl comparative labor. POSITION: Prof of Ind Rels, GMI Engineering & Mgmt Inst, Flint. ADDRESS: 5088 Cedardale Lane, Flushing, MI 48433. 313/762-7977

DEAR, JOSEPH A. Union. BA 1977, Evergreen State Coll. INT: govt labor policy, labor market econ, coll barg. POSITION: (since 1981) Res Dir, Washington State Labor Council, AFL-CIO, 2815 2nd Ave, Room 470, Seattle, WA 98121. 206/682-6002.

DEBONIS, JOHN R. Bus:Pers/Ind Rels. INT: arb/med, coll barg, personnel. ASSN: West VA IRRA, Upper Ohio Valley Pers Assn, ASPA, Ohio Valley Ind Rels Assn. POSITIONS: Member, Adjunct Faculty, West VA Northern Community Coll, 1980, and, since 1979, Pers Dir, Eagle Manufacturing Co, 24th & Charles Streets, Wellsburg, WV 26070. 304/737-3171

DECENZO, DAVID ANTHONY Acad: Bus Admin. POSITION: Dept of Mgmt, Univ of Baltimore, Charles At MT Royal, Baltimore, MD 21201. 301/659-2789

DECKER, ROBERT L. Acad: Ind Rels, Psych; Consulting. PhD 1953, Carnegie-Mellon U. INT: ind psych, empl/trng programs, labor educ. ASSN: West VA IRRA, Amer Psych Assn, West VA Psych Assn, Inter-Ameri Psych Assn. POSITION: (since 1977) Prof of Ind Rels, West Virginia Univ, PO Box 6025, Morgantown, WV 26506. 304/293-4495

DeCLERCQ, NEILL GERARD Acad: Education. 461 S Owen Dr, Madison, WI 53711. 608/-238-1181

DECOEN, EMILE G. Bus:Pers/Ind Rels. POSITION: Vice Pres, Employee Rels, Harsco Corp, PO Box 8888, Camp Hill, PA 17011. 717/-763-7064

DECRISTOFARO, MARYANN Health Care, Pers/Ind Rels. BS 1978, Long Island U; MBA 1981, Pace U. INT: health & hosp care, personnel, arb/med. ASSN: New York IRRA. POSITIONS: Labor Rels Rep, New York State Nurses Assn, 1981; and (since 1983) Labor Rels Manager, St. Vincent's Hospital and Medical Center. ADDRESS: 3640 Bronx Blvd, #2F, Bronx, NY 10467. 212/790-7890

DEEDS, RALPH E., JR. Bus:Pers/Ind Rels. BA 1957, Cornell; MBA 1960, Harvard. INT: coll barg, intl comparative labor, org beh. ASSN: Detroit IRRA. POSITIONS: Labor Rels Staff, 1960, and, currently, Asst Dir Intl Labor Relations, General Motors Corp, 9-212 General Motors Bldg, Detroit, MI 48202. 313/556-3778

DEEDS, WARREN DERRICK Student. BSIM 1982, Ga. Tech. ADDRESS: 101 Shannon Chase Way, Fairburn, GA 30213.

DEEL, KEN W. Student. ADDRESS: 2608 Lincoln Ave, Parkersburg, WV 26104. 304/485-2754

DEENY, RAY ASSN: Rocky Mt IRRA. 633 17th St, #2900 Denver, CO 80202. 303/893-2900

DEERY, STEPHEN JAMES Acad: Ind Rels. BEc 1971, Monash U; MComm 1979, Melbourne U, Australia. Publ: Australian Industrial Relations, (w D. Plowman & C. Fisher), McGraw Hill, Sydney, 1980; "Trade Unions, Technological Change and Redundancy Protection in Australia," J of Ind Rels, June 1982; "Trade Union Amalgamation and Government Policy in Austrilia," Australian Bull of Labor, 1983. INT: union org/admn, intl comparative labor. POSITIONS: Lecturer, Ind Rels, Phillip Inst of Tech, 1977, and (since 1982) Lecturer, Ind Rels, Univ of Melbourne, Parkville, Victoria, Australia. Phone: 3052

DeFREHN, RANDY G. Pension Funds. BASW 1974, U of Pittsburgh; MAIR 1981, St. Francis Coll. INT: ERISA/Pension health benefit programs, coll barg, arb/med. ASSN: Western Penna IRRA, ASPA. POSITIONS: Dir, Johnstown Field Serv Office, UMWA Health & Retirement Funds, 1978, Mediator, Johnstown Area Regional Industries, 1983, and, since 1983, Asst Dir for Eligibility Services, UMWA Health & Retirement Funds, Wash DC. ADDRESS: 18743 Cross Country Lane, Gaithersburg, MD 20879. 202/452--5050

DEFREITAS, GREGORY E. Acad: Econ. BA 1971, Stanford U; MA 1975, PhD 1979, Columbia U. PUBL: "Ethnic Differentials in Hispanic Unemployment," in G. Borjas & M. Tienda (eds) Hispanics in the U.S. Economy, Acad Press: 1983; "Occupational Mobility Among Recent Black Immigrants," Monthly Labor Rev, Apr 1981; "Labor Market Outcomes of Immigrants in the U.S., " in P. Cottingham, ed, The Labor Market Impact of Immigration, Rockfeller Found, forthcoming. INT: labor market econ, income maint, intl comparative labor. ASSN: AEA. POSITIONS: Supr, Labor Econ, Cambridge U, 1978; Asst Prof, Labor and Ind Rels, Mich State Univ, 1979; and (since 1980) Asst Prof of Econ, Dept of Econ, Barnard College, Columbia Univ, New York, NY 10027. 212/280-4369

DEITSCH, CLARENCE Acad: Ind Rels, Econ; Arbitration. BS 1965, Xavier U; MA 1967, PhD 1974, U of N. H. PUBL: "Arbitration Lost: The Public Sector Assault on Arbitration," (w D. A.Dilts), Labor Law J, vol 35, #3, Mar 1984, pp 182-188; "Bowen V. United States Postal Service: Preparing the Way for a More Active Labor Role in Contract Administration," The Arb J, vol 39, #1, Mar 1984, pp 57-59; "NLRB V. Yeshiva: A Positive Perspective," Monthly Labor Rev, vol 106, #7, July 1983, pp 34-37. INT: arb/med, coll barg, labor law. ASSN: AAA, SPIDR. POSITIONS: Asst Prof of Econ, Wilmington Coll (Ohio), 1968; Teaching Assoc, U of N. H. 1973; and (since 1974) Prof of Economics, Ball State Univ. ADDRESS: Rt 12, Box 275, Muncie, IN 47302. 317/285-5368

DELANEY, JEFFREY M. Bus:Pers/Ind Rels. BS 1980, LeMoyne Coll; AM 1982, U of Ill. INT: arb/med, coll barg, govt labor policy. POSITION: (since 1983) Pers Rep, Pacific Gas and Electric, Pittsburgh CA. ADDRESS: 320 Oakland Ave, Oakland, CA. 94611. 415/682-7400

DELANEY, JOHN T. Acad: Ind Rels. BS 1977, Le Moyne Coll; AM 1980, PhD, 1983, U of Ill. PUBL: "Strikes, Arbitration and Teacher Salaries: A Behavioral Analysis," Ind and Labor Rels Rev, 36, April 1983, 431-446; "Union Success in Hospital Representation Elections," Ind Rels, 20, Spring 1981, 149-161; "Bargaining, Arbitration, and Police Wages," (w. P. Feuille), in IRRA Proceedings, 1983. INT: coll barg, arb/med, union org/admn. ASSN: AEA, Acad of Mgmt. POSITION: (since 1983) Asst Prof, Grad School of Bus, Columbia Univ, 704 Uris Hall, New York, NY 10027. 212/280-4416

DELLA ROCCO, LUCIANO Student. ASSN: McGill Ind Rels Assn. POSITION: Student-McGill Univ. ADDRESS: 21 Thornton Drive, Dollard des Ormeaux, PQ H9B 1X7 Canada.

DELOOR, RUTH M. Government. RB, BSN 1969, Vanderbilt; MN 1976, Emory U. PUBL: Hematological Procedure; "To Care for Him Who Shall Have Borne the Battle." INT: coll barg, health & hosp care, mgmt/educ. ASSN: Amer Nurses Assn. POSITIONS: Head Nurse, 1974, Instructor, Nursing Ed, 1976, and, since 1981, Asst District Coordinator, Veterans Administration. ADDRESS: 1169 University Dr NE, Atlanta, GA 30306. 404/321-0862

DELORME, FRANCOIS Government. MA 1971, MSc, 1974, Univ of Montreal. PUBL: Les Licensiements Collectifs Au Quebec: Un Bilan Partiel DW Dispositif Public En Vigueur, (w R. Parent), Montreal, School of Ind Res, monograph #12, 1982; "La Concurrence Dans Un Contexte De Pluralisme Syndicat: Quelques Donnees Sur Le Quebec," Rels Industrielles, Vol 37, #3, 1982, 575-605; "Les Syndicats Independants Au Quebec: Un Apercu De Leur Situation," (w D Veilleux), Ministry of Labour and Manpower, Res and Statis Center on the Labour Market, Quebec, 1980. INT: govt labor policy, labor law, union org/admn. ASSN: Canadian Ind Rels Assn. POSITIONS: Res Analyst, 1977, Head, Coordination of Negotiations, Treasury Board, 1982, and, since 1983, Secretary, Ministry of Labour, Govt of Quebec. ADDRESS: 1319 De La Chatelaine, Charlesbourg PQ G2L 1A5, Canada. 418/643-3239

DEMERS, W.C. Union. INT: empl/trng programs, coll barg, arb/med. POSITION: Communication Workers of America, AFL-CIO, 6033 W Century Blvd, #600, Los Angeles, CA 90045. 213/387-3371

DEMPSEY, JOSEPH R. SJ Acad: Ind Rels; Arbitration. PhD 1958, U of Wis-Madison. PUBL: The Operation of the Right to Work Laws. INT: arb/med, coll barg, labor history. ASSN: NAA. POSITION: (since 1958) Prof, Univ of Detroit, 4001 W McNichols Rd, Detroit, MI 48221. 313/927-1000

DEMPSEY, MICHAEL LEE Bus: Pers/Ind Rels. AA 1973, Miami-Dade Community Coll; BA 1975, Fla Intl U; MLIR 1980, U of Ill. INT: personnel, govt labor policy, coll barg. POSITIONS: Reg Pers Specialist, 1980, Affirmative Action Specialist, 1981, and, since 1982, Pers Operations Specialist, Xerox Corp-Systems Marketing Div, El Segundo. ADDRESS: 22215 Ellinwood Dr, Torrance, CA 90905. 213/536-5816

DENACO, PARKER A. Government, Arbitration, Legal Practice. BA 1965, MBA 1975, U of Maine; JD 1968, Washington & Lee U. PUBL: "Conceptual Considerations for Unit Determinations" in Portrait of a Process, Labor Rels Press, 1980; "How Mediation and Fact Finding Break Deadlocks," Public Pers Admin," Prentice Hall, 1974; "Public Sector Perspectives on Scope of Bargaining, Maine Bar Bull, May 1975. INT: labor law, coll barg, arb/med. ASSN: ABA-Committee on State & Local Govt Bargaining, Maine Bar Assn, AAA-Natl Labor Panel. POSITIONS: Exec Bd Member, (part time) New England Consortium of State Labor Rels Agencies, 1979 to present; Pres, Assn of Labor Relations Agencies, 1978-79; and (since 1972) Exec Dir, Maine Labor Rels Board, State House #90, Augusta, Maine. 04333. 207/289-2016

DENENBERG, TIA SCHNEIDER Arbitration. BS 1967, NYSSILR-Cornell. PUBL: Alcohol and Drugs: Issues in the Workplace, BNA 1983; Dispute Resolutions: Settling Conflicts Without League Action; "Handling Prison Grievances: The 'Labor Model' in Practice," Monthly Labor Rev, vol 100, #3, March 1977. INT: arb/med, int'l comparative labor. ASSN: Albany, Conn and New York IRRA, NAA, SPIDR, AAA. POSITION: Arbitrator, (self-employed), RD 1, Box 357, Red Hook, NY 12571. 518/398-5193

DENISE, MALCOLM L. Consulting, Legal Practice. AB 1935 & JD 1937, U of Mich. POSITIONS: VP, Labor Rels, 1959-74 & VP, Labor Policy Planning, 1974-75 (Ret), Ford Motor Co; Of Counsel, Keller, Thoma, Schwarze & Schwarze, 1976. Retired. ADDRESS: 1 Stratford Pl, Grosse Pointe, MI 48230. 313/886-6234

DENKER, JOEL S. Acad: Labor Educ. POSITION: Labor Studies, University of District of Columbia, 1722 19th St NW #402, Washington DC 20009. 202/727-2326

DENNIS, BARBARA D. Acad: Ind Rels. BS 1940, MS 1959, U of Ill. INT: coll barg, labor law, labor market econ. ASSN: Wis IRRA. POSITIONS: Editor (Asst Prof), Inst of Labor and Ind Rels, Univ of Illinois, 1952, and (since 1967) Editor (Project Assoc), Univ of Wis-Madison, 4321 Social Science Bldg, Madison, WI 53706. 608/262-4867

DENNIS, BARBARA HANSON Government, Consulting, Org Beh/Pers. MSIR, BA, 1978, Loyola U of Chicago. INT: mgmt/educ, empl/trng programs, govt labor policy. ASSN: Chicago IRRA, Ill Trng and Development Assn, Women Employed, Women in Government Rels. POSITIONS: Administrative Coordinator of Trng and Compensation Admin, Art Inst of Chicago, 1980; Intructor, Mgmt Principles and Pers Admin, Northwestern Univ, 1982; and (since 1983) Legislative Aide, Ill State Senate and Leg Dist, Chicago. ADDRESS: 641 Judson Ave, Evanston, IL 60202. 312/764-2200

DENNIS, LESLIE Consulting. BS 1956, MSED 1957, Northern Ill U. INT: intl comparative labor, empl/trng programs, coll barg. POSITIONS: Teacher of Sociology & Amer History, Glenbrook High, 1959; Intl Vice Pres, Brotherhood of Railway & Airline Clerks, 1961; and (since 1976) President, D. C. Associates. ADDRESS: 641 Judson Ave, Evanston, IL 60202. 202/547-8600

DENNISON, CYNTHIA ELLEN Research. 6663 Witherington Ct, Norcross, GA 30093. 404/938-6042

DENSON, FRED L. Arbitration, Legal Prac. BCH 1959, RPI; JD 1966, Georgetown U. INT: arb/med, labor law. ASSN: NAA, ABA, New York State Bar Assn. POSITION: (since 1967) Attorney (self-employed), PO Box 801, 14 E Main St, Webster, NY 14850. 716/265-2710

DEOM-CAMIRE, ESTHER Acad: Ind Rels. BA 1978, MA, 1981, Univ Laval. PUBL: "Politique De Main D'Oeuvre Et Politiques Publiques," (w Sexton & Leclerq), Rels Industrielles, vol 35, #1, 1980; "La Negociation Collective Chez Les Fonctionnai Res et Les Enseignants Quebecois: 1975-1976," Rels Industrielles, Vol 37, #1, 1982; "L'Approche Sustemique En Relations Industrielles," Rels Industrielles, Vol 39, #1, 1984. INT: coll barg, ind sociol, union org/admn. ASSN: Canadian Ind Rels Assn, Corp des conseillers in rel inds du Quebec. POSITIONS: Adjointe au Dir Rels Ind, 1980, and since 1983, Prof-Substitut, Univ Laval, Ste Foy, Quebec. ADDRESS: 10 Jardins Merici #1206, Quebec G1S 4T1, Canada. 418/656-2704

DePREY, KENNETH W. Government. BS 1958, U of Wis. INT: personnel, coll barg, empl/trng programs. ASSN: Wisconsin IRRA, ASPA, Intl Pers Mgmt Assn, Wis Public Employers Labor Rels Assn. POSITIONS: Chief of Pers Services & Deputy State Pers Dir, Wis Dept of Admin, 1968, Division Admin, Mgmt Services, Wis Dept of Revenue, 1973, and, since 1978, Dir of Pers and Employment Rels, Wis Dept of Health and Social Services, Box 7850, 1 W Wilson St, Madison, WI 53702. 608/266-9862.

DERBER, MILTON Acad: Ind Rels. PhD 1940, U of Wis. PUBL: The American Idea of Industrial Democracy, 1970; "Management Organization for Collective Bargaining in the Public Sector," in IRRA Public Sector Bargaining, 1978; Research in Labor Problems in the U.S., 1967. INT: coll barg, labor history, govt labor policy. POSITION: (since 1947) Prof of Labor & Ind Rels, and, since 1983, Prof Emeritus, Labor & Ind Rels, Inst of Labor and Ind Rels, Univ of Ill, 504 E Armory St, Champaign, IL 61820. 217/333-2384

DERR, BARON W. Arbitration. POSITION: Executive Director, SMACNA West Washington, 1200 Westlake Ave 512, Seattle, WA 98109.

DESANTIS, NORA STEVENS Bus:Pers/Ind Rels. BA 1974, Queens Coll; MBA 1976, Pace U. ASSN: Ind Rels Soc, New York, New Jersey Arbitration Group. POSITION: Manager, Labor Rels, Consolidated Edison Co of New York, Inc, 4 Irving Place, Rm 915S, New York, NY 10009. 212/460-2098

DESCHENEAU, MICHAEL D. Business. 207 N Richardson, Vicksburg, MI 49097. 616/-349-8400

DESCHENES, GILBERT Pers/Ind Rels. POSITION: Dir of Pers, Le Droit, 375 Rue Rideau, Ottawa, K1N 5Y7, Canada. 613/560-2566

DESJARDINS, NORMAND J. Acad:Ind Rels. ASSN: La Corp professionelle des conseillers en rels ind-Quebec, Faculte de l'Education permanente, Univ of Mtl, Comite de retraite et des assurances collectives. POSITIONS: Dir du pers, Fed de Montreal, and since 1977, Vice Pres Human Resources, Fed des caisses populaires, Desjardins de Montreal et de l'Ouest, 1 Complexe du Quebec, Desjardins, C.P. 35, Succursale Desjardins, Montreal Quebec H5B 1E7, Canada.

DESOUZA, ANGELA C. Student. ADDRESS: 104 East 31st 2B, New York, NY 10016. 212/679-9035

DESPOL, JOHN A. Government, Arbitration, Investment Consulting. INT: labor law, arb/med, coll barg. ASSN: Los Angeles IRRA, Inst of Ind Rels-UCLA, LA Committee on Foreign Rels, LA World Affairs Council. POSITIONS: Intl Rep, United Steel Workers of America, 1937-68; Ind Rels Consultant, J. Despols & Assoc, 1973; and (since 1976) Deputy Labor Commissioner, State of Calif, Div of Labor. ADDRESS: 4717 Willis Ave #7, Sherman Oaks, CA 91403. 818/782-3862

DESS, SUSAN A. Bus:Pers/Ind Rels. BA 1979, Ind U; MLIR, 1981, Mich State U. INT: empl/trng programs, intl comparative labor, govt labor policy. ASSN: ASPA. POSITIONS: Pers Asst, Lindberg, 1981; Order Runner, Drexel Burnhan, 1982; and (since 1983) Position Analyst, Central States (Teamsters Pension Fund), Chicago. ADDRESS: 430 West Diversey, #404, Chicago, Il 60614. 312/693-5300 ext 210

DEUTERMANN, CYNTHIA Government. BA 1963, American U; MA 1966, U of Mo-Kansas City; PhD 1980, Univ of Southern Calif. INT: labor market econ, gvot labor policy, method/statis. POSITION: Empl Standards Admin, USDL. ADDRESS: 7004 Arandale Rd, Bethesda, MD 20817. 202/523-8288

DEUTERMANN, WILLIAM V., JR. Government. BA 1966, U of Mo-Kansas City; MA 1970, Georgetown U. INT: empl/trng programs, intl comparative labor, method/statis. POSITION: Economist, Intl Labor Affairs Bureau, USDL. ADDRESS: 7004 Arandale Rd, Bethesda, MD 20817. 202-523-7616

DEVEREUX, GREG D. Union. BA 1975, Duke U; MA 1979, U of Ill. INT: coll barg, govt labor policy, union org/admn. ASSN: Wash DC IRRA. POSITIONS: Field Examiner, Ill Office of Coll Barg, 1979, and (since 1980) Asst Dir of Corp Affairs, Food & Allied Service Trades, AFL-CIO, Wash DC. ADDRESS: 2610 Bryan Point Rd, Accokeck, MD 20607. 202/737-7200

DEVINO, WILLIAM STANLEY Acad: Univ Admin. BA 1951, U of Vt; MA 1953, U of Conn; PhD 1959 Mich State U. POSITION: Dean, Coll of Bus Admin, Univ of Maine, Orono, ME 04469. 207/581-1968

DEVOL, KAREN ROBERTS Student. ADDRESS: 299 River St, West Newton, MA 02165. 617/964-5406

DEWIT, GARRY DALE Bus:Mgmt/Admin. POSITION: Pers Mgr, Ore-Ida Foods Inc, PO Box 34, Greenville, MI 48838. 616/754-4631

DEYE, JAMES R. Arbitration. BA 1975, U of Calif-San Diego. INT: arb/med, coll barg, ind psych. ASSN: SPIDR. POSITIONS: Eligibility Supr, Dept for Human Resources, Commonwealth of Ky, 1975; Tribunal Administrator, Cincinnati, 1978, and, since 1979, Reg Dir, AAA, 510 Foshay Tower, Minneapolis, MN 55402. 612/332-6545

DIALI, AZUKA O. Bus:Pers/Ind Rels. PUBL: "Industrial Relations in Nigeria in the Seventies;" "Industry-wide Collective Bargaining: The Nigerian Bankers Employers Model;" "The Organization of Industrial Unions." INT: coll barg, labor educ, union org/admin. ASSN: IIRA, Nigerian Inst of Mgmt, Inst of Pers Mgmt of Nigeria. POSITIONS: Reg Staff Officer, Standard Bank of Nigeria Ltd, 1973-79; Deputy Gen Sec, 1966-70, and, since 1981, Sr Deputy General Secretary, Natl Union of Banks, Insurance and Financial Inst Employees, 310 Herbert Macaulay St, PMB 1139 Yaba, Lagos, Nigeria.

DIBBLE, RICHARD E. Acad: Ind Rels, Org Beh/Pers, Univ Admin. BA 1970, SUNY-Buffalo; MA 1973, PhD 1977, SUNY-Albany. PUBL: Labor Relations For Transit Managers; Occupational Employment Survey of Long Island. INT: org beh, mgmt/educ, intl comparative labor. ASSN: Long Island IRRA, Transportation Res Board. POSITIONS: Res Dir, 1980, Asst Dir, 1982, and, since 1983, Dean, Center for Labor and Ind Rels, New York Inst of Technology. ADDRESS: 135 Clinton St, Apt 1D, Hempstead, NY 11500. 516/686-7722

DICKENS, WILLIAM T. Acad: Econ. PhD 1981, MIT. PUBL: "The Effect of Company Campaigns on Representation Elections: Law and Reality Once Again," ILRR, July 1983; "The Economic Consequences of Cognitive Dissonance," (w G. Atorlot), AER, June 1982; "The Productivity Crisis: Secular or Cyclical?" Econ Letters, #6, 1982. INT: labor market econ, govt labor policy. ASSN: AER, Econometric Soc. POSITION: (since 1980) Asst Prof of Econ, Dept of Econ, Univ of Calif, Berkeley, CA 94720. 415/642-5452

DIEKHOFF, PAUL R. Student. ADDRESS: Rte 8, Box 73, Harrison, AR 72601.

DIEMER, BERNARD BA 1976, U of Tenn; MA 1980, U of Ill. ADDRESS: 72 Gordon St, Ridgefield Park, NJ 07660. 201/440-2561

DIGGELMAN, ROBERT E. Government. BS 1961, Bradley U. INT: labor law, coll barg, arb/med. ASSN: Wis IRRA. POSITION: Asst of Regional Dir, NLRB, 2824 E Hampshire, Milwaukee, WI 53211.

DIGGS, CECIL, JR. Acad: Student; Bus:Mgmt/-Admin. BS 1979, U of Dist Columbia. INT: labor educ, labor history, labor law. ASSN: Amer Mgmt Assn, Assn for Work Place Democracy. POSITIONS: Manager, Georgetown Station, 1978, Letter Sorting Machine Supr, 1982, and, since 1983, Employee Involvement Facilitator, United State Postal Service, Wash DC. ADDRESS: 7990 Aububon Ave, #102, Alexandria, VA 22306. 202/523-2575/78

DI IORIO, JAMES D. Sales. AB 1951, Miami U-Ohio; MA 1954, U of Ill. Int: ind psych method/statis, org beh. POSITION: Salesman, House of Business Forms, Chicago. ADDRESS; 9301 Central Park Ave, Evanston, IL 60203. 312/454-9526

DILALLO, MICHAEL Bus:Pers/Ind Rels. BS 1979, U of Ill; MS 1981, Purdue. INT: personnel, arb/med, coll barg. POSITIONS: Pers Advisor, 1982, and, since 1983, Pers Administrator, Consumers Power Co, Essexville. ADDRESS: 405 Old Orchard Dr, Essexville, MI 48732. 517/892-3551 ext 263

DILLARD, RICHARD B. Bus:Mgmt/Admin. POSITION: Professional & Ind Rels, Continental Resources Co, PO Box 44, Winter Park, FL 32790. 305/646-1305

DILLINGHAM, ALAN EDWARD Acad: Univ Admin. PhD 1979, Cornell. PUBL: "Effects of Labor Force Age Distribution on Workers' Compensation Costs," J Risk &Ins, June 1983; Estimates of Occupational Injury Risk and Compensation Wage Differential, NTIS; "Sex Differences in Labor Market Injury Risk," Ind Rels, 1981. INT: labor market econ, coll barg. ASSN: AEA, Natl Assn Bus Economists. POSITION: (since 1981) Chairperson, Dept of Econ, Ill State Univ, Normal, IL 61761. 309/483-8625

DILLON, CATHERINE M. Librarian. POSITION: Librarian, Jackson, Lewis & Schnitzler, 261 Madison Ave, New York, NY 10016. 212/697-8200

DILLON, PETER C. Bus:Pers/Ind Rels. BA 1970, MA 1972, U of Calif-Berkeley. INT: ind psych, coll barg, arb/med. POSITION: (since 1980) Manager of Labor Rels, McKesson Wine and Spirits, 155 E 44th St, New York, NY 10017. 212/573-0334

DILLON, WILLIAM A. Bus/Pers/Ind Rels. POSITION: Vice Pres, Ind Rels, Inland Steel Co, 30 W Monroe St, Chicago, IL 60603. 312/346-0300

DI LORENZO, GLORIA A. Acad: Ind Rels; Government. MA 1982, U of Ill. INT: labor law, coll barg, union org/admin. POSITION: (since 1972) Field Examiner, NLRB, Chicago. ADDRESS: Apt 1801, 1455 N Sandburg TR, Chicago, IL 60610. 312/353-7570

DILTS, DAVID A. Arbitration; Acad: Econ. BS 1974, MA 1975, Ball State U; PhD 1978, Ind State U. PUBL: Labor Relations, (co-authored), Macmillan, 1983; "Award Clarification: An Ethical Dilemma?" Labor Law J, vol 33, #6, June 1982, pp 366-370; "NLRB V. Yeshiva University: A Positive Perspective," Monthly Labor Rev, vol 106, #7, July 1983, pp 34-37. INT: arb/med, coll barg, labor market econ. ASSN: AAA, SPIDR. POSITIONS: Asst Prof, Dept of Econ, Ball State U, 1978; and (since 1980) Assoc Prof, Labor Rels, College of Bus Admin, Calvin Hall, Kansas State Univ, Manhatten, KS 66502. 913/532-6925

DION, GERARD Acad: Ind Rels. BA 1935, LTh, 1939, LPh, MS 1943, Laval U. PUBL: Glossary of Terms Used in Industrial Relations (English-French;) Dictionnaire Canadian des Relations du Travail. INT: ind sociol, labor history, union org/admin. ASSN: CIRA, CRI, Assn Intl de Soc de Langue Francaise. POSITION: Editor, Prof, Laval Univ, 1944-1980; Re-tired. ADDRESS: 909 Maz Grandin, Quebec G1V 3X8 Canada. 418/656-3358

DISSEN, RICHARD W. Arbitration, Legal Practice. BA 1975, Carnegie-Mellon U; JD 1978, U of Pittsburgh. PUBL: "Grievance Arbitration and the Regulation of Public Employee Life Style," (w I. J. Dean Jr.), Arbitration Issues for the 1980s, BNA 1982. INT: arb/med, coll barg, labor law. ASSN: Western Penna IRRA, AAA. POSITIONS: Natl Acad of Arbitrators, Intern to Irwin J. Dean, Jr. 1978; and (since 1980) Attorney-Arbitrator, 100 Ross St, Pittsburgh, PA 15219. 412/261-6798

DITTMER, ROGER A. Union. #1073, 13300 Village Park Dr, Southgate, MI 48195. 313/676-5583

DIXON, THOMAS J. Bus:Mgmt/Admin. BS & MBA 1973, SUNY-Buffalo. INT: coll barg, arb/med, personnel. ASSN: Syracuse IRRA. POSITIONS: Supr Salary Admin, Carborundum Co, 1973; Pers Mgr, Bos-Hatten Co, 1976; and (since 1977) Pers Mgr, Arm & Hammer Div, Church & Dwight Co Inc, 1416 Willis Ave, Syracuse, NY 13201. 315/488-2961.

DOBBELAERE, Arthur G., JR. Acad: Ind Rels. BA 1970, St. Benedicts Coll; MA 1973, PhD 1975, U of Notre Dame. PUBL: Deprived Urban Youth, Praeger; "Economic Value of the Housewife Trial," Diplomacy Journal; "Computer Application to Human Resource Function," Federal Mgrs Quart. INT: labor market econ, personnel, union org/admn. ASSN: AEA, Natl Acad of Mgmt. POSITIONS: Instructor, U of Notre Dame, 1974; Asst Prof, 1975, and since 1982, Assoc Prof, Loyola Univ of Chicago, 820 N Michigan Ave, Chicago, IL. 60611. 312/670-2752

DOBRY, STANLEY T. Arbitration. AB 1970, U of Mich; JD 1974, Detroit Coll of Law. INT: arb/med, govt labor policy, labor law. ASSN: Detroit, Mid Michigan IRRAs, SPIDR, State Bar of Mich (Labor Law Section), Detroit Bar Assn (Labor Law Committee). POSITIONS: Asst Supervising Attorney, Wayne County Neighborhood Legal Service, 1973; Staff Attorney, Mich Judicial Tenure Comm, 1976; and (since 1981) Attorney/Arbitrator (sole practitioner), Suite 1404 Lafayette Bldg, Detroit, MI 48226. 313/963-6850

DODD, RICHARD A. Bus:Pers/Ind Rels. AB 1964, Mich State U; MA 1971, U of Ill. INT: coll barg, personnel, empl/trng programs. POSITIONS: Mgr Ind Rels, Consolidated Aluminum Corp, 1970; Corp Ind Rels Staff, American Motors Corp, 1973; and (since 1982) Bus Consultant, Washtenaw County Government. ADDRESS: 2310 Churchill Dr, Ann Arbor, MI 48103.

DODT, HAROLD Union. POSITION: Local 675 IUOE, 1551 W Copans RD, Pompano Beach, FL 33064.

DOERING, BARBARA W. Arbitration. AB 1965, Cornell; MS 1969, NYSSILR-Cornell. INT: arb/med, coll barg, labor law. ASSN: Chicago IRRA, NAA, SPIDR, AAA. POSITION: (since 1973) Arbitrator, 2186 Tecumseh Pk Landing, West Lafayette, IN 47906. 317/463-7845

DOERING, RICK ROBERT Bus:Pers/Ind Rels. BS 1979, U of Calif-Berkeley; MS 1981, U of Wis-Madison. INT: grievance procedure, coll barg. POSITIONS: Board Agent, NLRB, 1981, and since 1982, Labor Rels Rep, Pacific Gas and Electric Co, Oakland. ADDRESS: 2622 Calhoun, Alameda, CA 94501. 415/835-8500

DOERINGER, PETER BRANTLEY Acad: Econ, Ind Rels; Arbitration. AB 1962, AM 1964, PhD 1966, Harvard. PUBL: Internal Labor Markets and Manpower Analysis; Industrial Relations in International Perspective; "Internal Labor Markets and Paternalism in Rural Areas." INT: labor market econ, coll barg. ASSN: Boston IRRA, AEA, NAA. POSITIONS: Lecturer, London School of Econ, 1971; Assoc Prof, Harvard, 1972; and (since 1974) Prof of Econ and Dir, Inst for Empl Policy, Boston Univ, 270 Bay State Rd, Boston, MA 02215. 617/353-4447

DOERR, ELAINE KAY Bus:Pers/Ind Rels. MA 1983, U of Ill. INT: coll barg, labor law, mgmt/educ. ASSN: ASPA. POSITION: Human Resources Assoc, GTE Corp, Des Plaines. ADDRESS: 1410 Chicago Ave #610, Evanston, IL 60201. 312/391-5187

DOHERTY, ROBERT E. Acad: Ind Rels. POSITION: Prof, ILR, Cornell Univ, Ithaca, NY 14853. 607/256-2024

DOHERTY, THOMAS G. Position: Deputy Dir Labor Rels, NYC Health and Hospital Corp, 222 W 255th St, New York, NY 10471.

DOIDGE, J. LLOYD Bus:Pers/Ind Rels. POSITION: Macmillan Bloedel Ltd, 1075 W Georgia St, Vancouver BC V6E 3R9 Canada. 604/683-6711

DOLAN-GREENE, COLLEEN Acad: Univ Admin; Bus:Pers/Ind Rels. BA 1970, Mount Scholastica Coll; MPA 1973, LBJ School of Publ Affairs, U of Tex-Austin. PUBL: What if the Faculty Member to be Laid Off is the Governor's Brother?" in Coping With Faculty Reductions, S.Hample ed, San Francisco-Jossey Bass Publishers, Spring 1984; Responding Constructively to Strikes and Threats of Strikes," in Handbook of Faculty Bargaining, Jossey-Bass Publishers, 1977; Environmental Impact Statements: Effects on Program Implementation, a report by the Environmental Impact Statement Policy Res Project, LBJ School of Publ Affairs, U of Tex-Austin, 1974. INT: personnel, mgmt/-educ, coll barg. ASSN: Detroit IRRA, Detroit Pers Mgmt Assn/ASPA, Coll and Univ Pers Assn, Academy for Academic Pers Admin. POSITIONS: Labor Rels and Equal Opportunity Mgr, Oakland Univ, 1973; Dir-Univ Pers, Univ of Detroit, 1976; and (since 1980) Pers Admin/-Asst Dir, Univ of Mich, 500 S State St/1020 LS&A Bldg, Ann Arbor, MI 48109. 313/764-1469

DOLAN, SHIMON Acad: Org Beh/Pers. BA 1971, Tel Aviv U; MA 1976, PhD 1977, U of Minn. PUBL: Stress, Health and Performance at Work; "Validity of an Assessment Center for Spotting Future Female Officers in the Military;" Determinants of Union Officers Militancy." INT: personnel, org beh, ind psych. ASSN: Academy of Mgmt. POSITIONS: Pres, Management Decisions Systems, Inc, 1980, and (since 1981) Assoc Prof, School of IR, Univ Montreal, PO Box 6128, Station A, Montreal PQ H3C 3J7, Canada. 514/343-7320

DOLIN, KEN R. Government. BA 1978, U of Wis-Madison; JD 1980, U of Ill; MILR 1981, NYSSILR-Cornell. INT: labor law. ASSN: ABA. POSITION: (since 1982) Field Attorney, NLRB. ADDRESS: Apt 305, 240 Mercer St, New York, NY 10012. 212/330-2852

DOLNICK, DAVID Arbitration. AB 1938, AM 1939, U of Chicago. PUB: "History and Theory of the Labor Movement," Empl Rels Res, H. Heneman et al, Harper Bros, 1960; "The Settlement of Grievances and Joint Consumers Theory," Labor Law J, April 1970, 240-247. INT: arb/med, coll barg, labor history. ASSN: Chicago IRRA, AEA, NAA, Intl Soc of Labor Law and Soc Security. POSITIONS: Res Dir, Amalgamated Meat Cutters, 1947, Consultant, Labor Mgmt Rels, 1956; and (since 1959) Arbitrator (self-employed), 333 N Michigan Ave, Chicago, IL 60601. 312/332-6750

DOLSKI, ERWIN R. Government. INT: arb/med, coll barg, labor educ. ASSN: Northeast Ohio IRRA. POSITIONS: United Brick & Clayworkers Intl Union, 1960, and (since 1968) Mediator, FMCS, Room 1525, Euperior Bldg, 815 Superior Ave, Cleveland, OH 44114. 216/522-4806

DOMITRZ, JOSEPH S. Acad: Admin. BS 1962, Central Mich U; MA 1966, W Mich U; PhD 1971, Southern Ill U. PUBL: "Collective Bargaining and Public Administration: The Role of Long-Term Contracts," Public Empl Rels Library, 1971; "Recruiting the Disadvantaged Worker: The Value of Vietnam Era Military Experience," Pers J, 1974. INT: coll barg, labor market econ, union org/admn. ASSN: Wis IRRA, Financial Exec Inst. POSITIONS: Assoc Prof, 1966-72 & Chairman, 1972-76, Econ Dept, Western Ill U; and (since 1976) Dean, Coll of Bus and Econ, U of Wis-Whitewater. ADDRESS: 467 Buckingham, Whitewater, WI 53190. 414/472-1343

DONALD, CARRIE G. Acad: Law. POSITION: Government Law Center, Belknap Campus, Univ of Louisville, Louisville, KY 40292. 502/588-6508

DONLEY, RAY N. Legal Practice. BS 1977, Abilene Christian U; JD 1982, U of Tex. PUBL: "Don't Shoot From the Hip," May 1983, Colorado Bus Magazine. INT: labor law, personnel. ASSN: Colorado Bar Assn. ABA, Amer Trial Layers Assn. POSITION: Attorney, Holland & Hart, Denver. ADDRESS: PO Box 8749, Denver, CO 80201. 303/295-8149

DONN, CLIFFORD B. Acad: Ind Rels. BS 1972, Cornell; PhD 1980, MIT. PUBL: The Australian Council of Trade Unions: History & Economic Policy, 1983; "Games Final-Offer Arbitrator Might Play," Ind Rels, Oct 1977; "Arbitration and the Incentive to Bargain," J of Labor Res, 1982. INT: coll barg, arb/med, intl comparative labor. ASSN: Central New York IRRA, AEA. POSITIONS: Lecturer in Econ, Macquarie Univ, 1976-78; Asst Prof-Econ, Univ of Tenn, 1979; and (since 1982) Assoc Prof and Chair, Dept of Ind Rels, Le Moyne Coll, Syracuse, NY 13214. 315/446-2882

DONNELLY, JOHN THOMAS Acad: Ind Rels. ADDRESS: 1417 Grand Ave, Iowa City, IA 52240. 806/742-6229

DONNELLY, LAWRENCE I. Acad: Econ & Ind Rels; Arbitration. AB 1955, Loyola U-Chicago, MBA 1957, Xavier U, Cincinnati; PhD 1964, U of Cincinnati. PUBL: "Reflections of an Arbitrator," Discipline & Grievances;

"Guidance on Grievances," CUPA Special Report; "Towards An Alliance Between Research & Practice in Collective Bargaining," Pers J. INT: coll barg, labor market econ, arb/med. ASSN: Greater Cincinnati IRRA, Assn for Soc Econ, Ohio Assn of Econ and Pol Scientists. POSITION: (since 1965) Prof of IR & Econ, Dept of Econ, Xavier Univ, 3800 Victory Parkway, Cincinnati, OH 45207. 513/745-3667

D'ONOFRIO, JOSEPH D. Bus:Pers/Ind Rels, Bus Mgmt/Admin. BS 1943, CCNY; IR Cert Prog 1961, NYU Mgmt Inst. INT: personnel, coll barg, health & hospital care. ASSN: ASTD, AHPA, ASPA. POSITIONS: Pers Dir, Digitronics Corp, 1966; Dir of Empl Rels, P.A.S.N.Y., 1972; and (since 1975) Dir of Personnel, Isabella Geriatric Center, 515 Audubon Ave, New York, NY 10040. 212/781-9800

DONOIAN, HARRY AVEDIS Consulting. BS 1961, NYU; MA 1968, Catholic U of America. PUBL: "Recent Changes in Federal Service Labor Management Relation," Labor Law J, March 1972; "Setting Federal Blue Collar Pay, Monthly Labor Rels Rev, April 1969. The Government Employee's Council, Government Empl Council, 1968. INT: coll barg, arb/med, labor educ. ASSN; Wis IRRA. POSITIONS: Res Dir, Allied Ind Workers, 1972-75; Assoc Dir, Dist Council 48, AFSCME, 1976-77, and (since 1978) Exec Dir, Allied Ind Workers, Reg 9, AFL-CIO, Health & Welfare Fund, 3540D N 126th St, Brookfield WI 53005. 414/781--1970

DONOVAN, CHARLES EDWARD Bus:Pers/-Ind Rels. INT: personnel, org beh, govt labor policy. ASSN: Inst of Pers Mgmt-UK, Assoc Member Inst of Gas Engineers-UK. POSITIONS: Sr Pers Officer Eng, West-Midlands Gas, 1966, Pers Dir,Southern Gas, 1975, and, since 1981, Board Member and Mgr Div Pers, British Gas, 152 Grosvenor Rd, London England SW1V 3JL. Phone: 01-821-1444

DONOVAN, DENNIS MICHAEL Bus:Pers/Ind Rels. BBA 1971, MSBA, 1972, U of Mass; JD 1978, Western New England Coll. INT: coll barg, labor law, arb/med. ASSN: ABA (Labor Law Sec). POSITION: Area Labor Rels Negotiator, 1978, Mgr, Labor Rels, Pittsfield, MA 1980, and, since 1982, Consultant, Union Relations, General Electric, Corp Office, , Fairfield. ADDRESS: Philo Curtis Rd, Sandy Hook CT 06482. 203/373-2248

DONOVAN, RONALD Acad: Ind Rels. POSITION: Prof Ind and Labor Rels, NYSSILR, Cornell Univ, Ithaca NY 14853. 607/256-4469

DOOM, G. PRESTON Bus:Mgmt/Admin. POSITION: President, Preston Industries, Box 188, Ledbetter, KY 42058.

DORAN, W. WILEY Legal Practice. ADDRESS: Mitchell & Doran, Suite 820, 1010 Jefferson, Houston, TX 77002. 713/652-2010

DORANZ, JEFFREY DAVID Government, Legal Prac, Arbitration. AB 1969, JD 1971, Rutgers U; MLIR 1968, Mich State U. INT: arb/med, govt labor policy, labor law. POSITIONS: Deputy Attorney General, New Jersey, 1971; Special Counsel, U.S. Senate Labor Committee, 1972, and (since 1978) Counsel, Office of the Solicitor, USDL, Wash DC. ADDRESS: 8200 Mockingbird Dr, Annandale, VA 22003. 703/235-1161

DORF, GERALD L. Legal Practice. POSITION: Counsellor at Law, 2376 St George Ave, Rahway, NJ 07065. 201/574-9700

DORNBAUM, CHARLES Government, Arbitration; Acad: Ind Rels. BS 1957, NYU. INT: arb/med, coll barg, personnel. ASSN: Long Island IRRA, AAA, New York State Bar Assn. POSITIONS: Labor Specialist, NYS Dept of Labor, 1958; V.P. Pers & Labor Rels, Lafayette Radio Electronics Corp, 1960; and (since 1976) Labor Mediator-Arbitrator, Suffolk County Dept of Labor. ADDRESS: 26 Sioux Dr, Commack, Long Island, NY 11725. 516/348-2025/2026.

DORNBAUM, MICHAEL L. Student. BA 1982, SUNY-Stony Brook. INT: labor law, arb/med, coll barg. POSITIONS: Sales Counselor, LaFayette Radio Electronics, Div of Wards, 1979; Legal Intern, New York State Supreme Court, Tenth Judicial Dist, 1984; and (since 1982) Law Student, Hofstra Univ. ADDRESS: 26 Sioux Dr, Commack, Long Island, NY 11725. 516/543-2527

DORR, JOHN VAN N., III Arbitration, Mediation/Fact Finding. BA 1970, U of Md; MA & JD 1975, St. Louis U. PUBL: "Labor Arbitrator Training: The Internship," Arbitration J, June 1981, vol 36 #2; "Factors To Consider When Negotiating A Grievance Procedure," Prentice Hall, Ind Rels Guide Service, Sept 1981. INT: arb/med, intl comparative labor, govt labor policy. ASSN: New England IRRA, N.H. Bar Assn, NAA, SPIDR. POSITIONS: Attorney, City of Manchester, NH, 1976; Attorney, 1978, and since 1978, Arbitrator and Mediator/Fact Finder (self-employed), 965 Union St, Manchester, NH 03104. 603/668-3612

DOUGLAS, JOEL M. Acad: Ind Rels. POSITION: NCSCBHE Dir, Baruch Coll, 17 Lexington Ave, Box 322, New York, NY 10010. 212/725-3390

DOUTY, HARRY MORTIMER Econ Research. AB 1932, Duke U; MA 1932, Columbia U; PhD 1936, U of N.C. PUBL: "The Slowdown in Real Wages in Postwar Perspective," Monthly Labor Rev, Aug 1977; The Wage Bargain and the Labor Market, Johns Hopkins Press, 1980; "Jevons, Labor and the State 100 Years Later-a Centennial Essay," Monthly Labor Rev, Mar 1982. INT: labor market econ, coll barg, labor history. ASSN: Wash DC IRRA, AEA, Southern Econ Assn. POSITIONS: Sr Res Consultant, USBL, 1967; Visiting Prof, NYSSILR-Cornell U, 1971-72; and currently, self-employed. ADDRESS: 4612 Butterworth Place NW, Washington DC 20016. 202/363-8343

DOWLING, PETER JOHN Acad: Org Beh/-Pers, Psych, Ind Rels. PhD 1979, Flinders U of South Australia. PUBL: "A Study of Economic Panic: The 'Run' on the Hindmarch Building Society," (w L. Mann & T. Nagel), Sociometry, 1976, 39, pp 223-235; "The Effects of Congruency Between Perceived and Desired Job Attributes Upon Job Satisfaction," (w G. E. O'Brien), J of Occupation Psych, 1980, 53, pp 121-130; "Executive Leasing: Career Path or Career Transition?" (w T. L. McVeigh), Human Res Mgmt Australia, 1983, 21, pp 29-34. INT: personnel, org beh, ind psych. POSITIONS: Asst Prof, School of Bus, Calif State Univ-Chico, 1978; and (since 1980), Lecturer, Grad School of Bus Admin, Univ of Melbourne, Parkville 3052, Australia.

DOWN, RICHARD JOHN Bus:Pers/Ind Rels. BS 1979, NYSSILR-Cornell. INT: coll barg, arb/med, org beh. ASSN: Atlanta IRRA. POSITION: Labor Rels Rep, Lockheed Georgia Co, Marietta. ADDRESS: 789 Adair Ave NE, Atlanta, GA 30306. 404/424-3029

DOWNER, BEVERLEY MARCIA Acad: Student, Ind Rels. BAIR 1984, McGill U. INT: labor law, personnel, govt labor policy. POSITION: Student-McGill Univ. ADDRESS: 7728 Bernard St, LaSalle, Montreal, PQ H8N 1V9 Canada. 514/392-5088

DOWNIE, BRYAN McKAY Acad: Ind Rels; Government. BA 1960, Concordia Coll; MBA 1963, PhD 1969, U of Chicago. PUBL: "Some Thoughts On Public Policy and Industrial Peace," Rels Industrielles, vol 35, #4, 1981; "Joint Union-Management Cooperation," in M.Anderson & J. Anderson, Union Mgmt Relations in Canada, Addison Wesley, 1981; "Collective Bargaining Under an Essential Services Disputes Commission," in G. Swimmer and M. Thompson (eds) Public Sector Ind Rels Ottawa Inst for Res on Public Policy, 1983. INT: coll barg, arb med, org beh. ASSN: Canadian: SPIDR, CIRA, ASAC. POSITION: (since 1965) Prof, School of Bus, Queens Univ, Kingston, Ontario K7L 3N6, Canada. 613/547-6198

DOYLE, JANE F. Government. BS 1972, Lock Haven State Coll. INT: govt labor policy, coll barg, personnel. ASSN: Western Penna IRRA, Amer Bus Women's Assn, Penna Elected Women's Assoc. POSITION: Revenue Investigator, Penna Dept of Revenue, Altoona. ADDRESS: PO Box 1883, Altoona, PA 16603. 814/946-7310

DOZIER, JANELLE B. Student. BS 1975, U of Mo; MBA 1979, Memphsis State U. INT: org beh, personnel, ind psych. ASSN: Academy of Mgmt. POSITIONS: Loan Review Analyst, 1980, Manager, Publ Rels, Union Planters Natl Bank, Memphis, 1981, and (since 1982) Student & Grad Res Asst, Ohio State Univ. ADDRESS: 1136 Shady Hill Dr, Columbus, OH 43221. 901/422-2809

DRACHMAN, ALLAN W. Legal Practice. AB 1958, Brandies U; LLB 1961, Harvard. PUBL: Municipal Negotiations: From Differences to Agreement. INT: coll barg, labor law, arb/med. ASSN: Boston IRRA, ABA, AAA. POSITION: Sr Attorney, Holland, Crowe & Drachman, 185 Devonshire St, Boston, MA 02110. 617/482-8250

DRAKE, CHARLES GOODLOE, Acad: Econ. AB 1935, Westminster Coll,Fulton Mo; MA 1952, Washington U; PhD 1965, U of Mo-Columbia. INT: income maint, labor market econ, coll barg. ASSN: AEA, Midwest Econ Assn, Mo Valley Econ Assn. POSITIONS: Assoc Prof of Econ, Southern Ill Univ-Edwardsville, 1965; Prof of Econ, Central Missouri State Univ, 1968, and (since 1979) Visiting Prof of Econ, Southwest Missouri State Univ. ADDRESS: 312 Johnson Ave, Warrensburg, MO 64093. 417/836-5589

DRAVES, EDWARD F. Union. BSILR 1978, Cornell. INT: union org/admin, labor history, labor educ. POSITION: (since 1979) Political and Legislative Dir, AFSCME, Albany. ADDRESS: Box 215, RD 1, Duanesburg, NY 12056. 518/465-4585

DRAYER, WENDY Student. BS 1980, U of Ill. INT: personnel, health & hosp care. ASSN: Univ of Ill IRRA. ADDRESS: Room 218, 909 South Fifth St, Champaign, IL 61820. 217/332-4653

DRAZNIN, ANNE L. Arbitration; Acad: Law. BA 1966, Earlham Coll; JD 1971, U of Ill. PUBL: "Arbitration-Available Alternative," Handling Bus and Commercial Litigation, ICLE; "Legal Clinics: Illegimate Children of Progressive Advertising Rules," ABA Monograph. INT: arb/med, empl/trng programs, intl comparative labor. ASSN: Chicago and Central Ill IRRA, SPIDR, AAA, ABA. POSITIONS: Dir of Legal Services, 1977, Reg Dir-Chicago, AAA, 1981, and (since 1982) Assoc Prof of Legal Studies, Public Affairs Center 482, Sangamon State Univ, Springfield, IL 62708. 217/786-6535

DRAZNIN, JULIUS N. Arbitration. PUBL: Pers J - column on Labor Rels, Monthly. POSITION: Arbitrator, 737 S Highland Ave, Los Angeles, CA 90036. 213/822-1944

DREIBLATT, DEAN M. Union. BA 1974, U of Wis-Madison; MILR 1976, Cornell. INT: coll barg, arb/med, health & hosp care. POSITIONS: Sr Editor, Prentice Hall, 1976; Field Rep, NY State Nurses Assn, 1979, and (since 1981) Field Rep, Wis Fed of Nurses and Health Professionals, Milwaukee. ADDRESS: 2628 N Prospect Ave, Milwaukee, WI 53211. 414/475-6065

DRISCOLL, JOHN J. Union. POSITION: President, Conn State Labor Council, PO Box 5278, Hamden CT 06518. 203/288-3591

DROEGE, JOHN D. L. Bus:Pers/Ind Rels, Bus:Mgmt/Admin, Arbitration. MS 1960, U of North Dakota. INT: coll barg, personnel, arb/med. ASSN: Tech Assn Pulp & Paper Industry, ASPA, AMA. POSITIONS: Faculty, UW-GreenBay/Madison, 1964; Production Mgr, 1967, and, since 1977, Vice Pres, Ind Rels, Green Bay Packaging Inc, PO Box 1107, Green Bay, WI 54305. 414/433-5120

DROGIN, IRA Acad: Law. LLB 1958, Cornell. INT: labor law, arb/med, coll barg. ASSN: New York IRRA, New York State and City Bar Assn. POSITION: (since 1966) Attorney, Leaf, Deull Drogin and Kramer, 730 Third Ave, New York, NY 10017. 212/573-9200

DROHAN, WILLIAM D. Government. POSITION: Exec Asst to Undersecretary of Labor, USDL, Room S-2018, Washington DC 20210. 202/523-6151

DROST, DONALD A. Acad: Org Beh/Pers. ADDRESS: School of Bus, Texas Christian Univ, PO Box 32868, Ft Worth, TX 76129. 817/921-7569

DROTNING, JOHN EVAN Acad:Ind Rels; Arbitration. BA 1958, U of Rochester; MBA 1959, PhD 1965, U of Chicago. INT: coll barg, govt labor policy, arb/med. ASSN: Northeast Ohio IRRA, NAA. POSITIONS: Prof, SUNY-Buffalo, 1963; Assoc Dean, IL & R, Cornell, 1972, and (since 1976) Head & Prof, Div of Ind Rels, Weatherhead School of Mgmt, Case Western Reserve Univ, Cleveland, OH 44106. 216/368-5971

DUBAY, CONSTANCE M. Bus:Pers/Ind Rels. #114B, 1415 E Central Rd, Arlington Heights, IL 60005.

DUBOIS, EILEEN C. Acad: Counseling. ASSN: Conn Valley IRRA. POSITION: Career Counselor, Yale School of Management. ADDRESS: 172 Exeter Rd, Hamden, CT 06518. 203/248-3027

DUFFE, WILLIAM C. Acad: Bus Admin, Econ. BA 1965, U of Minn; MA 1974, U of Mo-St Louis; MBA 1977, St. Louis U. INT: personnel, coll barg, health & hosp care. ASSN: Gateway IRRA, Intl Pers Mgmt Assn, ASPA, Natl Public Empl Rels Assn. POSITIONS: Pers Management Specialist, 1973, Pers Officer, Veterans Admin Reg Office-St. Louis, 1974, and (since 1978) Director of Pers, City of St.Louis, 1320 Market St, St Louis, MO 63110. 314/776-0905

DUFFY, CONSTANCE D. Government. MSIR 1978, Loyola U-Chicago. INT: empl benefits, health & hosp care, empl/trng programs. ASSN: Chicago IRRA. POSITIONS: Regional Trng, Federal Rep, Empl & Trng Admin, Region V, and, since 1983, Investigator, Chicago Area Office. Office of Pension, Welfare and Benefit Plans, USDL. ADDRESS: 212 N Scoville, Oak Park, IL 60302. 312/353-0900

DUFFY, JOHN F. Acad: Org Beh/Pers, Ind Rels; Consulting. PhD 1973, Iowa State U. PUBL: Canadian Personnel Management, Prentice Hall, 1984; "Social Forces in Negotiating Experiments," J of Conflict Res, 1983; "Program Evalution and BARS," Personnel Psych, 1979. INT: ind psych, personnel, coll barg. ASSN: APA, CPA, Acad of Mgmt. POSITION: Assoc Prof, Dalhousie Univ. ADDRESS: 2111 Poplar St, Halifax, NS, B3L 2Y6 Canada. 902/424-7080

DUFFY, WILLIAM E. Bus:Pers/Ind Rels. BBA 1965, Manhatten Coll, MBA 1970, Bernard Baruch Coll. POSITIONS: VP, Pers, Presbyterian Hosp, 1966, and currently, Director of Human Resources, Medical Center Hospital of Vermont, Colchester Ave, Burlington, VT 05401. 802/656-2825

DUFTY, NORMAN FRANCIS Acad: Univ Admin. AMBT 1938, Sheffield U; BA 1956, U of Western Australia; AM 1958, U of Ill; PhD 1961, MEd 1966, U of Western Australia. PUBL: Industrial Relations in the Public Sector- - the Fireman, St. Lucia: Univ of Queensland Press, 1979; Changes in Labor/Management-Relations in the Enterprise, Paris: OECD, 1975; Industrial Relations in the Australian Metal Industry, Sydney: West Publishing, 1972. INT: arb/med, intl comparative labor, ind sociol. ASSN: Ind Rels Soc of Western Australia, Australian Inst of Mgmt, Australian Coll of Educ. POSITIONS: Principal Member of Div, ILO, 1962; Asst Principal, Perth Tech Coll,1964, and (since 1967) Assoc Director, Western Australian Inst of Technology, Kent St, South Bentley, Western Australia 6102. Phone: 09-350-7280

DUNBERRY, FERNAND J. Union. POSITION: Economist Research Dept, Paperworkers, Suite 1501, 1155 Sherbrooke St W, Montreal H3A 2N3 Canada. 514/842-8931

DUNLAP, CHRIS R. Government. BA 1971, Penn State U. INT: arb/med, coll barg, personnel. ASSN: Central Penn IRRA. POSITION: Labor Rels Specialist, Bureau of Labor Rels, Commonwealth of Penn, 404 Finance Bldg, Harrisburg, PA 17109. 717/783-5160

DUNLOP, JOHN THOMAS Acad: Econ. AB 1935, PhD 1939, U of Calif-Berkeley. PUBL: Wage Determination Under Trade Unions, 1944; Industrial Relations System, 1958; Labor and the American Community, (w D. C. Bok) 1970. INT: coll barg, govt labor policy, arb/med. ASSN: NAA, Inst of Medicine, Amer Acad of Arts and Sciences. POSITION: Prof at Harvard since 1938,and, since 1970, Lamont Univ Prof, 208 Littauer Center, Harvard Univ, Cambridge, MA 02138. 617/495-4157

DUNN, J. D. Acad: Org Beh/Pers; Arbitration. PhD 1961, U of Ala. PUBL: Wage and Salary Administration; Personnel Management; Essentials of Management. INT: arb/med, personnel. ASSN: North Tex IRRA, NAA. POSITION: (since 1963) Prof of Bus Admin, North Texas State Univ, Box 5281, N.T. Station, Denton, TX 76203. 817/565-3158

DUNN, W. STEVEN Bus:Pers/Ind Rels. POSITION: Regional Pers Manager, Ground Round, 4247 George St, Shiller Park, IL 60176. 305/377-9000

DUNNING, JOHN C., JR. Bus:Pers/Admin. BA 1959, Colgate U. INT: personnel, empl/trg programs. ASSN: ASPA, Amer Compensation Assn, Ind Rels Assn of Greater St. Louis. POSITIONS: Reg Pers Mgr, Ins Co of North America, 1962; Eastern Zone Pers Mgr, Transamerica Ins Group, 1973, and (since 1976) Personnel Manager, Auto Club of Missouri, 12901 N Forty Dr, St. Louis, MO 63141. 314/576-7350

DURANKO, PETER Bus:Pers/Ind Rels, Arbitration, Bus:Mgmt/Admin. BA 1967, U of Notre Dame; MA 1978, St. Francis Coll. PUBL: "Experimental Negotiating Agreement, 'A Formula or Foundation.'" INT: personnel, empl/trng programs, coll barg. ASSN: Western Penn IRRA, ASPA, PA Employers Advisory Council, Natl Football League Players Assn. POSITIONS: Professional Athlete, Denver Broncs, 1967; Publ Rels Pers, Personalities Inc, 1974, and (since 1979) Personnel Manager, ABEX Corp, R.P.G., Hollsopple. ADDRESS: 417 S Clearfield, Johnstown, PA 15905. 814/479--2551

DURHAM, JOHN L. Union. POSITION: Bus Mgr, Local 1439 IBEW AFL-CIO, 2121 59th St, St Louis, MO 63110.

DURKAY, JOHN J. Legal Practice. BA 1968, Fordham Coll; JJD 1973, Harvard. INT: labor law. ASSN: Houston IRRA, Tex Board of Legal Specialization. POSITION: Attorney, Mehaffy,Weber, Keith & Consoulin, PO Box 16, Beaumont, TX 77704. 409/835-5011

DURSO, CAROLE G. Student; Bus:Pers/Ind Rels. BBA 1979, Baruch Coll. ASSN: ASPA (student). POSITIONS: Compensation Administrator, 1980, and, since 1982, Pers Administrator, Nabisco Brands Inc., East Hanover. Student: NY Inst of Tech. ADDRESS: Apt 2D, 234 E 77th St, New York, NY 10021. 201/884-3037

DUSSEY, CHARLES JEVENS Bus:Pers/Ind Rels. BBA 1953, Le Moyne Coll; MA 1955, Marquette U. INT: labor market econ, coll barg. ASSN: Detroit IRRA, Ind Rels of Detroit, Bus Res Advisory Council, BLS, Detroit Assn of Bus Economists. POSITIONS: Manager, Pers Admin, Latin Amer Operations, 1967, Mgr, Pers Res, 1973, and, since 1980, Manager, Res and Planning, Chrysler Corp, PO Box 1919, CIMS: 416-27-20, Detroit, MI 48288. 313/956-2726

DUZAK, THOMAS Health Plan/Admin. BA 1967, SUNY-Buffalo; MILR 1969, Cornell U. INT: health & hosp care, coll barg, union org/admin. POSITIONS: Dir, Insurance & Pension Dept, United Steelworkers of Amer, 1984; and (since 1984) Vice Pres, U. S. Administrators Inc, 3540 Wilshire Blvd, Los Angeles, CA 90010. 213/738-0235

DWORKIN, JAMES BARNET Acad: Ind Rels. BA 1970, MAIR 1971, U of Cincinnati; PhD 1977, U of Minn. PUBL: Owners versus Players: Baseball and Collective Bargaining, Auburn House Publ, 1981; "Final Offer Arbitration and the Naive Negotiator," (w A. DeNisi), ILRR Oct 1981; "Research on Unions and Productivity," Advances in Ind and Labor Rels," (w D. Ahlburg), 1984. INT: coll barg, arb/med, labor market econ. ASSN: SPIDR, AAA, Soc of Federal Labor Rels Professionals. POSITIONS: Assoc Prof (Visiting) U of Minn, 1981; Asst Prof, 1976, and, since 1983, Assoc Prof and Chairperson, Ind Rels Committee, 489 Krannert Grad School, Purdue Univ, West Lafayette, IN 47907. 317/494-5703

DWORKIN, JONATHAN Arbitration, Legal Prac; Student. BA 1960, LLB 1962, Western Reserve U. INT: arb/med, labor educ, labor law. ASSN: Northeast Ohio IRRA, NAA, SPIDR, Cleveland Bar Assn. POSITIONS: Lecturer, Advanced Arbitration, Cleveland State Univ, and (since 1971) Arbitrator (self-employed), 16828 Chagrin Blvd, Shaker Heights, OH 44120. 216/561-8400

DWYER, RICHARD E. Acad: Labor Studies. EdD 1975, Rutgers U. PUBL: Labor Education in the U.S.: An Annotated Bibliography, Metuchen, NJ: Scarecrow Press, 1977; "Labor Studies in Quest of Industrial Justice," Labor Studies J, 1977; "Labor Studies" in Encyclopedia of Educational Research, 1982. INT: labor educ, labor history, union org/admin. ASSN: Univ & Coll Labor Educ Assn. POSITIONS: Asst Prof, Rutgers U, 1972; and (since 1978) Dean, Center for Labor Studies, Empire State College-SUNY, 326 W 42nd St, New York, NY 10036. 212/279-7380

DYCK, R. GORDON Union. POSITION: Assistant Business Manager, Local 213, Intl Brotherhood of Electrical Workers, 4220 Norland Ave, Burnaby, BC V5G 3X2 Canada. 604/294-2361

DYER, LEE DOUGLAS Acad: Ind Rels, Org Beh/Pers. PhD 1971, U of Wis-Madison. PUBL: Personnel/Human Resource Management, (W H. Heneman, D.Schwab & J. Fossum), Irwin 1983 Rev Ed; Industrial Relations Research in the 1970's: Review and Appraisal, (co-editor w T. Kochan and D.J.B. Mitchell) IRRA, 1982; "On Studying Strategy in Human Resource Management: An Approach and an Agenda," Ind Rels, 23,2, 1984. INT: personnel. ASSN: Human Resource Planning Soc, Acad of Mgmt. POSITION: Asst Prof, 1971, and, since 1977, Assoc Prof, NYSSILR-Cornell Univ, Ithaca, NY 14853. 607/256-3279

DYKE, ANNMARIE K. Arbitration, Legal Practice. BSN 1964, St Louis U; JD 1968, Cleveland State U. ADDRESS: 28961 Turnbridge Rd, Cleveland, OH 44140. 216/696-4455

DYKE, THEODORE Arbitration, Legal Practice. BS 1941, JD 1947, Fordham U; LLM 1964, JSD 1965, NYU. ADDRESS: 28961 Turnbridge Rd, Cleveland, OH 44140. 216/696-4455

E

EAKLE, WILLIAM E. Government. BS 1945, U of S. C. INT: personnel, govt labor policy, mgmt/educ. ASSN: Maryland County Admin Officers, Public Sector Labor Rels Conf Board, Intl Pers Mgr Assn. POSITIONS: Corp Dir of Ind Rels, 1962, Corp Dir of Packaging, 1969, National Brewing Co, and (since 1975) County Administrator/Pers Office, Howard County Government, 3430 Courthouse Drive, Ellicott City, MD. 21043. 301/992-2020

EARL, LEWIS HAROLD Bus:Mgmt/Admin, Legal Practice, Consulting. BA 1939 Tex Tech-Lubbock; JD 1950, Georgetown U. PUBL: "Manpower Policy and Programs in 5 Western Counties;" "Reorganizating Advisory Planniing Councils;" Energy Manpower Assessment Fact Book, U. S. Dept of Energy, 1980. INT: labor market econ, personnel,govt labor policy. ASSN: Amer Soc for Trng and Develop, Tex Bar Assn, Soc for Intl Devel. POSITIONS: Staff Advisor, American Productivity Center, Houston, 1980; Lecturer, Texas Tech Univ, 1982; and, currently, Manager, Post Chamber of Commerce, Post, TX 79356. 806/495-3461

EATON, ADRIENNE E. Student. MLHR 1983, Ohio State U. INT: coll barg, union org/admin, labor educ. POSITION: Currently, PhD Candidate, IRRI-U Wis. ADDRESS: 460 N Few St, Madison, WI 53703. 608/262-1403.

ECKHARDT, CHRISTY A. Student. BS 1983, Loyola U-Chicago. INT: personnel, empl/-trng programs, org beh. POSITION: Student-Ind Rels, Loyola Univ. ADDRESS: 1218 W Albion St, Chicago, IL 60626.

EDELMAN, MILTON T. Acad: Econ; Arbitration. BS 1946, U of Chicago, MBA 1947, U of Penn; PhD 1951, U of Ill. POSITION: Professor, Dept of Economics, Southern Illinois Univ, Carbondale, IL 62901. 618/453-2332

EDELSTEIN, J. DAVID Acad: Sociology. PhD 1959, New York U. PUBL: Comparative Union Democracy: Organization and Opposition in British and American Unions, (co-author), Transaction Books, 1979; "The Origin, Structure and Problems of Four British Producers' Cooperatives," chapter in F. Lindenfeld & J. Rothschild-Whitt, eds, Porter Sargent, 1982; "Consumer Representation on Corporate Boards: The Structure of Representation," Participation & Self-Management, vol 2, 1972. INT: intl comparative labor, ind sociol, union org/admn. ASSN: Amer Sociol Assn. POSITION: (since 1968) Professor, Dept of Sociology, Syracuse Univ. ADDRESS: 206 Berkeley Dr, Syracuse, NY 13210. 315/423-2346

EDGINGTON, JOHN C. Union. INT: arb/med, coll barg, labor law. ASSN: San Diego IRRA. POSITIONS: Intl Rep, Newspaper Guild,AFL-CIO, 1965-68; Dist Mgr, Dispatch Printing Co, 1956-71, and (since 1971) Administrative Officer, San Diego Newspaper Guild, 1450 Frazee Rd #211, San Diego, CA 92108. 619/299-4083

EDMONDSON, JOHN J. Government. BS 1971, MD 1972, Purdue U. INT: personnel, coll barg, income maint. ASSN: Human Resource Mgmt Assn of Chicago, Amer Compensation Assn. POSITIONS: Ind Rels Specialist, Sr Contract Admin, and, since 1980, Chief, Ind Rels, Chicago Operations Office, U.S. Dept of Energy, 9800 S Cass Ave, Argonne, IL 60439. 312/972-2320

EDSTROM, THOMAS J. Union. ADDRESS: 1112 W Edwards, Springfield, IL 62701. 217/788-2800

EDWARDS, BRUCE H. Acad: Univ Admin; INT: ind psych, mgmt/educ, org beh. ASSN: Central New Jersey IRRA, CUPA, ASPA. POSITIONS: Dir of Pers, Plasma Physics Lab, 1962, Dir of Pers, Forrestal Res Center, 1967, and, since 1956, Deputy Dir, Pers, Princeton, Univ, Clio Hall, Princeton, NJ 08540. 609/452-3300

EDWARDS, CHARLES A. Legal Practice. AB 1967, Davidson Coll; JD 1970, U of N.C. PUBL: Georgia Employment Law, 1983; "Labor Relations and Attorney's Fees," 54 N.C.L. Rev, 1161, 1976; "The 'Squeaky Wheel' Employee," 32 Mercer Law Rev, 479, 1981. INT: labor law, personnel, intl comparative labor. ASSN: Atlanta IRRA, ABA, Intl Soc for Labor Law and Soc Security, Defense Res Inst. POSITIONS: Partner, Hunter, Houlihan et al, 1970; Partner, Constagny, Brooks & Smith, 1976, and (since 1982) Partner, Green, Buckley, DeRieux and Jones, Suite 1515, 225 Peachtree St, Atlanta, GA 30303. 404/522-3541

EDWARDS, HARRY T. Acad: Law; Government. BS 1962, Cornell; JD 1965, U of Mich. PUBL: Labor Relations Law in the Public Sector, Bobbs Merrill, 1979; Collective Bargaining & Labor Arbitration, Bobbs Merrill, 1979; Higher Education and the Law, Harvard, 1979. INT: labor law, arb/med, coll barg. ASSN: NAAM ABA, Amer Judicature Soc. POSITIONS: Prof of Law, Harvard, 1975-77; Prof of Law, Univ of Mich, 1970-75, 1977-78, and (since 1980) U.S. Circuit Judge, U.S. Court of Appeals, 5818 U.S. Courthouse, 3rd and Constitution Ave, Washington DC 20001. 202/535-3380

EDWARDS, LINDA Acad: Econ. BA 1963, U of Penn; PhD 1971, Columbia U. PUBL: "Wellington-Winter Revisited: The Case of Municipal Sanitation and Collection," ILRR, Apr 1982, pp 307-18; "Public Unions, Local Government Structure and the Compensation of Municipal Sanitation Workers," Econ Inquiry, July 1982, pp 405-21; "Income and Race Differences in Children's Health in the Mid-1960's," Medical Care, Sept 1982, pp 915-30. INT: labor market econ, union org/admn, method/statis. ASSN: AEA. POSITIONS: Asst Prof, 1970, Assoc Prof, and, since 1982, Professor, Queens Coll, CUNY. ADDRESS: 25 Fairview Rd, Scarsdale, NY 10583. 212/520-7361

EDWARDSON, RON W. Consulting. BS 1973, JD 1976, MSIR 1982, U of Oregon. INT: coll barg, arb/med, labor law. ASSN: Sacramento IRRA, Oregon State Bar. POSITIONS: Empl Rels Rep, Samsonite Corp-Denver, 1982-83; and (since 1984) Labor Rels Consultant, Blanning & Baker Assoc. ADDRESS: 1720 N Street #27, Sacramento, CA 95814. 503/673-5626

EGE, ROGER DONALD Government. BS 1970, MS 1972, Iowa State U. INT: arb/med, ind psych, personnel. ASSN: Central Ohio IRRA, SPIDR. POSITIONS: Pers Mgmt Specialist, U.S. Civil Service Commission, 1972; Labor Rels Officer, U.S. Army Finance Center, 1974, and (since 1978) Pers Mgmt Specialist, Defense Logistics Agency, 3990 E Broad St, Columbus. ADDRESS: 1480 Heisten Rd, Lancaster, OH 43130. 614/837-0687

EGGEMEYER, GERALD A. Legal Practice. ADDRESS: Riley & Roumell, 720 Ford Bldg, Detroit, MI 48226. 313/962-8255

EHRENBERG, RONALD G. Acad: Ind Rels, Econ, Univ Admin. BA 1966, Harper Coll-SUNY; MA 1970, PhD 1970, Northwestern U. PUBL: Regulatory Process and Labor Earnings, 1979; Modern Labor Economics: Theory and Policy, 1982; "Public Sector Labor Markets," 1984. INT: labor market econ, coll barg, empl/trng programs. ASSN: AEA, Econometric Soc, Evaluation Res Soc. POSITIONS: Editor, Res in Labor Econ, 1975; Res Assoc, Natl Bureau of Econ Res, 1981; and (since 1977) Prof of Econ and Labor Econ, and Dir of Research, NYSSILR-Cornell, Ithaca, NY 14853. 607/256-3026

EHRENHALT, SAMUEL M. Government; Acad: Econ. BA 1946, Brooklyn Coll; MA 1949, Columbia U. PUBL: "Some Perspectives on the New York City Economy In A Time of Change," in New York City's Changing Econ Base, 1981; "Recent New York City Trends and the Challenges To Development Policy," Pratt Planning Papers, Feb 1983; "What Lies Ahead for College Graduates?" Amer Demographics, Sept 1983. INT: labor market econ, method/statis, mgmt/educ. ASSN: New York IRRA, AEA, ASA, MEA. POSITIONS: Deputy Reg Commissioner, USBL, 1970, Adjunct Prof, 1975, and (since 1980) Regional Commissioner, Middle Atlantic Reg, U.S. Bureau of Labor Statis, 1515 Broadway, New York, NY 10036. 212/944-3117

EINBECKER, RICHARD C. Univ Admin. POSITION: Dean, College of Bus, U of West Florida, Pensacola, FL 32504. 904/476-9500

EISCHEN, DANA E. Arbitration;Acad: Ind Rels. AB 1966, Le Moyne Coll; MS 1968, Cornell; JD 1972, Georgetown U. PUBL: 50 Years Under the Railway Labor Act, (co-author). INT: arb/-med. ASSN: Central New York IRRA, Wash and New York Bar, NAA. POSITION: Arbitrator (self-employed), PO Box 877, Ithaca NY 14851. 607/257-4160

EISELE, C. FREDERICK Acad: Bus Admin, Uni Admin; Arbitration. BS 1942, Iowa State U; PhD 1971, U of Iowa. PUBL: "Plant Size and Frequency of Strikes," Labor Law J, vol 21, Dec 1970; "Organization Size, Technology, and Frequency of Strikes," Ind and Labor Rels Rev, vol 27, July 1974; "Consumer Price Index: Description and Discussion," Center for Labor & Mgmt, U of Iowa, 1975. INT: arb/med, coll barg, labor law. ASSN: SPIDR, AAA, Acad of Mgmt. POSITIONS: Factory Mgr, Omaha Steel Works, Omaha, 1946; VP & Gen Mgr, Mid-American Steel, Fargo, 1959, and (since 1971) Prof and Dir MBA Program, North Dakota State Univ, Fargo, ND 58105. 701/237-8804

EISENBERG, ARTHUR Government. BSS 1947, CCNY. INT: labor law, arb/med, coll barg. POSITIONS: NLRB, various offices since 1948, and (since 1973), Director, Reg 22, NLRB, Newark. ADDRESS: 288 Nob Hill, Roseland, NJ 07068. 201/645-3240

EISENBERG, HARRY H. Acad: Econ, Ind Rels; Arbitration. POSITION: Sr Examiner, SLRB, 2 World Trade Center, Room 3334, New York NY 10047

EISENBERG, WALTER L. Arbitration, Consulting; Acad: Ind Rels. PhD 1959, Columbia U. PUBL: "Toward More Effective Grievance Arbitration," 1983; "The Mechanics of Public Finance," 1979; "A Failure of National Policy: The Business Cycle as Usual," 1975. INT: arb/-med, coll barg, labor market econ. ASSN: New York IRRA, AEA, NAA SPIDR. POSITIONS: Dean of Grad Studies, Hunter Coll, 1947; Public Member, NYC Board of Coll Barg, 1969, and (since 1963 part time and 1976 full time) Arbitrator (self-employed), 939 E 24 St, Brooklyn NY 11210. 212/252-9835

EISENGA, LARRY C. Bus:Pers/Ind Rels. POSITION: Empl Rels Manager, Leon Plastics, 4901 Clay Ave SW, Grand Rapids, MI 49509. 616/531-7970

EISENHOWER, R. WARREN Government. AB 1961, George Washington U; ME 1969, U of Va; PhD 1979, U of Md. INT: personnel, coll barg, org beh. ASSN: Amer Assn of School Admin, Amer Assn of School Pers Admin, Phi Delta Kappa. POSITIONS: Labor-Mgmt Rels Examiner, NLRB, 1961; Dir, Empl Rels, 1968, and, since 1980, Asst Supt, Pers Services, Fairfax County Public Schools, 6815 Edsall Road, Springfield, VA 22151. 703/750-8450

EKSTROM, J. FREDRIK Acad: Univ Admin; Arbitration. BA 1951, Rutgers U; AM 1955, New York U; MA 1968, U of Penna. PUBL: Harvard Business Review Letters, March/April, 1980. INT: arb/med, coll barg, labor history. POSITION: (since 1951) Director, Registration Services, Camden Div U Coll, Rutgers Univ, 311 N 5th St, Camden, NJ 08102. 609/757-6002

ELBAUM, BERNARD LOUIS Acad: Econ, Ind Rels. BA 1971, U of Mich; PhD 1982, Harvard. PUBL: "The Making and Shaping of Job and Pay Structures in the Iron and Steel Industry," in P. Osterman (ed) Employment Practices Within Large Firms, MIT Press, 1984; "The Internalization of Labor Markets: Causes and Consequences," Amer Econ Rev, May 1983. POSITION: Dept of Economics, Boston Univ, 270 Bay State Rd, Boston, MA 02215. 617/353-4447

ELEGREET, FRANK J. Bus:Pers/Ind Rels. BA 1951, Ripon Coll. POSITION: Corporate Vice Pres-Human Resources, Chicago Rawhide Mfg Co, 900 N State St, Elgin, IL 60120. 312/-742-7840

ELKIN, RANDYL D. Acad: Ind Rels, Econ. BS 1965, PhD 1971, Iowa State U. PUBL: Labor and the Economy, (co-author), Cincinnati, Southwestern Publ, 1983; Succesful Arbitration, (co-author), Reston (VA) Publ, 1980. INT: coll barg, arb/med, health & hosp care. ASSN: W Va. IRRA, AEA, SPIDR. POSITIONS: Asst Prof, Illinois State Univ, 1970, and (since 1983) Prof of Econ/IR; Dir MSIR Program, West Virginia Univ, PO Box 6025, Morgantown, WV 26506. 304/293-5721

ELKIN, SOL M. Acad: Educ; Arbitration. EdD 1958, Wayne State U. PUBL: "Unchanging Schools," Intellect, Mar 1973; "Student Teacher Provisions in Collective Bargaining Agreements in Michigan," Secondary Educ Today, Spring 1973; "Prospects for Radical School Reform," Education, v 92, #4, April-May, 1972. INT: coll barg, arb/med. ASSN: Southwest Mich IRRA, AAUP, SPIDR. POSITION: (since 1968) Professor, Educ Dept, Albion Coll, Albion, MI 49224. 517/629-5511

ELKISS, HELEN Acad: Ind Rels. MLIR 1976, Mich State U; MPH 1981, U of Ill. INT: labor educ. ASSN: Chicago IRRA, Univ & Coll Labor Educ Assn, Ill Labor History Society. POSITION: Assoc Prof, Univ of Ill, Rice Bldg #214, PO Box 4348, Chicago, IL 60680. 312/996-2623

ELLARD, CHARLES J. Acad: Econ. PhD 1974, Uof Houston, INT: empl/trng programs, govt labor policy, labor market econ. ASSN: AEA, Southern Econ Assn, Western Econ Assn. POSITION: (since 1976) Assoc Prof, Pan American Univ. ADDRESS: 1901 Point West Drive, Edinburg, TX 78539. 512/381-3391

ELLENBERG, MARTIN Bus:Pers/Ind Rels. BS 1948, CCNY: MA 1949, Columbia U; JD 1954, NYU. INT: coll barg, personnel, arb/med. POSITION: (since 1960) Vice Pres Empl Rels, S&S Corrugated Paper Mach Co, 160 N 4th St, Brooklyn, NY 11211. 212/782-9700

ELLERBROCK, GERALDINE B. Acad: Ind Rels; Arbitration. PhD 1971, Ohio State U. PUBL: People Problems; People Problems, revised, 2nd ed. INT: coll barg, arb/med, personnel. ASSN: Central Coast IRRA, Acad of Mgmt, Western Acad of Mgmt, AAA. POSITION: (since 1973) Prof of Mgmt, Calif Polytech State Univ, San Luis Obispo, CA 93407. 805/544--9390

ELLERY, LAWRENCE FENN Bus:Pers/Ind Rels. BA 1953, Oberlin Coll; MS 1959, U of Ill; Grad Work, UCLA. POSITIONS: Asst Prof of Mgmt, Calif State U, San Diego, 1966; Corp Pers Dir, SER-Jobs for Progress, 1971, and Dir of Human Resources, Litton Fastening Systems, 1977. ADDRESS: 4131 Deeboyar Ave, Apt 12, Lakewood, CA 90712. 213/512-2010

ELLINGER, RUTH Union. BA 1940, Washington U/St. Louis. INT: labor educ, labor history, labor law. ASSN: South Tex IRRA. POSITION: Educ Director, Tex AFL-CIO, PO Box 12727, Austin, TX 78711. 512/472-0915

ELLIOTT, CLIFTON L. Legal Practice. JD 1963, Northwestern U. PUBL: "Sexual Harassment Hurts Productivity;" "Unionization of Hospitals in the Eighties;" "What Trustees Can Do To Maintain Nonunion Status." INT: labor law, coll barg, empl/trng programs. ASSN: Kansas City IRRA, ABA, Soc of Hospital Attorneys, Missouri Bar Assn. POSITIONS: Attorney, Spencer, Fane et a; Attorney, Roan & Grossman, 1979, and (since 1981) Attorney, Elliott & Kaiser, P.C., 1100 Main St, PO Box 26190, Kansas City, MO 64196. 816/471-3022.

ELLIS, GERALDINE Bus:Pers/Ind Rels. POSITION: Manager, Labor Rels, Southern Calif Gas Co, PO Box 3249, Terminal Annex, Los Angeles, CA 90051. 213/689-2281

ELLISON, MYRON K. Legal Practice. Stinson, May, Thomson, McEvers & Fizzell, 2100 Ten Main Center, Kansas City, MO 64105.

ELLSBURG, DONALD B. Legal Practice. ADDRESS: Connerton & Bernstein, 1899 L St NW, Suite 800, Washington DC 20036. 202/-466-6790

ELSON, BARRY R. Legal Prac. BS 1967, New York U; JD 1971, George Washington U. INT: labor law, health & hosp care, coll barg. ASSN: Philadelphia IRRA, ABA: Devel of Law Committee, Occupational Safety Comm, Amer Soc of Hosp Attorneys. POSITIONS: Mgmt Rels Specialist, 1969; Attorney, NLRB, 1971; and (since 1978) Partner, Cohen, Shapiro, Polisher, Shiekman & Cohen, 12 South 12th St, Philadelphia, PA 19107. 215/922-1300

EMANUELE, BENEDICT D. Bus:Pers/Ind Rels. BA 1967, JD 1971, NYU. INT: labor law, coll barg, arb/med. POSITIONS: Dir of Labor Rels, RKO General Inc, 1978; and (since 1984) Dir of Labor Rels, Electronic Systems, Sperry Inc, Lakeville Rd, MS:IV107, Great Neck, NY 11020.

EMER, WILLIAM HOWARD Legal Prac, Bus:Pers/Ind Rels; Acad: Law. AB 1969, JD 1972, UCLA. PUBL: "Advising California Employers," Affirmative Action Control Compliance, June 1982; "Hiring Handicapped," CCH Labor Law J, Sept, 1983. INT: labor law, arb/med, union org/admin. ASSN: ABA (Labor & Empl Law Section), L.A. County Bar Assn (Labor Law), Amer Mgmt Assn. POSITION: Assoc 1972, and, since 1979, Partner, Parker, Milliken, Clark, O'Hara & Samuelian, 333 S Hope St, 27th FL, LosAngeles, CA 90071. 213/683-6615

EMERSON, WAYNE Prof Assn. POSITION: Dir, Policy Analysis, Amer Nurses Assn, 1101 14th St NW, Suite 200, Washington DC 20005. 202/789-1800

EMERY, SUSAN K. Student; Bus:Pers/Ind Rels. BA 1982, U of Wis-Madison; MSIR 1983, U of New Haven. 2 Treat St, #15-C, West Haven, CT 06516. 203/932-6357

EMMETT, THOMAS A. Acad: Univ Admin. PhB 1952, MEd 1953, U of Detroit; DEd 1963, U of Mich; LLB 1965, U of Detroit. PUBL: The Academic Department or Divison Chairman: A Complex Role, Belamp Press, 1973; Collective Bargaining in Post Secondary Institutions, Educ Comm of the States, 1974; "Managing Collective Bargaining," Academic Leaders as Managers, Jossey Bass, 1981. INT: coll barg, mgmt/educ, arb/med. ASSN: Rocky Mountain IRRA, Assn of Amer Geographers, Natl Assn of Student Pers Admin, Academy of Academic Pers Admin. POSITIONS: Pres, Higher Educ Executive Assoc, McGraw Hill, 1967; Senior Advisor-CLDNE, Amer Council on Educ, 1979 to present, and (since 1971) Special Asst to Pres & Prof, Regis College, 50th & Lowell Blvd, Denver, CO 80221. 303/770-5317

ENCINO, PHILIP A. Arbitration, Bus:Mgmt/-Admin, Bus:Pers/Ind Rels. POSITION: Manager, Labor Relations, Univ of Calif, 2535 Channing Way, Berkeley, CA 94720. 415/642-3119

ENGELBRECHT, MARK ALAN Bus:Pers/Ind Rels. BA 1975, U of Tex-Austin; MA 1977, U of New Mexico; MLIR 1981, Mich State Univ. INT: coll barg, arb/med, personnel. ASSN: ASPA. POSITIONS: Empl Rels Assistant, 1981, and, since 1983, Analyst-Labor Rels, Texaco Inc, 2000 Westchester Ave, White Plains NY, 10650. 914/253-7201

ENGLE, DENNIS E. Acad: Ind Rels. BA 1981, Juniata Coll; MA 1983, Indiana U of Penn. INT: arb/med, coll barg, labor law. ASSN: Harrisburg IRRA, ASPA. ADDRESS: 14 Wintermere Rd, Lebanon, PA 17042. 717/272-6233

ENGLISH, LYNN H. Student; Bus:Pers/Ind Rels. BBA 1981, UGA; MSIR 1984, GSU. INT: personnel, health & hosp care, arb/med. ASSN: Atlanta IRRA. POSITION: Human Resource Asst, N. Fulton Medical Center, Roswell. ADDRESS: 2491 Overlook Way NE, Atlanta, GA 30345. 404/442-2230

EPSTEIN, IRA STEPHEN Arbitration, Legal Practice. BA 1963, Columbia Coll; MA 1965, ILIR, U of Ill; JD 1968; U of Wis. INT: arb/med, coll barg, labor law. ASSN: Wis IRRA, AAA, Intl Labor Law Soc. POSITIONS: Attorney, Region 33, NLRB, 1968; Attorney, Goldberg, Previant & Velmen, 1979, and (since 1982) self-employed. ADDRESS: 12533 N Jacqueline Ct, Mequon, WI 53092. 414/277-7077

ERB, CHARLOTTE M. Acad: Ind Rels. PhD 1969, U of Wis. INT: personnel, mgmt/educ, gerontology (retirement planning, mgmt of life care facilities.) POSITION: Prof of Mgmt and Ind Rels, Bus & Admin Sciences, Calif State Univ, Fresno, CA 93740. 209/294-2851

ERDHEIM, ANDREA RUTH Student. BA 1981, U of Penn; MLIR 1984, Mich State U. INT: coll barg, labor history, labor law. ASSN: Long Island IRRA, ASPA. ADDRESS: 830 Lawrence Ct, West Hempstead, NY 11552.

ERENBURG, MARK E. Acad: Econ, Ind Rels. AB 1963, U of Mich; MA 1966, PhD 1969, U of Wis. POSITION: (since 1970) Assoc Prof of Econ, Sangamon State Univ, Springfield IL 62708. 217/786-6571

ERICKSON, HERMAN Acad: Econ, Ind Rels; Union. INT: labor educ. POSITION: Professor Emeritus, U of Ill. ADDRESS: 816 W Columbia Ave, Champaign, IL 61820. 217/333-0981

ESKAY, HENRY H. Arbitration. Retired. ADDRESS: 24 Hutton Ave, West Orange, NJ 07052.

ESSELMAN, MARK STEVEN Bus:Pers/Ind Rels. BBA 1978, MS 1980, U of Wis-Madison. INT: labor law, personnel, union org/admin. ASSN: ASPA, ACA. POSITIONS: Compensation & Benefits Analyst, Empl Rels and Trng Supr, and, since 1983, Area Empl Rels Manager, PepsiCola Bottling Group. ADDRESS: 2017 Chestnut Hill Lane, Richardson, TX 75081. 214/324-8523

ESTENSON, JERRY D. Bus:Pers/Ind Rels; Acad: Ind Rels, Org Beh/Pers. BS 1971, U of San Francisco; MBA 1975, Portland State U. INT: coll barg, org beh, personnel. ASSN: Sacramento IRRA, Ind Rels Assn of Northern Calif. POSITIONS: Area Mgr, Timber Operators Council, 1972; Lecturer, Calif State Univ-Sacramento, 1980, and (since 1983) Asst General Manager, Sacramento Reg Transit Dist, 1400 29th St, PO Box 2110, Sacramento, CA 95810. 916/321-2980

ESTEY, MARTEN S. Acad: Ind Rels; Arbitration. BS 1940, Purdue; PhD 1952, Princeton. PUBL: The Unions: Structure, Development, and Management, 3rd ed, Harcourt, 1981; "The Grocery Clerks: Center of Retail Unionism," Ind Rels, vol 7 #3, May 1968, pp 249-261; "Trends in Concentration of Union Membership, 1897-1962," Quart J of Econ, vol LXXX #3, Aug, 1966, pp 243-360. INT: union org/admin, govt labor policy, arb/med. ASSN: Philadelphia IRRA, AAA. POSITIONS: Sr Staff Econ, Council of Econ Advisers, 1968-69; Visiting Prof, Univ of Otago, Dunedin, New Zealand, 1975, and (since 1956) Prof, Mgmt and Ind Rels, U of Penn, Philadelphia. ADDRESS: 730 Ogden Avenue, Swarthmore, PA 19081. 215/898-7734

ETUKUDO, AKANIMO JONATHON Bus:Pers/-Ind Rels, Bus:Mgmt/Admin. BA 1961, U of London. ASSN: IIRA. POSITIONS: Sr Pers Officer, Shell Oil of Nigeria, 1962-65; Secretary, Nigeria Bankers Employers Assn, 1966-75; and (since 1975) Regional Adviser on Employers Org, Regional Office for Africa, ILO, PO Box 2788, Addis Ababa, Ethiopia.

EVANS, EUGENE EMERSON Acad:Bus Admin. ADDRESS: Dept of Mgmt and Marketing, Western Kentucky Univ, Bowling Green, KY 42101. 502/745-5408

EVANS, RICHARD K. Government, Labor Mgmt Committees. BA 1950, Dickinson Coll, MGA 1973, U of Penn; PhD 1982, Union Grad School. INT: labor/mgmt committees, mgmt/-educ, org beh. ASSN: NPELRA, Lebanon Area Pers Assn. POSITION: Labor Rels Specialist, Dept of Community Affairs, Commonwealth of Penn, Harrisburg. ADDRESS: R 3, Box 410H, Old Forge Acres, Annville, PA 17003. 717/787-7149

EVANS, ROBERT, JR. Acad: Econ. PhD 1959, U of Chicago. PUBL: The Labor Economies of Japan and the United States, Praeger, 1971; "Changing Labor Markets and Criminal Behavior in Japan," J of Asian Studies, May 1977; "The Great Computer Bubble," Ind Rels, 1976. INT: intl comparative labor, labor market econ, govt labor policy. ASSN: AEA, Assn for Asian Studies. POSITIONS: Asst Prof, Ind Rels, MIT, 1959-65, and (since 1965) Atran Prof of Econ, Brandeis Univ, Waltham, MA 02254. 617/647-2776

EVANS, W. KENNETH Government, Mediation. LMR 1960, Penn State U. INT: arb/med, coll barg, labor history. ASSN: Northeast Ohio IRRA. POSITIONS: Mediator Asst, Penn Bureau of Mediation, 1960; Mediator, 1964, and, since 1983, District Director, FMCS, Room 508, Mall Bldg, 118 St. Clair Ave NE, Cleveland, OH 44114. 216/522-4800

EVERITT, ALICE LUBIN Arbitrator. ADDRESS: 3241D Sutton Pl NW, Washington DC 20016. 202/363-1424

EVERY, ALLYSON Bus:Mgmt/Admin/Union. BA 1973, Bridgewater State-MA. INT: coll barg, union org/admin, personnel. ASSN: Boston IRRA, Labor Guild of Boston. POSITIONS: Classified Sales, 1973, Dist Sales Mgr, 1974 to present, Boston Globe, and, since 1981, President, Boston Globe Employees Assn, 135 Morrissey Blvd, Boston, MA 02107. 617/929-3272

EVISTON, ROBERT J. Bus:Pers/Ind Rels. POSITION: Manager, Industrial Rels, The Kroger Company, 1014 Vine St, Cincinnati, OH 45201. 513/762-1308

EWING, DAVID FLAGG Bus:Pers/Ind Rels. BBA, 1981, MS 1982, U of Wis-Madison. INT: personnel, coll barg, empl/trng programs. ASSN: ASPA. POSITION: Human Resource Asst, Ohio Medical Anesthetics. ADDRESS: 2615 Madrid Lane #5, Madison, WI 53715. 608/-273-0019

EWING, DAVID W. Acad: Editor. PUBL: Do It My Way or You're Fired!, Wiley, 1983; Writing for Results," Wiley, 1979; The Human Side of Planning, Macmillan, 1969. INT: labor law, org beh, personnel. ASSN: Amer Assn for the Advancement of Sci. POSITION: (since 1949) Managing Editor, Harvard Business Review, Soldiers Field, Boston, MA 02163. 617/495-6174

EXO, SUSAN Acad: Univ Admin. PhD 1979, U of Wis-Madison. INT: method/statis, labor market econ, govt labor policy. ASSN: Assn for Institutional Research. POSITIONS: Dir, Office of Prog Evaluation & Review, UCLA, 1970; and, since 1978, Sr Staff Assoc, Univ of Wis System Admin, 1530 Van Hise Hall, Univ of Wisconsin, Madison, WI 53706. 608/263-7918

EXTEJT, MARIAN M. Acad: Bus Admin. BA 1975, John Carroll U; MSIA 1976, PhD 1980, Purdue U. PUBL: "New Strategies in Union Organizing," J of Labor Res, 1983; Impact of Arbitration on the Collective Bargaining Process, J of Collective Negotiations in the Public Sector, 1983; "An Analysis of Fringe Benefit Levels Among Teacher Bargaining Units," J of Coll Negotiations in the Public Sector, 1983. INT: coll barg, arb/med, personnel. ASSN: Academy of Mgmt, Pittsburgh Pers Assn. POSITION: (since 1980) Asst Prof of Business Admin, Grad School of Bus, Univ of Pittsburgh, 254 Mervis Hall, Pittsburgh, PA 15260. 412/624-6276

EZBIANSKY, DONALD Government. ADDRESS: 103 Fairway Dr, Mechanicsburg, PA 17055. 717/766-9515

EZRATTY, ARLENE Consulting, Home Health/Service. PUBL: "OSHA Study," J of Preventive Medicine, vol 7, #3, Sept, 1978. INT: coll barg, labor educ, empl/trng programs. ASSN: Long Island IRRA, Coalition for Labor Union Women. POSITION: Executive Vice-Pres, District 1199, 1967; and (since 1984) Partner, Resources for Labor Associates, 57-10 244 St, Douglaston, NY 11362. 516/829-6390

F

FABI, BRUNO C. Acad: Org Beh/Pers; Consulting, Bus:Pers/Ind Rels. DPs 1981, U of Montreal. PUBL: "Private vs Public: Choice and Transfer of Organizational Sector," "Validation of the 'Learning Ability Profile' Against GPA," "Improvement of the Productivity in Public Organizations." INT: ind psych, personnel, org beh. ASSN: Corp professionnelle des psych du Quebec, Canadian Council on Working Life, Assn of Sci Admin Canadian. POSITION: (since 1979) Prof, Dept of Admin and Econ, Case Post 500/Blvd Forges, Univ Quebec Trois Riviers, Quebec G9A 5H7 Canada. 819/376-5734

FADEM, JOEL ALAN Acad: Ind Rels, Org Beh/Pers. BA 1963, U of Calif-Berkeley; MA 1968, Yale. ADDRESS: Quality Working Life Center, Inst of Ind Rels, Univ of California, Los Angeles, CA 90024. 213/825-8862

FAHERTY, JOSEPH C. Union. INT: coll barg, arb/med, labor history. ASSN: BOSTON IRRA, Board of Dir United Community Planning Corp. POSITIONS: Natl Executive Board-AFL-CIO; Customer Relations, Boston Edison Co, 1954, and (since 1979) Pres and Bus Agent, Local 387, UWUA, AFL-CIO, 161 Massachusetts Ave, Room 310, Boston, MA 02115. 617/536-1940

FAIRCHILD, CHARLES Bus:Pers/Ind Rels. BS 1976, SUNY. INT: health & hosp care, arb/-med, coll barg. ASSN: Central New York IRRA, ASPA, Amer Compensation Assn, Amer Soc Hospital Pers Assn. POSITIONS: Empl Mgr, House of GoodSamaritan, 1974; Dir of Pers and Ind Rels, Northland Div, Scott Fetzer Co, 1979; and (since 1980) Director of Empl Rels, House of Good Samaritan, 830 Washington St, Watertown, NY 13601. 315/785-4152

FALKNER, MICHAEL J. Acad: Student IR 1984, Le Moyne Coll. INT: personnel, empl/-trng programs. POSITION: Student, LeMoyne Coll. ADDRESS: 3944 W Main St, Williamson, NY 14859. 315/589-2356. School: 315/446-2227

FALLON, WILLIAM JAMES Arbitration. AA 1949, St. Michael's Coll, Vt; JD 1953 Suffolk U. ADDRESS: 36 Florence Avenue, Arlington, MA 02174. 617/643-6699

FALVEY, PAMELA J. Government. BS 1966, MS 1975, U of Wis-Milwaukee. INT: org beh, personnel, compensation/benefits. ASSN: Wisconsin IRRA, Amer Comepnsation Assn, Intl Pers Mgmt Assn, Int Found of Empl Benefits. POSITIONS: Compensation Analyst, 1979, Compensation Manager, 1981, and, since 1983, Mgr, Human Resources Group, Milwaukee Metro Sewerage Dist, 735 N Water St, Milwaukee, WI 53202. 414/225-2075

FANNING, JOHN J. Government, Arbitration. BS 1974, CUNY; MS 1982, New York Inst of Tech. INT: govt labor policy, arb/med, labor law. ASSN: Long Island IRRA, AAA, SPIDR. POSITIONS: Asst Commissioner, NY State Dept of Labor, and, since 1983, Chairman, New York State Labor Rels Board, 400 Broome St, New York, NY 10013. 212/219-4132

FANNING, MARK STEPHEN Bus:Pers Ind Rels. POSITION: Manager Pers & Ind Rels, Xerox Corp, 1808 Swift Dr, Oak Brook, IL 60521. 312/654-8419

FANOK, STEPHEN Bus:Pers/Ind Rels. MSIR 1975, JD 1981, U of W Va. INT: arb/med, personnel, labor law. ASSN: West Va IRRA, AAA, ABA, Amer Mgmt Assn. POSITIONS: Prof/Dir Ind Rels, Salem Coll, 1981; Manager Human Resources, 1981, and, since 1983, General Manager Pers & Empl Rels, Eastern Associated Coal Corp, Box 70, Beckley, WV 25802. 304/255-0422

FARABEE, BARRETT B. Bus:Pers/Ind Rels. POSITION: Director of Pers, France, PO Box 300, Fairview, TN 37062. 615/799-0551

FARBER, DAVID J. Consulting. POSITION: Consulting Economist, 10611 Cavalier Dr, Silver Spring, MD 20901. 301/593-1424

FARBER. EVELYN W. Government. POSITION: Supervisory Labor Econ, Womens Bureau, USDL. ADDRESS: 10611 Cavalier Dr, Silver Spring, MD 20901. 202/523-6636

FARBER, HENRY E. Legal Practice. BS 1978, NYSSILR-Cornell; JD 1983, U of Calif-Berkeley. PUBL: "NLRB Procedures for Resolving Election Objections," Ind Rels Law J, vol 6, #2, Spring, 1984. INT: labor law, arb/med, coll barg. ASSN: ABA. POSITIONS: Field Examiner, NLRB, 1979; and (since 1983) Attorney, Mitchell, Silberberg & Knupp, 11377 West Olympic Blvd, Suite 800, Los Angeles, CA 90064. 213/312-2000

FARBER, HENRY S. Acad: Econ. BS 1972, Rensselaer Polytech Inst; MS 1974, Cornell U; PhD 1977, Princeton. PUBL: The Determination of the Union Status of Workers," Econetrica, Sept 1983; "Splitting the Difference in Interest Arbitration," ILRR, Oct 1981; "Individual Preferences and Union Wage Determination: The Case of the United Mine Workers," J of Political Economy, Oct 1978. INT: labor market econ, coll barg, method/statis. ASSN: AEA, Econometric Soc. POSITION: (since 1977) Assoc Prof, Dept of Econ, E52-172, MIT, Cambridge, MA 02139. 617/253-2678

FARKASH, ALEXANDER Acad: Org Beh/-Pers, Ind Rels. BS 1964, St Louis U; MS 1966, Columbia U; PhD 1977, U of Minn. PUBL: "Two Contrasting Explanations of Overall Job Satisfaction Among Production Employees," (w G. W. England), in Work Organization Research, Kent State U, pp 135-153, 1978; "An Empirical Investigation of Organization Development, Beliefs, Activities and Outcomes," Selected Paper #8, Org Devel Div, Amer Soc for Trng and Devel, Mar 1979. INT: org beh, personnel, mgmt/educ. ASSN: Western New York IRRA, Acad of Mgmt, Amer Assn for Trng and Devel, Admin Mgmt Soc. POSITIONS: Dir, Mgmt Trng, Israel Aircraft Industry-Israel, 1967-70; and (since 1975) Assoc Prof of Mgmt, Canisius Coll. ADDRESS: 167 Ponderosa Dr, Williamsville, NY 14221. 716/883-7000 ext 735.

FARLEY, JEFFREY A. Student. AA 1981, U of Cincinnati; BS 1983, Northern Ky U; MAIR 1984, U of Cincinnati. INT: arb/med, method/statis, labor market econ. ASSN: Cincinnati IRRA, Alpha Chi. POSITIONS: Res Asst, Tax Survey, Northern Ky Univ, 1983;

Deputy Recorder, Clermont County Recorder's Office, 1983; and (since 1983) Student, Res Asst, Dept of Econ, Univ of Cincinnati. ADDRESS: 2319 St, Rt 125, Amelia, OH 45102. 513/734-7451

FARRELL, ROBERT A. Bus/Mgmt Admin. INT: health & hosp care, coll barg, personnel. ASSN: Amer Soc of Assn Exec. POSITIONS: Manager-Empl & Community Rels, General Electric Co, 1961; Vice Pres-Labor Rels, 1968, and, since 1974, Exec Vice Pres, Massachusetts Hospital Assn, 5 New England Executive Park, Burlington, VT 01803. 617/272-8000

FARWELL, CAROL Government. BS 1981, Okla State U. INT: arb/med, labor law, personnel. ASSN: Amer Assn of Univ Women, Okla City Pers Assn. POSITIONS: Pers Specialist, State Pers Board, 1981, Empl Rels Specialist, Ethics and Merit Comm, 1982, and, since 1983, Pers Specialist, Office of Pers Mgmt, State of Oklahoma. ADDRESS: 9517 Essex, Okalahoma City, OK 73120. 405/521-3081

FASCHAN, KRISTINE M. Government, Bus:Pers/Ind Rels, Bus:Mgmt/Admin. BS 1980, ESC at Stonybrook U. PUBL: Fiscal Analysis of a Counseling Service Agency's Statistical Data & Service Unit Reports; "Section 504 of the Rehabilation Act of 1973, and Public Sector Laws on Promotional Opportunities;" "Analysis of Factor Ranking Methodologies For Salary Administration." INT: personnel, mgmt/educ, coll barg. ASSN: Long Island, New York IRRA, Advisory Board Labor Mgmt Studies @ Stonybrook U, Long Island Professional Women in Government. POSITIONS: Labor Rels Manager, Victims Information Bureau of Suffolk, 1980, and, since 1978, Deputy Director of Pers, Suffolk County Dept of Civil Service. ADDRESS: 19 Strongs Ct, Smithtown, NY 11787. 516/348-5412

FASHOYIN, TAYO Acad: Ind Rels. Consulting. AB 1972, MA 1974, U of Minn; D Phil 1981, U of Sussex. PUBL: Industrial Relations in Nigeria, London, Longman, 1980; Inflation and Incomes Policy in Nigeria, Longman 1984; "State Regulation of Trade Disputes in Essential Services," in Nigeria Rels Industrielles, vol 36, #1, 1981, pp 207-222. INT: coll barg, labor market econ, intl comparative labor. ASSN: IIRA.POSITION: Senior Lecturer and Acting Head, Dept Ind Rels and Pers Mgmt, Univ of Lagos, Lagos, Nigeria.

FAUMAN, S. JOSEPH Acad: Sociol; Arbitration, Legal Prac. AB 1939, AM 1940, PhD 1949, JD 1975, U of Mich. PUBL: "Jewish Mortality in the U.S. (w A.J. Mayer), Chapter 3 in Ethnic Groups in America: Their Morbidity, Mortality and Behaviour Disorders," vol I The Jews, ed by A. Shiloh (I.C. Selavan, Springfield 1973; "Presenting the Results of Social Research to the Public," (w H. Sharp), Public Opinion Quart, vol XXII, #2, 1958; "Status Crystallization and Interracial Attitudes," Social Forces, vol 47, #1, Sept 1968, pp 53-60. INT: arb/med, ind sociol, org beh. ASSN: Detroit IRRA, Amer Soc Assn, Law and Soc Assn, ABA. POSITIONS: Dir, Res and Community Rels, Jewish Community Council of Metro Detroit, 1947, and (since 1958) Prof of Sociology, Eastern Mich Univ. ADDRESS: 25685 York Rd, Royal Oak, MI 48070. 313/487-2330

FAVOR, LEDA FULLER Bus:Pers/Ind Rels, Consulting. BA 1979, Goucher Coll; MA 1981, U of Ill. INT: empl/trng programs, org beh, personnel. ASSN: Greater Baltimore Pers Assn, ASPA. POSITIONS: Empl & Trng Supr, General Cable Co, 1981; Program Evaluation Consultant, Provident Hosp, 1983; and (since 1984) Personnel Manager, Moldcraft, 3920 Buena Vista Ave, Baltimore, MD 21211. 301/338-4100

FAY, CHARLES H. Acad: Org Beh/Pers; Consulting. BA 1961, NYU; MBA 1962, Columbia U; PhD 1979, U of Wash. PUBL: Compensation: Theory and Practice; Administering Human Resources. INT: personnel, labor market econ, method/statis. ASSN: Cincinnati IRRA, Academy of Mgmt, Human Resource Planning Soc, Amer Compensation Assn. POSITION: Asst Prof, 345 H Commerce Bldg, Univ of Kentucky, Lexington, KY 40506. 606/257-2927

FEARN, ROBERT MORCOM Acad: Econ; Consulting. AA 1950, Boston U; BS 1952, MA 1955, Wash State U; PhD 1968, U of Chicago. PUBL: Labor Economics: The Emerging Synthesis, Winthrop 1981; "Employer-Employee Interaction and the Duration of Unemployment," QJE, Mar 1980; "Cylical, Seasonal and Structural Factors in Area Unemployment Rates," ILRR, April 1975. INT: labor market econ, empl/trng programs, income maint. ASSN: AEA, Southern Econ Assn. POSITIONS: Asst Prof, 1965, Assoc Prof, 1968, and, since 1975, Prof of Econ and Bus, North Carolina State Univ, Raleigh, NC 27650. 919/737-2605

FECHTER, ALAN E. Acad: Economics. BBA 1958, CUNY; AM 1962, U of Chicago. PUBL: Public Employment Programs, Amer Enterprise Institute, 1975; "Arab Scientific Manpower in the United States," in The Arab Basin Drain, A. B. Zahlan, ed, 1981; "Health Conditions and Earnings Capacity: A Human Capital Model," in Policy Analysis with Social Security Research Files, Soc Sec Admin, 1979. INT: labor market econ, empl/trng programs, method/statis. ASSN: Wash DC IRRA, AEA. POSITIONS: Sr Res Assoc, Urban Inst, 1972; Head, Scientific & Tech Pers Studies Section, Div of Science Resource Studies, Natl Science Found, 1978; and (since 1983) Executive Dir, Office Sci/Engineering Pers JH 604, National Academy of Sciences, 2101 Constitution Ave NW, Washington DC 20418. 202/334-2700

FEDRAU, RUTH Consulting, Ind Rels. BA 1951, U of Calif-Berkeley. INT: empl/trng programs, coll barg, org beh. POSITION: Project Director, Bus Consulting Service, National Alliance of Business, Wash. ADDRESS: 2727 29th St NW #121, Washington DC 20005. 202/289--2908

FEGATILLI, DIANE Professional Assn. ADDRESS: 9520 Marine Memorial Dr, Niagara Falls, NY 14304. 716/297-3425

FEIGENBUAM, ARMAND VALLIN, Bus: Pers/Ind Rels. BA 1942, Union Coll; MS 1948, PhD 1951, MIT. PUBL: Total Quality Control, 1983, 1961, 1951; Managment Programming, 1980; The Organization Process, 1980. INT: mgmt/educ, labor market econ, org beh. ASSN: AEA, IEEE, Intl Academy of Quality. POSITION: President & C.E.O., General Systems Co. ADDRESS: 123 Ann Dr, Pittsfield, MA 01201. 413/499-2880

FEIGENBAUM, CHARLES Arbitration. BA 1952, Brooklyn Coll, MA 1961, American U; MS 1974, Cornell U. PUBL: "Final Offer Arbitration: Better Theory Than Practice," in Ind Rels, Oct 1975; The Union Impact on Job Evaluation and Pay Administration," in Job Evaluation and Pay Administration in the Public Sector," H. Suskin, ed, IPMA, 1977; "The Relation of Arbitration and Administrative Procedure in the Discipline and Discharge of Federal Employees," in Labor Law J, Sept 1983. INT: arb/med, coll barg, labor law. ASSN: Wash DC and Maryland IRRAs, AAA, SPIDR, Soc of Federal Labor Rels Professionals. POSITIONS: Chief, Coll Barg Section, Internal Revenue Service, 1973; Deputy Asst Dir for Labor-Mgmt Rels, U.S. Office of Pers Mgmt, 1976, and (since 1982), Arbitrator (self-employed). ADDRESS: 14020 Breeze Hill Lane, Silver Spring, MD 20906. 301/460-7300

FEIN, MITCHELL Consulting. BSME 1937, NYU. PUBL: Industrial Engineering Handbook, Wiley 1982. INT: Productivity Mgmt. ASSN: New York IRRA, Inst of Ind Engineers, Inst of Mgmt Consultants. POSITION: (since 1942) President, Mitchell Fein, Inc., 202 Saddlewood Dr, Hillsdale, NY 07642. 201/664-2055

FEINAUER, DALE M. Acad: Org Beh/Pers, Bus Admin. BA 1978, MLHR, 1982, PhD 1983, Ohio State U. INT: personnel, empl/trng programs, labor market econ. POSITIONS: Grad Res Asst, Center for Human Resource Res, 1978, and (since 1983) Asst Prof, Coll of Bus Admin, Univ of Wis-Oshkosh. ADDRESS: 307 Fulton Ave, Oshkosh, WI 54901. 414/488-9236

FELDACKER, BRUCE S. Arbitration. 705 Olive St, Suite 500, St. Louis, MO 63101. 314/-231-2970

FELDMAN, LLOYD Government. INT: empl/-trng programs, govt labor policy, intl comparative labor. ASSN: Wash DC IRRA. POSITION: Director, Office of Planning and Policy Analysis, Empl and Trng Admin, USDL, Wash DC. ADDRESS: 7916 Maryknoll Ave, Bethesda, MD 20817. 202/376-6274

FELDMAN, MARVIN J. Arbitration, Legal Prac. BBA 1952, JD 1955, Western Reserve U. ADDRESS: 340 Western Reserve Bldg, 1470 W 9th St, Cleveland, OH 44113. 216/781-6100

FELHAUER, LARRY WAYNE Student. BSBA 1969, Mich Tech U. INT: labor law, EEO/AAP, arb/med. ADDRESS: 1733 Molitor Rd, Aurora, IL 60505. 312/898-4368

FELLER, DAVID E. Acad: Law, Ind Rels. AB 1938, LLB 1941, Harvard. PUBL: "A General Theory of the Collective Bargaining Agreement," 61 Calif L Rev 663, 1973; "Arbitration: The Days of Its Glory Are Numbered," 2 Ind Rels Law J, 97, 1977; "The Remedy Power In Grievance Arbitration," 5 Ind Rels Law J 128, 1982. INT: labor law, coll barg, arb/med. ASSN: San Francisco IRRA, NAA, AAUP, ABA (Labor & Empl Section). POSITIONS: General Counsel, Ind Union Dept, AFL-CIO, 1961, United Steelworkers of Amer, 1961, and (since 1967) John H. Boalt Prof of Law, School of Law, Univ of Calif, Berkeley, CA 94720. 415/642-0629

FELLMAN, GERRY L. Arbitration, Legal Prac. BSL 1954, LLR & JD 1956, U of Nebr; MAIR 1959, U of Minn. INT: arb/med. ASSN: Southern Calif IRRA, NAA, SPIDR, Calif State Bar Assn (Labor & Empl Law). POSITIONS: Field Attorney, NLRB, 1959; Lawyer, Dept of Ind Rels, Div of Labor Law, State of Calif, 1963, and (since 1967) Arbitrator of Labor/Mgmt Disputes, (self-employed), 1557 Beverly Blvd, Los Angeles, CA 90026. 213/250-8317

FERGUSON, TRACY H. Legal Prac.; Acad: Ind Rels. AB 1931, Syracuse U; LLB 1934, Harvard. INT: labor law, mgmt/educ, arb med. ASSN: Syracuse IRRA, ABA, New York State Bar, Onondaga County Bar. POSITION: Senior Partner, Bond Schoeneck & King, 1 Lincoln Center, Room 1720, Syracuse NY 13202. 315/422-0121

FERMAN, LOUIS A. 130 S First St, Ann Arbor, MI 48108.

FERNANDEZ, MANUEL Government. Cert-IR, 1981, BLS 1982, St. Louis U. INT: coll barg, arb/med, org beh. ASSN: Gateway IRRA. POSITIONS: Inland Steel, 1948; Staff Rep, United Steelworkers of Amer, 1965; and (since 1972) Commissioner, FMCS, 12140 Woodcrest, Suite 325, St. Louis, MO 63141. 314/576-3805

FERRARO, JEAN Bus:Pers/Ind Rels. POSITION: Director Human Resources, Bowen Tools Inc, PO Box 3186, Houston, TX 77253. 713/868-8867

FERREE, JAMES L. Government. BA 1969, Wesleyan U. INT: coll barg, labor law, public sector labor rels. ASSN: Cincinnati IRRA, ASPA. POSITIONS: Supervisory Examiner, Subregion 38, Peoria, 1971, Operations Examiner, Div of Operations Mgmt, Wash DC, 1973, and, since 1975, Asst to the Regional Director, Region 9, NLRB, 3003 Federal Office Bldg, 550 Main St, Cincinnati, OH 45202. 513/684-3625

FERRELL, DAVID LEE Bus:Pers/Ind Rels; Acad: Ind Rels, Student. BS 1983, W Va. Inst of Tech. INT: personnel, labor law, health & hosp care. POSITION: (since 1983) Personnel Asst, Charleston Area Medical Center Memorial Div. ADDRESS: PO Box 287, Glasgow, WV 25086. 304/595-2444

FERRIS, GERALD R. Acad: Org Beh/Pers. BS 1973, MS 1976, Ill State U; PhD 1982, U of Ill-Champaign. PUBL: Personnel Management, (w Rowland); "Social Facilitation: A Review & Alternative Conceptual Model," Academy of Mgmt Rev; "Casual Attributions and Expectations for a Day's Work Performance," Academy of Mgmt J. INT: personnel, org beh, method/-statis. ASSN: Academy of Mgmt, Amer Psych Assn, ASPA. POSITIONS: Assoc Dir of Org Res, Inst for Personality and Ability Testing, 1976-79; Asst Prof of Quantitative Methods, Ill State Univ, 1981; and (since 1982) Asst Prof of Mgmt, Dept of Mgmt, Texas A & M Univ, College Station, TX 77843. 409/845-4839

FERRIS, JOHN E. Legal Practice. ADDRESS: 110 Brentwood Dr, Syracuse, NY 13219. 315/488-2659

FESKO, ROBERT J. Bus:Pers/Ind Rels. POSITION: Director, Employee Rels Administration, American Motors Corp, 5626 25th Avenue, Kenosha, WI 53140. 414/658-6278

FEUILLE, PETER Acad: Ind Rels, Arbitration. BA 1967, Claremont Men's Coll; PhD 1973, U of Calif-Berkeley. PUBL: "Behavioral Research in Industrial Relations," (w D. Lewin), Ind & Labor Rels Rev, 36, 3, Apr 1983; "Equal Employment Opportunity Bargaining," (w D. Lewin) Ind Rels, 20, 3, Fall, 1981; "Selected Benefits and Costs of Compulsory Arbitration, Ind & Labor Rels Rev, 33, 1, Oct 1979. INT:

arb/med, coll barg, labor law. ASSN: Academy of Mgmt, AAA, SPIDR. POSITIONS: Asst Prof of Mgmt, Univ of Oregon, 1972; Asst Prof of Mgmt, SUNY-Buffalo, 1974; and (since 1977) Prof of Labor and Ind Rels, Univ of Illinois, 504 E Armory Ave, Champaign, IL 61820. 217/333-1489

FIBISH, NANCY CONNOLLY Government. BA 1957, St. Joseph Coll, MD. PUBL: "The Board of Inquiry: A New Dimension in Private Sector Health Care Collective Bargaining," Handbook of Health Care Pers Mgmt, Germantown & London, Aspen Systems Corp, 1981; "A Mediator's View of Federal Sector Labor Relations," Public Pers Admin & Labor Mgmt, Prentice Hall, 1974; "Is Mediation an Art or a Science?" IRRA Conference Working Paper, 1975. INT: foreign service, Dept of State, political cone. ASSN: Wash DC IRRA, ASPA, Soc of Federal Labor Rels Professionals, Sr Exec Assn. POSITIONS: Natl Mediator Rep; Health Care and Age Discrimination Act Coordinator, 1977, Asst Reg Dir, FMCS, 1981; and (since 1983) International Rels Officer, Foreign Service, Dept of State, Office of Intl Devel, Room 5333, Main State Bldg, Washington DC 20520. 202/632-1016

FIDANDIS, NICHOLAS ANDREW Mediator. AB 1961, George Washington U. INT: arb/med, coll barg, govt labor policy. ASSN: Wash DC IRRA, SPIDR, Assn of Labor Rels Agencies. POSITIONS: Mediator, 1966, Director, Mediation Services, FMCS, 1979; and (since 1983) Chairman, Joint Labor Mgmt Committee of the Retail Food Industry, Wash DC. ADDRESS: 7914 Jansen Dr, Springfield, VA 22152. 202/331-0950

FIEDLER, SUSAN Acad: Student, Ind Rels; Retail Sales. BSW 1983, U of Ill. INT: health & hosp care, empl/trng programs, labor law. ADDRESS: 608 S State St #1, Champaign, IL 61820.

FIGLER, ROBERT ALBERT Acad: Ind Rels, Org Beh/Pers, Bus Admin. BA 1976, Ind U of Penna; MA 1980, ABD 1982, W Va U. PUBL: "Work Interruptions in the Underground Coal Mining Industry: The Coal Miner's Perspective." INT: coll barg, org beh, arb/med. ASSN: AEA. POSITION: Asst Prof-Bus Admin, Eastern Kentucky Univ, 215 Combs Hall, Richmond, KY 40475. 606/622-3742

FILGUT, PAUL ROSS Acad: Student, Labor Studies. BS 1983, U of Wis-Madison. INT: arb/-med, govt labor policy, coll barg. POSITIONS: Student-Univ of Mass-Amherst. ADDRESS: 6500 N Keating, Lincolnwood, IL 60646. 413/546--1055

FILIPPELLI, RONALD LEE Acad: Labor Studies. PhD 1968, Penna State. INT: labor history, intl comparative labor. POSITION: (since 1982) Prof & Head, Dept of Labor Studies, Penna State Univ, 901 Liberal Arts Tower, University Park, PA 16802. 814/865-5425

FILLION, JOHN A. Acad: Law. BA 1950, Lawrence Coll; JD 1953, U of Mich. POSITIONS: General Counsel, 1973, and, since 1983, Special Counsel, Intl Union, UAW, 8000 E Jefferson, Detroit, MI 48214. 313/926-5216

FINA, PAUL J. Acad: Student, Econ. BA 1982, MA 1983, U of Ill. INT: labor law, labor econ, arb/med. ASSN: LIRA-U of Ill. POSITIONS: Grad Teaching Asst, U of Ill, 1982; and, currently, Student, ILIR-Univ of Ill, and Law Student, Washington Univ-St. Louis. ADDRESS: 222 Scottswood, Riverside, IL 60576. 217/333-1000

FINE, JOEL MARC Bus:Pers/Ind Rels. BA 1976, Albion Coll; MA 1983, U of Ill. INT: personnel, income maint, org beh. POSITIONS: Pers Specialist, General Foods Corp, 1979; and (since 1983) Compensation Analyst, Milgo, 8600 NW 41st St, Miami, FL 33166. 305/591-5490

FINE, NED ARNOLD Legal Practice. BA 1962, Tufts U; JD 1970, U of Calif-Berkeley. INT: labor law, arb/med, coll barg. ASSN: San Francisco IRRA. POSITIONS: Partner, Morrison & Foerster, 1970; and (since 1982) Fisher & Phillips, Hearst Bldg, 5 3rd St, Suite 925, San Francisco, CA 94103. 415/974-6160

FINEGAN, THOMAS ALDRICH Acad: Econ, Ind Rels. BA 1951, Claremont Men's Coll; PhD 1960, U of Chicago. PUBL: The Economics of Labor Force Participation, (w W. G. Bowen), 1969; "Discouraged Workers and Economic Fluctuations," Ind Rels and Labor Rels Rev, vol 35, Oct 1981, pp 88-102; "Hours of Work in the U.S.: A Cross Sectional Analysis," J of Political Econ, vol 70, Oct 1962, pp 452-470. INT: labor market econ, govt labor policy, coll barg. ASSN: AEA, Southern Econ Assn. POSITIONS: Asst Prof of Econ, Princeton Univ, 1960; Assoc Prof of Econ, 1965, and since 1970, Prof of Econ, Vanderbilt Univ, Nashville, TN 37235. 615/322-3445

FINSTON, HOWARD V. Acad: Human Resources Mgmt; Arbitration, Consulting. AB & AM 1948, PhD 1953, Stanford U. PUBL: Selected Cases in Labor Relations-An Experiential Approach, (w J. L. Porter), Reston Publ Co, 1983; Selected Cases in Labor Relations-Case Awards and Opinions, (w J. L. Porter), Reston Publ Co, 1984. INT: arb/med, org beh, mgmt/educ. ASSN: AAA. POSITIONS: Sr Partner, Management Devel Systems, 1965; and (since 1953) Prof, Human Resources Mgmt, Anderson Grad School of Mgmt, Univ of New Mexico, Albuquerque, NM 87131. 505/277-2639

FIORITO, JACK T. Acad:Ind Rels, Org Beh/Pers, Econ. BS 1974, AM 1976, PhD 1980, U of Ill. PUBL: "Determinants of U.S. Unionism: Past Research and Future Needs," (w C. P. Greer), Ind Rels, vol 21, #1, Winter 1982, pp 1-32; "The School to Work Transition of College Graduates," Ind & Labor Rels Rev, vol 35, #1, Oct 1981, pp 103-114; "The Determinants of Occupational Unionization," (w C. Dauffenbach) J of Labor Res, vol III, #4, Fall 1982, pp 473-485. INT: union org/admn, coll barg, labor market econ. ASSN: Academy of Mgmt. POSITIONS: Res Assoc, U of Ill, 1978; Asst Prof of Mgmt, Okla State Univ, 1979; and (since 1982) Asst Prof of Ind Rels, Univ of Iowa. ADDRESS: 3323 Shamrock, Iowa City, IA 52240. 319/353-4400

FIRESTONE, BERNARD J. Union. BA 1957, LB 1959, Wayne State U. ASSN: Detroit IRRA. POSITION: Secretary/Treas, Chicago and Central States Joint Board, ACTWU, AFL-CIO, 1550 Howard, Detroit, MI 48216. 313/961-3085

FIRESTONE, FREDERIC N. Adac: Law; Arbitration. BA 1948, Olivet Coll Mich; MS 1952, PhD 1958, U of Wis-Madison; MSL 1979, Yale; JD 1981, U of Va. PUBL: Marginal Aspects of Management Practices; "Economic Change: Newtonian or Darwinian?" "Paradigm and Analysis in Evolutionary Economics." INT: labor law, arb/med, coll barg. ASSN: AEA, ABA. POSITIONS: Prof of Econ, Ill State Univ, 1970; Visiting Prof of Econ, U of Va, 1979; and (since 1982) Assoc Prof of Law, Oklahoma City Univ, School of Law, 2501 N Blackwelder, Oklahoma, OK 73106. 405/521-5185

FISCHER, BEN Acad: Labor Rels, Public Policy; Arbitration. PUBL: "State of Labor Relations," CMU Conference, 1983; "New Challenges for Labor and Management Achieving a Cooperative Climate," NYU Conference, June, 1983; "Evaluating the Steel Industry Consent Decree," Rutgers U Symposium on EEO, Nov 1975. INT: arb/med, coll barg, empl/-trng programs. ASSN: Pittsburgh IRRA. POSITIONS: Intl Rep, 1941, Asst to Pres, United Steelworkers of America, 1960; and (since 1980) Director, Center for Labor Studies and Adjunct Prof of Ind Rels, School of Urban and Public Affairs, Carnegie Mellon Univ, Pittsburgh, PA 15213. 412/578-2177

FISCHER, LYDIA HELENA Union; Acad: Labor School. PhD 1971 U of Wis-Madison.PUBL: "Auto Crisis and Union Response", in Labor and Technology, Penn State U, 1981. INT: coll barg, govt labor policy, method/statis. ASSN: Union of Radical Political Econ, AEA. POSITION: Research Assoc, UAW Intl Union, 8000 E Jefferson, Detroit, MI 48214. 313/926-5256

FISCHER, RUDOLF L. Bus:Pers/Ind Rels. POSITION: Personnel, Bechtel Power Corp, 50 Beale St, San Francisco, CA 94105. 415/768-3862

FISCHNALLER, JOSEPH E. Legal Practice. BA 1968, Central Wash Coll; JD 1973, Gonzaga U. PUBL: "Technical Preparation and Exclusion of Photographic Evidence," Pers Injury Annual, M. Bender & Co, 1974. INT: labor law, coll barg, arb/med. ASSN: Northwest IRRA, ABA, Wash State Bar Assn, Wash State Trial Lawyers Assn. POSITIONS: Assoc, 1973, Partner, Reaugh, Hart, Allison, Prescott & Davis, 1977; and (since 1980) Founding Partner, Reaugh & Prescott, 3000 Westin Bldg, Seattle, WA 98121. 206/622-3000

FISH, HY Arbitration. MBA 1960, U of Chicago. INT: arb/med, coll barg, govt labor policy. ASSN: Chicago IRRA, AAA, Inst of Ind Engineers. POSITIONS: Asst Dir & Assoc Prof, Roosevelt Univ, 1947; Consulting Ind Engineer (self-employed), 1952; and (since 1948) Arbitrator, 5530 South Shore Dr, Chicago, IL 60637. 312/324-8420

FISHBURN, DREW H. Bus:Pers/Ind Rels. MA 1973, DAGS 1980, MLIR, 1983, Mich State U. INT: coll barg, arb/med, laborlaw. POSITIONS: Instructor, Lyman Briggs Coll, Mich State Univ, 1977, and (since 1981) Contract Administrator, Jones & Laughlin Steel Corp. ADDRESS: 2910 Jay Ave, Cleveland, OH 44113. 219/398-2416

FISHER, ANN D'ESTERRE Student-Docotoral Program, 407, Uris Hall, Columbia Univ, New York, NY 10027. 212/222-4558

FISHER, CARICIA J. Trade Assn, Attitudinal & Evaluation Res. BA 1976, Brown U; MSIR 1983, U of Wis-Madison. INT: labor market econ, empl/trng programs, labor history. ASSN: Washington DC IRRA. POSITIONS: Res Asst, Urban Inst, 1980; Project Asst, Intl City Mgmt Assn, 1981; and (since 1983) Res Assistant, American Council of Life Insurance. ADDRESS: 1851 Columbia Rd #509, Washington DC 20009. 202/862-4138

FISCHER, CLARENCE ROBERT Bus:Pers/Ind Rels. BS 1963, Mich Tech U. INT: coll barg, personnel, mgmt/educ. ASSN: Upper Peninsula Labor Mgmt Council, Edison Electric Inst Human Resource Planning & Develop Committee. POSITIONS: Sales Manager, 1973, Dir Consumer Rels, 1974, and, since 1975, Director of Pers and Ind Rels, Upper Peninsula Power Co, 616 Sheldon Ave, Houghton, MI 49931. 906/482-0220

FISHER, EDWARD GEORGE Acad: Ind Rels, Bus Admin, Econ. BA 1967, U of Colo, MA 1970, Ind U; PhD 1979, U of B.C. PUBL: "Police Bargaining in Canada: Private Sector Bargaining, Compulsory Arbitration and Mediation-Arbitration in Vancouver," (w H. Starek) in B. M. Downie and R. L. Jackson eds, Conflict and Cooperation in Police Labour Relations, Hull: Supply and Services, 1980, 35-61; "Strike Activity and Wildcat Strikes in British Columbia: 1945-75," Rels Industrielles, 37:2, 1982, 284-312; "The Impact of Unanticipated Output and Consumer Prices on Wildcat Strikes," Rels Industrielles, 38:2, 1983, 254-276. INT: arb/med, coll barg, labor law. ASSN: SPIDR, Canadian Ind Rels Assn, Canadian Econ Assn. POSITIONS: Teaching Asst, Dept of Economics, 1971-71, Sessional Lecturer, Faculty of Commerce, Univ of British Columbia, 1974; and (since 1977) Assoc Prof (1980-83) Faculty of Bus, Dept of Ind Rels and Legal Rels, Univ of Alberta, 3-21D Faculty of Bus Bldg, Edmonton, Alberta T6G 2G1 Canada. 403/432-3054

FISHER, PATRICK J. Arbitration. AB 1936, JD 1937, Notre Dame. INT: arb/med, coll barg. ASSN: NAA. POSITION: Arbitrator (self-employed, 107 N Pennsylvania St #907, Indianapolis, IN 46204. 317/637-1456

FISHER, PAUL Consulting; Acad: Econ, Ind Rels. JD 1930, U of Vienna. PUBL: Retirement Age: An International Perspective, (w S Rix), Pergamon Press, 1982; "The Social Security Crises-An International Dilemna," in Aging and Work, Winter 1978, ISSA-Geneva, 1978 and in French, German & Spanish; "Labor Force Participation of the Aged and the Social Security Systems in Nine Countries," Ind Gerontology, Winter 1978. INT: income maint, govt labor policy, intl comparative labor. ASSN: AEA, AAA, Editorial Advisory Board "Aging and Work". POSITIONS: Sr Res Econ, ILO, Geneva, 1968-1969; Chief, Intl Staff, Social Security Admin, HHS, 1963-1978; and (since 1978) Retired. ADDRESS: 7025 Bybrook Lane, Chevy Chase, MD 20815.

FISHER, STEPHEN TODD Government. BA 1963, Washington & Jefferson Coll; MBA 1965, Cornell. INT: mgmt/educ, health & hosp care, personnel. POSITIONS: Director of Mgmt Educ, Naval School of Hosp Admin, 1976, Executive Officer, Naval School of Health Sciences, 1979, and since 1982, Enlisted Community Mgr, Hosp Corpsmen & Dental Technicians, U.S. Navy. ADDRESS: 4301 Sheridan St, University Park, MD 20782. 202/694-5596

FISHMAN, HARRY Arbitration, Union; Acad: Sociology. BA 1938, Brooklyn Coll; MA 1965, New School for Social Res. PUBL: "Encyclopedia of Sociology-Collective Bargaining; "Analysis of Bridgeport Regional Economy in Event of Reduction of Defense Analysis." INT: arb/med, coll barg, ind sociol. ASSN:

Amer Sociol Assn. POSITIONS: Prof and Chairman, Dept of Sociol, Fairfield Univ, 1967; Staff Rep, Council #4, AFSCME,AFL-CIO, 1976; and (since 1982) Alternate Labor Member, Conn State Board of Mediation and Arbitration. ADDRESS: 10 Ermine St, Fairfield, CT 06430. 203/566-4394

FITCH, DAVID PAUL Student. MS 1976, Iowa State U. INT: labor law, coll barg. POSITION: Student, William Mitchell Coll of Law. ADDRESS: 1259 Avon St N, St. Paul, MN 55117.

FITCH, MARY Student. MS 1975, Iowa State U. PUBL: "Subjective Expected Utility and Academic Preferences," (w Paulm & Muchinsky) Organizational Behaviour and Human Performance, 14, pp 217-226, 1975. INT: compensation, org beh, personnel. ASSN: Amer Compensation Assn. POSITIONS: Human Resources Mgr, 1981, Org and Compensation Planner, Northern Telecom Inc, 1982; and (since 1982) Teaching Asst (Doctoral Grad student) Univ of Minn. ADDRESS: 1259 Avon St N, St. Paul, MN 55117. 612/376-2618

FITCH, STONA J. Bus:Pers/Ind Rels. BA 1955, U of Okla. POSITION: (since 1983) Manager, Ind Rels Div, Proctor & Gamble Co, Ivorydale Technical Center, Cincinnati, OH 45217. 513/627-6343

FITTON, PATRICIA A. Union. ADDRESS: 214 Laurel St, Hartford, CT 06105. 203/246-1828

FITZGERALD, MARK J. AB 1928, U of Notre Dame; MBA 1931, Harvard; PhD 1950, U of Chicago. Prof Emeritus, U of Notre Dame. ADDRESS: PO Box 476, Notre Dame, IN 46556. 219/239-6213

FITZGERALD, WILLIAM T. Acad: Law, Student. BIA 1983, General Motors Inst. INT: labor law, arb/med, labor market econ. ASSN: Amer Marketing Assn. Student Member of Bar. POSITIONS: Manufacturing Engineer, GM Assembly, 1978; and (since 1983) Student, Coll of Law, Univ of Okla. ADDRESS: 248 Hal Muldrow Court, Norman, OK 73069.

FITZPATRICK, ROBERT Acad: Psych, Org Beh/Pers; Consulting. PhD 1953, U of Pittsburgh. INT: ind psych, org beh, personnel. ASSN: Western Penn IRRA, Amer Psych Assn, Amer Educ Res Assn, Academy of Mgmt. POSITION: (since 1979) Assoc Prof, St. Francis Coll, 111 Wood St, Pittsburgh, PA 15222. 412/765-2246

FLAGLER, JOHN J. Acad: Ind Rels. 11810 54th Ave, Plymouth, MN 55442. 612/559-4644

FLAHERTY, BERNARD Bus:Pers/Ind Rels. POSITION: Cornell Univ, Conference Center, PO Box 1000, Ithaca, NY 14850. 607/256-2125

FLAMM, ARTHUR J. Legal Practice. BS 1948, Cornell U; LLB 1951, Harvard. INT: labor law, arb/med, coll barg. ASSN: ABA, AFL-CIO Lawyers Coordinating Committee. POSITION: (since 1951) Partner, Flamm & Birmingham, 50 Congress St, Boston, MA 02109. 617/720-3888

FLANAGAN, GEORGE JAY Government. BBA 1975, MSBA 1979, U of Mass. INT: labor rels-mass transit industry, arb/med, coll barg. ASSN: Washington DC IRRA. POSITIONS: Soc Insurance Rep, Soc Security Admin, 1975, and, since 1979, Ind Rels Specialist, USDL, Wash DC. ADDRESS: 112 W Marshall St, Falls Church, VA 22046. 202/357-0473

FLANAGAN, ROBERT JOSEPH Acad: Econ, Bus Admin, Law. BA 1963, MA 1966, Yale U; PhD 1970, U of Calif-Berkeley. PUBL: Unionism, Economic Stabilization and Incomes Policies, (w L. Ulman & D. Soskie), Brookings Inst, 1983; "Workplace Public Goods and Union Organization," Ind Rels, May 1983; "Wage Interdependence in Unionized Labor Markets," Brookings Papers on Econ Activity, 1976. INT: labor market econ, govt labor policy, coll barg. ASSN: AEA. POSITIONS: Senior Staff Econ, U.S. Council of Econ Advisers, 1978; Assoc Prof of Labor Econ, Stanford, 1975, and (since 1984), Senior Fellow, Brookings Inst, 1775 Massachusetts Ave NW, Washington DC 20036.

FLEGEL, JAMES RICHARD Student. BA 1969, Wash State U; BS 1982, MBA 1983, Oregon State U. INT: personnel, arb/med, labor law. ASSN: Oregon IRRA, Pacific Northwest Pers Mgmt Assn. POSITIONS: Supervisor, Charges and General Rev, Oregon State Empl Div, 1970; and (since 1981) Grad Student, Oregon State U. ADDRESS: 6264 13th NE, Salem, OR 97303.

FLEISCHLI, GEORGE ROBERT Arbitration. BS 1962, JD 1965, MA 1970, U of Ill. PUBL: "Some Problems with the Administration of Compulsory Final Offer Arbitration Procedures," 56 Chicago-Kent Law Rev, 559 1980; "The Uniformed Services," ch 24 in Portrait of a Process--Collective Negotiations in Public Employment, Labor Rels Press, 1979; "A Comparison of the Wisconsin and Federal Labor Relations Act," 2 Comparative Labor Law Rev, 1978. INT: arb/med, labor law, govt labor policy. ASSN: Wis IRRA, NAA, SPIDR, Wis Bar Assn. POSITIONS: Staff Mediator/Arbitrator, 1970, General Counsel, Wis Empl Rels Commission, 1975, and (since 1981) Arbitrator (self-employed). ADDRESS: 15 Hiawatha Circle, Madison, WI 53711. 608/255-7255

FLEISHMAN, WILLIAM E. Government. AB 1960, Rutgers U; PhD 1971, U of Mich, JD 1975, Fla State U. POSITION: Labor Rels Specialist, Federal Labor Rels Authority, 7612 14th St NW, Washington DC 20012. 202/653-7213

FLEISCHMANN, FRED L. Bus:Pers/Ind Rels. POSITION: Vice Pres-Pers, Alexander & Baldwin Co Inc, PO Box 3440, Honolulu, Hawaii 96801. 808/525-6684

FLEISCHMANN, ROSS A. Government, Consulting. BA 1955, Rollins Coll. INT: govt labor policy, personnel, mgmt/educ. ASSN: Intl Pers Mgmt Assn, Ill Labor History Soc, Southern Labor History Assn. POSITIONS: Dir, Ind Rels, Mil go Electronics Corp, 1968; Reg Pers Dir, Sonesta Intl Hotels, 1970; and (since) 1972) District Director, Empl and Labor Rels, U.S. Postal Service, Florida Dist. ADDRESS: 3609 Floyd Rd, Tampa, FL 33618. 813/228-2461

FLEMING, LORETTA A. Writing:worklife. MA 1931, Columbia. PUBL: "Work Humanization: Challenge or Threat?" Mgmt World, Mar 1975; "Let's Humanize the Unemployment Insurance System," Mgmt World, Nov 1980; "Success is a High I (P) Q-Improving the Quality of Worklife," J of Mgmt and Bus Consulting, Jan 1976. INT: quality of worklife. ASSN: The Improvement Inst, Natl Writers Club. POSITIONS: Occupational Analyst and Empl Specialist, 1952, Manager, Penn Bureau of Empl Security, 1967-1973; currently Writer/Worklife concerns. ADDRESS: 1240 Wyoming Ave, Exeter, PA 18643. 717/655-8072

FLETCHER, LOUISE J. Consulting. BE 1974, U of N. H.; MED 1983, Harvard. INT: peronnel, org beh, arb/med. POSITION: Consultant (self-employed), 85 Mt Auburn St, Watertown, MA 02172. 617/924-5294

FLORA, JUDITH A. Acad: Health Policy. BA 1975, Cornell. INT: health & hosp care, income maint, coll barg. ASSN: Coalition of Labor Union Women. POSITIONS: Ind Rels Specialist, USDL, 1975; Union Rep, United Steelworkers of Amer, 1980; and (since 1983) Policy Analyst, Health Policy Inst, Grad School of Public Health, Univ of Pittsburgh. ADDRESS: 340 S Highland, Pittsburgh, PA 15206. 412/624-6104

FLOREY, PETER Arbitration. LLB 1950, U of Penna. INT: arb/med. ASSN: Philadelphia IRRA, NAA, AAA, SPIDR. POSITION: (since 1962) Labor Arbitrator, 310 Evans Ave, Haddonfield, NJ 08033. 609/354-1033

FLORKEY, ELLEN M. Bus:Pers/Ind Rels, Consulting. MAIR 1982, Wayne State U. INT: health & hosp care, arb/med, labor law. ASSN: Detroit IRRA, Ind Rels Assn of Detroit. POSITIONS: Dir of Pers, North Detroit General Hosp, Asst Admin, Plymouth General Hosp, 1979; and (since 1982) Pers Rep, Univ of Mich Hospitals, Ann Arbor. ADDRESS: 17566 Muirland, Detroit, MI 48221. 313/763-4600

FLORKOWSKI, GARY WALTER Student. 120 A Kings Park Dr, Liverpool, NY 13088.

FLYNN, THOMAS F. Bus:Pers/Ind Rels. AB 1955, Iona Coll; MBA 1967, NYU. POSITION: Empl Rels, IBM Corp, Old Orchard Rd, Armonk, NY 10504. 914/765-5046

FOEGEN, JOSEPH HENRY Acad: Ind Rels, Org Beh/Pers, Bus Admin. BBA 1954, MBA 1955, PhD 1959, U of Wis-Madison. PUBL: "Fringe Benefits Are Being Diversified Too," Industry Week, Oct, 1982; "Big Motherism," (concerned day-care centers,) Bus and Soc Rev, Spring 1982; "The Creative Flowering of Employee Benefits," Bus Horizions, May-June 1982. INT: personnel, org beh, mgmt/educ. ASSN: ASPA, Soc for Advancement of Mgmt, World Future Soc. POSITION: (since 1958) Prof of Bus, Dept of Bus Admin and Econ, Winona State Univ, Johnson & Sanborn St, Winona, MN 55987. 507/457-5190

FOGEL, WALTER Acad: Ind Rels. BS 1954, N Dak State U; MA 1957, U of Minn; PhD 1962, MIT. POSITION: Prof of Ind Rels, UCLA. ADDRESS: 15340 Albright, #109, Pacific Palisades, CA 90272.

FOISSOTTE, COLETTE M. Student. 4801 Greenwich Ct, Rolling Meadows, IL 60008. 312/397-4363

FOLCARELLI, JOHN WALSH Bus:Pers/Ind Rels, Arbitration; Student. BA 1974, New York U; MPA 1976, U of R.I. INT: arb/med, coll barg, labor law. ASSN: New York IRRA, AAA, ABA (law student), ASPA. POSITIONS: Examiner, Labor Rels, 1979, Supr, Labor Rels, Consolidated Rails Corp, 1981; and (since 1983) Asst Manager-Labor Rels, Metro-North Commuter Railroad Co, 347 Madison Ave, Room 1805, New York, NY 10017. 212/340-2254

FOLEY, MARY COSGROVE Student. BA 1982, U of Colo. INT: health & hosp care, personnel, ind psych. ASSN: LIRA-U of Ill. ADDRESS: 1402 Grandview, Champaign, IL 61820.

FOLTMAN, FELCIAN N. Acad: Ind Rels. POSITION: Prof, Manpower Studies, NYSSILR-Cornell. ADDRESS: 140 Northview Rd, Ithaca, NY 14850. 607/256-2273

FORBES, PATRICIA Bus.Pers/Ind Rels; Acad: Bus Admin. EdD 1981, VA Polytech Inst & State U. PUBL: "Personnel Administrator," 3rd Annual IRRA Academic Seminar. INT: arb/med, labor law, personnel. POSITIONS: Lecturer, Va Tech, 1982; Asst Prof, U of North Fla, 1983; and (since 1983) Research Specialist, AT&T. ADDRESS: 12463 Attrill Rd, Jacksonville, FL 32223. 904/636-2286

FORD, LUCILLE G. Acad: Univ Admin. BS 1944, MBA 1945, Northwestern U; PhD 1967, Case Western Reserve. PUBL: Economics: Learning and Instruction; "Freedom is Not Free;" "Banking is Ideal Example of Government Regulation." INT: labor market econ, mgmt/-educ, personnel. ASSN: AEA, Amer Private Enterprise Assn, Amer Assn Pol Soc Scientists. POSITIONS: Dir, Gill Center Bus/Econ, 1970, Dean, Special Programs, 1977, and, since 1979, Vice Pres, Dean School of Bus, Ashland Coll, Ashland, OH 44805. 419/289-5132

FORKOSCH, MORRIS DAVID Acad: Ind Rels, Law; Arbitration. LLB 1930, 1932, St. John's U; BA 1936, MA 1938, JSD 1948, NYU; PhD 1952, MSSc 1956, New School for Soc Res. PUBL A Treatise on Labor Law, 2nd Ed,1969; Constitutional Law, 2nd Ed, 1968; Outer Space and Legal Liability, 1982. INT: arb/med, coll barg, labor law. ASSN: Assn of Bar-NYC, AEA, Amer Pol Sci Assn. POSITIONS: Prof, Chairman, Dept Public Law, Brooklyn Law School, 1949; Prof, Cardozo Law School, 1981; and (since 1931) Private Law Practice, 88 Bleeker St, #4N, New York, NY 10012. 212/475-8861

FORMAN, HOWIE Union. BA 1966, NYU; MA 1971, San Francisco State U. INT: coll barg, labor history, union org/admin. ASSN: AEA. POSITIONS: Res Assoc, United Electrical Workers, 1972; Ind Economist, Intl Div, IRS, U. S. Dept of Treasury, 1980; and (since 1984) Research Associate, UFCW, 1775 K St NW, Washington DC 10025. 202/223-3111

FORST, ROBIN ILENE Bus:Pers/Ind Rels. MS 1976, Cornell. INT: personnel, org beh. ASSN: Amer Compensation Assn, ASPA. POSITIONS: Compensation Specialist, 1970, Pers Mgr, 1978, and, since 1981, Assoc Director Compensation, American Broadcasting Co, Inc, 1345 Ave of the Americas, 27th Floor, New York, NY 10019. 212/887-5458

FORSYTHE, EDWIN J. Acad: Ind Rels. PhD 1956, U of Mo. INT: arb/med, coll barg, govt labor policy. ASSN: Detroit IRRA, NAA. POSITIONS: Professor 1956, and, since 1958, Assoc Dir, Inst of Labor & Ind Rels, Wayne State Univ, Detroit, MI 48202. 313/577-4552

FOSS, GARY CLARE Bus:Pers/Ind Rels. BA 1960, San Jose State U; MPA 1975, USC. INT: govt labor policy, coll barg, arb/med. ASSN: San Francisco IRRA, IPMA. POSITIONS: Dir Empl Rel/Pers, County of Santa Clara, 1973, Consultant, 1976; and (since 1980) Director,

Empl Rels, Envirotech Operating Services, One Waters Park Drive, San Mateo, CA 94403. 415/349-9291

FOSSUM, JOHN ANTHONY Acad: Ind Rels; Consulting. BA 1961, St. Olaf Coll; MA 1968, U of Minn; PhD 1975, Mich State. PUBL: Labor Relations: Developments, Structure, Process; Personnel/Human Resource Management, (co-author); The Collective Bargaining Process, (co-editor). INT: personnel, coll barg. ASSN: Acad of Mgmt. POSITIONS:Instructor, U of Wyo, 1972; Asst Assoc Prof, U of Mich, 1974; and (since 1983) Assoc Prof, Ind Rels Center, Univ Minnesota, 537 Mgmt/Econ Bldg, 271-19th Ave S, Minneapolis, MN 55455. 612/376-7-21

FOSTER, DONALD Bus:Pers/.Ind Rels. BA 1950, St. Lawrence U. INT: coll barg, empl/-trng programs, arb/med. ASSN: Central New York IRRA, Amer Soc of Safety Engineers, ASPA, North Country Pers Assn. POSITIONS: Pers and Safety Dir, Gouverneur Talc Co, 1950; Corp Dir of Pers, R. T. Vanderbilt Co, 1965; and (since 1971) Vice Pres, Empl Rels, New York Air Brake Co-General Signal, Starbuck Ave, Watertown, NY 13601 315/782-7000

FOSTER, HOWARD GEORGE Acad: Ind Rels. BA 1964, Brandeis U; MILR 1966, PhD 1969, Cornell. PUBL: Open Shop Construction; Manpower in Homebuilding. INT: coll barg, arb/med, labor law. ASSN: Western New York IRRA, AAA, NAA POSITIONS: Assoc Dean, 1976, and, since 1981, Prof and Chairman, Dept of Org and Human Resources, SUNY, Crosby Hall, Buffalo, NY 14214. 716/831-2358

FOSTER, JAMES D. Union. POSITION: Bus Manager, Sheet Metal Workers, Local #2, PO Box 8, Kansas City, MO 64141. 816/531-8021

FOTTLER, MYRON DAVID Acad: Bus Admin, Univ Admin, Ind Rels. BS 1962, Northeastern U; MBA 1963, Boston U; PhD 1970, Columbia U. INT: empl/trng programs, personnel. ASSN: Academy of Mgmt, Southern Mgmt Assn. POSITIONS: Prof of Health Care Mgmt, 1976, and, since 1983, Prof of Mgmt and Director of PhD Program in Admin Health Services, Grad School of Mgmt, Univ of Alabama, Univ Station, Birmingham, AL 35294. 205/934-5661

FOULKES, FRED KLEE Acad: Ind Rels, Org Beh/Pers; Consulting. AB 1963, Princeton U; MBA 1965, DBA 1968, Harvard Bus School. PUBL: Personnel Policies in Large Non Union Companies, Prentice Hall, 1980; Human Resource Management: Text v Cases, (w E. Livernash), Prentice Hall 1982; Employee Benefits Handboook, Editor, 1982. INT: personnel, coll barg, mgmt/educ. ASSN: Boston IRRA, Human Resources Council of Amer Mgmt Assn, ASPA, Amer Compensation Assn. POSITIONS: Asst Prof, 1970, Assoc Prof, Harvard Univ, 1975; and (since 1980) Prof of Mgmt Policy and Director of the Human Resources Policy Inst, School of Mgmt, Boston Univ, 621 Commonwealth Ave, Boston, MA 02215. 617/353-4281

FOX, EDWARD M. Union. INT: arb/med, coll barg, union org/admin. POSITIONS: Intl Rep, 1975, and, since 1976, Director, Grievance Dept, AFSCME, Council 13, AFL-CIO, 301 Chestnut St, 5th FL, Harrisburg, PA 17101.

FOX, MARION B. Acad: Empl Planning, Ind Rels; Research. MCP 1969, PhD 1979, U of Penn. PUBL: "Working Women and Transportation: The Access of Women to Work and to Community Facilities," J of the Amer Planning Assn, Spring 1983. INT: empl/trng programs, govt labor policy, coll barg. ASSN: Philadelphia IRRA, Amer Planning Assn, Policy Studies Org. POSITIONS: Prof, Labor Force Policy and Planning, Rutgers U, 1980; Prof Labor Force Policy and Coll Barg, Drexel Univ, 1982; and currently, Consultant and Researcher, Marion B Fox, Empl Planning and Research, 211 Marvin Rd, Elkins Park, PA 19117. 215/635-2516

FOX, MARY P. Acad: Educ. BA 1954, Rice Inst; MEd 1973, Texas A & M U. INT: coll barg, arb/med, labor educ. ASSN: Texas State Teachers Assn, Assn of Professional Educators. POSITIONS: Special Educ Admin, 1975, and, currently, fourth grade teacher, Bryan I.S.D. ADDRESS: PO Box 3151, Bryant, TX 77805.

FOX, MILDEN J., JR. Acad: Ind Engineering; Arbitration. BS 1949, MS 1953, Okla A & M Coll; PhD 1969, Tex A & M U. PUBL: Labor Relations and Collective Bargaining: A Bibliographic Guide to Doctoral Research, The Scarecrow Press; "The Scope of Teacher Bargaining," in Collective Bargaining Techniques in Education; "The Referral Policy Revisited..from Spielberg to Suburban Motor Freight." INT: arb/med, coll barg, labor law. ASSN: Greater Houston IRRA, SPIDR, Inst of Ind Engineers, AAA. POSITIONS: Reg Mgr, Clayton Manufacturing Co, 1962, and (since 1965) Prof, Industrial Engineering Dept, Texas A & M Univ. ADDRESS: PO Box 3151, Bryan TX 77805. 409/845-5531

FOY, MARY CHRISTINE Bus:Mgmt. ADDRESS: 1600 Filbert St #3, San Francisco, CA 94123.

FRANCIS, EDNA E.J. Legal Practice. ADDRESS: Suite 1155, 417 S Hill St, Los Angeles, CA 90065. 213/620-1748

FRANK, MURRAY W. Acad: Social Policy, Univ Admin. PhD 1974, Brandeis U. PUBL Job Training for the Poor; "University and the Community;" "Women and Poverty." INT: income maint, empl/trng policy, org beh. ASSN: Natl Assn of Social Workers, Mass Assn for Mental Health. POSITIONS: Prof, Rutgers Univ-Livingston Coll, 1971; Educ Dir, AFSCME Council 37, 1974; and (since 1979) Prof of Community Service, Univ of Mass, Boston, MA 02125. 617/929-7274

FRANK, ROBERT M. Bus:Mgmt. POSITION: General Manager, House of Ronnie, Route 9, Box 104A, Johnson City, TN 37601. 615/928-8261

FRANKE, ARNOLD Acad: Bus Admin, Org Beh/Pers; Arbitration. BS 1955, Eastern Ill U; MS 1960, Purdue U; PhD 1970, Sussex Coll. PUBL: "The Role of Personnel in Improving Productivity," Pers Admin, Mar 1982; "A New Look at Management Techniques," NACUBO Bus Office, Dec 1980. INT: arb/med, mgmt/educ, coll barg. ASSN: Gateway IRRA, ASPA, Acad of Mgmt. POSITIONS: Labor Rels Analyst, Shell Oil Co, 1960; Dir of Pers, Catalytic Construction Co, 1965, and (since 1970) Director, Small Bus Devlop Center, Southern Ill Univ, Edwardsville, IL 62026. 618/692-2929

FRANKE, WALTER H. Acad: Ind Rels, Univ Admin; Arbitration. BS 1950, St. Olaf Coll; MS 1951, PhD 1955, U of Wis-Madison.

PUBL: "The Changing Bargaining Structure in Construction: Wide-Area and Multicraft Bargaining," (w P,. Hartman), ILRR, 1980. INT: labor market econ, arb/med, coll barg. ASSN: AAUP. POSITIONS: Prof of Labor and Ind Rels, 1957, and, since 1981, Director (and Professor) Inst of Labor and Ind Rels, Univ of Illinois at Urbana-Champaign, 504 E Armory Ave, Champaign, IL 61820. 217/333-1480

FRANKLIN, LINDA ROBINS Arbitration. BA 1940, MA 1950, New York U. INT: arb/med, labor law, coll barg. ASSN: New York IRRA, AAA, SPIDR, New York Pers Mgmt Assn. POSITIONS: Dir of Pres and Labor Rels, Jewish Theological Seminary, 1950-62; Dir of Labor Rels, Community Service Society, New York, 1963-81; and, currently, Arbitrator, 580 W End Ave, New York, NY 10024. 212/799-2666

FRANKLIN, SAM Government. POSITION: FMCS, Room 5421, 230 North 1st Ave, Phoenix, AZ 85025.

FRANS, KLAAS JAN Government. BA 1970, MPA 1978, Queens Univ, Kingston, Ont. INT: govt labor policy, arb/med, coll barg. ASSN: Inst of Public Admin of Canada, Economic Soc of Alberta. POSITIONS: Admin Coordinator, Ind Rels Centre, Queens Univ, 1970; Progam Coordinator, Mediation Services Branch, 1979, and (since 1982) Manager, Statistical Information, Planning and Research Branch, Alberta Dept of Labour. ADDRESS: 18415-81 Avenue, Edmonton, Alberta T5T 1A6 Canada. 403/427-8531

FRANZ, VERL R.W. Acad: Sociol; Consulting, Bus:Pers/Ind Rels. BS 1953, MS 1956, U of Wis-Madison; PhD 1969, Mich State U. INT: org beh, personnel, ind sociol. ASSN: Amer Soc Assn, Rural Soc Assn, Midwest Soc Assn. POSITIONS: Owner, Franz & Assoc, 1958, and (since 1980) Asst Prof, Dept of Sociol, Univ of Wis, 231 Clow Faculty Annex, Oshkosh, WI 54901. 414/233-2030

FRASER, CHRISTOPHER R.P. Consulting; Acad: Ind Rels. PhD 1975, U of Wis. PUBL: "Vancouver: A History of Conflict," (w S. Angel) in G. Hebert, ed, Labour Rels in the Newspaper Industry. INT: coll barg. ASSN: British Columbia IRRA. POSITIONS: Asst Prof, Univ of B.C., 1975; IndRels Manager, Employers Council of B.C., 1979; and (since 1980) Consultant. ADDRESS: 4607 Puget Dr, Vancouver, BC V6L 2V9 Canada.

FRAUNDORF, MARTHA NORBY Acad: Econ. BA 1968, Carleton Coll; MA 1971, PhD 1976, Cornell. PUBL: "The Effect of the Davis Bacon Act on Construction Costs in Rural Areas," The Rev of Econ & Statis, Feb 1984; "The Labor Force Participation-of-Turn-of-the-Century Married Women, J of Econ History, June 1979; "Relative Earnings of Native and Foreign-Born Women," Explorations in Econ History, April 1978. INT: labor market econ, govt labor policy, coll barg. ASSN: AEA. POSITIONS: Instructor, Mount Union Coll, 1973; Asst Prof, 1975, and since 1983, Assoc Prof, Dept of Econ, Oregon State Univ, Corvallis, OR 97331. 503/754-2321

FREDIAN, ALAN J. Acad: Univ Admin, Org Beh/Pers; Consulting. BSS 1952, St. Mary's Coll of Winona, MA 1954, Loyola U of Chicago; PhD 1956, Ill Inst of Tech. PUBL: Creativity and Innovation in Organizations; The Dynamics of Black Employee Relations. INT: org beh, mgmt/educ, personnel. ASSN: Chicago IRRA, Amer Psych Assn, Academy of Mgmt, ASPA. POSITIONS: President, Alan J. Fredian & Assoc, 1965, and (since 1969) Dir, Inst of Ind Rels, Loyola U, 820 N Michigan Ave, Chicago IL 60611. 312/670-3134

FREEDMAN, AUDREY Business Analyst, Consulting. BA 1952, Wellesley. PUBL: "Last Rites for Pattern Bargaining," Harvard Bus Rev, Mar-Apr 1982; "Japanese Management of U.S.Workforces," The Conference Board, 1983; "Labor Outlook, 1984," The Conference Board, 1983. INT: labor market econ, mgmt/-educ, coll barg. ASSN: AEA. POSITIONS: Economist, USDL, 1961; Consultant, Organization Resource Counselors Inc, 1973; and (since 1975) Senior Research Assoc, The Conference Board. ADDRESS: 100 Ash Drive, East Hills, LI, NY 11576. 212/759-0900

FREEDMAN, MARCIA Acad: Human Resources. AB 1943, U of Mich; MS 1947 Columbia; PhD 1962, NYU. POSITIONS: Consultant, Pres Committee on Juvenile Delinquency & Youth Crime, 1962-64; Dir, Youth-Work Program Rev, Natl Comm on Employment of Youth, 1962-65, and currently, Senior Research Assoc, Conservation of Human Resources, Columbia Univ, 2880 Broadway, New York. NY 10025. 212/280-2301

FREEMAN, DAVE Arbitration, Consulting; Acad: Law. BBA 1952, U of Mich; JD 1955, Stanford U. Publ: "A Unified System for Employment Resources," 7 Inst Monograph Series, Northeastern Univ, 1969; "Professionlism Trends Toward Unionism," Calif Librarian, vol XXXVII, #4, Oct 1976; "Two Priorities For Public Managers," Sage Publ, The Bureaucrat, vol 5, #3, Oct 1976. INT: arb/med, govt labor policy, labor market econ. ASSN: Northern Calif IRRA, Soc of Fed Labor Rels Professionals, American and State Bar Assn (Labor & Empl Law Section). POSITIONS: Prof of Law, Willamette Univ, 1981; Prof of Law and Asst Dean, McGeorge School of Law, Univ of the Pacific, 1982, and, currently, Labor Arbitrator and Consultant Committee of Bar Examiners, State Bar of California, 209 Country Pl #162, Sacramento, CA 95831. 916/422-0400

FREILICHER, FREDERIC Legal Practice. 1637 Montague St NW, Washington DC 20011. 202/633-4510

FREILICHER, MIRIAM S. Legal Practice. 1637 Montague St NW, Washington DC 20011.

FREMONT, JOSEPH W. Bus:Mgmt/Admin. POSITION: Labor Rels Supr, City of Detroit, 304 City-County Bldg, Detroit, MI 48226. 313/224-3873

FRENCH, JOHN L. Acad: Org Beh/Pers, Ind Rels. BA 1965, Wesleyan U; MS 1971, MIT; PhD 1977, Cornell. PUBL: "Compensation of National Union Presidents," J of Labor Res, V 4, Summer 1983, pp 225-237; "Attitudes Toward Unionization In An Employee Owned Firm in the Southwest," Work and Occupations, 1984; "Role Allocation Processes in Public Bureaucracies," Administration & Society, v 12, Feb 1981, pp 399-426. INT: org beh, intl comparative labor, union org/admin. ASSN: Acad of Mgmt, Amer Sociol Assn, Latin Amer Studies Assn. POSITIONS: Asst Prof, Northwestern Univ, 1977; Asst Prof, 1978, and, since 1982, Assoc Prof of Management, Mgmt Dept, Univ of Texas, Arlington, TX 76019. 817/273-3852

FRENCH, WENDELL LOWELL BA 1948, MPS 1949, U of Colo, EdD 1956, Harvard. POSITION: (since 1958) Prof of Mgmt and Org, and Assoc Dean, Univ of Washington, Grad School of Bus. Retired. ADDRESS: 17364 Beach Drive NE, Seattle, WA 98155. 206/367-0538

FRENZEL, K. ARNOLD Acad: Econ, Ind Rels. MA 1964, U of Wash. PUBL: "Health Economics: A Subdiscipline?" (w D. J. McCready) Econ Devel & Cultural Change, Jan 1979; "Economics of Education: The Development of a Subdiscipline," (w D. J. McCready), Amer Economist, Spring 1982; "Introductory Economics Texts-A Differentiated Product?" Eastern Econ J, Apr-June 1983. INT: labor market econ, health & hosp care, coll barg. POSITIONS: Asst Prof, 1966, and, since 1969, Assoc Professor, Wilfrid Laurier Univ, Waterloo, Ontario N2L 3C5 Canada. 519/884-1970

FRIED, MORRIS L. Acad: Labor Educ, Sociology. BA 1951, U of Buffalo; MA 1959, PhD 1964, New School for Social Research. PUBL: "Expanding Options for Worker Education," (co-author) in P.E. Barton, ed, Implementing New Education-Work Policies, Calif, Jossey Bass, 1978; "Labor Looks At Lifelong Learning," Wash DC, Natl Inst of Educ, 1977; "Social Stratification and Mental Illness," in R. Konig & M. Tonnesmann, eds, Problems of Medical Sociology, Cologne, 1970. INT: labor educ, intl comparative labor, ind sociol. ASSN: Conn Valley IRRA, AAUP, Amer Sociol Assn, Univ & Coll Labor Educ Assn. POSITIONS: Assoc Prof, Sociol Dept, SUNY-Buffalo, 1964; Dir, Labor Educ Center & Prof of Sociol, Georgia State Univ, 1978; and (since 1981) Prof, Labor Education Center, Univ of Conn. ADDRESS: 6 Patriots Square, Freedom Green, RFD 3, Willimantic, CT 06226. 203/486-3417

FRIEDMAN, ABRAHAM Acad: Ind Rels. POSITION: School of Business Admin, Hebrew Univ, Jerusalem, Israel.

FRIEDMAN, BRUCE Consulting. BA 1962, MBA 1964, Univ of Chicago. PUBL: "Executive Compensation," 1973 Proceedings, Natl Conf, Amer Compensation Assn; "Stock Option Successes," (Comment), Harvard Bus Rev, Mar-Apr 1978. INT: Compensation, org planning, mgmt/educ. ASSN: Chicago IRRA, Inst of Mgmt Consultants, ASPA, Amer Compensation Assn. POSITIONS: Manager, Human Resource Consulting, Peat, Marwick, Mitchell & Co, 1969; Dir, Human Res Consulting, Coopers & Lybrand, 1975, and (since 1980) President and Chief Exec Officer, Bruce Friedman & Assoc, 3520 Lake Shore Drive, Suite 113, Chicago, IL 60657. 312/929-2379

FRIEDMAN, BRUCE L. Consulting. 264 Avenue B, Lake Ronkonkoma, NY 11779.

FRIEDMAN, CLARA H. Arbitration. PhD 1962, Columbia. PUBL: "Arbitration of Discipline for Abuse of Mental Patients," Arbitration J, Sept 1978; "Education of NYC Public School Teachers: An Economic Analysis," Ind and Labor Rels Rev, Oct, 1964. INT: arb/med, govt labor policy, labor law. ASSN: New York IRRA, NAA, AAA. POSITION: Arbitrator, 200 Central Park South, New York NY 10019. 212/541-8897

FRIEDMAN, HARVEY LEONARD Acad: Univ Admin, Ind Rels, Political Sci. JD 1947, Boston U. PUBL: "Trade Unions and the Politics of Pre-Retirement Education," in New Directions in Pre-Retirement Education, C. Phillipion ed, B. Johnson Found, England 1983; "Labor Education on College and University Campuses," in Labor Educ Workers; "The Role of the AFL-CIO in the Growth of Public Sector Collective Bargaining," in Sorry..No Government Today, R.E. Walsh, ed. INT: labor educ, arb/med, union org/admin. ASSN: Boston IRRA, Boston Bar Assn, AAA, Univ & Coll Labor Educ Assn. POSITIONS: Asst N E Dir, ACTWU, 1949-65; Asst Dir and Asst Prof, 1965-70 and, since 1970, Prof and Dir Labor Rels & Res Center, Univ of Mass, Draper Hall, Amherst, MA 01003. 413/545-2884

FRIEDMAN, JACK J. Consulting. BA 1953, NYU. INT: public information. ASSN: Intl Assn of Bus Communicators, Publicity Club of New York. ADDRESS: Martin E Segal Co, 730 5th Ave, New York, NY 10019. 212/586-5600

FRIEDMAN, PAMALA F. Government. ADDRESS: 53 Homecrest Ct, Oceanside, NY 11572. 212/488-6286

FRIES, HENRY WILLIAM Acad: Ind Rels. Retired. ADDRESS: 2539 SE 34th St, Portland, OR 97202. 503/236-4201

FRIES, ROBERT T. Legal Practice; Acad: Law. BA 1969, JD 1972, Stanford U. INT: labor law, personnel, arb/med. ASSN: ABA (Labor & Empl), Calif State Bar (Law Section), Bar Assn of San Francisco. POSITIONS: Law Clerk, US District Court-SF, 1972; and (since 1973) Partner, Steinhart & Falconer, 333 Market St, Suite 3200, San Francisco, CA 94105. 415/-777-3999

FROMM, GERARD P. Bus:Pers/Ind Rels. MS 1972, U of Mass. INT: empl/trng programs, coll barg, personnel. ASSN: Amer Mgmt Assn, ASPA. POSITIONS: Manager Labor Rels, Canteen Corp, 1976; Dir, Labor Rels, 1980, and, since 1982, Director Human Resources, Interstate United Corp, 120 S Riverside Plaza, Chicago, IL 60606. 312/930-2321

FROMM, KENNETH N. Bus:Pers/Ind Rels. POSITION: Vice Pres, Human Resources, GTE Network Systems, 2500 W Utopia Rd, Phoenix, AZ 85207. 602/582-7002

FROST, CARL F. Consulting; Acad: Psychology. PhD 1948 Clark U. PUBL: The Scanlon Plan for Organization Development: Identity, Participation and Equity, (w J. H. Wakely, & R. A. Ruh), Mich State U Press, 1974; "The Scanlon Plan: Anyone for Free Enterprise?" Mich State U Bus Topics, Winter 1978, pp 25-33; "The Scanlon Plan at Herman Miller, Inc: Managing An Organization by Innovation," in The Innovative Org: Productivity Programs in Action, Pergamon Press/Work in America Series 63-87. INT: ind psych, org beh. ASSN: Amer Psych Assn, Mid West and Mich Psych Assn. POSITIONS: Instructor, Ind Rels Sector, MIT, 1946; Prof, Mich State Univ, 1949; and (since 1980) Partner, Frost, Greenwood & Assoc, 217 N Clippert St, Lansing, MI 48912. 517/332-8927

FRYE, JACK G. Consulting. POSITION: Economic Consultant, Room 1702, 111 N Wabash Ave, Chicago, IL 60602. 312/263-6153

FRYER, JOHN LESLIE Union. ADDRESS: Natl Union of Provincial Government Employees, 204-2841 Riverside Drive, Ottawa, Ontario K1V 8N4 Canada. 604/291-9611

FUJIWARA, MICHIO Acad: Ind Rels. POSITION: Dept of Bus Admin, Nanzan Univ, 18 Yamazato-Cho, Showa-Ku, Nagoya 466, Japan

FUKAMI, CYNTHIA G. Acad: Org Beh/Pers. BA 1973, MA 1975, U of Ill; PhD 1979, Northwestern U. PUBL: "Organization Design and Adult Development," (w D.T. Hall) in Res in Org Behaviour, B. Staw, ed, Vol 1, 1979, pp 125-167; "The Effect of Dual Career Marriages on Work-Related Outcomes," Eastern Academy of Mgmt Proceedings, 1981; "Organizational Participation: A Cross Validation Study," (w E. Larson & J. Alutto), Acad of Mgmt Proceedings, 1983. INT: org beh, mgmt/educ. ASSN: Academy of Mgmt, Amer Psych Assn. POSITIONS: Asst Prof, SUNY-Buffalo, 1978; and (since 1983) Asst Prof of Management, Coll of Bus Admin, Univ of Denver, University Park, Denver, CO 80208. 303/753-2489

FUKAMI, FUMIO Acad: Ind Rels. POSITION: Dept of Education, Shizuoka Univ, Ohya Shizuoka-Shi 422, Japan

FULLER, DEWEY C. Executive Director, Urban League, 2400 Reading Rd, Cincinnati, OH 45202.

FULMER, WILLIAM E. Acad: Ind Rels. ADDRESS: College of Bus, University of Alabama, Box J, University, AL 35486

FULRATH, THOMAS A. Bus:Pers/Ind Rels. POSITION: Vice Pres Personnel, Miller Brewing Co, 3939 W Highland Blvd, Milwaukee, WI 53208. 414/931-2044

FUNK, CHRISTINE M. Student. ADDRESS: 44 Pomeroy Terr, Northampton, MA 01060. 413/586-3614

FURDYNA, MICHAEL ADAM Government. ADDRESS: 263 Myrtle Avenue, Albany, NY 12208. 518/434-1034

FYLPOWYCZ, TARAS Government; Student. BS 1971, Southern Ill U. INT: govt labor policy, govt non-labor rels. POSITION: (since 1978) Auditor, Ill Dept of Public Aid, Chicago. ADDRESS: 6140 N Drake, Chicago, IL 60659. 312/793-8366

G

GABA, RICHARD M. Legal Prac, Arbitration. BS 1951, U of Penn; LLB 1954, LLM 1957, NYU. INT: labor law, coll barg, arb/med. ASSN: Long Island IRRA, New York State & Nassau County Bar Assn. POSITION: (since 1959) Senior Partner, Richard M. Gaba-Attorney at Law, 1055 Franklin Ave, Garden City, NY 11530. 516/742-0242

GABEL, SUKHREET Government. ADDRESS: 400 E 89th St, New York, NY 10128. 212/876-0526

GADON, HERMAN Acad: Bus Admin; Arbitration. PhD 1953, MIT. PUBL: Alternative Work Schedules, Addison-Wesley; Effective Behavior In Organizations, R.D. Irwin. INT: arb/med, labor law, org beh. POSITIONS: Prof, U of New Hampshire, 1964, and (since 1980) Prof, Coll of Bus Admin, San Diego State Univ. ADDRESS: 2235 Calle Guaymas, La Jolla, CA 92037. 619/265-5306

GAFNI, MIRIAM L. Legal Practice. AB 1963, Barnard Coll; JD 1967, Villanova U. INT: labor law, health & hosp care, arb/med. ASSN: Philadelphia IRRA, Philadelphia Bar Assn. POSITIONS: Partner (Assoc) Markowitz & Kirschner, 1974; Partner, Gafni & Goldstein, 1979; and (since 1981), Associate, Freedman and Lorry, P.C., 800 LaFayette Bldg, Philadelphia, PA 19106. 215/925-8400

GAGHEN, HARRY W. Acad: Econ. ADDRESS: Dept of Econ, Eastern Montana Coll, 87 Mountain View, Billings, MT 59101. 406/259-2926

GALE, EDWARD R. Union. AB 1977, AM 1981, U of Ill. INT: arb/med, coll barg, labor educ. ASSN: Phi Alpha Theta. POSITION: (since 1982) Asst Director of Research, Amalgamated Transit Union, Wash DC. ADDRESS: 4915 Battery La, #202, Bethesda, MD 20814. 202/537-1645

GALFAND, S. HARRY, Legal Practice. ADDRESS: Galfand, Berger Senesky, Lurie & March, 1737 Chestnut St 1200, Philadelphia, PA 19103.

GALIN, AMIRA Acad: Ind Rels, Org Beh/-Pers. DSC 1972 Technion-Israel. PUBL: "Workers Participation in Management," (w G.Y. Tabb) Pergamon Press 1970; Wage Indexation and Industrial Relations in Israel, labor & Society, July 1977; "Evaluating the Israel: Mediation Service," Intl Labor Rev, July-Aug 1979. INT: coll barg, arb/med, personnel. ASSN: IRRA-Israel, Academy of Mgmt. POSITIONS: Chairperson, OB Studies, Faculty of Mgmt, Tel-Aviv Univ, 1982; and (since 1983) Assoc Researcher, Inst of Ind Rels, Univ of Calif-Berkeley, 2521 Channing Way, Berkeley, CA 94720. 415/642-5452

GALL, GILBERT Acad: Labor Educ; Arbitration. BA 1974, Wayne State U; MA 1979, Oakland U; PhD 1984, Wayne State U. PUBL: "Heber Blankenhorn: The Publicist As Reformer," The Historian, Aug 1983; "Constant Vigilance: The Heritage of the AFL's Response to Right-To-Work Legislation, 1943-49," Labor Studies J, 1984. INT: labor history, labor educ, arb/med. ASSN: Univ & Coll Labr Educ Assn, Org of Amer Historians. POSITIONS: Workers' Compensation Claim Adjuster, Liberty Mutual Ins Co, 1976-78; and (since 1983) Asst Prof, Tenn Learning Center, Tenn State Univ, 10th & Charlotte, Nashville, TN 37203. 615/251-1112

GALLAGHER, DANIEL GERARD Acad: Ind Rels; Arbitration. BA 1972, Boston State Coll; MA 1974, PhD 1977, U of Ill. PUBL: "Isoquants, College Bargaining and Resource Allocation," J of Econ and Bus, vol 31 #3, Spring 1979; "Impasse Behavior and Tri-Offer Arbitration," Ind Rels, vol 21, #2, Spring 1982; "Integrating Collective Bargaining and Human Resource Management," in Research in Pers and Human Resources Mgmt, JAI Press, 1983. INT: coll barg, personnel, labor law. ASSN: Academy of Mgmt, AAA. POSITIONS: Asst Prof, U of Iowa, 1977; Visiting Asst Prof, U of Minn, 1980; and (since 1981) Assoc Prof, Dept of Ind Rels & Human Resources, Phillips Hall, Univ of Iowa, Iowa City, IA 52242. 319/-353-5921

GALLAGHER, DANIEL J. Acad: Bus Admin. BA 1968, MA 1972, PhD 1979, U of Cincinnati. PUBL: "A Readability Analysis of Selected Introductory Economics Textbooks," J of Econ Educ; "Textbooks in Management, Marketing and Finance..." J of Bus Educ. INT: personnel, mgmt information systems, mgmt/educ. ASSN: Academy of Mgmt. POSITIONS: Asst Prof of Mgmt, Niagara Univ, 1975, and (since 1979) Assoc Prof of Mgmt, Dept of BUAD, Salisbury State Coll, Salisbury, MD 21801. 301/543-6315.

GALLAGHER, G. BUD Legal Practice. ADDRESS: 7672 Chiselhampton St, Burnaby BC V5E 2L7 Canada. 217/525-8422

GALLAGHER, JAMES J. Labor Education. POSITION: Labor Ed & Res Center, Univ of Oregon, 154 PR Lucien Campbell, Eugene, OR 97403. 503/686-5054

GALLAGHER, JOHN OWEN Acad: Econ, Ind Rels. BA 1943, MA 1946, PhD 1953, Tufts U. Retired. ADDRESS: Apt 3, 120 Washinton St, East Orange, NJ 07017.

GALLENTINE, ROGER J. Consulting. POSITION: Manager, Arthur Young Co, Suite 2100, 777 E Wisconsin Ave, Milwaukee, WI 53202. 414/273-3340

GALLERY, MAUREEN L. Labor Market Analysis. Pacific Maritime Assn, 635 Sacramento St, San Francisco, CA 94111. 415/576-3241

GALVIN, MILES EUGENE Acad: Labor Educ, Ind Rels. BA 1949, Mexico City Coll; MS 1961, Cornell; PhD 1972, U of Wis. PUBL: The Organized Labor Movement in Puerto Rico, Assoc Univ Presses 1979; "Labor Studies: In Quest of Industrial Justice," (w R. Dwyer & S. Larson), Labor Studies J, Fall 1977; "Reaching Out: New York's Hispanic Leadership Training Project," Labor Studies J, Spring 1982. INT: labor educ, intl comparative labor, labor history. ASSN: New Brunswick IRRA, Workers Educ Local #19. POSITIONS: Dir, Labor Rels Inst, Univ of Puerto Rico, 1960, and (since 1975) Assoc Prof, Rutgers Univ. ADDRESS: 39 Colburn Rd, East Brunswick, NJ 08816. 201/932-7303

GANDEL, MATTYE Arbitration. BS 1964, U of Md; MPA 1982, New York U. INT: arb/med, coll barg, govt labor policy. ASSN: New Brunswick IRRA, ASPA. POSITION: (since 1982) Apprentice Arbitrator, Research Asst. ADDRESS: 520 Melrose Pl, South Orange, NJ 07079. 201/763-3271

GANNON, FRANK ARTHUR Arbitration. POSITION: President, Frank A Gannon & Assoc, 3180 Cairncross, Lake Orion, MI 48035. 313/693-8129

GANT, JOCELIND Acad: Univ Admin. ADDRESS: Affirmative Action, Univ of Mass, Harbor Campus, Boston, MA 02125. 617/929-7075

GANZ, SAMUEL Consulting. BS 1932, MS 1932, CCNY. INT: empl/trng programs, health & hosp care, labor law. POSITIONS: Pres, Econ & Manpower Corp, 1969; Prof/Dir Coop Educ, New York Inst of Tech, 1979; and (since 1983) President, Samuel Ganz & Associates Inc, 6700-192 St, Fresh Meadows, NY 11365. 212/454-0777

GARBARINO, JOSEPH W. Acad: Ind Rels, Bus Admin; Arbitration. BA 1942, Duquesne; MA 1947, PhD 1949, Harvard. PUBL: Faculty Bargaining: Change and Conflict, McGraw Hill, 1975; Wage Policy and Long Term Contracts, Brookings, 1961; Health Plans and Collective Bargaining, UC Press 1959. INT: coll barg, intl comparative labor, arb/med. POSITION: (since 1949) Prof/Dir, Inst of Business and Econ Research, Univ of Calif, Berkeley, CA 94720. 415/642-2025

GARCHIK, JEROME Legal Practice. BE 1975, Cooper Union; MIA 1967, Yale, JD 1971, Harvard. INT: labor law, union org/admin, arb/med. ASSN: San Francisco IRRA. POSITION: (since 1972) Attorney At Law, 240 Stockton ST, 10th Floor, San Francisco, CA 94108. 415/-986-6489

GARCIA, DAVID A. Acad: Student, Univ Admin. BA 1975, Stanford U; MAIR 1984, U of Ore. INT: arb/med, coll barg, labor law. ASSN: Calif Teachers Assn, Stanford Alumni Assn. POSITION: (since 1983) Equal Education Specialist, Affirmative Action Office, Univ of Oregon. ADDRESS: 2129 W 17th Ave, Eugene, OR 97402. 503/686-3123

GARCIA, MARTHA A. Union. BS 1975, Northwestern U. INT: union org/admin, coll barg, health & hosp care. ASSN: Chicago IRRA. POSITION: (since 1975) Assoc Administrator, Illinois Nurses Assn, 20 N Wacker Dr, Suite 2520, Chicago, IL 60606. 312/236-9708

GARDNER, PHILIP M. Bus:Pers/Ind Rels. BA 1967, Claremont Men's Coll; MA 1968, U of Calif-Berkeley. INT: coll barg, personnel, union org/admin. ASSN: San Francisco IRRA, ASPA, North Calif Human Resources Council. POSITIONS: Pers Mgr, Pacific Telephone, 1970; Labor Rels Asst, City of San Diego, 1977; and (since 1979) Manager, Labor Rels Planning, Pacific Telesis Group, 140 New Montgomery Room 800, San Francisco, CA 94105. 415/542-2116

GARNEL, DONALD Acad: Econ. BS 1955, Queens Coll; PhD 1966, U of Calif-Berkeley. POSITION: (since 1958) Prof, Dept of Econ, San Jose State Univ, 1884 Kirkmont Dr, San Jose, CA 95124. 408/265-0751

GARNHOLZ, EDWARD W. Legal Practice. BS 1943, JD 1947, Washington U-St. Louis. ADDRESS: Suite 11 Oxford Bldg, 141 N Meramec Ave, Clayton, MO 63105. 314/725-5430

GARNIER, KATHERINE 9611 W Lorraine Pl, Milwaukee, WI 53222. 414/453-5056

GARNIER, ROBERT CHARLES Consulting, Bus Mgmt/Admin. BS 1939, Purdue U. PUBL: "Structuring the Work Force," Intl City Mgmt Assn, Green Book 1976; "Maintaining Good Labor-Management Relations," APWA Reporter, 1977. INT: personnel, coll barg, empl/trng programs. ASSN: Wis IRRA, Intl Pers Mgmt Assn, Amer Public Works Assn, Intl City Managers Assn. POSITIONS: Chief Labor Negotiator, 1965-67, City Pers Director, City of Milwaukee, 1958-1981; and (since 1981) Pres, Fastback Ltd & Pers Mgmt Consultant, 9611 W Lorraine Pl, Milwaukee, WI 53222. 414/453-5056

GARRETT, SYLVESTER Arbitration. AB 1933, Swarthmore; MB 1936, U of Penn. INT: arb/med, coll barg, govt labor policy. ASSN: NAA, ABA. POSITION: Chairman, Iron Ore

Industry, Board of Arbitration, Box 158, Stahlstown, PA 15687. 412/471-1558

GARST, JAMES D. Union. 100 W 94th St, New York, NY 10025.

GARST, VOLTAIRINE Government. 100 W 94th St, New York, NY 10025.

GARVEY, JOHN JOSEPH Mediation. BA 1982, Marquette U. INT: arb/mred, coll barg, personnel. POSITIONS: Mayor's Office for Cultural & Community Affairs, Springfield, 1982, Computer Center Staff Asst, Westfield State Coll, 1982, and (since 1983) Project Coordinator-Dispute Resolutions, City of Springfield, 31 Elm St, Suite 231, Springfield, MA 01103. 413/787-6480

GARWOOD, THOMAS CHASON JR., Legal Practice. PO Box 231, Orlando, FL 32802.

GASTWIRTH, JOSEPH L. Acad: Statistics, Econ. BS 1958, Yale; PhD 1963, Columbia U. PUBL: "The Estimation of the Lorenz Curve and Gino Index," Rev Econ Stat 1972; "Defining the Labor Market for Equal Employment Standards," (w S. E. Haber) Monthly Labor Rev, Mar 1976; "Estimating the Demographic Mix of the Available Labor Force," Monthly Labor Rev, Apr 1980. INT: method/statis, labor market econ, labor law. ASSN: Amer Statis Assn, Inst of Math Statis, Econometric Soc. POSITIONS: Assoc Prof, Johns Hopkins U, 1964-72; Visiting Faculty Adviser, Office of Mgmt & Budget, 1972; and, currently, Prof, Dept of Statistics, George Washington Univ, 2201 G St NW, Washington DC 20052. 202/676-6548

GAT, NERI Bus:Pers/Ind Rels. Head of Pers Div, Koor Foods Ind Ltd, POB 1597, Haifa, Israel.

GATTI, MICHAEL R. Student, LeMoyne College. 401 B Sr Residence, Syracuse, NY 13214. 315/445-1256

GAUBECA, MICHAEL JESS Student; Hosp Data. MBA 1982, MAIR, U of Cincinnati. INT: labor market econ, method/statis, mgmt/educ. POSITION: (since 1973) Computer Operator, St. Elizabeth Medical Center Data Center, Dayton. ADDRESS: 2410 Ohio Ave #506, Cincinnati, OH 45219. 513/229-6688

GAUTHIER, FERNAND Research. ADDRESS: Institut de Productivite, Bureau 1509 Tour Sud, 1 Complexe Desjardins, Montreal PQ H5B 1B3, Canada. 514/873-7601

GAVIN, MORTIMER HUGH S. J. Clergyman Educator, Retired. ADDRESS: 761 Harrison Ave, Boston MA 02118. 617/536-9440

GAYER, PAUL DAVID Government. Acad: Econ, Ind Rels. POSITION: Labor Economist. Evaluation Director OEO, 202 Woodmoor Dr, Silver Spring, MD 20901. 202/254-5664

GEARE, ALAN JAMES Acad: Ind Rels. POSITION: Management Dept, Univ of Otago, PO Box 56, Dunedin, New Zealand

GEETER, JOAN Acad: Univ Admin. BA 1959, Bennington Coll; MA 1961, U of Penn; PhD 1977, U of Conn. PUBL: "On Determining Faculty Workload," J of Coll and Univ Law, vol 8, #2, 1981-82; "How to Read a Collective Bargaining Contract," J of Allied Health, Summer 1982; "Managing Collective Bargaining with Non-Faculty Personnel," Coll and Univ Pers Assn monograph, 1984. INT: coll barg, personnel, arb/med. ASSN: Hartford, Conn IRRA, Coll and Univ Pers Admin, Academy for Academic Pers Admin. POSITION: (since 1976) Asst Vice Pres for Academic Affairs, U-86, Univ of Connecticutt, Storrs, CT 06268. 203/486-4038

GEIGER, MARTHA Arbitration, Legal Practice. BA 1969, U of Calif; MA 1976, JD 1980, U of Pacific. PUBL: "The Right to Strike and the Rodda Act: A Shift in Bargaining Power," 10 Pacific Law J, (971) 1979. INT: arb/med, labor law, coll barg. ASSN: San Francisco IRRA, AAA, ABA, Ind Rels Assn of Northern Calif. POSITIONS: Attorney, Littler, Mendelson et al, 1980, Berman Cassel & Carter, 1981, and (since 1982) Labor Arbitrator, (Office of Donald Wollett), 2020 29th St, Suite 200, Sacramento, CA 95817. 916/731-4370

GEISSNER, JAMES W. Government, Consulting. BS 1966, U of Wis-LaCrosse; MA 1970, Wayne State U. PUBL: "Presenting Your Case to the Arbitrators," Intl Assn of Fire Chiefs, Feb 1978; "Orientation of Elected Offficals, Supervisors Essential," LMRS Newsletter, May 1978; "City Employment and Payrolls: 1977" Urban Data Service Report, Intl City Mgmt Assn, Feb 1979. INT: coll barg, arb/med, labor law. ASSN: Wis IRRA, Natl Public Empl Labor Rels Assn, Intl Pers Mgmt Assn, Wis Public Employer Labor Rels Assn. POSITIONS: Dir of Empl Rels, Tampa, FL 1975; Deputy Comm of Empl Rels, State of Minn, 1979; and (since 1982) City Labor Negotiator, City of Milwaukee, City Hall #701, 200 E Wells St, Milwaukee, WI 53202. 414/278-2356

GELTMAN, OSCAR Arbitration. POSITION: Attorney, 505 East 79th St, New York, NY 10021. 212/628-7666

GENDEL, EUGENE B. Acad: Econ. 1970 U of Conn; MA 1972, PhD 1979, Boston U. INT: labor market econ, Empl/trng programs, govt labor policy. ASSN: AEA, Eastern & Atlantic Econ Assn. POSITION: Asst Prof of Econ and Bus, Dept of Econ, Lafayette Coll, Easton, PA 18042. 215/250-5301

GENTILE, CHARLES Union. BS 1970, St. Joseph's Coll. INT: union org/admn, coll barg, health & hosp care. ASSN: Philadelphia IRRA. POSITION: (since 1966) Vice Pres, UFCW Local #1357, 210 E Courtland St, Philadelphia, PA 19120. 215/457-5200

GENTILE, JOSEPH Arbitration. INT: arb/med. ASSN: Central New York IRRA, SPIDR, NAA. POSITIONS: Director, Dist 50, ATW, 1955, and (since 1971) Arbitrator/Mediator, New York State Mediation Board, 335 E Washington St, Syracuse, NY 13202. 315/428-4068

GENTILE, PATRICIA CONNOLLY Bus:Pers/-Ind Rels. BA 1976, Rutgers U; MBA 1978, New York U. INT: personnel. ASSN: New Brunswick IRRA. POSITION: Personnel Dir, New Brunswick Scientific Co, Inc. ADDRESS: Cokesbury Rd, Annandale, NJ 08801. 201/287-1200

GENTRY, JOHN NEWTON Arbitration. ADDRESS: Suite 414, 1211 Connecticutt Ave NW, Washington DC 20036. 703/435-1129

GEORGE, CHARLENE A. Union. POSITION: Teamster Joint Council 56, 5031 N Woodland, Kansas City, MO 64118.

GEORGE, DANNY Bus:Pers/Ind Rels. Labor Rels, Whitaker Cable, 2801 Rockcreek Pkwy, PO Box 7499, North Kansas City, MO 64116.

GEORGE, JACK R. 5925 Vogel Rd, Mobile, AL 36609.

GEORGE, SCOTT W. Bus:Pers/Ind Rels. AB 1975, U of Ga; MLIR 1977, Mich State U. INT: ind sociol, personnel, org beh. ASSN: Wisconsin Rapids Area Pers Club. POSITIONS: Pers Mgr, 1978, Compensation Mgr, 1980, and, since 1981, Empl Rels Manager, Ore-Ida Foods, PO Box 10, Plover, WI 54467. 715/421-3400

GEORGE, TIMOTHY Bus:Pers/Ind Rels. BA 1979 Xavier U; MAIR 1983, U of Cincinnati. INT: personnel, labor law. POSITIONS: Planner, Cincinnati Inst of Justice, 1980, and (since 1984) Manager of Assoc Relations, Shillito Rikes. ADDRESS: 4424 Clifford Rd, Cincinnati, OH 45236. 513/369-7544

GERAGHTY, WILLIAM V. Acad: Ind Rels, Org Beh/Pers, Univ Admin. BA 1971, MA 1973, Fairfield U; MA 1979, Rutgers U. INT: coll barg, personnel, mgmt/educ. ASSN: Trenton IRRA. POSITIONS: Dir of Pers and Labor Rels, Middlesex County Coll, 1972-78, and (since 1978) Asst Dir of Pers, Office of Personnel Services, Princeton Univ, Clio Hall, Princeton, NJ 08544. 609/452-3276

GERARD, IRWIN Government. BS 1941, CCNY; MA 1947, Columbia U; MA 1969, New School for Social Research. POSITION: Commissioner, FMCS, 26 Federal Plaza, Room 2937, New York, NY 10278. 212/264-1013

GERATY, JOHN M. Legal Practice. ADDRESS: Burns Intl Security Service, PO Box 400, Briarcliff Manor, NY 10510. 914/762-1000

GERBER, CARO JANET Bus:Pers/Ind Rels. MA 1979, U of Ore. INT: personnel, coll barg, arb/med. ASSN: ASPA, Intl Pers Mgmt Assn, Montana Arbitrators Assn. POSITIONS: Pers Specialist, Pers Div Dept, 1979, Hearing Examiner, Board of Pers Appeals, 1981, and (since 1982) Pers Officer, Dept of Admin, State of Montana, Capital Station. ADDRESS: 418 N Benton, Helena, MT 59601. 406/444-4613

GERHART, BARRY ALAN Acad: Ind Rels, Org Beh/Pers. BS 1979, Bowling Green U. INT: personnel, coll barg, labor market econ. ASSN: Acad of Mgmt. POSITION: Student, U of Wis Madison, IRRI, 4226 Social Sci, Madison, WI 53706. 608/262-3707

GERHART, PAUL F. Acad: Ind Rels, Univ Admin; Arbitration. AB 1963, Princeton; MBA 1966, Wharton-U of PA; PhD 1973, Chicago U. PUBL: "Public Sector Impasse Procedures," in Advances in Industrial and Labor Rels, D. Lipsky & J. Douglas, eds, vol 2, 1984; "Maintenance of the Union-Management Relationship," in Pers and Labor Rels Handbook, ed by Rabin et al, 1983; "The Emergence of Collective Bargaining in Local Government," Public Pers Mgmt, vol 9, #4, 1980. INT: coll barg, arb/med, wage & salary admin. ASSN: Northeast Ohio IRRA, AEA. POSITIONS: Res Assoc, Brooking Inst, 1968; Asst Prof of LIR, U of Ill, 1969; and (since 1977) Assoc Prof of IR, 614 Sears Library, Case Western Reserve Univ, Cleveland, OH 44106. 216/368-2045

GERLACH, KNUT Acad: Econ. ADDRESS: Liepmannstr 9 B, 3000 Hannover 91, West Germany.

GERMANI, PHILIP J. Bus:Pers/Ind Rels. MBA 1981, Cleveland State U. INT: personnel, employee benefits, coll barg. ASSN: Northeast Ohio IRRA. POSITIONS: Grad Asst, Ind Rels Center, Cleveland State U, 1979; Empl Rels Mgmt Trainee, 1981, and, since 1983, Empl Benefits Coordinator, Reliance Electric Co. ADDRESS: 3591 W 134th St, Cleveland, OH 44111. 216/266-7615

GERSHENFELD, GLADYS Acad: Ind Rels., Arbitration. BS 1946, Boston U; MS 1951, Cornell. PUBL: "The Scope of Collective Bargaining," (co-author), Handbook on Public Pers Admin and Labor Rels, NY:Marsell Dekker 1983; "Making Better Use of the Arbitration Process, Proceedings, Ind Rels Conference, McGill Univ, 1982; "Significant Developments in Public Employment Disputes Settlement," (co-author), NAA Proceedings, BNA 1980,1981. INT: arb/med, coll barg, personnel. ASSN: Philadelphia IRRA, NAA, SPIDR, AAA. POSITION: (since 1973) Assoc Prof, School of Bus Admin, Philadelphia Coll of Textiles and Science. ADDRESS: 6109 West Mill Rd, Flourtown, PA 19031. 215/951-2818

GERSHENFELD, WALTER J. Acad: Univ Admin, Ind Rels; Arbitration. BS 1948, Temple U; AM 1949, PhD 1964, U of Penna. PUBL: "State and Local Interest Arbitration," Proceedings Natl Academy of Arbitration, BNA 1984; "Officer, Member and Steward Priorities for Local Unions," (co-author) Proceedings, IRRA 1982; "Industrial Peacemaker: The Contribution of George W. Taylor to Industrial Relations, (co-editor), U of Penn Press, 1979. INT: coll barg, arb/med, govt & hosp care. ASSN: Philadelphia IRRA, NAA, SPIDR, AAA. POSITION: (since 1982) Acting Dean, Ambler Campus, Temple Univ. ADDRESS: 6109 West Mill Road, Flourtown,PA 19031. 215/643-1200

GERSUNY, CARL Acad: Sociology. PhD 1968, Western Reserve U. PUBL: Punishment and Redress In A Modern Factory, 1973; Work Hazards and Industrial Conflict, 1981; "From Contract to Status: Perspectives on Employment Seniority," Sociological Inquiry, 54 Feb 1984, pp 44-61. INT: ind sociol, labor history. POSITION: Prof, Dept of Sociology, Coll of Arts and Sciences, Univ of Rhode Island, Kingston, RI 02881. 401/792-4138

GEWIN. MICHAEL E. Bus:Pers/Ind Rels. BS 1974, MA 1978, U of Ala. INT: coll barg, labor law, arb/med. ASSN: St. Louis Ind Rels Assn. POSITIONS: Manufacturing Supr, Burlington Industries, 1974; Ind Rels Supr, American Cyanamid Co, 1979; and (since 1981) Labor Rels Superintendent, Monsanto Co. ADDRESS: 4223 Fatima Dr, St Louis, MO 63123. 314/622-1565

GHANI, TEMBON BIN Acad: Ind Rels; Consulting. BA 1971, U of Malaysia; DIR 1975, Inst of Soc Studies-The Hague; MLIR 1981, Mich State U. INT: mgmt/educ, labor educ, coll barg. POSITIONS: Tutor, Univ of Malaysia, 1971, and (since 1982) Head of Department, National Productivity Center, PO Box 64, Petaling Jaya, Malaysia. Phone: 03-563688

GHERSON, DIANE J. Student. Sloan School of Mgmt, 50 Memorial Drive, Cambridge, MA 02139.617/547-8589

GHILARDUCCI, TERESA Acad: Econ, Ind Rels. AB 1978, PhD 1983, U of Calif-Berkeley. PUBL: "Student Employees Under HEERA." INT: labor market econ, coll barg, income maint. ASSN: AEA. POSITIONS: Res Asst, Inst of Ind Rels, UC-Berkeley, 1979, and (since

1983) Asst Prof, Dept of Economics, Univ of Notre Dame, Notre Dame, IN 46556. 219/239-6335

GHITELMAN, STEVEN G. Government. BA 1974, SUNY-Binghamton; MA 1977, U of Wis. INT: coll barg, intl comparative labor. POSITION: (since 1983) Vice-Consul, Consulate General of the U.S.A., Mexico. ADDRESS: Level B, American Consulate, PO Box 3088, Guadalajara, Laredo TX 78041.

GIBBERMAN, CLIFFORD T. Bus:Pers/Ind Rels. BA 1976, Queens Coll; MSILR 1982, New York Inst of Tech. INT: coll barg, arb/med, labor law. ASSN: New York IRRA. POSITIONS: Bus Rep, Local 115 Nursing Home & Hosp Empl Union, 1978, and (since 1979) Corporate Labor Rels Rep, Allied Maintenance Corp, New York. ADDRESS: 88-04 632nd Dr, Rego Park, NY 11374. 212/868-5414

GIBBONS, JOHN E. Bus:Pers/Ind Rels. BS &ILR 1959, Cornell. INT: coll barg, labor market econ, labor law. POSITION: (since 1982) Vice President-Ind Rels, Guy F. Atkinson Company of Calif. ADDRESS: 246 El Granada Blvd, El Granada, CA 94018. 415/876-1396

GIBSON, E. L. Bus:Mgmt/Admin. POSITION: Executive Director, Guam Employers Council, PO Box BV, Agana Guam 96910.

GIBSON, GILES H. Union. ADDRESS: PO Box 6298, Santa Rosa, CA 95406. 707/545-7349

GIBSON, RANKIN MACDOUGAL Legal Practice, Arbitration; Acad: Law. LLB 1939, U of Mo; BSL 1949, St Paul Coll of Law; LLM 1951, George Washington U. INT: laborlaw, arb/med, coll barg. POSITIONS: Member, Public Utilities Commission of Ohio, 1962; Judge, Supreme Court of Ohio, 163-65; and (since 1965) Partner, Lucas, Pendergast, Albright, Gibson & Newmann, Columbus. ADDRESS: 7355 Feder Rd, Galloway, OH 43119. 614/228-5711

GIEBEL, RICHARD EARL Bus:Pers/Ind Rels. BA 1973, MLIR 1975, Mich State U. INT: empl relations, coll barg, personnel. POSITION: Supervisor, Labor Rels, Hourly Pers and Safety, Ford Motor Co, Dearborn Glass Plant. ADDRESS: 9377 Niver, Allen Park, MI 48101. 313/322-7781

GIFFORD, ADAM Acad: Econ; Consulting. BA 1943, U of Portland; MA 1947, Stanford; PhD 1955, U of Wash. PUBL: "Unionization Among Campus Auxiliary Employees," (w R. S. Frentz),. J of Collective Negotiations Public Sector, vol 11 #1 1982, pp 51-57; "The Impact of Socialism on Work Stoppages," Ind Rels, Vol 13, May 1974, pp 208-212; "Costs and Benefits of Higher Education-'A Comment'," J of Human Resources, Vol V Spring 1970, pp 227-229. INT: labor market econ, coll barg, intl comparative labor. ASSN: San Diego IRRA, AEA, Western and Atlantic Econ Soc. POSITION: (since 1954) Prof of Econ and Dir, Institute of Labor Econ, San Diego State Univ, San Diego, CA 92182. 619/265-5471

GIFFORD, NANCY PATON Bus:Pers/Ind Rels, Retail Mgmt. BA 1970, U of Colo; MS 1977 U of Utah. INT: personnel, org beh, coll barg. ASSN: Utah Univ IRRA, ASPA, Presidential Mgmt Intern Alumni Group. POSITIONS: Pres Mgmt Intern-Pers Mgmt, USDA Forest Service, Intermountain Region, 1978; Asst Manager, Jack Eckerd Corp, 1981. ADDRESS: 1406 30th Ave, Vero Beach, FL 32960.

GILES, ANTHONY JAMES Acad: Ind Rels, Sociol, Political Sci. BA 1978, Concordia U; MA 1980, Carleton U. PUBL: "The Canadian Labour Congress and Tripartism," Rels Industrielles, vol 37, #1, Jan 1982. INT: govt labor policy, intl comparative labor, political sociology. ASSN: Canadian Ind Rels Assn, Inst of Public Admin of Canada, Canadian Political Sci Assn. POSITION: Doctoral Student, School of Ind & Bus Studies, Univ of Warwick, 1980; and (since 1983) Asst Prof, Faculty of Admin, Univ of New Brunswick, Fredericton, NB E3B 6E5 Canada. 506/453-4869

GILLES, DONALD L., JR. Bus:Pers/Ind Rels. BA 1957, Monmouth Coll-Ill. POSITIONS: Div V.P.Ind Rels, RCA Corp, 1976; VP Empl Rels, 1980, and (since 1983) Senior Vice Pres Employee Rels, The Hertz Corp, 660 Madison Ave, New York, NY 10021. 212/980-2040

GILLIES, J.G. Consulting. MA 1973, Oxford U. PUBL: Human Relations in Industry: U.K. & USA; Communication in Trade Unions: U.K. & West Germany; The Management of Picketing. INT: empl/trng programs, intl comparative labor, labor educ. ASSN: British Univ Ind Rels Assn, Soc of Ind Tutors, Workers Educ Assn. POSITIONS: Asst Dir, I.R. Research, St. Edmund Hall, Oxford Univ, 1973; and (since 1983) Principal, J. G. Gillies & Assoc, Ind Rels Consultants, Redbrick House, NOKE, Oxford 0X3 9TX England. Phone: 08675 - 71405

GILLINGHAM, J. BENTON Acad: Ind Rels, Econ, Univ Admin, (Retired). BA 1939 Wash State U; MA 1942, U of Wis. PUBL: The Teamsters on the West Coast, Inst of Ind Rels-UC-Berkeley. INT: arb/med, coll barg, labor market econ. ASSN: Pacific Northwest IRRA, NAA, AAA. POSITIONS: Public Member & Chairman, U.S. Regional Wage Stabilization Board, 1951-53; Asst, Assoc & Full Prof of Econ, 1947-1977, (Retired), Emeritus Prof of Econ, Univ of Washington. ADDRESS: 17717 15th St NW, Seattle, WA 98177. 206/542-4765

GILLIS, MARILYN J. Bus:Mgmt/Admin, Bus:Pers/Ind Rels. BA 1957, Mich State U. INT: labor law, org beh, arb/med. ASSN: Chicago IRRA, Midwest Pers Managers Assn. POSITIONS: Manager, Empl Rels, Durkee Foods, 1978; Director Empl Rels, Spotnails, 1979, and, since 1983, Vice Pres, Administration, Veniculum Inc, Ace Fastener Co, 1100 Hicks Rd, Rolling Meadows, IL 60008. 312/259-1620

GILMAN, TAMARA ANN Acad: Bus Admin, Ind Rels; Arbitration. BA 1969, Northwestern U; MILR 1972, Cornell; MBA 1976, DBA 1981, Harvard. INT: coll barg, arb/med, union org/admin. ASSN: Boston IRRA, SPIDR, AAA, Acad of Mgmt. POSITIONS: Res Assoc, Harvard Bus School, 1976; Asst Prof, Northeastern Univ, 1980; and (since 1981) Lecturer, Babson College, Wellesley. ADDRESS: 4 Demar Rd, Lexington, MA 02173. 617/235-1200

GILMORE, CAROL BANKART Acad: Ind Rels, Bus Admin; Arbitration. BA 1962, Conn Coll; MS 1974, PhD 1979, U of Mass-Amherst. PUBL: "Education & Health Care: Does the Industrial Model Still Exist?" Labor Law J, vol 34, #5, May 1983; "Impact of Faculty Bargaining on the Management of Public Higher Educational Institutions," J of Coll Negotiations in the Public Sector, vol 10, #2, 1981; "Administrative Training & Collective Bargaining," J of the Coll & Univ Pers Assn, vol 31, #2, Summer 1980. INT: arb/med, labor law, personnel. ASSN: Acad of Mgmt, SPIDR, AAA. POSITIONS: Public Member-Chairman, Maine Board of Arbitration & Conciliation, 1982; and (since 1977) Assoc Prof of Mgmt, Univ of Maine at Orono, 24 South Stevens Hall, Orono, ME 04469. 207/581-1970

GILROY, CURTIS LLOYD Government. MA 1966, U of Toronto; MBA 1967, McMaster U; PhD 1973, SUNY-Binghamton. PUBL: "Time Series Evidence of the Effect of the Minimum Wage on Youth Employment and Unemployment," J of Human Resources, Winter 1983, pp 3-31; "The Effect of the Minimum Wage on Employment and Unemployment," J of Econ Literature, June 1982, pp 487-528; "The Effects of the Business Cycle on the Size and Composition of the U.S. Army," Atlantic Econ J, Mar 1983, pp 42-53. INT: labor market econ, method/statis. ASSN: AEA, Natl Economists Club. POSITIONS: Staff Economist, Natl Commission on Employment and Unemployment Statistics, 1977; Senior Economist, 1979, and, since 1981, Chief, Manpower & Pers Policy Research, U.S. Army Research Inst. ADDRESS: 10504 William Terry Dr, Vienna, VA 22180. 202/274-5610

GILSON, JAMES EDWARD Student. ADDRESS: 3324 Alabama Ave S, St Louis Park, MN 55416. 612/929-9756

GILSON, THOMAS QUINLEVAN Arbitration; Acad: Ind Rels, Org Beh/Pers. AB 1938, Princeton; MA 1942, Columbia; PhD 1954, MIT. PUBL: Executive Skills: Their Dynamics and Development, (w R. Bellows & G. Odiorne) P-H. 1962; "Public School Teacher Attitudes Toward Unionization," J of Collective Negotiations in the Public Sector, vol 11 #2, Aug 1982; "Employment Problems of Asian-Americans in Hawaii," 1st Conf on Empl Status of Asians-Americans, USDL 1978. INT: arb/med, coll barg, labor law. ASSN: Hawaii IRRA, NAA, AAA, Amer Psych Assn. POSITIONS: Prof & Chairman of Mgmt Dept, Rutgers U, 1952; Prof of Mgmt & Ind Rels, Coll of Bus Admin, U of Hawaii, 1964; and (since 1983) Arbitrator (and Prof Emeritus), Gilson Ltd, 2033 Nuuanu Ave, PH27-A, Honolulu, HI 96817. 808/536-6253

GINKEL, ALFRED OSCAR Acad: Univ Admin; Bus:Mgmt/Admin, Bus:Pers/Ind Rels. AB 1944, MS 1946, U of Rochester. INT: mgmt/-educ, org beh, intl comparative labor. ASSN: AEA. POSITIONS: Asia Area Manager, Sybron Corp, 1967; Vice Pres, Shinko Pfaudler Co, Japan, 1974; and (since 1983) President, Bacone College, Muskogee, OK 74403. 918/683-4581

GINSBURG, HELEN Acad: Econ. BA Queens Coll, MA & PhD 1947, New School for Social Res. PUBL: Full Employment and Public Policy: The United States and Sweden, Lexington Books 1983; Unemployment, Subemployment and Public Policy, New York Center for Studies in Income Maint Policy, 1975; Poverty, Economics and Society, Univ Press of America, 1981. INT: intl comparative labor, govt labor policy, income maint. ASSN: AEA, AFEA, Conference Group on Nordic Soc. POSITIONS: Asst Prof, Long Island Univ, Res Assoc Prof, New York Univ, 1977, and (since 1977) Assoc Prof, Dept of Econ, Brooklyn Coll of CUNY, Brooklyn. ADDRESS: 41-90 Frame Pl, Flushing NY 11355. 212/780-5317 (office); 212/358-2934 (home).

GINZBERG, ELI Acad: Econ. AB 1931, AM 1932, PhD 1932, Columbia U. PUBL: The Pluralistic Economy; The Human Economy; Good Jobs, Bad Jobs, No Jobs. INT: labor market econ, health & hosp care. ASSN: Inst of Medicine, AEA, Amer Acad of Arts and Sciences. POSITIONS: Director, Conservation of Human Resources, 1950, and, since 1979, Hepburn Prof Emeritus of Economics, Grad School of Bus, Columbia Univ, 525 Uris Hall, New York NY 10027. 212/280-3410

GIORDANO, DONALD A. Bus.Pers/Ind Rels, Bus:Mgmt/Admin. BS 1958, Rider Coll, NJ. INT: coll barg, personnel, labor law. ASSN: Central NJ and Lower Bucks County IRRA, Princeton Pers, NJ Bus & Industry, Delaware Valley Pers. POSITION: Vice Pres, Pers Rels, North American Philips Lighting Corp, 1 Westinghouse Plaza, Bloomfield, NJ 07003. 201/429-3000

GIROUX, MARIO Acad: Ind Rels. ADDRESS: 5275 Est St Zotique App 2, Montreal, Quebec H1T 1N7 Canada. 514/721-9330

GITELMAN, HOWARD M. Acad: Econ. AB 1954, U of Pittsburgh; MA 1957, PhD 1960, U of Wis. PUBL: In the Service of Millions, 1984; Workingmen of Waltham: Mobility in American Urban Industrial Development, 1850-1890, Johns Hopkins, 1974. INT: labor history, govt labor policy. ASSN: Econ History Assn, Labor Historians, Soc Sci History Assn. POSITIONS: Asst Prof, Brandeis Univ, 1960; Assoc Prof, Coll of William & Mary, 1966; and (since 1968) Professor, Dept of Econ, Adelphi Univ, Garden City, NY 11530. 516/746-3589

GITLOW, ABRAHAM L. Acad: Univ Admin, Ind Rels, Bus Admin. BA 1939, U of Penna; MA 1940, PhD 1947, Columbia U. PUBL: Labor and Manpower Economics, R. Dirwin, Homewood, Ill 1972, 3rd Ed; Economics, Oxford Press, NY 1962. INT: labor market econ, coll barg, labor law. ASSN: New York IRRA, AEA, Royal Econ Society, AAA. POSITIONS: Assoc Prof of Econ, 1954, Profof Econ, 1959, and since 1965, Dean, College of Bus and Public Admin, New York Univ. ADDRESS: Box 167, Spring Valley, NY 10977. 212/598-2235

GITTER, ROBERT J. Acad: Econ. Dept of Econ, Ohio Wesleyan Univ, Delaware, OH 43015.

GIUBILARO, PINA Student, McGill Univ. INT: personnel, coll barg, arb/med. ADDRESS: 4935 Burel, St. Leonard, PQ HIS 1H5 Canada.

GIUGNI, GINO Acad: Law. POSITION: Prof of Labor Law, Univ of Roma, Via Ronciglione 5, Roma Italy.

GLADSTONE, ALAN Acad: Ind Rels, Law; Consulting. BA 1951, Brooklyn Coll; JD 1954, Yale. PUBL: Employers Associations and Industrial Relations: A Comparative Study, (ed w Windmuller) Oxford Press, 1984; "Shop Floor Participation," (w Essenberg) in H.C. Jain (ed) Worker Participation: Success and Problems, Praeger, 1980; "Trade Unions, Growth and Development," Labour & Society, IILS, Geneva, Jan 1980. INT: intl comparative labor, labor law, coll barg. ASSN: Intl Soc for Labor Law and Soc Security, IIRA, Societe Geneviose de Droit et Legislation. POSITIONS: Senior Specialist, Labor Law and Rels, 1958, Counselor, Labor Law and Relations, ILO, 1968, and (since 1975) Head, Ind Rels Sector, Intl Inst for Labor Studies, Geneva. ADDRESS: 3 Avenue de Bude, 1202 Geneva, Switzerland. Phone 99-88-30

GLASER, ROBERT Union. BS 1980, Antioch Coll. ASSN: Wis IRRA. POSITION: Asst Dir, Dist #32, United Steelworkers of America, Room 205, 615 E Michigan St, Milwaukee, WI 53202. 414/276-2781

GLASSBERG, ELYSE J. Consulting. BA 1977, Bard Coll; MA 1980, U of Ill. PUBL: The Empowerment of Union Women Handbook; "Organizing Clerical Workers," Working Women Magazine, Apr 1984; "Absent From the Agenda: A Report on the Role of Women in American Unions." INT: arb/med, empl/trng programs, labor market econ. POSITIONS: Project Dir, Coalition of Labor Union Women Center for Educ and Res, 1979; NYC Human Resources Admin, 1981; and (since 1982) Consultant, 46 9th Ave, Sea Cliff, NY 11579. 516/676-8920

GLASSER, JOSEPH Arbitration, Factfinding Mediation. BS 1947, MBA 1948, U of Penn. PUBL: Fundamentals of Applied Industrial Management, Branden Press, 1975; "Impasse Resolution Procedures," J of Coll Negotiations in the Public Sector, vol #3, 1979; "Analysis of the Arbitration Procedure," Pers J, Nov 1973. INT: arb/med, mgmt/educ. ASSN: Conn IRRA, SPIDR, AAA. POSITIONS: Faculty School of Bus, Univ of Conn, 1955-81, since 1981, Emeritus Faculty; and, currently, Labor Rels Neutral (self-employed), 15 Westwood Rd, Storrs, CT 06268. 203/429-9486

GLAZER, JOSEPH Union, Labor Music. BA 1938, Brooklyn Coll. PUBL: Songs of Work & Protest. INT: labor history, union org/admin, indus sociol. ASSN: Wash DC IRRA, Amer Folklore Soc. POSITIONS: Labor Educator, United Rubber Workers Union, 195-61; Labor Specialist, U.S. Information Agency, 1961-81; and, currently, Labor's Troubador (freelance consultant/performer), 7307 Pomander La, Chevy Chase, MD 20815. 301/652-0393

GLAZER, MILDRED Government. BA 1944, U of Wis; MA 1948, NYU. INT: govt labor policy, personnel, ind sociol. POSITION: Pers-EEO, U.S. Commerce Dept, Wash DC. ADDRESS: 7307 Pomander La, Chevy Chase, MD 20815. 301/652-0393

GLEASON, ALAN HAROLD Acad: Econ. AB 1939, Princeton; MA 1941, Rochester; PhD 1950, MIT. PUBL: "Economic Growth and Consumption in Japan," in The State & Econ Enterprise in Japan, W.W. Lockwood, ed, Princeton U Press, 1965; "Post War Housing in Japan and the U.S.," in Studies on Economic Life in Japan, R.K. Beardsly, ed, Univ of Mich Press, 1964; "The Social Adequacy Method of International Level ofLiving Comparasions," J of Econ Behavior, April, 1961. INT: intl comparative labor. ASSN: AEA, Assn for Asian Studies. POSITIONS: Asst Prof of Econ, Univ of Rochester, 1946; Prof of Econ, Intl Christian Univ, Tokyo, 1956; and (since 1970) Prof of Econ, Dept of Econ, Univ of Toledo, Toledo, OH 43606. 419/537-2563

GLEASON, JOYCE G. Student, Econ. MA 1964, U of Mich; ABD 1982, U of Nebr. ADDRESS: Economic Education, CBA #305, Univ of Nebraska, Lincoln, NB 68588. 402/472-3442

GLEASON, SANDRA E. Acad: Econ. BA 1967, Smith Coll; MA 1968, PhD 1978, Northwestern U. PUBL: "The Decision to File a Sex Discrimination Complaint in the Federal Government: The Benefits and Costs of 'Voice;'" "The FTC and the Competitive Environment of the Professions;" "Hustling: The Inside Economy of A Prison." INT: labor market econ, govt labor policy, empl/trng programs. ASSN: AEA. POSITIONS: Asst Prof, Univ of Mich-Dearborn, 1977; Economist, Federal Trade Commission, 1979; and (since 1981) Asst Prof, School of Labor & Ind Rels, Mich State Univ. ADDRESS: 303 Chesterfield Parkway, East Lansing, MI 48823. 517/353-1807

GLENN, JIM Bus:Mgmt/Admin. POSITION: Employee Rels Manager, St. Joseph Hospital, 1919 LaBranch, Houston, TX 77002.

GLIDDEN, PRISCILLA A. Consulting. BA 1972, U of Mass; PhD 1979, MIT. POSITION: Pers Officer and Labor Rels Liaison, U of Mass at Boston, 1966-76. ADDRESS: 109 Beacon St, Boston, MA 02116. 617/266-4572

GLINSMAN, WILLIAM J. Government, Arbitration. BS 1968 Empire State Coll. POSITION: NY State Mediator, Room 3468, 2 World Trade Center, New York, NY 10047. 212/488-6694

GLOVER, BETTY E. Acad: Org Beh/Pers, Sociol. MA 1974, Roosevelt U. ADDRESS: 1153 E Hyde Park Blvd, Chicago, IL 60615. 312/667-4373

GLOVER, ROBERT W. Acad: Econ. BA 1965, U of Santa Clara; MA 1970, PhD 1972, U of Tex at Austin. PUBL: Training and Entry into Union Construction, (w Marshall & Franklin); Employment Discrimination: Impact of Legal Administrative Remedies, (w Marshall, Knapp & Liggett); Agricultural Labor and Public Policy: A Constructive View. INT: empl/trng programs, labor market econ, personnel. ASSN: South Tex IRRA, AEA, Amer Soc forTrng and Develop, Agricultural Pers Mgmt Assn. POSITION: (since 1977) Director, Center for Study of Human Resources, Univ of Texas, 107 West 27th St, Austin, TX 78712. 512/471-7891

GODARD, JOHN HAMILTON Acad: Sociol, Ind Rels, Org Beh/Pers. B Comm 1972, MBA 1975, U of Manitoba. PUBL: "Management Under Collective Bargaining," (w T. Kochan), in J. Anderson & M. Gunderson, eds, Union management Relations in Canada, 1982; "Labour Relations in Theory and Practice," in K. Sriniuas, Human Res Mgmt in Canada, 1984. INT: ind sociol, social theory, org beh. ASSN: Amer Soc Assn, Canadian Ind Rels Assn. POSITION: (since 1981) Asst Prof, School of Business, Queens Univ. ADDRESS: 123 King St, Apt 4, Kingston, Ontario K7L 2Z9 Canada. 613/547-5744

GOETZ, ALAN F. Bus:Pers/Ind Rels, Government. AB 1970, Rockhurst Coll; MPA 1975, U of Mo at Kansas City. INT: coll barg, personnel, union org/admin. ASSN: Greater Kansas City IRRA. POSITIONS: Labor Dept Program Officer, Amer Nurses Assn, 1972; Labor Rels Specialist, U.S. Dept of Housing and Urban Develop, 1975, and since 1983, Pers Rep, U. S. Dept of Commerce Kansas City. ADDRESS: 4504 Valley View Rd, Blue Springs, MO 64015. 816/374-7129

GOETZ, RAYMOND Acad: Law; Arbitration. JD 1950, MBA 1963, U of Chicago. PUBL: Tax Treatment of Pension Plans: Preferential or Normal, 1969; "Secondary Boycotts and the LMRA: A Path Through the Swamp," 19 Kansas Law Rev 651, 1979; "Arbitration after Termination of a Collective Bargaining Agreement," 63 Va Law Rev 693, 1977. INT: arb/med, labor law. ASSN: Greater Kansas City IRRA,

NAA, AAA,ABA(Labor & Empl Law section). POSITIONS: Assoc, 1950-75, Partner 1957-66, Seyfarth, Shaw, Fairweather, & Geraldson, Chicago, and (since 1966) Prof of Law, School of Law, Univ of Kansas, Lawrence, KS 66045. 913/864-4550

GOFF, NADINE A. Student-U of Wis. ASSN: Wis IRRA. ADDRESS: 344 W Dayton St, #1002, Madison, WI 53703.

GOLD, CHARLOTTE Arbitration. BA 1958, Smith Coll; MA 1970, Cornell. INT: arb/med, coll barg, empl/trng programs. ASSN: New York and Long Island IRRA, AAA, SPIDR. POSITIONS: Director, Publications Div, NYSS-ILR-Cornell, 1972; Vice Pres, AAA, 1977; and (since 1983) Arbitrator, 245 E 54th, Suite 14M, New York NY 10022. 212/935-8767.

GOLDBAUM, KAREN M. Student. ADDRESS: 7 Mohawk Pl, Latham, NY 12110. 518/785-6297

GOLDBERG, FRANK Acad: Univ Admin. BA 1967, CCNY; AM 1969, PhD 1975, U of Ill. INT: labor market econ. ASSN: AEA, Assn for Inst Res. POSITIONS: Instructor of Econ, U of Wis-Whitewater, 1971; Asst Prof of Econ, Roosevelt U-Chicago, 1975; and (since 1981) Asst Dean, The Graduate School, Northwestern Univ. ADDRESS: 811 Kingsbridge Way, Buffalo Grove, IL 60090. 312/492-7264

GOLDBERG, ISADORE Acad: Ind Rels, Psych; Consulting. BA 1955, Miami of Oh; MA 1957, PhD 1959, U of Md. INT: ind psych, arb/med, coll barg. ASSN: Wash DC IRRA, Amer Psych Assn, Univ & Coll Labor Educ Assn, Wash DC Psych Assn. POSITION: (since 1971) Prof, Univ of District of Columbia, and Labor Studies Consultant, C & G Assoc Inc, 3 Hearthstone Ct, Potomac, MD 20854. 301/-424-4060

GOLDBERG, JOSEPH P. Government. BSS 1937, CCNY; MA 1938, PhD 1950, Columbia U. PUBL: The Maritime Story, Harvard U Press, 1958; "Modernization of the Maritime Industry," in H.M. Levinson, C. Remus, J. Goldberg & M. Kahn, eds, Labor Mgmt Adjustments to Technological Change in the Transportation Industry, 1971; "The AFL and a National Bureau of Labor Statistics, pp 1881-1913," Monthly labor Rev, Mar 1982. INT: coll barg, govt labor policy, labor history. ASSN: Wash DC IRRA, AEA. POSITIONS: Res Assoc, Howard U, 1957; Res Assoc, U of Mich-Wayne State Ind Rels Inst, 1969; and (since 1955) Special Asst to U. S. Commissioner, BLS, USDL. ADDRESS: 707 Stonington Rd, Silver Spring, MD 20902. 202/272-5239

GOLDBERG, MICHAEL J. Acad: Law. AB 1971, Cornell; JD 1975, Harvard; LLM 1977, Georgetown. PUBL: "The Duty of Fair Representation: What the Courts Do In Fact," forthcoming 1984; "Affirmative Action in Union Government: The Landrum-Griffin Act Implications," 44 Ohio State Law J 649, 1983; "Implying Punitive Damages in Employment Discrimination Cases," 9 Harvard Civil Rights-Civil Liberties Law Rev 325, 1974. INT: labor law, union org/-admin. ASSN: Philadelphia IRRA, ABA(labor law section), AAUP. POSITIONS: Staff Attorney, Northwest Labor & Empl Law Office, Seattle, 1977; General Counsel, Teamsters for a Democratic Union, 1980; and (since 1981) Assoc Prof, Rutgers Law School, 5th & Penn Streets, Camden, NJ 08102. 609/757-6370

GOLDBERG, MILTON M. Arbitration; Acad: Ind Rels. BS 1934, St. Johns U; MA 1937, Columbia U. INT: arb/med, coll barg. ASSN: Western New York IRRA, NAA, AAA, SPIDR. POSITIONS: Labor Mediation-Arbitrator, 1954, Western NY Dist Dir, New York State Mediation Board, 1974; and (since 1954) Labor Arbitrator, 320 Windermere Blvd, Eggertsville, NY 14226. 716/833-1892

GOLDBERG, STANTON H. Bus:Pers/Ind Rels. BA 1959, MA 1960, Mich State U. INT: ind sociol, org beh, personnel. POSITION: (since 1977) Executive Director Human Resources, CIBA-GEIGY Corp, 556 Morris Ave, Summit NJ 07901. 201/277-7016

GOLDBERG, STEPHEN B. Acad: Law; Mediation, Arbitration. AB 1954, LLB 1959, Harvard. PUBL: "Grievance Mediation in the Coal Industry: A Field Experiment," (w J. M. Brett); "The Mediation of Grievances: An Alternate to Arbitration;" Union Representation Elections: Law and Reality, (w J. M. Brett, & J. Fetman). INT: arb/med, coll barg, labor law. ASSN: Chicago IRRA, NAA, SPIDR. POSITION: Prof of Law, Northwestern Univ Law School, 357 E Chicago Ave, Chicago, IL 60611. 312/649-8426

GOLDBERG, STEPHEN M. Acad: Univ Admin. BA 1971, Rutgers U; MS 1974, U of Utah; JD 1978, Seton Hall Law School. INT: coll barg, empl/trng programs. ASSB: New York IRRA, Coll & Univ Pers Assn, Amer Soc of Hosp Pers Admin, N.J. Soc of Hosp Pers Admin. POSITIONS: Asst Dir of Pers, Jersey City Medical Center, 1973; Assoc Dir of Pers, Beth Israel Medical Center, New York, 1975; and (since 1980) Vice Pres, Personnel Resources, Univ of Medicine and Dentistry of New Jersey, 100 Bergan St, Newark, NJ 07103. 201/456-6457

GOLDENBERG, SHIRLEY B. Acad: Ind Rels; Arbitration. BA 1944, MA 1966, McGill U. PUBL: Collective Bargaining in the Canadian Public Service: The Federal Experience, (w J. Finkelman), Montreal, Res on Public Policy, 1983; "Industrial Relations Research in Canada," (w H.D. Woods), in Ind Rels in Intl Perspective, P. B. Doeringer, ed, London. MacMillan 1981; Professional Workers and Collective Bargaining, Ottawa:Queens's Publisher, 1970. INT: govt labor policy, coll barg, arb/med. ASSN: Inst for Public Admin of Canada, Canadian Ind Rels Assn. POSITION: Prof of Ind Rels, McGill Univ, 1001 Sherbrooke St West, Montreal Quebec H3A 1G5 Canada. 514/392-5816

GOLDFARB, ROBERT STANLEY Acad: Econ. BA 1964, Columbia, MPhil, 1967, PhD 1968, Yale. PUBL: "A Model of Teenage Time Allocation," (w A. Yezar), J of Econ and Bus, Summer 1983; "Occupational Preferences' in the U.S. Immigration Law: An Economic Analysis," B. R. Chiswick ed, The Gateway: U.S. Immigration Issues and Policies, Wash: American Enterprise Inst, 1982; "The Davis-Bacon Act: An Appraisal of Recent Studies," (w J. Morrall), Ind & Labor Rels Rev, Jan 1981. INT: labor market econ, govt labor policy. ASSN: AEA, Western Econ Assn, Atlantic Econ Assn. POSITIONS: Asst Prof of Econ, Yale, 1968, and (since 1973) Prof of Econ and Chairman, Dept of Econ, George Washington Univ, Washington DC 20052. 202/676-7581

GOLDFIELD, MICHAEL H. Student, Political Sci. MA 1978, U of Chicago. PUBL: "The Decline of Organized Labor: NLRB Union Certification Results," Politics and Society, Spring, 1982. INT: coll barg, method/statis, labor history. POSITION: Currently Student, U of Chicago. ADDRESS: 5907 W Midway Park St, Chicago, IL 60644. 312/379-9187

GOLDMAN, ALVIN L. Acad: Law; Arbitration. AB 1959, Columbia; LLB 1962, NYU. PUBL: Labor Law and Industrial Relations in the U.S.A., BNA 1983; Legislation Protecting the Individual Employee, (w R. Covington) BNA 1982; Labour Law and Industrial Relations, chapter 16, R. Blanpain ed, Kluwer, 1982. INT: labor law, intl comparative labor, coll barg. ASSN: Cincinnati IRRA, Intl Society for Labor Law and Soc Security, NAA, The Labor Law Group. POSITIONS: Prof in Residence, NLRB-Zagoria Staff, 1967-68; Visiting Prof, Univ of Calif-Davis, 1977-78; and (since 1965) Prof of Law, Coll of Law, Univ of Kentucky. ADDRESS: 2063 Bridgeport Dr, Lexington, KY 40502. 606/257-3325

GOLDMAN, BARBARA S. Research-Econ. BA Conn Coll; MA & ABD, American U. ADDRESS: 6 Albert Ct, Great Neck, NY 11024. 516/829-6984

GOLDSMITH, STEVEN J. Arbitration. BS 1955, NYSSILR-Cornell; JD 1960, Columbia. PUBL: "The Attorney as Witness in Labor Arbitration," NYS Bar Assn, Labor & Employment Law Section, Proc, p 103, Fall 1982. INT: arb/med, govt labor policy, empl/trng programs. ASSN: New York IRRA, ABA (Labor Law), NYS Bar Assn (Committee on Arb), NY County Lawyers Assn (Committee on Labor Law.) POSITIONS: Assoc General Counsel, Dist Council #37, AFSCME, AFL-CIO, 1968-70; Labor Rels Councel, NYC Health & Hosp Corp, 1970-78; and (since 1978) Arbitrator, 10 Morgan Place, White Plains, NY 16505. 914/946-8656

GOLDSTEIN, ALLEN P. Government. POSITION: Deputy Dir, Governors Office of Empl Rels, 1115 11th St, Sacramento, CA 95814.

GOLDSTEIN, HAROLD Consulting. BA 1934, U of Ill, MA 1936, U of Chicago. PUBL: Employee Training: Its Changing Role and an Analysis of New Data, (w A.P. Carnevale), Wash:Amer Soc for Trng and Develop, 1983; "The Accuracy and Utilization of Occupational Forecasts," in Taylor, Rosen, and Pratzner, Responsiveness of Educ and Trng Invitations to Changing Demands for Labor, Columbus, OH, Natl Center for Res on Voc Educ, 1983; Training and Education by Industry, Wash:Natl Inst for Work and Learning, 1980. INT: labor market econ. ASSN: AEA, Amer Statis Assn. POSITIONS: Asst Commissioner for Manpower and Empl Statis, BLS,USDL, 1959, and (since 1972) Consultant (private practice). ADDRESS: 7012 Wilson Lane, Bethesda, MD 20817. 301/229-5088

GOLOB, HOWARD M. Arbitration. POSITION: Arbitrator. 58 Ross Hall Blvd. Piscataway, NJ 08854. 201/846-1966

GOLODNER, JACK Union. BS 1953, Cornell; JD 1958, Yale. POSITION: Director, Dept for Professional Employees, AFL-CIO, 815 16th ST NW, #608, Washington DC 20006.

GOMBERG, WILLIAM Retired. INT: arb/-med, govt labor policy, mgmt/educ. ASSN: Philadelphia IRRA, ASME, NAA. POSITION: Prof Emeritus, Wharton School, Univ of Penna, Philadelpha, PA 19104. 215/898-6598

GONAS, LENA KRISTINA Acad: Ind Rels. Phdr 1974, U of Uppsala-Sweden. PUBL: Plant Shutdown and Labour Market Policy, Uppsala, 1974; Population and Work, Lund 1981 (Swedish); "Structural Change, Consequences and Alternatives, IIRA 6th World Congress, 1983. INT: empl, ind sociol, ind policy. ASSN: Swedish IIRA. POSITIONS: Assistant, 1968, Research Asst, SW Inst for Social Research, 1972; and (since 1977) Ph. dr., Lena Gonas, Arbetslivscentrum, Box 5606, 11486 Stockholm, Sweden. Phone: 08/229980

GOODMAN, DONALD P. Arbitration; Acad: Ind Rels, Bus Admin. BS 1964, Syracuse U; MBA 1966, Northeastern U; MS 1977, Niagara U. PUBL: Collective Bargaining in the Public Sector, 1980; Labor Relations in the Netherlands-A Bibliography, 1979; " Do Deans Practice What They Teach?" Middle Atlantic Assn of Colleges of Bus Admin, Proceedings of Annual Meeting, 1981. INT: arb/med, coll barg, labor law. ASSN: Central and Western New York IRRA, NAA, SPIDR, ASPA. POSITIONS: (since 1975) Dean, Prof, 1968, Dean, Coll of Bus, 1975, and (since 1982) Prof Mgmt/Labor Rels, Niagara Univ, 3089 Malklem Ave, Niagara Falls, NY 14305. 716/285-1212

GOODSON, MICHAEL J. Student. MS 1984, U of Wis-Madison. INT: personnel, coll barg. ASSN: Wis IRRA, ASPA. ADDRESS: 1619 Jefferson, Madison, WI 53711. 608/255-9369

GOODSTEIN, BARNETT M. Arbitration, Legal Prac. BA 1942, MA 1942, U of Tex-Austin; JD 1957, Southern Methodist U. INT: arb/med, labor law, labor history. ASSN: North Tex IRRA, NAA, ABA, Texas & Dalls Bar Assn. POSITION: (since 1957) Attorney/Arbitrator, Goodstein & Starr P.C., 5925 Forest Lane, Suite 200, Dallas, TX 75230. 214/387-4303

GOODWIN, WILLIAM J. Student. BA 1976, Wadhams Hall Seminary-Coll; MILR 1984, Cornell. INT: arb/med, labor educ, mgmt/educ. ASSN: SPIDR. POSITIONS: Mediator (volunteer) Dist of Columbia Mediation Service, 1982; and (since 1983) Grad Asst and Student, NYSS-ILR-Cornell. ADDRESS: 415 E Seneca St, Ithaca, NY 14850. 607/272-3415

GORDON, JOHN G. Bus:Pers/Ind Rels. BSc 1972, London School of Econ; MBA 1974, Columbia U. INT: personnel, coll barg, org beh. ASSN: Boston IRRA, ASPA, Amer Compensation Assn, Machinery & Allied Products Inst. POSITIONS: Labor Rels Specialist, Citi-Bank, 1974; Ind Rels Mgr, Ciba-Geigy, 1975; Pers Mgr, 1978, and, since 1981, Director of Ind Rels, Brown & Sharpe Manufacturing Co, Precision Park, North Kingstown, RI 02852. 401/886-2215

GORDON, MARGARET S. Retired. BA 1931, Bryn Mawr Coll; MA 1933, PhD 1936, Radcliffe Coll. PUBL: The Economics of Welfare Policies, NY, Columbia U Press, 1963; Retraining and Labor Market Adjustment in Western Europe, DC, US off Mpr Automation and Trng, 1965; Higher Education and The Labor Market, (ed) NY McGraw Hill, 1974. ADDRESS: Inst of Ind Rels, Univ of Calif, Berkeley, CA 94720. 415/642-5452

GORDON, MICHAEL DAVID Legal Practice; Acad: Law. BS 1963, U of Wis; JD 1966 U of Mich. PUBL: "Synopsis of Other Labor Laws," Missouri Bar Handbook on Employer-Employee Law, 1984. INT: labor law, arb/med. ASSN:

Kansas City IRRA, Mo Bar Labor Committee, Intl Soc for Labor Law and Soc Security, ABA (labor section). POSITIONS: Lecturer in Ind Rels, Rockhurst Coll, 1971; Adjunct Prof, UMKC Law School, 1984, and (since 1969) Partner, Jolley, Moran, Walsh, Hager & Gordon, 1125 Grand Ave, Suite 1300, Kansas City, MO 64106. 816/474-1240

GORDON, MICHAEL E. Acad: Psych, Bus Admin. BA 1961, Lehigh U; MS 1963, Syracuse U; PhD 1969, U of Calif-Berkeley. PUBL: "Commitment to the Union: Development of a Measure and Examination of its Correlates;" "Psychological Approaches to the Study of Unions and Union-Management Relations;" "Seniority: A Review of Its Legal and Scientific Standing." INT: ind psych, org beh, union org/admin. ASSN: Amer Psych Assn. POSITIONS: Asst Project Dir, Life Insurance Agency Mgmt Assn, 1966, and (since 1968) Prof, Ind/Org Psychology, Coll of Bus Admin, Univ of Tenn, Knoxville, TN 37916. 615/974-3161

GORDUS, JEANNE PRIAL Acad: Ind Rels. POSITION: Ind Development Inst of Science & Tech, Univ of Mich, Ann Arbor, MI 48109. 313/763-0070

GORE, CHARLOTTE JEAN Student. ADDRESS: 502 W Main St, #314, Urbana, IL 61801.

GOSPEL, HOWARD F. Acad: Ind Rels. BA 1969, Oxford, PhD 1974, London School of Econ. PUBL: "An Approach to a Theory of the Firm in Industrial Relations," British J of Ind Rels, 1973; Managerial Strategies and Industrial Relations, London, 1983; "The Legal Obligation to Bargain: US, UK, Sweden," British J of Ind Rels, 1983. INT: coll barg, intl comparative labor, personnel. ASSN: British Univ Ind Rels Assn, Ind Law Soc. POSITIONS: Fellow, St. John's Coll, 1973; Fellow, Bus History Unit, London School of Econ, 1978, and (since 1974) Senior Lecturer, Keynes Coll, Univ of Kent, Canterbury, Kent, England.

GOSSELIN, LOUIS Acad: Law. POSITION: Univ Quebec/Rimouski, 300 Des Ursulines, Rimouski, PQ G5L 3A1 Canada.

GOTTESFELD, GARY I. Union/Data Processing, Consulting. BS 1973, SUNY-Buffalo; MA 1976, U of Mass-Amherst. INT: computers, labor educ, union org/admin. ASSN: Univ & Coll Labor Educ Assn. POSITIONS: Rep-Southwest Regions, ILGWU, 1976; Asst Prof, U of Missouri-Columbia, 1979; and (since 1983) Midwest Rep, Shared Union Systems, Inc, 1507 West Blvd Ct, Columbia, MO 65201. 314/449-8453

GOTTLIEB, BERTRAM Arbitration, Consulting. BA 1946, MS 1947, Ill Inst of Tech. PUBL: "Unions & Industrial Engineering," chapter in Handbook of Ind Eng & Mgmt, 2nd Ed, Prentice Hall, 1971; Stautory Obligation of an Employer to Furnish Information to a Union, (monograph), Amer Inst of Ind Engineers, revised 1975; The Art of Time Study: An Exercise of Personal Judgment, (monograph), Center for Labor & Mgmt, U of Iowa, Iowa City, 1966. INT: arb/med, coll barg, labor law. ASSN: Wash DC IRRA, Inst of Ind Engineers. POSITIONS: Asst Dir, Research, AFL-CIO, 1957; Dir of Research, Transportation Inst, 1974-78; and (since 1974) Arbitrator, 703 Hillsboro Dr, Silver Spring, MD 20902. 301/649-6814

GOTTSCHALK, IRVING E. Government. BA 1972, San Diego State U; MA 1974, U of Wis-Milwaukee. INT: labor law, coll barg, Federal sector labor rels law. ASSN: Soc of Federal Labor Rels Professionals. POSITION: (since 1976) Labor Management Rels Examiner, NLRB, Henry S. Reuss Federal Plaza, Suite 1240, 310 W Wisconsin Ave, Milwaukee, WI 53203. 414/291-3871

GOUKE, CECIL GRANVILLE Acad: Econ. BA 1956, CCNY; MA 1958, PhD 1967, New York U. PUBL: Amalgamted Clothing Workers of America, 1940-1966. INT: labor market econ. ASSN: AEA, Amer Statis Assn, Southern Econ Assn. POSITIONS: Asst to Assoc Prof, Grambling Coll, 1962-67; Prof and Chairman, Hampton Inst, 1967-1973; and (since 1973) Prof Dept of Economics, Ohio State Univ, Columbus, OH 43210. 624/422-2170

GOULD, WILLIAM B. Acad: Law, ADDRESS: 1-GCD-003, Stanford Law School, Crown Quadrangle, Stanford, CA 94305. 415/321-3128

GOULET, JANET C. Acad: Econ. POSITION: Dept of Economics, Wittenberg Univ, Springfield, OH 45501.

GOYET, FERNARD RENE Student. ADDRESS: Queens University, 251 Mack St, Kingston, Ontario Canada.

GRABER, NANCY R. Bus:Pers/Ind Rels. BS 1980 U of R.I.; MLIR 1982, Mich State U. INT: coll barg, arb/med., labor law. POSITIONS: Pers Generalist, Electrical Products Group, 1982, Employee Rels Rep, Communication Systems Div, 1982, and, since 1983, Labor Rels Administrator, Hawaiian Telephone CO (GTE), Po Box 2200, Honolulu, HI 96841. 808/-546-2018

GRABOWSKI, DONALD J. Arbitration, Government. BSIR 1955, LeMoyne Coll. PUBL: "Labor Relations and the Small Employer;" "Apprenticeship Today." INT: arb/med, govt labor policy, empl/trng programs. ASSN: AAA, Intl Assn of Pers in Empl Security. POSITIONS: Ind Rels Dir, N. J. Mgfrs Assn, 1958; Exec V.P., Oil Fuel Inst, 1965; and (since 1966) Director Employer Rels, NY State Labor Dept, Albany, NY 12211. 518/457-6820

GRAHAM, HARRY EDWARD Acad: Ind Rels; Arbitration. BA 1962, MA 1964, Hunter Coll; PhD 1967, U of Wis. PUBL: "Results of Arbitrations in the Public Sector," Public Pers Mgmt, Summer 1982; "Trends in Public Sector Arbitration Awards," Pers Administrator, April 1982; "The Experience of Wisconsin with State Provided Labor Arbitration Service, J of Coll Negotiations, Dec 1982. INT: arb/med, labor law, union org/admin. ASSN: Northeast Ohio IRRA, NAA, AAA. POSITIONS: Assoc Prof, School for Workers, 1972, Assoc Dir, Ind Rels Research Inst, U of Wis-Madison, 1975; and (since 1978) Professor of Ind Rels, College of Bus Admin, Cleveland State Univ, Cleveland, OH 44115. 216/687-3781

GRAHAM, JILL W. Acad: Org Beh/Pers, Ind Rels. BA 1968, Wellesley Coll; MM 1975, PhD 1983, Northwestern U. PUBL: "Dissent in Organizations as a Response to Perceived Injustice;" "The Role of Organizations in Sexual Conflict;" "Organizational Control From the Bottom Up." INT: org beh, ind sociol, ind psych. ASSN: Acad of Mgmt, Amer Psych Assn, Amer Sociol Assn. POSITIONS: Public Mgmt Program Coordinator, Northwestern U, 1976-79; and (since 1983) Asst Prof, Faculty of Commerce.

Univ of British Columbia, 2053 Main Mall, Vancouver BC V6T 1Y8 Canada. 604/228-6192

GRAMM, CYNTHIA L. Acad: Ind Rels. PhD 1983, U of Ill. INT: coll barg, labor market econ. POSITION: (since 1983) Asst Professor, Dept of Ind Rels and Human Resources, Univ of Iowa, Iowa City, IA 52242. 319/353-5471

GRANDE, JOSEPH A. Union. BS & BEd, 1960, Bryant Coll; MEd 1970, Rhode Island Coll. INT: arb/med, coll barg, union org/admin. ASSN: AAA Rhode Island Advisory Council. POSITIONS: Bus Teacher, 1960, and, since 1969, Executive Secretary, Providence Teachers Union, AFT #958, AFL-CIO, 199 Academy Ave, Providence, RI 02908. 401/421-4014

GRANT, ALICE B. Acad: Ind Rels; Arbitration. AB 1944, Wells Coll; AM 1946, Cornell. INT: arb/med, coll barg. ASSN: Western New York and Syracuse IRRA, NAA, SPIDR, AAA. POSITIONS: Extension Assoc, 1963, and, since 1970, Director, Rochester Area Office, NYSS-ILR, Cornell Univ, 305 Andrews St, Rochester, NY 14604. 716/428-9906

GRAY, CHARLES W. Consulting. BA 1948, MA 1949, U of Colo-Boulder. INT: personnel, org beh, mgmt/educ. ASSN: Northern Calif IRRA. POSITIONS: Vice Pres Pers, I. Magnin Co, 1966; Vice Pres Admin & Pers, Newhall Land & Farming Co, 1977; and (since 1979) Manager, Human Resources Consulting, Arthur Young and Co, Sacramento. ADDRESS: 2630 Willow Creek, Cool, CA 95614. 916/443-6756

GRAY, DAVID ALLEN Acad: Ind Rels. BBA 1967, MA 1969, U of Iowa; PhD 1974, U of Mass. PUBL: "The Compensation of National Union Presidents: Moderating Effects of Union Size," (co-authored), J of Labor Res, vol IV, Summer 1983, pp 225-237; "The Product Manager," (co-authored), Calif Mgmt Rev, vol 22, Fall 1980, pp 87-94; "From Conflict to Cooperation: A Joint Union-Management Goal Setting and Problem Solving Program," (co-authored), IRRA Proc, 34th Annual Winter Meeting, pp 26-32. INT: coll barg, personnel, labor law. ASSN: Acad of Mgmt, Southern Mgmt Assn. POSITIONS: Asst Prof, 1973, Assoc Prof, 1976, and, since 1981, Associate Dean, College of Bus Admin, #19467, Dept of Management, Univ of Texas, Arlington, TX 76019.

GRAY, GEORGE R. Acad: Ind Rels; Arbitration. BS 1964, Auburn U; MBA 1968, Scranton U; PhD 1975, U of Ala. PUBL: "Unionization in Virginiaian Analysis of Management Perceptions," Monograph, VCU Small Bus Inst, 1982; "Analysis of Power Factions in a Public Sector System," Southeastern AIDS, 1977; "Performance Evaluation: A Key to Employee Effectiveness," Mgmt World, 1980. INT: coll barg, arb/med, compensation. ASSN: Wash DC IRRA, AAA(labor panel). POSITION: (since 1977) Assoc Prof, School of Business, Virginia Commonwealth Univ, Floyd & Harrison St, Richmond, VA 23284. 804/257-1736

GRAY, LOIS SPIER Acad: Univ Admin. BA 1943, Park Coll; MA 1955, U of Buffalo; PhD 1965, Columbia. PUBL: Socio-Economic Profiles of Puerto Rican New Yorkers, published by USD-BLS, 1976; "Union Implementing Managerial Techniques," Monthly Labor Rev, June 1981; "Labor Management Cooperation: A Passing Fad or Permanent Change?" Labor Studies J, Winter 1984. INT: labor educ, labor market econ, union org/admin. ASSN: New York IRRA, Univ & Coll Labor Educ Assn, Natl Univ Extension Assn, Continuing Educ Assn of NYS. POSITIONS: Western District Dir, 1946, Metropolitan Director, 1956, and, since 1976, Assoc Dean and Director of Extension, NYSSILR, Cornell Univ, Ithaca, NY. ADDRESS: 7 E 43rd St, New York, NY 10017. 607/256-3281

GRAY, MARK L. Union. BA 1978, Mich State U; MS 1982, U of Mass. PUBL: Collective Bargaining In Education In Times of Fiscal Austerity and Declining Enrollments, (w S. Reardon & J. Young), U of Mass & Rutgers U: 1981; "Union Members Pitted Against Union Members: The Worst Possible Situation," Workplace Democracy, vol IX, #4, Summer 1982. INT: coll barg, labor law, labor educ. ASSN: Assn for Workplace Democracy. POSITIONS: Res Assoc, Center for Coll Barg in Educ, (Mass.), 1981; Dir of Res, 1982, and, since 1983, Labor Economist, AFSCME-Wash DC. ADDRESS: 1233 Briggs Chaney Rd, Silver Springs, MD 20904. 202/429-1225

GRAY, RUTH RUSSELL Legal Practice, Arbitration. BA 1943, U of Chicago; JD 1955, Rutgers. INT: arb/med, empl at will/law cases. ASSN: New Jersey, New York & Philadelphia IRRAs, New Jersey & Florida Bars, ABA, Assn of Women Lawyers. POSITION: (since 1956) Ruth Russell Gray, Esq., 60 Stirling Rd, Watchung, NJ 07060. 201/757-6800

GRAYSON, GERALD H. Acad: Econ, Ind Rels. BA 1961, Brooklyn Coll; MA 1963, U of Ill; PhD 1973, NYU. INT: coll barg, union org/-admin, arb/med. POSITION: (since 1966) Professor, Social Science Dept, New York City Technical College, CUNY, 300 Jay St, Brooklyn, NY 11201. 212/643-8154/5

GRECO, ALBERT NICHOLAS Bus:Pers/Ind Rels. POSITION: Executive Director, Metro Lithographers Assn, 21 E 73rd St, New York, NY 10021. 212/772-1027

GREEN, DANIEL H. Government, Consulting, Legal Practice. AA 1968, Catonsville Community Coll-Baltimore; BA 1970, Towson State U; JD 1983, U of Md. INT: labor law, arb/med, coll barg. ASSN: Maryland IRRA, SFLRP. POSITIONS: Meat Cutter, AMCBWNA Local #117, A & P Tea Co, 1967; Mgmt Intern, 1970, and, since 1972, Labor Rels Specialist (Sr Litigation), Social Security Administration. ADDRESS: 1901 Alto Vista Ave, #5, Baltimore, MD 21207. 301/594-4747

GREEN, GEORGE W. Bus:Mgmt/Admin. POSITION: General Motors Corp, 3421 Detroit St, Dearborn, MI 48124.

GREEN, RONALD M. Acad: Law; Legal Prac. BS 1965, NYU; JD 1968, Brooklyn Coll; LLM 1972, G.W.U. PUBL: "EEO and Affirmative Action for Balking Industry;" Executive's Guide to EEO Laws;" EEO in the Health Care Industry." INT: labor law. ASSN: ABA (EEO Committee), NY Bar Assn (trial lawyers). POSITIONS: Assoc General Counsel, USDL, 1969; Partner, Vedder Price et al, 1973; and (since 1978) Partner, Epstein, Becker, Borsody & Green PC, 250 Park Ave, New York, NY 10177. 212/370-9800

GREEN, WILLIAM F. Bus:Pers/Ind Rels. POSITION: Division Manager, Ind Rels, ZEP Manufacturing Co, 1310 Seaboard Ind Blvd, Atlanta, GA 30318. 404/352-1680

GREENBAUM, MARCIA L. Arbitration. BS 1962, NYSSILR-Cornell. PUBL: "Transit and Other Attempts to Arbitrate Contract Terms," in Arbitration Promise and Performance, Proceedings of the 36th Annual Meeting, NAA, BNA 1984, pp 202-220; "The Disciplinatrator, the Arbichiatrist and the Social Pyschotrator: An Inquiry into How Arbitrators Deal with a Grievant's Personal Problems and the Extent to Which They Affect the Award," Arbitration J, Dec 1982, pp 51-64; "Sexual Harrassment in the Workplace," (w B. Fraser), Arbitration J, Dec 1981, pp 30-41. INT: arb/med, coll barg, govt labor policy. ASSN: Boston IRRA, NAA, SPIDR, AAA. POSITIONS: Labor Arbitrator, Mediator and Fact Finder (self-employed), Apple St, Essex, MA 01929. 617/768-6337

GREENBERG-EDELSTEIN, RUTH Nursing. 206 Berkeley Dr, Syracuse, NY 13210. 315/473-6519

GREENBERG, BERNARD Union. Retired. ADDRESS: 474 Long Drive, Pittsburgh, PA 15241.

GREENBERG, DAVID HILLEL Acad: Econ. PhD 1966, MIT. "Inferences Concerning Labor Supply Behavior Based on Limited Duration Experiments," (w G. Burtless), Amer Econ Rev, June 1982; "Systematic Misreporting and Effects of Income Maintenance Experiments on Work Effort: Evidence from the Seattle-Denver Experiments," J of Labor Econ, Oct 1983; "An Analysis of Economic Efficiency and Distributional Effects of Alternative Program Structures: The Negative Income Tax Versus the Credit Income Tax," (w D. Betson & R. Kasten), I. Garfinkel, ed, Academic Press, 1982. INT: income maint, labor market econ, govt labor policy. ASSN: AEA, Assn for Public Policy Analysis and Mgmt. POSITIONS: Labor Economist (Acting Dir 1976-77), US Dept of Health and Human Services, 1975; Sr Economist and Assoc Dir, Socioeconomic Res Center, SRI Intl, 1975; and (since 1982) Visiting Professor, Univ of Maryland, Baltimore County, Cantonsville. ADDRESS: 1714 Maxwell Ct, Mc Lean, VA 22101. 301/455-2167

GREENBERG, LEON Retired. ASSN: Wash DC IRRA, Amer Statis Assn. ADDRESS: 10500 Rockville Pike #402, Rockville, MD 20852.

GREENBERG, RONALD Bus:Pers/Ind Rels. MA 1971, Columbia. PUBL: "Union Avoidance for Hospitals," J of the Amer College of Hospital Admin, Jan/Feb, 1983. INT: arb/med, coll barg, personnel. ASSN: Louisville Pers Assn, Louisville Hosp Pers Assn. POSITIONS: Dir of Pers, Long Island Univ-NY, 1977; and (since 1980) Vice Pres, Jewish Hospital, 217 E Chestnut St, Louisville, KY 40202. 502/587-4228

GREENDORFER, JEFFREY R. Union. BS 1971, Pacific U; MS 1973, U of Mass. INT: coll barg, empl/trng programs, arb/med.ASSN: San Francisco IRRA. POSITIONS: Bus Rep & Organizer, SEIU #250, 1973, Intl Rep, SEIU, 1978, and, since 1980, Asst to the Secretary-Treasurer, San Francisco Labor Council, AFL-CIO. ADDRESS: 451 Baden, San Francisco, CA 94131. 415/863-7011

GREENE, JAMES P. Bus.Pers/Ind Rels, Legal Practice, Consulting. BS 1973, U of Ore; MLIR 1975, Mich State U; JD 1981, U of Toledo. INT: labor law, coll barg, arb/med. ASSN: Detroit IRRA, Mich/Amer Bar Assns, Amer Mgmt Assn, Coll and Univ Pers Assn. POSITIONS: Labor Rels Consultant, Mich Assn of School Boards, 1974; Dir of Empl Rels, 1976, and, since 1981, Executive Director of Human Resources, Eastern Michigan Univ, 311 King Hall, Ypsilanti, MI 48197. 313/487-1052

GREENHALGH, LEONARD Acad: Org Beh/Pers, Bus Admin. BS 1968, MBA 1972, U of R. I.; PhD 1979, Cornell. PUBL: "Conjoint Analysis of Negotiator Preferences," J of Conflict Resolution, June 1981; 25(2): 301-327; "Job Insecurity: Toward Conceptual Clarity," Acad of Mgmt Rev, 1984; "Organizational Decline," Res in the Sociology of Organizations, Vol 2, 1983, 231-276. INT: org beh, ind psych, coll barg. ASSN: Acad of Mgmt, Amer Psychological Assn. POSITIONS: Res Dir, NYSSILR-Cornell, 1976; Asst Prof, 1978, and, since 1982, Assoc Prof, Amos Tuck School of Bus, Dartmouth College, Hanover, NH 03755. 603/646-2181

GREENHOUSE, SCOTT J. Bus:Pers/Ind Rels. BA 1977, Clark U; MS 1981, U of Wis-Madison. INT: personnel, arb/med, org beh. ASSN: Detroit IRRA. POSITION: Personnel Administrator, Consumers Power Co, 3201 E Court St, Flint, MI 48501. 313/235-1511 Ext 377

GREENSTEIN, FRED H. Bus:Pers/Ind Rels. POSITION: Personnel, Pacific Gas & Electric, 5555 Florin-Perkins Rd, Sacramento, CA 95822. 916/383-4141

GREER, CHARLES R. Acad: Ind Rels. MS 1971, Wichita State U; MBA, 1973, PhD 1975, U of Kans. PUBL: Personnel Management: Jobs, People, and Logic, (co-author), Prentice Hall, 1983; "Counter Cyclical Hiring as a Staffing Strategy for Managerial and Professional Personnel: Some Considerations and Issues," Acad of Mgmt Rev, April 1984; "Determinants of U.S. Unionism: Past Research and Future Needs," (co-author), Ind Rels, Winter 1982. INT: coll barg, personnel, arb/med. ASSN: Acad of Mgmt. POSITION: (since 1975) Professor of Management, Oklahoma State Univ, Stillwater, OK 74078. 405/624-5109

GREGORIO, COLEEN ANNE Student. 3225 History Dr, Oakton, VA 22124. 703/620-3170

GREGORY, GORDON A. Acad: Law. JD 1955, U of Wis. INT: labor law, arb/med, labor educ. ASSN: Detroit IRRA. POSITION: Senior Partner, Gregory, Van Lopik, Moore and Jeakle, 2042 First Natl Bank, Detroit, MI 48226. 313/-964-5600

GREIS, THERESA DISS Acad: Ind Rels, Management. BS 1977, Regis Coll-Denver; PhD 1982, Wharton-U of Penn. INT: coll barg, labor law. POSITIONS: C.P.A. Senior Auditor, Harris, Kerr Forster, 1977-79, and, since 1982, Asst Prof, Business School, Seton Hall Univ, South Orange. ADDRESS: 38 Samson Ave, Madison, NJ 07940. 201/761-9258

GRENIG, JAY EDWARD Acad: Law; Arbitration. BA 1966, Willamette U; JD 1971, U of Calif-Hastings Coll. PUBL: West's California Education Code Forms and Commentary; "Collective Bargaining: Exclusion of 'Confidential' Employees and 'Managerial' Employees," 22 Duquesne Law Rev 1, 1983; "The Statute of Limitations in Fair Representation Cases," 33 Labor Law J 483, 1982. INT: arb/med, labor law. ASSN: Wis IRRA, SPIDR, Wis/Amer Bar

Assn. POSITIONS: Asst Prof and Asst Dean, Willamette Coll of Law, 1971; Assoc Prof of Law, Pepperdine Univ School of Law, 1978; and (since 1980) Prof of Law, Marquette Univ, Milwaukee. ADDRESS: S56W23674 Maplewood Terr, Waukesha, WI 53186. 414/224-3799

GRESOCK, NICHOLAS F. Bus:Mgmt/Admin. POSITION: Market Relations J605, Blue Cross Blue Shield MI, 600 Lafayette E, Detroit, MI 48226. 313/225-8139

GRETZ, CLARE BURT Union. BSLA 1967, Georgetown U. INT: coll barg, arb/med. ASSN: New York IRRA. POSITIONS: Asst to Pres, 1978, and since 1980, National Bargaining Rep, Assoc of Flight Attendants, AFL-CIO, Wash DC. ADDRESS: 50 E 73rd St, New York,NY 10021. 212/794-9583; 202/328-5400

GRIESBACH, FERN C. Bus:Pers/Ind Rels. POSITION: Pers Admin, Consumer Power Corp, 3201 E Court St, Flint, MI 48501. 313/235-1511

GRIFFEN, LESLIE G. Acad: Ind Rels; Bus:-Pers/Ind Rels. BS 1970, Oakland U-Rochester, MI; MAIR 1981, Wayne State U. INT: personnel, mgmt/educ, preventative empl rels. ASSN: Detroit IRRA. POSITIONS: Empl Rels Admin, Dayton Hudson Corp, 1976; Regional Human Rels Mgr, Southern Pacific Communication Corp, and (since 1983) Manager, Employee Rels, GTE/SPRINT Communications Corp, 1818 Gilbreth, Suite 236, Burlingame, CA 94010. 415/375-4921

GRIFFIN, ELLEN E. Bus:Pers/Ind Rels. BA 1967, Wayne State U. INT: personnel, coll barg, empl/trng programs. ASSN: Detroit IRRA, ASPA, Mich State Chamber of Commerce. POSITIONS: Trng Dir, J. L Hudson, 1970; Pers Mgr, Montgomery Ward, 1971; and (since 1979) Personnel/Industrial Rels, Stone Container Corp, 6400 Harper Ave, Detroit, MI 48211. 313/925-1800 ext 24

GRIFFIN, MARY LOUISE Student. BA 1981, Western Md Coll; MSIR 1984, U of Wis-Madison. INT: union org/admin, emply/trng programs, coll barg. POSITIONS: Research Staff Intern, United Auto Workers, 1983, and (since 1982) Student, IRRI, U of Wis. ADDRESS: 221 N Livingston, #3, Madison, WI 53703. 608/262-1882

GRIFFITHS, HOWARD Acad: Bus Admin/-Mgmt. POSITION: Business Econ, Univ Witwatersrand, 1 Jan Smuts Ave, Johannesburg, 2001 South Africa.

GRIGGS, HOWARD S. Consulting. 824 Markdale, Lake Orion, MI 48035. 313/693-1297

GRIMES, JOHN A. Arbitration. BA 1948, Yale U. INT: arb/med, coll barg, labor history. ASSN: Greater Houston IRRA, AAA. POSITIONS: Chief Labor Reporter, Wall Street Journal, 1954-67; Exec Asst to Director, FMCS, 1977; and, currently, Arbitrator (self employed), 339 Bayridge Rd, La Porte, TX 77571. 713/471-6516

GRISE, SHERRY K. Student, Mich State U. MBA 1982, MLIR 1983, Mich State U. INT: labor law, arb/med, empl/trng programs. ADDRESS: 1572 C Spartan Village, East Lansing, MI 48823.

GROENIGER, LOUIS MARTIN Bus:Mgmt/-Admin, Bus:Pers/Ind Rels, Government. BS 1933, Xavier U-Cincinnati. INT: labor educ, coll barg, personnel. POSITIONS: Exec Officer, Res & Develop Corp, 1960; Regional Manager, Contract Compliance, U.S. Atomic Energy Commission, 1970, and (since 1973) Retired. ADDRESS: 9178 Dunbarton Ct, Knoxville, TN 37923. 615/691-4325

GROESBECK, JAMES D. Acad: Econ. POSITION: Assoc Prof of Econ, Huston-Tillotson College, 6616 Lexington Rd, Austin, TX 78731. 512/454-3670

GRONBACH, ROBERT CHARLES Bus:Pers/-Ind Rels; Acad: Bus Admin, Org Beh/Pers. BS 1950, MA 1951, CCNY. INT: personnel, empl/trng programs, mgmt/educ. ASSN: Conn IRRA, Conn Hosp Assn, Amer Soc for Hosp Pers Administrators. POSITION: (since 1958) Director of Employee Rels, Hartford Hospital, 80 Seymour St, Hartford, CT 06115. 203/524-2173

GROSLAND, DAVID A. Union, Arbitration, Coll Barg. BS 1964, Drake U. PUBL: Handbook for Master Contract Bargaining Preparation; Exhibit Preparation Handbook; "Salt in the Wound: A Classroom Teachers Viewpoint." INT: arb/med, coll barg, union org/admin. POSITIONS: UniServ Director-Unit One, 1970, Unit Five, 1979, and, since 1981, Impasse Specialist, Iowa State Education Assn, 4025 Tonawanda Dr, Des Moines, IA 50312. 515/279-9711

GROSS, ERNEST Legal Practice. POSITION: Counsellor at Law, 96 Bayard St, PO Box 241, New Brunswick, NJ 08904. 201/249-4002

GROSS, JAMES A. Acad: Ind Rels; Arbitration. BS 1956, La Salle Coll; MBA 1957, Temple U; PhD 1962, U of Wis. PUBL: The Reshaping of the NLRB: National Labor Policy in Transition, Albany: SUNY Press, 1981; The Making of the NLRB: A Study in Economics, Politics and the Law, 1933-1937," Albany: St Univ of New York Press, 1974; "Reflections on the Arbitrator's Responsibility to Provide a Full and Fair Hearing: How to Bite the Hands that Feed You," 24 Syracuse Law Rev 3, 879-899, 1978. INT: arb/med, labor law, govt labor policy. ASSN; Western New York IRRA, NAA, ASUP. POSITIONS: Res Asst, U of Wis, 1958; Asst Prof, Holy Cross Coll, Worcester, MA 1960; and (since 1966) Professor, NYSSILR-Cornell Univ, Ithaca, NY 14853. 607/256-3249

GROTY, CHARLES KEITH Acad: Univ Admin. BS 1962, MA 1964, PhD 1970, U of Mich. POSITION: Asst Vice Pres, Michigan State Univ, 140 Nisbet Bldg, East Lansing, MI 48824. 517/355-0290

GROVE, KATHRYN Health & Hosp Care. Pennsylvania Nurses Assn, 2515 N Front St, Harrisburg, PA 17110. 717/234-7935

GROVE, RICHARD LEE Union. BA 1960, MA 1966, U of Northern Iowa. INT: coll barg, arb/med, empl/trng programs. ASSN: Midwest IRRA, AAA. POSITIONS: Exec Dir, SE Idaho Educ assn, 1972; Aide, Congressman Wiley Mayne, 1974; and (since 1975) Executive Director, Geode Education Assn, 108 E Main, New London, IA 52645. 319/367-5923

GRUDE, JAN K. Acad: Student, Ind Rels, Org Beh/Pers. BA 1978, U of Alberta; Dip. C.S., 1979, U of British Columbia; MSc, 1983, London School of Econ. INT: org beh, personnel, intl comparative labor. POSITIONS: Lecturer in Econ & Bus Admin, Univ of Va-Clinch Valley College, 1980-82; and (since 1983) Tutor in

Ind Rels & Pers Mgmt and PhD Candidate, London School of Economics, Houghton St, Aldwych, London WC2A 2AE England. Phone: 01-405-7686

GRUENBERG, GLADYS W. Arbitration. Acad: Ind Rels, Econ. AB 1940, Marquette U; AM 1949, PhD 1952, St. Louis U. PUBL: Labor Peacemaker: The Life and Works of Father Leo C. Brown S.J., 1981. INT: arb/med, labor law, coll barg. ASSN: Gateway IRRA, NAA, Assn for Soc Econ. POSITIONS: Prof, Econ & I.R., 1969, Prof Emeritus, Econ & IR, St Louis Univ, 1983; and (since 1983) Arbitrator (self-employed), 801 Jackson Ave, St. Louis, MO 63130. 314/725-0793

GRUENBERG, HAROLD Legal Practice, Arbitration. AB 1945, George Washington U; JD 1951, St. Louis U. ASSN: Gateway IRRA, ABA, Mo Bar Assn. POSITIONS: Chief Examiner, NLRB, 1945, and (since 1952) Senior Partner, Gruenberg, Souders & Levine, 721 Olive St, Suite 905, St. Louis, MO 63101. 314/231-7440.

GRUENBERG, ROBERT Union. POSITION: NEA Communications, 1201 16th St NW Room 7, Washington DC 20036. 202/822-7200

GRUENDER, DANIEL F. Legal Practice. BA 1952, Antioch Coll; LLB 1955, U of Wis. INT: labor law, coll barg, arb/med. ASSN: Arizona IRRA, ABA, Maricopa & Ariz State Bar Assns, Wis Bar Assn. POSITIONS: Field Attorney, NLRB, 1958; Dir, 1960, and, since 1965, Vice Pres and Director, Shimmel, Hill, Bishop & Gruender PC. ADDRESS: 3329 Valencia Lane, Phoenix, AZ 85018. 602/224-9500

GRZYWACZ, ROSEMARY A. Bus:Pers/Ind Rels, Government, Bus:Mgmt/Admin. BS 1974, MAIR 1984, Wayne State U. INT: arb/med, coll barg, labor law. ASSN: Detroit IRRA, Mich Public Empl Labor Rels Assn, ASPA, Intl Pers Mgmt Assn. POSITIONS: Admin Asst, Labor Rels Bureau, 1966, and (since 1972) Personnel Officer, City of Detroit, Community and Econ Development Dept. ADDRESS: 7544 Nuernberg, Detroit, MI 48234. 313/224-2586

GUALTIERE, JAMES LAWRENCE Union. BS 1962, MBA 1969, U of S Calif. POSITIONS: Consultation Group, 1976, and (since 1976) President, Teamsters Local 572, 450 Carson Plaza Dr, Carson, CA 90746. 213/515-0601

GUDENBERG, HARRY R. Bus:Pers/Ind Rels. BS 1960, MBA 1964, NYU; JD 1970 Seton Hall. INT: coll barg, labor law, personnel. ASSN: New York IRRA, ABA. POSITION: Vice President-Emply Rels, Intl Telephone and Telegraph, 320 Park Ave, New York, NY 10022. 212/940-2772

GUERNSEY, SANDRA K. ADDRESS: 2622 N Farwell, Milwaukee, WI 53211.

GUJARATI, RUTH P. Acad: Univ Admin. AB 1960, Chatham Coll; MA 1971, New York U; MBA 1981, Pace Univ. INT: empl/trng programs, labor history, mgmt/educ. ASSN: New York IRRA, NY Soc of Assn Exec, Womens City Club of NY. POSITIONS: Assoc Dir, Executive Programs, 1976, and, since 1981, Director, The Corsi Inst for Labor Mgmt Rels, Pace Univ, Pace Plaza, New York, NY 10038. 212/-488-1943

GURDON, MICHAEL A. Acad: Bus Admin. BA 1970, U of Queensland; PhD 1979, Cornell. PUBL: "Patterns of Industrial Relations Research in Australia," J of Ind Rels, Dec 1978; "Is Employee Ownership the Answer to our Economic Woes?" Mgmt Rev, May 1982; "An American Approach to Self-Management," in Hem Jain (ed) Workers Participation: Success and Problems, New York, Praeger, 1980. INT: ind sociol, org beh, intl comparative labor. ASSN: Acad of Mgmt, Southern Mgmt Assn. POSITIONS: Trng and Development Manager, Australian Health Insurance Commission, 1975; Asst Prof, Univ of New Brunswick, 1978; and (since 1980) Asst Prof, School of Business Admin, Univ of Vermont, Burlington, VT 05405. 802/656-4015

GUSTAFSON, DONNA M. Union. ADDRESS: 6300 Stevenson Ave, #715, Alexandria, VA 22304.

GUTH, DENNIS JOSEPH Acad: Student. BA 1972, U of Pittsburgh. INT: ind sociol, mgmt/educ, labor law. POSITIONS: Dir of Human Resources Mgmt/Devlop, Bedford/Somerset Mental Health Org, 1973, and currently, Graduate Student, St. Francis Coll. ADDRESS: 242 W John St, Bedford, PA 15522. 814/623-8757

GUTTERIDGE, THOMAS GEORGE Acad: Univ Admin; Consulting, Arbitration. BS 1965, General Motors Inst; MS 1966, PhD 1971, Krannert-Purdue U. PUBL: Organizational Career Development: State of the Practice, ASTD Press, 1983; "Labor Market Adaptations of Displaced Technical Professionals," ILRR, July 1978; "Pervasiveness of Institutional Manpower Planning," Calif Mgmt Rev, Spring 1978. POSITIONS: Assoc Prof of Human Resources & Ind Rels, 1970-78, Assoc Dean for Org & Community Develop, School of Mgmt, SUNY-Buffalo, 1978; and, currently, College of Business, Southern Illinois Univ, Carbondale, IL 62901.

GWIAZDA, SUZANNE BUTLER Arbitration. BA 1964, Stanford U; MA 1968, PhD 1978, U of Chicago. INT: arb/med, coll barg, emply/-trng programs. ASSN: Boston IRRA, AAA, SPIDR, SFLRP. POSITIONS: Conciliator, EEOC, 1971; Field Examiner, NLRB, 1978, and (since 1979) Full time Labor Arbitrator, 44 Penniman Road, Brookline, MA 02146. 617/739-1309

H

HA, CHESTER CHIDUK Acad: Bus Admin, Ind Rels. BA 1960, Korea U; MS 1967, Ill State U; PhD 1974, Ohio State U. PUBL: A System for Program Planning & Coordination; "A Study of Relations Between Some Human Factors and Work Injuries;" "Union Participation in Company Decision Making: Its Implications for Labor Relations." INT: personnel, intl comparative labor, coll barg. ASSN: Acad of Mgmt, Amer Inst for Decision Sci. POSITIONS: President, S. R. Mgmt Intl Co, and, (since 1984) Prof of Bus Admin (visiting), Yeongnam Univ, Korea. ADDRESS: 11675 Pale Mesa Dr. Northridge, CA 91326. 213/360-2856

HABER, WILLIAM Acad: Univ Admin; Arbitration. BA 1923, MA 1926, U of Wis; PhD 1927, Harvard. PUBL: The Michigan Economy: Its Potential and Problems; The Impact of Technological Change: The American Experience; Unemployment Insurance in the American Economy. INT: arb/med, govt labor policy, income maint. POSITIONS: Chairman, Dept of Econ, Dean, College of Literature, Science & Arts, and, since 1969, Advisor to Executive Officers, Univ of Michigan. ADDRESS: 530 Hillspur Rd, Ann Arbor, MI 48105. 313/763-1355

HABERBERGER, MICHAEL J. Student; Consulting. BA 1982, MA 1983, U of Penna. PUBL: "The Arbitration of Worksharing Disputes: Developments and Implications," Labor Arbitration Information Systems: Perspectives, vol 10, #5, May 1983; "A Prospectus for Short-Time Compensation Research," Ind Univ of PA, Aug 1983. INT: labor educ, coll barg, govt labor policy. POSITIONS: Res Asst, Dept of Ind & Labor Rels, Ind Univ of Penna, 1982, and since 1983, University Fellow, Syracuse Univ, Skytop II, Room 312, Lambreth Lane, Syracuse, NY 13210. 315/423-3323

HACK, LINDA Legal Prac, Arbitration, Mediation. MA 1975 Roosevelt U; JD 1979, DePaul U. INT: arb/med, ind sociol, org beh. ASSN: North Texas IRRA, SPIDR, Acad of Family Mediators, Amer/Ill/Tex/Dallas Bar Assn. POSITIONS: Administrative Law Judge, Ill Dept of Labor, 1979; Attorney, Office of Ward Steinbach, 1981; and (since 1983) Staff Attorney, North Texas Mediation Center Inc., 3511 N Hall, Suite 306, Dallas, TX 75219. 214/-528-3018

HACKER, RICHARD BRUCE Arbitration, Consulting. BS 1949, Millersville State Coll, Penna. INT: arb/med, consulting Fed serv lab rels). ASSN: Wash DC IRRA, SPIDR, AAA, SFLRP. POSITIONS: Sr Employee-Mgmt Rel Officer, NASA, 1961; Dir, Labor Mgmt Rels Div, Office of the Secretary, US Dept of HEW, 1969; and (since 1982) Labor Rels Consultant/Grievance Examiner (self-employed), 10712 Gainsborough Rd, Potomac, MD 20854. 301/299-5511

HAEBIG, ROBERT C. Bus:Pers/Ind Rels. BBA 1967, U of Wis. INT: coll barg, org beh, mgmt/educ. ASSN: Wis IRRA, ASPA, MIMA. POSITIONS: Mgr Ind Rels, Babcock & Wilcox Co, 1967; Dir, Ind Rels, Waukesha Engine Div, 1979, and, since 1982, Director Human Resources, Intl Hough Div-Dresser Industries, East Sunnyside Ave, Libertyville, IL 60046. 312/367-2137

HAENER, AL Union. BBA 1949, Loyola U of Los Angeles; MA 1952, U of S Calif. INT: labor history, union org/admin. ASSN: Southern Calif IRRA. POSITION: (since 1981) Director, Walter and May Reuther Family Educ Center, Onaway, MI 49765. 517/733-8521

HAFERBECKER, GORDON Acad: Econ, Ind Rels, Retired. BE 1939, U of Wis-Stevens Point; MA 1942, Northwestern U; PhD 1952, U of Wis. PUBL: Wisconsin Labor Laws, 1958. INT: arb/med, coll barg, labor market econ. ASSN: North Central Wis Labor Mgmt Council, Service Corps of Retired Executives. POSITIONS: Member of Arbitration Panel, WERC, 1962 to present; Vice Chancellor Academic Affairs, 1956-74, Prof of Econ, 1956-80, Prof Emeritus, 1980. Univ of Wis-Stevens Point. ADDRESS: 1600 Brawley St, Stevens Point, WI 54481. 715/344-3867

HAGEN, JESSICA M. Student-MIRG, McGill Univ. ADDRESS: Staten Island, NY 10308. 212/984-1925

HAGEN, KAREN MARIE State Govern:Labor Rels, Arbitration, Government. MLIR 1983, Mich State U. INT: arb/med, coll barg, mgmt/-educ. POSITIONS: Trng Specialist, Oakdale Reg Center for Develop Disabilities, Dept Mental., 1977, and, since 1983, Labor Rels Rep, Dept of Social Services, State of Mich, East Lansing. ADDRESS: 4570 Blackstone, Okemos, MI 48864. 513/373-8866

HAGGLUND, GEORGE S. Acad: Ind Rels. BA 1957, U of Minn-Duluth; MA 1959, U of Minn-Minneapolis; PhD 1966, U of Wis-Madison. INT: coll barg, labor educ, industrial engineering. ASSN: Wis IRRA, Amer Public Health Assn, Univ & Coll Labor Educ Assn, Soc of Occupational and Environmental Health. POSITION: (since 1980) Professor and Director, School for Workers, Univ of Wis. ADDRESS: 1401 Longview St, Madison, WI 53704. 608/262-2111

HAGOOD, LEWIS R. Legal Practice. ADDRESS: Arnett, Draper & Hagood, Suite 2300, United American Plaza, Knoxville, TN 37929.

HAHN, ANA TERESA Bus:Pers/Ind Rels. 175 25th St, Copiague, NY 11726.

HAHN, LLOYD E. Bus:Mgmt/Admin, Bus:-Pers/Ind Rels. BME 1949, Cornell. INT: mgmt/-educ, coll barg, arb/med. ASSN: Western New York IRRA, American Gas Assn, Society of Gas Operators. POSITIONS: General Supt, 1963, Vice Pres, Iroquois Gas Corp, 1972; and (since 1974) Vice Pres, National Fuel Gas Distribution Corp, 10 Lafayette Square, Buffalo, NY 14203. 716/855-7145

HALAN, JOHN P. Bus:Pers/Ind Rels. BS 1952, Harpur Coll; MILR 1957, Cornell. INT: labor law, coll barg, arb/med. ASSN: New York IRRA. POSITIONS: Vice Pres-Admin, Philip Morris-Industrial Products, 1968; Vice Pres-Empl Rels, Citibank/Citicorp, New York, 1972; and (since 1975) Vice Pres-Employee Rels, Union Pacific Corp, 345 Park Avenue, New York, NY 10154. 212/826-8325

HALBACK, DONALD GORDON Government. BComm 1970, U of Alberta. INT: labor market econ, personnel, coll barg. POSITIONS: Pension Analyst, 1975, Compensation Res Officer, Pers Admin Office, Govt of Alberta, 1978, and (since 1981) Compensation Analyst, Govt of the Northwest Territories/Dept of Personnel. ADDRESS: PO Box 2486, Yellowknife NWT X1A 2P8 Canada. 403/873-7214

HALE, JUDITH A. Consulting. BA 1963, Ohio State U; MA 1965, Miami U. INT: empl/-trng programs, mgmt/educ, org beh. ASSN: Chicago IRRA, Amer Soc for Pers Admin, Amer Soc Trng & Develop, Natl Soc for Performance & Instruction. POSITION: (since 1974) President, Hale & Associates, 200 W Monroe, #1607, Chicago, IL 60606. 312/236-3122

HALE, KENNETH WADE Bus:Mgmt/Admin. POSITION: Employee Rels Admin, McEvoy Oil Field Equip Co, 3021 Mangum, Houston TX 77092. 713/683-4674

HALE, RANDOLPH M. Natl Trade Assn. AB 1951, U of Md, JD 1954, Georgetown Law School. INT: coll barg, intl comparative labor, labor law. PUBL: "The Impact of High Technology on Labor," George Mason Univ Spring Forum, 1983. ASSN: Wash DC IRRA, ASPA, Amer Soc Assn Exec. POSITION: (since 1977) Vice Pres, Ind Rels Dept, Natl Assn of Manufacturers, 1776 F St NW, Washington DC 20006. 202/626-3815

HALES, EDWARD E. Legal Practice, Arbitration, Consulting. BA 1955, Baldwin-Wallace Coll-OH; LLD 1962, U of Wis-Madison. INT: arb/med, coll barg, labor law. ASSN: Wisconsin IRRA, NAA, State Bar of Wis, ABA. POSITION: (since 1962) Attorney & Arbitrator, 1020 Washington Ave, PO Box 485, Racine, WI 53401. 414/632--1613

HALEVY, IRVING Acad: Ind Rels. BS 1947. MA 1948, Columbia. ADDRESS: 401 E 74th St, New York, NY 10021.

HALL, CHARLES ALBERT Acad: Ind Rels-Labor Studies. BA 1976, Fla Intl U. PUBL: "Grievance Handling and Standards Used by Arbitration;" "Public Sector Collective Bargaining." POSITION: Center for Labor, Florida Intl U, Tamiami Tr, Miami FL, 33199. 305/681-2122

HALL, GARY A. Bus:Pers/Ind Rels; Acad: Ind Rels, Econ. BA 1970, MA 1972, Middle Tenn State U; PhD 1976, U of Tenn-Knoxville. PUBL: "Wage Arbitration as a Bargaining Proxy: A Test of Split the Difference," Rev of Bus and Econ Res, Fall 1984; "Craft Requirements for Construction of Electric Power Plants," (w S. Paik), Growth and Change, vol 12, #4, Oct 1981; "Seasonal Employment Fluctuations in Contract Construction," (w S. Paik) Midsouth J of Econ, vol 5, #3, 1981. INT: coll barg, labor market econ, arb/med. ASSN: Tenn IRRA, AEA, Midsouth Acad of Econ. POSITIONS: Economist, Construction Labor Demand System, DOL, TVA, 1977; Assoc Prof of Econ, Middle Tenn State Univ, 1979; and (since 1983) Manager, Employee Rels, Samsonite Furniture, Samsonite Blvd, Murfreesboro, TN 37130. 615/893-0300

HALL, JOHN WESLEY Bus:Pers/Ind Rels. MA 1953. POSITION: (since 1973) Vice Pres, Human Resources/Ind Rels, Unitog Co, 101 W 11th, Kansas City, MO 64105. 818/474-7000

HALL, MARSHA KAY Bus:Pers/Ind Rels. BIA 1981, General Motors Inst. INT: personnel, coll barg, ind sociol. POSITION: (since 1981) Labor Rels Rep, General Motors Assembly Div, Ypsilanti. ADDRESS: 18103 Lister, Detroit, MI 48021. 313/485-5880

HALL, R. D. Government. BS 1949, Northwest Mo Teachers Coll; MPA 1964, U of Mo-Columbus. INT: mgmt/educ, coll barg, arb/med. ASSN: Greater Kansas City 'IRRA. POSITION: Reg Labor Rels Officer, GSA. Retired. ADDRESS: 3114 NE 48th Terr, Kansas City, MO 64119. 816/452-1629

HALLBERG, AL CARSTEN Bus:Pers/Ind Rels, Arbitration, Government. INT: coll barg, arb/med, govt labor policy. POSITION: Director-Labor Rels, Union Pacific Railroad Co, 406 West 1st South St, Salt Lake City, UT 84109. 801/363-1544

HALLER, ARCHIBALD O. Acad: Sociology. BA 1950, Hamline U; MA 1951, U of Minn; PhD 1954, U of Wis. PUBL: The Socioeconomic Macroregions of Brazil-1970, Nagoya Japan: United Nations Center for Regional Development, 1983; "Social Mobility Under Labor Market Segmentation," pp 113-140 (w R. B. Hauser, D. Mechanii, & T. S. Hauser) Social Structure and Behavior: Essays in Honor of William Hamilton Sewell, New York: Academic Press; "A Socioeconimc Regionalization of Brazil," Geographical Rev, 74:4 (Oct): 450-464. INT: social stratification, intl comparative labor, labor market econ. ASSN: Amer Sociol Assn, Amer Assn for the Advancement of Science, Rural Sociol Assn. POSITIONS: Assoc Prof-Prof Sociology, Mich State U, 1956; Distinguished Visiting Prof, Ohio State Univ, 1982-83, and, since 1965, Prof of Rural Sociology and Sociology, 3460 Agricultural Hall, Univ of Wis, Madison, WI 53706.

HALLOCK, MARGARET Union. PhD 1974, Claremont Grad School. INT: labor market econ, coll barg, empl/trng. POSITIONS: Asst Prof of Econ, U of Ore, 1974; Senior Econ, Oregon Exec Dept, 1982, and, since 1983, Economist, Oregon Public Employees Union, PO Box 12159, Salem, OR 97309. 503/581-1505

HALMOS, ANTHONY Trades Union. BA 1972, Oxford U; AM 1977, U of Ill. PUBL: Change in Trade Unions, (w R. Undy, V. Ellis & W. E. J. McCarthy), London: Hutchinson, 1980. INT: coll barg, govt labor policy, labor history. POSITIONS: Asst, Org & Ind Rels Dept, 1978, and, since 1982, Trades Union Officer, Social Democratic Party. ADDRESS: 14 Loftus Rd, Shepherd Bush, London W12 7EN England.

HALPERIN, SUSAN E. Arbitration, Legal Prac, Mediation. BA 1969, JD 1973, U of Conn. PUBL: New York PERB- "Selecting Neutrals for Public Sector Education." INT: arb/med, labor law, coll barg. ASSN: Conn IRRA, AAA-(labor panel), Conn Bar Assn (labor section). POSITIONS: Counsel to Gen Assembly Legislative Commissioners Office, 1973, Consultant Teacher Board Negotiations, Board of Education, State of Conn, 1976; and (since 1979) Owner/Sole Practitioner, Susan E. Halperin, 490 Prospect Ave, Hartford, CT 06105. 203/523-5782

HALPERIN, ZVI Bus:Pers/Ind Rels. POSITION: Pers Manager, Tambour Askar Paint Ltd, G7 Pinsker St, Haifa, Israel.

HALPIN, CHARLES A.J., JR. Acad: Ind Rels; Arbitration. BS 1943, LaSalle Coll; MA 1948, U of Penna; JD 1953, Temple U. INT: arb/med, coll barg, labor law. ASSN: Penna/-Philadelphia/ Amer Bar Assn, AAA. POSITION: Professor, Personnel and Labor Rels, LaSalle College, Philadelphia. ADDRESS: 111 Walnut St, Jenkinton, PA 19046. 215/951-1064

HALTER, PATRICK JOHN ADDRESS: 1245 4th St SW E405, Washington DC 20024.

HAMAI, ALBERT T. Union. POSITION: Secretary, AFSCME, AFL-CIO, 707 Alakea St, Honolulu, HI 96813. 808/521-6941

HAMEED, SYED M. A. Acad: Ind Rels. POSITION: Prof of Ind Rels, 300 AT, Faculty of Bus, Univ of Alberta, Edmonton, ALB T6G 2E8 Canada.

HAMERMESH, DANIEL S. Acad: Economics AB 1965, U of Chicago; PhD 1969, Yale U. PUBL: Economics of Work and Pay, 3rd Edition, 1984; "Social Insurance and Consumption," Amer Econ Rev, 1982; Jobless Pay and the Economy, 1977. INT: labor market econ, govt health policy, empl/trng programs. ASSN: AEA. POSITIONS: Asst Prof of Econ, Princeton, 1969; Assoc Prof of Econ, 1973, and since, 1976, Professor of Econ, Dept of Econ, Michigan State Univ, East Lansing, MI 48824. 517/355-7349

HAMES, DAVID SCOTT Student. MLIR 1979, Mich State U. INT: health & hosp care, arb/-med, coll barg. ASSN: Acad of Mgmt. POSITIONS: Pers Dir, Clinton Memorial Hosp, 1976; Empl Rels Rep, Standard Oil (Indiana), 1979; and (since 1983) Instructor, School of Bus Admin, Univ of North Carolina, Chapel Hill. ADDRESS: 400 Davie St #26, Carrboro, NC 27510. 919/962-3742

HAMLIN, TERESE A. Government, Bus.Pers/-Ind Rels. BA 1977, Eisenhower Coll; MPA 1978, Syracuse U. INT: personnel, arb/med, labor law. ASSN: Central NY IRRA, ASPA, Org of Mgmt Confidential Emply. POSITIONS: Sr Pers Administrator, 1978, and, since 1981, Assoc Pers Administrator, NY State Office of Mental Health-Rochester Psychiatric Center. ADDRESS: 1850 South Ave, Apt 10S, Rochester, NY 14620. 716/473-0135 ext 1643

HAMM, ELMER VAUGHAN Legal Practice. POSITION: Attorney, 107 Everett Avenue, Willow Grove, PA 19090. 215/657-1908

HAMMER, LAWRENCE I. Arbitration, Mediation/Fact Finding, Legal Prac. LLB 1950, Brooklyn Law School. INT: arb/med, coll barg, med/-fact finding. ASSN: New York & Long Island IRRA, NAA, SPIDR, NYS Bar Assn(labor section). POSITION: (since 1975) President, Lawrence I. Hammer, P.C.. 100 Veterans Blvd, Massapequa, NY 11758. 516/541-9623

HAMMER, TOVE HELLAND Acad: Psychology. BA 1969, Cornell, MA 1972, PhD 1973, U of Md. PUBL: " Employee Ownership: Implications for the Organizational Distribution of Power," (w R. N. Stern), Acad of Mgmt J, 23, 78-100, 1983; "Absenteeism When Workers Have A Voice: The Case of Employee Ownership," J of Applied Psych, 66, 561-573, 1981; "The Role of Non-Economic Factors in Faculty Union Voting," J of Applied Psych, 66, 415-421, 1981. INT: org beh, ind psych. ASSN: Amer Psych Assn, Acad of Mgmt, Intl Assn of Applied Psychologists. POSITIONS: Asst Prof, 1973, and, since 1982, Assoc Prof, NYSSILR, Cornell Univ, 383 Ives Hall, PO Box 1000, Ithaca, NY 14853. 607/256-5490

HAMMERMAN, HERBERT Government, Retired. 2125 S Culpepper St., Arlington, VA 22206.

HAMMON, DIANE LYNN Acad: Labor Educ. MA 1981, Mich State U. INT: labor educ. ASSN: Univ & Coll Labor Educ Assn. POSITIONS: Coordinator, Labor Studies Program, Black Hawk Coll, Moline, 1981; and (since 1983) Labor Education Specialist, Univ of Arkansas at Little Rock. ADDRESS: 8024 W 40th St, Little Rock AR 72204. 501/371-1971

HANCOCK, KEITH JACKSON Acad: Univ Admin, Econ. BA 1955, U of Melbourne, PhD 1959, U of London. INT: labor market econ, govt labor policy, arb/med. POSITION: Vice Chancellor, The Flinders Univ, Bedford Park, South Australia 5042.

HANCOX, ROBERT E. Bus:Pers/Ind Rels. BA 1965, Lycoming Coll, MBA 1970, Fairleigh Dickinson U. POSITIONS: Regional Pers Dir, State Farm Insurance Co, NJ, 1965, and, currently, Vice Pres Human Resources, Penn Mutual Life Ins Co, Independence Square, Philadelphia, PA 19172. 215/241-4090.

HANDSAKER, MARJORIE L. Res/Ind Rels. AB 1925, AM 1930, Radcliffe/Harvard. PUBL: Submission Agreement in Contract (Interest) Arbitration, (w M. Handsaker), U of Penna Press, 1952; "Remedies and Penalties for Wild-Cat Strikes," (w M. Handsaker), Catholic Univ Law Rev, Winter, 1973. INT: arb/med, coll barg, intl comparative labor. ASSN: AEA, SPIDR. POSITIONS: Instructor-Econ, Moravian Coll, 1963-64; and (since 1934) Res Assoc of Morrison Handsaker, 717 West Lafayette St, Easton, PA 18042. 215/258-3890

HANDSAKER, MORRISON Arbitration. AB 1929, Reed Coll; PhD 1939, U of Chicago. PUBL: Submission Agreement in Contract (Interest) Arbitration, (w M. Handsaker), U of Penna Press, 1952; "ILO Intervention and Japanese Public Unions," (w M. Handsaker), Ind Rels, Oct 1967; "Grievance Arbitration and Mediated Settlements," Labor Law J, 1966. INT: arb/med, coll barg, personnel. ASSN: NAA, IIRA, AEA. POSITIONS: Prof of Econ, Lafayette Coll, 1946-76; and (since 1941) Arbitrator of Labor Mgmt Disputes (self-employed), 717 West Lafayette St, Easton, PA 18042. 215/258-3890

HANES, WALTER W. Retired. JD 1940. Georgetown U. ASSN: Central Fla IRRA, District of Columbia Bar Assn. ADDRESS: 2869 Thistle Ct N, Palm Harbor, FL 33563 813/785-3205

HANEY, MARTIN D. Acad: Econ; Arbitration. BA/MA, Calif State U; MPA, PhD, Portland State U. INT: arb/med, labor educ, labor history. ASSN: Portland IRRA, SPIDR. POSITIONS: Arbitrator/Factfinder, Western Arbitration Assoc, 1983, and (since 1969) Portland Community Coll. ADDRESS: 3705 SW Canby St, Portland, OR 97219. 503/244-6111

HANEY, WILLIAM J. Government. POSITION: Conciliator, Calif State Med/Con Service, 2017 Heller Lane, Redding, CA 96001. 415/557-2426

HANKINSON, DAVID W. Bus:Pers/Ind Rels. BS 1976, MSM 1978, Frostburg State Coll; MSIR 1980, West Va U. INT: personnel, labor law, arb/med. POSITIONS: Res Asst, West Va U, Office of Res and Devel, 1979, and (since 1980) Supervisor of Pers, Newport News Shipbuilding and Dry Dock Co. ADDRESS: Apt 2, 974 Marcus Dr, Newport News, VA 23602. 804/380-2218

HANLON, MARTIN DANIEL Acad: Sociol; Consulting. PhD 1980, Columbia. PUBL: "Public Sector Productivity in an Era of Retrenchment;" "Primary Group Assistance During Unemployment;" "Quality of Work Life in Hospitals." INT: health & hosp care, org beh, personnel. ASSN: Acad of Mgmt, Amer Public Health Assn, Gerontological Soc of Amer. POSITION: Asst Prof, Dept of Urban Studies, Queens College, Flushing, NY 11367. 212/520-7510

HANNA, JAMES S. Government. POSITION: Employment Security Res, Nevada Empl Security, 500 E 3rd St, Carson City, NV 89713. 702/885-4550

HANNAH, RICHARD LLOYD Government, Union. BA 1973, U of TN at Chatanooga; BA 1974, MA 1976, Middle Tenn State U; Phd 1981, U of Utah. PUBL: "The Prospect for Occupational Bottlenecks in the Coal Industry," Intermountain Economic Rev, Spring 9 (1978) 78-92; "Human Relations and the Collective Bargaining Environment-With Special Reference to Underground Coal Mining," Human Res Mgmt, Winter, 1981, 2-7; "Coal Hungry-The Work Ethic of Underground Coal Miners," Pers J, 61, 746-751, Oct 1982. INT: coll barg, arb/med, union org/admin. POSITIONS: Group Rep-Chattanooga Sec, 1982, Pres-Chattanooga Section Eng Assn, 1983, and (since 1981) Fuels Economist, TVA. ADDRESS: 3607 Whitehead Ave, Chattanooga, TN 37412. 615/751-6757

HANNIGAN, THOMAS A. Bus:Mgmt/Admin, Bus:Pers/Ind Rels. PUBL: Realities of Metrication; "Metric Conversion: Unanswered Questions;" "How Labor Views Metrication." INT: union org/admin, mgmt/educ, personnel. ASSN: Natl Housing Conference, Labor Advisory Committee-NYSSILR, Natl Econ Club. POSITIONS: Res and Educ Dir, 1966, Admin Asst, 1972, and, since 1972, Admin Asst to the Intl Secretary, Intl Brotherhood of Electrical Workers, 1125 15th St NW, Washington DC 20005. 202/728-6030

HANSELMAN, KRISTEEN HUNT Union. MLIR 1974, Mich State U. INT: coll barg, union org/admin, union/org new members. POSITIONS: Negotiations Specialist, Mich Educ Assn, 1974, and (since 1980) Director Classified Public Emplys Assn, Wash Educ Assn. ADDRESS: 3758 53rd SW, Seattle, WA 98116. 206/941-6700

HANSEN, GARY B. Acad: Ind Rels, Univ Admin; Arbitration. BS 1957, MS 1963, Utah State U; PhD 1971, Cornell. INT: empl/trng programs, arb/med, coll barg. ASSN: AEA, SPIDR, Amer Soc for Trng and Devlop. POSITIONS: Asst Prof of Econ, 1967, and, since 1976, Prof of Econ and Director, Utah Center for Productivity and Quality of Working Life, Utah State Univ, Logan, UT 84322. 801/750-2283

HANSEN, GEORGE C. Business. POSITION: VP Remington Aluminum, PO 1035, 100 Andrews Rd, Hicksville, NY 11802. 516/681-9100

HANSEN, JEROME F. Publisher. BA 1950, Wayne State U. PUBL: Publisher: Labor Trends & Utility Trends. ASSN: Detroit IRRA, ASPA, Publ Rels Assn of America. POSITION: Publisher Labor Trends, 23100 Providence Dr, Suite 270, Southfield, MI 48075. 313/552-1175

HANSEN, W. LEE Acad: Econ, Ind Rels. BA 1950, MA 1955, U of Wis-Madison, PhD 1959, Johns Hopkins U. PUBL: "Forecasting the Market for New PhD Economists," (w others), Amer Econ Rev, Mar 1980; Effect of Tenured Faculty Exemption in the 1978 ADEA Amendments," Report of Select Committee on Aging, House of Reps, 97th Cong 1st Session; "Economic Growth and Equal Educational Opportunity," in E. Dean (ed) Education and Economic Growth, 1984. INT: labor market econ, empl/trng programs, health & hosp care. ASSN: AEA. POSITIONS: Asst & Assoc Prof of Econ, UCLA, 1958-65; Sr Staff Econ, President's Council of Econ Advisers, 1964-65; and (since 1963) Prof of Econ, (since 1983) Director of IRRI, Univ of Wis, 4226 Social Science Bldg, Madison, WI 53706. 608/263-3869.

HANSON, GREGORY A. Student. BA 1982, AM 1984, U of Ill. INT: personnel, org beh, gerontological studies. ASSN: ASPA, Natl Committee for Gerontology in Soc Work Educ. POSITION: (since 1981) Customer Rels Rep, Sears, Roebuck & Co. ADDRESS: 304 W Elm Apt 3, Urbana, IL 61801. 217/351-6400 ext 243

HARASIM, CHESTER Union. INT: union org/admin, labor law, labor educ. ASSN: Southwestern Mich IRRA. POSITIONS: Maintenance, Allied Paper Inc, Kalamazoo,MI, 1946, and (since 1961) Intl Rep, United Paperworkers Intl Union, Nashville. ADDRESS: 10405 Dewberry St, Kalamazoo, MI 49002. 615/834-8590

HARDBECK, GEORGE W. Acad: Univ Admin, Ind Rels, Econ. BS 1954, MS 1956, PhD 1958, U of Ill. PUBL: "Impact of the Nevada Consent Decree on the Employment Practice of Hotels and Unions," Cornell H.R.A. Quart, Nov 1973; "The Impact of Executive Order 10988 on Labor Mgmt Relations," Labor Law J, Nov 1969; "Status of Communist Dominated Unions Expelled from CIO," Marquette Bus Rev, Summer 1968. INT: arb/med, coll barg, empl/trng programs. ASSN: Southern Nevada IRRA, AAA, Western Assn of Coll Schools of Bus, Beta Gamma Sigma. POSITIONS: Assoc Dean, 1966, Dean, Coll of Bus Admin, Creighton Coll, 1968; and (since 1971) Dean Coll of Bus & Econ, Univ of Nevada. ADDRESS: 3659 Descanso, Las Vegas, NV 89121. 702/739-3362

HARDIMAN, KEVIN P. Bus:Pers/Ind Rels. BA 1972, Fordham U. INT: arb/med, coll barg, labor law. ASSN: Boston IRRA, Amer Gas Assn, New England Regional Utility Group, New England Labor Council. POSITIONS: Dir, Ind Rels, Philadelphia Coke Co; Mgr, Ind Rels, Boston Gas Co, One Beacon St, Boston, MA 02108. 617/742-8400

HARDIN, EINAR Acad: Labor Markets. BA 1945, Handelshogskolan, Goteborg, Sweden; MA 1947, PhD 1957, U of Minn. PUBL: Economic Benefits and Costs of Retraining, D.C. Heath, 1971; "Job Placement Services for Ex-Offenders: An Evaluation," J of Human Res, vol 11, #3, Summer 1976; "Disaggregating the Work Experience Measure in the Earnings Equation," Soc Statistics Sec Proceedings, Amer Statis Assn, 1978. INT: labor market econ, empl/trng programs, methodo/statis. ASSN: AEA, Amer Statis Assn. POSITIONS: Asst Prof, Econ & LIR, 1957-61, Assoc Prof, Dept of Econ, 1961-66, and (since 1967), Professor of Labor & IR, (Also Assoc Dir, SLIR, 1961-64 & 1968-73), Mich State U. ADDRESS: 304 Murphy Circle, East Lansing, MI 48824. 517/353-3905

HAREL, GEDALIAHU H. Acad: Ind Rels, Org Beh/Pers. PhD 1974, Mich State U. PUBL: "The Generic Reasons for Strikes: An Interpretative Analysis of the Israeli Case;" "Expectancy Theory Applied to the Process of Professional Obsolence;" "Combatting Sexual Harassment: The Michigan Experience." INT: personnel, coll barg, intl comparative labor. ASSN: Acad of Mgmt, Israel IRRA. POSITIONS: Visiting Assoc Prof, School of L&IR, Mich State U, 1980; Visiting Assoc Prof, UCLA, 1981; and (since 1974) Senior Lecturer, Technion, Israel Inst of Tech, Haifa, Israel. Phone: 04/292 854

HARKLESS, JAMES McCONNELL Arbitration. BA 1952, JD 1955, Harvard. INT: arb/med, coll barg, labor law. ASSN: Wash DC IRRA, NAA, AAA, Intl Soc of Labor Law and Soc Sec. POSITION: (since 1970) Labor Arbitrator, James M Harkless, 1053 31st St NW, Washington DC 20007. 202/965-3588

HARMON, CHERYL Acad: Ind Rels. BS 1973, Temple U; MS 1980, Drexel U. INT: arb/-med, labor law, method/statis. ASSN: Central Penna IRRA, Assn of Information and Image Mgmt, Coalition of Labor Union Women. POSITIONS: Librarian, Norristown Area School Dist, 1977; and (since 1979) Research Analyst, PA State Educ Assn, 400 N Third St, Harrisburg, PA 17105. 717/255-7040

HARNEY, JOHN ROBERT Union. BA 1978, U of Calif-Berkeley; MS 1981, U of Wis-Madison; INT: coll barg, health & hosp care, arb/-med. POSITION: Intl Res Specialist, SEIU. ADDRESS: 4533 N Newhall, Milwaukee, WI 53211. 414/463-3550

HARPAZ, ITZHAK Acad: Org Beh/Pers, Ind Rels, Bus Admin. BA 1972, U of Haifa; MA1975, PhD 1977, U of Minn. PUBL: Job Satisfaction: Theoretical Perspectives and a Longitudinal Analysis, 1983; "Assymetry of Cognitive Functioning as a Possible Predictor for Vocational Counseling and Personnal Classification,: J of Voc Beh, 1983; "Determinants of Continued & Discontinued Participation in Pre-Retirement Training: An Israeli Case Study," (w Kremer). J of Occupational Psych, 1981. INT: org beh, personnel, ind psych. ASSN: Acad of Mgmt, Ind Rels Res Assn (Israel), Israel Sociol Assn. POSITIONS: Lecturer, U of Haifa, 1977, and, since 1983, Assoc Prof, School of Mgmt, Boston Coll, Chestnut Hill, MA 02167. 617/552-8562

HARPER, HARRIETT J. Government. BS 1958, Penna State U. The Employment of Women: General Diagnosis of Developments and Issues, U.S. Report for OECD High Level Conf on the Employment of Women, April 1980; The Decision Making Process in the Federal System, (w H.H. White & others), 1974; "Economists' Perceptions of Minority Economic Problems: A View of Emerging Literature," (w Andres & Brimmer), J of Econ Lit, v 8, #3, Sept, 1970. INT: labor market econ, govt labor policy, intl comparative labor. ASSN: Wash DC IRRA, AEA, Amer Statis Assn, Natl Econ Assn. POSITIONS: Economist, Board of Governors of the Federal Reserve System, 1970, Supervisory Economist, US Equal Opportunity Comm, 1974, and, since 1978, Supervisory Labor Economist, Women's Bureau, USDL. ADDRESS: 2320 1st St NW, Washington DC 20001. 202/523-6601

HARPER, JOHN J. Legal Practice. POSITION: President, Harper & O'Brien, PO Box 198, Morris Plains, NJ 07950. 201/539-0226

HARPER, SHIRLEY F. Acad: Librarian. MA 1952 U of Chicago. ASSN: Amer Soc for Information Sci, Special Librarians Assn, Amer Library Assn. POSITIONS: Librarian, A. G. Bush Libr, 1949-75, and, since 1975, Director, Martin P Catherwood Libr, NYSSILR, Cornell Univ, PO Box 1000, Ithaca NY 14853. 607/256-5435

HARRAH, JEFFREY C. Student. ADDRESS: 416 E 5th St, Belle, WV 25015.

HARRINGTON, C. ROBERT Bus:Pers/Ind Rels. POSITION: Assoc Vice Pres Personnel, 408 U Serv Bldg, Temple Univ, 1601 Broad St, Philadelphia, PA 19122. 215/787-1319

HARRIS, DAWN A. Student, Bus Policy. BA 1976, Grinnell Coll; MLIR 1978, Mich State U; PhD 1984, Northwestern U. PUBL: "Interindustry Patterns in Unfair Labor Practice Cases," (w M. Roomkin) J of Labor Res, 1984. INT: labor market econ, personnel, methodol/statis. ASSN: AEA, Acad of Mgmt. POSITIONS: Res Analyst, Brandeis U, 1978; Instructor/Res Asst, 1981, and since 1980, Student, Northwestern Univ. ADDRESS: 6822 N Wayne, #2A, Chicago, IL 60626. 312/492-7415

HARRIS, JOY T. Student. ADDRESS: 1543 C Spartan Village, East Lansing, MI 48823.

HARRIS, PHILIP Acad: Ind Rels. ADDRESS: Baruch Coll, 17 Lexington Ave, New York, NY 10010. 212/725-7122

HARRIS, TIMOTHY A. Student. BA 1981, U of Ore, AM-ILIR, 1984, U of Ill. INT: coll barg, org beh, coll barg. ASSN: LIRA. ADDRESS: Inst of Labor and Ind Rels, Rm 17, Univ of Ill, 504 E Armory, Champaign, IL 61820.

HARRISON, CONSTANCE Bus:Pers/Ind Rels. BA 1975, Barnard Coll; MBA 1978, Columbia U. ASSN: ASPA, Lebanon Area Pers Assn. POSITIONS: Human Resources Assoc, The Continental Group, 1978; Asst Mgr-Empl Rels, 1980, and, since 1982, Employee Rels manager, Cleaver Brooks Div of Aqua-Chem, PO Box 150, Lebanon, PA 17042. 717/274-7763

HARRISON, EDWARD L. Acad: Ind Rels; Arbitration. BA 1960, Henderson Coll; MBA 1964, Southern Methodist U; PhD 1975, North Tex State U. PUBL: "Legal Restrictions on the Employer's Authority to Discipline," Pers J, Feb 1982; "The Role of the Supervisor in Representation Elections," Pers Admininstrator, Sept 1981; "Employee Attitudes Toward Mandatory Retirement," Midsouth Quart Bus Rev, May 1980. INT: arb/med, coll barg, personnel. ASSN: AAA, Acad of Mgmt, ASPA. POSITIONS: Mgr Pers & Ind Rels, Frito-Lay, 1964; Instructor, North Tex State U, 1972; and (since 1974) Professor of Ind Rels, College of Bus, Univ of South Alabama, Mobile, AL 36688. 205/460-6411

HART, WILLIAM S. Acad: Ind Rels, Org Beh/Pers; Arbitration. BS 1953, MS 1957, Emporia State Coll; PhD 1969, U of Fla. INT: arb/med, personnel, mgmt/educ. ASSN: ASPA, AAA, Southern Mgmt Assn. POSITIONS: Communications, U. S. Army-Germany, 1953; Assoc Prof, East Carolina U, 1958; and (since 1969) Assoc Prof, Univ of Miss. ADDRESS: 206 Stone Road, Oxford, MS 38655. 601/232-5463

HARTANTO, FRANS MARDI Student. 1207 Fifield Ave, St. Paul, MN 55108.

HARTER, LAFAYETTE G., JR. Acad: Econ. BA 1941, Antioch Coll; MA 1948, PhD 1960, Stanford U. POSITIONS: Instructor, Econ, Menlo Coll, Calif, 1948; Instructor, Econ, Coll of Marin, Calif; and (since 1960) Professor, Dept of Econ, Oregon State Univ, Corvallis, OR 97331. 503/752-4460

HARTER, PHILIP J. Consulting. 4801 Massachusetts Ave NW, Washington DC 20016. 202/966-0541

HARTFIELD, EDWARD F. Government, Mediation. BA 1972, Oberlin Coll. PUBL: "Becoming a Neutral," SPIDR Proc, 1982; "Mediation and Negotiation Skills," SPIDR Proc, 1982. INT: arb/med, coll barg, intl comparative labor. ASSN: Detroit IRRA, SPIDR, Natl Acad of Conciliators. POSITIONS: Mediator, Office of Dispute Settlement, State of New Jersey, 1976; and (since 1979) Commissioner, FMCS, 431 Federal Bldg, 231 W Lafayette St, Detroit, MI 48226. 313/226-2114

HARTLEY, WILLIAM B. Acad: Bus Admin. PhD 1969, U of Wis-Madison. INT: personnel, labor market econ, coll barg. ASSN: AEA, Acad of Mgmt. POSITIONS: Prof & Chairman, Dept of Bus Admin, Iowa Wesleyan Coll, 1972; Prof & Chairman, Dept of Bus Admin, Clinch Valley Coll, U of Va, 1974; and (since 1977) Prof of Management, SUNY-Fredonia, 3032 Thompson Hall, Fredonia, NY 14063. 716/673-3506

HARTSTEIN, RAYMOND E. Bus:Pers/Ind Rels. POSITION: Ind Rels, Brunswick Corp, One Brunswick Plaza, Skokie, IL 60077. 312/470-4645

HARVEY, SCOTT BARRETT Bus:Mgmt/Admin. 5121 Bradley Blvd, Chevy Chase, MD 20815. 301/656-1718

HARVEY, W. J. Bus:Pers/Ind Rels. POSITION: FMC Corp, PO Box 3091, Houston, TX 77001.

HASENSTAB, KAREN ANN Bus:Pers/Ind Rels. 2910 Jay Ave, Apt 4B, Cleveland, OH 44113. 216/566-1139

HASHIMOTO, RICHARD Business. POSITION: Sheraton Hawaii Corp, Box 8559, Honolulu, HI 96815. 808/948-8132

HASSON, EDWIN Acad: Public School Admin, Org Beh/Pers. BS 1973, Ind U of Penna; MEd 1977, DEd 1983, Penna State U. INT: mgmt/educ, org beh, personnel. ASSN: Western Penna IRRA, Natl Assn of Secondary School Principals, PA Assn of School Admin, PA Assn of Supervision & Curriculum Devel. POSITIONS: Teacher, Tyrone Area School Dist, 1973; and (since 1982) High School Principal, Southern Huntington Cty School Dist. ADDRESS: Box 94, Saltillo, PA 17253. 814/447-5529

HATCHER, W. J. Bus:Pers/Ind Rels. POSITION: (since 1959) Director, Industrial Relations, Pitney Bowes, Walter H. Wheeler Drive, Stamford, CT 06926.203/357-9111

HATHAWAY, GERALD T. Legal Practice. BA 1976, La Salle Coll; JD 1979, U of Pittsburgh. INT: labor law, arb/med, coll barg. ASSN: New York IRRA. ADDRESS: Holtzmann, Wise & Shepard, 745 5th Ave, New York, NY 10151. 212/753-4300

HAUCK, VERN E. Acad: Ind Rels; Arbitration, Consulting. BA 1967, U of Wash; MBA 1971, Seattle U; PhD 1974, U of Iowa. PUBL: "The Efficacy of Arbitrating Discrimination Complaints," Labor Law J, vol 35, #3, Mar 1984, p 175; "Employing Relatives in Government," J of Coll Negotiations, vol 12 (4), 1983, p 283; "Burdine: Sex Discrimination, Promotion and Arbitration," Labor Law J, vol 33, #7, July 1982, p 434. INT: arb/med, coll barg, empl/trng programs. ASSN: FMSC (Arb panel), AAA (panel of Arb), Acad of Mgmt. POSITIONS: Ind Rels Asst, Northwestern Glass Co, Seattle, 1967; Visiting Assoc Prof, School of Bus & Admin, Duquesne Univ, 1980; and (since 1975) Prof of Ind Rels, Univ of Alaska at Anchorage, 3210 Providence Dr, Anchorage, AL 99508. 907/786-1790

HAUSERMAN, BOB B. Bus: Pers/Ind Rels. POSITION: Vice-Pres, Corp Employee Rels, TRW Inc, 23555 Euclid Ave, Cleveland, OH 44117. 216/383-3370

HAUSMAN, LEONARD JOEL Acad: Econ. ADDRESS: Dept of Econ, Heller Grad School, Brandeis Univ, Waltham, MA 02154.

HAVEN, CHARLES P. Acad: Student, Ind Rels. BS 1984, LeMoyne Coll. INT: arb/med, coll barg, personnel. 7729 Lisa Lane, North Syracuse, NY 13212.

HAVENER, RONALD V. 5521 Loretto Ave, Philadelphia, PA 19124.

HAVLOVIC, STEPHEN J. Student. BA 1977, MLHR, 1979, Ohio State U. INT: coll barg, ind psych, intl comparative labor. POSITIONS: Labor Rels Rep, Ford Motor Co, 1978; Coordinator of Pers Rels, Ohio Edison Co, 1979; and (since 1983) Grad Admin Asst, Ohio State Univ. ADDRESS: 6364 Busch Blvd, #317, Columbus, OH 43229. 614/422-6024

HAWKINS, JOHN M. Arbitration, Consulting. AB 1957, U of Ala; MSIM 1974, Georgia Inst of Tech. INT: arb/med, coll barg, personnel. ASSN: Atlanta IRRA, AAA. POSITIONS: Member, House of Representatives, Georgia General Assembly, 1975-83, and (since 1974) Consultant (self-employed), 1360 Harvard Rd NE, Atlanta, GA 30306. 404/377-8352

HAWKINS, MICHAEL W. Legal Practice. ADDRESS: Dinsmore and Shore, 511 Walnut St, Cincinnati, OH 45242. 513/621-6747

HAWLEY, LANGSTON T. Acad: Ind Rels; Arbitration. BS 1932, MS 1933 U of Ala; PhD 1946, U of N.C. INT: arb/med, labor history, labor market econ. ASSN: NAA. POSITIONS: Instructor in Econ, U of North Caroline, 1939-42; Prof of Ind Rels, Univ of Alabama, 1946-74, and (since 1974) Retired. ADDRESS: K5 Woodland Trace, Tuscaloosa, AL 35405. 205/553-7305

HAWORTH, CHARLES T. Acad: Econ, Consulting. BS 1959, Stanford U; MA 1965, PhD 1967, U of Ore. PUBL: "Earnings, Productivity and Changes in Employment Discrimination During the Sixties," AER, Mar 1975; "Employer Costs and Discrimination," JPE, June, 1974; "Concentration and Interindustry Wage Determination," RE Statistics, 1978. INT: labor market econ. ASSN: AEA, Southern Econ Assn, Amer Statis Assn. POSITION: (since 1967) Prof of Econ, Econ Dept, Florida State Univ, Tallahassee, FL 32306.

HAYASHI, HIROKO Acad: Law, Ind Rels. LLB 1966, LLM 1968, Kyushu U; LLM 1970, Tulane U. POSITIONS: Asst, Kyushu U Law School, 1968-71; Visiting Prof, Yale Law School, 1976; and (since 1972) Professor, Kumamoto Univ of Commerce, 5-1, OE 2-Chome, Kumamoto-Shi 862, Japan.

HAYFORD, STEPHEN L. Acad: Ind Rels; Arbitration. BSBA 1970, U of Evansville; MBA 1971, U of Ariz; PhD 1975, U of Iowa. PUBL: "The Impact of Law and Regulation Upon the Remedial Authority of Labor Arbitration in the Federal Sector,: Arb J, Mar 1982; "Deferral to Grievance Arbitration in Unfair Labor Practice Matters: The Public Sector Treatment," Labor Law J, Oct 1981; "Bargaining Unit Determination Procedures in the Public Sector: A Comparative Evaluation," The Empl Rels Law J, Summer 1979. INT: arb/med, coll barg, labor law. ASSN: ASPA, SPIDR. POSITIONS: Asst Prof, Va Polytechnic & State U, 1975; and (since 1976) Assoc Prof of Labor Rels, School of Public & Environmental Affairs, Room 410G, Indiana Univ, Bloomington, IN 47405. 812/335-5971

HAYMAN, EUGENE J. Legal Practice. LLB 1948, JD 51, Cornell U. INT: labor law, coll barg, arb/med. ASSN: Wis IRRA, Amer/Wis Bar Assn, Amer Judicature Soc. POSITIONS: Dir of Ind Rels, New York Air Brakes, 1957-63; Vice Pres, Pers, Miller Brewing Co, 1964-72; and (since 1973) Senior Partner-Vice Pres, Lindner, Honzik, Marsack, Hayman and Walsh S.C., 700 N Water St, Milwaukee, WI 53202. 414/273-3910

HAYNES, GLENN M., JR. Union. ADDRESS: Suite #3010, 12440 E Firestone Blvd, Norwalk, CA 90650. 213/863-4821

HAYTHORNE, GEORGE VICKERS Consulting. BA 1930, MA 1932, U of Alberta; PhD 1949, Harvard. PUBL: "Industrial Relations in Canada-Internal and External Pressures," in Worker Militancy and Its Consequences, Praeger, 1983; Construction and Inflation, Information Canada, 1973; Labor in Canadian Agriculture, Harvard, 1960. INT: govt labor policy, mgmt/educ, empl/-trng programs. ASSN: Canadian Inst of Public Admin, Soc of Intl Develop, Canadian Agricultural Econ Soc. POSITIONS: Deputy Minister, Dept of Labor, Government of Canada, 1961; Founding Dir, Inst of Develop Mgmt, Botswana, Lesotho, Swaziland, 1974; and (since 1980) Adviser, Development Mgmt, Canadian Intl Develop Agency and Commonwealth Secretariat, 2190 Alta Vista Drive, Ottawa, K1H 7M1 Canada. 613/521-2905.

HAYWORTH, KELLY JOE Student. BBA 1983, U of Iowa. INT: personnel. ASSN: ASPA. ADDRESS: 636 Westgate #57, Iowa City, IA 52240. 319/354-8770

HAZARD, LELAND Consulting. ADDRESS: 5023 Frew Ave, Pittsburgh, PA 15213.

HEALY, JAMES J. Acad: Ind Rels; Arbitration. BA & MA 1936, U of Wis. POSITION: (since 1973) Prof of Ind Rels, Harvard Univ, 342 Beacon St, Boston, MA 02116. 617/495-6605

HEARNE, WILLIAM M. Arbitration, Legal Practice. BA 1937, JD 1939, U of Tex. INT: arb/med, labor law, personnel. ASSN: Dallas IRRA, Tex Bar Assn. POSITIONS: Attorney, Private Practice, 1939; Appeals Officer & Pers Mgmt Specialist, US Civil Service Comm, 1941; and (since 1972) Arbitrator, 3215 James St, Dallas, TX 75227. 214/381-1304

HEBEIN, PETER J. Government. BS 1961, Marquette U. POSITION: (since 1962) Economist, Bureau of Labor Statis, USDL, 230 S Dearborn St, 9th Floor, Chicago, IL 60604. 312/353-8080

HEBERT, GERARD Acad: Ind Rels, Econ, Law. BA 1942, U of Montreal; PhD 1963, McGill U. PUBL: Labour Relations in the Quebec Construction Industry, 2 vols. Econ Council of Canada, 1978; Strategic Factors in I.R. Systems: The Construction Industry in Canada, I.I.L.S., (ILO) 1981; Public Sector Bargaining in Quebec, Chapter in Public Sector Bargaining in Canada, I.R.P.P., 1983. INT: coll barg, labor market econ, labor law. ASSN: Montreal IRRA, Canadian Ind Rels Assn, Corp des conseillers en relations industrielles, SPIDR. POSITIONS: Lecturer, McGill Univ 1957; Directeur, Institut social populaire, 1960; and (since 1965) Professor titulaire, Universite de Montreal, Ecole de relations industrielles, C.P. 6128, Succ "A", Montreal, PQ, H3C 3J7, Canada. 514/744-1870

HEDGES, JANICE NEIPERT Research. BA 1941, U of Wis-Madison. PUBL: "Job Commitment: Is it Waxing or Waning?" in The Work Ethic-A Critical Analysis, IRRA, 1983; "Absence from Work: Measuring the Hours Lost," Monthly Labour Rev, Oct 1977; "A Look at the 4-Day Week," Monthly Labor Rev, Oct 1971. pp 33-37. INT: labor market econ, coll barg. ASSN: Wash DC IRRA. POSITIONS: Labor Economist, Women's Bureau, 1963, Supervisory Labor Economist, BLS, USDL, 1966; and (since 1972) Researcher (self-employed), 616 E Capitol St NE, Washington DC 20003. 202/546-6772

HEDRICK, CHARLES BARNHART Bus:Pers/-Ind Rels. AB 1942, Marshall U; MBA 1947, Wharton-School, U of Penna. INT: personnel, org beh, health & hosp care. POSITIONS: Assoc Dir, Empl-Trng-Editorial, 1954, Dir of Ind Rels, 1957, and, since 1967, Manager, Employee Relations, The Proctor & Gamble Co, PO Box 599, Cincinnati, OH 45201. 513/562-2817

HEE, HAROLD S.Y. Bus:Mgmt/Admin. POSITION: Vice President, C. Brewer & Co Ltd, 1051 Iiwi St, Honolulu, HI 96816. 808/737-9851

HEEKIN, WILLIAM C. Bus.Mgmt/Admin. ADDRESS: Charles Mullin Inc, 1301 Union Trust Bldg, Pittsburgh, PA 15220. 513/391-7154

HEGEDUS, DAVID M. Acad: Org Beh/Pers; Consulting. BS 1971, PhD 1981, MIT. INT: personnel, org beh, mgmt/educ. ASSN: Acad of Mgmt, ASTD. POSITION: (since 1980) Asst Prof, Faculty of Business, CAB 441, Univ of Alberta, Edmonton, Alberta T6G 2G1 Canada. 403/432-4683

HEIM, JOHN H. Student. BS 1981, Okla State U; MA 1983, U of Ill. INT: coll barg, labor law, personnel. ASPA. POSITION: Grad Res Asst, Univ of Illinois. ADDRESS: 6929 E 29th St, Tulsa, OK 74129.

HEIMBACH, WILLIAM WEBSTER Retired. BS 1940, Lehigh U. INT: coll barg, arb/med, govt labor policy. POSITIONS: Asst Dir, Labor Rels, Westinghouse, 1957; Deputy Dir Labor Rels, Federal Aviation Admin, 1964; Retired. ADDRESS: Box 533 Lake of The Woods, Locust Grove, VA 22508. 703/972-7308

HEINEN, MARK L. Legal Practice. BA 1968, Central Coll; MA 1972, U of Ariz; JD 1978, Harvard. INT: labor law, arb/med, union org/admin. ASSN: Detroit IRRA, ABA, Mich/-Detroit Bar Assn. POSITIONS: Res Analyst, Ariz Legislative Council, 1973, and (since 1978) Attorney, Gregory, Van Lopik, Moore and Jeakle, 2042 First National Bldg, Detroit, MI 48226. 313/964-5600

HEINSZ, TIMOTHY J. Acad: Law; Arbitration. AB 1969, St. Louis U; JD 1972, Cornell. PUBL: "The Assault on the Employment at Will Doctrine," 40 Mo. Law Rev 855, 1983; "The Partial Closing Conundrum," Duke Law J 71, 1981; "The Subpoena Power of Labor Arbitrators," Utah Law Rev 29, 1979. INT: labor law, arb/med, coll barg. ASSN: NAA, ABA, Phi Beta Kappa. POSITIONS: Attorney, Lewis & Rice, St. Louis, 1972; Law Prof, U of Toledo, 1975; and (since 1980) Prof of Law, Univ of Missouri Law School, Tate Hall, Columbia, MO 65211. 314/882-6487

HEISER, DAVID M. Arbitration, Legal Prac. BS 1969, U of Penna; JD 1972, New York U. INT: arb/med, coll barg, labor law. ASSN: ABA, NY State Bar Assn, Assn of the Bar of City of New York. POSITIONS: Attorney, NY State Labor Rels Board, 1972; Assoc General Counsel, Amalgamated Clothing & Textile Workers Union, 1975; and (since 1983) Labor Rels Attorney, Natl Broadcasting Co. ADDRESS: 205 West 89th St, New York, NY 10024. 212/-664-4178

HELBURN, ISADORE B. Acad: Ind Rels; Arbitration. BS 1960, MS 1962, PhD 1966, U of Wis-Madison. PUBL: Local Option Recognition and Bargaining: The Texas Fire Fighter and Police Experience, (w D. Barnum), Lubbock: CBA, Tex Tech Univ, 1976; "Effects of Incomes Policies on the Health Care Industrial Relations System in the United States," (w. R. Santos) in Industrial Rels and Health Services, A.S. Sethi (ed), London: Crown Helm, 1982; "Influencing the Electorate: Refernda on Public Employee Bargaining," Ind and Labor Rels Rev, 35, April 1982, pp 330-342. INT: coll barg, arb/med, labor law. ASSN: South Tex IRRA, NAA, SPIDR. POSITIONS: (since 1968) Asst Prof, and currently, The Bobbi and Coulter R Sublett Centennial Professor and Prof of Ind Rels, Grad School of Bus, Univ of Texas. ADDRESS: Dept of Mgmt, GSB 2.206, Univ of Texas, Austin, TX 78712. 512/471-9441

HELER, EDWARD Acad: Public & Environmental Affairs; Consulting. BS 1959, Ariz State U; MPH 1984, PhD 1984, Syracuse U. PUBL: "Compensation for Death from Asbestos;" "The Costs of Asbestos-associated Disease and Death;" "The Personel Economic Impact of Asbestos-related Disability." INT: health & hosp care, labor market econ, personnel. ASSN: ASPA, Amer Public Health Assn, AEA. POSITIONS: Consultant, Human Resource Consultants, Inc., 1971; Lecturer on Human Resources, Ariz State Univ, Center for Public Affairs, 1978; and (since 1983) Asst Prof of Public & Environmental Affairs, Indiana Univ Northwest, 3400 Broadway, Gary, IN 46408. 219/980-6762

HELFAND, RICHARD Legal Practice. BA 1973, Washington U; JD 1976, U of Kans. INT: labor law, arb/med, coll barg. ASSN: Greater Kansas City IRRA, ABA(labor law), Mo Bar Assn(labor law and worker's compensation committees), Amer and Mo Assn of Trial Attorneys. POSITION: Attorney, Panethiere & Helfand, 1301 Traders Bank Bldg, 1125 Grand Ave, Kansas City, MO 64106. 816/842-9700

HELFGOTT, ROY B. Acad: Econ; Consulting. BS 1948, CCNY; MA 1949, Columbia U; PhD 1957, New School for Social Res. PUBL: Labor Economics, Random House, 2nd Ed, 1980; "American Unions and Multinational Companies: A Case of Misplaced Emphasis," Columbia J of World Bus, Summer 1983; Management, Automation, and People, (w R. Beaumont), Ind Rels Counselors, 1964. INT: impact of technology, labor market econ, coll barg. ASSN: New York IRRA, AEA. POSITIONS: Ind Devel Officer, United Nations, 1966-67; Consultant, Organization Resources Counselors, Inc, 1968 to present, and (since 1968) Prof of Econ, New Jersey Inst of Tech, 323 High St, Newark, NJ 07102. 201/645-5271

HELFRICH, THOMAS GEORGE Bus:Pers/Ind Rels, Bus:Mgmt/Admin, Arbitration. BS 1964, Cornell U; MBA 1969. INT: coll barg, arb/med, mgmt/educ. ASSN: Harrisburg IRRA, ASPA, AAA. POSITIONS: Labor Rels Rep, Construction Empl Labor Rels Assn of NYS, 1971; Mediator-Arbitrator (self-employed), 1974; and (since 1978) Supervisor of Labor Rels, GPU Nuclear Corp, Middletown. ADDRESS: 400 Wetherburn Dr, Lancaster, PA 17601. 717/948-8110

HELIKER, GEORGE B. Acad: Econ. Retired. 1407 S 4th Ave, Boseman, MT 59715.

HELING, KEVIN J. Student. BA 1978, U of Wis-Madison. Currently, Student of IR at U of Wis. ADDRESS: 509 Fourth St, Waunakee, WI 53597

HELLQUIST, JAMES K. Arbitration, Bus:-Pers/Ind Rels. BA 1965, MA 1966, Drake U. INT: arb/med, coll barg, ind psych. ASSN: Chicago IRRA, AAA, Soc of Federal Labor Rels Professionals. POSITIONS: Pers Dir, General Motors Parts Div, 1967; Manager, Arbitration Branch, Labor Rels Div. 1972, and currently, General Mgr, Labor Rels Div, U.S. Postal Service, Central Reg, 433 West Van Buren, Room 1110, Chicago, IL 60699. 312/886-2959

HELMREICH, THEODORE C. Acad: Econ, Ind Rels. PhD 1936, U of Ill. INT: coll barg, govt labor policy, labor market econ. POSITION: Emeritus Prof of Econ, Purdue U. ADDRESS: 116 Rockland Dr, West Lafayette, IN 47906. 317/463-5824

HELSBY, ROBERT D. Acad: Ind Rels; Arbitration, Consulting. BS 1940, SUNY-Oswego; MA 1948, Ohio State U. DEd 1958, NYSSILR-Cornell. PUBL: Portrait of a Process-Collective Negotiations in Public Employment; "Commentary on Bargaining in American Higher Education," chapter in book; "One Man's View of the Taylor

Law-Thirteen Years Later." INT: arb/med, coll barg, govt labor policy. ASSN: ALRA, AAA. POSITIONS: Chairman, 1967-77, Director PERB, 1977-81; Natl Consultant-Pub Emp Labor Rels, Carnegie Corp, 1977-81; and (since 1981) Professor, Ind Rels, Univ of North Florida. ADDRESS: 4567 St. John's Bluff Rd, Jacksonville, FL 32216. 904/646-2780

HENDERSON, ROBERT D. Retired. BBA 1938, Westminster Coll (PA); MBA 1941, Ohio State U; PhD 1949, U of Pittsburgh. INT: mgmt/-educ, empl/trng programs, personnel. ASSN: Acad of Mgmt, Natl Assn of Purchasing Mgmt. POSITIONS: Prof of Mgmt, Bowling Green U, 1954-73; Dana Professor of Management, Univ of Tampa, 1973-1980, and, currently, Retired. ADDRESS: 11801 Lipsey Rd, Tampa, FL 33618. 813/961-0769

HENDRICKS, WALLACE Acad: Econ, Ind Rels. AB 1969, PhD 1973, U of Calif. PUBL: Wage Indexation in the United States, 1984; "Determinants of Bargaining Structure in U.S. Manufacturing," Ind and Labor Ed Rev, Jan 1982, pp 181-195; "Unionism Oligopoly and Rigid Wages," rev of Econ and Statis, May 1981, pp 198-205. INT: labor market econ, method/-statis, coll barg. ASSN: AEA. POSITIONS: Asst Prof, 1975, Assoc Prof of Econ and LIR, 1978, and, since 1982, Professor of Econ and Labor & Ind Rels, Inst of Labor and Ind Rels, Univ of Illinois, 504 E Armory, Champaign, IL 61820. 217/333-6028

HENDRICKSON, STEVEN J. Union. BA 1970, MA 1973, U of Wis-Madison. INT: coll barg, intl comparative labor. POSITION: (since 1978) Research Analyst, Industrial Union Department, AFL-CIO, 815 16th St NW, Washington DC 20006. 202/842-7866

HENDRIX, THOMAS C. Government. POSITION: Regional Director, National Labor Rels Board, 10439 Ash, Overland Park, KS 66207. 816/361-8233

HENEMAN, HERBERT G. III Acad: Org Beh/Pers. AB 1966, Wabash Coll; MS 1968, PhD 1970, U of Wis-Madison. PUBL: Personnel/-Human Resource Management, (w D. Schwab, J. Fossum and L.Dyer) rev ed. Homewood IL: Irwin, 1983; "Predicting the Outcome of Union Certification Elections: A Review of the Literature," (w M. Sandver), Ind and Labor Rels Rev, 36, 1983, pp 537-559; "Pay Satisfaction: Its Multidimensional Nature and Measurement," (w D. Schwab), Intl J of Psychology, in press. INT: personnel, union org/admin, org beh. ASSN: Wis IRRA, Acad of Mgmt. POSITIONS: Visiting Assoc Prof, U of Wash, 1976-77; Univ Distinguished Prof, Ohio State Univ, 1981, and (since 1978) Prof of Business, Grad School of Bus, Room 188A Bascom Hall, Univ of Wis, Madison, WI 53706. 608/263-3461

HENEMAN, HERBERT G., JR. Acad: Org Beh/Pers, Ind Rels, Econ. Retired. PhD 1948, U of Minn. PUBL: Handbook Personnel and Industrial Relations, (co-editor w D. Yoder), Amer Soc of Pers Admin; Labor Economics, (co-editor w D. Yoder); Employment Relations Research. INT: personnel, coll barg, labor market econ. ASSN: AEA, ASPA. POSITIONS: Visiting Prof of Econ and IR, U of Western Australia, 1973-78, and (since 1954) Prof Econ and Ind Rels, Univ of Minn. Retired. ADDRESS: 92 Norma St. Belen, NM 87002. 505/864-1988

HENEMAN, ROBERT LLOYD Acad: Ind Rels. MA 1978, U of Ill at UC; PhD 1984, Mich State U. PUBL: "The Effects of Time Delay in Rating and Amount of Information Observed on Performance Rating Accuracy," Acad of Mgmt J, 26, 1983, pp 677-686. INT: personnel, ind psych, coll barg. ASSN: Acad of Mgmt. POSITIONS: Pers Specialist, Pacific Gas & Electric Co, 1979; Grad Res Asst, Mich State Univ, 1980; and (since 1984) Asst Prof of Labor & Human Resources, Ohio State Univ, 319 Hagerty Hall, 1775 College Rd, Columbus, OH 43210. 614/422-2809

HENLE, PETER Arbitration, Consulting. BA 1940, Swarthmore Coll; MA 1947, Amer U. PUBL: "Reverse Collective Bargaining? A Look at Some Union Concession Situations," Ind and Labor Rev, April 1973; "The Worker and the Job: Coping With Change," Chapter 5 Economic Effects: Reviewing the Evidence, Prentice Hall, 1974; "The Distribution of Earned Income Among Men and Women, 1958-77," (w P. Ryscavage), Monthly Labor Rev, April 1980. INT: coll barg, govt labot policy, arb/med. ASSN: Wash DC IRRA, AEA, AAA. POSITIONS: Sr Specialist, Congrssional Res Serv, U.S. Library ofCongress; Deputy Asst Sec of Labor, USDL, 1977, and (since 1980) Arbitrator (self-employed), 3219 N Wakefield St, Arlington, VA 22207. 703/536-7917

HENNES, THOMAS M. Union. N 7822 Espe Rd, Spokane, WA 99207.

HENSON, THERESA M. Student. 7306 East Avenue, Turlock, CA 95380. 209/668-9017

HERCULES, DENNIS CHARLES Bus:Pers/Ind Rels. POSITION: Director of Ind Rels, Whitaker Cable Corp, 2801 Rockcreek Parkway, North Kansas City, MO 64116. 816/474-0300

HERCUS, TERRY F. Acad: Ind Rels, Bus Admin. POSITION: Professor, Dept of Bus Admin, Univ of Manitoba, Winnipeg, Manitoba R3T 2N2 Canada. 204/474-9662

HERDING, RICHARD GUNTHER Journalism. Dr 1971, Frankfurt (Germany). PUBL: Job Control and Union Structure, Rotterdan: Univ Press, 1972; Lohnarbeiter interessen, (w B. Kirchlechner), Frankfurt/New York: Campus 1978; Sozialdemokratie und Klassenkonflikte, (w D. Hoss), Frankfurt/New York Campus: 1975. INT: labor journalism, labor history, ind sociol. ASSN: Media Alliance, Deutsche journalistea-Union. POSITIONS: Res Sociologist, Inst for Sozialforschung, Frankfurt, 1969; and (since 1977) Journalist, Informations dienst: Zentrum fur alternative Medien, Cornelius Str 24, Frankfurt 1 West Germany. Phone: 0611/704352

HERGENHAN, ROBERT J. Arbitration. POSITION: Vice Pres Operations, National Acad of Conciliators, 5530 Wisconsin Ave #1250, Chevy Chase, MD 20815.

HERINGTON, CARL DAVID Bus:Pers/Ind Rels. BS 1963, St. John's U-Minn; MAIR, 1970, U of Minn. INT: personnel, labor law, arb/med. ASSN: Amer Compensation Assn. POSITIONS: Vice Pres-Cash Compensation, 1976, Vice Pres-Personnel Operations, 1979, and, since 1983, Vice Pres-Corp Employee Rels, Crocker National Corp & Bank, 79 New Montgomery, 4th FL, San Francisco, CA 94105. 415/477-5880

HERLIHY, H. MURRAY Acad: Econ, Ind Rels; Arbitration. Retired. PhD 1954, U of Chicago. INT: labor market econ, arb/med, coll barg. ASSN: Chicago IRRA, AEA. POSITION: Emeritus Prof of Econ, Lake Forest College. ADDRESS: 6007 Sheridan Rd, Apt 9A, Chicago, IL 60660. 312/234-3100

HERLING, JOHN Journalism. AB Harvard. POSITION: (since 1948) Editor, J. Herlings Labor Letter, 1411 K St NW, Suite 1234, Washington DC 20005. 202/737-2511

HERMAN, EDWARD EMIL Acad: Econ, Ind Rels. BComm 1958, MA 1962, PhD 1965, McGill U. PUBL: Labor Law, (co-author w G. S. Skinner), Random Houjse, Mar 1972; Collective Bargaining and Labor Relations, (co-author w A. Kuhn), Prentice Hall, 1981; "The Importance of Costing Labor Contracts," (w G. S. Skinner), IRRA Spring Proc & Labor Law J, Aug 1981. INT: coll barg, labor law, arb/med. ASSN: Cincinnati IRRA, AEA, Canadian Ind Rels Assn. POSITIONS: Assoc Prof of Econ, SUNY-Plattsburgh, 1964; and (since 1966) Prof of Econ, Dept of Econ, Univ of Cincinnati, 1200 Crosley Tower, Cincinnati, OH 45221. 513/475-3568

HERMAN, FRANCINE APRIL Acad: Bus Admin; Consulting, Communications. POSITION: Assoc Prof, School of Hotel Admin, Cornell Univ, Ithaca, NY 14853. 607/256-3846

HERNANDEZ-BENITEZ, F. Arbitration. BA 1965, U of Puerto Rico. INT: arb/med, labor law, coll barg. ASSN: Assn of Labor Rels Practitioners, P.R. & V.I., Assn of Labor Mediators and Arbitrators of P.R., AAA. POSITIONS: School Teacher, DPI-PR, 1965; Juvenile Probation Officer, Adm of Courts-P.R., 1966, and, since 1968, Labor Arbitrator, Dept of Labor, Munoz Rivera Ave, #505, Hato Rey, PR 00918. Phone: 7545309

HERNANDEZ, MICHELLE MARIE Student. BA 1982 UCLA. INT: coll barg, govt labor policy, arb/med. ASSN: PIRA. POSITION: Currently, Student, UCLA Grad School of Management. ADDRESS: 1516 Colby Ave, #9, Los Angeles, CA 90025.

HERRICK, CHRISTINE T. Arbitration. BA 1971, Sarah Lawrence Coll; JD 1975, Northwestern School of Law-Portland, OR. INT: arb/med, labor law. ASSN: Ore State Bar(labor law section), AAA(labor panel), SPIDR. POSITIONS: Hearing Examiner, Empl Rels Board, State of Oregon, 1975-82, and (since 1982) Arbitrator (self-emloyed), 1610 Winter St SE, Salem, OR 97302. 503/362-3351

HERRICK, NEAL Q. Consulting. BA 1953, U of N.H.; PhD 1976, UGS. PUBL: Improving Government Experiments with QWL Systems, ed, NY:Praeger, 1983; Where Have All the Robots Gone? (w H. Sheppard), NY: The Free Press, 1972; "The Means and End of Work," Human Rels, vol 34, #7, 1981, pp 611-632. INT: union org/admin, govt labor policy, coll barg. POSITIONS: Consultant, Ohio State U, 1978; Lecturer, U of Ariz, 1979; and (since 1984) Sr Assoc, Mgmt and Beh Science Center, The Wharton School. ADDRESS: 4701 Pine St, B11, Philadelphia, PA 19143. 215/898-1494

HERRNSTADT, IRWIN L. Acad: Econ. PhD 1964, MIT. PUBL: "Reaction of Three Local Unions to Economic Adversity," J of Pol Econ, Oct 1954; "The Boston Experience," in Metropolitan Inpact of Manpower Programs: A Four-City Comparison, (w G.L. Mangum & R. Thayne), Olympus Publishing, UT 1973; A Study of the Training of Tool and Die Makers, (Report) USDL, 1970. INT: labor market econ, empl/trng programs, coll barg. ASSN: AEA, Southern Econ Assn, Eastern Econ Assn. POSITIONS: Res Asst, Ind Rels Sec, Dept of Econ, MIT, 1954-55; Res Asst, Union-Mgmt Project, Harvard, 1955-58; and (since 1960) Prof of Econ, Dept of Econ, Northeastern Univ, 360 Huntington Ave, Boston, MA 02115. 617/437-2882

HERRNSTADT, OWEN EDWARD Student. BS 1980, MS 1982, U of Wis-Madison. INT: labor law, arb/med, coll barg. ASSN: ABA(section of empl and labor law). POSITIONS: Law Clerk to Natl Labor Rels Bd Member D. A. Zimmerman, 1983, and, currently, student. ADDRESS: 1008 Grant St, Madison, WI 53711.

HERSHEY, MARGARET L. Student. ADDRESS: 596 Fairfield, Elmhurst IL 60126. 312/530-7421

HERSHFIELD, DAVID CHARLES Acad: Bus Admin; Arbitration. BA 1962, CCNY; MA 1964, PhD 1970, Princeton U. PUBL: "Negotiating Away Narrow Skill Jurisdictions," IRRA Proceedings of the 32nd Annual Meeting, 1979; The Multinational Union Challenges the Multinational Company, The Conference Board, Inc, 1975; "The Choice Between Obstruction and Control in the New York City Newspaper Industry," IRRA, Proceedings of the 24th Annual Meeting, 1971. INT: coll barg, arb/med, labor market econ. ASSN: New York IRRA. POSITIONS: Res Assoc, Labor Rels Res, The Conference Board, 1972-77; Assoc Prof of Econ, Baruch Coll, CUNY, 1978-81, and, since 1981, Assoc Prof of Mgmt, College of Staten Island, CUNY. ADDRESS: 162 Abernathy Dr, Trenton, NJ 08618. 212/390-7991

HERZOG, PAUL M. Retired. SB 1927, Harvard; MA 1930, U of Wis; LLB 1936, Columbia. POSITIONS: Chmn, NLRB, 1945-53; and Pres, Salzburg Seminar, 1965-71. ADDRESS: 14 E 75th St, New York, NY 10020.

HESHIZER, BRIAN P. Acad: Ind Rels. BA 1971, Columbus Coll; MA 1976, Fla State U; PhD 1978, U of Wis-Madison. PUBL: "Discipline in the Non Union Company: Protecting Employer and Employee Rights," Pers 59, Mar-Apr, 1982, pp 71-78; "The Experience of Wisconsin with State Provided Labor Arbitration," J of Coll Negotiations in the Public Sector, 11, #4, 1982, pp 337-350; "The Effect of Contract Language on Low-Level Settlement of Grievances," Labor Law J, 30, #7, July 1979, pp 427-432. INT: coll barg, personnel, labor law. ASSN: Northeast Ohio IRRA, ASPA. POSITION: Asst Prof, Dept of Mgmt and Labor, Coll of Bus Admin, Cleveland State Univ, Cleveland, OH 44115. 216/687-4748/4754

HESSE, DANA L. Government. Acad: Bus Admin. BBA 1969, MA 1971, U of Wis-Madison. INT: labor law, coll barg, arb/med. ASSN: Wis IRRA, Wis Ind Rels Alumni Assn. POSITIONS: Part time Lecturer, Labor Rels, School of Bus Admin, U of Wis-Milwaukee, 1981, and (since 1971) Supervising Examiner, NLRB, Henry Reuss Fed Plaza, Suite 1240, 310 West Wisconsin Ave, Milwaukee, WI 53203. 414/291-3878

HETRICK, JERRY LYNN Bus:Pers/Ind Rels. BS 1964, Ind U; MA 1966, U of Ill. INT: coll barg, arb/med, labor law. POSITIONS: Labor

Rels/Safety Plant, 1970, Corp Labor Rels Rep, 1973, and, currently, Corporate Labor Rels Manager, Brunswick Corp, Skokie. ADDRESS: 602 W Hackberry, Arlington Heights, IL 60004. 312/470-4660

HEYSER, MARLENE K. Bus:Pers/Ind Rels, Consulting, Ind Rels. BS 1982, U of Redlands; Cert in Human Res Mgmt, 1983, Wharton School. INT: coll barg, mgmt/educ, labor law. ASSN: Orange County IRRA. POSITIONS: Admin Asst/Pers, Westinghouse, 1976; Lecturer, Loyola Marymount U, 1983, and (since 1978) Manager, Employee and Union Rels, Orange Cty Transit Dist, 11222 Acacia Pkwy, Garden Grove, CA 92642. 714/971-6319

HICKLING, M. ANTHONY Acad: Econ. Prof Faculty of Law, U of British Columbia, 1822 East Mall, Vancouver Canada, V6T 1Y1 Canada.

HIESTAND, DALE L. Acad: Human Resources. MA 1949, Washington U; PhD 1963, Columbia U. PUBL: Comparative Metropolitan Labor Markets; Changing Careers After 35; Economic Growth and Employment Opportunities for Minorities. INT: labor market econ, personnel, health & hospital care. ASSN: AEA. POSITIONS: Res Assoc 1955, Sr., Res Assoc, 1959, Asst Prof, 1964, and, since 1970, Professor of Business, Grad School of Bus, Columbia Univ, 116 & Broadway, New York, NY 10027. 212/280-3482

HIGDON, ROBERT B. Bus:Pers/Ind Rels. POSITION: Vice Pres, Human Resources, Chicago Sun Times, 401 N Wabash Ave, Chicago, IL 60611.

HIGGINS, GEORGE G. Arbitration. Acad: Theology. MA 1942, PhD 1944, Catholic U of Amer. PUBL: Syndicated columnist for N.C. News Service: "The Yardstick." INT: arb/med, labor history, coll barg. ASSN: Leadership Conf on Civil Rights. POSITIONS: Secretary for Special Concerns, U. S. Catholic Conference, 1944-1981; and, currently, Adjunct Lecturer, Dept/Theology, Catholic Univ and Chairman, UAW Public Review Board, United Auto Workers, Livonia, MI. ADDRESS: Curley Hall, Catholic Univ of America, Washington DC 20064. 202/635-5660

HIGGINS, JOHN E. Arbitration. Burdett Jr. Coll, 1929. INT: arb/med, health & hosp care. ASSN: Boston IRRA, NAA, SPIDR, Labor Guild Boston, MA. POSITIONS: Assoc Director of Labor Rels, John Hancock Insurance Co, 1959-74 (retired), and, since 1974, Arbitrator (self-employed), 33 Holland Road, Melrose, MA 02176. 617/665-8372

HIGGINS, NORMAN G. Bus:Pers/Ind Rels. AB 1959, Duke U. INT: coll barg, empl/trng programs, personnel. ASSN: ASPA, Pers Accreditation Inst. POSITIONS: Manager, Pers, 1981, and, since 1983, Manager, Employee/Labor Rels, Monsanto, 800 N Lindbergh, St. Louis, MO 63166. 314/694-2416

HIGGINS, RICHARD G. Arbitration. BS 1963, US Military Acad; MBA 1972, Harvard. INT: arb/med, labor history, labor market econ. ASSN: Boston IRRA, SPIDR, FMCS Panel. POSITION: Arbitrator, 87 Pillsbury Rd, Londonderry, NH 03053. 603/432-9225

HIGGINS, THOMAS JAMES Acad: Ind Rels; Bus:Pers/Ind Rels. BS 1978, Cornell U. INT: personnel, union org/admin, labor law. ASSN: New England Chapter, Cornell ILR Alumni, Amer Mgmt Assn. POSITIONS: Labor Res Specialist, Bond, Schoeneck & King, 1978; Labor Res Specialist, Stoneman, Chandler & Miller, 1980; and (since 1982) Corporate Dir of Human Resources, Spencer Press, Inc., Hingham. ADDRESS: 19 Valentine Rd, Framingham, MA 01701. 617/749-5000

HILDEBRANDT, ANN Legal Practice. BA 1969, U of Mich; JD 1976, U of Detroit. PUBL: "Michigan Construction Lien Statute Update," Detroit Lawyer, Oct 1979. INT: labor law, arb/med, coll barg. ASSN: Detroit IRRA, Women Lawyers Assn of Mich, Mich Trial Lawyers Assn, Detroit Bar Assn. POSITIONS: Architect, Nathan Johnson Assoc, 1975; Labor Attorney & Assoc, Klein & Bloom, P.C., 1976; and (since 1982) Attorney, Ann Hildebrandt, Attorney and Counselor, 975 E. Jefferson Ave, Detroit, MI 48207. 313/567-2333

HILL, HERBERT Acad: Ind Rels. ADDRESS: Humanities Bldg, Room 4225, Univ of Wis, 455 N Park St, Madison, WI 53706.

HILL, MARVIN F. Acad: Ind Rels. POSITION: Management and Ind Rels, Wirtz Hall, Northern Ill Univ, Dekalb, IL 60115.

HILL, RICHARD EMMETT Acad: Bus Admin. PhD 1970, Purdue. INT: coll barg, org beh, personnel. ASSN: Acad of Mgmt, ASPA, Northeast Indiana Pers Assn. POSITION: Assoc Prof, Indiana Univ at Fort Wayne, 2101 Coliseum Blvd E, Fort Wayne, IN 46805. 219/482-5289

HILL, SAMUEL ERVIN Retired. BA 1935, Ohio Wesleyan U, MA 1938, PhD 1940, Harvard. PUBL: Teamsters and Transportation; Manpower and Innovation in American Industry; Toward Fair Employment. INT: arb/med. ASSN: Conn IRRA, AEA. ADDRESS: 11 John Read Rd, West Redding, CT 06896.

HILLARY, TIMOTHY B. Bus:Pers/Ind Rels, Mgmt/Admin. BA 1967, Western Mich U. INT: personnel, coll barg, health & hosp care. ASSN: ASPA-Northern Calif Human Resource Council; Calif Hospital Pers Mgr Assn, Federated Employers-Ind Rels Round Table. POSITIONS: Empl Rels Mgr, Simplicity Pattern Co, Niles, MI, 1970; Dir of Ind Rels, Penn-Dixie Industries, Cement Div, Nazareth, PA, 1977; and (since 1981) Dir of Human Resources, Mt. Diablo Hospital Medical Center, 2540 East St, Concord, CA 94549. 415/674-2015

HILLS, STEPHEN MOORE Acad: Ind Rels. PhD 1975, U of Wis. PUBL: "The Long-Run effects of Job Changes and Unemployment Among Male Teenagers," (w B. Becker), J of Human Resources, Spring 1983; "Unemployment Compensation and the Duration of Unemployment-the Problem of Eligible Nonfilers," J of Human Resources, Summer 1982; "Youth Employment in the United States," Chapter 9 in B.G. Reubens Youth at Work: A Cross National Survey, Totowa NJ: Allenheld Osmun, 1983. INT: empl/trgn programs, income maint, ind sociol. POSITIONS: Asst Prof-Econ, U of Dubuque, 1970; Asst Prof, Ind Rels, U of British Columbia, 1974; and (since 1977) Assoc Prof, Labor & Human Resources, Ohio State Univ. ADDRESS: 196 W Jeffrey Pl, Columbus, OH 43214. 614/422-2809

HILZ, EDWARD RICHARD Government. BA 1968, U of Nebr; AM 1975, U of Ill. INT: coll barg, personnel. ASSN: Wash DC IRRA,

SPIDR, SFLRP. POSITIONS: Mgmt Trainee, 1981, Production Foreman, U. S. Steel, 1972; and (since 1980) Special Asst to the Chief Counsel, Federal Labor Rels Authority, Washington DC. ADDRESS: 3405-B S Stafford St, Arlington, VA 22206. 202/382-0876

HIMMELMAN, WILLIAM C. Union. INT: union org/admin, labor history, labor educ. ASSN: Denver IRRA, Council for Public TV, Urban League. POSITIONS: Technician, Mountain States Tel & Tel Co, 1956; Pres, Communications Workers of Amer, Local #8412, 1972, and, since 1977, President, Denver Area Labor Fed, AFL-CIO, 360 Acoma St, #202, Denver, CO 80223. 303/722-1306

HINDS, JULIE G. Bus:Pers/Ind Rels. POSITION: Ind Labor Rels & EEO, Ciba-Geigy Corp, Pharmaceutical Div, 556 Morris Ave, Summit, NJ 07901. 201/277-7240

HINKSON, ROBERT E. Bus:Mgmt/Admin, Bus:Pers/Ind Rels. BS 1958, Midwestern U. INT: personnel, mgmt/educ, coll barg. ASSN: Houston IRRA. POSITIONS: Mgr Operations, 1978, and, since 1980, Manager, Industrial Rels, Denka Chemical Corp. PO Box 87220, Houston, TX 77017. 713/477-8821 ext 300

HIROZAWA, BETTY F. Employer Assn. BS & ILR 1951, Cornell. INT: coll barg, personnel, labor law. ASSN: Hawaii IRRA, ASPA. POSITION: Vice Pres Admin/Secretary-Treas, Hawaii Employers Council, PO Box 29699, Honolulu, HI 96820. 808/836-1511

HIRSCHEY, K. DAVID Bus:Pers/Ind Rels, Mgmt/Admin, Consulting. BS 1972, MA 1974, U of Minn. INT: personnel, coll barg, health & hosp care. POSITIONS: Zone Pers Mgr/Sales, Frito-Lay Inc., 1977; Pres/Principal Consultant, Hirschey Assoc, Inc., 1979; and (since 1982) Personnel Director, General Mills, Inc. ADDRESS: PO Box 1113, Minneapolis, MN 55440. 612/540-3033

HIRSH, STEVEN J. Bus:Pers/Ind Rels. BS-BA 1975, U of Ill. JD 1984, Kent Coll of Law, Ill Inst of Tech. INT: EEO/Affirmative Action, labor law, coll barg. ASSN: Chicago IRRA, Delta Sigma Pi, ABA, Affirmative Action Soc of Chicago. POSITIONS: Asst Dir of Pers, Palmer House (Hilton Hotels), 1977; Plant Pers Labor Rep, 1977, and, since 1982, Corp EEO Coordinator, Zenith Radio Corp/Zenith Electronics Corp. ADDRESS: Apt 1, 2346 N Geneva Terr, Chicago, IL 60614. 312/745-4866

HIRSHORN, BARBARA Consulting. POSITION: Res Assoc, Vice Pres, SIH Inc, 3382 Bluett Dr, Ann Arbor, MI 48105.

HISATOMI, MINDY MIDORI Bus:Pers/Mgmt/-Admin. BA 1977, U of Calif-Berkeley, MS-IR 1979, U of Wis-Madison. INT: ind sociol, org beh, ind psych. POSITIONS: Placement Rep, 1980, College Rels Coordinator, 1981, and, since 1982, Business Admin, TRW Electronics & Defense, Redondo Beach. ADDRESS: 3515 Spencer St, Torrance, CA 90503. 213/370-2117

HOBART, CHRISTINE L. Acad: Ind Rels, Org Beh/Pers; Arbitration. BBA 1971, Harvard. PUBL: "Collective Bargaining with Professionals," Health Care Mgmt rev, Spring 1976; "Sex Roles Stereo Typing Among Future Managers," Women in Mgmt, Ed D. Jewell, 1977; "Can Faculty Unionism Boomerang on the Students?" Policy Issues in Contemporary Pers & Ind Rels, Miner & Miner Eds, Macmillan, 1977. INT: coll barg, health & hosp care, personnel. ASSN: Boston IRRA, Acad of Mgmt, Amer Public Health Assn. POSITION: (since 1971) Assoc Prof, Dept of Mgmt, Northeastern Univ. ADDRESS: 32 Webster Court, Newton Centre, MA 02159. 617/437-4728

HOCHNER, ARTHUR Acad: Org Beh/Pers, Ind Rels. BA 1970, Queens Coll, CUNY; PhD 1978, Harvard. PUBL: "Worker Ownership, Community Ownership, and Labor Unions: Two Examples," Econ and Ind Democracy, Fall 1983; "Plant Closings and Job Loss In Philadelphia: A Statistical Analysis," (w D. Zibman), in Raines, Berson and Grace (eds) Community and Capital in Conflict, Temple U Press, 1982; "Worker Ownership, Participation, and Control,(w R. Russell & S. Perry), Ind Rels, Fall 1979. INT: org beh, worker ownership, coll barg. ASSN: Philadelphia IRRA, Amer Sociol Assn, Intl Sociol Assn, Acad of Mgmt. POSITION: (since 1978) Asst Prof of Ind Rels and Org Beh, School of Bus Admin, Temple Univ. ADDRESS: 130 W Queen Lane, Philadelphia, PA 19144. 215/787-8133

HODES, NANCY L. Government. BS 1968, Cornell U. PUBL: "Casual Employees: Scabs or Saviors?" Natl Center for Coll Barg in Higher Educ, July 1983; "Ethics in Collective Bargaining in Higher Education," (co-authored w R. J. Kurach), in Ethical Principles, Practices and Problems in Higher Education, C. C. Thomas Publ, 1983. ASSN: Albany Dispute Mediation Prog, Natl Center for Coll Barg in Higher Educ, Intl Pers Mgmt Assn. POSITIONS: Asst Dir, 1979, Deputy Dir, 1981, and, since 1984, Executive Deputy Director, Governor's Office of Empl Rels, Empire State Plaza, Agency Bldg 2, 12th FL, Albany, NY 12223. 518/474-2350

HODGES, ANN C. Legal Practice. BSIR, 1973, U of N.C; MA 1974, U of Ill; JD 1981, Northwestern U. PUBL: "Extending Tree Fruits to Protect Picketing of Predominant Product-Secondaries," Retail Store Empl Union Local 1001U NLRB, (Safeco Title Ins Co). INT: labor law. ASSN: Chicago/Amer Bar Assn. POSITIONS: Field Examiner, NLRB, 1974, and (since 1981) Attorney, Katz, Friedman, Schur and Gagle, Chicago. ADDRESS: 815 W Newport 1 Front, Chicago, Il 60657. 312/263-6330

HOELLERING, MICHAEL F. Arbitration, Consulting, Legal Practice. BS 1956, JD 1959, Columbia. PUBL: Arbitration and the Law, Editor; Regular Contributor on Arbitration, New York Law J; Wide World of Arbitration - Selected Articles. INT: arb/med, coll barg, intl comparative labor. ASSN: ABA(Committee on Arb & Law of Coll Barg), Natl Construction Arb Committee, Assoc of the Bar, City of New York. POSITIONS: Vice Pres-Case Admins, 1972, and, since 1980, General Counsel, Amer Arb Assn, 140 W 51st St, New York, NY 10020. 212/484-4110

HOERR, JOHN P. Journalism. AB 1953, Penna State. PUBL: "The New Industrial Relations," Bus Week, May 14, 1981; "A Revolution in Work Rules," Bus Week, May 16, 1983. INT: labor journalism, org beh, coll barg. POSITIONS: Producer-Commentator, WQED (Public TV), Pittsburgh, 1969-74; and (since 1979) Assoc Editor, Business Week, 1221 Ave of the Americas, New York, NY 10020. 212/512-3292

HOEXTER, ELSIE GOODMAN Retired. ADDRESS: 703 Buccaneer Court, Silver Springs, MD 20904.

HOFFMAN, EILEEN BARKAS Government, Labor Mediation. BS 1969, NYSSILR-Cornell; MA 1970, Columbia. PUBL: "Mediation of Unfair Dismissal Grievances: The British Example," Proceedings of the 32 Annual Meeting, IRRA: Unionization of Professional Studies; Resolving Labor-Management Disputes: A Nine Country Comparison. INT: arb/med, intl comparative labor, coll barg. ASSN: Wash DC, New York IRRA, SPIDR, Intl Soc of Labor Law & Soc Security. POSITIONS: Research Specialist, The Conference Board, New York, 1971; Res Director, Mass Labor Rels Commission, 1974; and (since 1975) Commissioner (Labor Mediator), FMCS, Wash DC Office. ADDRESS: 2925 28th St NW, Washington DC 20008. 202/653-5230

HOFFMAN, EMILY P. Acad: Econ. BA 1965, U of Mass; MA 1968, Boston Coll; PhD U of Mass. PUBL: "Faculty Salaries: Is There Discrimination by Sex, Race, and Discipline? Additional Evidence," Amer Econ Rev 66, 1, Mar 1976, pp 196-8; "The Deeper Economics of Sleeping: Important Clues Toward the Discovery of Activity X," J of Pol Econ, vol 85, #3, June 1977, pp 647-9; "Economic Progress of Black Women," Econ Letters, vol 6 #2, 1980, pp 191-5. INT: labor market econ, govt labor policy, empl/trng programs. ASSN: Southwestern MI IRRA, AEA. POSITIONS: Visiting Prof, U of N.C., Chapel Hill, 1976; Asst Prof, Douglass Coll, Rutgers Univ, 1977; and (since 1981) Assoc Professor, Dept of Econ, Western Mich Univ, Kalamazoo, MI 49008. 616/383-1745

HOFFMAN, HELEN G. Acad: Ind Rels, Law; Arbitration. JD 1947, Columbia U. INT: arb/med, govt labor pollicy, labor law. ASSN: AAA, ASPA. POSITIONS: Asst Dean, Rutgers School of Law, 1962-78; Arbitrator, and, currently, Assoc Prof, Grad School of Public Admin, Florida Atlantic Univ, Boca Raton. ADDRESS: 150 Bradley Pl, Palm Beach, FL 33480. 305/655-4149

HOFFMAN, JOSEPH P. Union, Legal Prac. BS 1980, LeMoyne Coll; JD 1983, U of Minn. INT: arb/med, health & hosp care, union org/-admin. ASSN: Ramsey County/Minn/Amer Bar Assn. POSITION: Staff Attorney, Minnesota Nurses Assn, 1821 University Ave W, St. Paul, MN 55104. 612/646-6676

HOGAN, CURTIS J. Consulting. BS 1950, Rockhurst Coll. 434 S Newport Way, Denver, CO 80224. 303/388-9237

HOGLER, RAYMOND LOUIS Acad: Ind Rels.; Arbitration. BA 1967, Fort Lewis Coll; PhD 1972, JD 1976, U of Colo. PUBL: "Impasse Resolution in Public Sector Collective Bargaining: A Proposed Structure," Ind Rels Law J, vol 6, #4, 1984; "The Regional Transportation District Strike and the Colorado Labor Peace Act: A Study in Public Sector Collective Bargaining," U of Colo Law Rev, vol 54, #2, 1983; "Employee Discipline and Due Process Rights: Is There an Appropriate Remedy?" Labor Law J, vol 33, #12, 1982. INT: labor law, arb/med, coll barg. ASSN: Acad of Mgmt, ABA, Colo Bar Assn. POSITION: (since 1983) Asst Prof, Dept of Labor Studies, Pennsylvania State Univ, 901 Liberal Arts Tower, University Park, PA 16802. 814/865-5425

HOGUE, JAMES C. Bus:Pers/Ind Rels. POSITION: Vice Pres Ind Rels, Florida Steel Corp, PO Box 23328, Tampa, FL 33630. 813/251-8811

HOLIBER, CARYL LOIS Government. ADDRESS: 6414 Kenhowe Drive, Bethesda, MD 20817. 301/229-6414

HOLLAND, SUSAN S. Government. BS 1960, Cornell. INT: labor market econ. ASSN: San Francisco IRRA. POSITION: Asst Regional Commissioner, USDL-BLS. ADDRESS: 535 Pennsylvania Ave, San Francisco, CA 94107. 415/556-7384

HOLLEY, WILLIAM H., JR. Acad: Ind Rels; Arbitration. BS 1962, MBA 1965, Miss State U; PhD 1970 U of Ala. PUBL: Labor Relations Process; Personnel Management: Functions & Issues; "Relationship of Performance Appraisal System Characteristics to Verdicts in Selected Employment Discrimination Cases," Acad of Mgmt J, June 1982. INT: coll barg, arb/med, personnel. ASSN: Atlanta IRRA, SPIDR, Southern Mgmt Assn, Acad of Mgmt. POSITION: Lowder Professor, Auburn Univ. ADDRESS: 819 Winterhawk Dr, Auburn, AL 36830. 205/826-5381

HOLLISTER, SALLY Bus:Pers/Ind Rels. POSITION: Personnel Manager, Gordon Manufacturing Co, 5250 52nd St, Grand Rapids, MI 49508.

HOLM, LYNDA L. Bus:Pers/Ind Rels. POSITION: Supr of Human Relations, Continental Group, PO Box 3337, Hayward, CA 94540.

HOLMES, ALLAN RILEY Legal Practice. BS 1970, JD 1973, U of S. C. INT: labor law, empl/trng programs, mgmt/educ. ASSN: S.C. Bar Assn (Employment & Labor Law), S. C. Trial Lawyers Assn. POSITION: Partner-Attorney, Gibbs and Holmes, Suite 217, 145 King St, PO Box 1512, Charleston SC 29402. 803/722-0033

HOLOVIAK, STEPHEN JULIAN Acad: Ind Rels. 410 Overhill Dr, Chambersburg, PA 17201.

HOLT, KATHERINE E. Student. BES 1974, U of Minn. INT: ind psych, coll barg, labor educ. ASSN: ASTD, APA, Acad of Mgmt(student member). POSITIONS: Installation & Repair Supr, NW Bell, 1974; Pers Analyst, Ramsey Cty Civil Service, 1978, and (since 1982) Student and Res Asst, Ind Rels Center, U of Minn. ADDRESS: 1177 Thomas, St. Paul, MN 55104. 612/376-2422

HOLTGRAVE, RALPH R. Bus:Mgmt/Admin. POSITION: Vice Pres, Pacific Maritime Assoc, 635 Sacramento St, San Francisco, CA 94111. 415/362-7973

HOLTON, GARY Bus:Pers/Ind Rels. MLIR 1979, Mich State U. INT: org beh, ind psych. POSITION: Compensation Analyst, Advanced Micro Devices Inc, Sunnyvale. ADDRESS: 10194 Miner Pl, Cupertino, CA 95014. 408/749-2097

HOLTZMANN, HOWARD M. Arbitration. POSITION: Partner, Holtzman, Wise & Shepard, 745 5th Ave, New York, NY 10151. 212/753-4300

HOLZER, HARRY J. Acad: Econ. AB 1978, PhD 1983, Harvard. PUBL: Inner City Black Youth Unemployment, (w R. Freeman), Univ of Chicago Press, (forthcoming); "Black Youth

Unemployment: Duration and Job Search," in Freeman & Holzer eds; "Unions and the Labor Status of White and Minority Youth," Ind Rels Rev, Apr, 1982. INT: labor market econ, coll barg, empl/trng programs. ASSN: AEA, Natl Bureau of Econ Res. POSITION: Asst Prof, Dept of Econ, Michigan State Univ, 101 Marshall Hall, East Lansing, MI 48824. 517/355-8320

HOMANN, ANNE Y. Bus:Pers/Ind Rels. BA 1959, Lawrence U. INT: mgmt/educ, personnel, empl/trng programs. ASSN: Cincinnati IRRA, Admin Mgmt Soc, ASTD, IAPES (Assoc Member). POSITIONS: Office Mgr, Cordage Papers, Columbus, Div, 1978; and (since 1983) Human Resources Admin, Cincinnati Cordage & Paper Co, PO Box 17125, Cincinnati, OH 45217. 513/242-3600

HONGLADAROM, CHIRA Acad: Econ, Ind Rels. MA 1969, MSc 1970, U of Wis-Madison; PhD 1978, U of Wash. PUBL: "A Feasibility of Reducing the Population Growth Rate of Thailand to 1.5% Per Annum by the End of the Fifth Five-year Plan: An Analysis of Contraceptive Targets and Supply," Natl Econ and Social Develop Board, 1980; "Case Studies on Labor Relations at the Level of the Enterprise in Asia," Siam Cement Co, Human Res Inst, Thammasat Univ, Jan 1982; "The Effect of Child Mortality on Fertility in Thailand: The Test for the Magnitude and the Speed of the Response in Rural and Urban Thailand," Paper #32, Inst of Population Studies, Chulalongkorn Univ, Sept 1979. INT: coll barg, empl/trng programs. ASSN: Econ Assn of Thailand, Thai Population Assn. POSITIONS: Assoc Prof, Faculty of Econ, 1982, and, (since 1982) Director, Human Resource Inst, Thammasat Univ, Prachan Road, Bangkok 10200, Thailand. Phone: 2238286

HOOVER, DAVID J. Student. BA 1968, Covenant Coll, Tenn; MDiv 1971, Westminster Seminary, Penna. INT: personnel, method/statis, ind psych. ASSN: ASPA, Acad of Mgmt. POSITIONS: Dir of Pers, Virginia Transformer Corp, 1979; Consultant (self-employed), 1981; and (since 1981) PhD Student & Grad Res Asst, Virginia Polytechnic Inst & State Univ, Coll of Bus, Dept of Mgmt. ADDRESS: 300 Penn St, Apt #7, Blacksburg, VA 24060. 703/961-7376

HOOVER, JOHN J. Acad: Ind Rels, Law; Consulting. BS 1964, Villanova U; MS 1973, Drexel U; PhD 1978, U of Notre Dame. PUBL: "Workers Have New Rights to Health & Safety;" "Negotiating the Initial Union Contract;" "Union Organization Attempts: Management's Response." INT: coll barg, arb/med, labor law. ASSN: Acad of Mgmt, Southern Acad of Mgmt, Southern IRRA. POSITION: (since 1978) Asst Prof, College of Business, Va Polytech Inst & State Univ, Blacksburg. ADDRESS: Rte 4, Box 580, Christiansburg, VA 24073. 703/961-7372

HOPKINS, ARTHUR S. Bus:Pers/Ind Rels. POSITION: Assistant Vice Pres, Oster, 5055 Lydell, Milwaukee, WI 53217. 414/332-8300

HORAN, MARCIA D. Government. BS 1974, U of Ill; MAIR 1977, Cornell. INT: empl/trng programs, income maint, housing policy. ASSN: Natl Assn of Housing and Rehab Officials. POSITION: (since 1978) Program Admin, Community Develop, City of Lansing, 410 Abbott Rd, East Lansing, MI 48823. 517/337-1731

HORN, ROBERT N. Acad: Econ. PhD 1978, U of N.H. PUBL: "A Case Study of Labor Law in the Public Sector," J of Coll Neg in the Public Sector, 1982; "Work Stoppages by Teachers: An Empirical Analysis," J of Labor Rels, 1982; "A Case Study of the Dual Labor Market," J of Econ Issues, 1980. INT: labor market econ, coll barg, labor history. POSITION: (since 1978) Asst Prof of Econ, Dept of Econ, James Madison Univ, Harrisburg, VA 22807. 703/433-6232

HORN, THEODORE B. Government, Consulting; Acad: Ind Rels. BS 1965, UCLA; JD 1973, Southwestern Univ. INT: labor law, coll barg, arb/med. ASSN: Orange Cty IRRA, Calif/Southern Calif/Orange Cty School Pers Commissioners Assn. POSITIONS: Labor Rels Law Inst, Long Beach Community Coll, 1976; Chairman, Pers Commission, Los Alamitos Unified School Dist, 1980; and (since 1965) Supervisor, NLRB, Reg 21, Los Angeles. ADDRESS: 11322 Weatherby Rd, Los Alamitos, CA 90720. 213/688--5227

HOROWITZ, AVERY M. Acad: Student, Econ, Ind Rels. MA 1973, Brooklyn Coll. INT: labor market econ, coll barg, labor law. ASSN: Metro Econ Assn NYC, AEA. POSITION: Special Lecturer, NJ Inst of Tech, Newark. ADDRESS: 1633 E 13th St, Brooklyn, NY 11229. 201/645-5264

HOROWITZ, LOUISE M. Bus:Pers/Ind Rels. POSITION: Pers Director, Stardust Hotel, 3000 Las Vegas South, Las Vegas, NV 89109. 702/732-6301

HOROWITZ, MORRIS A. Acad: Econ; Arbitration. PhD 1954, Harvard. INT: labor market econ, arb/med, govt labor policy. ASSN: Boston IRRA. POSITION: (since 1956) Prof of Econ, Dept of Econ, Northeastern Univ, Boston, MA 02115. 617/437-2872

HORTON, JAMES W., JR. Bus:Pers/Ind Rels. BALS 1981 Penna State U. INT: empl/trng programs, org beh, personnel. POSITIONS: Co-Mgr, 1982, Empl Devel Specialist, 1983, and, since 1984, Field Skills Trainer, P+C Foods, Inc. ADDRESS: 5607 Bear Rd, Apt I-10, North Syracuse, NY 13212. 325/458-5283

HORTON, LEMUEL LEONARD Bus:Pers/Ind Rels. BS 1963, Fort Valley State Coll. INT: coll barg, arb/med, personnel. ASSN: Atlanta IRRA, Intl Assn of Quality Circles. POSITIONS: Human Res Planning, 1973, Employee Develop, 1977, and, since 1978, Manager, Empl Rels, Gold Kist Inc, PO Box 2210, Atlanta, GA 30301. 404/393-5297

HORVATH, ALEX Student. 785 Laurel Drive, Aurora, IL 60506

HORVITZ, WAYNE L. Consulting, Arbitration; Acad: Ind Rels. BA 1942, Bard Coll, Columbia; MS 1953, Alfred P Sloan Fellow, MIT. PUBL: "What's Happening in Collective Bargaining?" Proc of the Thirty First Annual Conference on Labor, 1978; "Labor Management Committees: Their Impact on Productivity," Chapter in Productivity: Prospect for Growth, Work in Amer Inst, mid-April, 1981; "Effects of the World Recession on the Application and Development of Labor Law," Intl Bar Assn, Toronto, Canada, Oct 1983. INT: arb/med, coll barg, labor educ. ASSN: Wash DC IRRA. POSITIONS: Chairman, Joint Labor-Mgmt

Committee of the Retail Food Industry, 1974; Dir, FMCS (appointed by Jimmy Carter), 1977; and (since 1981) Labor-Mgmt Consultant, 1333 H St NW, Suite 460, Washington DC 20005. 202/898-0047

HOSKA, LUKAS ERNEST, JR. Acad: Political Science. POSITION: Assoc Prof of Political Sci, Indus Coll Armed Forces, 3800 N Fairfax Dr, 711, Arlington, VA 22203.

HOTCHKISS, W. E. Acad: Ind Rels, Econ. MEc 1967, U of Sydney (Australia). POSITIONS: Res Officer, NSW Dept of Motor Transport, 1963; Visiting Scholar, Dept of Econ, U of Sierra Leone, and (since 1967) Sr. Lecturer, School of Econ, Univ of New South Wales, Kensington 2033 NSW, Australia.

HOTT, TIMOTHY R. Legal Practice. Hott, Kropf, Margolis & Hernandes, 591 Summit Ave, Jersey City, NJ 07306. 201/653-5000

HOTVEDT, RICHARD C. Legal Practice. 1800 M St 800, Washington DC 20036. 202/872-5075

HOUCHINS, JOSEPH ROOSEVELT Acad: Econ. POSITION: Prof, Howard Univ, 5708 14th St NW, Washington DC 20011.

HOULIHAN, WILLIAM C. Government, Arbitration, Legal Prac. BA 1972, SUNY-Oswego; MS 1974, JD 1978, U of Wis. INT: arb/med, coll barg, labor law. POSITION: (since 1978) Mediator III, Wis Empl Rels Commission. ADDRESS: Apt 123, 325 S Yellowstone Dr, Madison, WI 53705. 608/266-0147

HOUSE, MALCOLM G. Arbitration. ASSN: NAA, AAA, FMCS. POSITION: (since 1977) President, Malcolm G. House, Arbitrator, Inc., 10 N 3rd St, Niles, MI 49120. 616/684-3810

HOUSFELD, DANIEL R. Bus:Pers/Ind Rels. BS 1962, U of Wis-Stevens Point. INT: personnel, coll barg, arb/med. ASSN: Wis IRRA. POSITIONS: Mgr of Labor Rels, Phillip Morris 1978; and (since 1981) Director, Employee Rels, Oster, 5055 N Lydell Ave, Milwaukee, WI 53217. 414/332-8300

HOUSEHOLDER, ROBERT W. Government. BBA 1964, U of Pittsburgh. INT: arb/med, coll barg, intl comparative labor. ASSN: Pittsburgh Press Club. POSITION: (since 1965) U.S. Commissioner-Federal Mediator, FMCS, PO Box 2183, Pittsburgh, PA 15230. 412/644-2995

HOUSKA, MARY DITTMER Acad: Econ. BS 1954, Simmons Coll; PhD 1963, MIT. INT: labor market econ. ASSN: Wash DC IRRA, AEA, AAUP, Southern Econ Assn. POSITIONS: Asst Prof, Econ, Radford U, 1964; Asst Prof, 1966, and, since 1972, Assoc Prof of Econ, Hollins College. ADDRESS: 2301 Hollow La NW, Blacksburg, VA 24060. 703/362-6354

HOWARD, WAYNE E. Acad: Ind Rels; Arbitration. BS 1943, MBA 1949, Wharton School-U of Penna; PhD 1957, U of Penna. PUBL: Cases in Labor Relations, An Arbitration Experience, (w J. Abersold); The Missile Sites Labor Commission. INT: arb/med, coll barg, mgmt/educ. ASSN: Philadelphia IRRA, NAA, AAA. POSITION: Assoc Prof of Management & Ind Rels, Wharton School, Univ of Penn, Philadelphia, PA 19104. 215/898-7732

HOWLETT, ROBERT GLASGOW Arbitration, Government. BS 1929, JD 1932, Northwestern U. PUBL: "The Arbitrator, the NLRB, and the Courts," Proceedings of the 20th Annual Meeting, NAA, BNA Inc, 1967; "Contract Negotiation Arbitration in the Public Sector,: 42 Univ of Cinncinnati Law Rev, 1973; "The Forgotten Man," New Techniques in Labor Dispute Resolution, A Report of the 23rd Conference of the Assn of Labor Mediation Agencies, 1974. INT: arb/med. ASSN: Detroit IRRA, ABA, NAA SPIDR. POSITIONS: Member/Partner, Pruitt, Hale & Coursen, 1939; Partner, Schmidt, Howlett et al, 1949;, and (since 1983) Counsel, Varnum, Riddering, Schmidt & Howlett, 800 Mutual Home Bldg, Grand Rapids, MI 49503.

HOYER, DENISE TANGUAY Acad: Org Beh/Pers, Ind Rels, Bus Admin. BS 1975, SUNY-Brockport; PhD 1982, U of Mich. PUBL: "Relations By Objectives: A Method of Conflict Resolution." INT: arb/med, worker-ownership, union org/admin. ASSN: SPIDR, Acad of Mgmt, AAUW. POSITION: (since 1980) Asst Prof of Mgmt, Univ of North Carolina, One University Heights, Dept of Mgmt, Asheville, NC 28804. 704/258-6554

HOYMAN, MICHELE MATIS Acad: Ind Rels, Law. PhD 1978, U of Mich. PUBL: "Who Files Suits and Why: An Empirical Portrait of the Litigious Worker;" "State Correlates of Equal Employment Opportunity Commission Complaints;" "Arbitrating Discrimination Grievances in the Wake of Gardner Denver." INT: govt labor policy, labor law, equal emply. ASSN: St. Louis IRRA, Amer Pol Sci Assn. POSITIONS: Field Examiner (intern), NLRB, 1981, Asst Prof of Ind Rels, Inst of Labor & IR, U of Ill, 1981; and (since 1982) Asst Prof of Political Science, Univ of Missouri-St. Louis. ADDRESS: 7318 Pershing, #1W, St. Louis, MO 63130. 314/-553-5521

HOYT, DANIEL REXFORD Acad: Org Beh/-Pers; Consulting. BS 1965, U of Mo-Columbia; MBA 1969, Memphis State U; PhD 1976, U of Nebr-Lincoln. PUBL: "Techniques for Effective Time Management of Meetings," Nonprofit World Report, June/July 1983; "Investment in Human Capital," The Singapore Mgmt J, Oct 1982; "Planning Time for a Career in Personnal Management," The Pers Admin, Oct 1980. INT: personnel, transportation, coll barg. ASSN: ASPA, Acad of Mgmt. POSITIONS: Pres, DRH Mgmt Group, Jonesboro, AR, 1982-to present; and (since 1976) Assoc Prof of Mgmt, Arkansas State Univ, PO Box 115, State University, AR 72467. 501/972-2097

HOYT, RALPH B. Legal Practice. JD 1957, Hastings Coll. INT: labor law, coll barg. POSITION: President/Attorney, Hoyt, Hoyt & Walling, Suite 220, 1910 Olympic Blvd, Walnut Creek, CA 94596. 415/930-9255

HUBBARD, DEBRA ANN Student. BS 1982, Ga. Tech. INT: arb/med, coll barg, personnel. ASSN: Atlanta IRRA. POSITION: (since 1983) Student, Georgia State Univ. ADDRESS: 200 26th St, #4101, Atlanta, GA 30309.

HUBBARD, HARRY Union. POSITION: Texas AFL-CIO, PO Box 12727, Austin, TX 78711. 512/477-6195

HUBERT, BLAKE L. Student; Bus:Pers/Ind Rels. BS 1981, U of Ill. ASSN: U of Ill IRRA, Ill Student Soc Pers Admin. POSITION: Ind Rels Asst, Baldwin Assoc, 1981, and, currently,

Student. ADDRESS: 205 Stanage, Champaign, IL 61820.

HUBNER, WALTER FRANK Acad: Ind Rels, Org Beh/Pers. PhD 1969, U of Wis-Madison. PUBL: A Reformation of Maslow," monograph. INT: org psych, personnel, mgmt/educ. ASSN: Central New York IRRA, ASPA, ASTD. POSITIONS: Assoc Prof, Mgmt, Univ of South Florida, 1977; Assoc Prof, 1979, and, since 1982, Director, Inst of Ind Rels, Le Moyne Coll, Syracuse, NY 13214. 315/446-2882

HUDDLESTON, GARY Bus:Labor Rels. POSITION: Labor Rels Manager, Kroger Company, PO Box 1309, Houston, TX 77001.

HUDSON, HARRIET DuFRESNE Acad: Admin, Econ, Retired. AB 1933, Wellesley Coll; MA 1936, U of Chicago; PhD 1950, UCLA. INT: coll barg, labor history, personnel. ADDRESS: 3500 Bahia Blanca 1G, Laguna Hills, CA 92653.

HUEY, REGINALD T. Government. BS-BA 1976, Rockhurst Coll. INT: coll barg, labor law, union org/admin. ASSN: Greater Kansas City IRRA. POSITIONS: Social Insurance Claims Examiner, Social Sec Admin, 1976; and (since 1978) Executive Vice Pres, Amer Federation of Government Employees, Local 1336, PO Box 15281, Kansas City, MO 64106. 816/374-2286

HUFFMAN, JOHN Government.BA 1972, Ind Univ; MA 1975, U of Ill-UC. INT: coll barg, arb/med, personnel. ASSN: SFLRP. POSITIONS: Pers Mgmt Spec, Salisbury, N.C., 1977, and, since 1980, Supervisory Pers mgmt Specialist, Veterans Admin, Milwaukee. ADDRESS: 3939 W College, Milwaukee, WI 53221. 414/384-2000 ext 2756

HUGGINS, CHARLES D. Union. BA 1971, MS 1974, U of Wis-Madison. INT: coll barg, arb/med, labor educ. ASSN: Wis IRRA. POSITIONS: Field Rep, Wis Nurses Assn, 1975; and (since 1977) Exec Director, United Assn of Office, Sales and Tech Employees, 152 W Wisconsin Ave, Suite 703, Milwaukee, WI 53203. 414/276-5074

HUMPHREYS, RICHARD W. Acad: Ind Rels. BA 1948, Hamline U; MA 1950, U of Wis. PUBL: Work Measurement: A Review and Analysis; "Inflation, Disinflation Pensions." INT: union org/admin, coll barg. ASSN: West Va IRRA, Univ & Coll Labor Educ Assn, WV Econ Educ Assn. POSITIONS: Instructor, School for Workers, Univ of Wis, 1951; Admin Asst to the President, Allied Ind Workers Intl Union,AFL-CIO, 1958; and (since 1967) Director/-Professor, Inst for Labor Studies, West Virginia Univ, Morgantown, WV 26505. 304/293-3323

HUNDLEY, GREGORY S. Acad: Ind Rels. PhD 1981, U of Minn. PUBL: "Determinants of Certification and Decertification Activity;" The Economic and Structural Effects of the Aluminium Industry in Australia." INT: labor market econ, coll barg, personnel. ASSN: AEA. POSITION: (since 1983) Asst Prof, Grad School of Mgmt, Univ of Oregon, Eugene, OR 97405. 503/668-3347

HUNSUCKER, JOHN L. Acad: Ind Rels. BS 1963, Lamar U; MS 1965, PhD 1969, LSU; ME 1978, Tex A & M. INT: arb/med. ASSN: Houston IRRA, IIE. POSITION: (since 1979) Assoc Prof, Dept of Ind Engineering, Univ of Houston, Houston, TX 77004. 713/749-2545

HUNT, ALLAN Research. BS 1964, U of Wis-Madison; MS 1966, Lehigh U; PhD 1974, U of Calif-Berkeley. PUBL: "Human Resource Implications of Robotics," Kalamazoo, MI: W. E. Upjohn Inst for Empl Res, 1983; The Workers' Compensation System in Michigan: A Closed Case Survey, Kalamazoo, MI: W. E. Upjohn Inst for Empl Res, 1982. INT: income maint, empl/trng programs, labor market econ. ASSN: Southwest Mich IRRA, AEA, Intl Assn of Ind Accident Boards and Commission. POSITIONS: Asst Prof, U of Conn, 1974; Sr Res Economist, 1978, and, since 1982, Acting Manager of Research, W. E. Upjohn Inst for Empl Research, 300 S Westnedge Ave, Kalamazoo, MI 49007. 616/343-5541

HUNTER, STEPHEN BENNETT Government, Mediation, Legal Prac. POSITION: Labor Mediator, NJ Public Emp Rels Comm, 1 Delta Dr, Ocean, NJ 07712. 201/493-2409

HUOT, JOHN J. Ind Mining. BS 1969, Penna State U; MA 1983, Ind Univ of Penna. INT: empl supervision, personnel, arb/med. ASSN: Western Penna IRRA. POSITION: Employee, 1976, and, since 1983, Asst Mine Foreman, Keystone Coal Mining Corp. ADDRESS 402 Greenwood Ave, Punxsutawney, PA 15767.814/-838-3967

HURD, RICHARD W. Acad: Econ. POSITION: Asst Prof, Whittemore School of Bus and Econ, Univ of New Hampshire, Durham, NH 03824.

HURLEY, JOHN P. Legal Practice. JD 1965, Creighton U, Omaha. INT: labor law. ASSN: ABA, Mo Bar Assn. ADDRESS: Jolley, Moran et al, 1300 Traders Bank, 1125 Grand Ave, Kansas City, MO 64106. 816/474-1240

HUSSELMAN, PETER L. Government. AB 1975, U of Mass/Boston. INT: coll barg, org beh, arb/med. ASSN: Wash DC IRRA, SPIDR. POSITION: (since 1976) IndRels Specialist, Officeof Labor-Mgmt Relations Services, USDL. ADDRESS: 5117 1st St N, Arlington, VA 22203. 202/523-6098

HUTCHINSON, JOHN Acad: Ind Rels; Arbitration, Consulting. BSc 1950, LSE; MA 1952, UCLA; PhD 1964, LSE. PUBL: The Imperfect Union: A History of Corruption in American Trade Unions, New York: E.P. Dutton, 1970; "The Constitution and Government of the AFL-CIO," Calif Law Rev, 45, 5, 1958; "John L. Lewis: To The Presidency," Labor History, 19, 2, 1978. INT: govt labor policy, labor history, intl comparative labor. ASSN: AAA. POSITIONS: Coordinator of Labor Programs, Inst of Ind Rels, UC-Berkeley, 1955, and, since 1965, Professor of Ind Rels, Grad School of Mgmt, UCLA, Los Angeles, CA 90024. 213/825-3134/2505

HUTCHISON, KAY B. Arbitration. BA 1967, Wis State U-Oshkosh; MA 1970, U of Wis-Madison. ADDRESS: 5905 Timber Ridge Trail, Madison, WI 53711. 608/271-6513

HUTTER, DEAN E. Acad: Bus Admin. POSITION: Bus Admin, Chaminade Univ, 3140 Waialae Ave, Honolulu, HI 96816.

HUYBREGTS, GERARDUS AC. Student. 8448 Sharp Ave, Sun Valley, CA 91352. 213/767-1623

HYCLAK, THOMAS J. Acad: Econ. BA 1969, MA 1970, Cleveland State; PhD 1976, Notre Dame. PUBL: "Union-Nonunion Wage

Changes and Voting Trends in Union Representation Elections," IRRA Proceedings, 1982; "The Effect of Unions on Earnings Inequality in Local Labor Markets, ILRR 1979; "An Analysis of the Earnings Profiles of Immigrants," Rev of Econ and Statis, 1984. INT: labor market econ, coll barg, intl comparative labor. ASSN: Philadelphia IRRA, AEA, Polish Inst of Arts and Sci in America. POSITIONS: Asst Prof of Econ, Ball State Univ, 1976; Asst Profof Econ, 1979, and, since 1983) Associate Prof of Econ, Dept of Econ, Drown Hall #35, Lehigh Univ, Bethlehem, PA 18015. 215/861-3425

HYDE, PHILIP RALPH Legal Practice. BA 1976, Swarthmore U; JD 1979, Villanova U. ADDRESS: Holtzman, Wise & Shepard, 745 5th Ave, New York, NY 10151. 212/753-4300

I

ICHNIOWSKI, BERNARD E. Acad: Ind Rels. BA 1977, Harvard; MS 1981, PhD 1983, MIT-Sloan School. INT: coll barg, labor market econ, arb/med. POSITIONS: Res Dir, Mass Joint Labor Mgmt Committee for Police and Fire, 1978, and, currently, Deputy Dir, Labor Studies Program, Natl Bureau of Econ Res, and, Res Assoc, MIT Sloan School of Mgmt, 10 Ellery St, Cambridge, MA 02139. 617/253-2667.

IGBO, GREGORY A. Bus:Pers/Ind Rels. INT: coll barg, arb/med, personnel. ASSN: Nigerian Ind Rels, Nigerian Inst of Mgmt, Inst of Pers Mgmt, IIRA. POSITIONS: Registrar of Trade Unions, Federal Ministry of Labour, 1972, and (since 1975) Industrial Rels Adviser, First Bank of Nigeria Ltd, Unity House, PO Box 5216, 37 Marina, Lagos, Nigeria. Phone: 01-663879

ILIVICKY, JOAN Arbitration; Acad: sociology. MA 1974, NYU; BA 1960, Brooklyn Coll. INT: arb/med, ind sociol, labor law. ASSN: New York IRRA, AAA, Amer Sociol Assn. POSITIONS: Coll Barg Res, A. L. Goldstein Esq, 1974; and (since 1983) Arbitrator, 86 Walworth Ave, New York, NY 10583. 914/725-2795

ILYASHOV, ANATOLI Acad: Labor Studies. BA 1970, Mich State U; MA 1972, U of Mich. Publ: "Locations of International Labor Organizations," Intl Labor Working Class History, #23, Spring 1983, pp 70-77. INT: labor history, intl comparative labor, labor educ. ASSN: Amer Historical Assn, Univ & Coll Labor Educ Assn, Natl Capital Labor History Soc. POSITION: Asst Prof, Labor Studies Center, Univ of District of Columbia, 724 9th St NW, #528, Washington DC 20001. 202/727-2326

IMBERMAN, E. WOODRUFF Consulting. ADDRESS: Imberman & Deforest, Inc., 209 S LaSalle St, Chicago, IL 60604. 312/263-0422

IMES, SHARON K. Arbitration, Consulting; Acad: Political Science. BA 1969, MA 1980, U of Wis-Madison. INT: arb/med. ASSN: Wis IRRA. AA, SPIDR. POSITIONS: Dir, Disaster Housing Assistance, State of Wis, 1978; Instructor, Political Sci, 1979; and (since 1979) Arbitrator, 3465 Ebner Coulee Rd, LaCrosse, WI 54601. 608/782-0835

IMRI, ERNEST P. Bus:Pers/Ind Rels. POSITION: Personnel Mgr, Nash Engineering Co, 310 Wilson Ave, Norwalk, CT 06856. 203/852-3609

INGSTER, BERNARD Consulting. BA 1951, LaSalle Coll; EdM 1957, Temple U; EdD 1969, Rutgers U. PUBL: Industrial Peacemaker, The Contributions of George W. Taylor to Collective Bargaining, (w E. Shils, W. Gershenfeld & W. Weinberg), Phila, PA: Univ of Penna Press, Nov 1979; Scope of Public Sector Bargaining, (w W. Gershenfeld & J. Loewenberg), Lexington, Mass: D. C. Heath, Sept 1977; "Appraising Hourly Performance," in M. L. Rock, ed, Handbook of Wage and Salary Administration, 2nd Ed, New York: McGraw Hill, 1983. INT: personnel, coll barg, arb/med. ASSN: Philadelphia IRRA, Phi Delta Kappa. POSITIONS: Dir of Pers, IRC Inc, 1959-67; Dir, Special Educ/Government Services, Hay Assoc, World Headquarters, 1967-78; and (since 1978) Consultant, Human Res Mgmt, (Private Practice), 2226 Lombard St, Philadelphia, PA 19146. 215/735-7125

INSIDIOSO, RICARD C. Bus.Mgmt/Admin. BA 1957, Mich State U. POSITION: Du-Wel Products Inc, PO Box 160, Bangor, MI 49013. 616/427-7901

INSLEY, PATRICE J. Union. BS 1973, Ursinius Coll; MBA 1982, Temple U. PUBL: "Organizing Low-Income Women in New Ways: Who, When, and Why," IRRA Proc, 34th Annual Meeting. INT: union org/admin, coll barg, arb/med. ASSN: Philadelphia IRRA. POSITIONS: Social Worker, Penna Dept of Welfare, 1975; Res Asst, Temple Univ, 1981; and (since 1982) Director, Sales & Installations, Shared Union Systems, Ft. Washington. ADDRESS: Box 161, Ottsville, PA 18942. 215/628-2741

IORIO, TIMOTHY WILLIAM Bus:Pers/Ind Rels. BA 1975, U of Toledo; MA 1977, U of Ill. INT: personnel, empl/trng programs. ASSN: Empl Assn of Toledo, Toledo Pers Mgmt Assn. POSITIONS: Mgr, Ind Rels, Fundimensions-Div of General Mills, 1978; Labor Rels Rep, Seaway Food Town, Maumee, 1979; and (since 1981) Manager, Empl Rels, AP Parts Co, One John Goerlich Square, Toledo, OH 43696. 419/259-3254

IPAVEC, CHARLES FRANCIS Arbitration. POSITION: Arbitrator, 738 National City Bank, Cleveland, OH 44114. 216/241-1397

IRSAY, LEONARD Arbitration. BA 1938, NYU; MPH 1941, U of Wis. PUBL: Handbook of Wages, Hours & Fringe Benefits, GAIU, 1965-70; Background for Bargaining, GAIU, 1965-70; Arbitration Awards Under the OCB, NYC Office of Coll Barg. INT: arb/med, coll barg, govt labor policy. ASSN: New York IRRA, SPIDR, Soc of Fed CAM Rel Professionals. POSITIONS: Dep Exec Dir, NYC Bd of Educ, 1974; and (since 1977) Arbitrator (Private Prac), 66 Coleridge St, Brooklyn, NY 11235. 212/891-7290

IRWIN, DONALD M. Bus:Pers/Ind Rels. BA 1945, U of Calif-Berkeley. INT: coll/barg, health & hosp care, personnel. ASSN: Seattle IRRA, AEA. POSITIONS: Dir of Pers Res, Chrysler Corp, 1957-58; Administrator Wage & Salary Admin, Cost of Living Council, Wash DC, 1973-74; and (since 1974) Vice President Employee Rels, PACCAR INC, Bellevue. ADDRESS: 9531 SE 43rd St, Mercer Island, WA 98040. 206/455-7351

ISENBERG, HAROLD J.T. Union, Consulting, Arbitration. BA 1966, St. John's U; MS 1972, PhD 1974, Richmond Coll. PUBL: "A New Rate of Arbitration," Natl Catholic Reporter; "If You Want Us to Teach...," America Magazine; "Collective Bargaining in Church Related Institutions," Origins Magazine. INT: coll barg, arb/med, labor history. ASSN: New York City IRRA, SPIDR, Labor Press Council of Metro New York, NYS Mediation Board. POSITIONS: Social Studies Chairman, Archdiocese of New York School System, 1966, and, since 1976, President, Federation of Catholic Teachers, 342 Madison Ave, Room 951, New York, NY 10173. 212/953-1194

ISRAEL, DAVID Legal Practice. BS 1976, NYSSILR-Cornell; JD 1981, Seton Hall U. INT: labor law, EEO law, union org/admin. ASSN: ABA, La. Bar Assn. POSITIONS: Empl Rels Supr, Eaton Corp, 1976; and (since 1981) Attorney, Jones, Walker et al, 225 Baronne, 22nd FL, New Orleans, LA 70112. 504/581-6641

ITO, CARL S. Bus:Pers/Ind Rels. POSITION: Personnel Manager, Times Super Market Ltd, 2153 N King St, Honolulu, HI 96819. 808/847-0811

IWUJI, ELEAZAR Acad: Econ, Ind Rels. BA 1964, MA 1967, PhD 1970, Univ of Manchester, UK. PUBL: Employment Promotion Problems in the Economic and Social Development of Nigeria, (IEME), Intl Inst for Labour Studies, Geneve, 1972; "Wage Structure in Developing Countries: A Comparative Study of Six English-speaking African Countries," Labour and Society, vol 5, #2, Apr 1980, IILS, Geneva, pp 151-169; "Contemporary Developments in Industrial Relations in Nigeria," in A. A. Blum (ed) International Handbook of Ind Rels: Contemporary Developments and Research, Greenwood Press, Westport, Conn, pp 417-442, 1981. INT: labor market econ, arb/med, govt labor policy. ASSN: IIRA, Royal Econ Soc, Nigerian Econ Soc. POSITIONS: Sr Teaching Fellow, Intl Inst for Labour Studies, Geneva, 1972; Sr Lecturer in Econ, Univ of Nigeria, Nsukka, Anambra State, 1973; and (since 1977) Judge, Natl Industrial Court, 22 Oju Olobun Close, Victoria Island, P.M.B. 12768, Lagos Nigeria. Phone: Lagos 617068

IZUTSU, GLENN T. Acad: Univ Admin. BA 1965, U of Hawaii; MPA 1967, Maxwell School Syracuse U. INT: coll barg, arb/med, labor law. ASSN: New York IRRA, ASPA. POSITION: (since 1974) Labor Relations Assoc, City Univ of New York, 535 East 80 St, New York, N.Y. 10021. 212/794-5366

J

JABIN, NORMAN E. Bus:Mgmt/Admin. POSITION: Miller, Johnson Snell, 800 Calder Plaza Building, Grand Rapids, MI 49503. 616/459--8311

JACKSON, CAROLE ANN Bus:Mgmt/Admin, Arbitration; Acad: Student. BA 1980, Northwestern U; MBA 1984, Florida Intl U. INT: financial analysis, arb/med, labor market econ. ASSN: BetterBus Bureau-Volunteer Arb, Natl Assn of Bank Women, Econ Soc of South Fla. POSITIONS: General Develop Corp, 1980, and (since 1982) Supr and Sr Financial Analyst, The Bank of Miami. ADDRESS: 10250 Jamaica Dr, Miami, FL 33189. 305/579-3261

JACKSON, GEORGE Bus:Pers/Ind Rels. BBA 1956, St.Mary's U; MA 1958, U of Ill. INT: coll barg, arb/med, labor law. POSITION: Director-Human Resources, James River Corp, PO Box 790, Green Bay, WI 54305. 414/433-6469

JACKSON, ROBERT DEWITT Government, Mediator. BA 1952, Grinnell Coll; MS 1953, U of Wis. INT: coll barg, personnel, labor market econ. ASSN: Southwest Mich IRRA. POSITIONS: Bus Rep, Teamsters Joint Council #84, 1955; Pers Mgr, Spartex Inc, 1969; and (since 1974) Commissioner, FMCS, B96 Federal Building, 410 W Michigan Ave, Kalamazoo, MI 49007. 616/345-2409

JACOB, NANCY Government. BS 1973, U of Cincinnati; MA 1975, U of Ill. INT: labor law, coll barg, arb/med. POSITIONS: Field Agent, NLRB, 1972, Labor Rels Specialist, USDL, 1975, and, since 1979, Labor Rels Specialist, Federal Labor Relations Authority, Wash DC. ADDRESS: 9900 Georgia Ave, 213, Silver Spring, MD 20902. 202/382-0910

JACOBS, ARTHUR THEODORE Acad: Univ Admin; Arbitration. PhD 1951, U of Mich. PUBL: Manual of Industrial Relations, Natl Foreman's Inst; Collective Bargaining, Natl Foreman's Inst; How to Use Handicapped Workers, Natl Foreman's Inst. INT: arb/med, coll barg. ASSN: New York IRRA, SPIDR. POSITION: Vice Pres, Administration & Finance, Ramapo Coll of New Jersey. ADDRESS: Tamarac Tr, Harrison, NY 10528. 201/825-2800

JACOBS, DAVID C. Acad: Ind Rels. BA 1974, MA 1976, U of Mich; PhD 1983, NYSSILR-Cornell. INT: coll barg, labor history, intl comparative labor. ASSN: Amer Pol Sci Assn. POSITIONS: Res Dir, Americans for Democratic Action, 1980; Asst Prof of Mgmt, Kansas State Univ, 1982; and (since 1983) Asst Prof of Management, Univ of Mich-Flint, Flint, MI 48503. 313/762-3160

JACOBS, JAMES KEVAND Union. BA 1972, SUNY; BS 1981, MBA 1983, Calif State-Long Beach. INT: union org/admin, coll barg, arb/-med. ASSN: Orange Cty IRRA, Pers Ind Rels Assn, Orange Cty Ind Rels Assn. POSITIONS: Base Career Adviser, USAF, 1972-1980; Vice Pres, Local 774, CSEA, 1983, and, since 1983, Field Rep/Bus Agent, Calif State Employees Union, Los Angeles. ADDRESS: 9220 Brookshire Ave, 205, Downey, CA 90240. 213/383-1744

JACOBSEN, MAGGIE Government, Mediation. POSITION: FMCS, 525 Market St, 29th Floor, San Francisco, CA 94133. 415/974-9864

JACOBY, SANFORD MARK Acad: Ind Rels, Econ. AB 1974, U of Penna; PhD 1981, U of Calif-Berkeley. PUBL: Employing Bureaucracy: Management, Unions and the Transformation of Work in American Industry, 1910-1945, Columbia Univ Press, 1984; "Union-Management Cooperation in the United States: Lessons from the 1920s," Ind and Labor Rels Rev, Oct 1983; "The Duration of Indefinite Employment Contracts in the United States and England," Comparative Labor Law, Winter 1982. INT: labor market econ, coll barg, personnel. ASSN: AEA, IIRA, Acad of Mgmt. POSITIONS: Res Asst, Inst of Ind Rels, UC-Berkeley, 1976, and, since 1980, Asst Prof, Grad School of Management, UCLA, Los Angeles, CA 90024. 213/825-2505

JAFFE, IRA F. Arbitration, Acad: Law. BS 1974, NYSSILR-Cornell; JD 1977, George Washington U. INT: arb/med, coll barg, labor law. ASSN: Wash DC IRRA, AAA, Soc of Federal Labor Rels Professionals, ABA. POSITIONS: Attorney, Deutsch, Weintraub & Glazerman, 1977-1980, (since 1980) Adjunct Prof of Law, George Washington Law School, and Impartial Labor Arbitrator, 961 Farm Haven Drive, Rockville, MD 20852. 301/984-1112

JAFFEE, LUDWIG Union; Acad: Law. LLB 1926, U of Lvov; DCL 1928, U of Cracow, DJP 1934, U of Vienna. PUBL: Introduction to Philosophy of Law; Comparative Social Legislation; "Workers' Compensation Costs." INT: labor law, health & hosp care, coll barg. ASSN: Acad of Pol Sci. POSITION: (since 1952) Director of Research and Legislation, New York State AFL-CIO, 451 Park Ave S, New York, NY 10016. 212/689-9320

JAIN, HARISH C. Acad: Ind Rels. MBA 1962, Ind U; PhD 1970, U of Wis-Madison. PUBL: Equal Employment Issues: Race & Sex Discrimination in the United States, Canada and Britain, (w P.J. Sloane), New York: Praeger, 1981; "Micro-Electronics Technology and Industrial Relations in Canada," in Ind Rels, Laval Univ; "Human Resource Management Effectiveness." INT: personnel, govt labor policy, intl comparative labor. ASSN: Hamilton Dist IRRA, Acad of Mgmt, IIRA, Acad of Intl Bus. POSITIONS: Dir of Res, Nova Scotia Dept of Labour, 1964, and (since 1970) Professor, Faculty of Bus, Bldg KTH, Room 226, Mc Master Univ, Hamilton, Ont L8S 4M4 Canada. 416/525-9140

JAIN, HEM C. Acad: Ind Rels, Org Beh/-Pers. MS 1958, PhD 1968, U of Ill. PUBL: Worker Participation: Success & Problems, New York: Praeger, 1980; "Viability of the Japanese Ind Rels System in the Canadian Context," IIRA Sixth World Congress, vol 5, 1983; Canadian Labour and Ind Rels, McGraw Hill, Ont, 1975. INT: intl comparative labor, coll barg, mgmt/-educ. ASSN: Canadian Ind Rels, Acad of Mgmt, Acad of Intl Bus. POSITIONS: Visiting Prof, European Inst for Advanced Studies in Mgmt, Catholic U of Leuven, 1976-78; Visiting Prof, Chuo Univ, Tokyo, Japan, 1983, and (since 1973) Professor, Faculty of Admin, Univ of New Brunswick, Bag Service #45555, Fredericton, NB E3B 6E5 Canada. 506/453-4869

JAMES, ANTONIO Bus:Pers/Ind Rels. Diploma, Pers/LR 1979, Cert in Mgmt, 1980, U West Indies. INT: personnel, labor law, coll barg. ASSN: Pers Admin Soc-Trinidad. POSITIONS: Pers Officer, H. E. Robinson Co Ltd, 1980; Head: Empl/Ind Rels, Secondary Schools Trng Security Main Co, Ltd, 1982; and (since 1983) Pers Officer-Ind Rels, Dunlop Trinidad & Tobago Ltd. ADDRESS: Esmeralda Rd, Pole 54, Cunupia, Trinidad, West Indies.

JANECEK, MICHAEL J. Student. INT: coll barg, labor law, health & hosp care. ADDRESS: 21218 Kenyon Dr, Maple Heights, OH 44137. 216/475-2619

JANES, CLINTON S. III Military, Legal Practice. BS 1978,NYSSILR-Cornell; JD 1981, Emory U. INT: labor law, coll barg, arb/med. ASSN: ABA, Federal/Georgia Bar Assn. POSITIONS: Summer Intern, USDL, 1979, Summer Intern, NLRB, 1980, and since 1982, Judge Advocate, U. S. Marine Corps, Office of the Staff of Judge Advocate, Marine Corps Base, Camp Lejeune, NC 28542. 919/451-2321

JANICKI, NORMAN K., JR. Union. POSITION: Bus Mgr, Laborers Union Local 368, AFL-CIO, 1617 Palama St, Honolulu, HI 96817. 808/841-5877

JANTZEN, ROBERT H. Acad: Econ. PhD 1982, Northeastern U. PUBL: "Differential Impact of CETA Training," (w Sawhney & Herrnstadt), ILLR, Jan 1982; The Economic Impact of CETA Training: The Boston Experience, (w Sawhney & Darrah), 1981. INT: empl/-trng programs, labor market econ, poverty & discrimination. ASSN: AEA, Eastern Econ Assn. POSITIONS: Res Assoc, 1978, Instructor, Northeastern Univ, 1980; and (since 1982) Asst Prof of Econ, Iona Coll. ADDRESS: 201 Clove Rd, New Rochelle, NY 10801. 914/636-2000 ext 215

JAQUAY, JOSEPH N. Union. AB 1976, W Va Inst of Tech; AM 1982, U of Ill. PUBL: "Still Playing Catch-up," AFL-CIO Federationist, Mar 1980; "Incomes: Equity Slips Away," (w A. Cantor) AFL-CIO Federationist, May 1980. INT: coll barg, labor educ, labor market econ. ASSN: Wash DC IRRA. POSITIONS: Res Asst, Inst of Labor & IR, U of Ill, 1977; Res Assoc, AFL-CIO Res Dept, 1979, and, since 1980, Director of Res and Educ, Amalgamated Transit Union, 5025 Wisconsin Ave NW, Washington DC 20016. 202/537-1645

JARLEY, PAUL A. Student. ADDRESS: 3002 Patty Lane, #6, Middleton, WI 53562.

JASCOURT, HUGH DONALD Legal Prac, Government, Bus:Pers/Ind Rels. AB 1956, U of Penna; JD 1960, Wayne St U. PUBL: Government Labor Relations: Trends and Information for the Future; Labor Rels Editor, J of Law & Educ. INT: labor law, coll barg, arb/med. ASSN: Wash DC IRRA, SPIDR, ABA, SFLRP. POSITIONS: House Counsel & Dir of Serv, AFSCME, 1968; Dir, Public Empl Rels Res Inst, 1972; and (since 1982) Labor Law Counsel, U. S. Dept of Commerce. ADDRESS: 7 Maplewood Ct, Greenbelt, MD 20770. 703/557-3643

JASPER, DEBBIE ANN Teacher. BS 1979, U of Pittsburgh-Johnstown; MA 1982, St. Francis Coll. INT: personnel, empl/trng programs, health & hosp care. ASSN: Western Penna IRRA, Venture Club. POSITIONS: Placement Specialist, Goodwill Industries, 1979; and (since 1983) Nursery School Teacher, Little People Learning Center, Johnstown. ADDRESS: 613 Coleman Ave, Johnstown, PA 15902. 814/536-8141

JAUVTIS, ROBERT LLOYD Legal Practice. Epstein, Becker, Borsody & Green, 250 Park Ave, New York, NY 10177. 212/490-0994

JEDEL, MICHAEL JAY Acad: Ind Rels, Univ Admin, Arbitration. BS 1964, Cornell; MBA 1966, NYU; DBA 1972, Harvard. PUBL: "The Efficiacy of a Point-Scored Negotiation Exercise in a Graduate Collective Bargaining Course: A Multi-year Cooperative Analysis," IRRA 35th Annual Meeting, pp 343-351; "The Labor Practices of Foreign-Owned Manufacturing Companies in the U.S.," in The Shrinking Decimeter: Unionism & Labor Rels in Manufacturing, D. C. Heath; "Management and Employment Practices of Foreign Direct Investors in the U. S.," U. S. Dept of Commerce. INT: arb/med, intl comparative labor, personnel. ASSN: Atlanta IRRA, NAA, SPIDR, AAA. POSITIONS: Prof of Mgmt, 1971, and, since 1983, Interim Dir, Inst of Ind Rels, Georgia State Univ, University Plaza, Atlanta, GA 30303. 404/658-3404

JENKINS, MICHAEL E. Manufacturing Mgmt. BS 1968, U of Del. INT: coll barg, empl/trng programs, personnel. ASSN: Southwest Mich IRRA. POSITIONS: Operator Supr, 1979, Plant Mgr, 1980, and, currently, First Vice Pres, Hercules Inc, PO Box 1027, Kalamazoo, MI 49005. 616/343-6161

JENNINGS, JOHN PAUL Acad: Law. AB 1929, LLB 1932, Stanford U. INT: labor law. ASSN: San Francisco IRRA. POSITION: Attorney, (Regional-SF), NLRB, 1937-46; and, currently, Attorney. ADDRESS: Suite 440, 100 Bush St, San Francisco, CA 94104. 415/981-4400

JENNINGS, KENNETH M. Acad: Ind Rels; Consulting. BA 1965, Knox Coll; AM 1967, PhD 1973, U of Ill. PUBL: Personnel Management: Functions and Issues, (w W. Holley), Dryden Press, 1983; The Labor Relations Process, 2nd ed, (w W. Holley), Dryden Press, 1984; Labor Relations in a Public Sector Industry. INT: coll barg, personnel, labor history. POSITIONS: Recruiting Coordinator, Ind Rels Asst, Union Carbide Corp, 1967-71; and, currently, Prof of Mgmt and Ind Rels, Univ of North Florida. ADDRESS: 11533 Starboard Rd, Jacksonville, FL 32225. 904/646-2781

JENNINGS, THOMAS W. Legal Practice. BA 1968, U of Scranton; JD 1971, Georgetown U. PUBL: "Limited Right to Strike Laws-Can They Work When Applied to Public Education?" J of Law & Educ, 4, Oct 1973; "The Crossroads of the Future," Labor Law J, Aug 1980, pp 498-502. INT: arb/med, coll barg, labor law. ASSN: Philadelphia IRRA, ABA, Phila Bar Assn. POSITIONS: Asst Attorney General for Litigation, Commonwealth of Penna, 1971, and, since 1972, Senior Partner, Sagot & Jennings, 1300 Two Penn Center, Philadelphia, PA 19102. 215/-963-3212

JENSEN, ROBERT R. Union. PO Box 1701, Springfield, MA 01101.

JENSEN, VERNON H. Acad: Ind Rels; Arbitration. PhD 1938, U of Calif-Berkeley. PUBL: Strike on the Waterfront, Cornell Press, 1974; Hiring of Dockworkers, Harvard Press, 1971; Heritage of Conflict, Cornell Press, 1950. INT: coll barg, labor history, arb/med. POSITION: Retired. Prof Emeritus, Cornell, since 1973. ADDRESS: NYSSILR, Cornell Univ, Ithaca, NY 14850.

JERDEE, THOMAS HARLAN Acad: Org Beh/Pers; Consulting. PhD 1961, U of Minn. INT: ind psych, personnel. POSITION: Prof of Bus Admin, Carroll Univ of North Carolina, Carroll 012A, Chapel Hill, NC 27514. 919/962-3167

JETHRO, PAUL G. Human Resources, Bus:-Pers/Ind Rels. POSITION: Manager, Human Resources, Weyerhaeuser, PO Box 1830, Columbus, MS 39701. 601/243-4201

JEWELL, STEVEN CORBETT Acad: Student, Sociology. BA 1982 U of Minn-Duluth; MALIR 1983, Mich State U. PUBL: Right to Work Movement in the U.S. Labor Review (forthcoming). INT: empl/trng program, personnel, mgmt/educ. ASSN: M.S.U. Student Center IRRA, ASPA. Currently, student, MSU. ADDRESS: 1014 Marigold St, East Lansing, MI 48823.

JICK, TODD DAVID Acad: Org Beh/Pers. BA 1971, Wesleyan U; MS 1976, PhD 1978, Cornell. PUBL: "A Process Analysis of Labor-Management Committee Problem Solving," (w R.B. McKersie & L. Greenhalgh), Proceedings of 1982 IRRA Annual Meeting; "As the Ax Falls: Budget Cuts and the Experience of Stress in Organizations;" "A Theory and Empirical Examination of the Mediation Process,: J of Conflict Resolution, 1978. INT: org beh, ind psych, coll barg. ASSN: Acad of Mgmt, APA, OB Teaching Soc. POSITIONS: Visiting Assoc Prof, Columbia U School of Bus, 1982, and (since 1978) Assoc Prof, Faculty of Admin Studies, York Univ, 4700 Keele St, Downsview, Ont M3J 2R6 Canada. 416/667-2531

JIRIKOWIC, RALPH A. Union. INT: govt labor policy, labor history, labor market econ. POSITION: Vice Pres-Labor, Milwaukee County Labor Council AFL-CIO, 633 S. Hawley Rd, Milwaukee, WI 53214. 414/771-7070

JOHANSEN, ELAINE ADDRESS: U-106, Univ of Connecticut, Storrs, CT 06268. 203/486-4518

JOHNSON, ALTON C. Acad: Bus Admin. BA 1949, St. Olaf Coll; MBA 1953, PhD 1957, U of Wis-Madison. PUBL: Management of Hospitals, (w R. Schulz); "Intraorganizational Strategic Decision Model in Certificate of Need Application," (w M. Levy & M. Covaleski), Health & Mgmt Rev; "Participatory Management and Cost Containment in Hospitals," in Containment: A Selection of Papers, Intl Hosp Federation. INT: health & hosp care, personnel, mgmt/-educ. ASSN: Wis IRRA, ASPA, Amer Mgmt Assn. POSITION: Prof of Business Mgmt, U of Wis, 329 Commerce Bldg, Madison, WI 53706. 608/262-1943

JOHNSON, ARTHUR BRANNON Union. BEd 1956, Southwestern Coll, Kans. INT: govt labor policy, coll barg, labor law. ASSN: Kansas City IRRA. POSITIONS: Reconsideration Reviewer, SSA, 1956; and (since 1965) President, AFGE Local 1336, PO Box 15281, 601 E 12th St, Kansas City, MO 64106. 816/374-3885

JOHNSON, CASWELL L. Acad: Econ, Ind Rels. ADDRESS: Caribbean Development Bank, PO Box 408 Wildey, St. Michael, Barbados, West Indies.

JOHNSON, DAVID B. Acad: Ind Rels; Arbitration. BA 1942, Antioch Coll; PhD 1955, U of Wis. INT: govt labor policy, arb/med, coll barg. ASSN: Wis IRRA, NAA, SPIDR, AAA. POSITIONS: Field Examiner, NLRB, 1946, Chief Contractor, Pers Branch, U.S. Atomic Energy Commission, 1950; and (since 1957) Prof of Econ, Dept of Econ, Social Science Bldg, Univ of Wis, Madison, WI 53706. 608/262-3804

JOHNSON, GARY C. Legal Practice. BA 1972, Rider Coll; JD 1980, Case Western Reserve. INT: coll barg, labor law. ASSN: Northeast Ohio IRRA, Ohio Bar Assn, ABA, NPELRA & OHPELRA. POSITIONS: Coll Barg Specialist, Civil Service Empl Assn, 1970; Labor Rels Consultant (Partner), General Mgmt Assoc, 1977; and currently, Attorney At Law, (Partner), Reid, Johnson, Downes, Andrachik & Webster, 1300 Illuminating Bldg, 55 Public Square, Cleveland, OH 44113. 216/861-3086

JOHNSON, HARRY L. Arbitration, Church/-Minister, Family Therapy. BA 1952, Austin Coll; M Div, 1955, Auston Presbyterian Theological Seminary. INT: arb/med, labor law, govt labor policy. ASSN: Amer Assn for Marriage & Family, Acad of Parish Clergy, Intl Council of Sex Educ & Parenthood. POSITIONS: Stated Clerk/Coordinator of Staff, Highlands Presbytery, Presbyterian Church U.S., 1974; Texas Dir, Church World Services-Tex Conference of Churches, 1979; and (since 1983) Pastor, Presbyterian Church, Drawer 490, Edna, TX 77957. 512/782-3108

JOHNSON, HOWARD WESLEY Acad: Univ Admin, Bus Admin. MA 1947, U of Chicago. POSITIONS: President, 1966, Chairman of the Corp, 1972, and currently, Honorary Chairman of the Corporation and Professor, MIT, Cambridge, MA 02139. 617/253-6143

JOHNSON, LAURIE L. Bus:Pers/Ind Rels. BA 1978, U of Fla. INT: personnel, coll barg, labor law. ASSN: Cincinnati IRRA, Cincinnati Pers Assn, ASPA. POSITIONS: Pers Tech, City of Gainesville, 1978; Empl Supervisor, Stearns & Foster, 1979; and (since 1980) Director of Personnel, The Westin Hotel, Fountain - Square, Cincinnati, OH 45202. 513/621-7700

JOHNSON, MARVIN E. Mediation, Consulting; Acad: Ind Rels. MSIR 1974, U of Wis; JD 1980, Catholic U. ADDRESS: 1221 Smith Village Rd, Silver Spring, MD 20904.

JOHNSON, NANCY BROWN Student. BS 1975, Kansas State U; MBA 1980, U of Kansas. INT: labor market econ, coll barg, labor law. POSITIONS: Pers Mgt Trainee, Bendix-Kansas City, 1980; and (since 1983) Grad Teaching Asst, School of Bus, 3060 Summerfield Hall, Univ of Kans, Lawrence, KS 66045. 913/864-3117

JOHNSON, R. H. Bus:Pers/Ind Rels. BA 1952, U of Ill; MA 1955, UCLA. ASSN: coll barg, arb/med, govt labor policy. ASSN: Wis IRRA. POSITION: (since 1955) Vice Pres, Pers and Ind Rels, Oscar Mayer Foods Corp, PO Box 7188, Madison, WI 53707. 608/241-3311 ext 4656.

JOHNSON, RALPH ARTHUR Acad: Labor Educ; Consulting. PhD 1976, Ind U. PUBL: "Targeting the Political Image: The Case of Amendment 4," Labor Studies J, 8, Spring 1983, pp 34-47; "World Without Workers: Prime Time's Presentation of Labor," Labor Studies J, 5, Winter 1981, pp 199-207; "Practicing Rhetoric Without Speaking," J of Communications Assn of the Pacific, 8, 1979, pp 152-158. INT: labor educ, coll barg, union org/admin. ASSN: Southern IRRA, Speech Communications Assn, Univ & Coll Labor Educ Assn, Communication Assn of the Pacific. POSITIONS: Asst Prof Labor Studies, Ind Univ, 1976; Assoc Prof Labor Studies, 1980, and since 1983, Assoc Prof and Assoc Director, Center for Labor Educ & Res, Univ of Alabama, Birmingham, Al 35294. 205/234-2101

JOHNSON, ROGER J. Consulting, Bus:-Pers/Ind Rels, Acad: Ind Rels. BA 1976, John Jay Coll-NYC; MSW 1979, Hunter Coll, Univ of NY. INT: arb/med, empl/trng programs, mgmt/educ. ASSN: New York IRRA, Acad of Certified Soc Workers, SPIDR. POSITIONS: Deputy Dir, Inst for Mediation and Conflict Resolution, 1980; and (since 1983) Dir, Human Res Trng Systems, NYC, and Regional Coordinator of NYS Emply Supervisors, Trng Program, NYSSILR-Cornell. ADDRESS: 649 East 14th St 2D, New York, NY 10009. 212/473-5674

JOHNSON, RONALD D. Acad: Univ Admin. BS 1965, MBA 1967, DBA 1970, Ind U. INT: org beh, personnel, ind psych. ASSN: Amer Psych Assn, Acad of Mgmt, Amer Inst for Decision Sciences. POSITIONS: Head Dept of Mgmt/Mrkt, Northeast La. Univ, 1974; Visiting Assoc Prof, U of Wis-Madison, 1980; amd (since 1981) Asst Dean and Director of Masters Programs, Coll of Bus Admin, Texas A & M Univ, College Station, TX 77843. 409/845-4714

JOHNSON, WALTER L. Union. ASSN: San Francisco IRRA. POSITION: President, Dept Store Employees 1100, 1345 Mission St, San Francisco, CA 94103. 415/863-3823

JOHNSON, WILLIAM G. Acad: Economics. BS 1956, U of Penna; MA 1968, Temple U; PhD 1971, Rutgers U. PUBL: "Compensation For Death From Asbestos," (w E. Heler), Ind & Labor Rels Rev, 1984; "Robots to Reduce the High Cost of Illness and Injury," (w J. Lambrinos), Harvard Bus Rev, 1984; "The Disincentive Effects of Workers Compensation Insurance," in Worrall (ed) Safety and the Work Force, ILR Press (Cornell), 1983. INT: occupational health/safety, labor market econ, income maint. POSITION: (since 1981) Prof of Econ, The Maxwell School, Syracuse Univ. ADDRESS: Health Studies Program, Syracuse Univ, 712 Ostrem Ave, Syracuse, NY 13210.

JOHNSON, WILLIAM S. Bus:Pers/Ind Rels, Bus:Govt Rels, Bus:Mgmt/Admin. BA 1955, Mich State U. INT: personnel, bus/govt rels, govt labor policy. ASSN: Wash DC IRRA, ASPA. POSITIONS: Dir of Pers, IBM World Trade, 1969, Dir of Pers Develop, 1972, and, since 1978, Director of Government Programs, IBM Corp, Suite 1200, 1801 K St NW, Washington DC 20006. 202/833-6633

JOHNSTON, DONALD RICHARD Bus:Pers/Ind Rels, Bus:Mgmt/Admin. BSB 1959, MBA 1960, U of Minn. PUBL: "An Evaluation of the Business Decision Game," Trng Dir, May 1961; "The Impact of Waiving Compulsory Retirement," Hosp Progress, June 1978. INT: personnel, health & hosp care, org beh. ASSN: ASPA, ACA, ASTD. POSITIONS: Dir Human Resources, Holy Cross Health System, 1977; Vice Pres, Human Resources, St. John's Regional Medical Center, 1981; and (since 1983) Vice Pres Human Resources, Hospital Sisters Health

Systems Inc, PO Box 42, Sangamon Ave Rd, Springfield, IL 62705. 217/522-6969

JOHNSTON, THOMAS LOTHIAN Acad: Econ; Arbitration. 14 Mansionhouse Rd, Edinburgh 9 Scotland.

JOHRI, CHANDRA KUMAR Acad: Econ, Ind Rels, Consulting. PhD 1963, U of Mich. PUBL: Unionism in a Developing Economy, Asia Publishing House, 1967; India, monograph in the Intl Encyclopedia for Labor Law and Ind Rels, Kluwer, 1980; "Social Security in India," Labour & Society, vol 7, #2, 1982. INT: labor market econ, govt labor policy, labor law. ASSN: Royal Econ Soc U.K., India Soc of Labor Econ. POSITION: (since 1964) Professor, Shri Ram Centre for Ind Rels and Human Resources, 5 Sadhu Vaswani Marg, New Delhi 110005 India. Phone: 568261

JOLLEY, William A. Legal Practice. LLB 1963, St. Louis U. INT: labor law, coll barg, arb/med. ASSN: Kansas City IRRA, ABA, Mo/Kansas City Bar Assn. POSITIONS: Partner, Jolley, Moran, Walsh, Hager & Gordon, 1300 Traders Bldg, Kansas City, MO 64106. 816/474-1240.

JONES, DALLAS LEE Acad: Ind Rels; Arbitration. PhD 1954, Cornell. INT: arb/med, coll barg, intl comparative labor. ASSN: NAA. POSITION: (since 1956) Professor of Ind Rels, Grad School of Bus Admin, Univ of Michigan, Ann Arbor, MI 48109. 313/764-1396

JONES, DEREK C. Acad: Econ, Ind Rels; Consulting. BA 1968, Newcastle-upon-Tyne; MSc 1969, London School of Econ; PhD 1974, Cornell. PUBL: Participatory and Self Managed Firms: Evaluating Economic Performance, (w J. Svejnar, ed) Lexington, MA 1982; "American Producer Cooperatives and Employee Owned Firms: An Evaluation," in Worker Cooperatives in America, R. Jackall and H. Levin, eds., U of Calif Press, 1984; "Producer Cooperatives in Industrialized Western Economics," British J of Ind Rels, vol 18, July 1980, pp 141-154. INT: worker participation in decision making in owner ship and profits; intl comparative labor, labor market econ. ASSN: AEA, Intl Assn for Econ of Self Mgmt, Royal Econ Assn. POSITIONS: Chairman, Dept of Econ, Hamilton College, 1978-83, Visiting Fellow, Univ of Manchester, 1984-85, and (since 1979) Assoc Prof of Econ, Hamilton College, Clinton, NY 13323. 315/859-4381

JONES, EDGAR A., JR. Acad: Law; Arbitration. BA 1942, Wesleyan U; LLB 1950, Univ of Va. PUBL: "His Own Brand of Industrial Justice: The Stalking Horse of Judicial Review of Labor Arbitration," 30 UCLA Law Rev 881, 1983; "The Decisional Thinking of Judges and Arbitrators as Triers of Fact," BNA, Stern & Dennis, 1981; "'Truth' When the Polygraph Operator Sits as Arbitrator (or Judge): The Deception of 'Detection'," in the Diagnosis of Truth & Deception, BNA Stern ed, 1980. INT: labor law, arb/med, labor history. ASSN: NAA, ABA. POSITION: (since 1951) Professor of Law, School of Law, UCLA. ADDRESS: 405 Hilgard Ave, Los Angeles, CA 90024. 213/825-4841

JONES, ETHEL B. Acad: Univ Admin, Econ. AB 1952, Vassar Coll; MA 1954, PhD 1961, U of Chicago. PUBL: "ERA Voting: Labor Force Attachment, Marriage and Religion," J of Legal Studies, Jan 1983; "Union/Nonunion Differentials: Membership or Coverage," J of Human Resources, Spring 1982; "Review of Economics and Statistics," (w J. E. Long), Feb 1981. INT: labor market econ, govt labor policy, method/statis. ASSN: AEA, Southern Econ Assn, Western Econ Assn. POSITIONS: Prof of Econ, U of Ga., 1965; Prof of Econ, 1975, and, since 1982, Assoc Dean, School of Bus, Auburn Univ. ADDRESS: 606 Green St, Auburn, AL 36830.

JONES, HAROLD D., JR. Arbitration. ADDRESS: PO Box 28195, Atlanta, GA 30358. 404/255-9629

JONES, JAMES EDWARD, Jr. Acad: Law, Ind Rels; Arbitration. INT: EEO & affirmative action, arb/med. BA 1950, Lincoln U (Mo); MA 195, U of Ill; JD 1956, U of Wis. POSITIONS: Dir, Office of Policy Devel LMSA 1966-67, Assoc Soliciter, 1967-69; and (since 1979) Prof of Law, 608 Law School, Univ of Wisconsin, Madison, WI 53706. 608/262-2440

JONES, JOHN D. Bus:Mgmt/Admin. PhB 1948, U of Toledo; LLB 1951, Case Western Reserve. INT: mgmt educ, org beh. POSITIONS: VP-Ind Rels, Koppers Co, 1956; and (since 1969) Senior Vice Pres Admin, Mattel Inc, 5150 Rosecrans, MS117-1, Hawthorne, CA 90250. 213/978-6350

JONES, LAMAR BABINGTON Acad: Econ. PhD 1965, U of Tex at Austin. ADDRESS: Dept of Econ, Louisiana State Univ, 5666 Forsythia Dr, Baton Rouge, LA 70808. 504/766-2215

JONES, MAX B. Acad: Ind Rels; Arbitration. AB 1952, U of Va; MS 1955, PhD 1961, U of N.C. PUBL: "Models for Examining Organizations," (co-author), J of Systems Mgmt, vol 24, #9; "Business Horizons," The Commonwealth Series of monthly articles, Va State Chamber of Commerce; Virginia Business Index Report, 1963-64. INT: arb/med, coll barg, govt labor policy. ASSN: Acad of Mgmt, Southern Mgmt Assn. POSITIONS: Supply Corps Officer, U.S. Navy (Reserve), 1952; Assoc Prof, College of William & Mary, 1959; and (since 1965) Professor, School of Bus Admin, Old Dominion Univ, Norfolk, VA 23508. 804/440--3550

JONES, NANCY W. Bus:Pers/Ind Rels, Union, Arbitration. INT: coll barg, arb/med, personnel. ASSN: Penna IRRA, ASPA, Natl Assn of Female Exec, Amer Soc of Professional and Exec Women. POSITION: Manager, Ind Rels, Teledyne McKay, 850 Grantley Rd, Box 1509, York, PA 17405. 717/845-7581

JONES, RALPH THOMAS Consulting. ADDRESS: 190 Goden St, Belmont, MA 02178.

JONES, ROBERT A. Acad: Ind Rels. BSc 1970, MSc 1971, Lond School of Econ; PhD 1984, U of Witwatersrand. PUBL: "Manpower Shortages, Black Advancement, and Job Africanisation in South African Industry," South African J of Labour Rels, Dec 1979; "Mechanisation, Learning Periods and Productivity Change in the South African Coal Mining Industry," South African J of Econ, Dec 1983; Collective Bargaining in South Africa, Macmillan: 1st ed, 1982: 2nd Revised ed, 1984. INT: coll barg, union org/admin, ind sociol. ASSN: South Africa Ind Rels Res Assn. POSITION: Lecturer in Econ, U of Rhodesia, 1975; Statistician, Rhodesian Central Statistical Office, 1977; and (since 1978) Senior Lecturer in Bus Econ, Univ of Witwatersrand, 1 Jan Smuts Ave, Braamfontein, Johannesburg, South Africa.

JORDAN, JAMES HARRY Bus:Pers/Ind Rels, Arbitration. BA 1950, MA 1957, PhD 1966, Wharton School, U of Penn. POSITIONS: Asst Dir, Ind Rels, 1960, VP, USOP Empy Rels, 1966, and, currently, Vice Pres, Empl Rels, ICI Americas Inc, Wilmington DE 19897. 302/-575-8545

JOSEPH, MYRON L. Acad: Econ, Ind Rels; Arbitration. POSITION: Assoc Dean, Grad School of Ind Admin, Carnegie Mellon Univ, Schenley Park, Pittsburgh, PA 15213. 412/621-2600

JOURDAN, MICHELE MARIE Bus:Pers/Ind Rels. B Ind Adm 1983, GMI Eng & Mgmt Inst. PUBL: "Training an Effective Team Concept Organization," (Thesis). INT: personnel, coll barg, labor law. POSITIONS: Cooperative Student, 1978, and, since 1983, Pers Specialist, Assembly Div, GMC. ADDRESS: 404 Michael Ave, Wentzville, MO 63385. 314/327-2114

JOY, WILLIAM FRANCIS Legal Practice. AB 1940, JD 1943, MBA 1950, Boston U. POSITION: (since 1961) Partner, Morgan, Brown, Kearns & Joy, One Boston Place, Boston, MA 02108. 617/542-6666

JOYCE, R. D. Consulting. ADDRESS: Suite 702, 701 Evans Ave, Toronto, Ont M9C 1A3 Canada. 416/621-6221

JUDGE, JEROME JOSEPH Acad: Ind Rels; Arbitration. PhD 1955, Natl U-Ireland. INT: arb/med, coll barg, labor educ. ASSN: IRRA, SPIDR, AEA. POSITION: (since 1970) Executive Director, Inst of Ind Rels, College of the Holy Cross, Worcester, MA 01610. 617/793-2426

JUENGER, ROBERT Bus: Mgmt/Admin, Bus:Pers/Ind Rels. BE 1957, Rensselaer Poly U. INT: coll barg, labor law, personnel. ASSN: Chicago IRRA, IIRA, Intl Soc for Labor Law and Soc Security, Labor Policy Assn. POSITIONS: Dir, Ind Rels, Ingersoll-Rand Co, 1967-78; and (since 1978) Director, Ind Rels, FMC Corp, 200 E Randolph Dr, Chicago, IL 60601. 312/861-5983

JULIANO, JAN M. Bus:Pers/Ind Rels. 30805 Red Maple Lane, Southfield, MI 48076.

JULNES, THERESA EILEEN Student. BA 1979, MPA 1982, PhC 1984, U of Wash. INT: coll barg, govt labor policy, health & hosp care. ASSN: ASPA. POSITIONS: Council Res Analyst, City of Tukwila, 1981; and, currently, PhD Student, Univ of Wash. ADDRESS: 10514 14th Ave NW, Seattle, WA 98177.

JUNEMAN, RONALD C. Bus:Pers/Ind Rels. POSITION: Director of Personnel, Radisson Muehlebach Hotel, 12th & Baltimore, Kansas City, MO 64105.

JUNG, GEORGE T. Bus:Pers/Ind Rels. BS 1970, Long Island U. INT: personnel, mgmt/educ, emply/trng programs. ASSN: NY State Bankers Assn, Natl Assn of Drug Abuse Problems. POSITIONS: Pers Rels Officer, Chase Manhatten Bank, 1968; Mgr, Salary Admin Dept, Natl Bank of NA, 1978; and (since 1982) Vice Pres-Human Resource Dir, Citibank-NA, 100 Baylis Rd, Melville, NY 11747. 516/454-5792

JURIS, HERVEY A. Acad: Ind Rels; Consulting, Arbitration. AB 1960, Princeton; MBA 1962, PhD 1967, U of Chicago. PUBL: "The Shrinking Perimeter: Unionisms and Labor Relations," (co-author & co-editor), in The Manufacturing Sector, D. C. Heath, 1980; "A Critical Review of the Collective Bargaining Literature, 1970-1980," (co-author), in Kochan et al, ed, A Decade of Industrial Relations Research, IRRA 1982; "On the Existence of Unrecorded Human Assets: An Economoic Perspective," J of Accounting Res, Spring 1976. ASSN: Chicago IRRA, AEA. POSITIONS: Asst/Assoc Prof of Labor Educ, School for Workers, Univ of Wis, 1965; Assoc Prof, 1970, and, since 1975, Prof of Human Resources Mgmt, Kellogg Grad School of Mgmt, Northwestern Univ, Evanston, IL 60201. 312/492-3465

K

KADAU, GARY Bus:Pers/Ind Rels. MBA 1979, Wayne State U. INT: coll barg, personnel. POSITION: Supervisor, Labor Rels, Great Lakes Steel-Div Natl Steel, Ecorse. ADDRESS: 8452 Hampton, Grosse Ile, MI 48138. 313/297-2406

KADEN, ANDREA LYNN Government. POSITION: Labor RelsSpecialist, FLRA, 350 S Figuero, 10th FL, Los Angeles, CA 90071.

KADEN, LEWIS B. Acad: Law; Arbitration. POSITION: Law School, Columbia Univ, 435 W 116th St, New York, NY 10027. 212/280-2743

KAHL, ANNE S. Government. POSITION: Labor Economist, BLS, 4000 PH Bldg, Washington DC 20212. 202/272-5285

KAHN, LAWRENCE M. Acad: Econ, Ind Rels; Consulting. BS 1971, U of Mich; PhD 1975, U of Calif-Berkeley. PUBL: Wage Indexation in the United States: Cola vs. Uncola, (w w. Hendricks), Cambridge, Mass: Ballinger Publ Co, forthcoming; "The Relative Effects of Employed and Unemployed Job Search," (w S. Low), Rev of Econ & Statis, 64, May 1982, pp 234-241; "Unionism and Relative Wages: Direct and Indirect Effects," Ind & Labor Rels Rev, 32, July 1979, pp 520-532. INT: labor market econ, coll barg. ASSN: AEA. POSITIONS: Asst Prof, 1975-79, Assoc Prof, 1979-83, and, since 1983, Prof of Econ, Labor & Ind Rels, Univ of Illinois, 504 E Armory Ave, Champaign, IL 61820. 217/333-4295

KAHN, MARK L. Acad: Ind Rels; Arbitration. BA 1942, Columbia U; PhD 1950, Harvard. PUBL: "Airlines", Chapter 7 of G.G. Somers (ed) Collective Bargaining: Contemporary American Experience, IRRA, Madison, 1980, pp 315-372; "Labor-Management Relations in the Airline Industry," Chapter IV of C.M. Rehmus (ed) The Railway Labor Act at Fifty, Natl Med Board, Wash DC 1977, pp 97-128; "Seniority Problems in Business Mergers," Ind and Labor Rels Rev, vol 8, #3, Apr 1955, pp 361-378. INT: coll barg, arb/med, govt labor policy. ASSN: Detroit Area IRRA, NAA, SPIDR, AEA. POSITIONS: Dir, Case Analysis, U.S. Wage Stabilization Bd, Reg 6-B, 1952-53; Economics Faculty, 1949, and since 1978, Professor of Econ and Director,

M. A. Ind Rels Program, Wayne State Univ, 5165 Gullen Mall, Detroit, MI 48202. 313/577-4380

KAHN, MIRIAM K. Student. INT: arb/med, labor law, coll barg. ASSN: New York IRRA. ADDRESS: 76 Hampton Rd, Scarsdale, NY 10583.

KAHN, RUTH E. Arbitration. BA 1947 Radcliffe Coll-Harvard; JD 1974 Wayne State Univ. INT: arb/med, coll barg, labor law. ASSN: Detroit IRRA, NAA. POSITIONS: Attorney and Assoc Arb, Law Firm-Alspector, Sosin, Mittenthal & Barson, 1974, and, since 1975, Arbitrator, Ruth E. Kahn P.C., 17515 W Nine Mile Rd, Suite 130, Southfield, MI 48075. 313/-559-8282

KAHN, SHULAMIT Acad: Econ. PhD 1983, MIT. INT: labor market econ, govt labor policy, method/statis. ASSN: AEA, Western Econ Assn. POSITIONS: Res Assoc, Charles River Assoc, Cambridge, 1973; and (since 1981) Asst Prof, U of Calif/Irvine. ADDRESS: 34031 La Serena, Dana Point, CA 92629.714/856-5189

KAHNE, HILDA Acad: Econ. BA 1943, U of Wis; MA 1948, PhD 1953, Harvard. PUBL: "Economic Perspectives on Roles of Women in the American Economy," J of Econ Literature, Dec 1975; "Economic Security for Older Women: Too Little for Late in Life," Heller School Brandeis U, June 1981. INT: labor market econ, income maint, coll barg. ASSN: Boston IRRA, AEA. POSITIONS: Visiting Res Scholar, Wellesley Coll Center for Res, 1982 to present, and, since 1977, A. Howard Meneely Prof of Econ, Wheaton Coll, Norton, MA 02766. 617/-285-7722

KAISER, CHARLES M. Arbitration, Mediation. INT: arb/med, coll barg, labor law. ASSN: Central New York IRRA, SPIDR. POSITIONS: Labor Mediator-Arb, 1963, and, since 1970, Reg Dir, New York State Mediation Board, 333 E Washington St, Syracuse, NY 13202. 315/428-4068

KAISER, EARL H. Union. ILA Local 1351, 7524 Ave N, Houston, TX 77012.

KAISER, STACY S. Student. 318 Elmwood Ave, Ithaca, NY 14850. 716/634-0006

KAJANDER, JOHN Bus: Pers/Ind Rels. BS 1940, Tufts U. INT: mgmt/educ, empl/trng programs, org beh. POSITIONS: Vice Pres, Ind Rels, Warwick Electronics, Chicago, 1956; and (since 1968) Vice Pres, Empl Rels, Pennzoil Co. ADDRESS: 303 Yorkchester Rd, Houston, TX 77079.

KAKAZU, CHERYL K. Legal Practice. BA 1976, JD 1981, MBA 1982, Univ of Hawaii. INT: labor law, arb/med, coll barg. ASSN: Hawaii IRRA, Hawaii State Bar Assn. POSITIONS: Law Clerk, Chief Judge James Burns, Intermediate Court of Appeal, Hawaii, 1982; and (since 1983) Assoc Attorney, Kobayashi, Watanabe, Sugita & Kawashima, 745 Fort St, 8th FL, Honolulu, HI 96813. 808/544-8300

KALES, ROBERT G. Econ, Research, Foundations. POSITION: President, Kales-Kramer Investment Co, 1900 East Jefferson, Detroit, MI 48207. 313/963-3160

KALWA, RICHARD Student. MIR 1980, U of Toronto. PUBL: "Occupational Status Attainments of University Graduates," Canadian Rev of Sociol & Anthropology, (forthcoming). INT: coll barg, labor market econ, union org/admin. POSITION: PhD Candidate, NYSSILR-Cornell. ADDRESS: 320 North Aurora, Ithaca, NY 14850. 607/256-7622

KAMBER, FRAYDA Legal Practice. MA 1971, Occidental Coll; JD 1981, Dickinson School of Law. INT: coll barg, labor law, mgmt/educ. ASSN: Penna Bar Assn, Snyder & Northumberland Bar Assn, Natl Assn of Women Lawyers. POSITIONS: Lecturer, Susquehanna Univ, 1968; Staff Attorney, Penna Labor Rels Bd, 1981; and (since 1983) Partner, Kury & Kamber, 800 North Fourth St, Sunbury, PA 17801.286-5866

KAMBER, VICTOR S. Consulting, Union; Acad: Law. BA 1965, U of Ill; MA 1966, U of N. Mex; JD 1969, American U; LLM 1971, George Washington U. INT: labor communication, govt labor policy, labor law. ASSN: Wash DC IRRA. POSITIONS: Dir, AFL-CIO Task Force Labor Law, 1977-79, Asst to President, Building & Construction Trades Dept, AFL-CIO, 1973-80; and (since 1980) President, The Kamber Group, 1899 L St NW, #800, Washington DC 20036. 202/223-8700

KAMINSKI, DONALD BERNARD Bus:Mgmt/-Educ. BA 1980, Carnegie-Mellon Inst; MA 1982, Ind U of PA. INT: labor history, coll barg, org beh. POSITIONS: Trainee-Ind Rels, Jones & Laughlin Steel Corp, 1982; and (since 1983) #1 Stocker Foreman, Alleghany Ludlum Steel Corp, West Leechburg. ADDRESS: 978 Highview Rd, Pittsburgh, PA 15234. 412/224-1000 ext 552)

KAMM, RENNE Arbitration. BA 1965, NYU; JD 1968, Brooklyn Law School. INT: arb/med, coll barg, labor law. ASSN: New York IRRA, AAA, ABA. POSITIONS: Asst Dist Attorney, 1974; Dir, Labor Rels, Trans World Airlines, 1977; and (since 1983) Arbitrator (self-employed). ADDRESS: 340 East 74th St, New York, NY 10021. 212/288-3524

KAMPAS, BRADLEY W. Legal Practice. ADDRESS: 1335 Pacific Ave, Apt #420, San Francisco, CA 94109. 415/771-3186

KANE, ARTHUR FRANCIS Union. INT: labor educ, coll barg, arb/med. ASSN: AAUP. POSITIONS: Dept of Educ, AFL-CIO, & Amer Fed of Govt Emply, Wash DC, 1962, and, since 1978, Director of Educ, IBT, 25 Louisiana Ave NW, Washington DC 20001. 202/624-8117

KANE, E. LEONARD Bus:Pers/Ind Rels. POSITION: Vice Pres, Ind Rels, Raytheon Co, 141 Spring St, Lexington, MA 02173. 617/862-6600

KANE, EDWARD T., JR. Bus:Pers/Ind Rels, Consulting; Acad: Ind Rels. BS 1972, La Salle Coll-Philadelphia; MA 1973, St. Francis Coll. INT: health & hosp care, personnel, coll barg. POSITIONS: Pers Rep, Colonial Penn Group, 1973; Asst Dir of Pers, Albert Einstein Med Center, Daroff Div, 1975; and (since 1978) Director of Personnel, Holy Redeemer Hosp, Meadowbrook. ADDRESS: 26 East Pickering Bend, Richboro, PA 18954. 215/947-3000

KANE, STEVEN Bus:Pers/Ind Rels, Legal Prac. BSIR 1972, MBA 1973, Cornell; JD 1977, U of Akron. PUBL: "Current Developments in Expedited Arbitration," Labor Law J; "Summer Jobs And Pay Off as a Recruiting Tool," J of Coll Placement; "The Use of Bench Decisions in Labor Arbitration," Ind and Labor Rels Forum. INT: personnel, labor law, health & hosp care. ASSN: ABA. POSITION: Director, Empl Rels Div, American Hospital Supply Corp, One American Plaza, Evanston, IL 60201. 312/866-4864

KANG, MELVIN R. Government. BA 1967, Calif State-L.A., MD 1974, U of Ore; JD 1978, Antioch Law School INT: labor law, govt labor policy, union org/admin. ASSN: ABA. POSITION: Attorney, NLRB, Reg 19. ADDRESS: 7309 17th Ave NW, Seattle, WA 98117. 206/442-4532

KANNE, MARVIN G. Bus:Pers/Ind Rels. BS 1960, St. Louis U. INT: coll barg, personnel, emply/trng programs. ASSN: Gateway IRRA, Amer Assn Ind Mgmt, Amer Newspaper Publisher Assn, Newspaper Pers Rels Assn. POSITION: (since 1972) Asst to the Publisher & Dir of Ind Rels, St. Louis Post-Dispatch, 900 N Tucker Blvd, St. Louis, MO 63101. 314/-622-7466

KANNER, RICHARD L. Arbitration. LLB, JD 1950, Wayne State U. POSITIONS: Attorney, 1950-70, and (since 1970) Arbitrator, Suite 213, 24100 Southfield, Southfield MI 48075. 313/569-5740

KAPLAN, ALVIN I. Bus:Pers/Ind Rels, Bus:-Mgmt/Admin, Legal Prac. AB 1948, Cornell; LLB, New York U. PUBL: Contributor to The Developing Labor Law, 2nd Ed, BNA 1983. INT: coll barg, labor law, arb/med. ASSN: San Francisco IRRA, ABA (Labor & Empl Law Sec), Amer Soc for Corp Secretaries, Federal Bar Assn. POSITIONS: Group Vice Pres-Ind Rels, Diversified Apparel Enterprises, Inc, 1979, Asst General Counsel, Levi Strauss & Co, 1980; and (since 1982) Attorney, Archer Rosenak & Hanson, 130 Sutter St, San Francisco, CA 94104. 415/397-7667

KAPLAN, DAVID Union, Arbitration. MA 1933, U of Wis. INT: coll barg, arb/med, intl comparative labor. POSITIONS: Chief Economist, IBT, 1941-55; Pres, Economics of Distribution Foundation, 1955-66. ADDRESS: 6A Aspen Plaza, Clearbrook, Cranbury NJ 08512. 609/655-2397

KAPLAN, DAVID M. Arbitration, Legal Practice; Acad: Ind Rels. ADDRESS: 67-23 198th St, Flushing, NY 11365. 212/686-3640

KAPLAN, HERBERT Consulting. BA 1959. CCNY. INT: mgmt/educ, coll barg, arb/med. ASSN: Los Angeles IRRA, IPMA, NPELRA, Calif PELRA. POSITIONS: Chief Negotiator, Los Angeles County Govt, 1960-84; and (since 1984) General Partner, Creative Resources Intl, 33912 Cape Cove, Laguna Niguel, CA 92677 213/974-1331

KAPLAN, MICHELE Acad: Labor Educ. BA 1969, MA 1970, SUNY-Buffalo. INT: labor educ, occupational safety & health, labor history. ASSN: Western New York IRRA, Univ & Coll Labor Educ Assn, Genessee Reg Assn for Continuing & Community Educ, Coalition of Labor Union Women. POSITION: (since 1981) Extension Assoc, Dir of Labor Programs, NYSSILR-Cornell. ADDRESS: 305 Andrews St, Rochester, NY 14604. 716/428-9906

KAPNER, ALEX Mediation. BS 1949, MISR, 1962, Loyola U of Chicago. INT: coll barg, arb/med, labor educ. ASSN: Philadelphia IRRA. POSITIONS: Labor Contract Mgr, Goldblatt Bros, Chicago, 1950-59; and (since 1959) Commissioner, FMCS, 600 Arch St, Room 3456, Philadelphia, PA 19106. 215/597-7694

KAPSCH, FRANCIS E., SR. Arbitration. LLB 1942, Columbus U (now American U). INT: arb/med. ASSN: SPIDR, AAA. POSITIONS: Investigator, 1943-59, Labor/Mgmt Specialist-Investigator, USDL, 1959-73; and (since 1974) Arbitrator (self-employed) 6000 James Ave South, Minneapolis, MN 55419. 612/869-0368

KARAKO, JEFFREY J. Health & Hosp Care. ADDRESS: 12026 Wildshire Dr, N. Huntingdon, PA 15642.

KARDASH, JAMES D. Union. POSITION: Organization Specialist, UHPA, 1649 Kalakaua Ave, Honolulu, HI 96826. 808/947-3917

KARIM, AHMAD R. Acad: Bus Admin. PhD 1981, U of Iowa. PUBL: "Mediator Strategies," Ind Rels, vol 22, 1983; "Arbitrator Acceptability," Montana Arb Assn Quart, vol IV, 1981. INT: arb/med, coll barg, mgmt/educ. ASSN: Acad of Mgmt, Inst of Mgmt Science, Amer Inst of Decision Sci. POSITIONS: Asst Prof, U of Iowa, 1981-82; Asst Prof, U of Wis-La Crosse, 1982-83; and (since 1983) Asst Prof, Northern Illinois Univ, Dekalb, IL 60115. 815/-753-1124

KARPER, MARK D. Acad: Ind Rels. AB 1973, Georgetown U; MAIR 1976, PhD, 1980, U of Cincinnati. PUBL: "Changes in Ind Rels Climate," Proceedings of 34th Annual Meeting, IRRA, 1981; "Analysis of ULP's," Monthly Labor Rev, May 1982; "Impact of Ind Arb on Wages," Public Pers Admin, Sept 1976. INT: arb/med, coll barg, labor law. ASSN: Central New York IRRA, AAA (Labor Arb Panel) NYS Mediation Bd-Labour Arb Panel, NYS Public Empl Bd-Panel of Mediators and Fact Finders. POSITION: (since 1977) Asst Prof of Ind Rels, Le Moyne Coll. ADDRESS: 101 Roycroft Rd, Dewitt, NY 13214. 315/446-2882

KARSH, BERNARD Acad: Ind Rels, Sociol. PhD 1954 U of Chicago. PUBL: Workers and Employers in Japan; Diary of a Strike; The Worker Views His Union. INT: intl comparative labor, ind sociol, labor history. ASSN: Amer Sociol Assn, Assn for Asian Studies. POSITIONS: Asst Prof, Univ of Chicago, 1951-54, and, since 1954, Professor, Ind Rels, ILIR, Univ of Illinois, 504 E Armory Ave, Champaign, IL 61820. 217/333-1485

KARSTEN, MARGARET F. Acad: Org Beh/-Pers, Bus Admin, Ind Rels. BA 1977, Winona State U; MBA 1981, U of Wis-Madison. INT: personnel, women in mgmt, mgmt/educ. ASSN: ASPA, Natl Assn of Female Exec. POSITIONS: Res Analyst, U Of Wis-Oshkosh, 1977, and, since 1981, Instructor, Dept of Bus Admin, 515 Pioneer Tower, Platteville, WI 53818. 608/-342-1465

KARWOSKI, CARYN S. Student. POSITION: Food Service Manager, Bethany Methodist Terrace. ADDRESS: 1296 Washington St, #7, Des Plaines, IL 60016. 312/297-8136.

KASKA, EDWARD W. Government, Legal Prac. BA 1972, JD 1975, U of Tex-Austin; MLIR 1977, Mich State U. INT: labor law. ASSN: Natl Assn of Coll and Univ Attorneys, State Bar of Texas. POSITIONS: Staff Attorney, 1976, Assoc General Counsel, Texas A & M Univ, 1978; and (since 1980) General Counsel, Texas State Univ System. ADDRESS: 1304 Darter Lane, Austin, TX 78746. 512/475-3876

KASPER, HIRSCHEL Acad: Econ; Arbitration, Consulting. BA 1956, Boston U; MA 1959, PhD 1963, U of Minn. PUBL: "Toward Estimating the Incidence of Journey-to-Work Costs," Urban Studies, vol 20, #2, May 1983, pp 197-208; Final Offer Arbitration: The Effects on Public Safety Bargaining, (co-author), Lexington, Mass.: D.C. Heath, 1975; "The Effects of Collective Bargaining on Public School Teachers' Salaries," Ind and Labor Rels Rev, vol 25, #1, Oct 1970, pp 57-72. INT: labor market econ, income maint, coll barg. ASSN: Northeast Ohio IRRA, AEA, AAA, AAUP. POSITIONS: Visiting Prof, Univ of Glasgow, Scotland, 1975, Visiting Professor, School of Ind and Labor Rels-Cornell, 1977-78, and, since 1970, Prof of Econ, Dept of Econ, Oberlin College, Oberlin, OH 44074. 216/775-8483

KASSALOW, EVERETT M. Acad: Econ, Ind Rels. BA 1938, CCNY; MA 1964, American U. PUBL: Trade Unions and Industrial Relations: An International Comparison, Random House, 1969; "Concession Bargaining, Something Old, But Also Something Quite New," IRRA Proc, NY 1982; "Japan As An Industrial Relations Model," J of Ind Rels, Australia, June 1983. INT: intl comparative labor, coll barg, union org/admin. ASSN: Wis IRRA. POSITIONS: Special Consultant, ILO Geneva, 1974-75; Senior Labor Specialist, Cong Res Service, Library of Congress, 1977-80; and (since 1964) Prof of Econ and Ind Rels, Univ of Wis-Madison. ADDRESS: 7405 Tree Lane, Madison, WI 53717. 608/262-8910

KASSALOW, GERALD M. Government. BA 1973, MAIR 1976, U of Wis-Madison. PUBL: "Discussion: Developments in Equal Employment for the 1980's," Proc of the 34th Annual Meeting--IRRA, Dec 1981; "Unemployment: Costlier Than It Appears," Wis Econ Indicator, Dept of Ind, Labor & Human Rels, Nov 1976; "Social Indicators: Examining Prison Population," Wis Econ Indicators, Dept of Ind, Labor & Human Rels, March 1976. INT: labor market econ, method/statis, coll barg. ASSN: Wash DC IRRA, Intl Assn of Pers in Empl Security, Soc of Government Economists. POSITIONS: Res Analyst, Wis Dept of Ind, Labor & Human Rels, 1974; Instructor in Econ, Univ of Mo.-Columbia, 1977; and (since 1983) Economist, Equal Employment Opportunity Commission, Wash DC. ADDRESS: 6448 Blarney Stone Ct, Springfield, VA 22152. 202/634-6097

KASSALOW, SYLVIA D. Retired. BA 1945, George Washington U. ADDRESS: 7405 Tree Lane, Madison, WI 53717.

KATZ, ARNOLD Acad: Econ. AB 1952, Hamilton Coll; PhD 1961, Yale U. PUBL: "Nonexperimental Evaluation of the Employment Service," Annual Rev of Res in Voc Educ, vol 1, 1980; "Implications of Potential Duration Policies," Unemployment Compensation: Studies and Research, Natl Commission on Unempl Compensation, 1980; "Growth and Regional Trends in Unemployment in Yugoslavia: 1965-80," Carl Beck Papers on Russia and East Europe, 1983. INT: labor market econ, intl comparative labor, empl/trng programs. ASSN: Western Penna IRRA, AEA, Econometric Soc, Assn for Self-Mgmt. POSITION: (since 1967) Assoc Professor or Econ, Dept of Econ, Univ of Pittsburgh, 4350 Lydia St, Pittsburgh, PA 15207. 412/624-5712

KATZ, EDWARD C. Consulting. Johnson & Higgins, 95 Wall St, New York, NY 10005.

KATZ, HARRY C. Acad: Ind Rels. AB 1973, PhD 1977, U of Calif-Berkeley. PUBL: "Industrial Relations, Economic Performance and QWL: An Interplant Analysis," I.L.R.R., Oct 1983; "Interest Abritration, Outcomes and the Incentive to Bargain: The Role of Risk Preferences," I.L.R.R., Oct 1979; "The Municipal Budgeting Response to Changing Labor Costs: The Case of San Francisco," I.L.R.R., July 1979. INT: coll barg. POSITIONS: Asst Prof, 1977, and, since 1983, Assoc Prof, Sloan School of Mgmt, E52-564, MIT, Cambridge, MA 02139. 617/253-2667

KATZ, JEROME Arbitration. 4520 Westminster Rd, Great Neck, NY 11020. 516/412-3177

KAUFMAN, ADAM D. Legal Prac, Government, Arbitration. POSITION: Counsel, City School Dist, 131 W Broad St, Rochester, NY 14608. 716/325-4560

KAUFMAN, ANNE T. Bus:Pers/Ind Rels. BA 1976, MAIR 1979, Mich State U. INT: coll barg, arb/med, labor history. POSITIONS: Policy Analyst, Dept of Commerce, Dept of Labor, Mich State, 1979; and (since 1979) Sr Employee Rels Analyst, Shell Offshore Inc/Shell Oil Co, New Orleans. ADDRESS: 1901 D Faith Pl, Gretna, LA 70053. 504/588-4613

KAUFMAN, BRUCE E. Acad: Econ. PhD 1978, U of Wis-Madison. "Interindustry Trends in Strike Activity," Ind Rels, Winter 1983; "The Determinants of Strikes in the U.S., 1900-77," Ind & Labor Rels Rev, July 1982; "Bargaining Theory, Inflation and Cyclical Strike Activity in Manufacturing," Ind & Labor Rels Rev, Apr 1981. INT: labor market econ, coll barg. ASSN: Atlanta IRRA. POSITION: Assoc Prof, Dept of Econ, Georgia State Univ, Atlanta, GA 30303. 404/658-2773

KAUFMAN, FAY G. Legal Practice, Government. 1711 Commonwealth Ave, Brighton, MA 02135.

KAUFMAN, JACOB J. Acad: Ind Rels; Consulting. BA 1934, Brooklyn Coll; MS 1935, PhD 1952, Columbia U. PUBL: Collective Bargaining In The Railroad Industry, Russell & Russell, 1972; "Evolution of Work Rules in the Railroad Industry," in Productivity in U.S. Railroads, A. D. Kerr, ed, Pergamon Press, NY 1980. INT: coll barg, labor market econ, labor educ. ASSN: New York IRRA. POSITIONS: Asst Prof, U of Buffalo, 1947; Prof, Penna State Univ, 1956; and (since 1977) Professor, NYSSILR-Cornell Univ. ADDRESS: Apt 3C 211 E 53rd St, New York, NY 10022.

KAUFMANN, DENNIS R. Union; Student. AA 1976, Merratt Jr Coll-Oakland; AA 1980, Chabot Jr Coll-Hayward; BBA Calif State-Hayward. INT: union org/admin, arb/med, coll barg. ASSN: San Francisco IRRA, AAA.

POSITIONS: Asst Mgr-Retail, Safeway Stores Inc, 1972; Auditor, Amer President Lines Ltd, 1981; and (since 1983) Union Rep, Marine Engineers Beneficial Assn, 340 Freemont St, San Francisco, CA 94102. 415/421-9620

KAUPINS, GUNDAR E. Acad: Student, Org Beh/Pers. BA 1979, Wartburg Coll; MBA 1981, U of Northern Iowa. INT: personnel, method/statis, org beh. ASSN: Amer Mgmt Assn. POSITION: PhD Student/Teaching Asst, Univ of Iowa. ADDRESS: 126 N Clinton St, Iowa City, IA 52240. 319/353-3129

KAUT, JAMES I. Government, Arbitration. BS 1951, Rockhurst Coll; JD 1956, LLM 1974, U of Mo-Kansas City. INT: arb/med, labor law, labor educ. ASSN: Kansas City IRRA, Amer Judicaturory Soc, AAA (Natl Panel Member), Mo Bar Assn. POSITIONS: Claims Attorney, USF&G Ins Co, 1952; and (since 1961) Chief Administrative Law Judge, State of Missouri, 615 E 13th St, Kansas City, MO 64106. 816/274-6481

KAWAKAMI, STEVEN S. Bus:Pers/Ind Rels. 4732 W Cleveland St, Skokie, IL 60076.

KAYE, JAMES H. Union, Legal Prac. BS 1973, NYSSILR-Cornell; JD 1976, LLM 1980, New York U. INT: coll barg, union org/admin, arb/med. ASSN: New York IRRA, ABA, NYS Bar Assn, New York Cty Lawyers Assn. POSITIONS: Law Res Asst, Supreme Court of the State of New York, 1976; and (since 1978) Asst Exec Director, Writers Guild of America, East, Inc, New York. ADDRESS: 60 Remsen St, 7G, Brooklyn, NY 11201. 212/245-6180

KAZAZEAN, SUSAN JANE Registered Nurse. BS 1979, U of Utah. INT: coll barg, health & hosp care, union org/admin. ASSN: Amer Nurses Assn, New York State Nurses Assn. POSITIONS: Emergency Room Nurse, St. Mark's Hosp, Salt Lake City, 1979; Paralegal, Asbestos Litigation, Kreindler & Kreindler, 1983 to present, and, Registered Nurse, 1982 to present, St. Luke's-Roosevelt Hospital Center. ADDRESS: 540 West 112 St #1A, New York, NY 10025.

KEARNEY, WILLIAM J. Acad: Bus Admin. BS 1958, Western Mich U; MA 1959, PhD 1965, Mich State U. PUBL: "The Value of Behaviorally Anchored Rating Scales," Bus Horizons, June 1976; "Performance Appraisal: Which Way to Go?" Bus Topics, Winter 1977; "Improving Work Performance Through Appraisal," Human Resource Mgmt, Summer 1978. INT: empl/trng programs, org beh, personnel. ASSN: Acad of Mgmt. POSITION: Assoc Prof of Mgmt, Dept of Mgmt, Univ of Cincinnati, Cincinnati, OH 45221. 513/475-6421

KEARNS, OLIVER Arbitration; Acad: Ind Rels. BBA 1936, U of Wash-Seattle; MBA 1964, U of Toledo. INT: arb/med, govt labor policy, labor law. ASSN: Kennedy Labor Mgmt Rels Council, Pers Officers Assn, Kennedy Space Center. POSITIONS: Mediator, FMCS, 1957; Dir, Labor Rels, J.F. Kennedy Space Center, NASA, 1963; and (since 1974) Arbitrator (self-employed), 2085 South River Rd, Melbourne Beach, FL 32951. 305/723-6322

KEARSLEY, DORA F. Union. INT: union org/admin, arb/med, coll barg. ASSN: New York IRRA, Council of Concerned Black Exec Inc; Natl Assn of Negro Bus & Professional Women's Clubs Inc. POSITION: Field Rep, Public Empl Federation, AFL-CIO, New York. ADDRESS: PO Box 186, Ossining, NY 10562. 212/227-3132

KEAVENY, TIMOTHY J. Acad: Org Beh/Pers, Ind Rels. PhD 1971 U of Minn. PUBL: Contemporary Labor Relations. INT: personnel, union org/admin, org beh. ASSN: Acad of Mgmt, Amer Psych Assn. POSITION: Professor of Bus Admin, Univ of Wyoming, Laramie, WY 82071. 307/766-4244

KEEFE, JEFFREY H. Union. BA 1971, Villanova U; MA 1976, New School for Social Research. INT: labor market econ, coll barg, method/statis. POSITION: Student, Cornell ILR, and Chief Steward, CWA Local 2108. ADDRESS: 9909 Blundon Dr, #302. Silver Spring, MD 20902.

KEENAN, FRANK ARTHUR Arbitration. ASSN: Cincinnati IRRA. POSITION: Labor Arbitrator, 841 Ludlow Ave, Cincinnati, OH 45220. 513/861-7095

KEENAN, JOHN FRANCIS X. Bus:Pers/Ind Rels. 5221 Dorsett Dr, Madison, WI 53711.

KEIR, JEFFREY B. Government, Arbitration. AA 1971, Nassau Community Coll; BA 1973, Stony Brook Univ Center; MS 1975, U of Mass. INT: labor law, coll barg, arb/med. ASSN: Soc of Fed Labor Rels Professionals. POSITIONS: Labor Rels Specialist, Office of Labor-Mgm, Rel. LMSA, Dept of Labor, 1975, and, since 1979, Labor Rels Specialist, Federal Labor Rels Authority, Office of Chief Counsel, Wash DC. ADDRESS: 8674 Brae Brooke Dr, Lanham, MD 20706. 202/382-0938

KELL, PAUL G. Arbitration. BA 1949, MIE 1952, NYU. INT: arb/med, coll barg, labor law. ASSN: New York IRRA, NAA, AAA, SPIDR. POSITION: Arbitrator, 8300 1st Ave, North Bergen, NJ 07047.201/861-1600

KELLER, ANNA D. Librarian. BA 1976, U of Calif-Santa Cruz; MLS 1981, Catholic U of America. INT: labor educ, govt labor policy, intl comparative labor. POSITIONS: Reference Tech Asst, General Accounting Office, Wash DC, 1979; Reference Asst, Georgetown Univ, 1980; and (since 1982) Reference Librarian, Library of Congress. ADDRESS: 1725 Seaton Pl NW, Washington DC 20009. 202/287-5471

KELLER, ROBERT E. Bus:Pers/Ind Rels. BS 1970 Cornell; JD 1973, U of NC-Chapel Hill. INT: coll barg, labor law, arb/med. ASSN: Gateway IRRA, ABA, Mo Bar Assn (Labor Law Committee), Midwest Aerospace Ind Rels Council. POSITIONS: Special Union Rels, General Electric Co, 1973; Assoc Attorney, McCaul, Grigsby & Pearsall, 1975; and (since 1977) Corporate Mgr, Labor Rels, General Dynamics Corp, Pierre Laclede Center, St. Louis, MO 63105. 314/889-8443

KELLERMAN, STEPHEN H. Consulting; Acad: Org Beh/Pers, Ind Rels. BA 1964, Temple U; MS 1971, Calif State U-San Francisco. PUBL: "Perceived Importance of Pay and Managerial Style Orientations;" "Personnel Policies in San Francisco Bay Area Companies;" "Vacations, Holidays, Salary Continuation Policies and Practices of San Francisco Bay Area Companies." INT: ind psych, personnel, mgmt/educ. ASSN: San Francisco IRRA, ASPA, N Calif Human Resources Council. POSITIONS: Mgr,

Federated Employers of the Bay Area, 1966; and (since 1981) Exec Vice Pres, Human Resource Management Inst. ADDRESS: 452 Alvarado, San Francisco, CA 94114. 415/468-1650

KELLETT, NORMAN M. Bus:Pers/Ind Rels. BA 1957 USC; LLB 1974, La Salle U. INT: coll barg, arb/med, org beh. ASSN: Southern Calif IRRA, ASPA, Calif State Chamber of Commerce, Calif Manufacturers Assn. POSITION: (since 1942) Vice President, Ind Rels, NI Industries, One Golden Shore, Long Beach, CA 90802. 213/435-6676

KELLEY, MARYELLEN R. Acad: Ind Rels, Bus Admin. BA 1971, Brandeis U; MCP, 1976, Harvard U; PhD 1984, MIT. PUBL: "Discrimination in Seniority Systems: A Case Study," ILRR, 36 Oct 1982, 1: 40-55; "The Problems and Prospects of Computer Aided Manufacturing Systems For Cooperation and Conflict Between Unions and Management," J.F. Kennedy School of Govt Discussion Paper Series, Harvard, Fall 1983; "The Future of Sex Segregation Research: Analyzing Mobility Through Given Structure v. Studying Structural Transformation," in Sex Segregation In The Workplace: Trends, Explanation, Remedies, ed by Barbara F. Reskin, Wash DC Natl Acad Press, 1984. INT: sociol of work and org, labor market econ, coll barg. ASSN: Amer Sociol Assn, Soc for the Study of Social Problems. POSITIONS: Instructor, Sloan School of Mgmt, MIT, 1979-80; Research Fellow, J. F. Kennedy School of Govt, Harvard, 1982-83; and (since 1982) Lecturer, Dept of Mgmt, Coll of Mgmt, Univ of Mass-Boston. ADDRESS: 1514 Beacon St, Apt 48, Brookline, MA 02146. 617/929-7844.

KELLY, EILEEN PATRICIA Acad: Ind Rels, Bus Admin. BS 1978, U of Steubenville; MA 1979, PhD 1982, U of Cincinnati. PUBL: "Organizing in the Hospital Environment," Amer Inst for Decision Sciences Proceedings Kansas City, MO, Apr 1983; "An Evaluation of Union Risk-Taking in Concessionary Bargaining," (W J. Phillips), Midwest Bus Admin Assn, Insurance and Risk Proceedings, Mar 1983; "An Empirical Evaluation of the Effectiveness of Computer Assisted Instruction in Facilitating Learning of Business Statistics Concepts," Natl Acad of Mgmt, Dallas TX, Aug 1983. INT: coll barg, union org/admin, arb/med. ASSN: Natl Acad of Mgmt, Amer Inst For Decision Sciences, Univ & Coll Labor Educ Assn. POSITIONS: Lecturer on Mgmt, U of Cincinnati, 1981; and (since 1982) Asst Prof of Mgmt, Creighton Univer-Coll of Bus Admin, 2400 California St, Omaha, NB 68178. 402/280-2091

KELLY, ERWIN L., JR. Acad: Econ, Ind Rels; Consulting. AB 1954, U of Calif. INT: labor market econ, intl comparative labor, labor history. ASSN: Sacramento IRRA. POSITIONS: Asst Prof, Antioch Coll, 1965; Asst Prof, San Francisco State Univ, 1967; and (since 1971) Professor, Dept of Econ, Calif State Univ, 6000 Jay St, Sacramento, CA 95819. 916/454-6223

KELLY, JOSEPH T. Consulting. BS/ILR 1958, NYSSILR-Cornell. INT: coll barg, arb/med, labor law. ASSN: NPELRA. POSITIONS: Director of Pers, General Telephone & Electronics, 1958-63; Corp Labor Rels Mgr, Mohasco Industries Inc, 1963-67; and (since 1967) Consultant, Thealan Associates Inc., 5 Sunset Dr, Latham, NY 12110. 518/785-3271

KELLY, MATTHEW A. Acad: Ind Rels; Arbitration. AB 1936, Amherst Coll; MA 1940, PhD 1946, Princeton U. PUBL: Technological Change and Human Development, (Co-Editor w W. Hodges), NYSSIL-Cornell, 1970; Labor-Management Relations in the 1970's," (Monograph), NAM, 1970. "The Contract Rejection Problem: A Positive Labor Management Approach," Labor Law J, July 1969. INT: coll barg, arb/med, labor law. ASSN: New York IRRA, NAA, SPIDR, Acad of Political Sci. POSITIONS: Asst Prof of Econ, Princeton U, 1940; Dir of Ind Rels and Exec Dir, Printers League Printing Industries, NYC, 1950; and (since 1966) Professor of Ind Rels, NYSSILR-Cornell Univ, 3 East 43rd St, New York, NY 10017. 212/599-4550

KELLY, RANDALL M. Legal Practice. POSITION: Labor Attorney, R. H. Macy & Co Inc, 151 W 34th St, New York, NY 10001. 212/560-4058

KELTNER, JOHN WILLIAM Consulting. POSITION: Consultant, Consulting Associates, PO Box 842, Corvallis, OR 97339. 503/754-2461

KEMMERER, BARBARA E. Student. Univ of Nebraska-Lincoln, CBA Rm 224, Dept of Mgmt, Lincoln, NB 68588. 402/472-2317

KEMP, HOMER ROBERT, JR. Government. Retired. AB 1934, Lincoln U-Jefferson, MO. INT: coll barg, arb/med, labor history. ASSN: Wash DC IRRA. POSITION: Labor Economist, USDL 1965 until retirement. ADDRESS: 3169 Walbridge PL NW, Washington DC 20010. 202/-232-6170

KENDALL-ABBOTT, ROSEMARY Bus:Pers/-Ind Rels. MLIR 1974, U of Ill. INT: coll barg, empl/trng programs, mgmt/educ. ASSN: Houston IRRA, Tex Assn of Bus. POSITIONS: Labor Rels Admin, 1979, and, since 1981, Division Head, Employment and Salary Admin, Union Carbide Corp, Box 471, Texas City, TX 77059. 409/948-5586

KENDELLEN, GARY THOMAS Government. BS 1966, Boston Coll; MS 1969, NYSSILR-Cornell. INT: labor law, coll barg, labor history. ASSN: New Brunswick IRRA. POSITIONS: Field Examiner, 1971, Supervisory Examiner, 1977, and, since 1979, Asst Regional Dir, NLRB, 970 Broad St, Newark, NJ 07102. 201/645-3498

KENNEDY, FRANCIS, JR. Union. INT: coll barg, arb/med, govt labor policy. ASSN: Hawaii IRRA. POSITION: (since 1972) Business Manager, Hawaii Fire Fighters Assn, (IAFF Local 1463), 2305 S Beretania St, #202, Honolulu, HI 96826. 808/949-1566

KENNEDY, JOHN W. Arbitration. AB 1942, AM 1947, Duke U; PhD 1951, U of N.C. at Chapel Hill. PUBL: Economics: Principles and Applications, (w A. R. Olsen), Cincinnati: South-Western Publ Co, 9th Ed, 1978; A Problem Manual in Economic Theory, Dubuque: W. C. Brown Co, 6th Ed, 1974; "Compensation for Injured Local Employees," (w H. E. Steele & S. C. McIntyre), The Municipal South, Feb 1957, pp 16-28. INT: arb/med, coll barg, labor history. POSITIONS: Prof of Econ & Bus Admin, 1952-56, Auburn U; Prof of Econ, 1956, Vice Chancellor for Grad Studies, 1971, Univ of North Carolina at Greensboro; and (since 1984) Arbitrator, 2505 Fairway Dr, Greensboro, NC 27408. 919/379-5596

KENNEDY, KAREN M. Student. 18 W Gilman St, #3, Madison, WI 53703.

KENNEDY, RALPH WILKES Consulting, Bus:Pers/Ind Rels. BA 1981, U of N.C.-Chapel Hill; MA 1983, U of Ill-UC. POSITIONS: Teaching Asst, U of Ill-UC, 1981; and (since 1983) Research Assoc, Modern Management Inc, 2275 Half Day Rd, Bannockburn, IL 60015. 312/945-7400

KENNEDY, THOMAS MAYNARD Acad: Ind Rels; Arbitration. PhD 1947, U of Penna. PUBL: European Labor Relations, Lexington Books, D. C. Heath; Cases in Labor Relations, (w J. Stamm), Sherborn-Exeter Co. INT: coll barg, arb/med, intl comparative labor. ASSN: Boston IRRA, NAA. POSITIONS: Emeritus Prof of Labor Rels, Harvard Bus School, 1956-78; and (since 1978) Prof of Labor Relations, Babson College, Babson Park, Wellesley, MA 02157. 617/235-1200

KENNEY, KAREN RAE Government. BA 1971, Wilkes Coll; MS 1981, Rutgers U. INT: arb/med, coll barg, labor law. ASSN: New Brunswick and New York IRRA. POSITION: Mediator, NY St. Public Empl Rels Board, New York. ADDRESS: 500 Woodmere Ave, Neptune NJ 07753. 212/587-4111

KENNEY, LAWRENCE C. Union. POSITION: Secretary-Treasurer, Wash Labor Council AFL-CIO, 2815 2nd Ave, Seattle, WA 98121. 206/682-6002

KENNEY, THOMAS F. Bus:Pers/Ind Rels. BS 1970, Northeastern U. INT: coll barg, org beh, personnel. ASSN: Boston IRRA. POSITION: Vice Pres - Pers and Ind Rels, Boston Gas Company, One Beacon St, Boston, MA 02108. 617/742-8400 ext. 343

KENNY, ROBERT A. Consulting, Arbitration, Bus:Mgmt/Admin. AB 1960, Colgate U. PUBL: "Three Arbitration Awards in A.A.A.'s," Summary of Labor Arb Service; 117 Tailor Designed Training Problems in Management Education, Training Manuals. INT: arb/med, mgmt/educ, empl/trng programs. ASSN: Hawaii IRRA, AAA, NAA ASPA. POSITIONS: Foreign Service Officer, U.S. Dept of State, 1965; Dir, Mgmt Programs, Hawaii Employer's Council, 1969; and (since 1971) General Manager, Bob Kenny & Associates, PO Box 10367, Honolulu, HI 96818. 808/528-2555

KENT, ANDREW GRAHAM Arbitration, Research. BA 1982, U of Rochester. INT: arb/-med, labor law, coll barg. ASSN: AAA. POSITION: Research Assoc, R. C. Simpson, Inc, PO Box 567, Ridgewood, NJ 07451. 201/445-2260

KENT, RONALD CHARLES Union, Labor Educ. BA 1970, MS 1973, U of Wis-Madison. PUBL: "Employment Testing and the Law: A Critical Review," in Ind Social Cybernetics, ed K. U. Smith, 1974; "Labor History, A selected Reading and Resource Bibliography for Trade Unionists," 1983. INT: union org/admin, Marxism, labor history. ASSN: Wis IRRA. POSITIONS: Field Rep, AFSCME, 1974, Organizer, United Farm Workers, AFL-CIO, 1973-74, and, since 1977, Intl Education Representative, AFSCME, 5 Odana Ct, Madison, WI 53719. 608/271-8850

KEPPLER, MARK J. Student. BS 1979, State U of New York; MS, 1981, JD 1984, U of Wis. INT: arb/med, coll barg, labor law. ASSN: ABA, Nathan P. Feinsinger Labor Law Soc. POSITIONS: Law Clerk, Winston & Strawn and Michael, Best & Friedrich, 1982, and since 1983, Law Clerk, NLRB, Milwaukee. ADDRESS: Apt 112, 222 Randolph Dr, Madison, WI 53717. 608/833-6589

KERACHSKY, STUART H. Economics. POSITION: Senior Economist, Mathematica Policy Research, PO Box 2393, Princeton, NJ 08540. 609/799-2600

KERCHNER, CHARLES T. Acad: Education. BS 1962, MBA 1964, U of Ill; PhD 1976, Northwestern U. PUBL: "Collective Bargaining and Teaching Work," Chapter in Handbook of Teaching and Policy, Shulman & Sykes; "Impacts of Collective Bargaining on Governance," chapter in Teachers, Policy and Collective Bargaining..., Creswell & Murphy;"Impacts of Collective Bargaining on Policy and Governance," Amer J of Educ, 1981. INT: ind sociol, org beh, coll barg. POSITIONS: Assoc Dir, Ill Board of Higher Educ, 1971; Asst Prof, Northwestern Univ, 1975; and (since 1976) Assoc Prof, Education Dept, Claremont Grad School, Claremont, CA 91711. 714/621-8075

KERINS, PAUL T. Bus:Pers/Ind Rels. BS 1966, Northeastern U; MBA 1967, U of Mich. INT: personnel, org beh, intl comparative labor. POSITIONS: V.P. Personnel, M.S.P. Group, Pfizer Inc, 1972, and Pfizer Asia, 1973; and (since 1982) Vice Pres-Personnel, Howmedica Inc, 235 E 42nd St, New York, NY 10017. 212/-573-7488

KERNER, BENJAMIN A. Government; Acad: Ind Rels. BA 1970, Brandeis U; MPH 1972, U of Mich; JD 1978, Wayne State U. PUBL: "The Agency Shop After Aboud: No Free Ride But What's the Fare?" (w C. Rehmus) 34 Ind & Labor Rev, 70, 1980; "Labor Law," 1979 Annual Survey of Mich Law, 26 Wayne L. Rev 727, 1980. INT: arb/med, labor law, labor history. ASSN: Detroit IRRA, MICH Bar Assn. POSITION: Hearing Officer, Mich Employment Rels Commission, Detroit. ADDRESS: 2788 Wagner Ct, Ann Arbor, MI 48103. 313/662-2566

KERR, CLARK Consulting. AB 1932, Swarthmore Coll; MA 1933, Stanford U; PhD 1939, U of Calif-Berkeley. PUBL: Industrialism and Industrial Man, (w J.T. Dunlop, F. H. Harbison and C. A. Myers), 1960; Labor and Management in Industrial Society, 1977; The Future of Industrial Societies, 1983. INT: intl comparative labor, labor market econ, quality of work life. ASSN: AEA, Natl Acad of Educ, Amer Acad of Arts and Sciences. POSITIONS: Chair & Director, Carnegie Commission on Higher Education, 1967, Chair & Director, Carnegie Council on Policy Studies in Higher Educ, 1974; and (since 1974) President Emeritus/Prof/-Emeritus, Univ of Calif. ADDRESS: 8300 Buckingham Dr, El Cerrito, CA 94530. 415/642-8106

KERR, FREDERICK L. Bus:Pers/Ind Rels, Union; Acad: Ind Rels. BA 1959, Penna State; AM 1969 U of Ill. POSITION: Employee Ind Rels Vice Pres, Alloy Rods Div/Chemetron, Wilson Ave, Hanover, PA 17331. 717/637-8911

KERRISON, IRVINE L. H. Prof Emeritus. AB 1938, Albion Coll; MA 1941, Wayne State U; PhD 1951, Columbia U. PUBL: Workers' Education at the University Level, Rutgers U Press, 1951; Labor Leadership Education, (w H. A. Levine), Rutgers U Press, 1961; The Supervisor and the New Jersey Employer-Employee Relations Act, Rutgers Inst of Mgmt and Labor Rels, 1968. INT: arb/med, mgmt/educ, labor educ. ASSN: New Brunswick IRRA, NAA, AAA, SPIDR. POSITIONS: Dir of Develop, Inst of Mgmt & Labor Rels, 1959, Prof of Mgmt and Labor Rels, Rutgers Univ, 1964. ADDRESS: 18 Green St, Metuchen, NJ 08840.

KERSHEN, HARRY Arbitration; Acad: Public School Admin. BS 1950, State U of NY; MA 1953, Long Island U; PhD 1971, U of Sarasota. PUBL Journal of Collective Negotiations in the Public Sector, Exec Editor; Public Sector Contemporary Series, (books). INT: arb/med, coll barg, mgmt/educ. ASSN: Long Island IRRA. POSITIONS: Dir-Office of Employer-Employee Rels,NYS Dept of Educ, 1969; Asst Superintendent, Ardsley Public School, 1971; Asst Super, Seaford Public Schools, 1975, and, since 1984, Exec Dir, Consultation and Res Services, 25 E Shore Dr, Massapequa, NY 11758.

KERSTEN, EDWARD A. Union. MSIR 1984, U of Wis-Madison. INT: coll barg, labor law. ADDRESS: 104 Brown St, Valparaiso, IN 46383.

KERVIN, JOHN B. Acad: Ind Rels. ADDRESS: Ind Rels Centre, Univ of Toronto, 123 St. George St, Toronto, Ont M5S 1A1 Canada.

KESSING, STEPHEN L. Bus:Pers/Ind Rels. MILR 1971, Cornell. INT: labor law, coll barg, arb/med. POSITION: Director, Ind Rels, Domestic Tire Div, The General Tire and Rubber Co, One General St, Akron, OH 44329. 216/798-2154

KESSLER, FREDERICK P. Arbitration, Legal Prac, Circuit Judge. BA 1962, LLB 1966, U of Wis-Madison. INT: arb/med. ASSN: Wis IRRA, Wis Bar Assn, AAA, ABA. POSITIONS: State Representative, 10th Dist-Milw, 1964, Circuit Court Judge-Milw County, State ofWis, 1972; and (since 1983) Attorney, Silverstein, Halloran & Kessler, 744 N 4th St, Miwlaukee, WI 53203. 414/347-0650

KESSLER, PAUL Acad: Bus Admin, Ind Rels; Trng Consultant. BS 1948, CCNY; AM 1949, Columbia U; MA 1956 U of Penna. INT: empl/trng programs, govt labor policy, labor market econ. ASSN: Philadelphia IRRA. POSITIONS: Head, Empl Development, U.S. Navy Aviation Supply Office, 1958, (now retired); and (since 1959) Adjunct Asst Prof, The Evening College, Drexel Univ, Philadelphia. ADDRESS: 316A Sutton Apts, Collingswood, NJ 08107. 609/858-1334

KESSLER, RICHARD Bus:Mgmt/Admin. AAS 1960, Jamestown Community Coll; BS 1962, Ind U. INT: coll barg, personnel, labor market econ. ASSN: Kansas City IRRA, Wire Assn Intl. POSITIONS: Plant Mgr, Ithaca Gun Co, 1969; Manufacturing Mgr, 1975, and, since 1983, Manager Plant Operations, Wire Rope Corp of America Inc, Box 288, St. Joseph, MO 64502. 816/233-0287

KETCHAM, RAYMOND Bus:Pers/Ind Rels, Employee Rels. BSILR 1982, Cornell. INT: coll barg, org beh, ind psych. ASSN: Labor Rels Council, Ind Rels Assn of Philadelphia. POSITIONS: Staff Vice Pres, Employee Rels, Scott Paper Co, Scott Plaza 1, Philadelphia, PA 19113. 215/522-5837

KIDSTON, ROGER G. Legal Practice. Kidston-Peterson, 2915 W Main St, Kalamazoo, MI 49007.

KIENAST, PHILIP K. Acad: Ind Rels; Arbitration. BA 1963, U of Notre Dame; MLIR 1968, PhD 1972, Mich State Univ. PUBL: "Employing Conjoint Analysis in Making Compensation Decisions," Pers Psych, vol 36, #2, Summer 1983, pp 301-313; "The Modern Way to Redesign Compensation Packages," Pers Admin, vol 28, #6, June 1983, pp 127-133. INT: arb/med, coll barg, personnel. ASSN: NAA, AAA. POSITION: Assoc Prof, Univ of Washington, DJ-10, Grad School of Bus, Seattle, WA 98195. 206/543-7141

KIERS, PETER C. Government. BA 1968, St. Joseph's Coll; MA 1975, St. John's U. INT: arb/med, coll barg, labor law. ASSN: Long Island IRRA. POSITIONS: Teacher, Cardinal Spellman High School, 1976; Vice Pres, Lay Faculty Assn, 1980; and (since 1984) Coordinator Field Projects, NYC Dept of Corrections. ADDRESS: 345 North Broadway, Yonkers, NY 10701. 212/728-6592

KILGOUR, JOHN GRAHAM Acad: Univ Admin, Ind Rels. PhD 1972, Cornell. PUBL: Preventive Labor Relations, AMA COM, 1981; United States Merchant Marine: National Maritime Policy and Industrial Relations, Praeger, 1975; "Union Organizing Activity Among White-Collar Employees," Personnel, Mar-Apr 1983. INT: compensation, coll barg, intl comparative labor. ASSN: ASPA. POSITIONS: Asst Ind Rels Mgr, Container Corp of America, 1968; Professor, 1972, and, since 1980, Assoc Dean, School of Bus and Econ, Calif State Univ, Hayward, CA 94542. 415/881-3311

KILLINGSWORTH, CHARLES C. Acad: Ind Rels, Econ; Arbitration. BA 1938, Mo State U; MA 1939, Okla State U; PhD 1946, U of Wis. PUBL: State Labor Relations Acts;Trade Union Publications; Jobs and Income for Negroes. INT: arb/med, labor market econ, empl/-trng programs. ASSN: NAA. POSITIONS: Instructor in Pol Econ, 1941, and, since 1960, Professor, School of Labor & IR Michigan State Univ, East Lansing, MI 48823. 517/355-1800

KILLINGSWORTH, MARK R. Acad: Econ; Consulting. AB 1967, U of Mich; BPhil 1969, DPhil 1977, Oxford U-England. PUBL: Labor Supply, Cambridge U Press, 1983; "Union-Nonunion Wage Gaps and Wage Gains," Rev of Econ and Statis, 1983; "Pay Discrimination Research and Litigation,": (w D. E.Bloom), Ind Rels, 1982. INT: labor market econ. ASSN: Econometric Soc, Royal Econ Soc, AEA. POSITIONS: Asst Prof of Econ, Fisk U, 1969; Asst Prof of Econ, Barnard Coll, 1976; and (since 1978) Asst Prof of Econ, Rutgers Univ, New Brunswick. ADDRESS: 43 S Main St, Cranbury, NJ 08512. 201/932-8240

KILLION, LEO V. Legal Practice, Arbitration. INT: arb/med, labor law. ASSN: San Francisco IRRA, ABA, Calif Bar Assn, Federal Bar Assn. POSITION: Attorney-Arbitrator (self-employed). ADDRESS: 81 Cornelia Ave, Mill Valley, CA 94941. 415/479-1370

KILROY, W. TERRANCE Legal Practice. Shugart, Thomson & Kilroy, 922 Walnut, 9th FL, Kansas City, MO 64106.

KIM, HWANG JOE Acad: Econ, Ind Rels. BA 1962, MA 1965, Yonsei U-Korea; PhD 1973, U of Mass. PUBL: "The Competitive Market Hypothesis and the Movement of Interindustry Wage Structure in Korea," Soc Sci J, vol 14, Aug 1977; "A Comparative Analysis of the

Marxism and the Classical Theory of Wages," J of East and West Studies, vol VI, #2, Sept 1978; "Determinants of Collective Bargaining Structure of White-Collar Workers with Special Reference to Engineers," J of East and West Studies, vol VIII, #2, Sept, 1979. INT: labor market econ, coll barg, govt labor policy. ASSN: Korean Econ Assn, Korean Labor Econ Assn. POSITIONS: Assoc Prof 1977, Prof of Econ, 1980, Coll of Bus & Econ, and, since 1981, Assoc Dean, Grad School of Bus Admin, Yonsei Univ, Seoul, Korea 120. Phone: Seoul 392-0131 ext 2510

KIM, SOOKON Acad: Ind Rels, Econ Bus Admin. BA 1957, Korea U; MPA 1965, CUNY; PhD 1971, U of Minn. PUBL: Labor Force Behavior and Unemployment in Korea; Wages and Labor-Management in Korea; "Is the Japanese Lifetime Employment System Applicable to a Developing Country Such as Korea?" IIRA Sixth Congress Proc, 1983. INT: labor market econ, personnel, govt labor policy. ASSN: IIRA, Korean Econ Assn, Korean Labor Econ Assn. POSITIONS: Asst Prof, U of Saskatchewan, 1972; Sr Fellow, 1974, and, since 1983, Vice Pres, Korea Devel Inst, PO Box 113, Cheongryangri, Seoul, Korea.

KIMMETT, CHARLES T. Acad: Univ Admin. BA 1962, Seton Hall U; MA 1972, Kean Coll of NJ. INT: mgmt/educ, coll barg, personnel. ASSN: New Brunswick IRRA, Council for Advancement & Support of Educ. POSITION: Vice Pres for Campus Planning, Kean Coll of New Jersey, Union. ADDRESS: 77 Lincoln Ave, Florham Park, NJ 07932. 201/527-2220

KIMPAN, JEFFREY K. Bus:Pers/Ind Rels, Mgmt/Admin; Arbitration. BA 1974, Bowling Green U. INT: personnel, org beh, union org/admin. POSITIONS: Supr, Labor Rels, 1977, and, since 1982, General Supr of Salaried Pers, General Motors Div, Packard Elec. ADDRESS: 1144 Bennett NW, Warren, OH 44485. 216/373-3638

KINCAID, ELMER D. Mediator, Government. BS 1942, U of Pittsburgh. INT: coll barg, arb/-med, empl/trng programs. ASSN: Houston IRRA, SPIDR, AAA. POSITION: (since 1964) Commissioner, FMCS, 515 Rusk St, Houston, TX 77002. 713/229-2562

KING, CHARLES DOUGLAS Acad: Sociology. PHD 1968, SUNY-Buffalo. PUBL: Models of Industrial Democracy. INT: ind sociol, intl comparative labor, ind democracy/workers participation. ASSN: Amer Sociol Assn, Southwestern Sociol Assn. POSITIONS: Lecturer, SUNY-Buffalo, 1965-68; Asst Prof, Tex Tech Univ, 1968-72; and (since 1972) Professor, Indiana State Univ. ADDRESS: 7645 Mt. Vernon Dr, Terre Haute, IN 47802. 812/232-6311

KING, CHRISTOPHER T. Government. BA 1968, U of Tex-Austin; MA 1972, PhD 1976, Mich State U. INT: empl/trng programs, labor market econ, coll barg. ASSN: South Tex IRRA, AEA. POSITIONS: Labor Economist, ASPER, USDL, Wash DC, 1976; Res Asst, Center for Study of Human Resources, U of Tex-Austin, 1980; and (since 1983) Asst Dir for Research Demonstration, Tex Dept of Community Affairs. ADDRESS: 2108 Montclaire, Austin, TX 78704. 572/443-4100

KING, CLAY B. Acad: Econ. BA 1961, Whitman Coll, Walla-Walla; MA 1964, U of Ariz; PhD 1972, Wash State U. INT: coll barg, govt labor policy, labor law. ASSN: AEA, Western Econ Assn, Natl & State Council on Econ Educ. POSITIONS: Lecturer, Humboldt State U, 1972-75; and (since 1975) Assoc Prof of Econ, Dakota Northwestern Univ, Minot, ND 58701. 701/857-3133

KING, GEORGE SAVAGE Acad: Law, Arbitration. JD 1949, U of S.C.; LLM 1950, NYU. POSITIONS: Asst Prof of Econ, 1947-49, Prof of Law, 1962, and Professor Emeritus, Emory Univ. ADDRESS: 453 Emory Dr NE, Atlanta, GA 30307. 404/378-8773

KING, STANLEY P. Bus:Pers/Ind Rels. BA 1978, Shippensburg U. INT: coll barg, arb/-med, personnel. ASSN: Harrisburg IRRA, Harrisburg Area Pers Assn. POSITION: (since 1972) Pers Manager, Capitol Products Corp, PO Box 3070, Harrisburg, PA 17105. 717/766-7661.

KIRCHER, KRAIG KAY Acad: Ind Rels. BA 1975, U of Waterloo; MA 1977, New School for Social Res; PhD 1984, U of Ill. INT: govt labor policy, coll barg, labor law. ASSN: Canadian Ind Rels Assn, Acad of Mgmt. POSITIONS: Res Asst, U of Ill, 1978; Instructor, U of Wis-Parkside, 1981; and (since 1982) Asst Prof, Faculty of Admin, Univ of New Brunswick, Bag Service Number 45555, Fredericton, NB E3B 6E5 Canada. 506/453-4869

KIRKPATRICK, FORREST H. Consulting. INT: empl/trng programs, personnel, mgmt/educ. ADDRESS: PO Box 268, Wheeling, VA 26003.

KIRKPATRICK, GARY J. Professional Assn. ADDRESS: 413 Parkview, Dallas, TX 75223. 214/821-4380

KIRRANE, WILLIAM Union. POSITION: Intl Vice Pres, TWU AFL-CIO, 1980 Broadway, New York, NY 10023.

KIRSCH, CHARLES JOHN Student. 1403 Marcy, Iowa City, IA 52240.

KIRSCHKE, GERALD J. Bus:Pers/Ind Rels. BBA 1970, Western Mich U; MA 1979, Central Mich U. POSITION: Manager-Empl Rels, Capitol Products, PO Box 3070, Harrisburg, PA 17105. 717/766-7661

KISCH, VICTOR J. Acad: Student, Law. BBA 1980, U of Iowa, AM 1982, U of Ill. PUBL: "Union Liability for Illegal Strikes: The Mass Action Theory Redefined," (co-author), W. Va. Law Rev, Aug 1984. INT: labor law, coll barg. ASSN: Philadelphia IRRA, ABA. POSITION: Law Clerk, Robert J. Bray & Assoc, 1983, and Student, Temple U. ADDRESS: 1314 S 3rd St, Philadelphia, PA 19147. 215/557-9200

KISS, BERTHA Research. 711 W. San Antonio St, Fredericksburg, TX 78624.

KISS, JOSEPH S. Arbitration, Consulting. 711 W San Antonio St, Fredericksburg, TX 78624. 512/997-5662

KLAAS, BRIAN S. Student. 218 S Bassett, Apt 208, Madison, WI 53703.

KLAMPH, BEN JOSEPH Student. INT: arb/-med, mgmt/educ, union org/admin. ASSN: McGill IRRA. POSITION: Student, McGill U. ADDRESS: 136 Vivian Ave, Mount Royal, PQ H3P 1N7 Canada. 514/342-9788

KLASEN, GERALD U. Bus:Mgmt/Admin. POSITION: Manager of Personnel, Doboy Packaging Mach Inc, New Richmond, WI 54017. 715/-246-6511

KLASS, IRWIN E. Union. PhB 1930, MA 1958, U of Chicago. INT: coll barg, labor history, unin org/admin. ADDRESS: Chicago Fed of Labor and Ind Union Council, 300 S Ashland Blvd, Chicago, IL 60607. 312/829-2412

KLECKNER, WILLARD R. Bus:Pers/Ind Rels, Bus:Mgmt/Admin, Consulting. PhD 1980 Calif Western U. PUBL: "Smoking Habit Affects Workers' Compensation Award;" "Outplacement - Who? When? Why?" "How to Run A Successful Outplacement Program." INT: personnel, coll barg, mgmt/educ. ASSN: ASPA, Amer Soc of Ind Security, Amer Soci of Safety Engineers. POSITION: Dir of Ind Rels, Penn-Dixie Ind-Cement Div, 1978; Vice-Pres Admin, The Merrick Corp, 1981; and (since 1983) Director, Kleckner Assoc-Div of Kleckner Enterprises, Inc (established in 1961), 15 Colonial Rd, Lake Telemark, NJ 07866. 201/625-8626

KLEIMAN, BERNARD Legal Practice, Union. BS 1951, Purdue U; JD 1954, Northwestern U. PUBL: "Seniority Remedies Under Title VII: The Steel Consent Decree - A Union Perspective," Proceedings of the NYU 28th Annual Conf on Labor 177, 1975; "Collective Bargaining in Perspective," 13 Duquesne Law Rev 481, 1975; "The Landrum-Griffin Act," in Labor Law for the General Practitioner, Ch 15, IICLE 1976 & 1980 eds. INT: labor law, coll barg, govt labor policy. ASSN: Chicago & Pittsburgh IRRAs. ABA, Chicago Bar Assn, AFL-CIO Lawyer Coordinating Committee. POSITIONS: Partner, 1960, President, 1976, Kleiman & Whitney P.C.; and (since 1965) General Counsel, United Steelworkers of America, 1 E Wacker Drive, Chicago, IL 60601. 312/467-1995

KLEIN, BERNARD Acad: Public Admin; Arbitration. AB 1950, Brooklyn Coll-CUNY; MA 1954, U of Mo.; PhD 1966, Mich State U. PUBL: "Michigan Response to Reagonomics," Publious, 1983; "Administrative Agencies and the Publics They Serve," Publ Admin Rev, Sept 1966; "Impeachment in Michigan, Detroit Discovery, 1975. INT: arb/med, govt labor policy, coll barg. ASSN: Detroit IRRA, Amer Pol Sci Assn, ASPA, AAA. POSITIONS: Controller, City of Detroit, 1967-70; Provost, Wayne State Univ, 1980-81; and (since 1971) Prof of Political Science, Univ of Mich-Dearborn, 4901 Evergreen Rd, Dearborn, MI 48128. 313/-593-5282

KLEIN, JANICE A. Acad: Bus Admin. BSIE 1972, Iowa State U; MBA 1978, Boston U; PhD 1983, MIT. PUBL: "Productivity: The Industrial Relations Connection," (w R. B. McKersie); "First Line Supervisors: Past, Present & Future," (w L. A. Schlesinger). INT: production/operations mgt, ind sociol, org beh. POSITIONS: HRM, General Electric Co, 1972-81; and (since 1983) Asst Prof, Grad School of Bus Admin, Harvard Univ, Soldiers Field, Boston MA 02163. 617/495-6352

KLEIN, LAWRENCE R. Retired. 4771 Via Entrada, Tucson, AZ 835718. 602/299-3117

KLEINER, A. ROBERT Legal Practice. LLB 1938, JD 1941, U of Mich. INT: labor law, arb/med. ASSN: Western Mich IRRA. POSITION: (since 1946) Partner, Kleiner, De Young and Fayette, 1508 McKay Tower, Grand Rapids, MI 49503. 616/4590-3267

KLEINER, MORRIS MICHAEL Acad: Bus Admin; Consulting. BS 1971, Bradley U; AM 1972, PhD 1974, U of Ill. PUBL: "Barriers to Labor Migration: The Case of Occupational Licensing," in Ind Rels; "Employer Discrimination Against Employees: Determinants of 8(a) (3) Violations," in Ind Rels; "Metropolitan Area Labor Market Changes: Determinants and Comparisons by Industry," in Regional Studies. INT: labor market econ, coll barg, method/-statis. ASSN: AEA, Regional Sci Assn. POSITIONS: Examiner, NLRB, 1971; Assoc in Empl Policy, Brookings Institute, 1976; and (since 1974) Assoc Prof, School of Bus, Univ of Kansas, 307 Summerfield Hall, Lawrence, KS 66045. 913/864-4500

KLEINGARTNER, ARCHIE Acad: Ind Rels; Arbitration. BA 1959, U of Minn; MS 1961, U of Ore; PhD 1965, U of Wis. PUBL: "Academics and Unions," Contemporary Labor Issues; 'Professionalism and Salaried Worker Organization." INT: coll barg, personnel, mgmt/-educ. POSITIONS: Chair and Assoc Dean, Grad School of Mgmt, 1969, Vice Pres, Univ of Calif System, 1975-83, and (since 1965) Prof of Ind Rels, UCLA. ADDRESS: 500 Grizzly Peak, Berkeley, CA 94708. 415/526-1463

KLEYWEGT, C. JOHN Acad: Labor Studies. AA 1980, Des Moines Area Community Coll; BA 1982, Antioch U. INT: arb/med, coll barg, intl comparative labor. ASSN: Univ & Coll Labor Educ Assn, Iowa Higher Educ Assn. POSITIONS: County Program Dir, Amer Inst for Free Labor Development, 1965; Apprenticeship Specialist, Communications Workers of Amer, 1980; and (since 1976) Chairperson Labor Studies, Des Moines Area Community Coll, 1100 7th St, Des Moines, IA 50314. 515/244-4226

KLINEDINST, MARK A. Student. 373 Enfield Falls Rd, Ithaca, NY 14850.

KLINGER, ALLAN H. Legal Practice. PO Box 477, 25 E Salem St, Hackensack, NJ 07602.

KLINSHAW, ROBERT A. Government, Mediator. INT: arb/med, coll barg, labor educ. ASSN: Western NY and Central NY IRRA, SPIDR. POSITIONS: Employee (Machinist & Local Union Pres) Worthington Corp, 1942; Staff Rep, United Steelworkers of Amer, 1965; and (since 1974) Commissioner, FMCS, Syracuse. ADDRESS: 5 Jay Path, Liverpool, NY 13088. 315/423-5318

KLINSHAW, ROBERT J. Student. 7155 Northview Dr, Lockport, NY 14094. 716/433-2754

KLITZKIE, ALAN GEORGE Government. BS 1954, MS 1960, U of Wis-Madison. INT: personnel, org beh, coll barg. ASSN: Wis IRRA, Intl Pers Mgmt Assn. POSITION: (since 1960) Pers Specialist, Dept of Empl Rels, State of Wisconsin. ADDRESS: 1701 Vondron Rd, Madison, WI 53716. 608/266-1254

KNAPP, ANDRIA S. Acad: Law; Arbitration. BA 1970, Duke U; JD 1976, Harvard. INT: labor law, arb/med, coll barg. ASSN: Western Penna IRRA, ABA (Section on Empl Rels Law), AAA (Natl Labor Panel), FMCS Labor Panel. POSITION: (since 1978) Asst Prof, Law School, Univ of Pittsburgh, Pittsburgh, PA 15260. 412/624-6741

KNAUSS, KEITH D. Acad: Education. 1614 Oak Park, South Bend, IN 46617.

KNEZEK, LAVERNE D. Acad: Univ Admin. 4901 Racquet Club Dr, Arlington, TX 76017.

KNIGHT, HENRY S., JR. Legal Practice. BA 1970, Centre Coll of Ky; JD 1977, U of S.C. INT: labor law, coll barg, arb/med. ASSN: South Atlantic IRRA, ABA (Labor & Empl Law Section), S. C. Bar (Empl and Labor Law Sec), Defense Res Inst. POSITIONS: 1st Lt, U.S. Army, 1966; Plant Manager, Cowden Manufacturing Co, 1970; and (since 1977) Attorney, Nelson, Mullins, Grier & Scarborough, PO Box 11070, Columbia, SC 29211. 803/799-2000

KNIGHT, ROBERT EDWARD LEE Acad: Econ. POSITION: Assoc Prof, Dept of Econ, Univ of Maryland, College Park, MD 20742.

KNIGHT, THOMAS ROCKWELL Acad: Bus Admin, Ind Rels. BA 1976 Hampshire Coll; MS 1978, PhD 1982, Cornell U. INT: coll barg, arb/med, labor law. ASSN: British Columbia IRRA, Acad of Mgmt, Canadian Ind Rels Assn, SPIDR. POSITION: Asst Prof, Faculty of Commerce, 2053 Main Mall, Univ of British Columbia, Vancouver, BC V6T 1Y8 Canada. 604/228-5957

KNOBLOCH, RACHEL MARIE Student, Ind Admin. BIA 1984, GMI Eng & Mgmt Inst. INT: ind admin. ADDRESS: 3139 N 88th St, Milwaukee, WI 53222.

KNOPF, KENYON A. Acad: Econ, Ind Rels. AB 1942, Kenyon Coll; MA & PhD 1949, Harvard. PUBL: The Market System, (w R. Haveman) 4th Ed. INT: coll barg, labor market econ, arb/med. ASSN: AEA. POSITIONS: Jensen Prof of Econ, Grinnell Coll, 1949-67; Dean of the Coll & Provost, 1967-1980, and, since 1967, Prof of Econ, Whitman Coll, Walla Walla, WA 99362. 509/527-5127

KNOTT, ILDIKO Acad: Ind Rels. PO Box 328, Bloomfield Hills, MI 48013.

KNOX, ROBERT E. Union. INT: labor law, arb/med, coll barg. ASSN: Detroit Area IRRA. POSITION: President, Teamsters Local #1038, 2741 Trumbull, Detroit, MI 48216. 313/964-0720

KOBELL, GERALD Government. BS 1953, LLB 1966, U of Penna; LLM 1967, New York U. INT: labor law, coll barg, arb/med. ASSN: Western Penna IRRA, ABA, Federal Bar Assn. POSITIONS: Supervisory Attorney, Reg 22, Newark NJ, 1972, Asst General Counsel, Wash DC, 1976, and, since 1982, Regional Dir, NLRB, Reg 6, 1000 Grant St, Suite 1501, Pittsburgh, PA 15222. 412/644-2944

KOCH, DAVID H. Government. BA & MA 1970, S Ill U. INT: labor market econ, personnel. POSITIONS: Res Analyst, Job Service, 1971, Statis Res Specialist, Res Analyst, 1975, NBLS; and (since 1982) Accountant, VI Contributions, c/o Unemployment Ins, 90 N Port, Alton, Il 62002. 618/466-8221

KOCHAN, THOMAS ANTON Acad: Ind Rels. BBA 1969, MS 1971, PhD 1973, U of Wis. PUBL: Collective Bargaining and Industrial Relations; Dispute Resolution Under Factfinding and Arbitration, AAA, 1979; "Strategic Choice and Industrial Relations Theory and Practice," Ind Rels, 1984. INT: coll barg, org beh, arb/med. ASSN: Boston IRRA, SPIDR, Acad of Mgmt, The Labor Guild. POSITIONS: Asst Prof, 1973, Assoc Prof, Cornell School of Ind and Labor Rels, Cornell, 1978; and (since 1980) Professor of Ind Rels, Sloan School of Mgmt, MIT, 50 Memorial Dr, Cambridge, MA 02139. 617/253-6689

KOELLER, CHARLES TIMOTHY Acad: Econ, Bus Admin. AB 1971, Rutgers U; MS 1973, Auburn U; AM 1976, MPhil, 1977, PhD, 1979, Rutgers U. PUBL: "Structural Stability in Models of American Trade Union Growth," Quar J of Econ, Feb, 1981; "The Three Faces of Unionism," vol 14, Fall 1980; and "U. S. Unionism: Reply," Policy Rev, vol 18, Fall 1981; "Compact of Labor-Management Relations on Productivity: U.S. & Japan- A Comment," abstracted in Atlantic Econ J, vol 9, Mar 1981. INT: labor market econ, union org/admin, coll barg. ASSN: AEA, Eastern Econ Assn, IIRA. POSITIONS: Teaching Asst, Econ, 1973, Instructor of Econ, Rutgers Coll, 1976; and (since 1979) Asst Prof, Dept of Mgmt, Stevens Inst of Technology, Castle Point, Hoboken, NJ 07030. 201/420-5376

KOENIG, EDWARD C. Arbitration. BA 1947, Amherst Coll. INT: arb/med, coll barg, empl/-trng programs. ASSN: Houston IRRA, SPIDR. POSITIONS: Sec/Treas, Teamsters Local 310, Tucson, 1960; Mediator, FMCS, 1964; and (since 1982) Arbitrator, 209 Fairfield, La Porte, TX 77571. 713/471-9191

KOERNER, STEPHEN Union. 2690 Queenswood Dr, Victoria BC V8N 1X5 Canada.

KOHEN, ANDREW I. Acad: Econ. PhB 1963, Wayne State U; MA 1964, Yale U; PhD 1973, Ohio State U. PUBL: "Time Series Evidence of the Effect of the Minimum Wage on Teenage Employment and Unemployment," J of Human Resources, Winter 1983; "Changing Jobs: Moving Up or Out?" Thrust, Spring, 1980; "Factors Determining College Student Retention of Economic Knowledge After the Principles of Microeconomics Course," J of Econ Educ, Spring 1979. INT: labor market econ, govt labor policy, human capital econ. ASSN: AEA, Amer Educ Res Assn. POSITIONS: Assoc Project Dir, Natl Longitudinal Survey, Ohio State Univ, 1971-76; Sr Economist, U.S. Minimum Wage Study Comm., 1979-80; and (since 1983) Prof of Econ, Dept of Econ, James Madison Univ, Harrisonburg, VA 22807. 703/433-6605

KOHL, GEORGE H. Union. BA 1976, U of Tex. PUBL: "Changing Competitive and Technology Environments in Telecommunications;" "Unions in the Information Industry;" "Telecommunications in Transition: Its Impact on Work and Workers." INT: labor market econ, coll barg, labor educ. POSITIONS: Res Dir, Center for Development Policy, 1977; Program Res Dir, SANE, 1979; and (since 1980) Research Economist, Communication Workers of America, 1925 K St NW, Washington DC 20006. 202/728-2396

KOHLER, THOMAS C. Acad: Law. BA 1974, Mich State U; JD 1977, Wayne State U. PUBL: "Distinctions without Differences: Effects Bargaining," in Light of First Natl Maintenance, 5 Ind Rels L.J. 402, 1983; "Methods of Worker Participation in the United States," (w J. G. Getman), 34 Revue Intl de Droit Compare, Spring 1984. INT: labor law, coll barg, intl comparative labor. ASSN: Societe de Legislation Comparee. POSITIONS: Grad Fellow, Res Fellow, Yale, 1981-83; and (since 1983) Asst Prof of Law, Boston Coll Law School, 885 Centre St, Newton Centre, MA 02159. 617/552-4321

KOHN, EMANUEL LOUIS Retired. 445 N Wilmot, #146, Tucson, AZ 85711.

KOJIMA, NORIAKI Acad: Economics. POSITION: Faculty of Econ, Toyama Univ, 3190-Banchi Gofuku, Toyama-Shi 930 Japan

KOLB, DEBORAH M. Acad: Org Beh, Ind Rels; Consulting. BA 1965, Vassar; MBA 1973, U of Colo; PhD 1981, MIT. PUBL: The Mediators; "Strategy and the Tactics of Mediation," "Problem Definition and Policy Research." INT: arb/med, coll barg, ind sociol. ASSN: Acad of Mgmt, SPIDR. POSITION: Assoc Prof of Mgmt, Simmons Grad School of Mgmt, Boston. ADDRESS: 214 Buckminster Rd, Brookline, MA 02146. 617/536-8390

KOLB, JEAN Union. 4301 Beaumont Ct, Fairfax, VA 22030.

KOLMAN, JOHN ROBERT Student; Workers Comp. BA 1975, MA 1980, U of Ill; JD 1984, Brooklyn Law School. INT: labor law. ASSN: NY Bar Assn, ABA. POSITION: Hearing Representative, State Ins Fund. ADDRESS: 200 W 93rd St, Apt 4D, New York, NY 10025. 212/962-8900 ext 1658

KOLODRUBETZ, WALTER W. Government. BA 1952, St. Cloud State, MA 1953, Marquette U. POSITION: (since 1976) Economist, USDL, 9802 Cottrell Terr, Silver Spring, MD 20903. 202/523-9421

KONVITZ, MILTON R. Acad: Law, Ind Rels. BS 1928, JD 1930, NYU; PhD 1933, Cornell. PUBL: "The Constitution & Cicil Rights;" "Fundamental Rights of a Free People;" "Expanding Liberties." INT: arb/med, labor law, govt labor policy. ASSN: Law & Soc Assn, Amer Acad of Arts & Sciences (Fellow). POSITION: (since 1975) Prof Emeritus, Ind & Labor Rels & Law, Cornell, Ives Hall, Ithaca, NY 14850.

KOOP, DAVID H. Bus:Pers/Ind Rels. 563 Randolph St, #7, Meadville, PA 16335.

KOPELMAN, RICHARD E. Acad: Org Beh. BS 1965, MBA 1967, U of Penna; DBA 1974, Harvard. PUBL: "The Case for Merit Rewards," Pers Admin, Oct 1983; "A Model of Work, Family and Conflicts: A Construed Validation Study," Org Beh and Human Performance, 1983; "Parkinson's Law and Absenteeism: A Program to Rein In Sick Leave Cuts," Pers Admin, May 1981. INT: org beh, Ind psych, personnel. ASSN: New York IRRA, Acad of Mgmt, Amer Psych Assn, ASPA. POSITIONS: Asst Prof of Mgmt, 1974, Assoc Prof of Mgmt, 1978, and, since 1981, Prof of Mgmt, Baruch Coll, New York. ADDRESS: 65 Colgate Rd, Great Neck, NY 11023. 212/725-7136

KORECKIS, PAUL H. Government. BA 1981, Otterbein Coll. INT: govt labor policy, coll barg, arb/med. ASSN: Central Ohio IRRA, SFLRP, Natl Council on Alcoholism, Ohio, Assn of the U.S. Army. POSITIONS: Admin Officer, 1960, Supr Pers Mgmt Specialist, 1977, and, since 1982, Labor Rels Officer, Ohio Natl Guard, 2825 N Granville Road, Worthington, OH 43085. 614/889-7050

KORETZ, ROBERT F. Acad: Law; Arbitration. AB 1933, JD 1938, Syracuse; LLM 1939, Harvard. PUBL: Statutory History of the U.S. Labor Organizations, McGraw Hill, 1970; "Federal Regulation of Secondary Strikes and Boycotts," 59 Columbia Law Rev., 1959; "Employer Interference With Union Organization Versus Free Speech, 29 G. Wash Law Rev, 399, 1960. INT: labor law, arb/med, coll barg. ASSN: NAA, ABA, NYS Bar Assn. POSITIONS: Attorney, Trial Examiner, NLRB, 1939; and (since 1946) Professor of Law (now Emeritus), College of Law, Syracuse Univ, Syracuse, NY 13210. 315/423-3136

KORN, AMY Consulting. 15 Stratford Rd, Plainview NY 11803.

KORN, RICHARD HENRY Bus:Pers Ind Rels. POSITION: Vice Pres, Pers and Labor Rels, Ship'n Shore Div, General Mills, New York. ADDRESS: 15 Stratford Rd, Plainview, NY 11803. 212/398-7021

KORNFELD, MARC C. Union. BS 1963, Cornell. INT: arb/med, coll barg, union org/-admin. ASSN: Central Penna IRRA. POSITIONS: Research Officer, Electrical, Electronic, Telecommunications Union of Great Britain, 1967; Asst to the Pres and Rep, Retail Clerks Union Local 1436, 1969; and (since 1971) Representative, Pennsylvania State Educ Assn, Box 1724, 400 N 3rd St, Harrisburg, PA 17105. 717/255-7015

KOSS, J.J. Arbitration, Consulting, Bus:-Mgmt/Admin. BS 1948, MA 1951, U of Pittsburgh; MS 1978, Youngstown State U. INT: arb/med, income maint, coll barg. ASSN: AEA, Natl Board for Certified Counselors, Northwestern Oh Counselors Assn. POSITIONS: Asst Prof, Indiana State U; Assoc Prof, Youngstown State Univ, and J. J. Koss, Pres, Labor Rels Consultant and Marriage Counselor, 4055 South Ave, Youngstown, OH 44512. 216/788-9470

KOTIN, LEO Arbitration. POSITION: Arbitrator, Suite 105, 14200 Ventura Blvd, Sherman Oaks, CA 91423.

KOUTOUZOS, GEORGIA D. Acad: Student; Legal Practice. BA 1976, U of Ill-UC; JD 1980, Drake U. INT: labor law, coll barg. ASSN: ABA (Section on Labor & Empl Law), Iowa Bar Assn. POSITIONS: Legal Intern, Iowa Public Empl Rels Board, 1980; Field Agent Intern, Fed Labor Rels Authority, 1984; and (since 1983) Student/Res Asst, Inst of Labor & Ind Rels, Univ of Ill. ADDRESS: 909 S First, #2, Champaign, IL 61820. 217/333-0984

KOVACS, ARANKA EVE Acad: Econ. BA 1955, McMaster U; MA 1956, U of Toronto; PhD 1960, Bryn Mawr Coll. POSITIONS: Lecturer, McGill Univ, 1961; and (since 1961) Professor, Dept of Econ, Univ of Windsor, Windsor, Ontario, Canada. 519/253-4232

KOVAL, VITALINA Acad: Administration. ADDRESS: Academy of Sciences-Labor House GA Room 308, Kolpachney Pereulok, Moscow Center, USSR.

KOVENETSKY, SAM Government. POSITION: Member Unemployment Insurance Appeal Board, 2 World Trade Center, New York, NY 10047. 212/488-5802

KOWALCZYK, ROBERT S. Union. BA 1959, U of Detroit; MA 1973, Wayne State U; PhD 1983, U of Mich. PUBL: Local Teacher Organizations; "The Teacher's Advocate." INT: arb/med, coll barg, union org/admin. ASSN: Mich Exec Dir Assn, NEA, Mich Educ Assn. POSITIONS: Instructor, McComb Cty Community Schools, 1958, Exec Dir, Warren Educ Assn, 1968; and (since 1978) Exec Dir, Wayne-Westland Educ Assn and Affiliates, 29520 Munger Ave, Suite 1, Livonia, MI 48154. 313/421-1501

KOWALSKI, RONALD E. Acad: Ind Rels; Mediation, Arbitration. BA 1966, U of Rochester; MA 1968, Ohio U; PhD 1973, Syracuse U. PUBL: "The A.T.T.I. and the Question of TUE Affiliation," in Albion, Spring 1978. INT: arb/-med, coll barg, labor educ. ASSN: Central New York IRRA, SPIDR, Amer Historical Assn. POSITION: (since 1969) Director of Labor Studies, Onondaga Community College. ADDRESS: 102 Dewitt Rd, Syracuse, NY 13214. 315/469-7741

KOZIARA, KAREN SHALLCROSS Acad: Ind Rels. BA 1961, Penna State U; MS 1963, PhD 1965, U of Wis. PUBL: "The Impact of Flexible Automation Technology on Industrial Relations," chapter in Proceedings-Human Factors in Manufacturing, 1984; "Measuring Comparable Worth," chapter in The Comparable Worth Issue, Helen Remick, ed, 1984; "Collective Bargaining in Agriculture," chapter in Collective Bargaining: Contemporary American Experience, G. Somers ed, IRRA, 1980. INT: coll barg, union org/admin, govt labor policy. ASSN: Philadelphia IRRA, AAA. POSITION: (since 1966) Professor, Ind Rels, Org Behavior, Temple Univ, Philadelphia, PA 19122. 215/787-8138

KOZLOWSKI, RICK J. Bus:Pers/Ind Rels, Mgmt/Admin; Acad: Ind Rels. BA 1975, MS 1984, Northern Ill U. INT: coll barg, labor law, personnel. ASSN: Univ & Coll Labor Educ Assn, ASPA. POSITIONS: Intl Rep, Intl Brotherhood of Boilermakers, Iron Ship Builders, Blacksmiths, Forgers & Helpers, AFL-CIO, 1977; Labor Studies Coordinator, Black Hawk Coll-Moline, 1979; and (since 1981) Grad Asst/Mgmt Dept, Northern Ill Univ. ADDRESS: Apt 305, 1025 Crane Dr, De Kalb, IL 60115. 815/758-6375

KRAHN, DONALD E. Union. BS 1957, Carroll Coll, Waukesha. INT: union org/admin, coll barg, labor law. POSITIONS: Teacher, Biology, Fort Atkinson, 1961; Field Consultant & Dir of Field Services, 1968, and, since 1976, Director of Legal Services, Wis Education Assn Council, PO Box 8003, 101 West Beltline Hwy, Madison, WI 53708. 608/255-2971

KRAMER, JAY Government. POSITION: Chairman Emeritus, NY State Labor Rels Bd, 200 Grist Mill Lane, Great Neck, NY 11023. 516/487-8698

KRAMER, LYNDA H. Bus:Pers/Ind Rels. POSITION: Manager, Human Resources, Armco Building Systems Inc., PO Box 465622, Cincinnati, OH 45246. 513/782-5031

KRAMER, ROBERT E. Student. POSITION: General Services Manager, Clipper Express Company, 3401 W Pershing Rd, Chicago, IL 60632. 312/376-7400

KRANZ, HARRY Acad: Public Admin, Ind Rels, Org Beh/Pers. BLitt 1945, Rutgers U; JD 1962, PhD 1974, American U. PUBL: The Participatory Bureaucracy: Women & Minorities In A More Representative Public Service, D. C. Heath, 1976. INT: empl/trng programs, coll barg, personnel. ASSN: Wash DC IRRA, ASPA, Amer Pol Sci Assn, POSITIONS: Dir, Office of Migrant Farm Workers, 1978-79, Dir, Office of Special Projects, 1979-81, USDL, Retired. ADDRESS: 6527 Elgin Lane, Bethesda, MD 20817. 301/229-6943

KRASHEVSKI, RICHARD S. Union. PhD 1979, Georgetown U. PUBL: "Union Structure," (w R. Oswald), in Trade Unionism in the United States: A Symposium in Honor of Jack Barbash, J. Stern & B. Dennis, eds, IRRI-U of Wis, Oct 1981. ASSN: AEA. POSITION: (since 1980) Economist, AFL-CIO, Dept of Economic Res, 815 16th St NW, Washington DC 20006. 202/637-5313

KRAUSE, EDWARD FRANCIS Student. BS 1984, LeMoyne Coll. INT: personnel, labor law, org beh. ASSN: Central New York IRRA, ASPA. Student-Le Moyne Coll. Address: 51 Seymour St, Auburn, NY 13021. 315/252-7484

KRAUSE, MARY A. Student. 210 Riverdale Rd, Liverpool, NY 13088. 315/622-2061

KREBS, LINDA Bus:Pers/Ind Rels. BA 1970, Calif State U-Sacramento; MA 1978, U of Ill. INT: labor market econ, personnel, labor law. POSITIONS: Res Analyst, Chrysler Corp, 1978; and (since 1979) Administrator, Affirmative Action Compliance, ANR Pipeline Co, Detroit. ADDRESS: Apt B102, 2273 E Maple, Birmingham, MI 48008. 313/496-5724

KREBS, PAUL J. Arbitration. POSITION: Labor Arbitrator, 156 W Hobart Gap Rd, Livingston, NJ 07039. 201/992-5209

KREIDER, L. EMIL Acad: Econ; Consulting. BA 1960, Bethel Coll-Kans; PhD 1968, Ohio State U. PUBL: Development and Utilization of Managerial Talent, (Monograph & Dissertation), Dept of Commerce, Inst for Applied Tech, 1968; "Banana Cartel?" Inter-Amer Econ Affairs, 1977; "Elasticity of Demand for Bananas," Inter-Amer Econ Affairs, 1978. INT: coll barg, labor market econ, proof of econ loss. ASSN: Wis IRRA, Natl Assn of Bus Economists, Soc of Intl Devel, AEA. POSITIONS: Asst Prof, Dept of Econ, S Ill Univ, 1965-70; Economist, Planning & Devel Dept, Castle & Cooke Inc, 1976-77; and (since 1970) Prof of Econ & Mgmt, Beloit Colege, Beloit, WI 53511. 608/365-3391 ext 231.

KRENDEL, EZRA S. Acad: Research. ADDRESS: Wharton School DH/CC, Univ of Pennsylvania, Philadelphia, PA 19104.

KRESIN, GEORGE L. Bus:Pers/ Ind Rels, Arbitration. INT: arb/med, coll barg, labor law. ASSN: Detroit IRRA, IRAD. POSITIONS: Detroit Labor Rels Mgr, Excello Crop; and, currently, Corp Dir, Labor Relstions, Stroh Brewery Co, 1 Stroh Dr, Detroit, MI 48226. 313/446-2315

KRIDER, CHARLES E. Acad: Ind Rels, Bus Admin. BA 1963, Kalamazoo Coll; MBA 1966, PhD 1976, U of Chicago. ADDRESS: School of Business, University of Kansas, Lawrence, KS 66044.

KRINSKY, EDWARD B. Arbitration, Environmental Mediation. BA 1963, Antioch Coll; MA 1966, PhD 1969, U of Wis-Madison. PUBL: The Impact of Collective Bargaining on Hospitals, (W R. U. Miller and B. E. Becker), New York, Praeger, 1979; "The Effect of the Senate Bill 15 Amendments to the Municipal Employment Relations Act," Wis Legislative Council, Dec 1980; "The Impact of the Labor Management Reporting and Disclosure Act (LMRDA) on Union Administration and Leadership," report to U.S. Dept of Labor, RFPL/M 80-13, Mar 1982. INT: arb/med, coll barg, govt labor policy. ASSN: Wis IRRA, NAA, AAA. POSITIONS: Project Dir, Wis Center for Public Policy, 1976; Mediator, Inst for Environmental Mediation, 1982, and (since 1966) Arbitrator, 2021 Chamberlain Ave, Madison, WI 53705. 608/257-1060, 231-1898

KRISLOV, JOSEPH Acad: Econ. BS 1949, Ohio U; MA 1950, Western Reserve U; PhD 1954, U of Wis. POSITIONS: Fulbright Prof, Trinity Coll, Ireland, 1979-71; Visiting Prof, Tel-Aviv U, Israel, 1977-78; and (since 1964) Professor, Department of Economics, University of Kentucky, Lexington, KY 40506. 606/-212-3626

KRISTALL, WAYNE PAUL Government. BA 1971, Mich State U; MS & JD 1974, U of Wis. ASSN: Mich and Wis Bar Assn. POSITIONS: Attorney Private Practice, White and Maxwell, 1974; and (since 1978) Referee (Attorney), Oakland County Friend of Court, Admin Annex II, 1200 N Telegraph Rd, Pontiac, MI 48053. 313/858-0443

KROLIKOWSKI, RICHARD JOHN Bus:Pers/-Ind Rels. BA 1975, Penna State U; AM 1977, U of Ill. PUBL: "Bargaining Costs and Outcomes in Municipal Labor Relations," (w P. F. Gerhart), J of Coll Negotiations in the Public Sector, vol 9, #3, 1980. INT: coll barg, arb/med, labor law. POSITIONS: Res Asst, ILIR, Univ of Ill, 1975; Pers Interviewer, Pratt & Whitney Aircraft, 1978; and (since 1979) Labor Rels Rep, Ford Motor Co, Tulsa Glass Plant. ADDRESS: 9114-H South Urbana, Tulsa, OK 74137. 918/252-7555

KROPP, STEVEN H. Acad: Ind Rels; Arbitration. BA 1977, U of Mass-Amherst; JD 1981, Boston U. INT: arb/med, coll barg, labor law. ASSN: Boston IRRA. POSITION: Asst Prof of Business, Dept of Bus, Plymouth State Coll-Univ of New Hampshire, Plymouth, NH 03264. 603/536-1550

KROUL, RUSSELL Student. 212 E Armory, Champaign, IL 61820. 217/337-6373

KRUGER, ARTHUR MARTIN Acad: Econ, Ind Rels; Arbitration. BA 1955, U of Toronto; PhD 1959, MIT. POSITION: Professor, University Coll, University of Toronto, Toronto, Ont Canada. 416/978-3183

KRUGER, DANIEL H. Acad: Ind Rels. BA 1949, U of Richmond; MA 1951, PhD 1954, U of Wis. PUBL: Occupational Licensing Practices & Policies, (w Shinberg & Esser) Public Affairs Press, 1973; Collective Bargaining in the Public Sector, Random House, 1969; "Labor Relations and the Nurse," chapter in The Nurse as a Change Agent, Lancaster & Lancaster eds, C. V. Mosby Co, 1982. INT: coll barg, arb/med, empl/trng programs. ASSN: AAA, Mich Acad of Sci, Arts and Letters, Southern Econ Assn. POSITIONS: Asst Prof of Mgmt, Univ of Alabama, 1954; and (since 1957) Prof of Labor and Ind Rels, School of L & IR, Michigan State Univ, 428 S Kedzie Hall, East Lansing, MI 48823. 517/353-7231

KRUGLAK, GREGORY Intl Org. ADDRESS: ILO, Casse Postale 500, CH 1211, Geneva 22, Switzerland.

KRUMWIEDE, JERRY Bus:Pers/Ind Rels. BA 1974, Pacific Lutheran U; MS 1977, Ind State U. INT: personnel, emp/trng programs, health & hosp care. ASSN: North Texas IRRA, Dallas Pers Assn, Amer Soc of Safety Eng, Amer Ind Hygiene Assn. POSITIONS: Instructor, Dallas Independent School Dist; Safety Mgr, Dresser Ind, 1980; and (since 1983) Safety Manager, Peterbilt Motors Co, 3200 Airport Rd, PO Box 550, Denton TX 76201. 817/566-7100

KRUSE, ROY Union. POSITION: Hawaii Newspaper Guild, 451 Atkinson Dr, Honolulu, HI 96814.

KUCHEROV, TANYA L. Government. ADDRESS: 2216 King Pl NW, Washington DC 2007.

KUECHLE, DAVID Acad: Ind Rels; Arbitration. JD 1954, U of Wis. PUBL: "Yeshiva Shock Waves," Harvard Educ Rev, 1982; "The Art of Negotiation," Bus Quart, 1981; The Practice of Industrial Relations, McGraw Hill, 1975. INT: arb/med, mgmt/educ, coll barg. ASSN: Boston IRRA, SPIDR, Wis Bar Assn. POSITION: (since 1977) Professor, Harvard Univ, 989 Memorial Dr, Cambridge, MA 02138. 617/495-3405

KUEHN, DONALD H. Union. BSS 1965, Texas A & I U. INT: union org/admin, coll barg, empl/trng programs. POSITIONS: Teacher, School Dist of Kansas City, 1969; and (since 1974) Natl Rep, Amer Federation of Teachers, AFL-CIO, Wash DC. ADDRESS: 6800 Willow Lane NW, Kansas City, MO 64152. 202/797-4400

KUGLER, ISRAEL Arbitration. PhD 1954, NYU. INT: arb/med, coll barg, labor history. ASSN: New York IRRA. POSITION: Professor Emeritus, CUNY. ADDRESS: 21-66 33 Road, Long Island City, NY 11106. 212/274-1163

KUHL, WILLIAM OWEN Union. BA 1947, Iowa State U; MS 1949, PhD 1957, U of Wis. INT: labor educ, union org/admin, coll barg. ASSN: Kansas City IRRA, AEA. POSITION: Dir of Res and Educ, Intl Brotherhood of Boilermakers, 1960; and (since 1983) Retired. ADDRESS: 9401 Outlook Dr, Overland Park, KS 66207.

KUHN, JAMES WESLEY Acad: Bus Admin. BA 1949, Harvard; MA 1950, PhD 1954, Yale; LLD 1969, Linfield Coll. PUBL: Collective Bargaining, (w N. W. Chamberlain), 1984; "Electrical Products," chapter in Collective Bargaining: Contemporary American Experience, G.G. Somers, ed, IRRA 1984; "A Retrospective Analysis of Chamberlain's Scholarly Work," (w Lewin & McNulty), British J of Ind Rels, 21, 143, 1983. POSITION: Graduate School of Business, Columbia Univ, 706 Uris Hall, New York, NY 10027. 212/280-4424

KUHN, TED Legal Practice. BA 1968, U of Houston; LAW, 1971, S Tex Coll. INT: labor law, arb/med, union org/admin. ASSN: Houston IRRA, State Bar of Tex-Labor Law. POSITION: (since 1971) Attorney, Aldrich, Buttril & Kuhn, 2100 Travis #415, Houston, TX 77002. 713/654-1313

KUHR, M. I. Acad: Student, Communications. BA 1949, MA 1952, Temple U; PhD 1963, U of Mo-Columbia. PUBL: "Making the Transition to a Small College," ACA Bull, Jan 1984; "John Dickinson, Reluctant Revolutionist," Penna Heritage, June 1978; "Legal Speaking by Pennsylvania Lawyers," in A History of Public Speaking in Pennsylvania, 1971. INT: arb/med, org beh, labor educ. ASSN: Speech Communication Assn of Amer. POSITIONS: Instructor, Temple U, 1958; Prof, Slippery Rock U, 1961; and (currently) Student, Ind Univ of Penna.

ADDRESS: 100 Elise Dr, Butler, PA 16001. 412/794-7109

KUJAWSKI, KARL R. Government. 4651 Blaine SE, Kentwood, MI 49508.

KULASH, MARJORIE Consulting. BA 1966, Wellesley Coll; MA 1973, U of Md. PUBL: "Pension Plan Equity:The Unintended Consequences," J of Policy Analysis in Mgmt, vol 3, #1, Fall 1983; Tuition Tax Credits: The Policy Issues..., (monograph w Peterson, Foster & McCallum), The Urban Inst, Feb 1983. INT: pension/empl benefits, govt labor policy, health & hosp care. POSITIONS: Res Assoc, The Urban Inst, 1980; Sr Labor Policy Analyst, Government Res Corp, 1982; and (since 1983) Consultant, The Wyatt Company Research & Information Center, 1990 K St NW, Washington DC 20006. 202/857-9278

KULCHIN, BERNARD A. Bus:Pers/Ind Rels. AA 1952, U of Fla; BA 1954, BEE 1955, U of Miami. INT: coll barg, arb/med, empl/trng programs. ASSN: San Diego IRRA, Amer Electronics Assn, ASPA, Pers Mgmt Assn. POSITIONS: Mgr of Pers, 1970, Dir of Ind Rels, 1971, and, since 1983, Division Vice Pres, Ind Rels, General Dynamics Electronics Div, PO Box 85227, San Diego, CA 92138. 619/573-7116

KUMAR, PRADEEP Acad: Ind Rels, Econ, Univ Admin. PhD 1974, Queen's Univ. PUBL: The Current Industrial Relations Scene in Canada, (w W. D. Wood), Annual Vol; "Occupational Earnings, Compensating Differentials and Human Capital," CJE Aug 1982; Canadian Perspectives on Wage Price Guidelines, Queen's Univ, Kingston, 1976. INT: labor market econ, coll barg, personnel. POSITION: (since 1976) Asst Dir, Ind Rels Centre, Queen's Univ, Kingston, Ont K7L 3N6 Canada. 613/547-5871

KUMAR, PRAVEEN Bus:Pers/Ind Rels. MA 1980, Tata Inst of Soc Sci-Bombay. PUBL: "Industrial Relations in the Unorganized Sector," Vol IV, IIRA 6th World Congress, 1983. INT: intl comparative labor, union org/admin, personnel. ASSN: IIRA, Bombay Mgmt Assn. POSITION: (since 1980) Pers Exec, Siemens India Ltd, Kalwa Works, Maharashtra. ADDRESS: 21 Shirish, Makarand Hsg Soc, SB Marg, DADAR (W), Bombay, 400 028 India. Phone: 922-2307

KUNNECKE, BENTON F. Bus:Pers/Ind Rels, Bus:Mgmt/Admin. BBA 1951, U of Tex-Austin; MBA 1971, Pepperdine U. PUBL: "Do High Grades, Top School or an Advanced Degree Lead to Job Security and Extraordinary Salary Progression?" (w G. J. Schick), vol 11, #6: Interfaces, Inst of Mgmt Sci, Feb 1982. INT: personnel, coll barg. ASSN: Orange Cty IRRA, ASPA, PIRA, Reg 7. POSITIONS: Branch Mgr, Pers Serv Centers, McDonnell Douglas Astronautics, 1973, Mgr, Labor Rels, Long Beach, 1979, and, since 1982, Director-Labor Rels & Personnel Service Centers-West, Douglas Aircraft Co, 3855 Lakewood Blvd, Long Beach, CA 90846. 213/593-4353

KUPTZIN, HAROLD Acad: Econ, Labor Market Analysis; Government. BS 1941, CCNY; MA 1952, American U. PUBL: Chronic Labor Surplus Areas: Experience and Outlook; Handbook on Area Skill Survey; "Use of Employment Service Job Openings Data in the Measurement and Interpresentation of Job Vacancies." INT: labor market econ, empl/trng programs, method/statis. ASSN: Wash DC IRRA, Acad of Pol Sci, Regional Sci Assn, Intl Assn of Pers & Empl Security. POSITIONS: Dir, Office of Technical Support, US Empl Service, 1971; Part Time Econ & Res Consultant, 1978; Retired. 1316 Xaveria Court, Silver Spring, MD 20903.

KURCINA, JOYCE A. Bus:Pers/Ind Rels. BS 1979 U of Pittsburgh; MA 1982, Ind U of Penna. INT: personnel, empl/trng programs, labor law. ASSN: ASPA. POSITIONS: Labor Rels Specialist, 1980; and (since 1981) Empl Rels Assoc, Union Carbide, South Charleston. ADDRESS: 1516 Kanawha Blvd, E, Charleston, WV 25311. 304/747-2113

KUROMOTO, PERRY K. Bus:Pers/Ind Rels. BA 1959, U of Hawaii. INT: labor law, coll barg, arb/med. POSITIONS: Vice Pres, Times Super Market Ltd, 1963, and, currently, Director, Ind Rels, Dillingham Maritime Pacific Div, PO Box 3288, Honolulu, HI 96801. 808/543-9361.

KUROWSKI, DAVID STEVEN Acad: Student; Bus:Mgmt/Admin, Consumer/Arbitration. AA 1981, BA 1982, Penna State U. INT: personnel, arb/med, coll barg. ASSN: IIRA. POSITION: Asst Manager, Shehadi Stereo Inc, Throop. ADDRESS: 825-A Prospect Ave, Scranton, PA 18505. 717/961-2202

KURTH, EDMUND ANTHONY Acad: Economics. POSITION: Prof, Dept of Econ, Loras Coll, Dubuque, IA 52001.

KURTZ, CARY R. Union, Bus:Pers/Ind Rels. BA 1980, Bethany Coll-W. Va.; MALIR 1983, Ind U of Penna. INT: coll barg, arb/med, labor law. ASSN: Central Penna Chapter-Penna Interscholastic Athletic Assn Basketball Officials. POSITIONS: Grad Intern: Ind Rels, Season-All Industries, Inc., Indiana, PA, 1982; and (since 1983 Asst Dir of Contract Implementation, Assn of Penna State College and Univ Faculties (APSCUF), 319 N Front St, Box 787, Harrisburg, PA 17108. 717/236-7486

KUTCHINS, KAY OVERTON Consulting; Acad: Org Beh/Pers, Public Admin. BA 1962, U of Ill-UC; MA 1978, U of Tex-San Antonio. PUBL: "Improving Customer Communications," AWA J, 1982; "Plan for An Emergency Before It Happens," AWA J, 1978; "In-Service Training," Amer Water Works Mgmt Manual M-5, 1979. INT: mgmt/educ, org beh, personnel. ASSN: San Antonio IRRA, ASTD, Amer Water Works Assn, Women in Communications, Inc. POSITIONS: Communications Editor, Riegel Paper Corp, 1969; Trng Admin, San Antonio City Water Board, 1973; and (since 1979) Owner/Consultant, Personnel Services-Evaluation, Trng, Communications, 216 Garden View Dr, San Antonio, TX 78213. 512/349-4937

KYLE, JAMES T. Acad: Econ. MBA 1961, Ind U. INT: coll barg, arb/med. POSITIONS: Asst Prof, 1967, Assoc Prof, 1976, and, since 1979, Assoc Prof and Chairman, Dept of Econ, Indiana State Univ, Terre Haute, IN 47809. 812/232-6311 ext 5781

KYROUAC, RICHARD C. Bus:Pers/Ind Rels. POSITION: Manager EEO, Morton Thiokol Inc, 110 N Wacker Dr, Chicago, IL 60606. 312/-621-5200

L

LABIG, CHALMER E., JR. Acad: Student, Ind Rels, Org Beh/Pers. BA 1968, Ohio State U; MA 1971, U of Tenn; PhD 1984, U of Tex-Austin. INT: arb/med, personnel, union org/admin. ASSN: Acad of Mgmt, ASPA. POSITIONS: Pers Dir, Defiance Hosp, 1975; Pers Dir, Community Hosp, San Antonio, 1979; and (since 1980) Asst Instructor/Student, Dept of Mgmt, GSB2.206, Austin, TX 78712. 512/471-3676

LABOVITZ, TRUDY A. Student. 504 Sleepy Hollow Rd, Pittsburgh, PA 15228. 412/341-1516

LACKEY, GERALD B. Legal Practice. JD 1962, Ohio State U. ADDRESS: Lackey, Nusbaum, Phillips & Harris, Spitzer Bldg, Suite 330, Toledo, OH 43604. 419/243-1105

LAEDTKE, GLENN MARVIN Bus:Pers/Ind Rels. BBA 1953 U of Wis-Madison; MAIR 1974, U of Minn. PUBL: An Experimental Study of the Effects of Introducing Job Enrichment in Assembly Work. INT: personnel, org beh, opinion survey applications. ASSN: Human Resource Res Assn, Rochester Pers Assn. POSITIONS: Recruitment, Salary Adm, Pers Adm, 1956, Job Enrichment Consultant, 1970, and, since 1973, Manager, Pers Reseach & Planning, IBM. ADDRESS: 1232 6th St SW, Rochester, MN 55902. 507/286-2212

LAFFERTY, LINDA A. Government. MILR 1968, Cornell. INT: arb/med, coll barg, govt labor policy. ASSN: Wash DC IRRA, SPIDR. POSITION: Deputy Exec Director, Federal Service Impasses Panel, 500 C St SW, Washington DC 20424. 202/382-0981

LAFLAMME, GILLES Acad: Ind Rels, Sociol, Research. POSITION: Teacher, Dept Ind Rels, Faculte des Sci Sociales, Laval Univ, Quebec, G1K 7P4 Canada. 418/656-2235

LAGERQUIST, WALTER W. Consulting. BS 1957, U.S. Merchant Marine Acad; BA 1958, MA 1959, George Washington U. POSITION: Consultant, Wyatt Co, 200 First Natl Bldg, Detroit, MI 48226. 313/673-0804

LAGROTT, WAYNE A. Student. 468 Brock St, Kingston, Ont K76 1T6 Canada.

LAJOIE, MARIO Acad: Ind Rels, Law. BA & MA, Univ Laval. "Tensions Within the Labour Movement in Quebec: Relations Between the Public and Private Sectors," Inst for Res in Public Policy, Carleton Univ, 1983; Histoire des tramilleurs quebecus, Bull, RCHTQ, vol 9, #2, pp 33-62, La Monde ouvier au Quebec, vol a paraitre en 1984. INT: labor law, personnel, arb/med. ASSN: Canadian Ind Rels Assn, CPCRIQ, Soc Historique du Canada. POSITION: Res Asst, Univ Laval, 747 Chanoine Groulx #302, Ste-Foy, Quebec G1X 3V1 Canada. 418/-656-2794

LAKE, ANGELA L. Student. 505 E Jefferson, #5, Iowa City, IA 52240. 319/338-1923

LAKICH, STEVE Bus:Pers/Ind Rels, Government. Acad: Ind Rels. BS 1962 Cal Poly, Pomona. PUBL: "The Impact of Proposition 13 on Labor-Management Relations in Local Government. INT: coll barg, arb/med. ASSN: Northern Calif IRRA. POSITIONS: Empl Rels Officer, County of Sacramento, 1972; Deputy Dir, Governor's Office of Empl Rels, 1978; and (since 1980) Empl Rels Dir, City of Sacramento, 801 9th St, Room 105, Sacramento, CA 95814. 916/449-5924

LAMANNA, JUDITH Abritration, Legal Practice; Acad: Law. BA, LeMoyne; MPA & JD, Syracuse U. INT: arb/med, labor law, intl comparative labor. ASSN: Central New York IRRA, SPIDR, AAA, Natl Center for Dispute Settlement. POSITION: Arbitrator & Attorney (Private Practice), 709 Avery Ave, Syracuse, NY 13204. 315/488-1237

LaMARTINA, JAMES Government. POSITION: FMCS, Suite 325, 12140 Woodcrest Exec Dr, St. Louis, MO 63141.

LAMB, CYNTHIA ANN Bus:Pers/Ind Rels. POSITION: Senior Pers Admin, Harris Corp. ADDRESS: 2381 Eden Park Dr, Melbourne, FL 32953. 305/254-1834

LAMB, MARJORIE A. Professional Assn. BA 1953, Briar Cliff Coll, Sioux City, IA. POSITION: (since 1976) Staff Assistant, IRRA National Office, 7226 Social Science, Univ of Wis, Madison, WI 53706. 608/262-2762

LAMBERTI, THOMAS M. Acad: Law. AB 1952, Fordham Coll; LLB 1957, Harvard. INT: labor law, coll barg, arb/med. ASSN: Long Island IRRA, NYS Bar Assn, Nassau County Bar Assn. POSITION: Senior Partner, Cullen & Dykman, 1010 Franklin Ave, Garden City, NY 11530. 516/741-0900

LAMPMAN, ROBERT J. Acad: Econ. PhD 1950, U of Wis. INT: income maint, labor market econ, health & hosp care. ASSN: AEA, Natl Tax Assn, Conference on Res in Income and Wealth. POSITIONS: Asst and Assoc Prof of Econ, U of Wash, 1948; and (since 1958) Prof of Econ, Dept of Econ, Social Science Bldg, Univ of Wis, Madison, WI 53706. 608/262-8829

LANDO, MORDECHAI E. Government. BA 1959, Brooklyn Coll; MPh 1967, Columbia U. "Recent Trends in the SSDI Program," Soc Security Bull, Aug 1970; "Disablilty Benefit Application and the Economy,: Soc Security Bull, Oct 1977; "A Comparison of the Military and Civilian Health Systems," Inquiry, June 1971. INT: income maint, labor market econ, health & hosp care. ASSN: AEA, Soc of Govt Economists. POSITIONS: Instructor of Econ, Hofstra Univ, 1963; Senior Analyst, Center for Naval Analyses, 1968; and (since 1976) Chief, Disability Impact Studies Board, Social Security Admin, 3602 Clarks Lane, Baltimore, MD 21215. 301/594-0300

LANDSBERGER, HENRY A. Acad: Sociology. BSc 1948, London School of Econ; PhD 1954, Cornell U. PUBL: "Working Class Revolutionary Consciousness: Chile 1970:1973; Germany 1918-1920," pp 131-169 in R. L. Simpson and I. Simpson (eds) Research in the Sociology of Work, Greenwich CT, JAI Press, 1981; "The Trend Toward Citizen Participation in the Welfare State: Counterveiling Power to the Professions?" Chapter 17, pp 228-243 in C. R. Foster (ed) Comparative Public Policy and

Citizen Participation, Pergamon Press, 1980. INT: comparative social policy, health & hosp care, ind sociol. ASSN: Amer Sociol Assn, Latin Amer Studies Assn. POSITIONS: Asst/-Assoc/Prof, NYSSILR-Cornell, 1956; and (since 1968) Professor, Dept of Sociology, Univ of North Carolina, Chapel Hill, NC 27514. 919/962-1007

LANE, PEGGY ANN B. Student. BS 1976, MA 1982, New York U. INT: arb/med, coll barg, org beh. ASSN: New York IRRA, AAA, AERA, SPIDR. POSITION: Res Asst and Phd Candidate, New York Univ, Community Mediator, NYS Unified Court System. ADDRESS: 33 Franklin Pl, Rutherford, NJ 07070. 212/598-2918

LANG, KEVIN Acad: Econ. BA 1976, U of Oxford; MSc U of Montreal; PhD 1982, MIT. PUBL: "Unions, Firms and the Return to Seniority," J of Labor Res, Winter 1984. INT: labor market econ, govt labor policy, method/statis. ASSN: AEA, Canadian Econ Assn. POSITION: (since 1981) Asst Prof, School of Social Sciences, Univ of Calif-Irvine. ADDRESS: 34031 La Serena, Dana Point, CA 92629. 714/856-6205

LANG, THEODORE H. Arbitration; Acad: Org Beh/Pers, Ind Rels. BS 1936, MS 1939, CCNY; MPA 1942, PhD 1951, NYU. PUBL: "Emerging Role of the Public School Personnel Administrator," in Public Personnel Rev, Oct 1969; chapter on "Educational Accountability," in New Dimensions in Educational Leadership, D. Erger & B. Israel Eds, Corley Publishers, NY 1975, pp 149-188; "Teacher Tenure as a Management Problem," Phi Delta Kappa, Mar 1975, pp 459-462. INT: arb/med, coll barg, govt labor policy. ASSN: Long Island IRRA, AAA, SPIDR, Phi Delta Kappa. POSITIONS: Deputy Superintendent of Schools, NYC Board of Educ, 1965-71; Chairman, Port Authority Empl Rels Bd, Port Authority of NY & NJ, 1977-83; and (since 1971) Professor, Dept of Educ, Baruch Coll, CUNY. ADDRESS: 795 Addison St, Woodmere, NY 11598. 212/725-4481

LANGBAUM, ERIC Consulting. BA 1962, Queens Coll; MA 1964, U of Wis. INT: org beh, ind psych, coll barg. ASSN: Amer Marketing Assn. POSITION: (since 1977) President, Eric Langbaum & Assoc, 333 Sylvan Ave, Englewood Cliffs, NJ 07632. 201/567-2229

LANGE, CARL B. A., III Consulting, Arbitration. BA 1965, MA 1966, Utah State U. INT: arb/med, coll barg, labor law. ASSN: AAA, SPIDR. POSITIONS: Dir of Government Rels, Fla Educ Assn, 1973; Coordinator, Fla Public Empl Rels Commission, 1975; and (since 1977) Consultant, Labor Rels, School Legal Service. ADDRESS: PO Box 10329, Bakersfield, CA 93389. 805/398-3830

LANGE, JOHN PATRICK Bus:Pers/Ind Rels. POSITION: Director Labor Rels, Illinois Central Gulf RR, 517 Illinois St, Park Forest, IL 60466. 312/748-1536

LANIGAN, JOHN J. Student. Heller School, Brandeis University, Waltham. ADDRESS: 26 Porter St, Watertown, MA 02172. 617/923-0463

LANSBURY, RUSSELL D. Acad: Ind Rels, Bus Admin, Org Beh/Pers. MA 1969, U of Melbourne (Australia); PhD 1973, U of London. PUBL: Industrial Relations: An Australian Introduction, Longman Cheshire, 1982; Australian Labour Relations: Readings, Macmillan 1980; Organizational Behaviour: The Australian Context, Longman Cheshire, 1983. INT: ind sociol, intl comparative labor, personnel. ASSN: IIRA, Ind Rels Assn of Australia, Acad of Mgmt. POSITIONS: Res Fellow, British Airways, London, 1970; Senior Lecturer, Monash Univ, Australia, 1974; and (since 1981) Assoc Prof, Management Studies, Macquarie Univ, North Ryde, NSW 2113, Australia. Phone: 02-889535

LaPENTA, THOMAS M. Acad: Univ Admin, Ind Rels, Law. BA 1973, U of Del; JD 1977, Dickinson U. INT: empy/trng programs, coll barg, arb/med. ASSN: Philadelphia IRRA, Delaware Bar Assn. POSITIONS: Deputy Attorney General, Del Dept of Justice, 1977; and (since 1981) Empl Rels Administrator, Univ of Delaware. ADDRESS: 1920 Thomas Rd, Wilmington DE 19803. 302/738-2171

LAPERCH, WILLIAM J. Bus:Pers/Ind Rels, Consulting. MBA 1976, Pepperdine U. INT: personnel, empl/trng programs. POSITION: President, Bus and Professional Consultants Inc, 3255 Wilshire Blvd, Los Angeles, CA 90010. 213/380-8200

LAPIDUS, LAWRENCE SEARLE Legal Practice. AB 1967, George Washington U; JD 1970, American U; LLM 1976, Georgetown U. INT: labor law, arb/med, govt labor policy. ASSN: ABA, Wash DC Bar, SFLRP. POSITION: Partner, Sherman & Lapidus, 1801 K St NW, Suite 220, Washington DC 20006. 202/785-0382

LaPORTE, PHILIP ANTHONY Acad: Labor Studies. MA 1983, U of Minn. PUBL: "Bargaining for Safety and Health Contract Language;" "Gaining A Contractual Right to Refuse Unsafe Work;" "Utilization Patterns of Minnesota Arbitrators." INT: arb/med, coll barg, govt labor policy. ASSN: Atlanta IRRA, AAA, Univ of Minn Ind Rels Alumni Assn, Univ & Coll Labor Educ Assn. POSITIONS: Compliance Monitor, Empl Program, City of Minneapolis, 1978; Program Coordinator, Univ of Minn, 1979; and (since 1983) Asst Prof, Labor Studies Program-CPUA, Georgia State Univ, University Plaza, Atlanta, GA 30303. 404/658-3653

LARKIN, JOHN DAY Arbitration. AB 1923, Berea Coll, AM 1925 U of Chicago, PhD 1935, Harvard. POSITION: Arbitrator, Retired, 33 N La Salle St, Room 2129, Chicago, Il 60602.

LARNEY, GEORGE EDWARD Arbitration, Mediator. BS 1965, U of Ill-UC; MBA Northwestern U; PhD 1974, Ill Inst of Tech. PUBL: Series of Articles on Becoming a Labor Arbitrator - published in SPIDR Newsletter in 1983. INT: arb/med, coll barg, labor law. ASSN: Chicago IRRA, SPIDR, SFLRP, Ill Labor History Assn. POSITIONS: Exec Dir, Natl Commission for Ind Peace, 1973; Commissioner, FMCS, 1974; and (currently) Labor Arbitrator-Mediator (self-employed), 1721 Dobson St, Evanston, IL 60202. 312/864-9040

LaROUCHE, VIATEUR Acad: Ind Relsl; Arbitration, Consulting. BSc 1964, MSc 1966, U of Montreal; PhD 1972, U of Minn. PUBL: "La qualite de vie au trovoil et l'horaire aairoble," "L'approche systemique en relations industrielles," Formation et perfect imnement en milieu organisation nil. INT: ind psych, arb/med, personnel. ASSN: Counselors in Ind Rels in Quebec, Conference of Arbitrators in Quebec, Canadian Ind Rels Assn. POSITION: Professor, School of Ind Rels, Univ of Montreal, Montreal PQ H3C 3J7 Canada. 514/737-3701

LARSON, LENNART VERNON Acad: Law; Arbitration, Legal Practice. BS 1933, JD 1936, U of Wash; SJD 1942, U of Mich. PUBL: "Bulk Transfers," Article in Creditors' Rights in Texas, vol 1, State Bar of Tex, 1981; Texas Litigation Guide, (w Dorsaneo), Vol 16, Tex Probate Litigation, 1982; Labor Law Section Yearbook, Tex Bar Assn, 1948-1970, editor and contributor of several papers on Labor Law. INT: arb/med, labor law, govt labor policy. ASSN: North Texas IRRA, NAA, Tex Bar Assn, Amer Coll of Probate Counsel. POSITIONS: Legal Counsel, Natl War Labor Bd, 1944; Legal Counsel, Naval Ordnance Res Proj, U of New Mexico, 1945; and (since 1946) Professor, School of Law, Southern Methodist Univ, Dallas, TX 75275. 214/692-2634

LaSALVIA, MARIA C. Union. BA 1964, Kean Coll; MEd 1982, Rutgers U. INT: coll barg, arb/med, labor educ. ASSN: New Brunswick IRRA, NEA, Kappa Delta Pi. POSITIONS: Teacher, South Plainfield, 1970; and (since 1980) President, Middlesex County Educ Assn, 1014 Livingston Ave, North Brunswick, NJ 08902. 201/246-2335

LASALLE, JON G. Union. 1942 Neidhart, Marquette, MI 49855.

LATIMER, MURRAY WEBB Retired. 2951 Albemarle St NW, Washington DC 20008. 202/-244-7958

LATINO, MICHAEL T. Student; Union. BA 1982, Knox Coll; MA 1984, U of Notre Dame. INT: coll barg, arb/med, empl/trng programs. POSITIONS: Manager, Hardees of Streator Inc, 1972-78; Consultant, Streator Building Trades, 1981; and (since 1982) Grad Student, Dept of Econ, Univ of Notre Dame, Notre Dame, IN 46556. 219/282-1904

LATTA, GEOFFREY W. Consulting. BA 1968, Oxford U; MA 1969, Warwick U; MBA Wharton School, U of Penna. PUBL: Profit Sharing, Employee Stock Ownership, Savings, and Asset Formation Plans in the Western World, 1979; "Union Organization Among Engineers: A Current Assessment," Ind & Labor Rels Rev, vol 35, #1, Oct 1981; "Making the Corporation Transparent: A Prelude to Multinational Bargaining," (w J. R. Bellace) Columbia J of World Bus, Summer 1983. INT: intl comparative labor, coll barg, personnel. ASSN: New York and Philadelphia IRRA, Ind Law Soc. POSITIONS: Res Assoc, Ind Rels Unit, Wharton School, 1977; Manager, Intl Pers, Pennwalt Corp, 1979; and (since 1981) Consultant, Organization Resources Counselors Inc. NY. ADDRESS: 2501 Naudain St, Philadelphia, PA 19146. 212/-719-3400

LA VAN, HELEN Acad: Org Beh/Pers, Bus Admin. PhD 1978, Loyola U of Chicago. PUBL: "A Survey of the Human Resource Information Systems of Major Companies," in Human Resource Planning, vol 5, #2, 1982; "A Look at the Counseling Practices of Major U.S. Corporations," in Pers Admin, June 1983; "Litigation as a Forum for the Resolution of Employment Discrimination Against Hispanics," in Empl Rels Today, Winter 1984. INT: personnel, org beh, arb/med. ASSN: Chicago IRRA. POSITION: Assoc Prof of Mgmt, DePaul Univ, 25 E Jackson Blvd, Chicago, IL 60604. 312/321-7783

LAVANWAY, PAUL J. Bus:Mgmt/Admin. BA 1971, Wayne State U; MAIR 1975, U of Minn. INT: coll barg, arb/med, org beh. POSITIONS: Mgr, Labor Rels, Coco-Cola Co, 1978; Mgr, Human Resources, Weyerhaeuser Co, 1980; and (since 1982) Manager, Human Resources, Reed Lignin Inc., 100 Hwy 15 South, Rothschild, WI 54474. 715/355-3641

LAWLER, JOHN JOSEPH Acad: Ind Rels, Or Beh/Pers. BA 1972 U of Wis-Madison; AM 1976, U of Ill-UC; PhD U of Calif-Berkeley. PUBL: "Representation Elections in Higher Education: Occurence and Outcomes," (w J.M. Walker), J of Labor Resources, Winter 1984; "Determinants for Certification and Decertification Activity," (w G. Hundley), Ind Rels, Fall 1983; "Collective Bargaining and Market Uncertainty," Ind Rels, Winter 1982. INT: union org/-admin, coll barg, org beh. POSITIONS: Research Assoc, Gary Income Maint Experiment, 1972; Asst Prof, Ind Rels Center, U of Minn, 1979; and (since 1982) Asst Prof, Inst of Labor and Ind Rels, Univ of Ill, 504 E Armory, Champaign, IL 61820. 217/333-1482

LAWRENCE, DANIEL G. Consulting. PO Box 952, St. Charles, IL 60174.

LAWRENCE, DOREEN S. Bus:Mgmt/Admin. 4708 Ardmore, Sterling Heights, MI 48077.

LAWRENCE, JAMES B. Bus:Pers/Ind Rels. MLIR 1973, Mich State U. INT: ind sociol, org beh, arb/med. ASSN: Grand Rapids IRRA. POSITIONS: Provost Marshall 3rd IBDE, US Army-Europe, 1970; Labor Rels Mgr, Eaton Corp, 1973; and (since 1980) Pers Manager, Federal Mogul Corp, 510 E Grove St, Greenville, MI 48838. 616/754-5681

LAWRENCE, PAUL R. Acad: Org Beh/-Pers. BA 1943, Albion Coll; MBA 1947, DCS 1950, Harvard. PUBL: The Changing of Organizational Patterns; Organizational Environment, (w Loosch); Reviewing American Industry, (w Dyer). INT: org beh, ind sociol. ASSN: Acad of Mgmt, Amer Sociol Assn. POSITION: Donham Prof of Org Beh, Harvard Business School, Humphrey House, Boston, MA 02163. 617/495-6650

LAWSKY, PAUL JOHN Student; Consulting. BS 1973, MSLIR 1984, New York Inst of Tech. INT: org beh, ind psych, mgmt/educ. ASSN: Natl Soc for Internships & Experimental Educ, Assn of MBA Exec. POSITIONS: Production Supr, Faberge Inc, 1973; Pharmaceutical Packing Supr, Organon Inc, 1979; and (currently) Management Consultant, Bell and Co, Baltimore. ADDRESS: 11 Bender Place, Cliffside Park, NJ 07010. 301/544-4445

LAWSON, ERIC W., Jr. Arbitration, Legal Prac. BA 1963, Syracuse U; MA 1969, Colgate U; JD 1982, SUNY-Buffalo. PUBL: Collective Bargaining Law in the Public Sector, (co-author), Niagara U Press, 1981; "Arbitrator Acceptability: Factors Affecting Selection," Arb J, Dec 1981; "Super Conciliation in the Public Schools," J of NYS School Boards Assn, 1981. INT: arb/med, coll barg, labor educ. ASSN: Western NY IRRA, AAA, NYS Bar Assn. POSITIONS: Supr Public Empl Mediator, 1973, Chief Reg Mediator, NYS Public Employment Rels Bd, 1976; and, currently, Independent Labor Arbitrator (self-employed), 293 Center St, East Aurora, NY 14052. 716/655-1735

LAWSON, GARY MICHAEL Student. BS 1974, MBA 1976, U of Tenn. PUBL: Flexible Compensation: Past Results and Future Prospects. INT: personnel, arb/med, coll barg. ASSN: Atlanta IRRA, ASPA. POSITIONS: Corp Compensation & Benefits Mgr, Natl Data Corp, 1980; Human Resource Consultant, Ernst & Whinney, 1981; and (cur-rently) Doctoral Student-Ind Rels, Georgia State Univ. ADDRESS: 1700 Noble Forest Dr, Norcross, GA 30092. 404/658-2792

LAWSON, LUTHER D. Acad: Econ. BS 1967, MS 1970, Ind State U; PhD 1981, U of Tenn. INT: coll barg, arb/med, labor market econ. ASSN: Southern Econ Assn, Natl Assn of Econ Educators. POSITIONS: Asst Prof of Econ, Tuscukum Coll, 1970; Asst Prof, U of N.C.-Asheville, 1977, and, since 1983, Asst Prof of Econ, Univ of N. C.-Wilmington, 601 College Rd, Wilmington, NC 28403. 919/791-4330 ext 2226

LEACH, DONALD B. Arbitration. ADDRESS: 548 S 4th St, Columbus, OH 43206. 614/228-6252

LEADER, ALAN HOWARD Acad: Univ Admin, Bus Admin; Consulting. BS 1952, MS 1960, U of Rochester; DBA 1963, Ind U. PUBL: Introduction to Case Analysis, U of Guam, 3rd ed, 1983; Problems and Opportunities in Economic Development, New Issues Press, 1977; Modernizing Calhoun County Government, New Issues, 1975. INT: emp;/trng programs, mgmt/educ, org beh. ASSN: Acad of Mgmt, ASPA, Amer Inst for Decision Sci. POSITIONS: Prof of Mgmt, Western Mich Univ, 1963; Consultant, Leader Assoc, 1978; and (since 1978) Dean, Coll of Bus and Public Admin, University of Guam, UOG Station, Mangilao, Guam, 96913. 671/734-4110

LEAHY, WILLIAM HENRY Acad: Ind Rels; Arbitration. AB 1959, MA 1960, PhD 1966, U of Notre Dame. PUBL: New Directions in Labor Economics and Industrial Relations, 1981; "Evaluating Productivity Programs and Job Security, 1982; "Landmark Cases Involving Union Representatives," 1979. INT: arb/med, coll barg, labor law. ASSN: AAA, FMCS, SPIDR. POSITION: (since 1963) Professor of Economics, Dept of Econ, University of Notre Dame, Box 102, Notre Dame, IN 46556. 219/239-6335/-7238

LEAL, BEN C. Union. BCS 1950, Seattle U. INT: coll barg, health & hosp care, union org/admin. ASSN: San Francisco IRRA. POSITIONS: President, 1956, and, since 1982, Secretary-Treasurer, Teamster Local 856, 459 Fulton St, Suite 304, San Francisco, CA 94102. 415/-863-7607

LEASK, WILLIAM M. Bus:Pers/Ind Rels, Government. BS 1971, CCNY; MS 1981, NY Inst of Tech. INT: arb/med, personnel. ASSN: Long Island IRRA, Amer Soc for Ind Security. POSITION: Director Labor Rels, Emergency Medical Services, Maspeth. ADDRESS: 88-19 76th St, Woodhaven, NY 11421. 212/326-0600

LeCLERC, CLAUDINE Acad: Ind Rels; Consulting. BA 1978, MA 1981, Laval U. PUBL: Le placement et la securite d'emploi dans l'industrie de la construction au Quebec (w J. Sexton), 1983; "Politique de main-d'oeuvre et politiques publiques," (w J. Sexton & E. Deom), Rels Industrielles, Quebec, vol 35, #1, 1980,3-19. INT: coll barg, labor law, arb/med. ASSN: Canadian Ind Rels Assn. POSITION: (since 1981) Research Asst, Ind Rels Dept, Laval Univ. ADDRESS: App 514, 3600 Descompagnons, Ste-Foy, Quebec G1X 3Z4 Canada. 418/656-7643/656-7021

LEDGERWOOD, DONNA E. Acad: Bus Admin. POSITION: Dept of Management, College of Bus Admin, North Texas State Univ, Denton, TX 76203. 817/565-3157

LEDOUX, DEO Bus:Mgmt/Admin; Acad: Ind Rels. MAIR 1954, Montreal U. PUBL: "Canadian Labor Relations;" "Les Techniques d'Intervention o'ier Tiers," en Relations Industrielles; "Gestia du Personnel." INT: coll barg, personnel, health & hosp care. ASSN: Corp Prof du Admin Agries du Quebec, Corp Prof du Conseillers en Rels Ind, Inst Canadian de Admin Publique du Quebec. POSITIONS: Notre Dame Hosp, General Secretary, 1969; Prof, ENAP, 1978; and (since 1982) Dir, Admin Services, O.i.i.Q., 4200 Dorchester West, Montreal, PQ H3Z 1V4 Canada. 514/935-2501

LEE, BARBARA A. Acad: Law. PhD 1977, Ohio State U; JD 1982, Georgetown U. PUBL: "Balancing Confidentiality and Disclosure in Faculty Peer Review: Impact of Title VII Litigation," J of Coll and Univ Law, (9) 1982-83; "Faculty Role in Academic Governance and the Managerial Exclusion: Impact of the Yeshiva Univ Decision," J of Coll and Univ Law, (7) 1980-81; "Federal Court Involvement in Academic Decision Making," J of Higher Educ (forthcoming). INT: labor law, org behavior, coll barg. ASSN: New Brunswick IRRA, ABA, Natl Assn of Coll & Univ Attorneys, Assn for the Study of Higher Educ. POSITIONS: Policy Analyst, U.S. Dept of Educ, 1978; Dir, Data Trends Analysis, Carnegie Found for the Advancement of Teaching, 1980; and (since 1982) Asst Prof, Grad School of Education, Rutgers Univ, 10 Seminary Pl, New Brunswick, NJ 08903. 201/932-7531

LEE, EDGAR Acad: Labor Educ. MS 1973, Federal City Coll-DC. INT: govt labor policy, labor educ, union org/admin. ASSN: Wash DC IRRA, Amer Adult & Continuing Educ Assn, Intl Associates, Univ & Coll Labor Educ Assn. POSITIONS: Asst Dir Educ Dept, AFGE, 1969; Assoc Dir, Natl Acad for Voluntarism-United Way of America, 1972; and (since 1976) Asst Dir, Labor Studies Center, U.D.C., Wash DC. ADDRESS: 11 Farm Haven Ct, Rockville, MD 20852. 301/727-2326

LEE, JOSEPH SHING Acad: Economics. PhD 1970, U of Mass. PUBL: Manpower and Economic Development in Taiwan; "An Empirical Study of Labor Market in Taiwan," 1975; "Collective Bargaining and Collegiality: The Case of Mankato State University." INT: labor market econ, govt labor policy, arb/med. ASSN: AEA, IIRA, Midwest Econ Assn. POSITION: (since 1970) Professor of Economics, Dept of Econ, Mankato State Univ. ADDRESS: 5224 Lochloy Dr, Edina, MN 55436.507/387-2713

LEE, MICHAEL B. Acad: Student, Ind Rels. MLHR 1982, Ohio State. INT: coll barg, personnel, method/statis. POSITIONS: Res Asst, Center for Human Resources, 1981; Res Asst, 1982, and, since 1983, Teaching Asst, Ind Rels Center, 537 M & E Bldg, 271 19th Ave S, Univ of Minn, Minneapolis, MN 55455. 612/373-4126

LEES, THOMAS SUTTON Acad: Ind Rels. BS 1973, MLIR 1974, Mich State U. INT: coll barg, arb/med, labor law. POSITIONS: Labor Rels Asst, Waterville, 1974, Asst Pers Mgr,

Skowhegan, Me, 1976, and, since 1979, Human Resource Manager, Scott Paper Company, PO Box 925, Everett, WA 98206. 206/259-7451

LEFEBVRE, LINDA H. Student. 245 Orchard Point Dr, Zionsville, In 46077.

LEFF, IRWIN Legal Practice. SB 1947, LLB 1951, Harvard. POSITION: Attorney, Rosenthal & Leff Inc, 100 Bush St, San Francisco, CA 94104. 415/433-3870

LEFKOWITZ, JEROME Government; Acad: Law. BA 1952, NYU; JD 1955, Columbia U. PUBL: Public Employee Unionism in Israel, Inst of Labor & Ind Rels, U of Mich & Wayne State U, 1971; Portrait of a Process-Collective Negotiations in Public Employment, (co-editor), Labor Rels Press, Penna, 1979; "Unionism in the Human Services Industries," Albany Law Rev, vol 36, #4, p 603 et seq, 1972. INT: coll barg, labor law. ASSN: ABA, NYS Bar Assn, Assn of the Bar NYC. POSITIONS: Counsel & Deputy Commissioner, NY State Dept of Labor 1960-67; Lecturer at Law, Columbia School of Law, 1969 to present, and, since 1967, Deputy Chairman, NYS Public Empl Rels Board, 50 Wolf Rd, Albany, NY 12205. 518/457-2614

LEFTWICH, HOWARD M. Acad: Ind Rels. AB 1955, AM 1962, PhD 1965, U of Ill. PUBL: "An Analysis of Unionization in Agriculture," (w E. E. Herman), Sixth World Congress IIRA, Kyoto, Japan, 1983; "Organizing in the Eighties: A Human Resource Perspective," Proceedings of the 1982 Spring IRRA Meeting, Labor Law J, Aug 1982; Study Guide and Readings for Labor Relations in the Health Care Industry, Univ of Cincinnati, College of Community Services, 1982. INT: govt labor policy, union org/admin, coll barg. ASSN: Cincinnati IRRA, AEA, Ohio Assn of Econ and Political Scientists, IIRA. POSITION: (since 1964) Assoc Prof of Econ, Dept of Econ, M.L. 371, Univ of Cincinnati, Cincinnati, OH 45221. 513/475-3583

LEHMAN, MARY L. Student. BA 1981, Penn State U. PUBL: Labor & Technology: Union Response to Changing Technology, (co-author). INT: coll barg, labor history, labor educ. POSITION: Student-Cornell Univ. Apt 1-2A, 305 Highland Rd, Ithaca, NY 14850. 607/257-7955

LEHMANN, HANS J. Acad: Law, Ind Rels. PhD 1938, U of Wis. INT: labor law, arb/med, intl comparative labor. ASSN: Wash DC IRRA, Federal Bar Asssn DC. POSITIONS: Attorney & Statistician, 1938-58, and (1958-70) Appellate Atty, NLRB, Retired. ADDRESS: Apt 1015, 4000 Tunlaw Rd NW, Washington DC 20007. 202/337-7437

LEIFER, LORENZ A. Registered Professional Eng, Consulting. BS 1933, MS 1934, U of Wis-Madison. INT: Product Develop. ASSN: I.E.E.E. POSITIONS: Manager, Prod Design, Gisholt Machine Co, 1934-68; Dir Res & New Prod Devel, Gidding & Lewis Inc, 1968-71; and (since 1972) Pres, L & M Enterprises, 3730 W Karstens Dr, Madison, WI 53704. 608/-244-7329.

LEIFER, MARION J. Professional Assn. ASSN: Wis IRRA. POSITIONS: Exec Secretary, Wis Congress of Parents & Teachers, 1974; Staff Asst, 1978, and, since 1983, Executive Asst, National IRRA, 7226 Social Science Bldg, Univ of Wis, Madison, WI 53706. 608/262-2762

LEIFER, NANCY Government. BS 1976, U of Montana; MPA 1979, Woodrow Wilson School-Princeton. INT: status of women, govt labor policy. POSITIONS: Research (private practice) Wash DC 1979-80; Bureau Chief, 1981, and, since 1983, Div Admin, Development Bureau, Econ and Community Development, State of Montana. ADDRESS: 6 S Park, B13, Helena, MT 59620. 404/444-3757

LEIFER, RICHARD P. Bus:Mgmt/Admin. BS 1963 U of Wis; MA 1969 U of Southern Calif. INT: productivity, org beh, mgmt/educ. ASSN: Natl Mgmt Assn, Tech Marketing Soc of America. POSITIONS: Chief Maintenance Analysis Div, Strategic Air Command, USAF, 1964; Manager, Mgmt Systems, 1967, and, since 1983, Director of Productivity, Lockheed-Calif Co, Burbank. ADDRESS: 12603 Byron Ave, Granada Hills, CA 91344. 213/847-9465

LEIGL, KATHY Student. 2810 Curry Parkway, #8, Madison, WI 53713.

LELLING, BERNARD H. Union. BS 1960, Oswego State; MA 1966, Newark State. INT: union org/admin, arb/med, coll barg. ASSN: New Brunswick IRRA. POSITIONS: Teacher, Old Bridge Board of Educ, 1964; and (since 1972) Uniserv Rep, NEA/NJEA, 23 Rte 206, Box 397, Stanhope, NJ 07874. 201/347-5717

LEMELIN, MAURICE Acad: Ind Rels. POSITION: Hautes Etudes Commerciale, 5255 Ave Decelles, Montreal PQ H3T 1V6 Canada. 514/676--4716

LENART, SHARON ANN Acad: Education. RFD #4, Box 173F, Belle Vernon, PA 15012. 412/872-6440

LENGNICK-HALL, MARK L. Student. 419 Catherwood Dr, West Lafayette, IN 47906. 317/743-0070

LENIHAN, PATRICK M. Acad: Economics. BA 1959, Creighton U; PhD 1968, U of Wis. INT: labor market econ, income maint. ASSN: AEA, AFT. POSITIONS: Instructor, Marquette U, 1962; and (since 1967) Professor, Dept of Econ, Eastern Ill Univ, Charleston, IL 61920. 217/581-2719

LENTZ, BERNARD F. Acad: Economics. ADDRESS: Dept of Econ, Ursinus Coll, Collegeville, PA 19426.

LEONARD, ARTHUR S. Acad: Law. BS 1974, Cornell; JD 1977, Harvard. PUBL: "Specific Enforcement of Collective Bargaining Agreements," 52 Fordham Law Rev 193, 1983; "Post-Contractual Arbitrability After Nolde Brothers: A Problem of Conceptual Clarity," 28 NY Law School Law Rev #2, 1983; "Collective Bargaining on Issues of Health and Safety in the Public Sector: The Experience Under New York's Taylor Law," 31 Buffalo Law Rev 165, 1982. INT: labor law, arb/med, coll barg. ASSN: New York IRRA, Assn Bar of City of New York, (Committee on Sex & Law), ABA (Sections: Empl Law, Individual Rights), NY Bar Assn for Human Rights. POSITIONS: Assoc Attorney, Kelley, Drye & Warren, 1977; Assoc Attorney, Seyfarth, Shaw, Fairweather & Geraldson, NY, 1979; and (since 1982) Assoc Prof of Law, New York Law School. ADDRESS: 247 E 83rd St, New York, NY 10028. 212/431-2100

LEONARD, JOHNATHAN S. Acad: Ind Rels. BA 1976, MS 1980, PhD 1983, Harvard. PUBL: "Anti-Discrimination or Reverse Discrimination;" "Wage Expectations in the Labor Market;" "Unions and Equal Employment Opportunity." INT: govt labor policy, labr market econ, labor law. ASSN: San Francisco IRRA, AEA. POSITION: Asst Prof, School of Business Admin, Univ of Calif, 350 Barrows Hall, Berkeley, CA 94720. 415/642-7048

LEONARD, LORNE PETER Government. BA 1957, Sir George William Univ. POSITION: Res Office, Dept of Labour, Govt of Canada Labour Dept, Ottawa, Ontario Canada. 613/996-3838

LEONE, RICHARD DAVID Acad: Ind Rels; Arbitration, Consulting. AB 1956, Niagara U; MA 1959, Catholic U of America; PhD 1964, U of Penna. PUBL: The Operation of Area Labor Management Committees, (report); "Area Labor Management Committees: Where Do We Go From Here?" IRRA Proceedings, 1982; Program Impacts of Jobs for Delaware's Graduates, (report w M. J. Kelley). INT: empl/-trng programs, govt labor policy, labor market econ. ASSN: Philadelphia IRRA, AAA. POSITION: (since 1964) Professor and Director, Center for Labor and Human Resource Studies, School of Bus Admin, Temple Univ, Philadelphia, PA 19122. 215/787-6843

LEONG, RONALD Y. K. Legal Practice. BA 1969, Coe Coll; JD 1972, George Washington U. INT: labor law, arb/med, coll barg. ASSN: ABA, Hawaii Bar Assn. POSITION: (since 1979) Attorney, Kobayashi, Watanabe, Sugita & Kawashima, 745 Fort St, 8th FL, Honolulu, HI 96813. 808/544-8300

LEOPOLD, ANNA S. Acad: Sociology. MA 1962, U of Chicago. INT: ind sociol, ind & community, ind archeology/photography. ASSN: Eastern Sociol Soc, Amer Sociol Assn, Intl Visual Sociol Assn. POSITION: Asst Prof, Penn State Univ, Altoona Campus, 1957-70, now Retired. ADDRESS: 101 Halleck Place, Altoona, PA 16602. 814/943-2975

LEOPOLD, JOHN WATT Acad: Ind Rels. MA 1973, U of Edinburgh; MPhil 1983, U of Glasgow. PUBL: "The State of Workplace Health and Safety in Britain," (w P. B. Beaumont), Chapter 5 of C. Jones and J. Stevenson (eds), The Year Book of Social Policy in Britain, 1982, Routedge and Kegan Paul, London 1983; "Joint Health and Safety Committees in the United Kingdom: Participation and Effectiveness - A Conflict?" (w P. B. Beaumont), Economic and Ind Democracy, vol 3, #3, Aug 1982; "Arbitration Arrangements in the Public Sector in Britain," (P. B. Beaumont), in The Arb J, vol 38, #2, June 1983. INT: health & hosp care, union org/admin, health & safety at work. ASSN: British Univ Ind Rels Assn, Soc of Ind Tutors, Scottish Labour History Soc. POSITIONS: Workers' Educ Assn, West Scotland Dist, 1975; Sr Res Asst, 1980, and, since 1982, Research Fellow, Dept of Social and Econ Res, Adam Smith Bldg, Univ of Glasgow, Glasgow, Scotland G12 8RT. Phone: 041-339-8855 ext 662

LePAGE, FRANCOIS Student, McGill Univ, 6549 PIE IX, Montreal PQ H1X 2C5 Canada. 514/392-4311

LePAGE, LEON Bus:Pers/Ind Rels. POSITION: Director, Human Resources, Produits Chimiques Expro, CP 5520, Valleyfield, PQ J6S 4V9. 514/937-5711

LEQUIN, JACQUES A. Acad: Ind Rels. BBA 1973, MBA 1975, Ecole de hautes Etudes Commerciales de Montreal; PhD 1983, UCLA. INT: govt labor policy, coll barg, labor law. ASSN: Canadian Ind Rels Assn. POSITION: (since 1980) Professor, Ecole de Hautes Etudes Commerciale de Montreal. ADDRESS: 8220 Chateauneuf, Anjou PQ H1K 1E2 Canada. 514/354-9236

LERBINGER, OTTO Acad: Org Beh/Pers, Ind Rels; Bus:Pers/Ind Rels. PhD 1954 MIT. PUBL: Designs for Persuasive Communication; Manager's Public Relations Handbook. INT: org beh, personnel, ind psych. ASSN: Amer Assn for Public Opinion Res, AEA, Public Rels Soc of Amer. POSITION: Chairman, Public Rels Dept, School of Public Communications, Boston University, Boston, MA 02215. 617/353-3464

LERMAN, DAVID MIGEL Student. MA 1984, U of Wis-Madison. INT: arb/med, intl comparative labor, ind sociol. ASSN: Wis IRRA. POSITIONS: Community Worker, Interns for Peace, Israel, 1981; (since 1983) Law Clerk, Wis Empl Rels Commission and Student, U of Wis. ADDRESS: Route 1, 500 Sugar River Pkwy, Albany, WI 53502.

LEROY, DOUGLAS R. Government. 6424 Silver Ridge Cir, Alexandria, VA 22310.

LESLIE, ASTLEY NOEL Intl Organization. POSITION: ILO, 62 Regency Park, Christ - Church, Barbados, West Indies.

LESTER, RICHARD ALLEN Acad: Econ, Ind Rels. PhB 1929, Yale; AM 1930, PhD 1936, Princeton. PUBL: As Unions Mature, 1958; Economics of Labor, (2nd edition) 1964; Reasoning about Discrimination, 1980. INT: labor market econ, govt labor policy, arb/med. ASSN: AEA, Royal Econ Soc. POSITIONS: Assoc, Ind Rels Section, 1945, Prof of Econ, 1948, Dean of the Faculty (Emeritus), Princeton Univ, 1968, now retired. ADDRESS: Dept of Ind Rels, Princeton Univ, PO Box 248, Princeton, NJ 08544. 609/452-4777

LEUNG, CHO KIN Acad: Econ. POSITION: School of Management, William Patterson Coll, 300 Pompton Rd, Wayne, NJ 07470. 201/595-2407

LEVENSALER, WALTER L. Bus:Pers/Ind Rels; Acad: Sociology. BS 1961, MA 1976, Northwestern U. PUBL: "Can Hospital Managers Operate a Merit Pay System?" "Nurses May be Ready to Give Up Differentials and Premium Pay." INT: personnel, coll barg, ind sociol. ASSN: Mass Pers Dir Assn, AAA, Amer Mgmt Assn. POSITIONS: Pers Administrator, ITEK Corp, 1963; Pers Mgr for Male Support Service, MITRE Corp, 1966; and (since 1968) Administrator Pers and Labor Rels, University Hospital, Boston. ADDRESS: 25 Simon Willard Road, Acton, MA 01729. 617/247-5447

LEVENSTEIN, AARON Acad: Ind Rels, Law; Consulting. BA 1930, CCNY; JD 1934, New York Law School. PUBL: Labor Today and Tomorrow; Use Your Head-The Art of Problem Solving; Escape to Freedom-The Story of the International Rescue Committee. INT: coll barg, health & hosp care, ind psych. ASSN: Organizational Behavior Inst. POSITIONS: Practise of Labor Law (self-employed), 1934-40;

Dir, Labor Div, Res Inst of Amer, 1940-60; and (since 1981) Emeritus Prof of Mgmt, Baruch Coll, Univ of New York. ADDRESS: 3083 Uncas St, Mohegan Lake, NY 10547. 212/725-3390

LEVENTHAL, ROBERT MARK Arbitration. BS 1957, MBA 1960, UCLA. INT: arb/med, empl/trng programs. ASSN: Southern Calif IRRA, NAA, AAA, SPIDR. POSITION: Arbitrator Fact Finder, PO Box 2926, Culver City, CA 90230. 213/559-5382

LEVIN-EPSTEIN, MICHAEL Publishing. BA 1969, Union Coll; JD 1974, U of Ill; MEd 1978, American U. INT: coll barg, empl/trng programs, health & hosp care. ASSN: Wash DC IRRA, ABA, Wash DC and Md. Bar Assns. POSITION: (since 1974) Managing Editor, Employee Relations Weekly, Bureau of Natl Affairs, 1231 25th St NW, Washington DC 20037. 202/452/4510

LEVIN, DAVID ALLEN Acad: Sociology. BA 1964 U of Wis; Master's 1966, U of Ill. POSITION: Dept of Sociology, Univ of Hong Kong, Hong Kong.

LEVIN, DOUGLAS Union. INT: coll barg, union org/admin, labor educ. POSITIONS: Mgr-Secretary, Local 99, 1959, and, since 1968, Vice President, ILGWU, 275 7th Ave, New York, NY 10001. 212/741-6171

LEVIN, EDWARD Arbitration. BS 1961, Cornell-NYSSILR; MIA 1967, Yale. POSITIONS: Labor Rels Spec, Cornell U; Adjunct Prof, Pace U; and, currently, Arbitrator, 140 Riverside Dr, Apt 6A, New York, NY 10024. 212/787-6464

LEVIN, HENRY M. Acad: Econ. BS 1960, New York U; MA 1962, PhD 1966, Rutgers U. PUBL: Financing Recurrent Education, 1983; Producer Cooperatives in America, 1984; "Issues in Assessing the Comparative Productivity of Worker-Managed and Participatory Firms in Capitalist Societies." INT: empl/trng programs, labor market econ. ASSN: AEA, Amer Educ Res Assn. POSITIONS: Sr Res Assoc, NYU, 1965; Res Assoc, Brookings Inst, 1966; and (since 1968) Prof and Dir, Inst of Res on Educ Finance and Governance, Stanford Univ, CERAS Bldg, Stanford, CA 94305. 415/497-0840

LEVIN, NOEL A. Legal Practice. Morgan, Lewis & Bockius, 101 Park Ave, New York, NY 10178.

LEVIN, WILLIAM Arbitration. BS 1943, U of Pittsburgh; LLB 1949, Gerogetown U. INT: arb/med. ADDRESS: 12650 Riverside Dr, North Hollywood CA 91607. 714/295-1234

LEVINE, LOUIS L. Bus:Mgmt/Admin. ASSN: New York IRRA. POSITION: Vice Pres, Blue Cross/Blue Shield, 622 Third Avenue, New York, NY 10017. 212/481-4086

LEVINE, MARVIN JACOB Acad: BusAdmin, Consulting. POSITION: Professor, Dept of Bus Admin, Univ of Maryland, College Park, MD 20742. 301/454-4721

LEVINE, SOLOMON BERNARD Acad: Ind Rels, Econ, Bus Admin. AB 1942, MBA 1947, Harvard; PhD 1951, MIT. PUBL: Human Resources in Japanese Industrial Development, (co-author), 1980; Workers and Employers in Japan, (co-editor, co-author), 1973; Industrial Relations in Japan, 1958. INT: coll barg, intl comparative labor, arb/med. ASSN: AEA, Assn for Asian Studies, Acad of Intl Bus. POSITIONS: Prof of Ind Rels, U of Ill-UC, 1961; and (since 1969) Prof of Econ and Bus, School of Bus, 189 Bascom Hall, Univ of Wisconsin, Madison,WI 53706. 608/263-3459

LEVINSON, ALAN Union. BA 1973, U of Rochester; MS 1977, U of Wis-Madison. INT: union org/admin, coll barg, empl/trng programs. ASSN: San Francisco IRRA. POSITIONS: Program Dir, CETA Youth Programs, College of DuPage, Glen Ellyn, IL, 1978; Organizer, State Empl Trade Council Laborers #1268, Sacramento, 1980, and, since 1981, Bus Rep and Organizer, SEIU, Local 250, 2417 Mariner Sq Loop, #125, Alameda, CA 94110. 415/865-6688

LEVINSON, HAROLD MYER Acad: Econ. AB 1941, MBA 1942, PhD 1950, U of Mich. POSITION: Prof of Econ, Dept of Economics, Univ of Mich, Ann Arbor, MI 48109. 313/764-2366

LEVITAN, SAR A. Acad: Econ; Arbitration, Consulting. PhD 1949, Columbia. PUBL: Second Thoughts on Work; Programs In Aid Of The Poor; Working for the Sovereign: Federal Employee Relations. INT: Federal social & econ policy, labor market econ, arb/med. ASSN: Wash DC IRRA. POSITION: (since 1967) Director, Center for Social Policy Studies, George Washington Univ, 2000 K St, NW, Suite 454, Washington DC 20006. 202/833-2530

LEVY, ABE F. Acad: Law; Legal Prac. BA 1940, NYU; LLB 1942, USC. INT: labor law, coll barg, arb/med. ASSN: L.A. IRRA. POSITION: (since 1951) Senior Partner, Levy & Goldman, 3550 Wilshire Blvd, Suite 1020, Los Angeles, CA 90010. 213/380-3140

LEVY, BRUCE Bus:Pers/Ind Rels. MA 1972, St. Francis Coll. INT: coll barg, org beh, personnel. ASSN: Amer Compensation Assn, ASPA. POSITIONS: Plant Mgr, Piper Aircraft Corp, 1977; Mgr, Personnel, PA. House Furniture, 1981; and (since 1983) Manager, Compensation & Benefits, Armour Handcrafts Inc. ADDRESS: Box 222, Hazelton, PA 18201. 717/455-9980

LEVY, CLARA S. Bus:Mgmt/Admin, Consulting. INT: mgmt/educ, org beh, arb/med. ASSN: Assn of Information Processing Professionals, Amer Soc for Trng and Devlop. POSITIONS: Assoc Consultant, Harold D. Levy Consultants, 1965; Teacher, Jewish Fed, 1976; and (since 1979) Material Information Processing Coordinator, General Dynamics/Fort Worth Div. ADDRESS: 3712 Kelvin Ave, Fort Worth, TX 76133. 817/777-6469

LEVY, HAROLD DAVID Consulting, Retired. 3712 Kelvin Avenue, Forth Worth, TX 76133.

LEVY, JOE L. Legal Practice. LLB 1951, U of Kan. INT: arb/med, labor law, coll barg. ASSN: ABA, Kansas Bar Assn, Montgomery Cty (Kans) Bar Assn. POSITION: (since 1971) Vice Pres, Hall, Levy, Lively, Viets & DeVore, P.A., 815 Union, PO Box 9, Coffeyville, KS 67337. 316/251-1300

LEVY, ROBERT ALAN Bus:Mgmt/Admin. POSITION: Economist, W. Levy Cons Corp, 201 W 77th St, New York, NY 10024. 212/724-7155

LEWIN, DAVID Acad: Ind Rels. BS 1965, Calif State U at L.A.; MBA 1967, PhD 1971, UCLA. PUBL: "Behavioral Research In Industrial Relations," ILRR 1983; Theoretical Perspectives On The Modern Grievance Procedure,"

Res in Labor Econ, 1983; Public Sector Labor Relations: Analysis and Readings, 1981. INT: coll barg, personnel, arb/med. ASSN: New York IRRA, AEA, Amer Acad for the Advancement of Sci. POSITIONS: Visiting Prof, Grad School of Bus Admin, U of Calif-Berkeley, 1978-79; Assoc Prof, 1974, Prof of Bus, 1979, and, since 1982, Prof of Bus and Coordinator of the PhD Program, Grad School of Business, 708 Uris Hall, Columbia Univ, New York, NY 10027. 212/280-4418

LEWIS, ALBERT L. Communications. ADDRESS: 1203 E High St, Mt. Pleasant, NY 48858. 517/773-2438

LEWIS, DAWSON JAMES Arbitration. 8127 Colony Dr, Groose Ile, MI 48138.

LEWIS, H. NELSON, JR. Bus:Pers/Ind Rels. INT: coll barg, arb/med, govt labor policy. ASSN: Retail Food Ind Joint Labor Mgmt Committee, Assn of Private Pension & Welfare Plans, Intl Found of Empl Benefit Plans. POSITIONS: Dir of Pers & Ind Rels, 1971, Natl Dir of Ind Rels, 1974, and, since 1975, Vice Pres Ind Rels, The Great Atlantic & Pacific Tea Co, Inc. ADDRESS: 365 Stevens Ave, Ridgewood, NJ 07450. 201/652-3798

LEWIS, H. THERESA Bus:Pers/Ind Rels. BA 1983, Fordham U; MA 1985, New School for Social Res. INT: personnel, arb/med, health & hosp care. ASSN: Assn of Hosp Pers Admin. POSITIONS: Admin Officer, Dist 119, Natl Union of Hosp & Health Care Empl, 1977-80; Pers Asst, 1981, and, since 1983, Asst Pers Director, Montefiore-North Central Bronx Hosp Affiliation, 3424 Kossuth Ave, Bronx, NY 10467. 212/920-7467

LEWIS, HOWARD W. Bus:Pers/Ind Rels. BS, U of Calif-Berkeley. INT: arb/med, coll barg. ASSN: Houston IRRA. POSITIONS: Labor Rels Rep, Bay Area Rapid Transit, 1969; and (since 1983) Labor Rels Manager, Metro Transit Authority, 5700 Eastex Freeway, Houston, TX 77026. 713/635-0400

LEWIS, IRVING Consulting, Arbitration, Legal Prac. LLB 1934, New York Law School. INT: coll barg, arb/med, labor law. ASSN: New York IRRA. POSITIONS: Asst Exec Secretary, Amer Federation of Television and Radio Artists, 1953; and (since 1983) Consulting (self-employed), 345 8th Ave, New York, NY 10001. 212/675-5865

LEWIS, JEFFREY DEAN Union. BA 1979, U of Pittsburgh-Johnstown; MLIR 1981, Mich State U. INT: health & hosp care, coll barg, union org/admin. POSITIONS: Staff Asst, Mich Chapter of Sheet Metal and Air Conditioning Contractor's Natl Assn, 1980, Natl Rep, Natl Fed of Federal Empl, 1981; and (since 1982) Labor Rep, Pennsylvania Nurses Assn. ADDRESS: Bldg C, #22, 148 Cedar Ridge Dr, Monroeville, PA 15146. 717/234-7935

LEWIS, NANCY L. Bus:Pers/Ind Rels. 1203 E High St, Mt. Pleasant, MI 48848. 517/773-2438

LEYDEN, JOHN F. Union. POSITION: Public Empl Dept, AFL-CIO, 815 16th St NW, Washington DC 20006. 202/393-2820

L'HEUREUX, WAYNE D. Bus:Pers/Ind Rels. BS 1980, LeMoyne Coll; MILR 1981, Mich State U. PUBL: "Telco Loss Control," Telephony, June 13, 1983, pp 34-35. INT: personnel, labor law, arb/med. POSITIONS: Specialist, State Pers, Continental Telephone Co Of Arkansas, 1981, Division Coordinator Safety/Security, 1983, Continental Tel Co-West Central Div, 1983, and, since 1983, Coordinator Pers, Continental Telephone Co of Iowa, 1214 West Jackson, Knoxville, IA 50138. 515/828-8251

LIBERSON, DENNIS H. Bus:Pers/Ind Rels, BA 1978, Coll of William & Mary; MLIR 1980, Mich State U. PUBL: "The Arbitration of Sex Discrimination Grievances," (w B. Wolkinson), The Arb J, vol 37, #2, June 1982. INT: coll barg, ar/med, labor law. POSITIONS: Labor Rels Rep, 1980, Labor Rels Admin, 1981, and, since 1983, Asst to the Director, Empl Rels, Philip Morris U.S.A., Richmond. ADDRESS: 27 Muirfield Green Lane, Midlothian, VA 23113. 804/274-2628

LIDDLE, JEFFREY L. Legal Practice. BS 1971, Cornell; JD 1976, New York U. PUBL: "Review of the Law of Restrictive Covenants, Non Competition Agreements and Employee Loyalty," (co-author),6 Empl Rels Law J 601, 1981; "Proof of Damages for Breach of a Restrictive Covenant or Noncompetition Agreement," (co-authro), 9 Empl Rels Law J 455, 1984, "Disparate Treatment Claims Under ADEA: The Negative Impact of McDonnell-Douglas v. Green 5 Empl Rels Law J 549, 1980. INT: labor law. ASSN: New York IRRA, ABA, Assn of the Bar, NYC, ILR Alumni Assn. POSITION: Attorney, Liddle & Assoc, 80 Pine St, New York, NY 10005. 212/344-5790

LIDDLE, WALTER T. Bus:Pers/Ind Rels; Acad: Ind Rels. MLIR 1980, Mich State U. INT: personnel, coll barg, empl/trng programs. ASSN: ASPA. POSITION: Personnel Dir, United Cerebal Palsy Assn of Western NY, 7 Community Dr, Buffalo, NY 14225. 716/894-0132

LIEBERMAN, IRWIN MARTIN Arbitration. AB 1939, MA 1941, U of Chicago. INT: arb/med, coll barg, labor educ. ASSN: SW Conn IRRA, NAA, AAA, SPIDR. POSITIONS: Principal Field Dir, NLRB, 1946; Empl Rels Dir, Toni Div of Gillette Co, 1954; and (since 1972) Arbitrator, 91 Westover Ave, Stamford, CT 06902. 203/327-9958

LIEBERTHAL, MILFERD Acad: Labor Educ. BS 1950, MA 1956, U of Ill. POSITION: Professor, School for Workers, Univ of Wis, 432 N Lake St, Madison, WI 53706. 608/262-2111

LIEBES, RICHARD A. Union, Retired. 330 W Blithedale Ave, Mill Valley, CA 94941.

LIESS, MICHAEL T. Student. BS 1984, Cornell. INT: coll barg, govt labor policy, labor law. ASSN: ASPA. POSITIONS: Res Asst, Public Service Res Council, 1982; and (since 1983) Res Assoc, Natl Legal Center for the Public Interest, Wash DC. ADDRESS: 8702 Queen Elizabeth Blvd, Annandale, VA 22003. 202/296-1683

LIGGETT, MALCOLM HUGH Acad: Ind Rels; Arbitration, Consulting. BA 1957, U of Tex-Austin; PhD 1967, Cornell. Publ: Employment Discrimination: The Impact of Legal and Administrative Remedies, Praeger, 1978; "The Efficacy of State Fair Employment Practices Commissions," ILRR, 1969; "The World Aluminum Industry," in The Encyclopedia of Econ and Bus. INT: coll barg, arb/med, labor market econ. ASSN: AEA, AFEE, SPIDR. POSITIONS: Sr Res Economist, Center for Study of Human Resources, U of Tex-Austin, 1973; Supervisory Labor Economist, Council on Wage & Price Stability, DC, 1975; and (since 1983) Assoc Prof-Ind Rels, Div of Bus Admin, Penn State Univ, Capitol Campus, Olmsted Hall, Middletown, PA 17057. 717/948-6342

LILLICH, JOHN E. Acad: Ind Rels, Supr Managment; Arbitration. BSILR 1948, Cornell; MS 1971, Purdue U. INT: arb/med, mgmt/educ, intl comparative labor. ASSN: Chicago IRRA, AAA. POSITIONS: Vice Pres, Manufacturing, Shallcross Mfg. Co, Selma, NC, 1969; Plant Mgr, CentraLab Div-Globe Union, West Lafayette, 1964; and (since 1977) Assoc Prof, School of Technology, M.E. Annex, Purdue Univ, West Lafayette, IN 47907. 317/494-5598

LILORE, DOREEN Union. PhD 1982 Columbia. PUBL: The Local Union of Public Librarians. INT: union org/admin, labor educ, coll barg. ASSN: ALA. POSITIONS: Reference Librarian, Paterson Public Library, 1972; Teaching Asst, School of Library Services, Columbia Univ, 1978; and (since 1979) Dist Council Staff Rep, AFSCME, Council 52, Jersey City. ADDRESS: 51 Menzel Ave, Maplewood, NJ 07040. 201/435-0255

LINDAU, DAVID S. Legal Practice. BA 1948, Swarthmore Coll; LLB 1952, Yale. INT: labor law, arb/med, coll barg. ASSN: New York IRRA, ABA, New York State Bar Assn. POSITION: Partner, Holtzman, Wise & Shepard, 745 Fifth Ave, New York, NY 10151. 212/753-4300

LINDBERG, BONITA Bus:Pers/Ind Rels. BS 1979, LeMoyne Coll; MA 1981, U of Ill. INT: coll barg, arb/med, labor law. POSITION: (since 1981) Pers Rep, National Supply Co, PO Box 9163, Houston, TX 77011. 713/960-5938

LINDEMANN, A. J. Bus:Mgmt/Admin, Consulting; Acad: Ind Rels. BA 1971 U of San Francisco; MS 1973, U of Calif. PUBL: Health Care and Industrial Relations, "Cost, Conflict and Controversy," ed by R. N. Schwartz, Monograph Res Series, #28, Inst of Ind Rels, UCLA, 1981. INT: health & hosp care, labor law, org beh. ASSN: Los Angeles IRRA, Amer Soc for Hosp Pers Admin, Calif Hosp Pers Mgmt Assn, Inst of Ind Rels Assn-UCLA. POSITIONS: Res Assoc & Intl Res Specialist, 1972, Res Dir, S. Calif Joint Council, 1973, SEIU, AFL-CIO; and (since 1981) Vice Pres Corporate Human Resources, San Pedro Pension Health Services. ADDRESS: 2459 Ladoga Ave, Long Beach, CA 90815. 213/832-3311

LINDEN, NICHOLAS A. Legal Practice, Consulting. BS 1973, AM 1975, U of Ill. INT: coll barg, arb/med, labor law. POSITIONS: Asst Exec Dir, Madison Teachers Inc, 1975; Consultant (self-employed), 1981; and (since 1983) Legal Assistant, Cullen & Weston. ADDRESS: 3009 Gregory St, Madison, WI 53711. 608/251-0101

LINDNER, DENNIS G. Legal Practice. BA 1958, Stanford U; LLB 1963, Marquette U. INT: coll barg, labor law, arb/med. ASSN: Wis IRRA, ABA, State Bar of Wis. POSITION: (since 1977) President, Lindner, Honzik, Marsack, Hayman & Walsh, S.C., 700 N Water St, Milwaukee, WI 53202. 414/273-3910

LINDSAY, RICHARD E. Union. BSS 1981, Penn State-Capitol Campus. INT: arb/med, union org/admin, govt labor policy. POSITIONS: Staff Rep, 1973, Asst Council Dir, 1978, and, since 1984, Asst Director, Grievance Dept, AFSCME, Council 13, 301 Chestnut St, 5th FL, Harrisburg, PA 17101. 717/236-4051

LINVILLE, RONALD G. Legal Practice. Porter, Wright, Morris & Arthur, 37 W Broad St, Columbus, OH 43215. 614/227-2161

LIPPER, STUART J. Union. BSILR 1978, Cornell. INT: union org/admin, coll barg, labor market econ. POSITION: (since 1978) Asst to the Executive Vice Pres, ILGWU, 1710 Broadway, New York, NY 10019. 212/265-7000

LIPSKY, DAVID BRUCE Acad: Ind Rels; Consulting, Arbitration. BS 1961, Cornell; PhD 1967, MIT. PUBL: Advances in Industrial and Labor Relations, (co-editor), Greenwich, CT, JAI Press, 1983; The Labor Market Experience of Workers Displaced and Relocated by Plant Shutdowns, NY & London: Garland, 1979; Unfinished Business: An Agenda for Labor Management and the Public, (co-editor), Cambridge, MA: MIT Press, 1978. INT: coll barg, arb/med, empl/trng programs. ASSN: SPIDR, AEA. POSITIONS: Visiting Assoc Prof of Econ, Boston Univ, 1976-77; Visiting Assoc Prof of IR, Sloan School-MIT, 1976-77; Assoc Prof, 1969, and, since 1979, Professor, NYSSILR-Cornell, 293 Ives Hall, Ithaca, NY 14853. 607/256-3230

LIPTON, BENJAMIN B. Arbitration, Government; Acad: Law. JD 1943, St. John's U; LLM 1957, George Washington U. PUBL: "Misconduct in Concerted Activities," Labor Law J, (BNA). INT: Fed admin/law, arb/med, labor law. POSITIONS: Admin Law Judge (A.P.A.), NLRB, 1961-76, (Retired); Admin Law Judge (contract-indep), U. S. State Dept/EEO/Arms Control & Disarmament Agency, 1980; and (since 1977) Labor Arbitrator and Admin Law Judge (self-employed). ADDRESS: 2020 Yarmouth Court, Falls Church, VA 22043. 703/536-1642

LITTLE, ALFRED Bus:Pers/Ind Rels. BA 1968, Howard U; MBA 1979, Fairleigh Dickinson U. INT: coll barg, labor law, union org/admin. ASSN: Natl Petroleum Refiners Assn (IR Committee). POSITIONS: Labor Rels Analyst, Jones & Laughlin Steel, 1968; Ind Rels Rep, Inmont Corp, 1975; and (since 1982) Manager, Employee Rels & EEO, Sun Company, 1801 Market St, Philadelphia, PA 19103. 215/977-3261

LITTMAN, DANIEL ALAN Government. BA 1976, Brandeis U; MA 1979, Boston U. PUBL: "Plant Closings and Worker Dislocations," in R. McKensie, ed, Plant Closings: Public or Private Choices, CATO Inst, 1984; "Union Wage Concessions," Economic Commentary, Fed Reserve Bank of Cleveland, June 1982; "Collective Bargaining and Disinflation," Economic Commentary, Fed Reserve Bank of Cleveland, Feb 1984. INT: labor market econ, govt labor policy, coll barg. ASSN: Northeast Ohio IRRA, AEA. POSITIONS: Res Assoc, Inst for Empl Policy, Boston U, 1978; Planning Mgr, Penobscot Consortium T.E.A., Bangor, Me., 1979; and (since 1981) Economist, Federal Reserve Bank of Cleveland. ADDRESS: 8275 Stockholm Rd, Shaker Heights, OH 44120. 216/579-2039

LIVERNASH, EDWARD ROBERT Acad: Bus Admin. AB 1932, U of Colo; MA 1934, Tufts Coll; PhD 1940, Harvard. PUBL: Human Resource Management: Text and Cases, (w F. K. Foulkes), Prentice Hall, 1982; Impact of Collective Bargaining on Management, (w S. H. Slichter & J. J. Healy), Brookings Inst, Wash DC. ASSN: Boston IRRA. POSITION:

Prof Emeritus, Harvard Bus School. ADDRESS: 17 Venner, Arlington, MA 02174.

LIVINGSTON, FREDERICK R. Legal Practice. POSITION: Attorney, Kaye, Scholer, Fierman, Hays and Handler, 425 Park Ave, New York, NY 10022. 212/759-8400

LLOYD, KENNETH L. Consulting; Acad: Org Beh/Pers. AB 1967, U.C. Berkeley; MS 1969, PhD 1972; UCLA. INT: org beh, ind psych, personnel. ASSN: Amer Psych Assn, Calif State Psych Assn. POSITIONS: Mgmt Consultant, The McMurray Co, 1972; and (since 1977) Management Consultant (self-employed), Suite 500, 15233 Ventura Blvd, Sherman Oaks, CA 91403. 213/783-4461

LLOYD, WILLIAM V. Bus:Pers/Ind Rels, Consulting. BA 1941, T.C.U.-Ft.Worth; BS 1952, U of San Marcos-Lima, Peru. INT: personnel, mgmt/educ, coll barg. ASSN: ASPA, Pers & Ind Rels Assn of Southern Calif; Agricultural Pers Mgmt Assn of Calif. POSITIONS: Information Specialist, Office of Foreign Ag Res, 1947, Foreign Labor Service Rep, Bureau of Empl, USDL, 1958; and (since 1962) General Manager, Coastal Growers Assn. ADDRESS: 530 Lawnwood Way, Oxnard, CA 93030. 805/-483-0185

LOCIGNO, PAUL R. Union. POSITION: Government Affairs, Intl Brotherhood of Teamsters, 25 Louisiana Ave, Washington DC 20001. 202/624-6916

LOCKHART, JANET S. Government. AB 1968, Wittenberg U; MS 1971, Purdue U; PhD 1980, Mich State U. INT: empl/trng programs, income maint, labor market econ. ASSN: Southeastern Empl and Trng Assn. POSITIONS: Labor Economist, BLS-USDL, 1975; Supr Assessment and Evaluation, CETA Div, 1979, and, since 1982, Manager of Policy, Planning and Evaluation, Office of the Governor, Div of Empl and Trng, 1800 St. Julian Place, Columbia, SC 29204. 803/758-3130

LOCKHART, SHARON J. Bus:Mgmt/Admin. Apt 105, 900 Willowdale Rd, Morgantown, WV 26505.

LODATO, MICHAEL J. 925, Park Plaza Dr, Evansville, In 47715.

LOEB, BARRY L. Bus:Mgmt/Admin. BS 1964, MS 1971, U of Cincinnati. INT: mgmt/educ, coll barg, arb/med. ASSN: Cincinnati IRRA, Amer Inst of Chemical Eng. POSITIONS: Dir, Chemical Eng, 1974, Dir, Enginering Services, 1981, and, since 1983, Plant Manager, Emery Industries, Cincinnati. ADDRESS: 4900 Este Ave, Cincinnati, OH 45232. 513/482-2242

LOEWENBERG, J. JOSEPH Acad: Ind Rels; Arbitration. AB 1955, MBA, 1959, DBA, 1962, Harvard. PUBL: Compulsory Arbitration: An International Comparison; Scope of Public-Sector Bargaining; "U.S. Postal Service," in Collective Bargaining: Contemporary American Experience, Gerald Somers, ed, IRRA 1980. INT: coll barg, arb/med, intl comparative labor. ASSN: Philadelphia IRRA, NAA. POSITION: (since 1966) Professor of Ind Rels, Temple Univ. ADDRESS: 1364 Indian Creek Dr, Philadelphia, PA 19151. 215/787-8187

LOMBARDO, DAVID D. Government; Acad: Org Beh/Pers, Ind Rels. BA 1961, Albright Coll; MA 1964, PhD 1978, New York U. INT: personnel, empl/trng programs, coll barg. ASSN: ASPA, Amer Soc for Public Admin, Intl Pers Mgmt Assn. POSITIONS: Chief, Empl Rels, 1971, Chief, Pers, Soc Security Admin, DHEW, 1973; and (since 1977) Chief, Recruitment & Placement Officer, The Library of Congress, Wash DC. ADDRESS: 1741 Tarrytown Ave, Crofton, MD 21114. 202/287-6593

LONDA, JEFFREY C. Legal Practice. Butler & Binion, Allied Bank Plaza, Houston, TX 77002.

LONERGAN, WALLACE G. Acad: Org Beh/-Pers, Ind Rels; Consulting. MBA 1955, PhD 1960, U of Chicago. PUBL: Developing the Municipal Organization, Intl City Mgmt Assn, Wash DC,1974, 2nd ed, 1981; "Performance Appraisal," in Encyclopedia of Professional Mgmt, McGraw Hill, 1978, 2nd ed, 1984. INT: personnel, org beh, mgmt/educ. ASSN: Acad of Mgmt, Intl House of Japan. POSITIONS: Sr. Lecturer, Grad School of Bus, 1960, Director, Human Resources Center, Univ of Chicago, 1955, and, since, 1983, Retired. ADDRESS: 1404 East 55th St, Chicago, IL 60615. 312/324-8375

LONEY, TIMOTHY JOHN Bus:Pers/Ind Rels, Consulting; Acad: Org Beh/Pers. BS 1965, Southern Conn State U; MSA 1971, George Washington U; MPA 1981, DPA 1983, U of Southern Calif. PUBL: "Capitulate or Litigate in ULP Settlements: A New Try in the Federal Sector," Labor Law J, Nov 1982; "Realism in EEO," Acad of Mgmt Rev, Winter 1982;" "Mid-Term Bargaining in the Federal Government," Federal Services Labor Rels Rev, Summer, 1979. INT: org beh, personnel, ind psych. ASSN: San Francisco IRRA, ASPA, Into Pers Mgmt Assn, Acad of Mgmt. POSITIONS: Empl Rels Advisor, USDL, 1973; Lead Instructor, Human Resources/Org, Develop Div, U of San Francisco, 1983; and (since 1974) Regional Labor Rels Officer, General Services Admin, 525 Market St, San Francisco, CA 94105. 415/-974-9273

LONG, LYLE HERBERT Bus: Pers/Ind Rels. BA 1948, Harvard U; JD 1951, U of Mich. INT: org beh, mgmt/educ, ind sociol ASSN: Detroit IRRA, Ind Rels Assn of Detroit. POSITIONS: Mgr, Labor Rels, 1967, and, since 1982, Manager, Employee Involvement Systems, Federal-Mogul Corp, PO Box 1966, Detroit, MI 48235. 313/354-2686

LONGENECKER, KATHIE Bus:Mgmt/Admin. BS 1976, U of Wyo; MS 1977, U of Ore. ADDRESS: PO Box 391, Vail CO 81658. 303/476-7256

LORENZ, FRED J. Consulting. POSITION: F. J. Lorenz & Assoc, Health Res Bldg, Suite 101, 909 University St, Seattle, WA 98101.

LOSCHE, PETER Acad: Political Science. DrPhil 1966, Dr phil ham'l 1973, Free Univ of Berlin; PUBL: "Anarchismus," Wiss. Buchgemeinschaft, Darmstadt, 1977; "Politik in USA," Opladin, 1977; "Industriegewerkeshaften in Organisierten Kapitalismus, Westdeutsches Verlag, 1974. INT: labor history, intl comparative labor, union org/admin. ASSN: AHA, APSA, Deutsihe Vereinigung fur Politikwissennshaft. POSITIONS: Asst Prof, Free Univ of Berlin, 1971; and (since 1973) Professor, Political Sci Dept, Univ of Goettingen, Nikolausberger Weg 5C, 34 Gottingen, West Germany. Phone: 0551-397218

LOUGHRAN, CHARLES S. Bus:Pers/IndRels. BA 1959, Johns Hopkins U; MA 1961, U of Calif-Berkeley; JD 1971 Golden Gate U. PUBL: Negotiating a Labor Contract: A Management Handbook; Attorney's Guide to Damages (chapter on Labor Law.)INT: coll barg, arb/med, labor law. ASSN: San Francisco IRRA, ABA, Calif Bar Assn, Pacific Coast Assn of Pulp & Paper Mfgrs. POSITIONS: Mgr of Labor Rels, Crown Zellerbach Corp, 1967; Attorney, Pettit, Evers & Martin, 1972; and (since 1978) Dir, Corporate Ind Rels, Louisiana-Pacific Corp, 1243 Alpine Rd, Suite 116, Walnut Creek, CA 94596. 415/932-0814

LOVE, SHELLEY B. Student. INT: New York & Long Island IRRA. POSITIONS: Exec Asst, Memorial Sloan Kettering Center, and Doctoral Candidate, Rutgers Univ. ADDRESS: Apt 2B, 210 E 90th St, New York, NY 10028. 212/794-6885

LOVELACE, ROBERT F. Bus:Mgmt/Admin. POSITION: Director, Research Admin, The Graduate Hospital, 1 Graduate Plaza, Philadelphia, PA 19146. 215/893-7497

LOVELL, HUGH G. Acad: Econ; Arbitration. PhD 1951, MIT. INT: coll barg, arb/med, labor law. POSITION: (since 1955) Professor, Portland State Univ. ADDRESS: 0104 SW Lane St, Portland, OR 97201. 503/229-3915

LOWENSTEIN, DEBORAH J. Bus:Pers/Ind Rels. BS 1975, Southern Ill U; MA 1980, U of Ill-CU. INT: personnel, empl/trng programs, coll barg. ASSN: ASPA, Soc of Pers Admin of Greater Chicago, Midwest Ind Mgmt Assn. POSITIONS: Pers Mgr, Fischer Imaging Corp, 1981; Empl Rels Mgr, Wabash Data Tech Inc, 1981; and (since 1983) Ind Rels Mgmt Asst, Commonwealth Edison Co, Chicago. ADDRESS: 732 N Ridge Ave, Arlington Heights, IL 60004. 312/294-4321

LOWENSTEIN, HENRY Acad: Bus Admin; Consulting. BS 1975, Va Commonwealth U; MBA 1976, George Washington U; PhD, U of Ill-UC. PUBL: "The Need for Limitations on Federal Mass Transit Operating Subsidies: The Chicago Example," Transportation Law J, vol 13, Summer 1982; "CTA: Going Backward in Style," Chicago Tribune, Feb 16, 1982; "Management Has Wrecked RTA," Chicago Tribune, June 14, 1981. INT: mgmt/educ, empl/trng programs, labor law. ASSN: Acad of Mgmt, ASPA, Transportation Research Forum. POSITIONS: Exec Vice-Pres, Americana Furniture, Inc, 1976; Instructor in Mgmt, Virginia Commonwealth Univ, 1977; and (since 1980) Professorial Lecturer in Mgmt, Coll of Bus Admin, Dept of Mgmt, Univ of Illinois at Chicago. ADDRESS: 732 N Ridge Ave, Arlington Heights, IL 60004. 312/996-2799

LOWENSTERN, HENRY Government. LIT.B 1950, Rutgers U; MA 1951, U of Wis. INT: publishing, govt labor policy, coll barg. ASSN: Wash DC IRRA, AEA, Natl Assn of Government Communicators, Soc for Tech Communication. POSITIONS: Exec Editor, Monthly Labor Rev, 1968, and, since 1975, Assoc Commissioner, Bureau of Labor Statistics, USDL. ADDRESS: 3432 Gaddy Court, Falls Church, VA 22042. 202/523-1327

LOWREY, JAY Bus:Pers/ Ind Rels. BS 1971, U of Nebr; MLIR 1972, Mich State U. INT: personnel, org beh, mgmt/educ. POSITIONS: Pers Dir, Bankers Trust Co, Des Moines, 1980; and (since 1982) Vice Pres-Operations Human Resources, Chase Manhatten Bank, NA, New York. ADDRESS: 238 Park Ave, Belford, NJ 07718. 212/676-5650

LOWRY, DAVID R. Acad: Law. POSITION: Dean of Law School, Biscayne Coll, 16400 NW 32nd Ave, Miami, FL 33054.

LUBELL, SCOTT K. Union. 88 Walnut St, Brookline, MA 02146. 617/232-6370

LUBIN, STAN Legal Practice. AB 1963, JD 1966, U of Mich. PUBL: "Union Fines & Union Discipline," (w S. Schlossberg), 22nd NYU Conference of Labor Law Proceedings, 1971. INT: labor law, arb/med, govt labor policy. ASSN: ABA State Bar of Ariz, AAA. POSITIONS: Asst General Counsel, Intl Union UAW, 1968-1972; and (since 1975) Partner, McKendree & Lubin, 902 W McDowell Rd, Phoenix, AZ 85007. 602/252-5955

LUCAS-WALLACE, KATHLEEN Legal Practice. Wharfside Building, 680 Beach St, Suite 394, San Francisco, CA 94109.

LUCAS, FREDDIE H. Bus:Mgmt/Admin, Fed Govt/Liaison, Bus:Ind Rels. BS 1956, Morgan State Coll-Baltimore; MS 1958, Penna State U; PhD 1964, U of Iowa. INT: mgmt/educ, Fed govt liaison, empl/trng programs. ASSN: Program Specialist, Women's Job Corp Center, OEO, 1966; Washington Rep, J. C. Penny Co, 1968; and (since 1976) Sr Washington Rep, General Motors Corp, 1660 L St NW, Washington DC 20036. 202/775-5080

LUCAS, ROBERT Acad: Org Beh/Pers. PhD 1984, Cornell. INT: org beh, coll barg, ind sociol. POSITION: (since 1981) Asst Prof, Faculty of Admin Studies, York Univ, Downsview, Ont M3J 1P3 Canada. 416/667-2531

LUCCHI, GINA DIANE Student. 125 N Hagadorn, Apt 3, East Lansing, MI 48823.

LUDLOW, HOWARD T. Acad: Ind Rels, Univ Admin; Arbitration. BS 1947, MA 1949, PhD 1955, Fordham U. PUBL: "The Role of Trade Unions in Poland," in Political Sci Quart, Summer 1975; "Formal Education and Mediator Acceptability," in Labor Law J, Oct 1966; "Big Mediator is Watching You," America, June 6, 1964. INT: arb/med, coll barg, labor history. ASSN: New Brunswick IRRA, AAA, SPIDR, Assn of Labor Rels Agencies. POSITION: (since 1949) Professor of Ind Rels, School of Bus Admin, Seton Hall Univ. ADDRESS: 22 Martha Blvd, Parlin, NJ 08859. 201/762-9242

LUDWIG, LARRY G. Government; Acad: Grad Student Government Assn. AB 1963, U of Calif-Berkeley. PUBL: "Labor Requirements for Construction of Single Family Houses;" "Hydraulic Cement-Technological Change and Manpower Trends." INT: coll barg, empl/-trng programs, intl comparative labor. ASSN: Wash DC IRRA, Soc of Government Economists. Intl Assn of Pers Empl Specialists, Natl Notary Assn. POSITIONS: Economist, BLS, 1967, and, since 1975, Supervisory Economist, Deputy Administrative Officer, USDL, Employment & Trng Admin. ADDRESS: 1810 22nd St SE, Washington DC 20020. 202/376-6842

LUNDBERG, CRAIG CARL Acad: Org Beh/-Pers, Bus Admin; Consulting. MBA 1957, U of Washington; PhD-OB 1966, Cornell. PUBL: "The Informant Panel Technique," Group &

Org Studies, vol 8, #2, 1983; "Micro-Intervention in Team Development," in D. Warrick ed, Current Development in OD, Scott Foresman, 1983; "What's Wrong With OD?" in E. Parlock, ed, Org Development Managing Transition, ASTD, 1982. INT: org beh, mgmt/educ, ind sociology. ASSN: Acad of Mgmt, Org Beh Teaching Society, Certified Consultants Intl. POSITIONS: Dean, School of Mgmt, SUNY-Binghamton, 1979; and (since 1982) Chair & Professor, Dept of Mgmt and Org, School of Bus, Univ of Southern Calif, Los Angeles, CA 90007. 213/743-2437

LUNDEN, LEON E. Government. BA 1951, Queens Coll; MA 1952, PhD 1967, U of Wis. INT: coll barg, union org/admin, govt labor policy. ASSN: Wash DC IRRA. POSITIONS: Economist, 1960, Project Dir, Coll Barg Studies, Div of Ind Rels, OWIR/BLS, 1967, and, since 1976, Chief, Div of Research and Analysis, LMRS/LMSA, USDL. Wash DC. ADDRESS: 1018 Chiswell Lane, Silver Spring, MD 20901. 202/523-7481

LUNNIE, FRANCIS M., JR. Bus:Pers/Ind Rels. BS 1971, Ohio U. POSITION: Assistant Vice Pres, Ind Rels, Natl Assn of Manufacturers, 1776 F St NW, Washington DC 20006. 202/626-3813

LUOMA, VAENOE Acad: Ind Rels, Sociol, Econ. MA 1948, U of Turku (Finland), Lic Econ, 1952, U of Gothenburg (Sweden), PhD 1962, U of Turku. Publ: "On the Concept and Field of Industrial Relations," 1976; "Elementary Price Theory," 1969; Civil Servant Unionism in Finland," 1962. INT: union org/admin, coll barg, ind sociol. ASSN: Finnish Econ Soc, Finnish Pol Sci Assn. POSITIONS: Reader, U of Turku, 1963-70; Prof, 1967-75, and (since 1975) Prof Emeritus, The Turku School of Econ. Address: Tammitie 2, 20540 Turku 54, Finland.

LURIE, MELVIN Acad: Econ, Ind Rels. PhD 1958, U of Chicago. PUBL: "The Effect of Unionization on Wages in the Transit Industry," JPE, Dec 1961; "The Effects of Non-Vested Pension Plans on Mobility," ILRR, Jan 1965; "Racial Differences in Migration and Job - Search," (w E. Paepke), July 1966. INT: labor market econ, coll barg, empl/trng programs. ASSN: Wis IRRA, AEA. POSITION: (since 1966), Professor, Dept of Econ, Univ of Wis-Milw, PO Box 413, Milwaukee, WI 53201. 414/963-6536

LUSKIN, BERT L. Arbitration. JD 1932, DePaul U. INT: arb/med. ASSN: NAA, ABA, Chicago Bar Assn. POSITION: Attorney, 134 N La Salle St, Chicago, IL 60602. 312/372-1036

LYLE, JEROLYN R. Government; Acad: Econ. MA 1966, PhD 1970, U of Md. PUBL: The Dynamics of Recent Inflation in Latin America; "Use of the Input-Output System to Estimate the Employment Impact of Trade Deficits; "Assessment of Day Care Centers. INT: labor market econ, govt labor policy, intl comparative labor. ASSN: Amer Statis Assn, AEA, Soc of Government Economists. POSITIONS: Economist, Office of the President, Office of Mgmt and Budget, 1975, Economist/Sr Program Analyst, FEMA, & Prof of Econ-Univ of Maryland, 1976, and, Prof of Econ, U of Pittsburgh-Inst of Shipboard Educ. ADDRESS: 5512 Center St, Chevy Chase, MD 20815. 301/-986-1786

LYMAN, JAY RICH Acad: Econ. PhD 1972, U.C.-Davis. INT: coll barg, arb/med, labor market econ. ASSN: Northern Calif IRRA, SPIDR. POSITION: Prof, Dept of Econ, Calif State Univ, Chico, CA 95926. 916/895-5244

LYNCH, LISA M. Acad: Econ, Ind Rels. BA 1978, Wellesley Coll; MS, 1979, PhD 1983, London School of Econ. PUBL: "Job Search & Youth Unemployment," Oxford Econ Papers, Nov 1983, pp 271-282; "Unemployment of Young Workers in Britain," British J of Ind Rels, Nov 1982, pp 362-372; "Strike Frequency in British Coal Mining: 1950-1974," British J of Ind Rels, Mar 1978, pp 95-98. INT: labor market econ, intl comparative labor, coll barg. ASSN: Central Ohio IRRA, The Econometric Soc, AEA. POSITIONS: Asst Prof, Univ of Bristol, England, 1982; and (since 1983) Asst Prof, Ohio State Univ, 319C Hagerty Hall, 1775 College Ave, Columbus, OH 43210. 614/422-4589

LYNCH, MICHAEL P. Bus:Pers/Ind Rels. POSITION: Labor Rels Rep, Allied Maintenance Corp, 2 Penn Plaza, New York, NY 10001.

LYNCH, WILLIAM F. Acad: Law, ADDRESS: Niagara Univ, Niagara Univ, NY 14109. 716/285-1212

LYON, RICHARD MARTIN Legal Practice. LLB 1952, Brooklyn Law School; MS 1952, PhD 1954, Cornell. PUBL: The College Decision, 1967; The Labor Relations Law of Canada,, 1976. INT: laboı law. ASSN: Chicago IRRA, ABA (Section on Empl Law), Intl Bar Assn(Sect on Bus Law). POSITION: (since 1955) Partner, Seyfarth, Shaw, Fairweather & Geraldson, 42nd Floor, 55 East Monroe St, Chicago, IL 60603. 312/346-8000

LYONS, DEE Acad: Labor Studies. ADDRESS: K. Morris Labor Studies, 234 Varner Hall, Labor Educ, Oakland Univ, Rochester, MI 48063. 313/377-3125

LYONS, DONALD E. Bus:Pers/Ind Rels; Acad: Ind Rels. BS 1959, MS 1961, Purdue U. INT: coll barg, personnel, labor law. ASSN: ASPA, ASTD. POSITIONS: Div Dir, I.R., Chicago Rawhide Mfg Corp, 1970; Group Mgr, Empl Rels, Clow Corp, 1972; and (since 1977) Vice Pres-Empl Rels, Snap On Tools Corp, 2801 80th St, Kenosha, WI 53140. 414/656-5330

LYONS, ROBERT W. Union. BS 1966, U of Wis-Madison. INT: union org/admin, coll barg, arb/med. ASSN: Wis IRRA. POSITIONS: Staff Rep, 1970, and, since 1979, Executive Director, Wis Council 40. AFSCME. AFL-CIO, 5 Odana Ct, Madison, WI 53719. 608/274-9100

LYSAGHT, WALTER J. Bus:Pers/Ind Rels. POSITION: Director, Labor Rels, Long Island Railroad Co, Jamaica, NY 11435.

M

MACAROV, DAVID Acad: Social Work. BSc 1951, U of Pittsburgh; MSc 1954, Case Western Reserve; PhD 1968, Brandeis U. PUBL: Incentives to Work, Jossey-Bass, 1970; Work and Welfare: The Unholy Alliance, Beverly Hills: Sage, 1980; Worker Productivity: Myths and Reality, Beverly Hills: Sage 1982. INT: personnel, govt labor policy, income maint. ASSN: World Future Soc, Soc for the Reduction of Human Labor, Intl Assn for Soc Econ. POSITIONS: Sr Lecturer, 1972, and, currently, Assoc Prof, School of Social Work, Hebrew Univ, Nayot 8, Jerusalem, 93704, Israel.

MACCOBY, MICHAEL Acad: Psych, Ind Rels; Consulting. PUBL: The Leader, Simon & Schuster, NY, 1981; The Gamesman, Simon & Schuster, 1976; Social Character in a Mexican Village, (w E. Fromm), Prentice Hall, 1970. ASSN: Amer Psych Assn, Amer Anthropological Assn. POSITION: Director, Project on Tech, Work & Character, 1710 Connecticut Ave NW, Washington DC 20009. 202/462-3003

MacDONALD, DONALD M. Arbitration, Consulting, Bus:Mgmt/Admin. BS 1949, Rutgers U; MS 1975, NJ Inst of Tech. ADDRESS: 31 Fleetwood Rd, Woodbridge, NJ 07095. 201/636-3195

MacDONALD, J. RANDALL Bus:Pers/Ind Rels. POSITION: Dir, Employee Rels, GTE Service Corp, One Stamford Forum, Stamford, CT 06904. 203/965-2740

MacDONALD, JEFFREY A. Union. POSITION: Asst Res Dir, Allied Industrial Workers, 3520 W Oklahoma Ave, Milwaukee, WI 53215.

MacDONALD, RAYMOND WILBUR Union. BS 1964, San Diego State U. POSITIONS: Res Dir, Graphic Arts Intl Union, AFL-CIO, 1972; Economist, Asian-Amer Free Labor Inst, AFL-CIO, 1972-74; and (since 1975), AIW, AFL-CIO, 3520 W Oklahoma Ave, Milwaukee, WI 53215. 414/645-9500.

MacEACHERN, J. ANGUS Government. MPA 1979, U of Nev-Las Vegas. INT: coll barg, arb/med, health & hosp care. ASSN: Southern Nevada IRRA, NPELRA, Southern Nev Pers Assn. POSITION: Chief, Labor Relations, City of Las Vegas, 400 East Stewart Ave, Las Vegas, NV 89101. 702/386-6315

MacGREGOR, ROBERT W. Arbitration. ADDRESS: 284 Breton Woods Drive, Coram,NY 11727.

MacKELL, THOMAS JAMES, JR. Investment Mgmt. BA 1964, Seton Hall U; MPS 1975, Long Island U; EdD 1981, Rutgers U. INT: investment mgmt of empl benefit funds, coll barg, arb/med. ASSN: Long Island & New York IRRA, SPIDR, Assn of Benefit Admin, Intl Found of Empl Benefit Plans. POSITIONS: Admin, Dist 2 Marine Eng Beneficial Assn, Assoc Maritime Officers-AFL-CIO, 1966; Professor, Long Island Univ, 1980; and (since 1981) Senior Vice Pres, M.D. Sass Assoc Inc, 475 Park Ave South, New York, NY 10016. 212/532-6010

MacKENZIE, HELEN R. MS 1974, WVU. INT: coll barg, govt labor policy, arb/med. ASSN: Wash DC IRRA, SPIDR. POSITIONS: Labor-Mgmt Rels Specialist, Internal Revenue Service, 1974; Labor Mgmt Rels Spec, Dept of Labor, 1977; and (since 1978) Labor-Mgmt Rels Spec, Agency for Intl Development, Wash DC. ADDRESS: 8608 Grant St, Bethesda, MD 20817. 202/632-7454

MacKENZIE, JOHN ROBERT Acad: Univ Admin, Labor Studies. MS 1972, West Va U. PUBL: "Labor Education," Serving Personal and Community Needs Through Adult Education, E/. J. Boone, R. W. Sherman, E. E. White & Assoc, editors, Jossey-Bass 1980; "U.S. Labor Education: How It Started, Where It Is, Where It's Going," U.S. Labor Bull, 1980-2; "Union Education and Training Programs, " The Terrain of Postsecondary Education, Natl Comm on Student Financial Assistance, 1983. INT: labor educ, intl comparative labor, coll barg. ASSN: Wash DC IRRA, Univ and Coll Labor Educ Assn. POSITIONS: Asst Dir for Labor Educ, Inst for Labor Studies, WVU, 1964; Dir, Labor Studies Center, American Univ, 1967; and (since 1971) Assoc Prof and Director, Labor Studies Center, Univ of District of Columbia. ADDRESS: 8608 Grant St, Bethesda, MD 20817. 202/727-2324

MacKENZIE, MALCOLM R. Consulting. BA 1945, Tufts U, Medford, MA. INT: personnel, mamgt/educ, arb/med. ASSN: Intl Pers Mgmt Assn, Amer Soc for Pers & Admin, Amer Soc for Trng Develop. POSITIONS: Civilian Pers Dir, Commanding Gen, U.S. Army Electonics Command, 1969; Command Civilian Pers Mgr, Chief, Naval Educ & Trng, U.S. Navy; 1976, and (since 1981) Personnel Mgmt Consultant (self-employed), 2652 Venetian Way, PO Box 280, Gulf Breeze, FL 32561. 904/932-6367

MACKIN, MARIAN C. Bus:Pers/Ind Rels. BA 1981, SUNY-Potsdam; MLIR 1983, Mich State Univ. INT: personnel, arb/med, empl/trnt programs. ASSN: ASPA. POSITION: (since 1984) Human Resources Assoc, GTE Service Corp, One Stamford Forum, Stamford ADDRESS: 4201 St John Dr, Syracuse, NY 13215. 203/965-3162

MACKLAN, RICHARD Student. D.E.C. 1983, Vanier Coll. INT: arb/med, coll barg, labor law. ASSN: McGill Ind Rels Assn. POSITION: Student, McGill Univ. ADDRESS: 890 Alexis Nihon, St. Laurent, PQ H4M 2B7 Canada.

MACKRAZ, JAMES AUGUSTINE Government. BA 1949, MA 1950, U of Wis. INT: coll barg, arb/med, labor history. ASSN: West Mich IRRA. POSITION: (since 1953) Mediator, FMCS. ADDRESS: 7303 Grachen S.E., Grand Rapids, MI 49506. 616/456-2401

MacLACHLAN, GRETCHEN E. Acad: Public Policy. BA 1958, Douglass Coll. PUBL: Making CETA-PSE Work: A Case Study of Public Service Employment under Atlanta's CETA Program, (booklet) 1978; Labor Markets: Segments and Shelters (assistant to M. Freedman), 1976; The Other Twenty Percent: A Statistical Analysis of Poverty in the South. INT: method/statis, labor market econ, emply/trng programs. ASSN: Atlanta IRRA. POSITIONS: Res Statistician, Columbia U, 1966; Program Officer, Southern Reg Council, 1973; and (since 1975) Res Assoc, Clark College, 240 Chestnut St, SW, Atlanta, GA 30307. 404/752-6422

MacLEOD, ANGUS G.S. Acad: Ind Rels. AB 1939, Amherst; MBA 1948, Columbia U. INT: mgmt/educ, personnel, health & hospital care. POSITIONS: Ind Rels Mgr, Continental Group (Can Co), 1948; and (since 1959) Asst Dir Center for Mgmt Res & Educ, Inst of Ind Rels, 9244 Bunche Hall, UCLA, Los Angeles, CA 90024. 213/825-8034

MacNETT, KATHRYN S. Government. POSITION: House Majority Legal Staff, Main Capitol, Rm 113, Harrisburg, PA 17120.

MacNETT, STEPHEN G. Government. POSITION: General Counsel, Senate Minority Caucus, Penna Senate, Harrisburg, PA 17120.

MacQUEEN, WILLIAM J. Acad: Univ Admin, Law; Arbitration. BA 1965, U of Mich; JD 1968, Detroit Coll of Law. INT: labor law, coll barg, arb/med. ASSN: Detroit IRRA, State Bar of Mich(Labor Rels Section). Mich Publ Empl Labor Rels Assn, Mich Community Coll Pers Assn. POSITIONS: Partner, Shapiro, MacQueen, Attorneys-at-Law, 1971; Asst Corp Counsel (Labor), Wayne County, 1973; and (since 1979) Director of Empl Rels, Macomb Community Coll. ADDRESS: 14500 12 Mile Rd. Warren, MI 48093. 313/286-2116

MACY, BARRY A. Acad: Org Beh/Pers, Ind Rels, Bus Admin. BBA 1966, MBA 1968, Ohio U-Athens; PhD 1974, Ohio State U. PUBL: "Organizational Change Efforts: Methodologies for Assessing Organizational Effectiveness and Program Costs versus Benefits," (w P.H. Mirvis), Evaluation Rev, 1982,6(3), 301-372; "The Bolivar Quality of Work Life Program: Success or Failure?" in R. Zager & M.P. Rosow (eds), The Innovative Organization: Productivity Programs in Action, New York: Work In Amer Inst, Pergamon Press, 1982, 184-221; "Assessing Unions and Union-Management Collaboration, (w R. J. Bullock & P.H. Mirvis), in S. E. Seashore, E. E. Lawler, P.H. Mirvis & C. Cammann (Eds), Assessing Organizational Change: A Guide to Methods, Measures, and Practice, NY:Wiley Interscience, 1983, 369-413. INT: org beh, mgmt/educ, ind psych. ASSN: Acad of Mgmt, Amer Psych Assn, U.S.Consortium of Productivity Centers. POSITIONS: Org/-Change-Org Design, Ind Rels, Aluminum Co of Amer, 1968; Asst Res Scientist-Org Beh Program, Inst for Soc Res, U of Mich, 1974; and (since 1980) Assoc Prof, Org Beh and Director, Texas Center for Productivity and QWL, Coll of Bus, Texas Tech Univ, PO Box 4320, Lubbock, TX 79409. 806/742-1530

MADDEN, JOHN V. Acad: Law. ADDRESS: PO Box 1310, Marshfield, MA 02050. 617/837-1567

MADDEN, STANFORD C. Arbitration, Legal Practice. LLB 1939, U of Mo-Kansas City. INT: arb/med. ASSN: Kansas City IRRA, AAA, FMCS. ADDRESS: Room 239, 6225 Brookside Blvd, Kansas City, MO 64113. 816/363-4822

MADIGAN, ROBERT M. Acad: Org Beh/Pers, Ind Rels. PhD 1982, Mich State U. INT: personnel, mgmt/educ. ASSN: Acad of Mgmt, ASPA. Human Resources Planning Soc. POSITIONS: Pers Dir, Whirlpool Corp, 1974; Pers Dir, Medrex Corp, 1976; and (since 1981) Asst Prof, Virginia Tech. ADDRESS: 712 Circle Dr, Blacksburg, VA 24060. 703/961-7376

MADISON, JOSEPH JAMES Union. BBA 1958, Manhatten Coll. INT: coll barg, method/-statis, labor market econ. ASSN: Wash DC IRRA. POSITION: Res Director, Transport Workers Union, 1126 16th St NW, Suite 404, Washington DC 20036. 202/467-5610

MADKOUR, M. TAHA Bus:Pers/Ind Rels, Bus Admin. BCom 1951, Cairo U. PUBL: Interpretation and Analysis of Kuwait Labour Law; Oil Workers, Their Rights and Duties; "The Reasons for theCurrent Instability Which Characterizes Labour Relations In Kuwait." INT: coll barg, labor law, abr/med. ASSN: IIRA, Arab Mgmt Soc, Assn of Labor Med Agencies. POSITIONS: Labour Expert, Ministry of Soc Affairs of Labour, 1960; and (since 1970) Ind Rels Advisor, Kuwait Oil Co, Ahmadi, Kuwait. Phone: 984-201

MAESHIMA, IWAO Acad: Ind Rels, Sociology. LLB 1958, Chuo U-Tokyo; Diploma-Christian Soc Sci 1963, Westfalische Wilhelms U-Munster. PUBL: Trade Unions and Political Activities, (co-author), Tokyo, 1978; Pension Scheme for Aged People, (co-author), Tokyo, 1975; Enterprises in the World, Bd 4, Tokyo, 1975. INT: intl comparative labor, ind sociology, union org/admin. ASSN: Japan Ind Rels Res Assn, Assn for Soc Policy of Japan, Labour Legislation Res Assn. POSITIONS: Res Officer, Friedrich-Ebert-Found, Tokyo, 1977; Assoc Prof, 1977, and, since 1983, Prof, Div of Intl Studies, Tokai Univ, 1117 Kita Kaname, Hiratsuka-Shi, Kanagawa Pref. Japan

MAETZOLD, THOMAS O. Professional Assn. BBAIR 1951, U of Minn. INT: empl/trng programs, org beh, ind psych. ASSN: Minnesota IRRA, Assn of Mgmt Consultants. POSITIONS: VP-Human Resources, Dayton's, 1965; VP-Human Resources, NW Corp, Minneapolis, 1969; and (since 1972) Pres-Principal, Maetzold Assoc Inc, 3822 County Rd 73, Minnetonka, MN 55343. 612/933-7505

MAFFEO, MARIO R. Government, Acad: Ind Rels. BSD 1953, U of Tampa; MA 1956, George Peabody Coll. INT: labor educ, govt labor policy, coll barg. ASSN: Penna Soc of Assn Exec, Amer Mgmt Assn. POSITIONS: Labor Rels Dir, 1977, and, since 1983, Deputy Auditor General, Dept of Auditor General, State of Penna, Room 318, Finance Bldg, Harrisburg, PA 17120. 717/783-5067

MAGDON, MAIDA S. Arbitration. Libby Dr, Biddeford, ME 04005. 207/282-3992

MAGENAU, JOHN M. III Acad: Ind Rels, Psych, Org Beh/Pers. AB 1971, Case Western Reserve U; PhD 1981, SUNY-Buffalo. PUBL: "Value Dilemmas in Law Enforcement: A Study of Administrative Decision Making in a Police Department," (W R. Hunt), Law & Police Quart, vol 5, Oct 1983; "The Impact of Alternative Impasse Procedures on Bargaining: A Laboratory Experiment," ILRR, vol 36, Apr 1983; "The Social Psychology of Bargaining: A Theoretical Synthesis," in G. Stephenson & C. Brotherton (eds), Industrial Relations: A Social Psychological Approach, Wiby, Chichester, England, 1979. INT: arb/med, coll barg, org beh. ASSN: Detroit IRRA, Amer Psych Assn, Soc for Psych Study of Soc Issues, Acad of Mgmt. POSITIONS: Visiting Asst Prof, SUNY-Buffalo, 1979; and (since 1980) Asst Prof, School of Bus Admin, Wayne State Univ. ADDRESS: 17519 Melrose, Southfield, MI 48075. 313/577-4565

MAGGIOLO, WALTER A. Arbitration; Acad: Ind Rels. BA 1930, Holy Cross Coll; JD 1933, Harvard. PUBL: Techniques of Mediation in Labor Disputes, Oceana Publs. INT: arb/med, labor educ. ASSN: Federal Bar Assn, SFLRP, NAA. POSITIONS: General Counsel and Asst to Dir, 1952, Dir of Mediation Activity, FMCS, 1957; and (since 1973) Arbitrator-Fact Finder (self-employed), 1619 N Nicholas St, Arlington, VA 22205. 703/538-5776

MAGNUSEN, KARL O. Acad: Ind Rels, Org Beh/Pers; Arbitration. BS 1963, MS 1967, PhD 1970, U of Wis-Madison. PUBL: Organizational Design, Development, & Behavior, Scott Foresman, 1977. INT: coll barg, org beh, arb/-med. ASSN: Acad of Mgmt, SPIDR. POSITIONS: Chairperson Bus, Dept of Mgmt, 1977-79, Assoc Dean, Bus, 1979-82, and, since 1974, Assoc Prof, College of Bus Admin, Florida Intl Univ, Tamiami Trail, Miami, FL 33199. 305/554-2791

MAHER, ROGER EDWARD Arbitration. MS 1982, New York Inst of Tech. INT: arb/med, coll barg, labor market econ. ASSN: Long Island IRRA, FMCS, AAA, SPDIR. POSITION: (since 1979) Labor Mediator-Arbitrator, NYS Mediation Board. ADDRESS: 327-82nd St, Brooklyn, NY 11209. 212/219-4113

MAHER, WILLIAM J. Bus:Pers/Ind Rels. BBA 1964, Manhatten Coll. INT: human resources, coll barg, empl/trng programs. ASSN: New York IRRA, Res Advisory Group-Wharton School, Labor Policy Assn. POSITIONS: VP Human Res, Kayser-Roth Corp, 1981, VP-Human Res, GTW Consumer Products Group, 1982, and, since 1983, Vice-Pres, Human Resources, G+W Consumer & Ind Products Group, One Gulf Western Plaza, New York, NY 10023. 212/333-2962

MAHLER, MERLE E. Bus:Pers/Ind Rels. BS 1970, Ind U. INT: personnel, coll barg, org beh. ASSN: West Va. IRRA, ASPA, Chamber of Commerce. POSITIONS: Pers Supr, 1974, Pers Supt, 1976, and, since 1979, Supt Personnel, Monsanto Co, Nitro, WV 25143. 304/755-3341

MAHLER, WALTER ROBERT Consulting, Bus:Pers/Ind Rels, Bus:Mgmt/Admin. AD 1939, North Colo U; MA 1947, PhD 1950, Columbia U Teachers Coll. PUBL: Succession Planning at the Executive Level, 1983; How Executives Interview, 1979; Executive Continuity, 1973. INT: mgmt/educ, org beh, personnel. ASSN: Amer Psych Assn, Amer Soc Adv Sci, Amer Mgmt Assn. POSITIONS: President, 1954, and, since 1982, Chairman, Mahler Assoc Inc, Midland Park. ADDRESS: 392 Pathway Manor, Wyckoff, NY 07481. 201/447-1130

MAHON, CLYDE JOHN Consulting. Rd 1, Danser Hill Road, Easton, PA 18042. 215/252-2528

MAHONEY, CARYL B. Health Care:Human Res/Ind Rels. BA, Coll of New Rochelle. INT: personnel, health & hosp care. ASSN: New York IRRA, NY Pers Mgmt Assn, Amer Soc of Hosp Pers Admin, Ass of Hosp Admin of NY. POSITIONS: Mgmt Trainee, Martin Marietta Corp, 1966; Pers Mgr, Albert Einstein Coll of Medicine, 1969; and (since 1982) Dir of Human Resources/Ind Rels, Manhatten Eye, Ear, Throat Hospital, 210 East 64th St, New York, NY 10021. 212/605-3754

MAHONEY, DONALD L. Union. INT: labor law, labor educ, organizing. ASSN: Chicago IRRA. POSITION: (since 1958) Intl Representative, IBEW, AFL-CIO, 10041 S Oakley, Chicago, IL 60643. 312/445-6544

MAILLOUIX, NOEL Acad: Psychology. ADDRESS: 2715 Chemin St Catherine, Montreal PQ H3T 1B6, Canada.

MAJOR, LEE F. III Legal Practice. Smith, Gill, Fisher & Butts, 14th FL Commerce Bank Bldg, Kanses City, MO 64106.

MAKI, DENNIS R. Acad: Econ. BA 1964, U of Minn-Duluth; PhD 1967, Iowa State U. PUBL: "The Effects of Unions and Strikes on the Rate of Total Factor Productivity - Growth in Canada," Applied Econ, 15:1, 1983, pp 29-42; "An Estimate of the Value To Unions of Compulsory Membership Clauses," (w S. Christenson), Ind & Labor Rels Rev, 36:2, 1983, pp 230-8; "A Note on the Output Effects of Canadian Postal Strikes," Canadian J of Econ, 16:1, 1983, pp 149-54. INT: labor market econ. ASSN: AEA, Canadian Econ Assn, Canadian Ind Rels Assn. POSITION: Professor, Dept of Econ, Simon Fraser Univ, Burnaby BC V5A 1S6, Canada. 604/291-3707

MALAMUD, SHERWOOD Arbitration. BA 1965, CCNY; BHL, 1966, Jewish Theological Seminary. JD 1969, U of Wis. INT: arb/med, coll barg, govt labor policy. ASSN: Wis IRRA, State Bar of Wis, Penna Bar. POSITIONS: Attorney, Neighborhood Legal Services, Pittsburgh, 1969; Mediator III, Wis Empl Rels Comm, 1973; and (since 1983) Private Arbitrator, Sherwood Malamud, Suite 21, 222 S Hamilton, Madison, WI 53703. 608/251-3400

MALIN, MARTIN H. Acad: Law; Arbitration. BA 1973, Mich State U; JD 1976, George Washington U. PUBL: Legal Environments of Business: Public Law & Regulation, (w Blackburn & Klayman), R. D. Irwing, Inc, 1982; "Protecting the Whistleblower From Retaliatory Discharge," 16 U Mich J Law Reform, 277, 1983; "Student Employees & Collective Bargaining," 60 Kentucky Law J 1, 1980. INT: labor law, arb/med, coll barg. ASSN: Chicago IRRA, State Bar of Mich (Labor Law Sect), Soc of Federal Labor Rels Professionals. POSITIONS: Law Clerk Hon. Robert DeMascio, U.S. Dist Judge, 1976; Asst Prof of Bus Law, Ohio State Univ, 1978; and (since 1980) Asst Prof, Ill Inst of Tech;/Chicago Kent Coll of Law, 77 S Wacker Dr, Chicago, IL 60606. 312/567-5056

MALIN, SUSANN Arbitration. BA 1966, MA 1967, NYU. POSITION: (since 1969) Program Director, American Arbitration Assn, 140 W 51st St, New York, NY 10020. 212/977-2973

MALINOWSKI, ARTHUR A. Acad: Ind Rels; Arbitration. BS 1956, De Paul U; MSIR, 1958, Loyola; JD 1960, De Paul; PhD 1971 Ill Inst of Tech; LLM 1981, Chicago Kent Coll of Law. PUBL: An Empirical Analysis of Discharge Loss and the Work History of Employees Reinstated by Arbitration," The Arb J, Mar 1981, vol 36, #1; "The Teamsters 703(b) Exemption: Does it Apply to Non Union Employees?" Empl Rels Labor J, vol 7, #2, Autumn, 1981. INT: arb/med, coll barg, labor law. ASSN: Chicago IRRA, ABA, NAA, Ill State Bar Assn. POSITION: (since 1982) Professor, Ind Rels, Loyola Univ, 9240 Major Ave, Morton Grove, IL 60053. 312/670-2751

MALKIN, JULIUS L. Arbitration, Legal Practice. LLB 1934, New Jersey Law School, JD 1970, Rutgers U. INT: arb/med. ASSN: New York IRRA, SPIDR. POSITIONS: Judge, River Edge Municipal Court, 1962, and (since 1934) Attorney (self-employed), 301 Princeton Dr, PO Box 116, River Edge, NJ 07661. 201/487-6111

MALMO, DIANE M. Union. POSITION: Union Rep, Michigan Education Assn, 130 Maple, Big Rapids, MI 49307.

MALONE, RENEE H. Union. BS 1966, Villa Maria Coll. INT: arb/med, coll barg. ASSN: Capital District IRRA, Professional Staff Assn. POSITIONS: Teacher, Freeport (NY) School Dist, 1966, and, since 1970, Field Rep, New York State United Teachers, Box 15-008, 159 Wolf Rd, Albany, NY 12212. 518/459-7740

MALONEY, EMILY Arbitration. POSITION: Arbitrator/Attorney, Trust Building, 105 Soquel Ave, Santa Cruz, CA 95060. 408/426-8334

MAMER, JOHN W. Acad: Bus Admin, Econ. ADDRESS: 319 Giannini Hall, Univ of Calif, Berkeley, CA 94720.

MANAUSA, KATHLEEN R. Bus:Pers/Ind Rels, Mgmt/Admin. POSITION: (since1976) Personnel Mgr, United Centrifugal Pumps, 1132 N 7th St, San Jose, CA 95112. 408/298-0123

MANDEL, ELLIOT J. Government. NLRB Region 29, 16 Court St, 4th Floor, Brooklyn, NY 11241.

MANDRELL, ROBERT ROY Bus:Pers/Ind Rels, Consulting. MA 1979, SIU-E; BA 1950 SIU-C. INT: ind psych, arb/med, org beh. ASSN: ASPA. POSITIONS: Mgr, Empl Rels, Freeman United Coal Mining Co, Illinois, 1975; VP Human Res, UNC Mining and Milling, New Mexico, 1980; and (since 1983) Base Manager, McDonnell Douglas Services Inc, MDS Box R, APO New York, NY 09671. Phone: Saudi Arabia: 11-966-07-222-0101

MANGUM, GARTH L. Acad: Econ, Ind Rels, Arbitration. PhD 1960, Harvard. PUBL: Human Resources and Labor Markets; Job Market Futurity; Employability, Employment and Income. INT: labor market econ, empl/trng programs, arb/med. POSITION: (since 1969) Professor of Econ & Mgmt, and Director, Inst for Human Resources Mgmt, 413 Coll of Bus Bldg, Univ of Utah, Salt Lake City, UT 84112. 801/-581-6127

MANGUM, STEPEHN L. Acad: Econ. BA 1978, MS 1979, U of Utah; PhD 1984, George Washington U. PUBL: A Search for Synthesis: Contemporary Reinterpretations of Classicism, the 'Neoclassical Synthesis', and Post Keynesian Economics, Olympus Publ, 1983; "Can Remittances Compensate for Manpower Outflows: The Case of Phillipine Doctors," (w B. Goldfarb & O. Havrylyshya), J of Develop Econ; "Recruitment and Job Search: Improving the Labor Exchange," Pers Admin, 1982. INT: labor market econ, empl/trng programs, govt labor policy. ASSN: AEA. POSITIONS: Res Scientist, Public Policy Program, George Washington Univ; and (since 1983) Asst Prof, Academic Faculty of Mgmt and Human Resources, Ohio State Univ-Columbus. ADDRESS: 2494 Cranford Rd, Columbus, OH 43221. 614/422-3834

MANKOFF, CHARLES HOWARD Bus:Pers/Ind Rels. BA 1970, U of Ill. INT: personnel, arb/med, coll barg. POSITIONS: Empl Rels Mgr, Champion Intl, Hoerner Waldorf Div, 1973; Mgr, Ind Rels, Anchor Coupling Co, Div Amerace Corp, 1977; and (since 1979) Personnel Manager, Research-Cottrell Inc, Somerville. ADDRESS: 2 Guildford Ct, Annandale, NJ 08801. 201/685-4957

MANN, J. KEITH Acad: Law. BS 1948, LLB 1949, Ind U. POSITION: Professor, School of Law, Stanford Universiyt, Stanford, CA 94305. 415/497-4523

MANN, SEYMOUR Z. Acad: Public Admin & Public Sector Pers & LR, Univ Admin; Consulting. BE 1942 Northern Ill U; MA 1948, PhD 1951, U of Chicago. PUBL: "Taft Hartley and the 80th Congress," and The Background of the Taft Hartley Act, " Chapters 9 & 10 in From the Wagner Act to the Taft-Hartley Act, H. Mills & E. Brown eds, U of Chicago Press, 1950; "Bargaining & Labor Relations-Issues and Trends in the Public Sector," Natl Civic Rev, Sept 1978; "The Politics of Productivity; The State & Local Focus," Public Productivity Rev, Vol IV, #4, Dec 1980. INT: coll barg, govt labor policy, union org/admin. ASSN: New York IRRA, ASPA, Amer Pol Sci Assn, Fulbright Alumni Assn. POSITIONS: Prof and Chair - Dept of Urban Affairs, Hunter Coll-CUNY, 1967; Deputy to the Executives, Dist Council 37, AFSCME, AFL-CIO, 1977; and (since 1980) Prof of Public Admin and Assoc Dir, Natl Center for Public Productivity, John Jay College-CUNY, 445 W 59th St, New York, NY 10019. 212/489-5028.

MANNING, NORA JEAN Student; Consulting. MBA 1983, North Tex State. INT: personnel, arb/med, empl/trng programs. ASSN: Natl Acad of Mgmt, Southwestern Acad of Federated Disciplines, Soc of Consumer Affairs Professionals. POSITIONS: Res Asst/Teaching Asst, North Tex State, 1982; and (since 1983) full time student/part time consultant, Tex Consulting and Applied Research, Dallas. ADDRESS: 2402 Jacqueline, Denton, TX 76201. 214/350-5799

MANNIX, THOMAS M. Acad; Univ Admin. POSITION: Manager, Coll Bargaining Services, Univ of Calif, 2199 Addison St, Berkeley, CA 94720. 415/642-6264

MANTILLA, ENRIQUE SANTAGO Business. ADDRESS: Beatrice A Diaz, Av L N Alem 1067, PISO 27, 1001 Buenos Aires, Argentina.

MANZANORES, ANDY J. Bus:Pers/Ind Rels. ADDRESS: Ind Rels, Molycorp Inc, Questa NM 87556. 505/586-0212

MAPP, MILTON MARVIN Union. ADDRESS: 375 Bellevue, Apt 202, Oakland, CA 94610. 415/444-7281

MARANTO, CHERYL LYNN Acad: Ind Rels. MLIR 1978, PhD 1982, Mich State U. INT: coll barg, labor market econ. POSITION: Asst Prof, Dept of Ind Rels, Univ of Iowa. ADDRESS: 1607 E Court St, Iowa City, IA 52240. 319/353-4847

MARCEAU, LEROY Arbitration. JD 1931, Ohio State U. POSITION: Labor Council, Exxon Corp, 1959-72 (Retired). ADDRESS: 208 Sturges Road, Fairfield, CT 06430.203/255-1606

MARCELLO, FRANK E. Bus: Pers/Ind Rels, Consulting. INT: coll barg, labor educ, labor law. ASSN: Northern Calif IRRA. POSITIONS: Associate, Tulare Kings Empl Council, 1961, and, since 1973, General Manager, Employers Labor Relations Service, 1104 8th St, Sacramento, CA 95814. 916/443-1957

MARCHANT, J. DOUGLAS Government. BA 1968, Tufts U; MS 1970, Iowa State U. INT: coll barg, govt labor policy, org beh. ASSN: Wash DC IRRA. POSITIONS: Mgmt Intern, 1971, Ind Rels Specialist, 1973, and, since, 1983, Labor Economist, Labor-Mgmt Admin, Div Research & Analysis, USDL. ADDRESS: 536 Fort Williams Pky, Alexandria, VA 22304. 202/523-6481

MARCOTTE, MARILEE ANN Student. 401 Princess Street, #1200 Kingston, Ontario K7L 5C9 Canada. 613/542-1715

MARCOU, ROSS A. Government, Consulting. AB 1967, Boston Coll; PhD 1977, Princeton U. PUBL: "Federal Employee Compensation: Past Experience and Future Prospects," Eastern Econ J, VI (2), Apr 1980; "Comparing Federal and Private Employee Benefits," Civil Service J, Oct/Dec 1978; "Estimating the Cost of Total Compensation," U.S. Civil Service Comm, 1978. INT: empl benefits, income maint, labor market econ. ASSN: Wash DC IRRA, AEA, Royal Econ Assn. POSITIONS: Federal Exec Fellow, Brookings Inst, 1978; Dir, Total Compensation Comparability Div, 1979, and, since 1980, Chief, Benefit Analysis Div, U.S. Office of Pers Managment. ADDRESS: 6441 Dahlonega Rd, Bethesda, MD 20816. 202/632-4614

MARCUS, LEONARD Bus: Pers/Ind Rels, Arbitration, Legal Prac. BA 1954, JD 1962, Brooklyn Coll. INT: coll barg, arb/med, labor law. ASSN: Maryland IRRA, AAA, ASHPA, Amer Mgmt Assn. POSITIONS: Mgr, Ind Rels, Inland Steel Co, 1936; Dir of Empl Rels, Yale Univ, 1966; and (since 1976) Vice Pres-Human Resources, Sinai Hosp of Baltimore, 2401 West Belvedere Ave, Baltimore, MD 21215. 301/578-5138

MARCUS, SUSAN E. Union, Contract Admin. BA 1981, MBA 1983, Pace Univ. INT: coll barg, union org/admin, ind sociol. ASSN: New York IRRA. POSITION: (since 1983) Contract Administrator, Doctors Council, New York. ADDRESS: 165 Langham St, Brooklyn, NY 11235. 212/532-7690

MARETT, PAMELA C. Acad: Ind Rels, Org Beh/Pers, Econ. BA 1972, Mich State U; MA 1977, Clemson U; PhD 1982, U of Tenn. PUBL: "The Japanese in the U.S.-Are They Labor Law Violaters?" Report on the Proc of the 4th Annual IRRA Southern Reg Acad Seminar, 1983; Book Review on From Skygirl to Flight Attendant, by G. P. Nielson in J of Econ History, June 1983; "Loser Pays Arbitration," Labor Law J, May 1979. INT: coll barg, arb/med, intl comparative labor. POSITION: (since 1980) Asst Prof, North Carolina State Univ, Dept of Bus & Econ. ADDRESS: PO Box 50235, Raleigh, NC 27650. 919/737-3881

MARGADONNA, J. ROBERT Bus:Pers/Ind Rels. POSITION: Director Corporate Labor Rels, Johnson & Johnson, 501 George St, New Brunswick, NJ 08903.

MARK, JEROME A. Government. BS 1948, Carnegie Inst of Tech; MA 1957, U of Chicago. PUBL: Trends in Multifactor Productivity, BLS Bull 2178, Sept 1983; "Measuring Productivity in Service Industries," Monthly Labor Rev, June1982; "Meaning and Measurement of Productivity," Public Admin Rev, Nov 1972. INT: productivity measurement & analysis, intl comparative labor, labor market econ. ASSN: Wash DC IRRA, AEA, Amer Statis Assn, Natl Economists Club. POSITION: (since 1967) Assoc Commissioner for Productivity & Tech, BLS, USDL. ADDRESS: 11207 Lombardy Rd, Silver Spring, MD 20901. 301/593-3693

MARKLE, JOHN, JR. Legal Practice. BA 1953, Yale U; LLB 1958, Harvard. INT: labor law. ASSN: Philadelphia IRRA, ABA, Penna Bar Assn, Ind Rels Assn. POSITIONS: Assoc, 1958, and, since 1964, Partner, Drinker, Biddle & Reath, 1100 Phila Natl Bank Bldg, Philadelphia, PA 19107. 215/988-2922

MARKOVITCH, GEORGE JOHN Bus:Pers/Ind Rels, Arbitration, Mgmt/Admin. BSILR 1978, Cornell. INT: personnel, arb/med, labor law. ASSN: Regional Safety Committee-A.I.S.I. POSITIONS: Dir of Safety/Workers Comp, Cooper Energy Serv, Div of Cooper Industries, 1978; and (since 1980) Manager, Ind Rels, Valley Mould, Div of Microdot, 526 Bessemer Ave, Grove City, PA 16127. 216/534-1191

MARKOVITZ, JEROME L. Legal Practice. POSITION: Attorney, WSB Suite 1004, 1346 Chestnut St, Philadelphia, PA 19107. 215/545-4414

MARKOWITZ, IRVING R. Arbitration. Retired. 989 James St, #4-B, Syracuse, NY 13203. 315/479-5759

MARKOWITZ, JAMES R. Acad: Ind Rels; Arbitration. BA 1964, Dartmouth; JD 1970, Yale; MPA 1974, Syracuse. INT: arb/med, coll barg, labor law. ASSN: NAA, SPIDR, ABA. POSITION: (since 1972) Assoc Professor, School of Bus, Ithaca Coll, Ithaca, NY 14850. 607/274-3940

MARLATT, ERNEST E. Legal Prac, Arbitration. JD 1953, Southern Methodist U. INT: labor law, arb/med. ASSN: Houston IRRA, NAA, SPIDR, AAA. POSITIONS: Colonel, U. S. Army (Retired), and, currently, Arbitrator, PO Box 13199, Houston, TX 77219. 713/961-1594

MARLOW, NANCY AILEEN Student. 120 Campbell Cres, Kingston, Ontario K7M 1Z5 Canada. 613/548-7659

MARMO, MICHAEL J. Acad: Ind Rels. BA 1965 Brooklyn Coll; MA 1968, U of Ill; PhD 1971 U of Ill. PUBL: "Arbitrators View Problem Employees: Discipline or Rehabilitation," J of Contemporary Law, vol 9, 1983; "Multilateral Bargaining in the Public Sector: A New Perspective," Proc of the 35th Annual IRRA Meeting, Dec 1982; "Arbitrating Sex Harassment Cases," Arb J, Mar 1980. INT: coll barg, arb/med, labor law. ASSN: Greater Cincinnati IRRA, Mid-West Economics Assn. POSITIONS: (since 1970) Professor of Ind Rels, Xavier University, Hinkle Hall, Victory Parkway, Cincinnati, OH 45207. 513/745-3598

MARSH, ARTHUR IVOR Acad: Ind Rels, Law, Org Beh/Pers. MA 1948, U of Oxford. PUBL: Employee Relations Policy and Decision Making, Gower Press and Confederation of British Ind, 1982; "Trade Union Journals Revisited," (w G. Gillis),Ind Rels J, vol 14, #2, Summer 1983; Concise Encyclopedia of Industrial Relations, Gower Press, 1979. INT: arb/med, empl/tnrg programs, personnel. ASSN: British Universities Ind Rels Assn. POSITIONS: Staff Tutor in Ind Rels, Oxford Univ, 1949, and, since 1964, Fellow in Ind Rels, St. Edmund Hall, Oxford, England OX14AR. Phone: (0865) 721296

MARSH, MILAN Union. POSITION: President, Ohio AFL-CIO, 271 E State St, Columbus, OH 43215.

MARSHALL, F. RAY Acad: Econ, Public Affairs; Arbitration. BA 1949, Millsaps Coll; MA 1959, La State U; PhD 1954, U of Calif-Berkeley. PUBL Lagging Productivity Growth in the U.S.: Lessons From Abroad, (w D. Werneke & V. Adams), John Wiley & Sons, forthcoming; Basic Trends Affecting Womens Jobs and Job Opportunities, Women's Research & Educ Inst, 1983; Labor Economics: Wages Employment and Trade Unionism, (w V. Briggs & A.G. King), Richard D. Irwin, 5th ed, 1984. INT: govt labor policy, labor market econ, empl/trng programs. ASSN: Texas IRRA, AEA, SEA, Acad of Public Admin. POSITIONS: Secretary of Labor, U.S. Government, 1977; Pres, Natl Policy Exchange, 1981; and (since 1981) Bernard Rapoport Centennial Professor of Econ and Public Affairs, L.B. J. School of Public Affairs, Univ of Texas. ADDRESS: 6400 Lost Horizon Drive, Austin, TX 78759. 512/471-4962

MARTIN, JAMES E. Acad: Ind Rels, Org Beh/Pers. BA 1966, Antioch Coll; MBA 1968, PhD 1973, Washington U-St. Louis. PUBL: "Federal Union-Management Relations: A Longitudinal Study," Public Admin Rev, Sept/Oct 1980; "Joint Union-Management Committees: A Comparative Longitudinal Study," Admin and Soc, May 1983; "Dual Allegiance in Public Sector Unionism: A Case Study," Intl Rev of Applied Psych, April 1981. INT: coll barg, personnel, union org/admin. ASSN: Detroit IRRA, Acad of Mgmt, SPIDR, Amer Inst of Decision Sci. POSITIONS: Asst Prof of Admin, Antioch Coll, 1969; Asst Prof of Admin, Sangamon State Univ, 1972; and (since 1976) Assoc Professor of Management and Ind Rels, Wayne State Univ. ADDRESS: 21670 Winchester Dr, Southfield, MI 48076. 313/577-4515

MARTIN, PHILIP L. Acad: Econ, Ind Rels, Ag Econ. PhD 1975, U of Wis-Madison. PUBL: "Labor Intensive Agriculture," Scientific American, Oct 1983; Labor Displacement and Public Policy, Lexington, 1983; Guestworker Programs: Lessons From Europe, Lexington, 1981. INT: ag econ, govt labor policy, labor market econ. ASSN: Amer Ag Econ Assn, AEA, Ag Pers Mgmt Assoc. POSITIONS: Staff Assoc, Brookings Inst, Wash DC, 1978-79; and (since 1975) Assoc Prof, Dept of Ag Econ, U of Calif-Davis. ADDRESS: 802 Valencia Ave, Davis, CA 95616. 916/752-1530

MARTIN, RAYMOND M. Bus:Pers/Ind Rels. BA 1952, U of Maine; MBA 1955, Northwestern U. INT: arb/med, coll barg, labor law. ASSN: Wis IRRA, ASPA, ASTD. POSITIONS: Dir, Ind Rels, American Motors Corp, 1966; Dir Ind & Community Rels, Wagner Castings, 1975; and (since 1976) Manager, Human Resources, Eaton Corp-Milwaukee Facilities, 4201 N 27th St, Milwaukee, WI 53216. 414/449-6764

MARTIN, ROBERTA M. Business. UTC Harding Machine, 13060 St Rte 287, PO Box 97, East Liberty, OH 43319.

MARTINI, BARRY E. Student. ADDRESS: 701 Millar Cir, Indiana, PA 15701. 412/349-5584

MARTYN, ROBERT G. Consulting, Bus:Pers/-Ind Rels. BA 1952, MEd 1959, Linfield Coll. INT: personnel, labor educ, mgmt/educ. ASSN: ASPA, Amer Electronics Assn, Assoc Oregon Industries. POSITION: Pers Dir, 1975, Ind Rels Mgr, 1980, Textron Inc; and (since 1983) Partner, Sloan, Silver, Floren & Martyn, 13535 N.W. Science Park Dr, Portland, OR 97229. 503/626-7527

MARUTANI, HERBERT K. Government. POSITION: Spec-Coop Extension Service, Univ of Hiawaii-Tropical Ag, 875 Komohana St, Hilo, HI 96720.

MARX, HARRIET S. Conflict Mgmt, Consulting. BA 1957, George Washington U; MS 1984, George Mason U. INT: arb/med, mgmt/educ, empl/trng programs. ASSN: SIETAR-Intl, The Possible Society. POSITIONS: Dir of Community Res, Mt. Vernon Center for Community Mental Health, 1973; Resource Coordinator, Women's Room & Res Center, Alexandria Community "Y", 1983; and (since 1984) Associate, Conflict Management Assoc, 3102 Wessynton Way, Alexandria, VA 22309. 703/360-2228

MARX, HERBERT L., JR. Arbitration; Acad: Ind Rels. AB 1943, Dartmouth Coll; MBA 1955, NYU. PUBL: "Expecting the Unexpected in Arbitration," chapter in The Arbitration and Grievance Process, Aspen Systems, 1983; "Arbitration," chapter in Handbook of Health Care Personnel Management, Aspen Systems, 1981; "Arbitration as an Ethical Institution in our Society," Arb J, Sept 1982. INT: arb/med, coll barg. ASSN: New York IRRA, NAA, SPIDR, Soc of Silurians. POSITIONS: Assoc Editor and Natl Affairs Editor, Scholastic Magazines, 1945; Vice-Pres, Ind Rels, General Cable Corp, 1951; and (since 1975) Arbitrator, 20 Waterside Plaza, New York, NY 10010. 212/685-3501

MASAKAME, YOSHIZO Acad: Ind Rels. POSITION: Faculty of Econ, Toyama Univ, 3190-Banchi, Gofuku, Toyama-shi 930 Japan.

MASCOLA, FRANCIS X. Bus:Mgmt/Admin. Management Consultants, 11 Stokum Lane, New City, NY 10956. 914/638-0122

MASKIN, NORMAN H. Student. BA 1974, Northern Ill U; MSW 1977, U of Ill. INT: health & hosp care, empl asst/programs, personnel. ASSN: Human Res Mgmt Assoc of Chicago, Natl Assoc of Soc Workers, Acad of Certified Soc Workers. POSITIONS: Social Worker, St. Francis Hosp, 1978; Social Worker, Columbus Hosp, 1979; and, currently, Student-Loyola Univ. ADDRESS: 2837 W Summerdale, Chicago, IL 60625.

MASON, FRANK A. Government. BA 1953, NYSSILR-Cornell; MBA 1958, NYU. POSITIONS: Asst VP, Pers, Johnson & Johnson, 1955-69; and (since 1969) Dir, Empl Rels Office, State of New Jersey, 134 W State St, Trenton, NJ 08608. 609/292-6180

MASON, KENNETH BRIAN Bus:Pers/Ind Rels. 66 Clearfield Dr, Williamsville, NY 14221.

MASON, MARIANNE Bus:Mgmt/Admin. 290 River Rd F4, Piscataway, NJ 08854.

MASON, ROBERT H. Union. Local 111, IBEW, 360 Acom St, Rm 305, Denver, CO 80223.

MASONDO, JAMES LINCOLN S. Bus:Pers/Ind Rels; Acad: Ind Rels. Dip Soc Wk, 1972, U of Zululand; Dip Pers Mgmt 1977, Dip Ind Rels 1979, U of South Africa; MA 1984, U of Warwick. INT: intl comparative labor, ind sociol, personnel. ASSN: IIRA, Inst for Pers Mgmt (Britain), Council for Social and Assoc Workers (South Africa). POSITIONS: Social Worker, Pietermaritzburg Child and Family Welfare Soc 1973; Pers Officer, Nestle (SA) 1973; and (since 1979) Ind Rels Officer, Shell & BP SA Petro Refineries LTD, PO Box 3179, Durban, South Africa 4000

MASSAGLI, MARK TULLY Union. INT: coll barg, arb/med, health & hosp care. ASSN: Southern Nevada IRRA. POSITION: President, Musicians Union Las Vegas, 5020 Stacey Ave, Las Vegas, NV 89108. 702/739-9369

MASSARIK, FRED Org Beh/Pers; Consulting. PhD 1957, UCLA. PUBL: Leadership and Organization, (co-author); "Seeking Essence in Executive Mind;" Participative Management. INT: org beh, personnel, mgmt/educ. ASSN: Amer Psych Assn, Amer Sociol Assn, Amer Assn for Public Opinion Res. POSITION: Professor of Behavioral Science and Ind Rels, Grad School of Mgmt, UCLA. ADDRESS: 6245 Scenic Ave, Hollywood, CA 90068. 213/469-4976

MASSAROS, ANTHONY G. Student. 36 Corona Rd, East Brunswick, NJ 08816.

MASSERY, R. DAVID Bus:Pers/Ind Rels. BA 1981, U of San Francisco; MLIR 1982, Mich State U. INT: empl/trng programs, arb/med, mgmt/educ. POSITION: (since 1983) Pers/Employee Rels Specialist, Systematics Inc, 4001 Rodney Parham Rd, Little Rock, AR 72212. 501/223-5461

MASTERS, MARICK FRANCIS Acad: Ind Rels. POSITION: Dept of Mgmt, College of Bus Admin, Texas A & M Univ, College Station, TX 77843. 409/845-1456

MASTERS, STANLEY H. Acad: Econ. BA 1961, Amherst Coll; PhD 1965, Princeton. PUBL: Black-White Income Differentials; Estimating Labor Supply Effects of Income Maintenance Alternatives, (w I. Garfinkel), 1977; "Wages and Plant Size," Rev of Econ & Statis, Aug 1969. INT: labor market econ, empl/trng programs, income maint. ASSN: AEA. POSITIONS: Assoc Prof, U of Notre Dame, 1972; Res Assoc, Inst for Res on Poverty, U of Wis, 1974; and (since 1981) Professor Econ, SUNY-Binghamton. ADDRESS: 2641 Lynnhurst Dr, Vestal, NY 13850. 607/798-2297

MASTERS, W. FRANK Union. MS 1981, ILR-Cornell. INT: coll barg, labor history, org beh. ASSN: Wash DC IRRA. POSITIONS: Teacher, Alexandria Public Schools, 1964; Negotiator, 1969, and, since 1981, Director of Research Services, Natl Educ Assn, Wash DC. ADDRESS: 5823 Jane Way, Alexandria, VA 22310. 202/822-7433

MATER, PATTI R. Bus:Pers/Ind Rels. BBA 1979, U of Wis-Eau Claire; MSIR 1981, Purdue U. INT: personnel, empl/trng programs, coll barg. ASSN: Newark Area Pers Assn, Newark Safety Council, Mental Health Assn. POSITIONS: Empl Standards Specialist, 1981, Ind Operating Div-Pers Specialist, 1983, and, currently, Safety Supervisor, Owens-Corning Fiberglas, Case Avenue, Newark, OH 43055. 614/349-3261

MATHER, E. BRUCE Legal Practice. ADDRESS: Constangy, Brooks & Smith, 2400 Peachtree Center, 230 Peachtree St, Atlanta, GA 30303. 404/525-8622

MATHYS, NICHOLAS J. Acad: Bus Admin/-Mgmt. POSITION: Dept of Management, De Paul Univ, 25 E Jackson, Blvd, Chicago, IL 60604.

MATLACK, R.E. Bus:Pers/Ind Rels. BS 1967, Penn State. INT: personnel, ind psych, empl/trng programs. POSITIONS: Pers Rels Asst, 1970, Mgr, Pers Practices & Benefits, 1978, and, since 1981, Manager, Human Resources, Westinghouse Elec Corp, PO Box 920, South Boston, VA 24592. 804/575-7971

MATT, EUGENE C. Government, Bus.Pers/Ind Rels. BA 1972, U of Wash. INT: personnel, arb/med, coll barg. ASSN: Northwest IRRA. POSITION: Manager of Pers & Labor Rels, Municipality of Metro Seattle, 821 Second Ave, Seattle, WA 98104. 206/447-6731

MATTERN, THOMAS R. Bus:Mgmt/Admin. POSITION: Human Resources, Central Bank of Denver, 2445 W 37th St, Denver, CO 80211. 303/893-3456

MATTHEWS, DANIEL E. Arbitration, Legal Prac. AB 1937, Canisius Coll; JD 1954, Amer U; LLM 1956, Georgetown U. PUBL: "Federal Labor Relations: A Program in Transition," 21 Catholic L Rev, 512, 1972; "Federal Tort Claims Act: Proper Scope of the Discretionery Functions Exception," 6 Amer U Law Rev 22, 1957.INT: arb/med, labor law, coll barg. ASSN: ABA, AAA, SFLRP. POSITIONS: Dir of Pers, NLRB, 1959; Legal Practice (self-employed), 1971, and, since 1974, Labor Arbitrator (self-employed), 5109 Western Ave NW, Washington DC 20016. 202/362-2043

MATTHEWS, KEITH B. Bus:Pers/Ind Rels. BS 1953, Brigham Young U; Cert IR 1963, U of Utah. INT: coll barg, arb/med, personnel. ASSN: Amer Mining Congress Ind Rels Committee, Calif State Chamber of Commerce, Naval Reserve Assn. POSITIONS: Captain, U.S. Navy, 1953-57; Supr of Ind Rels, Kennecott Corp, 1957-67; and (since 1967) Manager of Ind Rels, Utah Intl Inc, 550 California St, San Francisco, CA 94104. 415/981-1515

MATTHEWS, MARILYN S. Union. BS 1984, Empire State Coll. INT: union org/admin, govt labor policy, arb/med. ASSN: New York IRRA. POSITION: Exec Secretary, Westchester Local 80, of CSEA Local 1000, AFSCME, AFL-CIO, 196 Maple Ave, White Plains, NY 10601. 914/428-6452

MATTILLA, JOHN P. Acad: Econ, Ind Rels. BA 1965, U of Mich; PhD 1969, U of Wis. PUBL: "Determinants of Male School Enrollments: A Time Series Analysis," "The Impact of Minimum Wages on Teenagers;" "G. I. Bill Benefits and Enrollments: How Did Vietnam Veterans Fare?" INT: labor market econ, govt labor policy, coll barg. ASSN: AEA. POSITIONS: Asst Prof of Econ, Ohio State Univ, 1969; Asst/Assoc Prof of Econ, 1973, and, since 1983, Professor Econ, Dept of Econ, Heady Hall, Iowa State Univ, Ames, IA 50011. 515/294-2701

MAUK, ELLEN SCHULER Union. MA 1970, Purdue. INT: coll barg, arb/med, labor law. ASSN: Long Island IRRA. POSITIONS: Prof of English, 1970, and, since 1978, President, Faculty Assn of Suffolk County Community Coll, Suffolk County Comm Coll, Selden, NY 11784. 516/451-4151

MAURER, ANN H. Union. MBA 1976, Wayne State U. INT: union org/admin, arb/med, coll barg. ASSN: Detroit IRRA. POSITIONS: UAW Intl Rep, UAW Intl Union, 1972; Staff Economist, Gregory, VanLopik and Korney, 1975; and (since 1979) Labor Economist/Bus Agent, Police Officers Assn of Michigan. ADDRESS: 29255 Laurel Wood Dr, Southfield, MI 48034. 313/569-8077

MAURER, GEORGE C. Bus:Pers/Ind Rels, Consulting, Bus:Mgmt/Admin. BA 1955, The Citadel. INT: method/statis, mgmt/educ, labor law. ASSN: Wis IRRA, ASPA, Amer Compensation Assn. POSITIONS: Vice Pres, Human Resources, National Forge Co, 1978; Dir, Human Resources, DEC Intl, 1981; and (since 1984) Executive Director, Employees Assn of Greater Wis, Inc, 6414 Copps Ave, Madison, WI 53716. 608/222-3342

MAURO, MARTIN JOHN Econ Forecasting. BS 1975, Fordham; PhD 1981, Cornell. PUBL: "Strikes as a Result of Imperfect Information." INT: labor market econ, method/statis, coll barg. POSITIONS: Economist, USDL, 1980; and (since 1981) Senior Economist, Merrill Lynch Economics Inc, New York. ADDRESS: 98 Manhatten Ave, Waldwick, NJ 07463. 212/-637-6232

MAXEY, CHARLES Acad: Univ Admin, Ind Rels, Arbitration. AM 1975, PhD 1981, U of Ill. INT: coll barg, health & hosp care, org beh. ASSN: Acad of Mgmt. POSITION: (since 1983) Asst Dean, Faculty Development & Res, Grad School of Bus Admin, Univ of Southern California, Los Angeles, CA 90089. 213/743-5273

MAXWELL, EUGENIA Arbitration. BA 1964, Fla State U; JD 1968, Stetson Coll of Law. INT: arb/med. ASSN: Southern Calif IRRA, SPIDR, AAA. POSITIONS: Deputy County Counsel, L.A. County Counsel, 1970; Manager, Labor Rels, Continental Airlines, 1976; and (since 1981) Arbitrator, 555 Pier Ave, Suite 4, Hermosa Beach, CA 90254. 213/372-4636

MAXWELL, NAN L. Acad: Econ. PhD 1983, Fla State U. INT: labor market econ, empl/trng programs. POSITION: Asst Prof, Dept of Econ, Denison Univ, Granville,OH 43023. 614/887-6404

MAYER, STEVEN J. Student. ADDRESS: PO Box 1375, Eugene, OR 97440.

MAYNARD, REBECCA Research. POSITION: Senior Economist, Mathematica Policy Research, PO Box 2393, Princeton, NJ 08540. 609/799-2600

MAZA, MIGUEL A. Student. ILR Dept, Indiana Univ of Penna, 411 John Sutton Hall, Indiana, PA 15701. 412/357-4470

MAZZOCCHI, G. CARLO Acad: Econ. POSITION: Professor, Dept of Econ, Universita Cattolica, Largo Gemelli 1, Milano, Italy.

McALINDEN, SEAN PAUL Acad: Research. 1452 Bemidiji, Ann Arbor, MI 48103.

McALLISTER, PETER JOHN Bus:Pers/Ind Rels, Bus:Mgmt/Admin, Government. BA 1970, McMaster U. INT: coll barg, health & hosp care, ind sociol. ASSN: British Columbia IRRA, Ind Rels Mgmt Assn of B.C., Inst of Association Executives, Vancouver Bd of Trade. POSITIONS: Labour Rels Officer, Ont, 1970; Mgr, Labour Rels Div, 1974, and , since 1981, President & C.E.O., Health Labor Rels Assoc of B.C., 1212 W Broadway, Vancouver B.C. V6H 3V1 Canada. 604/736-8221

McALLISTER, ROBERT W. Arbitration. BS 1955, JD 1959, Boston Coll. INT: arb/med, health & hosp care, labor law. ASSN: Chicago IRRA, AAA, Economics Club of Chicago, ABA. POSITION: (since 1979) Robert W. McAllister, Ltd. Suite 1607, 200 West Monroe St, Chicago, IL 60606. 312/782-0596

McAULEY, DONAN B. Bus:Pers/Ind Rels. JD 1974, U of Minn. INT: labor law, arb/med, coll barg. POSITIONS: Mgr, Labor Rels, Thomson Newspapers Inc, 1974; and (since 1982) Manager of Labor Rels, Interstate United Corp, 120 South Riverside Plaza, Chicago, IL 60606. 312/930-2334

McAULLIFFEE, CORNELIUS J. Arbitration. Acad: Law. BS 1959, St. Louis U; JD 1963, Boston Coll. INT: arb/med, labor law, labor educ. ASSN: Chicago & Gateway IRRAs, Assn of Trial Lawyers in Amer, ABA (Labor Committee), SPIDR. POSITIONS: Attorney (Private Prac), 1963; Exec Dir, Ill Office of Coll Barg, 1978; and (since 1975) Attorney-Arbitrator (self-employed), 220 Elmwood Ave, Providence, RI 02907. 401/277-2741

McAULIFFE, PAUL S. Bus:Pers/Ind Rels. POSITION: Director, Ind Rels, The Standard Oil Co, 1521 Midland Building, Cleveland, OH 44115. 216/575-5936

McBREARTY, JAMES CONNELL Acad: Ind Rels, Econ; Arbitration. AB 1963, La Salle Coll; MA 1965, PhD 1968, U of Ill. PUBL: American Labor History and Comparative Labor Movements: A Representative Bibliography, Tucson: Univ of Ariz Press, 1973; Grievances: From Prevention Through Arbitration, (w G. M. Parent), Old Pueblo Printers, 1973; "Legality of Employment Tests: The Impact of the Duke Power Co," Labor Law J, July, 1971, pp 387-393. INT: coll barg, arb/-med, labor history. ASSN: Arizona IRRA, NAA, SPIDR, AEA. POSITIONS: Teaching Asst, Econ, U of Ill, 1963; Asst Prof, Econ, 1968, and, since 1973, Assoc Prof of Econ and Ind Rels, Dept of Econ, Coll of Bus and Public Admin, Univ of Arizona, Tucson, AZ 85721. 602/621-1639/6224

McCABE, DOUGLAS M. Acad: Bus Admin, Ind Rels; Consulting. BA 1971, Marquette U; MS 1973, Loyola U of Chicago; PhD 1977, Cornell. PUBL: The Crew Size Dispute in the Railroad Industry, Wash DC: U.S.Dept of Transportation, Fed Railroad Admin, 1978; "Problems in Federal Sector Labor-Management Relations Under Title VII of the Civil Service Reform Act of 1978," Labor Law J, vol 33, #8, Aug 1982, pp 560-565; "Mediation Techniques in the Federal Sector: Labor and Management Viewpoints," Federal Service Labor Rels Rev, vol 3, #2, 1981, pp 36-52. INT: coll barg, arb/-med, personnel. ASSN: Wash DC IRRA, IIRA, SPIDR, SFLRP. POSITIONS: Asst Prof of Ind Rels and Labor Rels, Georgetown U, 1976; Principal Investigator/Project Res Dir/Exec Dir, Federal Sector Mediation, FMCS, 1978; and (since 1982) Assoc Prof of Ind & Labor Rels, School of Bus Admin, Georgetown Univ, Washington DC 20057. 202/625-3225

McCAFFERTY, JOHN K. Government. MSIR 1967, Loyola U of Chicago. INT: personnel, govt labor policy, empl/trng programs. ASSN: Chicago IRRA. ADDRESS: 6055 N Kilpatrick, Chicago, IL 60646.

McCAFFREE, KENNETH M. Arbitration; Acad: Ind Rels, Econ. PhD 1950, U ofChicago. INT: arb/med, health & hosp care, labor market econ. ASSN: Northwest IRRA, NAA, AEA. POSITIONS: Prof, 1949, and, since 1981 Prof Emeritus, Univ of Washington, and, Arbitrator (self-employed), 7020 NE Twin Spits Rd, Hansville, WA 98340. 206/638-2426

McCANN, RICHARD A. Bus:Mgmt/Admin, Government. BA 1967, U of N. H.; MBA 1980, Rivier Coll. INT: coll barg, arb/med. ASSN: ASBO INTL, NHAASA, AAA. POSITIONS: Account Exec, W. E. Hutton & Co, 1969; Sr Mgmt Analyst, N. H. Hospital, 1974; and (since 1975) Bus Admin, Nashua School Dist #42, 6 Main St, Nashua, NH 03061. 603/883-7791

McCARGER, GEORGE L. Government. BA 1963, U of Ore. INT: coll barg, govt labor policy, labor law. ASSN: Northwest IRRA, Pacific Northwest Labor History Assn. POSITIONS: Pers Dir, George Lawrence Co, 1968; Suprervisory Examiner, 1972, and, since 1983, Asst to the Regional Dir, NLRB, Region 19, 2948 Federal Bldg, 912 2nd Ave, Seattle, WA 98174. 206/442-0220

McCARTHY, PAUL F. Consulting/Organized Labor. BS 1966 Boston Coll; MS 1968, U of Mass. INT: coll barg, union org/admin, coll barg. POSITION: President, Collective Bargaining Assoc, 9 Carolyn Cir, Marshfield, MA 02050. 617/834-7863

McCARTHY, ROBERT JOSEPH Bus:Pers/Ind Rels. AB 1954, Niagara U; MILR 1959, Cornell. INT: personnel, coll barg. ASSN: ASPA. POSITION: Dir, Ind Rels, Akzo Chemie America, 300 S Wacker Dr, Chicago, IL 60606. 312/786-0400

McCAUSLAND, ALLAN STUART Arbitration, Consulting; Acad: Econ. BA 1967, Amer Intl Coll-MA; MA 1969, Whittemore School-U of N.H.; PhD, 1975, Clark U. PUBL: "Using Statistics To Assess Affirmative Action Progress," Papers & Proceedings, NEB&EA, Fall 1982; "The Ripple Effect (?) in Minimum Wage Legislation," Atlantic Econ J, vol III, #4, p 92, Dec 1979; "Fair Labor Standards Amendments of 1975," 94 Congress, U.S. House of Rep, Nov 1975. INT: arb/med, labor market econ, affirmative action. ASSN: Boston IRRA, AAA, AEA, SFLPR. POSITIONS: Asst Prof, Econ and Finance, 1969, Prof: Econ and Finance, New Hampshire Coll, 1974; and (since 1976) President, McCausland Econ Assoc, RD 1, Box 126, Warner, NH 03278. 603/456-2393

McCLOSKEY, MARGARET M. Union. BA 1980, MA 1982, Wayne State U. INT: union org/admin, coll barg. ASSN: Detroit IRRA. POSITIONS: Secretary, Detroit Public Schools, 1970, and, since 1983, Admin Secretary, Detroit Assn of Educational Office Employees-AFT. ADDRESS: 7707 Reuter, Dearborn, MI 48126. 313/963-3380

McCLURE, DWIGHT I. Bus:Pers/Ind Rels. BA 1973, MBA 1984, Memphis State U. INT: coll barg, arb/med, personnel. ASSN: Natl Public Employers Labor Rels Assn, Ind Pers Council. POSITIONS: Foreman, Water Operations, 1977, Labor Rels Asst, 1978, and, since 1979, Manager of Labor Rels, Memphis Light, Gas & Water, 220 S Main, Memphis, TN 38101. 901/528-4609

McCOLLUM, JAMES KENNETH Acad: Ind Rels, Bus Admin. BS 1960, USMA West Point-NY; MA 1968, U of Dayton; MA 1971, U of Cincinnati. PUBL: "Politics and Labor Relations in Virginia: The End to Public Sector Labor Relations," Empl Rels Law J, Winter 1981-82; "Decertification of the Northern Virginia Public Sector Unions: A Study of Its Effect," J of Coll Negotiations in the Public Sector, I, 1982. INT: labor law, govt labor policy, coll barg. ASSN: Acad of Mgmt, Inter Univ Seminar on Armed Forces and Soc, Alpha Kappa Psi. POSITIONS: Major, U.S. Army, 1968; Instructor, VPI & SU, 1975; and (since 1979) Asst Prof, Dept of Management, Auburn Univ, Auburn, Al 36849. 205/826-5290

McCONNELL, JOHN W. Acad: Ind Rels; Arbitration. PhD 1937, Yale. PUBL: Economic Needs of Older People, (w J. Carson)., 1956; America's Needs and Resources, (w others), 1955. INT: arb/med, health & hosp care, income maint. ASSN: NAA. POSITIONS: Dean & Prof, ILR School, Cornell, 1946-62; Pres, U of N.H., 1962-71, and (since 1971) Adjunct Prof, Cornell U. ADDRESS: 21 Cayuga St, Trumansburg, NY 14886. 607/256-4401

McCONNELL, ROBERT C. Acad: Ind Rels; Bus:Mgmt/Admin. BS 1938, ML 1949, U of Pittsburgh. INT: mgmt/educ, coll barg, personnel. POSITIONS: VP-Ind Rels, 1968, Dir of Ind Rels Corp, Diamond Shamrock Corp, 1978; and (since 1978) Instructor (self-employed), Ind Rels Instruction, 118 Eaton Square, Mobile, AL 36608. 205/342-2874

McCORKLE, LOIS PAKE Consulting, Arbitration. AB 1947, Oberlin Coll; MD 1951, Western Reserve U; MBA 1982, Case Western Reserve U. PUBL: "Duration of Hospitalization Prior to Surgery," Health Serv Res 5:114-131, Summer 1970; "Utilization of Facilities of a University Hospital: Length of Inpatient Stay in Various Hospital Departments," Health Serv Res 1:91-114, Summer 1966; " A Study of Illness in a Group of Cleveland Families VIII: the Relation of Tonsillectomy to the Incidence for Common Respiratory Diseases in Children," New England J Med, 1066, June 1955. INT: health & hosp care, arb/med. ASSN: Amer Public Health Assn, Amer Soc for Advancement of Sci, Amer Medical Women's Assn. POSITIONS: Biostatistician, Dir Div of Biostatistics, Univ Hosp of Cleveland, 1970; Consultant in health care, Physicians Peer Review Org of Cuyahoga County, 1978; and (since 1981) Independent Consultant, Health Care, Assessment & Data Interpretation, 2245 Harcourt Dr, Cleveland Heights, OH 44106. 216/721-2423

McCORMACK, JOSEPH H. Bus:Pers/Ind Rels. BA 1952, Mich State U. POSITIONS:

Ind Rels Asst, Bethlehem Steel, 1965; Mgr, Ind Rels, Copperweld Steel, 1970; and (since 1971) Vice Pres, Penn-Dixie Steel Corp, 1111 S Main St, Kokomo, IN 46901. 317/452-0976

McCORMICK, THOMAS PATRICK Legal Practice. BBA 1973, MS 1975, JD 1983, U of Wis-Madison. PUBL: "Unemployment Compensation-An Examination of Wisconsin's 'Active Progress' Labor Dispute Disqualification Provision," 1982 Wis L Rev, 907. INT: labor law, coll barg, personnel. ASSN: Wis IRRA, State Bar of Wis, ABA. POSITIONS: Bus Studies Lecturer (U.S. Peace Corps), Fiji Inst of Tech, 1976; Ind Rels/Org Develop Mgr, Burns Philp (South Sea) Co Ltd, Suva, Fiji, 1979; and (since 1983) Attorney, Michael, Best & Friedrich, 250 E Wisconsin Ave, Milwaukee, WI 53202. 414;271-6560

McCOY, WALTER D. Acad: Bus Admin, Ind Rels. PhD 1982, U of Tex at Arlington. PUBL: "Comparison of School Superintendents and City Managers in Politics;" "Executive Women in Management." INT: coll barg, arb/-med, labor educ. POSITIONS: Dean of Student Serv, Univ of Tex-Arlington, 1974; Coordinator of Public Admin, 1976, and, since 1976, Asst Prof of Mgmt, Corpus Christi State Univ, 6300 Ocean Dr, Corpus Christi, TX 78412. 512/991-6810 ext 379

McCULLOCH, FRANK W. Arbitration; Acad: Law. AB 1926, Williams Coll; LLB 1929, Harvard. PUBL: The National Labor Relations Board, (w T. Bornstein), Praeger, 1974. INT: labor law, intl comparative labor, arb/med. ASSN: ABA, AAA. POSITIONS: Chairman, NLRB, 1961-70; Prof of Law, 1971, and, since 1976, Scholar in Residence, Univ of Virginia Law School, and, currently, Part time Arbitrator, Public Review Bd-UAW & Committee of Experts-ILO, Geneva. ADDRESS: 104 Falcon Dr, Charlottesville, VA 22901. 804/295-7371

McCUTCHEON, AUBREY V., JR. Bus:Mgmt/-Admin. POSITION: President, McCutcheon Assoc Inc, 815 Fisher Bldg, Detroit, MI 48202. 313/871-3939

McDADE, ROBERT JOSEPH Acad: Law. AB 1950, Niagara U; JD 1953, St. John's U; LLM 1956, NYU. INT: coll barg, arb/med, labor law. POSITION: Director-Ind Rels, Hanna Mining Co, 100 Erieview Plaza, Cleveland, OH 44114. 216/589-4250

McDERMOTT, THOMAS JOSEPH Arbitration. BBA 1939, MBA 1941, PhD 1955, Boston U. PUBL: "Survey on Availability and Utilization of Arbitrators in 1972," Proceedings Natl Acad of Arbitrators, BNA 1974; "Discharge, Reinstatement: What Happens Thereafter," ILR Rev, July 1971; "Arbitrability: The Courts versus the Arbitrator," The Arb J, vol 23, #1, 1968. INT: arb/med, coll barg, labor history. ASSN; NAA, AAA, Assn for Soc Econ. POSITIONS: Assoc Prof ofEcon, Holy cross Coll, 1948; Prof of Econ, Duquesne Univ, 1959, and (currently) Labor Arbitrator(self-employed), 4826 Bohill Dr, San Antonio, TX 78217. 512/657-0775

McDONALD, JOHN MICHAEL Union. BA 1981, U of Mass; MA 1982, U of Wis-Madison. INT: coll barg, labor educ, labor law. POSITION: (currently) Exec Bd, Bargaining Committee, Intl Longshoremen's Assn, Local #1066, AFL-CIO. ADDRESS: 11 Abbott St, Medford, MA 02155. 617/395-6230

McDONNELL, FRANK S., JR. Arbitration. INT: arb/med, empl/trng programs. ASSN: Boston IRRA, NAA, AAA, SPIDR. POSITIONS: Commissioner, FMCS, 1952; and, currently, Arbitrator (self-employed), PO Box 605, Avon, MA 02322. 617/587-2403

McELROY, KATHLEEN Government. PhD 1974, Case Western Reserve. INT: empl/trng programs, labor market econ, income maint. ASSN: Union of Radical Pol Econ. POSITION: (since 1975) Program Manager, Planning & Evaluation, Wis Dept of Ind, Labor & Human Rels. ADDRESS: 118 W Lakeside, Madison, WI 53715. 608/267-9519

McFARLAND, C. K. Acad: Ind Rels, Labor History. PhD 1965, U of Ariz. PUBL: Roosevelt, Lewis and the New Deal, 1933-1940, 1970; "Crusade for Child Laborers: 'Mother" Jones and the March of the Mill Children," Penna History, vol 38, #3, July 1971; "20 Years of a Successful Labor Paper: The Working Man's Advocate, 1829-49," (co-author), Journalism Quart, vol 60, #1, Spring, 1983, 35-40. INT: labor history, coll barg, labor educ. ASSN: Univ& Coll Labor Educ Assn, Labor Historians, Org of Amer Historians. POSITIONS: Asst Prof of History, U of Southwestern La, 1965; Assoc Prof of History, Tex Christian Univ, 1966; and (since 1971) Professor of History and Ind Rels, Arkansas State Univ, PO Box 1890, State University, AR 72467. 501/972-3046

McGANN, F. MICHAEL Bus:Mgmt/Admin. ADDRESS: Fram Corp, 105 Pawtucket Ave, E. Providence, RI 02916. 401/434-7000

McGILL, WILLIAM R. Government. ADDRESS: 1365 Jerusalem Rd, Mechanicsburg, PA 17055. 717/761-3919

McGINNIS, JAMES ROBERT Bus:Mgmt/-Admin; Acad: Ind Rels. BS 1950, Fordham U. ASSN: Greater Houston IRRA, ASPA. POSITIONS: Labor Rels Mgr, Petro-Tex Chemical Corp, 1950; and (since 1977) General Mgr, Corporate Services, Denka Chemical Co, 8701 Park Place Blvd, Houston, TX 77017. 713/477-8821

McGINNIS, JEANETTE M. Consulting. BS, Glassboro State Coll. POSITION: McGinnins & Assoc, McGinnis Bldg, 25 W 45th St, Brant Beach, NJ 08008. 609/494-0785

McGINNIS, WILLIAM JOHN JR. Consulting. BS 1967, La Salle Coll-Phila; MS 1982, Rutgers U. PUBL: "Employee Relations Management," CAI Inst; Successful Negotiations, Mgmt Educ Inst, Ship Bottom NJ; Developing & Managing A Successful Consulting Practice, Mgmt Educ Inst, Ship Bottom, NJ. INT: coll barg, mgmt/educ, empl/trng programs. ASSN: ASPA, SPMC, IMC. POSITIONS: CEO, W. J. McGinnins & Assoc, Consultants, 1965; and (since 1982) Vice-Chairman, Natl Advisory Council on Voc Educ & Mgmt Trng, Wash DC. ADDRESS: 25 W 45th St, Brant Beach, NJ 08008. 202/376-8873

McGINTY, IAN GREGORY Bus:Pers/Ind Rels. Ind Admin, 1983, GM Inst. INT: personnel, arb/med, empl/trng programs. ASSN: Amer Marketing Assn, Amer Foundrymen Soc. POSITION: (since 1983) Labour Rels Rep, General Motors of Canada Ltd. ADDRESS: 6 Kingsway Crescent, St. Catharines, Ontario L2N 1A6 Canada. 416/685-2764

McGIVERN, EDWARD J. Union, Bus:Pers/Ind Rels. BA 1979, Rutgers U; MLIR 1980. Mich State U. INT: coll barg, org beh, personnel. Natl Rep, Natl Federation of Federal Employees, 1981. ADDRESS: 24 Orchard St, Bloomfield, NJ 07003.

McGLONE, PATRICK DANIEL Acad: Teacher, Ind Rels. BS 1979, SUNY-Brockport; MSIR 1983, Coll of Grad Studies Inst-W Va. INT: personnel, empl/trng programs, mgmt/educ. ASSN: West Va IRRA, Wyoming Cty AFT, AFL-CIO. POSITIONS: Pers Mgr, County Seat Construction, Mayville, NY 1979; Adjunct Faculty Member, Mgmt/Pers, Bluefield State Coll, W Va., 1984, and, since 1981, Special Educ Teacher, Wyoming County Bd of Educ. ADDRESS: Box 372, Pineville, WV 24874. 304/294-6839

McGOWAN, WILLIAM H. Bus:Pers/Ind Rels. MBA 1977, Temple U. INT: personnel, labor law, labor history. POSITION: (since 1982) Director, Empl Rels, The Allentown Hospital. ADDRESS: 4131 Broadway, Cetronia, PA 18104. 215/376-5081

McGRATH, MARIE DOROTHEA Acad: Ind Rels, Univ Admin, Org Beh/Pers. BA 1974, MBA 1980, Temple U. INT: coll barg, arb/med, personnel. ASSN: Philadelphia IRRA, Ind Rels Assn. POSITIONS: Pers Data Serv, ARA Services, 1979; labor Rels Asst, Bethlehem Steel Co, 1980; and (since 1982) Labor Rels Supr, Woodhaven Center, Temple Univ, 2900 Southampton Rd, Philadelphia, PA 19154. 215/671-7577

McGUIRE, JAMES J. Bus:Mgmt/Admin. BSILR 1960, Cornell; MBA 1974, Rochester Inst of Tech. INT: coll barg, arb/med, personnel. ASSN: Natl Assn of Manufacturers (Labor Rels Committee). POSITIONS: Dir Ind Rels, Corp Headquarters, 1970, Vice Pres, Ind Rels, Medical Products Div, 1979, and, since 1982, Vice Pres Operations, Sybron Ritter-Tycos Div, Arden, NC 28704. 704/684-8111

McILVAIN, CHARLES L. Government. B/BA 1975, New Mex State U. INT: org beh, labor market econ. POSITIONS: Marketing VP, Odessa, Tx Chamber of Commerce, 1975, Exec VP, Las Cruces, New Mexico, Chamber of Commerce, 1977; and (since 1979) Director of Marketing, City of Farmers Branch, PO Box 34435, Farmers Branch, TX 75234. 214/247-3131

McINERNEY, MARJORIE L. Acad: Org Beh/Pers, Bus Admin, Ind Rels. BSBA 1975, U of Akron; MBA 1977, Marshall U; PhD 1983, Ohio State U. INT: personnel, coll barg, arb/-med. ASSN: Amer Mgmt Assn, Omicron Delta Epsilon, Phi Delta Gamma. POSITIONS: Asst Natl Bank Examiner, U.S. Treasury Dept, Comptroller of the Currency, 1977; Adjunct Faculty, Wesleyan Coll, 1979; and (since 1982) Asst Prof, Univ of North Carolina. ADDRESS: 3307-8 Wickslow Dr,Wilmington, NC 28403. 919/392-3721

McINTIRE, WARREN W., JR. Acad: Ind Rels, Org Beh/Pers; Consulting. PhD 1972, U of Wis. INT: coll barg, org beh, personnel. ASSN: Acad of Mgmt, ASPA, Midwest Bus Admin Assn. POSITIONS: Asst Prof, Penna State Univ-Harrisburg, 1971; Assoc Prof, U of Wis-Oshkosh, 1973; and (since 1978) Professor, Dept of Bus Admin, College of St. Thomas, St. Paul, MN 55105. 612/647-5164/5650

McINTOSH, BARBARA R. Acad: Ind Rels; Consulting. BS 1965, U of Ill; MLIR 1972, Mich State U; PhD 1979, Purdue U. INT: personnel, govt labor policy, labor market econ. ASSN: Acad of Mgmt, Human Resources Planning Soc, Southern Mgmt Assn. POSITIONS: Admin Asst, Grad School of Bus, Purdue, 1972; Instructor, 1976, and, since 1979, Asst Prof, Rutgers Univ, Inst of Mgmt & Labor Rels, Ryders Lane, New Brunswick, NJ 08903. 201/932-9874

McINTOSH, STEPHEN SCOTT Bus:Pers/Ind Rels. BS 1968, MS 1970, Purdue; PhD 1978, Kent State U. POSITION: PPG Industries Inc, Chemical Division-US, PO Box 191, New Martinsville, WV 26155. 304/455-2200

McKECHNIE, GRAEME H. Acad: Ind Rels; Arbitration, Mediation-Fact Finding. BCom 1961, U of Toronto; MSc 1963, PhD 1965, U of Wis. PUBL: Federalism & Policy Developments: The Case of Adult Occupational Training in Ontario, U of Toronto Press, 1973. INT: arb/med, coll barg, labor market econ. ASSN: Canadian Ind Rels Assn, SPIDR, AEA. POSITION: Assoc Prof/Chairman, Dept of Econ, York Univ, 4700 Keele St, Downsview, Ont M3J 1P3 Canada. 416/667-2362

McKEE, CLIVE B. Arbitration. ADDRESS: 5931 Marine Dr, West Vancouver, BC V7W 2S1 Canada. 604/921-9812

McKEE, WILLIAM L. Acad: Ind Rels, Econ; Arbitration. BS 1968, Southwest Mo U; MA 1970, PhD 1975, U of Mo-Columbia. PUBL: Identifying Emerging Job Opportunities, The W. E. Upjohn Inst for Empl Res, 1983; "Value Judgements Inherent in Criticisms of CPS Measurement of Unemployment," Soc Sci Quart, Sept 1980; "Labor Market Information and Career Planning," Joint Council on Econ Educ, 1984, (forthcoming bookchapter). INT: arb/med, labor market econ, coll barg. ASSN: North Texas IRRA, AEA, Southwestern Econ Assn, Southwestern Soc of Economists. POSITIONS: Asst Prof, Kentucky State Univ, 1976; Staff Assoc in Empl Policy, Brookings Inst-Wash DC, 1977; and (since 1978) Assoc Prof and Director, Labor and Ind Rels Inst, North Texas State Univ. ADDRESS: 1320 Churchill, Denton, TX 76201. 817/565-3445

McKELVEY, JEAN T. Acad: Ind Rels; Arbitration, Government. BA 1929, Wellesley Coll; MA 1931, PhD 1933, Radcliffe Coll. PUBL: AFL Attitudes Toward Production; The Duty of Fair Representation, (editor); "Arbitrators on Arbitration," (chapter). INT: arb/med, coll barg, labor law. ASSN: NAA, Intl Soc for Labor Law and Soc Legislation, SFLRP. POSITIONS: Member, Public Rev Bd, UAW, 1968 to present; Member, Federal Serv Impasses Panel, 1979 to present; and (since 1946) Professor, NYSSILR, Cornell Univ. ADDRESS: 53 Aberthaw Rd, Rochester, NY 14610. 716/428-9906

McKENNA, ALEX Bus:Pers/Ind Rels. BS 1962, U of Buffalo; MS 1983, Niagara U. INT: coll barg, mgmt/educ, empl/trng programs. ASSN: Western New York IRRA. POSITIONS: Ind Rels Supr, Continental Can, 1962; and (since 1970) Vice Pres Ind Rels, Monogram Industries Inc, 1299 Ocean Ave, Santa Monica, CA 90401.213/451-0681

McKERSIE, ROBERT B. Acad: Ind Rels. ADDRESS: Sloan School of Management, MIT, Cambridge, MA 02139. 617/253-2671

McKEW, JOHN J. Bus:Mgmt/Admin. BA 1955, Manhatten Coll; LLB 1958, NYU. INT: coll barg, personnel, labor history. ASSN: New York IRRA, NYS Bar Assn, New York Pers Mgmt Assn. POSITION: Director, Admin Services, New York Zoological Society, 185th St & Southern Blvd, Bronx, NY 10460. 212/220-5113

McKINNEY, EDWARD C. Public School Admin. BA 1951, Grinnell Coll; MAT 1955, Harvard. INT: personnel, coll barg, arb/med. ASSN: Mid-Mich IRRA, Mich Assn of School Admin, Mich Negotiators Assn, AAA. POSITIONS: Supt of Schools, Baldwin, Mich, Community School, 1971; Supt of Schools, Yellow Springs Schools, Ohio, 1975; and (since 1980) Asst Supt, Waverly Community Schools, 515 Snow Rd, Lansing, MI 48917. 517/321-7265

McKONE, FREDERICK W. Arbitration, Legal Prac. BS 1940, Conn State U; PhD 1955, Yale U; JD 1968, U of Conn. INT: arb/med, labor law. ASSN: Conn Valley IRRA, ABA (Commission on Airline & Railroad Law), Conn Bar Assn (Empl & Labor Law), SPIDR. POSITIONS: Prof, 1949, Prof Emeritus, 1971, Connecticut State U-Science Dept; and (since 1969) Attorney (sole practitioner), 25 Maple St, PO Box 267, Rockville, CT 06066. 203/871-2898

McLAIN, JAMES M. Acad: Econ, Ind Rels. BA 1940, U of Akron; MA 1942, Western Reserve U; PhD 1959, Ohio State U. POSITION: Prof Emeritus, U of Akron. ADDRESS: 2192 Coon Road, Copley, OH 44321.

McLAUCHLAN, J. MICHAEL Acad: Economics. INT: labor market econ, empl/trng programs, coll barg. ASSN: AEA, Southern Econ Assn, Assn for Evolutionary Sciences. POSITIONS: Asst Prof of Econ, U of Louisville, 1979; and (since 1981) Asst Prof of Econ and Finance, Univ of Southwestern Louisiana, Box 44570, Lafayette, LA 70504. 318/231-5727

McLAUGHLIN, DORIS B. Acad: Ind Rels, Labor History. PhD 1973, U of Mich. PUBL: Michigan Labor, A Brief History From 1818 To The Present; "Putting Michigan Back to Work: Bill Haber Remembers the 1930's;" "Electronics & The Future of Work." INT: coll barg, technology & jobs, labor history. ASSN: Econ History Soc, Mich Labor History Soc. POSITION: (since 1973) Assoc Res Scientist, ILIR, Univ of Mich, Benz Bldg, 130 S 1st, Ann Arbor, MI 48103. 313/763-9427

McLAUGHLIN, FRANCIS M. Acad: Econ, Ind Rels. BS 1954, MA 1957, Boston Coll; PhD 1964, MIT. PUBL: "Findings of a Process Evaluation of the STIP Program," N.E. J of Emp & Trng, Winter 1981; "CETA and the Private Sector," in Harrington P.E. et al, Current Issues in Emp & Training Policy, 1980; Evaluating The Performance of Emp & Training policy at th Local Level, (A. Sum et al) 1978. INT: labor market econ, empl/trng programs, coll barg. ASSN: Boston IRRA, AEA. POSITION: (since 1968) Assoc Prof of Econ, Boston College, Carney 130, Chestnut Hill, MA 02167. 617/552-3675

McLEAN, BETH MAIR 1983, St. Francis Coll. INT: labor law, arb/med, coll barg. ADDRESS: 12 Highland Park, Massena, NY 13662. 518/472-4821

McLENNAN, KENNETH Foundations. BSc 1957, U of London; MBA 1961, U of Toronto; PhD 1965, U of Wis. POSITION: (since 1968) Director, Ind Studies, Committee for Econ Develop, 1700 K St NW, Suite 700, Washington DC 20006. 202/296-5860

McMAHON, BERNARD J. Bus:Ind Rels. POSITION: Corporate Director, Emp Rels and Services, Aerospace Corp A-2-1005, PO Box 92957, Los Angeles, CA 90009. 213/648-6730

McMAHON, JUNE Union. INT: arb/med, labor market econ. POSITION: Research Dir, Service Empl Intl Union, 2020 K St NW, Washington DC 20006. 202/452-8750

McMANEMIN, JOSEPH P. Legal Prac. BS 1948, Manhatten Coll; MA 1949, Columbia U; DJ 1957, Wayne State U; LLM 1962, NYU. PUBL: Article: CCH Labor Law J-Subject Matter of Coll Barg; Article: Personnel-Labor Turnover. INT: labor law, coll barg, arb/med. ASSN: New York IRRA, New Jersey State Bar Assn, Passaic County Bar Assn. POSITIONS: Dir of Ind Rels, Amer Home Products Corp, 1959; and (since 1972) Attorney (self-employed), Suite 505, 45 N Broad St, Ridgewood, NJ 07450. 201/444-0654

McMILLAN, WILLIAM R. Acad: Retired; Consulting. BS 1948, Cornell; MA 1949, Columbia. INT: health & hosp care, labor market econ, arb/med. ADDRESS: 2701 N Martin Ave, Tucson, AZ 85719.

McMONIGLE, BERNARD Arbitration; Student. BBA 1971, U of Ga; MS 1977, American U; JD 1984, U of the Pacific. PUBL: "Solar-Energy of the Future," The AFL-CIO Amer Federalist, Mar 1978. INT: arb/med, labor law, coll barg. ASSN: AAA. POSITIONS: Assoc Res Dir, Sheet Metal Workers Intl Assn, 1972; Mediator, FMCS, 1977; and (since 1983) Arbitrator. ADDRESS: 1100 Silver Lake Dr, Sacramento, CA 95831. 916/392-8327

McMULLAN, JAMES Arbitration. BA 1983, Antioch U. INT: arb/med, coll barg, labor law. ASSN: Philadelphia IRRA, SPIDR. POSITION: (since 1981) Arbitrator, 5018 Copley Rd, Philadelphia, PA 19144. 215/438-2814

McNAMARA, BERTRAM N. Union. Coll Work: 1931-33, Fort Wayne Art School; 1933 Beau Arts Inst of Design. INT: coll barg, union org/admin, labor educ. ASSN: Wis IRRA, Betta Gamma Sigma Bus & Commerce Honor Soc. POSITIONS: Labor Tech Officers, US Aid Mission to India, 1961-63; Staff Rep, 1963-65, and, 1965, Dir Dist #32, United Steelworkers of Amer, Retired. ADDRESS: 4646 N Sheffield Ave, Milwaukee, WI 53211. 414/964-9468

McNEIL, PAUL J., JR. Union, Writer/Journalism. INT: coll barg, labor educ, labor history. ASSN: Greater Rhode Island IRRA, Intl Assn on Soc Welfare, R.I. Conference on Soc Work. POSITIONS: Treasurer, New England Chapter, Local 189 Workers Educ,; Claims Examiner, R.I. Dept of Empl Security, 1979; and (since 1980) Recording Sec, Local 401, R. I. Empl Security Alliance, SEIU, PO Box 945, Annex Station, Providence, RI 02901. 401/831-2081

McNICHOLS, JAMES F. Bus:Pers/Ind Rels. BA 1973, U of Notre Dame; MBA 1975, U of Mich. INT: coll barg, arb/med, mgmt/educ. ASSN: ASPA. POSITIONS: Mgr, Professional Staffing, B. F. Goodrich Co, 1978; Labor Rels Supr, 1979, and, since 1981, Pers Superintendent, Monsanto Co, 5045 W Jefferson Ave, Trenton, MI 48183. 313/676-4400

McPHEE, JOAN MELVILLE Acad: Bus Admin/Mgmt. POSITION: Sr Lecturer, Chisholm Inst, David Syme Bus School, PO Box 197, Caulfield East, Victoria 3145 Australia.

McPHERSON, DONALD S. Acad: Ind Rels; Arbitration, Consulting. BA 1969, MA 1971, Ind U of Penna; PhD 1977, U of Pittsburgh. PUBL: Resolving Grievances, Reston Publ Co, 1983; "Union Leader Responses to California's WSUI Program," BNA Daily Labor Report, 102, May 28, 1981, D1-D10; "Unionism's Effect on Faculty Pay," Monthly Labor Rev, 103, June 1980, 34-36. INT: arb/med, labor history, personnel. ASSN: Western Penna IRRA, IIRA, Penna Labor History Soc, Assn of Penna State Coll and Univ Faculty. POSITIONS: Dir of Residence Life/Asst Prof, 1969, and, since 1977, Prof of Ind and Labor Rels, Indiana Univ of Penna. ADDRESS: 240 Oriole Ave, Indiana, PA 15701. 412/357-4470

McPHERSON, WILLIAM HESTON Arbitration. AB 1923, Harvard; MA 1924, Ohio State U; PhD 1935, U of Chicago. PUBL: Labor Relations in the Automobile Industry; The French Labor Courts: Judgement by Peers (w F. Ungers); Public Employee Relations in West Germany. INT: arb/med, coll barg, intl comparative labor. ASSN: AEA, NSS, IIRA. POSITIONS: Principal Economist, War Manpower Comm, 1942; Chairman. Shipbuilding Comm, War Labor Bd, 1943; and (since 1971) Professor Emeritus ILIR, Univ of Ill, 504 E Armory Ave, Champaign, IL 61821. 217/333-2381

McPHILLIPS, DAVID C. Acad: Ind Rels. POSITION: Univ of British Columbia, 203-2053 Main Mall, Vancouver BC V6T 1W5 Canada. 604/734-5493

McSHANE, STEVEN L. Acad: Bus Admin. POSITION: School of Bus, Queen's Univ, Kingston, Ont K7L 3N6 Canada.

McWILLIAMS, SHAUN W. Acad: Student; Health Care, Compensation/Salary Admin. BSLE 1981, U of Akron; MLIR 1983, Mich State Univ. INT: health & hosp care, compensation, personnel. ASSN: Amer Soc of Hosp Pers Admin. POSITION: (since 1983) Wage & Salary Analyst, Timken Mercy Medical Center, Canton. ADDRESS: 1818 Stabler Rd, Akron, OH 44313. 216/489-1025

McWOLD, RONALD R. Government. INT: health & hosp care; arb/med, empl/trng programs. ASSN: New Brunswick IRRA, NJ Hosp Pers Officers Assn. POSITIONS: Asst Pers Officer, 1974, and, since 1976, Personnel Officer, VA Medical Center, Lyons. ADDRESS: PO Box 352, White House Station, NJ 08889. 201/-647-0180

MEAD, JOHN FORD Acad: Econ. POSITION: Professor, Econ Dept, School of Business, Univ of Louisville, Louisville, KY 40292.

MEAD, JOHN P. Arbitration. BA 1934, U of Ill; JD 1937, U of Mich. INT: arb/med, govt labor policy, labor law. ASSN: Fla IRRA, AAA, NAA. POSITIONS: V.P., Ind Rels, Transworld Airlines, 1945, V.P. Ind Rels, Eastern Airlines, 1964-75 (Retired); and, currently, Arbitrator, 550 Ocean Dr, Key Biscayne, FL 33149. 305/361-9489

MEADER, LELAND V. Bus:Pers/Ind Rels. POSITION: Vice Pres, Empl Rels, Schwinn Bicycle Co, 1856 N Kostner Ave, Chicago, IL 60639. 312/227-3000

MEALS, RUTH L. Bus:Pers/Ind Rels. 495 Cherry Ct, Pittsburgh, PA 15237.

MEANY, PETER MICHAEL Bus:Pers/Ind Rels. BA 1971, Canisius Coll; MS 1974, Purdue U. INT: coll barg, arb/med, labor law. ASSN: New York IRRA. POSITIONS: Ind Rels Analyst, Intl Paper, 1974; Asst VP Ind Rels, Anchor Motor Freight, 1978; and (since 1979) Manager Labor Rels, The Nestle Co, 100 Bloomingdale Rd, White Plains, NY 10605. 914/682-6715

MECK, JUDITH Bus:Pers/Ind Rels. POSITION: Senior Labor Rels Rep, Kaiser Permanente Medical, 4747 Sunset Blvd, Los Angeles, CA 90027. 213/667-8481

MEDOFF, JAMES L. Acad: Econ. POSITION: Dept of Econ, Harvard Univ, Cambridge, MA 02138. 617/495-4209

MEEKS, JOHN R. Bus:Pers/Ind Rels. POSITION: Pers Dir, B. J. Hughes Machinery Div, 10777 NW Freeway, Suite 500, Houston, TX 77092.

MEER, CLAUDIA GAILLARD Acad: Ind Rels. BS 1973, Cornell; MA 1974, U of Ill; EdD 1982, Rutgers U. PUBL: Customer Education, Nelson-Hall, 1984; "Company Sponsored Tuition Assistance Programs: A Review of the Research and Literature," Lifelong Learning: The Adult Years, col IV, #4, Dec 1980; Sex Role Stereotyping in Occupational Choices, Rutgers U, 1982. INT: adult educ, empl/trng programs, mgmt/educ. ASSN: New Brunswick IRRA, Amer Assn of Adult and Continuing Educ, Amer Soc for Trng & Develop, Natl Univ Continuing Educ Assn. POSITION: (since 1974) Assoc Extension Specialist, Rutgers Univ, Inst of Mgmt and Labor Rels. ADDRESS: 742 Butternut Dr F, Franklin Lakes, NJ 07417. 201/932-9232

MEGLEY, JOHN E. Acad: Ind Rels. AB 1957, U of Ill; MBA 1963, Roosevelt U-Chicago; PhD 1970, U of Mo-Columbia. INT: arb/med, coll barg, personnel. ASSN: AIDS. POSITIONS: Prof, Southern Ill Univ-Edwardsville, 1969; Prof, Sangamon State Univ, 1980; and (since 1981) Professor, Univ of Scranton, Scranton, PA 18510. 717/344-7475

MEHL, DEBORAH KAY Bus:Pers/Ind Rels. BA 1976, Wichita State U; MA 1979, U of Ill. INT: personnel, coll barg, org beh. ASSN: ASPA. POSITIONS: Ind Rels Mgr, General Cable Co, 1978; and (since 1982) Regional Personnel Mgr, Pizza Hut Inc, Suite 380, 6445 Powers Ferry Rd, Atlanta, GA 30339. 404/955-3030

MEIER, ANNE L. Legal Counsel. BA 1974, Hanover Coll; JD 1979, U of Cincinnati. INT: arb/med, coll barg, labor law. ASSN: Wis IRRA, Wis Bar Assn, ABA, Southeastern Wis Assn of School Dist Negotiators. POSITIONS: Attorney, Nieman, Aug, Elder & Jacobs, Cincinnati, 1979; Asst Admin/Empl Rels, Kenosha Public Schools, 1979; and (since 1982) Asst Exec Dir/-Employee Rels, Milwaukee Public Schools, PO Drawer 10K, Milwaukee, WI 53201. 414/475-8381

MEIER, ELIZABETH L. Government. 1647 Bentano Way, Reston, VA 22090.

MEISLER, GEORGE Acad: Adjunct Prof. BA 1976, Thomas A. Edison State Coll. INT: arb/med, labor educ, labor history. ASSN:

New Brunswick IRRA, SPIDR, AAA, Assn of Labor Rels Agencies. POSITIONS: Board Member, NJ State Bd of Mediation, 1969; Pres-Chief Exec Officer, United Food & Commercial Workers Union Local 21, AFL-CIO, 1958-76, Pres Emeritus, (Retired) UFCWU Local 21. ADDRESS: 21 Deerfield Ave, Piscataway, NJ 08854.201/463-9195

MELAMED, JEROME Government. BS 1948, Temple U; MBA 1951, U of Penna. POSITIONS: Secy-Treas, Loca 190, ILGWU, 1953-67; and (since 1967) Dir, Labor Rels, School Dist of Phila. ADDRESS: 6632 Greene St, Philadelphia, PA 19119. 215/438-3884

MELAS, NICHOLAS J. Government. BS 1948, MBA 1950, U of Chicago. PUBL: "The Prairie Plan-The First Decade, The Second Decade-The United States'Longest Recycling System," Prog Wat Tech, Vol 11, #5, pp 331-340, Pergamon Press, 1980. INT: govt labor policy, coll barg. ASSN: Chicago IRRA, Amer Acad of Pol and Soc Sci. POSITIONS: Res Assoc and Project Dir, Ind Rels Center, Univ of Chicago, 1951; Commissioner of Weights and Measures, 1961, and, since 1975, President, Board of Commissioners, Metropolitan Sanitary Dist of Greater Chicago, 100 E Erie St, Chicago, IL 60611. 312/751-5700

MELI, JOHN THOMAS Acad: Univ Admin. MBA 1961, PhD 1971, U of Penna. INT: coll barg, empl/trng programs, labor history. ASSN: AEA, Acad of Mgmt. POSITIONS: Asst Prof, St. Joseph's Univ, 1957; Asst Prof, 1966, and, since 1971, Dean, School of Management, Widener Univ. ADDRESS: 505 Cricket LA, Media,PA 19063. 215/499-4300

MELIS, PATRICIA A. Bus:Pers/Ind Rels. INT: personnel, mgmt/educ, empl/trng programs. ASSN: Long Island IRRA, Assn of Hosp Pers Admin, Amer Soc Hosp Pers Admin. POSITIONS: Dir of Pers, North Shore Univ Hosp, 1973; Dir of Pers, St. John's Episcopal Hosp, 1980; and (since 1982) Director of Pers, Consolation Residence, 111 Beach Dr, West Islip, NY 11795. 516/587-1600 ext 29

MELNICK, HAROLD H. Union. POSITION: Exec Asst, City Employees Union #237, 216 W 14th St, New York, NY 10011.

MELNYK, ANTON M. Legal Practice. BA 1961, LLB 1962, U of Alberta; LLM 1963, Harvard. INT: arb/med, labor law. ASSN: SPIDR. POSITION: Partner, Melnyk, McCord & Meiklejohn, 11054 86th Ave, Edmonton, Alberta T6G 0W9 Canada. 403/432-7464

MELOON, JAMES ALLEN Dispute Resolution, Consulting/Trng. BA 1968, SUNY-Buffalo; MILR 1969, NYSSILR-Cornell. INT: arb/med/negotiations, org beh/HRD/QWL, Labor Mgmt Committees/Empl Participation. ASSN: ASTD. POSITIONS: Consultant, SUNY Res Foundation, Buffalo, 1982; Adjunct Prof/Community Educ, Niagara Cty Community Coll, Sanborn, NY 1983, and, since 1983, Dispute Settlement Specialist, The Dispute Settlement Center, Buffalo. ADDRESS: 11 Wellington Ave, Buffalo, NY 14223. 716/842-1416

MELTZ, NOAH MOSHE Acad: Econ, Ind Rels, Org Beh/Pers. BCom 1957, U of Toronto; AM 1960, PhD 1964, Princeton U. PUBL: Economic Analysis of Labour Shortages: The Case of Tool and Die Makers in Ontario, Toronto: Ont Econ Council, 1982; Shaping The Work: An Analysis of the Issues in Worksharing and Jobsharing, (w F. Reid & G. Swartz), Toronto: Univ of Toronto Press, 1981; Personnel Management in Canada, (w T. Stone), Toronto: Holt, Rinehart & Winston, 1983. INT: labor market econ, empl/trng programs, personnel. ASSN: Canadian Ind Rels Assn, Canadian Econ Assn, Amer Econ Assn. POSITIONS: Economist, Econ and Res Branch, Dept of Labour, Government of Canada, 1969; and (since 1964) Professor of Econ and Ind Rels and Dir, Centre for Ind Rels, Univ of Toronto, 123 St. George St, Toronto, Ont M5S 1A1 Canada. 416/978-5398

MELTZER, BERNARD D. Acad: Law. POSITION: Distinguished Service Professor, Univ of Chicago Law School, 1111 E 60th St, Chicago, IL 60637. 312/753-2448

MENARD, ARTHUR Legal Practice. Morgan, Brown & Joy, 1 Boston PL, Boston, MA 02108.

MENEFEE, MICHAEL L. Acad: Org Beh/Pers. POSITION: Dept of Business Mgmt, Tennessee Technological Univ, Campus PO Box 5022, Cookeville, TN 38501. 615/528-3727

MENEZ, JOSEPH ROBERT Government. BA 1970, Oglethorpe Coll; MS 1974, U of Utah. INT: labor market econ, labor law, empl/trng programs. POSITIONS: Field Operations Officer, 1977, Deputy Asst Reg Admin, Pension & Welfare Benefit Programs, and, since 1983, Area Admin, Labor Mgmt Services Adm, USDL, Ft. Wright. ADDRESS: 2712 Wesley Dr, Villa Hills, KY 41017. 513/684-2227

MERCER, WALTER JAMES Government. POSITION: Regional Attorney, Federal Bldg, 29th Floor, 915 Second Ave, Seattle, WA 98174. 206/442-7543

MERCHANT, CHRISTINA SICKLES Mediation. BS 1971, NYSSILR-Cornell. INT: arb/med, coll barg, labor law. ASSN: Philadelphia IRRA, SPIDR, SFLRP, Cornell Club. POSITIONS: Fed Labor Mgmt Rels Specialist, USDL, 1971; and (since 1975) Federal Mediator, FMCS, Room 3456, Wm. J. Green Bldg, 600 Arch St, Philadelphia, PA 19106. 215/597-4796

MERCIER, JACQUES Acad: Ind Rels. BA 1972, U of Ottawa; MA 1975, Laval U; PhD 1983, U of Ill-UC. INT: empl/trng programs, labor market econ. ASSN: Canadian Ind Rels Assn. POSITION: Asst Prof, Dept Rels Ind, University Laval, Quebec, PQ G1K 7P4 Canada. 418/656-5787

MERCIER, PIERRE Acad: Student; Union. DEC 1979, CEGEP Saint-Laurent. INT: govt labor policy, labor history, labor law. POSITION: Student, McGill Univ. ADDRESS: 3125 Barclay, Apt 3, Montreal PQ H3S 1K2 Canada.

MERICLE, KENNETH Acad: Labor Educ, Ind Rels; Consulting. BS 1967, MS 1969, Iowa State U; PhD 1974, U of Wis-Madison. PUBL: The Political Economy of the Latin American Motor Vehicle Industry, (co-editor and author); "Physical Fatigue and Stresses in Warehouse Operations;" "Corporatist Control of the Working Class: Authoritarian Brazil Since 1964." INT: labor educ, coll barg, intl comparative labor. ASSN: Univ and Coll Labor Educ Assn. POSITIONS: Asst Prof Ind Rels, Sloan School-MIT, 1973; and (since 1979) Asst Prof Labor Educ, School for Workers, Univ of Wis. ADDRESS: 2325 E Dayton, Madison, WI 53704. 608/262-2111

MERISALO, CARL B. Bus:Pers/Ind Rels. BS 1948, U of Wis; MBA 1952, U of Chicago. INT: coll barg, personnel. ASSN: Wis IRRA, Natl Foundry Assn. POSITIONS: Asst Pers Dir, Rheem Mfg Co, 1955; Ind Rels Mgr, Wm Kratt Co, 1959; and (since 1973) Manager, Ind Rels and Pers, Quality Aluminum Casting Co, 1242 Lincoln Ave, Waukesha, WI 53187. 414/542-0731

MERKER, GEORGE E. Legal Practice. BS 1974, Ill State U; MBA 1976, U of Neb-Lincoln; JD 1980, U of Ill. INT: labor law, coll barg, union org/admin. ASSN: Northwest IRRA, ABA, Wash State Bar Assn, Amer Trial Lawyers Assn. POSITIONS: Attorney, Goddard & Wetherall, Inc. P.S., 1981; and (since 1983) Attorney, Reaugh & Prescott, P.S., 3000 Westin Bldg, 2001 6th Ave, Seattle, WA 98121. 206/622-3000

MERLO, THEODORE C., JR. Bus:Mgmt/-Admin. AB 1981, Lafayette Coll. INT: ind sociol, org beh, ind psych. ASSN: Amer Production & Inventory Control Soc. POSITION: Production Scheduler, 1983, and, since 1984, Senior Production Planner, Teradyne Inc, Boston. ADDRESS: 36 Hillside Rd, Wellesley Hills, MA 02181. 617/482-2700

MERRIFIELD, LEROY S. Acad: Law, Ind Rels; Arbitration. LLB 1941, U of Minn; MPA 1942, SJD 1956, Harvard. PUBL: Labor Relations Law, (w Smith & St. Antoine); Collective Bargaining & Labor Relations, (w Rothschild & Edwards). INT: labor law, arb/med, intl comparative labor. ASSN: Wash DC IRRA, ABA(Labor & Empl Law Section), IIRA, Intl Soc for Labor Law and Soc Security. POSITION: (since 1947) Lobingier Prof of Jurisprudence and Comparative Law, Natl Law Center, George Washington Univ, Washington DC 20052. 202/676-6745

MESCH, CRAIG R. BA 1969, MSIR 1971, Loyola U; JD 1978, Lewis U. ADDRESS: 1326 W Wincrest, Winona, MN 55987.

METCALF, CHARLES E. Consulting. POSITION: Director of Research, MPR Inc, PO Box 2393, Princeton, NJ 08540.

METZGER, NORMAN Bus:Mgmt/Admin; Acad: Ind Rels. BBA 1948, Baruch Coll-CCNY; MA 1954, Columbia U. PUBL: Handbook of Health Care Human Resources Management; The Arbitration and Grievance Process; The Health Care Supervisor's Handbook, Second Ed. INT: coll barg, health & hosp care, mgmt/-educ. ASSN: New York IRRA, Amer Soc of Hosp Admin, Assn of Hosp Pers Admin, Medical Center Empl Rels Assn. POSITIONS: VP-Pers, 1960, and, since 1970, Vice Pres for Labor Rels, Mount Sinai Medical Center, 1 Gustave L Levy Pl, New York, NY 10029. 212/650-6226

MEYER, DAVID GLENN Acad: Bus/Mgmt POSITION: Dept of Management, Univ of Alabama, University, AL 35486. 205/348-6090

MEYER, GORDON WILLIAM Acad: Student, Org Beh/Pers, Ind Rels; Consulting. BA 1973, U of Del; MOB 1979, Brigham Young U. PUBL: "Organization Development: A Closer Scrutiny," (w W. Woodworth, & W. N. Smallwood), Human Rels, 35, pp 307-319, 1982. INT: org beh, union org/admin, ind sociol. ASSN: Acad of Mgmt. POSITIONS: Org Devel Intern, Clark Equip Co, 1978; QWL Consultant, General Motors Corp, 1980; and (since 1981) Grad Student, NYSSIRL-Cornell. ADDRESS: 1021 E State St, Ithaca, NY 14850. 607/272-5498

MEYER, RICHARD F. Bus:Labor Rels. POSITION: Labor Rels/Risk Mgmt, Mass Port Authority, 99 High St, 14th Floor, Boston, MA 02110. 617/482-2930

MEYERS, FREDERIC Acad: Ind Rels; Arbitration. PhD 1941, U of N.C. PUBL: Ownership of Jobs, Los Angeles, UCLA Inst of Ind Rels; "The Analytic Meaning of Seniority," Proceedings, IRRA 1965; "France," chapter in A. A. Blum (ed) International Handbook of Ind Rels, Greenwood Press, 1981. INT: intl comparative labor, coll barg, arb/med. POSITIONS: Asst/-Assoc Prof of Econ, U of Tex-Austin, 1948; Prof of Ind Rels, 1958, and, since 1980, Prof Emeritus, UCLA. ADDRESS: 529 Marsh Cir, St. Simons Island, GA 31522. 912/638-8370

MICALLEF, CHARLES N. Arbitration. 320 W Woodruff, #222, Toledo, OH 43625.

MICELI, MARCIA PARMERLEE Acad: Org /Beh/Pers, Ind Rels. DBA 1982, Ind U. PUBL: "Beliefs, Position Characteristics and Whistle-Blowing Status," Proceedings, IRRA, Dec 1983; "Why Realistic Job Previews Cannot Meet Our Unrealistically High Expectations," Proceedings, Acad of Mgmt, Aug 1983; "Correlates of Whistle-Blowers Perception of Organizational Retaliation," Admin Sci Quart, 1982. INT: pers, org beh, ind psych. ASSN: Central Ohio IRRA, Acad of Mgmt, Amer Psych Assn, ASPA. POSITIONS: Tax Law Specialist, Empl Plans, Internal Revenue Serv, 1975; Lecturer of A & BS, Indiana Univ, 1977; and (since 1981) Asst Prof, MHR Dept, Ohio State Univ, 1775 College Rd, Columbus, OH 43210. 614/422-2809

MICHAELSON, RITA C. Arbitration. AB 1950, Brown U. INT: arb/med, labor educ. ASSN: Greater Rhode Island IRRA, AAA, R.I. Advisory Council, Inst for Labor Studies & Res. POSITIONS: Commissioner, R. I. Human Rights Commission, 1972; and (since 1973) Arbitrator, 78 Lorraine Ave, Providence, RI 02906. 401/861-3056

MIHARA, YASUHIRO Acad: Ind Rels. MB 1964, Kobe Univ. INT: coll barg, personnel, org beh. POSITIONS: Asst Prof, 1967; Assoc Prof, 1971, and, since 1980, Professor, Faculty of Econ, Nagasaki Univ, 4 Katafuchi, Nagasaki 850 Japan. Phone: 0958/26-8231

MIKAN, KURT W. Acad: Org Beh/Pers, Ind Rels. BA 1967, Mich State U; MBA 1974, Cleveland State U. INT: empl/trng programs, org beh, method/statis. ASSN: Acad of Mgmt, Southern Mgmt Assn, AIDS. POSITION: (since 1980) Asst Prof, Univ of Montevallo. ADDRESS: 2350 Mountain Oaks Ln, Birmingham, AL 35226. 205/665-2521

MIKRUT, JOHN JOSEPH JR. Acad: Econ; Arbitration. MLIR 1968, U of Mass; EdD 1976, U of Mo-Columbia. INT: arb/med, labor educ. ASSN: St. Louis and Kansas City IRRA, SPIDR, NAA, Univ/Coll Labor Educ Assn. POSITIONS: Asst Prof of Labor Studies, Penna State Univ, 1968; and (since 1969) Assoc Prof, Labor Program, Univ of Missouri, 1004 Elm St, Columbia, MO 65201. 314/882-4074

MILES, RAYMOND EDWARD Acad: Bus Admin. BA 1954, MBA 1958, North Tex State; PhD 1963, Stanford. PUBL: Organizational Strategy, Structure and Process; Theories of Management; Organizations by Design. INT: org beh, personnel, mgmt/educ. ASSN: Acad of Mgmt. POSITIONS: Prof & Assoc Dir, 1970, Prof & Dir Inst of Ind Rels, 1982, and, since 1983, Dean, School of Business, 350 Barrows Hall, Univ of California, Berkeley, CA 94720. 415/642-3860

MILJUS, ROBERT C. Acad: Ind Rels. BA 1955, Augustana Coll-Rock Island; MA 1957, U of Ill; PhD 1963, U of Wis. PUBL: Union-Management Relations in the Nation's Bituminous Coal Industry: Lessons for the Future, (w. A.C. Campagna, J. Kim, & C. J. Slanicka), Published O.S.U. Res Found, 1982. INT: coll barg, personnel, org behavior. ASSN: Central Ohio IRRA, Acad of Mgmt. POSITION: Professor, Management & Human Resources, Ohio State Univ, 1775 S College Rd, Columbus, OH 43210. 614/422-4587

MILKE, TOM Consulting. MA 1977, U of Ill. INT: empl/trng programs, method/statis, labor market econ. POSITIONS: Systems Analyst, Center for Advanced Computation, U of Ill, 1970; and (since 1979) Senior Systems Analyst, Westat Inc, 1650 Research Blvd, Rockville, MD 20850. 301/251-1500

MILKOVICH, GEORGE THOMAS Acad: Org Beh/Pers. PhD 1970 U of Minn. PUBL: Compensation, (w J. Newman), BPI Plano, Tex, 1983; Personnel Management: A Diagnostic Approach, BPI, Plano, Tex, 1982. INT: personnel. ASSN: Acad of Mgmt, Human Resources, Planning Soc. POSITION: Prof & Chairman, ILR School, Pers/Human Resources Dept, Cornell Univ, Ithaca, NY 14853. 607/256-7785

MILLEN, BRUCE H. Government. Apt 308, 3601 Connecticut Ave NW, Washington DC 20009.

MILLER, ALICE R. Acad: Univ Admin, Org Beh/Pers. BS 1975, NYSSILR, MS 1976, Cornell. INT: personnel, org beh, empl/trng programs. ASSN: Empl Mgmt Assn, CUPA, Amer Compensation Assn. POSITIONS: Pers Supr, Operations, SCM Corp, 1978; Mgr, Staffing Services, 1979, Asst Dir, Univ Pers Services, Cornell Univ, 130 Day Hall, Ithaca, NY 14853. 607/256-5226

MILLER, CHRISTOPHER S. Acad: Ind Rels, Law, Econ. Student. BS 1978, JD 1981, Syracuse U. PUBL: "Evaluating the Older Worker: Use of Employee Appraisal Systems in Age Discrimination Litigation," Aging and Work, 4(4), 229-243, Fall 1981; "Performance Evaluations As Evidence in HDEA Cases," Empl Rels Law J, 6(4) 561-583, Spring 1981; "A Study of Union-Management Cooperation in the United States," USDL (in press). INT: labor law, coll barg, personnel. ASSN: Central New York IRRA, Acad of Mgmt, ABA(section on Labor & Empl Law), Natl Council on Aging. POSITION: (since 1981) Res Asst/PhD Candidate, School of Mgmt, Syracuse Univ, Syracuse, NY 13210. 315/423-2601

MILLER, DONALD E. Bus:Pers/Ind Rels, Arbitration, Bus:Mgmt/Admin. BS 1967, U of Pittsburgh; MIR 1984, St. Francis. INT: personnel, arb/med, coll barg. ASSN: Pittsburgh Pers Assn. POSITIONS: Super, Columbia Gas of Penna, Inc, 1971; Owner, Miller-Snyder Remodeling Inc, 1974; and (since 1977) Dist Pers Mgr, Columbia Gas of Penna, Inc., 107 West Main St, Uniontown, PA 15401. 412/439-7915

MILLER, EDWARD J. Bus:Pers/Ind Rels; Acad: Ind Rels. BS/BA 1959, MBA 1962, Xavier U. PUBL: "First-Line Supervisors: The Key to Improved Performance," Mgmt Rev, Dec 1980. INT: coll barg, personnel, arb/med. ASSN: San Francisco IRRA. POSITIONS: Pers Mgr, Union Hardware Operations, 1963; Ind Rels Mgr, Brunswick Corp, 1964; and (since 1968) Vice Pres, Ind Rels/Pers, Tri/Valley Growers, PO Box 3327, Modesto, CA 95353. 209/526-4676

MILLER, EDWIN LEROY Acad: Org Beh/Pers. PUBL: Management of Human Resources, Prentice Hall, 1980: "Managerial Qualifications of Personnel Occupying Overseas Positions," J of Intl Bus Studies, 1977; "Influences on Overseas Subsidiary Decision Making," Mgmt Intl Rev, 1981. INT: personnel, intl human res mgmt, org beh. ASSN: Acad of Mgmt, Amer Psych Assn, Acad of Intl Bus. POSITION: (since 1964) Professor, Grad School of Bus Admin, Univ of Mich, Ann Arbor, MI 48109. 313/764-1408

MILLER, GLENN W. Acad: Econ, Ind Rels. BEd 1934, Southern Ill U; AM 1935, PhD 1939, U of Ill. PUBL: Government Policy Toward Labor; The Practice of Local Union Leadership, (joint author); Problems of Labor. INT: govt labor policy, coll barg, arb/med. ASSN: Columbus IRRA. POSITIONS: Prof, Ohio State U, 1939; Prof, Wichita State U, 1969; Retired. ADDRESS: 1822 Ardleigh Rd, Columbus, OH 43221. 614/457-4463

MILLER, JAMES GORMLEY Acad: Librarian. AB 1936, U of Rochester; BS 1938, Columbia. PUBL: Collection Development and Management at Cornell: A Concluding Report, Cornell U Libraries, 1981; An Assessment and Reviews of the Programme of the Information Systems Unit of the Department of International Economic and Social Affairs, New York: United Nations, 1983. INT: information/library services, mgmt/educ. ASSN: Amer Soc for Information Sci, Amer Library Assn, New York Library Assn. POSITIONS: Deputy Chief, Central Library & Documentation, ILO, 1970; Dir of Libraries, 1975, and, since 1979, Prof Emeritus, Cornell U. ADDRESS: 7D Eastwood Commons, Ithaca, NY 14850. 607/256-7724

MILLER, JOHN WADE, JR. Consulting. AB 1941, Washington & Jefferson; PhD 1948, MIT. INT: personnel, coll barg, org beh. POSITIONS: VP, Central Serv, Dewey & Almy Chemical Div, W. R. Grace Co, 1950; VP, Corp Rels, B. F. Goodrich Co, 1963; and (since 1974) Exec Vice Pres, Organization Resources Counselors. ADDRESS: 425 E 58 St, 7C, New York, NY 10022. 212/719-3400

MILLER, JOYCE D. Union. POSITION: Vice Pres, ACTWU Social Services, 15 Union SQ, New York, NY 10003.

MILLER, KATHRYN S. Student. BA 1978, Allegheny Coll; MSIR 1979, West Va U. INT: labor & mgmt cooperative projects, personnel, org beh. ASSN: Central Ohio IRRA. POSITIONS: Assoc Pers Rep, Armco-Specialty Div, 1979-82; and (since 1982) PhD Candidate/Teaching Assoc, MHR Dept, Ohio State Univ. ADDRESS: 1649 Wyandotte Rd, Columbus, OH 43212. 614/422-2809

MILLER, LYNN 15906 Pasadero Dr, Houston, TX 77083.

MILLER, MOLLIE A. Government; Acad: Sociology. BA 1958, MA 1960, Boston U. INT: ind sociol, intl comparative labor, labor history. ASSN: New York IRRA, The Circle (Ind Rels), English-Speaking Union, Intl Assn of Pers in Empl Security. POSITIONS: Admin Asst,

John Rock Found, Medical School-Harvard, 1960; and (since 1980) Admin Asst-Secretary, New York State Dept of Labor. ADDRESS: 102-21 63rd Rd, Apt 25B, Forest Hills, NY 11375. 212/488-6721

MILLER, MONA Acad: Ind Rels; Arbitration. BA 1957, MA 1961, U of Rochester. INT: arb/-med, mgmt/educ, personnel. ASSN: Central NY & Western IRRAs, AAA, SPIDR, ASTD. POSITION: (since 1973) Ext Assoc, ILR, School, Cornell U, 305 Andrews St, Rochester, NY 14604. 716/428-9906

MILLER, R. BERKELEY Acad: Student, Sociology. AB 1974, U of Calif-Santa Cruz; MA 1979, PhD 1984, Brown Univ. INT: intl comparative labor, govt labor policy, ind sociology. ASSN: Amer Sociological Assn. POSITIONS: PhD Candidate & Teaching Asst, Brown U, 1977; and (since 1984) Asst Prof, New Coll of the Univ of South Florida. ADDRESS: 88 Pitman St, Providence, RI 02906. 401/863/2367

MILLER, RICHARD ULRIC Acad: Ind Rels; Arbitration. BBA 1958, U of Miami; MS 1960, PhD 1966, Cornell. PUBL: Collective Bargaining in Hospitals, (co-author), 1979; Canadian Labour in Transition, (co-author), 1971; "Patterns & Determinants of Union Growth in the Hospital Industry," (co-author), J of Labor Res, 1981. INT: coll barg, arb/med, intl comparative labor. ASSN: Wis IRRA, SPIDR. POSITIONS: Asst Prof of Ind Rels, School of Bus, SUNY-Buffalo, 1065-66; Dir, Ind Rels Res Inst, 1973-77, and, since 1971, Professor of Bus and Ind Rels, Grad School of Bus, Univ of Wis, 181 Bascom Hall, Madison, WI 53706. 608/263-7979

MILLER, ROBERT W. Acad: Psych. POSITION: Res Professor, 410 Knapp Hall, West Virginia Univ, Morgantown, WV 26506. 304/293-4201

MILLER, VERA Union. AB 1938, AM 1940, PhD 1947, U of Chicago. INT: coll barg, method/-statis, ind sociol. ASSN: New York IRRA, Amer Sociol Assn, Amer Assn for Public Opinion Res. POSITION: (since 1943) Vice Pres, Dir of Research, ACTWU, 15 Union Square, New York, NY 10003. 212/242-0700

MILLER, WALDO G. Bus:Pers/Ind Rels. BA 1949, Jamestown U. INT: coll barg, empl/-trng programs, arb/med. POSITIONS: Factory Pers Mgr, 1958, Asst Mgr, Ind Rels, 1972, Mgr, Ind Rels Research, 1976, and, since 1980, Manager, Pers/Labor Rels Research, Brown & Williamson Tobacco Corp, 1600 West Hill St, Louisville, KY 40232. 502/774-7703

MILLMAN, BRUCE R. Legal Practice. AB 1970, Princeton; JD 1973, Columbia U. INT: labor law, coll barg, arb/med. ASSN: Long Island IRRA, ABA, NY Bar Assn. POSITION: (since 1973) Partner, Rains & Pogrebin, P.C., 210 Old Country Rd, Mineola, NY 11501. 516/742-1470

MILLS, DANIEL QUINN Acad: Bus Admin; Consulting. BA 1963, Ohio Wesleyan U; MA 1965, PhD 1968, Harvard. PUBL: Labor Management Relations; Labor, Government and Inflation; "Human Resource Challenges of the 1980's." INT: coll barg, empl/trng programs, mgmt/educ. ASSN: AEA. POSITIONS: Chairman, Construction Industry Stabilization Committee, US Govern, 1971; Prof, MIT, 1968; and (since 1976) Prof of Bus Admin, Bus School, Harvard Univ, Morgan Hall 326, Soldiers Field Rd, Boston, MA 02163. 617/495-6206

MILLS, MIRIAM K. Acad: Ind Rels; Arbitration. BA 1964, CCNY; MPA 1969, PhD 1978, NYU. PUBL: "Impact of the Energy Laws on Labor Relations," Arb J, 12/80; "Containing Conflict: Teleconferencing & Labor Rels," Arb J, 6/83; "Luddits at the Terminal & Other Renegades Computer Generated Conflict Areas," J of Computers & the Law, 3/84. INT: arb/med, govt labor policy, health & hosp care. ASSN: New York IRRA, ASPA, AAA, World Futures Soc. POSITIONS: Pers Dir, Jewish Home & Hosp for Aged, 1965; Dir, Manpower & Labor Rels, Jersey City Medical Center, 1972; and (since 1975) Assoc Prof, NJ Inst of Tech, 323 High St, Newark, NJ 07102. 201/645-4977

MILMET, MORRIS Legal Practice. POSITION: Stern, Milmet, Vecchio, & Goll, Suite 700, 400 Renaissance Center, Detroit, MI 48243. 313/259-7070

MINAMOTO, JENNIFER N. Union. BS 1971, Colo State U; MBA 1979, George Washington U. INT: union org/admin, ind engineering. ASSN: Wash DC IRRA. POSITION: (since 1976) Assoc Dir of Res, Eastern Conf of Teamsters. ADDRESS: Apt 817, 4242 East-West Hwy, Chevy Chase, MD 20815. 301/656-6006

MINCER, JACOB Acad: Econ. BA 1950, Emory U; PhD 1957, Columbia U. PUBL: Schooling, Experience, and Earnings, Columbia Press 1974; "Labor Force Participationof Married Women," NBER, 1962; "Labor Mobility and Wages," NBER, 1981. INT: labor market econ. ASSN: AEA, ASA, ES. POSITIONS: Professor, 1964, and, since 1979, Buttenwieser Prof of Econ, Columbia Univ, SIA, New York, NY 10027. 212/280-3676

MINER, JOHN BURNHAM Acad: Org Beh/-Pers, Ind Rels, Psych. MA 1952, Clark U; PhD 1955, Princeton U. PUBL: Personnel and Industrial Relations: A Managerial Approach, 4th Ed, Macmillan, 1985; Theories of Organizational Structure and Process, Dryden, 1982; Theories of Organizational Behavior, Dryden, 1980. INT: personnel, org beh, ind psych. ASSN: Atlanta IRRA, Acad of Mgmt, Amer Psych Assn, Soc for Personality Assessment. POSITIONS: Prof, U of Oregon, 1960; Professor, Univ of Maryland, 1968; and, since 1973, Res Prof of Mgmt and Ind Rels, Georgia State Univ, University Plaza, Atlanta, GA 30303. 404/658-3404.

MINER, MARY GREEN Publishing. BA 1950, Cornell U. PUBL: Employee Selection Within the Law, BNA Books, 1978; Personnel and Industrial Relations, 3rd Ed, Macmillan, 1977; "Job Absence and Turnover: A New Source of Data," Monthly Labor Rev, Oct 1977. INT: intl comparative labor, personnel, EEO. ASSN: Wash DC IRRA, Acad of Mgmt, ASPA. POSITIONS: Dir, BNA Surveys, 1972, Mgr, BNA Books, 1979, and, since 1982, Director, BNA Books and Conferences, Bureau of Natl Affairs, 1231 25th St NW, Washington DC 20037. 202/-452-4130

MING, LEO HEZEKIAH JR. Bus:Pers/Ind Rels, Arbitration. BA 1980, Empire State Univ. INT: govt labor policy, labor history, coll barg. ASSN: Gateway IRRA. POSITIONS: VP, Chief Spokesman, Fed of Postal Security Police, 1973; Fed Counselor, Inspection Serv, 1979, and, since 1981, Labor Rels Rep, U.S. Postal Data Center, St. Louis. ADDRESS: 7840 Stanford, University City, MO 63130. 314/425-6145/-5431.

MINTER, MILTON M. Bus:Pers/Ind Rels. BA 1965, U of Ga. INT: coll barg, personnel, arb/med. ASSN: New Brunswick IRRA. POSITIONS: Pers mgr, 1973, Admin Staff Asst Labor Rels, 1976, and, since 1980, Senior Staff Rep, Nabisco Brands Inc, East Hanover. ADDRESS: 27 Molly Stark Dr, Morristown, NJ 07960. 201/884-4016.

MIRE, JOSEPH Acad: Ind Rels. PhD 1930, U of Vienna. POSITION: (currently) Exec Dir, Natl Inst of Labor Educ, 2944 University Terr NW, Washington DC 20016.

MIRENGOFF, WILLIAM Consulting. BA 1938, Brooklyn Coll; MA 1946, American U. PUBL: CETA: Accomplishments, Problems, Solutions; CETA: Manpower Programs Under Local Control; Transition to Decentralized Manpower Programs. INT: empl/trng programs, labor history, labor market econ. ASSN: ASPA. POSITION: Retired. Address: 4986 Sentinel Dr, Apt 202, Bethesda, MD 20816.

MIRON, YESHAYAHU Bus:Mgmt/Admin, Bus:Pers/Ind Rels. BA 1975, Bar-Ilan Univ. INT: coll barg, mgmt/educ, personnel. POSITION: Israel Ports Authority, POB 20121, Tel Aviv 67215, Israel.

MIRSKY, JOE Bus:Mgmt/Admin, Legal Prac; Acad: Bus Admin. BS 1961, JD 1966, U of Houston. INT: arb/med. ASSN: Houston IRRA, ABA, AAA, Tex Bar Assn. POSITIONS: Staff Attorney, NLRB, 1966; Gen Counsel, Jas. L. Dunn & Assoc, 1968; and (since 1972) President, Beckman Office Supply Co, 1953 W Gray, Houston, TX 77019. 713/526-8981

MISA, KENNETH F. Consulting. BS 1961, Fairfield U; MS 1963, Purdue U; PhD 1966, St. John's U-Jamaica, NY. PUBL: "Management's Involvement in the Strategic Utilization of the Human Resource, Mgmt Rev, Oct 1983, pp 13-17; "Strategic HRM and the Bottom Line," Pers Admin, Oct 1983, pp 27-32; "Back to Basics: Managing People Effectively," The Private Carrier, Apr 1983, pp 18-21. INT: ind psych, org beh, personnel. ASSN: Amer Psych Assn, Inst of Mgmt Consultants, Acad of Mgmt. POSITION: Assoc, 1968, Principal, 1975, and, since 1983, Vice Pres, A. T. Kearney, Inc, One Wilshire Blvd, Suite 2501, Los Angeles, CA 90017. 213/627-0721

MISHEL, LAWRENCE R. Union. POSITION: UAW Research, 8000 E Jefferson Ave, Detroit, MI 48243.

MITCHELL, AMY LYNN Unit 401, 49 Park Ave, Georgetown Ont L7G 3H9 Canada.

MITCHELL, DANIEL J. B. Acad: Ind Rels, Univ Admin. AB 1964, Columbia Coll; PhD 1968, MIT. PUBL: Unions, Wages and Inflation, Brookings, 1980; "Recent Union Wage Concessions," Brookings Papers on Econ Activity, 1:1982; "Should the Consumer Price Index Determine Wages?" Calif Mgmt Rev, Fall 1982. INT: labor market econ, coll barg. ASSN: Southern Calif IRRA, AEA, Inst of Ind Rels. POSITIONS: Senior Fellow, Brookings Inst, 1978; Prof, Grad School Mgmt, 1968, and, since 1979, Director, Inst of Ind Rels, UCLA, Los Angeles, CA 90024. 213/825-4339

MITCHELL, J. M. ADDRESS: Texas Oil Company, PO Box 52332, Houston, TX 77010.

MITCHELL, JAMES L. Acad: Bus Admin. BA 1950, MBA 1960, DBA 1967, Mich State U. INT: mgmt/educ, empl/trng programs. ASSN: Northeast Mich IRRA, Amer Accounting Assn. POSITIONS: Assoc Prof of Accounting, Western Mich Univ, 1964; Prof of Accounting, 1977, and, since 1980, Dean School of Bus and Mgmt, Saginaw Valley State Coll, University Center, MI 48710. 517/790-4064

MITCHELL, JOHN J. IV Acad: Ind Rels, Org Beh/Pers. AB 1950, Harvard, MBA 1961 U of Pittsburgh; MS 1979, Temple U. ASSN: Western Penna IRRA, Pittsburgh Pers Assn. POSITION: Lecturer, Point Park College. ADDRESS: 4716 Ellsworth Ave, Pittsburgh, PA 15213. 412/391-4100

MITCHELL, OLIVIA S. Acad: Econ, Ind Rels. BA 1974, Harvard; MA 1976, PhD 1978, U of Wis. PUBL: Retirement Pensions and Social Security; "The Economics of Retirement Behavior," JOLE, 1984; "Fringe Benefits and the Costs of Changing Jobs," ILR Rev, 1983. INT: labor market econ, govt labor policy, method/statis. ASSN: AEA. POSITIONS: Visiting Scholar in Econ, Harvard Univ, 1981-82, and, since 1978, Asst Prof, Labor Econ, NYSSILR-Cornell Univ, 167 Ives Hall, Ithaca, NY 14853. 607/256-4561

MITRANI, ROBERT L. Arbitration. BBA 1950, CCNY; MSILR 1951, Cornell.INT: arb/med, coll barg, labor law. ASSN: New York and New Brunswick IRRA, AAA, NAA, SPIDR. POSITIONS: (since 1978) Arbitrator (self-employed), 775 Highview Dr, Wyckoff, NJ 07481. 201/891-5931

MITTENTHAL, RICHARD Arbitration. AB 1948, Cornell; LLB 1951, NYU. PUBL: "Past Practices and This Administration of Collective Bargaining Contracts, Mich Law Rev, 1961; "Joys of Being An Arbitrator," Proceedings of the Natl Acad of Arb, 1979; "Credibility, A 'Will-o-the-Wisp'," Proceedings of NAA, 1971. INT: arb/med, coll barg, labor law. ASSN: Detroit IRRA, NAA, AAA, SPIDR. POSITION: (since 1954) Arbitrator, Suite 302, 30100 Telegraph Rd, Birmingham, MI 48010. 313/642-3200

MIXER, MADELINE CODDING Government. Regional Dir, Women's Bureau, USDL, 76 Bonnie Lane, Berkeley, CA 94708. 415/556-2377

MOBERG, DAVID Journalism. BA 1965, Carleton Coll; MA 1971, PhD 1978, U of Chicago. INT: coll barg, govt labor policy, ind sociol. POSITION: Senior Editor, "In These Times." ADDRESS: 5731 S Blackstone, Chicago, IL 60637. 312/493-0996

MOBERLY, GARY L. Government. INT: govt labor policy, ind psych, org beh. POSITIONS: Restaurant Mgr, Jerrco Inc, 1970; Empl Standards Inspector, 1975, and, since 1984, Executive Director, Kentucky Labor Cabinet, US 127 South, Franfurt, KY 40601. 502/564-3070

MOBERLY, ROBERT B. Acad: Law; Arbitration. BS 1963, JD 1966, U of Wis. PUBL: Arbitration and Conflict Resolution, (w E. Teple), BNA, 1979; Public Employment Labor Relations, (w C. Mulcahy), 1974. INT: arb/med, labor law, intl comparative labor. ASSN: South Central Florida IRRA, NAA, ABA, Intl Soc for Labor Law and Soc Security. POSITION: (since 1977) Professor of Law, College of Law, Univ of Florida, Gainesville, FL 32611. 904/392-2211

MOBERLY, RUSSELL L. Acad: Bus Admin; Arbitration, Consulting. BM 1931, MA 1934, PhD 1939, U of Wis. INT: mgmt/educ, arb/med, personnel. ASSN: Wis IRRA, Amer Soc for Pers Mgmt, NEA, Amer Soc for Trng and Develop. POSITION: Educator, Arbitrator and Consultant (self-employed), 4260 Lake Dr, West Bend, WI 53095. 414/644-5065

MOFFETT, KENNETH E. 1906 Fox St, Adelphi, MD 20783.

MOHR, COENRAAD LUTTIG Acad: Bus Admin, Org Beh/Pers, Ind Rels. BComm 1949, U of Stellenbosch (So Africa); MA 1955, PhD 1969, U of Minn. INT: personnel, coll barg, org beh. ASSN: Acad of Mgmt, AAUP. POSITIONS: Asst Prof, Bradley Univ, 1959; Assoc Prof of Mgmt, St. Louis Univ, 1964; and (since 1970) Prof of Mgmt, Dept of Mgmt, Illinois State Univ, Normal, IL 61701. 309/438-5606

MOLINI, PAUL JOSEPH JR. Acad: Student, Ind Rels. BS 1983, Le Moyne Coll. INT: personnel, labor law. POSITIONS: United Parcel, 1976; Intern-IR Dept, Carrier Corp, 1983; and (since 1983) Student in IR Program, Univ of Cincinnati. ADDRESS: 413 Branchwood Dr, Liverpool, NY 13088.

MOLNER, ERNEST Bus:Mgmt/Admin, Bus:-Pers/Ind Rels, Consulting. INT: coll barg, magmt/educ, org beh. ASSN: Northwest Ohio IRRA, ASPA, Amer Soc of Assn Exec, Amer Soc of Mechanical Eng. POSITIONS: Ind Rels Dir, Cleveland Pneumatic Tool Co, 1950; and (since 1968) Executive Dir, Mechanical Contractors Assn of Cleveland, 1737 Euclid Ave, Cleveland, OH 44115. 216/575-0770

MONACO, ANGELO G. Bus:Pers/Ind Rels. POSITION: Personnel Manager, NY Zoological Society, Bronx Zoo, New York, NY 10460.

MONAT, JONATHAN S. Acad: Ind Rels; Arbitration. BS 1965, UCLA; MS 1967, San Diego State; PhD 1972, U of Minn. PUBL: "A Perspective on the Evaluation of Training," Pers Admin J, 1981; "Effectiveness and Value Consideration in Bargaining Emp. and Design," OB Teaching Conf, USC, June 1980; Instructors Manual to Accompany Belcher Compensation Administration, Prentice-Hall, 1977. INT: arb/-med, coll barg, personnel. ASSN: Orange County & Southern Calif IRRA, SPIDR, AAA, Acad of Mgmt. POSITIONS: Asst Prof of Bus Admin, Western Wash Univ, 1972; and (since 1978) Assoc Prof, Dept of Mgmt/HRM, Calif State Univ, Long Beach, CA 90840. 213/498-4753

MONET, STEVEN A. Student. MAIR 1983, Wayne State U. INT: coll barg, arb/med, personnel. ASSN: Detroit IRRA, Better Bus Bureau-Arb Program. POSITION: (since 1975) Probation/Parole Officer, Mich Dept of Corrections. ADDRESS: 29560 Ann Arbor Tr, Westland, MI 48185. 313/831-0800 ext 52

MONITTO, ANGELO Bus:Pers/Ind Rels, Arbitration. Cert Law, 1939, St. John's U-Brooklyn. INT: arb/med, coll barg, labor law. ASSN: Conn Valley IRRA, Manufacturing Assn of Hartford Cty, New Britain Area Empl Mgrs Assn, Conn Pers Mgr Assn. POSITIONS: Wage & Salary Admin, 1964, Vice Pres Labor Rels, 1978, Emhart Corp, Hardware Div; and (since 1978 by Governor's appointment) State Arbitrator, State Bd of Arb and Mediation, 29 Steele St, New Britain, CT 06052. 203/225-3204

MONROE, CHARLES RICHARD Bus:Pers/Ind Rels, Data Processing. BGS 1977, U of Mich; MLIR 1979, Mich State U. INT: pers systems/-data processing, personnel, empl/trng programs. POSITIONS: Pers Rep, 1981, Compensation Analyst, 1982, and, since 1983, Project Coordinator, Human Res Mgmt Systems, Armco-National Supply Co. ADDRESS: 13407 Bridgewalk Lane, Houston, TX 77041. 713/966-4247

MONTGOMERY, B. RUTH Student. AB 1977, Grinnell Coll. INT: coll barg, personnel. ASSN: Acad of Mgmt. POSITION: PhD Student, Univ of Mich. ADDRESS: 2261 Stone Dr, Ann Arbor, MI 48105. 313/763-5165

MONTROSS, WILLIAM Union. AB 1968, Rutgers U; JD 1971, Stanford. INT: coll barg, govt labor policy, labor history. POSITION: Res Assoc, United Food & Commercial Workers Intl Union, 1775 K St NW, Washington DC 20006. 202/223-3111 ext 483

MONTY, GERALD A. Bus: Pers/Ind Rels. BA 1956, U of Denver. INT: coll barg, arb/med, labor law. ASSN: Orange Cty IRRA, NMA, NSTD, Hughes Mgmt Club. POSITIONS: Dir of Pers, 1976, Dir Labor Rels, Rockwell Intl-Space Group, 1973; and (since 1982) Dir, Employee and Labor Rels, Hughes Aircraft, PO Box 1042, (MSB-173), El Segundo, CA 90245. 213/414-6378

MOON, GARY LEE Union. INT: arb/med, coll barg, labor law. POSITION: President, U.P.I.U. Local #1161, Route 1, Box 268, Rogersville, AL 35652. 205/247-3781

MOONEY, MARTA J. Acad: Bus Admin/-Mgmt. POSITION: Graduate School of Bus, Fordham Univ, Lincoln Center, New York, NY 10023. 212/675-6517

MOORE, ALGER Bus:Pers/Ind Rels. POSITION: Personnel Manager, Gifford-Hill Co Inc, PO Box 47127, Dallas, TX 75211. 214/637-3860

MOORE, CHARLES COTY ILO. BSc 1955, MA 1961, U of Ill. PUBL: Multinational Enterprises and Social Policy, 1973. INT: intl comparative labor, govt labor policy, labor history. ASSN: Intl Inst of Lab Rels. POSITIONS: Tech Assistance Programming Officer, Caribbean Port of Spain, Trinidad & Tobago, 1972, Cooperative Tech Assistance Projects Officer, Geneva, 1975, and, since 1982, Deputy Director, Office for the South Pacific, Intl Labour Office, PO Box 1546, Suva, Fiji. Phone 313 866

MOORE, DAVID G. Acad: Bus Admin, Org Beh/Pers, Sociol. PhD 1954, U of Chicago. PUBL: Human Relations in Industry, R. D. Irwin, 4th ed; The Enterprising Man, Mich State; SRA Employee Inventory, Science Res Assoc. INT: mgmt/educ, bus policy. ASSN: Amer Sociol Assn, Soc for Applied Anthro, Acad of Mgmt. POSITIONS: Dean, NYSSILR-Cornell, 1963; Exec VP, The Conference Board, 1971; and (since 1983) Special Asst to the President, Univ of North Florida, Jacksonville. ADDRESS: PO Box 1905, Ponte Verde Beach, FL 32082. 904/646-2700

MOORE, EDGAR Acad: Labor Educ, Ind Rels, Sociol. MA 1975, U of Minn. INT: labor educ, arb/med, ind sociol. ASSN: Detroit IRRA, Univ & Coll Educ Assn, Workers Educ Local 189, AAUP. POSITIONS: Teacher, Detroit Public School, 1961; Res Asst, U of Minn, 1973;

and (since 1974) Assoc Prof, Ohio State Univ, 310 W Woodruff, Suite 222, Toledo, OH 43624. 419/242-2151

MOORE, ERNEST C. III Legal Practice. ADDRESS: Torkildson et al, AMFAC Bldg, 15 Floor, 700 Bishop, Honolulu, HI 96813. 808/-521-1051

MOORE, GARY A. Acad: Ind Rels, Econ; Arbitration. BS 1968, Nebr Wesleyan U; MA 1973, PhD 1974, U of Nebr-Lincoln. PUBL: Labor and the Economy, (w R. Elkin), Southwestern Publishing Co, 1983; "The Effect of Collective Bargaining on Internal Salary Structures in the Public School," Ind & Labor Rels Rev, April 1976; "Equity Effects of Higher Education Finance and Tuition Grants in New York State," J of Human Resources, Fall 1978. ASSN: AEA, Eastern Econ Assn, Amer Bus Law Assn. POSITIONS: Asst Prof, 1974, and, since 1980, Assoc Prof, SUNY-Geneseo, School of Bus, Welles 221, Geneseo, NY 14454. 716/245-5363

MOORE, GREGORY LEE Bus:Mgmt/Admin. POSITION: Section Manager-Staffing, Oglethorpe Power Corp, 2888 Woodcock Blvd, Atlanta, GA 30341.

MOORE, JIM L. Bus:Pers/Ind Rels. BS 1965, Okla State U. INT: arb/med, coll barg, labor law. ASSN: St. Louis IRRA. POSITIONS: Marketing Mgr, AT&T, New York, 1974; Div Directory Sales Mgr, Southwestern Bell Telephone Co, Houston, 1977; and (since 1980) Director, Corporate Labor Relations, Southwestern Bell Publications, Inc., 112 N 4th St, Room 1515, St. Louis, MO 63102. 314/247-4716

MOORE, JOHN COCHRANE Arbitration. POSITION: President, Australian Council & Arbitration Comm, Law Courts Bldg, Queens SQ, Sydney NSW 2000 Australia.

MOORE, LESTER L. Bus:Mgmt/Admin. POSITION: Southern Union Co, Suite 1800, 1st Intl Bldg, 1201 Elm St, Dallas, TX 75270.

MOORE, MAUREEN F. Legal Practice. BBA 1980, North Tex State U; JD 1983, Southern Methodist U. INT: labor law, coll barg, empl laws. POSITION: (since 1983) Associate, McCalla, Thompson, Pyburn & Ridley, 1001 Howard Ave, Suite 2800, New Orleans, LA 70113. 504/-524-2499

MOORE, MICHAEL LEE Acad: Org Beh/Pers. BA 1964, Kalamazoo Coll; MBA 1966, PhD 1970, U of Mich. PUBL: "Use of Modern Organization Designs as a Basis for Motivational and Productivity Programs," chapter in The Handbook of Modern Pers Admin, J. Famularo, Ed, McGraw Hill, 1984; "Installing Management by Objectives in a Public Agency: A Comparison of Black and White Managers, Supervisors and Professionals," (w D. Scott), Publ Admin Rev, Mar-April 1983, vol 2, pp 121-126; "Training Needs Analysis: Review and Critique," Acad of Mgmt Rev, vol 3, #3, July 1978; 532-545.INT: personnel, org beh, ind psych. ASSN: Acad of Mgmt, ASPA, Org Beh Teaching Soc. POSITIONS: Ind Rels Analyst, Ford Motor Co, 1964-66; Assoc Dir for the Academic Program, 1973-79, and, since 1969, Prof of Org Beh, Pers Mgmt and Ind Rels, School of Labor and Ind Rels, Michigan State Univ. ADDRESS: 4351 Wausau Rd, Okemos, MI 48864. 517/353-3896

MOORE, THOMAS F. Union, Firefighter, Consulting. INT: coll barg, arb/med, labor law. ASSN: Intl Assn of Firefighters, Minn Professional Firefighters, Richfield Professional Firefighters. POSITIONS: Captain, 1969, Vice Pres/Bus Rep, 1978, and, since 1974, President, Richfield Firefighters, IAFF 1215. ADDRESS: 6115 15th Ave South, Minneapolis, MN 55423. 612/869-7521 ext 316

MOORE, WILLIAM J. Acad: Econ, Ind Rels. BA 1964, MA 1966, PhD 1970, U of Tex - Austen. PUBL: "A Quality Adjustment Model of the Academic Labor Market," Econ Inquiry, 1983; "A Time Series Analysis of the Growth and Determinants of Union/Nonunion Relative Wage Effects, 1967-1977," J of Labor Res, 1983; "A Comparative Analysis of Strike Models During Periods of Rapid Inflation," 1967-1977," J of Labor Res, 1982. INT: labor market econ, union org/admin, coll barg. ASSN: AEA. POSITIONS: Asst Prof of Econ, Univ of Okla, 1968; Assoc Prof of Econ, Univ of Houston, 1975; and (since 1981) Julian G. Lange Prof of Econ, Dept of Econ, Miami Univ, Oxford, OH 45056. 513/529-3136

MOORING, KELLEY D. Bus:Pers/Ind Rels. BBA 1974, Temple Univ. INT: org beh, personnel, coll barg. ASSN: Philadelphia IRRA, AAA, ASPA Princeton Pers Assn. POSITIONS: Special Asst V.P. of Human Resources, 1971, Dir, Labor Rels, 1974, Temple Univ; and (since 1981) Director, Empl Rels, Educational Testing Service, Princeton, NJ 08541. 609/734-1645

MORAN, MICHAEL L. Bus:Pers/Ind Rels. BA 1975, St. Michael's Coll; MLIR 1976, St. Francis Coll. INT: labor law, coll barg, arb/med. ASSN: New Jersey Pers Group. POSITIONS: Bus Rep, Intl Union of Operating Engineers, Local 106, 1978; Ind Rels Mgr, United Technologies-Inmont, 1981; and (since 1983) Asst Manager-Labor Rels, Lever Brothers Co, Edgewater. ADDRESS: 7 Hoffman Ct, East Brunswick, NJ 08816. 201/945-8550

MORAND, MARTIN J. Acad: Ind Rels. BS 1948, Cornell. PUBL: Short-Time Compensation: A Formula for Worksharing; "Back to Basics, A Call For Accuracy in Research on Collective Bargaining's Effects on Faculty Compensation," (w D. S. McPherson), IRRA Proc, 1979 "Colloquiality and Collective Bargaining, Rutgers, Camden Law Rev, 1978. INT: labor educ, coll barg. ASSN: Western Penna IRRA, SPIDR, AAUP, AFI. POSITIONS: Dir, State Assn of Penna State Coll and Univ, 1973; Dir/Prof, Penna Center for the Study of Labor Rels, 1976, and, since 1976, Professor, Indiana Univ of Penna, Indiana, PA 15705. 412/357-2645

MORGAN, BILL E. Union. POSITION: Negotiations Consultant, Calif Teachers Assn #102, 235 N Rancho Santa Fe RD, San Marcos, CA 92069.

MORGAN, CELIA A. Acad: Econ. PhD 1971, U of Houston. PUBL: "An Analysis of Interregional Migration in Texas, Rev of Reg Studies, vol 6:2. INT: labor market econ, health & hosp care, govt labor programs. POSITION: (since 1971) Professor, Dept of Econ, Southwest Texas State Univ, San Marcos, TX 78666. 512/245-2547

MORGAN, CHARLES A. Legal Practice. AB 1942, Case Western Reserve U; JD 1947, U of Mich. POSITION: (since 1947) Partner, Amerman, Burt & Jones Co, 624 Market Ave N, Canton, OH 44702. 216/456-2491

MORGAN, GARY R. Arbitration. POSITION: NYC Board of Education, 69-38 112th St, Forest Hills, NY 11375. 212/263-9798

MORGAN, HOWARD J. Arbitration, Consulting. NBA 1981, Simon Fraser U. PUBL: Recruiting Techniques for Small Businesses; Decision Making Within Accredited Bargaining Associations. INT: arb/med, labor educ, personnel. ASSN: Vancouver IRRA, ASPA. POSITIONS: Dir of Empl Rels, Shared Hosp Services, 1978; and (since 1981) Director of Pers/Ind Rels, Labatt Breweries, 976 Richards St, Vancouver, BC V6B 3C1 Canada. 604/669-5050

MORGENBESSER, LEONARD IRA Government. BA 1971, Queens Coll-CUNY; MA 1974, SUNY-Albany; MA 1975, SUNY-Binghamton. PUBL: "Pilot EAP Within NYS Department of Correctional Services," Corrections Compensation, May 1981; "The Battering of Women: Bringing Data to the Discussion," (book review) J of Pers Assessment, Oct 1979, pp 554-57; "Program Evaluation: Recidivism Research Involving Sex Offenders," (co-author), chapter in Sexual Aggressor-Current Perspective on Treatment (ed by J. Greer and I. Stuart). Van Nostrand Reinhold Co, 1983. INT: ind psych, ind sociol, quality of worklife. ASSN: New York Capital Dist IRRA, Amer Sociol Assn, Amer Correctional Assn. POSITION: (since 1975) Program Research Specialist III, NYS Dept of Correctional Services. ADDRESS: 219 Tampa Ave, Albany, NY 12208. 518/457-2144

MORISHIMA, MOTOHIRO Student. BA 1980, MA 1982, Keio Univ, Tokyo. PUBL: Information In Japanese Labor Markets, (co-authored, in Japanese) Keio Univ Press, 1981. INT: org beh, ind psych, method/statis. ASSN: Beh Soc of Japan, Japan Assn of Org Sci. POSITION: Grad Student (PhD Program), ILIR, Univ of Ill-UC, 504 E Armory, Champaign, IL 61820. 217/333-0984

MORRIS, CHARLES JACOB Acad: Law; Arbitration. AB 1944, Temple U; LLB 1948, Columbia U. PUBL: The Developing Labor Law,(editor-in chief), 1st ed, 1971, 2nd ed, 1983; "The Role of Interest Arbitration in a Collective Bargaining System, in Future of Labor Arbitration Bargaining in America, AAA 1976, and in 1 Ind Rels Law J 427, 1976; "The Role of the NLRB and the Courts in the Collective Bargaining Process: A Fresh Look at Conventional Wisdom and Unconventional Remedies," 30 Vanderbilt Law Rev, 661, 1977. INT: labor law, arb/med, intl comparative labor. ASSN: North Tex IRRA, ABA(labor & Empl Law Section), NAA, SPIDR. POSITIONS: Visiting Prof Monash Univ, 1974, Visiting Prof, ILR & Law School-Cornell, 1977-79, and, since 1966, Professor of Law, Southern Methodist Univ, Dallas, TX 75275. 214/692-2571

MORRIS, JOHN P. Union. POSITION: Teamsters Local 115, 2833 Cottman Ave, Philadelphia, PA 19149.

MORRISON, DAVID D. Bus:Pers/Ind Rels. BA 1973, Rutgers. PUBL: Long Island Railroad Trial Officers Manual. INT: arb/med, coll barg, labor law. ASSN: Long Island IRRA, Natl Railway History Assn. POSITION: Manager, Labor Rels, Long Island Railroad, Jamaica Station, Jamaica, NY 11435. 212/526-0900 ext 405.

MORRISON, MALCOLM H. Acad: Org Beh/-Pers, Ind Rels, Econ. MPA 1968, U of Mich; PhD 1974, Brandeis U. PUBL: Economics of Aging: The Future of Retirement, Van Nostrand, 1982; "The Aging of the U. S. Population: Human Resource Implications," Monthly Labor Rev, May 1983; "Retirement and Human Resource Planning for the Aging Workforce," Pers Admin, 1984. INT: personnel, labor market econ, mgmt/educ. ASSN: Wash DC IRRA, Intl Soc of Pre-retirement Planners, Gerontological Soc of Amer. POSITIONS: Assoc Professorial Lecturer, George Washington U, 1979; Dir, Natl Studies of Mandatory Retirement, USDL, 1979; and (since 1983) Res Assoc in Public Policy and Management, The Wharton School, Dept of Policy & Mgmt, Univ of Pennsylvania, Steinberg Dietrich Hall, Philadelphia, PA 19104. 215/898-3013

MORSE, JENNIFER B. Bus:Pers/Ind Rels. 327 Gordon Pky, Syracuse, NY 13219.

MORTON, CHARLES WILLIAM Bus:Mgmt/-Admin, Bus:Pers/Ind Rels. BA & BBA 1957, New Mexico. INT: coll barg, personnel, labor law. POSITIONS: Reg Labor Rels Mgr, Armour & Co, 1967-68; Ind Rels Mgr, ARMIRA Corp, 1968-77; and (since 1979) Vice Pres, Human Resources & External Rels, Universal Foundry, 495 Pearl Ave, Oshkosh, WI 54901. 414/235-9200

MORTON, HERBERT CHARLES Government, Consulting. PhD 1964, U of Minn. PUBL: Public Contracts and Private Wages, Brookings, 1965; An Introduction to Economic Reasoning, (co-author), 5th ed, Doubleday, 1980; Energy Today and Tomorrow, (co-author), Prentice Hall, 1983. INT: govt labor policy, method/statis, labor market econ. ASSN: Wash DC IRRA, AEA, AAAS. POSITIONS: Assoc Commissioner, U.S. Bureau of Labor Statistics, 1968; Sr Fellow, Resources for the Future, 1974; and (since 1983) Consultant, 7106 Laverock Lane, Bethesda, MD 20817. 301/229-1718

MOSER, COLLETTE H. Acad: Econ, Ag Econ. BS 1962, Ill State U; MS 1966, PhD 1971, U of Wis-Madison. POSITIONS: Lecturer, Rutgers U, 1967-69; Lecturer, Ind Univ, S Bend, 1969-71; and, currently, Dept of Agricultural Econ, Mich State Univ, East Lansing, MI 48824. 517/353-3298

MOSES, EVELYN B. Government. 3801 Ct Ave NW, Apt 320, Washington DC 20008. 202/362-9063

MOSES, MARY HELEN Acad: Law; Legal Practice. BA 1975, Furman U; JD 1978, U of Ga; LLM 1981, Georgetown U. PUBL: "Nonmajority Bargaining Orders: A Study in Indecision," 46 Albany Law Rev, 363, 1982; "Deferral to Arbitration in Individual Rights Cases: A Reexamination of Spielberg," Tenn L Rev, Apr 1984. INT: labor law, govt health policy, arb/-med. ASSN: New York Capitol Dist IRRA, Dist of Columbia Bar, State Bar of Georgia, ABA. POSITIONS: Asst Prof of Law, N.C. Central Univ, Durham, 1978-79; Counsel to Mbr. John A Penello, NLRB, 1979-81; and (since 1981) Assoc Prof of Law, Albany Law School of Union Univ, 80 New Scotland Ave, Albany, NY 12208. 518/445-2311

MOSKOW, MICHAEL H. Bus:Mgmt/Admin. AB 1959, Lafayette Coll; MA 1962, PhD 1965, U of Penna. PUBL: Collective Bargaining in Public Employment, (co-author), Random House, 1970; Labor Relations in the Performing Arts: An Introductory Survey," Associated Councils for the Arts, 1970; Strategic Planning in Business and Government, Committee on Econ Develop, 1978. INT: coll barg, govt labor policy, arb/med. ASSN: Natl Bureau of Econ Res, Center for Intl Mgmt Studies, Econ Club of Chicago. POSITIONS: Vice Pres, Corp Develop & Planning, Esmark Inc, 1977, Exec Vice Pres, Estronics (Div of Esmark), 1980; and (since 1982) President and Chief Executive Officer, Velsicol Chemical Corp, 341 East Ohio, Chicago, IL 60611. 312/670-4572

MOSKOWITZ, LEON DAVID Bus:Mgmt/-Admin. BS 1947, CCNY; MS 1948, U of Wis. INT: mgmt/educ, health & hosp care, group AWD soc ins programs. POSITION: (since 1983) Vice Pres, Corp Planning and Develop, Metropolitan Life Ins Co, One Madison Ave, New York, NY 10010. 212/578-3148

MOTIUK, I. LEO Legal Practice; Acad: Ind Rels. JD 1969, Duquesne U; LLM 1980, NYU. INT: labor law, arb/med, coll barg. ASSN: New Brunswick IRRA, ABA(Labor Law Committee), NJ State Bar Assn(Labor Law Committee). POSITION: Partner, Schaff, Motiuk, Hornby, Gladstone & Knox, Trenton. ADDRESS: PO Box 996, Flemington, NJ 08822. 609/695-5511

MOTSEPE, OSCAR W.E. Acad: Student, Org Beh/Pers, Ind Rels. BA 1966, BA 1968, MA 1980, U of South Africa; MS 1983, Purdue U. PUBL: Organizational Behavior-Readings for Management, (w M. Nasser, E. Schmikl & C. Van Veijeren), 1976; South Africa's Urban Blacks: Problems and Challenges, (w G. Marais & R. Van Der Kooy), 1978. INT: org beh, coll barg, ind psych. ASSN: Acad of Mgmt, Soc for Ind and Org Psych, South African Psych Assn. POSITIONS: Pers Officer, Asea Elec Ltd, S.A., 1968; Sr Lecturer, Univ of South Africa, 1974; and (since 1980) Doctoral Student, Krannert Grad School, Purdue Univ, West Lafayette, IN 47907. 317/743-9085

MOUNTS, PHILIP HARRY Acad: Org Beh/-Pers, Ind Rels, Bus Admin. BS 1940, Iowa State; MS 1965, PhD 1972, UCLA. INT: personnel, org beh, mgmt/educ. ASSN: Wis IRRA, Acad of Mgmt, ASPA, AAUP. POSITIONS: Dir of Operations, Collins Radio, 1957; VP Operation, Redcar Corp, 1964; and (since 1971) Prof of Management, Coll of Bus Admin, Univ of Wis-Oshkosh, Oshkosh, WI 54902. 414/424-1457

MOWRY, CHRISTINE B. Acad: Univ Admin. BA 1971, MA 1976, JD 1984, Rutgers. POSITIONS: Assoc Dir, Dir, 1981, and, since 1983, Asst Vice Pres for Staff Affairs and Director, Office of Empl Rels, Rutgers, The State Univ, 60 College Ave, New Brunswick, NJ 08901. 201/-932-7162

MROZAK, JACK LAWRENCE Government, Bus:Pers/Ind Rels, Union. ASSN: NY Capital Dist IRRA. POSITION: Chief Investigator, NYS Div of Labor Standards, 50 Windmill Dr, Glenmont, NY 12077. 518/767-9210

MROZEK, JOHN S. Government; Acad: Ind Rels. INT: govt labor policy, coll barg, labor law. ASSN: Rocky Mountain IRRA. POSITIONS: Dir, Denver Construction Coordinating Committee, USDL, 1979; Exec Vice-Pres, Rocky Mountain Investors, 1981; and (since 1983) Mgr of Public Works/Deputy Mayor, City and County of Denver. ADDRESS: 3959 S. Boston, Denver, CO 80237. 303/575-2561

MUESSIG, ECKEHARD Arbitration. BS 1949, Ohio State U. INT: arb/med, coll barg, personnel. ASSN: Wash DC IRRA, SPIDR, SFLRP. POSITIONS: Program Evaluation Dir, U.S. Civil Service Comm, 1973, Deputy Asst Secretary, USDL, 1976; and (since 1981) Arbitrator, 3450 N Venice St, Arlington, VA 22207. 703/538-4716

MUIR, NORMAN WILLIAM Union. POSITION: Regional Director, PSEA, 1005 Penllyn Pike, Spring House, PA 19477.

MULCHAHEY, TERRY S. Bus:Pers/Ind Rels. BS 1970, Mich State U. INT: personnel, org beh. POSITIONS: Pers Specialist, Federal Reserve Bd, Wash DC, 1973; Empl Rels Mgr, Mobil Chemical Co, Woodland, CA, 1976, and, since 1981, Manager, Personnel Services, Mobil Research & Devel Corp, Princeton, NJ. ADDRESS: 309 Robin Hood Dr, Yardley, PA 19067. 609/737-5074

MULKERN, PAUL VINCENT Government. AB 1938, MS 1940, Boston Coll. INT: arb/med, coll barg, labor market econ. POSITION: Bureau of Labor Statistics, USDL, Boston Reg Office, Retired. ADDRESS: 11 Spafford Rd, Milton, MA 02186.

MULLADY, SARAH F. Bus:Pers/Ind Rels. BA 1952, St. Joseph's Coll-Brooklyn; MA 1955, Fordham U. INT: labor law, personnel, ind psych. ASSN: ALMACA, NY Pers Mgmt Assn, NY Acad of Women Achievers. POSITIONS: Benefits Supr, Olin Corp, 1955; Benefits Mgr, 1977, and, since 1981, Manager, Empl Assistance Program, Champion Intl Corp, One Champion Plaza, Stamford, CT 06921. 203/358-7385

MULLALY, EDWARD J., S. J. Acad: Ind Rels. POSITION: Director, Comey Inst of Ind Rels, St. Joseph's Univ, Philadelphia, PA 19131. 215/879-7660

MULLAN, BRIAN FRANCIS Acad: Sociol, Admin. POSITION: Institutional Planner, Univ of Puerto Rico, 395 San Genaro St, Rio Piedras, PR 00926. 809/767-7370

MULLEN, CHARLENE H. 1808 Woodcove Pl, Pittsburgh, PA 15216.

MULLEN, MARY ANN Government. BA 1973, Blackburn U; MA 1981, George Washington U. INT: arb/med, empl/trng programs. ASSN: Wash DC IRRA. POSITION: (since 1973) Ind Rels Specialist, USDL. ADDRESS: 2302 Highland Ave, Falls Church, VA 22046. 703/357-0473

MULLENNIX, GRADY LEE Acad: Econ, Ind Rels; Arbitration. BS & MS 1942, North Tex State; PhD 1955, U of Tex. PUBL: "Wage-Productivity Comparisons," ILRR, 7/55; "Labor USA," Reviewed in ILRR, Oct, 1960; "Farmers Under Wage Controls," Colo Farmer, 1952. INT: arb/med, labor history, coll barg. ASSN: Central Calif IRRA, AAA, Assn for Evolutionary Econ. POSITIONS: Asst Dir of Res & Educ, Oil, Chemical & Atomic Workers Intl Union-Denver, 1954; Asst Prof, Mich State U, 1956; and (since 1958) Prof of Econ, Calif State Univ-Fresno. ADDRESS: 135 La Verne Ave, Clovis, CA 93612. 209/294-3916

MULLINS, CAROL M. Government. BA 1980, Mary Washington Coll; MA 1982, Penna State U. INT: labor market econ, manpower planning and forecasting. POSITION: (since 1983) Economist, Navy Pers Research and Develop Center, San Diego. ADDRESS: #17-208, 10737 San Diego Mission, San Diego, CA 92108. 619/225-7388

MUNCHUS, GEORGE III Acad: Ind Rels; Arbitration. BBA 1972, MBA 1973, PhD 1976, North Tex U. PUBL: "Collective Bargaining and the Future of the FederalMerit System of Human Resource Administration," J of Coll Negotiations in the Public Sector, vol 11, #4, 1982, pp 297-303; "Public Employee Labor Relations In A Legislative Dilemma: The Alabama Case," Alabama Bus and Econ J, vol 6, #2, Jan 1983, pp 25-36; "A Review of Employer-Employee Based Quality Circles in Japan: A Human Resource Management Policy Implication for American Firms," Acad of Mgmt Rev, vol 8, #2, April 1983, pp 255-261. INT: personnel, coll barg, arb/med. ASSN: Atlanta IRRA, SPIDR, AAA, Pers Accreditation Inst. POSITIONS: Teaching Asst, North Tex State Univ, 1973-76; Asst Prof, 1976-82, and, since 1982, Assoc Prof of Mgmt, School of Business, Univ of Alabama, Birmingham, AL 35294. 205/934-3481

MUNNS, VICTOR GEORGE Government. BA 1951, U of London. INT: empl/trng programs, coll barg, labor law. ASSN: Wash DC IRRA. POSITIONS: Secretary, Shipbuilding Ind Trng Board, London, 1963; Secretary, Health & Safety Comm, London, 1974; and (since 1983) Counselor (Labor), British Embassy, 3100 Massachusetts Ave NW, Washington DC 20008. 202/462-1340

MURASE, JERRY L. Association Executive. BS 1972, UCLA. INT: arb/med, coll barg, empl/trng programs. ASSN: Southern Calif IRRA, Amer Mgmt Assn, SPIDR. POSITION: (since 1969) Regional Director, AAA, 443 Shatto Place, Los Angeles, CA 90020. 213/383-6516.

MURBACH, ILENE 2196 Northampton Dr, San Jose, CA 95124. 408/266-6424

MURBACH, RICHARD T. Consulting, Bus:-Per/Ind Rels, Bus:Mgmt/Admin. AB 1952, Colgate U; MBA 1956, Dartmouth Coll; Cert/Prod Mgmt, General Motors Inst. INT: outplacement, career develop, personnel. ASSN: San Francisco IRRA, ASPA, Northern Calif Human Resources Council, Career Planning Network. ADDRESS: 2196 Northampton Dr, San Jose, CA 95124. 408/266-6424

MURCH, KEN Union. INT: govt labor policy, coll barg, arb/med. POSITION: (since 1981) Operations Division Administrator, Calif State Employees Assn, 1108 O St, 4th FL, Sacramento, CA 95814. 916/444-8134

MURPHY, CHARLES J. Acad: Ind Rels, Bus Admin. PhD 1980, U of Wis. INT: unionorg/-admin, arb/med, intl comparative labor. ASSN: Acad of Mgmt, Assn of Soc & Beh Sci. POSITIONS: Asst Prof, Ohio State U, 1972; Dir, Inst for Labor Rels, 1981, and, since 1982, Assoc Prof of Mgmt, School of Bus & Public Admin, Howard Univ, 2014 Franklin St NE, Washington DC 20018. 202/832-1158

MURPHY, FRANK J. S. J. Rockhurst Coll, 5225 Troost Ave, Kansas City, MO 64110.

MURPHY, JAY W. Arbitration. BA 1933, U of Ill; MD 1943, LLM 1944, George Washington U. PUBL: Labor Relations and the Law. (cooperating editor, Wollett & Aaron), 2nd Ed, 1950; Legal Education In A Developing Nation: The Korea Experience. INT: arb/med, labor law. ASSN: NAA, Distric of Columbia Bar, Alabama Bar. POSITIONS: Prof, 1947-81, Prof Emeritus of Law, 1981, School of Law, Univ of Alabama; and (since 1951) Labor Arbitrator (self-employed), Murphy & Murphy, 921 3rd Ave East, Suite 101, Tuscaloosa, AL 35401. 205/349-1444

MURPHY, JOHN MICHAEL Acad: Econ, Ind Rels. BA 1953, Coll of Sante Fe; MA 1958, Boston Coll. INT: labor educ, coll barg, union org/admin. ASSN: Appalachian Mountain Club, Mass Teachers Assn. POSITIONS: Instructor in Econ, Gannon Coll, Erie PA, 1958-59; Instructor in Econ, Niagara Univ, 1960-66; and (since 1966) Assoc Prof of Econ, Dept of Econ, North Shore Community Coll, Beverly, MA 01915. 617/927-4850 ext 211

MURPHY, JOSEPH ANTHONY Government. 33 Wayne Dr, East Lyme CT 06333.

MURPHY, KEVIN R. Union. BA 1976, Oberlin; MILR 1980, Cornell. PUBL: "Technological Change Clauses in Collective Bargaining Agreements." INT: coll barg, ind sociol, ind psych. POSITION: (since 1980) Economist, AFSCME, Wash DC. ADDRESS: 413 Boyd Ave, Takoma Park, MD 20912. 202/429-1227

MURPHY, WILLIAM PATRICK Acad: Law; Arbitration. BA 1941, Southwestern Coll-Memphis; LLB 1948, U of Va; JSD 1960, Yale. INT: arb/med, labor law, govt labor policy. ASSN: NAA, ABA. POSITIONS: Prof of Law, Univ of Miss, 1953; Prof of Law, Univ of Mo, 1962; and (since 1971) Professor of Law, Univ of North Carolina, Chapel Hill, NC 27514. 919/902-4124

MURRMANN, KENT F. Acad: Ind Rels. BS 1967, Purdue U; MBA 1971, Ind U; PhD 1979, Mich State U. PUBL: "The Scanlon Plan Joint Committee and Section 8(A)(2)," Labor Law J, vol 31, #5, May 1980; "Attitudes of Professionals Towards Arbitration," Arb J, vol 37, #2, June, 1982; "Productivity Measurement in Manufacturing Firms," J of Cost and Mgmt, Jan-Feb, 1983. INT: govt labor policy, coll barg, arb/med. ASSN: Acad of Mgmt, ASPA. POSITIONS: Field Examiner, NLRB, 1971-74; Res Asst, SLIR-Mich State Univ, 1974-78; and (since 1979) Asst Prof, Virginia Polytechnic Inst, I.R. Center, Dept of Mgmt. ADDRESS: 1111 Horseshoe Lane, Blacksburg, VA 24060. 703/961-6353

MURRMANN, SUZANNE K. Acad: Ind Rels. 1111 Horseshoe Lane, Blacksburg, VA 24060. 703/953-1178

MUSHKIN, PHYLLIS Consulting, Home Health Care Service. INT: coll barg, labor educ, empl/trng programs. ASSN: Long Island IRRA. POSITIONS: Elected Admin Organizer, District 1199, 1974; and (since 1984) Partner, Resources for Labor Assoc, 57-10 244 St, Douglaston, NY 11362. 516/829-6390

MUSSER, STEVEN J. Acad: Org Beh/Pers, Ind Rels, Econ. AB 1975, Albright; MA 1977, Temple U. PUBL: "A Brief Application of Dialectical Theory to the Study of Union Organizations," Annual IRRA Proceedings, 1982, "A Model for Predicting the Choice of

Conflict Management Strategies by Subordinates in High Stakes Conflicts," Org Beh and Human Performance, April, 1982, 257-269. INT: org beh, union org/admin, labor market econ. ASSN: Acad of Mgmt Amer Mgmt Assn. POSITION: (since 1977) Asst Professor, Messiah College, Grantham, PA 17027. 717/766-2511

MUSTO, J. N. Union/Public Sector. BS 1967, Hillsdale Coll; AM 1970, PhD 1973, U of Mich. PUBL: "Implications for Research on Public Sector Wage Determination and Labor Relations--a discussion," IRRA, 1983; "The Supreme Court Beyond Sinderman and Roth, NCSCBHE, Baruch Coll, 1979; "Merit Determination as Basis for College and University Faculty Compensation," NCSCBHE, Baruch Coll, 1984. INT: coll barg, arb/med, public sector labor rels. ASSN: Hawaii IRRA, AAA, Phi Delta Kappa, NEA. POSITIONS: Asst Prof, Northern Mich U, 1973; Exec Dir for Higher Educ, Mich Educ Assn, 1975; and (since 1980) Executive Director, Univ of Hawaii Professional Assembly, 1649 Kalakaua Ave, Honolulu, HI 96826. 808/-947-3917

MUTH, LAWRENCE WILLIAM Bus:Pers/-Ind Rels. BS Rutgers U. PUBL: "Wage and Salary Admin Handbook," Edition 1; "Wage and Salary Administration Handbook," Edition 2. INT: coll barg, health & hosp care, income maint. ASSN: New York IRRA, NJ Bus and Ind Assn, Governor's Mgmt Improvement Plan Task Force, Amer Mgmt Assn. POSITION: (since 1971) Director, Corporate Economic Research, Johnson & Johnson, One Johnson and Johnson Plaza, New Brunswick, NJ 08933. 201/524-6361

MUTHUCHIDAMBARAM, S.P. Acad: Ind Rels. POSITION: Professor, Faculty of Admin, Univ of Regina, Regina, Saskatchewan S4S 0A2 Canada. 306/584-4713

MYERS, A. HOWARD Arbitration, Retired. AB 1926, Cornell, MA 1932, PhD 1933, Columbia. ADDRESS: Apt 401E, 2121 N Ocean Blvd, Boca Raton, FL 33431. 305/391-3143

MYERS, CHARLES ANDREW Acad: Ind Rels; Arbitration. BA 1934, Penna State U; PhD 1939, U of Chicago. PUBL: Personnel Administration, (co-author), 9th ed, 1981; Industrialism and Industrial Man, (co-author), 1960; Education, Manpower and Economic Growth, (co-author), 1964. INT: labor market econ, intl comparative labor, personnel. ASSN: NAA. POSITION: Prof of Mgmt, 1939, and, since 1981, Prof Emeritus, Sloan School of Mgmt, MIT. ADDRESS: 1403 Seton Hall Dr, Sun City, FL 33570. 813/634-3957

MYERS, HOWARD N. Legal Practice. BA 1961, Ripon Coll; LLB 1964, U of Wis. INT: labor law, arb/med, coll barg. Wis IRRA, Wis Bar Assn. POSITIONS: Attorney, NLRB-Pittsburgh, 1964; and (since 1966) Attorney-Partner, Shneidman, Myers, Dowling, Blumenfield & Albert, 735 W Wisconsin Ave, Milwaukee, WI 53233. 414/271-8650

N

NA, BOON CHONG Student. c/o Gary Benson, 102 E 19th St, #111, Minneapolis, MN 55403.

NADLER, CHARLES H. Student. AB 1962, Columbia U; JD 1984, U of Iowa. PUBL: "Issues in Fact Finding and Arbitration: Higher Education," in Public Sector Bargaining in Iowa: A Seven Year Perspective, R. Pegnetter, ed, Iowa Empl Rels Bd, Spring 1982; "The Dynamics of Collective Bargaining: Challenge of the Future," (w H. B. Weston & S. Klinefelter), New Directions for Community Colleges, Jossey--Bass, Winter 1978-79; "Criticism and Comment: Faculty Union Activity in Higher Education-1976," Ind Rels, vol 16, #3, Oct 1977. INT: coll barg, arb/med, labor law. ASSN: AAA, ABA(Labor & Empl Law Section), Assn of Trial Lawyers of Amer. POSITIONS: Asst Prof, Central Wash Univ-Ellesnburg, 1969; UniServ Dir, Iowa Higher Educ Assn-Iowa State Educ Assn, 1975; and (since 1983) Res Asst, College of Law, Univ of Iowa. ADDRESS: 715 River St, Iowa City, IA 52240. 319/337-9845

NADWORNY, MILTON J. Acad: Ind Rels. BS 1947, CCNY; MA 1948, Columbia; PhD 1952, U of Wi. ADDRESS: 33 Balsam St, Burlington, VT 05401. 802/862-1603

NAGATOMO, LAWRENCE M. Government. PhB 1956, U of N. Dak.; MSIR 1966, Loyola U-Chicago. INT: empl/trng programs, govt labor policy, contract mgmt. ASSN: Chicago IRRA, ASPA, Affirmative Action Assn. POSITIONS: Dir of Public Serv Employment Program, 1980, and, since 1983, Manpower Planning Supr, Private Ind Council (Branch of Mayor's Office of Empl and Trng). ADDRESS: 2130 Lincoln Park W, Chicago, IL 60614. 312/236-4522

NAIMARK, RICHARD Arbitration. BA 1975, U of R.I.; MS 1983, Columbia. PUBL: New York: No-Fault Abritration Reports. INT: arb/med, labor market econ, mgmt/educ. ASSN: New Brunswick IRRA. POSITION: (since 1977) Regional Director, AAA, One Executive Dr, Somerset, NJ 08873. 201/560-9560

NAJITA, JOYCE M. Acad: Ind Rels; Arbitration. BBS 1954, MBA 1955, U of Hawaii; MTP Cert, 1955, Radcliffe Coll. PUBL: The Mandatory Agency Shop in Hawaii's Public Sector," ILRR, April 1974; "When A University Faculty Rejects A Contract," Ind Rels, Feb 1976. INT: arb/med, coll barg, affirmative action. ASSN: Hawaii IRRA, AAA, SPIDR. POSITIONS: Assoc Researcher, 1974-77, Researcher, 1978, and, since 1983, Director, Ind Rels Center, Univ of Hawaii at Manoa, 2425 Campus Rd, Honolulu, HI 96822. 808/948-8132/8165

NANGERONI, JILL E. Union. POSITION: Office & Professional Employees Intl Union, 265 W 14th St, New York, NY 10011.

NAPIER, NANCY K. Acad: Org Beh/Pers, Ind Rels. PhD 1981, Ohio State U. PUBL: "Putting Human Resource Management Where It Belongs: At the Line Manager Level," Bus Horizons, 1984. INT: personnel, intl comparative labor, empl/trng programs. ASSN: Acad of

Mgmt, Acad Intl Bus. POSITION: (since 1981) Asst Prof, Mgmt & Org, School of Bus Admin, Univ of Washington, DJ-10, Seattle, WA 98195. 206/543-5909

NAPLES, MICHELE I. Acad: Economics. POSITION: Dept of Econ, Winants Hall, Rutgers Univ, New Brunswick, NJ 08903. 201/932-7363

NATHANSON, LESLIE Consulting. Acad: Org Beh/Pers. BS 1968, Tufts U; MS 1975, PhD 1979, Northwestern U. PUBL: Small Group Problem Solving: Aid to Organizational Effectiveness, Addison-Wesley, 1981. INT: org beh, union org/admin, mgmt/educ. ASSN: Chicago IRRA, Acad of Mgmt. POSITION: (since 1980) Principal, CCN Consulting Inc. ADDRESS: 1733 Highland, Wilmette, IL 60091. 312/256-3533

NAY, LESLIE A. Student. 522 N Pinckney St, Madison, WI 53703. 608/251-4236

NAYLON, JAMES A. Bus:Pers/Ind Rels. AS 1974, Honolulu Comm Coll, U of Hawaii; BGS 1974, Chaminade U; MA 1975, Central Mich U. INT: personnel, coll barg, mgmt/educ. ASSN: Hawaii IRRA, ASPA, ASTD, Intl Pers Mgmt Assn. POSITIONS: Major, Pers Officer, 1967, Inspector, Internal Affairs, 1978, Honolulu Police Dept; and (since 1982) Asst Vice Pres, Dir of Pers, Servco Pacific Inc, 89 King St, Honolulu, HI 96813. 808/521-6511

NAYLOR, PETER GEOFFRY Bus: Mgmt. ADDRESS: Bestobell Place, 16 Bath Rd, Slough, Berkshire, England, SL1355.

NAZZARO, STEWART E. Bus:Pers/Ind Rels. POSITION: Manager, Ind Rels Planning, General Electric WABA, 3135 Easton Trunpike, Fairfield, CT 06431. 203/373-2231

NEAL, RICHARD G. Consulting; Acad: School Admin. BA 1952, Md. U; MA 1957, George Washington U; Adv Degree, 1964, Ohio State U. PUBL: School and Government Relations; Bargaining Tactics, Vol 1 & 2; Countering Strikes in School and Government Service. INT: coll barg, mgmt/educ. ASSN: Assn of Negotiators & Contract Admin, Amer Assn of School Admin, Phi Delta Kappa. POSITIONS: Asst Dir, Educ Service Bureau, 1968; Empl Rels Dir, 1972, and, since 1980, Special Programs Dir, Prince William Co School Board, Box 389, Manassas, VA 22110. 703/369-8707

NEALE, WILLIAM S. Acad: Univ Admin. 12068 Riverbend Dr, Grand Blanc, MI 48439

NEAS, RUSSELL C. Arbitration. BS 1941, MS 1951, Kans State Coll-Pittsburgh. INT: arb/med, labor law, govt labor policy. ASSN: Kansas City IRRA, SPIDR, AAA. POSITION: (since 1970) Labor Arbitrator, (self-employed), 3377 East Kelly Dr, #106, Tulsa, OK 74135. 918/742-4846

NEFT, DARRELL K. Union. BSEE 1970, U of Calif-Irvine. INT: labor law, coll barg, union org/admin. POSITIONS: Electrical Engineer, 1970, and (since 1980) Chairman, Chapter 3, IFPTE Local 174, Long Beach Naval Shipyard. ADDRESS: 2700 Peterson Place, 15B, Costa Mesa, CA 92626. 213/547-8404

NEIDORFF, MICHAEL F. Bus:Mgmt/Admin. BS 1965, Trinity U; MBA 1966, St. Francis U. POSITIONS: Ind Rels, Canada, Dir Planning and Org, and Dir, Intl Marketing, Miles Laboratories, Inc. ADDRESS: 1565 Greenleaf Blvd, Elkhart, IN 46514. 219/264-8503

NEIGH, CHARLOTTE Arbitration; Acad: Student-Law. BA 1964, Grove City Coll; MA 1966, Mich State U. INT: arb/med, coll barg, govt labor policy. ASSN: SPIDR, Community Mediation Center. POSITIONS: Regional Dir, AAA, 1969; Arb Assoc, Leonard Lindquist, 1976; and (since 1978) Arbitrator, 1106 Summit Ave, St. Paul,MN 55105. 612/293-9230

NEIMEISER, MARK M. Union. INT: union org/admin, govt labor policy, coll barg. ASSN: New Brunswick IRRA. POSITIONS: Staff Rep, 1972, Exec Dir, Council #63, 1973, and, since 1973, Assoc Director, AFSCME, AFL-CIO, Council #1, Trenton. ADDRESS: 4134 S Broad St, T21, Yardville, NJ 08620. 609/396-3707

NELSON, ELINOR Acad: Educ Admin; Arbitration. BA 1974, Marshall U; MA 1976, PhD 1980, U of Minn. PUBL: "Organizational and Process Characteristics Determining Collective Bargaining in Public Education: A Comparative Analysis," U of Minn, 1980. INT: coll barg, personnel, arb/med. ASSN: Gateway IRRA, NASSP-MASSP, AAUP, PDK. POSITIONS: Researcher, U of Minn, 1976; School Admin, Dist #742 Community School, 1980; and (since 1981) Asst Prof of Educ Admin, Dept of Educ, St. Louis Univ, 221 N Grand Blvd, St. Louis, MO 63103. 314/658-2487/2508

NELSON, NELS E. Acad: Ind Rels; Arbitration. BA 1965, MA 1967, PhD 1972, U of Conn. PUBL: Arbitrator Characteristics and Arbtrel Decisions," Ind Rels, Fall 1981; "Grievance Rates and Technology," Acad of Mgmt J, Dec 1979; "Union Dues and Political Spending," Labor Law J, Feb 1977. INT: coll barg, arb/med, labor market econ. ASSN: Northeast Ohio IRRA. POSITIONS: Dir Ind Rels Program, LeMoyne Coll, 1975; Dir, Ind Rels Center, 1978, and, since 1981, Assoc Prof of Mgmt and Labor, Cleveland State Univ. ADDRESS: 13510 Fox Den East, Novelty, OH 44072. 216/-687-4742

NELSON, PAMELA K. Student. 303 E Michigan, #4, Urbana, IL 61801. 217/384-0120

NENNER, RODNEY ANDREW Student. 8 Juniper Dr, Great Neck, NY 11021. 516/466-8764

NESS, DEBRA L. Union. AB 1977, Drew U; MS Columbia, 1979. INT: empl/trng programs, org beh, labor educ. ASSN: Amer Public Health Assn, Natl Assn of Social Workers, Women's Equity Action League. POSITION: (since 1979) Natl Dir, Lifelong Ed & Development Program, SEIU, AFL-CIO, CLC, 2020 K St NW, Washington DC 20006. 202/452-8750.

NESSELROTH, SAUL H. Acad: Labor Educ, Ind Rels. POSITION: Labor Ed Center, Univ of Conn. ADDRESS: 157 Hillyndale Road, Storrs, CT 06268. 203/429-7882

NESTOR, OSCAR W. Acad: Ind Rels; Consulting, Arbitration. BS 1947, Thiel Coll, Greenville, PA; MBA 1948, Wharton School-U of Penna; PhD 1954, U of Penna. PUBL: The Strike as an Investment to Increase Productivity, Rutgers U, Inst of Mgt and Labor Rels, 1980; "Improving the Effectiveness of Home Health Care through Better Management," Career Planning Workbook, Advisor Press, 1980. INT: arb/med, health & hosp care, mgmt/educ. ASSN: New York IRRA, New York City Pers Assn. POSITIONS: Ind Rels Mgr, Sperry Corp, 1959; President, Pittsburgh Tech Inst, 1967; and (since 1981)

Dir, Doctoral Program and Prof of Ind Rels, Lubin Grad School of Bus, Pace Univ, Pace Plaza, New York, NY 10038. 212/488-1988

NEUFELD, MAURICE FRANK Acad: Ind Rels, Labor History; Consulting. PhD 1935, U of Wis. PUBL: Italy: School for Awakening Countries: The Italian Labor Movement in It's Political, Social, and Economic Setting from 1800 to 1960, NYSSILR-Cornell, 1961; Poor Countries and Authoritarian Rule, NYSSILR-Cornell, 1965; "The Persistence of Ideas in the American Labor Movement: The Heritage of the 1830's," Ind and Labor Rels Rev, vol 35, #2, Jan 1982. INT: union org/admin, intl comparative labor, labor history. ASSN: Org of Amer Historians, Study Group on Intl Labor and Working Class History, Soc for Italian Historical Studies. POSITIONS: Deputy Commissioner of Commerce, NYS Dept of Commerce, 1941, Dir, NYS Bureau of Rationing, 1941; and (from 1945-1976) Prof of Ind Rel, and, since 1976, Prof Emeritus, NYSSILR-Cornell. ADDRESS: 25 Cornell St, Ithaca, NY 14850. 607/-256-2266/2240

NEUMAN, GEORGE R. Acad: Econ, Ind Rels. BA 1968, LeMoyne Coll; MA 1969, PhD 1974, Northwestern U. INT: labor market econ, coll barg, method/statis. ASSN: Econometric Soc, AEA, Amer Statis Assn. POSITIONS: Asst Prof, Penn State Univ, 1972; Asst/Assoc Prof, Univ of Chicago, 1975; and (since 1982) Assoc Professor, Dept of Econ, Northwestern Univ. ADDRESS: 2418 Hastings Ave, Chicago, IL 60201. 312/492-5140

NEUMEIER, ELIZABETH Arbitration. BA 1972, New York U; JD 1975, Boston U. "Will Federal Arbitration Survive the Decade of the 80's?" 4 Fed Serv Labor Rels Rev 21, 1981. INT: arb/med, labor law, intl comparative labor. ASSN: SPIDR. POSITIONS: Dir-Legal Dept, Assn of Flight Attendants, 1975; Attorney-Adviser, Fed Labor Rels Authority, 1980; and (since 1983) Asst to the Chairman, Board of Arbitration, United States Steel Corp and United Steelworkers of America, 530 Oliver Bldg, Pittsburgh, PA 15222. 412/471-1558

NEVINS, DAVID C. Arbitration. BA 1962, U of Wis; JD 1967, George Washington U. INT: arb/med, laborlaw. ASSN: San Francisco IRRA, AAA, State Bar of Calif (Labor & Empl Section). POSITIONS: Attorney, NLRB, 1967; Admin Law Officer, Calif Agricultural Labor Rels Bd, 1975; and (since 1979) Arbitrator, 212 Frederick St, San Francisco, CA 94117. 415/665-1754

NEWELL, REGINALD Union. BA 1957, U of Buffalo; MA 1964, American U. POSITION: (since 1958) Dir of Research, IAM. ADDRESS: 2525 E Meredith Dr, Vienna, VA 22180. 202/857-5242

NEWMAN, HAROLD R. Government. PUBL: "Portrait of a Process," chapter in Public-Sector Bargaining; "In Higher Education", chapter in Collective Bargaining; Author of Monthly Bull for Mediators and Arbitrators. INT: arb/med, coll barg, labor history. ASSN: Capital Dist IRRA, Assn of Labor Rels Agencies, SPIDR, AAA. POSITIONS: Partner, Image Inc, 1963; Dir of Conciliation, 1967, and, since 1977, Chairman, NYS Public Empl Rels Board, 50 Wolf Rd, Albany, NY 12205. 518/457-2578

NEWMAN, JACK B. Fed Grievances, Equal Empl. PUBL: The Ubiquitous Series Code, Fed Occupations; Thirteen Volume Career Guide, HEW. INT: Fed grievances & complaints. ASSN: Wash DC IRRA, SPIDR. POSITIONS: Chief Pers Mgmt Inspector, Dir Long-Range Manpower Planning, HEW, 1974-77, and, since 1977, Grievance Examiner-EEO Investigator, Fed Govt Agencies (self employed contractor). ADDRESS: 9806 Dilston Rd, Silver Spring, MD 20903. 301/434-7172

NEWMAN, JERRY M. Acad: Org Beh/Pers. BA 1969, U of Mich; MAIR 1973, PhD 1974, U of Minn. PUBL: Compensation, BPI, 1984; "Discrimination in Recruitment: An Empirical Analysis," 1979; "Quantified Job Analysis," 1979. INT: personnel, govt labor policy, ind psych. POSITION: Assoc Prof, SUNY-Buffalo, 317 Crosby, Buffalo, NY 14214. 716/831-3326

NEWMAN, LLOYD N. Bus:Pers/Ind Rels, Consulting. BA 1952, U of Penna. INT: ind psych, org beh, bus strategies. ASSN: Public Rels Soc of Amer. POSITION: (since 1970) Exec Vice-Pres, Manning, Selvage, & Lee Inc, 3rd Floor, 99 Park Ave, New York, NY 10016. 212/599-6911

NEWMAN, STEPHEN J. Union. BA 1966, Long Island U; MA 1967, U of Ill. INT: coll barg, govt labor policy, intl comparative labor. POSITION: Research Assoc, United Steelworkers of Amer, 2568 N Lightwood Ave, Bethel Park, PA 15102. 412/562-2474

NEWMAN, TED E. Acad: Econ. POSITION: Asst Prof, Econ Dept, Northern Illinois Univ, DeKalb, IL 60115. 815/758-3713

NEWMAN, THEODORE Bus:Pers/Ind Rels. BA 1953, CCNY; MS 1956, Cornell. INT: coll barg, personnel, health & hosp care. POSITION: Macy's, 1958, and, since 1979, Senior Vice Pres Personnel, Macy's New York. ADDRESS: 350 Central Park W, New York, NY 10025. 212/560-4317

NEWMANN, WINN Union. ADDRESS: Suite 1205, 1000 Cennecticut Ave NW, Washington DC 20036. 202/331-8505

NEWMARK, MELVIN L. Legal Practice. JD 1936, Washington U-St. Louis. PUBL: "Reflections of An Arbitrator," Discipline and Grievances Issue, #499, Natl Foremen's Inst, Oct 1982. INT: arb/med. ASSN: Gateway IRRA, Metro Bar Assn of St. Louis, State of Mo Bar Assn. POSITIONS: Judge, Municipal Court of Olivette, 1962-66. ADDRESS: 2020 Ry Exch Bldg, 611 Olive St, St. Louis, MO 63101. 314/231-1312

NEWTON, DAVID Acad: Univ Admin. POSITION: Vice Chancellor, Long Island Univ, University Center, Greenvale, NY 11545. 511/-299-2510

NICHOLAS, CHARLES E. Bus:Pers/Ind Rels. BS 1960, Rider Coll. INT: personnel, org beh, mgmt/educ. ASSN: Central NJ & New Brusnwick IRRA, RMA Ind Rels Committee, Del Valley Pers Assn. POSITION: (since 1962) Asst Vice President, Goodall Rubber Co, Whitehead Rd, Trenton, NJ 08650. 609/587-4000

NICHOLS, GEORGE N. Arbitration. Cummings & Lockwood, 855 Main St, Bridgeport, CT 06604.

NICHOLS, HENRY W. Government. POSITION: Commissioner, FMCS, 739 US Court House, 920 W Riverside, Spokane, WA 99201.

NICHOLSON, PERCIVAL L. Bus:Empl/Labor Rels. POSITION: Empl/Labor Rels/EEO, US Postal Service, 107-18 Pinegrove St, Jamaica, NY 11435. 212/291-8560

NICHOLSON, ROBERT PAUL Acad: Student; Bud:Mgmt/Admin. AAS 1981, Montgomery Cty Community Coll,Penna; BSBA 1983, Shippensburg. INT: coll barg, arb/med, labor law. ASSN: Central Penna IRRA. POSITIONS: Asst Mgr, 1982, Manager, McLeans Restaurant, Haven Crest, NJ; and (since 1984) Grad Student, St. Francis Coll-School of Ind Rels. ADDRESS: RF 1 Box 78, Apt 7, Loretto, PA 15940. 814/472-4176

NICKL, CARL E. Bus:Mgmt/Admin. ADDRESS: 412 Hazelnut Dr, Monroeville, PA 15146. 412/372-0910

NICOLAI, DAVID Acad: Student, Ind Rels. BA 1975, Grinnel; MA 1983, U of Ill-UC. INT: labor educ, labor history. POSITIONS: Workers Compensation Specialist, USDL, 1977; and (since 1980) Res Asst, Inst of Labor and Ind Rels, Univ of Ill, 504 E Armory, Champaign, IL 61820. 217/333-0984

NICOLAU, GEORGE Arbitration, Legal Prac. BA 1944, U of Mich; JD 1951, Columbia U. ADDRESS: 125 E 10th St, New York, NY 10003. 212/777-5032

NICOSON, JOHN PATRICK Bus:Mgmt/Admin. 460 Mapleton Ave, Pittsburgh, PA 15228.

NIELSEN, PAUL B. Acad: Ind Rels. POSITION: Ind Rels, OSHAWA Group Ltd, 302 The East Mall, Islington, Toronto, Ont M9B 6B8 Canada.

NIEMIC, JOAN City Council Member. MAIR 1983, U of Minn. INT: govt labor policy, personnel, empl/trng programs. ASSN: Twin Cities Pers Assn. POSITION: Council Member, City of Minneapolis. ADDRESS: 4239 Harriet Ave, Minneapolis, MN 55409. 612/348-2210

NIKAIDO, ROY SAICHI Bus:Pers/Ind Rels, Labor Rels. POSITION: Health Labour Rels Assn, #500, 1212 W Broadway, Vancouver, BC V5Z 1G1 Canada.

NILAND, JOHN R. Acad: Ind Rels. BCom 1964, MCom 1967, U of New South Wales; PhD 1970, U of Ill. PUBL: Australian Labour Economics: Readings, (co-edited),Macmillan, 1984; Industrial Relations in Australia, (co-authored), Allen & Unwin, 1981; Collective Bargaining and Compulsory Arbitration, New South Wales Univ Press, 1978. INT: coll barg, labor market econ, govt labor policy. ASSN: Ind Rels Soc of Australia, IIRA. POSITIONS: Asst Prof, Cornell Univ, 1970; Reader in Econ, Australian Natl Univ, 1972; and (since 1974) Professor and Dir, Ind Rels Research Centre, Univ of New South Wales, PO Box 1, Kensington, NSW, Australia 2033. Phone: 662 3526

NITTA, MICHIO Acad: IndRels. BA 1971, MA 1974, U of Tokyo. PUBL: "'Self Management' in the Iron and Steel Industry," (Nibon, Rodo, Kyolgai, Sasshi), J of the Japan Inst of Labor; "Joint Labor-Management Conference in the Japanese Steel Industry," (Shakai Kagaku Kenkyu) The J ofSoc Sci. INT: coll barg, intl comparative labor, personnel. ASSN: Japan Ind Rels Research Assn. Soc for theStudy of Soc Policy. POSITIONS: Asst, Inst of Soc Sci, Univ of Tokyo, 1978; Asso Prof, Faculty of Econ, Musashi Univ, 1980; and (since 1983) Visiting Scholar (Fulbright Scholar), Sloan School of Mgmt, MIT, E52-564, 50 Memorial Dr, Cambridge, MA 02139. 617/253-2602

NIXON, KATHLEEN A. Government. #407, 3221 Connecticut Ave NW, Washington DC 20008.

NOBILI, RONALD B. Union. BA 1969, Sacred Heart U; IE Cert 1974, Central Conn State U. INT: union org/admin, arb/med, labor law. ASSN: Southwestern Conn IRRA. POSITIONS: Ind Arts Educ Instructor, Shelton Public Schools, 1975; Field Rep, 1979, and, since 1983, Bus Manager, Laborer's Intl Union, Local 665, AFL-CIO, Bridgeport. ADDRESS: 73-B Riverbend, Stratford, CT 06497. 203/335-7943

NOBLE, ALBERT CHARLES Acad: Univ Admin; Consulting, Retired. BS 1932, U of Ill; MA 1964, East Tenn State U. INT: empl/trng programs, mgmt/educ, personnel. POSITION: Coordinator Non Degree Programs, East Tenn State Univ, Retired. ADDRESS: 156 Indian Trail, Bristol, TN 37620. 615/968-1534

NOLAN, DENNIS R. Acad: Law; Arbitration. AB 1967, Georgetown U; JD 1970, Harvard; MA 1974, U of Wis-Milwaukee. PUBL: Labor Arbitration Law and Practice in a Nutshell, West Pub Co, 1979; "American Labor Arbitration: The Early Years," (w R. Abrams),35 Univ of Fla Law Rev, #3, 1983; "The Common Law of the Labor Agreement: Vacations," (w R. Abrams), 5 Ind Rels Law J, 301, 1983. INT: arb/med, labor law, labor history. ASSN: South Carolina Bar, Intl Soc for Labor Law and Soc Security, Southern Labor Studies Assn. POSITIONS: Visiting Assoc Prof of Law, Univ of Wash School of Law, 1979-80; Fulbright Visiting Prof of Law, Univ Coll Galway, Ireland, 1981-82; and, since 1980, Prof of Law, School of Law, Univ of South Carolina, Columbia, SC 29208. 803/777-4155

NOLAN, TERRANCE J. Legal Practice, Bus:Pers/Ind Rels; Acad: Univ Admin. BA 1971, St. Francis Coll; JD 1974, St. John's U; LLM 1982, New York U. PUBL: "The Unfavorable Arbitration Award: Is He Who Hesitates Lost?" NYS Bar Assn Labor and Empl Law Sec Newsletter, Summer 1983. INT: labor law, arb/med, coll barg. ASSN: New York IRRA, ABA, NYS Bar Assn, Natl Assn of Coll and Univ Attorneys. POSITIONS: Attorney, NYC Transit Authority, 1974; Labor Rels Specialist, Pepsi-Cola Co, Purchase, NY, 1977; and (since 1980) Staff Counsel and Asst Dir of Labor Rels, New York Univ, 70 Washington Square South, New York, NY 10012. 212/598-7567

NOLLEN, STANLEY D. Acad: Bus Admin, Ind Rels, Org Beh/Pers. MS 1965, Cornell U; MBA 1970, PhD 1974, U of Chicago. PUBL: New Work Schedules in Practice, NY:Van Nostrand Reinhold, 1982; "Does Flexitime Increase Productivity?" Harvard Bus Rev, Sept-Oct 1979; "Paid Educational Leave of Absence," IRRA Proceedings, 1979. INT: personnel, empl/trng programs, labor market econ. ASSN: AEA, Acad of Mgmt. POSITIONS: Asst Prof, 1973, and, since 1983, Assoc Prof and MBA Program Dir, School of Bus Admin, Georgetown Univ, Washington DC 20057. 202/625-4704

NORDLANDER, AKE Employer Org. POSITION: President, Sveriges Verkstadforening, Box 5510 S-11485, Stockholm, Sweden

NORGREN, PAUL HERBERT Acad: Org Beh/Pers. Retired. POSITION: Assoc Prof Emeritus, University College, Rutgers Univ. ADDRESS: 90 Crestwood Dr, Stamford, CT 06905

NORMAN, RICHARD CALHOUN Bus:Pers/Ind Rels. BA 1974, U of N.C; MA 1978, U of Minn. INT: coll barg, personnel, arb/med. ASSN: South Atlantic IRRA, ASPA. POSITIONS: Pers Adm Rep, 1978, Labor Rels Rep, 1981, and, since 1982, Labor Rels Supervisor, Celanese Fibers Operations, Cherry Road Station, Rock Hill, SC 29730. 803/366-3897

NORTHROP, JAMES B. Government. POSITION: Director, Work Force Planning Unit, Agency Bldg 2, 13th Fl, Empire State Plaza, Albany, NY 12223. 518/474-2350

NORTHRUP, HERBERT ROOF Acad: Ind Rels; Research, Consulting. AB 1939, Duke U; AM 1941, PhD 1942, Harvard U. PUBL: Economics of Labor Relations, 9th ed, Irwin, 1981; Multinational Collective Bargaining Attempts, Wharton School, U of Penna, 1979; "The Rise and Demise of PATCO," Ind & Labor Rels Rev, Jan 1984. INT: coll barg, multinational ind rels, ind race rels. ASSN: AEA, ASPA. POSITIONS: Vice-Pres, Penn-Tex Corp, 1953; Mgr, Empl Rels, General Electric Co, 1957; Prof of Ind, 1961, Dir, Ind Research Unit, 1964, and, since 1968, Chairman, Labor Rels Counsel, The Wharton School, Univ of Penna. ADDRESS: 517 Thornbury Rd, Haverford, PA 19041. 215/-898-7729

NORTON, DANIEL JAY Bus:Mgmt/Admin. 3882W N Wood Lake Dr, Columbus, IN 47201.

NORWOOD, JANET L. Government. BA 1945, Douglas Coll; MA 1948, PhD 1949, Tufts U. INT: labor market econ, coll barg, method/-statis. ASSN: AEA, Amer Statis Assn, Natl Econ Club. POSITION: (since 1979) Commissioner of Labor Statistics, US Bureau of labor Statistics, 441 G St NW, Washington DC 20212. 202/-523-1092

NOTARO, SALVATORE A. Acad: Univ Admin. BS 1972, MS 1973, U of Wis; EdSp, 1977, Mich State U. INT: empl/trng programs, mgmt/-educ, labor educ. ASSN: Wis IRRA, Adult Educ Assn, P.D.K., ASTD. POSITIONS: Ind Shop Worker, A. O. Smith, 1963; Inst Labor Rels, Milw Area Tech Coll, 1977; and (since 1979) Asst Dir of Continuing Educ and Summer Sessions, Marquette Univ, 1918 W Wisconsin Ave, Milwaukee, WI 53233. 414/225-7507

NOUNE, MICHAEL ANTHONY Bus:Mgmt/-Admin. BSBA 1972, MAIR 1980, Wayne State U. INT: mgmt/educ, personnel, empl/trng programs. ASSN: Detroit IRRA, AICPPSA, MACPA. POSITIONS: Supr-Financial Info and Controls, City of Detroit, 1978; Controller, Book Cadillac Hotel, 1982; and (since 1983) Controller, The Michigan Inn, 16400 J. L. Hudson Dr, Southfield, MI 48075. 313/559-6500

NOVAK, HENRY LINTON Acad: Bus:Admin/Mgmt. ADDRESS: 124 Taylor, Dwight, IL 60420. 815/584-2874

NOVICK, DAVID S. Bus:Pers/Ind Rels. BS 1970, Cornell U; MA 1982, New York U. INT: ind psych, org beh, personnel. ASSN: Human Resource Planning Soc, ASPA, ASTD. POSITIONS: Labor Rels Assoc, Western Electric Co, 1970; Empl Rels Mgr, Pepsi Co, Inc, 1973; and (since 1977) Director of Human Resources, The Nestle Co, 100 Bloomingdale Rd, White Plains, NY 10605. 914/687-6896

NOVIT, MITCHELL SHELDON Acad: Org Beh/Pers, Ind Rels. AB 1954, U of N.C.-Chapel Hill; MBA 1959, PhD 1966, U of Mich. PUBL: Essentials of Personnel Management, Prentice Hall, 1979; "Employer Liability for Employee Misconduct: Two Common Law Doctrines," PERSONNEL, Jan-Feb 1982; "Employees, Too, Have Legal Obligations," S.A.M. Advanced Mgmt J, Summer 1983. INT: personnel, coll barg, mgmt/educ. ASSN: Acad of Mgmt, ASPA. POSITIONS: Asst Empl Mgr, F. & R. Lazarus Co, 1959; Lecturer, Univ of Mich, 1965; and (since 1966) Assof Prof of Pers & Org Beh, Grad School of Bus, Indiana Univ, Bloomington, IN 47405. 812/335-2755

NOVOGRODSKY, DAVID Union; Acad: Ind Rels. BA 1955, Reed Coll; MA 1959, U of Ore. INT: union org/admin, govt labor policy, labor educ. ASSN: San Francisco IRRA. POSITIONS: (since 1976 and currently, Instructor, Labor Studies, San Francisco Community College, and, since 1981, Bus Manager, Intl Fed of Professional & Technical Engineers, #21. ADDRESS: 1404 Willard, #4, San Francisco, CA 94117. 415/673-0220

NOWAKOWSKI, MICHAEL G. Government. Acad: Ind Rels. AB 1972, Harvard; JD 1975, Wayne State U. INT: arb/med, coll barg, labor law. ASSN: Detroit IRRA, SPIDR, ABA, Mich Bar Assn. POSITIONS: Instructor-Part Time, currently, Wayne State Univ, and (since 1975) Commissioner, FMCS, 431 Federal Bldg and Courthouse, 231 W Lafayette, Detroit, MI 48226. 313/226-7769

NOWICKI, HENRY H. Retired. BA 1929, JD 1932, U of Mich. POSITIONS: Chmn, Trucking Panel & Hearings Officer, War Labor Bd, 1944-47; Dir of Labor Rels, Intl Multifood, 1947-74. Retired. ADDRESS: 1536 E River Terrace, Minneapolis, MN 55414.

NSIAH-YEBOAH, RICHARD Student. 1441 J Spartan Village, East Lansing, MI 48823. 517/355-1155

NULTY, LESLIE E. Union. POSITION: UFCW Intl Union, 1775 K St NW, Washington DC 20006. 202/223-3111

NYE, DAVID PAUL Bus:Mgmt/Admin. POSITION: manager/Union Relations, Trane Company, 2231 E State St, Trenton, NJ 08619. 609/587-3400

NYGREN, JAMES WILLIAM Bus:Pers/Ind Rels. BA 1968, Regis Coll. INT: coll barg, health & hosp care, labor law. POSITIONS: Pers Mgr, King Soopers, Inc., Denver, 1971; and (since 1977) Director of Personnel, Frys Food Stores of Ariz, 6101 W Washington, Phoenix, AZ 85005. 602/269-3171

NYSTROM, PAUL CLIFDON Acad: Org Beh/Pers, Ind Rels. BS 1962, MA 1966, PhD 1970, U of Minn. PUBL: Handbook of Organizational Design, Vols 1 & 2, Oxford Univ Press, 1981; Prescriptive Models of Organizations, TIM's Studies in Mgmt Sci, vol 5, 1977; "Nursing Jobs and Satisfaction": Nursing Mgmt, 1984.

INT: org beh, personnel, ind psych. ASSN: Acad of Mgmt, Amer Psych Assn, Inst of Mgmt Sci. POSITION: (since 1978) Professor, School of Bus Admin, Univ of Wis-Milwaukee, PO Box 742, Milwaukee, WI 53201. 414/963-4337

O

OAXACA, RONALD L. Acad: Econ. BA 1961, Calif State U-Fresno; MA 1969, PhD 1971, Princeton U. PUBL: "Opportunity Costs of the Minimum Wage," (w J.C. Cox), Research in Labor Econ, 1983; "The Political Economy of Minimum Wage Legislation," (J.C. Cox), Econ Inquiry, Oct 1982; "Identification of Supplier Induced Demand in the Health Care Sector," (w R.D. Auster), J of Human Res, Summer 1981. INT: labor market econ, govt labor policy, method/statis. ASSN: AEA, North Amer Econ & Finance Assn. POSITIONS: Asst Prof of Econ, U of Mass, 1973; Assoc Prof of Econ, Univ of Ariz, 1976; and (since 1983) Visiting Assoc Prof of Econ, Grad School of Bus, Stanford Univ, Palo Alto, CA 94303. 415/497-2158

OBERHOLTZER, DAWN M. Student. 611 S Lincoln Ave, Lebanon, PA 17042. 717/273-0675

OBERMAYER, PETER EARLE Government. BA 1960 St. Olaf Coll; MA 1963, EdD 1977, U of Minn. INT: arb/med, coll barg, govt labor policy. ASSN: Assn of Labor Rels Agencies, SPIDR, AAA. POSITION: (since 1979) Mediator, Bureau of Mediation Services, State of Minnesota. ADDRESS: 5913 Hansen Rd, Edina, MN 55436. 617/296-2525

OBERSTEIN, ROBERT F. Bus:Pers/Ind Rels, Arbitration; Acad: Ind Rels. BA 1971, St. John's U; MS 1977, Long Island U. PUBL: Apprenticeship On The Move, History of the Joint Industry Board (50 Years). INT: coll barg, labor law, arb/med. ASSN: AAA, Maricopa County Part Time Faculty Assn, I.B.E.W. POSITIONS: Pers Mgr, Continental Connector Corp, 1978; Labor Rels Rep, EBASCO Services/St. Lucie II & Waterford III Nuclear Projects, 1979; and (since 1980) Senior Labor Rels Admin, Salt River Project, PO Box 1980, Phoenix, AS 85001. 602/273-5643

O'BRIEN, FABIUS PRINCE Acad: Bus Admin; Consulting. BS 1976, MS 1980, PhD 1984, Va Tech. PUBL: "Are There Grievances Against Your Non-Union Grievance Procedure?" (w D. Drost),Pers Admin, 28,1 Jan 1983, pp 36-46. INT: union org/admin, personnel, org beh. ASSN: Acad of Mgmt, Amer Psych Assn. POSITIONS: Asst Prof of Admin, School of Commerce, Econ and Pol, Wash & Lee Univ, 1982; and (since 1983) Asst Prof of Mgmt, College of Bus, Western Ill Univ, Macomb, IL 61455. 309/298-1018

O'BRIEN, FRANCIS D. Government. BS 1968, MSIR 1975, Loyola U-Chicago; MPA 1983, Harvard. INT: coll barg, labor law, personnel. ASSN: Chicago IRRA, Intl Pers Mgmt Assn, ASPA. POSITIONS: Personnel Analyst, Metro Sanitary Dist-Chicago, 1970; Pers Dir, Milwaukee Metro Sewerage Dist, 1978; and (since 1983) Chief Labor Negotiator, Metropolitan Sanitary Dist of Greater Chicago, 100 E Erie St, Chicago, IL 60611. 312/751-5600

O'BRIEN, FRANCIS T. Acad: Ind Rels; Arbitration, Consulting. BSBA 1955, MA 1957, Boston Coll. INT: arb/med, coll barg, labor law. ASSN: Boston IRRA, SPIDR, AAA, AEA. POSITION: (since 1973) Director, Quirk Inst of Ind Rels, Providence College, Providence, RI 02918. 401/865-2156

O'BRIEN, JAMES J., JR Bus:Pers/Ind Rels, Consulting; Acad: Ind Rels. BMgt 1969, Bucks County Community Coll; BS 1971, MPA 1978, Rider Coll. INT: arb/med, coll barg, personnel. ASSN: Philadelphia IRRA, ASPA, Phila Survey Group. POSITIONS: Pers Supr, Ind Rels Specialist, and, since 1980, Superintendent Labor Rels and Pers, Southeastern Penna Transportation Authority, Philadelphia. ADDRESS: 2 Briaroot La, Levittown, PA 19054. 215/456-4541

O'BRIEN, RAE ANN Acad: Ind Rels; Consulting. MILR 1978, NYSSILR-Cornell. PUBL: Directory of Labour Organizations, vol I Intl and European Regional Bodies, (w. H. R. Northrup, & R. L.Rowan), Mgmt Centre Europe, 1980; Multinational Union Organizations in the Manufacturing Industries, (w R. L. Rowan & H. R. Northrup), Phila: Ind Rels Unit, Wharton School-Univ of Penna, 1980. INT: coll barg, intl comparative labor, arb/med. ASSN: Boston IRRA, SPIDR, AAA, ILR Alumni Assn. POSITIONS: Dir of Placement, NYSSILR-Cornell, 1977; Res Specialist, Ind Res Unit, Wharton School-Univ of Penna, 1979; and (since 1983) Assoc in Research, Harvard Grad School of Bus Admin. ADDRESS: 1742 Beacon St, #4, Brookline, MA 02146. 617/495-6902

O'BRIEN, ROBERT M. Arbitration. ADDRESS: 50 Congress St, Boston, MA 02109. 617/225-0768

O'BRIEN, THOMAS H. Government, Consulting. PUBL: "Futuristics: An Aid to Decision Makers," Trends, Mar 1971; "Environmental Hazards Faced by Management Analysts," The Office, Mar 1972; "Working Smarter--Through Process Improvement Teams," Interest Publ, USDL, Sept 1981. INT: employee participation, mgmt/educ, org beh. ASSN: ASTD, ASPA, World Future Soc. POSITIONS: Internal Consultant, Commonwealth of Penna, 1958; Internal Consultant, US-HEW, 1965; and, since 1967, Internal Consultant,USDL, 200 Constitution Ave NW, Washington DC 20210. 202/523-6341

O'BRIEN, THOMAS M. Government; Acad: Labor/Mgmt Rels. BA 1975, Webster Coll-St. Louis. INT: arb/med, labor educ, coll barg. ASSN: Gateway IRRA, Speakers Bureau. POSITIONS: Supr, Boston Securities Inc, 1965; Bus Rep, OPEIU, Local #13, AFL-CIO, 1970; and (since 1977) Federal Mediator, FMCS, 12140 Woodcrest Exec Dr, St. Louis, MO 63141. 314/-576-3977

OCKERT, ROY ANTHONY Union; Acad: Econ, Ind Rels. AB 1941, U of Calif-Berkeley. POSITION: Coord Dept of Res Ed & CB, IWA, 1622 N Lombard St, Portland, OR 97217. 503/-285-5281

O'CONNELL, EDWARD J. Arbitration, Legal Prac. BA 1956, JD 1959, Villanova U. INT: arb/med, labor law, coll barg. ASSN: Western Penna IRRA, ABA, Penna Bar Assn, Allegheny Cty Bar Assn. POSITIONS: Counsel Empl Rels, Allegheny Ludlum Ind Inc, 1974, Sr Counsel & Asst to V.P. Empl Rels, Allegheny Ludlum Steel Corp, 1980; and (since 1981) Arbitrator (self-employed), 1301 Union Trust Bldg, Pittsburgh, PA 15219. 412/391-1067

O'CONNER, FRANK Bus:Pers/Ind Rels. POSITION: Industrial Relations, Arcata Graphics, TC Industrial Park, Depew, NY 14043.

O'CONNER, PAULA Union; Acad: Student. BA 1961 Antioch Coll. INT: union org/admin, labor educ. POSITIONS: Editor, Child Herald (Newsletter), 1971; and (since 1974) Asst Dir/Office of the Sec-Treas, Amer Fed of Teachers, AFL-CIO, 11 Dupont Circle NW, Washington DC 20036. 202/797-4457

ODELL, WILLIAM LUCIEN Consulting. BA 1962, Stanford U; MPA 1963, Syracuse U. PUBL: "Negotiations Preparation," Assn of Educ Negotiators J, Sep-Oct 1977. INT: coll barg, labor law, arb/med. ASSN: Sacramento IRRA, ASPA, Calif School Admin Assn, Intl Pers Mgmt Assn. POSITIONS: Asst Pers Dir, San Mateo High School Dist, 1967; Pers Dir, Santa Cruz School Dist, 1972; and (since 1974) Consultant, Public Empl Rels Consulting, 6858 Whispering Canyon Rd, Anderson, CA 96007. 916/357-3417

O'DONNELL, JOSEPH PATRICK Acad: Univ Admin; Arbitration. BA 1944, JD 1949, Boston U. INT: arb/med, coll barg, govt labor policy. ASSN: Boston IRRA. POSITION: Executive Dir, Harvard Univ Trade Union Program, GSED Appian Way, Cambridge, MA 02138. 617/495-9265

O'DONNELL, LIGUORI A. Acad: Econ. AB 1949, U of Notre Dame; MSIR, 1953, Loyola U-Chicago; PhD 1961, U of Wis-Madison. PUBL: "Rationalism, Capitalism and the Entrepreneur," History of Pol Economy, Spring 1973; "From Limerick to the GoldenGate: Odyssey of An Irish Carpenter," Studies :An Irish Quart Rev, Spring-Summer, 1979; "Should We Repeal 14(b)?" America, April 1977. INT: labor market econ, coll barg, labor history. ASSN: AEA, Penna Labor History Soc. POSITIONS: Asst Prof, Univ of San Francisco, 1959; Labor Economist, US BLS, 1962; and (since 1967) Assoc Prof, Dept of Econ, Villanova Univ. ADDRESS: 16 Stonehedge Lane, Malvern, PA 19355. 215/-645-4359

O'DONNELL, THOMAS L. P. Legal Practice. AB 1947, LLB 1949, Harvard. INT: labor law. ASSN: Boston IRRA, ABA, Boston Bar Assn, Amer Judicature Soc. POSITION: (since 1949) Partner, Ropes & Gray, 225 Franklin St, Boston, MA 02110. 617/423-6100

ODZA, RANDALL M. Legal Practice. BS 1964, LLB 1967, Cornell. INT: coll barg, labor law. ASSN: Western New York IRRA, ABA-(Labor Section), NYS Bar Assn(Labor Section), Erie County Bar Assn(Labor Committee). POSITION: (since 1969) Attorney, Jaeckle, Fleischman & Mugel, 700 Liberty Bank Building, Buffalo, NY 14202. 716/856-0600

OECHSLIN, JEAN-JACQUES Empl Org. Grad, Inst d'Etudes Politiques, Paris; Doctor, Faculte de Droit, U de Paris. POSITION: Council-French Employers, 31 Ave Pierre I de Serbie, 75784 Paris Cedex 16, France.

OETTINGER, MARTIN P. Acad: Econ. BBA 1952, CCNY; MA 1956, Brown U; PhD 1960, Harvard. POSITIONS: Inst, Harvard U, 1960; and (since 1961) Dept of Econ, U of Calif, Davis CA 95616. 916/752-1574

OFONG, CHIGBO Acad: Ind Rels, Intl Rels; Union. BA 1976, SUNY-Buffalo; MA 1978, PhD 1982, Johns Hopkins U. PUBL: Unions in Politics: Nigeria; "Trade Unionism in Africa;" "Legal Aspects of Trade Unionism in Nigeria." INT: coll barg, intl comparative labor, labor market econ. ASSN: Amer Soc of Intl Law, World Soc Prospects Assn. POSITIONS: Consultant in Intl Affairs, Natl Alliance of Postal and Fed Empl, 1979; Consultant, UNIPOL Rising Sun Pub Co, 1982; and (since 1983) Acting Dir, Inst for Labor-Mgmt Rels, School of Bus and Public Admin, Howard Univ, Washington DC 20059. 202/636-7449

O'GRADY, JAMES P. Acad: Ind Rels; Arbitration. BS 1958, MS 1963, PhD 1969, St. Louis U. PUBL: Elements of Business; Labor Relations; "Grievance Mediation Usage by Selected States." INT: arb/med, personnel, coll barg. ASSN: Gateway IRRA, AAA, SPIDR. POSITIONS: Health/Pension Specialist, General American Life Ins Co, 1958; Pers/Labor Rels Specialist, Ernst & W. Linney, 1963; and (since 1964) Prof of Ind Rels, St.Louis Community Coll at Florissant Valley. ADDRESS: 12054 Greenwalk Dr, Creve Coeur, MO 63141. 314/595-4336

O'GRADY, JOHN P. Bus:Mgmt/Admin, Bus:Pers/Ind Rels. BSLE, 1973, U of Akron; MSIR 1980, Rutgers U; PhD 1981, Calif Western U-Santa Anna. INT: coll barg, arb/med, labor law. ASSN: SPIDR, ASPA. POSITIONS: Dir Compensation & Benefits, ITT Europe Inc-Brussels, 1980, Dir Admin, ITT Fluid Handling Div-Chicago, 1981, and, since 1983, Vice Pres-Dir Admin, ITT Federal Electric Corp, 621 Industrial Ave, Paramus, NJ 07652. 201/967-2983

OKUBAYASHI, KOJI Acad: Org Beh/Pers, Ind Rels, Bus Admin. MB 1968, DR-Bus Admin, 1975, Kobe U. PUBL: Humanization of Work, Yuhikaku, Tokyo, 1981; Ideas of Worker's Participation in Management, Yuhikaku, Tokyo, 1979; Theories of Personnel Management. Yuhikaku, Tokyo, 1974. INT: org beh, coll barg, personnel. ASSN: Acad of Mgmt, Japan Soc for Pers and Labor Research, IIRA. POSITIONS: Asst Prof, 1969, and, since 1975, Assoc Prof, School of Bus Admin, Kobe Univ, Rokkodai, Nada, Kobe, 657 Japan. Phone: 078-881-1212.

OLAYIWOLA, PETER OLU Acad: Econ. BBA 1979, M Admin, 1980, Penna State U. PUBL: "Job Satisfaction Among the Data Processing Professionals in a Large Service Organization." INT: empl/trng programs, intl comparative labor, mgmt/educ. ASSN: Philadelphia IRRA, British Inst of Mgmt, IIRA. POSITIONS: Res Asst 1981, and, since 1982, Doctoral Candidate, Univ of Delaware, PO Box 25247, Wilmington, DE 19899. 302/999-1523

OLBRICH, RICHARD Government. JD 1967, U of Wis-Madison. INT labor law.: POSITION: Senior Counsel, NLRB. ADDRESS: 4627 Butterworth St NW, Washington DC 20016. 202/254-9043

O'LEARY, JOHN Union. BS 1963, Cornell U. INT: coll barg, labor law, union org/admin. ASSN: New York & Long Island IRRA. POSITION: (since 1980) Dir of Organizing, New York State United Teachers, 410 Jericho Turnpike, Jericho, NY 11753. 516/938-4871

OLIN, BRUCE KEVIN Bus:Pers/Ind Rels. 201 Hawthorne Ave, Apt 64, Central Islip, NY 11722.

OLIVA, HENRY Bus:Pers/Ind Rels. POSITION: Pers Manager, Dole Company, POB D, Lanai, HI 96763. 808/565-6922

OLIVEIRA, MYRA Bus:Pers/Ind Rels. POSITION: Personnel & Ind Rels, Kapiolani/Child Medical Center, 1319 Punahou St, Honolulu, HI 96826.

OLIVER, ANTHONY THOMAS JR. Legal Practice. BS 1951, JD 1953, U of Santa Clara. PUBL: "Affirmative Action Programs and Compliance," (w W. E. Emer), chapter 3 in Advising Calif Employers, CEB 1981; "The Disappearing Right to Terminate Employees at Will," Pers J, Dec 1982; "Labor Relations," Pers J, Aug 1983. INT: labor law, arb/med, coll barg. ASSN: South Calif, Orange County, Arizona & South Nevada IRRA, Calif Bar Assn, ABA, Town Hall of Calif. POSITION: (since 1963) Partner, Parker, Milliken, Clark, O'Hara & Samuelian, 333 S Hope St, 27th Fl, Los Angeles, CA 90071. 213/683-6618.

OLIVER, HOWARD WAYNE Union. BA 1947, Harvard; MA 1958, UCLA; MA 1966 U of South Calif. INT: arb/med, coll barg. ASSN: Southern Calif IRRA. POSITION: Exec Secretary, Amer Fed of TV and Radio Artists, 1717 N Highland Ave, Hollywood, CA 90028. 213/461-8111

OLIVER, WALTER L. Union. Position: Secretary-Treasurer, Mich State AFL-CIO, 419 S Washington Ave, Lansing, MI 48933.

O'LOUGHLIN, WILLIAM Arbitration. INT: arb/med, labor law, labor market econ. ASSN: New York IRRA. POSITIONS: Field Rep, NLRB, 1941, Asst Reg Dir, USDL, 1960; and (since 1979) Arbitrator, 250 W 57th St, New York, NY 10107. 212/581-3816

OLSEN-TJENSVOLD, REYNOLDS Consulting; Acad: Bus Admin. PhB 1935, U of Wis-Madison; MS 1970, U of Wis-Milwaukee; PhD 1946, Northwestern U. PUBL: How To Select & Train New First Line Supervisors, Dartwell, 1980. INT: personnel, memt/educ. ASSN: Wis IRRA. POSITIONS: Mgr/Ind & Community Rels, Inland Steel Products Co, 1957; Mgr, Trng & Devel, Kearney & Trecker Co, 1965; and since 1975, President, Triangle T Corp, Mequon, WI 53092. 414/241-5638

OLSON, CRAIG Acad: Ind Rels, Bus Admin. PhD 1979, U of Wis. PUBL: "The Impact of Rescheduled School Days in Teacher Strikes," ILRR, vol 37, #4, July 1984; "Sex Discrimination in the Promotion Process," (w Becker),ILRR, vol 36, #4, July 1983; "The Effects of Unions on Job Satisfaction: The Role of Work Related Values and Perceived Outcomes," (w Berger & Boudreau), Org Beh & Human Performance, vol 32, Dec 1983. INT: coll barg, govt labor policy, labor market econ. POSITION: (since 1980) Asst Prof, School of Mgmt, SUNY-Buffalo, 312 Crosby Hall, Buffalo, NY 14214. 716/831-3327

OLSON, JULIE EILEEN Bus:Mgmt/Admin, Bus:Pers/Ind Rels; Acad: Ind Rels. BA 1980 North Park Coll; MSIR 1984, Loyola U-Chicago. INT: govt labor policy, health & hosp care, labor law. POSITION: Operations Manager, Pelam Inc-Health Systems Div. ADDRESS: 2625 W Farragut, Chicago, IL 60625. 312/271-7354

ONANIAN, EDWARD DONALD Government. AB 1958, Brown U; PhD 1963, U of Ill. INT: govt labor policy, labor law, coll barg. POSITION: (since 1974) Chief, Div of Legislative Analysis, Labor-Mgmt Services, USDL. ADDRESS: 13010 Hathaway Dr, Wheaton, MD 20906. 202/523-6487

O'NEAL, KEITH ALAN Acad: Student, Univ Admin. BA 1978, MLIR 1984, Mich State U. INT: coll barg, labor law, empl/trng programs. POSITIONS: Retail Div Mgr, Sears, Roebuck & Co, 1977; and (since 1980) Resident Student Life Dir, Mich State Univ. ADDRESS: A-101 Butterfield, East Lansing, MI 48825. 517/355-1509

O'NEILL, JOHN N. Union. POSITION: AFSCME Council #13, 301 Chestnut St, 5th FL, Harrisburg, PA 17101. 717/236-5978

ONI, I. O. Acad: Ind Rels; Bus:Mgmt/Admin. BSc 1979, M.ED 1983, U of Ibadan, Nigeria. PUBL: "When Industrial Disputes May Lead to Political Instability," Daily Sketch, Apr 7, 1983; "Workers Must Be Happy," Nigerian Tribune, July 5, 1983; "Who Can Lead Nigeria Labour Congress?" Nigerian Tribune, Dec 27, 1983. INT: mgmt/educ, union org/admin, coll barg. ASSN: Pol Sci Assn, U. I. Chapter, Alumni Assn, U. I. Chapter. POSITIONS: Confidential Secretary, 1975, and, since 1982, Adminstrative Officer, Univ of Ibadan, Ibadan, Nigeria.

ONO, TSUNEO Acad: Ind Rels. 56-214 Nakazawa-Cho, Asahi-Ku Yokohama, Japan.

OPARA, ROSE UJUNMA Government, Arbitration, Union. BSc 1977, U of Nigeria; MSc 1983, U of Benin, Nigeria. PUBL: Feudalism in Nigeria: A Comparative Study of NUPE and OYO Kingdoms, 1977; Industrial Conflict in Nigerian Medical Profession: A Case Study of the Strike Action Of Medical Doctors in Southern Nigeria, 1982. INT: arb/med, coll barg, org beh. POSITIONS: Labour Officer Grade II, 1978, Labour Officer Grade I, 1981, and, since 1982, Senior Labour Officer, Federal Ministry of Employment, Labour & Productivity, PMB 1017 Warri, Bendel State, Nigeria. Phone: 053-231348

OPPENHEIMER, MARGARET ANN Acad: Econ. PhD 1974, Northwestern U. PUBL: "Arbitration Awards in Discrimination Disputes: An Empirical Analysis," Arb J, Mar 1979, pp 12-16. INT: labor market econ, arb/med, govt labor policy. ASSN: Chicago IRRA, AEA. POSITION: Assoc Prof of Econ, De Paul Univ, 25 E Jackson Blvd, Chicago, IL 60604. 312/321-7839/7781

ORCHARD, ROBERT Bus:Pers/Ind Rels. POSITION: Personnel Manager, Boyle-Midway Inc, South Ave & Hale St, Cranford, NJ 07016.

O'REILLY, ANNE B. Student. ADDRESS: 832 Lavergne Ave, Wilmette, IL 60091. 312/256-5230

O'REILLY, JAMES MICHAEL Arbitration, Labor/Mgmt Committees. MS 1969, St. Louis U. INT: arb/med, coll barg, labor/mgmt committees. ASSN: Gateway IRRA, SPIDR, AAA. POSITIONS: Pers Dir, Hunter Engineering Co, 1970; Federal Mediator, FMCS, 1972; and (since 1980) Executive Director, New Spirit of St. Louis Labor/Mgmt Committee. ADDRESS: 9251 Roger Lee La, Crestwood,MO 63126. 314/231-0260

O'REILLY, JOHN F. Legal Practice. POSITION: Labor Rels Counsel, NYC Health & Hospitals, 125 Worth St, #418, New York, NY 10013.

ORENSTEIN, SIDNEY Legal Practice, BSS 1938, CCNY, LLB 1943, New York U. INT: arb/med, coll barg, labor law. ASSN: New York IRRA. POSITION: (since 1943) Partner, Solomon, Rosenbaum, Drechsler & Leff, 100 E 42nd St, New York, NY 10017. 212/867-5720

ORESON, KEITH A. Bus:Pers/Ind Rels. BA 1978, MLIR 1980, Mich State U. INT: coll barg, mgmt/educ, org beh. ASSN: ASPA. POSITIONS: Human Res Assoc, GTE Service Corp, 1981, and, since 1982, Supr-Human Resources, GTE Bus Communication Systems, 12502 Sunrise Valley Dr, Reston, VA 22091. 703/435-7465

ORNATI, OSCAR A. Acad: Bus Admin; Arbitration. PhD 1955, Harvard. PUBL: Jobs and Workers in India; Poverty Amid Affluence; Transportation Needs of the Poor. INT: labor market econ, arb/med, personnel. ASSN: New York IRRA, NAA, AEA. POSITION: (since 1966) Prof of Manpower Mgmt, Grad School of Bus, New York Univ. ADDRESS: Apt 5A, 100 Bleeker St, New York, NY 10012. 212/285-6063

ORR, ANDREW Bus:Pers/Ind Rels; Acad: Health Care. BA 1959, Rutgers; MBA 1978, U of Chicago. INT: personnel, health & hosp care, ind sociol. POSITION: Administrative Staff, St. Francis Hosp. ADDRESS: 2333 Lincoln St, Evanston, IL 60201. 312/492-2455

ORR, LOIS BRANDS Government. BS 1957, Beaver Coll; MA 1959, U of Minn. INT: govt labor policy, labor market econ, method/statis. ASSN: Chicago IRRA, Amer Statis Assn. POSITION: Asst Regional Commissioner, Bureau of Labor Statis, Chicago. ADDRESS: 2333 Lincoln St, Evanston, IL 60201. 312/353-1884

ORR, MARSHA J. Consulting, Mediation. BA 1974, Mich State U; MS 1984, NYSSILR-Cornell. PUBL: Subcontracting NYS Public Sector Experience, (w R. Donovan), monograph. INT: arb/med, coll barg, empl/trng programs. POSITIONS: SEIU Res Dir, Local 660, 1978; Ext Assoc, Cornell Univ, 1979-82; and (since 1980) President, LMC Consultants Inc, 2060 Dryden Rd, Freeville, NY 13068. 607/844-4784

ORSATTI, ERNEST B. Arbitration. ADDRESS: Jubelirer, Pass, Intrieri, 219 Fort Pitt Blvd, Pittsburgh, PA 15222. 412/281-3850

ORTIZ, KATHERINE Government, Bus:Pers/-Ind Rels; Acad: Ind Rels. BA 1973, Northeastern U. INT: arb/med, labor law, labor educ. ASSN: Hispanic Alliance for Career Enhancement. POSITIONS: Para-Prof Investigator, Comm on Human Relations, City of Chicago, 1972; Exec Dir, Latin Amer Task Force, 1974; and (since 1977) Equal Opportunity Specialist, USDL. ADDRESS: 1342 N Monticello Ave, Chicago, IL 60651. 312/353-1930

ORTON, ELIOT SMITH Acad: Econ. PhD 1971, Cornell U. INT: labor market econ, empl/-trng programs, labor history. ASSN: AEA. POSITION: (since 1970) Assoc Prof, Econ Dept, Box 3CQ, New Mexico State Univ, Las Cruces, NM 88003. 505/646-3800

OSA, JOSEPH M. Union. BA 1976, Lew & Clark Coll. ADDRESS: PO Box 14747, Portland, OR 97214. 503/233-8861

OSCADAL, MARTIN G. Bus:Pers/Ind Rels. BA 1975, SUNY-Buffalo; MLIR 1976, Mich State U. INT: health & hosp care, arb/med, coll barg. ASSN: ASPA. POSITIONS: Asst Pers Officer, State Prison of Southern Mich, 1977; Labor Rels Rep, 1978, and, since 1981, Manager, Labor Rels, Michael Reese Hosp and Medical Center, Chicago. ADDRESS: 827 Mulford (Upper), Evanston, IL 60202. 312/791-3003

OSIKA, THOMAS Bus:Pers/Ind Rels. POSITION: Personnel Admin, Freezer Queen/United Food, PO Box 948, New York, NY 14240. 716/-826-2500

OSOFSKY, DEBRA Student. INT: coll barg, labor law, arb/med. POSITIONS: Intern, AAA, Wash DC, 1983; and (since 1981) Student, School of Ind and Labor Rels, Cornell Univ. ADDRESS: 157-23 14th Ave, Whitestone, NY 11357.

OSTERMAN, PAUL S. Acad: Econ, Ind Rels; Government. PhD 1976, MIT. PUBL: Internal Labor Markets, MIT Press, 1983; The Youth Labor Market, MIT Press, 1980; "Affirmative Action and Opportunity," Rev of Econ and Statis, 1982. INT: labor market econ, empl/trng programs, org beh. POSITIONS: Asst Prof of Econ, Boston Univ, 1976; Deputy to the Assoc Sec of Econ Affairs, Commonwealth of Mass, 1983; and (since 1983) Assoc Prof of Econ, Dept of Econ, Boston Univ, 270 Bay St Rd, Boston, MA 02215. 617/353-4447

OSTRY, SYLVIA Government; Acad: Econ. PhD 1954, McGill U. PUBL: Labour Economics in Canada, (w M. Zaidi), 3rd Ed, 1979; "Government Intervention in Democratic Economies: Canada-U.S. Comparison," IRPP and Brookings, 1978; "Energy and Growth," Econ Interests in the 1980's, Atlantic Inst, Paris, 1982. ADDRESS: Apt 1201, 40 Boteler St, Ottawa, Ont K1N 9C8 Canada.

OSWALD RUDOLPH ALPHONSUS Union. BA 1954, Holy Cross Coll; MS 1958, U of Wis; PhD 1965, Georgetown Univ. PUBL: "Labor's Agenda for 1980's Research," IRRA Annual Proceedings, 1980; "Fair Labor Standards," Chapter 5 in Federal Policies and Worker Status Since the Thirties," IRRA Series, 1976; "Bargaining and Productivity in the Public Sector: A Union View," Collective Bargaining and Productivity, Chapter 5, IRRA Series, 1975. INT: govt labor policy, coll barg, empl/-trng programs. ASSN: Wash DC IRRA, AEA, Amer Statis Assn. POSITIONS: Economist, AFL-CIO, 1963; Res Dir, Service Empl Natl Union, 1972; and (since 1976) Director, Dept of Econ Res, AFL-CIO, 815 16th St NW, Washington DC 20006. 202/637-5160

OVERTON, CRAIG E. Acad: Ind Rels; Arbitration. BS 1965, MBA 1967, Northeastern U; PhD 1971, U of Mass. PUBL: "The Climate for Collective Bargaining in General Purpose Local Governments in the 1980's," IRRA Annual Meeting-Denver, 1980; "Significant Management Rights Clauses in Municipal Police Contracts;" "Criteria in Grievance and Interest Arbitration in the Public Sector." INT: arb/med, coll barg, personnel. ASSN: Boston IRRA, NAA, AAA, FMCS. POSITION: (since 1969) Prof of Labor Rels, College of Bus Admin, Univ of Rhode Island. ADDRESS: PO Box 828, North Kingston, RI 20852. 401/294-9678

OWEN, JOHN PIPKIN Acad: Admin, Bus Admin/Mgmt. BA 1941, MBA 1944, PhD 1949, La. State U. PUBL: Anatomy of a Work-Force Reduction, An Analysis of the Social, Psychological and Economic Impact of a Major Gulf Coast Work Force Reduction, (co-author) Center for Res, U of Houston, 1965; What's Wrong With Workmen's Compensation in the United States," in Tex Houston Studies in Bus and Econ, #4, Bureau of Bus & Econ Research, Univ of Houston, 1956. INT: arb/med. ASSN: AEA, Southwestern Soc Sci Assn, NAA. POSITIONS: Dean, 1967, and, since 1983, Distinguished Prof of Mgmt, College of Bus Admin, Univ of Arkansas, Fayetville, AR 72701. 501/-575-4908/521-2133

OWENS, STEPHEN DENNIS Acad: Ind Rels, Org Beh/Pers; Arbitration. PhD 1981, North Tex State U. PUBL: "Arbitral Reaction to Alexander & Gardner-Denver Co: An Analysis of Arbitrator's Awards, 1974-1980;" "A Review and Analysis of Behavioral Research of Project Management;" "Leadership Theory and Project Management: Which Approach is Applicable?" INT: coll barg, arb/med, personnel. ASSN: Acad of Mgmt, Project Mgmt Inst, ASPA. POSITIONS: Asst Prof of Mgmt, LSU in Shreveport, 1974; and (since 1981) Asst Prof of Mgmt/-IR, Dept of Mgmt, Western Carolina Univ, Cullowhee, NC 28723. 704/227-7401

OWLEY, CANDICE Union. ASSN: Wis IRRA. POSITION: President, AFT, 6333 W Bluemound Rd, Milwaukee, WI 53213. 414/259-1832

OXNAM, DESMOND W. Acad: Ind Rels, Econ, Ind Sociol. BA 1940, MA 1942, U of New Zealand; APD 1976, Accreditation Inst. PUBL: "Industrial Relations in Australia: Its Effects on Unions and Wages," Ind and Labor Rels Rev, vol 9, #4, July, 1956; "International Comparisons of Industrial Conflict: An Appraisal," J of Inds Rels, vol 7, #2, July 1965; "The Incidence of Strikes in Australia," Chapter 1 in Australian Labour Relations: Readings, ed by J. E. Isaac and S. W. Ford, Sun Books, Melbourne, 1966 & 1971. INT: coll barg, intl comparative labor, ind sociol. ASSN: Ind Rels Soc of Western Australia, Australian Inst of Pol Sci, Economic Soc of Australia and New Zealand. POSITIONS: Visiting Lecturer, Ind Rels Center, Univ of Minn, 1970; Senior Lecturer of Econ, 1955, Assoc Prof in Econ, 1971-79, Univ of Western Australia, Retired. ADDRESS: 55 Phillip Rd, Dalkeith, Western Australia 6009.

OYAGA, GLADYS T. DE Student. 5508 Kenneylane Blvd, Columbus, OH 43220.

OZANNE, ROBERT Acad: Labor Educ, Econ. BS 1936, MS 1941, PhD 1954, U of Wis. PUBL: The Wisconsin Labor Movement: A History, Wis State Historical Soc, Oct 1984; A Century of Labor Management Relations at International Harvester, Univ of Wis Press, 1967; "Trends in American Labor History," Labor History, Fall 1980. INT: labor history, labor educ, labor econ. ASSN: Wis IRRA, AEA, Univ & Coll Labor Educ Assn. POSITION: (since 1954) Prof, Labor Educ, Econ, Univ of Wis. ADDRESS: 210 S Owen Dr, Madison, WI 53705. 608/262-2111

P

PACE, STANLEY D. Legal Practice. Spieth, Bell, McCurdy & Newell, 2000 Union Commerce Bldg, Cleveland, OH 44115. 216/696-4700

PADILA, TARCISIO M. Acad: Univ Admin. PUBL: Negociacao e Relacoes de Trabalho; A Pratica das Relacoes Industriais no Estado do Rio de Janeiro; Politica de Emprego. POSITION: Inst Euvaldo Lodi NL/AIR, Rua S Luzia 685-110 Andar, 20030 Rio de Janeiro RJ, Brazil.

PADULA, CHERYL A. Bus:Pers/Ind Rels. MLIR 1977, Mich State U. INT: coll barg, personnel, labor law. POSITION: Empl Rels Rep, Shell Oil Co. ADDRESS: 15903 Tumbling Rapids Dr, Houston, TX 77084. 713/241-4247

PAGENSTECHER, ULRICH Acad: Ind Rels. DR 1955, U of Koln-Germany. INT: coll barg, govt labor policy, labor market econ. POSITION: (since 1966) Professor, Universitat, Erlangen-Nurnberg, Sozialwissenschaftiches Institut. ADDRESS: Ginsterweg 67, 8500 Nurnberg-Mogeldorf, West Germany.

PALIWODSINSKI, ROBERT L. Union; Acad: Ind Rels. MS 1967, SUNY. INT: union org/admin, coll barg, arb/med. ASSN: Capital Dist IRRA. POSITION: (since 1976) Dir, Affiliated Services, NEA of New York, 217 Lark St, Albany, NY 12210. 518/462-6451

PALOMBA, CATHERINE A. Consulting. BBA 1965, CCNY-Baruch School; PhD 1969, Iowa State U. PUBL: "Right-to-Work Laws: A Suggested Economic Rationale," J of Law & Econ, Oct 1971; "Snowball & Other Control Groups," J of Voc Beh, vol 6, 1975; "Some Economic Factors Affecting Safety in Underground Bituminous Coal Mines, A Comment," Southern Econ J, Oct 1975. INT: labor market econ, govt labor policy. ASSN: AEA, Amer Statis Assn. POSITIONS: Asst Prof of Econ, 1972, Assoc Prof of Econ, West Va Univ, 1976; and (since 1981) Res Analyst, Center for Naval Analyses, 2000 N Beauregard St, Alexandria, VA 22311. 703/998-3810

PALOMBA, NEIL ANTHONY Acad: Univ Admin. BBA CCNY-Baruch School; PhD 1966, U of Minn. PUBL: Manpower Economics, Addison Wesley, 1973; "Unemployment Compensation Program: Stabilizing or Destabilizing," J of Pol Econ, Jan-Feb, 1968; "Accreditation of Personnel Administrators: Theory and Reality," Pers Admin, Jan 1981. INT: labor market econ, govt labor policy, labor educ. ASSN: AEA, Amer Statis Assn. POSITIONS: Asst Prof-Econ, Iowa State Univ, 1966; Chairman, Dept of Econ, West Va Univ, 1975; and (since 1980) Assoc Dean, Bus & Mgmt, Tydings Hall, Univ of Maryland, College Park, MD 20742. 301/454-5297

PANERAL, ALLEN J. Bus:Pers/Ind Rels; Acad: Ind Rels. BS 1952, DePaul U; MS 19658, Loyola U. INT: coll barg, empl/trng programs, mgmt/educ. ASSN: ASPA. POSITION: (since 1968) Employee Rels Manager, I.M.C. Carlsbad Operations, PO Box 71, Carlsbad, NM 88220. 505/887-2871

PANFIL, JAMES F. Union. INT: govt labor policy, arb/med, labor educ. ASSN: Wis IRRA. POSITION: (since 1982) Business Agent, Intl Union of Operating Engineers, Local #317, 3152 South 27th St, Milwaukee, WI 53215. 414/-671-3258

PANZERA, DONALD P. Government. BSFS 1969, Georgetown U; PhD 1980, Northwestern U. INT: labor history, intl comparative labor, coll barg. ASSN: Amer Historical Assn. Amer Library Assn. POSITION: (since 1975) Subject Cataloger, Library of Congress. ADDRESS: 7602 Highland St, Springfield, VA 22150. 703/-569-5360

PAPIER, WILLIAM BERNARD Retired. BSc 1932, MA 1933, Ohio State U. PUBL: "Perspectives on Employment and Unemployment in Ohio;" "Men and Women in Ohio's Labor Force;" "Should Unemployment Benefits Be Extended?" INT: labor market econ, unempl insurance, empl/trng programs. ASSN: Central Ohio IRRA. POSITION: Dir, Div of Research and Statis, Ohio Bureau of Empl Services, 1934-1983; Retired. ADDRESS: 1023 S Remington Rd, Columbus, OH 43209. 614/231-0408

PAPINI, FRANK E. Union; Student. INT: union org/admin, arb/med, coll barg. POSITIONS: Machine Operator-Temp Foreman, Technical Tape Corp, Wheeling, 1969; Dept Mgr, Fishers Big Wheel, Wheeling, 1971; and (since 1972) Steelworker, Wheeling-Pittsburgh Steel Corp. ADDRESS: Four Gracie Dr, Wheeling, WV 26003. 304/234-3212.

PAPROCKI, JOHN L. Arbitration, Consulting/Career/Work Crisis, Counseling. MA 1964, Seton Hall. INT: arb/med, work crisis issues, ind psych. ASSN: SPIDR, Amer Soc for Counseling & Devel, N.J. Professional Counselors Assn. POSITION: Rev. John L. Paprocki (private practice, 340 Main St, Fort Lee, NJ 07024. 201/944-2727

PARENT, GUY M. Arbitration, Consulting, Mediation. BA 1952, Montreal U; BA 1983, Prescott Coll-Ariz. PUBL: Grievances: From Prevention Through Arbitration, (co-author w J. C. McBrearty), Old Pueblo Press-Tucson, 1973. INT: arb/med, ind psych, coll barg. ASSN: Ariz IRRA, SPIDR. POSITIONS: Dir of Corp Ind Rels, Dominion Glass Co, 1968; Mediator, FMCS, 1970; and (since 1981) Arbitrator (self-employed), 1035 W Mission Lane, Phoenix, AZ 85021. 602/997-1213

PARGUEL, NORBERT Bus:Pers/Ind Rels; Acad: Sociol. PhD, U of Paris. PUBL: "New Forms of Work Organization: Logic vs Enthusiasm," Sociol du travial, #4, 1981 INT: ind sociol, labor history, method/statis. ASSN: Paris IRRA. ADDRESS: 5 Allee du Prunier Hardy, 92220 Bagneux, France.

PARIGI, SAM F. Acad: Econ, Ind Rels. BS 1954, St. Edwards U-Austin; MBA 1957, PhD 1964, U of Tex-Austin. PUBL: A Case Study of Latin American Unionization in Austin, Texas, Arno Press 1977; "The Unionization of Lawyers: The East Texas Legal Services," (w H.C. Owens), Papers & Proceedings of the Southwestern Soc of Econ, 1983; "Police and Firefighter Collective Bargaining in Beaumont: The Texas Precedent," Papers & Proceedings for the Southwestern Soc of Econ, 1982. INT: coll barg, labor educ, arb/med. ASSN: Houston IRRA, Tex Assn of Coll Teachers, Omicron Delta Epsilon, Southwestern Soc of Econ. POSITIONS: Project Dir, Southern Rural Trng Project, 1965; Project Dir, Manpower Educ and Trng Inc, 1968; and (since 1961) Prof of Econ, Lamar Univ. ADDRESS: 5256 Lakeshore Dr, Port Arthur, TX 77640. 409/838-8652

PARKER, CARL D. Acad: Econ, Empl Rels. PhD 1971, Okla State U. INT: coll barg, arb/med, labor market econ. POSITION: (since 1977) Dir of Empl Rels and Prof of Econ, Fort Hayes State Univ, Hays, KS 67601. 913/628-5805

PARKS, WALTER J. Consulting; Acad: Ind Rels, Org Beh/Pers. MBA 1970, U of Toronto. PUBL: "Job Redundancy;" "Unwritten Probation;" "Training Programs Needed." INT: arb/-med, mgmt/educ, personnel. ASSN: SPIDR. POSITIONS: Dir of Examinations, Soc of Mgmt Accountants of Canada, 1970; Prof of Ind Rels, Seneca Coll of A.A.&T., 1973; and (since 1983) President, Walter Parks Inc, Lower Concourse Level, 40 Orchard View Blvd, Toronto, Ont M4R 1G9 Canada. 416/489-3402

PARNELL, EDWARD J. Government. AB 1950, MA 1953, U of Calif-Berkeley. INT: labor law, govt labor policy, coll barg. ASSN: Hawaii IRRA. POSITIONS: Bus Rep, Local 400, SEIU, San Francisco, 1955; Fulbright Scholar, London School of Econ, 1962; and (since 1970) Senior Examiner, NLRB, Sub Region 37. ADDRESS: 1310 Heulu St, Suite 1701, Honolulu, HI 96822. 808/546-5100

PARNES, HERBERT S. Acad: Econ. AB 1939, MA 1941, U of Pittsburgh; PhD 1950, Ohio State U. PUBL: Work and Retirement, (Editor & contributor), MIT Press, 1981; Policy Issues in Work and Retirement, (Ed & contributor), W. E. Upjohn, 1983; Unemployement Experience of Individuals Over the Decades, W. E. Upjohn, 1982. INT: labor market econ, govt labor policy, income maint. ASSN: Amer Econ Assn, Gerontological Soc, AAUP. POSITIONS: Prof of Econ, Ohio State Univ, 1947-80; Prof of Ind Rels and Human Res, Rutgers, 1981-1983; and (since 1980) Prof Emeritus of Econ, Ohio State Univ. ADDRESS: 302 E. Beaumont Rd, Columbus, OH 43214.

PARRA, A. FERNANDO IGNACIO Acad: Law, Ind Rels; Legal Prac. LLB 1958, LLD 1962, Univ of Catolica Andres Bello-Caracas. PUBL: Venezuelan Labor Law Precedents, 1830-1928; Venezuelan Labor Law Precedents 1916-1928; "Considerations on Union Security Clauses," 1981. INT: coll barg, labor law, labor history. POSITION: (since 1978) Chief of the Social Law Dept, Law School, Univ Central de Venezuela. ADDRESS: PO Box 64538, Caracas 1064A Venezuela.

PARRY, JAMES Acad: Univ Admin, Law. POSITION: State Univ System Florida, 107 W Gains, Talahassee, FL 32301. 904/488-5480

PARSH, STEVEN FRANCIS Bus:Pers/Ind Rels. ADDRESS: 348 Sunset NW, Grand Rapids, MI 49504. 616/453-8074

PARSONS, WILLIAM F., JR. Acad: Student, Sociology, Ind Rels. BA 1973, MLIR 1977, Mich State U. PUBL: "Participative Decision-Making at Work," Labor Studies J, (forthcoming); "QWL-EI Orientation Pamphlet," Lansing Joint Labor-Mgmt Committee, 1983. INT: ind sociol, labor educ, org beh. ASSN: Univ & Coll Labor Educ Assn. POSITIONS: Assembler-Auto worker, Fisher Body Div, GMC, 1971; Coordinator of Labor Studies, Lansing Community Coll, 1980;

and (since 1982) Res Dir, Lansing Area Joint Labor-Mgmt Committee. ADDRESS: 2800 West Rd, Lansing, MI 48912. 517/482-1654

PASEK, JEFFREY IVAN Legal Practice. BA 1973, U of Pittsburgh; JD 1976, U of Penna. PUBL: "Employment Discrimination," (w A.M. Lerner), PA Bar Inst 1983; "Statistics: The Name of the Game in EEO Cases," (w A.M. Lerner), PA Chamber of Commerce, 1980. INT: labor law, coll barg, arb/med. ASSN: Philadelphia IRRA, Amer/Penna/Philadelphia Bar Assn. POSITION: (since 1976) Assoc Attorney, Cohen, Shapiro, Polisher, Shiekman & Cohen, 12 South 12th St, 22nd Floor, Philadelphia, PA 19107. 215/922-1300

PASSANT, GREG S. Consulting. POSITION: Labor Rels Consultant, Human Resource Mgmt, 3350 Scott Blvd, #2401, Santa Clara, CA 95051. 408/727-9670

PASSMORE, SANDRA BETTY Bus:Pers/Ind Rels. BS 1971, Northeastern Coll. INT: personnel, empl/trng programs. ASSN: Natl Assn Female Executives. POSITIONS: Dir of Pers, Oahu, 1980, and, since 1983, Director of Personnel, Hyatt Regency Buffalo. ADDRESS: 939 Delaware Ave #104, Buffalo, NY 14209. 716/856-1234

PASTORE, JOSE Government; Acad: Sociol. PhD 1968, U of Wis-Madison. PUBL: Inequality and Social Mobility in Brazil, U of Wis Press, 1982; Pobreza e Mudanca Social uo Brasil, IPE Pioneira, Sao Paulo, 1983; Profissionais Espeoalizados uo Mercado de Trobella, IPE, Sao Paulo, 1980. INT: coll barg, empl/trng programs, govt labor policy. ASSN: Amer Sociol Assn, Amer Acad of Pol Sci, Intl Rural Sociol Assn. POSITIONS: Prof of Sociol, Univ of Sao Paulo, 1964; and (since 1979), Head of the Technical Staff, Ministry of Labor. ADDRESS: R Barao de Sao Gabriel 122, Sao Paulo-SP, 05085 Brazil. Phone: (011) 212-5471

PATERACKI, JOHN A., JR. Acad: Law; Arbitration. AB 1939, LLB & JD 1942, Fordham. INT: labor law, arb/med, coll barg. ASSN: New York and Conn IRRA, ABA, New York/-Westchester County Bar Assn. POSITION: (since 1950) Senior Partner, Whitman & Ransom, 522 Fifth Ave, New York, NY 10036. 212/575-5800

PATINO, ANTONIO J. Union. Assoc Applied Sci 1971, Manhatten Community Coll; BBA 1974, CCNY; MS 1982, NY Inst of Tech. INT: coll barg, arb/med. ASSN: AAA, Assn of Colombian Professionals, Amer Marketing Assn. POSITION: (since 1964) Administrator, Production, Maintenance & Serv Empl Union, Local #3 Welfare Fund. ADDRESS: 1129 Braxton St, Uniondale, NY 11553. 516/483-0221

PATRICK, JAMES R. Bus:Pers/Ind Rels, Bus.Mgmt/Admin. INT: arb/med, labor law, personnel. ASSN: Amer Public Transit Assn. POSITIONS: Supt of Safety and Trng, 1976, Supt of Base Operations, 1978, and, since 1981, Personnel, Dept of Metro, Municipality of Seattle, 821 2nd Ave MS/91, Seattle, WA 98104. 206/447-5821

PATRUDU, B.V.S. Acad: Ind Rels. POSITION: Dept of IR & PM, College of Arts, Andhra Univ, Waltair 530 003 India.

PATTEN, THOMAS HENRY JR. Acad: Org Beh/Pers. AB 1953, Brown; MS 1955, PhD 1959, Cornell. PUBL: A Manager's Guide to Performance Appraisal, NY Free Press, 1982; Organizational Development Through Teambuilding, NY: Wiley, 1981; Pay: Employee Compensation and Incentive Plans, NY Free Press, 1977. INT: personnel, org beh, ind sociol. ASSN: Detroit IRRA, Amer Sociol Assn, NTL Inst for Applied Beh Sci, Amer Compensation Assn. POSITIONS: Ind Rels Exec, Ford Motor Co, 1957; Prof of Mgmt and Soc, U of Detroit, 1965; and (since 1967) Prof of Org Beh and Pers Mgmt, School of Labor and Ind Rels, Univ of Mich. ADDRESS: 2599 Woodhill Rd, Okemos, MI 48864. 517/351-7252

PATTERSON, ELAINE FELDMAN Bus:-Pers/Ind Rels. BS 1976, Trinity Coll; MILR 1979, Cornell U. INT: personnel, org beh, labor law. ASSN: Southern Calif IRRA. POSITIONS: EEO Serv Coordinator, 1980, Univ Rels Coordinator, 1981; and, since 1982, Pers Coordinator, Union Oil Company of Calif-Oil and Gas Div, PO Box 7600, Los Angeles, CA 90051. 213/977-5208

PATTERSON, R. A. Acad: Org Beh/Pers, Ind Rels. BSA 1943, U of Toronto; MBA 1967, U of Western Ontario; PhD 1975, U of Minn. INT: personnel, coll barg. ASSN: Canadian Ind Rels Assn, Admin Sci Assn of Canada, Acad of Mgmt. POSITIONS: Empl Mgr-Winnipeg Store, The T. Eaton Co Ltd, 1963; Lecturer, School of Bus and Admin, U of Western Ontario, 1967; and (since 1974) Assoc Prof, Faculty of Admin Studies, Univ of Manitoba, Winnipeg, Manitoba R3T 2N2 Canada. 204/474-8184

PATTON, DAVID B. Acad: Labor Studies. BA 1959, Coll of Wooster, MA 1964, Ohio State U. PUBL: "The Impact of Labor Endorsements," Labor Studies J, Spring 1984. INT: labor educ, union org/admin, labor & politics. ASSN: Central Ohio IRRA, Amer Assn of Public Opinion Res, AAUP. POSITION: (since 1973) Assoc Prof, Ohio State Univ, Room 2, Page Hall, 1810 College Rd, Columbus, OH 43210. 614/422-8157

PAUL, KATHLEEN M. Bus:Pers/Ind Rels. BA 1973, Marion Coll-Indpl,IN. INT: coll barg, arb/med, personnel. POSITIONS: Bus Agent, AFSCME Council 40, 1978; Empl Rels Rep, 1981, and, since 1983, Manager, Empl Relations, Cummins Engine Co. ADDRESS: 4705 Chapel Dr, Columbus, IN 47203. 812/379-6451

PAUL, MELINDA M. Student. 511 Goodale Ct, Clawson, MI 48017. 313/583-4033

PAUL, ROBERT D. Consulting. POSITION: Vice-Chairman, Martin E. Segal Co, Inc, 730 Fifth Ave, New York, NY 10019. 212/586-5600

PAULSON, GARY D. Bus:Pers/Ind Rels. MSIR 1975, Cornell U. INT: personnel, org beh, mgmt/educ. ASSN: Empl Mgmt Assoc. POSITIONS: Pers Mgr, Harris Corp, Ft. Lauderdale, 1975; and (since 1978) Manager, Employment & Employee Rels, Compugrahic Corp, 80 Industrial Way, Wilmington, MA 01886. 617/944-6555

PAULSON, STEVEN Union. POSITION: Uniserv Director, Wash Educ Assn, 203 Palouse, #205, Wenatchee, WA 98801. 509/662-8145

PAVLINSKY, NANCY MARIE Bus: Pers/Ind Rels. BS 1981 Shippensberg U. INT: personnel, labor law, arb/med. POSITION: (since 1981) Corporate Recruiter, Kidder Peabody and Co Inc. ADDRESS: Apt 3, 46 First Place, Brooklyn, NY 11231. 212/510-8350

PAYNE, J. MICHAEL Bus:Pers/Ind Rels. BS, Cleveland State U. INT: ind psych, personnel. ASSN: ASPA. POSITIONS: Supr Human Resources, Mobil Oil, 1980; Staff Compensation Coordinator, 1983, and, since 1984, Manager of Employee Rels, Exxon Chemical Americas, 8230 Stedman St, Houston, TX 77029. 713/671-8612

PEACE, NANCY E. Librianship; Abritration. BA 1968, Ohio Wesleyan U; AMLS 1969, U of Mich, DLS 1981, Columbia U. INT: arb/med, coll barg. POSITION: Assoc Professor, Simmons Coll, Boston. ADDRESS: 41 Melville Ave, Boston, MA 02124. 617/738-2223

PEACH, DAVID ALAN Acad: Bus Admin, Ind Rels, Org Beh/Pers. BSC 1962, MBA 1964, Ohio State U; DBA 1969, Harvard. PUBL: Grievance Initiation and Resolution, (w E. R. Livernash), Boston, Harvard U Press, 1974; The Practice of Ind Rels, (w D. Kuechle), McGraw Hill Ryerson, 1975; "The CandAir-I.A.M. Productivity Improvement Plan," Rels Industrielle, vol 37, #1, 1982. POSITION: Professor, School of Bus Admin, U of Western Ontario, London, Ont N6A 3K7 Canada.519/679-3216

PEARCE, JOHN J. JR. Arbitration. AB 1947, MA 1948, Rutgers U. PUBL: The Joint Employee Rating Plan of the P.J. Ritter Company and Local 56, Amalgamated Meat Cutters and Butcher Workmen of North Amer, IMLR, Rutgers, 1950. INT: abr/med, coll barg, labor law. ASSN: New Brunswick IRRA. POSITIONS: Ext Specialist/Prof, IMLR-Rutgers Univ, 1969; Exec Dir, NJ State Bd of Mediation, 1972; and (since 1976) Arbitrator (self-employed), 135 N Lakeside Dr, Piscataway, NJ 08854. 201/463-8140

PEARCE, THOMAS G. Acad: Ind Rels, Law; Arbitration. MBA 1980, U of Alaska. INT: labor law, arb/med, personnel. ASSN: Tulsa Pers Assn, ASPA. POSITIONS: Secondary Teacher, Anchorage Alas. Public Schools, 1975; Student, U of Washm 1980; and (since 1983) Asst Prof, College of Bus Admin, Oklahoma State Univ, Stillwater, OK 74074. 405/-624-5116

PEARSON, DONALD W. Acad: Econ. PhD 1970, U of Tex-Austin. INT: coll barg, labor educ, intl comparative labor. POSITION: (since 1969) Dir of Labor Studies/Prof, Dept of Econ, Eastern Michigan Univ, Ypsilant, MI 48197. 313/487-0008

PECKHAM, JAMES D. Bus:Mgmt/Admin. BA 1980, MLIR 1982, Mich State U. INT: personnel, arb/med, empl/trng programs. POSITION: (since 1984) Senior Personnel Specialist, Motorola Inc, PO Box 20903, Phoenix, AZ 85036. 602/244-3781

PEDEVILLANO, MARY THERESA Bus:-Pers/Ind Rels. BS 1976, U of Md; MILR, 1978, Cornell U. INT: personnel. ASSN: ASPA. POSITIONS: Coordinator of Empl Rels, American Can Co, 1979; Supr of Empl, 1980, and, since 1982, Dept Head, Human Resource, Clairol, Inc. ADDRESS: 187 Grand Blvd, Emerson, NJ 07630. 201/845-7400 ext 46

PEEVEY, MICHAEL ROBERT Trade Assn. AB 1959, MA 1961, U of Calif-Berkeley. INT: labor market econ, govt labor policy, ind sociol. ASSN: San Francisco IRRA. POSITIONS: Research Dir, Calif AFL-CIO, 1965; and (since 1973) President, Calif Council for Environment and Econ Balance. ADDRESS: 365 Margarita Dr, San Rafael, CA 94901. 415/495-5666

PEGNETTER, RICHARD C. Acad: Ind Rels. 330 W Park Road, Iowa City, IA 52240.

PEIRCE, WILLIAM SPANGAR Acad: Econ. AB 1960, Harvard; PhD 1966, Princeton U. PUBL: Technological Progress and Industrial Leadership (w Gold, Rosegger and Perlman); Bureaucratic Failure and Public Expenditure; "Bureaucratic Politics and the Labor Market," Public Choice, 1981. INT: labor market econ, org beh, govt labor policy. ASSN: AEA, Public Choice Soc, Intl Assn of Energy Economists. POSITIONS: Asst Prof, 1966, Assoc Prof, 1972, and, since 1983, Chairman of Econ Dept, Case Western Reserve Univ, Cleveland, OH 44106. 216/368-4112

PELHAN, RALPH E. Arbitration. MSIR 1976, West Va. U. INT: arb/med, labor law, coll barg. ASSN: AAA. POSITIONS: Coal miner, Consolidated Coal Co-UMWA; Dir, Bus-Mgmt Program, Seton Hall Coll; and (since 1978) Labor Arbitrator, 7002 Mallgate Pl B2, Louisville, KY 40207. 502/897-6665

PELLE, MICHAEL A. Bus/Pers/Ind Rels. POSITION: Director, Ind Rels, Fairchild Weston Systems, 300 Robbins Lane, Syosset, NY 11791. 516/349-2221

PELLOW, DAVID Legal Practice; Acad: Ind Rels. BS 1972, Boston Coll; JD 1975, U of Mich. INT: labor law, coll barg, arb/med. ASSN: Central New York IRRA, ABA & New York Bar Assn(Labor & Empl Law Committees). POSITIONS: Adjunct Asst Prof, Labor Law, LeMoyne Coll, 1981; and (since 1975) Attorney, Bond, Schoeneck & King, One Lincoln Center, Syracuse, NY 13202. 315/422--0121.

PELTIER, JAMES W., JR. Bus:Pers/Ind Rels. POSITION: Director, Ind Rels, Interisland Resorts Ltd, PO Box 8539, Honolulu, HI 96815.

PENDERGAST, JOHN J. III Legal Practice; Acad: Ind Rels. BA 1957, JD 1960, Yale. INT: labor law, arb/med, coll barg. ASSN: ABA (Labor Law Section). POSITIONS: Lecturer in Health Care Labor Law, Providence Coll, 1983, and, since 1960, Partner, Hinckley & Allen, 2200 Fleet Natl Bank Bldg, Providence, RI 02903. 401/861-2069

PENDLETON, EDWIN CHARLES Acad: Bus Admin (Retired). POSITIONS: (since 1975) Prof Emeritus, Coll of Bus Admin, U of Hawaii. ADDRESS: 2123 Armstrong St., Honolulu, HI 96822.

PENFIELD, ROBERT VERDON Acad: Univ Admin. BA 1951, Brigham Young U; MBA 1960, U of Utah; PhD 1966, Cornell U. PUBL: "A Study in Predicting Voluntary Labor Turnover with A Weighted Application Blank," Marquette Bus Rev, Spring 1977, pp 1-8; "The Double-Breasted Operation in the Construction Industry," Labor Law J, Feb 1976, pp 89-93; "A Guide to the Computation and Evaluation of Direct Labor Costs," Pers J, June 1976, pp 285-288. INT: coll barg, arb/med, personnel. ASSN: Gateway IRRA, SPIDR, ASPA, Acad of Mgmt. POSITIONS: Dir of Grad Studies, 1976, Asst Dean, 1983, and, since 1983, Assoc Dean, Coll of Bus & Public Admin, Univ of Missouri. ADDRESS: 402 Hullen Dr, Columbia, MO 65201. 314/882-2750

PERELES, EDWARD A. Arbitration, Consulting; Acad: Ind Rels. BS 1961, Cornell; JD 1964, U of Wis. INT: arb/med, coll barg, labor law. ASSN: Philadelphia IRRA, AAA, SPIDR. POSITIONS: Dir-Empl Rels, Astronautics Corp of Amer, 1970; Assoc Dir Admin, The Wistar Inst, 1973; and (since 1976) Principal, Pereles & Assoc, 1016 Clinton St, Suite B, Philadelphia, PA 19107. 215/627-5678

PEREZ, ARVELO HUMBERTO Bus:Pers/-Ind Rels. BS 1971, Catholic U "Andres Bello-Venezuela, MLIR, 1974, Mich State U. PUBL: The Personnel Function in the Middle Size Industry in Caracas; A Collective Contract Analysis of Banks in Caracas. INT: personnel, coll barg, empl/trng programs. ASSN: IIRA, Venezuela Natl Ind Rels Assn. POSITIONS: Asst of Dir of Pers, Sudamtex de Venezuela, Subsidiary of United Merchant, 1974; Dirof Human Resources, Otis Elevator Co, 1977; and (since 1979) Vice Pres of Human Resources, CITIBANK-Venezuela, Citibank, Apartado 1289, Caracas 1010A, Venezuela. Phone: 81.79.63

PERICH, GEORGE H. Bus:Pers/Ind Rels. BA 1977, U of Pittsburgh; MA 1979, St. Francis Coll; JD 1983, Duquesne U. INT: coll barg, labor law. ASSN: ABA(Labor/Empl Law Section), Penna Bar Assn, Pittsburgh Pers Assn. POSITION: (since 1980) Empl Rels Rep, Westinghouse Airbrake Div, Amer Standard Inc, PO Box 1, Wilmerding, PA 15148. 412/825-1606

PERKEL, GEORGE Consulting, Union; Acad: Econ. BA 1939, Brooklyn Coll; MA 1952, New York U. PUBL: "A Labor Leader's Viewpoint," Govern Regulation: New Perspectives, U of Pittsburgh, 1980; "Collective Bargaining: Another Approach to Job Safety and Health," (co-author), Protecting People at Work, 1980; "A Labor View of the OCC Safety & Health Act," Proceedings, IRRA Spring Meeting, 1972. INT: health & hosp care, union org/admin, coll barg. ASSN: Soc for Occ and Env Health. POSITIONS: Dir of Research, 1963, Dir Occupational Safety and Health, Amalg Clothing & Textile Workers of Amer, 1976; and (since 1980) Consultant (self-employed), 56 Allenwood Rd, GreatNeck, NY 11023. 516/773-4383

PERKINS, CHARLES WILBUR Consulting:-Pers/Ind Rels, Arbitration. MBA 1952, Boston U. INT: arb/med, coll barg. ASSN: Rhode Island IRRA, Inst of Ind Engineers. POSITION: (since 1977), Owner, Charles Perkins & Assoc, 52 Houston Dr, Warwick, RI 02886. 401/739-7569

PERL, PETER Journalism. AB 1972, Brown U. INT: coll barg, labor history, health & hosp care. ASSN: The Newspaper Guild. POSITIONS: Reporter, Providence Journal, 1975; and (since 1981) Labor Reporter, Washington Post, 1150 15th St NW, Washington DC 20071. 202/334-7461

PERLEY, JAMES DWIGHT Arbitration, Consulting; Acad: Mgmt. BSME 1932, Penna State U; Grad Work,1932-33, Wharton School. PUBL: Arb Award, AAA Case #31-30-0080-83 Fieldcrest Mills Inc & ACTWU, Sept 1983. INT: arb/med, mgmt/educ, coll barg. ASSN: AAA. POSITIONS: Asst Vice-Pres Pers, Westinghouse Air Brake Co, 1953; Vice Pres, Empl Rels, (Retired) Consolidated Natural Gas Co, 1959; and (since 1974) Part Time Prof, Mgmt Dept, Walker Coll of Bus, Appalachian State U. ADDRESS: 256 Rhodendron Dr, Beech Mountain, Banner Elk, NC 28064. 704/262-2163

PERLINE, MARTIN MICHAEL Acad: Econ. BA 1960, Ariz State; MA 1962, PhD 1965, Ohio State. PUBL: "A Sporting Alternative to Tenure: A Comment," Academe, Feb 1980; "Mobility of Unemployed Engineers: A Case Study," (w R. Presley), Monthly Labor Rev, May 1973; "The Trade Union Press: An Historical Analysis," Labor History, Winter 1969. INT: coll barg, govt labor policy, labor market econ. ASSN: AEA, AAUP. POSITION: (since 1971) Prof of Econ, Dept of Econ, Wichita State Univ, Wichita, KS 67208. 316/683-3220

PERLMAN, SEYMOUR W. Legal Practice. BA 1949, Penna State U; JD 1952, Rutgers U. INT: labor law, arb/med, coll barg. ASSN: Central NJ, Lower Buck Cty IRRA, NJ Bar Assn, Amer Trial Lawyers Assn, Compensation Assn of NJ. POSITIONS: Board Counsel, Mercer Cty Bd of Social Services, 1969; Labor Negotiator, Ewing Township, 1975; and (since 1952) Attorney, Rothbard, Harris & Oxfeld, 28 West State St, Trenton, NJ 08608. 609/394-3171

PERNA, NICHOLAS S. Bus:Mgmt/Admin. 273 Wilton Rd East, Ridgefield, CT 06877

PERRY, CHARLES R. Acad: Ind Rels. BA 1960, U of Mich; MBA 1962, PhD 1968, U of Chicago. PUBL: Collective Bargaining and the Decline of the United Mine Workers; Operating During Strikes; "Teacher Bargaining: The Experience in Nine Systems." INT: coll barg, govt labor policy, labor law. POSITIONS: Spec Asst to the Assoc Dir, 1970, Exec Asst to the Dir, Office of Mgmt & Budget of the U.S. Govt, 1971; and (since 1966) Assoc Prof of Mgmt and Ind Rels, Wharton School, Univ of Penna, 3733 Spruce St, Philadelphia, PA 19104. 215/898-5605

PERRY, HERBERT ANTHONY Acad: Econ; Arbitration, Consulting. BSC 1954, Cornell; MA 1960, U of Calif-Berkeley; PhD 1965, U of London. PUBL: "Jerry Brown and the ALRB-A Good Idea Gone Bad," Calif J, vol XIV, #12, Dec 1983; "San Francisco Longshoremen Work on Rotterdam Docks," Monthly Labor Rev, Aug 1976; "Building Trades Training-Another Mirage?" Ind and Commercial Trng-Mgmt of Human Res vol 5, #6, June 1973. INT: labor market econ, arb/med, intl comparative labor. ASSN: Northern Calif IRRA, AAA, Calif Conciliation & Med Serv-Arb Panel, Fed Med Serv-Arb Panel. POSITIONS: Chairman, Sacramento Reg Transit Auth and Amalgamated Transit Union Accident Grading Bd, 1973; Board Member, Calif Ag Labor Rels Bd, 1977; and (since 1965) Prof of Econ, Calif State Univ-Sacramento. ADDRESS: 4166 American River Dr, Sacramento, CA 95825. 916/454-6223

PERRY, JAMES B. Legal Practice. BA 1974, U of Mich; JD 1977, Emory U. INT: labor law, arb/med, coll barg. ASSN: Detroit IRRA, ABA(Labor & Empl Law Section), State Bar of Mich(Labor Law Section), Detroit Bar Assn. POSITIONS: Attorney, Cox and Hooth P.C., 1977; and (since 1983) Attorney, Abbott, Nicholson, Ouilter, Esshaki & Youngblood P.C., 1840 Buhl Bldg, Detroit, MI 48226. 313/963-2500

PERRY, JAMES LEE Acad: Org Beh/Pers, Public Admin. BA 1970, U of Chicago; MPA 1972, PhD 1974, Syracuse. PUBL: "Reforming the Upper Levels of the Bureaucracy: A Longitudinal Study of the Senior Executive Service," (w P.S. Ring),Admin and Society, 15 May 1983, pp 119-144; "Federal Merit Pay: A Longitudinal Analysis," (w J.L. Pearce), Publ Admin Rev

43, July;Aug 1983, 315-325; "Labor Management Relations and Organizational Performance: The Case of Public Transit," (w H. L. Angle), J of Coll Negotiations in the Public Sector, 12 Nov 1983, 271-282. POSITION: Grad School of Mgmt, Univ of California, Irvine, CA 92717. 714/833-5840

PERRY, MICHAEL S. Community Rels. BA 1976, U of Va; MA 1979, U of Ill. INT: empl/trng programs, union orb/admin, govt labor policy. POSITIONS: Staff Rep, AFSCME, 1978, Field Coordinator, AFL-CIO Great Lakes Reg Council, 1979; and (since 1981) Area Director, Jewish Labor Committee. ADDRESS: 2112 Walnut St, Philadelphia, PA 19103. 215/568-4770

PERRY, SAMUEL STRODE Arbitration, Legal Prac, Consulting. BBA 1949, Case Western Reserve U; JD 1954, Cleveland Marshall Coll of Law. INT: arb/med, labor law, health & hosp care. ASSN: Northeast Ohio IRRA, Bar Assn of Greater Cleveland, NAA, SPIDR. POSITIONS: Wage-Hour Investigator, USDL, 1950; and (since 1955) Attorney/Arbitrator, Samuel S. Perry & Assoc Co, L.P.A., 118 St. Clair Ave, Cleveland, OH 44114. 216/771-3700

PERSELAY, GERALD Acad: Bus Admin, Org Beh/Pers, Ind Rels. BA 1949, Rutgers U; MBA 1961, Syracuse U; DBA 1970, George Washington U. PUBL: "Military Unions: Advent, Demise & Future," Govern Union Rev, Fall 1981; "Executive Training and Development" chapter in Management: Theory and Concept, F. Brown ed, Lomand Publ, 1977; "The Realities of Military Union" chapter in Military Unions vs Trends, Issues and Alternatives, W. J. Taylor et el eds, Sage Publ, 1977. INT: coll barg, personnel, org beh. ASSN: ASPA, IPMA, Acad of Mgmt. POSITIONS: Dir of Precommissioning Programs, Dept of Defense, 1971, Faculty Member, Ind Coll of Armed Forces, 1974; and (since 1978) Assoc Prof, School of Bus Admin, Winthrop Coll, Rock Hill, SC 29733. 803/323-2186

PETERFREUND, STANLEY Consulting. POSITION: President, S. Peterfreund Assoc Inc, 10 McKinley St, Closter, NJ 07624. 201/-767-6100

PETERMAN, MARY C. Bus:Mgmt/Admin. POSITION: Personnel Manager, Interbake Foods Inc, 207 Lois Dr, Battle Creek, MI 49017.

PETERS, RONALD J. Acad: Ind Rels. PhD 1976, Mich State U. PUBL: "Roots of Public Support for Labor Education 1900-1945," Labor Studies J, Fall 1976. POSITION: ILIR, Univ of Illinois, 504 E Armory, Champaign, IL 61820.

PETERSEN, DONALD J. Acad: Ind Rels; Arbitration. BBA 1962, MSIR 1964, Loyola U of Chicago; PhD 1970, Ill Inst of Tech. PUBL: Arbitration in Health Care, Aspen Systems, 1981; "Arbitration Decision Writing: Selected Criteria," Arb J, June 1983; "Strategies of Arb Selection," 70 LA 1307-1320. POSITION: Prof, School of Bus Admin, Loyola Univ, 820 N Michigan Ave, Chicago, IL 60611. 312/670-3167

PETERSEN, RALPH C. Bus: Pers/Ind Rels. POSITION: Personnel & Ind Rels, CPC International Inc, Intl Plaza, PO Box 8000, Englewood Cliffs, NJ 07632. 201/894-2371

PETERSON, DAVID A. Arbitration. BA 1973, U of Ky; JD 1976, Duquesne U; MBA 1981, U of Pittsburgh. INT: arb/med. POSITION: (since 1980) Asst to the Chairman, USS/USWA Board of Arbitration, 530 Oliver Bldg, Pittsburgh, PA 15222. 412/471-1558

PETERSON, RAYMOND A. Union. POSITION: President, NJSFT, AFT, AFL-CIO, 128 W State St, Trenton, NJ 08608.

PETERSON, RICHARD BYRON Acad: Bus Admin. MA 1956, U of Ill; PhD 1966, U of Wash. PUBL: Conflict Management and Industrial Relations, (co-edited w G.B.J. Bomers), Boston:Kluwer-Nijhoff, 1982; Systematic Management of Human Resources, (w L.N. Tracy), Addison-Wesley, 1979; "The Relationship Between Conflict Resolution and Trust - A Cross Cultural Study," Acad of Mgmt J, Dec 1981, pp 803-815. INT: coll barg, intl comparative labor, personnel. ASSN: Acad of Mgmt. POSITION: (since 1966) Professor, Dept Mgmt & Org, School of Bus Admin, DJ-10, Univ of Wash, Seattle, WA 98195. 206/543-7695

PETIT, ANDRE Acad: Org Beh/Pers, Bus Admin, Ind Rels. MSc 1972, Laval U; PhD 1982, Cornell U. PUBL: La gestion des ressources humaines: uno approche," globale et intiquie, G. Morin ed, 1983; "The Performance Appraisal Process..." Acad of Mgmt Rev, vol 3, #3, July 1978, 635-647; "Evaluating QWL Projects," Working Papers, Univ of Sherbrooke, 1982. INT: personnel, org beh, coll barg. ASSN: Acad of Mgmt, Assn of Human Resources Professionals of the Prov of Quebec, Canadian Ind Rels Assn. POSITION: (since 1980) Assoc Prof of Human Res Mgmt, School of Bus Admin, Univ of Sherbrooke, Sherbrooke, Quebec J1K 2R1 Canada. 819/565-3406/3470

PETRACK, MICHAEL J. Bus:Pers/Ind Rels. BA 1971, MLIR 1972, Mich State U. INT: coll barg, personnel, org beh. ASSN: ASPA. POSITIONS: Pers Mgmt Specialist, U.S. Civil Serv Comm, 1972; Pers Dir, City of Southfield, 1974; and (since 1979) Dir of Labor Rels, Schoolcraft College. ADDRESS: 19010 Hilton Dr, Southfield, MI 48075. 313/591-6400

PETRALIA, JEAN Bus:Pers/Ind Rels. POSITION: Boston Health/Hospitals, 35 Northampton St, Boston, MA 02118. 617/646-7480

PETREE, DANIEL L. Student. BSBA 1973, MBA 1980, Rockhurst Coll. INT: arb/med, coll barg, labor law. POSITIONS: Staff Accountant, 1977, Regional Contracting Officer, 1981, U.S. Dept HUD, Kansas City, MO; and (since 1982) Res Assoc, Inst for Bus and Econ Res, Univ of Kansas. ADDRESS: 445 Arkansas, Lawrence, KS 66044. 913/864-3123

PETTENGILL, MARIAN M. Acad: Nursing Admin. BS 1964, U of Ill; MS 1967, Rutgers U. INT: health & hosp care, method/statis, mgmt/educ. ASSN: Sigma Theta Tau, Amer Nurses Assn. POSITION: (since 1982) Research Asst, College of Nursing, U of Illinois at Chicago. ADDRESS: 23 S Bodin, Hinsdale, IL 60521. 312/996-2112

PETTY, RAYMOND D., SR. Bus:Pers/Ind Rels. BA 1952, Emory U; MBA 1971, Ga State U. INT: arb med, coll barg, empl/trng programs. ASSN: Atlanta IRRA, ASPA, Intl Assn of Quality Circles, Amer Mgmt Assn. POSITIONS: Labor Market Analyst, Georgia Dept of Labor, 1954; Safety Trng Mgr, 1957, and, since 1962, Ind Rels Mgr, William L.Bonnell Co, Inc, 25 Bonnell St, PO Box 428, Newman, GA 30263. 404/253-2020

PHELPS, JAMES C. Arbitration, Consulting. AB 1932, JD 1935, Harvard. INT: arb/med. ASSN: San Francisco IRRA, ABA. POSITIONS: Vice Pres, Great Lakes Steel Corp, 1957; Dir, Ind Rels, Fibreboard Corp, 1965; Retired. ADDRESS: 3234 Rossmoor Pkwy, Apt 4, Walnut Creek, CA 94595.

PHILIP, JOSEPH PAUL Bus:Pers/Ind Rels. BBA 1971, MBA 1973, U of Wis. INT: empl/trng programs, health & hosp care, org beh. POSITIONS: Dir Mgmt Develop, Lifemark Corp, 1980; and (since 1984), Manager, Mgmt Develop, American Medical Intl, 16800 Greenspoint Park Dr, Houston, TX 77060. 713/445-6900

PHILIPPI, MARILYNN R. Student. POSITION: PhD Candidate, Columbia U. ADDRESS: 104 West 70th St, 6B, New York, NY 212/595-8182

PHILLIPS, BARBARA ASHLEY Mediator. AB, U of Calif-Berkeley; LLB, Yale U. PUBL: "Mediation: A New Tool for Resolving Disputes," San Francisco Atty, Feb/Mar 1983; "Using Mediation to Resolve Disputes," (w A. Piazza), Calif Lawyer, Oct 1983; "The Role of Mediation in Litigation Practice," (w A. Pizza), CEB Civil Litigation Reporter, Apr 1983. INT: arb/-med, empl/trng programs. ASSN: San Francisco IRRA, SPIDR, ABA(Labor & Litigation Sections) San Francisco Bar Assn. POSITIONS: Partner, Carter,Cook, Phillips & Voltz, 1975; Principal, Barbara Ashley Phillips, P.C., 1977; and (since 1983) President & Founder, American Intermediation Service, 126 Post St, Suite 600, San Francisco, CA 94108. 415/788-6252

PHILLIPS, DACE Bus:Pers/Ind Rels; Acad: Languages. BA 1979, U of Toronto. INT: coll barg, empl/trng programs, arb/med. ASSN: Pers Assn of Toronto. POSITIONS: Div Mgr, Ontario N/E, 1979, Div Mgr, Metro, 1980, and, since 1982, Director, Labour Rels, Bell Canada, 393 University Ave, 9 Floor, Toronto, Ont M5G 1W9 Canada. 416/599-2629

PHILLIPS, GARY T. Bus:Pers/Ind Rels. POSITION: Dir-Human Res, GTE Mobilnet Inc, 616 FM 1960 West #400, Houston, TX 77090. 713/583-9051

PHILLIPS, JACK J. Bus:Pers/Ind Rels. AE 1966, Southern Tech Inst-Marietta; BS 1969, Oglethorpe U; MD 1973, Ga State U. PUBL: Handbook of Training Evaluation and Measurement Methods, Gulf Publ Co, 1983; The Handbook of Human Resource Development, (contributing author), John Wiley, 1984; "Training Programs: Results-Oriented Model for Managing the Development of Human Resources," Personnel, May-June 1983. INT: coll barg, org beh, personnel. ASSN: ASPA, Amer Soc for Trng and Develop, Natl Mgmt Assn. POSITIONS: Mgr, 1974, Pers Mgr, Stockholm Valves and Fittings, 1978; and (since 1980) Manager, Human Resources and Admin, Vulcan Materials Co, Southern Div, P.O. Box 7324-A, Birmingham, AL 35253. 205/877-3610

PHILLIPS, MARK B. Union. PO Box 25074, Lansing, MI 48909.

PHINIOTIS, STELIOS P. Public Utility. Coll Work: 1963, NYSSILR-Cornell and 1971, Scientific Ind Mgmt Sci School-Nicosia. POSITIONS: Deputy Section Head, 1967, and, since 1977, Section Head, Electrcity Auth of Cyprus. ADDRESS: 2 Dragoumi St, Acropolis, 142 Nicosia Cyprus.

PICULIN, LAURETTE Government. POSITION: National Mediation Board, #101, 1711 Massachusetts Ave NW, Washington DC 20036. 202/483-1252

PIERCE, CAROLYN F. Trade Assn. INT: coll barg, mgmt/educ, union org/admin. ASSN: Inland Empire IRRA, Natl Assn of Women in Construction. POSITION: (since 1965) Office Manager, Associated General Contractors, PO Box 3266, Spokane, WA 99220. 509/535-0391

PIERCE, DANIEL Bus:Pers/Ind Rels. MA 1966, U of Mich. INT: coll barg, arb/med, labor law. ASSN: Detroit IRRA, Ind Rels Assn of Detroit, Detroit Pers Mgmt Assn. POSITIONS: Pers Mgr/Asst, Whitehead & Kales Co, 1960; Pers Mgr, Indianhead Inc, 1968; and (since 1973) Employee Rels Manager, Aetna Industries Inc, 24331 Sherwood, Center Line, MI 48015. 313/536-0240

PIERCE, THOMAS J. Bus:Pers/Ind Rels. BA 1951, MA 1958, U of Tex-Austin; PhD 1964, U of Tex-Houston. INT: personnel, ind psych, org beh. ASSN: Amer Psych Assn, Texas Psych Assn, ASPA. POSITIONS: Senior Consultant-Manpower Planning, Control Data Corp, 1966; Dir, Manpower Planning and Develop, Super Valu Stores, Inc, 1969; and (since 1975) Vice Pres, Human Resources, H. E. Butt Grocery Co, PO Box 9216, Corpus Christi, TX 78469. 512/881-1223

PIERSON, FRANK COOK Acad: Econ. BA 1934, Swarthmore Coll; MA 1938, PhD 1942, Columbia. POSITIONS: Vice Chmn, Regional War Labor Bd, 1944-45; Inst of Ind Rels, UCLA, 1948-50; Joseph Wharton Prof of Pol Econ, 1940, and currently, Prof Emeritus, Swarthmore Coll, 740 Ogden Ave, Swarthmore, PA 19081.

PIETRANTON, ANTHONY F. Bus:Pers/Ind Rels. BS 1981, MSIR 1983, West Va U. INT: personnel, empl/trng programs. ASSN: West Virginia IRRA. POSITIONS: Mgr, Claudio's Pizza; Assoc Dir, C.H.A.N.G.E., Inc, 1983; and (since 1984) Employment/Staff Services Specialist, Federated Investors, Pittsburgh. ADDRESS: 110 Phillips St, Weirton, WV 26062. 412/288-1252

PIGAGE, LEO C. Acad: Engineering. ME 1936, MME 1938, Cornell U. INT: work standards & job evaluation. ASSN: Amer Inst of Ind Engineers, Amer Soc of Mechanical Engineers. POSITION: Prof of Ind Engineering, Univ of Illinois. ADDRESS: 206 Elmwood Rd, Champaign, IL 61821. 217/333-1466

PIGANIOL, CLAUDE Acad: Ind Rels, Org Beh/Pers; Consulting. Dr d'Etat, 1976, U of Paris. "Techniques et politiques d'amelioration des conditions de travail," Ed: Enterprise Moderne d'Edition, Paris 1980; "Comparison of Quality of Worklife Attitudes of Samples of American and French Word-Processing/Data Processing Operators," (w W. D. Torrence), Communications Congress, AIRP Kyoto, Mar 1983; "La 'grievance procedure'aux USA et en France," (w W. D. Torrence) Revue Francaise des Affaires Sociales, #2, 1984. INT: intl comparative labor, org beh, personnel. ASSN: Assn Francaise de Rels Professionnelles. POSITIONS: Maitre-Asst, Conservatore Natl des Arts et Metiers, 1972; Chargee d'un Seminaire do doctorat, 1976, and, since 1984, Chargee d'un seminaire de 3c Cycle, Univ of Paris. ADDRESS: 60 Rue Edouard Manet, 78730 Plaisir France. Phone: 271 24 14

PIGORS, PAUL Acad: Ind Rels. PhD 1927, Harvard. PUBL: Personnel Administration, 9th Ed, 1981; The Pigors Incident: Process of Case Study, 1980. INT: arb/med, mgmt/educ, personnel. POSITION: Prof Emeritus, Ind Rels, MIT. ADDRESS: 385 Salem-End Rd, Framingham, MA 01701. 617/872-0945

PILENZO, RONALD C. Professional Assn, Bus:Pers/Ind Rels. BBA 1961, MBA 1964, U of Detroit. PUBL: "Placement by Objectives," Pers J. INT: empl/trng programs, intl comparative labor, mgmt/educ. ASSN: Amer Compensation Assn, Amer Soc Trng and Develop, OD Network. POSITIONS: VP-Human Res, Evans Products Co, 1971; Corp Dir, Compensation & Mgmt Devel, Intl Multifoods Corp, 1975; and (since 1980) President and C.O.O., Amer Soc for Pers Admin, 606 N Washington St, Alexandria, VA 22314. 703/548-3440

PINCUS, DAVID M. Arbitration, Empl Involvement. MS 1977, Ga Inst of Tech; MLIR 1980, PhD 1984, Mich State U. INT: arb/med, coll barg, empl involvement. ASSN: Mid-Mich IRRA, AAA, FMCS, (Arb Panel), Amer Mgmt Assn. POSITION: Arbitrator (self-employed), 5771 Bois Isle, Haslett, MI 48840. 517/339-2983

PINCUS, S. RICHARD Acad: Law. BA 1958, George Washington U; JD 1961, U of Chicago. PUBL: "Labor Relations Considerations: Summary of the Taft-Hartley Act," Chap 12 in Organizing and Advising Ill Businesses, Ill Inst for Continuing Legal Educ, 1975-Rev 1978; "The Common Law Contract and Tort Rights of Union Employees: What Effect After the Demise of the 'At Will' Doctrine?" Chicago-Kent Law Rev, Winter 1983. INT: labor law, union org/admin, coll barg. ASSN: Chicago IRRA, Chicago/Ill Bar Assns, ABA. POSITIONS: Supervising Attorney, NLRB, Chicago & Peoria, 1961; and (since 1969) Partner, Fox and Grove, Chartered, 233 S. Wacker Dr, Suite 7818, Chicago, IL 60606. 312/876-0500

PINEAU, CHARLES A. Bus:Pers/Ind Rels. Rawlings Sporting Goods, 2300 Delmar Blvd, St. Louis, MO 63166.

PINKUS, EDWARD C. Arbitration. 89 Pinckney St, Boston, MA 02114.

PINTO, E. NICHOLAS Legal Practice. POSITION: Attorney, 5 Roger Ave, Lincroft, NJ 07738.

PINTO, NICHOLAS F. Union. BA 1952, Tex Western Coll. INT: union org/admin, coll barg, arbitration. ASSN: New York & Capital Dist IRRA. POSITIONS: Exec Dir, Council 31, Ariz, 1960, Exec Dir, NY Council 66, 1970, and, since 1975, Staff Rep-Bargaining Specialist, AFSCME, Council 82, AFL-CIO, Albany. ADDRESS: 215 Mallard Dr, Camillus, NY 13031. 518/489-8424.

PIRKEY, NANCY L. Legal Practice. INT: coll barg, arb/med, labor law. POSITION: (since 1981) Res Assoc, Mulcahy & Wherry, S.C., 815 E Mason St, Suite 1600, Milwaukee, WI 53202. 414/278-7110

PISEGNA, DOMINCK Government. BS 1971. INT: coll barg, arb/med, personnel. ASSN: Central New York IRRA, AAA, NYS Public Empl Labor Rels Assn, Natl Public Empl Labor Rels Assn. POSITION: (since 1978) Dir, Onondaga County Div of Empl Rels, 421 Montgomery St, 14th Floor Civic Center, Syracuse, NY 13202. 315/425-3455

PIZARRO, ZOSIMO Q. Professional Assn. POSITION: Intl Rice Institute, Pers & Legal Dept, PO Box 933, Manila, Phillipines.

PIZZURRO, ROBERT D. Bus:Pers/Ind Rels. 1760 Kirts, #106, Troy, MI 48084.

PLAMBECK, DONALD L. Professional Assn. PO Box 632, Vienna, VA 22180. 703/281-1509

PLANTZ, FREDERICK DAVID Student. BSSW 1979, U of Wis-Madison. INT: Affirmative Action/EEO, personnel, empl/trng programs. ASSN: Madison Urban League, NAACP-Madison. POSITIONS: Dir of Soc Services, 1982, Asst Affirmative Action Officer, Allen Hall, 1982; and (since 1983) Student, U of Wis-Madison. ADDRESS: 2818 Curry Parkway, #23, Madison, WI 53713.

PLATT, HARRY H. Legal Practice. POSITION: Attorney, 22505 Providence Dr, #101, Southfield, MI 48075.

PLOSCOWE, STEPHEN A. Legal Practice. BSIR 1962, LLB 1965, Cornell U. INT: coll barg, arb/med, labor law. ASSN: New York & New Jersey IRRAs, New Jersey Bar Assn, ABA. POSITION: Attorney, Grotta, Glassman & Hoffman, 65 Livingston Ave, Roseland, NJ 07086. 201/992-4800

PLOWMAN, DAVID H. Acad: Ind Rels. BEc 1974, U of Western Australia; MA 1976, U of Melbourne. PUBL: Wage Indexation, Allen & Unwin, 1982; Australian Industrial Relations, McGraw Hill, 1980; "Unions and Income Policies," in Ford & Plowman (ed) Australian - Unions, Macmillan, 1983. INT: arb/med. ASSN: Ind Rels Soc-Australia, IIRA, Econ Soc-Australia. POSITIONS: Tutor, Melbourne U, 1975; Lecturer, South Australian Inst Tech, 1976; and (since 1978) Senior Lecturer, Univ of New South Wales, PO Box 1, Kensington, NSW, Australia 2033. Phone: (02) 66220 26

PODGURSKY, MICHAEL JOHN Acad: Econ, Ind Rels. PhD 1980, U of Wis-Madison. PUBL: "Unions and Family Income Inequality;" "Labor Market Policy and Structural Adjustment." INT: govt labor policy, labor market econ, empl/trng programs. ASSN: AEA. POSITIONS: Lecturer, Dept of Econ, Notre Dame Univ, 1979; and (since 1980) Asst Prof of Econ, Dept of Econ, Thompson Hall, Univ of Mass, Amherst, MA 01375. 413/545-2590

POE, LAWRENCE J. Acad: Ind Rels; Consulting, Bus/Pers Ind Rels. BA 1975, MLIR 1979, Mich State U. INT: coll barg, arb/med, labor law. ASSN: Detroit IRRA, ASPA. POSITIONS: Labor Rels Consultant, Mich Assn of School Boards, 1979; and (since 1982) Asst Prof, School of Labor & Ind Rels, Mich State U. ADDRESS: 3745 E Beard Rd, Morrice, MI 48857. 517/355-9591

POFF, FRANK M. Acad: Student. Bus:Pers/-Ind Rels. BS-BA 1984, Shippensburg U. INT: personnel, labor law, coll barg. ASSN: Harrisburg IRRA, Pers Labor Rels Club. POSITION: Student, Shippensburg U of Penna, 129 Allen Drive, Beaver, PA 15009. 412/774-9483

POGLIANICH, ANTONIO Government, Empl Trng, Consulting. BSILR 1983, Cornell. INT: empl/trng programs, coll barg, arb/med. ASSN: IIRA. POSITIONS: (since 1983) Job Search Program Coordinator, Dept for the Aging, City of New York. ADDRESS: Apt 3RW, 138 West 10th St, New York, NY 10014. 212/577-8424

POLCA, ROBERT FRANCIS Bus:Pers/Ind Rels. BA 1974, U of Pittsburgh-Johnstown; MA 1981, St. Francis Coll. INT: safety, personnel. ASSN: Pacific NW Pers Mgmt Assn (ASPA). POSITIONS: Pers Trainee, 1981, and, since 1983, Safety Mgr, Reynolds Metals Co. ADDRESS: 3100 Rowe Pl, Fremont, CA 98632

POLK, ROBERT C. Bus:Mgmt/Admin. BA 1962, Dillard U. PUBL: Transit Manager's Handbook-Preparing for Negotiations, Implementing the Contract and Contract Administration. INT: coll barg, arb/med, mgmt/educ. ASSN: Houston IRRA, AAA, Houston Pers Assn, Amer Public Transit Assn. POSITIONS: Dir Transportation, 1981, Acting Asst General Mgr-Transit Operations, 1981, and, since 1983, Deputy Asst General Mgr-Transit Operations, Metro Transit Authority, 5700 Eastex Freeway, Houston, TX 77208. 713/635-6337

POLLAND, HARRY Consulting. Beeson, Taylor & Silbert, 100 Bush St, Suite 1500, San Francisco, CA 94104. 415/986-4060

POLLARD, DENNIS R. Legal Practice. BA 1965, JD 1968, U of Detroit. ASSN: Natl School Board Assn, Empl Assn of Detroit, State Bar of Mich. POSITION: (since 1972) Partner, Clark, Hardy, Lewis, Pollard and Page, P.C.,555 S Woodward Ave, 7th Floor, Birmingham, MI 48011. 313/645-0800

POLLARD, HINDA GREYSER Acad: Ind Rels; Legal Practice. BA 1959, Tufts Univ; JD 1964, U of Calif-Berkeley. INT: coll barg, labor law, personnel. ASSN: Member RI Bar, Acad of Mgmt, Amer Mgmt Assn. POSITION: (since 1979) Assoc Prof and Chairperson-Mgmt Dept, Bryant College, Smithfield, RI 02917. 401/231-1200 ext 390.

POLLEY, IRA Arbitration; Acad: Pol Sci, Org Beh/Pers. BA 1938, Ind U; PhD 1954, U of Minn. PUBL: Wage Stabilization in Region 8: A Case Study, 1954; "Collective Negotiations-A View from a State Department of Education," State Govern, Spring 1969; "What's Right With American Education?" Phi Delta Kappan, Sept 1969. INT: arb/med, personnel, govt labor policy. ASSN: Mid-Michigan IRRA, SPIDR, AAA(Labor Panel), Amer Civil Liberties Union. POSITIONS: State Controller and Dir of Dept of Admin, 1960-62, State Supt of Public Inst, Dept of Educ, Mich State Govern, 1966-69; and (since 1970) Prof of Political Science, Mich State Univ. ADDRESS: 935 Audubon Rd, East Lansing, MI 48823. 517/353-5336/365-6590

POLLO, STEVE A. Acad:Ind Rels. ADDRESS: 732 Princeton Ave, Lansing, MI 48915. 517/484-0253

POMER, MARSHALL I. Acad: Sociology. POSITION: Sociology & Econ, Merrill College, Univ of California, Santa Cruz, CA 95064.

POMNICHOWSKI, ALEX S. Acad: Bus Admin. POSITION: Management Dept, Ferris State College, Big Rapids, MI 49307.

PONAK, ALLEN M. Acad: Ind Rels; Arbitration, Consulting. BA 1970, McGill U; MLIR, Mich State U; PhD 1977, U of Wis-Madison. PUBL: "Unionized Professionals and the Scope of Bargaining: The Case of Nurses," ILR Rev; Canadian Bank Unionism, Rels Industrielles; "Choice of Procedures in Canada and the United States," Ind Rels. INT: coll barg, arb/med, public sector labor rels. ASSN: Canadian Ind Rels Assn. POSITIONS: Visiting Prof, McGill Univ, 1980, and, since 1982, Assoc Prof, Faculty of Mgmt, Univ of Calgary, 2500 University Dr NW, Calgary, Alberta T2T 4X4 Canada. 403/284-7584.

PONCINI, CONCHITA Intl Org, Pers/Ind Rels. MSIR 1964, U of Wis-Madison. PUBL: Editor IRRA Bulletin; "New Approaches and Trends in Personnel management in the U.S. and Some Western Countries: An Overview," forthcoming. INT: personnel, coll barg, intl comparative labor. ASSN: IIRA. POSITIONS: Exec Officer, 1976, Editor, 1980, IIRA; and (since 1976) Research and Tech Officer, ILO, Labour Law and Labour Rels Branch. ADDRESS: 7 Chemin Champ Carre, 1256 Troinex-Geneva, Switzerland. Phone: (022) 99 78 78

POOL, C. Allen Arbitration; Acad: Ind Rels. EdD, 1981, U of Houston. INT: arb/med, coll barg, labor educ. ASSN: San Francisco IRRA, AAA, SPIDR. POSITIONS: Project Dir, Near East South Asia Grad Overseas Program, U of Houston, 1976; Lecturer, Golden Gate U, 1983; and (since 1981) Arbitrator (self-employed), PO Box 2591, Monterey, CA 93940. 408/372-4138

POORE, K. E. Bus:Labor Rels. INT: ind psych, org beh, arb/med. POSITIONS: Worker's Compensation Admin, 1979, and, since 1981, Labor Rels Rep, Ford Motor Co, PO Box 1600, Dearborn, MI 48121. 313/322-8030

PORTER, ARTHUR R., JR. Arbitration. BS 1940, Washington & Lee U; MA 1947, PhD 1955, U of Penna. PUBL: Sub Property Rights, Columbia Univ Press, 1954. INT: arb/med, coll barg. ASSN: NAA. POSITIONS: Dean & Prof of Econ, Heidelberg Coll, 1967; and (since 1979) Arbitrator, 2520 East Township Road 122, Tiffin, OH 44883.

PORTER, KAREN D. Union. BBA 1978, Detroit Inst of Tech. ASSN: Detroit IRRA, Coalition of Labor Union Women, Black Office & Professional Empl Caucus. POSITION: (since 1982) President, OPEIU Local 494, AFL-CIO/-CLC, PO Box 15308, Detroit, MI 48215. 313/822-0059

PORTER, ROBERT GERARD Bus:Mgmt/Admin. B/Ind Admin 1978, General Motors Inst. ADDRESS: 2613 Parsifal, Springfield, IL 62704.

PORTER, THOMAS B. Student. BA 1983, Drake U. INT: personnel, empl/trng programs, labor market econ. ASSN: ASPA. ADDRESS: 1361 W Downer, Aurora, IL 60506. 312/896-0263

PORTIS, BERNARD Acad: Bus Admin. PhD 1962, Harvard. PUBL: Reducing Labour Turnover in the Canadian Shoe Industry; Effect of Advance Notice in a Plant Shutdown; Analysis of Attitudes Toward Unemployment Insurance. INT: empl/trng programs, method/statis, ind sociol. ASSN: Amer Sociol Assn, Amer Assn for Public Opinion Res, Canadian Ind Rels Assn. POSITIONS: Asst Prof, 1961-63, Harvard U; and (currently) Assoc Prof, Univ of Western Ontario. ADDRESS: 1190 Richmond St, London, Ont N6A 3L2 Canada. 519/679-3217

PORTNER, DAVIS A. Retired. BA 1938, MA 1939, U of Ariz. INT: income maint, intl comparative labor, labor market econ. POSITIONS: Asst Admin, Bus & Defense Services, US Dept of Commerce, 1967, Dir, Manpower Planning, USDL, 1970. Retired. ADDRESS:

Apt 904, 5200 Brittany Dr S, St. Petersburg, FL 33715.

PORTWOOD, JAMES D. Acad: Org Beh/Pers. POSITION: Dept of IROB, Temple Univ, 1822 Park Mall, Philadelphia, PA 19122.

PORTZ, JOHN H. Student. ADDRESS: 127 Proudfit, Madison, WI 53715.608/255-2541

POST, WILLIAM B. Arbitration. BS 1935, New York U. INT: arb/med. ASSN: Conn IRRA. POSITION: Labor Arbitrator, 75 Mumford Road, New Haven, CT 06515. 203/397-3097

POSTHUMA, RICHARD A. Government, Bus:Pers/Ind Rels. BA 1976, Calvin Coll; MLIR 1977, Mich State U. INT: personnel, coll barg, empl/trng programs. ASSN: West Mich IRRA, ASPA, Natl & Mich Public Employer Labor Rels Assn. POSITIONS: Pers Dir, Cutler Mfg Copr, 1977; Pers Mgr, Kindel Furniture Co, 1979; and (since 1980) Labor Rels Supervisor, City of Grand Rapids. ADDRESS: 1730 Stilesgate S.E., Grand Rapids, MI 49508. 616/456-3105

POTASH, SIDNEY Acad: Bus Admin. BS 1968, Utica Coll; MBA 1971, PhD 1978, SUNY-Buffalo. INT: org beh, personnel. ASSN: Acad of Mgmt, Beta Gamma Sigma. POSITION: Assoc Prof, Dept of Mgmt, Marietta Coll, Marietta, OH 45750. 614/374-4623

POTTER, EDWARD E. Legal Practice, Arbitration. BA 1968, Mich State U; MILR, 1972, Cornell; JD 1978, American U. PUBL: Employee Selection: Legal and Practical Alternatives to Compliance and Litigation, 1983. INT: labor law, arb/med, coll barg. ASSN: Wash DC IRRA, ABA, Fed Bar Assn, SPIDR. POSITIONS: Ind Rels Advisor, USDL, 1972; Staff Assoc, Fed Service Impasse Panel, 1973, and (since 1979) Partner, McGuiness & Williams, 1015 15th St NW, Washington DC 20005. 202/789-8600

POTTER, RICHARD H. Acad: Univ Admin; Arbitration. MBA 1966, Central Mich U; MLIR & PhD, 1981, Mich State U. INT: arb/med, coll barg, labor law. ASSN: Detroit IRRA, AAA, SPIDR, Coll & Univ Pers Assn. POSITION: Asst Dir, IPCD, Central Mich Univ. ADDRESS: 1309 Highland, Mt. Pleasant, MI 48858. 517/774-3865

POTTS, ANNE M. Bus.Pers/Ind Rels. POSITION: Labor Rels, NJ Inst of Tech, 323 High St, Newark, NJ 07716. 201/645-5172

POWELL, WALTER H. Arbitration. BS 1938, JD 1940, NYU; MA 1948, U of Penna. PUBL: Handbook on Faculty Bargaining, Josey-Bass; Collective Bargaining, AAA; Negro and Employment Opportunity, U of Mich. INT: arb/med, labor law, personnel. ASSN: Philadlaphia IRRA, NAA. POSITIONS: Vice Pres, IRC (Div of TRW), 1953-1970; Vice Pres, Temple Univ, 1973-77; and (since 1977) Arbitrator, S-1705, 2200 B. Franklin Hwy, Philadelphia, PA 19130. 215/561-3197

POWER, DONALD F. Government. ADDRESS: 1307 Ramblewood Dr, East Lansing, MI 48823. 517/337-7665

POWER, JAMES F. Government. FMCS, 2100 K St NW, Washington DC 20427.

POWERS, EDWARD W. Acad: Univ Admin. BS 1953, NYSSILR-Cornell; JD 1956, Mich Law School. POSITIONS: Assoc Dir of Personnel, Harvard, 1968-73; Dir of Civil Service, Comm of Mass, 1973-751 and (since 1975) Assoc General Counsel, Harvard Univ, 1350 Massachusetts Ave, Rm 646, Cambridge, MA 02138. 617/495-2798

POWERS, KATHLEEN JAY Acad: Ind Rels, Org Beh/Pers, Bus Admin. BA 1974, MBA 1975, Fla Intl U. PUBL: "The Quantitative Assessment of Content Validity," (w C. A. Schriesheim), Acad of Mgmt, Southwest Div Proceedings, Mar 1983, pp 103-107; "Union Participation and Perceptions of the Employing Organization," (w J. M. Jermier & J. Gaines), Acad of Mgmt Southern Div, Proceedings, Nov 1982, pp 91-93; Collective Bargaining Simulation For the Private Sector, Bus Publication Inc, forthcoming. INT: coll barg, org beh, labor law. ASSN: Acad of Mgmt, Amer Bus Law Assn, Amer Psych Assn. POSITIONS: Res Assoc, 1980, Teaching Assoc, Dept of Mgmt, 1981, and, since 1983, Doctoral Candidate, Univ of Florida, School of Bus. ADDRESS: 4511 NW 28th St, Gainesville, FL 32605. 904/392-0163

POWERS, ROBERT S. Acad: Pers/Ind Rels; Govt Pers/Ind Rels. BS 1967, McMurray Coll; MS 1970, USC; MA 1976 U of North Tex. INT: health & hosp care, mgmt/educ, org beh. ASSN: ASPA.POSITIONS: Postal Operations Officer, USAF, 1968; Pers Dir, Flaw Memorial Hosp, 1973; and (since 1974) Pers Officer, Denton State School. ADDRESS: 2305 Yorkshire Rd, Denton TX 76201. 817/387-3831

PRASSE, FRED C. Bus:Pers/Ind Rels. POSITION: Director, Union Rels, Cleveland Electric Co, PO Box 5000, Cleveland, OH 44101.

PRELI, SORINE Government. INT: admin generalist, coll barg, arb/med. ASSN: SPIDR. POSITIONS: Assoc Dir, 1973, Asst Dir, Budget and Finance, 1975, and, since 1980, Program Analyst and Oper Analysis, Audit Div, FMCS, Wash DC. ADDRESS: 1213 North Wayne St, Arlington, VA 22201. 202/653-6136

PREMACK, STEVEN Student. BS 1978, Fla State U; MLIR 1982, Mich State U. PUBL: The Unionization Process: A Review of Literature, (w R. N. Block), chapter in D.B. Lipsky and J. M. Douglas (Eds), Advances in Industrial and Labor Relations, vol 1, JAI Press, in press. INT: personnel, org beh, coll barg. ASSN: Acad of Mgmt, IIRA, Amer Psych Assn. POSITION: PhD Candidate, School of Labor Rels, Mich State Univ. ADDRESS: PO Box 1452, East Lansing, MI 48823. 517/353-3398

PRENTING, THEODORE O. Acad: Bus Admin; Consulting. MBA 1960, U of Chicago. PUBL: "Job Enrichment: How Important is the Work Itself?" U of Mich Bus Rev, Jan 1976; Humanism and Technology in Assembly Line Systems, Hayden Book, Rochelle Park, NJ, 1974; "Some Missing Links In Improving Assembly Productivity," Assembly Engineering, Nov 1973. INT: mgmt/educ, labor market econ, arb/med. ASSN: ASPA, Amer Inst of Ind Eng, SPIDR. POSITIONS: Systems Analyst, IBM, 1960; Mgr, Operations Res, IIT Res Inst, 1963; and (since 1976) Prof of Bus, Marist Coll. ADDRESS: 2 Alden Rd, Poughkeepsie, NY 12603. 914/471-3240

SER, RICHARD A. Union. POSITION: ...n of Machinists and Aerospace Workers, Dist 10, 624 N 24th St, Milwaukee, WI 53233. 414/933-5720

PRESTON, VALERIE KNOX Union. POSITION: Field Representative, MSTA/NEA. ADDRESS: 112 Colony Ct, Walkersville, MD 21793. 301/662-9077

PREVIANT, DAVID Legal Practice. LLB 1935, U of Wis. INT: arb/med, coll barg, labor law. ASSN: Wis IRRA. POSITION: Chairman of Board, Goldberg, Previant, Uelmen et al S.C., 788 N Jefferson St, Milwaukee, WI 53202. 414/271-4500

PRIBBLE, EDWARD DAVID Arbitration, Fact Finding/Mediation. BBA 1966, JD 1969, U of Wis-Madison. INT: arb/med, health & hosp care, govt labor policy. ASSN: AAA, SPIDR, ABA, WIs & Federal Bar Assns (Labor Rels Sections). POSITIONS: Attorney, Labor, NLRB, Region 17, 1969-80; Arbitrator (Labor) Pribble Arbitration & Mediation Services, Inc., 621 S Cedar Lake Rd, Minneapolis, MN 55405. 612/377-6319

PRIEBJRIVAT, VUTHIPHONG Thammasat Univ, 177 Charkrapong St, Banglampoo Bangkok, Thailand 10200.

PRIGGINS, GEORGE M. Bus:Pers/Ind Rels. BA 1968, Lafayette Coll; MBA 1974, Penna State U. INT: coll barg, arb/med, personnel. ASSN: ASPA. POSITIONS: Mgr, Supervisory Devel, Daniel Intl, 1974; Mgr, Ind Rels, Dresser Ind Inc, 1976; and (since 1979) Manager, Labor Rels, Ericsson, Inc, GOP #3, PO Box 3110, Greenwich, CT 06836. 203/625-7254

PRINS, JOHN ROBERT Consulting. BA 1978, U of Conn; MALR 1981, Rutgers U. INT: arb/med, health & hosp care, coll barg. ASSN: New Brunswick & Central NJ IRRA. POSITIONS: Labor Rep, NJ State Nurses Assn, 1980; and (since 1982) Labor Consultant, Ind Labor Relations Consultants Inc, E. Orange. ADDRESS: 272 Ward Ave, Apt 24A, Bordentown, NJ 08505. 609/298-0284

PRIOR, JOHN J. Bus:Pers/Ind Rels. POSITION: Labor Relations, Super-Valu Stores Inc, PO Box 990, Minneapolis, MN 55440. 612/828-4001

PRITZKER, MALCOLM L. Legal Practice. BA 1957, Penna State U; JD 1968, Temple U. PUBL: "Arbitration of Employer Withdrawal Liability," Empl Benefits J, Dec 1982. INT: arb/med, coll barg, labor law. ASSN: ABA, DC Bar, SPIDR. POSITION: Attorney, Zimmerman, Semler and Pritzker, 1511 K St NW, Suite 623, Washington DC 20005. 202/783-5500

PROCELLI, MATTHEW S. Bus:Mgmt/Admin. BE 1949, RPI; MBA 1953, Hofstra U. INT: arb/med, coll barg, health & hosp care. ASSN: Long Island IRRA. POSITION: (since 1979) Vice Pres, Long Island Lighting Corp, 175 East Old Country Rd, Hicksville, NY 11801. 516/733-4274

PROCOPIO, MARIO A. Arbitration. LLB 1950, New York U. INT: arb/med. ASSN: New York and Long Island IRRA, NAA, AAA. POSITIONS: Practice of Law, 1952; Labor Mediator, NYS Mediation Bd, 1961; and, currently, Arbitrator, 41 Hollywood Ct, Rockville Centre, NY 11570. 516/536-8198

PROCTOR, WILLIAM McKENZIE Government. POSITION: FMCS, 250 Federal Bldg, Grand Rapids, MI 49503.

PROSPER, PETER ANTHONY JR. Acad: Econ, Ind Rels; Arbitration. BS 1958, Penna State; PhD 1970, Cornell. PUBL: Rate of Change of Money Wages in the U.S.; "Geographical Mobility in Three Southern States;" "Conglomerate Merges and Public Policy." INT: arb/med, coll barg, labor market econ. ASSN: Capital Dist IRRA, AEA, SPIDR. POSITION: Assoc Prof, 1964, and, since 1980, Professor, Dept of Econ, Union College, Schnectady, NY 12308. 518/370-6219

PROSTEN, RICHARD M. Union, Ind Rels; Acad: Econ. PUBL: "Organized Labor and the National Guidelines," Ohio U J of Bus Admin, Spring, 1979; "Industrial Unions in the 1980's," chapter in The Shrinking Perimeter: Unionism and Labor Relations in Manufacturing, D.C. Heath 1980; "Multinational Companies and Labor-A Union View of the Multinational Problem," chapter in Labor Relations in Advanced Industrial Societies, Kassalow & Martin, eds, Carnegie Endow. 1980. INT: coll barg, union org/admin, transnationals and empl. ASSN: Wash DC IRRA. POSITIONS: Instructor, Labor Educ Div, Roosevelt U, 1961-64; Coordinator of Coll Barg, 1964-70, and (since 1970) Director of Research, Industrial Union Dept, AFL-CIO, 815 16th St NW, Washington DC 20006. 202/842-7860

PROUTY, E. KEITH Government. AB 1942, Dartmouth Coll; MA 1956, Yale. PUBL: "Dialogue or Diatribe: A Current View of Labor-Management Relations in Transportation;" "DOT and the Unions;" "Organizational Options For Owner-Operators in Over-The-Road Trucking." INT: coll barg, govt labor policy, labor market econ. ASSN: Wash DC IRRA, AEA, Assn for Workplace Democracy, Transportation Res Board. POSITIONS: Dir of Develop and Res, CWA, 1966; Dir of Res, AFSCME, 1970; and (since 1975) Transportation Labor Specialist, Office of the Secretary, US Dept of Transportation. ADDRESS: 9714 Rutley Rd, Bethesda, MD 20817. 202/426-4386

PRYOR, GRACE T. Bus:Mgmt/Admin. ASSN: Baltimore IRRA. POSITION: Manager, Compensation, Sinai Hospital of Baltimore, 2401 W Belvidere Ave, Baltimore, MD 21215. 301/578-5662

PUCCINI, NANCY ANN Student. BS 1983, Va Polytech Inst & State U. INT: personnel, labor law. POSITION: (since 1984) Grad Asst, Inst of Labor & Ind Rels, Univ of Illinois. ADDRESS: 2053 Swan's Neck Way, Reston, VA 22091. 217/333-0984

PUFF, HAROLD FREDERICK Acad: Bus Admin, Org Beh/Pers, Ind Rels. BS 1938, Miami U; MBA 1948, U of Mich; DBA 1957, Ind U. INT: mgmt/educ, personnel, org beh. ASSN: Acad of Mgmt, Natl Assn of Purchasing Mgmt, Inst of Ind Eng. POSITIONS: Asst Supt, Bldg & Ground, Western Coll, Oxford, OH, 1941; Sales Purchasing Agent, Specialty Envelope & Bag Co, Cincinnati; Prof of Mgmt, 1948, and, since, 1983, Prof Emeritus, School of Bus Admin, Miami Univ, Oxford, OH 45056. 513/529-4215

PULHAMUS, AARON R. Acad: Univ Admin, Student. BA 1960, West Va Wesleyan; MA 1962, New York U; MPA 1977, Rutgers U. INT: coll barg, labor history, personnel. ASSN: New

Brunswick IRRA, ASPA, Coll & Univ Pers Assn, Acad for Academic Pers Admin. POSITION: (since 1968) Exec Dir, Empl Rels, New Jersey Inst of Tech. ADDRESS: 68 Minnisink Road, Totowa, NJ 07512. 201/645-5122

PULICH, MARCIA A. Acad: Ind Relsl; Arbitration, Consulting. BS 1966, Texas Woman's U; MS 1974, PhD 1979, North Tex U. PUBL: "Train First-Line Supervisors to Handle Discipline;" "The Supervisor's Role in an Employee's On-The-Job Development;" "Effective Listening: A Key to Better Communications." INT: arb/med, labor law, coll barg. ASSN: Wis IRRA, AAA, Blackhawk Pers Assn. POSITIONS: Instructor, North Tex State U, 1974; Asst Prof, Northern Ariz U, 1977; and (since 1978) Asst Prof, Mgmt Dept, Univ of Wis-Whitewater, Whitewater, WI 53190. 414/472-3983

PULLEN, ROBERT WHITE Retired. PhD 1949, MIT. ADDRESS: Emerald Pointe C-303, 1612 E Marion Ave, Punta Gorda, FL 33950. 813/637-1886

PURCELL, THEODORE VINCENT Acad: Bus Admin. AB 1933, Dartmouth, AM 1946, Loyola U-Chicago; PhD 1952, Harvard. PUBL: The Worker Speaks His Mind HU Press, 1953; Blacks in the Industrial World, Free Press, 1973; Cases in Business Ethics, Appleton Century Crofts, 1968. INT: mgmt/educ, ind psych, org beh. ASSN: Amer Psych Assn, Assn for Soc Econ. POSITION: (since 1972) Res Prof, Jesuit Center for Soc Studies, Georgetown Univ, Washington DC 20057. 202/625-4634

PUTNAM, DAVID ROSS Bus:Pers/Ind Rels. ADDRESS: 1477 Ridge Rd, Ontario Center, NY 14520. 315/524-3683

PYLE, DONALD G. Government. POSITION: Public Service Staff Rels Bd, PO Box 1525, Station B, Ottawa, Ont K1P 5V2 Canada. 613/995-9083

Q

QUALLS, JOHN ROBERT Bus:Pers/Ind Rels. BA 1974, JD 1977 U of Cincinnati. INT: arb/med, labor law, coll barg. ASSN: Ohio Bar Assn, Cincinnati Bar Assn, Ohio Self Ins Assn. POSITIONS: Staff Attorney, Legal Aid Soc of Cincinnati, 1977; Asst Supr, Labor Rels, 1981, and, since 1982, Supr, Labor Rels, Hamilton Mill, Champion International, 601 North B St, Hamilton, OH 45013. 513/868-5235

QUARLES, MARY VIRGINIA Union. BA 1962, Miss Coll; MA 1970, Fla State U. INT: coll barg, arb/med, union org/admin. POSITIONS: Teacher, Brevard County School Board, 1962, UniServ Director, Fontana/Chaffey UniServ, 1976, and, since 1978, UniServ Director, Central Wis UniServ Council-West, PO Box 1606, Wausau, WI 54401. 715/675-3305

QUEEN, LLOYD J. Bus:Pers/Ind Rels. BA 1975, NYU; JD 1978, John Marshall Law School (Atlanta); MSIR 1981, Ga State U. INT: labor law, govt labor policy, health & hosp care. ASSN: Southern Calif IRRA. POSITION: (since 1981) Assistant Area Personnel Director, Kaiser-Permanente Medical Care Program. ADDRESS: 127 Vista Pl #1, Venice, CA 90291. 213/399-4391

QUICK, D.L. Bus:Pers/Ind Rels. AB 1948, MA 1953, U of Mo, Kansas City. POSITION: Vice Pres-Personnel, Western Auto Supply Co, 2107 Grand Ave, Kansas City, MO 64108. 816/346-4500

QUIGLEY, ROBERT J. Bus:Pers/Ind Rels, Consulting. BA 1954, Baldwin-Wallace Coll; MS 1968, U of Mo. INT: coll barg, union org/-admin, arb/med. ASSN: ASPA. POSITIONS: Dir-Pers/Labor Rels, Milgram Food Stores, 1966; VP-Labor Rels, Cook United, Inc, 1969; and (since 1975) Dir-Ind Rels, Wickes Companies Inc, 3340 Ocean Park Blvd, Santa Monica, CA 90405. 213/452-9471

QUINET, FELIX Government. MA 1955, U of Montreal. PUBL: The Content and Role of Collective Agreements in Canada; Collective Bargaining in the Canadian Context; Dimensions of Canadian Collective Bargaining. INT: coll barg, govt labor policy, method/statis. ASSN: Canadian Ind Rels Assn. POSITION: (since 1969) Dir of Research, Pay Research Bureau, PO Box 1525, Station "B", Ottawa, Ont K1P 5V2 Canada. 613/995-8889

QUINN, FRANCIS X. Arbitration, Consulting, Editor. MA 1956, Fordham U; MSIR 1966, Loyola Coll; PhD 1976, Calif Western. PUBL: The Ethical Aftermath of Automation; Ethics-Advertising and Responsibility; Population Ethics. INT: arb/med, health & hosp care, labor law. ASSN: Dallas & Philadelphia IRRAs, NAA, SPIDR, Assn of Social Economists. POSITIONS: Special Asst to Dean, School of Bus, Temple Univ, 1968-76; Foreign Service Grievance Board, US State Dept, 1976-81; and (currently) Arbitrator-Mediator, F. X. Quinn Inc, 230 Hazel Blvd, Tulsa, OK 74114. 918/742-8181

R

RADCLIFFE, JOHN H. Union. BA 1965, U of Wis. INT: coll barg, arb/med. ASSN: Hawaii IRRA, Hawaii State Central Labor Council. POSITIONS: UniServ Dir, Indiana State Teachers Assn, 1972; Exec Dir, Fairfax Educ Assn, 1974; and (since 1976) Executive Director, Hawaii State Teachers Assn, 2828 Paa St, Honolulu, HI 96819. 808/833-2711

RADER, JENETTE S. Acad: Econ, Bus Admin. AB 1951, Duke U; MA 1957, U of Ill,U-C; MA 1972, Rosary Coll. ASSN: Chicago IRRA, Special Libraries Assn, Amer Library Assn. POSITIONS: Reference Librarian, 1972, Librarian, Ind Rels Center, 1975, and, since 1980, Business-Econ Librarian, Univ of Chicago, 1100 East 57th St, Chicago, IL 60637. 312/962-8718

RADER, WILMA R.K. Legal Practice. ADDRESS: 570 Santa Clara Ave, Berkeley, CA 94707. 415/527-6676

RADINE, LAWRENCE B. Acad: Sociology; Arbitration. BA 1967, MA 1968, San Jose State U; PhD 1973, Washington U-St. Louis. PUBL: Taming of the Troops, Social Control in the US Army; "Pangolins and Advocates, Vulnerability and Self Protection in a Mental Patient's Rights Agency;" "Assessing Compliance with Legal Reform in Psychiatric Hospitals." INT: ind sociology, arb/med, health & hosp care. ASSN: Amer Sociol Assn, Evaluation Network & Evaluation Res Soc, Law and Soc Assn. POSITIONS: Assoc Prof of Sociology and Dir, U of Mich-Dearborn, 1973; and (since 1977) NIMH Post-Doctoral Fellow in Social Policy and Evaluation, Univ of Mich. ADDRESS: 2400 Geddes Ave, Ann Arbor, MI 48104. 313/-593-5520

RADLE, JANICE ANN Student. 242 Curtner Ave, Apt F, Palo Alto, CA 94306.

RADOM, MATTHEW Acad: Bus Admin; Arbitration, Consulting. BS 1928, U.S. Naval Academy; MA 1937, NYU; PhD 1966, Columbia U. PUBL: The Social Scientist in American Industry. INT: arb/med, personnel, org beh. ASSN: SW Conn IRRA, AAA, Columbia Univ Seminar on Labor. POSITIONS: Professor, Rutgers, Univ, 1961, Consultant, Work in American Inst, 1975; Chairman, Voluntary Action Center of Greater Norwalk 1981; (Retired.) ADDRESS: 13 Buckthorn Rd, Norwalk CT 06851. 203/852-0850

RADTKE, ROBERT C. Bus:Pers/Ind Rels. POSITION: Ind Rels Manager, B. F. Goodrich Co, PO Box 9077, Long Beach, CA 90810. 213/549-8210

RAELIN, JOSEPH A. Acad: Org Beh/Pers, Ind Rels; Consulting. EdM 1971, Tufts U; CAGS 1973, Boston U; PhD 1977, SUNY-Buffalo. PUBL: Building a Career: The Effect of Initial Job Experiences and Related Work Attitudes on Labor Employment, Kalamazoo, MI: The W. E. Upjohn Inst for Empl Res, 1980; "A Comparative Analysis of Female-Male Early Youth Careers," Ind Rels, 21 (2): 231-247, Spring 1982; The Salaried Professional: How to Make the Most of Your Career, New York: Prager, 1984. INT: personnel, org beh, empl/trng programs. ASSN: Academy of Mgmt, Policy Studies Organization. POSITIONS: Teaching and Res Assoc, SUNY-Buffalo, 1974; Director, Inst for Public Service, 1978, and, since 1976, Assoc Prof of Mgmt, Boston College. ADDRESS: 294 Nehoiden St, Needham, MA 02192. 617/552-4090

RAFFAELE, GARY CHARLES Acad: Ind Rels, Org Beh/Pers, Bus Admin. BS 1960, SUNY--Maritime Coll; MBA 1965, U of Tex; DBA 1973, Harvard. INT: arb/med, coll barg, personnel. ASSN: Alamo Area IRRA, AAA, Academy of Mgmt. POSITION: Assoc Prof of Mgmt, Division of Mgmt and Marketing, Univ of Texas at San Antonio, San Antonio, TX 78285. 512/691-4310

RAGAN, JAMES F. Acad: Econ. PhD 1975, Washington U-St. Louis. PUBL: "Minimum Wages and the Youth Labor Market," Rev of Econ and Statis, May 1977; "Investigating the Decline in Manufacturing Quit Rates," J of Human Resources, Winter, 1984; "The Voluntary Leaver Provisions of Unemployment Insurance and Their Effect on Quit and Unemployment Rates," Southern Econ J, july, 1984. INT: labor market econ, govt labor policy. ASSN: AEA, Southern Econ Assn, Midwest Econ Assn. POSITIONS: Research Economist, Federal Reserve Bank of New York, 1977; Asst Prof, 1977, and, since 1980, Assoc Prof, Dept of Economics, Kansas State Univ, Manhatten, KS 66506. 913/532-6702

RAINS, HARRY H. Arbitration, Mediation. LLB 1932, St. Laurence U; MPA 1947, MLL 1954, NYU. PUBL: "Title v Seniority Based Layoffs," Hofstra U Law Rev, 1975; Dispute Settlement in the Public Sector, Buffalo Law Rev, 1969-70. INT: arb/med, labor law. ASSN: New York and Long Island IRRA, NAA, ABA, ASPA. POSITIONS: Senior Partner, Rains & Pogebrin P.C., 1947; and (currently) Arbitrator-Mediator, 31 Frost Creek Dr, Locust Valley, NY 11560; 2685 Coconut Dr, Sanibel FL 33957.

RAISIAN, JOHN Government. BA 1971, Ohio U; PhD 1978, UCLA. PUBL: "Contracts, Job Experience, and Cyclical Labor Market Adjustments," J of Labor Econ, Vol 1, #2, pp 152-170, April 1983; "Union Dues and Wage Premiums," J of Labor Research, Vol 4, #1, pp 1-18, Winter 1983; "Cyclic Patterns in Weeks and Wages," Econ Inquiry, Vol 17, #4, pp 475-495, Oct 1979. INT: labor market econ, method/-statis, income maintenance. ASSN: AEA, Econometric Soc, Western Econ Assn. POSITIONS: Asst Prof, Dept of Econ, U of Houston, 1976; Senior Economist, Office of Res and Evaluation, 1980, and, since 1981, Director of Pers, Office of Policy, USDL. ADDRESS: 1000 N Beverly Glen Blvd, Los Angeles, CA 90077.

RAJAN, G.S. Acad: Ind Rels. MA 1955, Annamalai U-India; MS 1960, PhD 1965, U of Wis-Madison. PUBL: A Study of Wisconsin State Apprenticeship Programs 1900-1965; A Study of Canada's Independent Unions. INT: coll barg, intl comparative law, labour & society. POSITION: Assoc Prof of Ind Rels, Concordia Univ. ADDRESS: PO Box 1776, Station 'H', Montreal PQ H3G 2N6 Canada. 514/879-2881

RALLIS, JOHN J. Government. 38 Belleview Heights, Ashland, MA 01721. 617/801-3027

RAMLOCHAN, MOOTOOR Bus:Pers/Ind Rels. POSITION: Pers/Ind Rels, Abel-Clay & Concrete Div, Longdenville, Trinidad, West Indies.

RAMOS, ELIAS T. Acad: Ind Rels. BA 1962, Silliman U; MA 1972, PhD 1976, U of Wis-Madison. PUBL: Philippine Labor Movement in Transition; "Industrial Relations Strategies of Trade Unions in Southeast Asia," Agenda for Ind Rels in Asian Development, Tokyo: Inst of Labour, 1981; "Viability of the Japanese Trade Union Model in Singapore and the Philippines," 6th World Congress, IIRA, Kyoto, Japan, Vol V, pp 132-43, March, 1983. INT: intl comparative labor, labor market econ, coll barg. ASSN: Hawaii IRRA, IIRA, Assn for Asian Studies Inc. POSITIONS: Res Asst, U of Wis-Madison, 1970; Asst Prof, 1976, and, since 1982, Assoc Prof of Ind Rels, Univ of Hawaii at Manoa, Dept of Mgmt and Ind Rels, 2404 Maile Way, Honolulu, HI 96825. 808/948-8536

RAMSUBEIK, GEORGE Acad: Ind Rels; Bus: Pers/Ind Rels. BA 1970, Lakehead U-Canada; MSS 1979 Utah State U. INT: arb/med, coll barg, govt labor policy. POSITIONS: (since 1971) Senior Labour Relations Officer, Ministry of Labour, Port-of-Spain. ADDRESS: 8 St. Vincent St, Tunapuna, Trinidad, West Indies. Phone: 62 38446

RANDALL, GERALDINE M. Arbitration. AB 1970, U 0f Calif-Berkeley; JD 1973, U of Calif-Davis. PUBL: "California FEPA Remedies for Sex Discrimination: Are They Working?" U.C. Davis Law Rev, 1972; "Understaffed FEPC Finds Popularity a Mixed Blessing," Calif J, May 1972. INT: arb/med, empl/trng programs, labor law. ASSN: San Francisco IRRA, Calif State Bar and Labor Law Section, SPIDR, ABA(Labor Law Section.) POSITIONS: Counsel (Labor), Kaiser Ind, 1974-76; Counsel (Labor), Bank of America, 1976-77; and (since 1977) Arbitrator/Mediator/Factfinder, Geraldine M. Randall, PO Box 1540, San Anselmo, CA 94960. 415/459-2148

RANDALL, ROGER L. Arbitration, Consulting. BA 1942, Reed Coll. INT: arb/med, labor educ, mgmt/educ. ASSN: San Francisco IRRA, SPIDR, SFLRP. POSITIONS: Mediator, Asst to Reg Dir, FMCS, 1965, and (since 1983) Retired. ADDRESS: 24208 Ox Bow Lane N, Sonora, CA 95370.

RANDLES, DAVID C. Arbitration, Factfinder, Mediation. BA 1957, SUNY-Albany; STM 1960, Yale-Berkeley Divinity School; Cert 1968, R.P.I. Mgmt Devel Program. INT: arb/med, labor educ, Bd Member. ASSN: Capital Dist IRRA, NAA, AAA, SPIDR. POSITIONS: Asst, St. Stephen's Episcopal Church, 1960-63; Rector, St. George's Episcopal Church, 1963-78; and (since 1978) Member NY State PERB and Arb. ADDRESS: PO Box 500, Clifton Park, NY 12065. 518/371-5353

RANDOL, GEORGE C. Union. BS 1954, U of San Francisco. INT: arb/med, coll barg, health & hosp care. POSITIONS: Wire Editor, Fresno Bee, 1968; Intl Rep, The Newspaper Guild, 1974; and (since 1976) Administrative Officer, Central Calif Newspaper Guild, Local 92, 1330 21st St #103, Sacramento, CA 95814. 916/446-4885

RANDOLPH, ROBERT D. Legal Practice. BA 1951, Westminster Coll; LLB 1957, Harvard U. INT: labor law, coll barg, arb/med. ASSN: Western Penna IRRA, ABA, Federal Bar Assn, Allegheny Cty Bar Assn. POSITION: (since 1974) Labor Lawyer, Labor and Empl Law Section Chairman, Buchanan Ingersoll, P.C., Suite 5700, 600 Grant St, Pittsburgh, PA 15219. 412/562-8933

RANHAND, SAMUEL Acad: Ind Rels; Arbitration, Bus:Pers/Ind Rels. BBA 1940, CCNY; CPA 1942, MBA 1954, PhD 1958, NYU. INT: arb/med, coll barg, labor history. ASSN: New York, Long island and New Brunswick IRRA, NAA, SPIDR, Center for Coll Barg in Higher Educ & Professions. POSITION: (since 1946) Professor, Dept of Mgmt, Baruch College-CUNY. ADDRESS: 33-39 80th St, Jackson Heights, NY 11372. 212/725-7124

RAO, M. GANGADHARO Acad: Ind Rels, Org Beh/Pers. BComm, 1961, MComm 1962, PhD 1970, Andhra U-India. PUBL: Industrial Relations in Indian Railways; "Wage and Salary Levels in Indian Railways," Indian J of Ind Rels, Vol 17, #3, 1982; "Negotiating Machinery in Indian Railways," Indian J of Labour Econ, vol XXVm # 1 & 2, Apr-July 1982. INT: personnel, org beh, union org/admin. ASSN: Visakhapatnaje Mgmt Assn, Natl Inst of Pers Mgmt (India), Indian Commerce Assn. POSITIONS: Lecturer, 1963, Reader, 1972, and, since 1975, Prof and Dean, Dept of Commerce and Mgmt Studies, Andhra Univ, Waltair 530 003 India. Phone: 64871-242

RAPPAPORT, CYRIL M. Bus:Pers/Ind Rels. BSS 1942, CCNY; MS 1943 Columbia. POSITIONS: Dir, Pers, St. Joseph's Hosp; Dir, Pers, Edgewater Hosp; and (currently) Director of Personnel, Jewish Vocational Service, 4939 W Coyle Ave, Skokie, IL 60076. 312/346-6700

RAPPAPORT, LOIS A. Arbitration. BA 1959, Brown U; MA 1969, Columbia U. INT: arb/med. ASSN: New York Philadelphia & New Brunswick IRRA, SPIDR, AAA. POSITIONS: Director, Domestic Empl Rels, Chase Manhatten Bank, 1969-77; Research Faculty, Wharton School, Univ of Penna, 1977-1981; and (since 1980) Labor Arbitrator. ADDRESS: 525 West End Dr, New York, NY 10024. 212/362-8423

RAPPAPORT, MICHAEL D. Arbitration; Acad: Law, Univ Admin. BS 1965, JD 1968, U of Wis. INT: arb/med, labor law. ASSN: Los Angeles IRRA, NAA, SPIDR, UCLA Inst for Ind Rels Assn. POSITIONS: Peace Corps Volunteer Attorney, Micronesia, 1968; and (since 1970), Asst Dean, Law School, UCLA. ADDRESS: 15957 Ventura Blvd, #338, Encino, CA 91436. 213/825-4105

RASKIN, ABRAHAM HENRY Journalism. BA 1931, CCNY. PUBL: David Dubinsky: A Life With Labor, (co-author). INT: govt labor policy, labor history, labor law. POSITIONS: Asst Ed, Editorial Page, 1961, Labor Columnist, The New York Times, 1976; and (since 1978) Assoc Director, National News Council. ADDRESS: 136 E 64th St, New York, NY 10021. 212/319-1008

RATNER, ROBERT A. Acad: Univ Admin, Engineering; Arbitration. BS 1947, MS 1951, Iowa State U INT: arb/med, ind psych, coll barg. ASSN: Wisconsin IRRA, Inst of Ind Eng, Amer Soc for Engr Educ, AAUP. POSITIONS: Dir, Engr Institutes, Univ Ext Div, 1954, and, since 1964, Assoc Dean/Prof, Ind Engr, College of Engineering, Univ of Wis. ADDRESS: 2141 Chamberlain Ave, Madison, WI 53705. 608/262-3484

RAUDABAUGH, JOHN N. Legal Practice. BS 1968, U of Penna; MS 1974, NYSSILR-Cornell; JD 1977, U of Va. INT: labor law, labor market econ, govt labor policy. ASSN: AAA, State Bar of Georgia, Atlanta State Bar Assn. POSITION: (since 1977) Attorney, Powell, Goldstein, Frazer & Murphy, 1100 C & S Natl Bank Bldg, 36 Broad St, Atlanta, GA 30335. 404/572-6600

RAY, PHILLIP EVERETTE Labor-Mgmt Committee. BS 1970, U of N.C; MS 1971, U of Ore. PUBL: "Specific Experiences of Labor-Management Committees," IRRA Spring Proceedings, 1981; "Industrial Relations in a Job Loss Environment: The Labor Relations Impact of Store Closings in the Retail Food Industry," IRRA Spring Proceedings, 1980; "A Joint Labor Management Voluntary Approach to Workplace Exposure Research," Hazardous Materials Mgmt J, Spring 1980. INT: coll barg, govt labor policy, arb/med. ASSN: Wash DC IRRA. POSITION: (since 1975) Executive Dir, Joint Labor-Mgmt Committee of the Retail Food Industry, 2120 L St NW, Suite 245, Washington DC 20037. 202/331-0950

RAY, STEVEN ERIC Student. RD 1, Box 314, Indiana, PA 15701. 412/465-5864

RAY, WENDELL F. Bus:Mgmt/Admin. BS 1971, BA 1972, Mich State U. INT: personnel, coll barg, arb/med. ASSN: West Mich IRRA, ASPA, ASTD. POSITIONS: Dir, Labor Rels, 1975, Dir, Pers/Labor Rels, 1979, and, since 1969, Senior Vice Pres, Meijer Inc, 2727 Walker Ave NW, Grand Rapids, MI 49504. 616/453-6711

RAYMAN, DALE M. Student. 3720 North 250 West, West Lafayette, IN 47906. 317/-463-2157

RAZA, M. ALI Acad: Ind Rels, Bus Admin, Org Beh/Pers. BA 1953, LLB 1955, U of Panjam-Pakistan; MBA 1959, U of Wash; PhD 1962, U of Ore. INT: coll barg, labor law, personnel. ASSN: Northern Calif IRRA. POSITIONS: Sr Advisor, ILO-Sri Lanka, 1972-74, and, since 1969, Professor, School of Bus and Public Admin, Calif State Univ, 6000 J St, Sacramento, CA 95819. 916/454-6463

READDEAN, SHIRLEY Government. POSITION: Regional Planning Center, Albany BOCES, 1015 Watervliet/Shaker Rd, Albany, NY 12205. 518/456-9281

READER, MARK M. Union. BS 1973 Cornell U. INT: union org/admin, coll barg, arb/med. ASSN: Philadelphia IRRA, Professional Empl Dept, AFL-CIO; Natl Operations Committee, AFL-CIO, A Phillip Randolph Inst. POSITIONS: Natl Organizer, 1199RWDSU, 1973, Int Rep, OPEIU, AFL-CIO, 1976, and, since 1980, Dir of Organization, Office and Professional Empl Union, 265 W 14th St, New York, NY 10011. 212/675-3210

REAGAN, PAUL MARION Bus:Pers/Ind Rels. ADDRESS: 1997 Lake Lansing Rd, #6, Haslett, MI 48840. 517/339-3781

REARDON, JACK E. Student. ADDRESS: Dept of Econ, Univ of Notre Dame, Notre Dame, IN 46556.

REBER. ROBERT ALLEN Acad: Org Beh/-Pers; Consulting. BA 1977, West Va U; MA 1979, PhD 1982, La. State U. PUBL: "The Effects of Training, Goal Setting, and Knowledge of Results on Safe Behavior: A Component Analysis," (co-author), Acad of Mgmt; "An Applied Behavioral Analysis Approach to Occupational/Industrial Safety," (co-author),Ind Rels (in press); "Validation of a Behavioral Measure of Occupational Safety," J of Org Beh Mgmt, (in press.) INT: personnel, org beh, ind psych. ASSN: Acad of Mgmt, Amer Psych Assn, Southeastern Psych Assn. POSITIONS: Grad Asst, La State Univ, 1977; Consultant, Cameco Inc, Thibodeaux, LA, 1980-82; and (since 1982) Asst Prof of Mgmt, Dept of Mgmt and Marketing, Western Kentucky Univ, Bowling Green, KY 42101. 502/745-5408

REDWOOD, ANTHONY LEO Acad: Ind Rels, Econ, Univ Admin. BEcon 1964, BCom 1967, U of Queensland; MA 1971, PhD 1973, U of Ill,U-C. PUBL: "An Economic-Demographic Approach to Forecasting National and Subnational Birth Rates," Socio-Econ Planning Sciences; "Population and Labor Force Issues for Australia: The Barrie Report Projections in Retrospect," Australian and New Zealand J of Sociology; "Wage Indexation and Wage Differentials," IRRA Proceedings. INT: labor market econ, empl/trng programs, arb/med. ASSN: AEA, Population Assn of Amer, Western Econ Assn. POSITIONS: Chief of Div, Res and Planning, Papua-New Guinea Dept of Labor, 1960-1969; Asst Secretary (Manpower & Econ Policy), Australian Dept of Labor & Immigration, 1974-1976; and (since 1972) Prof of Bus and Dir, Inst for Econ and Bus Res, University of Kansas, Lawrence, KS 66045. 913/864-3123.

REED, JAMES E. Arbitration. BGS 1976, U of Nebr-Omaha; MLIR 1977, Mich State U. INT: arb/med, govt labor policy, labor law. POSITION: (since 1978) Labor Arbitrator (self employed), 965 Boise Ave, Idaho Falls, ID 83402. 208/526-0459

REED, JEFFREY A. Acad: Econ; Consulting. BA 1971, Western Wash State Coll; PhD 1976, La. State U. PUBL: Wage Standards, Wages & Employment in the North Dakota Farm Labor Market, (monograph) U.N.D. 1979; "Right-to-Work Laws: The Issues and Evidence," Louisiana Bus Rev, Dec 1978; Labor Force Participation and Unemployment in Louisiana, (monograph) Baton Rouge: Public Affairs Res Council, 1976. INT: labor market econ, govt labor policy, method/statis. ASSN: AEA, Western Econ Assn, Southern Econ Assn. POSITIONS: Instructor of Econ, La. State Univ, 1975; Asst Prof of Econ, Univ of Richmond, 1976; and (since 1978) Assoc Prof of Econ, Gamble Hall, Univ of North Dakota, Grand Forks, ND 58201. 701/777-3350

REED, TED Government. POSITION: Asst Chief Administrative Officer, Los Angeles County, 500 W Temple, Room 713, Los Angeles, CA 90012. 213/974-1104

REED, THEODORE E. Union. BA 1955, Northeastern U. PUBL: Articles for the Operating Engineers, 1971 to present; Articles for Stanford Res Inst, 1965-70; Articles for ORD and Martin Marietta, 1959-64. INT: union org/-admin, empl/trng programs, intl comparative labor. ASSN: Wash DC IRRA, AEA, Amer Inst of Plant Engineers, Operations Res Soc of Amer. POSITIONS: Sr Cost Analyst, Stanford Res Inst, 1965; Dir, Dept of Statis, Western Conference of Operating Engineers-Calif, 1971, and, since 1979, Director, Dept of Res, Intl Union of Operating Engineers, 1125 17th St NW, Washington DC 20036. 202/429-9100

REED, THOMAS FRANCIS Student. BA 1979, New School for Social Res; MPH 1984, Columbia U. INT: coll barg, health & hosp care. ASSN: AEA, Amer Public Health Assn. POSITION: (since 1984) Doctoral Student, Division of Corp Rels and Public Affairs, Columbia Univ. ADDRESS: 531 W 162nd St, New York, NY 10032. 212/694-3924

REES, ALBERT E. Foundation. BA 1943, Oberlin Coll; MA 1948, PhD 1950, U of Chicago. PUBL: The Economics of Trade Unions; The Economics of Work and Pay; Striking a Balance: Making National Economic Policy. INT: labor market econ, coll barg, income maintenance. ASSN: AEA, Amer Assn for Advancement of Science. POSITIONS: Prof of Econ, Univ of Chicago, 1948; Prof of Econ, Princeton Univ, 1966; and (since 1979) President, Alfred P. Sloan Foundation, 630 Fifth Ave, New York, NY 10111. 212/582-0450

REESMAN, CILLA J. Evaluation Research. MS 1970, PhD 1975, U of Wis-Madison. PUBL: "Risk Factors and High School Completion Rates Among Low Income Youth", (w R. Cook), in Assessments of the Youth Incentive Entitlement Pilot Projects, New York City, Manpower Demonstration Res Corp, Fall, 1983; "Coordination and Cooperation Between CETA and the Senior Community Service Employment Program," (w K. Rupp and R. Montovani), in Natl Empl Policy and Older Americans, ed. S. Sandell, Wash DC Natl Commission for Empl Policy, 1983; "Job Search and Relocation Assistance Pilot Project: Final Report," (w. J. K. Herzog), Report to USDL, 1981. INT: empl/-trng programs, income maintenance, labor market econ. ASSN: Wash DC IRRA. POSITIONS: Evaluation Research Consultant, (self-employed), 1972; and (currently) Senior Research Associate, Westat Inc, Rockville. ADDRESS: 10309 Green Holly Terrace, Silver Spring, MD 20902. 301/681-5116

REEVES, T. ZANE Acad: Univ Admin. POSITION: Director, Public Admin, Univ of New Mexico, 3059 Mesa Vista, Albuquerque, NM 87131. 505/277-3312

REFIOR, EVERETT LEE Acad: Econ, Ind Rels. BA 1942, Iowa Wesleyan Coll; MA 1955, U of Chicago; PhD 1962, U of Iowa. PUBL: Estimating the Labor Supply in a Rural Community, (monograph); "Income-Leisure Preferences of College Teachers." INT: labor market econ, coll barg, ind sociol. ASSN: Wisconsin IRRA, AEA, Midwest Econ Assn. POSITIONS: Assoc Prof-Econ, Simpson Coll, 1952; Asst Prof, 1955, Assoc Prof, 1962, Prof, 1964, and, since 1983, Emeritus Prof of Econ, Univ of Wis-Whitewater. ADDRESS: 205 N Fremont St, Whitewater, WI 53190. 414/473-5209

REHMUS, CHARLES MARTIN Acad: Univ Admin, Ind Rels; Arbitration. AB 1947, Kenyon Coll; PhD 1955, Stanford U. PUBL: Labor and American Politics, Univ of Mich Press, 1978, 2nd ed; Final Offer Arbitration, D. C. Heath, 1975; The Railway Labor Act at Fifty, U.S. Government Printing Office, 1976. INT: govt labor policy, arb/med, labor law. ASSN: Northern NY IRRA, NAA, IIRA, Amer Pol Sci Assn. POSITIONS: Chairman, Mich Empl Rels Commission, 1976; Prof of Pol Sci, Univ of Mich, 1962; and (since 1980) Dean, NYSSILR, Cornell Univ, Ithaca, NY 14853. 607/256-2185

REICHENBACH, ROBERT R. Consulting. BS 1952, U of Nebr; MS 1954, Cornell U. INT: coll barg, labor law, org beh. POSITION: (since 1963) Vice Pres, Organization Resources Counselors, Inc, New York. ADDRESS: 37 Keats Rd, Millington, NJ 07946. 212/719/3400

REICHENBACHER, MARK C. Government, Labor-Mgmt Rels. AB 1975, Ind U; MS 1977, U of Mass-Amherst. INT: coll barg, mgmt/third party procedures, mgmt/educ. ASSN: Wash DC IRRA, SFLRP. POSITIONS: Labor-Mgmt Rels Specialist, Fed Labor Rels Authority, 1977, Labor Mgmt Rels Specialist, Agricultural Marketing Service, 1979, and, since 1980, Labor Mgmt Rels Specialist, Food Safety and Inspection Service, U.S. Dept of Agriculture. ADDRESS: 11975 Barrel Cooper Ct, Reston, VA 22091. 202/447-4819

REID, FRANK Acad: Econ, Ind Rels. BA 1970, U of BC, MSc 1971, London School of Econ; PhD 1975, Queen's U. PUBL: "UI-Assisted Worksharing as an Alternative to Layoffs: The Canadian Experience," Ind Labor Rels Rev, vol 35, Apr 1982, pp 318-29; "Control and Decontrol of Wages in the U.S.: An Empirical Analysis," Amer Econ Rev, Mar 1981, pp 108-20; Sharing the Work: An Analysis of the Issues in Worksharing, Jobsharing and Part-Time Employment, Univ of Toronto Press, 1981. INT: labor market econ, govt labor policy, coll barg. ASSN: Canadian Ind Rels Assn, Canadian Econ assn, IIRA. POSITION: (since 1974) Assoc Prof, Centre for Ind Rels, Univ of Toronto, 123 St. George St, Toronto M5S 1A1 Canada. 416/978-5366

REID, HENRY O. III Bus:Mgmt/Admin. Monsanto Chemicals, PO Box 1311, Texas City, TX 77590.

REIFF, SIDNEY Bus:Ind Rels. BS/ILR 1950, Cornell U. INT: coll barg, arb/med. POSITIONS: Pres, Halmar Dress Corp, 1956; Assoc Exec Dir, Natl Dress Mfgr Assn, 1971; and (since 1973) Executive Dir, Sportswear Apparel Assn Inc, 519 8th Ave, New York, NY 10018. 212/244-6625

REIFLER, ELIZABETH ANN Arbitration, Legal Practice. BA 1978, Lone Mt. Coll, U of San Fran; JD 1983, U of Calif. INT: arb/med, labor law. ASSN: San Francisco IRRA, State Bar Assn, SPIDR, ABA. POSITIONS: Asst to Arbitrator G.M. Randall, 1982; Extern to Justice J. R. Gredin, Calif Supreme Court, 1983; and (since 1983) Arbitrator/Mediator; Attorney (self employed), 331 Olema Rd, Fairfax, CA 94930. 415/459-3330.

REILLY, RICHARD MENTON Arbitration. BA 1967, Fordham U; MA 1972, St. John's U-NYC. PUBL: "Neutrals Response to a Society in Dispute: Will Collective Bargaining in the 1980's Turn into Starwars?" SPIDR Proceedings, 1980; "Labor Arbitrator-Is It Really the Job for You?" NY State Bar Assn, Mar 1980. INT: arb/med, empl/trng programs, labor history. ASSN: Boston IRRA, SPIDR, SFLRP, New England Soc of Assn Exec. POSITIONS: Tribunal Admin, 1970-72, Program Dir-Educ Dept, 1972-75, and, since 1975, Regional Dir, Amer Arbitration Assn, 60 Staniford St, Boston, MA 02114. 617/367-6800

REINERTH, MICHAEL W. Acad: Ind Rels. MLIR 1982, Mich State U. INT: org beh, coll barg, personnel. POSITIONS: Benefits Administrator, Chrysler Corp, 1977; Benefits Admin, 1981, and, since 1983, Attendance Coordinator, Oldsmobile, Div of General Motors Corp. ADDRESS: 2766 Hawthorne Lane, Okemos, MI 48864. 517/377-6760

REINHOLD, ROBERT Bus: Pers/Ind Rels. BA 1976, Lebanon Valley Coll. INT: personnel, arb/med, coll barg. ASSN: Central Penna IRRA. POSITIONS: Div Pers Mgr, 1980, and, since 1983, Pers Mgr, Empl/Labor Rels, United Telephone System-Eastern Group, PO Box 1170, Carlisle, PA 17013. 717/245-6379

REISMAN, MARSHALL M. Bus:Mgmt/Admin. POSITION: President, Wine Merchants Ltd., PO Box 2309, Syracuse, NY 13220.

REITMAN, SIDNEY Legal Practice. JD 1937, Rutgers U. INT: arb/med, labor law. ASSN: New Jersey IRRA, ABA, Essex Cty Bar Assn, Federal Bar Assn. POSITION: (since 1982) Partner, Reitman, Parsonnet, Maisel and Duggan, 744 Broad St, Room 1807, Newark, NJ 07102. 201/642-0885

RELLINI, GIAMPIERO Professional Assn. POSITION: Principal Admin OECD, 2 Rue Andre Pascal, 75775 Paris Cedex 16, France.

REMBOLD, CHRIS J. Union. BA 1965, U of Northern Iowa; MA 1975, Western Ill U. INT: union org/admin. ASSN: SPIDR. POSITIONS: UniServ Dir, Iowa State Educ Assn, 1972, and, since 1973, UniServ Dir, Mississippi Bend UniServ, ISEA/NEA, Box 474, Route 3, Mt. Joy, Davenport, IA 52804. 319/391-9122

REMINGTON, JOHN Acad: Ind Rels; Arbitration. AB 1964, Gustavus Adolphus Coll; MA 1965, U of Wyo; PhD 1975, U of Mich. PUBL: Collective Bargaining Dispute Resolution; "The Retention of Women and Minorities in Apprenticeship Programs;" "The Determination of Issues by the Arbitrator." INT: arb/med, labor educ, empl/trng programs. ASSN: UCLEA, IPMA, AAA. POSITIONS: Res Assoc, B & P Assoc, Ann Arbor, 1971; Assoc Prof of Ind Systems, 1972, and, since 1973, Dir, Center for Labor Res Studies, Florida Intl Univ, Tamiami Campus, Miami, FL 33199. 305/552-2371

RENNELS, MARLINE Union. POSITION: UniServ Director, Washington Educ Assn, PO Box 460, Poulsbo, WA 98370.

RENNER, DONNA L. WILSON 1931 Plumb Creek Circle, Knoxville, TN 37922

RENNISON, RALPH Union. POSITION: Bookbinders Union 60, Suite 701, 818 Grand, Kansas City, MO 64106. 816/842-5234

RENS, LAVERNE GENE Legal Practice. ADDRESS: 401 Old Town ct, Alexandria, VA 22314.

RENTON, GEORGE G. Bus:Pers/Ind Rels. POSITION: Asst Dir, Employee Rels, NYU Medical Center, 445 E 14th St, New York, NY 10009.

REPAR, GEORGE Research. POSITION: Director, Plan & Development H-2, Niagara Coll, Woodlawn Rd, PO Box 1005, Welland, Ont L3B 5S2 Canada.

RETTIG, JACK L. Acad: Bus Admin. PhD 1962, UCLA. PUBL: Careers: Exploration and Decision, Prentice-Hall, 1974; "On the Meaning of Work," Productivity and Motivation, June 1982. INT: personnel, coll barg, org beh. ASSN: ASPA. POSITION: (since 1961) Prof of Bus Admin, Dept of Mgmt, School of Bus, Oregon State Univ, Corvallis, OR 97331. 503/754-3688

REUTLINGER, BLOSSOM M. Government. POSITION: Dept of Labor, Manpower Admin, 601 D St, Room 9412, Washington DC 20213.

REVELL, JOHN M. Union. BS 1971, MEd 1973, Calif State U of Penna; MA 1982, Ind State U of Penna. INT: union org/admin, personnel, coll barg. ASSN: Western Penna IRRA, Va Professional Staff Assn/NSO. POSITIONS: Ind Rels Rep, Season-All Industries, 1982; Special Projects Organizer, Penna School Service Pers Assn, 1983; and (since 1983) UniServ Director, Central Va UniServ. ADDRESS: 409-F Kerry Lane, Lynchburg, VA 24502. 804/-846-0748

REVELL, JOSEPH J. Government, Bus:-Labor Rels. POSITION: PEI Labour Rels Board, PO Box 2000, Charlottetown, PEI C1A 7N8 Canada. 902/892-3416

REVITTE, JOHN LAWRENCE Acad: Labor Educ, Ind Rels. BGS 1972, U of Mich; MS 1976, U of Mass-Amherst. INT: labor history, labor educ. ASSN: Workers Educ Local 189, Univ and Coll Labor Educ Assn. POSITION: (since 1977) Assoc Prof, School of Labor & Ind Rels, Mich State Univ. ADDRESS: 528 Everett Dr, Lansing, MI 48915. 517/355-5070

REY, MICHAEL W. Acad: Labor Studies. BA 1982, U of Puerto Rico; MA 1984, Rutgers U. INT: coll barg, labor law, arb/med. POSITIONS: Grad Student, Rutgers Univ, 1983-84; and (since 1984) Professor, Univ of Puerto Rico-Rio Piedras. ADDRESS: Box 311, Guarbo, Puerto Rico 00658.

REY, SALVADOR Acad: Law. POSITION: Facultad de Ciencias, Economicas Y Empresariale Avenida Ramon Y Cajal S/N, Sevilla, Spain.

REYNAERTS, WIM H.J. Acad: Ind Rels. Dr. Econ, 1975, Tilburg U. PUBL: Industrial Relations, Theory and Practice, I and II, 1982 & 1983; Social Economics, 1979; The Investment Wage. INT: coll barg, intl comparative labor, union org/admin. ASSN: IIRA, Ned Verensfin voor Arbeidsverhoudingen. POSITIONS: Econ Adviser, Dutch Catholic Labor Movement, 1958; and (since 1975) Prof of Ind Rels, Tilburg Univ, Burg Damsstraat 44, Tilburg, S037NR Netherlands.

REYNOLDS, BENNY L. Union. INT: union org/admin, coll barg, arb/med. ASSN: Houston IRRA, GE Electrical EM-5 Systems Council. POSITION: (since 1974) Asst Business Manager, Intl Brotherhood of Electrical Workers, Local 716, 1475 North Loop West, Houston, TX 77008. 713/869-8900

REYNOLDS, CALVIN Consulting. Organization Resources Counsellors Inc, 1211 Ave of Americas, New York, NY 10036

REYNOLDS, J.C. Union. POSITION: President, Local 732, 250 Tenth St NE, Suite 208, Atlanta, GA 30309. 404/892-1590

REYNOLDS, JOY K. Government. BA 1966, Swarthmore Coll. INT: govt labor policy, labor law, coll barg. ASSN: Wash DC IRRA. POSI-

TIONS: Labor Law Admin Adviser, 1966, and, since 1971, Ind Rels Specialist, Labor Mgmt Services Admin, USDL. ADDRESS: 3420 39th St NW, #706D, Washington DC 20016. 202/523-6487

REYNOLDS, LLOYD GEORGE Acad: Econ. BA 1931, Alberta U; MA 1933, McGill U; PhD 1936, Harvard. PUBL: The Structure of Labor Markets, Harper 1952; The Evolution of Wage Structure, Yale, 1956; Labor Economics and Labor Relations, Prentice Hall, Eighth Ed, 1982. INT: labor market econ, coll barg, arb/-med. ASSN: AEA, Royal Econ Soc. POSITION: (since 1945) Sterling Prof of Econ Emeritus, Yale Univ, Box 1972. Yale Station, New Haven, CT 06520. 203/436-8549

REYNOLDS, ROY R. Acad: Ind Rels, Org Beh/Pers, Bus Admin. BA 1946, U of Alberta; MA 1947, Yale; PhD 1951, MIT. POSITIONS: Dir, Ind Rels Planning, Kaiser Ind Corp, 1964-67; Pers Dir, Kaiser Foundation Medical Care Program, 1967-72; and (since 1973) Prof of Mgmt, School of Bus Admin, Central Mich Univ, Mt. Pleasant, MI 48859. 517/774-3534

REZLER, JULIUS Arbitration, Acad: Ind Rels. PhD 1938, U of Szeged (Hungary); PhD 1941, U of Pecs (Hungary). PUBL: Arbitration in Health Care, (co-author), Aspen, 1981; "Strategies of Arbitrator Selection," (co-author), Labor Arbitration Reports, BNA, vol 70, pp 1307-20, 1978; Automation and Industrial Labor, Random House, 1969. INT: arb/med, intl comparative labor, labor market econ. ASSN: NAA, AAA. POSITIONS: Dir, Inst of Ind Rels, 1965-69, Prof of Ind Rels, Loyola Univ of Chicago, 1957-76; and (since 1972) Arbitrator, 22W765 Tamarack Dr, Glen Ellyn, IL 60137. 312/858-1284

RHODES, GARY BOYD Acad: Labor Education. POSITION: Acting Director, Labor-Mgmt Center, College of Urban/Public Affairs, Univ of Louisville, Louisville, KY 40292. 502/588-7177

RICE, WILLIAM V., JR. Acad: Ind Rels, Econ. BS 1949, USMA-West Point; MBA 1958, Air Force Inst of Tech-Dayton; PhD 1974, La State U. PUBL: Introduction to Labor Relations for Air Force Supervisors in the Decades of the 80's; "Joint Union-Management Training-Improving the Relationship; Supersimulation-An Advanced Collective Bargaining Exercise. INT: coll barg, labor educ, arb/med. ASSN: Houston IRRA, AEA, Southern Econ Assn, Case Res Assn. POSITIONS: Dir, Labor Mgmt Rels Div, Air Univ, Maxwell AFB, 1969; Assoc Prof, 1978, and, since 1982, Professor, Univ of Houston/Clear Lake, 2700 Bay Area Blvd, Houston, TX 77058. 713/488-9420

RICE, ZEL S. Arbitration, Legal Practice. BS 1948, JD 1950, U of Wis. INT: arb/med, coll barg. ASSN: Wisconsin IRRA, NAA, AAA, SPIDR. POSITIONS: Secretary, Dept of Transportation, 1975, Secretary, Dept of Labor, Industry and Human Rels, State of Wis, 1977; and (since 1950) Attorney, Rice & Abbott, 112 West Oak St, Sparta, WI 54656. 608/269-2174

RICH, JOSEPH M. Arbitration. Acad: Ind Rels, Org Beh/Pers. BA 1941, Dartmouth Coll; MA 1943, U of Ill; EdD 1959, Temple U. PUBL: "Why Not Fire the Personnel Manager?" Human Resource Mgmt, Summer 1975; "Program Evaluation-Demonstration Training Program for Upgrading Present Employees-Educating the Disadvantaged for Upgrading," Wharton School, 1974; "Selection and Development is the Line Executive's Primary Job," Empl Rels Bull, June 1967. INT: arb/med, personnel, org beh. ASSN: Philadelphia, Trenton, and New Brunswick IRRA, Acad of Mgmt, AAA, South Jersey Pers Assn. POSITIONS: Pers Dir, American Pulley Co, 1956; Corp Pers Dir, St. Regis Paper Co, 1959; and (since 1969) Prof of Mgmt and Ind Rels, Rutgers Univ. ADDRESS: 225 Westover Dr, Cherry Hill, NJ 08034. 609/429-3171

RICHARDS, EMORY H. Acad: Bus Admin. AB 1941, Denison U; MBA 1943, Harvard U; PhD 1971, Ohio State U. INT: personnel, org beh, mgmt/educ. ASSN: Acad of Mgmt, Amer Mgmt Assn. POSITIONS: Prof, East Tenn State U, 1964; Prof, Armstrong State Coll, 1972; and (since 1979) Professor, School of Bus and Econ, Mercer Univ, Macon, GA 31207. 912/744-2840

RICHARDSON, DOUGLAS A. Union. BA 1970, U of Wis-Madison, MA Studies, 1976-77, U of Ill. INT: union org/admin, labor market econ, health & hosp care. ASSN: AFL-CIO Field Rep Federation. POSITIONS: Manpower Planning Specialist, Governor's Office of Manpower and Human Develop, State of Ill, 1977; Field Rep, Dept of Org and Field Services, Natl AFL-CIO, 1978 to present, and, since 1982, Div Coordinator, Public Employees and Health Care Division, Houston Organizing Project, AFL-CIO, 1445 N. Loop West, Suite 160, Houston, TX 77092. 713/869-0265

RICHARDSON, GERALD Union. BA 1971, Western Mich U; MA 1974, U of Ill. INT: labor law, arb/med, union org/admin. POSITIONS: Field Rep, Amer Nurses Assn, 1974; and (since 1978) Natl Representative, American Federation of Teachers, AFL-CIO, 11 Dupont Circle NW, Washington DC 20036. 202/797-4400

RICHARDSON, REED C. Acad: Ind Rels; Arbitration. BS 1945, Utah State U; MA 1947, U of Calif-Berkeley; PhD 1955, Cornell. PUBL: Brotherhood of Locomotive Engineers-100 Years Work Rules and Collective Bargaining; Collective Bargaining by Objectives; "Arbitration Decisions", BNA and CCH. INT: coll barg, arb/med, mgmt of conflict. ASSN: NAA, SPIDR, AAA. POSITION: (since 1947) Professor of Ind Rels, Kendall Garff Bldg 209, Univ of Utah, Salt Lake City, UT 84112. 801/581-7778

RICHMAN, HYMAN Government, Consulting; Acad: Govt Labor Rels. AB 1939, ML 1954, U of Pittsburgh. INT: arb/med, coll barg, labor standards. ASSN: Western Penna IRRA, Intl Pers Mgmt Assn, AAA (labor panel). POSITIONS: Adjunct Prof, U of Pittsburgh & Penna State U, 1954-present; Area Dir, USDL Wage and Hour Div, 1941-74; and (since 1974) Labor Mediator, Bureau of Mediation, Commonwealth of Penna. ADDRESS: 3 Bayard Rd, Apt 61, Pittsburgh, PA 15213. 412/682-7912

RICHTER, DAVID JAMES Arbitration. POSITION: Management Services, AAIM Management Assoc, 1600 S Hanley Rd, St. Louis, MO 63144.

RICKER, EDWIN D. Bus:Mgmt/Admin. POSITION: President, PLRS, 210 McFarland, Grand Blanc, MI. 48439

RICO, LEONARD Acad: Ind Rels; Consulting, Arbitration. POSITION: Assoc Prof Mgmt Dept, W-187 Dietrich Hall, Wharton School, Univ of Penn, Philadelphia, PA 19174. 215/898-7727

RIDENOUR, KAREN SUE Bus:Pers/Ind Rels. POSITION: Personnel, Lansing General Hosp, 2800 Devonshire, Lansing, MI 48909. 517/387-8335

RIDEOUT, MARC P. Bus:Pers/Ind Rels. BS 1977, MLIR 1980, Mich State U. INT: org beh, personnel, ind sociol. ASSN: ASPA. POSITIONS: Empl Rels Rep, 1979, Mgr, Human Resources, Advanced Energy Dept, 1980, and, since 1982, Manager, Organization and Staffing, General Electric Aircraft Engine Group, Mail Drop 14511, 1000 Western Ave, Lynn, MA 01910. 617/594-3517

RIDGEL, GUS TOLIVER Acad: Econ, Ind Rels. BS 1950, Lincoln U (MO); MA 1951, PhD 1957, U of Wis. INT: labor history, labor market econ, labor law. ASSN: AEA, Natl Econ Assn, Kentucky Econ Assn. POSITIONS: Chairman, Dept of Bus & Econ, 1960, and, since 1978, Dean, School of Bus, Kentucky State Univ, Frankfort, KY 40601. 502/227-6714

RIKARD, DOROTHY J. Bus:Pers/Ind Rels. INT: empl/trng programs, mgmt/educ, coll barg. ASSN: ASPA, Tombigbee Ind Club. POSITIONS: Pers Dir, Winter Garden, Inc, Div United Foods, 1970; Dir Ind Rels, Salante and Salante, Div Salante Corp, 1978; and (since 1982) Employee Rels Mgr, Belwood Div U. S. Industries, PO Drawer A, Ackerman, MS 39735. 601/285-6281

RIKER, WILLIAM E. Arbitration; Acad: Bus Admin, Ind Rels. BA 1958, Niagara U; MBA 1970, Golden Gate U. INT: arb/med, coll barg, labor law. ASSN: San Francisco IRRA, AAA, Intl Found of Empl Benefit Plans, ASPA. POSITIONS: Ind Rels Advisor, Golden Gate Highway & Trans Dist, 1970; Asst Admin, Carpenters Trust Funds, Calif, 1979; and (since 1982) Arbitrator (self-employed), 15 Santa Paula Ave, San Francisco, CA 94127. 415/664-1538

RIMER, J. THOMAS Arbitration. BS 1933, U of Pittsburgh. POSITIONS: VP, Ind Rels, Cyclops Corp, 1943-60; Dir, Labor Rels, Glass Container Mfrs Inst, 1961-70; and (since 1970) Arbitrator (self-employed), Suite 1010, 1447 Peachtree St, Atlanta, GA 30309. 404/892-6548

RITCHIE, J. BONNER Acad: Org Beh/Pers. PhD 1968, U of Calif-Berkeley. PUBL: Organization and People, (w P. Thompson). INT: org beh. POSITIONS: Asst Prof of Ind Rels, Univ of Mich, 1967; and (since 1973) Prof of Org/Beh, Brigham Young Univ, Provo, UT 84602. 801/378-2902

RITT, DONALD D. Bus:Pers/Ind Rels. BA 1973, Dartmouth Coll; MBA 1975, U of Minn. INT: personnel, coll barg, arb/med. ASSN: ASPA. POSITIONS: Ind Rels Mgr, 1978, Labor Rels Mgr, 1981, and, since 1983, Pers Administration Manager, Miller Brewing Company, 405 Cordele Rd, Albany, GA 31708. 912/888-3000

RITTENOURE, R. LYNN Acad: Econ. PhD 1970, U of Tex. PUBL: The Consequences of Cuts: The Effects of the Reagan Domestic Program on State and Local Government, (contributor), Richard Nathan et.al; Reductions in U.S. Domestic Spending: How They Affect State and Local Governments, John Ellwood et.al; Black Employment in the South: The Case of the Federal Government. INT: govt labor policy, income maintenance, labor market econ. ASSN: Assn for Inst Thought, Southwestern Soc Sci Assn, Western Soc Sci Assn. POSITIONS: Res Assoc, Woodrow Wilson School-Princeton U, 1981 to present, Assoc Prof, 1977, and, since 1983, Professor, Dept of Econ, Univ of Tulsa, 600 S College, Tulsa, OK 74104. 918/592-6000

RIZZO, JAMES M. Bus:Pers/Ind Rels. POSITION: Personnel, Foxmoor, PO Box 855, Brockton, MA 02403.

ROACH, BONNIE L. Student. BA 1979, Vassar; MLHR 1980, Ohio State U. INT: personnel, org beh, coll barg. ASSN: Acad of Mgmt. POSITIONS: Grad Res Asst, 1979, Grad Intern, 1980, and, since 1980, Grad Res Asst-Data Center, Ohio State Univ. ADDRESS: 1991 N 4th St, Apt E, Columbus, OH 43201. 614/422-1741

ROADLEY, C. ROBERT Arbitration. POSITION: Arbitrator (self-employed), 314 Littletown Quarter, Williamsburg, VA 23185. 804/229-4087

ROBBINS, MICHAEL ARLEN Legal Practice. AB 1975, San Diego State U; JD 1978, UCLA. PUBL: The Developing Labor Law, (contributing editor) Morris, BNA 1983. INT: labor law, coll barg, arb/med. ASSN: ABA (Labor Law section), LA Cty and Beverly Hills Bar Assns, (Labor Law Sections). POSITIONS: Attorney, CBS Inc, 1979; Dir of Labor Rels and Labor Counsel, Golden West Broadcasters/TV Inc, 1981; and (since 1983) Attorney, Pepper, Hamilton & Scheetz, City Natl Bank Bldg, 20th Floor, 606 S. Olive St, Los Angeles, CA 90014. 213/617-8151

ROBERTS, B. C. Acad: Ind Rels. MA 1950, Oxford U. POSITION: London School Econ-Pol Sci, Univ of London Ind Rels, Houghton St, London England WC2A 2AE.

ROBERTS, HIGDON C., JR. Acad: Ind Rels, Econ, Univ Admin. BA 1960, MEd 1962, U of Cincinnati; MA 1965, Miami U; PhD 1971, Ohio State U. PUBL: Labor Law and the Local Union; Workers Guide to Unemployment and Workmens Compensation; Local Central Labor Bodies. INT: labor educ, coll barg, union org/-admin. ASSN: Univ and Coll Labor Educ Assn. POSITIONS: Instructor, Ohio State U, 1965; Asst-Assoc Prof, Indiana U, 1967; and (since 1972) Dir/Professor, Center for Labor Educ and Res, Univ of Alabama, U Station, Birmingham, AL 35294. 205/934-2101

ROBERTS, JOHN F. Bus:Pers/Ind Rels. POSITION: Director of Econ Res, Natl Railway Labor Conference, 1901 L St NW, Washington DC 20036. 202/862-7222

ROBERTS, MARKLEY Union. Acad: Econ. AB 1951, Princeton U; MA 1960, PhD 1970, American U. INT: labor market econ, coll barg, empl/trng programs. ASSN: Wash DC IRRA, AEA, Assn for Evolutionary Econ, Amer Pol Sci Assn. POSITIONS: Reporter, Washington Star Newspaper, 1952-57; Legislative Asst, Office of Senator Hubert Humphreys, 1958-61; and (since 1962) Economist, AFL-CIO. ADDRESS: 4931 Albemarle St NW, Washington DC 20016. 202/637-5171

ROBERTS, RAY C., JR. Acad: Econ; Arbitration, Consulting. AB 1950, Duke U; MS 1957, PhD 1961, U of NC. POSITIONS: Chmn, Dept of Econ, Old Dominion U, 1963-67; Dean, School of Bus Admin, Winthrop Coll, 1967-69; and (currently) F. W. Symmes Prof, Dept of Econ and Bus Admin, Furman Univ, Greenville, SC 29613. 803/294-2132

ROBERTS, THOMAS T. Arbitration. BBA 1952, JD 1957, Loyala U. POSITION: Attorney, Suite 307, 827 Deep Valley Dr, Rolling Hills Estate, CA 90274. 213/377-6969

ROBERTSON, JUAN P. Mfg Systems Res/-Develop. BS 1963, MBA 1970, San Jose State; PhD 1978, UCLA. PUBL: The Assessment of Production Technologies, Univ Microfilm, 1978. INT: ind psych, ind sociol, mgmt/educ. ASSN: Computer & Automated Systems Assn of Soc for Mfg Engineers, Assn for Computing Machinery, Amer Statis Assn. POSITIONS: Resident Consultant, Rand Corp, 1974; Consultant, Consulting Div, 1978, and, since 1980, Res Specialist, Manufacturing & Development, Boeing Commercial Airplane Co. ADDRESS: 4330 S 263rd, Kent, WA 98032. 206/931-3505

ROBERTSON, THOMAS HENRY Bus:Pers/Ind Rels. POSITION: Supt, Ind Rels, Bethlehem Mining Corp, 64 N Watson Ave, East Washington, PA 15301. 412/222-2410

ROBINS, EVA Arbitration. LLB 1932, St. John's U. PUBL: Guide for Labor Mediation, U of Hawaii. INT: arb/med, coll barg, govt labor policy. ASSN: New York IRRA, NAA, SPIDR, ABA. POSITION: Arbitrator, 155 W 68th St, New York, NY 10023. 212/724-0700

ROBINSON, DEREK Acad: Econ, Government. BA 1959, MA 1963, Oxford U. POSITIONS: Deputy Chmn, Pay Board, 1973-74, Chmn, UK Social Sci Res Council, 1975-78; and (since 1961) Senior Research Officer, Inst of Econ and Statis, Oxford Univ, St. Cross Bldg, Manor Rd, Oxford, England OX1 3UL.

ROBINSON, DONALD JOHN Student. BSED 1972, MSED 1973, Western Ill U; C.A.S. 1976, Northern Ill U. INT: mgmt/educ, arb/med, union org/admin. ASSN: AAA (Commercial Panel), ASPA. POSITION: Student-Loyola U of Chicago I.I.R. Program. ADDRESS: 395 Tarrington Way, Bolingbrook, IL 60439. 312/739-3353

ROBINSON, EDWARD W., JR. Acad: Ind Rels; Bus:Mgmt/Admin. BS 1970, U of Pittsburgh; MA 1979, St. Francis Coll. INT: coll barg, arb/med, mgmt/educ. ASSN: Western Penna IRRA. POSITIONS: Part Time Faculty, LaRoche Coll and Robert Morris Coll, 1981, and, since 1953, Manager-T.C., Bell of Penna. ADDRESS: 2626 Broad St, Bethel Park,PA 15102. 412/673-1546

ROBINSON, JAMES WILLIAM Acad: Univ Admin; Arbitration, Consulting. AB 1960, Johns Hopkins U; PhD Econ, Duke U. PUBL: Introduction to Labor, 2nd ed, Prentice-Hall, 1984; The Grievance Procedure and Arbitration: Text and Cases, rev. ed. Washington: Univ Press of Amer, 1984; Labor Economics and Labor Relations, New York, Ronald Press, 1967. INT: arb/med, personnel, labor market econ. ASSN: SPIDR, AAA, ASPA. POSITIONS: Dean, School of Bus, Shippensburg State Coll, 1977; Dean, Coll of Bus Admin and Prof of Mgmt, Univ of Arkansas, 1979; and (since 1984) College of Business, Montana State Univ, Bozeman, MT 59717.

ROBINSON, JERALD FRANCIS Acad: Ind Rels. POSITION: Ind Rels Center, Dept of Mgmt, Virginia Polytechnic Inst, Blacksburg, VA 24061.

ROBINSON, LISA G. Student. General Delivery, Crown Hill, WV 25052. 304/595-1814

ROBINSON, SARAH A. Government. Apt 516, 1711 Massachusetts Ave NW, Washington DC 20036.

ROBSON, R. THAYNE Acad: Univ Admin. POSITION: Dept Econ & Finance, Univ of Utah. ADDRESS: 3548 Westwood Dr, Salt Lake City, UT 84109. 801/581-7274

ROCHA, JOSEPH RAMON JR. Acad: Ind Rels, Econ; Arbitration. 15 Dakota Dr, Chelmsford, MA 01824. 617/452-5000

ROCHELEAU, DENNIS W. Bus:Pers/Ind Rels. BS 1964 Northwestern U; JD 1967, Harvard U. INT: coll barg, arb/med, govt labor policy. POSITIONS: Mgr, Union Rels Planning, 1975, Mgr, Legislative Liaison, 1977, and, since 1978, Consultant, Union Rels, General Electric Co, Easton Turnpike, Fairfield, CT 06431. 203/373-2415

ROCK, CHARLES P. Acad: Econ. BA 1970, Williams Coll; MA 1979, Ohio U; PhD 1984, Cornell U. INT: coll barg, labor market econ, participation & labor. ASSN: Intl Assn for the Econ of Self Mgmt, Assn for Workplace Democracy. POSITIONS: Teaching Asst, Econ Dept, Cornell, 1979; and (since 1983) Instructor, Wells Coll, Dept of Econ. ADDRESS: Dept of Econ-PPLMS, Uris Hall, Cornell Univ, Ithaca, NY 14853. 315/364-3320

RODERICK, ROGER DUANE Acad: Ind Rels, Univ Admin; Arbitration. BS 1960, Eastern Ill U; MS 1963, PhD 1970, U of Ill. INT: arb/med, coll barg, personnel. ASSN: Boise ID IRRA, AEA, Acad of Mgmt, ASPA. POSITIONS: Faculty Res Assoc, Ohio State U, 1969; Asst Prof Ind Rels, Loyola U of Chicago, 1973; and (since 1976) Dir of Research, Boise State Univ, PO Box 6653, Boise, ID 83707. 208/385-1394

RODGERS, ROBERT CHARLES Acad: Ind Rels. PhD 1981, Mich State U. INT: coll barg, method/statis, personnel. ASSN: Austin IRRA, AIDS, Acad of Mgmt. POSITION: (since 1981) Asst Prof, Management Dept, School of Bus, Univ of Texas. ADDRESS: 504 Pecan Grove Rd, Austin, TX 78704. 512/471-3676

RODGERS, THOMAS J. Union. ASSN: San Diego IRRA. POSITION: (since 1976) Secretary-Treasurer, Teamsters Local 542, PO Box 23217, San Diego, CA 92123. 619/278-1920

ROESER, JOHN F., JR. Bus:Mgmt/Admin, Bus:Pers/IndRels. Dedicated Carriage Services, PO Box 1791, Wilmington, DE 19899.

ROGERS, ART Bus:Pers/Ind Rels. POSITION: Manager, Personnel Mfg, Schlumberger Well Service, PO Box 4595, Houston, TX 77210.

ROGERS, DANIEL C. Legal Practice. POSITION: Chairman, Missouri State Board of Mediation, 207 Adams St, Jefferson City, MO 65101. 314/751-3614

ROGERS, DAVID E. Acad: Econ. BA 1976, U of Mass; MS 1979, PhD 1982, Cornell U. INT: labor market econ, govt labor policy, coll barg. ASSN: Central NY IRRA, AEA, Econometric Soc. POSITIONS: Instructor, U of Wis-Milwaukee, 1980; and (since 1983) Asst Prof, Dept of Econ, LeMoyne College, Syracuse, NY 13214. 315/446-2882

ROGERS, JOEL E. Acad: Pol Sci, Law. BA 1972, JD 1976, Yale; MA 1978, PhD 1984, Princeton U. PUBL: The Hidden Election: Politics and Economics in the 1980 Presidential Campaign, (co-editor),NY: Pantheon, 1981; On Democracy, (co-author), NY: Penquin, 1983; The Political Economy: Readings in the Politics and Economics of American Public Policy, (co-editor), NY: M. E. Sharpe, 1984. INT: govt labor policy, labor law, labor market econ. ASSN: Amer Pol Sci Assn, Conference Group on the Pol Economy of Advanced Ind Societies. POSITION: (since 1980) Asst Prof of Political Science, Rutgers Univ, 720 Hill Hall, Newark, NJ 07102. 201/648-5753/5819

ROGOW, ROBERT Acad: Bus Admin, Ind Rels, Econ. POSITION: Faculty of Bus Admin, Simon Fraser Univ, Burnaby BC V5A 1S6 Canada. 604/291-3746

ROHDE, DIANE M. Student. BBA 1984, U of Iowa. INT: arb/med, coll barg, personnel. POSITIONS: Accounting Clerk, Monsanto Corp, 1974; and (since 1980) Student. ADDRESS: PO Box 846, Wilton, IA 52778.

ROHRER, JENNIFER Journalism. Kartemquin Films Ltd, 1901 W Wellington, Chicago, IL 61657.

ROHRLICH, GEORGE F. Acad: Econ, Soc Policy. Dr Jur 1937, U of Vienna; PhD 1943, Harvard. PUBL: "Environmental Hazards and Collective Liability: A Comparative Analysis," Outlook Environmental Law J, Vol II, 1983, pp 30-36; "John M. Clark's Unmet Challenge," Rev of Social Econ, vol 39, #3, Dec 1981, pp 343-348; "Maintaining Social Security Programs Adequate and Solvent--A Transnational Synopsis of Problems and Policies," Intl Soc Sec Rev, Vol XXXIII, #2, ISSA, Geneva, 1980, pp 119-154. INT: income maint, empl/trng programs, environmental problems. ASSN: Philadelphia IRRA, Assn for Soc Econ, Assn for Risk and Insurance, Intl Soc for Labor Law and Soc Sec. POSITIONS: Sr. Staff Member, Soc Sec Div, ILO, 1959-64; Visiting Prof of Econ & Soc Policy, School of Soc Service Admin, U of Chicago, 1964-67; Prof, 1967, and, since 1981, Prof Emeritus of Econ and Social Policy, Temple Univ. ADDRESS: 7913 Jenkintown Rd, Cheltenham, PA 19012. 215/379-4108

ROITMAN, HAROLD B. Legal Practice. BA 1935, Dartmouth; LLB 1942, Harvard. INT: labor law, arb/med, coll barg. ASSN: Boston IRRA, ABA, Boston Bar Assn. POSITION: (since 1970) Lawyer-Partner, Segal, Roitman & Coleman, 11 Beacon St, Boston, MA 02108. 617/742-0208

ROJOT, JACQUES R. Acad: Ind Rels, Bus Admin; Consulting. LLB 1965, JD, 1969, U of Paris; PhD 1976, UCLA. PUBL: "International Collective Bargaining: An Analysis and Case Study for Europe," Kluwer, Deventer, Pays-Bas, Mar 1978; "The International Encyclopedia for Labor Law and Industrial Relations," Ed en chef, R. Blanpain, Kluwer, DeVenter, Holland, 1980; "Job Security and Industrial Relations in France," Comparative Ind Rels Bull, U of Louvain, #11. INT: intl comparative labor, coll barg, labor law. ASSN: Paris IRRA, Assn Francoise & Etude des Relations Professionelle, IIRA. POSITIONS: Asst Prof of I.R., 1976, Assoc Prof of I.R., INSEAD (France), 1978; and (since 1982) Prof of Management and Ind Rels, Univ of Rennes-France. ADDRESS: 5 Avenue Courteline, Paris 12 75012 France.

ROLDAN, PEDRO Student, Law. BSILR, 1984, Cornell. INT: labor law, coll barg. ADDRESS: Orinoco St, #1710, Rio Piedras, PR 00926.

ROLE, THEODORE Arbitration; Acad: Arb, Ind Rels. CERT ME 1937, MIT-Lowell Inst; BBA 1943, Boston U; AMP 1958, Harvard. PUBL: "Avoiding Discipline/Discharge Disputes Under the Labor Agreement," AAA Educ Div, Prentice Hall, 1978. INT: arb/med, labor law, labor market econ. ASSN: Boston IRRA, SPIDR, AAA, SFLRP. POSITIONS: Lecturer (Part-Time), School of Ind Rels, Labor Guild of Boston, Instructor (Part-Time), Northeastern U; and (since 1974) Arbitrator (self-employed), 1021 Metropolitan Ave, Milton, MA 02186. 617/333-0858

ROLLE, LAVERNE Arbitration, Alternate Dispute Resolution. BS 1974, Cornell U. POSITION: Regional Director, AAA, 205 N. Wacker, Suite 1100, Chicago, IL 60606. 312/346-2282

ROMAN, PAUL MICHAEL Acad: Sociology. POSITION: Prof of Sociology, 220 Newcomb Hall, Tulane Univ, New Orleans, LA 70118. 504/865-5822

ROMERO, JOSE RAMON Bus:Pers/Ind Rels. POSITION: Personnel Manager, USA, Iberian Airlines, 97-77 Queens Blvd, Rego Park, NY 11374. 212/793-5000

ROMNEY, SUE I. Acad: Education. 702 Highland, Helena, MT 59601. 406/443-3578

RONDEAU, CLAUDE Acad: Econ; Consulting, Arbitration. POSITION: Dept Relations Industrial, Univ of Laval, Quebec, G1K 7P4 Canada.

RONNER, WALTER VALENTIN Legal Practice, Arbitration, Bus:Pers/Ind Rels. LLB 1935, Fordham U. INT: coll barg, labor law, personnel. ASSN: New York IRRA, ABA, ASPA. POSITION: (since 1938) Attorney in Labor Rels (self employed), 300 Garden City Plaza, Garden City, NY 11530. 516/248-0210

RONY, VERA Acad: Univ Admin. POSITION: Labor Management Studies, SUNY-Stony Brook, Stony Brook, NY 11794.

ROOMKIN, MYRON Acad: Ind Rels; Arbitration. BS 1967, Cornell; MS 1969, PhD 1971, U of Wis. PUBL: The Shrinking Perimeter: Unions and Collective Bargaining in the Manufacturing Industries, (w. H. Juris); "A Quantitative Study of Unfair Labor Practice Cases," Ind and Labor Rels Rev, 34, July 1981, pp 245-256; "Case Processing Time and the Outcome of NLRB Elections," (w R. Block), U of Ill Law Rev, 1981, pp 75-98. INT: govt labor policy, coll barg. ASSN: Chicago IRRA, Intl Soc of Labor Law and Soc Security. IIRA. POSITIONS: Asst Prof, U of Chicago, 1971; Assoc Prof, Case Western U, 1975; and (since 1976) Professor, Kellogg Grad School of Mgmt, Northwestern Univ, Leverone Hall, Evanston, IL 60201. 312/-492-3465

ROOT, KENNETH Acad: Sociology. BA 1960, St. Olaf Coll; MSW 1962, U of Wis; PhD 1970, U of Iowa. POSITIONS: Asst Prof, U of Nebr (Omaha), 1966-70; and (since 1970) Assoc Prof and Dept Head, Sociology Dept, Luther College, Decorah, IA 52101. 319/387-1280

ROOT, LAWRENCE S. Acad: Social Work. BA 1968, Haverford Coll; MSS 1971, Bryn Mawr Coll; PhD 1980, U of Chicago. PUBL: Fringe Benefits: Social Insurance in the Steel Industry; "Employee Benefits and Income Security: Private Policy and the Public Interest;" "Income Sources of the Elderly." INT: govt labor policy, income maintenance, ind sociology. ASSN: Council on Soc Work Educ. POSITION: (since 1978) Asst Prof, School of Social Work, Univ of Michigan, 4064 Frieze Bldg, Ann Arbor, MI 48109. 313/763-6581

ROPELLA, MYRON EDWARD Legal Practice, Arbitration, Bus:Pers/Ind Rels. BA 1941, U of Wis; JD 1948, Marquette U; MBA 1954, U of Wis. INT: labor law, intl comparative labor, coll barg. ASSN: Wisconsin IRRA, ABA, ASPA, Intl Soc of Law and Soc Security. POSITION: (since 1957) Senior Partner, Ropella & Van Horne, 1 Plaza E Suite 431, 330 E Kilbourn Ave, Milwaukee, WI 53202. 414/276-7290

ROSE, IRWIN A. Legal Practice (Retired). 183 Tahoe Dr, Carson City, NV 89701.

ROSE, JOSEPH BARKER Acad: Ind Rels. BBA 1966, Adelphi U; MBA 1968, U of Calif; PhD 1971, SUNY-Buffalo. PUBL: Public Policy, Bargaining Structure and the Construction Industry; "The Structure and Growth of the Canadian National Unions;" "Some Notes on the Building Trades-Canadian Labour Congress Dispute." INT: govt labor policy, coll barg, arb/med. ASSN: Hamilton IRRA, Canadian Ind Rels Assn, Acad of Mgmt. POSITIONS: Asst, Assoc Prof, U of New Brunswick, 1971; and (since 1979) Prof of Ind Rels, Faculty of Business, McMaster Univ, Hamilton, Ontario L8S 1R2 Canada. 416/525-9140 ext 4435

ROSE, LEO M. Government. POSITION: NYS Board of Mediation, 1180 Raymond Blvd, Room 830, Newark, NJ 07102. 201/648-2860

ROSE, MICHAEL L. Acad: Bus Admin, Ind Rels. BA 1971, Miami of Ohio; MA 1973, PhD 1981, Ohio State U. INT: coll barg, arb/med, mgmt/educ. ASSN: Acad of Mgmt. POSITION: (since 1980) Asst Prof of Mgmt, Drake Univ. ADDRESS: 3909 Waveland Dr, Des Moines, IA 50311. 515/271-3943

ROSEN, HOWARD Consulting, Government, Bus:Pers/Ind Rels. BA 1939, Rutgers U; MA 1942, NJ State Teachers Coll; PhD 1956, American U. PUBL: Responsiveness of Training Institutions to Changing Labor Market Demands; Job Training for Youth; One Third of a Nation, (monograph). POSITION: (since 1963) Dir, Office of Res & Development, Empl & Trng Admin, USDL. ADDRESS: 5204 Wyoming Rd, Bethesda, MD 20816. 301/229-0413

ROSEN, MARK I. Acad: Student, Org Beh/-Pers, Ind Rels. MLIR 1980, Mich State U. PUBL: Instructors Manual to accompany Personnel/Human Resource Management by Heneman, Schwab, Fossum and Dyer. INT: personnel, org beh, method/statis. ASSN: Acad of Mgmt. POSITIONS: Training Instructor, Manufacturing Data Systems Inc, Consultant (self-employed), and, since 1981, PhD Student, Ind Rels Res Inst, 4226 Social Science, 1180 Observatory Dr, Madison, WI 53706. 608/262-3707

ROSEN, SHERMAN D. Bus:Pers/Ind Rels. BS 1950, MA 1952, U of Ill. INT: org beh, personnel, mgmt/educ. ASSN: ASPA, Amer Compensation Assn. POSITIONS: Principal, Cresap, McCormick & Paget, 1967; Dir, Compensation & Benefits, 1977, and, since 1981, Vice Pres Human Resources, Hartmarx Corp, 101 N Wacker Dr, Chicago, IL 60600. 312/372-6300

ROSEN, STANLEY Labor Educator; Acad: Ind Rels. BA 1956, MA 1960, Rutgers U. INT: coll barg, labor educ, mass transit I/R. ASSN: Chicago IRRA, Univ & College Labor Educ Assn, Workers Educ L-189. POSITIONS: Ext Assoc, IMLR, Rutgers, 1956; Dir, Education, Textile Workers Union of Amer-AFL-CIO, 1960; and (since 1965) Prof of Labor & Ind Rels, Inst of Labor and Ind Rels, Labor Educ Programs, U of Ill-Chicago. ADDRESS: 2918 West Toughy, Chicago, IL 60645.

ROSEN, STEPHEN J. Acad: Ind Rels, Econ; Arbitration. BA 1962, William Paterson Coll; MA 1967, Fairleigh Dickinson U; EdD 1979, Rutgers U. PUBL: "How Arbitrators View Just Cause," IRRA Proceedings, May, 1983; "'Ethics of Discharge,' Legal and Moral Implications," FDU Conference, Oct 1982. INT: arb/med, coll barg, labor law. ASSN: New York IRRA, AEA, Western Econ Assn, Eastern Econ Assn. POSITION: (since 1968) Professor of Econ, Fairleigh Dickinson U. ADDRESS: 76 Sherman Ave, Cedar Grove, NJ 07009. 201/692-2675

ROSEN, SUMNER MAURICE Arbitration; Acad: Ind Rels. PhD 1959, MIT. PUBL: Economic Power Failure, 1975, McGraw Hill; "After Reagan-Alternatives for the 80's," (chapter) Gartner et al, 1984; "Worker Militance and Its Consequences," (chapter) Barkin, ed; Praeger, 1983. INT: union org/admin, govt labor policy, empl/trng programs. ASSN: New Brunswick, New York IRRA. POSITIONS: Sr Res Assoc, Inst of Public Admin, New York, 1969; Social Work Faculty, Columbia U, 1976; and (since 1983) Dir of Grad Studies, Rutgers Labor Educ Center, Ryders Lane,Clifton Ave, New Brunswick, NJ 08903. 201/932-9502

ROSENBAUM, EDWARD Acad: Bus Admin. 29485 Bermuda La, Southfield, MI 48076.

ROSENBAUM, RENE P. Acad: Econ. POSITION: Econ Dept, Univ of Wis, Whitewater, WI 53190. 414/472-1355

ROSENBERG, EMILY J. Union. BA Boston U; MA Wheelock Coll; MS 1978, U of Mass-Amherst. INT: labor educ, coll barg, arb/-med. ASSN: Connecticut IRRA. POSITIONS: Teacher, Town of Foxboro, MA, 1972-76; Labor Rels Specialist, Internal Revenue Service, 1977; and (since 1978) Field Rep, Connecticut Federation of Teachers, AFL-CIO. ADDRESS: 60 Davis St, New Haven, CT 06515. 203/828-1400

ROSENBERG, HOWARD R. Acad: Org Beh/-Pers, Bus Admin. BS 1968, MS 1969, Rennselaer Polytechnic Inst; PhD 1980, U of Calif-Berkeley. PUBL: "The Human Resource Approach to Management: Second Generation Issues," (w R. E. Miles); "Involving Workers in Decisions on the Farm," (w G. E. Billikopf); "Personnel Management of Lettuce Harvest Crews." INT: personnel/agriculture, org beh, mgmt/educ. ASSN: Acad of Mgmt, ASPA, Agriculture Pers Mgmt Assn. POSITIONS: Mgmt Analyst, San Francisco Housing Authority, 1971; Lecturer, Calif State U-Hayward, 1980; and (since 1981) Ext Specialist, Human Resource Mgmt, Cooperative Ext, 320 Giannini Hall, Univ of Calif, Berkeley, CA 94720. 415/642-7103

ROSENBERG, MAX Arbitration. BA 1948, CCNY; JD 1949, Columbia U. INT: arb/med, govt labor policy, labor law. ASSN: AAA, Federal Bar Assn, FMCS. POSITIONS: Chief Counsel, 1959, Administrative Law Judge, NLRB, Wash DC, 1963; and (since 1980) Arbitrator, Mediator, Fact Finder (self employed) 5500 Holmes Run Parkway #1207, Alexandria, VA 22304. 703/370-1099

ROSENBERG, REUBEN Arbitration, Union; Acad: Ind Rels. BA 1969, MBA 1971, Columbia U. INT: arb/med, coll barg, union org/admin. ASSN: New York & New Jersey IRRAs. POSITIONS: Assoc Dir, Res & Negotiations, 1973, Assoc Admin, Health & Security, Dist Council 37, AFSCME, New York, 1978; and (since 1983) Arbitrator, 60 Ardsley Rd, Montcliar, NJ 07042. 201/744-0336

ROSENBERG, SAMUEL Acad: Econ. BA 1970, Brandeis U; PhD 1975, U of Calif-Berkeley. PUBL: "Reagan Social Policy and Labour Force Restructuring," Cambridge J of Econ, vol 7, #2, June 1983; "Male Occupational Standing and the Dual Labor Market," Ind Rels, vol 19, #1, Winter 1980; "A Conflict Theory Approach to Inflation in the Postwar U. S. Economy," (w T. Weisskopf), Amer Econ Rev, vol 71, #2, May 1981. INT: labor market econ, govt labor policy. ASSN: AEA, Assn for Evolutionary Econ. POSITIONS: Asst Prof of Econ, Williams Coll, 1975; Visiting Asst Prof of Econ, Univ of Calif-Davis, 1979; and (since 1982) Asst Prof of Econ, Dept of Econ, Roosevelt Univ, 430 S Michigan Ave, Chicago, IL 60605. 312/341-3697

ROSENBLATT, ANNALEE Z. Consulting. BA 1966, MA 1969, Ariz State U. INT: coll barg, arb/med, empl/trng programs. ASSN: Natl Public Empl Labor Rels Assn, Amer Bus Women Assn, AAA. POSITIONS: Grievance Admin, Senate Professional Assn-SUNY, 1971; Labor Negotiator, Thelan Assoc Inc, 1973; and (since 1978) Owner, Annalee Z. Rosenblatt, Labor Negotiator/Mgmt Consultant, 18 Tall Pines Rd, Scarborough, ME 04074. 207/883-9025

ROSENBLUM, MARC J. Government; Acad: Bus Admin. PhD 1972, U of Minn. PUBL: "Evolving EEO Decision Law and Applied Research," Ind Rels 21, 1982, pp 340-51; "Age Discrimination in Employment and the Permissibility of Occupational Age Restrictions," Hastings Law J, 32, 1981, pp 1261-83. INT: EEO law & policy, labor market econ. ASSN: Wash DC IRRA, Soc of Government Economists. POSITIONS: Staff Economist, Natl Commission on Empl and Unempl Statis, 1977-78; Adjunct Prof of Mgmt & Policy, Amer Univ, 1979, and, also since 1979, Chief Economist, U. S. EEO. ADDRESS: Apt 1405, 309 Yoakum Pkwy, Alexandria, VA 22304. 202/634-6750

ROSENBLUM, PAUL Consulting. 66 W 94th St, Suite 19A, New York, NY 10025. 212/663-5099

ROSENSTEIN, ELIEZER Acad: Ind Rels. POSITION: Faculty of Ind Engineering/Mgmt, Technion Israel Inst Tech, Haifa 32000, Israel.

ROSOFSKY, ROSE G. Government (Retired Labor Economist-USDL). BA 1938, Brooklyn Coll; MA 1942, New School for Social Res. ADDRESS: 530 N Street SW, Washington DC 20024.

ROSOW, JEROME M. Non Profit Res Inst. BA 1942, U of Chicago. PUBL: Work In America: Decade Ahead, (editor w C. Kerr); Productivity: Prospects for Growth; "Punch Out the Time Clocks." INT: coll barg, org beh, personnel. POSITIONS: Asst Secretary of Labor, US Dept of Labor, 1969; Mgr, Public Affairs, Exxon Corp, 1952; and (since 1975) President, Work in America Inst, 700 White Plains Rd, Scarsdale, NY 10583. 914/472-9600

ROSS, KATY Bus:Pers/Ind Rels. POSITION: Shell Oil Co, PO Box 100, Deer Park, TX 77536.

ROSS, MARCIA E. Student. 488 Littleton St, West Lafayette, IN 47906. 317/743-2595

ROSS, RICHARD J. Government; Acad: Ind Rels. BS 1958, U of Buffalo; MA 1966, St. Francis Coll. INT: labor law, labor history, coll barg. ASSN: Intl Assn of Chiefs of Police, Assn Federal Investigators, Reserve Officers Assn. POSITION: (since 1981) Director-Eastern Div, Office Organized Crime and Racketeering. ADDRESS: 6301 Stevenson Ave, #806, Alexandria, VA 22304. 202/523-7290

ROSST, WARREN A. Bus:Pers/Ind Rels, Bus:Mgmt/Admin. BA 1973, U of Northern Iowa. INT: personnel, coll barg, ind sociol. ASSN: ASPA, Bluegrass Pers Assn, Lexington Chamber of Commerce. POSITIONS: Mgr, Ind Rels, 1976, Plant Superintendent, Lordin Div, Koehring Co, Chattanooga, 1978; and (since 1979) Manager, Pers & Ind Rels, WABCO Fluid Power Div, American Standard Inc, 1953 Mercer Rd, Lexington, KY 40505. 606/254-8031

ROSTOV, STANLEY DAVID Legal Practice. 1240 W 71st Terrace, Kansas City, MO 64114.

ROTH, HERRICK S. Consulting. 2887 S Monroe, Denver, CO 80210.

ROTH, JEREMEY ALAN Student. BS 1982, Iowa State U; MLIR 1983, Mich State U. INT: labor law, arb/med, coll barg. POSITION: Student, Boston Univ. ADDRESS: 293 Beacon St #6, Boston, MA 02116.

ROTH, THOMAS R. Arbitration, Consulting. MS 1973, U of Wis-Madison. INT: arb/-med, coll barg, govt labor policy. ASSN: Wash DC IRRA, AAA, Intl Foundation of Empl Benefit Plans. POSITION: (since 1974) President-Consulting Economist, The Labor Bureau Inc, 1346 Connecticut Ave NW, Washington DC 20036. 202/296-7420

ROTH, WILLIAM Government. POSITION: Attorney, 19 Lxn Crest Dr, Monsey, NY 10952. 212/488-3806

ROTHBAUM, MELVIN Acad: Ind Rels. AB 1949, AM 1951, PhD 1955, Harvard U. INT: intl comparative labor, govt labor policy, empl/trng programs. POSITIONS: (since 1967) Prof of Labor & Ind Rels, ILIR, Univ of Illinois, 504 East Armory Ave, Champaign, IL 61820. 217/333-1487

ROTHE, HAROLD FREDERICK Bus:Pers/-Ind Rels; Acad: Org Beh/Pers. AB 1939, Bates Coll; MA 1941, PhD 1944, U of Minn. PUBL: "Output Rates Among Industrial Employees," J Applied Psych, 63, 1978, 40-46; "Does Higher Pay Bring Higher Productivity?" Pers, 37, 4, 1960, 11-15; "Matching Men to Job Requirements," Pers Psych, 1951, 4, 291-301. INT: ind psych, org beh. ASSN: Amer Psych Assn, Midwest Psych Assn. POSITIONS: Pers Mgr, Fairbanks Morse Co, 1953-60; Cor Staff Asst, Beloit Corp, 1961-1975; Retired. 2013 E Ridge Rd, Beloit WI 53511.

ROTHENBERG, MARTIN R. Legal Practice. BS 1965, JD 1969, U of Ill. ASSN: Chicago IRRA, AAA, CBA, IBJ. POSITION: (since 1981) President, Martin R. Rothenberg Ltd, Suite 2101, 180 N La Salle St, Chicago, IL 60601. 312/236-2305

ROTHROCK, CLIFFORD D. Bus:Pers/Ind Rels. POSITION: Personnel/Labor Rels, Metropolitan Hospital, 1800 Tuxedo Ave, Detroit, MI 48206.

ROTHSTEIN, MICHAEL F. Arbitration, Legal Practice. BSILR 1965, JD 1968, Cornell U; MSW 1980, U of Wis. INT: arb/med, coll barg, labor law. ASSN: Wis State Bar Assn. POSITIONS: Attorney (self-employed), 1971; Arbitrator/Mediator/Hearing Examiner, Wis Empl Rels Comm, 1977; and (since 1981) Arbitrator/Attorney Self-employed, 217 S. Hamilton, Suite 300, Madison, WI 53703. 608/257-4151

ROTHSTEIN, WILLIAM G. Acad: Sociology. BS 1959, MIT; MA 1961, U of Minn; PhD 1965, Cornell U. PUBL: American Physicians in the Nineteenth Century, 1972; "Significance of Occupations in Work Careers," J Voc Beh, 1980; "Pathology: The Evolution of a Speciality," Medical Care, 1979. INT: ind sociol, org beh, health & hosp care. ASSN: Amer Sociological Assn, Amer Assn of History of Medicine. POSITION: (since 1966) Assoc Prof of Sociology, U of Maryland, Baltimore Cty, 5401 Wilkens Ave, Baltimore, MD 21228. 301/455-2000/2078

ROTTER, NAOMI G. Acad: Org Beh/Pers. BA 1963, Skidmore Coll; PhD 1974, New York U. PUBL: "Image of Engineering and Liberal Arts Students," J of Voc Behavior, 1982. INT: ind psych, org beh, personnel. ASSN: Amer Psych Assn, Acad of Mgmt, Eastern Evaluation Soc. POSITION: (since 1983) Assoc Prof of Soc Sci and Assoc Chair of Org & Soc Sci Dept, New Jersey Inst of Tech. ADDRESS: 36 Frederick St, Montclair, NJ 07042. 201/645-5073

ROUGEUX, NANETTE I. 400 Elm Ave, Clearfield, PA 16830. 814/765-5813

ROUKIS, GEORGE S. Arbitration. 198 Continental Dr, Manhasset Hills, NY 11040.

ROUMASSET, CHARLES Government, (Retired). 151 Wildwood Ave, San Carlos, CA 94070.

ROWAN, RICHARD LAMAR Acad: Ind Rels, Univ Admin. AB 1953, Birmingham Southern Coll; PhD 1961, U of NC-Chapel Hill. PUBL: Multinational Collective Bargaining Attempts: The Record, the Cases and the Prospects, U of Penna, Ind Res Unit, 1979; Multinational Union Organizations in the Manufacturing Industries, U of Penna Ind Res Unit, 1980; Multinational Enterprises and the OECD Industrial Relations Guidelines, U of Penna Ind Res Unit, 1983. INT: union org/admin, intl comparative labor, coll barg. ASSN: Southern Econ Assn. POSITION: (since 1961) Prof of Industry and Co-Dir, Ind Research Unit, The Wharton School, Univ of Penna, 317 Vance Hall-CS, Philadelphia, PA 19104. 215/898-7906

ROWE, ROBERT H. Legal Practice. 30045 Summit, #204, Farmington Heights, MI 48018.

ROWLAND, CLIFFORD V. Government/-Pers Ind Rels. BS 1953, Cornell U. INT: arb/med, coll barg, personnel. ASSN: New York IRRA. POSITIONS: VP Ind Rels, Grace Line Inc, 1965; and (since 1971) Director, Empl and Labor Rels, U.S. Postal Service, Newark Mgmt Sectional Center. ADDRESS: 122 Southern Blvd, Chatham, NJ 07928. 201/596-5220

ROY, WAYNE PAUL Union, Labor Empl & Develop. INT: empl/trng programs, labor market econ, health & hosp care. POSITION: L.E.A.D. Field Rep, Manpower Div, Mich State AFL-CIO, 315 South Front St, Marquette, MI 49855. 906/228-3211

ROZEK, B. J. Student. POSITION: Grad Asst, Loyola U of Chicago. ADDRESS: 599 Park Plaza #4, Glen Ellyn, IL 60137. 312/790-4319

RUBEN, ALAN MILES Acad: Law. POSITION: Cleveland-Marshall Law College, Cleveland State Univ, Cleveland, OH 44115.

RUBENFELD, STEPHEN A. Acad: Ind Rels. BA 1970, Becknell U; MS 1973, PhD 1977, U of Wis-Madison. PUBL: "Data on the Marlowe-Crowne and Edwards Social Desirability Scales," Psych Reports, v 53, 1984; "Employment Agencies: Are They Jeopardizing Your Selection Process?" Personnel, v 58, 1982; "The Uniform Guidelines: A Framework for Personnel Decision Making," Empl Rels Law J, v 7, 1981. INT: coll barg, personnel, union org/admin. ASSN: Acad of Mgmt, ASPA, Southern Mgmt Assn. POSITIONS: Asst Prof of Mgmt, Coll of Bus Admin, Tex Tech U, 1976; and (since 1981) Assoc Prof of Pers and Ind Rels, School of Bus and Econ, Univ of Minnesota, Duluth, MN 55812. 218/726-7531

RUBENSTEIN, BENJAMIN Arbitrator. 4430 Bathurst St, #505, Downsview, Ont M3H 3S3 Canada.

RUBENSTEIN, JEROME S. Acad: Law; Arbitration, Legal Prac. AB 1953, Cornell U; AM 1954, Columbia U; LLB 1957, Yale U. PUBL: "The Emerging Antitrust Implications of Mandatory Bargaining," 50 Marquette L Rev 50, 1966; "Some Thoughts on Labor Arbitration," 49 Marquette L Rev 695, 1966; "The Legal Fiction of Obscenity," XVII #47, The New Leader, Dec 1959, p 15. INT: arb/med, labor law, coll barg. ASSN: Boston & New York IRRAs, SFLRP, SPIDR. POSITIONS: Attorney , Rubenstein & Rubenstein, 1958; Trial Examiner, New York State Labor Rels Bd, 1973; and (since 1974) Labor/Arbitrator, PO Box 135, North Marshfield, MA 02059. 617/837-6728

RUBIN, HAROLD Government. BSS 1949, CCNY; MPA 1956, PhD 1963, Syracuse U. PUBL: "Labor Relations in State and Local Government", in Unionization of Municipal Employees, Proceedings of the Acad of Pol Sci, Dec 1970. INT: labor rels in public sector, coll barg, govt labor policy. ASSN: NY Capital Dist IRRA. POSITIONS: Empl Compensation and Rels Unit, Div of the Budget, 1967-71, Deputy Dir, Office of Empl Rels, 1979-1981, and, since 1981, Chief Budget Examiner, New York State Div of the Budget. ADDRESS: 156 Chestnut St, Albany, NY 12210. 518/474-6324

RUBIN, MILTON Arbitration. BA 1938, MA 1946, NYU. INT: arb/med, intl comparative labor, coll barg. ASSN: New York IRRA, NAA, AEA, SPIDR. POSITION: (since 1946) Arbitrator, 54 Sunset Dr, Croton-On-Hudson, NY 10520. 914/271-4660

RUBINSTEIN, SIDNEY P. Consulting. POSITION: President, Participative Systems Inc, PO Box 18, Princeton, NJ 08549.

RUBY, DONALD P. Bus:Pers/Ind Rels. Michigan Sugar Co, PO Box 1348, Saginaw, MI 48605.

RUFFO, PHILIP J. Acad: Law; Arbitration, Government. BLL 1947, Brooklyn Law School. PUBL: "The Law of Labor-Management Relations in Flux," NY Law Rev, Fall 1983; "The Residue of Sovereignty in New York Public Employment," Albany Law Rev, vol 39, #2, 1975; "Sovereignty Revisited and Modelled in New York Public Employment," 416 NYS 2d #2, June 27, 1979, p 31. INT: arb/med, labor law, coll barg. ASSN: New York & Long Island IRRA, SPIDR, NY State Bar Assn, Brooklyn Bar Assn. POSITIONS: General Counsel-Deputy Dir, NY City Office of Coll barg, 1971; and (since 1983) NY Member, Port Authority Labor Rels Bd, NY-NJ Port Authority. ADDRESS: NY Law School, 20 Harvard Ave, Rockville Centre, NY 11570. 212/982-2308

RULE, WILLIAM S. Arbitration. AB 1948, Stanford U; MBA 1950, Harvard U. INT: arb/-med. ASSN: San Diego IRRA, NAA, SPIDR. POSITION: (since 1972) Arbitrator, PO Box 3229, Rancho Santa Fe, CA 92067. 619/756-4662

RUNCIE, JOHN F. Bus:Pers/Ind Rels. BA 1964, Lehigh U; MA 1966 U of Conn; PhD 1971, Rutgers U. PUBL: "By Days I Make the Cars," Harvard Bus Rev 58(3) May-June 1980, pp 106-115; "Dynamic Systems and the Quality of Work Life," Pers 57 (6) Nov-Dec 1980, pp 13-24; Experiencing Social Research, Red Ed, Homewood, IL: Dorsey, 1980. INT: ind sociol, org beh. ASSN: Amer Soc Assn, OD Network. POSITIONS: Dir of Soc & Market Res, Development Analysis Assoc, 1978; Sr Researcher, Public Systems Evaluation, Cambridge, MA 1980; and (since 1982) Senior O.D. Specialist, Anheuser-Busch Co, Inc., 1 Busch Place, St. Louis, MO 63118. 314/577-4483

RUNGELING, BRIAN SCOTT Acad: Econ. PhD 1969, U of Ky. PUBL: Role of Unions in the American Economy, (co-author), JCEE, 1983; Public Service Employment in the Rural South, (co-author), U of Tex Bureau of Bus & Econ Develop, 1983; Employment, Income and Welfare in the Rural South, (co-author), Praeger Publ, 1979. INT: empl/trng programs, labor market econ, govt labor policy. ASSN: AEA, SEA, WEA. POSITIONS: Asso Prof of Econ, 1973, Chairman & Prof of Econ, U of Miss, 1978; and (since 1981) Chairman and Professor of Economics, Univ of Central Florida, PO Box 25,000, Orlando, FL 32816. 305/275-2465

RUNYAN, JOHN ROBERT, JR. Legal Prac; Acad: Law. AB 1968, U of Mich; JD 1972, Wayne State U. PUBL: "Employment Decision-Making in Educational Institutions," 26 Wayne Law Rev 955, 1980. INT: equal empl opportunity. ASSN: Detroit IRRA, ABA (Section of Local Government Law), State Bar of Mich (Section on Labor Rels), Federal Bar Assn. POSITIONS: Adjunct Prof of Law, Wayne State Univ Law School, 1974; Visiting Prof, School of Labor & Ind Rels, Mich State U, 1978; and (since 1979) Partner (Attorney), Sachs, Nunn, Kates, Kadushin, O'Hare, Helveston & Waldman, P.C., 1000 Farmer St, Detroit, MI 48226. 313/-965-3464

RUNYON, ARCH H. Arbitration, Bus:Pers/Ind Rels, Consulting. AB 1964, Berea Coll. INT: arb/med, personnel. ASSN: Southern WV Pers Assn, Big Sandy Area Mgmt-Labor Org. POSITIONS: Pers mgr, Pittston Co-Ky Div, 1970; and (since 1979) Group Pers & Labor Rels Director, Rawl Sales and Processing Co, PO Box 31, Lobata, WV 25677. 304/235-4290

RUSH, FRANCIS MICHAEL JR. Government. AB 1956, Drake U; MPA 1975, Auburn U. PUBL: "Getting the Most Out of Meetings," Bus Horizons, 1974. INT: ind sociol, personnel. ASSN: Inter-Univ Seminar on Armed Forces and Society. POSITIONS: Professional Staff Member, Privacy Protection Study Commission, 1976; Chief Officer Promotion Policy, Headquarters, US AirForce, 1978, and, since 1983, Director, Manpower and Pers, Office of Asst Secretary of Defense (Reserve Affairs). ADDRESS: 4816 Twinbrook Rd, Fairfax, VA 22032. 202/697-4334

RUSH, KEVIN Government. POSITION: Exec Asst, New York State Legislative Commission on Critical Transportation Choices. ADDRESS: 103 Inwood Ave, Point Lookout, NY 11569. 516/546-4100

RUSSELL, BEVERLY ANN Bus:Pers/Ind Rels. BS 1975, Ind U of Penna; MSIR 1976, MBA 1981, West Va U. INT: arb/med, coll barg, personnel. ASSN: Amer Mgmt Assn. POSITIONS: Turn Supr, Wheeling-Pittsburgh Steel Corp, 1976; Labor Contract Admin, 1978; and, since 1982, Procedure Analyst, Weirton Steel Div. ADDRESS: 104 Bridle Blvd, New Cumberland, WV 26047. 304/797-3613

RUSSELL, GARY PETER Student. 1111 E Johnson St, #4, Madison, WI 53703. 608/258-8842

RUSSELL, LUCAS G. Union. Local 50, SEIU, 4108 Lindell Blvd, St. Louis, MO 63108.

RUSSO, CHARLINE S. Acad: Mgmt Educ. BA 1972, MBA 1974 Rutgers U. INT: mgmt/educ, ind psych, org beh. ASSN: ASTD, ASPA, NSPI. POSITION: (since 1974) Asst Extension Specialist, Rutgers Univ Inst of Mgmt and Labor Rels. ADDRESS: 29 Ivyhill Dr, Aberdeen, NJ 07747. 201/932-9836

RUTHERFORD, WILLIAM T. Acad: Law. POSITION: Prof, Dept of Mgmt & Bus Law, Georgia State Univ, University Plaza, Atlanta, GA 30303.

RUTLEDGE, IVAN C. Acad: Law; Arbitration. MA 1940, LLB 1946, Duke U; LLM 1952, Columbia U. PUBL: "Manipulating Forum Jurisdiction," 32 Mercer Law Rev, 457, 1981; "Administrative Review and The Modern Courts Amendment," 35 Ohio State Law J, 41, 1974; "Justice Black and Labor Law," 14 U of Calif L Rev 501, 1967. INT: labor law, arb/med, govt labor policy. ASSN: NAA, Amer Law Inst. POSITIONS: Prof of Law, Indiana U, 1954; Dean, Coll of Law, Ohio State U, 1965; and (since 1979) Walter F. George Distinguished Professor, School of Law, Mercer Univ, Macon, GA 31207. 912/744-2641

RUTT, FRED JR. Government. BA, 1951, East Wash U. INT: coll barg, govt labor policy, labor law. POSITION: (since 1951) Chief, Labor Relations, U.S. Dept of Energy, 224 Armistead, Richland, WA 99352. 509/376-7221

RUTTENBERG, STANLEY H. Consulting. BS 1933, U of Pittsburgh. PUBL: Federal State Employment Service: A Critique, (w J. Gutchess); Manpower Challenge of the 1970's, (w J. Gutchess). INT: coll barg, empl/trng programs, labor market econ. ASSN: AEA. POSITIONS: Dir of Research, AFL-CIO, 1948-55; Asst Sec of Labor, Manpower Admin, USDL, 1966; and (since 1961) Chairman of the Board (Retired) Ruttenberg, Friedman, Kilgallan & Assoc Inc. ADDRESS: 6310 Maiden Lane, Bethesda, MD 20817. 202/293-1756

RYAN, EDWARD F. Legal Practice. LLB 1951, St. John's Law School; LLM 1956, New York U. INT: arb/med, coll barg. ASSN: New Brunswick IRRA, ABA, New Jersey Bar Assn, Natl Center for the Study of Coll Barg in Higher Educ and the Professions. POSITIONS: Field Attorney, NLRB, 1956; and (since 1959) Senior Partner, Carpenter, Bennett & Morrissey, 744 Broad St, Newark, NJ 07102. 201/622-7711

RYAN, EDWARD WILLIAM Acad: Econ. BS 1955, Wharton School-U of Penna; MA 1957, Duke U. INT: labor market econ, govt labor policy, mgmt/educ. ASSN: AEA. POSITION: (since 1958) Chairman of Department of Econ and Management, Manhattanville College. ADDRESS: 25 Jefferson Rd, Scarsdale, NY 10583. 914/694-2200

RYAN, HUBERT B. Trade Assn. BS 1966, Western Ky U. INT: coll barg, arb/med, health & hosp care. POSITION: (since 1980) Vice Pres, Michigan Beer & Wine Wholesalers Assn, 332 Townsend, Lansing, MI 48933. 517/482-5555

RYAN, JOHN M. Legal Practice, Bus:Mgmt/-Admin; Acad: Law. AB 1958, Dartmouth Coll; LLB 1963, U of Va. PUBL: The Teenager and the Law, (w A. Ayars), St. Christopher Press. INT: labor law, coll barg, arb/med. ASSN: ABA (Labor Law Section), Maritime Law Assn of U.S.A. POSITIONS: Chairman of the Board, Coastal Communications Ltd, 1980; and (since 1964) Partner, Vandeventer, Black, Meredith & Martin, 500 World Trade Center, Norfolk, VA 23510. 804/622-4381

RYAN, STEVE M. Nuclear Ind Trng. JSO 1981, Sangamon State U. PUBL: "R.I.C.S. Intervention Counselling in Sexual Assault." INT: labor psychology. ASSN: AAAS, IRT. POSITIONS: Rehabilitation Counsellor, A. MacFarland Mental Health Center, Instructional System Design (Faculty), Lakeland Community Coll, 1981; and (since 1982) Training Supr, Baldwin Assoc, PO Box 306, Clinton, IL 61727. 217/937-1111

RYNECKI, STEVEN B. Legal Practice. BS 1970, U of new Haven; MA 1974, JD 1973, U of Iowa. PUBL: Preparing and Presenting A Grievance Arbitration Case, (co-author w M. Hiss Jr.), Intl Pers Mgmt Assn, 1979; "What to Do Before the Pickets Arrive," Public Mgmt, Feb 1976; "Experience With Binding Arbitration in Education," J of Law and Educ, 1980. INT: labor law, coll barg, arb/med. ASSN: Wisconsin IRRA, ABA (Mgmt Member Comm on State & Local Govt), Wis Bar Assn (Labor Law Section), Illinois Bar. POSITIONS: Attorney, Intl Pers Mgmt Assn, 1973; and (since 1977) Attorney, von Briesen & Redmond, S.C., 757 N Broadway, Milwaukee, WI 53202. 414/276-1122

S

SABATINI, VICKI B. Legal Practice. AB 1975, AM 1982, U of Ill. INT: coll barg, arb/med, intl comparative labor. POSITIONS: Staff Rep, Office & Professional Empl,AFL-CIO, 1978; Instructor, Public Sector Barg, Community Coll of Allegheny Cty, 1981; and (since 1982) Legal Asst, Eckert, Seamans, Cherin & Mellott, 42nd Floor, 600 Grant St, Pittsburgh, PA 15219. 412/566-6000

SABGHIR, IRVING H. Acad: Ind Rels; Arbitration, Consulting. BS 1949, Cornell U; MPA 1951, PhD 1956, Harvard U. PUBL: "Sub-Contracting and Obligations to Bargain Under the Taylor Act," Labor Law J, Dec 1978; "Taylor Act-a Brief Look After Three Years," in 1970 Supplement to Report of Task Force on State & Local Government Labor Rels, Natl Governor's Conference, Mar 1971. INT: coll barg, arb/med, labor market econ. ASSN: New York Capital Dist IRRA, AEA. POSITIONS: Labor Econ, USDL, 1952; Staff Analyst, Ford Motor Co, 1954; and (since 1965) Professor, Labor & IR, SUNY-Albany, 1400 Washington Ave, Albany, NY 12222. 518/457-8515

SACHS, THEODORE Legal Practice. POSITION: Sachs Nunn Kates et al, 1000 Farmer, Detroit, MI 48226. 313/965-3464

SACK, J. ERICA Government. BA 1977, Brandeis U; MILR 1980, NYSSILR-Cornell U. INT: labor law, coll barg, arb/med. POSITION: (since 1980) Field Examiner, NLRB. ADDRESS: 275 Park St, Upper Montclair, NJ 07043. 201/645-6616

SACK, JEFFREY Legal Practice. BA LIB, 1965, U of Toronto. PUBL: Ontario Labor Board Law. INT: labor law. ASSN: Canadian Bar Assn, Intl Bar Assn. POSITION: (since 1967) Lawyer, Sack, Charney, et al 181 University Ave, Suite 800, Toronto, Ontario M5H 2E5, Canada. 416/864-9140

SADINSKY, MATTHEW L. Acad: Ind Rels, Org Beh/Pers, Psychology. BS 1979, Cornell U. INT: ind psych, labor law, govt labor policy. ASSN: East Tex Pers Assn, Global Res Inst, ASPA. POSITIONS: Legislative Asst, New York State Legislature, 1977; Political Action Specialist, Committee on Pol Educ, Colorado AFL-CIO, 1978; and (since 1979) Manager of Human Resources, Continental Can Co, Continental Group Inc, 901 Fisher Rd, Longview, TX 75604. 214/759-9416

SAINT ANTOINE, THEODORE J. Acad: Law; Arbitration. AB 1951, Fordham Coll; JD 1954, U of Mich; Post Grad, 1957-58, U of London (Fulbright Grant). PUBL: Labor Relations Law: Cases and Materials, Michie, 1979; "Free Speech or Economic Weapon: The Persisting Problem of Picketing," 16 Suffolk U Law Rev: 883, Winter 1982; "Protection Against Unjust Discipline: An Idea Whose Time Has Long Since Come," Proceedings of 34th Annual Meeting, NAA, pp 43-62, BNA 1982. INT: labor law, arb/med, coll barg. ASSN: Detroit IRRA, ABA (Labor Empl Law), State

Bar of Mich, NAA. POSITIONS: Prof of Law, 1969, Dean, 1971-78, and, since 1981, Degan Prof of Law, Univ of Mich Law School, Ann Arbor, MI 48109. 313/764-9348

SAINT LAURENT, JACQUES Acad: Ind Rels. ADDRESS: CP 738, 214 Chemin Tour du Lac, Lac Beauport, Quebec G0A 2C0 Canada.

SALANDRIA, VINCENT J. Legal Practice. AB 1948, LD 1951, U of Penna. INT: labor law. ASSN: Philadelphia IRRA, Phila Bar Assn, Justinian Soc. POSITIONS: Labor Rels Asst, 1967, Acting Dir Grievances & Disputes, 1974, and, since 1975, Asst General Counsel, School District of Philadelphia, 21st & Parkway, Philadelphia, PA 19103. 215/299-8925

SALERNO, GEORGE P. Acad: Univ Admin. MA 1966, U of Ill. INT: coll barg, arb/med, personnel. ASSN: San Francisco IRRA, Coll and Univ Pers Assn, Acad for Academic Pers Admin, Assn of Independent Calif Coll and Univ. POSITIONS: Mgr, Pers and Labor Rels, R. H. Macy's Inc, 1970; Div Labor Rels Mgr, Dutch Boy Paint, Div of N. L. Industries, 1974; and (since 1977) Director, Empl and Labor Rels, Univ of San Francisco, 2130 Fulton St, San Francisco, CA 94117. 415/666-6707

SALIPANTE, PAUL F., JR. Acad: Ind Rels, Pers. BSEE 1966, MIT, MBA, 1971, PhD 1975, U of Chicago. PUBL: "The Role of Organizational Procedures in the Resolution of Social Conflict," (w J. Aram), Human Org, Spring 1984; Job Satisfaction and Productivity: an Evaluation of Policy-Related Research," (w S. Srivastra and others), Kent State Univ Press, 1977; "A Matrix Approach to Literature Reviews," (w W. Notz & J. Bigelow), in L. L. Cummings & B. Staw (ed) Research in Organizational Behavior,4, 321-48, 1982. INT: empl due process, personnel, empl/trng programs. ASSN: Northeast Ohio IRRA, Acad of Mgmt. POSITIONS: Asst Prof of IR, 1977, and, since 1980, Assoc Prof of Ind Rels, Case Western Reserve Univ. ADDRESS: 3001 E Overlook Rd, Cleveland Heights, OH 44118. 216/368-2077

SALMON, DAVID W. Consulting. PhD 1946, Stanford U. INT: arb/med, coll barg, intl comparative labor. Retired. 959 Altos Oaks Dr, Los Altos, CA 94022.

SALMON, KARL Bus:Pers/Ind Rels; Acad: Ind Rels. BS 1974, Penna State U; MA 1981, St. Francis Coll. INT: personnel, coll barg, arb/med. ASSN: Ind Rels Council of York; Ind Mgmt Club of York. POSITIONS: Trng Coordinator, Penna Dept of Transportation, 1975; Dir of Pers, County of York, 1976; and (since 1979) Director of Pers & Ind Rels, Teledyne Readco, 901 S Richland Ave, York, PA 17405. 717/848-2801

SALSBERG, RICHARD M. Legal Practice; Acad: Law, Ind Rels. BS 1967 Cornell; JD 1970, SUNY-Buffalo. INT: coll barg, arb/med, labor law. ASSN: NJ State Bar Assn, Bergen Cty Bar Assn, Cornell Alumni Assn. POSITION: (since 1979) Partner, Aron & Salsberg, Esqs., 684 Passaic Ave, Nutley, NJ 07110. 201/667-3600

SALSBURG, SIDNEY W. Consulting, Bus:Pers/-Ind Rels. BA 1946, Mich State U; MA 1947, PhD 1954, U of Wis. INT: coll barg, personnel, health & hosp care. ASSN: Chicago IRRA, AEA, Human Resource Mgmt Assn. POSITIONS: Mgr, Research, Systems & Planning, Ind Rels Office, Chrysler Corp, 1959; and (since 1980) Senior Assoc, Bauer/Lawrence Assoc. ADDRESS: 248 Benham Court, St. Charles, IL 60174. 312/584-7440

SALTEN, DAVID G. Acad: Univ Admin. POSITION: Exec Vice Pres & Provost, NY Inst of Technology, Old Westbury, NY 11568.

SALTZMAN, ARTHUR WILLIAM Bus: Manpower. POSITION: Consultant, 30630 Woodside Dr, Franklin, MI 48025. 313/626-1153

SALTZMAN, GREGORY MARTIN Acad: Ind Rels, Econ. SB, SM 1976, MIT; PhD 1982, U of Wis-Madison. INT: coll barg, govt labor policy, health & hosp care. ASSN: Boston IRRA, Acad of Mgmt. POSITIONS: Instructor, Faculty of Labor & Human Resources, Ohio State U, 1981; and (since 1982) Asst Prof, The Heller School, Brandeis Univ, Waltham, MA 02254. 617/647-2116

SAMMIS, ROBERT LYLE Union. 630 E Garfield Ave, #12, Glendale, CA 91205.

SAMOFF, BERNARD L. Acad: Univ Admin; Arbitration. EdM 1937, Temple U; MA 1961, PhD 1963, U of Penna. PUBL: Unionizing the Armed Forces, (co-editor w E. Krendel), U of Penna Press, 1977; "Appointing NLRB Regional Directors," LLJ, 1975; "What Lies Ahead for the NLRB," LLJ 1974. INT: labor law, mgmt/educ, arb/med. ASSN: Philadelphia IRRA, ASPA, Acad of Mgmt, Amer Pol Sci Assn. POSITIONS: Field Examiner, 1942, Regional Dir, NLRB, 1963; and (since 1974) Adjunct Prof and Assoc Chairman, Wharton School, Univ of Penna. ADDRESS: 7966 Gilbert St, Philadelphia, PA 19150. 215/898-7740

SAMPSON, MERLE A. Bus:Mgmt/Admin. BA 1970, MAIR, 1972, U of Minn. INT: health & hosp care, org beh, ind psych. ASSN: Twin Cities Pers Assn. POSITIONS: VP-Trust Systems, Northwest Bank Corp, 1980, VP-Natl Accounts, Northwest Bank, 1981; and (since 1983) Director, Finance and Admin, Good Neighbor Services, 2177 Youngman Ave, St. Paul, MN 55116. 612/698-6544

SANCHEZ, JULIAN P. Bus:Pers/Ind Rels; Acad: Ind Rels. BA 1978, U of N. Mex; MBA 1980, Ohio State U. INT: labor rels, labor law, personnel. ASSN: Ohio IRRA, Amer Compensation Assn. POSITIONS: Empl Rep, Pacific Gas & Electric, 1980; Sr. Job Analyst, 1981, and, since 1983, Labor Rels Specialist, Sandia Natl Laboratories, also, currently, Prof of Pers & Labor Rels, Webster Coll. ADDRESS: 11108 Orr NE, Albuquerque, NM 87111. 505/844-4336

SANDERS, ELLEN M. Union. BA 1976, Marymount Manhatten Coll; RN 1963, Mt. Sinai Hosp School of Nursing. PUBL: "Statewide," Publ of NYSNA E & GW Program; "Vital Signs, "Publ of NYSNA E & GW Program. INT: coll barg, health & hosp care, union org/admin. ASSN: New York IRRA, Amer Nurses Assn, NY State Nurses for Political Action, Amer Soc of Law & Medicine. POSITIONS: Nursing Rep, 1977, Regional Coordinator, 1978, and, since 1981, Assoc Dir, Econ & General Welfare Program, New York State Nurses Assn. ADDRESS: 15 West 72nd St, New York, NY 10023. 212/460-5990

SANDERS, KENNETH M. Bus:Mgmt/Admin, Pers/Ind Rels, Consulting. BS 1969, Jackson State U-Miss; JD 1977, De Pawl U. INT: labor law, mgmt/educ, coll barg. ASSN: Amer Mgmt Assn, Ind Rels Assn of Chicago; Conference of Pers Officers. POSITIONS: Mgr, Labor Rels, Lynchburg Foundry Co, 1979; Corp Mgr, Labor Rels, 1981, and, since 1982, Corporate Director Labor Rels, Interstate United Corp, 120 South Riverside Plaza, Chicago, IL 60606. 312/930-2333

SANDLER, MELVIN Acad: Ind Rels. MA 1947 Northwestern U. INT: personnel, empl/trng programs, coll barg. ASSN: ASTD, ASPA, AICPA. POSITIONS: Dir Pers, FMC Corp, 1947; Consultant, Amer Hotel/Motel Corp, 1967; and (since 1972) Assoc Prof, School Bus & Econ, McConnell Hall, Durham, NH 03824. 603/862-2352

SANDVER, MARCUS H. Acad: Ind Rels. BA 1970, Pacific Lutheran U; MS 1973, U of Colo; PhD 1976, U of Wis-Madison. PUBL: "Factors Associated with Outcomes in NLRB Election," (w H.G. Heneman III), ILRR, July, 1983; "Arbitrators Background and Behavior," (w H.G. Heneman III), JLR, Dec 1983; "Time and Cost Savings Through Expedited Arbitration Procedures," Arb J, Dec 1981. INT: coll barg, labor law, arb/med. ASSN: Central Ohio IRRA, Acad of Mgmt, Assn for Bus Simulation and Experiential Learning. POSITIONS: Res Asst, U of Wis, 1973; Asst Prof, 1976, and, since 1982, Assoc Prof of Mgmt and Human Resource, Ohio State Univ. ADDRESS: 1961 Berkshire Rd, Columbus, OH 43221. 614/422-2809

SANO, JOSEPH B. Union, Bus:Pers/Ind Rels, Mgmt/Admin. BA 1970, MA 1973, SUNY-Albany. INT: union org/admin, coll barg, personnel. ASSN: Capital Dist IRRA. POSITIONS: Field Rep, 1982, and, since 1983, Executive Dir, Public Employees Federation, AFL-CIO, 159 Wolf Rd, Albany, NY 12205. 518/459-5412

SANTER, MARK Arbitration. BS 1938, Boston U. PUBL: "Municipal Collective Bargaining," Chapter VII, Boston Coll, 1968. INT: arb/med, coll barg, labor history. ASSN: Boston IRRA, NAA, SPIDR, AAA. POSITIONS: Inspector, Wage-Hour/USDL, 1941-47; Mediator, Mass Board of Con & Arb, 1947-67; and, currently, Arbitrator, 101 Chestnut St, K-6 Foxboro, MA 02035. 617/784-5343

SANTOS, RICHARD Acad: Econ, Ind Rels; Consulting. BA 1969, U of Tex; MLIR, 1975, PhD 1977, Mich State U. PUBL: "Estimating Youth Employment and Unemployment," Rev of Public Data use, 10:1982, 127-35; "Earnings Among Spanish Origin Males in the Midwest," Soc Sci J, Apr 1982; "Measuring the Employment Status of Youth-CPS vs the NLS," IRRA, Sept, 1980. INT: labor market econ, empl/trng programs, coll barg. ASSN: Austin IRRA. POSITIONS: Sr Res Assoc, Center for Human Resource Res, Ohio State Univ, 1979-82; and (since 1976) Asst Prof, Dept of Econ, Univ of Texas, Austin, TX 78712. 512/471-3211

SANTOS, SCOTT STUART Bus:Pers/Ind Rels. BS 1977, LeMoyne Coll; MLIR 1980, Mich State U. 8734 Bellanca Ave, Los Angeles, CA 90045.

SAPIRO, BERNARD L. Union. INT: union org/admin. ASSN: Los Angeles IRRA. POSITION: (since 1970) President, Printing Specialities & Paper Products Union Local #388, 12440 Firestone Blvd, East Bldg #3010, Norwalk, CA 90650. 213/863-4821

SARIANO, JOHN P. Government. BA 1968, St. Mary Coll; MA 1976, St. Francis Coll. INT: arb/med, coll barg, labor law. ASSN: Harrisburg IRRA. POSITION: (since 1979) Labor Rels Coordinator, Penna Dept of Labor & Industry, 7th & Forest Sts, Harrisburg, PA 17121. 717/787-8769

SATO, FRANCES F. Bus:Mgmt/Admin. POSITION: Employee Rels Officer, CSU Sacramento, 6000 Jay St, Sacramento, CA 95819.

SAUERESSIG, ROBERT Acad: Org Beh/Pers, Ind Rels. PhD 1969, U of Wis-Madison. INT: personnel, coll barg, org beh. ASSN: Acad of Mgmt, Inst of Mgmt Sciences, Midwestern Psych Assn. POSITIONS: Visiting Prof, Mgmt Studies, Univ of Leeds, England, 1983, and, since 1965, Prof of Mgmt, Coll of Bus & Econ, Univ of Wis, Whitewater, WI 53190. 414/472-3983

SAUNDERS, CHERYL S. Bus:Pers/Ind Rels. PO Box 917, Chewelah, WA 99109.

SAUNDERS, W. PHILLIP JR. Acad: Econ. BA 1956, Penna State U; MA 1957, U of Ill; PhD 1964, MIT. INT: labor market econ, labor history, union org/admin. ASSN: AEA. POSITIONS: Instructor in Econ, Bowdoin Coll, 1961; Asst & Assoc Prof, Carnegie-Mellon U, 1962; and (since 1970) Prof of Econ, Indiana Univ, Bloomington, IN 47401. 812/335-4050

SAUTER, JEROLD B. Union. Carpenters Local 1226, 1226 W Southmore, Pasadena, CA 77502.

SAVAS, D. THOMAS Bus:Mgmt/Admin; Acad: Ind Rels, Org Beh/Pers. PhD 1947 U of Wis. INT: coll barg, ind sociol, labor market econ. POSITIONS: VP, Pers & Ind Rels, Walker Mfg Co, 1986; VP, Pers & Ind Rels, 1972, and, since 1975, Senior Vice-Pres, Corporate Rels, Newport News Shipbuilding and Dry Dock Co, 4101 Washington Ave, Newport News, VA 23607. 804/380-2200

SAVOIE, ERNEST J. Bus:Pers/Ind Rels. MSIR 1955, Cornell U. PUBL: "The New Ford-UAW Agreement: Its Worklife Aspects," Work Life Rev, vol 1, #1, 1982; "A Progress Report on the UAW-Ford Employe Development and Training Program," Amer Productivity Center, 1982; "A Company and A Union Run a Program (The UAW-Ford Center)," In The Dislocated Worker, W. H. Kolberg, ed, 1984. INT: coll barg, empl/trng programs, org beh. POSITION: (since 1979) Dir, Labor Rels Planning & Employment Office, Labor Rels Staff, Ford Motor Co, The American Rd, Dearborn, MI 48121. 313/322-6593

SAWKA, JACOB R. Bus:Pers/Ind Rels. BS 1968, Wayne State U. POSITION: Division Manager, Labor Rels, Michigan Bell Telephone Co, 444 Michigan Ave, Room 1620, Detroit, MI 48226.

SAXBERG, BORJE OSVALD Acad: Org Beh/Pers; Government. BA 1950, Swedish School of Bus & Econ; BS 1952, Ore State U; MS 1953, PhD 1958, U of Ill. PUBL: Personality and Leadership Behavior (w H.P. Knowles); "University Interdisciplinary Research," (w Newell), Environmental Sci & Tech; "Human Relations and the Nature of Man," (w H. P. Knowles), Harvard Bus Rev. INT: mgmt/educ, ind sociol, org beh. ASSN: Acad of Mgmt, Amer Sociol Assn, Soc for Applied Anthropology. POSITION: (since 1962) Prof of Mgmt and Org, Grad School of Bus, Univ of Washington, DJ-10, Seattle, WA 98195. 206/543-4470

SAXTON, WILLIAM M. Legal Practice. AB 1949, JD 1952, U of Mich. INT: labor law, coll barg, arb/med. ASSN: Detroit IRRA, Amer Coll of Trial Lawyers, ABA (Labor Law Section), AAA. POSITIONS: Assoc Attorney, Love, Snyder & Lewis, 1952; and (since 1953) Vice Pres, Butzel, Long, Gust, Klein & Van Zile, P.C., 1881 First Natl Bldg, Detroit, MI 48226. 313/963-8142

SCALONE, JOHN A. J. Scalone & Assoc, 60 Loma Vista Dr, Orinda, CA 94563.

SCANNELL, RAYMOND MATTHEW Trade Assoc. BSC 1957, Loyola U-Chicago. INT: govt labor policy. ASSN: Chicago IRRA. POSITIONS: Dir, Empl Services, Chicago Commission on Human Rels, 1964-74; and (since 1975) Director, EEO Programs, Construction Employers Assn, 203 N Wabash, Chicago, IL 60601. 312/-782-6152

SCARPELLO, VIDA Acad: Ind Rels, Org Beh/Pers, Sociology. PhD 1980, U of Minn. PUBL: "Who Benefits from Participation in Long Term Human Process Interventions?" Group and Org Studies, 1983, 8, 21-44; "Job Satisfaction: Are All the Parts There?" (w J. P. Campbell), Pers Psych, 1983, 36,3, 577-600; "Toward Understanding the Contents of the Black Box for Predicting Complex Decision Making Outcomes," (w R. N. Holt & R. J. Carroll, Decision Sciences, 1983, 14, 253-269. INT: personnel, org beh, arb/med. ASSN: Amer Psych Assn, Acad of Mgmt, Amer Inst for Decision Sciences. POSITION: (since 1979) Asst Prof, College of Bus Admin, Univ of Georgia, Athens, GA 30602. 404/542-1294

SCAVUZZO, ROSEMARY T. Bus:Pers/Ind Rels. BA 1983, U of Hawaii. INT: ind psych, empl/trng programs, personnel. ASSN: ASPA, ASTD. POSITION: (since 1976) Pers Asst, Theo. H. Davies & Co, Ltd., 841 Bishop St, Honolulu, HI 96813. 808/531-8531

SCHAEFER, STEPHEN C. Acad: Bus Admin. BBA 1967, U of Cincinnati; MA 1970, U of Ill. POSITION: (since 1973) Instructor & Chairman, Bus Dept, Contra Costa College, San Pablo, CA 94806. 415/235-7800

SCHAFFER, BEVERLY K. Acad: Econ; Arbitration. AB 1961, Wilson Coll; PhD 1967, Duke U. PUBL: "Negotiation Impasses: The Road to Resolution," J of Air Law and Commerce, Southern Methodist U School of Law, June 1982. INT: arb/med, coll barg, labor law. ASSN: Atlanta IRRA, SPIDR, SFLRP, Intl Soc for Labor Law and Soc Legislation. POSITION: (since 1965) Prof of Econ, Dept of Econ, Emory Univ, Atlanta, GA 30322. 404/329-6361

SCHANO, JOHN F. Arbitration. POSITION: Regional Dir, AAA, 221 Gateway 4, Pittsburgh, PA 15222.

SCHAUPP, DIETRICH L. Acad: Management, Ind Rels. Armstrong Hall, West Virginia Univ, Morgantown, WV 26506. 304/293-4092

SCHEER, ALAN I. Legal Practice. ASSN: Hartford IRRA. POSITION: Principal, Updike, Kelly & Spellacy, One State St, PO Box 31, Hartford, CT 06103. 203/548-2600

SCHELL, CATHERINE ANN Acad: Student; Consulting, Union. BS 1974, U of Wis-Milwaukee. INT: health & hosp care, union org/admin, coll barg. ASSN: Amer Nurses Assn. POSITIONS: Consultant, UW-School for Workers, 1982 to present, and, grad student, U of Wis-Madison. ADDRESS: 150 Lakewood Garden Ln, Madison, WI 53704. 608/244-4558

SCHELLACE, FRANK N. Government. BA 1975, SUNY-Stony Brook; JD 1978, Hofstra U. INT: labor law, arb/med, govt labor policy. ASSN: Long Island IRRA, ABA, New York State Bar Assn, Florida Bar Assn. POSITIONS: Consultant, Inter-City Testing & Consulting Corp, 1978; Law Asst to Justices, 1980, and, since 1984, Law Clerk to Justice Kenneth D. Molloy, New York State Supreme Court. ADDRESS: 59 Wellington Rd S, West Hempstead, NY 11552. 516/535-2870

SCHEMANSKE, JANE MARIE Student. BA 1983, U of Mich-Dearborn. INT: labor law, coll barg, arb/med. ASSN: Detroit IRRA, ASPA, Amer Soc for Public Admin. POSITIONS: Sales Asst, Welcor Inc, 1980; Labor Rels Res Asst (Internship), Livonia Civil Service Comm, 1982; and (since 1981) Pharmaceutical Technician, Specialized Pharmacy Services, Inc. ADDRESS: 12914 Hazelton, Detroit, MI 48223. 313/422-3310

SCHENONE, RONALD JOSEPH Bus:Pers/-Ind Rels. BS 1952, U of Santa Clara. INT: coll barg, arb/med, labor law. ASSN: San Francisco IRRA, Calif State Bar (Labor & Empl Law), SF Peninsula Empl Rels Council. POSITIONS: Chief Pers Rep, United Technology Center Div, United Aircraft Corp, 1970; and (since 1980) Manager, Empl Rels, United Technologies Chemical Systems. ADDRESS: 1493 Los Rios Dr, San Jose, CA 95120. 408/778-4196

SCHER, MARTIN H. Legal Practice. BA 1955, Yale U; JD 1960, Harvard U. INT: labor law, coll barg, arb/med. ASSN: Long Island IRRA, NYS Bar Assn, Nassau Cty Bar Assn, Nassau Lawyer's Assn. POSITIONS: Partner, Rains, Pogrebin & Scher, 1962-79; and (since 1979) Attorney, (own firm) 1 Old County Rd, Carle Place, NY 11514. 516/746-5040

SCHEUCH, RICHARD Acad: Econ; Mutual Funds. SB 1942, MA 1948, PhD 1952, Princeton. PUBL: Labor in the American Economy; "Labor Policies in Residential Construction." INT: coll barg, labor history, labor market econ. ASSN: Connecticut Valley IRRA, AEA, SPIDR, IIRA. POSITION: G. Fox & Co, Prof of Econ, Trinity College, 54 Westwood Road, Hartford, CT 06117. 203/527-3151

SCHIEMANN, WILLIAM A. Consulting, Bus:Pers/Ind Rels. PhD 1976, U of Ill. PUBL: Managing Human Resources: 1983 and Beyond; "Leader-Member Agreement: A Vertical Dyod Linkage Approach," J of Applied Psych, 63,(2) 1978, 206-212; "Why Internal Communications is Failing." INT: org beh, ind psych, personnel. ASSN: Amer Psych Assn, Acad of Mgmt, Intl Assn of Applied Psychologists. POSITIONS: Asst Prof, Ga Inst of Tech, 1976; Project Mgr, A T & T, 1977; and (since 1981) Vice Pres, Opinion Research Corp, Box 183, N Harrison St, Princeton, NJ 08540. 609/924-5900

SCHIMEL, RUTH MARA Consulting, Government; Acad: Org Beh/Pers. BS 1961, Cornell U; MA 1977, George Washington U. PUBL: "Testimony on Human Aspects of Office Automation," House Committee on Sci and Tech;

"Making Performance Evaluation Work Better: A Supervisor's Viewpoint," Public Pers Mgmt J, Winter 1982; Book Review on Role Transitions in Later Life in The Geronotologist, Vol 21, #4, 1981. INT: mgmt/educ, empl/trng programs, health & hosp care. ASSN: ASPA, SPIDR, Gerontological Soc of Amer. POSITIONS: Foreign Service Officer, Dept of State, 1963; Professional Lecturer, American Univ, 1983; and (since 1982) Founder, Evergreen Group. ADDRESS: Apt 514, 2555 Pennsylvania Ave NW, Washington DC 20037. 202/223-6274

SCHINELLA, MICHAEL R. Bus:Pers/Ind Rels. BS 1978, Ind State U; MA 1982, Central Mich U. INT: personnel, arb/med, coll barg. POSITIONS: Safety Engineer, 1981, Pers Planning/Recruitment Rep, 1981, and, since 1983, Labor-Rels Rep, Ford Motor Co. ADDRESS: 3832 Far Hill Dr, Bloomfield Hills, MI 48013.

SCHLENDER, WILLIAM E. Acad: Bus Admin. AB 1941, Valparaiso U; MBA 1947, U of Denver; PhD 1955, Ohio State U. PUBL: Elements of Managerial Action, (w M. J. Jucius), R.D. Irwin Co; Management in Perspective: Readings, (w W. G. Scott & A. G. Filley), Houghton Mifflin Co. INT: bus policy, org beh, coll barg. ASSN: Northeast Ohio IRRA, Amer Mgmt Assn, Acad of Mgmt, Intl Council of Small Bus Mgmt. POSITIONS: Prof & Chairman, Dept of Mgmt, U of Tex-Austin, 1965-68; Dean & Prof of Mgmt, James J. Nance Coll of Bus Admin, Cleveland State U, 1968-1976; and (since 1976) Richard E. Meier Prof of Mgmt, Coll of Bus Admin, Valparaiso Univ, Valparaiso, IN 46383. 219/464-5020

SCHLESINGER, CARL T. Training Production Empl; Acad: Labor Mgmt. BS 1981, Empire State Coll-SUNY. PUBL: Union Printers and Controlled Automation, (co-author), Kelber-Schlesinger, Free Press, 1967; "Interrelationship Between Advances in Newspaper Technology, Worker Satisfaction and Changing Requirements for Future Jobs," ILO Conference, Geneva, 1982. INT: empl/trng programs, labor educ, ind sociol. ASSN: New York IRRA, Natl Academy of TV, Arts and Sciences, Amer Printing History Assn, Intl Graphic Arts Educ Assn. POSITIONS: Information Officers, African Medical Res Found, Nairobi, Kenya, 1973; Chief Technical Advisor, Printing Trng Prog, African-Amer Labor Center, Wash DC/Nairobi, 1967; and (since 1977) Trainer, Production Employees, Composing Room, The New York Times. ADDRESS: 39 Myrtle St, Rutherford, NJ 07070. 212/556-7484

SCHLIEP, R. L. Bus:Pers/Ind Rel, Mgmt/-Admin. BS 1966, Colo State U. POSITIONS: Mgr, Bus Centers-Empl Rels, 1977, Mgr Chemical Products, Empl Rels, 1979, and, since 1981, Manager, Industrial Rels, Shell Oil Co, PO Box 100, Deer Park, TX 77536. 713/476-6854

SCHMIDMAN, JOHN T. Acad: Labor Studies. PhD 1968, U of Wis. PUBL: Unions in Postindustrial Society, Penn State Press, 1979; Labor Law, Union Leadership Acad, 1980; "Entrepreneurship or Autonomy: Truckers and Cabbies," in P. L. Stewart & M. G. Cantor (eds) Varieties of Work, Sage Publ, 1982. INT: labor educ, union org/admin, labor law. ASSN: Atlanta IRRA, Univ & Coll Labor Educ Assn, Assn for Evolutionary Econ. POSITION: (since 1982) Director and Prof of Labor Studies, Georgia State Univ, University Plaza, Atlanta, GA 30303. 404/658-3653

SCHMIDT, CHARLES T., JR Acad: Ind Rels; Arbitration. BS 1958, U of Mass; MBA 1962, Northeastern U; MILR 1964, Cornell U; PhD 1968, Mich State U. PUBL: A Guide to Collective Negotiations in Education, Mich State U, Soc Sci Center, 1967; Collective Bargaining in the Public Sector, Random House, 1969; Fact-Finding and Ad. Arbitration in Conn Public Labor Disputes, U of Conn, 1974. INT: coll barg, arb/med, intl comparative labor. ASSN: SPIDR, AEA, IIRA. POSITIONS: Asst Prof/Lecturer, Ind Rels, SLIR, Mich State U, 1964-67; Sr. Tech Advisor, Ind Rels, ILO/-Republic of Zambia, 1975-78; and (since 1968) Prof of Ind Rels, Univ of Rhode Island. ADDRESS: 57 Ann La, North Kingston, RI 02852. 401/792-2068

SCHMIDT, ROBERT F. Acad: Univ Admin. BS 1965, U of Wis-Milwaukee. INT: personnel, org beh, health & hosp care. ASSN: Wisconsin IRRA, Coll & Univ Pers Assn, ASPA, Admin Mgmt Soc. POSITIONS: Pers Coordinator, 1965, Manager of Pers, Univ of Wis-Milw, 1972; and (since 1976) Director of Personnel/Affirmative Action Officer, Medical Coll of Wisconsin, 8701 W Watertown Plank Rd, Milwaukee, WI 53226. 414/257-8244

SCHMIDT, STUART MAXWELL Acad: Org Beh/Pers, Ind Rels; Consulting. BA 1965, MS 1969, PhD 1973, U of Wis. PUBL: "Patterns of Managerial Influence," Organizational Dynamics, Winter 1984; "An Influence Perspective on Bargaining Within Organizations," in Bazerman & Lewick (eds) Negotiating in Organizations, Sage 1983; "Why Do I Like Thee?" J of Applied Psych, 1981. INT: org beh, union org/admin, ind psych. ASSN: Acad of Mgmt. POSITION: (since 1973) Professor, IROB Dept/-SBA, Temple Univ, Philadelphia, PA 19122. 215/787-1621

SCHMIDT, THOMAS J. Bus:Pers/Ind Rels. BBA 1979, MSBA 1984, Temple U. INT: labor law, coll barg, arb/med. POSITIONS: Labor Rels Examiner, Consolidated Rail Corp, 1979; and (since 1983) Labor Rels Officer, New Jersey Transit Rail Operations Inc. ADDRESS: 807 Longshore Ave, Philadelphia, PA 19111. 201/648-7768

SCHMITT, JOHN W. Union. ASSN: Wisconsin IRRA. POSITION: (since 1966) President, Wisconsin State AFL-CIO, 6333 W. Bluemound Rd, Milwaukee, WI 53213. 414/771-0700

SCHNECK, DAVID M. Arbitration. INT: arb/med. ASSN: AAA, SPIDR. POSITION: Arbitrator, 2030 S 2nd St, Allentown, PA 18103. 215/797-5394

SCHNEIDER, BETTY V. H. Acad: Ind Rels. AB 1949, U of Calif-Berkeley; PhD 1954, U of London. PUBL: "Public Sector Labor Legislation-An Evolutionary Analysis," in Public Sector Bargaining, BNA & IRRA, 1978; California Public Employee Relations, (editor); As B. V. Humphreys, Clerical Unions in the Civil Service, Oxford: Basil Blackwell, 1958. INT: coll barg, labor law, arb/med. ASSN: San Francisco IRRA, SPIDR, Intl Soc for Labor Law and Soc Security. POSITIONS: Lecturer, Labor Econ, Mills Coll, 1968; Res Economist, 1954, and, since 1968, Director, Calif Public Employees Rels Program, Inst of Ind Rels, Univ of Calif, Berkeley, 2521 Channing, Berkeley, CA 94720. 415/642-0323

SCHNEIDER, DONALD J. Consulting. BA 1979, Hamilton Coll; MA 1980, U of Warwick. PUBL: "Self-Help Cooperatives," in Worker Cooperatives in America, ed by Jackall & Levin, 1984; "Canadian and U. S. Brands of Unionism Have Distinctly Different Nationalities," Mgmt Rev, Oct 1983. INT: org beh, coll barg, intl comparative labor. ASSN: New York IRRA. POSITION: (since 1981) Consultant, Organization Resources Counselors, Inc. ADDRESS: 112 W 72nd St, Apt 12F, New York, NY 10023. 212/7193400

SCHNEIDER, KENNETH B. Consulting. BGS 1976, U of Nebr-Omaha; MA 1977, U of Nebr-Lincoln. INT: union org/admin, labor educ, health & hosp care. ASSN: Acad of Mgmt, AEA. POSITIONS: Instructor, Creighton Coll, 1978; Asst Prof, Canisius Coll, 1980; and (since 1982) President, K. B. Schneider, Consultant, 114 Elmwood Park East, Tonawanda, NY 14150. 716/695-3220

SCHNEIDER, STEPHEN A. Consulting, Bus:Mgmt/Admin. BSIM 1971, MBA 1972, U of Cincinnati; PhD 1965, U of Penna. PUBL: Alternative Mechanisms for Financing Public Social Services; CETA Program Analysis Guide; The Availability of Minorities and Women for Professional and Managerial Positions, 1970-1985. INT: labor market econ, govt labor policy, empl/trng programs. POSITIONS: Staff Assoc in Empl Policy, Brookings Inst, 1977; St Assoc & Chief Economist, CSR, Inc. 1978; and (since 1984) Managing Assoc, Robert R. Nathan Assoc Inc. ADDRESS: 649 A St NE, Washington DC 20002. 202/393-2700

SCHNELL, JOHN F. Acad: Econ, Ind Rels. PhD 1983, U of Ill. INT: coll barg, labor market econ. POSITION: (since 1983) Asst Prof, Dept of Econ, 206 Maxwell Hall, Syracuse Univ, Syracuse, NY 13210. 315/423-2262

SCHNIPKE, GREGORY C. Bus:Pers/Ind Rels. BIA 1983, GMI Eng & Mgmt Inst. INT: personnel, empl/trng programs, coll barg. POSITIONS: Cooperative Student, 1978, Mfg Supr, General Motors Corp, 1983. ADDRESS: 392B Great Rd, Acton, MA 01720.

SCHOEBERLEIN, WILLIAM F. Legal Practice. INT: labor law, arb/med, coll barg. POSITION: Partner, Sherman & Howard, 2900 Intrawest Tower, 633 17th St, Denver, CO 80202. 303/893-2900

SCHOEN, STERLING H. Acad: Org Beh/-Pers, Ind Rels, Bus Admin. MA 1941, U of Wis; MBA 1943, PhD 1953, U of Mich. PUBL: Labor Relations Negotiations Simulator, 1983; Cases in Collective Bargaining and Industrial Relations, 1982; Cases and Policies in Human Resources, 1982. POSITION: Prof of Mgmt, Grad School of Bus Admin, Washington Univ, St. Louis, MO 63130. 314/725-7908

SCHOLTZ, EDWARD Arbitration. BS 1961, MBA 1963, JD 1967, U of Calif-Berkeley. INT: arb/med. ASSN: Southern Calif, Orange Cty IRRA, AAA, Natl Mediation Board. POSITIONS: Attorney, Reich, Adell & Crost; Labor Attorney, CBS Inc; and (since 1980) Arbitrator, 205 38th St, Manhatten Beach, CA 90266. 213/546-6529

SCHOR, ROBERT M. Arbitrator, PO Box 21, West Hartford, CT 06107.

SCHRAMM, CARL JUDE Acad: Law, Public Health. BS 1968, LeMoyne U; MS, 1969, PhD 1973, U of Wis; JD 1978, Georgetown U. INT: health & hosp care. ASSN: Maryland IRRA, AEA, AAA, ABA. POSITION: (since 1972) Assoc Prof & Dir, Center for Hospital Finance and Mgmt, Johns Hopkins Univ. ADDRESS: Room 302, Hampton House, 624 N Broadway, Baltimore, MD 21205. 301/955-2300

SCHRAMM, LEROY H. Acad: Univ Admin, Law, Ind Rels. MA 1968, SUNY-Albany; PhD 1972, Cornell; JD 1977, W. Mitchell School of Law. PUBL: "Job Rights of Strikers in the Public Sector," 31 ILRR 322, 1978; "Is Teacher Tenure Negotiable?" 6 J of Coll Neg, 245, 1977; "Authorization Cards as Valid Indicator of Union Majorities," 20 Syracuse L.R. 577, 1968. INT: labor law, coll barg, labor history. ASSN: Montana Arb Assn, Natl Assn of Coll & Univ Attorneys. POSITIONS: Labor Committee Counsel, Minn House of Rep, 1973-78; Chief State Labor Negotiator, 1978, and, since 1981, Chief Legal Counsel, Montana Univ System. ADDRESS: 1000 9th Ave, Helena, MT 59601. 406/449-3024

SCHRAMM, STEVEN EDWARD Bus:Pers/-Ind Rels. MSIR 1982, U of Wis-Madison. INT: coll barg, labor law, personnel. POSITION: (since 1983) Pers Rep, Pacific Gas & Electric Co, 1401 Fulton St, Fresno, CA 93760. 209/268-0441 ext 270

SCHRAUF, JEREMY P. Government. BS 1961, RensselaerPolytech Inst, MA 1975, SUNY-Albany. INT: labor market econ, coll barg, intl comparative labor. ASSN: NY Capital Dist IRRA, IPMA, TORCH Intl, State Acad for Public Admin. POSITIONS: Asst Chief Budget Examiner, Div of the Budget, 1975, and, since 1979, Research Dir, NYS Governor's office of Empl Rels, 2 Empire State Plaza, Albany, NY 12223. 518/473-7233

SCHRIESHEIM, CHESTER A. Acad: Org Beh/Pers, Ind Rels, Bus Admin. BS 1967, MBA 1968, Mich State U; PhD 1978, Ohio State U. PUBL: "Job Satisfaction, Attitudes Toward Unions, and Voting in a Union Representation Election," J of Applied Psych, 63, 548-552, 1978. INT: union org/admin, personnel, method/-statis. ASSN: Amer Psych Assn, Amer Sociol Assn, Acad of Mgmt. POSITIONS: Asst Prof, Kent State U, 1976; Assoc Prof, U of Southern Calif, 1978; and (since 1982) Assoc Prof, Dept of Mgmt, Coll of Bus Admin, Univ of Florida, Gainesville, FL 32611. 904/392-0163

SCHRIVER, WILLIAM RAGAN INT: empl/trng programs, coll barg, labor market econ. POSITIONS: Dir, Center for Manpower Studies, Memphis State U, 1970; Mgr, Cons't Labor Demand System, TVA, 1973; and (since 1980) Research Dir, Construction Resources Analysis, Room 9GBA, Univ of Tenn, Knoxville, TN 37996. 615/974-4422

SCHROEDER, HAROLD H. Arbitration, Consulting. EE 1931, U of Akron. PUBL: Arbitration J, AAA, 1982. ASSN: Florida IRRA, AAA, SPIDR. POSITIONS: Asst VP-Pers, AT&T Co, 1924-1968; Labor Arbitrator (self employed), 389 Bob White Dr, Sarasota, FL 33577. 813/366-8168

SCHULMAN, ROSALIND SADOFF Acad: Econ. AB 1934, Smith Coll; MA 1937, Columbia; PhD 1964, U of Penna. POSITIONS: Dir of Research (Natl) IUMSWA, AFL-CIO, 1943-64;

Econ Consultant, Joint State Govt Comm, General Assn of Penna; and Prof; Dept of Econ, Drexel Univ. Retired. ADDRESS: Suite 8-B-25, 2401 Pennsylvania Ave, Philadelphia, PA 19130.

SCHULTZ, L. LAWRENCE Arbitration, Consulting; Acad: Law. BA 1941, Centre Coll; Cert, 1956, Ind Coll of Armed Forces; LLB 1962, LaSalle. PUBL: Conciliation of Labour Disputes, ILO Geneva; "Arbitration Trends: An Agency Perspective," LLJ V29, #8; "Problems Related to Remedy Powers," Annual Proceedings ALRA. INT: arb/med, labor law, coll barg. ASSN: SPIDR, SFLRP, AAA. POSITIONS: Exec Dir, Assn of Professional Engr Pers, 1957; Dir, Office of Arb Sevices, FMCS, 1961; and (since 1973) Adjunct Prof of Law, Washington Coll of Law, American Univ. ADDRESS: 3331 Reservoir Rd NW, Washington DC 20007. 202/337-8756

SCHUMACHER, A. REBECCA Acad: Economics. POSITION: School of Business, San Francisco State Univ, 1600 Holloway, San Francisco, CA 94132.

SCHUMANN, PAUL L. Acad: Ind Rels. BS 1977, Ill State U; MS 1980, PhD 1983, Cornell U. PUBL: Longer Hours or More Jobs? An Investigation of Amending Hours Legislation to Create Employment (w R. G. Ehrenberg), Ithaca, NY: ILR Press, 1982; "Compliance with the Overtime Pay Provisions of the Fair Labor Standards Act," (w R. G. Ehrenberg), J of Law and Econ, Apr 1982; "The Overtime Pay Provisions of the Fair Labor Standards Act," (w R. G. Ehrenberg), in S. Rottenberg (ed) The Economics of Legal Minimum Wages, AEI 1981. INT: labor market econ, method/statis, coll barg. ASSN: AEA, Econmetric Soc. POSITIONS: Instructor, 1981, and, since 1982, Asst Prof, Ind Rels Center, Univ of Minn, 549 Mgmt & Econ Bldg, 271 19th Ave South, Minneapolis, MN 55455. 612/373-0366

SCHUSTER, MICHAEL H. Acad: Ind Rels; Arbitration. BA 1972, U of RI; MS 1974, U of Mass; JD 1977, PhD 1979, Syracuse U. PUBL: Union-Management Cooperation: Structure, Process and Impact, W. E. Upjohn Inst of Empl Res, 1984; "The Impact of Union-Management Cooperation on Productivity and Employment," Ind and Labor Rels Rev, vol 36, #3, 1983, pp 415-430; Managing An Aging Workforce, (w M. Doering & S. Rhodes), Sage Publ, 1983. INT: coll barg, personnel, labor law. ASSN: Central New York IRRA, Acad of Mgmt. POSITION: (since 1979) Assoc Prof, School of Mgmt, Syracuse Univ. ADDRESS: 853 Livingston Ave, Syracuse, NY 13210. 315/423-7601

SCHUSTER, RICHARD N. Union, Consulting. AB 1962, Central Mission State. INT: coll barg, arb/med, labor law. POSITIONS: Consultant, Imperial Valley, 1976, Exec Dir, South Cty Teachers, 1979, and, since 1981, Consultant/Field Rep, Calif Teachers Assn/NEA, 630 J St, Eureka, CA 95501. 707/443-6341

SCHUTTE, ROBERT M. Government. 405 Kurt Dr, Pittsburgh, PA 15243.

SCHWAB, DONALD P. Acad: Ind Rels. BBA 1960, MS 1964, PhD 1968, U of Minn. PUBL: "Systematic Bias in Job Evaluation and Market Wages: Implications for the Comparable Worth Debate," J of Applied Psych, 1983, 68, 60-69; "Construct Validity in Organizational Behavior," in Staw, B & Cummings, L. L. (Eds.), Research in Organizational Behavior, (vol 2), Greenwich, CT, JAI Press, 1980, 3-43; "Between Subject Expectancy Theory Research: A Statistical Review of Studies Predicting Effort and Performance," (w Olian-Gottlieb, J.D. & Heneman, H.G. III), Psych Bull, 1979, 86, 139-147. INT: personnel, method/statis, ind psych. ASSN: APA, Acad of Mgmt, Soc of Org Beh. POSITION: (since 1982) Slichter Research Prof, Grad School of Bus, Univ of Wis, Madison, WI 53706. 608/263-3463

SCHWAB, ROBERT M. Union. ASSN: Miami IRRA. POSITION: Asst Business Manager, Hotel Employees Union, Local 355. ADDRESS: 3200 Collins Ave, #94, Miami Beach, FL 33140. 305/532-2476

SCHWAPPACH, ROY A., JR. Bus:Pers/Ind Rels. INT: arb/med, personnel, org beh. ASSN: Inland Empire IRRA, ASPA, Twin Cities Pers Admin. POSITIONS: Computer Tech, Dataserv Inc, Hopkins, MN, 1981; Prod Scheduler, 1983, and, since 1983, Ind Rels Rep, Kaiser Aluminum & Chemical Corp, PO Box 15108, Spokane, WA 99216. 509/927-6405

SCHWARTZ, ALLEN D. Legal Practice. POSITION: Attorney, Robbins, Schwartz, Nicholas, Lifton & Taylor, 29 S La Salle St, Chicago, IL 60603. 312/332-7760

SCHWARTZ, ARTHUR R. Acad: Econ, Ind Rels. MA 1972, PhD 1978, U of Mich. PUBL: "The Changing of the Guard: The New American Labor Leader;" "Labor Turnover: A New Measure;" "The Falling Share of Corporate Taxation." INT: coll barg, labor market econ, intl comparative labor. ASSN: AEA. POSITION: (since 1978) Asst Res Scientist, Univ of Mich. ADDRESS: 1256 Westport, Ann Arbor, MI 48103. 313/-763-4466

SCHWARTZ, GEORGE WILLIAM Union. Acad: Ind Rels. POSITION: Asst Dir Research Dept, United Auto Workers, Box 207, Chelsea, MI 48118. 313/926-5256

SCHWARTZ, HERB A. Mediation, Arbitration, Legal Practice. BA 1962, U of Chicago; JD 1966, Hastings Coll of Law. INT: arb/med, org beh, psychotherapy. ASSN: SPIDR, AAA, NLG. POSITIONS: Vice-Pres, Bernstein & Schwartz, 1970; Staff Attorney, Marcois, Chatsny & Dunnett, 1975; and (since 1983) Partner, Team Mediation. ADDRESS: 1524 Arch St, Berkeley, CA 94708. 415/644-8326

SCHWARTZ, MARVIN Legal Practice. 243 Waverly Place, New York, NY 10014. 212/242-1844

SCHWARTZ, ROSALIND M. Acad: Ind Rels. AB 1960, U of Mich; MEd 1962, Leslie Coll; MBA 1976, UCLA. PUBL: "EEO for the Handicapped," in 1980 Report: EEO and Affirmative Action, G. Leshin, UCLA Inst of Ind Rels, 1980, 297-348; Employee Discipline (co-author w Spitz & Miller), UCLA, IIR, 1981; Health Care and Industrial Rels (editor), UCLA IIR, 1981. INT: personnel, coll barg, mgmt/educ. ASSN: Southern Calif IRRA. POSITIONS: Senior Editor, 1977, and, since 1983, Coordinator, Inst of Ind Rels, Center for Mgmt Res and Educ, UCLA, 9244 Bunche Hall, Los Angeles, CA 90024. 213/825-3089

SCHWARTZ, SHARRON Bus:Mgmt/Admin. BA 1982, McGill U; MSIR 1984, U of New Haven. INT: arb/med, labor law, personnel. POSITIONS: Grad Student, 1982, U of New Haven; and (currently) Self-employed, 11 Woodlawn Ave, Ottawa, Ont K1S 2S8 Canada. 613/235-4462

SCHWARTZ, STANLEY J. Acad: Ind Rels; Arbitration, Consulting. BS 1950, MS 1951, U of Penna; EdD 1978, Temple U. PUBL: "Governance-Another View," Labor Law J, Oct 1980; "How to Dehire: A Guide for the Manager," Human Res Mgmt, Winter 1980; "Different Views of the Duty of Fair Representation," Labor Law J, July 1983. INT: coll barg, arb/med, labor law. ASSN: Philadelphia, Central New Jersey IRRA, AAA. POSITIONS: Dir of Ind Rels, Elco Corp, 1969; Pers Dir, Temple U, 1970; and (since 1978) Asst Prof of Mgmt and Ind Rels, Rider Coll. ADDRESS: 409 Glenway Rd, Erdenheim, PA 19118. 215/233-5085

SCHWARZ, JOSHUA L. Acad: Student, Ind Rels, Econ. BA 1979, SUNY-Binghamton; MS 1983, NYSSILR-Cornell. PUBL: "Public Sector Labor Markets," (co-author w R. G. Ehrenberg), in Handbook of Labor Econ, forthcoming; "Unions and Productivity in the Public Sector: The Case of Municipal Libraries," (w R. Ehrenberg & D. Sherman), Ind and Labor Rels Rev 34, Jan 1983, 199-220; "The Effect of Unions on Productivity in Municipal Public Libraries," (co-author w R. Ehrenberg) in Economics of Municipal Labor Markets, W. Hirsh & A. Rufolo, eds, UCLA Press, 1983. INT: coll barg, arb/med, labor market econ. POSITIONS: (since 1983) Adjunct Lecturer, School of Mgmt, SUNY-Binghamton. ADDRESS: 433 N Cayuga St, Ithaca, NY 14850. 607/798-2402

SCHWEINBERG, JOSEPH Student. 117 Delaware Ave, Oakmont, PA 15139. 412/828-2382

SCHWENK, ALBERT ERNEST Government. BA 1962, U of N Dak. PhD 1969, Washington State U. PUBL: "Effect of Unions on Wages in Hospitals," (w G. Cain et al, Res in Labor Econ, 1981; "Profit Rates and Negotiated Wage Changes," Quart Rev of Econ & Bus, Spring 1980; "Wage Rate Variation by Size of Establishment," (w W. R. Bailey), Ind Rels, Spring 1980. INT: labor market econ, coll barg, health & hosp care. POSITION: (since 1969) Economist, Office of Wages and Ind Rels, BLS, GAO Bldg, Room 1913, Washington DC 20212. 202/523-1220

SCHWINDT, ROBERT F. Bus:Pers/Ind Rels. AB 1951, U of Cincinnati; MBA 1953, U of Mich. POSITIONS: Dir, Admin, Sao Paulo, Brazil, 1972-73, Managing Dir, Columbia, SA-Bogota, 1974-76, Vice Pres, Empl Rels, 1979, and, currently, Corp Dir, Union Carbide Corp, Old Ridgebury Rd, Danbury, CT 06817.

SCHWOCHAU, SUSAN GERTRUDE Student. BS 1980, U of Minn. INT: coll barg, ind sociol, method/statis. ASSN: LIRA-U of Ill. POSITION: Teaching Asst, Inst of Labor & Ind Rels, Univ of Ill, 504 E Armory, Champaign, IL 61820.

SCIARRA, SILVANA Acad: Law. Law Degree 1972, U of Bari (Italy). PUBL: Democrazia Politica E Democrazia Industriale, (Ed) De Donato Bari, 1978; "The Rise of the Italian Shop Stewards," Ind Law J, 1977; Il Pluralisolo E Il Dirito Del Lavoro, Essays on O. Kahan-Freund, (Ed w Balandi), Roma 1982. INT: coll barg, labor law, intl comparative labor. ASSN: Assn Italiana di Diritto del Lavoro, Assn Italiana Studi de Relazion Ind. POSITION: (since 1983) Assoc Prof, Univ of Siena, Via Degli Alfani 63, 50121 Firenze, Italy. Phone 055/218464

SCOBEL, DONALD Consulting, Labor/Mgmt Cooperation. MSIR 1953, Cornell. PUBL: Creative Worklife, Gulf Publ, 1981; "Business and Labor: From Adversaries to Allies," Harvard Bus Rev, 1982; "Doing Away With Factory Blues," Harvard Bus Rev, 1975. INT: org beh, labor/mgmt cooperation, mgmt/educ. ASSN: ASTD, Org Development Inst, Certified Consultants Intl. POSITIONS: Mgr, Empl Rels Develop, Eaton Corp, 1955; and (since 1979) Director, Creative Worklife Center, 8925 Mentor Ave, Mentor, OH 44060. 216/255-4191

SCOTT, CURTIS ANTHONY Bus:Pers/Ind Rels. MA-LIR 1982, U of Ill-UC. INT: labor law, personnel, arb/med. POSITIONS: Grad Res Asst, Inst for Labor & IR, U of Ill, 1981; Human Resources Assoc, GTE Service Corp-Stamford, 1982, and, since 1983, Human Resource Administrator, GTE Telenet Communications Corp. ADDRESS: 2426 Ridge Hampton Ct, Reston, VA 22091. 703/442-1726

SCOTT, GEROLD G. Union. POSITION: Secretary-Treasurer, Teamsters Union Local 952, 140 S Marks Way, Orange, CA 92668.

SCOTT, HUGH THOMAS Bus:Mgmt/Admin, Consulting. BS 1980, St. Joseph's U. INT: labor law, org beh, labor market econ. ASSN: Philadelphia IRRA. POSITIONS: Dist Office Mgr, VASCO, Wynnwood, PA, 1970; Mgr, Customer Service Dept, Colonial Penn Ins Co, 1972; and (since 1981) Management Consultant, Alexander Proudfoot Co, Chicago. ADDRESS: Apt A24, 914 South Ave, Secane, PA 19018. 215/328-5994

SCOTT, MARY THOMAS Arbitration; Acad: Ind Rels. BS 1976, SUNY-Buffalo; MS 1982, Carnegie-Mellon U. INT: arb/med, coll barg, labor law. ASSN: Western New York IRRA. POSITIONS: Consultant/Intern, Buffalo-Erie County Labor-Mgmt Council, 1982; Instructor-Labor Seminar, Erie County Community Coll, 1983; and (since 1983) Arbitrator, PO Box 301, Grand Island, NY 14072. 716/773-1424

SCOTT, WILLIAM S. Bus:Pers/Ind Rels. INT: laborlaw, coll barg, arb/med. POSITIONS: Dist Op Mgr, 1943, and, since 1978, Asst Dir, Labor Rels, Bell Canada, F9 393 University Ave, Toronto, Ont M5G 1W9 Canada. 416/599-2008

SCOVILLE, JAMES GRIFFIN Acad: Ind Rels. AB 1961, Oberlin Coll; AM 1963, PhD 1965, Harvard U. PUBL: The Job Content of the U.S. Economy. 1969; The International Labor Movement in Transition, 1973; "A Review of International and Comparative Research," 1982 IRRA Res Rev Volume. INT: intl comparative labor, labor market econ. ASSN: AEA. POSITIONS: Asst Prof of Econ, Harvard, 1966; Assoc Prof and Prof, Labor & Ind Rels, U of Ill, 1969; and (since 1979) Prof of Ind Rels, 537 Bus Admin Bldg, Univ of Minn, 271 19th Ave S, Minneapolis, MN 55455. 612/373-5737

SCRUGGS, T.J. Bus:Pers/Ind Rels. POSITION: Manager Pers Rels, GAF Corp, PO Box 2141, Texas City, TX 77590.

SEARS, KELLY D. Legal Practice. Stubb & Mann, 435 Westport Rd, Kansas City, MO 64111.

SECKINGER, WILLIAM Bus:Pers/Ind Rels. POSITION: Manager, Human Resources, National Pipe & Tube, PO Box 1267, Liberty, TX 77575.

SEDGWICK, W. STEWART Retired. BS 1948, Ohio State U. INT: personnel, coll barg, arb/-med. ADDRESS: 7 Scott Rd, Newport News, VA 23606. 804/595-2196

SEDLMEIER, EDWARD JOHN Government, Acad: Econ. PhD 1973, Cornell U. INT: arb/med, coll barg. POSITIONS: Asst Prof of Econ, U of Ga, Athens, 1969; and (since 1973) Commissioner, FMCS. ADDRESS: 420 Augusta National Way, Knoxville, TN 37922. 615/558-1315

SEDWICK, THOMAS Acad: Ind Rels; Arbitration. BS 1964, Syracuse U; MA 1974, PhD 1978, Maxwell School-Syracuse U. PUBL: State Employee Labor Relations; "C. B. In The Public Sector-A Focus on States." INT: personnel, arb/med, coll barg. ASSN: Western Penna IRRA, ASPA, AAA. POSITIONS: Asst Prof, Pol Sci, Hartwick Coll, 1978; Asst Prof, Pol Sci, U of Scranton, 1979; and (since 1981) Assoc Prof, Ind & Labor Rels, Indiana Univ of Penna. ADDRESS: 79 Shady Dr, Indiana, PA 15701. 412/357-4471

SEE, KIM MARIE Bus:Pers/Ind Rels, Health Care;Pers/Labor Rels. BA 1977, MLIR 1983, Mich State U. INT: health & hosp care, personnel, labor law. ASSN: ASPA, West Central Fla Hosp Pers Dir Assn, Fla Hosp Assn/Pers Admin Council. POSITIONS: Labor Rels Rep, Ford Motor Co, 1977; Pers Dir, Three Rivers Area Hosp, 1979; and (since 1983) Personnel Director, Doctors Hosp of Sarasota. ADDRESS: 3421 Clark Rd, #222, Sarasota, FL 33581. 813/-366-1411

SEEBER, RONALD L. Acad: Ind Rels. BS 1975, Iowa State U; AM 1977, PhD 1980, U of Ill. PUBL: "Union Organizing in Manufacturing: 1973-76;" "The Decline in Union Success in NLRB Representation Elections;" "Concession Bargaining." INT: coll barg, union org/admin, arb/med. POSITION: (since 1980) Asst Prof, NYSSILR, Cornell Univ, PO Box 1000, Ithaca, NY 14853. 607/256-2240

SEEBORG, MICHAEL C. Acad: Economics. POSITION: Dept of Econ, Ball State Univ, Muncie, IN 47306.

SEGAL, ROBERT M. Legal Practice; Acad: Law. AB 1936, Amherst; LLB 1942, Harvard. PUBL: "Economics of Legal Profession;" "Labor Union Lawyers;" "Labor and the Media in the 80's." INT: labor law, coll barg, arb/med. ASSN: Boston IRRA, ABA, Boston Bar Assn, AM Judicature Soc. POSITIONS: Lecturer on Labor Law, Harvard Bus School, 1960-1980; and (since 1955) Senior Partner, Labor Law Firm, Segal, Roitman & Coleman, 11 Beacon St, Boston, MA 02108. 617/742-0208

SEGALLA, MICHAEL Acad: Student, Ind Rels; Bus:Pers/Ind Rels. INT: coll barg, arb/med, union org/admin. POSITION: Teaching Asst, Univ of Iowa, 651 Phillips Hall, Iowa City, IA 52242. 319/353-5090

SEGUR, W.H. Acad: Econ. 1274 W Monterey Ave, Stockton, CA 95204.

SEHAM, MARTIN C. Legal Practice. BA 1954, Amherst Coll; LLB 1957, Harvard U. PUBL: Federal Wage and Hour Laws, Prentice Hall, 1962; Law and Policy in International Business, Vol 6, #2, 1974; "Limitations Upon a Union's Right to Discipline Its Members," Proceedings of NYU 25th Conference on Labor, New York Univ, 1973. INT: labor law, coll barg, arb/med. ASSN: New York IRRA, NY City Bar Assn (Labor Law Committee), ABA (Committee on Railway Labor Act), New Jersey State Mediation Board. POSITIONS: Partner, Kopple & Seham, 1963, Partner, Surrey, Karasik, Morse & Seham, 1966, and, since 1979, Partner, Seham, Klein & Zelman, 485 Madison Avenue, New York, NY 10022. 212/935-6020

SEIBEL, LAURENCE E. Arbitration; Acad: Law. BS 1940, CCNY; JD 1946, George Washington U; LLM 1951 Harvard. INT: arb/med, coll barg, labor law. POSITION: Arbitrator, 5523 Uppingham St, Chevy Chase, MD 20815.

SEIDENBERG, JACOB Arbitration. BS 1937, Temple U; LLB 1940, U of Penna; PhD 1951, Cornell U. POSITION: Labor Arbitrator, 6318 Cavalier Corridor, Falls Church, VA 22044. 703/256-4467

SEIDMAN, BERT Union. BA 1938, MA 1941, U of Wis. INT: health & hosp care, income maintenance. ASSN: Wash DC IRRA. POSITIONS: European Econ Rep, 1962, Dir, Dept of Social Security, 1966, and, since 1983, Dir, Dept of Occupational Safety, Health and Social Security, AFL-CIO, 815 16th St NW, Washington DC 20006. 202/637-5200

SEIDMAN, MARSHALL J. Arbitration. BS 1947, Wharton School-U of PA; JD 1950, LLM 1970, Harvard. PUBL: The Law of Evidence in Indiana, Bobbs Merrill, 1977; "Federalism & Labor Relations," (w A. Cox), Harvard Law Rev, 1950; "The Duty of Fair Representation," AAA, 1983. INT: arb/med, labor law, coll barg. ASSN: NAA, ABA, Indiana Bar Assn. POSITIONS: Prof of Law, 1970-80, Assoc Dean, 1977-80, Indiana Univ School of Law; and (since 1980) Arbitrator (self-employed), 3215 Citadel Court, Indianapolis, IN 46268. 317/875-0164

SEIM, DOUGLAS ROCCO Student. 190 Pleasant Grove Rd, C-3, Ithaca, NY 14850.

SEINSHEIMER, WALTER G. Arbitration. POSITION: Arbitrator, State of Ohio, 105 E 4th St, Cincinnati, OH 45202. 513/421-0800

SEITZ, REYNOLDS C. Arbitration; Acad: Law. BA 1929, Notre Dame; MA 1932, Northwestern U; JD 1935, Creighton U. PUBL: Yearbook of School Law; Numerous articles as listed in index to legal periodicals. INT: arb/-med, labor education, labor law. ASSN: NAA, Natl Org on Legal Problems in Educ; Wis & Amer Bar Assn. POSITIONS: Assoc Prof, Northwestern U, 1943; Dean, Marquette Law School, 1953-66, and, since 1953, Prof of Law Emeritus, Marquette Univ Law School, 1103 W Wisconsin Ave, Milwaukee, WI 53233. 414/-224-3880

SEKAS, MARIA HELENE Acad: Student; Bus: Ind Rels. BS 1984, NYSSILR-Cornell. PUBL: "Dual Career Couples: A Corporate Challenge," Pers Admin, Apr 1984, pp 37-45. INT: coll barg, pers/human rels, mgmt/devel/relocation. POSITIONS: Labor Rels Asst, League of Voluntary Hosp & Homes of NY, 1982; specialist, Professional Rels, General Electric Co, 1982; and (since 1984) Labor Rels Staff Supr, AT&T Communications. ADDRESS: 122 Kensington Rd, Garden City, NY 11530.

SELBY, MARY E. Consulting. BSN 1972, Marillac Coll. INT: org beh, mgmt/educ, ind psych. ASSN: Human Resource Mgmt Assn of Chicago, IRRI Alumni Assn-U of Wis. POSITIONS: Dir of Educ Services, St. Vincent Hosp-Green Bay, 1977; Org Consultant, Intl Harvester, Chicago, 1981; and (since 1983) Consultant, Bauer & Assoc, Utica, NY. ADDRESS: 5325 N Wayne, Chicago, IL 60640.312/784-5859.

SELDIN, GILBERT J. Arbitration. BA 1934, CCNY, LLB-JD 1937, Brooklyn Law School. INT: arb/med, coll barg. POSITIONS: Asst Dir of Mediation Activity, FMCS, 1964; P.G. Co, PERB-Mediation Panel, 1975; and 9since 1972) Arbitrator (self-employed), 9346 Our Time Lane, Columbia, MD 21045. 301/997-0942

SELIGMAN, SIDNEY DAVID Bus:Pers/Ind Rels. AB 1971, MS 1975, Rutgers U. INT: coll barg, health & hosp care, labor law. ASSN: New Brunswick IRRA, Amer Soc for Hosp Admin. POSITIONS: Dir of Labor Rels, Bronx Municipal Hosp, 1977; Dir of Pers, St. Joseph's Med Center, 1980; and (since 1980) Vice Pres, Human Resources, Long Island Coll Hosp, Brooklyn. ADDRESS: 308 Sharon Ct, Woodbridge, NJ 07095. 212/780-1500

SELTZER, GEORGE O. Acad: Ind Rels. 1917 E River Rd, Minneapolis, MN 55414. 612/-332-8277

SELTZER, LOUIS E. Arbitration, Legal Practice. AB 1948, U of Penna; JD 1951 Harvard. INT: arbitration. ASSN: Philadelphia IRRA, Amer, Penna, Phila Bar Assns, Phila Trial Lawyers Assn, SPIDR. POSITION: (since 1951) Arbitrator/Attorney, 916 One E Penn Sq, Philadelphia, PA 19107. 215/563-9901

SEMERAD, DAVID Bus:Pers/Ind Rels. BSBA 1977, U of Nebr-Omaha. PUBL: "The Union Mechanical Contracting Industry: An Industry in Need of Reform," Construction Data and News, Jan 29, 1982, pp 6-8; "Eatin' Hotdogs, Drinkin Beer and Talkin' Loud," Contractor Daily, Feb, 1983, pp 1-2. INT: coll barg, org beh/pers, labor market econ. ASSN: Amer Soc of Heating, Refrigeration, and Air Conditioning Engineers. POSITIONS: Safety Dir, Univ Nebr Medical Center, 1975; Ind Rels Mgr, J. A. Jones/Boecon, 1976; and (since 1979) Executive Vice Pres, Mechanical Contractors Assn of Wash, 200 W Mercer, Seattle, WA 98119. 206/284-6291

SEN, JOYA Acad: Ind Rels, Org Beh/Pers; Consulting. PhD 1983, U of Toronto. PUBL: Youth Unemployment: Importance of Education in Canadian Labour Market Adjustment, O.I.S.E. Press, Toronto, June 1982; "The Price of Canadian Experience: Income and Wage Differentials Between Native Canadians and Immigrants by Education and Skill," RIKKA J, Autumn/Winter, vol IV; Women's Participation in the Canadian Labour Market and Barriers to Their Unionization," 1984. INT: union org/-admin, empl/trng programs, labor market econ. ASSN: Canadian Ind Rels Assn, AEA, Canadian Assn of Studies in Asia. POSITIONS: Visiting Asst Prof, Faculty of Bus, U of Alberta, 1981; and (since 1984) Asst Prof, Faculty of Commerce/Admin, Mgmt Dept, Concordia Univ, 7141 Sherbrooke St West, Montreal PQ H4B 1R6, Canada.

SENIOR, KENT RICHARD Bus:Pers/Ind Rels. BS 1975, Georgetown U. INT: intl comparative labor, coll barg, union org/admin. ASSN: San Francisco IRRA. POSITIONS: Special Asst to Pres, Building & Construction Trades Dept, 1978, Asst to the Reg Dir, Dept of Intl Affairs, AFL-CIO, 1979; and (since 1982) Ind Rels Rep, Guy F Atkinson Co of Calif, PO Box 593, South San Francisco, CA 94083. 415/876-1169

SENS, JAMES F. Bus:Pers/Ind Rels, Union. Associated, 1981, Cuyahuga Comm Coll. INT: health & hosp care, union org/admin, coll barg. ASSN: Lake County Professional Communicators Club. POSITIONS: Empl Benefit Rep, White Motor Co, 1963; and (since 1978) Dist Enrollment Mgr, Kaiser Foundation Health Plan of Ohio, PO Box 5309, Cleveland, OH 44101. 216/621-5600

SEREDIAK, MARTIN S. Acad: Ind Rels, Econ; Consulting. BA 1969, Simon Fraser U; MA 1970, U of Calgary; PhD 1978, U of Mich. PUBL: "Impact of Micro Electronic Technology on Labour-Management Relations in the White Collar Occupations;" "Bargaining and the Professional Employee: Alberta;" "The Quality of Working Life at the Alberta Childrens Hospital." INT: coll barg, arb/med, intl comparative labor. ASSN: Canadian Ind Rels, Assn, Econ Soc of Alberta, Canadian Labour Studies Committee. POSITIONS: Assoc Program Coordinator, U of Mich, 1978; Dir, Centre for Labour-Mgmt Rels, 1979, and, since 1981, Cordinator, Dept of Econ, Mount Royal College, 4825 Richard Rd SW, Calgary, Alberta T3E 6K6 Canada. 403/240-6535

SERRA, ANTHONY T. Bus:Mgmt/Admin. BA 1967, U of Pittsburgh; MA 1983, U of Penna. INT: labor history, union org/admin, arb/med. ASSN: Western Penna IRRA, ILO, Amer Production and Inventory Control Soc. POSITIONS: Teacher, St. James School, Sewickley, 1970, Teacher, SS Simon and Jude School, Blairsville, 1971; and (since 1973) Inv Control Supr, Season-All Industries. ADDRESS: Rte 2, Box 205, Indiana, PA 15701. 412/349-4600

SERUMGARD, JOHN R. Trade Assn, Pers/Ind Rels. AB 1966, JD 1969, LLM, Georgetown U. INT: coll barg, govt labor policy, labor law. ASSN: Washington DC IRRA, ABA, Fed Bar Assn, Dist of Columbia Bar Assn. POSITION: (since 1975) Vice-Pres, Ind Rels & Treasurer, Rubber Manufacturers Assn Inc, 1400 K St NW, Suite 900, Washington DC 20005. 202/828-7752

SEXTON, JEAN Acad: Ind Rels, Assoc Editor; Arbitration. MA 1969, Laval U; PhD 1974, Cornell U. PUBL: La Securite D'emploi Dans L'industrie de la Construction au Quebec, PUL, 1983; Le Comite Syndical-Patronal de L'industrie Lanadienne des Textiles, Labour Canada, 1982; "Positions syndicales relatives aux licenciements collectifs," Document P, Montreal, vol 6, #8-9, Apr-May 1982. INT: coll barg, arb/med, labor market econ. ASSN: IIRA, Conference des Arbitres du Quebec, Canadian Ind Rels Assn. POSITION: (since 1972) Professor, Dept of Ind Rels, Laval Univ, St. Foy, Quebec G1K 7P4 Canada. 418/656-2641

SHAFFER, DONALD T. Bus:Pers/Ind Rels. BS 1967, MS 1970, U of Akron; MBA 1977, Kent State U. INT: coll barg, labor market econ, personnel. POSITIONS: Conference Leader, 1969, Ind Engineer, 1970, and, since 1974, Manager, Ind Rels Research, The Goodyear Tire & Rubber Co, 1144 E Market St, Dept 103-A, Akron, OH 44316. 216/796-2948

SHAFFER, DORIS Acad: History & Pol Sci; Union. MA 1955, Brooklyn Coll. INT: labor history, union org/admin, coll barg. ASSN: Long Island IRRA, AAUP. POSITION: (since 1961) Professor-History and Political Science, Nassau Community Coll. ADDRESS: 6 Old Colony Lane, Great Neck, NY 11023. 516/222-7198

SHAIR, DAVID I. Bus:Pers/Ind Rels. BSS 1940, CCNY; MBA 1950, NYU. PUBL: "In Unions There is Strength," Billboard, Aug 9, 1980; "Able, Experienced-and 59 Years Old," NY Times, 7/13/80. INT: personnel, org beh, coll barg. ASSN: New York IRRA, NYPMA, ASPA. POSITIONS: Mgmt Consultant, B. Werne and Assoc, 1955; Dir of Labor Rels, London Records Inc, 1970; and (since 1980) Vice Pres Personnel, Carl Fischer Inc, 62 Cooper Sq, New York, NY 10003. 212/777-0900

SHALLEY, CHRISTINA E. Student. BA 1980, SUNY-ALBANY, MA 1983, U of Ill-UC. INT: org beh, personnel, empl/trng programs. POSITION: Student-PhD Candidate, U of Ill, Dept of Bus Admin. ADDRESS: 401 E Chalmers St, #110, Champaign, IL 61820. 217/333-0500

SHAPIRO, SUMNER Bus:Mgmt/Admin, Arbitration; Ind Rels. BSME 1949, Lowell Tech Inst; MS 1955, Columbia U. INT: coll barg, arb/med, labor market econ. ASSN: Capital Dist IRRA. POSITION: Executive Vice Pres, Star Textile & Research, 136 Fullner Rd, Box 500 B, Albany, NY 12205. 518/459-1080

SHARMA, BASU D. Acad: Ind Rels, Econ. MA 1974, Tribuvan U-Nepal; AM 1979, PhD 1983, U of Ill. PUBL: "Multinational Corporations and Industrialization in Southeast and East Asia," in Contemporary Southeast Asia; "Foreign Direct Investment, Foreign Aid, Economic Growth and Employment in Selected Asian Countries," (w K. Taira), Asian Econ, Sept 1982. INT: IR theory, intl comparative labor, labor market econ. ASSN: AEA, Atlantic Econ Soc, Western Econ Assn Intl. POSITIONS: Res Fellow, Inst of Southeast Asian Studies, Singapore, 1983; and (since 1984) Asst Prof, Faculty of Commerce. Univ of Saskatchewan, Saskatoon, Sask. Canada.

SHARP, WALTON HENRY Acad: Econ, Ind Rels. BBA 1964, Lamar U; MA 1969, U of New Orleans; PhD 1983, U of Houston. INT: labor educ, labor law, method/statis. ASSN: Greater Houston IRRA, Acad of Mgmt. POSITIONS: Dir, ILIR, 1978, Instructor, Org Beh & Mgmt, 1981, U of Houston; and (since 1983) Director, Inst for Labor and Ind Rels, North Texas State Univ, N. T. Box 5427, Denton, TX 76203. 817/565-3439

SHARPE, CALVIN W. Acad: Law. BA 1967, Clark Coll; JD 1974, Northwestern U. PUBL: "A Reappraisal of the Barg. Order," 69 NW L Rev #4; "Standards of Proof in the Admissibility of Other Crimes Evid," 59 Notre Dame Law Rev; "Impeachment in the Administrative Case," Litigation Mag. INT: arb/med, govt labor policy, intl comparative labor. ASSN: Amer Assn of Law Schools, Lawyer's Alliance for Nuclear Arms Control, Amer Trial Lawyer's Assn. POSITIONS: Field Attorney, NLRB-Winston-Salem, 1977; Asst Prof of Law, U of Virginia, School of Law, 1981; and (since 1984) Assoc Prof of Law, Case Western Reserve Univ, School of Law, 11075 East Boulevard, Cleveland, OH 44106. 216/368-5069

SHARPE, MARJORIE JOHNSTON Assn Mgmt. BA 1951, U of Toronto. INT: org beh, mgmt/educ, personnel. ASSN: Chicago IRRA, Amer Soc of Assoc Executives, Acad of Mgmt. POSITIONS: Exec Dir, Amer Dental Hygienists' Assoc, Chicago, 1981; and (since 1977) President, Marjorie J. Sharpe & Assoc, 224 Timber Ridge, Barrington, IL 60010. 312/440-8911

SHATZ, SANFORD Acad: Student, Law, Econ. BA 1981, U of Mich. INT: labor law, arb/med, labor market econ. POSITION: Student-Cornell U. ADDRESS: 395 Sunrise Blvd, Williamsville, NY 14221. 716/632-8468

SHAULIS, P. A. Bus:Pers/Ind Rels. POSITION: Employee Rels Manager, Mobil Oil Credit Corp, PO Box 600, Kansas City, MO 64141.

SHAW, KIMBALL Consulting. POSITION: President, Kimball Shaw Assoc, 3 Pleasant St, Hingham, MA 02043.

SHAW, PAUL F. Arbitration, Consulting. PUBL: Checkpoints to Sound Collective Bargaining, 1957; "Worker Participation American Style," Empl Rels Law J, 1977; Manual of Labor Policies and Practices in Brazil, 1980-81. INT: arb/med, coll barg, labor law. ASSN: New York IRRA, IIRA, Ind Rels Soc, New York Pers Mgmt Assn. POSITIONS: Vice Pres, World Wide Labor Rels, Chase-Manhatten Bank, N.A., 1965; Empl Rels Consultant, 1977, and, since 1983, Arbitrator-Consultant (self-employed), 240 Broad St, Williston Park, NY 11596. 516/742-4282

SHAW, ROGER D. Bus:Pers/Ind Rels. BS 1963, Bowling Green State U. INT: coll barg, org beh, personnel. ASSN: Northeastern Mich IRRA, Ind Mgmt Assn-Saginaw Chapter. POSITIONS: Dir of Labor Rels, 1977, and, since 1983, Dir of Empl Services, Central Foundry, Div G.M.C., 77 W Center St, Saginaw, MI 48605. 517/776-3210

SHAW, SUE OLINGER Arbitration; Acad: Ind Rels, Econ. PhD 1967, Harvard U. INT: arb/med, coll barg, labor educ. ASSN: AAA, AEA, SPIDR. POSITION: (since 1979) Visiting Prof, North Carolina State U-Raleigh. ADDRESS: Rte 2, Box 106, Apex, NC 27502.

SHEA, DENNIS F. Bus:Pers/Ind Rels. BA 1973, SUNY-Stony Brook; MS 1975 U of Wis-Madison. INT: personnel, compensation, org beh. ASSN: North Jersey Pers Assn, New York Assn of Compensation Admin, Amer Compensation Assn. POSITIONS: Dir, I.R., Eastern Ops Center, 1979, Dir, Pers, Car Leasing Div, 1980, and, since 1981, Director, Compensation, The Hertz Co, 660 Madison Ave, New York, NY 10021. 212/980-2422

SHEA, GEORGE R. Union. POSITION: General Counsel, Mass Teachers Assn, 20 Ashburton Pl, Boston, MA 02108. 617/742-7950

SHEA, GREGORY P. Org Beh/Pers, Psychology; Consulting. AB 1974, Harvard; MSc 1976, London School of Econ; PhD 1981, Yale. PUBL: "The Study of Bargaining and Conflict Behavior: Broadening the Conceptual Arena;" "Work Design Committees." INT: org beh, mgmt/educ, union org/admin. ASSN: APA, Philadelphia IRRA, Acad of Mgmt. POSITIONS: Special Asst to Dir of Professional Studies, Yale, 1977; Mgr of Org Develop, Westinghouse, 1981; and (since 1982) Asst Prof, Wharton School of Bus, Univ of Penna, 2015 SA-OH/CC, Philadelphia, PA 19104. 215/898-3031

SHEARER, JOHN C. Acad: Econ; Arbitration, Government. BS 1952, Cornell; AM 1958, PLO 1960, Princeton U. PUBL: "Fact and Fiction Concerning Multinational Labor Relations," Vanderbilt J of Transnational Law, vol 10, #1, Winter 1977; "Do Foreign Owned U.S. Firms Practice Unconventional Labor Relations?" (w C. Greer), Monthly Labor Rev, vol 104, #1, Jan 1981, pp 44-48; "Dispute Settlement in the South," Proceedings of the 1981 IRRA Spring Meeting, pp 550-556, Labor Law J, vol 32, #8, Aug, 1981, pp 550-556. INT: empl/-trng programs, arb/med, govt labor policy. ASSN: NAA, AEA, Soc for Intl Development. POSITIONS: Prof/Economist, Econ Commission for Latin America, United Nations, 1962; Assoc Prof of Econ, Penna State U, 1965; and (since 1967) Prof of Econ, College of Bus Admin, Oklahoma State Univ, Stillwater, OK 74078. 405/624/5105

SHEIFER, VICTOR J. Government. BA 1947, MA 1949, PhD 1979, New York U. PUBL: "Collective Bargaining and the CPI: Escalation vs. Catch-up," Proceedings of 31st Annual Meeting, IRRA, Aug 29-31, 1978; "Employment Cost Index," in Encyclopedia of Statistical Sciences, vol 2, New York: J. Wiley & Sons, 1982; "The Relationship Between Changes in Wage Rates and in Hourly Earnings," Monthly Labor Rev, Aug 1970. INT: method/statis, labor market econ, coll barg. ASSN: Washington DC IRRA, AEA, Amer Statistical Assn. POSITIONS: Research Asst, Natl Bureau of Econ Res, 1957; Labor Economist, 1959, and, since 1981, Asst Chief, Div of Occupational Pay and Empl Benefit Levels, USDL, Bureau of Labor Statis. ADDRESS: 8705 Hickory Bend Trail, Potomac, MD 20854. 202/523-1910

SHEMKE, RAYMOND A. Arbitration, Legal Practice. JD 1951, Wayne State U. INT: arb/med, labor law, govt labor policy. ASSN: Detroit IRRA, SPIDR, Mich State Bar Assn. POSITIONS: Attorney, NLRB, 1961; Dir, Hearings Div, Civil Service Dept, State of Mich, 1979; and (since 1951) Attorney-Arbitrator (self-employed), 31310 Grandon, Livonia, MI 48150. 313/421-0529

SHERER, PAMELA DARLENE Student. 21-5 Eagle Head Terrace, Shrewsbury, MA 01545. 617/256-0785

SHERER, PETER D. Acad: Student, Ind Rels, Org Beh/Pers. BA 1977, U of Buffalo; MS 1981, U of Wis-Madison. INT: personnel, coll barg, org beh. ASSN: IIRA. POSITION: PhD Student, IRRI, 4226 Social Sci, U of Wis, Madison, WI 53706. 608/262-1403

SHERIDAN, PHILIP J. Consulting. PUBL: Labor Relations Manual; Labor Arbitration Manual; "Preparation and Presentation of Arbitration Cases." INT: arb/med, empl/trng programs, coll barg. ASSN: Connecticut Valley IRRA, AAA, Intl Platform Assn. POSITION: (since 1970) President/Treasurer, Sheridan and Assoc, Inc, PO Box 4995, 276 High St, Holyoke, MA 01041. 413/536-8504

SHERMAN, JAMES JOSEPH Acad: Ind Rels; Arbitration. BA 1949, Canisius Coll; LLB/JD 1952, U of Buffalo; PhD 1967, SUNY-Buffalo. INT: arb/med, labor educ, labor law. ASSN: Florida IRRA, NAA, ABA, SPIDR. POSITIONS: VP Ind Rels, Bell Aircraft, 1952; Lawyer, Owens, Turner & Sherman, 1961; and (since 1967) Professor, Univ of South Florida. ADDRESS: 14333 Lake Magdalene Blvd, Tampa, FL 33612. 813/-974-4155

SHERMAN, PATRICIA JOAN Student. 4 Caton Dr, Apt 8B, Dewitt. NY 13214. 315/446-8107

SHERR, MITCHELL AVRUM Legal Practice. 4809 Live Oak Ct, Fort Wayne, IN 46804. 219/432-7363

SHIBOTA, ATSUO Acad: Student; Government. BL 1977, U of Tokyo. 10983 Palms Blvd, #2, Los Angeles, CA 90034. 213/202-0831

SHIEBER, BENJAMIN M. Acad: Law; Arbitration. JD 1953, Columbia U. INT: labor law, arb/med. ASSN: NAA, ABA. POSITION: (since 1964) Professor, Louisiana State Univ Law School. ADDRESS: 338 Stanford Lane, Baton Rouge, LA 70808. 504/388-8846

SHIELDS, JANICE CHRISTINE Acad: Bus Admin. BSBA 1973, MBA 1974, Clarion State Coll; PhD 1983, Penna State U. PUBL: "Foreign Language and Accounting Expertise: A Marketable Combination;" "Transnational Auditing Standards: Constraints and Progress." INT: intl comparative labor, coll barg, labor educ. ASSN: Acad of Intl Business. POSITIONS: Auditor, Navy Audit Service, 1975; Auditor, Federal Home Loan Bank Board, 1976; and (since 1982) Asst Prof, Dept of Marketing, Univ of Toledo, Toledo, OH 43606. 419/537-2970

SHIMADA, HARUO Acad: Econ, Ind Rels. BA 1965, MA 1967, Keio U-Japan; PhD 1974, U of Wis-Madison. PUBL: Contemporary Industrial Relations in Japan, U of Wis Press, 1983; "Japan's Postwar Industrial Growth and Labor Management Relations," IRRA Proceedings 35th Annual Meeting, Dec 1982; "Japan", in Dunlop & Galenson eds, Labor in the Twentieth Century, 1979. INT: intl comparative labor, labor market econ, mgmt/educ. ASSN: IIRA. POSITIONS: Visiting Res Officer, Econ Planning Agency, Japan, 1978; and (since 1980) Professor, Econ Dept, Keio Univ, Mita, Minato-ku, Tokyo, Japan. Phone (03) 453-4511

SHINDELL, ANNE B. Legal Practice. 815 E Mason St, #1500, Milwaukee, WI 53202.

SHIROM, ARIE Acad: Ind Rels. BSol SC 1962, MSol SC, Hebrew U-Jerusalem; PhD 1968, U of Wis-Madison. PUBL: The Israeli System of Industrial Relations, 1983; "Toward A Theory of OD Intervention in Unionized Work Settings," Human Rels, 1983; "What is Organizational Stress?" J of Occ Beh, 1982. INT: ind psych, org beh. ASSN: Acad of Mgmt, Amer Psych Assn. POSITION: (since 1982) Professor, Dept of Labor Studies, Tel Aviv Univ, Tel Aviv, Israel.

SHISTER, JOSEPH Acad: Ind Rels; Arbitration. PhD 1943, Harvard U. PUBL: "The Direction of Unionism, 1947-1967," Ind & Labor Rels Rev, July 1967; "The Outlook for Union Growth," Annals of American Acad of Pol & Soc Sci, Nov 1963; Public Policy and Collective Bargaining, (editor), Harper & Row, 1962. INT: arb/med, coll barg, labor market econ. ASSN: AEA, NAA. POSITION: Professor Emeritus, SUNY-Buffalo. ADDRESS: 310 Brantwood Rd, Buffalo, NY 14226. 716/831-3327

SHOGREN, MARSHALL A. Bus:Pers/Ind Rels. POSITION: Director of Personnel, Bostitch Division of Textron, East Greenwich, RI 02818.

SHORE, HENRY Arbitration. LLB 1934, U of Pittsburgh. INT: arb/med, labor law. ASSN: Western Penna IRRA, Federal Bar Assn, Penna Bar Assn, ASPA. POSITION: Regional Attorney, (Reg 6) 1937, Reg Dir (Reg 6), NLRB, 1947-1981. Retired. ADDRESS: 764 Highvue Rd, Pittsburgh, PA 15228.

SHOWELL, CHARLES H., JR. Military; Acad: Org Beh/Pers, Ind Rels. PhD 1975, Ohio State U. INT: arb/med, coll barg, org beh. ASSN: Amer Mgmt Assn. POSITIONS: Asst Prof, 1981, and, since 1983, Asst Dept Chairman, Air Force Inst of Technology, Wright-Paterson AFB. ADDRESS: 2287 Jacavanda Dr, Dayton, OH 45431. 513/255-4848

SHROUT, ETHEL H. Acad: Org Beh/Pers. EdD 1970, Okla State U-Stillwater. POSITION: Mgmt, Business and Econ Dept, Missouri Western Coll, 4525 Downs Dr, St. Joseph, MO 64507. 816/271-4351

SHULENBURGER, DAVID E. Acad: Ind Rels, Univ Admin; Arbitration. MA 1968, PhD 1974, U of Ill-UC. PUBL: "Union-Nonunion Wage Differential," Ind Rels, Spring, 1982; "Evaluating the Earnings Impact of the Employment Service," Ind Rels, Winter, 1979; "Labors Share by Sector and Industry," Ind and Labor Rels Rev, July 1971. INT: labor market econ, coll barg, empl/trng programs. ASSN: AEA, Western Econ Assn. POSITIONS: Asst Prof, 1974, Assoc Prof, 1978, and, since 1983, Prof of Bus, Univ of Kansas. ADDRESS: 3101 Campfire Dr, Lawrence, KS 66044. 913/864-4500

SHULTZ, GEORGE P. Government. BA 1942, Princeton U; PhD 1949, MIT. POSITIONS: Secretary of the Treasury, US Government, 1972-74; Pres, Bechtel Corp, 1974; and, currently, Secretary of State, Dept of State, 2201 C Street NW, Washington DC 20520. 202/632-4910

SHUPE, PHILIP B. Bus:Pers/Ind Rels. POSITION: Employee Relations Director, East Ohio Gas Co, PO Box 5759, Cleveland, OH 44101.

SHUSTER, FRANK BARRY Legal Practice. 116 E Howard Ave, Decatur, GA 30030.

SICKLER, A. DAVID Union. "Factory of the Future," School of Mgmt, U of Minn; "Coors Boycott-(Lie Detectors)," Federationist, AFL-CIO. INT: union org/admin, labor history, labor educ. ASSN: Southern Calif IRRA, Inst of Ind Rels Assn. POSITIONS: Bus Manager, Brewery Workers, 1973-76, Natl Coordinator, Coors Boycott Committee, Natl AFL-CIO, 1977, and, since 1978, Coordinator, L. A.-Orange Cty Organization Committee, AFL-CIO, 724 S Park View St, Los Angeles, CA 91740. 213/-387-7281

SIEGEL, ABRAHAM J. Acad: Ind Rels. POSITION: Dean, Sloan School of Management, 50 Memorial Dr, RM E52474A, MIT, Cambridge, MA 02139. 617/253-7158

SIEGEL, BOAZ Acad: Law; Legal Prac, Arb. ADDRESS: Suite 2656, 30700 Telegraph Rd, Birmingham, MI 48010. 313/642-2190

SIEGEL, JAY S. Legal Practice, Journalism. BA 1950, LLB 1954, New York U. PUBL: The Developing Labor Law, (co-editor), First Ed 1971. INT: labor law, govt labor policy, coll barg. ASSN: New York & Central Conn IRRA, ABA. POSITION: (since 1977) Senior Principal and President, Siegel, O'Conner & Kainen, P.C., 370 Asylum St, Hartford, CT 06103. 203/547-0550

SIEGENTHALER, JURG K. Acad: Sociology. MA 1963, PhD 1966, U of Berne-Switzerland. PUBL: The Politics of Labor Unions, Berne, 1968; "Current Problems of T.V.-Party Relations in Switzerland," ILR Rev, 1975; Social Consequences of Industrialization, 1984. INT: labor history, ind sociol. ASSN: Amer Sociol Assn, Amer Hist Assn, Council of European Studies. POSITIONS: Asst Prof, Rutgers U, 1969; Asst Prof, 1974, and, since 1977, Assoc Prof, Dept of Sociology, The American Univ. ADDRESS: 2012 Luzerne Ave, Silver Spring, MD 20910. 202/686-2414

SIEGENTHALER, LINDA Government. 2012 Luzerne Ave, Silver Spring, MD 20910. 301/-585-1429

SIENGTHAI, SUNUNTA Acad: Student, Econ. BA 1975, Chulalongkorn U; MS 1979, U of Ill-UC. INT: intl comparative labor, labor market econ. ASSN: AEA, IIRA. ADDRESS: 401 E. Chalmers, #120, Champaign, IL 61820. 217/344-3697

SILVER, JONAS Arbitration. BSS 1939, CCNY; LLB 1944, George Washington U. ADDRESS: 1212 Parkwood Dr, North Merrick, NY 11566. 516/481-3715

SILVERBLATT, RONNIE Acad: Ind Rels, Org Beh/Pers. BS 1968, CUNY; MSBA 1974, U of Mass; PhD 1982, Ga. State U. INT: coll barg, personnel, union org/admin. ASSN: ASPA, Acad of Mgmt. POSITIONS: Asst Prof, Wayne State U, 1980; and (since 1983) Asst Prof, Florida Intl Univ, Bay Vista Campus, North Miami, FL 33181. 305/940-5870

SILVERMAN, HARRY Arbitration. BA 1976, LLB 1979, New York U. INT: arb/med, coll barg, labor law. ADDRESS: 0-62 Pine Ave, Fair Lawn, NJ 07410. 212/279-5475

SILVERSTEIN, EILEEN L. Acad: Law. JD 1972, U of Chicago. PUBL: Collective Bargaining in Public Employment, BNA 1978. POSITIONS: Assoc Prof, Indiana U; and (currently) Law School, Univ of Connecticut, West Hartford, CT 06117. 203/523-4841

SILVIA, STEPHEN J. Student. BS 1981, Cornell; MA 1983, MPh 1984, Yale U. INT: intl comparative labor, coll barg, govt labor policy. ASSN: Amer Pol Sci Assn. POSITION: Student, Yale Univ. ADDRESS: 126 Mansfield St, New Haven, CT 06511.

SIMMELKJAER, ROBERT Arbitration; Acad: Univ Admin. PhD 1972, MBA 1977, Columbia U; JD 1978, Fordham U. POSITIONS: Proj Dir, Inst for Educ Develop, 1969-71; Principal, Jr High School, 1971-74; and, currently, Prof, CCNY, 135th St & Convent Ave, New York, NY 10031. 212/690-5333

SIMMONS, ROBERT L. Bus:Pers/Ind Rels. POSITION: VP Ind Rels, Glass Containers Corp, 535 N Gilbert, PO Box 4118, Fullerton, CA 92634.

SIMON, KENNETH MARSHALL Legal Practice. Suite 512, 9465 Wilshire Blvd, Beverly Hills, CA 90212.

SIMON, S. FANNY Consultant (Retired). 160 West End Avenue, New York, NY 10023.

SIMON, SHARON Acad: Labor Educ. JD 1977, SUNY-Buffalo. PUBL: "Libel and Copyright Law," Editor's Guide, Intl Labor Press Assn, AFL-CIO, 1984; "Plant Closings and the Law of Collective Bargaining," Labor and Reindustrialization, D. Kennedy ed, Penna State U Press, 1983; Wisconsin Workers Compensation: A Manual for Unions, School for Workers, U of Wis Extension, 1983. INT: labor educ, labor law, coll barg. ASSN: Univ & Coll Labor Educ Assn, Coalition of Labor Union Women. POSITIONS: General Counsel and Staff Rep, AFSCME, Council 66, AFL-CIO, 1977-79; and (since 1979) Asst Prof of Labor Educ, School for Workers, 422 Lowell Hall, 610 Langdon St, Madison, WI 53703. 608/262-2111

SIMONETTI, JOAN E. Bus:Mgmt/Admin, Consulting; Acad: Ind Rels. BS 1974, Bethany Coll. INT: arb/med, empl/trng programs, labor law. ASSN: New Brunswick IRRA, ASPA, NAFE. POSITIONS: Partner, Elizabeth T. Lyons & Assoc-New Brunswick, 1975; Dept Mgr, Manufacturing, Ethicon Inc-Somerville, 1980; and (since 1982) Department Manager, Manufacturing, Johnson & Johnson Production. ADDRESS: 2212 Ridgewood Rd, Sherman, TX 75090. 214/-892-2191

SIMONS, MARK N. Legal Practice. POSITION: Attorney, Brauer, Simons, Buescher P.C., 1563 Gaylord St, Denver, CO 80206. 303/333-7751

SIMPKINS, JOHN PAUL Acad: Law; Arbitration, Consulting. AB 1964, Lincoln U; JD 1970,. Howard U. INT: arb/med, labor law, labor educ. ASSN: Philadelphia IRRA, NAA, AAA, ABA (Labor & Arb Sections). POSITION: Attorney-Arbitrator, 1300 Robinson Bldg, 15th & Chestnut St, Philadelphia, PA 19102. 215/568-8040

SIMPSON, KARL FRANKLIN JR. Retired. BA 1946, Baker U; MA 1946, Northwestern U; PhD 1954, U of Wis. POSITIONS: Labor Economist, Paperboard Packing Council, 1956-64; Exec Secretary, Paper Industry Mgmt Assn, 1964-68; Prof of Mgmt and Econ, Chicago City-Wide Coll, 1968. Retired. ADDRESS: 2410 Anderson, Newton, KS 67114. 316/284-2236

SIMSARIAN, ARAX Consulting, Bus:Pers/Ind Rels. BA 1983, Mount Holyoke Coll. INT: health & hosp care, income maint, labor market econ. ASSN: New York IRRA, NY Pers Mgmt Assn. POSITIONS: Economist and Manpower Planning, Exxon Corp, 1956; Coordinator, Subsidiary Operations, Equitable Life Assurance Co, 1974; and (since 1981) Consultant, Hirschfeld, Stern, Moyer & Ross. ADDRESS: 235 E 22nd St, New York, NY 10010. 212/582-2524

SINCLITICO, JOSEPH A. AB 1936, Holy Cross Coll; JD 1939, Harvard. ADDRESS: 7607 Calle Modero, LaCosta, CA 92008.

SINGER, PAULA Union, Consulting, Bus:-Mgmt/Admin. BS 1973, Cornell U; MAS 1976, Johns Hopkins U. PUBL: "Mandate: Minority Business Enterprise Utilization," IRRA, 1978; "Adjusting to the Fiscal & Demographic Constraints in Primary and Secondary Education;" "Counseling the Troubled Employee." INT: coll barg, union org/admin, personnel. ASSN: Baltimore IRRA, Md. Public Sector Labor Rels Conference Board. POSITIONS: Exec Dir, Classified Municipal Empl Assn of Baltimore City, Inc, 1978; Manager, Human Res, Bendix Communications Div, 1980; and (since 1982) Executive Director, Maryland Nurses Assn. ADDRESS: 2385 Flax Ter, Baltimore, MD 21209. 301/242-7300

SINGH, VISHWANATH PRASAD Consulting, Bus; Acad: Ind Rels. POSITION: Bus Consultant, Kendan Mfg Ltd, 3582 Huntington Ave, Windsor, Ont Canada. 519/966-1770

SINGLETARY, CARY ROBIN Legal Practice. BS 1968, U of Tampa; MCS 1970, Rollins Coll; JD 1973, Stetson U. INT: arb/med, coll barg, empl/trng programs. ASSN: Central Florida IRRA, ABA, Florida Bar Assn, Hills Cty Bar Assn. POSITION: Attorney/Partner, Singletary & Singletary, 315 E Madison St, Suite 500, Tampa, FL 33602. 813/229-0191

SINICROPI, ANTHONY V. Acad: Ind Rels; Arbitration. BA 1956, St. Bonaventure; MILR, 1958, NYSSILR-Cornell; PhD 1968, U of Iowa. PUBL: Evidence in Arbitration, BNA; Remedies in Arbitration, BNA; "Revisiting an Old Battleground: The Subcontracting Dispute," Arb of Subcontracting and Wage Incentive Disputes, Proceedings of 32nd Annual Meeting of NAA, J. Stern & B. Dennis, eds, BNA 1980. INT: arb/med, coll barg, empl discrimination. ASSN: NAA, SPIDR. POSITIONS: Dir of Grad Studies in Bus & Chairman, Dept of Bus Admin, 1972, Chairman, Dept of Ind Rels, 1979-83, and, since 1978, John F. Murray Prof of IR & Dir, Ind Rels Inst, Coll of Bus Admin, Univ of Iowa, Phillips Hall, Iowa City, IA 52242. 319/-353-5639

SIPORIN, DAVID Bus:Pers/Ind Rels. BA 1976, MLIR 1978, Mich State U. INT: personnel, org beh, ind psych. ASSN: ASPA. POSITIONS: Field Rep/Job Developer, Greater Lansing Urban League, Inc, 1978; and (since 1979) Senior Empl Rels Rep, Amoco Production Company. ADDRESS: 8923 W 81st Ln, Arvada, CO 80005. 303/830-4758

SIRUTIS, DONNA Government. BA 1968, U of Calif-Berkeley; MS 1974, U of Mass-Amherst; JD 1982, Suffolk U. INT: arb/med, labor law, personnel. ASSN: Boston IRRA, Mass Bar Assn. POSITIONS: Bus Agent, SEIU, Local 254, 1974; Asst Commissioner, Labor & Industries, Mass Dept of Labor & Industries, 1979, and, since 1981, Vice Chairman, Mass Board of Conciliation and Arbitration. ADDRESS: 38 Ransom Rd, #11, Brighton, MA 02135. 617/727-3466

SISSON, JEFFREY D. Bus:Pers/Ind Rels. MLIR 1983, Mich State U. INT: labor law, arb/med, coll barg. POSITION: (since 1983) Ind Rels Rep, Pacific Gas and Electric CO-SF. ADDRESS: 2712 Oak Rd, #52, Walnut Creek, CA 94596. 415/781-4211

SKANES-TAYLOR, J. Student. INT: arb/med, org beh, personnel. POSITION: (since 1983) B.Com Student, McGill Univ. ADDRESS: PO Box 905, Snowdon Post Office, Montreal, Quebec H3X 3Y1 Canada.

SKELTON, B. R. Acad: Ind Rels. POSITION: Dept of Economics, Clemson Univ, Clemson, SC 29631.

SKIDMORE, ROBERT W. Government. BA 1947, U of Puget Sound; LLB 1950, U of Wash. PUBL: "Jurisdiction of New Bankruptcy Court," CLE 1980, Wash State Bar Assn Convention;

"The New Federal Bankruptcy Code," Summer Meeting for Presenting Attorneys; "Overview of the Bankruptcy Code: the Courts Prospective," CLE Wash State Bar Assn, May 1983. INT: bankruptcy, arb/med. ASSN: ABA, Natl Conference of Bankruptcy Judges, Commercial Law League of Amer. POSITIONS: Partner, Girdlami & Skidmore, Attorneys-at-Law, 1964; and (since 1974) United States Bankruptcy Judge, U.S. Bankruptcy Court for the Western Dist of Wash at Tacoma, Room 224, U.S. Post Office Bldg, PO Box 1797, Tacoma, WA 98401. 206/593-6345

SKINNER, EDWARD E. Bus:Labor Rels. POSITION: Director-Labor Rels, Sherwin-Williams Co, 101 Prospect Ave NW, Cleveland, OH 44115. 216/566-2370

SKINNER, GORDON S. Acad: Econ, Ind Rels. BS 1948, Boston U; MS 1949, PhD 1953, U of Wis-Madison. PUBL: Labor Law: Cases, Text and Legislation, Univ Press, Random House 1972; "The Importance of Costing Labor Contracts," Labor Law J, Aug 1981; "A Survey of Faculty Attitudes Toward Collective Bargaining," Proceedings of the 1975 Annual IRRA Meeting. INT: labor market econ, income maint, labor law. ASSN: Greater Cincinnati IRRA, AEA. POSITIONS: Instructor of Econ, U of Wis, 1952-53; Res Assoc, U of Calif, 1961-62; and (since 1953) Prof, Dept of Econ, Univ of Cincinnati, Cincinnati, OH 45221. 513/-475-2095

SKOWRONSKI, AUDREY M. Union. 922 E Eden Pl, Milwaukee, WI 53221. 414/483-0540

SKRATEK, SYLVIA P. Union, Arbitration. BS 1971, Wayne State U; MLS 1975, Western Mich U; PhD Candidate, U of Mich. INT: arb/-med, labor law, coll barg. ASSN: Northwest IRRA, Women's Bus Exchange-Seattle, AAA. POSITIONS: Contract Specialist, Jackson County Educ Assn, 1976, UniServ Dir, Mich Educ Assn, 1979; and (since 1981) Contract Administration Field Rep, Wash Educ Assn, 33434 8th Ave S, Federal Way, WA 98003. 206/941-6700

SLATER, COURTENAY M. Consulting. PhD 1968, American U. PUBL: "Maintaining the Quality of Economic Data;" "A Budget Policy for Economic Recovery." INT: labor market econ, method/statis. ASSN: Wash DC IRRA, AEA, Amer Statis Assn, Natl Assn of Bus Economists. POSITIONS: Senior Economist, Congressional Jt Econ Committee, 1969, Chief Economist, U.S. Dept of Commerce, 1977; and (since 1981) President, CEC Assoc, Inc, 1804 N Harvard St, Arlington, VA 22201.

SLATER, WALTER Retired. BA 1951, Occidental Coll. ASSN: San Francisco IRRA. ADDRESS: 315 San Benito Way, San Francisco, CA 94127. 415/556-0538

SLEISTER, MICKEY KAY Government. BA 1974, Knox Coll. INT: labor law, coll barg, personnel. POSITIONS: Pers mgmt Specialist, US Dept of Agriculture, 1974, and, since 1977, Labor Mgmt Rels Field Examiner, NLRB, Reg 33, 411 Hamilton Blvd, Peoria, IL 61602. 309/671-7049

SLOAN, STANLEY Consulting. BS 1964, Temple U; MS 1966, Kansas State U; PhD 1969, U of Wis-Madison. PUBL: "New Context of Personnel Appraisal," Harvard Bus Rev, Nov-Dec, 1968; "Conceptual Framework for Employee Appraisal Decisions," Trng & Develop J, Jan, 1970; Hospital Management...An Evaluation, (monograph #4), Bureau of Bus Res & Service, Grad School of Bus, U of Wis, Oct 1971. INT: personnel, mgmt/educ, org beh. ASSN: Amer Psych Assn, ASPA. POSITION: (since 1974) Hay Associates, 57 Exec Park South, NE, Atlanta, GA 30329. 404/321-4996

SLOANE, ARTHUR ALLEN Acad: Ind Rels; Arbitration, Consulting. AB 1953, Harvard; MBA 1958, Columbia; DBA 1963, Harvard. PUBL: Personnel: Managing Human Resources, Prentice-Hall, 1983; Labor Relations, (w F. Whitney), 4th Ed, Prentice Hall, 1981; "Collective Bargaining in Major League Baseball," Labor Law J, Apr 1977. INT: coll barg, arb/med, personnel. ASSN: Philadelphia IRRA, AAA, NJ State Board of Mediation. POSITIONS: Asst Prof, Indiana U, 1963; Assoc Prof, 1966, and, since 1970, Prof of Ind Rels, Dept of Bus Admin, 305 Purnell Hall, Univ of Delaware, Newark, DE 19711. 302/738-2555

SLYE, JOANN MERTENS Union. BA 1973, U of Wash; MBA 1983, City U. INT: coll barg, union org/admin, ind sociol. ASSN: Northwest IRRA, State Educ Res Staff Assn. POSITIONS: Bargaining Analyst, 1979, and, since 1982, Field Rep-Research, Wash Educ Assn, 33434 8th Ave S, Federal Way, WA 98003. 206/941-6700 ext 246.

SMALL, FRANCIS X. Acad: Univ Admin. AB 1958, U of Calif-Berkeley, INT: personnel, org beh, arb/med. ASSN: San Francisco IRRA. POSITIONS: Mgr-Labor Rels, 1970, and, since 1978, Asst Vice-Chancellor, Employee Affairs, Univ of Calif-Berkeley, 200 California Hall, Berkeley CA 94720. 415/642-5666

SMEDINGHOFF, MARY LYNN Bus:Pers/Ind Rels. 14500 Dallas Pkwy #2080, Dallas, TX 75240

SMEDLEY, LAWRENCE THOMAS Union. BA 1952, Bowling Green State U; MA 1957, U of Mich, PhD 1972, American U. POSITIONS: Research Assoc, AFSCME, 1957-62, and, since 1962, Asst Dir, Dept of Social Security, AFL-CIO, 1616 Winding Waye Lane, Silver Spring, MD 20902. 202/637-5202

SMITH, ANNA D. Acad: Ind Rels; Arbitration. BA 1977, MBA 1978, Case Western Reserve U. INT: coll barg, arb/med, ind sociol. ASSN: Wis IRRA, SPIDR, Acad of Mgmt. POSITION: (since 1982) Asst Prof, Div of Bus & Admin Science, Box 2000, Univ of Wis-Parkside, Kenosha, WI 53141. 414/553-2193

SMITH, BRIAN J. Union. INT: coll barg, union org/admin, arb/med. ASSN: Detroit-IRRA, Mich Fraternal Order of Police Labor Council, Intl Pers Mgmt Assn, Israel Histadrut Assn. POSITIONS: Police Sergeant-Labor Rels Specialist, City of Detroit Police Dept, 1977, and, since 1981, Field Rep, Mich Fraternal Order of Police Labor Council, 6735 Telegraph Rd, Suite 395, Birmingham, MI 48010. 313/642-4440

SMITH, BRUCE E. Bus:Pers/Ind Rels. BS 1965, U of Kans; PhD 1972, Harvard U. POSITION: Corp Dir, Ind Rels, Cooper Tire & Rubber Co, Box 550, Findlay, OH 45840. 419/423-1321

SMITH, CHARLES L. Government. AB 1960, Albright Coll. INT: govt labor policy, union org/admin, mgmt/educ. ASSN: SFLRP. POSITIONS: Deputy Asst Reg Admin, Fed Labor

Mgmt Rels, 1975, Asst Reg Admin, Fed Labor Mgmt Rels, 1977, and, since 1978, Regional Admin, USDL, Labor Mgmt Services Admin, 1515 Broadway, Room 3515, New York, NY 10036. 212/944-3408

SMITH, CLIFFORD ELLSWORTH Acad: Ind Engineering; Arbitration. PhD 1964, Iowa State U. PUBL: "The Right to Union Representation During Investigatory Interviews," Arb J, vol 33, #2, June 1978; "The Donkey and the Stick Revisited," Pers Admin, vol 19, #7, Oct 1974. INT: arb/med, org beh, personnel. POSITIONS: General Supr, Production Control, Packard Electric Div, GM, 1959-62; Arbitrator, 1968-Present; Prof of Ind Eng, Indus Eng Dept, Iowa State Univ, Ames, IA 50010. 515/294-8727

SMITH, DOROTHY F. Union. POSITION: Ohio Educ Assn, 3587 Commerce Dr, Franklin, OH 45005. 513/423-9441

SMITH, EDWARD A. Business. 295 North Maple Ave, Basking Ridge, NJ 07920.

SMITH, FREDERICK D. Acad: Psychology. POSITION: Dept of Psychology, 350 Moore Bldg, Penna State Univ, University Park, PA 16802.

SMITH, JAMES R. Bus:Pers/Ind Rels. ABA 1958, BSBA 1960, MA 1963, MSBA 1964, Eastern Mich U; DBA 1969, Indiana Northern U. PUBL: Hardcore: The Unemployables in Contemporary Amer Society; "Training the Hardcore;" Ypsilanti Job Opportunity Program." INT: coll barg, empl/trng programs, personnel. ASSN: Amer Soc for Trng & Develop, ASPA, Acad of Mgmt. POSITIONS: Chairman, Dept of Mgmt, Cleary Coll, 1962; Mgr, Salaried Pers Admin, Hydra-Matic Div, GMC, 1960; and (since 1969) Vice Pres-Pers, Borman's Inc, PO Box 446, Detroit, MI 48232. 313/270-1280

SMITH, JOEL A. Legal Practice. Abato & Abato, 2360 W Joppa Rd, #308, Lutherville, MD 21093.

SMITH, JUDITH CANTRELL Student. 1126 Maple Ave, Evanston, IL 60202. 312/328-9578

SMITH, JULES Legal Practice. BS 1969, JD 1971, Syracuse U. PUBL: "New Antitrust Developments Affecting Labor Law," (co-author),33 Syracuse Law Rev, 945, 1982; "Labor Relations and Antitrust: Developments After Connell," 3 Ind Rel L.J., 1979. INT: labor law, litigation(labor), arb/med. ASSN: Central New York IRRA, NY State Bar Assn(Labor & Emply Law), ABA(EEO Committee). POSITION: (since 1971) Partner, Blitman & King, 500 Bldg, Suite 1100, 500 S Salina St, Syracuse, NY 13202. 315/422-7111

SMITH, KIRBY J., JR. Arbitration. JD 1949, U of Iowa. INT: arb/med, personnel. ASSN: Iowa State Bar Assn, Natl Assn of Govt Employees. POSITIONS: Chief Appeals Officer, U.S. Civil Service Commmission, 1955; Reg Dir, Merit Systems Protection Board, 1979; and (since 1982) Labor Arbitrator (self-employed), 54 Webster Acres, Webster Groves, MO 63119. 314/962-6378

SMITH, LEWIS H. Acad: Econ. BS 1963, PhD 1971, U of Tenn. PUBL: Employment, Income and Welfare in the Rural South, Praeger; "Wage and Occupational Difference Between Black and White Men," Southern Econ J; "On Moving the Poor: Subsidizing Relocation," Ind Rels. INT: labor market econ, empl/trng programs, govt labor policy. ASSN: AEA, Southern Econ Ass, Western Econ Assn. POSITION: (since 1971) Prof of Econ and Dir, Center for Manpower Studies, Univ of Miss, University, MS 38677. 601/232-5843

SMITH, LOUIS WARREN Government. BS 1976, New York Inst of Tech; MA 1978, U of Okla; MS 1982, New York Inst of Tech. INT: abr/med, govt labor policy, labor law. ASSN: New York IRRA. POSITION: (since 1981) Chief Regional Mediator, New York State Publ Empl Rels Board. ADDRESS: 11 Dikeman St, Hempstead, NY 11550. 212/587-4111

SMITH, MAURICE R. Bus:Pers/Ind Rels. BS 1974, U of Nebr. INT: labor law, empl/trng programs, org beh. ASSN: ASPA, Amer Soc of Engineering Educ, Council on Union-Free Environment. POSITIONS: Mgr, Professional Empl, 1968, Mgr, Personnel, Aviation Operations, 1973, and, since 1982, Director, Personnel, Sundstrand Advanced Tech, (Div of Sundstrand Corp), 4747 Harrison Ave, Rockford, IL 61125. 815/226-5232

SMITH, MICHAEL K. Consulting; Acad: Org Beh/Pers, Psychology. PhD 1972, U of Southern Calif. MA 1976, Goddard Coll. PUBL: "Managing Interpersonal Conflict Between Buddy Divers," Undercurrent IV, Aug 1979, pp 5-9; "Managing Predive Stress," Undercurrent (in press). INT: arb/med, org beh, personnel. ASSN: San Francisco IRRA, Calif Assn of Marriage and Family Therapists, Northern Calif Council of Mediators, SPIDR. POSITIONS: Clinical Dir, Youth & Family Serv Bureau, Hayward Police Dept, 1977; and (since 1979) Lecturer, Publ and Bus Admin, Calif State U, Hayward. ADDRESS: 1029 Hubert Rd, Oakland, CA 94610. 415/881-3282

SMITH, NATHAN Bus:Mgmt/Admin, Pers/Ind Rels, Consulting. BA 1950, Brooklyn Coll; MA 1951, New York U. PUBL: "Long Term Disability," Pension and Welfare News; "Cost Control on Benefit Plans," Empl Benefit Cost Control, Amer Mgmt Assn; "Maximizing Employee Benefits," Personnel News, Natl Retail Merchants Assn. INT: mgmt/educ, health & hosp care, labor market econ. POSITIONS: Mgr, Empl Benefits Planning, J. C. Penny Co, 1966; and (since 1975) Asst Vice Pres, Dir of Empl Benefits, American Home Products Corp-NY. ADDRESS: 5 Frost Pond, North Hills, NY 11576. 212/878-6601

SMITH, NEAL F. Bus:Pers/Ind Rels. AB 1960, Coll of Holy Cross; JD 1969, Georgetown U. INT: coll barg, labor law, mgmt/educ. ASSN: Boston IRRA, ABA, Va State Bar, Boston Labor Guild. POSITIONS: Attorney, NLRB-Wash DC, 1969-70; and (since 1970) Second Vice Pres & Dir of Ind Rels, John Hancock Companies, PO Box 111, Boston, MA 02117. 617/421-4391

SMITH, OSCAR S. Retired. BS 1929, Antioch U. POSITIONS: Dir of Ind Rels, US Atomic Energy Comm, 1947-65; and Dir, Non-Academic Pers, U of Ill, 1965-73, (Retired). ADDRESS: PO Box 360, Lusby, MD 20657.

SMITH, RALPH ELY Acad: Econ; Government, Res Inst. AB 1965, Dickinson Coll; PhD 1971, Georgetown U. PUBL: The Subtle Revolution: Women At Work, Wash: The Urban Inst, 1979; "A Simulation Model of the Demographic Composition of Employment, Unemployment, and Labor Force Participation," Res in Labor

Econ, I, 1977, pp 259-203; "The Persistence of the Discouraged Worker Effect," (w S. O. Schweitzer), Ind and Labor Rels Rev, XXVII, Jan 1974, pp 249-260. INT: labor market econ, govt labor policy, empl/trng programs. ASSN: AEA, Soc of Government Economists, Economic Soc of Australia. POSITIONS: Senior Res Assoc, The Urban Inst, 1973; Deputy Dir, Natl Comm for Empl Policy, 1979; Sr. Research Fellow, Dept of Econ, Inst of Advanced Studies, Research School of Soc Sci, Australian Natl Univ, 1983-84. ADDRESS: 4438 Davenport St NW, Washington DC 20016.

SMITH, ROBERT C. Bus:Pers/Ind Rels. BS 1974, Maine Maritime Acad; MSIR 1981, Pace U. INT: coll barg, arb/med, personnel. ASSN: New York IRRA. POSITIONS: Safety Engineer, 1976, Asst Supt of Ind Rels, 1978, Bethlehem Steel Corp; and (since 1982) Dir of Ind Rels, Alpha Metal Inc, Jersey City. ADDRESS: 799 Summit Ave, Hackensack, NJ 07601. 201/434-6778

SMITH, ROBERT EDWARD JR. Bus:Pers/Ind Rels. BA 1976, U of Mich; MLIR 1979, Mich State U. INT: coll barg, arb/med, labor law. POSITIONS: F.C.G.T.P., Ford Motor Co, 1979; Empl & Community Rels, 1980, and, since 1983, Empl Rels Specialist, General Electric Co, Tell City, IN. ADDRESS: Apt 37, R 1, Box 720, Lewis Port, KY 42351.

SMITH, ROBERT STEWART Acad: Econ. PhD 1971, Stanford. PUBL: Modern Labor Economics: Theory and Public Policy, (w R. Ehrenberg); The Occupational Safety and Health Act. INT: govt labor policy, labor market econ. POSITIONS: Asst Prof of Econ, U of Conn, 1971; Economist, Asst Secretary for Policy, Evaluation & Res, USDL, 1973; and (since 1974) Prof of Labor Econ, NYSSILR-Cornell Univ, Ithaca, NY 14853. 607/256-7650

SMITH, RUSSELL EDWARD Acad: Econ, Ind Rels; Consulting. BA 1969, U of Calif-Santa Cruz; MA 1978, San Francisco State U; PhD 1984, U of Ill-UC. PUBL: "Changes in the Source of Personel Income By Industry," Ill Bus Rev, May 1981. INT: intl comparative labor, labor market econ, emppl/trng programs. ASSN: AEA, Latin Amer Studies Assn, Assn of Borderland Scholars. POSITIONS: Res Asst, Olympus Res Corp, San Francisco, 1977; Grad Asst, U of Ill-Urbana, 1978; and (since 1984) Asst Prof of Econ, Washburn School of Bus, Washburn Univ of Topeka. ADDRESS: PO Box 5586, Main Office, Walnut Creek, CA 94596. 913/295-6307

SMITH, STERLING E. Acad: Ind Rels; Arbitration, Bus:Mgmt/Admin. INT: personnel, arb/med, coll barg. ASSN: Central Penna IRRA, Amer Soc of Safety Engineers, Amer Soc of Ind Engineers, Amer Soc of Ind Security. POSITIONS: Chief Ind Eng, Pittman Mfg Co, 1961; Production Control Mgr, 1968, and, since 1971, Safety Dir, Teledyne McKay, 850 Grantley Rd, York, PA 17405. 717/845-7581

SMITH, WENDY ANNE Acad: Anthropology, Ind Rels. BA 1972, Monash U-Australia. PUBL: "Japanese Factory-Malaysian Workers," Southeast Asia Chronicle, #88, Feb 1983, pp 19-22; "Understanding 'Japanese Society' Through Research on the Japanese Overseas-An Anthropological Study of Japanese Enterprise in Malaysia," NUSANTARA, #9, July 1982, pp 15-42; "The Relevance of the Japanese Model of Industrial Relations for the Analysis of Management-Labour Relations: A Case Study of a Japanese-Malaysian Venture," Proceedings of the IIRA, Kyoto, vol 5, 1983. INT: ind anthropology, intl comparative labor, coll barg. ASSN: Asian Studies Assn of Australia, Malaysian Soc Sci Assn, Ind Rels Assn of Australia. POSITIONS: Post-Grad Student, 1973, Tutor, Dept of Anthropology and Sociol, Monash U, 1978; and (since 1984) Res Assoc, Dept of Anthro & Sociol, Natl Univ of Malaysia, Bangi, Selangor, Malaysia. Phone: 03 (350) 001 ext 2232

SMITH, WIL J. Acad: Ind Rels, Econ. BS 1959, Alderson-Broadus Coll; MS 1962, U of Wis-Madison. PUBL: "The Impact of Federal Manpower Training Programs on the Employment and Earnings Experiences of Special Problem Groups of the Unemployed;" The Poor and the Hardcore Unemployed: Recommendations for New Approaches, (ed); Public Welfare..Right or Privilege: A System Under Attack. INT: empl/trng programs, labor market econ, income maint. ASSN: West Va IRRA, Mt. State Econ Assn, AEA, Natl Tax Assn. POSITIONS: Staff Economist, Northern Wis Develop Center, 1964; Asst Prof, 1967, and, since 1978, Assoc Prof of Econ and Ind Rels, Dept of Econ and Ind Rels, West Virginia Univ, Mortantown, WV 26505. 304/293-4201

SMITH, WILLIAM E. Bus:Pers/Ind Rels. POSITION: Industrial Relations Manager, Lubriquip Div Houdaille, 18901 Cranwood Pky, Cleveland, OH 44128.

SNIADECKI, ALAN F. Bus:Pers/Ind Rels. MLIR 1975, Mich State U. INT: personnel, org beh, ind psych. ASSN: Dallas/Ft. Worth IRRA, ASPA ACA, ASTD. POSITIONS: QWL Mgr, 1981, Reg Pers Mrg, 1982, Xerox-Office Products Div; and (since 1983) Director, Human Resources, Wangtek Inc, 41 Moreland Rd, Simi Valley, CA 93065. 805/583-5255

SNOOK, JOHN LLOYD JR. Acad: Ind Rels, Org Beh/Pers; Consulting. AB 1949, Antioch; LLB 1952, Harvard. INT: mgmt/human resources, org beh, personnel. POSITIONS: Empl Rels Assoc, Exxon (Standard Oil Co of NJ). 1952; and (since 1961) Prof of Bus Admin, Darden School, Univ of Virginia, PO Box 6550, Charlotsville, VA 22903. 804/924-4818

SNOW, CARLTON J. Acad: Law; Arbitration. BA 1962, Taylor U; M Div, 1966, Fuller Theological Seminary; JD & MA 1969, U of Wis. POSITIONS: School of Law, Loyola U-Louisiana; and (since 1971) Prof of Law, Willamette U, Salem, OR 97301. 503/370-6382

SNOW-GODFREY, JANET Bus:Pers/Ind Rels. MILR 1983, U of Ill. INT: personnel, union org/admin. POSITION: (since 1983) Empl Rels Rep, Pepsi-Cola Bottling Group. ADDRESS: 3472 Chelsea Circle, Ann Arbor, MI 48104. 313/326-7300

SNYDER, RUSSELL A. Acad: Econ. PhD 1964, U of Ill-UC. PUBL: "Omaha Unemployment Study;" "What to Expect in Armour Closing in Omaha;" "Public Welfare Board of North Dakota." INT: empl/trng programs, govt labor policy, income maint. ASSN: Inland (Spokane) IRRA, AEA. POSITIONS: Assoc Prof of Econ, ND State Univ, 1962; Assoc Prof of Econ, U of Nebr at Omaha, 1966; and (since 1969) Prof of Econ, Eastern Washington Univ, 304L Patterson Hall, Cheney, WA 99004. 509/359-2424

SNYDER, WILLIAM C. Government, Bus:-Pers/Ind Rels, Mgmt/Admin. BS 1969, Central Mo State U. INT: arb/med, coll barg, labor law. ASSN: Iowa IRRA. POSITIONS: Hearing Officer/Mediator, Iowa Publ Empl Rels Bd, 1975, and, since 1980, Asst Dir of Employee Relations, State of Iowa. ADDRESS: 515 14th Ave NW, Altoona, IA 50009. 515/281-5760

SOBEL, IRVIN Acad: Econ. Position: Dept of Economics, Florida State Univ, Tallahassee, FL 32306.

SOCHA, JOHN L. Librarian. AA 1964, Suffolk Community Coll; BA 1966, Adelphi U; MLS 1970, Pratt Inst. PUBL: Editor, USORT Newsletter (of NY Library Assn.) INT: coll barg, labor history, union org/admin. ASSN: New York Library Assn, NY State Labor History Assn. POSITION: (since 1968) Branch Librarian, Queens Borough Public Library, Seaside Branch. Address: 102-26 127th St, Richmond Hill, NY 11419. 212/990-0700

SOCKELL, DONNA Acad: Ind Rels. BA 1977, Union Coll; MILR 1979, PhD 1982, Cornell U. PUBL: "Legal Obstacles to Employee Participation Plans in Unionized Enterprises," ILR Rev, forthcoming; "Toward a Theory of the Union Role," chapter in D. B. Lipsky (ed) Advances in Industrial Relations, Greenwich, CT: JAI Press, 1983. INT: coll barg, govt labor policy, labor law. ASSN: Acad of Mgmt. POSITIONS: Asst Prof, School of Mgmt, SUNY-Binghamton, 1981; and (since 1982) Asst Prof, Grad School of Bus, Columbia Univ. ADDRESS: 16 Eldridge Ave, Ossining, NY 10562. 212/280-4403

SOCKNAT, JAMES A. Acad: Manpower. BS 1961, Iowa State U; JD 1966, Georgetown U. PUBL: Manpower and International Labor Migration in the Middle East and North Africa, (co-author), Oxford U Press, 1983; "Progress and Problems in the Development and Utilization of Human Resources in the Arab Gulf States," AL-ABATH, Quart J of Amer Univ of Beirut. INT: intl comparative labor, labor market econ, empl/trng programs. ASSN: ABA. POSITIONS: Manpower Specialist, Ford Found, 1969; Adjunct Assoc Prof Econ, U of Utah, 1975; and (since 1976) Senior Manpower Specialist, World Bank-Wash DC. ADDRESS: 6711 Weaver Ave, Mc Lean, VA 22101. 202/473-2650

SOETAERT, LYNN A. Bus: Pers/Ind Rels; Acad: Org Beh/Pers. BLA 1982, Ottawa U. INT: empl/trng programs, personnel, unionorg/-admin. ASSN: ASPA/PMA, AMA. POSITIONS: Empl Rels Mgr, Old American Ins Co, 1979; Sr Pers Specialist, PACCAR, 1981; and (since 1983) Personnel Manager, C. J. Patterson Co, 3947 Broadway, Kansas City, MO 64111. 816/561-9050

SOFFER, BENSON Government. BA 1949, Queens Coll; MA 1951, PhD 1956, Princeton U. PUBL: "A Theory of Trade Union Development: The Role of the Autonomous Worker," Labor History 1960; "Effect of Cost-of-Living Escalator Clause on General Wage Level Movements," Quar J of Econ, 1959; "On Union Rivalries and Minimum Differentiation of Wage Patterns," Rev of Econ & Statis, 1959. INT: govt labor policy, intl comparative labor, income maint. ASSN: Wash DC IRRA, AEA, IIRA, Soc of Government Economists. POSITIONS: Asst Prof of Industry, Grad School of Bus, 1958, Assoc Prof of Industry, Wharton School/Univ of Penna, 1961; and (since 1966) Labor Economist, US Dept of Commerce. ADDRESS: 11228 Bybee St, Silver Spring, MD 20902. 202/377-5703

SOLANA, LUCILLE Union. BA 1968, Moravian Coll. INT: union org/admin, coll barg, arb/med. POSITIONS: Local Council Rep, 1976, and, since 1982, MEC Secretary/Treas, Assn of Flight Attendants, AFL-CIO, Rosemont, IL. ADDRESS: 1101 Castile Ave, Coral Gables, FL 33134. 312/297-7170

SOLIE, ELSIE E. Consulting. 4549 Wood River Dr, Fairbanks, AK 99701. 907/479-2719

SOLIE, RICHARD JOHN Acad: Ind Rels, Econ. BS 1955, U of Wis-Superior; PhD 1965, U of Tenn. PUBL: "Employment Effects of Retraining the Unemployed," Ind & Labor Rels Rev, 1968; "The Transportation Model," and "Estimating the Benefits of Tourism and Recreation," chapters in Mineral Ind Res Lab, U of Alaska, 1973; "The Impact of the Trans Alaska Oil Pipeline on Fairbanks, Alaska," (w M. E. Thomas & S. R. Fison), NW Reg Econ Conf, 1977. INT: labor market econ, labor law, arb/med. ASSN: AEA, Western Econ Assn, AAA (Natl Panel of Arbitrators). POSITIONS: Assoc Prof of Econ, U of ND, 1966-70; Visiting Prof of Ind Rels, U of Minn, 1978-79; and (since 1970) Prof of Econ, Dept of Econ, Univ of Alaska. ADDRESS: 4549 Wood River Dr, Fairbanks, AK 99701. 907/474-6523

SOLOMON, JANET STERN Acad: Bus Admin; Consulting. BA 1965, Syracuse U; MBA 1976, U of Mo-KC; DBA 1983, George Washington U. PUBL: "Performance Benefits: An Idea for the 1980s;" "Reentry Occupations for Mature Women: Are They Predictable?" "Enterprise Zones in the Inner Cities: A Supply Side Proposal." INT: personnel, coll barg, empl/trng programs. ASSN: Wash DC IRRA, Acad of Mgmt. ASSN: Asst Prof of Bus Admin, Baker U, Baldwin, Kans, 1976-1977; Assoc Prof of Bus Admin, Marymount Coll-Arlington, Va., 1977-1983; and (since 1983) Assoc Prof of Bus Admin, Towson State Univ. ADDRESS: 3720 Alton Pl NW, Washington DC 20016. 301/321-3235

SOLOMON, MARK Bus:Pers/Ind Rels. BA 1965, Adelphi U. INT: coll barg, arb/med, personnel. ASSN: Southern Nevada IRRA, ASPA, Southern Nevada Pers Assn. POSITION: (since 1977) Director of Human Resources, Flamingo Hilton Hotel, 3555 Las Vegas Blvd South, Las Vegas, NV 89109. 702/733-3220

SOLOMON, NORMAN A. Acad: Ind Rels. BS 1973, Cornell U; MA 1974, PhD 1980, U of Wis. INT: coll barg, govt labor policy, arb/-med. ASSN: Detroit IRRA, Canadian Ind Rels Assn, SPIDR. POSITION: (since 1982) Asst Prof, Faculty of Bus Admin, Univ of Windsor. ADDRESS: 373 Detroit St, #507, Windsor, Ont N9C 4B4 Canada. 519/253-4232

SOLTES, CYNTHIA YVONNE Government. BS 1967, Ill Inst of Tech. INT: coll barg, arb/-med, personnel. ASSN: Chicago IRRA, SFLRP, Natl Federal of Bus and Professional Women. POSITIONS: Pers Mgmt Specialist, U. S. Civil Service Comm, 1972; Labor Rels Officer, Internal Revenue Service-Chicago, 1974; and (since 1976) Labor Rels Officer, U. S. Dept of Health & Human Services, Region V. ADDRESS: 593 Ranger Dr, Chicago Heights, IL 60411. 312/353-4876

SOLTOW, MARTHA JANE Acad: Ind Rels Librarian. PHB 1946, Dickinson Coll; MLS 1953, Pratt Inst. PUBL: Women in the American Labor Movement 1825-1935, an annotated bibliography, 1976; Industrial Relations and Personnel Management, Selected Reference Sources, 1979; American Labor History: A Guide to Sources in the Michigan State University Libraries, (monograph), 1980. INT: labor history, labor law, personnel. ASSN: Amer Library Assn, Committee of Ind Rels Librarians. POSITIONS: Corporation Records Librarian, Baker Libr, Harvard U, 1959; and (since 1962) Librarian, School of Labor and Ind Rels, Mich State Univ. ADDRESS: 520 Wildwood Dr, East Lansing, MI 48823. 517/355-4647

SONG, KYE-CHUNG Acad: Student. BBA 1973, MBA 1975, Seoul Natl U-Korea; MBA 1981, Northeast La U. INT: org beh, ind sociol, intl comparative labor. ASSN: Acad of Mgmt, Amer Psych Assn. POSITIONS: Asst Prof, 1976, Chungman Natl Univ, Korea, 1976, and (since 1981) Grad Teaching Asst, Ohio State Univ. ADDRESS: 2600 Muskingum Ct, Columbus, OH 43210. 614/422-2959

SONNENFELD, JEFFREY A. Acad: Org Beh/Pers. ADDRESS: Baker 109, Harvard Business School, Soldiers Field, Boston, MA 02163.

SOPER, DAVID E. Bus:Pers/Ind Rels. BA 1968, Blackburn Coll. INT: arb/med, coll barg, labor law. ASSN: Rubber Manufacturer's Assn. POSITIONS: Cost Acct, 1979, Assist Mgr, Labor Rels, 1981, and, since 1982, World Tire Group, Labor Rels Rep, Firestone Tire & Rubber Co, 1200 Firestone Parkway, Akron, OH 44317. 216/379-7390

SORCINELLI, EUGENIO G. Acad: Labor Educ. BA 1973, MS 1975, U of Mass. POSITION: Div of Labor Studies, Owen Hall #101, Indiana Univ, Bloomington, IN 47405. 812/337-9082

SOUTAR, DOUGLAS H. Bus:Pers/Ind Rels. PHB & LLB U of Wis. ASSN: New York IRRA. POSITION: Senior Vice Pres, Ind Rels & Personnel, ASARCO Inc, 120 Broadway, New York, NY 10271. 212/669-1310

SOUTAR, PATRICIA L. Bus:Mgmt/Admin. 49 Mayo Ave, Greenwich, CT 06830.

SOUTHON, PRISCILLA JEANNE Government. POSITION: Labor Rels Office, NY Public Library, Room 113, 5th Ave at 42nd St, New York, NY 10018. 212/930-0539

SPALDING, FRANCIS O. Arbitration, Legal Practice; Acad: Law. BA 1950, Yale U; JD 1964, Northwestern U. PUBL: "One Zambia, One Judiciary," The Lower Courts of Zambia, 2 Zambia Law J, 1-300, 1970. INT: arb/med, labor law. ASSN: San Francisco IRRA, SPIDR, Amer Law Inst. POSITIONS: Prof of Law, Northwestern U, 1965; Visiting Prof, Hastings Coll of Law, UC, 1983-84; and (since 1982) Arbitrator-Attorney, PO Box 217, Sea Ranch, CA 95497. 707/785-2744.

SPANGLER, THOMAS JAMES Union. 11200 Lockwood Dr, #1714, Silver Spring, MD 20901.

SPARGO, PAUL Bus:Pers/Ind Rels. BS 1979, Cornell U. INT: personnel, org beh, coll barg. ASSN: ASPA, Ind Rels Assn of Western NY. POSITIONS: Director of Services, Master Printers of Amer, 1979; and (since 1981) Corp Mgr, Empl Rels, Greater Buffalo Press, 302 Grote St, Buffalo, NY 14207. 716/876-6410

SPARKS, JOAN KEE Student. 3704 Melody Lane E, Kokomo, IN 46902. 317/453-7254

SPARROUGH, MICHAEL E. Union, Bus:-Mgmt/Admin. BS 1965, U of Md; MBA U of Penna. INT: coll barg, org beh, personnel. ASSN: AEA, Amer Finance Assn, Wash Soc of Investment Analysts. POSITIONS: Economist, USDL-BLS, 1966; Research Assoc, Ind Res Unit, Wharton School, U of Penna, 1973; and (since 1974) Research Director, Air Line Pilots Assn Intl. ADDRESS: 6401 Western Ave NW, Washington DC 20015. 202/797-4090

SPARROW, DOROTHY G. Arbitration; Acad: Econ, Ind Rels. AB 1951, Wellesley Coll; AM 1955, Radcliffe; PhD 1965, Harvard. PUBL: "Firm Training Policy in France," Monthly Labor Rev, June 1980; "Changing Market Structures: Union Wage Gains." ASSN: Boston IRRA, AEA, Amer Pol Sci Assn. POSITIONS: Arbitrator, Fact-Finder, 1973-74; Lecturer, Ind Rels, School of Mgmt, Boston Coll, 1973; and (since 1982) Visiting Prof-Dept of Econ, Wheaton Coll, 15 Homestead St, Newton, MA 02168. 617/332-6559

SPELLMAN, DAVID J. III Legal Practice. BS 1977, JD 1980, Cornell U. PUBL: 'Future Shock and the NLRB," ALI-ABA; "EEO Update," ALI-ABA; "Employment At Will in New York," ABA Labor Section. INT: labor law, arb/med, coll barg. ASSN: ABA. POSITION: (since 1980) Attorney, Parker, Chapin, Flattan and Klimpe. ADDRESS: 105 Coachlight Sq, Montrose, NY 10548. 212/840-6200

SPELLMAN, WILLIAM E. Acad: Econ, Ind Rels; Arbitration. AB 1965, Baker U; MA 1966, PhD 1970, Kansas State U. PUBL: "Monopsonistic Market: Major League Baseball, Ind Rel, 1983; "Backward Glance at AEA Presidents," Am Economist, 1984; "Academic Origins of Economists," Am Econ Rev. INT: arb/med, coll barg, labor law. ASSN: AAA, AEA, Iowa Acad of Arb. POSITIONS: Instructor & Res Assoc, Kansas State U, 1968; Visiting Prof of Ind Rels, U of Iowa, 1983; and (since 1970) Prof of Econ and Bus Admin, Coe College, Cedar Rapids. ADDRESS: Rte 4, Box 474-F, Solon, IA 52333. 319/399-8573

SPENCE, MARY OTTO Bus:Pers/Ind Rels. BM 1971, U of Mo-Kansas City; MA 1981, Central Mich U. INT: coll barg, arb/med, org beh. ASSN: Kansas City IRRA, ASPA, Amer Compensation Assn. POSITIONS: Empl Rels Rep, General Serv Admin, 1976; Labor Rels Rep, Kansas City Power & Light Co, 1979; and (since 1981) Vice Pres, Human Resources, Libby Welding Co, 5800 Stilwell, Kansas City, MO 64120. 816/231-6039

SPENCER, DAVID C. Acad: Labor Studies. BS 1962, U of Wis-LaCrosse; MA 1963, U of Wis; MAIR 1982, U of Minn. INT: labor educ, coll barg, labor history. ASSN: Org of Amer History, UCLEA. POSITION: (since 1972) Assoc Prof, Room 336, Poplars Res Center, Indiana Univ, Bloomington, IN 47405. 812/335-9082

SPENCER, JANET M. Acad: Law; Arbitration. BA 1959, Cornell U; LLB 1962, Harvard. POSITION: (since 1974) Assoc Prof of Law, St. John's Univ Law School. ADDRESS: 1112 Park Ave, New York, NY 10028. 212/969-8000

SPERKA, SHLOMO Government. LLB 1958, Brooklyn Law School. PUBL: Dealing Effectively With Public Sector Labor Relations Agencies, Intl Pers & Mgmt Assn, 1980; "Unfair Labor Practice Remedies and Judicial Review," in Portrait of a Process, Collective Negotiations in Public Employment, Publ Empl Rels Service, 1979; Compiled Opinions of the Michigan Employment Relations Commission, 1965-75, Opinions Press, 1976, Volume II, 1976-81, Opinions Press, 1983. INT: labor law, arb/med, coll barg. ASSN: Detroit IRRA, SPIDR, Mich State Bar (Labor Law Section). POSITIONS: Attorney, NLRB, 1962; Administrative Law Judge, 1969, and, since 1983, Director, Michigan Employment Relations Commission, Bureau of Empl Rels, 1200 Sixth Ave, 14th Floor, Detroit, MI 48226. 313/256-3540

SPERLING, HERMAN J. Union. POSITION: Economist-Statistician, Joint Council of Teamsters, 17089 Bollinger Drive, Pacific Palisades, CA 90272.

SPERRY, JOHN C. Union. POSITION: President, UFCW Union Local 324, 8530 Stanton Ave, Box 5004, Buena Park, CA 90622. 714/995-4601

SPEYER, DAVID BLAIR Student. BS 1983, NYSSILR-Cornell; MSC 1984, London School of Econ. INT: arb/med, coll barg, intl comparative labour. ASSN: Wash DC IRRA, SPIDR. ADDRESS: Croton Dam Rd, Croton-on-Hudson, NY 10520. 914/271-9359.

SPICHTIG, JOHN J. Bus:Pers/Ind Rels. BS 1974, Calif State U-Fresno; MBA 1978, Calif State U-Sacramento. INT: labor law, personnel, coll barg. ASSN: Orange County IRRA, ASPA. POSITIONS: Sr. Pers Rep, McDonnell Douglas Astronautics Co, 1971, and, since 1981, Administrator-Pers Services, McDonnell Douglas Automation Company (McAuto), 3855 Lakewood Blvd, M/S K19-81, Long Beach, CA 90846. 714/952-5571

SPILKER, KATHLEEN JONES Arbitration. BA 1975, U of Notre Dame; JD 1978, U of Pittsburgh. INT: arn/med, coll barg, labor law. ASSN: Western Penna IRRA, AAA, FMCS, Penna Bar Assn. POSITIONS: Staff Asst, Labor Rels, Westinghouse Electric Co, 1978; and (since 1980) Arbitrator (self-employed), 1301 Union Trust Bldg, Pittsburgh, PA 15219. 412/281-2736

SPIRN, STEVEN Acad: Ind Rels; Consulting, Government. PhD 1974, U of Ill; 1979 JD, U of Toledo. PUBL: Handbook on Ohio Collective Bargaining Act; The Labor Relations Experience: Cases and Exercises; Issues in Health Care Administration. INT: coll barg, labor law. ASSN: Northeast Ohio IRRA, ASPA, Acad of Mgmt, ABA. POSITIONS: Dir of Labor Rels, Lucas County Board of Commissioners, 1980; and (since 1973) Prof of Labor Rels, Coll of Bus, Univ of Toledo, 2801 W Bancroft, Toledo, OH 43606. 419/537-2380

SPITZ, HERBERT Acad: Economics. 175 W 93rd St, New York, NY 10025. 201/645-5265

SPITZ, RUTH SACHERE Acad: Econ. BA 1938, Brooklyn Coll; MA 1948, U of Wis. PUBL: Dual Careers: A Longitudinal Study of Labor Market Experiences of Women, (co-author), Ohio State U, 1970; Career Thresholds: A...Study of Male Youth, (co-author), 1969; The Pre Retirement Years: A...Study of Men, (co-author), 1968. INT: labor educ, women at work, govt labor policy. ASSN: AEA, Univ & Coll Labor Educ Assn. POSITIONS: Research Assoc, Ohio State U, 1966-70; Labor Economist, 1970-75; and (since 1975) Assoc Prof, Empire State College. ADDRESS: 372 Central Park W 19N, New York, NY 10025. 212/279-7380

SPREHE, J. TIMOTHY Government, Arbitration. BA 1962, St. Louis U; MA 1963, PhD 1967, Washington U-St. Louis. INT: arb/med, method/-statis, ind sociol. ASSN: Wash DC IRRA, Amer Statis Assn, Intl Statis Inst, SPIDR. POSITION: (since 1981) Office of Information & Regulatory Affairs, Office of Mgmt and Budget-Wash DC. ADDRESS: 5504 Surrey St, Chevy Chase, MD 20815. 202/395-4814

SPRING, ELLAN H. Government. AB 1968, Randolph-Macon Woman's Coll; MBA 1970, U of Penna. INT: empl benefits, mgmt/educ, govt labor policy. ASSN: Wash DC IRRA, Women in Employee Benefits. POSITION: (since 1975) Program Analyst, Pension Benefit Guaranty Corp-Wash DC. ADDRESS: 3930 Forrest School Rd, Smithsburg, MD 21783. 202/254-6138

SPRING, H. CHARLES Government. AB 1965, U of N.C.; JD 1969, U of Md. INT: union org/admin, govt labor policy. ASSN: Wash DC IRRA. POSITION: Asst Division Chief, USDL, LMSA Div of Research and Analysis-Wash DC. ADDRESS: 3930 Forrest School Rd, Smithsburg, MD 21783. 202/523-7481

SPRINGER, BEVERLY J. Acad: Political Science. BA 1960, MA 1962, Ohio State U; PhD 1971, U of Colo. INT: intl comparative labor, govt labor policy, labor history. ASSN: Southwest Labor Studies, Soc for Intl Development, European Studies. POSITION: (since 1974) Prof of Intl Studies, American Grad School of International Mgmt, Glendale, AZ 85306. 602/978-7011

SPRITZER, ALLAN D. Acad: Univ Admin. BA 1963, CCNY; MA 1964, U of Ill; PhD 1971, Cornell U. PUBL: "Private Sector Industrial Relations in the South," (w T. Bain), Labor Law J, vol 32, #8, Aug 1981, pp 536-544; "Administrators' Attitudes Toward Faculty Unionism," (w C. A. Odewahn), Ind Rels, vol 15, #2, May 1976, pp 206-215; "Equal Employment Opportunity Versus Protection for Women: A Public Policy Dilemma," Alabama Law Rev, vol 24, #3, Summer 1972, pp 567-606. INT: higher educ admin, arb/med, coll barg. ASSN: SPIDR, Southern Mgmt Assn, Acad of Mgmt. POSITIONS: Asst/Assoc/Prof of Ind Rels, 1968, Asst Dean, Coll of Commerce and Bus Admin, U of Alabama-Tuscaloosa, 1976-1981; and (since 1981) Dean, College of Bus, East Tennessee State Univ, PO Box 23470 A, Johnson City, TN 37614. 615/929-4289

SPROAT, KEZIA Acad: Human Resource Research. AB 1959, Vassar Coll; MA 1963, PhD 1975, Ohio State U. PUBL: The National Longitudinal Surveys: An Annotated Bibliography of Research, Lexington, MA: Lexington Books, 1984; Tomorrow's Workers, (w M. Borus), Lexington, 1983; "How Do Families Fare When the Breadwinner Retires?" Monthly Labor Rev, vol 106, #12, Dec 1983, pp 44-44. INT: communications, govt labor policy. ASSN: Central Ohio IRRA, Modern Language Assn of Amer, Intl Assn of Bus Communicators. POSITIONS: Visiting Asst Prof of English, Ohio Wesleyan U, 1978; Director, Univ Center Ministries, Inc, 1978; and (since 1979) Editor, Center for

Human Resource Research, Ohio State Univ, 5701 North High St, Worthington, OH 43085. 614/888-8238

SQUILLACOTE, GEORGE F. Government. BA 1945, JD 1947, U of Chicago. INT: labor law, govt labor policy, coll barg. ASSN: Wisconsin IRRA, ABA, Federal Bar Assn, State Bar Assn. POSITION: (since 1964) Regional Dir, NLRB, Region 30. ADDRESS: 2628 N Lake Drive, Milwaukee, WI 53211. 414/291-3870

SRIKRISHNA, BELLUR N. Legal Practice. BSc, 1960, LLB 1962, LLM 1974, U of Bombay-India. INT: labor law, coll barg, labor history. ASSN: Labor Law Practitioners' Assn-Bombay. POSITION: (since 1962) Advocate, Supreme Court, 46 Shyamala, Behind Don Bosco School, Matunga, Bombay 400019 India. Phone: Bombay 471488

STAATS, CHARLES E., JR. Union. 11 Frantone LA, Londonville, NY 12211.

STABLEIN, RALPH E. Acad: Org Beh/-Pers. BA 1975, Ill Benedictine Coll; MA 1976, Western Ill U; PhD 1984, Northwestern U. INT: org beh, mgmt/educ, method/statis. ASSN: AOM, APA, ASA. POSITION: Asst Prof, Faculty of Commerce, Univ of British Columbia, 2053 Main Mall, Vancouver, BC V6T 1Y8 Canada. 604/228-5043

STALLER, JEROME M. Consulting, Arbitration. BA 1967, PhD 1975, Temple U. PUBL: Structural Settlements/The Art of Advocacy in Settlements, Matthew Bender. ADDRESS: 4536 Hornbeam Dr, Rockville, MD 20853. 215/732-4464

STALLWORTH, LAMONT EDWARD Acad: Ind Rels; Arbitration. BSBA 1970, Northeastern U; MS 1972, U of Mass; PhD 1980, NYSSILR-Cornell. PUBL: "Who Files Suits and Why: An Empirical Portrait of the Litigious Worker," Ill Law Rev; "Arbitrating Discrimination Grievances in the Wake of Gardner-Denver," Monthly Law Rev; "Federal and State Mediators and Grievance Mediation Process: An Empirical Inquiry,"Proceedings of Annual Spring Meeting, IRRA. INT: arb/med, labor law, intl comparative labor. ASSN: Chicago IRRA, SPIDR, AAA & FMCS-Arb Panels. POSITIONS: Labor-Mgmt Field Examiner, NLRB, 1972; Asst Prof, Inst Labor & Ind Rels, U of Ill, 1978; and (since 1981) Asst Prof, Inst of Ind Rels, Loyola Univ-Chicago. ADDRESS: 1853 N Cleveland Ave, Chicago, IL 60614. 312/787-4145

STANDRIFF, DONALD M. Bus:Mgmt/Admin. ASSN: Cincinnati IRRA, Soc of Advancement of Mgmt, ASPA. POSITIONS: Dir-Pers, D. H. Baldwin Co, 19 years; Dir-Ind Rels, Harvey Husbell Inc, 2 years; and (since 1974) Executive Mgr, Cincinnati Industrial Inst, 2495 Langdon Farm, Cincinnati, OH 45237. 513/731-2211

STANLEY, DOUGLAS C. Legal Prac, Arbitration. BBA 1967, LLB 1971, U of New Brunswick; LLM 1973, Osgoode Hall. PUBL: "Stumbling Blocks to Developing a National Human Resources Strategy," Canadian Bus Rev, 1981; "Out of the Quicksand (Review Social-Economic Policy)," vol 3, #3, 1982, Policy Option Inst for Res on Publ Policy; "Res Judicata in Administrative Law," U.N.B. Law J 221, 1983. INT: arb/med, coll barg, labor law. ASSN: Canadian Bar Assn, AAA, SPIDR. POSITIONS: Chairman, Public Service Labour Rels Bd, 1981;and (since 1981) Partner, Stanley & Levesque Law Firm, PO Box 65, Fredericton, NB E3B 4Y2 Canada. 606/454-4662

STAPP, MICHAEL Legal Practice. BS 1979, MBA & JD 1983, U of Kans. PUBL: "Ten Years After: A Legal Framework of Collective Bargaining in the Hospital Industry." INT: labor law, labor market econ, arb/med. ASSN: Kansas Bar Assn. POSITION: (since 1983) Attorney, Blake & Uhlig, 475 New Brotherhood Bldg, 8th & State Ave, Kansas City, KS 66101. 913/-321-8884

STARK, ARTHUR Arbitration. BA 1939, MA 1941, U of Chicago. INT: arb/med, coll barg, govt labor policy. ASSN: New York IRRA, NAA, SPIDR. POSITION: (since 1957) Arbitrator, 115 Central Park West, New York, NY 10023. 212/489-0080

STARK, DOROTHY C. 115 Central Park West, New York, NY 10023.

STARK, HARRY F. Acad: Ind Rels. PhD 1958, Rutgers U. INT: labor mgmt/educ, coll barg, union org/admin. ASSN: New Brunswick, New York IRRA, AEA, ASPA, SPIDR. POSITION: (since 1949) Professor, Inst of Mgmt and Labor Rels, Rutgers Univ. ADDRESS: 350 North Fourth Ave, Highland Park, NJ 08904. 201/932-9022

STASSEN, MARJORIE A. Student. 245 Upson Downs Rd, Newark, OH 43055. 614/366-4463

STATHAM, C. GORDON Legal Practice, Arbitration. BS 1950, Ga Inst of Tech; LLB 1965, Emory U. POSITION: Attorney at Law, 119 E Maple St, Decatur, GA 30030. 404/377-9277

STAUDOHAR, PAUL DAVID Acad: Ind Rels; Arbitration. BA 1962, U of Minn; MBA 1966, MA 1968, PhD 1969, U of Southern Calif. PUBL: Public Employment Disputes and Dispute Settlement, Honolulu: Ind Rels Center, U of Hawaii, 1972; Grievance Arbitration in Public Employment, Inst of Ind Rels, U of Calif-Berkeley, 1977; Personnel Management and Industrial Relations, (w D. Yoder), Englewood Cliffs, NJ: Prentice Hall Inc, 1982. INT: arb/med, coll barg, personnel. ASSN: AEA, AAA, Roster of Arbitrators, FMCS. POSITIONS: Administrative Officer, United Calif Bank, Trust Dept, 1964; Instructor of Econ, Univ of Southern Calif, 1967; and (since 1969) Prof of Bus Admin, School of Bus and Econ, Calif State Univ, Hayward, CA 94542. 415/881-3080

STAUDTER, DONALD V. Arbitration, Consulting. BSIE 1959, U of Dayton; MBA 1964, Xavier U; Cert OSHA 1975, USDL. PUBL: "Summary of Labor Arbitration Awards," New York, AAA, #298-8, Jan 15, 1984; "Labor Arbitration Awards," vol 81-2, 1981, Commerce Clearing House, Chicago; "Labor Arbitration Reports," 79LA508, BNA, Wash DC. INT: arb/med, coll barg, empl/trng programs. ASSN: Dayton IRRA, AAA, Amer Inst of Ind Engineers, FMCS. POSITION: Foreman, Inland Div-General Motors, 1959; Asst Prof, Ind Eng Tech, U of Dayton, 1966; and (since 1971) Arbitrator, 3115 Lenox Dr, Dayton, OH 45429. 513/298-6935

STAVROS, DEMO Acad: Industrial Engineering. POSITION: Engineering Technology, Texas A & M Univ, College Station, TX 77841.

STAWNYCHY, PETRO R. Legal Practice; Acad: Ind Rels. BA 1976, MA 1978, Rutgers U; JD 1981, New York Law School. PUBL:

"Municipal Bargaining in New Jersey;" "Interest Arbitration in New Jersey-Who's Winning?" (w E. Gross); "First Experience With Mediation By Arbitration Under Chapter 85 Laws of 1977." INT: labor law, coll barg, arb/med. ASSN: New Brunswick IRRA. POSITION: Pincus, Gordon & Zuckerman, 79 Paterson St, POB 1173, New Brunswick, NJ 08882. 201/247-6677

STAYT, JOHN Professional Assn, Bus: Ind Rels/Mgmt. POSITION: Penn Mfgs Assn, 925 Chestnut St, Philadelphia, PA 19107. 215/629-5080

STEADMAN, WALLACE PATRICK Bus:-Pers/Ind Rels. POSITION: Vice Pres-Human Resources, Standard Brands Paint Co, 4300 W 190th St, Torrance, CA 90509. 213/542-5901

STEALEY, PATRICIA Bus:Pers/Ind Rels, Legal Practice. BBA, Cleveland State U; JD 1980, Marshall School of Law-CSU. INT: personnel, org beh, arb/med. ASSN: Cleveland IRRA, ASPA, ABA, Ohio State Bar Assn. POSITIONS: Tribunal Supr, AAA, 1956; Pers Mgr, L & B Manufactore Inc, 1978; and (since 1978) Director of Pers, Dinner Bell Meats, Inc, 2699 East 51st St, Cleveland, OH 44104. 217/361-5400

STEENKAMP, THOMAS I. Bus:Mgmt/Admin, Pers/Ind Rels. BA 1956, Potchefstroom U. PUBL: Industrial Relations, 1974; Transformation Phase Two, 1983; Reintrenchment, 1982. INT: mgmt/educ, coll barg, govt labor policy. ASSN: Afkrikaanse Handelsinstituut. POSITIONS: Manpower Mgr, 1970, and, since 1979, Chief Exec (Manpower), GENCOR, PO Box 61820, Marshalltown 2107, South Africa. Phone: 836-1121

STEHLING, DONALD J. Student. Box 33, Ripview Ct, Cambridge, WI 53523. 608/423-3945

STEIN, BARRY A. Consulting. 330 Broadway, Cambridge, MA 02139.

STEIN, BRUNO Acad: Econ, Ind Rels; Arbitration. AB 1950, AM 1952, PhD 1959, New York U. PUBL: Social Security and Pensions in Transition; Work and Welfare in Britain and the USA; "Management Rights and Productivity." INT: arb/med, income maint, labor market econ. ASSN: New York IRRA, AEA, AAA, SPIDR. POSITIONS: Assoc Prof of Econ, 1963, Prof of Econ, 1968, and, since 1973, Dir, Inst of Labor Rels, New York Univ, 259 Mercer St, New York, NY 10003. 212/598-7796

STEIN, JOSEPHINE C. Government. BS 1941, Simmons Coll. POSITIONS: USDL-Retired. ADDRESS: 6512 Bannockburn Dr, Bethesda, MD 20817. 301/229-4991

STEIN, KENNETH L. Government, Legal Prac; Acad: Law. MA 1971, JD 1954, Temple U. PUBL: "The Fair Labor Standards Act," in Phila Lawyer, July 1981. INT: labor law, govt labor policy, labor market econ. ASSN: Philadelphia IRRA, ABA, AEA, Federal Bar Assn. POSITIONS: Adjunct Prof of Labor Law, Master's Program, Temple U; 1976; and (since 1967), Deputy Regional Soliciter, USDL, Office of the Soliciter. ADDRESS: 235 Holmecrest Rd, Jenkintown, PA 19046. 215/596-5171

STEIN, LEON Union. BS 1934, CCNY. PUBL: The Triangle Fire; The Education of Abraham Cahan; Out of the Sweatshop. ASSN: Amer Historical Assn, Org of Amer Historians. POSITIONS: Sr Advisory Editor, Arno Press, 1972; Natl Council for the Humanities, 1978; and (since 1976) Editor Emeritus, Intl Ladies Garment Workers' Union. ADDRESS: 448-A Dahlia Place, Cranbury, NJ 08512.

STEIN, ROBERT GARY Bus:Mgmt/Admin. 700 Brooksedge Blvd, Westerville, OH 43081. 614/891-6466

STEINBERG, HARVEY A. Acad: Econ, Law, Bus Admin. JD 1958, Brooklyn Law School. INT: labor law, personnel, coll barg. POSITIONS: Natl Vice Pres, Res Dir, United Hatters Intl Union, AFL-CIO, 1958; General Deputy Dir, Hoboken Model Cities, 1968; and (currently) Adjunct Prof, various colleges. ADDRESS: Apt C-2, 161 Franklin Corner Rd, Lawrenceville, NJ 08648. 609/896-2470

STENMARK, JOHN H. Bus:Pers/Ind Rels. POSITION: Vice Pres, Ind Rels, American Iron/Steel Inst, 1000 16th St NW, Washington DC 20036. 202/452-7210

STEPHAN, PAULA ELIZABETH Acad: Econ, Ind Rels. BA 1967, Grinnell Coll; MA 1968, PhD 1971, U of Mich. PUBL: "The Allocation of Employment & Training Funds Across States," Policy Analysis, vol 6, #4, 1980; "Career Commitment and Labor Force Participation of Married Women," (w L. Schroeder) in Women in the Labor Force, ed by Lloyd, Gilmore & Andrews; "Labor Service and Training Over the Life Cycle," (w H. Ryder & F. Stafford), Into Econ Rev, Oct 1976. Int: labor market econ, govt labor policy, union org/admin. ASSN: Atlanta IRRA, AEA, Southern Econ Assn, Southern Sociol Assn. POSITIONS: Asst Prof, 1971, Assoc Prof, 1976, and, since 1981, Prof of Econ, Georgia State Univ, Univ Plaza, Atlanta, GA 30303. 404/658-2774

STEPHENS, DAVID B. Acad: Ind Rels. POSITION: Dept of Bus Admin, College of Bus, Univ of Texas, El Paso, TX 79968.

STEPHENS, ELVIS CLAY Acad: Ind Rels. BBA 1958, MBA 1959, North Tex State U; DBA 1966, Ind U. PUBL: Management of Personnel: Manpower Management and Organization Behavior, McGraw Hill, 1972; "A Supervisor Performs Bargaining Work: Is the Contract Violated?" Labor Law J, Nov 1980; "Do No-Strike Clauses Prohibit Sympathy Strikes," Labor Law J, May 1982. INT: arb/med, coll barg, personnel. ASSN: North Texas IRRA, ASPA, Acad of Mgmt. POSITIONS: 1st Lt, U.S. Army Corps of Engineers, 1953; Instructor, Austin Coll, 1959; and (since 1963) Professor Bus Admin, College of Bus, North Texas State Univ, Box 5021, N.T. Station, Denton, TX 76203. 817/565-3159

STEPHENSON, JAMES R. Health & Hosp Care. POSITION: Charter Medical Corp, 577 Mulberry St, PO Box 209, Macon, GA 31202.

STEPINA, LEE P. Acad: Bus Admin, Org Beh/Pers, Ind Rels. BS 1973, MA 1976, PhD 1981, U of Ill-UC. INT: personnel, coll barg, org beh. ASSN: ASPA, APA. POSITION: (since 1981) Asst Prof of Mgmt & Labor Rels, College of Bus, Florida State Univ, Tallahassee, FL 32306. 904/644-6762

STERLING, WILLIAM P. Bus:Mgmt/Admin. POSITION: Economist, General Motors Corp, 3044 W Grand Blvd, 9-113, Detroit, MI 48202. 313/556-2489

STERN, BERNARD WOLF Consulting. BS 1933 CCNY. PUBL: "The Factors Determining Hawaii's Industrial Relations Climate," IRRA Proceedings, 1983 Spring Meeting. ADDRESS: 2196 Halekoa Dr, Honolulu, HI 96821.

STERN, JAMES L. Acad: Ind Rels, Econ; Arbitration. BS 1943, Antioch Coll, PhD 1954, U of Calif-Berkeley. PUBL: Arbitration Issues for the 1980s, (co-editor), 1982; Public Sector Bargaining, (co-editor & chapter author), 1979; Final Offer Arbitration, (co-author), 1975. INT: arb/med, coll barg, govt labor policy. ASSN: Wisconsin IRRA, NAA, AAA, AEA. POSITION: (since 1962) Prof of Econ and Ind Rels, 7434 Social Science Bldg, Univ of Wisconsin, Madison, WI 53706. 608/262-8789

STERN, ROBERT N. Acad: Org Beh/Pers, Sociol, Ind Rels. AB 1970, Washington U; MS, 1972, PhD 1974, Vanderbilt U. PUBL: "Resource Mobilization and the Creation of U.S. Producer's Cooperatives 1835-1935," (w H. Aldrich), Economic and Industrial Democracy, Aug 1983; "Competitive Influences on the Interorganizational Regulation of College Athletes," Administrative Sci Quart, Mar 1981. INT: org beh, ind sociol, govt labor policy. ASSN: Amer Sociol Assn, Southern Sociol Assn, Amer Assn for the Advancement of Sci. POSITIONS: Asst Prof, 1974, and, since 1980, Assoc Prof, NYSSILR-Cornell Univ, Ithaca, NY 14853. 607/256-3048

STERNSTEIN, HERMAN Consulting, Retired. 976 E 19th St, Brooklyn, NY 11230.

STESSIN, LAWRENCE Journalism. PhD 1958, New York U. PUBL: "Labor Arbitration," Harvard Bus Rev, Nov 1982; The Practice of Industrial Relations, BNA; Employee Discipline, BNA 1060. INT: ind psych, mgmt/educ, org beh. ASSN: New York IRRA. POSITIONS: Prof Emeritus, Hofstra Univ, 1958, and, currently, Syndicated Columnist, Miami Rev Syndicate. ADDRESS: Rodney Plaza 1209, 2301 Collins Ave, Miami Beach, FL 33139. 305/673-9121

STEVENS, CARL MANTLE Acad: Econ; Consulting, Arbitration. PhD 1951, Harvard U. PUBL: Strategy and Collective Bargaining Negotiation, McGraw Hill, 1963, reprinted Greenwood Press Inc, 1978; "Medical Malpractice: Some Implications of Contract and Arbitration in HMOs," Milbank Memorial Fund Quart, Health and Soc, vol 59, #1, 1982; "Is Compulsory Arbitration Compatible with Bargaining," Ind Rels, Feb 1966. ASSN: AEA, Amer Public Health Assn, AAUP. POSITION: (since 1954) Prof of Econ, Reed College, Portland, OR 97202. 503/771-1112

STEVENS, DAVID W. Arbitration, Bus:Pers/Ind Rels. BS 1970, MLIR 1974, Mich State U. INT: arb/med, coll barg. POSITIONS: Labor Rels Staff Asst, 1975, Labor Rels Rep, 1978, and, since 1981, Arbitration Rep, Caterpillar Tractor Co, Peoria. ADDRESS: 1027 Marshall, Morton, IL 61550. 309/263-8663

STEVENS, DAVID WALTER Acad: Econ. BA 1962, Calif State U at Sacramento; PhD 1965, U of Colo. POSITION: Prof, Dept of Econ, Univ of Missouri, Columbia, MO 65211. 314/882-3210

STEVENS, DONALD M. Bus:Pers/Ind Rels. POSITION: Employee Rels, Yale Univ, PO Box 2964, Yale Station, New Haven, CT 06520. 203/436-2310

STEVENS, JOHN E. Acad: Bus Admin. POSITION: Dept of Mgmt & Finance, Drown Hall 35, Lehigh Univ, Bethlehem, PA 18015. 215/861-3447

STEVENSON, ANN FRANCES Bus: Pers/-Ind Rels. MAIR 1983, Wayne State U. INT: govt labor policy, labor market econ, mgmt/-educ. POSITIONS: Intern-NLRB, Reg 7, Detroit, 1983; and (since 1984) Employee Rels Rep, Zilog-an affiliate of Exxon, Campbell. ADDRESS: 1674 Derose Way #4, San Jose, CA 95126. 408/370-8000 ext 4629

STEVENSON, THOMAS MARTIN Acad: Economics. RR 1, 61 Carla Dr, Granite City, IL 62040.

STEWARD, PHYLLIS R. Bus:Pers/Ind Rels, Mgmt/Admin; Student. BS 1965, Southern Ill U. INT: personnel, coll barg, arb/med. ASSN: ASPA. POSITIONS: Personnel Officer, 1973, and, since 1978, Pers Manager, Univ of Ill Operation and Maintenance Div, 1501 S Oak, Champaign, IL 61820. 217/333-7946

STEWART, JOANN PHELPS Acad: Econ. PhD 1969, Boston U. INT: labor market econ, coll barg, govt labor policy. ASSN: AEA, Atlantic Econ Assn, AAUP. POSITIONS: Prof-Econ, Boston State Coll, 1967-81; and (since 1982) Professor of Economics, Univ Mass/Boston. ADDRESS: 111 Hill St, Apt 8, Stoneham, MA 02180. 617/929-7435

STIEBER, JACK Acad: Ind Rels; Arbitration. BSS 1940,. CCNY; MA 1948, U of Minn; PhD 1956, Harvard U. PUBL: Protecting Unorganized Employees Against Unjust Discharge, (ed.) Mich State Univ, 1983; U.S. Industrial Relations 1950-1980: A Critical Assessment, (ed) IRRA 1981; Public Employee Unionism, Brookings Inst, 1973. INT: coll barg, arb/med, intl comparative labor. ASSN: Mid-Michigan IRRA, AEA, NAA, AAUP. POSITIONS: Exec Secretary, President's Labor Mgmt Advisory Committee, 1962; Res Assoc, Harvard Bus School, 1954; and (since 1956) Prof and Dir, School of Labor and Ind Rels, Mich State Univ, East Lansing, MI 48824. 517/355-1800

STILLER, W. A. Bus:Pers/Ind Rels. BS 1973, Cornell U. POSITIONS: Regional Mgr, Ind Rels American Cyanamid Co, 1980; and (currently) Manager, Labor Rels, Lederle Laboratories, One Cynanmid Plaza, Wayne, NJ 07470. 201/831-4634

STIMMELL, THOMAS W. III Bus:Pers/Ind Rels. BS 1975, Mich State U. INT: coll barg, arb/med, labor law. ASSN: Saginaw IRRA, Saginaw Valley Safety Council, AAPA, Saginaw Ind Mgmt Assn. POSITIONS: Labor Rep, Mich State Employees Assn, 1975; and (since 1980) Manager, Labor Rels, Baker Perkins Inc, 1000 Hess St, Saginaw, MI 48601. 517/752-4121

STOBER, RICHARD P. Union. BA 1969, Penna State; MLIR 1971, Mich State U. PUBL: "Comparable Worth: The Basis of the Controversy;" "Comparable Worth: Measuring Comparability." INT: labor educ, health & hosp care, method/statis. ASSN: Amer Health Planning Assn. POSITIONS: Staff Assoc, George Meany Center for Labor Studies, 1972; Labor Rep, 1976, and, since 1983, Educ/Research Dir, Penna Nurses Assn, 2515 Front St, Harrisburg, PA 17110. 717/234-7935

STOCHAJ, JOHN M. Acad: Ind Rels; Arbitration. BA 1951, Boston U; MA 1955, Rutgers U; PhD 1963, NYU. POSITION: Prof of Econ, NJ Inst of Technology. ADDRESS: 65 Riceman Rd, Berekely Heights, NJ 07922. 201/645-5270

STOCKER, NORMAN JAMES Consulting. Bus:Pers/Ind Rels, Arbitration. INT: coll barg, arb/med. ASSN: Western New York IRRA. POSITION: Consultant, Associated Labor Consultants. ADDRESS: Town of Tonawanda Labor Rels, PO Box 710, Buffalo, NY 14217. 716/877-1974.

STODGHILL, WILLIAM Union. POSITION: SEIU #50, 4108 Lindell Blvd, St. Louis, MO 63108.

STOESS, ALFRED WILLIAM Acad: Org Beh/Pers, Bus Admin; Bus:Mgmt/Admin. BA 1956, BBA 1957, U of Minn; MBA 1961, Wash State U; PhD 1967, U of Ore. PUBL: "Conformity Behavior of Managers and Wives of Managers," Acad of Mgmt J. INT: org beh, coll barg, mgmt/educ. ASSN: Acad of Mgmt. POSITIONS: Prof of Mgmt, 1963; Dir of Admin, U of Nevada System, 1975, and, since 1983, Prof of Mgmt, Univ of Nevada. ADDRESS: 1600 Royal Dr, Reno, NV 89557. 702/784-6824

STOIKOV, JUDITH Consulting. BS 1963, Cornell U; PhD 1970, London School of Econ. PUBL: "Affected Class Analysis in 1980," in American Banker, Oct 13, 1980; "Factors Influencing Hours of Work," in Manpower Policy and Employment Trends, 1966. INT: labor market econ, method/statis, personnel. ASSN: AEA. POSITIONS: Assoc Prof of Econ, SUNY-Cortland, 1970; Vice Pres, Natl Econ Res Assoc Inc, 1976; and (since 1983) President, Employment Economics Inc, 250 Park Ave, New York, NY 10177. 212/692-9711

STOKES, MICHAEL LEE Union, Labor. AB 1981, U of Mich-Dearborn; MA 1983, Wayne State U. INT: arb/med, labor law, contract admin. ASSN: Detroit IRRA. POSITION: (since 1978) Preloader, United Parcel Service. ADDRESS: Teamsters Local 243, 1756 Cardwell, Garden City, MI 48135. 313/422-3692

STONE, BRYCE DOUGLAS JR. Acad: Org Beh/Pers, Psych, Ind Rels. AB 1949, George Washington U; MS 1958, PhD 1963, U of Tenn-Knoxville. INT: personnel, ind psych, mgm/-educ. ASSN: Amer Psych Assn, ASPA, Acad of Mgmt. POSITIONS: Mgr, Corp Pers Info, Texas Instruments Inc, 1965; Professor of Mgmt, 1968-83 (Retired) Texas A & M Univ. ADDRESS: 1305 Glade St, College Station, TX 77840. 409/693-3779

STOREY, DONALD R. Arbitration. BA 1947, Antioch Coll. INT: arb/med. POSITIONS: Dir, Pers and Admin, Monsanto Research Corp, 1975, Personnel Manager, Monsanto Co, 1978; and (since 1981) Arbitrator (self employed), 731 Winged Foot Dr, Aiken, SC 29801. 803/649-6968

STOUT, JAMES S. Consulting. PO Box 5189, Charleston, WV 25311. 304/343-1544

STOUT, LARRY A. Union. MSW 1977, U of Ill-UC. PUBL: Plant Closings: A Worker Handbook. INT: empl/trng programs, ind social work. ASSN: NASW. POSITION: Executive Director, AFL-CIO Great Lakes Council, 500 W Central Rd, #205A, Mt. Prospect, IL 60056. 312/392-8304

STOVALL, J. R. Bus:Pers/Ind Rels. POSITION: Employee Rels Manager, Mobil Oil Credit Corp, PO Box 600, Kansas City, MO 64141.

STOVER, THOMAS Government. AAS 1953, SUNY; BS 1961, Cornell U. INT: mgmt/educ, arb/med, coll barg. ASSN: Greater Kansas & Vicinty IRRA, Amer Soc for Trng and Develop, SPIDR, Amer Mgmt Assn. POSITIONS: Dir, Arkansas Dept of Labor, 1967; Dir, Los Angeles Office, 1971, and, since 1975, Asst Regional Dir, USDL-Labor Mgmt Services, 2200 Federal Bldg, 911 Walnut St, Kansas City, MO 64106. 816/374-5131

STOVER, WALTER F. Acad: Univ Admin, Org Beh/Pers. BA 1952, San Jose State; MBA 1961, USC; PhD 1972, UCLA. POSITION: Asst Vice Pres Administrative Services, Univ of Calif, 192 University Hall, Berkeley, CA 94720. 415/642-2492

STRAIT, DORCAS L. Acad: Univ Admin. POSITION: Contract Administrator, Wm Patterson College, 300 Pompton Rd, Wayne, New Jersey 07470.

STRAND, KENNETH T. Acad: Econ, Ind Rels. BA 1953, Wash State Coll; MS 1956, PhD 1959, U of Wis. POSITIONS: Economist, OECD, 1964-66; Pres, 1968-74, and (since 1966) Prof, Simon Fraser U. ADDRESS: RR1, Box 9C, Port Moody BC V3H 3C8, Canada. 604/291-4641

STRANGER, CHARLES E. Groth Equipment Co, PO Box 15293, Houston, TX 77020.

STRASSER, ARNOLD Government. 106 Julian Court, Greenbelt, MD 20770. 202/254-8880

STRASSHOFER, ROLAND JR. Arbitration; Acad: Law. AB 1948, JD 1950, Case Western Reserve. INT: arb/med, labor law, health & hosp care. ASSN: Northeast Ohio IRRA, NAA, Amer Coll of Legal Medicine, AAA. POSITION: (since 1950) Arbitrator & Attorney (self-employed), 2520 Stratford Rd, Cleveland, OH 44118. 216/321-7022

STRAUSS, GEORGE Acad: Ind Rels, Org Beh/Pers, Univ Admin. BA 1947, Swarthmore; PhD 1952, MIT. PUBL: Personnel: The Human Problems of Management; Organizational Behavior: Research and Issues; The Local Union: Its Place in the Industrial Plant. INT: coll barg, union org/admin, personnel. ASSN: San Francisco IRRA, Acad of Mgmt. POSITIONS: Res Assoc, New York School of Ind & Labor Rels, 1951; Prof of Ind Rels, U of Buffalo, 1954; and (since 1960) Prof of Bus Admin, Univ of Calif-Berkeley. ADDRESS: 1468 Grizzly Peak, Berkeley, CA 94708. 415/843-6024

STRAW, RONNIE J. Union. BA 1957, Geneva Coll; MA 1958, Syracuse U; ABD 1968, George Washington U. PUBL: "Technology and Employment in Telecommunications, (w L. E. Foged), The Annals, 470, Nov 1983, pp 163-170; "Job Evaluation: One Union's Experience," (w L. E. Foged), ILR Report, XIX, Spring 1982, 124-26. INT: coll barg, technology, org beh/QWL. ASSN: AEA, Consumer Federation of Amer. POSITIONS: Staff Economist, Natl Rural Electric Cooperative Assn, 1961; Asst Exec Mgr and Staff Economist, Natl Telephone Cooperative Assn, 1968; and (since 1970) Director, Development and Res Dept, Communications

Workers of America, 1925 K St NW, Washington DC 20006. 202/728-2400

STROBER, MYRA HOFFENBERG Acad: Econ. BS 1962, Cornell U; MA 1965, Tufts U; PhD 1969, MIT. POSITIONS: Lecturer in Econ, U of Calif-Berkeley, 1970-72; Asst Prof, Grad School of Bus, 1972, and, currently, Center Research on Women, Serra House, Stanford Univ, Stanford, CA 94305. 415/497-0387

STUBBS, DANIEL G. Bus:Mgmt/Admin, Consulting. BA 1965, West Virginia U. ADDRESS: PO Box 9219, Glendale, CA 91206.

STURMTHAL, ADOLF F. Acad: Ind Rels. Dr pol, 1925, U of Vienna, Austria. PUBL: Tragedy of European Labor, 1918-1939, Col U Press; Left of Center: European Labor Since World War II, U of Ill Press; Workers Council, Harvard U Press. INT: intl comparative labor, labor history, coll barg. ASSN: U of Ill IRRA. POSITION: Prof Emeritus, ILIR, Univ of Ill, 504 E Armory, Champaign, IL 61821. 217/333-2381

STUTEVILLE, WALTER M. Union. POSITION: Washington State Nurses, 2615 4th Ave, Seattle, WA 98121.

SUAREZ, HERTA A. Student. BA 1971, U of Puerto Rico. INT: arb/med, labor law, union org/admin. POSITIONS: Evaluation Analyst, Housing & Urban Develop, Puerto Rico, 1971-72; and (currently) Student, Univ of Cincinnati. ADDRESS: 1798 Muskegon Dr, Cincinnati, OH 45230.513/474-0504

SUBBARAO, AREMANDA V. Acad: Ind Rels. LLB 1967, DBM 1970, Osmania U-India; PhD 1975, U of Minn. PUBL: "The Impact of Binding Interest Arbitration on Negotiation Process and Outcome," J of Conflict Resolution, vol 22, #1, Mar 1978; "The Impact of Two Dispute Resolution Processes on Negotiations," Ind Rels (Laval), vol 32, #2, 1977; "Impasse Choice and Wages in the Canadian Federal Service," Ind Rels (Berkeley) vol 18, #2, 1979. INT: arb/med, coll barg, personnel. ASSN: Acad of Mgmt, Admin Sciences Assn of Canada, Canadian Ind Rels Assn. POSITIONS: Labor Officer (Conciliation), 1962, Secretary, Central Wage Boards, Government of India, 1967; and (since 1974) Assoc Prof, Faculty of Admin, Univ of Ottawa, 135 Wilbrod St, Ottawa, K1N 9B5, Canada. 613/231-2221

SUCHARD, HAZEL Acad: Ind Rels, Econ. D Phil, 1979, U of Pretoria. PUBL: "Women in Trade Unions," Equal Opportunities Intl, vol 1, #4, Nov, 1982, pp 10-15; "Decentralisation in South Africa," South Africa Intl, vol 13, #2, Oct 1982, pp 112-120; "The Poverty Problem in the Black Township of Soweto. Major Results of a Survey," Development Studies on Southern Africa, vol 1, #4, July 1979; pp 431-456. INT: coll barg, income maint, labor market econ. ASSN: South African IRRA, Development Soc of South Africa, South African Econ Soc, AEA. POSITIONS: Visiting Full Professor, Univ of Hawaii at Manoa, 1983; Part Time Lecturer Economics, Dept Town Planning, 1976, and, since 1981, Full Time Lecturer, Dept Business Econ, Univ of Witwatersrand, 1 Jan Smuts Ave, Johannesburg 2001 South Africa. Phone: 716 3487

SULLIVAN, ANNE R. Union. POSITION: President, Local 2871 AFSCME, R. I. Dept of Health Union, 50 Orms St, Providence, RI 02909. 401/274-1011

SULLIVAN, EDWARD T. Union. BS 1960, Calvin Coolidge Coll; MPA 1975 Suffolk Univ. INT: coll barg, arb/med. ASSN: Boston IRRA, Assn of Governing Boards of Univ & Colleges. POSITIONS: Member, Mass Board of Regents of Higher Educ, 1982; Intl Exec Assn, SEIU, 1970,and, since 1958, Bus Manager, Secretary-Treas, SEIU Local 254, 59 Temple Place, Room 1000, Boston, MA 02111. 617/482-6148

SULLIVAN, FRANCIS W., JR. Student. INT: personnel, arb/med, labor law. POSITIONS: Supervisor, Dept of Youth, Buffalo, 1983; and (since 1981) Student, LeMoyne Coll (BS expected 1985). ADDRESS: 205 Whitfield Ave, Buffalo, NY 14220. 315/445-2600

SULLIVAN, JOHN F. Bus:Mgmt/Admin. POSITION: The Sullivan Group Inc, Suite 2007, 505 N Lake Shore Dr, Chicago, IL 60611. 312/-329-0409

SULLIVAN, KATHLEEN ANN Student. BA 1976, U of Mich; MSIR 1984, Loyola U-Chicago. INT: arb/med, labor law, coll barg. ASSN: SPIDR, Human Resource Mgmt Assn of Chicago. POSITIONS: Pers Research Consultant, Harris Bank, 1983; and Student, Inst of Ind Rels, Loyola. ADDRESS: 2020 W Farwell, #507, Chicago, IL 60645. 312/761-9731

SULLIVAN, MICHAEL FULLER Acad: Bus Admin, Econ, Ind Rels. BA 1950, U of Denver; MS 1961, U of Wis-Madison; PhD 1972, U of Colo-Boulder. INT: arb/med, coll barg, production methods. ASSN: Western Econ Assn, American Production & Inventory Control Soc. POSITIONS: Commercial Engineer-Rate & Tariff, 1951, Communications Rep-Sales, 1953, Mountain States Tel & Tel Co; and (since 1965) Assoc Prof, Div of Bus & Econ, Univ of Wisconsin, Stevens Point, WI 54481. 715/346-2156

SULZNER, GEORGE T. Acad: Political Science. POSITION: Dept of Political Sci, 306 Thompson Hall, Univ of Mass, Amherst, MA 01003.

SUMMERLOTT, PAUL N. Union. INT: union org/admin, arb/med, coll barg. ASSN: Southwest Mich IRRA. POSITIONS: Press Operator, Grand Rapids Packaging, 1978; Employee, State of Mich, 1980; and (since 1983) Regional Membership Services Rep, Mich State Employees Assn, Lansing. ADDRESS: 608 Axtell, Kalamazoo, MI 49008. 517/394-5900

SUNTRUP, EDWARD L. Acad: Ind Rels; Arbitration. PhD 1975, U of Minn. PUBL: "Union-Management Contracts in Higher Education," (w M. Bognanno and D. L. Estenson), Ind Rels, 17, 1978, 189-203; "New Dimensions in Sunshine Bargaining," Pers J 58, 1979, 157-59, 177-79; "The NLRB v. Yeshiva University and Unionization in Higher Education," Ind Rels Law J, 4, 1981, 287-307. INT: arb/med, coll barg, labor law. ASSN: Chicago IRRA, SPIDR, AAA. POSITION: (since 1976) Assoc Prof of Labor Rels, U of Illinois at Chicago, College of Bus Admin, Box 4348, UH2002, Chicago, IL 60680. 312/492-9523/996-4481

SUOJANEN, WAYNE WILLIAM Legal Practice. BA 1972, Northwestern U; SM 1974, PhD 1977, MIT; JD 1980, U of Penna. INT: labor law, org beh. ASSN: Philadelphia IRRA, ABA, Penna Bar Assn, Phila Bar Assn. POSITIONS: Asst Prof, Northeastern Univ, 1976; Instructor, Temple Univ, 1978; and (since 1980) Assoc

Attorney, Pepper, Hamilton & Scheetz, Philadelphia. ADDRESS: 970 La Fayette Rd, Bryn Mawr, PA 19010. 215/893-8806

SUPPES, DAVID E. Bus:Pers/Ind Rels. POSITION: Asst to VP, Bethlehem Steel Corp, 826 Hawthorne Rd, Bethlehem, PA 18018.

SUSMAN, GERALD ISAIAH Acad: Org Beh/-Pers, Bus Admin. BA 1963, MA 1965, PhD 1968, UCLA. PUBL: "Action Research: A Sociotechnical Perspective," in G. Morgan (ed) Beyond Method: Strategies for Social Research, Beverly Hills, CA: Sage 1983; "Planned Change: Prospects for the 1980s," Mgmt Sci, Feb 1981, pp 139-154; "The Scientific Merits of Action Research," Admin Sci Quart, Dec 1978. INT: org beh, empl/trng programs. ASSN: Natl Acad of Mgmt. POSITION: (since 1969) Prof of Organizational Behavior, Pennsylvania State Univ, 609L Business Administration Bldg, University Park, PA 16865. 814/863-2382

SWANSON, ROBERT Government. BS 1950, Cornell U. INT: arb/med, coll barg, health & hosp care. ASSN: Long Island IRRA, Cornell ILR Alumni Assn. POSITION: Reg Director, Dist 50, United Mineworkers of America, 1950; and (since 1960) Commissioner, FMCS, 175 Fulton Ave, Hempstead, L.I., NY 11550. 516/538-3232

SWEENEY, JOHN G. Acad: Econ. MA 1949, MPH 1973, Columbia U. INT: labor history, coll barg. ASSN: AEA, Assn for Social Econ. POSITION: (since 1983) Asst Prof and Acting Chair, Dept of Econ, John Carroll Univ, University Heights, OH 44118. 216/491-4393

SWEENEY, JOHN J. Union. POSITION: International President, SEIU, AFL-CIO, 2020 K St NW, Washington DC 20006.

SWENSON, CHARLES E. Arbitration. POSITION: Arbitrator, 21944 Jason Ave N, Forest Lake, MN 55025. 612/464-5141

SWERBILOW, SALLY PARKER Government. 303 W 66th St, New York, NY 10023. 212/362-8683

SWIERCZ, PAUL MICHAEL Acad: Ind Rels, Org Beh/Pers, Bus Admin. MPH 1976, U of Mich; MS 1980, PhD 1983, Va Polytechnic Inst & State U. PUBL: "Labor Law and Physician's Privileged Position: An Example of Structural Interest Influence," (w J. K. Skipper), Intl J of Health Services 12(2) 1982, pp 249-261; "Professional Associations and the Law," (w J. K. Skipper), Intl Soc Sci Rev, Fall 1983. INT: health & hosp care, coll barg, arb/med. ASSN: Northeastern Mich IRRA, SPIDR. POSITION: (since 1982) Chairman, Dept of Mgmt/-Marketing, Saginaw Valley State Coll. ADDRESS: 2317 Patton, Saginaw, MI 48602. 517/-790-4356

SWIFT, MARIS STELLA Legal Prac; Acad: Student. JD 1979, Cooley Law School; MILR 1983, Mich State U. INT: arb/med, coll barg, labor law. ASSN: Mich Bar Assn, Young Lawyers Assn. POSITION: Clerk for Dist Court Judge Gee, 53rd D.C., 1976; Law Clerk for County Prosecutor, Livingston Cty, Mich, 1977; and (since 1979) Asst City Attorney, Grand Rapids. ADDRESS: 222 Fountain NE, Grand Rapids, MI 49503. 616/456-3181

SWINEHART, DAVID P. Acad: Ind Rels. POSITION: Purdue Univ, 2101 Coliseum Blvd, Ft. Wayne, IN 46805. 219/482-5780

SYDNEY, LEONARD F. Consulting. POSITION: Dew Line Inc, Plant Mgmt/Labor Rels, 1245 Park Ave, New York, NY 10028. 212/831-2868

SYMKOWIAK, RONALD J. Government. BA 1972, MLIR 1973, Mich State U. INT: coll barg, govt labor policy, labor history. POSITIONS: Labor Economist, USDL, BLS, 1973; and (since 1974) Field Examiner, NLRB, 411 Hamilton Blvd, Peoria, IL 61602. 309/671-7046

T

TAGGART, JOHN DAVID Union. 2755 Daybreak Ave, Coquitlam BC V3C 2E8 Canada.

TAGGART, KARIN E. Government. 1611 S Klein, Reedley, CA 93654. 209/638-9322

TAIRA, KOJI Acad: Econ. BA 1953, U of New Mexico; MA 1954, U of Wis; PhD 1961, Stanford U. PUBL: "Industrial Policy and Employment in Japan," Current History, 82, 487, Nov 1983: 362-365, 392-393; "Japan's Unemployment: Economic Miracle or Statistical Artifact?" Monthly Labor Rev, 106, 7, July, 1983: 3-10; An Outline of Japanese Economic History 1603-1940, Tokyo: Univ of Tokyo Press, 1979. INT: intl comparative labor, govt labor policy, labor history. ASSN: AEA, Assn for Asian Studies. POSITIONS: Official, ILO, 1972; Assoc Prof of Econ, Stanford Univ, 1966; and (since 1970) Prof of Econ, Inst of Labor & Ind Rels, Univ of Illinois, 504 E Armory Ave, Champaign, IL 61820. 217/333-1483

TAKESHI, INAGAMI Acad: Sociology. POSITION: Dept of Sociology, Hosei Univ, 2-17-1 Fujimi, Chiyoda-Ku, Tokyo, Japan F102.

TALOS, EARL V. Bus:Pers/Ind Rels, Consulting. BA 1972, Wayne State U; MA 1978, Central Mich U. INT: personnel, org beh, coll barg. ASSN: ASPA. POSITIONS: Labor Rels Rep, Ford Motor Co, 1973; and (since 1981) Personnel Advisor, Arabian American Oil Company - (ARAMCO). ADDRESS: c/o D. Berger, 5401 Chimney Rock, Apt 630, Houston, TX 77081.

TAM, RICHARD Union. POSITION: Hotel/-Restaurant Employee Union, 615 Pikoi St, Honolulu, HI 96814.

TAMA-TROUTMAN, CATHERINE Bus:Pers/-Ind Rels. BSE 1978, U of Penna. INT: coll barg, empl/trng programs, personnel. ASSN: Central Penna IRRA. POSITIONS: Labor Specialist, Taylor-Wharton Div, Harsco Corp, 1978; and (since 1983) Ind Rels Rep, RCA Corp, UC & D Div, Lancaster. ADDRESS: 2405 Garrison Ave, Harrisburg, PA 17110. 717/397-7661 ext 2026

TAMOUSH, PHILIP P. Arbitration. BS 1959, MBA 1961, UCLA. PUBL: Local Option in Public Sector Employment Relations, (monograph), UC-Berkeley, 1977; "Professional Standards in Training and Retraining of Neutrals," Proceedings of the Inaugural Convention of SPIDR, 1974; "Views of Legal Guidelines: California

Public Employee Relations," USDL, 1974. INT: arb/med, empl/trng programs, coll barg. ASSN: Southern Calif IRRA, NAA, IIRA, AAA. POSITIONS: Personnel Admin, County of Los Angeles, 1961-70; Admin, Res & Educ, UCLA, 1970-76; and (since 1976) Arbitrator-Factfinder (self-employed), 2907 Oakwood Lane, Torrance, CA 90505. 213/325-6873

TANN, CHARLES JOHN Arbitration. BS 1962, Gannon U-Erie, PA. INT: arb/med, labor law, personnel. ASSN: AAA (Panel of Arb), FMCS (Panel of Arb), ASPA. POSITIONS: Pers Mgr, Bucyrus Erie Co-Erie, 1965; Ind Rels Mgr, Castings Services, Div of Marley Corp-Erie, 1974; and (since 1982) Arbitrator (self-employed), 607 Beverly Dr, Erie, PA 16505. 814/459-5195

TANNER, LUCRETIA DEWEY Government. BA 1962, U of Conn; MS 1964, U of Wis. PUBL: "Women in Labor Unions," Monthly Labor Rev, Feb, 1971; "Collective Bargaining in the Health Care Industry," Monthly Labor Rev, Feb 1980; "The Voluntary Pay Standard," Labor Law J, Mar 1981. INT: coll barg, govt labor policy. ASSN: Wash DC IRRA, Natl Economist Club, SPIDR. POSITIONS: Dir of Research, FMCS, 1974; Deputy Assistant Dir, Office of Pay Monitoring, Council on Wage and Price Stability, 1979; and (since 1982) Exec Dir, Advisory Committee on Federal Pay. ADDRESS: 14300 Baden Westwood Rd, Brandywine, MD 20613. 202/653-6193

TANZMAN, DAVID S. Government. POSITION: Assistant Regional Director, FMCS, 433 Federal Court Bldg, Detroit, MI 48226. 313/226-7765

TAPPER, GORDON A. Bus:Mgmt/Admin. POSITION: Manager, Research & Comp, The Employers Assn, 103 Pearl St NW, Grand Rapids, MI 49502.

TAPPER, OWEN A. Acad: Labor Educ. BS 1964, MS 1966, U of Wis. POSITIONS: Field Organizer, Electrical Workers, 1957; Lecturer, School for Workers, U of Wis, 1965; and (since 1968) Asst Director for Educ Labor Studies, 710 Knapp Hall, West Virginia Univ, Morgantown, WV 26506. 304/293-3323

TARANTELLI, EZIO ISEL, Via Dei Villini 13, 00161, Roma RM, Italy.

TARCZALI, EDWARD R. Bus:Pers/Ind Rels. BS 1962 U of Bridgeport. INT: personnel, coll barg, empl/trng programs. ASSN: Southwestern Conn IRRA, Southern Conn ASPA, Conn Pers Assn, Amer Compensation Assn. POSITIONS: Pers Assistant, Perkin-Elmer Corp, 1957-59; Dir of Pers, Barnes Engineering Co, 1959-72; and (since 1975) Vice-Pres, Ind Rels, Nash Engineering Co, 310 Wilson Ave, PO Box 5130, Norwalk, CT 06856. 203/852-3610

TAROLLI, MARIO P. Bus:Mgmt/Admin. BA 1977, Syracuse U. INT: empl/trng programs, ind psychology, mgmt/educ. ASSN: Manufacturing Assn of Central NY, Intl Mgmt Council, Natl Fire Prevention Assn. POSITIONS: Maintenance Manager, 1972, and (since 1978) Production Mgr, (Arm & Hammer Div), Church & Dwight Co, Inc, 1416 Willis Ave, Syracuse, NY 13204. 315/488-2961

TATUM, JAMES E. Trade Assn, Labor Rels. BSBA 1967, La. Tech U. INT: coll barg, arb/med, mgmt/educ. POSITION: (since 1970) Division Manager, Southeast Texas Chapter, Natl Electrical Contractors Assn, PO Box 37366, Houston, TX 77237. 713/669-0094

TAUSKY, CURT Acad: Sociology, Org Beh/-Pers. PUBL: Work Organizations, Peacock Pubs, 1978; Work and Society, Peacock Pubs, 1983; "Has Job Satisfaction Declined?" Monthly Labor Rev, Nov 1982. INT: org beh, ind sociol, intl comparative labor. ASSN: Amer Sociological Assn. POSITION: (since 1965) Professor, Dept of Sociology, Univ of Mass, Amherst, MA 01003. 413/545-2523

TAYLOR, CHARLES M. Bus:Mgmt/Admin. POSITION: B. J. Hughes Inc, 10777 Northwest Freeway, #500, Houston, TX 77092. 713/957-5700

TAYLOR, DAVID P. Internationl Org. BS 1956, Cornell U; MBA 1960, PhD 1966, U of Chicago. INT: intl comparative labor, labor market econ, personnel. POSITIONS: Asst Secretaryof Defense, Dept of Defense, 1976; Partner, Hay Assoc, 1977; and (since 1983) Deputy Director General, Intl Labour Office, Case Postale 500 CH 1211, Geneva 22, Switzerland.

TAYLOR, DOUGLAS Legal Practice, Union. MM 1974, Northwestern G.S.M.; JD 1977, Loyola-Chicago. INT: labor law, health & hosp care, coll barg. ASSN: Wash DC IRRA, ABA. POSITIONS: Field Rep, Ill Nurses Assn, 1974; Instructor, Amer Univ-KOGOD School, 1981; and (since 1977) Attorney/Economist-Consultant, Gromfine, Sternstein, Rosen & Taylor, P.C./Labor Bureau Inc, 1346 Connecticut Ave NW, Washington DC 20036. 202/296-7420

TAYLOR, G. STEPHEN Student. BA 1974, MA 1976, U of Va; MBA 1981, Va Polytechnic Inst. INT: personnel, coll barg, meth/statis. ASSN: Southern Mgmt Assn. POSITIONS: Buyer, Leggett Dept Stores, 1977; and (since 1983) Instructor, Virginia Polytechnic Inst, 207 Pamplin Hall, Blacksburg, VA 24060. 703/961-6353

TAYLOR, JAMES C. Bus:Pers/Ind Rels. BS 1977, Ind U; MA 1979, U of Ill. POSITIONS: Ind Rels Analyst, Ford Motor Co, 1978; and (since 1984) North American Van Lines, PO Box 12668, Ft Wayne, IN 46864. 219/429-2511

TAYLOR, JOHN R. Arbitration. INT: arb/-med, empl/trng programs, coll barg. ASSN: San Diego IRRA, Government Labor Rels Assn. POSITIONS: Federal Mediator, FMCS, 1962; and (since 1982) Arbitrator, PO Box 524, Julian, CA 92036. 619/765-2128

TAYLOR, MARLA Acad: Ind Rels. POSITION: Asst Editor, Inst of Ind Rels, Univ of Calif, 2521 Channing Way, Berkeley, CA 94720.

TAYLOR, MERLIN L. Union. PUBL: The Bricklayer, Brick and Block Construction; "New Industrial Worker," 1969. INT: labor law, govt labor policy, mgmt/educ. ASSN: Wash DC IRRA. POSITIONS: Exec Dir, Human Resources Develop Inst, AFL-CIO, 1968; Asst to the Pres, 1970, and, since 1979, Director, Dept of Apprenticeship and Trng, Intl Union of Bricklayers & Allied Craftsmen, 815 Fifteenth St NW, Washington DC 20005. 202/783-3788

TAYLOR, RICHARD B. Arbitration. BS 1938, Va. Polytech Inst. INT: arb/med, coll barg, empl/trng programs. ASSN: SPIDR, AAA.

POSITIONS: Commissioner, FMCS, 1961; Chief, Labor Rels, Thiokol Chemical Corp, 1968; and (since 1981) Arbitrator (self employed), 1035 Papworth Ave, Metairie, LA 70005. 504/-834-2703

TAYLOR, VICKY Bus:Mgmt/Admin. ASSN: San Antonio IRRA. POSITION: Personnel Dept, Coca Cola Bottling Co, PO Box 58, San Antonio, TX 78291. 512/229-0485

TENER, BARBARA ZAUSNER Arbitration, Acad: Ind Rels. MA 1977, Rutgers U. INT: arb/med, coll barg. ASSN: Central New Jersey/-Bucks, New Brunswick, Philadelphia and New York IRRAs, NAA, SPIDR. POSITION: Arbitrator, PO Box 124, Bordentown, NJ 08505. 609/-298-7722

TENER, JEFFREY BOOTH Arbitration. BA 1963, Yale U; MA 1968, U of Wis. PUBL: "The Public Employment Relations Commission: The First Decade," Rutgers Camden Law J, vol 9, #4, Summer, 1978; "New Jersey Supreme Court Interprets 1974 Amendments to New Jersey Employer-Employee Relations Act," Rutgers Camden Law J, vol 11, #2, Winter, 1980; "Interest Arbitration in New Jersey," The Arb J, vol 37, #4, Dec 1982. INT: arb/med, coll barg, govt labor policy. ASSN: New York City, Philadelphia, New Brunswick and New Jersey/Bucks County IRRAs, SPIDR, Assn of Labor Rels Agencies. POSITIONS: Chairman, New Jersey Public Employment Rels Commission, 1976; Assoc Prof, Inst of Mgmt & Labor Rels, Rutgers Univ, 1980; and (since 1983) Arbitrator (self-employed), 697 Prospect Ave, Princeton, NJ 08540. 609/929-6629

TEPER, LAZARE Union. PhD 1931, Johns Hopkins U. Retired. 650 West End Ave, New York, NY 10025.

TEPPER, ALLAN ARTHUR Legal Practice. POSITION: Partner, Snyder, Tepper, Berlin & Katz, 73 Tremont St, Boston, MA 02108.

TERRILL, T. E. Acad: History; Arbitration. BA 1957, Westminster Coll-Mo.; MA 1963, PhD 1966, U of Wis-Madison. PUBL: The Tariff, Politics, and American Foreign Policy, 1874-1901, 1973; Such As Us: Southern Voices in the Thirties, (w J. Hirsch), 1978; "Eager Hands: Textile Workers in the Antebellum South," J of Econ History, 1976. INT: labor history, arb/med. ASSN: South Atlantic IRRA, Southern Labor Studies Assn, Southern Historical Assn, Econ History Assn. POSITIONS: Asst Prof of History, 1966, Assoc Prof of History, 1970, and, since 1980, Professor of History, Univ of South Carolina. ADDRESS: 114 Saluda Ave, Columbia, SC 29205. 803/777-6026/5195

THAKER, HARSHADRAY H. Union. BA 1947, LLB 1967, U of Bombay, India; MA 1969, Appalachian State U. PUBL: Wage Setting & Evaluation: Economic Principles for Registered Nurses, (monograph in a series), Amer Nurses Assn. INT: health & hosp care, coll barg, labor market econ. ASSN: Kansas City (Mo) IRRA, AEA. POSITIONS: Manager Admin, Sarabhai Chemicals, India, 1955; Instructor in Econ, Clemson Univ, 1969; and (since 1972) Labor Policy Analyst, American Nurses Assn-Kansas City. ADDRESS: 12920 W 105th Terr, Overland Park, KS 66215. 816/474-5720

THAL, RICHARD L. Student. 306 L Eagle Heights, Madison, WI 53705. 608/233-6399

THAYER, RALPH IRA Acad: Economics BS 1937, Northwestern U, MA 1944, U of Wash; PhD 1947, Stanford U. POSITIONS: Asst Prof of Econ, U of Wash, 1945-48; Prof of Econ, Wash State U, 1948-78; Salesman, Tifft Agency, 1977, and, currently, Retired. ADDRESS: PO Box 694, Sandpoint, ID 83864. 208/263-7192

THEDE, KAY ANDERSON Government. MSIR 1982, Iowa State U. INT: personnel, labor market econ, empl/trng programs. ASSN: ASTD, Acad of Mgmt. POSITION: (since 1984) Manpower Research Economist, Iowa Dept of Job Service-Des Moines. ADDRESS: 724 Lincoln Ave, Boone, IA 50036.

THEEKE, HERMAN ARTHUR Acad: Ind Rels, Labor Educ, Manpower. ADDRESS: 9640 N Territorial, Plymouth, MI 48170. 313/459-1878

THEEP, RAYMOND T. Legal Practice. BS 1963, U.S. Naval Academy; JD 1972, U of San Diego. INT: labor law, arb/med, coll barg. ASSN: San Diego IRRA, AAA (Commercial Panel), State Bar of Calif, ABA. POSITIONS: General Counsel, Big Bear Super Market No 3, 1972; and (since 1980) Partner, Spievak & Theep, Attorneys at Law, 1629 Columbia St, Ste 100, San Diego, CA 92101. 619/233-7306

THEISS, JERRY L. Bus:Pers/Ind Rels, Mgmt/-Admin. BS 1973, Stephen F. Austin State U. INT: personnel, labor law, ind psychology. ASSN: Greater Houston IRRA, ASPA, Houston Pers Assn, Amer Mgmt Assn. POSITIONS: Pers Asst, 1973, Human Resource Mgr, Murray Rubber, a Mead Company, 1977; and (since 1983) Personnel Director, Houston Engineers Inc, PO Box 567, Houston, TX 77001. 713/237-3050

THEULE, BERNARD L. Bus:Pers/Ind Rels. BA 1968, Calif State U-Northridge. INT: coll barg, labor law, personnel. ASSN: San Diego IRRA. POSITIONS: Labor Rels Supervisor, Lockheed Calif Co, 1968; and (since 1980) Manager, Ind Rels, Solar Turbines Inc, PO Box 80966, 2200 Pacific Hwy, San Diego, CA 92138. 619/238-5809

THIBODEAU, GILLES Business. POSITION: Dominion Textile Inc, 1950 0 Sherbrooke W, Montreal, PQ H3H 1E7 Canada. 514/937-5711

THOMAS, BENJAMIN F. Acad: Univ Admin. POSITION: Dean, School of Bus, Ferris State Coll, Big Rapids, MI 49307.

THOMAS, JAMES EDWARD Bus:Mgmt/Admin. BSc 1968, Roosevelt U; MA 1970, U of Ill. INT: coll barg, arb/med, labor law. ASSN: Personnel Assn of Toronto; Calgary Pers Assn. POSITIONS: Division Pers Mgr, Consumers Glass Co, 1972; Dir of Pers and Ind Rels, Guthrie Canadian Investments Ltd, 1978; and (since 1981) Director of Human Resources, Bralorne Resource Ltd. ADDRESS: 815 Parkwood Way SE, Calgary, Alberta T2J 3V3 Canada. 403/261-9060

THOMAS, JAMES R. Acad: Ind Rels; Consulting. BA 1952, Duquesne U; MPM 1984, Carnegie Mellon U. PUBL: "Data Processing in Major Unions," IMF Bull, 1966; "Robotics in Penna," (co-author), Penna Milrite Council, 1983. INT: coll barg, union org/admin, labor history. ASSN: Western Penna IRRA. POSITIONS: Dir, Contract Dept, United Steelworkers of Amer, 1952; Part-Time Instructor, Duquesne Univ, 1983. ADDRESS: 1018 Sullivan Dr, West Homestead, PA 15120. 412/434-6226.

THOMAS, JOHN C. Labor Rels. BEcon 1981, Franklin & Marshall Coll. INT: arb/med, coll barg, labor educ. POSITIONS: Asst Labor Rels Rep, Limerick Generating Station, 1982, Labor Rels Rep, St. Lucie Nuclear Project, 1982, and, since 1983, Labor Rels Rep, Limerick Generating Station, Bechtel Power Corp, PO Box A, Sanatoga Branch, Pottstown, PA 19464. 215/327-4755

THOMAS, KENNETH W. Acad: Org Beh/Pers. BA 1965, Pomona Coll; PhD 1971, Purdue U. PUBL: Producing Useful Knowledge for Organizations, (co-editor), Praeger, 1983; "Conflict and Conflict Management," in Dunnette's Handbook of Ind and Org Psychology, Rand McNally, 1976; "Necessary Properties of Relevant Research," (w W. Tymon Jr.), Acad of Mgmt Rev, vol 7, 1982, pp 345-352. INT: org beh, conflict mgmt. ASSN: Acad of Mgmt, Amer Psychological Assn, Inst of Mgmt Sciences. POSITIONS: Asst Prof, Grad School of Mgmt, UCLA, 1969; Assoc Prof, School of Bus Admin, Temple U, 1977; and (since 1981) Assoc Prof of Bus Admin, Grad School of Bus, Univ of Pittsburgh, Pittsburgh, PA 15260. 412/624-0317

THOMAS, NANCY M. Acad: Student; Bus:-Pers/Ind Rels. MSIR 1983, U of Oregon. INT: personnel, labor law, empl/trng programs. ASSN: Pacific Northwest Pers Mgmt Assn. POSITION: Grad Student, Univ of Oregon. ADDRESS: 647 26th Ave #2, San Francisco, CA 94121.

THOMAS, PATRICK H. Union. POSITION: General Secretary, BCIT Staff Society, 3700 Willingdon Ave 1A269, Burnaby, BC V5G 3H2 Canada. 604/438-8033

THOMAS, PETER B. Bus:Pers/Ind Rels. BS 1967 LaSalle Coll; MBA 1975, Temple U. INT: personnel, labor market econ, govt labor policy. ASSN: Philadelphia IRRA, Labor Rels Council-Wharton School; Phila Ind Rels Assn, ASPA. POSITIONS: Ind Rels Mgr, Milprint Inc, 1972; Ind Rels Mgr, 1973, and, since 1979, Vice Pres, Ind Rels, Foote Mineral Co, Route 100, Exton, PA 19341. 215/363-6500

THOMAS, RITA E. Consulting, Legal Practice. BA 1971, Mich State U; JD 1978, Thomas Cooley Law School. INT: labor law, coll barg, labor history. ASSN: Detroit IRRA, ABA, Mich Bar Assn, Mich Public Employer Labor Rels Assn. POSITIONS: Attorney (Private Practice), Ann Arbor, MI, 1983; and (since 1980) Labor Rels Consultant, Mich Assn of School Boards, 421 W. Kalamazoo, Lansing, MI 48923. 517/371-5700

THOMAS, WADE L. Acad: Economics. POSITION: Dept of Econ & Finance, Coll of Bus Admin, Northeast Louisiana Univ, Monroe, LA 71209.

THOMAS, WILLIAM Bus:Pers/Ind Rels. BA 1978, Ohio Northern U; MA 1982, St. Francis Coll. INT: personnel, empl/trng programs, labor market econ. ASSN: West Va IRRA, ASPA, Ohio Valley Ind Rels Assn. POSITION: (since 1978) Human Resource Rep, Weirton Steel Co. ADDRESS: 2109 Commerce St, Wellsburg, WV 26070. 304/797-3521

THOMAS, WILLIAM WALTER Acad: Ind Supervision/Mgmt. BS 1951, MS 1982, Marshall U. INT: mgmt/educ, personnel, coll barg. ASSN: Southern Mgmt Assn, West Va Community Coll Assn. POSITIONS: Labor Rels Mgr, 1970, General Supt-Manufacturing, Huntington Alloys Inc-Inco Ltd, 1974; and (since 1983) Asst Prof Industrial Supervision, Community College of Marshall Univ, Huntington, WV 25701. 304/-696-3646

THOMPSON, ALLEN RUPERT Acad: Econ, Bus Admin. PhD 1973, U of Texas-Austin. INT: coll barg, empl/trng programs, labor market econ. ASSN: AEA. POSITIONS: Asst Prof, 1974, and, since 1978, Assoc Prof, Whittemore School, Univ of New Hampshire, Durham, NH 03824. 603/862-2771

THOMPSON, ANN R. Union. BA 1971, American U; MS 1975, Catholic U. PUBL: Teamsters All, Pictorial Highlights in Our History. INT: coll barg, organizing campaigns, labor history. ASSN: Wash DC IRRA, Coalition of Labor Union Women, Washington Union Women. POSITION: Director, Information Center, Intl Brotherhood of Teamsters, 25 Louisiana Ave NW, Washington DC 20001. 202/624-6927

THOMPSON, JAMES T. Government. BA 1952, U of N Mex. INT: labor market econ. ASSN: Intl Assn Pers in Empl Security. POSITION: Chief, Economic Res & Statis, Employment Security Dept of New Mexico, 1952-82, Retired. ADDRESS: 1209 Lafayette Dr NE, Albuquerque, NM 87106.

THOMPSON, MARK E. Acad: Bus Admin; Arbitration. BA 1961, Notre Dame; MS 1963, PhD 1966, Cornell U. PUBL: Public Sector Industrial Relations, (M. Thompson & G. Swimmer, eds), 1984; "International Unionism in Canada: The Move to Local Control," Ind Rels, Winter, 1983; "Elections and Union Democracy in Mexico: A Comparative Perspective," Br. J of IR, 7/82. INT: coll barg, arb/med, intl comparative labor. ASSN: British Columbia IRRA, CIRA, LASA, SPIDR. POSITIONS: Programme Analyst, ILO, 1969; Asst Prof, 1971, and, since 1973, Assoc Prof, Faculty of Commerce, 2053 Main Mall, Univ of British Columbia, Vancouver, BC V6T 1Y8 Canada. 604/228-4819

THOMPSON, STEPHEN L. Student. BA 1975, Drake U. INT: labor law, govt labor policy, health & hosp care. POSITIONS: Staff Respiratory Therapist, 1977, Shift Supervisor, Northwestern Memorial Hosp, 1977, and, since 1979, Instructor, Northwestern Univ Medical School, Respiratory Therapy Program. ADDRESS: 2533 N Springfield, Chicago, IL 60647. 312/649-2935

THOMSON, A. W. J. Acad: Ind Rels. POSITION: Dept Management Studies, Glasgow Univ, Glasgow G12 8RT Scotland.

THOMSON, LOUIS MILL, JR. Arbitration. POSITION: Adm Director, Toledo Labor-Mgmt Citizens Committee, 1806 Madison Ave, Room 208, Toledo, OH 43624.

THONG, GREGORY TIN SIN Acad: Bus Admin, Org Beh/Pers. BE 1961, U of Malaya, MBA 1968, U of British Columbia; PhD 1979, U of Malaya. PUBL: "An Empirical Research on Corporate Social Responsibilities Underwritten by Malaysian Companies," (w T. Hai Yap) Malaysian Mgmt Rev; "Reliability Index for Employee Job Performance," The Malaysian Accountant; Wage Incentive Schemes, (monograph). INT: mgmt/educ, org beh, personnel. ASSN: British Inst of Mgmt, Inst of Production

Control (England), Inst of Ind Managers (England). POSITIONS: Lecturer, 1968, Assoc Prof, 1977, and, since 1980, Prof of Bus Admin, Faculty of Econ and Admin, Univ of Malaya, Kuala Lumpur, 22-11, Malaysia. Phone: 03-554111

THORN, JERRY Consulting, Arbitration. BA 1950, Willamette U. INT: arb/med, coll barg, ind sociology. ASSN: AAA. POSITIONS: Union Rep, United Food & Commercial Workers, 1956; Dir of Pers & Labor Rels, Carrs Quality Centers, 1967; and (since 1979) Consultant, Ind Rels, 2421 Lee St, Anchorage, AK 99504. 907/337-0456

THORNA, SANDRA LEE Student. BS 1982, SUNY-Geneseo; AM 1984, U of Ill-UC. INT: personnel, coll barg, empl/trng programs. ASSN: U of Ill IRRA, ASPA, Intl Youth in Achievement. POSITIONS: Personnel Intern, Gannett Corp, 1981; Pers/Labor Rels Intern, Whirlpool Corp, 1983; and (currently) Student, Univ of Illinois. ADDRESS: 612 W Church St, #43, Champaign, IL 61820. 217/398-6402

THORNTON, JOHN A. Union. BE 1961, Jersey City State Teacher Coll. INT: arb/med, union org/admin, coll barg. ASSN: New Brunswick IRRA. POSITIONS: Teacher, Scotch Plains Fonwood Bd of Educ, 1961; and (since 1970) Field Rep, New Jersey Educ Assn-NEA, 47 E Main St, Flemington, NJ 08822. 201/782-2168

THORNTON, ROBERT J. Acad: Economics. PhD 1970, U of Ill. PUBL: "Teacher Unionism and Collective Bargaining in England," ILRR, 1982; "Licensing in the Barbering Profession," ILRR, 1979; Reindustrialization: Implications for Industrial Policy, JAI Press, 1984. INT: labor market econ, coll barg, labor history. ASSN: AEA. POSITION: Professor of Econ, Lehigh Univ, Drown Hall 35, Bethlehem, PA 18103. 215/861-3420

THURSCHWELL, HUBERT Legal Practice, Bus:Pers/Ind Rels. BA 1951, JD 1954, U of Chicago. INT: arb/med, labor law, coll barg. ASSN: Philadelphia IRRA, Phila Bar Assn, Penna Bar Assn. POSITION: General Attorney, Bell Telephone Co of Pennsylvania, Law Dept, One Parkway, 16th Floor, Philadlephia, PA 19102. 215/466-4551

TILLEM, JACK D. Arbitration. 20 W Marie ST, Hicksville, NY 11801.

TILLES, C. EVANS Arbitration, Legal Practice. BBA 1957, CCNY; LLB 1962, Brooklyn Law School. INT: arb/med, labor law, coll barg. ASSN: Long Island IRRA, AAA, SPIDR. ADDRESS: 1205 Franklin Ave, Garden City, NY 11530. 516/294-8012

TIMMONS, RICHARD LEE Union. POSITION: AFSCME Local 1550, 2030 Suffolk Dr, Houston, TX 77027.

TIPTON, JOHN B. Government. MA 1958, U of Ill. PUBL: U.S. Participation in the International Labor Organization. INT: intl comparative labor, govt labor policy, labor history. ASSN: Wash DC IRRA. POSITION: (since 1958) Foreign Service Officer, U.S. Dept of State. ADDRESS: 2400 41st NW, Apt 513, Washington DC 20007. 202/632-4799

TISSUE, DOROTHY Union. POSITION: OPEIU Local 129, 5638 Meadow Creek, Houston, TX 77017.

TITTLE, JOSEPH O. Bus:Pers/Ind Rels. BS 1960, Northern Ariz U. INT: coll barg, labor law, arb/med. ASSN: Arizona Ind Rels Assn. POSITIONS: Dir-Ind Rels, Southwest Forest Homes, Inc, 1970; Management Consultant, Arthur Young & Co, 1972; and (since 1973) Manager, Labor Rels, Salt River Project, PO Box 1980, Phoenix, AZ 85001. 602/273-2731

TOKARZ, JOEL C. Bus:Pers/Ind Rels. BA 1980, Susquehanna U. INT: personnel, coll barg, labor law. ASSN: Manufacturing Assn of Hartford, ASPA. POSITIONS: Employee Rels Rep, Leed & Northrup Co, 1981, and, since 1983, Supervisor Employee Rels, O. Z./-Gedney Co, a unit of General Signal Corp, Main St, Terryville, CT 06786. 203/584-0571

TOLAND, MARY M. Bus:Pers/Ind Rels. BA 1982, Trinity Coll; MLIR 1983, Mich State U. INT: personnel, org beh, ind psychology. ASSN: ASPA. POSITION: Human Resources Assoc, GTE Corporation. ADDRESS: 84 Maher Rd, Stamford, CT 06902. 203/965-3704

TOM, LINDA Acad: Univ Admin. POSITION: Personnel & Employee Rels, Hullihen Hall, University of Delaware, Newark, DE 19711. 302/738-2769

TOMEY, E. ALLAN Acad: Urban Affairs. POSITION: Instructor, Center for Urban Programs, St. Louis Univ, 221 N Grand Blvd, St. Louis, MO 63103. 314/535-3300

TOMKIEWICZ, JOSEPH Acad: Ind Rels, Org Beh/Pers. PhD 1978, Temple U. PUBL: "Work Stoppages by Teachers: An Empirical Analysis," J of Labor Res, Winter, 1982. INT: coll barg, personnel, org beh. ASSN: ASPA. POSITIONS: Controller, Berean Inst, 1971; Asst Prof, James Madison Univ, 1977; and (since 1981) Assoc Prof, East Carolina Univ. ADDRESS: 114 Hunters LN, Pineridge, Greenville, NC 27834. 919/757-6364

TOMLINSON, WILLIAM H. Acad: Bus Admin, Org Beh/Pers. BS 1943, U.S. Military Acad; MBA 1960, U of Alabama; MS 1966, George Washington U; PhD 1974, American U. PUBL: Assessment of National Defense Executive Reserve, U.S. Dept of Commerce, Natl Technical Information Service, 1975; "Southeastern Shipyards," in Rogers & Rolfe, eds, Corporate Strategy and Planning, Columbus, OH Grid Publishing, 1981; "History of the National Defense Executive Reserve," NDER Program Overview, Fed Emergency Mgmt Agency, Wash DC, 1983. INT: personnel, mgmt/educ, org beh. ASSN: Acad of Mgmt, Acad of Intl Mgmt, ASPA. POSITIONS: Commander, 7th Infantry Div Artillery, South Korea, 1965, Resident Faculty Dir Defense, Mgmt Program, Ind Coll of the Armed Forces, Wash DC, 1966; and (since 1983) Assoc Prof of Mgmt, Dept of Bus Admin, Univ of North Florida, PO Box 17074, Jacksonville, FL 32216. 904/646-2781

TONTI, DON G. Bus:Mgmt/Admin. POSITION: Walbro Corp, 6246 Garfield Rd, Cass City, MI 48726. 517/872-2131

TOROSIAN, HERMAN Government, Employee Rels. BS 1963, JD 1967, U of Wis. INT: arb/med, coll barg, mediation. ASSN: Wisconsin IRRA, NAA, SPIDR, State Bar of Wis. POSITIONS: Trial Examiner, Mediator, Arbitrator, 1963, Commissioner, 1975, and, since 1983, Chairman, Wisconsin Employment Rels Commission. ADDRESS: 1745 Camelot Dr, Madison, WI 53705. 608/266-1381

TORRENCE, WILLIAM DAVID Acad: Ind Rels, Bus Admin. BA 1953, MA 1954, PhD 1962, U of Nebr-Lincoln. PUBL: "The Impact of Compulsory Arbitration on Municipal Budgets," (co-author), J of Collective Negotiations in the Public Sector, 1983; "Age and the Job Hunting Methods of the Unemployed," (co-author), Monthly Labor Rev, 1979; "Public Employee Work Stoppages in the United States: 1968-1977," Government Union Rev, 1980. INT: coll barg, govt labor policy, intl comparative labor. ASSN: IIRA. POSITIONS: Ind Rels Admin, Marathon Corp-Div of American Can Co, 1954-57; Prof of Mgmt, 1957, and, since 1970, Regents Professor of Management, College of Bus Admin, Univ of Nebraska, Lincoln, NE 68588. 402/472-2313

TOSHOKAN, SAPPORO DAIGAKU Acad: Ind Rels. ADDRESS: Nishioka 3-JO 7-Chome, Toyohira Ku Sapparo, 062 Japan-Nau.

TOTTEN, JAN LAUBE Professional Assn. POSITION: Calif Assn Employers, 1553 Grove, San Francisco, CA 94117. 415/982-6901

TOWARNICKY, JOHN M. Bus:Pers/Ind Rels; Acad: Bus Admin, Law. BBA 1977, MBA 1979, Cleveland State U. INT: labor market econ, method/statis, health & hosp care. POSITIONS: Research Systems Advisor, Federal Reserve Bank of Cleveland, 1978; Personnel Analyst, Marathon Oil Co, Findlay, OH, 1979; and (since 1982) Employee Rels Administrator, Tenneco Oil Exploration and Production. ADDRESS: Apt T24, 5830 S Lake Houston Parkway, Houston, TX 77049. 713/757-8736

TOWNLEY, ROSEMARY A. Government. Empl Rels Dir, Ardlsey Union Free High School, 500 Farm Rd, Ardsley, NY 10502.

TRACHTENBERG, BRUCE S. Arbitration, Legal Practice. AS 1973, Orange Cty Community Coll; BS 1975, Cornell; JD 1978, Union U. INT: arb/med, labor law, govt labor policy. ASSN: New York Capitol Dist IRRA, ABA, New York State & Schnectady County Bar Assns. POSITIONS: Paralegal Instructor, Schnectady Cty Community Coll, 1978; Asst Corp Counsel, City of Schnectady, 1979; and (since 1980) Attorney/Arbitrator, 230-A State St, Schenectady, NY 12305. 518/382-7815

TRACY, LANE Acad: Ind Rels, Org Beh/-Pers. AB 1959, Cornell U; MA 1962, SUNY-Albany; PhD 1971, U of Wash. PUBL: Systematic Management of Human Resources; "Testing A Behavioral Theory of Labor Negotiations;" "Tackling Problems Through Negotiation." INT: coll barg, org beh, personnel. ASSN: Acad of Mgmt, ASPA, Society for General Systems Research. POSITION: (since 1971) Professor, Dept of Management Systems, Copeland Hall, Ohio Univ, Athens, OH 45701. 614/-594-5078

TRASK, THOMAS EDWARD Union. POSITION: (since 1978) Regional Director, ILWU, 451 Atkinson Dr, Honolulu, HI 94814.

TREASEH, RONALD L. Bus:Mgmt/Admin. MBA 1974, DePaul U. INT: personnel, mgmt/-educ, empl/trng programs. ASSN: Chicago IRRA, Natl Assn of Black MBA's, Hyde Park Businessman's Assn, Natl Assn of Accountants. POSITIONS: Branch Credit Mgr, 1979, Mgr of Operations, Xerox Finance Center, 1982, and, since 1983, Manager, Xerox Finance Center Admin, Xerox, 3000 Des Plaines Ave, Des Plaines, IL 60018. 312/635-2593

TREASURE, MARTIN G. Bus:Pers/Ind Rels. MA 1978, St. Francis Coll. INT: labor law, arb/med, coll barg. POSITIONS: Labor Rels Asst, Florence Mining Co, 1976; Mgr, Pers and Ind Rels, 1978, and, since 1980, Labor Rels Coordinator, North American Coal Corp, PO Box 351, Seward, PA 15954. 412/676-4703

TREVINO, ROSE I. Bus:Pers/Ind Rels. POSITION: Associate Personnel Rep, National Supply Co, 1455 W Loop S, Houston, TX 77027.

TREZISE, DAVID L. Bus:Pers/Ind Rels. BS 1947, Miami U-Ohio; JD 1950, U of Mich. INT: coll barg, labor law, personnel. ASSN: ABA, Federal Bar Assn, Mich Bar Assn. POSITIONS: Supervisor Attorney, NLRB, 1953; Partner-Law Firm, Humphleys & Hutcheson, 1974; and (since 1979) Vice Pres, Ind Rels, Westinghouse Elec Corp, Westinghouse Bldg, Pittsburgh, PA 15222. 412/642-3898

TRIPLETT, JACK E. Government. POSITION: Associate Commissioner, US Bureau of Labor Statistics, 441 G ST NW, Room 2021, Washington DC 20212.

TRIPP, L. REED Arbitration; Acad: Econ, Ind Rels. BA 1934, Union Coll; PhD 1942, Yale U. PUBL: Labor Problems and Processes, Harper, 1960; Wage Reopening Arbitration, (monograph), U of Penna, 1951; "The Economics of Dis-development," Il Politico, U of Pavia, Italy, 1966. INT: arb/med, coll barg, govt labor policy. ASSN: Philadelphia IRRA, NAA, AEA. POSITIONS: Prof of Econ, U of Wis, 1949; Prof of Econ, Lehigh Univ, 1964; and (since 1979) Labor Arbitrator (self employed), 577 Bierys Bridge Rd, Bethlehem, PA 18017. 215/861-0202

TRONT, MARIE A. Bus:Pers/Ind Rels. BBA 1978, MAIR 1982, Wayne State U. INT: coll barg. ASSN: Detroit IRRA, AAUW, DPMA. POSITIONS: Labor Rels Rep, 1978, Gen Supervisor-Pers Services, Cadillac Motor Car Div, 1980, and, since 1984, Supervisor of Ind Rels, General Motors Assembly Div-GMC, Detroit. ADDRESS: 23861 Lawrence, Dearborn, MI 48128. 313/556-9339

TROY, LEO Acad: Econ, Ind Rels; Arbitration. BA 1949, Penna State U; MA 1950, PhD 1958, Columbia. POSITIONS: Prof of Econ, 1958-68, Chairman, 1968-78, and, currently, Dept of Econ, Rutgers Univ. ADDRESS: 5 Lakeview Dr, West Orange, NJ 07052. 201/731-1554

TROYER, STEVEN ALAN Student; Legal Practice, Bus:Pers/Ind Rels. AB 1977, Harvard; MILR 1981, Cornell; JD 1984, UCLA. INT: labor law, arb/med, govt labor policy. POSITIONS: Systems Engineer, IBM, 1979; Associate, Shearmon & Stearling, New York, 1984; and (currently) Student, UCLA Law School. ADDRESS: 855 10th St, Santa Monica, CA 90403.

TRUELL, GEORGE F. Consulting. BS 1951, Cornell. PUBL: Coaching and Counseling: Key Skills for Managers; Performance Appraisal: Current Issues and New Directions; Building and Managing Productive Work Teams. INT: personnel, mgmt/educ, org beh. ASSN: Western New York IRRA, Inst of Mgmt Consultants, Intl Consultant Foundation, ASPA. POSITIONS: Pers Supervisor, Welch Foods Inc, 1953; Vice Pres-Ind Rels, Graphic Controls Corp, 1959; and (since 1971) President, G. Truell Assoc, 495 N. Forest Rd, Williamsville, NY 14221. 716/634-3491

TRUESDALE, JOHN C. Government. AB 1942, Grinnell Coll; MS 1948, Cornell U; JD 1972, Georgetown U. INT: labor law, arb/med, coll barg. ASSN: Wash DC IRRA, SPIDR, ABA, Federal Bar Assn. POSITIONS: Deputy Exec Secretary, 1968-72, Member, 1977-81, and, since 1972, Exec Secretary, NLRB, 1717 Pennsylvania Ave NW, Washington DC 20570. 202/-254-9430

TRUMBLE, ROBERT R. Government, Consulting; Acad: Ind Rels. BA 1962, Hamline U; MA 1963, PhD 1971, U of Minn. INT: empl/-trng programs, govt labor policy, labor market econ. POSITIONS: Dir, Div of Resources Analysis, Natl Inst of Health, 1972; Head, Manpower Studies Section, 1975, and, since 1978, Deputy Dir, Div of Policy Research and Analysis, Natl Science Foundation. ADDRESS: 8508 Cottage St, Vienna, VA 22180. 202/634-4787

TRUPIANO, JOHN Health & Hosp Care. POSITION: Manager, BCBSM, 600 LaFayette East, Detroit, MI 48066. 313/225-8416

TSUDA, MASUMI Acad: Ind Rels. POSITION: Professor, Dept of Sociology, Hitotsubashi Univ, 4-18-20, Kugahara Ohta-Ku, Tokyo, Japan 145

TUCK, KENNETH W. Union. INT: union org/admin, coll barg, arb/med. ASSN: Greater Houston IRRA. POSITIONS: Business Rep, 1975, and, since 1983, President and Directing Bus Rep, Intl Assn of Machinists and Aerospace Workers, Lodge 15, AFL-CIO, 6640 Long Point, Houston, TX 77055. 713/686-9464

TURNBULL, JOHN G. Acad: Econ. AB 1938, Dennison U; PhD 1947, MIT. PUBL: Economic and Social Security, 5th Ed, (w C. A. Williams, Jr. and E. F. Cheit). INT: labor market econ, income maint, coll barg. POSITION: (1949-1982) Prof of Economics, Univ of Minn. Retired. ADDRESS: 186 A Wentworth Ave W, West St. Paul. MN 55118.

TURNBULL, WILLIAM O. Acad: Elementary School Teacher; Union. BA 1969, U of Wash. INT: coll barg, labor law, govt labor policy. ASSN: Northwest IRRA, Retired Officers Assn, U.S. Naval Inst. POSITIONS: U.S. Naval Officer, U.S. Navy, 1938; and (since 1970) Elementary School Teacher, Bremerton School Dist. ADDRESS: 2503 Ridgeway Dr NW, Bremerton, WA 98312. 206/478-5080

TURNER, MARJORIE S. Acad: Econ, Ind Rels; Arbitration. PhD 1954, U of Tex-Austin. PUBL: Prices, Profits and Production, How Much Is Enough? (w J. W. Leasure)., U of New Mexico Press, 1974; "Wages and the Cambridge Theory of Distribution," ILRR, Cornell, 1966; Women and Work, UCLA Inst of Ind Rels, 1963. INT: arb/med, intl comparative labor, labor history. ASSN: Assn for Evolutionary Economists. POSITION: Professor Emeritus, San Diego State U. ADDRESS: Box 8005, Black Butte Ranch, Sisters, OR 97759.

TURNQUIST, DAN E. Government. POSITION: Deputy Coordinator, 5/IL Room 4234, Department of State, Washington DC 20520.

TUTTLE, PAMELA MAE Student. 3631 Collins Ferry Rd, Morgantown, WV 26505. 304/599-2993

TWOHEY, JERILOU COSSACK Arbitration. BA 1965, MS 1968, UCLA. INT: arb/med, labor law, coll barg. ASSN: San Francisco IRRA, AAA, SPIDR, Calif Bar Assn (Labor & Emp Law Section). POSITIONS: Supervisory Examiner, NLRB, 1972; Member, Calif Public Empl Rels Board, 1976; and (since 1979) Arbitrator, 3231 Quandt Rd, Lafayette, CA 94549. 415/937-6045

TWOMEY, TIMOTHY Union. POSITION: Executive Secretary, Hospital and Inst Workers Local 250, 240 Golden Gate Ave, San Francisco, CA 94102. 415/441-2500

TYER, CHARLES WILLIAM Acad: Ind Rels, Org Beh/Pers; Arbitration. BSC 1953, Tex Christian U; MBA 1975, PhD 1980, North Tex State U. PUBL: A Practical Guide to Labor Negotiations; Labor Relations for the Non-Union Company; New Hope-New Growth. INT: arb/-med, mgmt/educ, personnel. ASSN: North Texas IRRA, NAA, AAA, ASPA. POSITIONS: Corp Dir of Ind Rels, Automation Ind, 1964; Dir of Pers, Amerace Corp, EMCOVITE Div, 1969; and (since 1976) Assoc Prof of Mgmt, Tarrant County Jr. College. ADDRESS: 7016 Declaration, Ft. Worth, TX 76148. 817/232-2900

U

UBER, ARTHUR E., JR. Bus:Mgmt/Admin. BSEE & BSME, 1949, Carnegie Mellon U; JD 1953, Duquesne U. INT: labor law, mgmt/-educ, intl comparative labor. ASSN: ABA, Penna Bar Assn, Society for Advancement of Mgmt. POSITIONS: Sr Consultant, Corp Devel, 1972, Dir, Bus Devel, Public Systems Co, 1976, and, since 1981, Director, Special Studies, Corp Planning, Westinghouse Electric Corp, 4137 Northampton Dr, Allison Park, PA 15101. 412/255-3666

UDIS, BERNARD Acad: Economics. BA 1949, Penna State; MA 1951, Penna; PhD 1959, Princeton. PUBL: "Enlistments in the All-Volunteer Force: A Military Personnel Supply Model and Its Forecasts," (w C. Ash & R. J. McNown), Amer Econ Rev, Mar 1983, pp 145-155; "Prospects for Rationalization in NATO Via Collaborative Lessons From Aerospace," ORBEIS, Spring 1981; From Guns to Butter: High Technology Organizations and Reduced Military Spending in Western Europe,Cambridge, MA: Ballinger, 1978. INT: labor market econ, coll barg, govt labor programs. ASSN: AEA, Regional Sci Assn, Intl Inst of Strategic Studies. POSITION: Professor of Econ, Dept of Econ, Campus Box 256, Univ of Colorado, Boulder, CO 80309. 303/492-8872

UEHLEIN, JULIUS Union. INT: govt labor policy, labor law, labor educ. ASSN: Central Penna IRRA, Penna Humanities Council, Penna Human Rels Council, Penna Legal Services, Inc. POSITIONS: Staff Rep, USWA Dist 28, Ohio, 1956, Secretary-Treasurer, USWA Legislative Committee of Penna, 1967, and, since 1982, President, Penna AFL-CIO, 101 Pine St, Harrisburg, PA 17101. 717/238-9351

UEHLEIN, MARY LOU Journalism. 101 Pine St, Harrisburg, PA 17101.

UHLINGER, CHARLES W. Bus:Pers/Ind Rels; Bus Admin. BA 1941, Hofstra Coll; BS U.S. Merchant Marine Acad, 1947; MA 1948, Columbia U; PhD 1956, Fordham U. ADDRESS:

611 Berwick Rd, Wilmington, DE 19803. 302/-429-5267

ULLMAN, DONNA Union. BA 1961, Beloit Coll; MS 1969, U of Wis-Madison. INT: coll barg, arb/med. POSITION: (since 1981) Director of Collective Bargaining, Wis Educ Assn Council, PO Box 8003, Madison, WI 53708. 608/255-2971

ULLMAN, JOSEPH C. Acad: Bus Admin. BS 1951, Northwestern U; MBA 1962, PhD 1965, U of Chicago. PUBL: Women of Steel: Female Blue Collar Workers in Basic steel Industry; "Description and Use of an Empirical Approach to Organization Design;" A Study of the Local Job Bank Program. INT: coll barg, empl/trng programs, govt labor policy. ASSN: Acad of Mgmt. POSITIONS: Prof of Mgmt, Purdue U, 1965; and (since 1981) Program Dir and Prof of Mgmt, Univ of South Carolina. ADDRESS: 7 Fairway LN, Blythewood, SC 29016. 803/777-7410

ULMAN, LLOYD Acad: Econ, Ind Rels. AB 1940, Columbia; AM 1941, U of Wis; PhD 1950, Harvard. PUBL: Unionism, Economic Stabilization, and Incomes Policy: European Experience, (w R. J. Flanagan & D. Sobrice), 1983; The Government of the Steelworkers Union; The Rise of the National Trade Union. INT: coll barg, intl comparative labor, labor market econ. ASSN: San Francisco Bay Area IRRA, AEA. POSITIONS: Assoc Prof of Econ, 1952, Prof of Econ and Ind Rels, U of Minn, 1956; and (since 1958) Prof of Econ and Ind Rels, Univ of California, Berkeley, CA 94720. 415/525-8341

UMETANI, SHUNICHIRO Acad: Econ, Ind Rels. MS 1968, PhD 1977, U of Wis-Madison. POSITIONS: Res Assoc, The Japan Inst of Labor, 1969; Assoc Prof of Labor Econ, Tokyo Gakugei U, 1974; Visiting Sr Lecturer, Dept of Econ, U of Hong Kong, 1978. ADDRESS: 1-5-9 Harayama, Apt 401, Urawa Saitama 336, Japan.

UMHOEFER, GARY Bus:Pers/Ind Rels. MS-IR 1983, U of Wis. INT: personnel, empl/-trng programs. POSITION: Senior Pers Administrator, Harris Corp. ADDRESS: 2381 Eden Park Dr, Melbourne, FL 32953. 305/254-1834

UNDERHILL, RICHARD SANDS Consulting. AB 1950, AM 1951, U of Mich; DBA 1965, Ind U. INT: mgmt/educ, org beh, ind psychology. ASSN: Acad of Mgmt, Assn for Humanistic Psyc, Intl Transitional Analysis Assn. POSITIONS: Exec V.P., Battle Creek Equip Co, 1953; Prof of Mgmt, U of Richmond, 1963; and (since 1981) President, RCM Intl, 3507 Warner Rd, Richmond, VA 23225. 804/320-5781

UNGER, WILLIAM R. Union. POSITION: Grievance Specialist, Iowa State Education Association, 4025 Tonawanda Dr, Des Moines, IA 50312.

URQUHART, WARREN GEORGE Bus:Pers/Ind Rels. POSITION: Industrial Rels Manager, Alberta Govt Telephones, 10020 100th St C-32nd Fl, Edmonton, Alberta T5J 0N5 Canada. 403/-425-3402

USERY, WILLIAM J. Consulting. PUBL: "The American Labor Movement in the 1980's," (w D. Henne), Employees Rels Law J, vol 7, #2, 1981. INT: coll barg, arb/med. ASSN: Wash DC IRRA. POSITIONS: Dir, FMCS, 1973-76; U.S. Secretary of Labor, US Dept of Labor, 1976; and (since 1977) President, Bill Usery Assoc Inc, Suite 301, 1730 Rhode Island Ave NW, Washington DC 20036. 202/466-6260

V

VAAS, FRANCIS J. Legal Practice. AB 1938, Holy Cross Coll; LLB 1948, Harvard. "Title VII: Legislative History," chapter in Boston Coll Ind and Commercial Law Rev; "The Percentage Lease-Its Functions and Drafting Problems," Harvard Law Rev. INT: labor law, coll barg, arb/med. ASSN: ABA, Boston Bar Assn, Mass Bar Assn. POSITIONS: Sales Administration, General Tire and Rubber Co, 1938-41; and (since 1948) Partner, Ropes and Gray, 225 Franklin St, Boston, MA 02110. 617/-423-6100

VACCARO, VINCENT A. Bus:Pers/Ind Rels. BS 1964, Wash U-St. Louis; MBA 1975, Golden Gate U. INT: arb/med, labor law, coll barg. ASSN: Central Ohio IRRA, Ind Rels Assn of Central Ohio, ASPA, Central Ohio Pers Assn. POSITIONS: Warehousing and Shipping Mgr, 1971, Ind Rels Asst Mgr, 1977, and, since 1980, Ind Rels Manager, Anheuser-Busch, Inc, 700 East Schrock Rd, Columbus, OH 43229. 614/888-6644

VALENZUELA, DANY Bus:Pers/Ind Rels. POSITION: Director of Personnel, Kaiser Permanente, 615 S. Pepper, Anaheim, CA 92802. 213/920-6902

VALLONE, PETER D. Government. POSITION: Pers and Labor Rels, State of Illinois, 503 Stratton Bldg, Springfield, IL 62706. 217/-782-6191

VALORIS, BRUCE W. Bus:Pers/Ind Rels. BA 1966, Penna State U; MBA 1978, Ind U. INT: coll barg, arb/med, labor law. ASSN: Wash DC IRRA. POSITIONS: Asst Supervisor, Labor Rels, Jones & Laughlin Steel Corp-Pittsburgh, 1969; Mgr, Pers Rels, National Standard Co, Niles, MI, 1974; and (since 1979) Manager, Employee Rels, Martin Marietta Corp, 6801 Rockledge Dr, Bethesda, MD 20817. 301/897-6223

VALTIN, ROLF Arbitration. BA 1948, Swarthmore Coll; MA 1950, U of Penna. PUBL: "Judicial Review Revisited-The Search for Accommodation Must Continue;" "Hair and Beards in Arbitration;" "Preventative Mediation Grievance Disputes and the Taft-Hartley Act." INT: arb/med, coll barg, intl comparative labor. ASSN: Wash DC IRRA, NAA, Intl Society for Labor Law and Social Security. POSITIONS: Federal Mediator, FMCS, 1952; and (since 1956) Arbitrator (self-employed), 1319 Woodside Dr, McLean, VA 22102. 703/356-1930

VAN ALSTYNE, CARY BROWNELL Arbitration, Research. BA 1977, U of Rochester. INT: arb, labor law, coll barg. ASSN: AAA. POSITION: R. C. Simpson Inc, PO Box 567, Ridgewood, NJ 07451. 201/445-2260

VAN ALSTYNE, VANCE B. Arbitration, Consulting, Mgmt. BA 1948, U of Rochester; LLB 1964, Blackstone Coll of Law. INT: arb, labor law, coll barg. ASSN: Amer Mgmt Assn,

AAA. POSITIONS: Secretary, 1956, Vice Pres, 1961, and, since 1975, Chairman and Pres, R. C. Simpson Inc, PO Box 567, Ridgewood, NJ 07451. 201/445-2260

VAN CLEVE, ROY R. Acad: Univ Admin, Bus Admin. BS 1961, U of Omaha; MS 1966, WAUM Post Grad School; PhD 1976, U of Tex-Austin. INT: org beh, personnel. POSITION: (since 1983) Assoc Dean and Prof, School of Bus Admin, Univ of Pacific. ADDRESS: 6325 Savannah Pl, Stockton, CA 95209. 209/946-2476

VAN HELDEN, RONALD M. Government, Union; Acad: Ind Rels. BA 1966, Bucknell U; MA 1967, U of Grenoble; PhD, Amer U. PUBL: What You Should Know About the Pension and Welfare Law; Annual Report on the Construction Industry; Seasonality in the Construction Industry. INT: govt labor policy, intl comparative labor, union org/admin. ASSN: Wash DC IRRA. POSITIONS: Special Asst to the Asst Secretary for Labor Mgmt Rels, 1977-80, Dir, Office of Construction Industry Services, 1979-81, and, since 1981, Asst Administrator, Pension and Welfare Benefit Programs, USDL, 2418 39th PL, Washington DC 20007. 202/523-9218

VAN LAAN, RICK Student. BA 1982, MLIR 1983, Mich State U. INT: coll barg, arb/med, labor law. ASSN: Mich State U IRRA. ADDRESS: 1450 Yorkshire, Grand Rapids, MI 49508.

VAN WART, ARTHUR THOMAS Arbitration, Legal Prac; Acad: Law. BS 1966, Boston U; JD 1970, Suffolk U. INT: arb/med, labor law, intl comparative labor. ASSN: NJSB, ABA. POSITION: Arbitrator-Mediator (self employed), 75 Market St, Salem, NJ 08079.

VANA, ROBERT JOSEPH Arbitration. BS 1971, Kent State U; JD 1977, Akron U. INT: arb/med. ASSN: AAA (Labor Panel), ABA, Ohio State Bar Assn. POSITIONS: Educator, Streetsboro Bd of Educ, 1971; Attorney, Hogle & Kirkwood, 1977; and (since 1978) Arbitrator/-Attorney, LaPorte & Ipavec Co, LPA, 738 National City Bank Bldg, Cleveland, OH 44114. 216/241-1397

VANDE VORD, NEIL Acad: Labor Education. POSITION: Assoc Prof. ADDRESS: 1818 Wood, Lansing, MI 48912.

VARGA, PAUL V. Arbitration. BS 1967, St. Joseph's Coll-Phila. INT: arb/med. ASSN: Chicago IRRA, AAA, ASPA, SPIDR. POSITIONS: Member of Board, 1978, Vice-Chairman, Fourth Div, 1981, and, since 1982, Chairman, Fourth Div, Natl Railroad Adjustment Board, 10 W Jackson Blvd, Room 251, Chicago, IL 60604. 312/886-7321

VASA-SIDERIS, SANDRA Acad: Student, Org Beh/Pers; Consulting. BA 1971, MA 1976, U of Tenn; MBA, Ga State U. PUBL: "The Efficacy of a Point-Scored Negotiation Exercise in a Graduate Collective Bargaining Course: A Multi Year Comparative Analysis," (w M. J. Jedel, & D. P. Crane), IRRA 35th Annual Proceedings. INT: personnel, intl comparative labor. ASSN: Atlanta IRRA, ASPA. POSITIONS: Pers and Training Mgr, Lord & Taylor, 1977; and (since 1982) Grad Teaching Assistant and PhD Candidate, Management Dept, Georgia State Univ. ADDRESS: 2103 Mitchell Ct, Marietta, GA 30062. 404/658-3400

VATTENDAHL, OBERT J. Union. POSITION: Director, United Steelworkers, 615 E Michigan St, Milwaukee, WI 53202. 414/276-2781

VAUGHN, WILLIAM M. Bus:Pers/Ind Rels. BA 1962, Williams Coll; PhD 1970, MIT. INT: coll barg, labor market econ, labor law. ASSN: Boston IRRA. POSITION: (since 1979) Vice Pres, Labor Rels, Stop and Shop Companies, PO Box 369, Boston, MA 02101. 617/770-8270

VAUSE, WILLIAM GARY Acad: Law; Arbitration. BA 1967, JD 1970, U of Conn; LLM 1981, U of Va. PUBL: Labor Arbitration in State and Local Government, 1981. INT: arb/med, labor law. ASSN: Central Florida IRRA, AAA (Arb Panel). POSITIONS: Partner, private law practice, 1970; Assoc Dean, 1975, and, since 1983, Dir, Center for Labor Management Dispute Resolution, College of Law, Stetson Univ, 1401 61st St So, St. Petersburg, FL 33707. 813/343-3837

VECELLIO, DENISE McDONALD Ind Engineering. BACH-Ind Admin, 1981, General Motors Inst. INT: intl comparative labor, ind sociol, org beh. POSITIONS: Student CO-OP, 1976, Production Supervisor, 1981, and, since 1981, Ind Engineer, GM Truck and Bus Division of General Motors. ADDRESS: 2471 Buckingham, Birmingham, MI 48008. 313/456-3767

VELOTTA, CHARLES V. Union, Government. BS 1979, NY Inst of Tech; MBA 1982, Manhatten Coll. INT: coll barg, arb/med, union org/admin. ASSN: Long Island IRRA, AAA. POSITION: (since 1981) Director of Res Negotiations, TBTA Bridge and Tunnel Officers Benevolent Assn. ADDRESS: 1897 S. Railroad Ave, Staten Island, NY 10306. 212/233-1590

VENDITTO, JOHN G. Bus:Mgmt/Admin. POSITION: Warwick School Dept, 34 Warick Lake Ave, Warwick, RI 02889. 401/737-3300

VENERI, DARREN A. Student. 410-1 Pierpont Apts, Morgantown, WV 26505. 304/598-2153

VENEZIANI, BRUNO Acad: Law, Ind Rels. LAW 1965, U of Bari-Italy. PUBL: Mediation On Collective Disputes in Italy-(1950-1972); Trade Unions Comparative Law (Italy-U.K.-France-Sweden-Germany); Collective Bargaining in Italy (1945-1977). INT: labor law, coll barg, arb/med. ASSN: Italian Ind Rels Assn, Italian Labour Law Assn. POSITION: (since 1975) Professor on Labour Law, Dept Labor & Ind Rels, Univ of Bari. ADDRESS: Via Michele Mitolo 5, 70100 Bari, Italy. Phone: 216909

VENICK, CHARLES Student. AA 1970, Community Coll-Baltimore; BA 1972, U of Md-Baltimore Cty; MS 1983, U of Dist of Columbia. INT: arb/med, govt labor policy, personnel. POSITIONS: Transportation Analyst, New Jersey Dept of Trans, 1976; and (since 1978) Ground Transportation Supr, Intl Airport, Airway Limousine Service Inc, Baltimore. ADDRESS: 320 Highland Dr, #201, Glen Burnie, MD 21061. 301/859-7550

VER PLOEG, CHRISTINE D. Acad: Law; Arbitration. BA 1971, U of Mass; JD 1974, Drake U; LLM 1977, Georgetown U. INT: arb/-med, labor law, coll barg. ASSN: SPIDR, AAA, ABA (Labor Law & Empl Section). POSITIONS: Trial Attorney, US Dept of Justice, 1974; Labor Arbitrator, 1978; and (since 1977) Prof of Law, William Mitchell College of Law, 875 Summit Ave, St. Paul, MN 55105. 612/227-9171

VERBIN, SHELLEY C. Bus:Mgmt/Admin. POSITION: Planning Rep, Pacific Gas & Electric, 215 Market St, San Francisco, CA 94106.

VERMA, ANIL Acad: Bus Admin. B Tech,- 1971, Indian Inst of Tech-Kanpur; MBA 1976, U of Saskatchewan; PhD 1983, MIT. PUBL: "Negotiations in Organizations: Blending Industrial Relations and Organizational Behavior Approaches," (w T. A. Kochan), in M. H. Bazerman & R. J. Lewicki (eds) Negotiating in Organizations, Beverly Hills, CA: Sage Publ, 1983. INT: coll barg, org beh, personnel. ASSN: AEA, Acad of Mgmt. POSITIONS: Asst Mgr-Subcontracting, G.K.W. Ltd, Calcutta, 1976-78; Lecturer, Mgmt Science and Ind Rels, Univ of Saskatchewan, 1978-80; and (since 1983) Asst Prof, Faculty of Bus and Commerce, Univ of British Columbia, 2053 Main Mall, Vancouver, BC V6T 1Y8 Canada. 604/228-6798

VERNON, GIL Arbitration. PO Box 241, Eau Claire, WI 54701.

VERRASTRO, DOMINIC N. Bus:Pers/Ind Rels. BBA 1961, St. John's U-Brooklyn. INT: coll barg, labor law, arb/med. ASSN: Denver IRRA. POSITIONS: Labor Rels Mgr, ITT World Communications Inc-NY, 1961; Pers Mgr, Computer Machinery Corp-CA, 1972; and (since 1979) Manager Employee/Labor Rels, Martin Marietta Aerospace, PO Box 179, Denver, CO 80201. 303/977-5734

VEYSEY, VICTOR V. Government. MBA 1938, Harvard. PUBL: Manual for Conducting an Employee Opinion Poll, Caltech IRC, 1983; The New World of Managing Human Resources, Caltech IRC, 1980. INT: govt labor policy, productivity improvement, QWL. ASSN: Los Angeles IRRA, ASPA, Soc for Advancement of Mgmt. POSITIONS: Asst Secretary, U. S. Army, 1975; Dir, Ind Rels Center, Calif Inst of Technology, 1977; and (since 1983) Director for Ind Rels, State of California, 525 Golden Gate Ave, San Francisco, CA 94102. 415/557-3356

VIA, EMORY F. Acad: Labor Education. BA 1946, Emory U; MA 1956, PhD 1964, U of Chicago. INT: labor educ. ASSN: Amer Political Sci Assn. POSITIONS: Dir, Labor Program, Southern Reg Council-Atlanta, 1968; Visiting Prof, Georgia State Univ, 1976; and (since 1978) Dir/Prof, Labor Educ and Res Center, Univ of Oregon. ADDRESS: 1935 Sylvan, Eugene, OR 97403. 503/686-5054

VIANE, NICOLE KRISTINE Student. 3985 Hereford, Detroit, MI 48224. 313/886-1575

VIANI, ALAN R. Union. BS 1958, Kans State U. INT: coll barg, govt labor policy, personnel. ASSN: New York IRRA, ASPA. POSITION: Dir of Res and Negotiations, Dist Council 37, AFSCME, AFL-CIO, 125 Barclay St, New York, NY 10007. 212/766-1032

VIGIL, PATRICK R. Union. BA 1977, Fort Lewis Coll; MA 1982, Antioch U; Trade Union Program, 1980, Harvard. INT: labor educ, labor law, arb/med. POSITIONS: Local Union Positions, CWA, Local 8611; and (since 1983) Executive Director, New Mexico Public Employees Council #18, AFSCME. ADDRESS: 7724 Spencer NE, Albuquerque, NM 87109. 505/265-8533

VILLERE, MAURICE FRANCOIS Acad: Bus Admin. PhD 1971, U of Ill. PUBL: Transactional Analysis at Work, Prentice Hall, 1981; Successful Personal Selling Through TA, Prentice Hall, 1980. POSITION: (since 1971) Assoc Prof, Univ of New Orleans. ADDRESS: 7626 Willow St, New Orleans, LA 70118. 504/861-1361

VINTON, KAREN LYNN Acad: Org Beh/-Pers, Bus Admin, Ind Rels. AB 1971, MBA 1974, Ind U; PhD 1983, U of Utah. PUBL: "Assessment of Training Needs for Supervisors: Current Issues and a Survey of the Literature;" "Humor in the Workplace." INT: org beh, personnel, ind psych. ASSN: Acad of Mgmt, ASPA, Intl Council for Small Business. POSITIONS: Mgmt Employment Coordinator, Indiana Bell Telephone Co, 1971; Utah Employment Mgr, Mountain Bell Telephone Co, 1977; and (since 1983) Asst Prof, Mgmt and Marketing Dept, Montana State Univ. ADDRESS: 2915 Secor, Boseman, MT 59715. 406/994-6187

VITALIS, EARL L., JR. Acad: Org Beh/Pers. BBA 1962, MA 1964, U of Minn. INT: mgmt/-educ, org beh, personnel. POSITIONS: Instructor, U of Minn, 1963; Lecturer, U of Toronto, 1968; and (since 1976) Professor of Bus Admin, Ryerson Polytechnical Inst, 50 Gould St, Toronto M5B 1E8 Canada. 416/979-5000

VLADEK, JUDITH P. Legal Practice, Labor Educ. POSITION: Vladeck, Waldman, Elias and Engelhard , PC, 1501 Broadway, New York, NY 10036. 212/354-8330

VOELKER, KEITH EMERY Acad: Econ. BBA 1961, MSIR 1964, PhD 1969, U of Wis-Madison. POSITIONS: Asst Prof, Carthage Coll, 1965; and (since 1970) Assoc Prof, Dept of Econ, Univ of Wisconsin-Oshkosh. ADDRESS: 1311 Maricopa Dr, Oshkosh, WI 54901. 414/233-6093

VOGEL, MICHAEL S. Professional Recruiting & Search. BS 1965, Temple U. INT: empl/trng programs, personnel, mgmt/educ. ASSN: ASPA, Amer Comepnsation Assn, ASTD. POSITIONS: Ind Rels Mgr, Chilton PrintingCo, 1972; Labor Rels Mgr, Certainteed Corp, 1977; and (since 1978) Mgr, Pers Div, The Andre Group, 2000 Valley Forge Towers, King of Prussia, PA 19406. 215/783-5100

VOOS, PAULA BETH Acad: Ind Rels, Econ. AB 1971, Whittman Coll; MA 1976, Portland State; PhD 1982, Harvard. PUBL: "Union Organizing Programs: Costs and Benefits," Ind and Labor Rels Rev, July 1983; "Labor Union Organizing Programs: Past Research and Future Needs-A Comment," forthcoming, Ind Rels; Review of Richard Blandy and Sue Richardson, eds, How Labour Markets Work, forthcoming, J of Econ Literature. INT: coll barg, union org/admin, labor market econ. ASSN: AEA. POSITIONS: Res Asst, Natl Bureau of Econ Res, 1978; Instructor, Univ of Mass, 1978; and (since 1981) Asst Prof, Univ of Wis. ADDRESS: 2710 Willard, Madison, WI 53704. 608/-263-3866

VORYS, GAIL ARCH Student. BA 1974, Wheaton Coll; MA 1981, Ohio State U. INT: coll barg, labor educ, org beh. ASSN: Ohio State IRRA. POSITION: (since 1982) Grad Teaching Asst, Ohio State Univ. 406 W 6th Ave, Columbus, OH 43701. 614/422-2809

VOSBURGH, DONALD F. Bus:Pers/Ind Rels. BS 1958, Rider Coll; MBA 1965, Fairleigh Dickinson U. ASSN: Central NJ IRRA, ASPA, Amer Compensation Assn. POSITIONS: Mgr, Ind

Rels, Thiokol Chemical Corp, 1961-72; and, currently, Asst Prof, Rider Coll, School of Mgmt, and, (since 1972) Corp Manager Ind Rels, Transamerica Delaval, 3450 Princeton Pike, Lawrenceville, NJ 08648. 609/896-7681

VROMAN, WAYNE Non-Profit Research; Acad: Econ. PhD 1967, U of Mich. INT: labor market econ, income maint, coll barg. POSITION: (since 1977) Sr Research Assoc, Urban Inst, 2100 M St NW, Washington DC 20037. 202/223-1950

VYGANTAS, PETER VYTAUTAS Bus:Mgmt/-Admin. BA 1951, Brooklyn Coll; MA 1953, Fordham U; PhD 1956, U of Ill. INT: org beh, coll barg, personnel. ASSN: Amer Psych Assn. POSITION: (since 1980) Sr Vice Pres Administration, Sky Chefs, American Airlines, PO Box 619777, Dallas/Ft. Worth Airport, TX 75261. 817/792-2303

W

WACHTER, MICHAEL L. Acad: Economics. BS 1964, Cornell U; MA 1967, PhD 1970, Harvard U. PUBL: "A Production Function-Nonaccelerating Inflation Approach to Potential Output: Is Measured Potential Output Too High?" (w J. M. Perloff), Carnegie-Rochester Conference Series on Publ Policy, ed K. Brunner & A. H. Meltzer, 10 1979: 113-163; "Economic Changes Posed by Demographic Changes," in Work Decisions in the 1980's (Boston: Auburn House, 1982), pp 35-75; Toward a New U.S. Industrial Policy? (co-editor with S.M. Wachter), Phila: Univ of Penna Press, 1982. INT: labor market econ, coll barg, govt labor policy. ASSN: AEA, Amer Econometric Soc. POSITION: (since 1980) Prof of Econ and Mgmt, Dept of Econ, Univ of Pennsylvania, 3718 Locust Walk CR, Philadelphia, PA 19104. 215/898-7719

WADA, MARY MATSUKO BA 1970, MS 1974, U of Wis-Madison. INT: personnel, coll barg, labor law. POSITION: Specialist, Equal Opportunity, U of Wis-Madison, 1974-79. ADDRESS: 60 Flicker Ct, Naperville, IL 60565.

WAGNER, EDWIN M. Acad: Ind Rels. Apt 2, RD 1, Box 243, Patton, PA 16668. 814/678-3309

WAGNER, FRANK E. Acad: Economics. 6418 Main, Kansas City, MO 64113. 816/276-1313

WAGNER, MARLIN O. Union. POSITION: Rep, Grievance Dept, AFSCME Council #13, 301 Chesnut St, 5th Floor, Harrisburg, PA 17101. 717/236-5978

WAGNER, MARTIN Acad: Ind Rels; Arbitration. AB 1933, MA 1935, U of Mich; BA 1937, Oxford U. INT: arb/med, coll barg, govt labor policy. ASSN: Chicago IRRA, NAA, SPIDR. POSITIONS: Regional Dir, NLRB, 1943; Exec Dir, Louisville Labor-Mgmt Committee, 1948; Prof of Labor & Ind Rels, 1958, and, currently, Prof Emeritus, Univ of Illinois, 504 East Armory, Champaign, IL 61820. 217/333-2383

WAGO, SHARON F. Bus:Pers/Ind Rels. BA 1970, MBA 1972, U of Hawaii. INT: hotel industry, personnel, empl/trng programs. ASSN: Hawaii IRRA, ASPA, BPW (Manoa-Kai). POSITIONS: Dir of Pers, Hawaiian Regent Hotel, 1971-1973; Director, Career Information Center, 1973-1976; and (since 1976) Dir of Personnel, Hyatt Regency Waikiki, 2424 Kalakaua Ave, Honolulu, HI 96815. 808/922-9292

WAKIN, THOMAS Government. 9909 Blundon Dr, Silver Spring, MD 20902. 202/272-5483

WAKS, JAY W. Legal Practice. POSITION: Kaye, Scholer, Fierman, Hayes and Handler, 425 Park Ave, New York, NY 10022. 212/407-8558

WALD, MARTIN Legal Practice. Schnader, Harrison, Segal & Lewis, 1719 Packard, 15th & Chestnut, Philadelphia, PA 19102.

WALDMANN, PAUL J. Bus:Pers/Ind Rels. MS 1975, U of Nebr-Omaha. INT: coll barg, arb/med, labor law. ASSN: Omaha Assn of Bus Economist. POSITIONS: Sr Analyst, 1979, Asst Dir, 1981, and, since 1983, Asst Dir-Operating Crafts, Union Pacific Railroad, Room 332, 1416 Dodge St, Omaha, NE 68179. 402/271-3351

WALDRON, WILLIAM AUGUSTUS Legal Practice. AB 1935, Union Coll; AM 1937, LLB 1941, Harvard U. Retired Lawyer since 1981. 15 Larch Rd, Cambridge, MA 02138. 617/876-1096

WALKER, BRADLEY J. Bus:Mgmt/Admin. POSITION: Honeywell Inc, MN12-2141, Honeywell PZ, Minneapolis, MN 55408. 612/870-2803

WALKER, DARLENE 5227 Poinciana, Houston, TX 77092.

WALKER, DONALD P. Union. POSITION: National Education Assn, 1201 16th St NW, Washington DC 20036. 202/833-5463

WALKER, FRANCISCO Acad: Ind Rels. POSITION: Dept of Ind Rels, Univ of Chile, Rancagua 257/10 Piso, Santiago, Chile.

WALKER, J. MALCOLM Acad: Bus Admin. MBA 1960, U of Detroit; PhD 1970, U of Calif-Berkeley. PUBL: "Representation Elections in Higher Education: Occurrence and Outcomes," (w J. Lawler), J of Labor Rels, 5, Winter 1984; "University Administrators and Faculty Bargaining," (w J. J. Lawler), Res in Higher Educ, 16, Aug 1982; "Dual Unions and Political Processes in Organizations," (w J. J. Lawler), Ind Rels, 18, Feb 1979. INT: org beh, org theory, mgmt/educ. ASSN: Acad of Mgmt, Assn of Voluntary Action Scholars, Amer Sociol Assn. POSITION: (since 1968) Prof of Org and Mgmt, San Jose State Univ. ADDRESS: 10 Wilson Cir, Berkeley, CA 94708. 408/277-3338

WALKER, KENNETH FREDERICK Acad: Bus Admin, Ind Rels, Org Beh/Pers. MA 1939, U of Sydney; PhD 1952, Harvard. PUBL: Industrial Relations Australia, 1956; Australian Industrial Relations Systems, 1970; Research Needs in Industrial Relations, 1964. INT: intl comparative labor, coll barg, ind psych. POSITIONS: Dir, Intl Inst for Labour Studies, 1972; Prof, European Inst of Bus Admin, 1975; and (since 1981) Prof, School of Bus, Univ of Kansas, Lawrence, KS 66045. 913/864-4500

WALKER, ROGER WILLIAMS Acad: Econ, Ind Rels; Consulting. BBA 1953, MA 1954, U of Miami; PhD 1959, NYSSILR-Cornell. POSITIONS: Prof of Mgmt & Ind Rels, Va Poly Tech Inst, 1967-79; Fulbright Lecturer,

Royal Univ of Malta, 1976; and, currently, Prof, Dept of Econ, Hamline Univ, St. Paul, MN 55104. 612/641-2436

WALL, CHARLES Bus: Pers/Ind Rels. INT: coll barg, labor/mgmt relations, personnel. ASSN: Western New York IRRA, Internal Benefits Found. POSITIONS: Pers Mgr, Manufacturing Div, Stop & Shop Co Inc-Boston, 1969; Mgr, Empl Rels, Victory Markets Inc-Norwich, 1974; and (since 1979) Vice Pres of Labor Rels, Peter J. Schmitt Inc-New York. ADDRESS: 355 Harlem Rd, West Seneca, NY 14224. 716/821-1415

WALL, ROBERT JOHN Trade Assn. AB 1941, St. Anslem Coll-New Hampshire; MPA, New York U. INT: coll barg, arb/med, mgmt/-educ. POSITIONS: L-M Rels Examiner, NLRB, 1951; Ind Rels Administrator, Westvaco Corp-Charleston, 1957; and (since 1976) Manager, Empl Rels, American Paper Institute, 145 King St, Charleston, SC 29401. 803/722-4121

WALLACE, LAWRENCE A. Bus:Mgmt/Admin. BA 1942, Wichita State U; MBA 1950, U of Calif-Berkeley. INT: coll barg, labor law, arb/med. ASSN: Wash DC IRRA, Newspaper Pers Rels Assn. POSITIONS: Exec Secretary, Detroit Newspaper Publishers Assn, 1962; Labor Rels Dir, Detroit Free Press, 1966; and (since 1973) Vice Pres, Ind Rels, The Washington Post, 1150 15th St NW, Washington DC 20071. 202/334-7867

WALLACE, PAUL Union, Arbitration. BA 1973, U of Hartford; MS 1975, U of Mass, Intl Intern, ILO. INT: coll barg, intl comparative labor, arb/med. POSITIONS: Legal Res Assoc, Labor Law & Ind Rels Branch, United Nations-ILO; 1974; Asst Exec Dir, Penna Nurses Assn, 1975; and (since 1982) Staff Representative, AFSCME, Council #4, AFL-CIO. ADDRESS: 106 Kenwood Ave, Fairfield, CT 06430. 203/828-0537

WALLACE, PHYLLLIS A. Acad: Econ, Ind Rels. POSITION: Sloan School of Management, MIT, 50 Memorial Dr, Cambridge, MA 02139.

WALLICK, FRANKLIN Union. POSITION: Editor, UAW Washington Report, 1757 N St NW, Washington DC 20036. 202/828-8500

WALLMARK, CARLTON F. Government. INT: arb/med, coll barg, personnel. ASSN: Greater Kansas City IRRA, SPIDR. POSITIONS: Truck Driver, Pima Mining Co-Tucson, 1955; Secretary-Treas, Teamster Local 310-Tucson, 1961; and (since 1968) Commissioner, FMCS, 324 E 11th St, 23rd Floor, Kansas City, MO 64106. 816/374-3027

WALMSLEY, PETER YATES Acad: Bus Admin; Arbitration. POSITION: College of Commerce, Univ of Saskatchewan, Saskatoon, Sask S7N 0W0 Canada. 306/343-4165

WALSH, WILLIAM DAVID Acad: Econ. BCom 1958, U of British Columbia; MA 1960, PhD 1967, Yale. PUBL: "Employment and Labour Supply Effects of the Minimum Wage: Some Pooled Time-Series Estimates From Canadian Provincial Data," (w J. Schaafsma),Candian J of Econ, XVI, #1, Feb 1983, 86-97; "A Time Series Analyses of Female Labour Force Participation Rates Disaggregated By Marital Status," Rels Ind, vol 37, #2, 1982, 367-384; "The Supply of Canadian Physicians and Per Capita Expenditures For Their Services," (w J. Schaafsma), Inquiry, vol 18, Summer 1981; 185-190. INT: labor market econ, coll barg, health & hosp care. ASSN: Canadian Econ Assn, AEA. POSITIONS: Sr Consultant, Woods, Gordon & Co, 1969; Asst Prof, 1970, and, since 1976, Assoc Prof, Dept of Econ, Univ of Victoria, Victoria, BC Canada. 604/721-8542

WALT, ALAN Arbitration. Honeywell Bldg, 17515 W 9 Mile Rd, Southfield, MI 48075.

WALTON, EDWARD A. Bus:Pers/Ind Rels. BS 1959, North Tex State U. INT: coll barg, personnel, labor law. ASSN: North Texas IRRA, Tex Assn of Bus, AAA, Natl Mgmt Assn. POSITIONS: Supr, Benefits Admin, 1976, Supr, Bargaining Unit Wage Admin, 1977, and, since 1978, Manager, Labor Rels, Rockwell Intl-CTSD, PO Box 10462, M/S 406-131, Dallas, TX 75207. 214/996-6413

WALTON, LAMONT M. Acad: Law; Arbitration. BS 1972, U of Ill; JD 1975, U of Mich. PUBL: "Resolving Real Estate Valuation Disputes by Arbitration;" "Commercial Arbitration, A Tool for Dispute Resolution." INT: arb/med, labor law, coll barg. ASSN: Mid-Mich IRRA, AAA, Amer Business Law Assn, State Bar of Mich. POSITIONS: Asst City Attorney-Ann Arbor, 1978; Partner, Spaulding, Walton & Assoc, 1979; and (since 1981) Asst Prof, Mich State Univ, 109 Olds Hall, East Lansing, MI 48824. 517/355-0252

WANN, ANDREW JACKSON Acad: Political Science; Arb. AB 1940, Drury Coll; Grad Work, 1942, Johns Hopkins U; PhD 1961, U of Mo. PUBL: The President as Chief Administrator, Public Affairs Press, 1968; The AFL and International Affairs, (monograph), IULEC Project, 1952. INT: arb/med, coll barg, govt and labor. ASSN: Utah IRRA, Amer Pol Sci Assn, ASPA, AAUP. POSITIONS: Assoc Prof, ILIR, U of Ill, 1957-64; Prof & Dir, Labor Educ & Research, Ohio State U, 1964-68; and (since 1968) Prof, Dept of Political Science, Univ of Utah, 2628 E 13th St S, Salt Lake City, UT 84108. 801/581-7137

WARBURTON, REX M. Government, Union. BA 1965, Mich State, MA 1974, USIU, Cert in Mgmt, 1976, UCSD-Ext. INT: union org/admin, method/statis. ASSN: San Diego IRRA. POSITION: (since 1971) Deputy Probation Officer, San Diego County. ADDRESS: 4425 Promesa Circle, San Diego, CA 92124. 619/236-3407

WARD, JOHN T. Union. POSITION: Exec Dir, Jefferson County Educ Assn, 1050 Wadsworth, Lakewood, CO 80215. 303/232-6405

WARD, RANDALL P. Consulting, Union. BA 1972, U of Mont. INT: ind sociol, labor educ, arb/med. ASSN: Mid Mich IRRA, Natl Org of Nurses Organizers. POSITIONS: Field Rep, Montana Nurses Assn, 1974; and (since 1977) Field Rep, Michigan Nurses Assn, 120 Spartan Ave, East Lansing, MI 48823. 517/337-1653

WARD, ROBERT J. Union. 444 S Kingsley Dr, #235, Los Angeles, CA 90020. 213/382-4420

WARMAN, DAVID S. Bus:Pers/Ind Rels. POSITION: John Wiley & Sons Inc, 1 Wiley Dr, Somerset, NJ 08873. 201/469-4400

WARNER, AARON W. Acad: Univ Admin. Consulting. AB 1929, New York U; LLB 1932, Harvard; PhD 1956, Columbia U. INT: intl comparative labor, govt labor policy, arb/med.

ASSN: AEA, Political Sci Acad. POSITIONS: Prof of Econ, 1962, Dean, School of General Studies, 1968, and, since 1978, Dir, Columbia Univ Seminars, 606 Dodge Hall, Columbia Univ, New York, NY 10027. 212/280-2389

WARNOCK, JOHN A. Government. POSITION: Deputy Coordinator S/IL, Intl Labor Affairs, Dept of State, Washington DC 20520.

WARNS, MARIAN KINCAID Arbitration. Warns & Warns, 312 Brunswick Rd, Louisville, KY 40207.

WARTERS, RICHARD ADAM Acad: Student, Ind Rels. BS-ILR 1984, NYSSILR-Cornell. INT: coll barg, arb/med, intl comparative labor. ADDRESS: 922 S Main St, Horseheads, NY 14845. 607/739-9629

WARTMAN, DAVID B. Bus:Pers/Ind Rels. BA 1973, U of Saskatchewan; MS 1982, NYSSILR-Cornell. INT: coll barg, labor law, mgmt/-educ. ASSN: Acad of Mgmt, Canadian Ind Rels Assn, Pers Assn of Toronto. POSITIONS: Dir, Admin and Pers, Saskatchewan Dept of Labor, 1976; Asst Prof of Admin, U of Regina, 1980; and (since 1982) Director, Human Resources Div, Saskatchewan Wheat Pool, 2625 Victoria Ave, Regina, Victoria S4T 7T9 Canada. 306/569-4234

WARY, CURT Profession Assn. BA 1975, MPA 1978, Penna State U. PUBL: Costing Out the Labor Agreement; An Analysis of Teachers' Contracts in New Jersey 198-81/1981-82; Collective Bargaining Data 1980-81/1981-82. INT: coll barg, arb/med, labor law. ASSN: New Brunswick IRRA, Natl Assn of Educ Negotiators, Amer Society of School Pers Administrators. POSITIONS: Labor Analyst, 1979, Assoc Dir of Labor Rels, 1982, and, since 1984, Dir of Labor Rels, New Jersey School Boards Assn, 315 W State St, PO Box 909, Trenton, NJ 08605. 609/695-7600

WASHBURN, LYNN ANN Student. MS-IRHR 1984, Rutgers U. INT: govt labor policy, labor law, arb/med. ASSN: Newark IRRA. POSITION: (since 1983) Examiner, NLRB. ADDRESS: 515 Mt. Prospect Ave, Apt 5M, Newark, NJ 07104. 201/645-6223

WASHINGTON, JOHN LEVI Arbitration. POSITION: Arbitrator/Mediator, IMCR Dispute Resolution Center, 425 W 149th St, New York, NY 10031. 212/866-7530

WASMUTH, WILLIAM J. Acad: Ind Rels; Consulting. POSITION: Professor, Extension Div, NYSSILR, Cornell Univ, Ithaca, NY 14850. 607/256-3054

WASSER. LEONARD Journalism. POSITION: Exec Dir, Writers Guild Amer East, 555 W 57th St, New York, NY 10019.

WASSERMAN, DONALD S. Union. BS 1952, Temple U; MBA 1956, U of Penna. PUBL: "Collective Bargaining and Dispute Settlement in the Public Sector," Proceedings, Intl Inst for Labor Studies, ILO, U of Tel Aviv, 1979; "Problems in Public Sector Bargaining," Proceedings of New York U 33rd Annual Conf on Labor, 1979; "Parties View of the Neutral," Proceedings, SPIDR Tenth Intl Conf, 1982. INT: coll barg, arb/med, union org/admin. ASSN: Wash DC IRRA, Natl Bureau of Econ Res. POSITIONS: Labor Economist, CWA, 1957-61; Labor Economist, Intl Assn of Machinists, 1961-67; and (since 1967) Dir of Coll Barg Services, AFSCME, 4513 46th St NW, Washington DC 20016. 202/429-1219

WATKINS, DAVID W. Bus:Pers/Ind Rels. BS 1971, Cornell. PUBL: "Proposition 13: The California Experience," Labor Rels Press. INT: arb/med, coll barg, health & hosp care. ASSN: Philadelphia IRRA, Delaware Valley Cornell ILR Alumni Club. POSITIONS: Bus Agent/Reg Supr, SEIU, Hosp Workers Union-San Francisco, 1971-77; Hearing Examiner, Penna Labor Rels Board, 1978-80; and (since 1980) Labor Rels Supervisor, Personnel Office, Temple Univ, Broad and Oxford St, Philadelphia, PA 19122. 215/787-7177

WATKINS, THOMAS D. Legal Practice; Acad: Law. JD 1971, U of Mo-Columbia. ASSN: Heart of Amer Ind Rels Assn. POSITIONS: Attorney, Strop, Watkins, Roberts & Hale, 1971; and (since 1977) President, Watkins, Boulware, Lucas & Miner, Suite 302 Robidoux Center, St. Joseph, MO 64501. 816/364-6666

WATKINS, THOMAS L. Acad: Ind Rels; Arbitration. BBA 1965, mBA 1966, PhD 1971, U of Cincinnati. PUBL: "Public Sector Bargaining in an Austere Environment," Labor Law J, (27:8); "The Effects of Community Environment on Negotations," J of Coll barg Negotiations in the Public Sector, (1:3); Negotiating the Agreement, The Mich Public Empl Rels Manual, 1972. INT: arb/med, coll barg, intl comparative labor. ASSN: Rocky Mt IRRA, SPIDR, AAA. POSITIONS: (since 1974) Assoc Prof of Empl Rels, Coll of Bus Admin, Univ of Denver, Denver, CO 80208. 303/753-3444

WATROBA, DAVID R. Union. INT: coll barg, arb/med. ASSN: Detroit IRRA. POSITION: President, Detroit Police Officers, 2990 W Grand Blvd, Detroit, MI 48202. 313/224-4266

WATSON, J. PETER Bus:Pers/Ind Rels, Mgmt/Admin. BSc 1950, U of London. INT: coll barg, personnel, arb/med. ASSN: ASPA, AMA. POSITIONS: Pers Mgr, Simplot Chemical Co Ltd-Manitoba, 1966; and (since 1969) Pers Director, J. R. Simplot Co, PO Box 912, Pocatello, ID 83201. 208/232-6620

WATSON, JAMES R., JR. Legal Prac, Labor Law, Union. INT: labor law, arb/med, coll barg. ASSN: Houston IRRA. POSITION: (since 1983) President, Watson, Flynn & Bensik, Suite 800, 1445 N Loop W, Houston, TX 77008. 713/-861-6163

WATSON, WILFRED H. Acad: Org Beh; Consulting, Bus:Pers/Ind Rels. PhD 1960, U of Tex-Austin. INT: personnel, org beh, mgmt/-educ. ASSN: Central Tex IRRA, Acad of Mgmt, Amer Mgmt Assn, Amer Assn of Social and Political Science. POSITIONS: Assoc Dean & Prof of Mgmt, Emeritus, Univ of Texas at Austin. ADDRESS: 4201 Shoalwood Ave, Austin, TX 78756. 512/459-9782

WATTS, BRIDGET E. Student; Government. BS 1981, U of Rochester. INT: coll barg, arb/-med, union org /admin. POSITIONS: Examiner, Dept of Social Services-Rochester, 1979; Grad Student, NYSSILR-Cornell, 1982; and (since 1984) Intern, Federal Service Impasses Panel-Wash DC. ADDRESS: 75 East Blvd, Apt 7, Rochester, NY 14610. 202/382-0981

WAUCK, LAWRENCE ANDREW Government. 6525 Clayton Ave, St. Louis, MO 63139. 314/647-4137

WAUGH, DAVID A. Intl Organization. BA 1955, U of Ill; MBA 1964, Southern Methodist U. PUBL: "The ILO and Human Rights," Comparative Labor Law, Spring 1982, vol 5, #2. INT: intl comparative labor, labor educ, labor history. ASSN: Wash DC IRRA, Univ & Coll Labor Educ Assn, Intl Labor Press Assn, Amer Mgmt Assn. POSITIONS: Pers Office, Chrysler Corp, 1957; Trng Officer, Labor Mgmt Services, USDL, 1962; and (since 1967) Deputy Director, Washington Branch, ILO (United Nations), 1750 New York Ave NW, Washington DC 20006. 202/376-2315

WAX, HARVEY I. Legal Practice, Arbitration. BA 1957, U of Mich; JD 1960, Harvard. PUBL: "The Student-Employee at the University," PLI, 1972. INT: labor law, arb/med, coll barg. ASSN: Detroit IRRA, Mich State Bar Assn, (Labor Rels Law Section), Natl Assn of Teacher Attorneys, ABA. POSITION: (since 1968) Attorney (Partner), Levin, Levin, Garvett & Dill, 3000 Town Center, Suite 1800, Southfield, MI 48075. 313/352-8200

WAXMAN, BRUCE I. Arbitration. BS 1964, NYSSILR-Cornell; JD 1967, Columbia. PUBL: Moving the Apart Together: Alternative to Litigation," District Lawyer, Mar/Apr 1983. INT: arb/med, coll barg, labor law. ASSN: Wash DC IRRA. POSITIONS: Exec Dir, Wash DC PERB, 1972; Dir of Coll Barg, Assn of Flight Attendants, 1980; and, currently U. S. Patent and Trademark Office. ADDRESS: 1325 Jonquil St NW, Washington DC 20012.

WAY, PHILIP KEITH Student. BA 1976, Cambridge U-England; MA 1977, U of Warwick-England. PUBL: "Official Pay Inquiries: The Houghton Committee on Teachers Pay," Ind Rels J, Jan/Feb 1981; "Cash Limits and Public Sector Pay," Publ Admin, Winter 1981. INT: coll barg, govt labor policy, labor market econ. ASSN: British Univ Ind Rels Assn. POSITIONS: Res Officer, Nuffield Coll, Oxford, 1977; Frank Knox Memorial Fellow, 1982, and, since 1983, Teaching Asst, Dept of Econ, Harvard Univ. ADDRESS: 42 Dana St, Cambridge, MA 02138. 617/495-5350

WAYLAND, WILLIAM F. Bus.Mgmt/Admin, Pers/Ind Rels. AB 1958, Providence Coll. INT: personnel, coll barg, mgmt/educ. ASSN: New York IRRA. POSITIONS: Dir, Ind Rels, Schering Plough Corp, 1975; Dir, Intl Ind Rels, Chrysler Corp, 1973; and (since 1977) Vice Pres, A. Johnson & Co, Inc, 110 East 59th St, New York, NY 10022. 212/758-3200

WEBB, ROBERT L. Bus:Pers/Ind Rels; Acad: Org Beh/Pers. BA 1965, Northeastern U; MEd 1976, Suffolk U. INT: arb/med, coll barg, org beh. ASSN: Boston IRRA. POSITIONS: (since 1977) Dir, Ind Rels, Boston Gas Co, One Beacon St, Boston, MA 02018. 617/742-8400 ext 332

WEBER, ARNOLD R. Acad: Univ Admin. BA 1950, MA 1951, U of Ill; PhD 1958, MIT. PUBL: The Pay Board's Program, Brookings; In Pursuit of Price Stability; The Rewards of Public Service. POSITION: President, Univ of Colorado, Campus Box B-35, Boulder, CO 80309. 303/492-6201

WEBER, CHARLES T. Acad: Econ, Ind Rels. PhD 1977, Wayne State U. INT: coll barg, arb/med, labor market econ. ASSN: AEA, ASPA. POSITION: (since 1979) Asst Prof, Dept of Econ, Univ of Michigan-Flint, MI 48503. 313/762-3280

WEBER, DAVID CHRISTIAN Bus:Mgmt/Admin. BS 1958, Xavier U; MBA 1974, U of Cincinnati. INT: org beh, ind psych, ind sociol. ASSN: Intl Materials Mgmt Assn. POSITIONS: Dir, Empl Rels, Providence Hosp, 1967; Supr Quality Audit, Square D, 1973; and (since 1975) Operations Mgr, Positrol Inc. ADDRESS: 5663 Julmar Dr, Cincinnati, OH 45238. 513/272-0500

WEBER, R. S. Bus:Pers/Ind Rels, Arbitration, Bus:Mgmt/Admin. BA 1971, Central Methodist Coll-Fayette, Mo. INT: personnel, arb/med, ind sociol. ASSN: Kansas City IRRA, PMA. POSITIONS: Labor Rels Supr, 1979, and, since 1980, Pers Manager, Certainteed Corp, 3000 Chrysler Rd, Kansas City, KS 66115. 913/342-6624

WECKSTEIN, DONALD T. Acad: Law; Arbitration. BBA 1954, U of Wis; JD 1958, U of Tex; LLM 1959, Yale. PUBL: Professional Responsibility in a Nutshell, (w R. Atunson) 1980; "Should the Right of Collective Bargaining and Strike Be Extended to Public Employees?" in Siegan, Government, Regulation and the Economy, 47-57, 1980; Diversity Jurisdiction," (w J. W. Moore), in Moore's Fed Practice, 2nd Ed, 1964 to Date. INT: arb/med, labor law, intl comparative labor. ASSN: San Diego IRRA, ABA, SPIDR, Texas Bar Assn. POSITIONS: Labor Arbitrator, 1968 to present; Dean, School of Law, 1972-81, and, since 1972, Professor of Law, Univ of San Diego, San Diego, CA 92110. 619/291-6480 ext 4365

WEEKS, D. A. Research. POSITION: Vice Pres Research, The Conference Board, 845 Third Ave, New York, NY 10022. 212/759-0900

WEIKEL, FRANK K. Bus:Pers/Ind Rels. AB 1950, U of Louisville. INT: coll barg, personnel, empl/trng programs. ASSN: West Mich IRRA, ASPA, Cadillac Area Manufacturer's Assn. POSITIONS: Ind Rels Mgr, Peter Ekrich & Sons, Div Beatrice Foods, 1969; Ind Res Mgr, Bradford-White, Inc, 1972; and (since 1975) Vice Pres, Ind Rels, CMI Intl Inc, 230 10th St, PO 40, Cadillac, MI 49601. 616/775-2453

WEIKLE, ROGER DALE Student. MBA 1972, Marshall Univ; PhD 1984, U of S.C. PUBL: Technological Change and Industrial Relations in the U.S.," (w H. Wheeler), Bull of Comparative Labor. INT: coll barg, arb/med, ind psych. ASSN: Acad of Mgmt, Amer Psych Assn. POSITIONS: Instructor, Marshall U, 1973; Res Assoc, U of S.C. 1980, and (since 1982) Asst Prof of Mgmt, Winthrop Coll. ADDRESS: 1446 - Sprouse St, Rock Hill, SC 29730. 803/323-2186

WEIL, DAVID Student. BS 1983, NYSSILR-Cornell. INT: govt labor policy, labor market econ, coll barg. POSITION: (since 1983) Grad Student, Kennedy School of Govt, Harvard Univ. ADDRESS: 766 Mt. Auburn, Watertown, MA 02172. 617/926-5092

WEINBERG, EDGAR Consulting. BSS 1937, CCNY; MA 1952, American U. PUBL: Employment Security In A Changing Workplace; Labor-Management Cooperation for Productivity; Labor-Management Cooperation: The American Experience, (co-author). INT: coll barg. ASSN: Wash DC IRRA, Natl Economist Club. POSITIONS: Asst Dir, Natl Center for Productivity and QWL, 1971; Sr Economist, USDL, Office of Asst Secy for Policy, 1978-1980; and (since 1980) Consulting Economist (self-employed), 9302 Ewing Dr, Bethesda, MD 20817. 301/530-5782

WEINBERG, NAT Union, Consulting; Acad: Econ. BA 1942, New York U. PUBL: Adjusting to Technological Change, (co-editor), IRRA, Harper & Row, 1963; Additional Views of Commissioner Weinberg on Indicative Planning, (report), Natl Commission on Supplies and Shortages, Government Printing Office, Dec 1976; "The Death of the United States Guideposts," Chapter in The Labor Market and Inflation, Proceedings of Symposium, Intl Inst for Labor Studies, St. Martins Press, 1968. INT: coll barg, income maint, intl comparative labor. ASSN: Wash DC IRRA, AEA. POSITIONS: Special Projects Dir, UAW, 1947; Member (Presidential Appt), Natl Commis on Supplies and Shortages, 1975; and (since 1974) Consultant (self-employed), 4948 Sentinel Dr, #404, Bethesda, MD 20816. 301/229-0143

WEINBERG, PAUL Bus:Pers/Ind Rels. BS 1966, Cornell U; MA 1970, McGill U; PhD 1977, New York U. PUBL: European Labor and Multinationals, Praeger. INT: arb/med, coll barg. POSITIONS: Mgr, Empl Rels, 1972, Dir, Empl Rels, 1974, and, since 1976, Vice Pres, Employee Rels, American Express Co, 125 Broad St, New York, NY 10004. 212/323-3591

WEINBERG, WILLIAM M. Acad: Ind Rels; Arbitration. BS 1943, Glassboro State Coll; MA 1947, Temple U; PhD 1964, U of Penna. PUBL: "Cooperation Broke Out and Is Here To Stay," Proceedings, 35th Conf on Labor, NYU, 1983; Teacher Strikes in New Jersey, Weinberg et al, New Brunswick, NJ: 1982; Industrial Peacemaker: George Taylor, Phila, PA: U of Penna Press, 1979. INT: coll barg, arb/med, labor history. ASSN: New Brunswick and Philadelphia IRRAs, NAA, SPIDR. POSITIONS: Chairman, New Jersey State Bd of Mediation, 1970-73; Asst to Pres, 1965-73, and, since 1972, Prof, Ind Rels, Rutgers Univ, Ryders Lane, New Brunswick, NJ 08903. 201/-932-9022

WEINER, HERBERT Consulting, Government; Acad: Ind Rels. BSS 1941, CCNY; MA 1943, PhD 1957, Columbia U. PUBL: British Labor and Public Ownership; "The Peaceful Revolution: British Trade Unions and Nationalization;" "The Reduction of Communist Power in the Australian Trade Unions." INT: intl comparative labor, coll barg, govt labor policy. ASSN: Wash DC IRRA, Amer Foreign Service Assn. POSITIONS: Counselor for Labor Affairs, U.S. Embassy, London, 1977; and (since 1981) Consultant, Dept of State. ADDRESS: 4500 43rd PL NW, Washington DC 20016. 202/632-2806

WEINMANN, RICHARD A. Arbitration, Legal Practice. LLB 1948, Brooklyn Law School; LLM 1953, NYU. INT: arb/med, labor law, union org/admin. ASSN: New York IRRA, NY State Bar Assn, NY County Lawyers Assn, Assn of Trial Lawyers of America. POSITIONS: Partner, Sipser, Weinstock & Weinmann, 1952; and (since 1958) Attorney (self-employed), 9 E 40th St, New York, NY 10016. 212/685-4773

WEINSTEIN, DAVID Acad: Law; Arbitration. BA 1959, Yale; JD 1962, Harvard. INT: arb/med, coll barg, labor law. ASSN: Philadelphia IRRA, AAA, ABA. POSITION: (since 1976) Prof of Law, School of Law, Temple Univ, 1719 Broad St, Philadelphia, PA 19122. 215/787-8807

WEINSTEIN, HARRIET G. Government. PhD 1975, U of Penna. INT: coll barg, govt labor policy, method/statis. ASSN: Wash DC IRRA, AEA. POSITION: (since 1980) Project Dir, Current Wage Developments, BLS-USDL. ADDRESS: 7601 Whittier Blvd, Bethesda, MD 20817. 202/523-1308

WEINSTEIN, HOWARD GARY Bus:Pers/Ind Rels. BS 1979, SUNY-Binghamton; MA 1981, U of Ill. INT: coll barg, arb/med, govt labor policy. ASSN: Maryland IRRA, Pers Assn of Greater Baltimore. POSITIONS: Field Examiner-Intern, NLRB, Reg 33, 1980; and (since 1981) Pers Rep, ARMCO, Inc, 3501 E Biddle St, Baltimore, MD 21213. 301/563-5619

WEINSTEIN, PAUL A. Acad: Econ, Ind Rels; Arbitration. BA 1954, William & Mary; MA 1957, PhD 1961, Northwestern U. INT: labor market econ, arb/med, empl/trng programs. ASSN: Maryland IRRA, AEA, IIRA. POSITIONS: Exec Asst, Governor of Maryland, 1969-71; Assoc Prof of Econ, 1965 to present, and, since 1980, Acting Dir, Ind Rels and Labor Studies Center, Univ of Maryland, College Park, MD 20742. 301/454-5236

WEINTRAUB, NORMAN A. Union. BS 1958, Penna State U; MA 1969, Northwestern U. INT: coll barg, labor market econ, health & hosp care. ASSN: Wash DC IRRA, AEA, Natl Assn of Bus Economists, Transportation Res Forum. POSITIONS: Asst Dir of Res, OIL, Chemical Atomic Workers Intl Union, 1966; Dir of Res, Airline Pilots Assn, 1971; and (since 1974) Chief Economist, Dir, Dept of Econ, Intl Brotherhood of Teamsters, 25 Louisiana Ave NW, Washington DC 20001. 202/624-8100

WEISBERGER, JUNE Acad: Law; Arbitration. AB 1951, Swarthmore Coll; MA 1953, Johns Hopkins; JD 1963, U of Chicago. POSITION: Law School, Univ of Wis, Madison, WI 53706. 608/263-7407

WEISENFELD, ALLAN Arbitration. BS 1933, Rutgers; MBA 1938, NYU. INT: arb/med, coll barg. ASSN: NAA. POSITION: Prof, Grad School of Educ, Rutgers U, 1969-72; Distinguished Visiting Prof, Seton Hall, School of Bus, 1972-83. ADDRESS: 27 Lessing Rd, West Orange, NJ 07052.

WEISINGER, ROBERT S. Consulting, Arbitration. BS 1950, Rutgers U. INT: coll barg, arb/-med, mgmt/educ. ASSN: New York IRRA, Soc of Professional Mgmt Consultants. POSITIONS: Vice Pres Ind Rels, Pyro Plastics-Union, NJ, 1957; and (since 1963) President, R. S. Weisinger Assoc, 2204 Morris Ave, Suite One, Union, NJ 07083. 201/964-3830

WEISMAN, ROBERT D. Legal Practice; Acad: Law. PUBL: Contributing Editor to Developing Labor Law, BNA. INT: labor law, arb/med, govt labor policy. POSITION: Schottenstein, Zox & Dunn, 250 E Broad St, Columbus, OH 43215. 614/221-3211

WEISS, DIMITRI Acad: Ind Rels, Bus Admin. PhD Bus Admin 1969, U of Paris; PhD Mgmt Sci, 1975, U of Paris I Pantheon-Sorbonne. PUBL: Les Relations Du Travial: Employeurs, Personnel, Syndicats Etat, 5th Ed entirely rewritten, Paris, Dunod Editeur, 1983; Pratique de la Fonction Personnel, le Mgmt des Res Humaines, Paris, Les Editions d'Organisation, 1982; Relations Industrielles, 2nd Ed, Paris, Editions Sirey, 1980. INT: intl comparative labor, personnel, ind sociol. ASSN: Acad of Mgmt, IIRA, Amer Bus Communication Assn. POSITIONS: Asst Prof, 1962, Assoc Prof, 1969, and, since 1981, Professor of Bus Admin, Institut d/Admin des Enterprises, Univ de Paris I Pantheon-Sorbonne, 20 Rue De Gramont, 75002 Paris France. Phone: 558.00.21

WEISS, HARRY Retired. BA 1929, U of Pittsburgh; PhD 1933, U of Wis. Box 74, Old County Rd, West Tisbury, MA 02575.

WEISS, MICHAEL H. Legal Prac, Admin Law, Arbitration. BBA 1960, JD 1963, U of Mich. INT: labor law, admin law/judge, arb/-med. ASSN: San Francisco IRRA, Calif Med and Conciliation Service, CA Publ Empl Rels Bd-Panel of Neutrals. POSITIONS: Attorney, Center on Soc Welfare Policy & Law, Columbia U, 1969; Admin Law Judge, State of Calif Agric Labor Rels Act, 1977; and (since 1970) Attorney At Law, 1182 Market St, #320, San Francisco, CA 94102. 415/626-5433

WEISS, RICHARD MARK Acad: Org Beh/-Pers, Sociol, Ind Rels. PhD 1981, Cornell U. PUBL: "Max Weber on Bureaucracy," Acad of Mgmt Rev, 1983; "The Work-Leisure Relationship," Human Rels, 1982; Dealing With Arbitration in the Workplace, New York: The Conference Board, 1980. INT: org beh, ind sociol, health & hosp care. ASSN: Amer Sociol Assn, Acad of Mgmt, Southern Mgmt Assn. POSITIONS: Res Assoc, The Conference Board, 1977; Asst Prof of Mgmt, Northern Ill U, 1978; and (since 1980) Asst Prof of Bus Admin, Univ of Delaware, Newark, DE 19716. 302/451-2555

WEISSENBERG, PETER Acad: Univ Admin, Org Beh/Pers, Ind Rels. AB 1951, Syracuse U; BIE 1958, Ga Inst of Tech; MS 1965, PhD 1967, Cornell U. PUBL: Introduction to Organizational Behavior, Inr. Educ Publ, 1971; "A Comparison of Life Goals of Austrialian, German, Swiss and West German Managers," Econ & Soc, 1979; "Role Perceptions and Supervisory Behavior," (w L. W. Gruenfeld), J of Applied Psych, 1974. INT: org beh, personnel, leadership. ASSN: Amer Psych Assn, Acad of Mgmt, Intl Assn of Applied Psych. POSITIONS: Assoc Prof, Dir, Evening Grad Programs, 1974, Prof of Mgmt & Dir Ext Programs, School of Mgmt, SUNY-Binghamton; and (since 1981) Assoc Dean, Faculty of Bus Studies, Rutgers State Univ, Victor Hall, Camden, NJ 08102. 609/757-6217

WEISZ, MORRIS Acad: Ind Rels; Consulting. BSE 1934, CCNY. PUBL: "Employment Adjustment Implications of Changing International Trade," Incomes and Empl Policies-OECD, 1978; "Administration and Organization of Labor Resources in Developing Countries," Proceedings of World Congress of Engineers & Technicians, 1976, Intl Technical Training Centre, Tel Aviv, 1977; Manpower Administration in Austrialia (co-author), OECD, 1974. INT: coll barg, intl comparative labor, labor history. ASSN: Wash DC IRRA. POSITIONS: Dir, Ind Rels Div, OECD, Paris, 1975; Visiting Prof of Ind Rels, U of Wis-Madison, 1977-79; and (since 1979) Ind Rels Consultant (self-employed), 7106 Wilson LA, Bethesda, MD 20817. 301/229-0683

WEITZ, PETER R. Foundation Admin. MA 1967, Harvard U; BA 1965, Brown U. INT: empl/trng programs, govt labor policy, intl comparative labor. POSITION: (since 1972) Dir of Programs, German Marshall Fund-U.S., 11 Dupont Circle NW, Washington DC, 20036. 202/745-3950

WEIZENBAUM, SHARON K. Arbitration, Legal Prac. BA 1956, Vassar Coll; MA 1972, U of Dayton; JD 1977, U of Ariz. INT: arb/-med, labor law, coll barg. ASSN: Arizona IRRA, AAA (Labor Panel), SPIDR, ABA. POSITIONS: Law Clerk, Ariz Court of Appeals, 1977; and (since 1978) Attorney (Private Practice), 920 Corinth Ave, Tucson, AZ 85710. 602/885-1970

WELSH, ROBERT Union. BA 1969, U of Va; MPA 1979, Amer U. ASSN: Wash DC IRRA. POSITIONS: Social Security Dept, AFL-CIO, 1972, Asst to Exec Secretary, 1973-76, and, since 1976, Exec Asst to the President, SEIU, 2020 K St NW, Washington DC 20006. 202/452-8750

WEND, JARED SCUDDER Acad: Econ. AB 1942, Middlebury; MA 1948, PhD 1952, U of Mich. INT: labor market econ, govt labor policy, labor law. ASSN: Southwest Mich IRRA. POSITIONS: Instructor, U of Detroit, 1949; Asst Prof, Carroll Coll-Waukesha, WI, 1951; and (since 1955) Assoc Prof, Dept of Econ, Western Michigan Univ, Kalamazoo, MI 49008. 616/383-1875

WENDLING, WAYNE ROGER Foundation. BA 1971, MA 1973, PhD 1977, U of Wis-Milwaukee. PUBL: The Plant Closing Policy Dilemma, Upjohn Inst; "Health Manpower Programs to Affect Physician Location," J of Health Politics & Law, 1981; "Compensating Wage Differentials for Hazardous Work," Quart Rev of Econ & Bus, 1978. INT: labor market econ, coll barg, health & hosp care. POSITIONS: Res Assoc, AMA, 1977; Economist, Educ Comm of the States, 1979; and (since 1980) Sr Res Economist, W. E. Upjohn Inst for Employment Res, 300 Westnedge Ave, Kalamazoo, MI 49007. 616/343-5541

WENDT, ANN C. Acad: Ind Rels, Pers; Arb/Consulting. BS-Pol Sci & BS Psych 1977, MS 1980, PhD 1984, U of Utah. 4823 Naniloa Dr, Salt Lake City, UT 84117. 801/581-5572

WENIG, JEROME Legal Practice. 5 Lamplight Lane, Westport, CT 06880.

WENZLER, O. FRITZ Bus:Pers/Ind Rels. BA 1960, John Carroll U; LLB 1963, LLM 1973, Georgetown U. INT: coll barg, govt labor policy, labor law. ASSN: New York IRRA, ABA. POSITION: Vice Pres, Labor Rels Worldwide, Johnson & Johnson, One Johnson Plaza, New Brunswick, NJ 08933. 201/524-6522

WENZLER, RICHARD ARTHUR Bus:Pers/Ind Rels, Legal Prac. BS 1949, JD 1953, Fordham U. INT: labor law, coll barg, org beh. ASSN: New York IRRA, Empl Assn of NJ, ABA (Labor Law Committee). POSITION: (since 1957) Vice Pres Ind Rels, BOCG Inc, 85 Chestnut Ridge Rd, Montvale, NJ 07645. 201/573-0800

WERNER, HERBERT DENNIS Acad: Econ. BS 1953, Northwestern U; PhD 1964, U of Calif-Berkeley. INT: labor market econ, method/statis, coll barg. ASSN: Gateway IRRA, AEA. POSITIONS: Instructor/Asst Prof, Lewis & Clark Coll, 1961-66; Post Doctoral Fellow, Maxwell School, Syracuse U, 1966-67; and (since 1967) Assoc Prof, Dept of Econ, Univ of Missouri, St. Louis, MO 63121. 314/453-5351

WERTHER, WILLIAM B., JR. Arbitration, Consulting; Acad: Bus Admin. BSBA 1968, MA 1969, PhD 1971, U of Fla. PUBL: Personnel Management and Human Resources, (w K.

Davis), New York: McGraw Hill, 1981; Labor Relations in the Health Professions, (w C. Lockhart), Little, Brown & Co: 1976. INT: empl/trng programs, arb/med, mgmt/educ. ASSN: Arizona IRRA, Acad of Mgmt. POSITION: (since 1971) Prof of Mgmt, College of Bus Admin, Arizona State Univ, Tempe, AZ 85287. 602/965-3431

WESMAN, ELIZABETH CLAIRE Acad: Ind Rels, org Beh/Pers. AB 1966, Smith Coll; MA 1969, Northwestern U; PhD 1982, Cornell U. PUBL: "Labor Unions and Title VII: A Case Study of Organizational Response to Environmental Change;" "A Critique of the Study of Unions: Intraorganizational Communication as Analog;" "Chasing the Workplace Chimera: Definition of Sexual Harassment is as Difficult as Prevention." INT: empl/labor rels, intl comparative labor, personnel. ASSN: Central New York IRRA, Acad of Mgmt, AAUP, Human Resources Planning Society. POSITIONS: Instructor, Econ Dept, LeMoyne Coll, Syracuse, 1970; Lecturer, Human Resources Studies, NYSSILR-Cornell, 1980; Asst Prof, School of Mgmt, Syracuse Univ. ADDRESS: 308 Siena Dr, Ithaca, NY 14850. 315/423-2601

WESSE, DAVID JOSEPH Bus:Mgmt/Admin. POSITION: General Services Manager, Northwestern University, 710 N Lake Shore Dr, Chicago, IL 60611. 312/649-8129

WEST. DAVID H. Bus:Pers/Ind Rels. BS 1973, NYSSILR-Cornell. INT: labor law, coll barg, personnel. POSITIONS: Res Analyst, Div of Labor Statistics and Res, 1978, and, since 1980, Labor Rels Specialist, State Compensation Ins Fund, State of Calif, 1275 Market St, San Francisco, CA 94103. 415/565-1588

WEST, JUDE P. Acad: Org Beh/Pers, Bus Admin, Ind Rels. PhD 1969, U of Iowa. PUBL: "Relationship Between Work Environment Attributes and Burnout," (co-author), J of Leisure Res, Summer 1983; "Perceptions of Work Environments and Job Dimensions by High and Low Burnout of Park and Recreation Professionals," J of Park and Recreation Admin, vol 1, #3, July 1983.; Role of Correctional Industries , (co-author), Center for Labor & Mgmt, U of Iowa, 1971. INT: personnel, org beh, mgmt/educ. ASSN: Acad of Mgmt, ASTD. POSITIONS: Dir of Trng and Educ, Motorola-Franklin Park, IL 1963; and (since 1963) Assoc Prof, Dept of IR/HR, Phillips Hall, Univ of Iowa. ADDRESS: 326 Windsor Dr, Iowa City, IA 52240. 319/353-5901

WEST, MICHAEL D. Labor Mediation. AA 1963, San Jose City Coll; BA 1965, San Jose State U. INT: arb/med, labor law, labor history. ASSN: San Francisco IRRA, AAA, SPIDR. POSITIONS: (since 1976) Mediator, State of Calif, and (since 1979) Arbitrator, Arbitration West-Arb & Med Services. ADDRESS: 9 Chestnut Ave, Los Gatos, CA 95030. 415/557-2426

WEST, ROBIN KAY Student, Labor/Ind Rels. BSBA 1983, U of N.C.-Chapel Hill. INT: personnel, org beh, ind psych. ASSN: LIRA-U of Ill IRRA. POSITIONS: Exec Asst, Rachel Carson Council, Inc-Chevy Chase, 1980-81; Intern-Pers Dept, Fairchild Space Co-Germantown, 1982-83; and (since 1983) Res Asst, Inst of Labor & IR, Univ of Ill. ADDRESS: 1507 N Kiler Dr, #302, Champaign, IL 61820. 217/-333-0984

WESTERKAMP, PATRICK Legal Practice. BA 1965, Hofstra U; MSIR 1971, Loyola U-Chicago; JD 1981, Seton Hall School of Law. PUBL: "Obscure Lines - The Ridgefield Park Decision," Arb J, June 1980; "Barrentine: Milestone or Detour?" Labor Law J, Jan 1983; "Employment at Will: The New legal Definition of Just Cause," Proceedings of the 35th Annual Meeting, IRRA, 1983. INT: labor law, arb/med, coll barg. ASSN: New York IRRA, SPIDR, New Jersey Bar Assn. POSITIONS: Reg Dir, New Jersey Office AAA, 1971-77; Arbitrator, 1878-83, and, (since 1983) Attorney, Epstein Becker Borsody & Green, P.C.-New York. ADDRESS: 102 Stokes St, Freehold, NJ 07728. 212/370-9800

WESTERKAMP, PAUL R. Health & Hosp Care, Engineering. POSITION: Consolidated Edison Employees Mutual Aid Society, 4 Irving PL, New York, NY 10003. 212/460-2135

WESTMAN, CARL R. Government. BS 1951, MBA 1954, Syracuse U. INT: coll barg, arb/med, personnel. ASSN: South Central Alaska Ind Rels Assn. POSITION: (since 1982) Labor Rels Officer, Alaska Railroad. ADDRESS: 530 W 19th Ave, Anchorage, AK 99503. 907/765-2436

WESTON, JOSEPH A. Arbitration. BS 1942, MBA 1946, Wharton School-U of Penna. INT: arb/med. ASSN: West Central Florida IRRA, AAA. POSITIONS: Supr, NLRB, 1948-75; and (since 1979) Arbitrator. ADDRESS: 103 16th St, Belleair Beach, FL 33535. 813/596-2584

WETTLAUFER, JOHN J. Acad: Bus Admin, Ind Rels; Consulting. POSITION: School of Bus Admin, Univ of Western Ontario, London, Ont N6A 3K7 Canada. 519/679-3205

WETZEL, EVA Acad: Bus Admin. Coll of Commerce, Univ of Saskatchewan, Saskatoon, Saskatchewan, Canada.

WETZEL, KURT Acad: Ind Rels. PhD 1978, U of Ill. INT: coll barg, health & hosp care, govt labor policy. POSITION: (since 1976) Assoc Prof, College of Commerce, Univ of Saskatchewan, Saskatoon, Sask S7N 0W0 Canada. 306/343-2208

WEVER, KIRSTEN R. Student, Ind Rels, Human Resource Mgmt. BA 1980, MA 1981 U of Calif-Berkeley. PUBL: "Concession Bargaining 1979-83: Not Just the Same Old Thing," MIT Sloan School W. P., #1478-83-A; "Human Resource Planning for Information Systems Personnel: Skills, Mixes and Technological Trends," MIT Sloan W.P. #1478-83; "Productivity, Industrial Relations and Human Resource Management," MIT Sloan School W.P. #1358-82. INT: coll barg, govt labor policy, personnel. POSITION: Third year grad student, MIT. ADDRESS: 25 Laurel St, #1, Somerville, MA 02143. 617/253-5227

WEYLS, RICHARD C. Student. 510 Riddle Rd, #1, Cincinnati, OH 45220. 513/221-2441

WHALEY, GEORGE L. Acad: Org Beh/Pers, Ind Rels; Consulting. DBA 1974, U of Colo. PUBL: "Controversy Swirls Over Comparable Worth Issue," Pers Admin, 1982; "Use of Advisory Services in Affirmative Action Programs," Assn of Social & Behavioral Scientists, 1983; "Impact of Robotics Technology Upon Human Resource Management," Pers Admin, 1982. INT: personnel, org beh, method/statis. ASSN: Acad of Mgmt, FEHC, Assn of Social and

Behavioral Scientists. POSITIONS: Long Range Planner/Financial Analyst, Boulder, 1968, Financial Planner, San Jose, 1976, IBM Corp; and (since 1982) Prof of Organization & Mgmt, School of Bus, San Jose State Univ, San Jose, CA 95195. 408/277-3324

WHEELER, GARY R. Bus:Pers/Ind Rels, Government; Acad: Org Beh/Pers. BAS 1959, MCS 1972, Rollins Coll-FL. INT: org beh, empl/-trng programs, coll barg. ASSN: Florida IRRA, F/PELRA, N/PERLA, FPPA. POSITIONS: Asst Pers Dir, 1972; Labor Rels Officer, Broward County, 1979; and (since 1981) Dir, Employee Rels, Pinellas County, 315 Court St, 6th FL, Clearwater, FL 33516. 813/462-3506

WHEELER, HOYT NOLAND Acad: Ind Rels; Arbitration. BA 1958, Marshall U; JD 1961 U of Va; PhD 1974, U of Wis. PUBL: "Technological Change and Industrial Relations in the United States," (w R. D. Weikle)Bull of Comparative Labour Rels, Bull #12, 1983, pp 15-34; "Choice of Procedures in the United States and Canada," (w A. Ponak) Ind Rels, vol 19, #2, Fall 1980, pp 292-308; "Punishment Theory and Industrial Discipline," Ind Rels, vol 15, #2, May 1976, pp 235-43. INT: coll barg, arb/med, intl comparative labor. ASSN: ABA, Acad of Mgmt, IIRA. POSITIONS: Partner, Kay, Casto and Chancey, Attorneys-at-Law, 1961; Assoc Prof, Ind Rels Center, Univ of Minn, 1976; and (since 1981) Prof of Mgmt & Ind Rels, Coll of Bus Admin, Univ of South Carolina, Columbia, SC 29208. 803/777-5959

WHEELER, KENNETH GERALD Acad: Ind Rels. POSITION: Dept of Mgmt & Org Beh, Univ of Texas, Arlington, TX 76019.

WHELLAN, FLOYD Bus:Mgmt/Admin. BA 1959, CCNY; MA 1961, U of Ill. PUBL: "The Evolution of a Staff Development System." INT: mgmt/educ, org beh, personnel. ASSN: Amer Society for Pers Administrators. POSITIONS: Compensation Mgr, Armour Co, 1965; and (since 1971) Vice Pres, Human Resources, Newspaper Operations, Harte-Hanks Communications, PO Box 269, 237 Parklane Dr, San Antonio, TX 78212. 512/344-8000

WHIPPLE, C. DAVID Legal Prac, Union. BA 1950, Baker U-KS; JD 1952, U of Mo-Kansas City. INT: arb/med, coll barg, labor law. ASSN: Kansas City IRRA, Missouri Bar Assn, Kansas City Bar Assn. POSITION: President & Partner, Whipple & Kraft, P.C., 1111 Grand, Suite 200, Kansas City, MO 64106. 816/842-6411

WHITE, DONALD JOSEPH Acad: Univ Admin, Ind Rels. BS 1943, Boston Coll; MA 1946, PhD 1949, Harvard U. PUBL: New England Fishing Industry, Harvard U Press, 1954; "The Council on Industrial Relations," Proceedings IRRA, 1971. INT: arb/med, coll barg, labor history. ASSN: Boston IRRA, NAA, SPIDR, AEA. POSITIONS: Assoc Prof of Econ, 1950, Prof of Econ, 1955, and, since 1971, Dean, Grad School of Arts & Sciences, Boston College. ADDRESS: 25 Pilgrim Rd, Milton, MA 02186. 617/552-3268

WHITE, HAROLD CLIFFORD Acad: Org Beh/Pers, Ind Rels; Arbitration. BS 1959, MS 1960, U of Oregon; PhD 1966, U of Fla. PUBL: "The Three Faces of Personnel," (w. G. Bohlander & M. Wolfe), Pers, July-Aug, 1983, vol 60 (4); "Personnel Administration and Organizational Productivity: An Employee View," Pers Admin, vol 26 (8), Aug 1981; "The Arizona Farm Labor Law: A Supreme Court Test," (w W. Gibney), Labor Law J, Feb 1980, vol 31 (2). INT: org beh, personnel, coll barg. ASSN: Arizona IRRA, ASPA, Acad of Mgmt, AAA. POSITIONS: Instructor of Bus Admin, Idaho State U, 1960; Interim Inst of Mgmt, U of Florida, 1963; and (since 1966) Prof of Mgmt, College of Bus Admin, Arizona State Univ, Tempe,. AZ 85287. 602/968-0026

WHITE, LEE FRANCIS Retired. INT: labor law, personnel, coll barg. ASSN: Radio TV News Directors Assn. ADDRESS: Editorial Consultant, Clinton Herald, 730 6th Ave S, Clinton, IA 52732.

WHITE, LUTHER GLENN Acad: Ind Rels, Bus Admin, Org Beh/Pers. BS 1967, U of N.C.; MBA 1969, East Carolina U; PhD 1984, U of S.C. POSITIONS: Asst Prof, U of South Carolina, 1975; Asst Prof, Ind Mgmt, Clemson Univ, 1977; and (since 1979) Assoc Prof, Dept of Mgmt, Marshall Univ, 316 Corbly Hall, Huntington, WV 25705. 304/696-5423

WHITE, RUDOLPH A. Acad: Ind Rels. PhD 1958, U of Ala. INT: union org/admin, labor market econ, coll barg. ASSN: Southern Econ Assn, Southern Mgmt Assn. POSITIONS: Instructor, U of Ala-Birmingham, 1951; Dir of Instruction, Coll of Bus Admin, Miss State U, 1958; and (since 1969) Professor, Dept of Econ, Coll of Bus Admin, Univ of Georgia, Athens, GA 30602. 404/542-1311

WHITEHEAD, J. DAVID Acad: Bus Admin. ADDRESS: School of Business Administration, Univ Western Ontario, London, Ont N6A 3K7, Canada. 519/679-6059

WHITFORD, ANN M. Union. BS 1960, Columbia U. INT: org beh, arb/med, coll barg. ASSN: New Brunswick IRRA, CLUW, Natl Staff Org. POSITION: (since 1972) Field Representative, NJEA, 300 South Ave, Garwood, NJ 07901. 201/789-2355

WHITING, BASIL JOHN Prof Assn. MPA 1967, Woodrow Wilson School-Princeton. INT: QWI/EI, org beh, ind psych. ASSN: Detroit IRRA. POSITIONS: Sr Program Officer, Ford Found-NY, 1968; Dept Asst Secretary, USDL, 1977; and (since 1981) Executive Dir, Mich Quality of Work Life Council. ADDRESS: 1412 Nicolet PL, Detroit, MI 48207. 313/362-1611

WHITTINGTON, D.B. Bus:Labor Rels. POSITION: Employee Relations-Chemical & Plastics, Union Carbide, PO Box 471, Texas City, TX 77590. 713/945-7411

WHYTE, WILLIAM FOOTE Acad: Org Beh/-Pers. BA 1936, Swarthmore Coll; PhD 1943, U of Chicago. PUBL: Worker Participation & Ownership: Cooperative Strategies for - Strengthening Local Economies, (co-author), Ithaca: ILR Press, 1983; Money & Motivation, (co-author), New York: Harpers & Bros, 1955; Street Corner Society, Chicago: U of Chicago Press, 1943, 1955, 1981 (3 editions). INT: org beh, ind sociol, coll barg. ASSN: Amer Sociological Assn, Society for Applied Anthropology, Amer Anthropological Assn. POSITIONS: Asst Prof, U of Chicago, 1944; Professor, 1948, and, since 1979, Professor Emeritus, NYSSILR-Cornell Univ, Ithaca, NY 14853. 607/256-4531

WIANT, REX HARLAN II Bus:Pers/Ind Rels. MLIR 1979, Mich State U. INT: coll barg, arb/med. POSITION: (since 1981) Labor Rels Specialist, Iowa Assn of School Boards. AD-

DRESS: 1201 Office Park Rd, #307, West Des Moines, IA 50265. 515/288-1991

WICK, MARGIE Union. POSITION: Secretary-Treasurer, OPEIU Local 56, 9224 N 5th St, Phoenix, AZ 85020.

WIDICK, B. J. Acad: Ind Rels. Prof, 1969, Sr Lecturer, 1979, Columbia Univ Grad School of Bus. Retired. 1411 White St, Ann Arbor, MI 48104.

WIEDEMANN, HERBERT P. Legal Practice. BA 1949, LLB 1952, Yale. INT: coll barg, arb/-med, govt labor policy. ASSN: Wisconsin IRRA. POSITION: (since 1952) Partner, Foley & Lardner, 777 E. Wisconsin Ave, Milwaukee, WI 53202. 414/289-3581

WIETING, JOHN LEWIS Government. 515 S Chestnut St, Westfield, NJ 07090. 201/232-1889

WIGGINS, RONALD LUTHER Acad: Ind Rels, Bus Admin. Arbitration. 732 Kimball Rd, Fort Collins, CO 80521. 303/482-6561

WILBERG, WILLIAM R. Bus:Pers/Ind Rels. POSITION: Vice-Pres, Wis Assn of Manafacturers and Commerce, 111 E Wisconsin Ave, Milwaukee, WI 53202. 414/271-9428

WILCOX, JEAN Arbitration. JD 1974, Golden State U. INT: arb/med, govt labor policy, personnel. ASSN: Northern Calif IRRA, SPIDR, Bar Assn, AAA. POSITION: Arbitrator (sole practice), 1900 Vallejo #402, San Francisco, CA 94123. 415/563-5976

WILCOX, MARY ELIZABETH Government, Retired. 1282 Anthony Dr, Portsmouth, RI 02871.

WILENSKY, HAROLD L. Acad: Political Science, Sociology, Ind Rels. AB 1947, Antioch Coll; MA 1949, PhD 1955, U of Chicago. PUBL: The Welfare State & Equality: Structural and Ideological Roots of Public Expenditures, Berkeley: U of Cal Press, 1975; Organizational Intelligence: Knowledge and Policy in Government and Industry, New York: Basic Books, 1967, paperback, 1969; "Job Assignment in Modern Society," (w A. T. Lawrence), Societal Growth ed. A. H. Hawley, NY Free Press-Macmillan, 1979, pp 202-248. INT: comparative political econ, ind sociol, intl comparative labor. ASSN: Amer Pol Sci Assn, Amer Sociol Assn, Council for European Studies. POSITIONS: Prof of Sociology, 1962, Prof of Political Science and Research Sociologist, Inst of Ind Rels, Univ of Calif. ADDRESS: 638 Gravatt Dr, Berkeley, CA 94705. 415/642-1434

WILHELM, CROUS Bus:Mgmt/Admin. POSITION: Exec Dir, IPM Southern Africa, PO Box 31390 Braamfontein, Republic of South Africa.

WILHELM, JULIAN AUGUSTUS Legal Practice, Acad: Law. AB 1936, LLB 1939, Harvard U. PUBL: The Failure of American Peace Groups to Prevent War, 1914-17; "Duress as Rebuttal to Strike Participation." INT: labor law, govt labor policy, coll barg. ASSN: Wash DC IRRA, ABA & Federal Bar Assn (Labor & Empl Law Sections), D. C. Bar Assn (Div-Labor Law & Judicial Admin). POSITIONS: Labor Counsel & Asst General Attorney, Celanese Corp-New York, 1955; Supervisory Attorney & Sr Counsel, NLRB-Wash DC, 1959; and since 1982) Vice Pres & Treasurer, Burch, Wilhelm & McDonald, P.C. ADDRESS: 5908 Anniston Rd, Bethesda, MD 20817. 202/833-8400

WILLEA, CLIFF Union. 1015 W Norton, Muskegon, MI 49441.

WILLETT, TERESA LYNN Bus:Pers/Ind Rels. BA 1982, U of Mich; MILR 1984, Mich State U. ASSN: South Central Indiana Pers Assn. POSITION: (since 1984) Personnel Admin, Otis Elevator Co, Inc-UTC. ADDRESS: 120 Kingston PL #5, Bloomington, IN 47401. 812/339--2281

WILLIAMS, DONALD R. Acad: Econ. BBA 1977, U of Wis-Milwaukee. PUBL: "Racial Differences in the Propensity to Return to School," Proceedings of the Twelfth Annual Meeting of the Ill Econ Assn, 1982; "Evidence on the Racial Difference in the Discouraged Worker Effect among Male Teenagers," Proceedings of the 36th Annual IRRA Meeting, 1984. INT: labor market econ, govt labor policy, empl/trng programs. ASSN: AEA, Midwest Econ Assn. POSITIONS: Instructor, Dept of Econ, Roosevelt U, 1981; Instructor, Dept of Econ, Northwestern U, 1982; and (since 1983) Asst Prof, Dept of Econ, Kent State Univ, Kent OH 44240. 216/672-2366

WILLIAMS, DOUGLAS A. Acad: Bus Admin/-Mgmt. PO Box 572, Houston, TX 77001.

WILLIAMS, J. EARL Arbitration, Consulting. BA 1949, Carson-Newman Coll; MA 1950, U of Tenn; PhD 1961, U of Wis. PUBL: Plantation Politics: The Southern Economic Heritage; Agriculture To Automation: History of the American Labor Movement; "Manpower Programs and the New Federalism," Proceedings of North Amer Conference on Labor Statistics, Florida, June 1973. INT: arb/med, coll barg, empl/trng programs. ASSN: Houston and Atlanta IRRAs, NAA, AAA, SFLRP. POSITIONS: Dir, Inst of Ind Rels, U of Houston, 1966-78; Dir, Inst of Ind Rels, Georgia State U, 1978-81; and (since 1981) Labor-Management Arbitrator, 7530 Del Monte Dr, Houston, TX 77063; 3050 Margaret Mitchell Dr, #36, Atlanta, GA 30327. 404/352-3770

WILLIAMS, JERRY J. Arbitration; Acad: Law, Ind Rels. AB 1953, JD 1961, UCLA. PUBL: "Pre-Emption-Sears and After," Symposium, L.A. Bar Assn, 1981; "Retail Installment Sales Act; Usury Doctoring," UCLA L. Rev, 1961. ADDRESS: 1850 Fifth Ave, San Diego, CA 92101. 619/696-0655

WILLIAMS, RICHARD C. Acad: Ind Rels, Org Beh/Pers; Arbitration. BA 1972, Cleveland State U; MPA 1974, Syracuse U. INT: coll barg, personnel, union org/admin. ASSN: Acad of Mgmt. POSITIONS: Pers Dir, City of Champaign, 1978; Research Asst, Inst of Labor and Ind Rels, U of Ill, 1981; and (since 1983) Asst Prof of Labor and Ind Rels, Dept of Mgmt & Marketing, Murray State Univ. ADDRESS: 1617 Locust, Murray, KY 42071. 502/762-3009

WILLIAMS, ROY L. Union. POSITION: Manager, Labor Rels, MFA Inc, 201 S 7th St, Columbia, MO 65201.

WILLIAMS, TIM Arbitration; Acad: Bus Admin. PhD 1970, U of Minn. POSITION: Western Arbitration Assn, 4350 W Galewood St, PO Box 2029, Lake Oswego, OR 97034.503/635-9915

WILLIAMSON, B. G. Union. INT: union org/-admin, coll barg, arb/med. ASSN: Cincinnati IRRA. POSITIONS: Bus Manager, Local 972, 1951, Intl Rep, 1956, and, since 1972, Intl Vice President, District 4, Intl Brotherhood of Electrical Workers, 7710 Reading Rd, Suite 9, Cincinnati, OH 45237. 513/821-5480

WILLIAMSON, THOMAS Bus:Pers/Ind Rels. BA 1973, Calif State U-Fullerton. INT: coll barg, mgmt/educ, labor market econ. ASSN: Southern Calif IRRA, Amer Compensation Assn, Amer Society for Hosp Pers Admin, Amer Mgmt Assn. POSITIONS: Empl Rels Rep, 1977, Sr. Labor Rels Rep, 1979, and, since 1980, Manager, Labor Rels & Compensation, Kaiser Permanente Medical Care Program, 4747 Sunset Blvd, Los Angeles, CA 90027. 213/667-8481

WILLIARD, DAVID M. Student. Apt 314, Essex House, 1300 Oakland, Indiana, PA 15701. 412/349-7659

WILLMAN, PAUL Acad: Ind Rels. BA 1974, MA 1977, Cambridge U; DPhil 1978, Oxford U. PUBL: Fairness, Collective Bargaining and Incomes Policy, Oxford U Press, 1982; Power Efficiency and Institutions, Heinemann, 1983; Technological Change & Industrial Relations, Oxford U Press, 1984. INT: coll barg, labor market econ, org beh. ASSN: British Univ Ind Rels Assn. POSITIONS: Lecturer, Imperial Coll-London, 1978; and (since 1983) Lecturer, Cranfield Mgmt School, Cranfield, Bedfordshire M43 0AL UK.

WILSON, ANDREA Arbitration. BA 1943, Mount Holyoke Coll; MBA 1946, PhD 1971, NYU. PUBL: "Recent Trends in Arbitration in the Schools," Labor Rels Press, Wash PA, Feb 1982, pp 16-19; "How Powerful is Schooling?" NYU Educ Quart, vol XI #3, Spring 1980, pp 28-31; "Two Partnership Models Aimed at Easing Transition from School to the World of Work," Urban School in Urban Systems, Selected Papers, Phila: The Assn for Urban Educ, 1979. INT: arb/med, coll barg. ASSN: New York and Long Island IRRAs, Amer Educ Res Assn, New York Society of Security Analysts. POSITIONS: Asst Dean, New York Univ, 1973; and (since 1980) Arbitrator, 133 Wooster St, New York, NY 10012. 212/982-2286

WILSON, ANDREW A Government, Consulting. POSITION: Economist, AID, Rte 2, Box 89, Scottsville, VA 24590. 202/632-9282

WILSON, DUANE M. Bus:Mgmt/Admin. POSITION: Duane Wilson & Assn, W 4020 Weile, Spokane, WA 99208. 509/328-5299

WILSON, STEVEN F. Acad: Bus Admin/-Mgmt. 6 Austin Terr Upper, Toronto, Ont M5R 1X9 Canada. 416/468-3947

WINDMULLER, JOHN P. Acad: Ind Rels; Consulting, Arbitration. BA 1948, U of Ill; PhD 1951, Cornell U. PUBL: Employers Associations and Industrial Relations: A Comparative Study, (co-editor), Oxford U Press, 1984; The International Trade Union Movement, Netherland: Kluwer Publ, 1980; "Concentration Trends in Union Structures: An International Comparison," Ind & Labor Rels Rev, Oct 1981. INT: intl comparative labor, union org/admin, labor history. POSITION: Professor, NYSSILR, Cornell Univ, PO Box 1000, Ithaca, NY 14853. 607/256-4436

WINEGAR, CYNTHIA Legal Practice. BA 1970, Stephens Coll; JD 1976, U of Hawaii. INT: arb/med, coll barg, labor law. ASSN: Hawaii IRRA, Hawaii State Bar Assn, ABA, Hawaii Women Lawyers. POSITIONS: Deputy Attorney General, State of Hawaii, 1978; Empl Rels Admin, U of Hawaii, 1980; and (since 1982) Associate, Kobayashi, Watanabe, Sugita & Kawashima, 745 Fort St, 8th Floor, Honolulu, HI 96813. 808/544-8300

WINERITER, GAYLE Government. POSITION: FMCS, PO Box 50022, Honolulu, HI 96850. 808/546-6532

WINKLER, RALPH Arbitration. BA 1935, U of Scranton; JD 1938, U of Mich. INT: arb/-med, labor law. ASSN: Federal Bar Assn. POSITIONS: Chief Counsel to Board Member, 1961, Admin Law Judge, NLRB, 1972; and (since 1981) Arbitrator, 7801 Beech Tree Rd, Bethesda, MD 20817. 301/229-5969

WINOGRAD, DANIEL M. Legal Practice. BA 1970, Colorado Coll; JD 1973, U of Chicago. INT: arb/med. ASSN: Colorado IRRA, Colorado Bar Assn, El Paso County Bar Assn, Illinois Bar Assn. POSITIONS: Attorney, Elson, Lassers & Wolff, 1973; Attorney (solo practice), 1978; and (since 1979) Attorney, Makepeace & Winograd, P.C., 606 South Tejon St, Colorado Springs, CO 80903. 303/632-6644

WINTERS, B. C. Acad: Econ. BA 1955, UCLA; MA 1958, USC. POSITION: (since 1959) Instructor, Los Angeles City College. ADDRESS: 855 N Vermont Ave, Los Angeles, CA 90029. 213/-893-1235

WINTON, JEFFREY B. Arbitration. MA 1978, U of Ill. INT: arb/med, coll barg, labor law. ASSN: Chicago IRRA, AAA, NAA. POSITION: (since 1972) Arbitrator/Mediator, 2525 W Moffat, Suite 100, Chicago, IL 60647. 312/-252-3402

WIRPEL, ESTELLE M. Economics. 1167 Asbury Ave, Winnetka, IL 60093. 312/446-6112.

WIRPEL, SANDER W. Arbitration, Consulting, Bus:Pers/Ind Rels. AA 1940, Woodrow Wilson Jr. Coll; AB 1942, Grad Work, 1946-47, 1951-53, U of Chicago. PUBL: "Adequacy of an Employee Group Insurance Program," Proc 10th Annual IRRA, 1955; "Health Plans in Collective Bargaining: Responsibilities of Mgmt and Labor for Medical Care--A Commentary,: Proc 12th IRRA, 1959; "Benefit Trends in Industry Today," J of Coll & Univ Pers Assn, vol 16, #1, Nov 1964. INT: arb/med, coll barg, health & hosp care. ASSN: Chicago IRRA, AAA, AEA. POSITIONS: Asst to Exec Dir, Airlines Pers Rels Conf, 1947-50; Asst Mgr Labor Rels, Inland Steel Co, 1950-82; and (since 1982) Arbitrator, Mediator, Fact-Finder, 1167 Asbury Ave, Winnetka, IL 60093. 312/446-6112

WISNIEWSKI, STANLEY C. Legal Practice. BA 1969, Allentown Coll of St. Francis de Sates, MA 1971, PhD 1975, Catholic U of Amer; JD 1982, U of Md. PUBL: "Achieving Equal Pay for Comparable Worth Through Arbitration," Empl Rels Law J, Autumn 1982. INT: coll barg, arb/med, labor law. ASSN: Wash DC IRRA, AEA, ABA, SPIDR. POSITIONS: Res Dir, SEIU, 1975; Economist, Intl Assn of Machinists and Aerospace Workers, 1980; and (since 1983) Attorney, Conneston & Bernstein-Wash DC. ADDRESS: 6589 Quiet Hours, #102, Columbia, MD 21045. 202/466-6790

WITHAM, DENNIS Bus:Pers Ind Rels. AA 1968, Musk. Co. Comm Coll, BS 1971, Mich State U. INT: coll barg, personnel, empl/trng programs. POSITIONS: Asst Pers Mgr, Sparta Foundry, 1976; and (since 1978), Director, Ind Rels, Hastings Mfg Co, 325 N Hanover St, Hastings, MI 49058. 616/945-2491

WITKOWER, PHILIP Union. PhD 1982, U of Wis-Madison. INT: coll barg, health & hosp care, arb/med. ASSN: New York IRRA. POSITIONS: (since 1974) Research Director, Natl Union of Hosp and Health Care Employees, 330 W 42nd St, New York, NY 10036. 212/947-1944

WITNEY, FRED Acad: Econ, Ind Rels. BA 1940, MA 1941, PhD 1947, U of Ill. PUBL: Labor Relations, (co-author), Prentice Hall, 1984; Labor Relations Law, Prentice Hall, 1983; Labor Policies and Practices in Spain, Praeger, 1965. INT: arb/med, coll barg, govtlabor policy. ASSN: NAA, AEA, AAUP. POSITIONS: (since 1947), Prof of Econ, Ballantine Hall, Indiana Univ, Bloomington, IN 47401. 812/335-2288

WITT, RAY E. Bus:Pers/Ind Rels. BS 1969, U of Colo. POSITION: Ideal Basic Industries, 950 17th St, PO Box 8789, Denver, CO 80201. 303/623-5661.

WITTENBERG, CAROLE A. Acad: Univ Admin, Ind Rels; Arbitration. BS 1965, NYSS-ILR-Cornell; MS 1975, Hunter Coll. INT: arb/-med, empl/trng programs, labor educ. ASSN: New York IRRA, AAA, SPIDR. POSITIONS: Dir, Westchester Office, 1977, Assoc Dir, New York Office, 1982, and, since 1983, Metropolitan Dir, NYSSILR-Cornell Univ. ADDRESS: 19 Gray Rock LA, Chappaqua, NY 10514. 212/-340-2800

WITTERIED, GEORGE C. Acad: Ind Rels, Bus Admin,; Arbitration. BSC 1949, U of Notre Dame, MBA 1956, U of Chicago; JD 1952, Northwestern U. PUBL: The Developing Labor Law, Five Year Cumulative Supplement, Chapter 29, BNA, Wash DC, 1975; Labor Relations and Collective Bargaining: Text and Cases, Boston: Allyn Bacon, 1969; Labor Relations and Collective Bargaining: Instructor's Manual, Boston: Allyn Bacon, 1969. INT: personnel, coll barg, mgmt/educ. ASSN: Gateway IRRA, Acad of Mgmt, Amer Bus Law Assn, ABA. POSITIONS: Assoc Prof-Mgmt, Eastern Mich U, 1958; Visiting Prof-Mgmt & Pers, Mich State U, 1962; and (since 1965) Assoc Prof, Mgmt and Ind Rels, School of Bus Admin, Univ of Missouri, 8001 National Bridge, St. Louis, MO 63121. 314/553-6134

WOLCHOK, HAROLD Acad: Labor/Mgmt Rels; Union, Radio Host. AB 1957, Hunter Coll; MA 1966, New York U. PUBL: The Real World of Work, An Introduction to Labor Management Relations, First and Second Editions. INT: coll barg, labor educ/history, media. ASSN: New York IRRA. POSITIONS: Secretary-Treasurer, Local 917, IBT, 1953; and (since 1961) Assoc Prof, New York City Coll-CUNY. ADDRESS: 33 Claire Ct, Staten Island, NY 10301. 212/643-8154

WOLF, ANDREW J. Student. MLIR 1983, Mich State U. INT: coll barg, arb/med, personnel. 53 Silver Birch Lane, Pearl River, NY 10965. 914/623-5640

WOLF, CHARLES M. Bus:Pers/Ind Rels. BS 1956, Penna State U. INT: arb/med, coll barg, empl/trng programs. ASSN: Central Penna IRRA. POSITIONS: Assoc, Charles Minner Assoc Consulting, 1977; and (since 1979) Administrator, Employee Rels, Harsco Corp, Camp Hill, PA 17011. 717/763-7064

WOLFE, KATIE J. Acad: Law, Ind Rels. BA 1972, JD 1976, MS 1979, U of Wis-Madison. INT: labor law, admin law, empl regulation. ASSN: State Bar of Wis, ABA, Amer Bus Law Assn. POSITIONS: Legal Counsel/Project Coordinator, Police Policy Develop Project-Oshkosh, WI, 1978; Asst Prof, Dept Bus Law & Regulation, Central Mich U, 1980; and (since 1982) Asst Prof, Dept of Ind Rels and Human Resources, Univ of Iowa. ADDRESS: PO Box 768, West Branch, IA 52358. 319/353-3799

WOLFE, KENNETH B. Consulting, Arbitration. AB 1951, Lycoming Coll; MED 1963, U Rochester. INT: arb/med, labor law, mgmt/educ. ASSN: Southern Conn IRRA, AAA. POSITIONS: VP, Ind Rels, Lorac Corp, 1968-70; VP Organization, Kentucky Fried Chicken, 1970-72; and (since 1972) Consultant, (self-employed), 905 King St, Greenwich, CT 06830. 203/531-4498

WOLFF, HELMUT O. Arbitration, Bus:Mgmt/-Admin. BBA 1955, North Tex State U. PUBL: "The Development of Arbitration in Texas," Baylor Law Rev, 1983. INT: arb/med, labor/-mgmt trng programs. ASSN: North Texas IRRA, Dallas/Ft Worth Assn Executives. POSITION: (since 1961) Regional Dir, Amer Arb Assn, 1607 Main St, RM 1115, Dallas, TX 75201. 214/748-4979

WOLFMEYER, PAMELA V. Acad: Bus Admin. BA 1966, Grinnell Coll; MA 1969, ABD, U of WisMadison. INT: personnel, coll barg, org beh. POSITION: (since 1969) Assoc Prof, Dept of Bus Admin, Winona State College, 656 Dacota St, Winona, MN 55987. 507/457-8159

WOLITZ, LOUISE BERMAN Acad: IndRels, Econ; Arbitration. PhD 1974, U of Calif/Berkeley. PUBL: Access of Hispanics to Professional Technical & Managerial Jobs; Analysis of the Labor Market for Policeman. INT: labor market econ, govt labor policy, arb/med. ASSN: South Texas IRRA, AEA, AAA, ASPA. POSITIONS: Asst Prof, Hunter Coll-CUNY, 1974; Asst Prof, U of Tex, San Antonio, 1976, and, since 1983, Asst Prof, Dept of Government, Univ of Texas-Austin. ADDRESS: 4007 Edgerock, Austin, TX 78731. 512/471-5121

WOLKINSON, BENJAMIN W. Acad: Ind Rels; Arbitration. BA 1966, George Washington U; MA 1969, U of Chicago; PhD 1972, Cornell U. PUBL: Blacks, Unions The EEO, D. C. Heath, 1973, 1975, (2nd printing); "NLRB and Alternative Situs Picketing," Ind Rels Law J, vol 3, 1979, pp 643-670; "Arbitration and the Rights of the Mentally Handicapped," Monthly Labor Rev, vol 103, #3, Apr 1980, pp 41-47. INT: govt labor policy, labor law, coll barg. ASSN: SPIDR. POSITIONS: Industrial Analyst, NLRB, 1969-71; Conciliator, EEO Commission, 1970-71; and (since 1971) Professor, School of Labor and Ind Rels, Mich State Univ, East Lansing, MI 48824. 517/353-1696

WOLKOFF, REGINA LOIS Student. 2119 Old Oak Dr, West Lafayette, In 47906. 317/-463-7162

WOLLETT, DONALD H. Acad: Law. POSITION: McGeorge School of Law, Univ of the Pacific, 3200 5th Ave, Sacramento, CA 95817.

WOLOZIN, HAROLD Professor, Univ of Massachusetts. ADDRESS: 22 Garden St, Boston, MA 02114. 617/367-1094

WOLTERS, ROGER S. Acad: Ind Rels, Org Beh/Pers, Bus Admin. PhD 1981, U of Ill. PUBL: "Union-Management Ideological Frames of Reference," J of Mgmt, 8(2), 1982, 21-33; "Doctoral Education and Research in Industrial Relations," (w J. Dworkin & P. Feuille), Ind Rels, 19(1), 1980, 74-80; "Discharge Cases Reconsidered," (w K. Jennings), Arb J, 31(3) 1976, 164-180. INT: coll barg, labor law, personnel. ASSN: Acad of Mgmt, Southern Mgmt Assn. POSITIONS: Instructor/Acad & Career Advisor, Dept of Mgmt, Mar, & Bus Law, U of North Fla, 1976; Grad Res Asst, ILIR, U of Ill, 1977; and (since 1980) Asst Prof, Dept of Mgmt, Auburn Univ, Auburn, AL 36849. 205/826-4522

WOOD, DAVID P. Legal Practice. Clark, Klein & Beaumont, 1600 1st Federal Bldg, Detroit, MI 48226.

WOOD, W. DONALD Acad: Ind Rels, Econ. BA 1950, McMaster U; MA 1952, Queens U; A.M. 1954, PhD 1959, Princeton. PUBL: "The Industrial Relations Scene in Canada," Senior Editor, published by Queens U. INT: coll barg, govt labor policy, labor market econ. ASSN: AEA, CIRRA, IIRA. POSITIONS: R.C.A.F. (Admin), 1940-45; Dir/E.R. Research, Imperial Oil Ltd, 1955-60; and (since 1960) Director, School of Ind Rels, and Prof of Econ, Queens Univ, Kingston, Ont K7L 3N6 Canada. 613/546-4448

WOODBRIDGE, HENRY SEWALL Consulting. POSITION: Consultant, PO Box 156, Pomfret, CT 06258. 203/928-7979

WOODBURY, STEPHEN A. Acad: Econ. AB 1975, Middlebury Coll; MS 1977, PhD 1981, U of Wis. PUBL: "Methodological Controversy in Labor Economics," J of Econ Issues 13, Dec 1979, 933-955; "Substitution between Wage and Nonwage Benefits," Econ Rev, 73 Mar 1983, 166-182. INT: arb/med, govt labor policy, labor market econ. ASSN: AEA, Midwest Econ Assn, Assn for Evolutionary Econ. POSITIONS: Res Analyst, Wis Council 40, AFSCME, 1978; Instructor/Asst Prof of Econ, Penna State U, 1977; and (since 1982) Asst Prof of Econ, Marshall Hall, Mich State Univ, East Lansing, MI 48824. 517/355-4587

WOODHAM, BRENT A. Student. 439A S River Rd, West Lafayette, IN 47906. 317/-743-5462

WOODHOUSE, ROBERT J. Bus:Pers/Ind Rels. BS-ILR 1964, Cornell; MBA 1980, Pace U. INT: personnel, mgmt/educ, org beh. POSITIONS: Dir of Human Resources, Butler Automatic-Canton, 1980; Mgr of Human Resources, Gould Madison-Andover, 1982; and (currently) Director of Human Resources, Tau Tron Div of General Signal, 27 Industrial Ave, Chelmsford, MA 01824. 617/256-9013

WOODS, LESLIE EARLE Acad: Ind Rels, Retired. INT: mgmt/educ, org beh, personnel. ASSN: Boston IRRA, NAA. POSITIONS: Raytheon Co, Lexington, 1960 to retirement, and, currently, Lecturer, Grad School of Engineering, Northeastern Univ, 1716 Cambridge St, Cambridge, MA 02138.

WOODWORTH, WARNER P. Acad: Org Beh/Pers. POSITION: Org Beh Dept, Brigham Young Univ, Provo, UT 84602.

WOOL, HAROLD Consulting. PhD 1965, American U. PUBL: The Military Specialist, Johns Hopkins Press, 1968; The Labor Supply for Lower Level Occupation, Praeger, 1976; The Labor Outlook for the Bituminous Coal Industry, Electric Power Res Inst, 1980. INT: empl/trng programs, labor market econ, military manpower. ASSN: Wash DC IRRA, AEA, IIRA, Natl Economists Club. POSITIONS: Project Dir, Natl Planning Assn, 1972; Program Dir, Energy Manpower Res, The Conference Board, 1979; and (since 1980) Economic-Consultant (self-employed), 6716 Brigadoon Dr, Bethesda, MD 20817. 301/229-0545

WOOL, MURIEL B. Acad: Econ, Ind Rels. INT: labor market econ, labor history, intl comparative labor. ASSN: Wash DC IRRA, AEA, Wash Economist, Society of Govt Economists. Retired. 6716 Brigadoon Dr, Bethesda, MD 20817. 301/229-0545

WOOLEY, THOMAS R. Bus:Pers/Ind Rels. BS 1951, Evansville Coll-Ind; MS 1964, San Jose State Coll. INT: personnel, labor law, govt labor policy. ASSN: New York IRRA, ASPA. POSITIONS: Personnel Positions, 1956; and, since 1974, Employee Relations Advisor, IBM Corp, Old Orchard Rd, Armonk, NY 10504. 914/765-5792

WOOLF, ANN HOLMAN Arbitration. BA 1951, Wellesley Coll; MS 1955, Cornell U. PUBL: "Back Pay Awards in Arbitration;" "Management Rights and Arbitration." INT: arb/med, coll barg, labor law. ASSN: SPIDR, AAA. POSITIONS: Visiting Asst Prof, Hofstra U, 1959; Visiting Prof, U of Okla, 1964; and (since 1972) Arbitrator, 4922 Stonehenge LA, Norman, OK 73071. 405/329-6653

WOOLF, DONALD AUSTIN Acad: Ind Rels, Bus Admin.; Arbitration. BS 1952, Kansas State U; MPA 1956, Wayne State U; PhD 1962, Cornell U. INT: admin process, labor rels, psychology. POSITION: (since 1962) Assoc Prof, Dept of Mgmt, Univ of Oklahoma, Adams Hall, Norman, OK 73071. 405/325-2651

WORDEN, ROBERT G. Professional Assn. POSITION: President, West Virginia Manufacturers, 1313 Charleston Natl Plaza, Charleston, WV 25301. 304/342-2123

WORLAND, DAVID Acad: Ind Rels. BComm 1962, U of Melbourne; MEcon 1974, LaTrobe U. PUBL: "Variations in Award Rates of Pay and the Absorption of Overaward Payments," JIR 14(4), 1972, 396-412; "Survey of Wage Rates and Their Effects on Employment," NILS W.P. Series #40. INT: labor market econ, arb/med. ASSN: Ind Rels Soc of Victoria, Econ Soc of Aust and New Zealand, IIRA. POSITIONS: Res Asst, La Trobe U, 1967; and (since 1979) Principal Lecturer, Footscray Inst of Tech. ADDRESS: 87 Locksley Rd, Ivanhoe, Victoria, Australia 3079. Phone: 6884325

WORLEY, G. THOMAS Government. BA 1976, MPA 1978, Ohio State U; JD 1983, Capital U Law School. INT: govt labor policy, labor law, arb/med. ASSN: Central Ohio IRRA, Columbus Bar Assn, Ohio Bar Assn. POSITIONS: Ind Rels Admin, City of Columbus, 1977; and (since 1984) Labor Rels Specialist, State Empl Rels Bd of Ohio. ADDRESS: 2338 Hardesty Ct, Columbus, OH 43204. 614/462-8573

WORTMAN, MAX S., JR. Acad: Org Beh/-Pers; Consulting. BSCE 1956, Iowa State U; PhD 1962, U of Minn. PUBL: "An Overview of the Research on Women in Management: A Typology and a Prospectus," in Women and Work, ed J. Bernardin, New York: Praeger, 1982, pp 1-28; Defining the Managers Job, New York: AMACUM, 1975; Administrative Policy, (2nd edition) New York: John Wiley, 1980. INT: personnel, strategic mgmt, health & hosp care. ASSN: Acad of Mgmt, Amer Inst for Decision Sciences, Amer Mgmt Assn. POSITIONS: Prof, U of Mass, 1968; Prof, Va Polytechnic Inst & State U, 1968; and (since 1981) The William B.Stokely Prof of Mgmt, and Dir, Inst for Strategic Mgmt, Coll of Bus Admin, Univ of Tenn, Knoxville, TN 37916. 615/974-3161

WRATHALL, LEILA Union. BA 1976, U of Calif-Santa Barbara; MLIR 1980, Mich State U. INT: coll barg, union org/admin, arb/med. POSITIONS: Program Admin, Center for Labor Educ & Res, U of Kentucky, 1978-80; Instructor, Labor Educ & Res Center, U of Oregon, 1980-82; and (since 1983) Bus Agent, SEIU, Local 503. ADDRESS: PO Box 252, Pendelton, OR 97801. 503/276-4983

WRIGHT, GERALD W. Bus:Pers/Ind Rels. BSBA 1957, U of Fla. INT: coll barg, personnel, arb/med. ASSN: Central Florida IRRA, ASPA, Newspaper Pers Rels Assn, Greater Tampa Pers Admin Assn. POSITION: (since 1966) Dir of Pers and Ind Rels, The Tribune Co, 202 S Parker St, Tampa, FL 33601. 813/272-7751

WRIGHT, JOHN C., JR. Legal Practice. AB 1961, Princeton U; LLB 1964, U of Penna. INT: labor law, coll barg, arb/med. ASSN: Philadelphia IRRA, ABA, Penna Bar Assn, Phila Bar Assn. POSITIONS: Assoc, McCulloch, et al, Portland, OR, 1965-69; and (since 1969) Partner, Montgomery, McCracken, Walker & Rhoades, 3 Parkway, 20th Floor, Philadelphia, PA 19102. 215/563-0650

WRIGHT, KENNETH B. Government. POSITION: Office of Labor Rels, Room 401, City County Bldg, Madison, WI 53710.

WRIGHT, SUE ELLEN Student. BA 1983, MLIR, 1984, Mich State U. INT: org beh, empl/-trng programs, ind psych. ASSN: ASPA. POSITION: Student-Mich State U. ADDRESS: 28051 Stuart, Southfield, MI 48076. 313/557-3219

WRONG, ELAINE Acad: Ind Rels, Econ. PhD 1980, NYU. PUBL: "Arbitrators, The Law & Women's Job Bids," Labor Law J, Dec 1982; "Selecting An Abrbitrator for a Discrimination Grievance," Pers Admin Jan 1983; "The Social Responsibilities of Arbitrators in a Title VII Dispute," Labor Law J, Sept 1981. INT: coll barg, labor law, arb/med. ASSN: New York IRRA, Metropolitan Econ Assn, Eastern Econ Assn. POSITIONS: (since 1980) Asst Prof, CUNY. ADDRESS: 24 W 69th ST, New York NY 10023. 212/725-7133

WUSLICH, GARY L. Bus:Pers/Ind Rels. Mgmt/Admin, Government. BA 1967, Youngstown U. INT: coll barg, empl/trng programs, govt labor policy. POSITIONS: Asst Supt, Ind Rels, 1975, Superintendent, Ind Rels/Empl Serv, 1977, and, since 1981, Sr Manager, Ind Rels, Jones & Laughlin Steel Corp, 3 Gateway Center, Pittsburgh, PA 15263. 412/227-4028

WYKERT, TIMOTHY R. Union; Acad: Student. BA 1973, Oakland U; MLIR 1983, Mich State U. INT: coll barg, arb/med, labor law. ASSN: Mid-Mich IRRA, Natl Troopers Coalition. POSITIONS: Trooper, 1973, and, since 1981, Vice Pres, Mich State Police Troopers Assn, 23527 N Rockledge, Novi, MI 48050. 313/477-4671

WYMAN, EARL J. Acad: Ind Rels; Consulting, Arbitration. BS 1950, MS 1964, U of Wis-Madison. INT: arb/med, personnel, mgmt/educ. ASSN: Wisconsin IRRA, AAA (roster of Arbritrators), NCHRC. POSITIONS: Dir of Empl Rels, UOP, 1965; Assoc Prof, U of Wis-Ext, 1968; and (since 1981) Chairman, Center for Mgmt Programs, Univ of Calif-Berkeley. ADDRESS: PO Box 4788, Berkeley, CA 94704. 415/642-0323

WYNNE, DAVID JEFFREY Acad: Consulting, Bus:Pers/Ind Rels, Government. BS 1955, MBA 1968, Temple U. PUBL: Guidelines for the Development of an Affirmative Action Plan; Equal Opportunity Programs for State and Local Governments; "Pensions-Relation to Employee Mobility." INT: personnel, govt labor policy, empl/trng programs. POSITIONS: Regional Merit Systems Rep, USDHEW, 1970; Chief, Merit Systems and Tech Asst, US Civil Service Comm, 1971; and (since 1979) Chief, Intergovernmental Rels, US Office of Pers Mgmt-Philadelphia. ADDRESS: 502 Queen Anne Rd, Cherry Hill, NJ 08003. 215/597-0920

YAGER, PAUL Government. BA 1942, NYU; MSILR, 1949, NYSSILR-Cornell. PUBL: "The Role of the Mediator in Health Care Collective Bargaining,: in the Handbook of Health Care Human Resources Mgmt, Aspen System Corp, 1981, pp 767-770; "Mediation: Conflict Resolution Techniques in the Industrial, Community and Public Sector," New Techniques in Labor Dispute Resolution, BNA, Wash DC, Chapter 10, pp 122-219; "Collective Bargaining Strategies in Context of Unemployment and Inflation: A Mediator's View," Proceedings of 1976 IRRA Spring Meeting, pp 475-479. INT: arb/med, labor history, intl comparative labor. ASSN: New York IRRA, SPIDR, Advisory Council NYSSILR. POSITIONS: Mediator, 1951, Asst Reg Dir, 1962, and, since 1973, Dir, Eastern Regions, FMCS, New York. ADDRESS: 8 Lexington Dr, Metuchen, NJ 08840. 212/264-1000

YAGODA, LOUIS Arbitration. BS 1933, MPA 1945, NYU. INT: arb/med, coll barg, ind sociol. ASSN: New York IRRA, NAA, SPIDR, IIRA. POSITIONS: Arb/Mediator, New York State Board of Mediation, 1945; and (since 1960) Arbitrator, (self-employed), 15 Earle PL, New Rochelle, NY 10801. 914/632-9591

YANCY, DOROTHY COWSER Acad: Political Science, Ind Rels; Arbitration. AB 1964, Johnson C. Smith U; MA 1965, U of Mass, PhD 1978, Atlanta U. PUBL: The Federal Government Policy and Black Enterprise, (w R. J. Yancy),Cambridge, MA: Ballinger Publ Co, 1974; "Public Sector Bargaining in the South: A Case Study of Atlanta and Memphis," in Ind Rels Assn Proc, 1979, 300-310; "Perceptions of the AFSCME and IAFF Rank and File Towards the City of Atlanta's Labor Relations Policy," Labor Studies J, Winter 1981, 222-232. INT: arb/med, coll barg, govt labor policy. ASSN: Atlanta IRRA, AAA, SPIDR, Assn for the Study of Afro-Amer Life and History. POSITIONS: Dir of Afro-Amer Studies, Barat Coll, Lake Forest, IL, 1971-72; and (since 1972) Acting Assoc Dir School of Social Sciences and Assoc Prof, Georgia Inst of Tech, Atlanta, GA 30332. 404/894-3195

YAROWSKY, SOL M. Arbitration. BS 1941, U of Wis-Madison. JD 1941, Drake Univ. INT: arb/med, labor law, ind sociol. ASSN: Kansas City IRRA, AAA, NAA, Amer Judicature. POSITIONS: Reg Attorney, Natl War Labor Board, 1943; Attorney, 1946; and (since 1970), Labor Arbitrator, Power & Light Bldg, Suite 2308, 106 W 14th St, Kansas City, MO 64105. 816/842-7294

YEE, KENNETH Consulting. INT: health & hosp care, coll barg, arb/med. ASSN: Mid-Mich, Detroit, NE Michigan IRRAs. POSITION: (since 1959) Market Rels, Blue Cross Blue Shield of Mich. ADDRESS: 2123 Heights Ave, Lansing, MI 48912. 517/374-8594

YODER, DALE Acad: Ind Rels. MA 1926, PhD 1929, State Univ of Iowa. PUBL: Personal Mgmt and Industrial Relations. Retired. 3002 Salmon Dr, Los Alamitos, CA 90720. 213/430-9560

YONEDA, KIYOTAKA Acad: Ind Rels, Bus Admin. BA 1934, MA 1935, Wesleyan U. PUBL: Personnel Administration; "An Appropriate Bargaining Unit in the U.S.A.;" "An Appropriate Bargaining Unit in U.S. Health Care Industry." INT: intl comparative labor, coll barg, personnel. ASSN: Japan Ind Rels Res Assn, Japan Mgmt Assn, AEA. POSITIONS: Prof of Mgmt and Ind Rels, Rokkyo Univ, Tokyo, 1944; Asst Dir, Brotherhood of Railway and Airline Clerks (USA), 1968; and (since 1975) Prof of Mgmt and Labor Rels, Kokusai Shoka Coll, Kawagoe-Shi, Saitama-Ken, 350 Japan. Phone: 0492-32-1111

YOST, EDWARD B. Acad: Org Beh/Pers. BSIM 1975, MBA 1976, U of Akron. PUBL: Management Education and Development; Functional Business Concepts. INT: personnel, org beh. ASSN: Acad of Mgmt. POSITIONS: Independent Consultant, 1982, and, since 1982, Asst Prof, Dept of Mgmt Systems, Copeland Hall, Ohio Univ, Athens, OH 45701.

YOUNG, DALLAS M. Acad: Ind Rels; Arbitration, Consulting. BEd 1936, Southern Ill U; AM 1937, PhD 1941, U of Ill. PUBL: Understanding Labor Problems, (Text and Trade Editions), McGraw Hill, 1959; "Fifty Years of Labor Arbitration in Cleveland Transit," Monthly Labor Rev, May 1960; "Understanding and Managing Changes in University Labor Relations," CWRU W.P. Series on Mgmt, #106, Feb 1974. INT: arb/med, govt labor policy, labor history. ASSN: Northeast Ohio IRRA, NAA. POSITIONS: President, Dallas Young & Assoc, 1972; Permanent Arbitrator, General Dynamics & Intl Assn of Machinists, Ft.Worth, TX, 1982-82; and, (since 1965) Prof of Labor Rels, Case Western Reserve Univ, 638 Library Bldg, Cleveland, OH 44106. 216/368-2063

YOUNG, EDWIN Acad: Univ Admin. BS 1940, MA 1942, U of Me; PhD 1950, U of Wis. INT: trade unions, economic development. POSITIONS: Pres, Univ of Maine; Pres, Univ of Wis System, President Emeritus and Rennebohm Professor of Applied Economics, U of Wis, Helen White Hall, Madison, WI 53706. 608/263-2930

YOUNG, FREDERICK JOHN L. Arbitration; Acad: Ind Rels. MA 1950, St. Andrews-Scotland; MA 1952, Queen's U-Canada. PUBL: "The Labor Market," in Labor and Industrial Relations in New Zealand, (Editor & Contributor), Pitman, 1973; The Contenting Out of Work, Queens U, Kingston, Ont, 1963. INT: arb/med, coll barg, intl comparative labor. ASSN: New Zealand Assn of Economists, ANZ Assn of Econ. POSITIONS: Sr. Lecturer, Econ Dept, 1963, Dir, Ind Rels Center, Victoria Univ of Wellington, 1970; and (since 1983) Permanent Arbitrator, Ministry of Employment and Ind Rels, Suva, Fiji Island. Phone: 25-461

YOUNG, JOHN C. Bus:Pers/Ind Rels. BA 1969, Divine World Coll-Iowa; MA 1973, Ohio U-Athens; MA 1976, U of Cincinnati. INT: coll barg, arb/med, personnel. ASSN: Cincinnati IRRA, ASPA. POSITIONS: Empl Supr, Hayes Albion Corp-Tiffin, 1977; Empl Rels Mgr, Emery-Cincinnati, 1981; and (since 1984) Employee Relations Manager, U.S.I. Chemicals Co, PO Box 848, Port Arthur, TX 77641. 409/724-3927

YOUNG, JOSEPH A. Law Enforcement. MILR 1983, Mich State U. INT: coll barg, arb/med, labor history. ASSN: Amer Society for Industrial Security. POSITION: (since 1976) Detective Lieutenant, Dept of Mich State Police. ADDRESS: 943 Eugenia, Mason, MI 48854. 517/337-6115

YOUNG, ROBERT C., JR. Consulting. BA 1976, U of Ill-Chicago; MA 1978, Northwestern U; CAS 1981, SUNY-Albany. INT: coll barg, mgmt/educ, org beh. ASSN: Western New York IRRA. POSITIONS: (since 1981) Labor Rels Specialist, Multi-BOCES Labor Rels Office, 4232 Shelby Basin Rd, Medina, NY 14103. 716/-798-4800

YOUNGBLOOD, STUART A. Acad: Org Beh/Pers, Ind Rels, Bus Admin. PhD 1978, Purdue U. PUBL: "Work, Nonwork, and Withdrawal," J of Applied Psych, 1984; "The Impact of Work Environment, Instrumentality Perceptions, Labor Union Image, and Subjective Norms on Union Voting Intentions," Acad of Mgmt J, 1984; "A Longitudinal Analysisof the Turnover Process," J of Applied Psych, 1983. INT: personnel, org beh, method/statis. ASSN: Acad of Mgmt, Amer Psychological Assn, Amer Inst of Decision Sciences. POSITIONS: Instructor, Purdue U, 1974; Asst Prof, U of S.C., 1977; and (since 1981) Asst Prof of Management, College of Bus Admin, Texas A & M Univ, College Station, TX 77843. 409/845-4882

YOUNGLOVE, PEGGY C. Bus:Mgmt/Admin. MLIR 1980, Mich State U. INT: personnel, org beh, empl/trng programs. POSITION: (since 1981) Computer Systems Manager, Casciani Communications, Inc. ADDRESS: 1527 Jerico Rd, Jackson, MI 49203. 517/787-1450

YURKO, SUSAN Acad: Student, Ind Rels. BS 1977, U of Ark; MS 1964, W Va U. INT: coll barg, arb/med. ASSN: West Virginia IRRA. POSITIONS: Dist Mgr, W Va American Future Systems, Inc, 1982; Volunteer Coordinator, Rape & Domestic Violence Information Center, 1983; and, currently, Student, W. Va Univ. ADDRESS: PO Box 4162, Morgantown, WV 26505. 304/296-7462

Z

ZACK, ARNOLD MARSHALL Arbitration. AB 1953, Tufts; LLB 1956, Yale; MPA 1961, Harvard. PUBL: The Agreement in Negotiations and Arbitration, BNA 1983; Understanding Grievance Arbitration in the Public Sector, USDL, 1974; Understanding Fact Finding Arbitration in the Public Sector, USDL, 1974. INT: arb/med, empl/trng programs, intl comparative labor. ASSN: Boston IRRA, NAA, AAA. POSITIONS: Member, Foreign Service Labor Rels Board, Wash DC, 1981-; and (since 1968) Arbitrator-Mediator, Arnold M. Zack Inc, 170 W Canton St, Boston, MA 02118. 617/262-1193

ZAIDI, MAHMOOD A. Acad: Econ, Ind Rels. BA 1957, UCLA; MA 1958, PhD 1966, U of Calif-Berkeley. PUBL: "Human Capital and Earnings: Some Evidence from Brazil and Mexico," (w R. U. Miller), Proceedings of IRRA, 1981; Labour Economics in Canada, (w S. Ostrey), Toronto: Gage Publ, 1979; "Benefit-Cost Analysis in the Healthcare," (w C.D. Siebert), Biosciences Communications, vol 1, #4, 1975. INT: labor market econ, intl comparative labor, health & hosp care. ASSN: Canadian Ind Rels Assn, IIRA, Australian Econ Society. POSITIONS: Acting Dir, Ind Rels Center, U of Minn, 1976; Visiting Prof, Australian Grad School of Mgmt, U of New South Wales, 1979; and (since 1980) Prof and Dir of Grad Study, Ind Rels Center, Univ of Minn, 537 Mgmt & Econ Bldg, 271 19th Ave S, Minneapolis, MN 55455. 612/373-3827

ZALUSKY, JOHN LUCAS Union, Research. POSITION: Research Dept, AFL-CIO, 815 16th St NW, Washington DC 20006. 202/637-5173

ZAMBONI, RICHARD A. Union. POSITION: Representative/Grievance Dept, AFSCME Council #13, 301 Chestnut St, 5th FL, Harrisburg, PA 17101. 717/236-5978

ZANDER, JACK Union. POSITION: Business Manager, AFGW Local #558, 6301 Rockhill Rd, Room 309, Kansas City, MO 64131.

ZAPPIN, BRUCE I. Bus:Pers/Ind Rels; Acad: Ind Rels. BA 1963, JD 1966, U of Cincinnati. INT: coll barg, labor law, personnel. ASSN: Labor Rels Council, Org Res Council, AAA. POSITIONS: Dir, Labor Rels, 1971, Dir, Ind Rels, 1976, and, since 1980, Staff Vice Pres, Ind Rels, ARA Services Inc, 6th & Walnut St, Curtis Bldg, Philadelphia, PA 19106. 215/-574-5348

ZECHAR, R. DALE Arbitration. BS 1956, Calif State U at Los Angeles. POSITIONS: Mgr, Ind Rels, Anchor Hocking Glass Corp, 1964; Dir, Ind Rels, Davis Walker Corp, 1968. ADDRESS: 8326 Croydon Ave, Westchester, CA 90045.

ZEFFIRO, JAY A. Acad: IndRels, Econ, Bus Admin. BA 1950, Wash & Jefferson Coll; MA 1970, Duquesne U. INT: coll barg, arb/med, labor educ. ASSN: Western Penna IRRA, Amer Mgmt Assn. POSITIONS: V.P., Gen/Mgr, Zeffiro Transfer Inc. 1953: Pres. Donora Lumber Co. 1968; and (since 1970) Assoc Prof, Labor Rels & Econ, Calif U of Penna, California, PA 15419. 412/938-4372

ZELLER, FREDERICK ANTHONY Acad: Ind Rels, Econ; Consulting. BSC 1955, MA 1956, U of N Dak; PhD 1963, Ohio State U. PUBL: Leadership in Trade Unions; Manpower in Appalachia; "Grievance Procedure in the U.S. Postal Service." INT: labor market econ, org beh, labor educ. ASSN: Rural Sociological Society, AEA. POSITIONS: Instructor, 1959, Asst Prof, Econ, Ohio State U, 1963; and (since 1965) Prof, Econ and Ind Rels, 411 Knapp Hall, West Virginia Univ, Morgantown, WV 26505. 304/293-4201

ZELLERS, JAMES ANTHONY Union. POSITION: Pres, Service Employees Union #399, 1247 W 7th St, Los Angeles, CA 90017.213/680-9567

ZERVANOS, CHRIST J. Government. BS 1951, Albright Coll; MGA 1953, U of Penna. INT: coll barg, personnel, labor law. ASSN: Central Penna IRRA, ASPA, Intl Pers Mgmt Assn, Natl Public Empl Labor Rels Assn. POSITIONS: Asst Dir of Pers, 1960, Dir of Pers, 1971, and (since 1971) Director of Labor Rels, Commonwealth of Penna, 404 Finance Bldg, Harrisburg, PA 17120. 717/787-5837

ZEYTINOGLU, ISIK F. Student. MA 1979, Bogazici U; MSAE 1983, Wharton-U of Penna. INT: intl comparative labor, coll barg, labor law. ASSN: Philadelphia IRRA, IIRA. POSITIONS: Econ Adviser to the Pres, Turkish Civil Aviation Union, 1979; Research Asst and PhD Candidate, The Wharton School-Univ of Penna. ADDRESS: 2001-D Orchard St, Urbana, IL 61801.

ZIMAROWSKI, JAMES B. Acad: Law; Legal Practice. BS 1974, W Va Inst of Tech; MBA 1976, MA 1977, Marshall U; JD 1982, W Va U; LLM 1984, U of Ill-UC. PUBL: "The Limits Upon A Labor Unions' 'Duty' To Control Wildcat Strikers," 84 W Va Law Rev, 933, 1982; "Into The Mire Of Uncertainty: Union Disciplinary Fines and NLRA 8(b) (1) (A)," 84 W Va L Rev 411, 1982; "Abusive Discharge and Employment at Will," 5 W Va. Pub Int L Rep 4, 1982. INT: coll barg, labor law, arb/med. ASSN: ABA, Assn of Trial Lawyers of Amer, Illinois State Bar Assn. POSITION: (since 1982) Asst Prof, Eastern Illinois Univ. ADDRESS: 216 Polk Ave, Charleston, IL 61920. 217/581-6119

ZIMMERMAN, DAVID ROY Research Firm. BS 1969, U of Wis-Oshkosh; MS 1971, PhD 1975, U of Wis-Madison. PUBL: "Public Sector Job Creation for Youth: Some Observations on its Role and Effectiveness;" "Impact of Public Service Employment on Public Sector Labor Relations;" "Measuring Costs of Employment and Training Programs." INT: empl/trng programs, health & hosp care, arb/med. ASSN: Wisconsin IRRA, IIRA. POSITIONS: Sr Researcher, 1975, Vice Pres, 1978, and (since 1983) Sr Fellow, Mathematica Policy Research, 905 University Ave, Madison, WI 53715. 608/-255-1900

ZIMMERMAN, STEVEN ARTHUR Bus:Pers/-Ind Rels. BS 1972, Ohio U. INT: coll barg, arb/med, labor law. POSITIONS: Ind Rels Mgr, Portsmouth Div, Dayton Walther Corp, 1979; and (since 1983) Labor Rels, Asst Supr, Champion Intl Corp, 601 North B St, Hamilton, OH 45013. 513/868-5234

ZIPP, GLENN ARTHUR Government. BS 1961, Wis State Coll-Stevens Point; AM 1966, U of Ill. PUBL: "Rights and Responsibilities of Parties to a Union-Security Agreement," Labor Law J, 1982. INT: labor law, coll barg, govt labor policy. ASSN: Senior Exec Assn. POSITIONS: Budget Analyst, Commodity Credit Corp, U.S. Dept of Agriculture, 1961-63; Labor-Economist, BLS-USDL, 1963-64; and (since 1978) Regional Dir, NLRB, Region 33, Savings Center Tower, 16th FL, Peoria, IL 61602. 309/-671-7083

ZIRKEL, PERRY A. Acad: Law/Educ. PhD 1972, JD 1976, U of Conn; LLM 1983, Yale. PUBL: Legal Issues in Public School Employment; "Profile and Grievance Arbitration Cases;" "Procedural Arbitrability of Grievance Arbitration Cases." INT: arb/med, labor law. ASSN: Philadelphia IRRA, AAA, SPIDR, Amer Educ Res Assn. POSITIONS: Dean, School of Educ, 1977, and, since 1983, Univ Professor, Lehigh Univ. ADDRESS: 3906 Walbert Ave, Allentown, PA 18104. 215/861-3241

ZISKIND, DAVID Arbitration, Legal Practice. JD 1925, U of Chicago; PhD 1937, Johns Hopkins U. PUBL: One Thousand Strikes of Government Employees, Columbia Univ Press; "Fringe-Points on Labor Law: Capitalist and Communist," Comparative Labor Law, Spring 1981; "U.S. Constitutional Norms and Their Offspring," Amer J of Comparative Law, 1982. INT: labor law, govt labor policy, arb/med. ASSN: Los Angeles IRRA, NAA, AEA, ABA. ADDRESS: 2339 Silver Ridge Ave, Los Angeles, CA 90039.

ZOLADZ, JOSEPH M. Acad: Student, Ind Rels, Econ. BS 1984, Cornell U. INT: govt labor policy, labor market econ, coll barg. ADDRESS: 38 Eltham Dr, Amherst, NY 14226. 716/836-0984

ZOLLER, JOHN HARRY Acad: Bus Admin. BBA 1948, U of Minn; MBA 1968, U of N.Mex; PhD 1977, U of Ariz. INT: mgmt/educ. POSITION: (since 1971) Prof of Bus Admin, Fort Lewis College, Durango, CO 81301. 303/247-7265

ZOLOT, NORMAN Legal Practice. BS 1941, JD 1947, Yale. INT: arb/med, health & hosp care, labor law. POSITION: Attorney, 9 Washington Ave, PO Box 5278, Hamden, CT 06518. 203/288-3591

ZUBRENSKY, RUTH J. Consulting. BA 1949, Antioch Coll; MA 1984, U of Wis-Milwaukee. INT: empl/trng programs, affirmative action, org beh. ASSN: Wisconsin IRRA, Governor's Equal Rights Council. POSITIONS: School for Workers Project Coordinator, Ext Div, 1972, Specialist, Empl & Trng Inst, Univ of Wis-Milwaukee, 1976; and (since 1983) Consultant, 3404 N Summit Ave, Milwaukee, WI 53211. 414/332-1492

ZUCKERMAN, JOHN V. Consulting. 5107 Del Monte, #8, Houston, TX 77056.

ZUMAS, NICHOLAS H. Arbitration, Legal Practice. POSITION: Arbitrator/Attorney, Suite 712, 1140 Connecticut Ave NW, Washington DC 20036. 202/223-4455

ZUMBOLO, ANTHONY Government; Acad: Econ, Ind Rels. MA 1981, SUNY-Albany. INT: mediation, coll barg. ASSN: New York Capitol Dist IRRA. POSITIONS: Bus Rep, SEIU, AFL-CIO, 1978; and, currently, Mediator, New York State Public Empl Rels Board. ADDRESS: 242 Manning Blvd, Albany, NY 12206. 518/457-6015

ZURVALEC, DAVID STANLEY Bus:Pers/Ind Rels. BGS 1974, U of Mich; JD 1977, T. M. Cooley Law School; MLIR 1978, Mich State U. INT: govt labor policy, labor law, coll barg. ASSN: Mid-Mich & Detroit IRRAs, Ingham Cty Bar Assn, State Bar of Mich, ABA. POSITIONS: Labor Rels Law Researcher, Mich Supreme Court, 1977; and (since 1979) Director of Ind Rels, Michigan Manufacturers Assn, 124 East Kalamazoo St, Lansing, MI 48933. 517/372-5900

ZURVALEC, SUSAN H. Bus:Pers/Ind Rels, Arbitration, Consulting. BA 1974, U of Mich, MA 1977, MLIR 1982, Mich State U. INT: coll barg, arb/med, labor law. ASSN: Mid Mich & Detroit IRRAs, Mich Public Employers Labor Rels Assn. POSITIONS: Teacher, Lansing School Dist, 1975; Labor Rels Consultant, Mich Assn of School Boards, 1982; and (currently) Asst Employee Rels, Lansing School Dist, 519 W Kalamazoo St, Lansing, MI 48933. 517/374-4068

ZWERLING, HARRIS L. Acad: Student, Law, Ind Rels. MS 1979, U of Mass-Amherst. INT: labor law, coll barg, arb/med. ASSN: Wisconsin IRRA. ADDRESS: 1750 Fordem Ave, #601, Madison, WI 53704.

ZYLBERSTAJN, HELIO Student. BE 1979, U of Sao Paulo-Brazil. INT: arb/med, coll barg, labor market econ. POSITIONS: Economist, Econ Res Inst/Univ of Sao Paulo; Technical Staff, Dept of Labor-Brazil, 1980; and (since 1982) PhD Candidate, IRRI, Univ of Wis. ADDRESS: 105C Eagle Heights Apts, Madison,WI 53705.

GEOGRAPHIC LIST OF MEMBERS

Members in the geographic section are listed alphabetically, categorized by country, state (or province), and city. In the United States, cities within the state are in zip code order. Current mailing addresses are used, and the business or professional affiliation of members is also indicated.

UNITED STATES

ALABAMA

Birmingham 35226-35294
Fottler, M. D., U of Alabama
Johnson, R. A., U of Alabama
Mikan, K. W.
Munchus, G. III, U of Alabama
Phillips, J. J., Vulcan Materials Co
Roberts, H. C. Jr., U of Alabama

Tuscaloosa 35404-35405
Clarke, J.
Hawley, L. T.
Murphy, J. W., Murphy & Murphy

University 35486
Bain, T. U of Alabama
Fulmer, W. E., U of Alabama
Meyer, D. G. U of Alabama

Rogersville 35652
Moon, G. L.

Mobile 36608-36688
George, Jack R.
Harrison, E. L., U of South Alabama
McConnell, R. C.

Auburn 36830-36849
Benson, P. G., Auburn U
Holley, W. H. Jr., Auburn U
Jones, E. B., Auburn U
McCollum, J. K., Auburn U.
Wolters, R. S., Auburn U.

ALASKA

Anchorage 99503-99508
Hauck, V. E., U of Alaska
Thorn, J., Industrial Relations
Westman, C. R., Government

Fairbanks 99701
Solie, R. J., Industrial Relations
Solie, E. E., Consultant

ARIZONA

Phoenix 85001-85034
Bush, R. W., Maricopa Community College
Davies, A., Marathon Steel
Franklin, S., FMCS
Fromm, K. N., GTE Network Systems
Gruender, D. F., Shimmel, Hill & Bishop P.C.
Lubin, S., McKendree & Lubin
Nygren, J. W., Frys Food Stores of Arizona
Oberstein, R. F., Salt River Project
Parent, G. M., Arbitration
Peckham, J. D., Motorola Inc
Tittle, J. O., Salt River Project
Wick, M., OPEIU Local 56

Mesa 85202-85281
Bohlander, G. Industrial Relations
Hoffner, Paul E. Acad Administration

Tempe 85281-85287
Burgess, P. L., Arizona State U
Werther, W. B. Jr., Arizona State U.
White, H. C., Arizona State U.

Glendale 85306
Springer, B. J., Amer Grad School Intl Mgmt

Tucson 85703-85726
Bongiovanni, A., St. Mary's Hospital
Klein, L. R., Retired
Kohn, E. L. Retired
McBrearty, J. C., U of Arizona
McMillan, W. R., Retired
Weizenbaum, S. K., Arbitrator/Attorney

ARKANSAS

Little Rock 72204-72212
Hammon, D. L., Labor Education
Massery. R. D., Systematics Inc
Robinson, J. W., U of Arkansas

State University 72467
Hoyt, D. R., Arkansas State U
McFarland, C. K., Arkansas State U.

Harrison 72601
Diekhoff, P. R., Student

Fayetteville 72601-72701
Curington, W. P., U of Arkansas
Owen, J. P., U of Arkansas

CALIFORNIA

Los Angeles 90009-90089
Aaron, B. UCLA
Adler, S. Arbitrator
Anderson, C.S., Student-UCLA
Bailer, L. H., Arbitrator
Baek, G. G., Student. UCLA
Bernstein, I., UCLA
Berry, J. H. Jr., Jones, Day, Reavis & Pogue
Berry, J. E. Academic
Betcherman, G., Student
Bodle, G. E., Arbitration
Bullock, P., UCLA
Burstein, G., California State Univ
Busman, G. B., UCLA
Byrne, J. C., Gibson, Dunn & Crutcher
Collins, R. D., City of Los Angeles

Counts, J. C., Consulting
Davidson, M. B., Industrial Relations
Demers, W. C., AFL-CIO
Draznin, J. N., Arbitration
Duzak, T. F., U. S. Administrators Inc
Ellis, G., Southern Calif Gas Co
Emer, W. H., Parker, Milliken, Clark & O'Hara
Fadem, J.A., UCLA
Farber, H. E., Mitchell, Silverburg et al
Fellman, G. L., Attorney/Arbitrator
Francis, E. E. J., Arbitrator
Hernandez, M. M., Student
Hutchison, J., UCLA
Jacoby, S. M., UCLA
Jones, E. A. Jr., UCLA
Kaden, A. L., FLRA
Kaplan, H., Creative Resources Intl
LaPerch, W. J., Business/Prof Consultants
Levy, A. F., Attorney
Logan, C. M., State of California
Lundberg, C. C., Univ of Southern Calif
MacLeod, A. G. S., UCLA
Massarik, F., UCLA
Maxey, C. University of Southern Calif
McMahon, B. J., Aerospace Corp
Meck, J., Kaiser Permanente Medical
Misa, K. F., A. T. Kearney Inc
Mitchell, D. J. B., UCLA
Murase, J. L., American Arbitration Assn
Oliver, A. T. Jr., Parker, Milliken et al
Oliver, H. W., Amer Fed TV/Radio Artists
Patterson, E. F., Union Oil/Oil & Gas Div
Peterson, A. J., Hughes Aircraft Co
Reed, T., Los Angeles Admin Office
Robbins, M. A., Pepper, Hamilton & Scheetz
Salmon, R. F., Bus-Personnel
Santos, S. S., Bus Admin
Schwartz, R. M., UCLA
Shibota, A., Student
Sickler, A. D., AFL-CIO
Ward, R. J., Union
Williamson, T., Kaiser Health Plan
Winters, B.C., Los Angeles City College
Zechar R. D., Arbitration
Zellers, J. A., Service Employees #399
Ziskind, D., Arbitrator

Beverly Hills 90212
Simon, K. M., Attorney

Culver City 90230
Leventhal, R. M., Arbitrator Fact Finder

Downey 90240
Jacobs, J. K., Student

El Segundo 90245
Monty, G. A.,

Hawthorne 90250
Jones, J. D., Mattel Inc

Hermosa Beach 90254
Maxwell, E. Attorney

Manhattan Beach 90266
Scholtz, E. Arbitrator

Pacific Palisades 90272
Adelson, Y. C., Arbitration
Fogel, W., Academic
Sperling, H. J., Joint Council of Teamsters

Palos Verdes Estates 90274
Anderson, D. A., Arbitration
Anderson, J., Academic

Rolling Hills Estate 90274
Roberts, T. T., Attorney

Venice 90291
Queen, L. J., Industrial Rels

Santa Monica 90401-90405
Cloke, K., Arbitration
Troyer, S. A.

Torrance 90503-90509
Bistline, W. J., Martin Marietta Aluminum
Corley, S., Business Personnel
Dempsey, M. L., Business-Personnel
Hisatomi, M. M., Business Management
Steadman, W. P., Standard Brands Paint Co
Tamoush, P. P., Arbitrator

Buena Park 90622
Sperry, J. C., UFCW Union Local 324

La Habra Heights 90631
Blunt, K. R. Calif State Univ

Norwalk 90650
Haynes, G. M. Jr., Union
Sapiro, B. L., Printing Specialties

Lakewood 90712
Ellery, L. F., Litton Fastening Systems

Los Alamitos 90720
Horn, T. B., FMCS
Yoder, D., Retired

Carson 90745-90746
Culp, B. C., Instructor Negotiations
Gualtier, J. L., Teamsters Local 572

Long Beach 90802-90846
Cassidy, G. W., Academic
Kellett, N. M., NI Industries Inc
Kunnecke, B. F., Douglas Aircraft Co
Lindemann, A. J.
Monat, J. S., Calif State University-LB
Radtke, R. C.,, B. F. Goodrich Co
Spichtig, J. J., McDonnell Douglas Automat.

Glendale 91202-91206
Sammis, R. L., Union
Stubbs, D. G., Consultant

Canoga Park 91304
Austin, H. M., Consulting

Encino 91316
Cotler, M. P., Student
Rappaport, M. D., Aribtrator

Northridge 91326
Ha, C. C., Academic

Granada Hills 91344
Leifer, R. P., Lockheed California

Sun Valley 91352
Huybregts, G. A. C., Student

Sherman Oaks 91403-91423
Bell, L., Business Management
Despol, J. A., Government
Kotin, L., Arbitrator
Lloyd, K. L., Consulting

North Hollywood 91607
Levin,W., Arbitration

Claremont 91711
Kerchner, C. T., Claremeont Grad School

Pomona 91765-91768
Coombs, W. P., Calif State Polytechnic
Dale, L. A. Calif State Polytechnic

LaCosta 92008
Sinclitico, J. A., Arbitrator

Julian 92036
Taylor, J. R., Arbitration

LaJolla 92037
Gadon, H., Academic

Poway 92064
Blakey, M. M., Government

Rancho Santa Fe 92067
Rule, W. S., Arbitration

San Marcos 92093
Morgan, B. E., California Teachers Assn

San Diego 92101-92181
Atchison, T. J., San Diego State Univ
Belcher, D. W., San Diego State Univ
Bowen, W. S., Solar Turbines Inc
Bullen, F. H., Kaye, Scholer, Fierman et al
Cheaney, N. N., Business Industrial Rels
Edgington, J. C. San Diego Newspaper Guild
Gifford, A., San Diego State Univ
Kulchin, B. A., General Dynamics-Electronics
Mullins, C. M., Government
Rodgers, T. J., Teamsters Local 542
Theep, R. T., Speivak & Theep
Theule, B. L., Solar
Warbutron, R. M., Government
Weckstein, D. T., University of San Diego
Williams, J. J., Arbitration.

Costa Mesa 92626
Neft, D. K., Union

Dana Point 92629
Kahn, S., Academic
Lang, K., Academic

Fullerton 92634
Bakken, G. M., California State Univ
Bickner, M. L., California State Univ
Simmons, R. L., Glass Containers Corp

Garden Grove 92642-92645
Aden, I., Student
Heyser, M. K., Orange County Transit

Huntington Beach 92646-92647
Begley, C. L., Busines Management
Castrey, B. P., FMCS
Castrey, R. T., Arbitration

Laguna Hills 92653
Hudson, H. D., Retired

Newport Beach 92660
Bloss, B. H., The Irvine Co

Orange 92668
Acosta, R. A., Council of Carpenters
Crost, P., Reich, Adell & Crost
Scott, G. G., Teamsters Union Local 952

Laguna Niguel 92677
Kaplan, H., Creative Resources Intl

Santa Ana 92706
Brisco, C. C., Arbitrator & Attorney

Fountain Valley 92708
Colinsky, E. G., Orange County Transit Dist

Irvine 92717
Perry, J. L., Univ of California

Anaheim 92802-92806
Christianson, V. J., Business Industrial Rels
Valenzuela, D., Kaiser Permanente

Oxnard 93030
Lloyd, W. V., Coastal Growers Assn

Simi Valley 93065
Sniadecki, A. F., Wangtek

Bakersfield 93389
Lange, C. B. A. III, Consulting

San Luis Obispo 93407
Adams, J. P. Jr., Calif Polytech State Univ
Aussieker B., Calif Polytech State Univ
Brewer, C. H., Student
Ellerbrock, G. B., Calif Polytech State Univ

Clovis 93612
Mullennix, G. L., Academic

Reedley 93654
Taggart, K. E., Business Management

Fresno 93704-93760
Anthony, C., Business Management
Ashe, J. L., Consulting
Bergmann, R. H., California State Univ
Carrig, K. J., Labor Relations
Erb, C. M., California State Univ
Schramm, S. E., Pacific Gas & Electric
Tombleson, C. M., R. T. French Co

Monterey 93940-93943
Boynton, R. E., Naval Post Grad School
Pool, C. A., Arbitration.

Burlingame 94010
Griffen, L. G., GTE Sprint

El Granada 94018
Gibbons, J. E., Business-Personnel

Los Altos 94022
Salmon, D. W., Retired

San Carlos 94070
Roumasset, C., Retired

South San Francisco 94080
Senior, K. R., Guy F. Atkinson Co

San Francisco 94101-94132
Abers, J. H., Academic
Allen, E. W., Calif State Med & Concil Serv
Amsler, T., Arbitration
Balanis, F. A., San Francisco State Univ
Bargmann, J. M., NABET
Barrett, E., Academic
Blank, D. L., Arbitration
Boss, A. C., SJ., Univ of San Francisco
Bradley, G. W., San Francisco State Univ
Burgeson, G. F., FMCS
Cooper, C. A., Amer Arbitration Assn
Cornford, D. N., Hotel Employers Assn
Crowley, J. F., SF Labor Council, AFL-CIO
Fine, N. A., Attorney
Fischer, R. L., Bechtel Power Corp
Foy, M. C., Business-Management
Fries, R. T., Steinhart & Falconer
Gallery, M. L., Pacific Maritime Assn
Garchik, J., Attorney
Gardner, P. M., Pacific Telesis Group
Greendorfer, J. R., Union
Herington, C. D., Crocker National Bank
Holland, S. S., Government
Holtgrave, R. R., Pacific Maritime Assn
Jacobsen, M., FMCS
Jennings, J. P., Attorney

Johnson, W. L., Dept Stores Employees 1100
Kaplan, A. I., Archer, Rosenak & Hanson
Kampas, B. W., Attorney
Kaufman, D. R., Marine Engineers Benefcl.
Kellerman, S. H., Consulting
Kohn, D. Z., Guadalupe Health Center
Leal, B. C., Teamster Local 856
Leff, I., Rosenthal & Leff Inc
Loney, T. J., GSA M23
Lucas-Wallace, K., Attorney
Matthews, K. B., Utah Intl Inc
Nevins, D. C., Arbitrator
Novogrodsky, D., Union
Phillips, B. A., Amer Intermediation Serv
Polland, H., Beeson, Taylor & Silbert
Riker, W. E., Arbitrator
Salerno, G. P., Univ of San Francisco
Schumacher, A. R., San Francisco State Univ
Slater, W., Retired
Thomas, N. M., Student
Totten, J. L., California Assn Employers
Twomey, T., Hosp & Inst Workers Local 250
Verbin, S. C., Pacific Gas & Electric
Veysey, V. V., State of Calif
Weiss, M. H., Attorney
West, D. H., State Compensation Insurance
Wilcox, J., Arbitration.

Palo Alto 94303-94306
Davis, J. R., Bus-Management
Oaxaca, R. L., Stanford University
Radle, J. A., Student

Stanford 94305
Gould, W. B., Stanford Law School
Levin, H. M., Stanford University
Mann, J. K., Stanford Law School
Strober, M. H., Stanford University

San Mateo 94402-94403
Berkley, G. W., Amer Arbitration Assn
Clinton, J. H., San Mateo Times
Foss, G. C., Envirotech Operating Servs

Alameda 94501
Doering, R. R., Labor Relations
Levinson, A., SEIU

El Cerrito 94530
Kerr, C., Consultant

Fremont 94536
Polca, R. F.

Hayward 94540-94542
Holm, L. L., Continental Group
Kilgour, J. G., Calif State University
Staudohar, P. D., Calif State University

Hercules 94547
Bargmann, R. M. Jr., Union

Lafayette 94549
Cox, D. R., Food Employers Council
Twohey, J. C., Arbitration.

Concord 94549
Hillary, T. B., Mt. Diablo Medical Center

Orinda 94563
Anderson, A. O., Arbitrator
Anderson, R., Arbitrator
Blandford, L., Bus-Industrial Relations
Scalone, J. A., J. Scalone & Assoc

Union City 94587
Badella, M. E., Bus-Industrial Relations

Walnut Creek 94595-94598
Behman, S., Academic
Hoyt, R. B., Professional Corp
Loughran, C. S., Louisiana-Pacific Corp
Phelps, J. C. Retired
Sisson, J. D., Bus-Industrial Relations

Oakland 94606-94643
Ames, C. D., Attorney
Chisholm, L., Union
Corbett, L. P., Attorney
Delaney, J. M., Business-Personnel
Mapp, M. M., Union
Sellheim, L.
Smith, M. K., Calif State Univ/Hayward

Berkeley 94704-94720
Aller, C. C., San Francisco State Univ
Bogue, B., Univ of Calif
Bridgewater, B., Arbitration.
Brown, C., Univ of Calif
Concepion, D.A., Arbitration
Dickens, W. T., Univ of Calif
Encinio, P. A., Univ of Calif
Estenson, D. L., Univ of Calif
Feller, D. E., Univ of Calif
Galin, A., Univ of Calif
Garbarino, J. W., Univ of Calif
Gordon, M. S., Univ of Calif
Kleingartner, A., Univ of Calif
Leonard, J.S., Univ of Calif
Mamer, J. W., Univ of Calif
Mannix, T. M., Univ of Calif
Miles, R. E., Univ of Calif
Mixer, M. C., USDL
Rader, W. R. K., Attorney
Rosenberg, H. R., Univ of Calif
Schneider, B. V. H., Univ of Calif
Schwartz, H. A., Mediation/Legal Services
Small, F. X., Univ of Calif
Stover, W. F., Univ of Calif
Strauss, G., Univ of Calif
Taylor, M., Univ of Calif
Ulman, L., Univ of Calif
Walker, J. M., Academic
Wilensky, H. L., Univ of Calif
Wyman, E. J., Univ of Calif

San Pablo 94806
Schaefer, S. C., Contra Costa College

San Rafael 94901
Peevey, M. R., Calif Labor Federation

Tiburon 94920
Kocin, H., AFTRA

Fairfax 94930
Reifler, E.A., Arbitrator

Mill Valley 94941
Killion, L. V., Attorney
Liebes, R. A., Union.

San Anselmo 94960
Randall, G. M., Arbitrator

Cupertino 95014
Holton, G., Bus-Industrial Relations

Los Gatos 95030
West, M. D., Arbitration

Santa Clara 95051-95053
Coz, R. T., Univ of Santa Clara
Passant, G. S., Human Resource Mgmt

Santa Cruz 95060-95064
Maloney, E., Arbitrator/Attorney
Pomer, M. I., Univ of Calif-Merrill Coll

San Jose 95112-95195
Boner, P. J., Arbitrator
Garnel, D., San Jose State Univ
Manausa, K. R., United Centrifugal Pumps
Murbach, I. G.
Murbach, R. T., Consulting
Schenone, R. J., Business-Ind Rels
Stevenson, A. F., Business-Ind Rels
Whaley, G. L., San Jose State Univ

Stockton 95204-95211
Blum, A. A., Univ of the Pacific
Segur, W. H., Academic
Van Cleve, R. R., Academic

Modesto 95353
Miller, E. J., Tri/Valley Growers

Sonora 95370
Randall, R. L., Student

Turlock 95380
Crist, W. D., Calif State Coll-Stanislaus
Henson, T. M., Student

Santa Rosa 95406
Gibson, G. H., SEIU Local 707

The Sea Ranch 95497
Spalding, F. O., Arbitration

Eureka 95501
Schuster, R. M., Calif Teachers Assn

Cool 95614
Gray, C. W., Consulting.

Davis 95616
Bartosic, F., Univ of Calif
Martin, P.L., Univ of Calif
Oettinger, M. P., Univ of Calif

Dutch Flat 95714
Cassady, P. A., Labor Arbitrator

Sacramento 95810-95831
Bonebrake, D., County of Sacramento
Brown, G. A., Arbitrator
Budlong, C.A., Calif Dept of Ind Rels
Edwardson, R. W., Bus-Personnel
Estenson, J. D., Business
Freeman, D., Arbitrator
Geiger, M., Arbitration
Goldstein, A.P.,Governors Office Empl Rels
Greenstein, F. H., Pacific Gas & Electric
Kelly, E. L. Jr., Calif State Univ
Lakich, S., City of Sacramento
Marcello, F.E.,Employers Labor Rels Service
McMonigle, B., Student
Murch, K., Calif State Employees Assn
Perry, H. A., Academic
Randol, G. C., Calif Newspaper Guild
Raza, M. A., Calif State Univ
Sato, F. F., Calif State Univ
Wollett, D. H., Univ of the Pacific

Chico 95926-95929
Cambridge, C. D., Calif State Univ
Lyman, J. R., Calif State Univ

Redding 96001
Haney, W. J., Calif State Med/Conc Svc

Anderson 96000
Odell, W. L., Consulting.

Shingletown 96088
Garvey, J.
Garvey, J.J., Retired

COLORADO

Arvada 80005
Siporin, D., Bus-Management

Aurora 80014
Byrnes, L., Union

Denver 80201-80237
Bransted, Z. N., Colorado AFL-CIO
Brauer, W. C. III. Attorney
Deeny, R.
Donley, R. N., Attorney
Emmet, T. A., Regis College
Fukami, C. G., Univ of Denver
Himmelmann, W. C., Denver Area Labor Fed
Hogan, C. J., Consulting
Mattern, T. R., Central Bank of Denver
Mrozek, J. S., Government
Roth, H. S., Consulting
Schoeberlein, W. F., Sherman & Howard
Simons, M. N., Brauer, Simons, Buescher P.C.
Verrastro, D. N., Martin Marietta Aerospace
Ward, J. T., Jefferson County Educ Assn
Watkins, T. L., Univ of Denver
Witt, R. E., Ideal Basic Industries

Boulder 80309-80401
Mason, R. H., IBEW Local 111
Udis, B., Univ of Colorado
Weber, A. R., Univ of Colorado

Fort Collins 80521-80523
Culley, J. F., Colorado State U
Wiggins, R. L., Academic

Colorado Springs 80903
Winograd, D. M., Makepeace & Winograd

Durango 81301
Zoller, J. H., Fort Lewis College

Vail 81658
Longenecker, K., Bus-Management

CONNECTICUT

Bristol 06010
Conte, M. R., Superior Electric Co

New Britain 06052
Monitto, A., Arbitration.

Rockville 006066
McKone, F. W. Attorney Arbitrator

Sharon 06069
Beaumont, R. A., Organization Research Counselors

Windsor 06095
Czerbinski, J. P., Union

Hartford 06103-06106
Barrington, K., Amer Arbitration Assn
Blum, P. R., Attorney
Darcy, W. R., Attorney
Fitton, P. A., Union
Halperin, S. E., Attorney
Scheer, A. I., Updike, Kelly & Spellacy
Siegel, J. S., Attorney

West Hartford 06107-06117
Beaudin, B. V., Mfgrs Assn
Gronbach, R. C., Hartford Hospital
Scheuch, R., Trinity College
Schor, R. M., Arbitrator
Silverstein, E. L., Univ of Connecticut

Willimantic 06226
Fried, M. L., Academic
Boardman-Free, R., Eastern Conn State Univ

Pomfret 06258
Woodbridge, H. S., Consultant

Storrs 06268
Geeter, J., Univ of Conn
Glasser, J., Academic
Johansen, E., Academic
Nesselroth, S. H., Univ of Conn

East Lyme 06333
Murphy, J. A., Government

Branford 06405
Prins, J. R., Consulting.

Clinton 06413
Busca, M. J.

East Hampton 06424
Childers, K. L, Bus-Personnel

Fairfield 06430-06431
Fishman, H., Arbitration.
Marceau, L., Retired
Nazzaro, S. E., General Electric WABA
Rocheleau, D. W., General Electric
Wallace, P., Union

Newton 06470
Priggins, G. M., Anaconda-Ericsson Inc

Sandy Hook 06482
Donovan, D. M., Bus-Ind Relations

Huntington 06484
Cureton, J. P., Bus-Industrial Relations

Stratford 06497
Nobili, R. B., Union.

New Haven 06511-06515
Annunziato, F., Union
Horvath, V. B., Government.
Post, W. B., Labor Arbitrator
Rosenberg, E. J., Union.
Silvia, S. J., Student

West Haven 06516
Emery, S. K., Student

Hamden 06518
Driscoll, J. J., Conn State Labor Council
Dubois, E. C.
Zolot, N., Attorney

New Haven 06520-06525
Brody, D. P., Retired
Reynolds, L. G., Yale University
Stevens, D. M., Yale University

Bridgeport 06604
Nichols, G. N., Cummings & Lockwood

Terryville 06786
Tokarz, J. C., O-Z/Gedney Co

Danbury 06817
Schwindt, R. F., Union Carbide

Greenwich 06830
Soutar, P. L., Management
Wolfe, K. B., Management

Norwalk 06851-06856
Imri, E. P., Nash Engineering Co
Radom, M., Retired
Tarczali, E. R., Nash Engineering Co

Ridgefield 06877
Perna, N.S., Management

Westport 06880
Wenig, J., Attorney

West Redding 06896
Hill, S. E., Retired

Stamford 06901-06926
Asher, W. S., Xerox Corporation
Benjamin, D. L., GTE Service Corp
Bloomquist, C. A., Peabody International
Cooleen, J. P., Singer Company
Hatcher, W. J., Pitney-Bowes
Lieberman, I. M., Arbitration
MacDonald, J. R., GTE Service Corp
Mullady, S. F., Champion Intl Corp
Norgren, P. H.
Toland, M. M., Student

DELAWARE

Newark 19711-19717
Bierlein, M. A., Government
Collyer, R. J., Business-Ind Rels
Sloane, A. A., Univ of Delaware
Tom, L., Univ of Delaware
Weiss, R. M., Univ of Delaware

Wilmington 19803-19899
Andrisani, P. J., Temple Univ
Jordan, J. H., ICI Americas Inc
La Penta, T. M., Academic
Olayiwola, P. O., Academic
Roeser, J. F. Jr., Dedicated Carriage Services
Uhlinger, C. W., Bus-Industrial Relations

DISTRICT OF COLUMBIA

Washington DC 20001-20570
Aldrich, E. I., Government
Andris, V. O., Coopers & Lybrand
Axelrod, J. G., Bein, Axelrod & Osborn
Azzan, C. C., Consulting
Baldwin, S. E., Natl Commission for Empl Policy
Barone, D. V., Government
Barth, M. C., Consulting
Becker, J. P., Department of State
Belitsky, A. H., Government
Benecki, S., Theological College
Bensinger, S. C., Government
Bier, J. V., Natl Railway Labor Conference
Bliss, K. S., Communications Workers
Bliss, R. C., Bricklayers Union
Blitzstein, D. S., United Mineworkers
Bloch, R. I., Arbitration
Bredhoff, E., AFL-CIO
Brickman, E. S., Union
Brooks, B. M., NAM
Burns, W. L., UFCW Intl Union
Cain, L. F., Academic
Carter, R. W., South African Embassy
Casey, E., Union Labor Life Ins Co
Christovich, L. J., Student
Clague, E., Consultant
Cohen, G. H., Bredhoff & Kaiser
Coleman, F. T., Boothe, Prichard & Dudley
Collins, A. M., IUOE
Colosi, T. RI., American Arbitration Assn
Confer, S. H., CWA
Connolly, W. B. Jr., Piper & Marbury
Conway, J. E., Air Conference
Coppess, J. B., CWA
Crane, L., Bureau of National Affairs
Cunningham, J. D., Univ of DC
Czarnecki, E. R., AFL-CIO
David, H., Consulting
Denker, J. S., Univ of DC
Douty, H. M., Research
Drohan, W. D., USDL
Edwards, H. T., U. S. Court of Appeals
Ellsburg, D. B., Connerton & Bernstein

Emerson, W., American Nurses Assn
Everitt, A. L., Arbitration
Fechter, A. E., Natl Academy of Sciences
Fedrau, R. H., Consulting
Fisher, C. J., Economics
Flanagan, R. J., Brookings Inst
Fleischman, W. E., Fed Labor Rels Authority
Fornam, H., CWA
Freilicher, F., Law
Freilicher, M. S., Law
Gastwirth, J. L., George Washington Univ
Gentry, J. N., Arbitration
Goldfarb, R. S., George Washington Univ
Golodner, J., AFL-CIO
Gruenberg, R., NEA
Hale, R. M., Natl Assn Manufacturers
Halter, P. J., Government
Hannigan, T. A., Intl Brotherhood of Elec Workers
Harkless, J. M., Arbitration
Harper, H. J., Government
Harter, P. J., Consulting
Hedges, J. N., Labor Economist
Hendrickson, S. J., AFL-CIO
Herling, J., J. Herlings Labor Letter
Higgins, G. G., Catholic Univ of America
Hoffman, E. B., Government
Horvitz, W. L., Consultant
Hotvedt, R. C., Attorney
Houchins, J. R., Howard Univ
Ilyashov, A., Univ of DC
Jaquay, J. N., Amalgamated Transit Union
Johnson, W. S., IBM Corp
Kahl, A. S., Bureau Labor Statistics
Kamber,V., The Kamber Group
Kane, A. F., IBT
Keller, A. D., Government
Kemp, H. R. Jr., Government
Kohl, G. H., CWA
Krashevski, R. S., AFL-CIO
Kucherov, T. L., Government
Kulash, M., Wyatt Company
Lafferty, L. A., Fed Service Impass Panel
Lapidus, L.S., Sherman & Lapidus
Latimer, M. W., Consulting
Lehmann, H. J., Retired
Levin-Epstein, M., Bureau of Natl Affairs
Levitan, S. A., Social Policy Studies
Leyden, J. F., AFL-CIO
Locigno, P. R., IBT
Ludwig, L. G., U. S. Dept of Labor
Lunnie, F. M. Jr., Natl Assn of Manufacturers
Maccoby, M., Academic
Màdison, J. J., Union
Martin, B., Government
Matthews, D. E., Arbitration
McCabe, D. M., Georgetown Univ
McLennen, K., Comm for Econ Development
McMahon, J., AFL-CIO
McNally, G. B., Consultant
Merrifield, L. S., George Washington Univ
Millen, B. H., Government
Miner, M. G., Bureau of Natl Affairs
Mire, J., Natl Inst of Labor Educ
Montross, W., UFCW Intl Union
Moses, E. B., Government
Munns, V. G., British Embassy
Murphy, C. J., Academic
Ness, D. L., SEIU, AFL-CIO
Newman, W., Union
Nixon, K. A., Government
Nollen, S. D., Georgetown Univ
Norwood, J. L., Bureau of Labor Statistics
Nulty, L. E., UFCW Intl Union
O'Brien, T. H., USDL
O'Connor, P., American Fed of Teachers
Ofong, C., Howard Univ
Olbrich, R., NLRB
Osofsky, D.
Oswald, R. A., AFL-CIO
Perl, P., The Washington Post
Piculin, L., Natl Mediation Board
Potter, E. E., McGuiness & Williams
Power, J. F., FMCS
Pritzker, M. L., Zimmerman, Semler, Pritzker
Prosten, R. M., AFL-CIO
Purchell, T. V., Georgetown Univ
Raisian, J., USDL
Ray, P. E., Joint Labor-Mgmt Comm Retail Food Ind
Reed, T. E., IUOE, AFL-CIO
Reutlinger, B. M., Dept of Labor
Reynolds, J. K., Government
Roberts, J. F., Natl Railway Labor Conf
Roberts, M., AFL-CIO
Robinson, S. A., Government
Rosofsky, R. G., USDL
Roth, T. R., The Labor Bureau Inc
Schimel, R. M., Consulting
Schmitz, J. G., AFSCME
Schneider, S. A., CSR Inc
Schultz, L. L., Arbitration
Schwenk, A. E., Bureal of Labor Statistics
Seidman, B., AFL-CIO
Serumgard, J. R., Rubber Manufacturers Assn
Shultz, G. P., Department of State
Solomon, J. S., Academic
Sparrough, M. E., Union
Stenmark, J. H., American Iron/Steel Inst
Straw, R. J., CWA
Sweeney, J. J., SEIU, AFL-CIO
Taylor, D., Gromfine, Sternstein et al
Taylor, M. L., IUBAC, AFL-CIO
Thompson, A. R., IBT
Tipton, J. B., Government
Triplett, J. E., Bureau of Labor Statistics
Truesdale, J. C., NLRB
Turnquist, D. E., Dept of State
Usery, W. J., Consulting
Van Helden, R. M., USDL
Vroman, W., Urban Institute
Walker, D. P., NEA
Wallace, L. A., The Washington Post
Wallick, F., UAW Washington Report
Warnock, J. A., Dept of State
Wasserman, D. S., AFSCME
Waugh, D. A. ILO
Waxman, B. I., Arbitration
Weiner, H., Government
Weintraub, N. A., IBT
Weitz, P. R., German Marshall Fund-U.S.
Welsh, R., SEIU
Zalusky, J. L., AFL-CIO
Zumas, N. H., Arbitrator/Attorney

FLORIDA

Ponte Vedra Beach 32082
Moore, D. G., Academic

Jacksonville 32212-3225
Forbes, P. C., Bus-Industrial Relations
Helsby, R. D., Univ of North Florida
Jennings, K. M., Academic
Tomlinson, W. H., Univ of North Florida

Tallahassee 32301-32308
Anthony, W. P., Florida State Univ
Auzenne, G. R., Academic
Haworth, C. T., Florida State Univ
Parry, J., State Univ System
Sobel, I., Florida State Univ
Stepina, L. P., Florida State Univ

Pensacola 32504
Einbecker, R. C., Univ of West Florida

Gulf Breeze 32561
MacKenzie, M. R., Consulting

Gainesville 32605-32611
Moberly, R. B., Univ of Florida
Powers, K. J., Student
Schriesheim, C. A., Univ of Florida

Winter Park 32790
Dillard, R. B., Continental Resource Co

Orlando 32802-32855
Garwood, T. C. Jr., Attorney
Rungeling, B. S., Univ of Central Florida

Melbourne 32953
Corradino, B. P., Bus-Personnel
Lamb, C., Harris Corp
Umhoefer, G., Harris Corp

Melbourne Beach 32951
Kearns, O. E., Arbitration

Vero Beach 32960
Gifford, N. P., Manpower

Pembroke Pines 33026
Boyajian, H. M., Bus-Industrial Relations

Key Biscane 33149
Mead, J. P., Arbitrator

Miami 33054-33199
(includes Coral Gables, Miami Beach & Pompano Beach)
Altman, S., Florida Intl Univ
Dodt, H., IUOE Local 675
Fine, J. M., Bus-Industrial Relations
Hall, C.A., Florida Intl Univ
Jackson, C. A., Bus-Management
Lowry, D. R., Biscayne College
Magnusen, K. O., Florida Intl Univ
McVay, G. R., Consulting
Remington, J., Florida Intl Univ
Schwab, R. M., Hotel Employees Union
Silverblatt, R., Florida Intl Univ
Solana, L., Union
Stessin, L., Professional Assn

Sunrise 33313
Bornman, J. W., Bus-Management

Boca Raton 33431-33432
Abbott, J. G., Florida Atlantic Univ
Myers, A. H., Retired

Palm Beach 33480
Hoffman, H. G., Academic

Homes Beach 33510
Bell, J. F., Attorney-Arbitrator

Clearwater 33516
Wheeler, G. R., Pinellas County

Belleair Beach 33535
Weston, J. A., Arbitration

Largo 33540
Bowman, G. J., Paradyne Corp

Lutz 33549
Balfour, G. A., Academic

Palm Harbor 33563
Hanes, W. W., Retired

Sun City Center 33570
Myers, C. A., Retired

Sarasota 33577-33583
Bressler, R., Consulting
Schroeder, H. H., Arbitration
See, K. M., Bus-Industrial Relations

Tampa 33601-33630
Bowers, P. A., Hillsborough County
Cohen, C. F., Univ of South Florida
Fleischmann, R. A., US Postal Service
Henderson, R. D., Academic
Hogue, J. C., Florida Steel Corp
Sheppard, H. L., Univ of South Florida
Singletary, C. R., Singletary & Singletary
Wright, G. W., The Tribune Co

St. Petersburg 33702-33715
Peckham, J. D., Student
Portner, D. A., Retired
Vause, W. G., Academic

North Fort Meyers 33903
Adams, L. P., Retired

Punta Gorda 33950
Pullen, R. W., Retired

GEORGIA

Decatur 30030
Anderson, W. G., Arbitrator
Shuster, F. B., Attorney
Statham, C. G., Attorney

Marietta 30062-30063
Akins, J. R. Jr., Lockheed
Vasa-Sideris, S., Student

Norcross 30092-30093
Dennison, C. E., Research
Lawson, G. M., Student

Woodstock 30188
Bradford, W. S., Federal Mediator

Newnan 30264
Petty, R. D. Sr., William L. Bonnell Co

Atlanta 30301-30335
(includes College Park & Dunwoody)
Adoma, O. J., St. Regis Corp
Barnes, J. B., Southern Bell Center
Blalock, M. L., Bus: Industrial Rels
Blicksilver, J., Georgia State Univ
Byars, L. L., Academic
Cavanaugh, V. A., Swift, Currie, BcGhee & Hiers
Chiappetta, C. L., Coca Cola Company
Conti, A. J., Student
Crane, D. P., Georgia State Univ
Crawford, J. F., Academic
Dallas, S. F., Arbitration
Deloor, R. M., Government
Down, R. J., Lockheed-Georgia
Edwards, C.A., Greene, Buckley et al
English, L. H., Student
Green, W. F., Zep Manufacturing Co
Hawkins, J. M., Arbitrator
Horton, L. L., Gold Kist Co
Hubbard, D. A., Student
Jedel, M. J., Georgia State Univ
Jones, H. D. Jr., Arbitration
Kaufman, B. E., Georgia State Univ
King, G. S., Academic
LaPorte, P. A., Georgia State Univ
MacLachlan, G. E., Clark College
Mather, E. B., Constangy, Brooks & Smith
Meers, R. M., Printing Specialities
Mehl, D. K., Pizza Hut Inc
Miner, J. B., Georgia State Univ
Moore, G. L., Oglethorpe Power Corp
Raudabaugh, J. N., Powell, Goldstein et al
Reynolds, J.C. ATU Local 732
Rimer, J. T., Arbitration
Roberts, G. C., Arbitration
Rutherford, W. T., Georgia State Univ
Schaffer, B. K., Emory University
Schmidman, J. T., Georgia State Univ
Sloan, S., Hay Assoc
Stephan, P. E., Georgia State Univ
Williams, J. E., Arbitration

Yancy, D. C., Georgia Inst of Technology

Athens 30602
Beadles, N. A., Univ of Georgia
Scarpello, V., Univ of Georgia
White, R. A., Univ of Georgia

Macon 31202-31207
Richards, E. H., Mercer University
Rutledge, I. C., Mercer University
Stephenson, J. R., Charter Medical Corp

Savannah 31402
Carter, J. N., Union Camp Corp
Campbell, J. Jr., Savannah State College

St. Simons Island 31522
Meyers, F.

Albany 31708
Ritt, D. O., Miller Brewing Co

HAWAII

Ewa Beach 96706
Corley, S., Reynolds Metal Co

Hilo 96720
Marutani, H. K., Univ of Hawaii

Lanai 96763
Oliva, H., Dole Company

Honolulu 96801-96850
Alicen, B., UHPA
Armitage, G. Nelson, UHPA
Damon, C. F. Jr., Damon, Ley Char & Bocken
Fleischmann, F. L., Alexander & Baldwin
Gilson, T. Q., Arbitration
Graber, N. R., Hawaiian Telephone
Hamai, A. T., AFSCME
Hashimoto, R., Sheraton Hawaii Corp
Hee, H. S. Y., C. Brewer & Co Ltd
Hirozawa, B. F., HI Employers Council
Hutter, D. E., Chaminade Univ
Ito, C. S., Times Super Market Ltd
Janicki, N. K. Jr., Laborers Union #368
Kakazu, C. K., Kobayshi, Watanabe et al
Kardash, J. D., UHPA
Kennedy, F. Jr., Hawaii Fire Fighters Assn
Kenny, R. A., Bob Kenny & Assoc
Kruse, R., Hawaii Newspaper Guild
Kuromoto, P. K., Dillingham Maritime
Leong, R. Y. K., Kobayashi, Watanabe et al
Moore, E. C. III, Torkildson et al
Musto, J. N., UHPA
Najita, J. M., Univ of Hawaii
Naylon, J. A., Servco Pacific Inc
Oliveira, M., Kapiolani/Child Med Ctr
Parnell, E. J., NLRB
Peltier, J. W. Jr., Interisland Resorts
Pendleton, E. C., Retired
Radcliffe, J. H., Hawaii Teachers Assn
Ramos, E. T., Univ of Hawaii
Scavuzzo, R. T., Theo H. Davies & Co
Stern, B. W., Consulting
Tam, R., Hotel/Restaurant Empl Union
Trask, T., ILWU
Wago, S. F., Hyatt Regency Waikiki
Winegar, C., Kobayshi, Watanabe et al
Wineriter, G., FMCS

IDAHO

Pocatello 83201
Watson, J. P., J. R. Simplot

Idaho Falls 83402
Reed, J. E., Arbitration

Boise 83707
Roderick, R. D., Boise State Univ

Sandpoint 83864
Thayer, R. I., Retired

ILLINOIS

Arlington Heights 60004-60005
Dubay, C. M., Bus-Industrial Relations
Hetrick, J. L., Brunswick Corp
Lowenstein, D. J., Bus-Industrial Relations
Lowenstein, H., Academic

Elk Grove 60007
Balanoff, T., UCLGAW

Rolling Meadows 60008
Foissotte, C. M., Student
Gillis, M. J., Spotnails

Barrington 60010
Sharpe, M. J., M. J. Sharpe & Assoc

Bannockburn 60015
Kennedy, R. W., Modern Management Co

Des Plaines 60016-60018
Cripe, L. E., UOP Inc
Karowski, C. S., Student
Treaseh, R. L., XEEP

Libertyville 60048
Haebig, R. C., Intl Hough/Dresser Industries

Morton Grove 60053
Malinowski, A. A., Loyola Univ

Mt. Prospect 60056
Stout, L. A., AFL-CIO Great Lakes Council

Skokie 60076-60077
Hartstein, R. E., Brunswick Corp
Kawakami, S. S., Bus-Personnel
Rappaport, C. M., Jewish Vocational Service
Skyer, B. S., Student

Buffalo Grove 60090
Goldberg, F., Academic

Wilmette 60091
Nathanson, L., Consulting
O'Reilly, A. B., Student

Winnetka 60093
Wirpel, E. M.
Wirpel, S. W., Arbitration

DeKalb 60115
Hill, M. F., Northern Illinois Univ
Karim, A. R., Northern Illinois Univ
Kozlowski, R. J., Bus-Industrial Relations
Newman, T. E., Northern Illinois Univ

Elgin 60120
Elegreet, F. J., Chicago Rawhide Mfg Co

Elmhurst 60126
Hershey, M. L., Student

Glen Ellyn 60137
Corpora, A. J., Arbitration
Rezler, J., Retired
Rojek, B. J., Student, Loyola-Chicago

Westchester 60153
Burki, F. A., UFCW Local 881

St. Charles 60174
Lawrence, D. G., Bauer & Assoc
Salsburg, S. W., Bauer & Assoc

Schiller Park 60176
Dunn, W. S., Ground Round

Evanston 60201-60204
Alden, J. R., Packaging Corp of America
Bies, R. J., Northwestern Univ
Brett, J. M., Northwestern Univ
Cassell, F. H., Northwestern Univ
Cummings, L. L., Northwestern Univ
Dennis, B. H., Government
Dennis, L. E.
DiIorio, J. D.,House of Business Forms
Doerr, E. K.
Juris, H. A., Northwestern University
Kane, S., American Hosp Supply Corp
Larney, G. E., Labor Arbitrator
Neumann, G. R., Academic
Orr, A., Industrial Rels
Orr, L. B., Government
Oscadel, M. G., Bus-Personnel
Roomkin, M., Northwestern Univ
Smith, J. C., Student

Chicago Heights 60411
Soltes, C. Y., Government

Dwight 60420
Novak, H. L., Academic

Argonne 60439
Edmondson, J. J., US Dept of Energy

Bolingbrook 60439
Robinson, D. J., Student

Orland Park 60462
Boddy, D. C., Bus-Industrial Rels

Park Forest 60466
Lange, J. P., Illnois Central Gulf RR

Aurora 60505-60506
Felhauer, L. W., Student
Horvath, A., Student
Porter, T. B., Student

Oak Brook 60521
Fanning, M. S., Xerox Corp

Hinsdale 60521
Pettengill, M. M., Student

Naperville 60540-60565
(Includes Riverside 60546)
Beaty, J. W., USDL
Braun, T. M., Bus-Industrial Rels
Fina, P. J., Student
Wada, M. M., Academic

Chicago Area 60601-60699
Abowd, J. M., Univ of Chicago
Adams, J. S., Student
Annable, J. E. Jr., Economics
Arndt, C. C., Univ of Chicago
Asher, L., Asher, Pavalon, Gittler et al
Bjurman, G. L., Bus-Industrial Rels
Bhattacharya, P. K., Student
Booth, P. R., AFSCME, AFL-CIO
Bottorf, R. N., Student
Burrows, S. J., Retired
Caples, W. G., Vedder, Price, Kaufman & Kammholz
Christopher, M. K, Student
Cloney, J. C.
Cohen, M. A., Illinois Inst of Tech
Cook, A. J., Arbitration
Cooper, C. G., Loyola Law School
Cullerton, J. E., Hilton Hotels Corp
D'Alba, J. A., Asher Pavalon et al
Davidson, M. E., Student
Dess, S. A., Bus-Personnel
Dillon, W. A., Inland Steel Co
DiLorenzo, G., Government
Dobbelaere, A. G. Jr., Loyola Univ
Dolnick, D., Arbitrator
Drayer, W., Student
Duffy, C. D., USDL
Eckhardt, C. A., Student
Elkiss, H., Univ of Illinois
Fish, H., Arbitrator
Filgut, P. R., Student
Fredian, A. J., Loyola Univ
Friedman, B., Friedman & Assoc
Fromm, G. P., Interstate Service Corp
Frye, J. G., Economic Consultant
Fylypowycz, T., Professional Assn
Garcia, M. A. Illinois Nurses Assn
Glover, B. E.
Goldberg, S. B.,Northwestern Univ Law School
Golden, K. M., Student
Hale, J. A., Hale & Assoc
Harris, D. A., Student
Hebein, P. J., Bureau of Labor Statistics
Hellquist, J. K., US Postal Service
Herlihy, H. M., Retired
Higdon, R. B., Chicago Sun-Times
Hirsh, S. J.
Hodges, A. C., Attorney
Imberman, E. W., Imberman & Deforest Inc
Juenger, R., FMC Corp
Klass, I. E., Fed of Labor & Indus Council
Kleiman, B., Kleiman & Whitney PC
Kramer, R. E., Clipper Express Co
Kyrouac, R. C., Morton Thiokol Inc
Larkin, J. D., Arbitrator
La Van, H., De Paul University
Lonergan, W. G., Retired
Luskin, B. L., Attorney
Lyon, R. M., Seyfarth, Shaw et al
Mahoney, D. L., IBEW
Malin, M. H., Ill Inst of Tech
Maskin, N. H., Student
Mathys, N. J., De Paul Univ
McAllister, R. W., Attorney
McAuley, D. B., Interstate United Corp
McCarthy, R. J., Akzo Chemie America
McCafferty, J. K.,Illinois State Pers Dept
Meader, L. V., Schwinn Bicycle Co
Melas, N. J., Metro Sanitary Dist
Meltzer, B. D., Univ of Chicago
Moberg, D., In These Times
Moskow, M. H., Velsicol Chemical Corp
Nagatomo, L. M., Mayors Office Empl & Trng
O'Brien, F. D., Chicago Metro Sanitary Dist
Olson, J. E., Student
Oppenheimer, M. A., De Paul Univ
Ortiz, K., Government
Petersen, D. J., Loyola Univ
Pincus, S. R., Fox & Grove
Price, D. L., Student
Rader, J. S., Univ of Chicago
Rohrer, J., Kartemquin Films Ltd
Rolle, L., Amer Arbitration Assn
Rosen, S. D., Hartmax Corp
Rosen, S., Academic
Rosenberg, S., Roosevelt Univ
Rothenberg, M. R., Attorney
Sanders, K. M., Interstate United
Scannell, R. M., Construction Emplrs ASSA
Schwartz, A. D., Robbins, Schwartz et al
Selby, M. E., Consulting
Stallworth, L. E., Academic
Sullivan, J. F., Sullivan Group Inc
Sullivan, K. A., Student
Suntrup, E. L., Univ of Illinois
Terepin, L. K., Student
Thompson, S. L., Student

Varga, P. V., Natl Railroad Adjustment Board
Wesse, D. J., Northwestern University
Winton, J. B., Arbitrator

Rockford 61125
Smith, M. R., Sundstrand Corp

Moline 61265
Davis, J. D., Deere & Company

Macomb 61455
O'Brien, F. P., Western Illinois Univ

Morton 61550
Stevens, D. W., Bus-Industrial Rels

Peoria 61601
Chester, R. W., NLRB
Sleister, M. K., NLRB
Symkowiak, R. J., NLRB
Zipp, G. A., NLRB

Normal 61761
Dillingham, A. E., Illinois State Univ
Mohr, C. L., Illinois State Univ

Urbana 61801
Beller, A. H., Univ of Illinois
Gore, C. J., Student
Hanson, G. A., Student
Nelson, P. K., Student

Champaign 61820-61821
Anderson, C. S., Student
Bartter, N. E., Student
Blau, F. D., Univ of Illinois
Cappelli, P. H., Univ of Illinois
Craver, C. B., Univ of Illinois
Day, D. R., Univ of Illinois
Derber, M., Univ of Illinois
Erickson, H., Univ of Illinois
Feuille, P., Univ of Illinois
Fiedler, S., Student
Foley, M. C., Student
Franke, W. H., Univ of Illinois
Harris, T. A., Student
Hendricks, W., Univ of Illinois
Hubert, B. L, Student
Kahn, L. M., Univ of Illinois
Karsh, B., Univ of Illinois
Kroul, R., Student
Koutouzos, G. D., Student
Lawler, J. J., Univ of Illinois
Lyons, S. L., Student
McPherson, W. H., Univ of Illinois
Morishima, M., Student
Nicolai, D. A., Student
Peters, R. J., Univ of Illinois
Pigage, L. C., Retired
Puccini, N. A., Student
Rothbaum, M., Univ of Illinois
Schwochau, S. G., Student
Shalley, C. E., Student
Siengthai, S., Student
Smith, R. E., Student
Steward, P. R., Univ of Illinois
Sturmthal, A. F., Retired
Taira, K., Univ of Illinois
Thorna, S. L., Student
Wagner, M., Univ of Illinois
West, R. K., Student
Zeytinoglu, I. F., Student

Charleston 61920
Lenihan, P. M., Eastern Illinois Univ
Zimarowski, J. B., Eastern Illinois Univ

Alton 62002
Koch, D. H., Unemployment Insurance

East Alton 62024
Bartareau, E., Olin Corp

Edwardsville 62026
Franke, A., Southern Illinois Univ

Granite City 62040
Stevenson, T. M., Academic

Decatur 62526
Ryan, S. M.

Springfield 62701-62708
Draznin, A. L., Sangamon State Univ
Edstrom, T. J., Union
Erenburg, M. E., Sangamon State Univ
Johnston, D. R., Hospital Sisters System
Porter, R. G., Bus-Management
Vallone, P. D., State of Illinois

Carbondale 62901
Edelman, M. T., Southern Illinois Univ
Gutteridge, T. G., Southern Illinois Univ
Mandrell, R. R., Bus-Industrial Relations

INDIANA

Zionsville 46077
Lefebvre, L. H., Student

Indianapolis 46208-46268
Bonifield, W. C., Butler Univ
Fisher, P. J., Arbitrator
Seidman, M. J., Arbitrator

Michigan City 46360
Brady, T. F., Purdue Univ-N. Central

Valparaiso 46383
Kersten, E.A., Union
Schlender, W. E., Valparaiso Univ

Gary 46408
Barnum, D. T., Indiana Univ Northwest

Elkhart 46514
Neidorff, M. F., Miles Laboratories Inc

Notre Dame 46556
Fitzgerald, M. F., Retired
Ghilarducci, T., Univ of Notre Dame
Latino, M. T., Student
Leahy, W. H., Univ of Notre Dame
Reardon, J. E., Student

South Bend 46617
Bella, S. J., Univ of Notre Dame
Knauss, K. D., Academic

Ft. Wayne 46804-46805-46864
Allison, J. M., Labor Relations
Hill, R. E., Indiana Univ
Sherr, M. A., Attorney
Swinehart, D. P., Purdue Univ
Taylor, J. C., North American Van Lines

Kokomo 46901-46902
Amba-Rao, S. C., Indiana U at Kokomo
McCormack, J. H., Penn Dixie Corp
Sparks, J. K., Student

Columbus 47201-47203
Norton, D. J., Bus-Management
Paul, K. M., Bus-Industrial Rels

Muncie 47302-47306
Deitsch, C., Ball State Univ
Seeborg, M. C., Ball State Univ

Bloomington 47401-47405
Cobb, J. J., Kendall Company
Hayford, S. L., Indiana Univ
Novit, M. S., Indiana Univ
Saunders, W. P. Jr., Indiana Univ
Sorcinelli, E. G., Indiana Univ
Spencer, D. C., Indiana Univ
Willett, T., Otis Elevator
Witney, F., Indiana Univ

Booneville 47601
Cooksey, J. P., Amax Coal Company

Evansville 47715
Lodato, M. J., Bus-Management

Terre Haute 47802-47809
Azar, E. R., Student
Conant, J. L., Indiana State Univ
King, C. D., Indiana State Univ
Kyle, J. T., Indiana State Univ

West Lafayette 47906-47907
Berger, C. J., Purdue Univ
Doering, B. W., Arbitrator
Dworkin, J. B., Purdue Univ
Helmreich, T. C., Retired
Lengnick-Hall, M. L., Student
Lillich, J. E., Purdue Univ
Motsepe, O. W. E., Purdue Univ
Rayman, D. M., Student
Ross, M. E., Student
Wolkoff, R. L., Student
Woodham, B. A., Student

IOWA

Ames 50010-50011
Chacko, T. I., Iowa State Univ
Matilla, J. P., Iowa State Univ
Smith, C. E., Iowa State Univ

Boone 50036
Thede, K. A., Government

West Des Moines 50265
Wiant, R. H. II, Academic

Des Moines 50311-50314
Grosland, D. A., Iowa State Educ Assn
Kleywegt, C. J., Des Moines Comm College
Rose, M. L., Academic
Unger, W. R., Iowa State Educ Assn

Decorah 52101
Root, K., Luther College

Iowa City 52240-52242
Blaser, A. C., Student
Camp, S. L., Student
Carlson, T. E., Student
Carnevale, C. M., Student
Donnelly, J. T., Academic
Fiorito, J. T., Univ of Iowa
Gallagher, D. G., Univ of Iowa
Gramm, C. L., Univ of Iowa
Hayworth, K. J., Student
Kaupins, G. E., Student
Kirsch, C. J., Student
Lake, A. L., Student
Maranto, C. L., Univ of Iowa
Nadler, C. H., Student
Pegnetter, R. C., Univ of Iowa
Segalla, M., Student
Sinicropi, A. V., Univ of Iowa
West, J. P., Univ of Iowa

Solon 52333
Spellman, W. E., Academic

Toddville 52341
Bergstrom, R. B. Sr., FMCS

West Branch 52358
Wolfe, K. J., Academic

New London 52645
Grove, R. L., Geode Education Assn

Clinton 52732
White, L. F., The Clinton Herald

Wilton 52778
Rhode, D. M., Student

Davenport 52803-52804
Buckley, L. F., Retired
Rembold, C. J., Mississippi Bend Uniserv

KANSAS

Lawrence 66044-66045
Baderschneider, J. A., Univ of Kansas
Cunningham, E. P., Quaker Oats Co
Goetz, R., Univ of Kansas
Johnson, N. B., Student
Kleiner, M. M., Univ of Kansas
Krider, C. E., Univ of Kansas
Petree, D. L., Student
Redwood, A. L., Univ of Kansas
Shulenburger, D. E., Univ of Kansas
Walker, K. F., Univ of Kansas

Kansas City 66101-66115
Stapp, M., Blake & Uhlig
Weber, R. S., Certaineed Corp

Shawnee Mission 66202
Brown, M., Strategic Mgmt Services Inc

Fairway 66205
Richardson, G., Union

Overland Park 66207-66215
Hendrix, T. C., NLRB
Kuhl, W. O., Union
Thaker, H. H., Arbitration

Manhattan 66502-66506
Dilts, D. A., Kansas State Univ
Ragan, J., Kansas State Univ

Newton 67114
Simpson, K. F. Jr., Retired

Wichita 67208
Perline, M. M., Wichita State Univ

Coffeyville 67337
Levy, J. L., Attorney

Hays 67601
Parker, C. D., Fort Hays State Univ

KENTUCKY

Louisville
Beckman, D. L., Arbitrator
Donald, C. G., Academic
Greenberg, R., Jewish Hospital
Mead, J. F., Univ of Louisville
Miller, W. G., Williamson Tobacco Corp
Moberly, G. L.
Pelhan, R. E., Arbitrator
Rhodes, G. B., Univ of Louisville
Warns, M. K., Warns & Warns

Richmond 40475
Figler, R. A., Eastern Kentucky Univ

Lexington 40502-40511
Cabe, C., Arbitration
Christian, V. L. Jr., Univ of Kentucky
Fay, C. H., Univ of Kentucky
Goldman, A. L., Academic
Krislov, J., Univ of Kentucky
Rosst, W. A., Wabco Fluid Power

Frankfort 40601
Ridgel, G. T., Kentucky State Univ

Villa Hills 41017
Baker, H. E., Student
Menez, J. R., Government

Highland Heights 41076
Barrett, J. T., Northern Kentucky Univ

Ledbetter 42058
Doom, G. P., Bus-Industrial Rels

Murray 42071
Williams, R. C., Academic

Bowling Green 42101
Ayres, R. C., Academic
Evans, E. M., Western Kentucky Univ
Reber, R. A., Western Kentucky Univ

Lewis Port 42351
Smith, R. E. Jr., Labor Relations

LOUISIANA

Metairie 70005
Taylor, R. B., Arbitrator

Gretna 70053
Kaufman, A. T., Bus-Industrial Rels

New Orleans 70112-70118
Anderson, C. J., Loyola Univ
Barron, P., Tulane Law School
Israel, D., Attorney
Moore, M. F., Attorney
Roman, P. M., Tulane Univ
Villere, M. F., Univ of New Orleans

Lafayette 70504
Brannen, D. E., Academic
McLauchlan, J. M., Univ of SW Louisiana

Baton Rouge 70808
Jones, L. B., Louisiana State Univ
Shieber, B. M., Louisiana State Univ

Monroe 71209
Bethke, A. L, Northeast Louisiana Univ
Thomas, W. L., Northeast Louisiana Univ

MAINE

Biddeford 04005
Magdon, M. S., Abritration

Scarborough 04074
Rosenblatt, A. Z., Labor Negotiator

Augusta 04333
Denaco, P. A., Maine Labor Rels Board

Orono 04469
Devino, W. S., Univ of Maine

MARYLAND

Accokeck 20607
Devereux, G. D., Union

Brandywine 20613
Tanner, L. D., Labor Economist

Lusby 20657
Smith, O. S., Retired

Lanham 20706
Keir, J. B., Government

Laurel 20708
Balog, J. Jr., USDL

College Park 20742
Knight, R. E., Univ of Maryland
Levine, M. J., Univ of Maryland
Palomba, C. A., Univ of Maryland
Palomba, N. A., Univ of Maryland
Weinstein, P.A., Univ of Maryland

Greenbelt 20770
Jascourt, H. D., Attorney
Strasser, A., Government

University Park 20782
Fisher, S. T., Government

Adelphi 20783
Moffett, K. E.

Chevy Chase 20815
Brandwein, E.
Brandwein, S., USDL
Fibish, N. C., Government
Fisher, P., Retired
Glazer, J., Union
Glazer, M., Government
Harvey, S. B., Bus-Management
Lyle, J. R., Emergency Mgmt Agency
Minamoto, J. N., Union
Seibel, L. E., Arbitrator
Sprehe, J. T., Government

Bethesda 20816-20817
Behr, A., Government
Brumm, J. M., Retired
Cantfil, A. F., Retired
Deutermann, C., US Office of Education
Deutermann, W. V. Jr., USDL
Feldman, L., Government
Gale, E. R., Union
Goldstein, H., Consulting
Holiber, C. L., Government
Kranz, H., Retired
MacKenzie, H. R., Government
MacKenzie, J. R., Univ of DC
Marcou, R. A., US Office-Pers Mgmt
Mirengoff, W., Retired
Morton, H. C., Government
Prouty, E. K., Government
Rosen, H., Consulting
Ruttenberg, S. H., Ruttenberg & Assoc
Stein, J. C., Retired
Stewart, C. D., Academic
Valoris, B. W., Martin Marietta Corp
Weinberg, E., Consulting
Weinberg, N., Retired
Weinstein, H. G., Government
Weisz, M., Retired
Wilhelm, J. A., Attorney
Winkler, R.
Wool, H., Retired
Wool, M. B.

Rockville 20850-20853
Greenberg, L., Retired
Jaffe, I. F., Arbitration
Lee, E., Academic
Milke, T., Westat Research
Staller, J. M., Consulting

Potomac 20854
Bauman, A., Bureau of Labor Statistics
Goldberg, I., C & G Assoc
Hacker, R. B., Arbitration
Sheifer, V. J., Government

Upper Marlboro 20870
Burkhardt, F. X., IBPAT

Gaithersburg 20879
Buchen, J. F., Government
DeFrehn, R. G., UMWA

Kensington 20895
Cohany, H. P., Government

Silver Spring 20901-20910
Albriton, J. W., Student
Allen, R. W., Academic
Bloch, J. W., Retired
Brophy, J. A., George Meany Center Labor Study
Cantor, A. B., AFL-CIO
Coyne, S. E., Student
Cushman, B., Arbitrator
Farber, D. J., Consulting Economist
Farber, E. W., USDL
Feigenbaum, C., Arbitration
Gayer, P. D., OEO
Goldberg, J. P., Bureau of Labor Statistics
Gottlieb, B., Arbitration
Hoexter, E. G., PBGC
Jacob, N., Government
Johnson, M. E., Mediation
Keefe, J. H., CWA Local 2108
Kolodrubetz, W. W., USDL
Kuptzin, H., Government
Lunden, L. E., USDL
Mark, J. A., USDL
Newman, J. B., Consulting
Onanian, E. D., USDL
Reesman, C. J., Westat Inc
Siegenthaler, J. K., Academic
Siegenthaler, L. A., Government
Smedley, L. T., AFL-CIO
Soffer, B., Retired
Spangler, T. J., Union
Wakin, T., Government.

Takoma Park 20912
Murphy, K. R., AFSCME

Ellicott City 21043
Eakle, W. E., Howard County

Columbia 21045
Ahmuty, A. L., Government
Seldin, G. J., Arbitrator/Mediator
Wisniewski, S. C., Attorney

Glen Burnie 21061
Venick, C., Student

Lutherville 21093
Smith, J. A., Attorney

Millersville 21108
Blake, C. A., Government

Crofton 21114
Lombardo, D. D., Government

Baltimore 21201-21237
Berkeley, A. E., Academic
Decenzo, D. A., Univ of Baltimore
Carmel, A. S., Academic
Favor, L. F., Moldcraft
Feeney, D. J., Bendix Corp
Green, D. H., Social Security Admin
Lando, M. E., Social Security Admin
Marcus, L., Sinai Hospital
Pryor, G. T., Sinai Hospital
Rothstein, W. G., Univ of Maryland
Schramm, C. J., Academic
Singer, P., Union
Weinstein, H. G., ARMCO Inc

Hagerstown 21740
Hankinson, D. W., Bus-Industrial Relations

Smithsburg 21783
Spring, E. H., Government
Spring, H. C., Government

Walkersville 21793
Preston, V. K., MSTA/NEA

Salisbury 21801
Gallagher, D. J., Salisbury State College

MASSACHUSETTS

Amherst 01002-01003
Blackman, J. L. Jr., Retired
Bornstein, T. L., Univ of Massachusetts
Brock, P. E., Student
Conlon, J. T., Univ of Massachusetts
Friedman, H. L., Univ of Massachusetts
Podgursky, M. J., Univ of Massachusetts
Sulzner, G. T., Univ of Massachusetts
Tausky, C., Univ of Massachusetts

Holyoke 01041
Sheridan, P. J., Sheridan & Assoc

Leverett 01054
Barkin, S., Retired

Northampton 01060
Funck, C., Student

Springfield 01101-01103
Garvey, J. J., Arbitration
Jensen, R. R., Union

Pittsfield 01201
Feigenbaum, A. V., General Systems Inc

Shrewsbury 01545
Sherer, P. D., Student

Worchester 01610
Chaison, G. N., Clark Univ
Judge, J. J., Holy Cross College

Framingham 01701
Higgins, T. J., Bus-Personnel
Pigors, P., Retired

Acton 01720
Schnipke, G. C.

Ashland 01721
Rallis, J. J., Retired

Concord 01742
Bloom, E. J. Jr., Consulting

Burlington 01803
Farrell, R. A., Mass Hospital Assn

Chelmsford 01824
Ames, M., Attorney
Cederlund, A. M., Univ of Lowell

Rocha, J. R. Jr., Academic
Woodhouse, R. J., Tau Tron

Reading 01867
Castellano, J. J., Suffolk Univ

Wilmington 01887
Paulson, G. D., Compugraphia Corp

Lynn 01910
Rideout, M. P., GE Co Aircraft Engine

Beverly 01915
Murphy, J. M., N Shore Commuity College

Essex 01929
Greenbaum, M. L., Labor/Arbitrator

Canton 02021
Riedell, G. D., Bus-Personnel

Foxboro 02035
Santer, M., Arbitrator

Hingham 02043
Shaw, K., Kimball Shaw Assoc

Marshfield 02050
Madden, J. V., Academic
McCarthy, P. F., Collective Bargaining Assoc

North Marshfield 02059
Rubenstein, J. S., Arbitration

Boston-Cambridge Area 02101-02215
Abraham, K. G., MIT
Alexander, J., Babson College
Allison, E. K., Data Resource Inc
Austin, D. G., Raytheon Company
Barocci, T. A., MIT
Barr, S. W., Kendall Co
Barres, S. L., Retired
Barry, J. C., Arbitration
Bazerman, M. H., MIT
Berry, D. J., Arbitrator
Bloom, D. E., Harvard University
Bloom, G. F., Attorney
Bloom, S., Student, Harvard
Boyle, E. F., Archdiocese of Boston
Brown, D. V., MIT
Brown, S. R., Arbitrator
Butler, J. B., Consulting
Carpenter, G. E. Jr., MA Labor Council
Cohane, J. J., Eastern Gas & Fuel Assn
Coleman, R. W., Segal, Roitman & Coleman
Cooke, J. R., Union
Cooper, M. R., Student
Dadalt, A. M., MA Labor Relations Comm
Devol, K. R.
Doeringer, P. B., Boston Univ
Dunlop, J. T., Harvard University
Elbaum, B. L., Boston University
Every, A., Boston Globe Empls Assn
Ewing, D. W., Harvard Business Review
Faherty, J.C.,Boston Edison Clerical Wrks Union
Fallon, W. J., Arbitrator
Farber, H. S., MIT
Flamm, A. J., Flamm & Birmingham
Fletcher, L. J., Consultant
Foulkes, F. K., Boston University
Frank, M. W., CPCS
Gant, J., Univ of Massachusetts
Gavin, M. H., Retired
Gherson, D. J., Student, MIT
Gilman, T. A., Harvard
Glidden, P. A., Univ of Massachusetts
Goldfield, M. H., Student
Gwiazda, S. B., Arbitration
Hardiman, K. P., Boston Gas Co
Harpaz, I., Boston College
Hausman, L. J., Brandeis University
Healy, J. J., Harvard University
Herrnstadt, I. L., Northeastern University
Higgins, J. E., Arbitrator
Hobart, C. L., Northeastern University
Horowitz, M. A., Northeastern University
Ichniowski, B. E., Student, MIT
Johnson, H. W., MIT
Jones, R. T., Arbitrator
Joy, W. F., Morgan, Brown, Kearns & Joy
Kane, E. L., Raytheon Company
Katz, H. C., MIT
Kaufman, F. G., Attorney
Keating, S. P., Student
Kelley, M. R., Academic
Kennedy, T. M., Babson College
Kenney, T. F., Boston Gas Co
Klein, J. A., Harvard University
Kochan, T. A., MIT
Kohler, T. C., Academic
Kolb, D. M., MIT
Kuechle, D., Harvard University
Lanigan, J. J., Student, Brandeis Univ
Lawrence, P. R., Harvard University
Lerbinger, O., Boston University
Levensaler, W. L., University Hospital
Livernash, E. R., Academic
Lubell, S. K., Union
McDonald, J. M.,Union
McKersie, R. B., MIT
McLaughlin, C. G., Tufts University
McLaughlin, F. M., Boston College
Medoff, J. L., Harvard University
Merlo, T. C. Jr., Bus-Management
Meyer, R. F., Mass Port Authority
Menard, A. P., Morgan, Brown & Joy
Mills, D. Q., Harvard University
Mulkern, P. V., Retired
Nitta, M., MIT
O'Brien, R. A., Academic
O'Brien, R. M., Arbitrator
O'Donnel, J. P., Trade Union Program
O'Donnell, T. L. P., Ropes & Gray
Osterman, R. S., Boston University
Peace, N. E.
Petralia, J., Boston Health/Hospitals
Pinkus, E. C., Arbitrator
Powers, E. W., Harvard University
Raelin, J. A., Boston College
Reilly, R. M., Amer Arbitration Assn
Role, T., Arbitrator
Roth, J. A., Student
Roitman, H. B., Segal, Roitman & Coleman
Segal, R. M., Segal, Roitman & Coleman
Shea, G. R., Mass Teachers Assn
Siegel, A. J., MIT
Sirutis, D., Government
Smith, N. F., John Hancock Insurance
Sonnenfeld, J. A., Harvard University
Sparrow, D. G., Wheaton College
Stein, B. A., Consulting
Stewart, J. P., Academic
Sullivan, E. T., Building Service Local 254
Tepper, A. A., Snyder, Tepper, Berlin & Katz
Vaughn, W. M., Stop & Shop Companies
Waldron, W. A., Retired
Wallace, P. A., MIT
Way, P. K., Student
Webb, R. L., Boston Gas Co
Weil, D., Student
Wever, K. R., Student
White, D. J., Boston College
Wolozin, H., Univ of Massachusetts
Woods, L. E., Northeastern University
Zack, A. M., Arbitrator

Waltham 02254
Evans, R. Jr., Brandeis University
Saltzman, G. M., Brandeis University

Avon 02322
McDonnell, F. S. Jr., Arbitrator

North Easton 02356
Burtt, E. J. Jr., Retired

Randolph 02368
Burgess, B. S., Mass Teachers Assn

Brockton 02403
Rizzo, J. M., Foxmoor

West Tisbury 02575
Weiss, H., Retired

Norton 02766
Kahne, H., Wheaton College

Raynham 02767
Burbine, H. W., Mass Teachers Assn

MICHIGAN

Birmingham 48008-48011
Abrams, N. D., Attorney
Krebs, L., Bus-Industrial Rels
Mittenthal, R., Arbitrator
Pollard, D. R., Clark, Hardy, Lewis & Pollard
Siegal, B., Attorney
Smith, B. J., Police Labor Council
Vecellio, D. M., Economics

Bloomfield Hills 48013
Buratto, R. J., Matheson, Bieneman, Parr et al
Knott, I., Academic
Schinella, M. R., Labor Relations
Wallisky, T. J., ITT Automotive Products

Center Line 48015
De Morris, R. S., Aetna Industries Inc
Pierce, D., Aetna Industries Inc

Clawson 48017
Paul, M. M., Student

Farmington Hills 48018
Austermiller, C. J., Academic

Farmington Heights 48018
Rowe, R. H., Attorney

East Detroit 48021
Hall, M. K., Bus-Industrial Rels

Farmington 48024
Benjamin, E., Academic

Franklin 48025
Saltzman, A. W., Consultant

Southfield 48034
Maurer, A. H., Union

Lake Orion 48035
Gannon, F. A., Frank A Gannon & Assoc
Griggs, H. S., Consulting

Novi 48050
Wykert, T. R., Union

Pontiac 48053
Kristall, W. P., Office of Friend of the Court

Rochester 48063
Barclay, L. A., Oakland University
Carillon, J. W., Parke-Davis
Coyle, J. B., Arbitrator
Lyons, D., Oakland University

Royal Oak 48070-48073
Chester, H. L., Retired
Faumann, S. J., Academic

Southfield 48075-48076
Alexander, G. N., Arbitrator
Beitner, E. I., Attorney
Brams, S. H., Intermedia Group Inc
Hansen, J. F., Labor Trends
Juliano, J. M.
Kahn, R., Arbitration
Kanner, R. L., Arbitrator
Magenau, J. M.III, Wayne State Univ
Martin, J. E., Wayne State Univ
Petrack, M. J., Industrial Relations
Platt, H. H., Arbitration
Rosenbaum, E., Academic
Walt, A.,Arbitration
Wax, H. I., Levin, Levin, Garvett & Dill
Wright, S. E., Student

Sterling Heights 48077
Lawrence, D. S., Business

Troy-Warren 48082-48098
Andren, M. D., Student
Clinton, D. J., Bundy Tubing
Comerford, J. K, Ameritech Publishing Co
MacQueen, W. J., Macomb County Comm College
Pizzurro, R. D., Labor Relations

Allen Park 48101
Giebel, R. E., Labor Relations

Ann Arbor 48103-48109
Boonin, R. A., Student
Cohen, M. S., Univ of Michigan
Cooke, W. N., Univ of Michigan
Dodd, R. A., American Motors Corp
Dolin-Greene, C., Univ of Michigan
Ferman, L. A., Univ of Mich
Goldman, E., Ann Arbor Public Schools
Gordus, J. P., Univ of Michigan
Haber, W., Retired
Hirshorn, B., SIH Inc
Jacobs, D. C., Univ of Mich
Jones, D. L., Univ of Michigan
Kerner, B. A., Government
Levinson, H. M., Univ of Michigan
McLaughlin, D. B., Univ of Michigan
McAlinden, S. P., Academic Research
Miller, E. L., Univ of Michigan
Montgomery, B. R., Student
Radine, L. B., Univ of Michigan
Root, L. S., Univ of Michigan
Schwartz, A. R., Univ of Michigan
Snow-Godfrey, J., Student
St.Antoine, T. J., Univ of Michigan
Widick, B. J., Academic

Chelsea 48118
Schwartz, G. W., United Auto Workers

Dearborn 48121-48128
Banas, P. A., Ford Motor Co
Chiesa, M., Arbitrator
Clark, R. W., Ford Motor Co
Crowell, E., Univ of Mich-Dearborn
Green, G. W., General Motors Corp
Klein, B., Univ of Mich-Dearborn
McCloskey, M. M., Union
Poore, K. E., Ford Motor Co
Schwartz, G. W., United Auto Workers

Garden City 48135
Stokes, M. L., Teamsters Local 243

Grosse Ile 48138
Kadau, G. S., Bus-Industrial Relations
Lewis, D. J., Arbitration

Livonia 48150-48154
Breitenbeck, J. T., Bus-Personnel
Kowalczyk, R. S., Union
Shemke, R. A., Attorney/Arbitrator

Plymouth 48170
Amar, J. C., Government
Blake, W. E., Ford Motor Co Steel Div
Theeke, H. A., Academic

Romulus 48174
Bachman, A., Federal-Mogul Copr

Trenton 48183
McNichols, J. F., Monsanto Co

Westland 48185
Monet, S. A., Student

Canton 48187
Clayton, S. L.

Southgate 48195
Dittmer, R. A., Union

Ypsilanti 48197
Andrews, F. W., Eastern Mich Univ
Greene, J. P., Eastern Mich Univ
Huszco, G. E., Eastern Mich Univ
Pearson, D. W., Eastern Mich Univ

Detroit 48202-48288
Angell, H. T., Angell, Wolney & Lech
Antczak, K., Hutzel Hospital
Bedikian, M., Amer Arbitration Assn
Berry, E., Government
Botan, C. H., Student
Bouknight, B. E., Government
Boyd, I. R., Alexander & Alexander
Brown, P. H., Student
Brown, R. C., Federal Mogul Corp
Cheek, R. N., Detroit Police Dept
Cordtz, SEIU Local 79
Curry, C. A., Student
Cushman, E. L., Wayne State Univ
Dansby, E. R., Arbitration
Deeds, R. E. Jr., General Motors Corp
Dempsey, J. R. SJ, Univ of Detroit
Denise, M. L., Retired
Dobry, S. T., Arbitrator
Dussey, C. J., Chrysler Corp
Eggemeyer, G. A., Riley & Roumell
Fillion, J. A., UAW
Firestone, B. J., Union
Fischer, L. H., Intl Union UAW
Florkey, E. M., Bus-Industrial Rels
Forsythe, E. J., Wayne State Univ
Fremont, J. W., City of Detroit
Gregory, G. A., Gregory, VanLopik, Moore & Jeakle
Gresock, N. F., Blue Cross Blue Shield-Mich
Griffin, E. E., Stone Container Corp
Grzywacz, R. A., City of Detroit
Hartifield, E. F., FMCS
Heinen, M. L., Attorney
Hildebrandt, A., Attorney
Kahn, M. L., Wayne State Univ
Kales, R. G., Kales Kramer Invest Co
Knox, R. E., Teamsters Local 1038
Kresin, G. L., Stroh Brewery
Kretschmar, F., Information Service Inc
Lagerquist, W. W., Wyatt Co
Long, L. H., Federal Mogul Corp
McCutcheon, A. V. Jr., McCutcheon Assoc Inc
Milmet, M., Stern, Milmet, Vecchio & Goll
Mishel, L. R., UAW
Noune, M. A., City of Detroit
Nowakowski, M. G., FMCS
Perry, J. B., Abbott, Nicholson et al
Porter, K. E., OPEIU
Porter, K. B., Employers Assoc Detroit
Rothrock, C. D., Metropolitan Hosp
Runyan, J. R. Jr., Marston, Sachs, Nunn et al
Sachs, T., Sachs, Nunn, Kates et al
Salton, R. F., Mich Bell Telephone
Savoie, E. J., Ford Motor Co
Sawka, J. R., Michigan Bell Telephone
Saxton, W. M., Butzel, Long, Gust et al
Schemanske, J. M., Student
Schiller, S. R., Student
Smith, J. R., Bormans Inc
Sperka, S.,Mich Employment Rels Comm
Sterling, W. P., General Motors Corp
Summerlott, P. N., Mich State Empl Assn
Tanzman, D. S., FMCS
Trupiano, J., BCBSM
Viane, N. K., Student
Watroba, D. R., Detroit Police Officers
Whiting, B. J. Jr., Professional Assn
Wood, D. P., Clark, Klein & Beaumont

Flushing 48433
Deane, R. G., GM Institute

Grand Blanc 48439
Neale, W. S., Academic
Ricker, E. D., PLRS

Flint 48501-48503
Allen, R. K., Employee Rels
Barton, D. R., Hurley Medical Center
Greenhouse, S. J., Consumers Power Co
Griesbach, F. C., Consumers Power Co
Weber, C. T., Univ of Mich-Flint

Saginaw 48601-48605
Basil, T. A., Luce, Basil & Collins Inc
Ruby, D. P., Michigan Sugar Co
Shaw, R. D., Central Foundry Div
Stimmell, T. W. III, Baker Perkins Inc
Swiercz, P. M., Academic

University Center 48710
Mitchell, J. L., Saginaw Valley State College

Cass City 48726
Tonti, D. G., Walbro Corp

Essexville 48732
Dilallo, M., Bus-Industrial Rels

East Lansing 48823-48825
Bandelow, R. T., Student
Banks, R. F., Mich State Univ
Block, R. N., Mich State Univ
Brazier, J. E.
Brickner, D. G., Mich State Univ
Brown, B. C., McGinty, Halverson et al
Castelli, R. J., Student
Culver, W. D., Mich Educ Assn
Curry, T. H. II, Academic
Gleason, S. E., Mich State Univ
Grise, S. K., Student
Groty, C. K., Mich State Univ
Hamermesh, D. S., Mich State Univ
Hardin, E., Mich State Univ
Harris, J. T., Student
Holzer, H. J., Mich State Univ
Horan, M. D., East Lansing City Hall
Jewell, S. C., Student
Killingsworth, C. C., Mich State Univ
Kruger, D. H., Mich State Univ
Lange, S. M., Student
Lau, K. K., Academic
Lucchi, G. D., Student
Moser, C. H., Mich State Univ
Nsiah-Yeboah, R., Student
O'Neal, K.A., Mich State Univ
Opdyke, M. C., Student
Pincus, D. M., Mich State Univ
Polley, I., Arbitration

Power, D. F., Government
Premack, S., Student
Soltow, M. J., Mich State Univ
Stieber, J., Mich State Univ
Walton, L. M., Mich State Univ
Ward, R. P., Mich Nurses Assn
Wolkinson, B. W., Mich State Univ
Woodbury, S. A., Mich State Univ

Greenville 48838
Dewit, G. D., Ore-Ida Foods
Lawrence, J. B., Bus-Industrial Rels

Haslett 48840
Corbitt, L. F., Student
Lawson, D. B., SMACNA
Reagan, P. M., Industrial Relations

Mason 48854
Young, J. A., Professional Assn

Morrice 48857
Poe, L. J., Mich Assn of School Boards

Mt. Pleasant 48858-48859
Bomzer, D. J., Student
Dayal, S., Central Mich Univ
Lewis, A. L., Academic
Lewis, N. L., Bus-Industrial Rels
Potter, R. H., Academic
Reynolds, R. R., Central Mich Univ

Okemos 48864
Hagen, K. M., Government
Moore, M. L., Mich State Univ
Patten, T. H. Jr., Mich State Univ
Reinerth, M. W., Academic

Williamston 48895
Carrigan, B. O., Bus-Industrial Rels

Lansing 48906-48933
Akarakcian, A. A., Student
Benca, T. J., Civil Service
Berkowitz, N., Arbitration
Connors, E. O., Mich Dept Labor
Frost, C. F., Academic
McKinney, E. C., Waverly Community Schools
Parsons, W. F. Jr., Student
Phillips, M. B., Union
Pollo, S. A., Academic
Revitte, J. L., Mich State Univ
Ridenour, K. S., Lansing General Hosp
Ryan, H. B., Bus-Management
Thomas, R. E., Mich Assn School Boards
Vande Vord, N., Mich State Univ
Yee, K., Consulting
Zurvalec, D. S., Mich Manufacturer's Assn
Zurvalec, S. H., Lansing School Dist

Kalamazoo 49001-49008
Beinhauer, M. T., Retired
Blaustein, S. J., W. E. Upjohn Institute
Buford, T. G., Howard & Howard
Buskirk, P. A. R., W. E. Upjohn Institute
Copps, J. A., Western Mich Univ
Davia, A. B., Allied Indus Workers of Amer
Harasim, C., Union
Hoffman, E. P., Western Mich Univ
Hunt, A., W. E. Upjohn Institute
Jackson, R. D., FMCS
Jenkins, M. E., Hercules Inc
Kidston, R. G., Kidston-Peterson
Wend, J. S., Western Mich Univ
Wendling, W. R., W. E. Upjohn Institute

Bangor 49013
Insidioso, R. C., Du-Wel Products

Battle Creek 49017
Peterman, M. C., Inerbake Foods Inc

Hastings 49058
Witham, D., Hastings Mfg Co

Marshall 49068
Daffara, J. C., Clarke Equipment Co

Vicksburg 49097
Descheneau, M. D., Business

Niles 49120
House, M. G., Arbitrator

Jackson 49203
Younglove, P. C., Bus-Management

Albion 49224
Elkin, S. M., Albion College

Big Rapids 49307
Curtis, F. J. Jr., Ferris State College
Malmo, D. M., Mich Educ Assn
Pomnichowski, A. S., Ferris State College
Thomas, B. F., Ferris State College

Grand Haven 49417
Burnell, S. E., MEA-NEA

Muskegon 49441
Willea, C., Union

Spring Lake 49456
Brocci, J. F., Sealed Power Corp

Grand Rapids 49501-49509
Broas, L. C., Leon Plastics
Eisenga, L. C., Leon Plastics
Hollister, S., Gordon Manufacturing Co
Howlett, R. G., Varnum, Riddering et al
Jabin, N. E., Miller, Johnson & Snell
Kleiner, A. R., Attorney
Kujawski, K. R., Government
Mackraz, J. A., Government
Parsh, S. F., Union
Posthuma, R. A.
Proctor, W. M., FMCS
Ray, W. F., Meijer Inc
Swift, M. S., Student
Tapper, G. A., The Employment Assn
Van Laan, R., Student

Wyoming 49509
Witte, W. J., Mediation

Cadillac 49601
Weikel, F. K., CMI International

Onway 49765
Haener, A., UAW Family Educ Center

Marquette 49841-49855
LaSalle, J. G., Union
Roy, W. P., Mich AFL-CIO

Houghton 49931
Alexander, K. O., Mich Tech Univ
Chaubey, M. D., Mich Tech Univ
Fisher, C. R., Upoper Peninsula Power Co

MINNESOTA

Forest Lake 55025
Swenson, C. E., Arbitrator

St. Paul Area 55103-55117
Anderson, W. C., State Mediator
Fitch, D. P., Student
Fitch, M., Student
Hartanto, F. M., Student

Hofmann, J. P., Minnesota Nurses Assn,
Holt, K. E., Student
Leeds, R. J., State of Minnesota
McIntire, W. W. Jr., College of St. Thomas
Mesch, C. R., Attorney
Neigh, C., Arbitration
Sampson, M. A., Good Neighbor Services
Turnbull, J. G., Retired
Ver Ploeg, C. D., Wm. Mitchell College of Law
Walker, R. W., Hamline Univ

Minnetonka 55343
Maetzold, T. O., Maetzold Assoc Inc

Minneapolis Area 55402-55480
Ahlburg, D. A., Univ of Minnesota
Angle, H. L., Univ of Minnesota
Azevedo, R. E., Univ of Minnesota
Bailey, B., McQuay Inc
Bates, C. W., General Mills
Bjerke, P.
Bloom, G. R., Industrial Rels Assoc Inc
Bognanno, M. F., Univ of Minnesota
Deye, J. R., Amer Arbitration Assn
Flagler, J. J., Academic
Fossum, J. A., Univ of Minnesota
Gilson, J. E., Student
Hirschey, K. D., General Mills Inc
Kapsch, F. E. Sr., Arbitration
Lee, J. S., Academic
Lee, M. B., Student
Mattson, J. N., Intl Multifoods
Moore, T. F., Union
Na, B. C., Student
Niemic, J., City Council Member
Nowicki, H. H., Retired
Obermeyer, P. E., Government
Pribble, E. D., arbitrator
Prior, J. J., Super-Valu Stores Inc
Schumann, P. L., Univ of Minnesota
Scoville, J. G., Univ of Minnesota
Seltzer, G. O., Univ of Minn
Tremiti, J. F., Attorney
Walker, B. J., Honeywell Inc
Zaidi, M. A., Univ of Minnesota

Duluth 55812
Boyer, J. W. Jr., Univ of Minn-Duluth
Rubenfeld, S. A., Univ of Minn-Duluth

Rochester 55902
Laedtke, G. M., Bus-Personnel

Winona 55902-55987
Foegen, J. H., Winona State Univ
Wolfmeyer, P. V., Winona State Univ

MISSISSIPPI

Oxford 38655
Hart, W. S., Univ of Mississippi

University 38677
Smith, L. H., Univ of Mississippi

Columbus 39701
Jethro, P. G., Weyerhaeuser

Ackerman 39735
Rikard, D. J., Belwood Div, US Industries

MISSOURI

St. Louis Area 63101-63166
Bernstein, M. C., Washington Univ
Bingman, M. B., Missouri Natl Educ Assn
Blank, I. L., Attorney
Boyer, G. P., Metro St. Louis Sewer Dist
Bynum, T. R., Missouri Educ Assn
Cannon, R. S., Hager Hinge Co
Clark, J. H., Government
Duffee, W. C., City of St. Louis
Dunning, J. C. Jr., Auto Club of Missouri
Durham, J. L., IBEW, AFL-CIO
Feldacker, B. S., Arbitration
Fernandez, M., Government
Garnholz, E. W., Attorney
Gewin, M. E., Bus-Industrial Rels
Gruenberg, G. W., Arbitration
Gruenberg, H., Gruenberg, Souders & Levine
Higgins, N. G., Monsanto
Hoyman, M. M., Academic
Kanne, M. G., St. Louis Post Dispatch
Keller, R. E., General Dynamics
La Martina, J., FMCS
Ming, L. H. Jr., Bus-Industrial Rels
Moore, J. L., Southwestern Bell Pub Inc
Nelson, E., St. Louis Univ
Newmark, M. L., Attorney
O'Brien, T. M., Government
O'Grady, J. P., St. Louis Community College
O'Reilly, J. M., Arbitrator
Pineau, C. A., Rawlings Sporting Goods
Richter, D. J., AAIM Management Assoc
Runcie, J. F., Anheuser-Busch Companies
Russell, L. G. SEIU Local 50
Schoen, S. H., Washington Univ
Smith, K. J. Jr., Arbitrator
Stodghill, W., SEIU 50
Tomey, E. A., St. Louis Univ
Wauck, L. A., Government
Werner, H. D., Univ of Missouri
Witteried, G. C., Univ of Missouri

St. Charles 63301-63302
Carvalho, D. M., Bus-Personnel
L'Heureux, W. D., Continental Telephone Co

Wentzville 63385
Jourdan, M. M., Bus-Industrial Relations

Blue Springs 64015
Goetz, A. F., Bus-Personnel

Grandview 64030
Bennett, D. J., ITT Continental Baking Co

Warrensburg 64093
Drake, C. G., Academic

Kansas City 64105-64196
Anderson, S. L., Whitaker Cable Corp
Berger, M., Univ of Missouri
Cassidy, W. J., Antiquarian Bookman
Clark, C. H., Whitaker Cable Corp
Clark, C. E., Arbitrator
Elliott, C. L., Elliott & Kaiser PC
Ellison, M. K., Stinson, May, Thomson et al
Foster, J. D., Sheet Metal Work Local #2
George, C. A., Teamster Joint Council 56
George, D., Whitaker Cable
Gordon, M. D., Jolley, Moran, Walsh et al
Hall, J. W., Unitog Co
Hall, R. D., Government
Helfand, R., Panethiere & Helfand
Hercules, D. C., Whitaker Cable Corp
Huey, R. T., AFGE Local 1336
Hurley, J. P., Jolley, Moran et al
Johnson, A. B., AFGE Local 1336
Juneman, R. C., Raddison Muehlbach Hotel
Kaut, J. I., State of Missouri
Kilroy, W. T., Shughart, Thomson & Kilroy
Kuehn, D. H., Union
Madden, S.C., Arbitration
Major, L. F. III, Smith, Gill, Fisher & Butts
Murphy, F. J. SJ, Rockhurst College
Quick, D. L., Western Auto Supply
Rennison, R., Bookbinders Union 60
Rostov, S. D., Attorney
Sears, K. D., Stubb & Mann

Shaulis, P. A., Mobil Oil Credit Corp
Soetaert, L. A., C. J. Patterson Co
Spence, M. O., Libby Welding
Stovall, J. R., Mobil Oil Credit Corp
Stover, T., USDL
Wagner, F. E., Academic
Wallmark, C. F., FMCS
Whipple, C. D., Whipple & Kraft
Yarowsky, S. M., Attorney & Arbitrator
Zander, J., AFGW Local 558

Maryville 64468
Brown, R. E., Northwest Missouri St Univ

St. Joseph 64501-64507
Clemens, J. P., St. Joseph Light & Power
Kessler, R., Wire Rope Corp of America
Shrout, E. H., Missouri Western College
Watkins, T. D., Watkins, Boulware & Lucas

Jefferson City 65101
Rogers, D. C., MO State Bd of Mediation

Columbia 65201-65211
Belcher, A. L., Arbitrator
Boyle, G. V., Univ of Missouri
Gottesfeld, G. I., Shared Union Systems Inc
Heinz, T. J., Univ of Missouri
Mikrut, J. J. Jr., Univ of Missouri
Penfield, R. V., Univ of Missouri
Stevens, D. W., Univ of Missouri
Williams, R. L., MFA Inc

Sedalia 65301
Copas, W. H., IBEW 814

Springfield 65802
Davis, C. H., Academic

MONTANA

Billings 59101
Gaghen, H. W., Eastern Montana College

Helena 59601
Gerber, C. J., State of Montana
Leifer, N. L., State of Montana
Romney, S. I., State of Montana
Schramm, L. H., State of Montana

Bozeman 59715
Heliker, G. B., Retired
Vinton, K. L., Academic

NEBRASKA

Omaha 68178-68179
Bannister, R.S., UPRR Company
Kelly, E. P., Creighton Univ
Waldmann, P. J., Union Pacific RR

Lincoln 68516-68588
Bourne, R. M., Retired
Gleason, J. G., Student
Kemmerer, B. E., Student
Torrence, W. D., Univ of Nebraska

Wayne 68787
Cook, R. A., Wayne State College

NEVADA

Las Vegas 89101-89121
Agonia, R. J., US Dept of Energy
Andriani, R. N., Bus-Industrial Rels
Burns, M. C., IB Teamsters Local 995
Hardbeck, G. W., Academic
Horowitz, L. M., Stardust Hotel
MacEachern, J. A., City of Las Vegas
Massagli, M. T., Musicians Union
Solomon, M., Flamingo Hotel

Reno 89557
Stoess, A. W., Academic

Carson City 89701-89703
Hanna, J. S., NV Employment Security
Rose, I. A., Retired

NEW HAMPSHIRE

Londonderry 03053
Higgins, R. G., Arbitrator

Nashua 03061
McCann, R. A., Nashua School Dist 42

Manchester 03104
Dorr, J. V. N. III, Arbitration

Northwood 03261
Chase, T. C.,Organization Dev Network

Plymouth 03264
Kropp, S. H., Univ System New Hampshire

Warner 03278
McCausland, A. S., Arbitration

Marlborough 03455
Bourassa, D. W., Student

Hanover 03755
Greenhalgh, L., Dartmouth

Durham 03824
Barlow, R. F., Univ of New Hampshire
Hurd, R. W., Univ of New Hampshire
Sandler, M., Univ of New Hampshire
Thompson, A. R., Univ of New Hampshire

NEW JERSEY

Bloomfield 07003
Giordano, D. A., NA Philips Lighting
McGivern, E. J., Union

Cedar Grove 07709
Rosen, S. J., Fairleigh Dickinson Univ

Cliffside Park 07010
Lawsky, P. J., Student

Cranford 07016
Orchard, R., Boyle-Midway

East Orange 07017
Gallagher, J. O., Retired

Ft. Lee 07024
Allan, P., Academic
Paprocki, J. L., Church of the Madonna

Garwood 07027
Whitford, A. M., NJEA/NEA

Hoboken 07030
Ballantine, J. W., Stevens Institute
Koeller, C. T., Stevens Inst

Livingston 07039
Krebs, P. J., Labor Arbitrator

Maplewood 07040
Lilore, D., Union

Montclair 07042
Rosenberg, R., Arbitration
Rotter, M. G., NJ Inst of Tech

Upper Montclair 07043
Sack, J. Erica, NLRB

North Bergen 07047
Kell, P. G., Arbitrator

West Orange 07052
Eskay, H. H.
Troy, L., Rutgers Univ
Weisenfeld, A., Arbitration

Watchung 07060
Gray, R. R., Arbitrator

Rahway 07065
Dorf, G. L., Counsellor at Law

Roseland 07068
Eisenberg, A., Government
Ploscowe, S. A., Grotta, Glassman & Hoffman

Rutherford 07070
Lane, P. A. B., Student
Schlesinger, C. T., New York Times

South Orange 07079
Gandel, M., Research

South Plainfield 07080
Brandon, D. J., Cassetta, Brandon & Taylor
Cassetta, R. A., Cassetta, Brandon & Taylor

Union 07083
Weisinger, R. S., Weisinger Assoc

Lake Telemark 07088
Kleckner, W. R., Kleckner Associates

Westfield 07090
Wieting, J. L., Government

Woodbridge 07095
MacDonald, D. M., Bus-Management
Seligman, S. D., Bus-Industrial Rels

Newark 07102-07104
Blumrosen, A. W., Rutgers Univ
Goldberg, S. M., Univ Med & Denistry
Helfgott, R. B., New Jersey Inst of Tech
Kendellen, G.T., NLRB
Reitman, S., Reitman, Parsonnet, Maisel & Duggan
Rogers, J. E., Rutgers Univ
Rose, L. M., NYS Board of Mediation
Ryan, E. F., Carpenter, Bennett & Morrissey
Washburn, L. B., Student

Nutley 07110
Salsberg, R. M., Aron & Salsberg

Jersey City 07306
Hott, T. R., Hott, Kropf, Margolis & Hernadez

Fair Lawn 07410
Silverman, H., Arbitration

Franklin Lakes 07417
Meer, C. G., Academic

Ridgewood 07450-07451
Lewis, H. N. Jr., Bus-Industrial Rels
Kent, A. G., R. S. Simpson Inc
McManemin, J. P., Attorney
Van Alstyne, V. B., R. C. Simpson

Waldwick 07463
Mauro, M. J., Bus-Econ.

Wayne 07470
Leung, C. K., William Patterson College
Stiller, W. A., Lederle Laboratories
Strait, D. L., William Patterson College

Wyckoff 07481
Mahler, W. R., Mahler Assoc Inc
Mitrani, R. L., Arbitrator

Totowa 07512
Pulhamus, A. R., Academic

Hackensack 07601-07602
Klinger, A. H., Attorney
Smith, R. C., Arbitration

Closter 07624
Peterfreund, S., S. Peterfreund Assoc Inc

Emerson 07630
Pedevillano, M. T., Bus-Industrial Rels

Englewood Cliffs 07632
Langbaum, E., Eric Langbaum Assoc Inc
Petersen, R. C., CPC International Inc

Hillsdale 07642
Fein, M., Mitchell Fein Inc

Montvale 07645
Wenzler, R. A., BOCG Inc

Paramus 07652
Comerford, R. D., Bergen Community College
O'Grady, J. P., Federal Electric Corp
Rarey, R. J., Federal Electric Corp

Ridgefield Park 07660
Diemer, B.

River Edge 07661
Malkin, J. L., Attorney

Teaneck 07666
Cull, C. P., Arbitrator

Ocean 07712
Hunter, S. B., NJ Public Empl Rels Comm

Newark 07716
Mills, M. K., NJ Inst of Tech
Potts, A. M., NJ Inst of Tech

Belford 07718
Lowrey, J., Bus-Industrial Rels

Freehold 07728
Westerkamp, P., Arbitrator

Lincroft 07738
Connerty, R. A., Retired
Pinto, E. N., Attorney

Little Silver 07739
Bulsiewicz, K. A., Labor Attorney

Aberdeen 07747
Russo, C. S., Academic

Stanhope 07874
Lelling, B. H., Union

Summit 07901
Goldberg, S. H., Ciba-Geigy
Hinds, J. G., Ciba-Geigy

Basking Ridge 07920
Smith, E. A., Business

Berkeley Heights 07922
Stochaj, J. M., NJ Inst of Tech

Chatham 07928
Rowland, C. V., US Postal Service

Florham Park 07932
Burns, R. T., Ohaus Scale Co
Kimmett, C. T., Kean College of NJ

Madison 07940
Greis, T. D., Academic

Millington 07946
Reichenbach, R. R., Org Res Counselors Inc

Morris Plains 07950
Harper, J. J., Harper & O'Brien

Morristown 07960
Butler, G. L., Allied Chemical Corp
Minter, M. M., Bus Management

Cherry Hill 08003
Wynne, D. J., Consulting

Brant Beach 08008
McGinnis, J. M., McGinnis Assoc
McGinnis, W. J. Jr., McGinnis Assoc

Haddonfield 08033
Florey, P., Labor Arbitrator

Cherry Hill 08034
Rich, J. M., Arbitration

Camden 08102
Coleman, C. J., Rutgers Univ
Ekstrom, J. F., Rutgers Univ
Goldberg, M. J., Rutgers Univ
Weissenberg, P., Rutgers Univ

Collingswood 08107
Kessler, P., Academic

Belle Mead 08502
Chu, P. B. J., Retired

Bordentown 08505
Tener, B. Z., Arbitrator

Cranbury 08512
Kaplan, D., Retired
Killingsworth, M. R., Rutgers Univ
Stein, L., Retired

Florence 08518
Christ, P. E.,Transamerica Delaval Inc

Hightstown 08520
Brown, J. D., Retired

Princeton 08540-08544
Ashenfelter, O., Princeton Univ
Cook, R. F., Princeton Univ
Edwards, B. H., Princeton Univ
Geraghty, W. V., Princeton Univ
Kerachsky, S. H., Mathematica Policy Res
Lester, R. A., Princeton Univ
Maynard, R. A., Mathematica Policy Res
Metcalf, C. E., Mathematica Policy Research
Mooring, K. D., Educational Testing Service
Rubinstein, S. P., Participative Systems Inc
Schiemann, W. A., Opinion Research Corp
Tener, J. B., Arbitrator

Trenton 08605-08619
Hershfield, D. C., Baruch College
Mason, F. A., State of New York
Nye, D. P., Trane Company
Perlman, S. W., Rothbard, Harris & Oxfeld
Peterson, R. A., NJSFT
Wary, C., NJ School Boards Assn

Yardville 08620
Neimeiser, M. M., Union

Lawrenceville 08648
Ben-Asher, D. L., Government
Steinberg, H. A., Academic
Vosburgh, D. F., Transamerica Delaval Inc

Trenton 08659
Nicholas, C. E., Goodall Rubber Co

Lakewood 08701
Berman, M. B., Government

Annandale 08801
Gentile, P. C., Bus-Industrial Relations
Mankoff, C. H., Bus-Industrial Rels

East Brunswick 08816
Galvin, M. E., Rutgers Univ
Moran, M. L., Academic

Edison 08817
Brown, A. B., Bus-Personnel

Flemington 08822
Motiuk, I. L., Attorney
Thornton, J. A., NJEA-NEA

Jamesburg 08831
Brent, A. H., Arbitration

Metuchen 08840
Chernick, J., Retired
Kerrison, I. L. H., Retired
Restaino, G., New Jersey Educ Assn
Yager, P., FMCS

Piscataway 08854
Golob, H. M., Arbitrator
Mason, M., Bus-Management
Meisler, G., Arbitration
Pearce, J. J. Jr., Arbitrator

Parlin 08859
Ludlow, H. T., Seton Hall Univ

Somerset 08873
Naimark, R., Amer Arbitration Assn
Warman, D. S., John Wiley & Sons Inc

Somerville 08876
Champi, P. L., Bus-Personnel

New Brunswick Area 08882-08933
Aranoff, A. M., Rutgers Univ
Begin, J. P., Rutgers Univ
Berkowitz, M., Rutgers Univ
Borus, M. E., Rutgers Univ
Chelius, J. R., Rutgers Univ
Gross, E., Attorney
La Salvia, M. C., Middlesex County Educ Assn
Lee, B. A., Rutgers Univ
Margadonna, J. R., Johnson & Johnson
McIntosh, B. R., Rutgers Univ
McWold, R. R., Government
Mowry, C. B., Rutgers Univ
Muth, L. W., Johnson & Johnson
Naples, M. I., Rutgers Univ
Stark, H. F., Academic
Stawnychy, P. R., Pincus, Gordon, Zuckerman
Weinberg, W. M., Rutgers Univ
Wenzler, O. F., Johnson & Johnson

NEW MEXICO
Belen 87002
Heneman, H. G. Jr., Retired

Albuquerque 87106-87131
Cohen, S., Univ of New Mexico
Finston, H. V., Univ of New Mexico
Gregory, P., Univ of New Mexico
Reeves, T. Z., Univ of New Mexico
Sanchez, J. P., Bus-Industrial Rels
Thompson, J. T., Retired
Vigil, P. R., Union

Questa 87556
Manzanores, A. J., Molycorp Inc

Las Cruces 88003
Orton, E. S., New Mexico State Univ

Carlsbad 88220
Paneral, A. J., IUOE #317

NEW YORK
New York City 09021-10475
(Includes Staten Island and the Bronx)
Ahern, E., Retired
Akabas, S. H., Columbia Univ
Akselrod, L. J., Government
Anderson, A., Office of Collective Barg
Anderson, B. E., Rockefeller
Bailey, T. R., Academic
Baitsell, J. M., Mobil Oil Corp
Balk, M. Attorney
Barbash, J., Debevoise & Plimpton
Barnes, A. W., CBS Inc
Bassen, H. R., Attorney
Bassen, N. H., Kelley, Drye & Warren
Bell, D. E., Union
Berenblum, M. B., Continental Grain Co
Berger, R. B., National Maritime Union
Berger, S. L., Freelance Writer
Berkelhamer, L., Lipkowitz & Plaut
Bernstein, S., Group Health Inc
Billett, L. M., Gulf Western Industries
Birnbaum, R., Columbia Univ
Bishow, H., New York Times
Blair, S. S., Union
Bogart, A., Equitable Life Assurance
Borba, P. S., Natl Council on Comp Ins
Borden, W. S., Trans World Airlines
Bremer, C. E., A. Philip Randolph Educ Fund
Brossman, M. E., Grutman, Miller et al
Bullard, C. K., Student
Burstein, H., Attorney
Cahn, S. L., Attorney/Arbitrator
Carey, P. A. SJ, Fordham Univ
Carroll, B., Attorney
Chamberlain, N. W., Retired
Chandler, M. K. Columbia Univ
Christensen, A. S., Kaye, Scholer et al
Christensen, T. G. S., Attorney
Clarke, C. L., Girl Scouts of the USA
Coburn, K., ASARCO Inc
Coffin, D. C., Continental Grain Co
Cohen, L. B., Columbia Univ
Coleman, P. T., US Army 21 SUPCOM
Colosi, M. L., Bronx-Lebanon Hosp
Corvino, A. J., Continental Grain Co
Coulson, R., Amer Arbitration Assn
Crannan, H. J., Government
Crea, M., Merrill Lynch & Co Inc
Dabney, H. L., Am Textile & Clothing Wrks Union
Daniels, W., ILGWU
Day, V. B., VPKK & Day
Dean, J. P., New School for Social Research
Decristofaro, M., St. Vincent's Hosp Med Center
DeFreitas, G. E., Columbia Univ
Delaney, J. T., Columbia Univ
Desantis, N. S., Consolidated Edison Co
Desouza, A. C., Student
Dillon, C. M., Jackson, Lewis & Schnitzler
Dillon, P. C., Foremost-McKesson Wines
Doherty, T. G., NYC Health/Hosp Corp
D'Onofrio, J. D., Isabella Geriatric Center
Douglas, J. M., Baruch College
Durso, C. G., Student
Drogin, I., Leaf, Kurzman, Duell & Drogin
Dwyer, R. E., Empire State Coll
Ehrenhalt, S. M., USDL
Fanning, J. J., NYS Labor Rels Board
Fisher, A. D., Student, Columbia Univ
Folcarelli, J. W., Bus-Personnel
Forkosch, M. D., Academic
Forst, R. I., Bus-Industrial Rels
Franklin, L. R., Arbitration
Freedman, M., Columbia Univ
Friedman, C. H., Arbitration
Friedman, J. J., Martin E Segal Company
Gabel, S., Government
Garst, J. D., Union
Garst, V. W., Government
Gazetas, G. A., Academic
Geltman, O., Attorney
Gerard, I., FMCS
Gilles, D. L. Jr., Hertz Company
Ginzberg, E., Columbia Univ
Glinsman, W. J., NY State Mediator
Gold, C., Arbitration
Gray, L. S., Cornell Univ
Greco, A. N., Metro Lithographers Assn
Green, R. M., Epstein, Becker, Borsody et al
Gretz, C. B., Union
Gudenberg, H. R., Intl Telephone & Telegraph
Gujarati, R. P., Pace University
Hagen, J. M., Student
Halan, J. P., Union Pacific Corp
Halevy, I., Academic
Harris, P., Baruch College
Hathaway, G. T., Holtzmann, Wise & Shepard
Hausman, L. J., Brandeis Univ
Heiser, D. M., Attorney
Herzog, P. M., Retired
Hiestand, D. L., Columbia Univ
Hoellering, M. F., Amer Arbitration Assn
Hoerr, J. P., Business Week
Holtzmann, H. M., Holtzmann, Wise & Shepard
Hyde, P. R., Holtzmann, Wise & Shepard
Isenberg, H. J. T., Fed of Catholic Teachers
Izutsu, G. T., City Univ of New York
Jaffe, L., NYS AFL-CIO
Jauvtis, R. L., Epstein, Becker, Borsody et al
Johnson, R. J., Consulting
Kaden, L. B., Columbia Univ
Kamm, R. E., Attorney
Katz, E. C., Johnson & Higgins
Kaufman, J. J., Cornell Univ
Kazazean, S. J., St. Lukes Hospital
Kerins, P. T., Howmedica Inc
Kelly, R. M., R. H. Macy & Co Inc
Kenney, K. R., NYS PERB
Kirrane, W., TWU
Kolman, J. R., Economics
Kovenetsky, S., Unempl Ins Appeal Board
Kuhn, J. W., Columbia Univ
Leonard, A. S., Academic
Levin, D., ILGWU Local 99
Levin, E., Academic
Levin, N. A., Morgan, Lewis & Bockius
Levine, L. L., Blue Cross/Blue Shield NY
Levy, R. A., W. Levy Cons Corp
Lewin, D., Columbia Univ
Lewis, H. T., Montefiore
Lewis, I., Arbitration
Liddle, J. L., Liddle & Assoc
Lindau, D. S., Holtzman, Wise & Shepard
Lipper, S. J., ILGWU
Livingston, F. R., Kaye, Scholer, Fierman et al
Love, S. B., Student

Lynch, M. P., Allied Maintenance Corp
MacKell, T. J. Jr., M. D. Sass Assoc Inc
Maher, W. J., G+W Consumer/Indus Product
Mahoney, C. B., Manhatten Eye/Ear Hosp
Malin, S., Amer Arbitration Assn
Mann, S. Z., CUNY
Marx, H. L. Jr., Arbitrator
Mascola, F. X., Management Consultants
Melnick, H. H., City Employees Union #237
Metzger, N., Mt. Sinai Medical Center
Miller, J. W. Jr., Consulting
Miller, J. D., ACTWU Social Services
Miller, V., ACTWU
Mincer, J., Columbia Univ
Monaco, A. G., NY Zoological Society
McKew, J. J., NY Zoological Society
Mooney, M. J., Fordham Univ
Moskowitz, L. D., Metropolitan Life Ins Co
Nangeroni, J. E., Office & Professional Empl Union
Nestor, O. W., Pace University
Newman, L. N., Manning, Selvage & Lee Inc
Newman, T., Business
Nicolau, G., Consulting
Nolan, T. J., New York Univ
O'Laughlin, W., Arbitration
O'Reilly, J. F., NYC Health & Hosp
Orenstein, S., Solomon, Rosenbaum et al
Ornati, O., A., Academic
Pateracki, J. A. Jr., Whitman & Ransom
Paul, R. D., Martin E. Segal Co Inc
Philippi, M. R., Student, Columbia Univ
Poglianich, A., Government
Rappaport, L.A., Univ of Penna
Raskin, A. H., Journalism
Reader, M. M., Office & Professional Empl Union
Reed, T. F., Student
Rees, A. E., Alfred P. Sloan Foudnation
Reiff, S., Sportswear Apparel Assn
Renton, G. G., NYU Medical Center
Reynolds, C., Org Res Counsellors Inc
Rosen, S. M., Columbia Univ
Rosenblum, P., Consulting
Robins, E., Arbitrator
Sanders, E. M., Professional Assn
Schneider, D. J., Consulting
Schwartz, H. A., Student
Schwartz, M., Attorney
Seham, M. C., Seham, Klein & Zelman
Shair, D. I., Carl Fischer Inc
Shea, D. F., Hertz Co
Simmelkjaer, R., CCNY
Simon, S. F., Retired
Simsarian, A., Consulting
Smith, C. L., USDL
Soutar, D. H., ASARCO Inc
Southon, P. J., NY Public Library
Spencer, J. M., Academic
Spitz, H., Academic
Spitz, R. S., Empire State College
Stark, A., Arbitrator
Stark, D. C.
Stein, B., New York Univ
Stoikov, J., Employment Economics Inc
Sweriblow, S. P., Government
Sydney, L. F., Dew Line Inc
Teper, L., Retired
Velotta, C. V., Union
Viani, A. R., AFSCME Dist Council 37
Vladeck, J. P., Vladeck, Waldman, Elias et al
Warner, A. W., Columbia Univ
Washington, J. L., IMCR Dispute Resolution Center
Wasser, L., Writers Guild Amer East
Waks, J. W., Kaye, Scholer, Fierman et al
Wayland, W. F., A. Johnson & Co Inc
Weeks, D. A., The Conference Board
Weinberg, P., American Express Co
Weinman, R. A., Attorney
Westerkamp, P. R., Con Edison Mutual Aid Soc
Wilson, A., Arbitration
Witkower, P., Natl Union Hosp Employees
Wolchok, H., Education
Wrong, E., Academic
Zimet, M., Manhatten College

Ardsley 10502
Townley, R. A., Ardsley Union Free School

Armonk 10504
Flynn, T. F., IBM Corp
Wooley, T. R., IBM Corp

Briarcliff 10510
Geraty, J. M., Burns Intl Security Service

Chappaqua 10514
Wittenberg, C. A., Academic

Croton-On-Hudson 10520
Rubin, M., Arbitrator

Harrison 10528
Jacobs, A. T., Ramapo College of NJ

Larchmont 10538
Kelly, M. A., Cornell Univ

Mohegan Lake 10547
Levenstein, A., Baruch College

Montrose 10548
Spellman, D. J. III, Attorney

Ossining 10562
Kearsley, D. F., Union
Sockell, D., Academic

Rye 10580
Blank, D. S., AFT Local #2934

Scarsdale 10583
Brecher, C., Professional Assn
Buzbee, E. W., Arbitration
Edwards, L. N., Academic
Ilivicky, J., Arbitrator
Kahn, M. K., Student
Rosow, J. M., Work in American Institute
Ryan, E. W., Manhattanville College

White Plains 10601-10650
Engelbrecht, M. A., Texaco Inc
Goldsmith, S. J., Arbitrator
Matthews, M. S., Westchester Local 860 CSEA
Meany, P. M., Nestle Enterprises
Novick, D. S., Nestle Co Inc

Yonkers 10701
Kiers, P. C., Archdiocese of New York

New Rochelle 10801
Jantzen, R. H., Academic
Yagoda, L., Arbitrator

Monsey 10952
Roth, W., Attorney

New City 10956
Anderson, J. K., County of Rockland
Bluth, A., Student

Pearl River 10965
Wolf, A. J., Academic

Piermont 10968
Bordwell, C., Arbitration

Spring Valley 10977
Gitlow, A. L., New York Univ

Franklin Square 11010
Barr, K. A., Chase Manhatten Bank

Great Neck 11020-11024
Brook, R., Attorney
Emanuele, B. D., Sperry Electronic System
Goldman, B. S., Economics
Katz, J., Arbitrator
Kopelman, R.E., Academic
Kramer, J., NYS Labor Rels Board
Labita, A. M., AVX Corp
Nenner, R. A., Student
Perkel, G., Consulting
Shaffer, D., Academic

Manhasset 11030
Cusack, J. J., North Shore Univ Hosp

Manhasset Hills 11040
Roukis, G. S., Arbitrator

Long Island City 11101-11106
Armiger, S. S., LaGuardia Community College
Kugler, I., CUNY

Brooklyn 11201-11241
Berger, R. S., Arbitration
Bigler, E. R., NYC Bureau of Labor Serv
Blumengarten, L. H., Government
Brody, M., Brooklyn Jewish Hosp
Eisenberg, W. L., Arbitration
Ellenberg, M., S & S Corr Paper Mach Co
Grayson, G. H., NYCTC
Horowitz, A. M., Student
Irsay, L., Arbitrator
Kaye, J. H., Union
Maher, R. E., Government
Mandel, E. J., NLRB
Marcus, S. E., Academic
Pavlinsky, N. M., Bus-Personnel
Sternstein, H., Retired

Bayside 11346
Bienstock, H., CUNY

Flushing 11352-11367
Bowman, Y. M., Bus-Labor Rels
Camerano, F., Booth Memorial Med Center
Ginsburg, H., Academic
Hanlon, M. D., Queens College
Kaplan, D. M., Attorney

Douglaston 11362
Ezratty, A., Resources for Labor
Mushkin, P., Resources for Labor

Fresh Meadows 11365
Ganz, S., Samuel Ganz & Assoc Inc

Jackson Heights 11372
Ranhand, S., Baruch College

Rego Park 11373-11374
Gibberman, C. T., Bus-Labor Rels
Romero, J. R., Iberian Airlines

Forest Hills 11375
Benjamin, J., Government
Bumas, L. O., Polytech Inst of NY
Charonis, V., USDL
Miller, M. A., NYS Dept of Labor
Morgan, G. R., NYC Board of Educ

Richmond Hills 11419
Socha, J. L.

Woodhaven 11421
Leask, W. M., Bus-Industrial Rels

Queens Village 11427
Eisenberg, H. H., Academic

Jamaica 11435
Lysaght, W. J., Long Island Railroad Co
Morrison, D. D., Long Island Railroad Co
Nicholson, P. L., US Postal Service

Mineola 11501
Bee, P. A., Attorney
Millman, B. R., Rains & Pogrebin
Rains, H. H., Arbitrator

Freeport 11520
Alers, B., Seaview Hosp & Home
Browne, D., Union

Garden City 11530
Gaba, R. M., Arbitration
Gitelman, H. M., Adelphi Univ
Lamberti, T. M., Cullen & Dykman
Ronner, W. V., Attorney
Sekas, M. H., Student
Tilles, C. E., Arbitration

Glen Cove 11542
Burnett, P. O., Bus-Labor Relations

Greenvale 11545
Newton, D., Long Island Univ

Hempstead 11550
Dibble, R. E., Academic
Smith, L. W., Arbitration
Swanson, R., FMCS

West Hempstead 11552
Erdehim, A. R., Student
Schellace, F. N., NYS Supreme Court

Uniondale 11553
Patino, A. J., Union

North Merrick 11566
Silver, J., Arbitration

Point Lookout 11569
Rush, K., Government

Rockville Center 11570
Procopio, M. A., Arbitration
Ruffo, P. J., Arbitration

Oceanside 11572
Friedman, P. F., Government

East Hills 11576
Freedman, A., The Conference Board

North Hills 11576
Smith, N., Bus-Management

Sea Cliff 11579
Glassberg, E. J., Consutling

Williston Park 11596
Shaw, P. F., Arbitrator

Woodmere 11598
Lang, T. H., Baruch College

Central Islip 11722
Olin, B. K., Bus-Industrial Rels

Commack 11725
Dornbaum, C., Arbitration
Dornbaum, M. L, Student

Copiague 11726
Hahn, A. T., Bus-Industrial Rels

Coram 11727
MacGregor, R. W., Arbitrator

Melville 11747
Jung, G. T., Citibank

Jericho 11753
Carey, T., Arbitrator
O'Leary, J., NYS United Teachers

Levittown 11756
Cullinan, M. J., AFT Local 1383
Cypin, J. G., Retired

Massapequa 11785
Hammer, L. I., Arbitration
Kershen, H., Academic

Northport 11768
Ahern, J. T., Arbitration

Lake Ronkonkoma 11770
Friedman, B. L., Union

Selden 11784
Mauk, E. S., Suffolk County Community College

Smithtown 11787
Faschan, K. M., Government

Hauppauge 11788
Allmendinger, R. C., Suffolk County

Syosset 11791
Pelle, M. A., Fairchild Weston Systems

Stony Brook 11794
Rony, V., SUNY-Stony-Brook

West Islip 11795
Melis, P. A., Bus-Industrial Rels

Hicksville 11801-11802
Hansen, G. C., Remington Aluminum
Procelli, M. S., Long Island Lighting Co
Tillem, J. D., Arbitration

Plainview 11803
Cohen, N., Arbitrator
Korn, A., Consulting
Korn, R. H., Bus-Industrial Rels.

Delmar 12054
Bers, M. K., SUNY

Duanesburg 12056
Draves, E. F., AFSCME

Clifton Park 12065
Randles, D. C., Arbitration

Glenmont 12077
Mrozak, J. L., NY Div of Labor Standards

Latham 12110
Beach, D. S., Academic
Goldbaum, K. M., Student
Kelly, J. T., Thealan Assoc Inc

Albany 12203-12230
Bress, J. M., Governors Office Empl Rels
Caropreso, A. C., Eastern Contractors Assn
Furdyna, M. A., Government
Grabowski, D. J., Arbitrator
Hodes, N. L., Governors Office of Empl Rels
Lefkowitz, J., NYS Public Empl Rels Board
Malone, R. H., NYS United Teachers
Moses, M. H., Academic
Morgenbesser, L. I., Government
Newman, H. R., Public Empl Relations Board
Northrop, J. B., State of New York
Paliwodzinski, R. L., NEA/New York
Readdean, S., Albany BOCES
Rubin, H., Government
Sabghir, I. H., SUNY
Sano, J. B., Public Empl Fed, AFL-CIO
Schrauf, J. P., Governors Office EE Rels
Shapiro, S., Star Textile & Research
Staats, C. E. Jr., Union
Zumbolo, A., Arbitration

Schnectady 12303-12308
Brennan, J. P., Bus-Personnel
Prosper, P. A. Jr., Union College
Trachtenberg, B. S., Arbitration

Red Hook 12571
Denenberg, T. A., Arbitrator

Poughkeepsie 12601-12603
Campion, D. L., Civil Serv Empl Assn

Prenting, T. O., Marist College

Auburn 13021
Barnes, S. D., Cayuga Community College
Colella, J. M., Student
Krause, E. F., Student

Camillus 13031
Pinto, N. F., Union

Freeville 13068
Orr, M. J., LMC Consultants Inc

Liverpool 13088
Florkowski, G. W., Student
Klinsahw, R. A., Government
Krause, M. A., Student
Molini, P. J. Jr., Student

Marcellus 13108
Carlton, J. M., NY Labor Advisory Services
Clarke, P. L., Student

Syracuse 13202-13221
Bova, D., IBEW
Brown, D. A., Amer Arbitration Assn
Carlson, C. K., P & C Food Markets Inc
Cutler, S. O. SJ, Le Moyne College
Dixon, T. J., Church & Dwight Co
Donn, C. B., Le Moyne College
Edelstein, J. D., Academic
Ferguson, T. H., Bond, Schoeneck & King
Ferris, J. E., Attorney
Gatti, M. R., Student
Gentile, J., NY State Mediation Board
Greenberg-Edelstein, R. Academic
Haberberger, M. J., Student
Haven, C. P., Student
Horton, J. W. Jr., Bus-Personnel
Hubner, W. F., Le Moyne College
Johnson, W. G., Syracuse Univ
Kaiser, C. M., NYS Mediation Board
Karper, M. D., Academic
Koretz, R. F., Syracuse Univ
Kowalski, R. E., Academic
Lamanna, J., Arbitration Office
Lancaster, J. J., Dept Public Works
Mackin, M. C., Student
Markowitz, I. R., Retired
Miller, C. S., Syracuse Univ
Morse, J. B., Bus-Personnel
Pellow, D., Bond, Schoeneck & King
Pisegna, D., Onandaga County
Reisman, M. M., Wine Merchants Ltd
Rogers, D. E., Le Moyne College
Schnell, J. F., Syracuse Univ
Schuster, M. H., Academic
Sherman, P. J., Student
Smith, J., Blitman & King
Tarolli, M. P., Church & Dwight Co Inc

Williams, J. P., Student

Clinton 13323
Crisafulli, V. C., Retired
Jones, D. C., Hamilton College

Utica 13501
Horton, J. W. Jr., Bus-Management

Watertown 13601
Benedetto, F., Intl Assn of Machinists
Fairchild, C., House of Good Samaritan
Foster, D., New York Air Brake

Potsdam 13676
Bakhtiara, P., Academic

Oneonta 13820
Baum, J., Academic

Vestal 13850
Masters, S. H., Academic

Depew 14043
O'Connor, F., Arcata Graphics

East Aurora 14052
Lawson, E. W. Jr., Arbitrator

Fredonia 14063
Hartley, W. B., SUNY-Fredonia

Grand Island 14072
Scott, M. T., Arbitration

Lockport 14094
Klinshaw, R. J., Student

Medina 14103
Young, R. C. Jr., Orleans-Niagara BOCS
Lynch, W. F., Niagara Univ

Tonawanda 14150
Schneider, K. B., Consulting

Buffalo 14202-14220
Ahern, R. W., Buffalo Labor Mgmt Council
Foster, H. G., SUNY-Buffalo
Hahn, L. E., Natl Fuel Gas Co
Liddle, W. T., United Cerebral Palsy
Newman, J. M., SUNY-Buffalo
Odza, R. M., Jaeckle, Fleischmann & Mugel
Olson, C., SUNY-Buffalo
Osika, T., Freezer Queen/United Foods
Passmore, S. B., Bus-Personnel
Shister, J., SUNY-Buffalo
Spargo, P., Greater Buffalo Press
Stocker, N. J., Consultant
Sullivan, F. W. Jr., Student

Williamsville 14221
Alexander, J. B., Attorney
Becker, B., Academic
Dansereau, A. E. Jr., Academic
Farkash, A., Canisius College
Mason, K. B., Bus-Industrial Rels
Truell, G. F., George Truell Assoc

Kenmore 14223
Atlas, C. M., Student
Meloon, J. A., Economist

West Seneca 14224
Wall, C., Bus-Industrial Rels

Eggertsville 14226
Alutto, J. A., SUNY-Buffalo
Goldberg, M. M., Labor Med/Arbitrator

Amherst 14226-14260
Atleson, J. B., SUNY-Buffalo
Butler, A. D., SUNY-Buffalo
Zoladz, J. M., Student

Niagara Falls 14302-14305
Carey, J. F., Union Carbide Corp
Fegatili, D., Academic
Goodman, D. P., Academic

Geneseo 14454
Moore, G. A., State Univ College

Ontario Center 14520
Putnam, D. R., Bus-Personnel

Webster 14580
Denson, F. L., Arbitration

Williamson 14589
Falkner, M. J., Student

Rochester 14589-14627
Bernstein, P., Rochester Inst Tech
Brophy, J. M., Retired
Campbell, A. E., Business
Grant, A. B., Cornell Univ
Hamlin, T. A., Government
Kaplan, M., Labor Education
Kaufman, A. D., City School District
McKelvey, J. T., Cornell Univ
Miller, M., Cornell Univ
Watts, B. E., Student

Bath 14810
Bennett, J. C. Jr., Bus Management

Ithaca 14850-14853
Aronson, R. L., Cornell Univ
Bauer, S. C., Student
Benson, F., Cornell Univ
Block, J. M., Student
Boudreau, J. W., Cornell Univ
Briggs, V. M. Jr., Cornell Univ
Broderick, R. F., Student
Burton, J. F. Jr., Cornell Univ
Cook, A. H., Retired
Cullen, D. E., Cornell Univ
Doherty, R. E., Cornell Univ
Donovan, R., Cornell Univ
Dyer, L. D., Cornell Univ
Ehrenberg, R. G., Cornell Univ
Eischen, D. A., Arbitration/Attorney
Fields, G. S., Cornell Univ
Flaherty, B., Cornell Univ
Foltman, F. F., Cornell Univ
Goodwin, W. J., Student
Gross, J. A., Cornell Univ
Hammer, T. H., Cornell Univ
Harper, S. F., Cornell Univ
Herman, F. A., Cornell Univ
Jensen, V. H., Cornell Univ
Kaiser, S. S., Student
Kalwa, R. W., Student
Klinedinst, M. A., Student
Konvitz, M. R., Cornell Univ
Lehman, M. L., Student
Lipsky, D. B., Cornell Univ
Markowitz, J. R., Ithaca College
Meyer, G. W., Student
Milkovich, G. T., Cornell Univ
Miller, A. R., Cornell Univ
Miller, J. G., Retired
Mitchell, O. S., Cornell Univ
Neufeld, M. F., Retired
Rehmus, C. M., Cornell Univ
Rock, C. P., Student
Schwarz, J. L., Student
Seeber, R. L., Cornell Univ
Smith, R. S., Cornell Univ

Stern, R. N., Cornell Univ
Wasmuth, W. J., Cornell Univ
Wesman, E. C., Academic
Whyte, W. F., Cornell Univ
Windmuller, J. P., Cornell Univ

Newfield 14867
Brooks, G. W., Retired

Trumansburg 14886
McConnell,J. W., Arbitrator

NORTH CAROLINA
Reidsville 27320
Andrews, J. F., Miller Brewing Co

Greensboro 27408
Kennedy, J. W., Arbitration

Apex 27502
Shaw, S. O., Arbitration

Carrboro 27510
Hames, D. S., Student

Chapel Hill 27514
Aldrich, H. E., Univ of North Carolina
Bigoness, W. J., Univ of North Carolina
Jerdee, T. H., Univ of North Carolina
Lansberger, H. A., Univ of North Carolina
Murphy, W. P., Univ of North Carolina

Raleigh 27607-27650
Allen, S. G., North Carolina State Univ
Carson, R. G. Jr., Arbitration
Fearn, R. M., North Carolina State Univ
Marett, P. C., Academic

Greenville 27834
Tomkiewicz, J., Academic

Charlotte 28210
Calvasina, G. E., Academic

Wilmington 28403
Lawson, L. D., Univ of North Carolina
McInerney, M. L., Academic

Camp Lejeune 28542
Janes, C. S. III, OSJA MCB

Banner Elk 28604
Perley, J. D., Arbitration

Arden 28704
McGuire, J. J., Sybron Corp, Ritter-Tycos

Cullowhe 28723
Owens, S. D., Western Carolina Univ

Ashville 28804
Hoyer, D. T., Univ of North Carolina

NORTH DAKOTA
Fargo 58105
Eisele, C. F., North Dakota State Univ

Grand Forks 58201
Reed, J. A., Univ of North Dakota

Minot 58701
King, C. B., Dakota Northwestern Univ

OHIO
Delaware 43015
Gitter, R. J., Ohio Wesleyan Univ

Granville 43023
Maxwell, N. L., Denison Univ

Newark 43055
Mater, P. R., Owens Corning Fiberglas
Stassen, M. A., Student

Westerville 43081
Buckingham, M. H., Ohio School Board Assn
Stein, R. G., Ohio School Board Assn

Worthington 43085
Bishop, J. H., Academic
Gagen, M. G., Student
Kindig, F. E., Arbitrator
Koreckis, P. H., Ohio Army Natl Guard
Sproat, K., Ohio State Univ

Galloway 43119
Gibson, R. M., Gibson, Newman & Gee

Lancaster 43130
Ege, R.D., Government

Columbus 43201-43229
Burchett, H. D., Burchett & Assoc
Campagna, A. F., Ohio State Univ
Casey, J. F., Casey Co LPA
Dozier, J. B., Student
Gouke, C. G., Ohio State Univ
Havlovic, S. J., Student
Heneman, R. L., Ohio State Univ
Hills, S. M., Ohio State Univ
Leach, D. B., Arbitration
Linville, R. G., Porter, Wright, Morris et al
Lynch, L. M., Ohio State Univ
Mangum, S. L., Ohio State Univ
Marsh, M., Ohio AFL-CIO
Mendicino, M., Student
Miceli, M. P., Ohio State Univ
Miljus, R. C., Ohio State Univ
Miller, G. W., Retired
Miller, K. S., Student
Oyaga, G. T. De, Student
Papier, W. B., Retired
Parnes, H. S., Ohio State Univ
Patton, D. B., Ohio State Univ
Roach, B. L., Student
Sandver, M. H., Ohio State Univ
Song, K. C., Student
Vacarro, V. A., Anheuser-Busch Inc
Vorys, G. A., Student
Weisman, R. D., Schottenstein, Zox & Dunn
Worley, G. T., Government

East Liberty 43319
Martin, R. M., UTC Harding Machine

Toledo 43604-43659
Gleason, A. H., Univ of Toledo
Iorio, T. W., Business
Lackey, G. B., Lackey, Nusbaum et al
Micallef, C. N., Arbitration
Moore, E., Ohio State Univ
Shields, J. C., Univ of Toledo
Spirn, S., Univ of Toledo
Thomson, L. M. Jr., Labor-Mgmt Citizens Comm

Mentor 44060
Scobel, D., Creative Worklife Center

Novelty 44072
Nelson, N. E., Cleveland State U

Oberlin 44074
Kasper, H., Oberlin College

Cleveland Area 44101-44140
Brandt, G., UAW Region 2
Cotabish, M. I., Consulting Services
Dolski, E. R., FMCS
Drotning, J. E., Case Western Reserve U
Dworkin, J., Arbitration
Dyke, A. K., Attorney
Dyke, T., Arbitration
Evans, W. K., FMCS
Feldman, M. J., Attorney
Fishburn D., Business
Gerhart, P. F., Case Western Reserve U
Germani, P. J., Labor Rels
Graham, H. E., Cleveland State Univ
Hasenstab, K. A., Bus-Industrial Rels
Hauserman, B. B., TRW Inc
Heshizer, B. P., Cleveland State U
Ipavec, C. F., Arbitrator
Janecek, M. J., Student
Johnson, G. C., Attorney
Laughlin, D. K., Roulston & Co
Littman, D.A., Government
McAuliffe, P. S., Standard Oil Co
McCorkle, L. P., Consulting
McDade, R. J., Hanna Mining Co
Molner, E., Mechanical Contr Assoc
Pace, S. D., Spieth, Bell, McCurdy et al
Peirce, W. S., Case Western Reserve U
Perry, S. S., Arbitration
Prasse, F. C., Cleveland Elec Co
Ruben, A. M., Cleveland State Univ
Salipante, P. F. Jr., Case Western Reserve U
Sens, J. F., Kaiser Foundation
Sharpe, C. W., Case Western Reserve U
Shupe,P.M., East Ohio Gas Co
Skinner, E. E., Sherwin Williams Co
Smith, W. E., Lubriquip Div Houdaille
Stealy, P., Dinner Bell Meats Inc
Strasshofer, R. Jr., Arbitration
Sweeney, J. G., John Carroll Univ
Vana, R. J., La Porte & Ipavec Co
Young, D. M., Case Western Reserve U

Kent 44240-44242
Bruning, N. S., Kent State Univ
De Blander, W. B., Academic
Williams, D. R., Kent State Univ

Akron 44308-44329
Ahern, L. J., Intl Chem Workers Union
Clem, C. S., United Rubber Workers
Kessing, S. L., General Tire & Rubber Co
McLain, J. M., Retired
Shaffer, D. T., Goodyear Tire/Rubber
Soper, D. E., Firestone Tire & Rubber

Warren 44485
Kimpan, J. K., Bus-Personnel

Youngstown 44512-44514
Daly, J. H., Youngstown State Univ
Koss, J. J., Labor Rels Consultant

Wooster 44691
Baird, W. M., College of Wooster

Canton 44702
Morgan, C. A., Amerman, Burt & Jones

Ashland 44805
Ford, L. G., Ashland College

Tiffin 44883
Porter, A. R. Jr, Arbitrator

Franklin 45005
Smith, D. F., Ohio Educ Assn

Hamilton 45005-45013
Qualls, J. R., Champion Intl
Smith, D. F., Ohio Educ Assn
Zimmerman, S. A., Champion Intl

Middletown 45043
Burns, S. R., ARMCO Middleton Works

Oxford 45056
Box, J. R., Miami Univ
Moore, W. J., Miami Univ
Puff, H. F., Miami Univ

Amelia 45102
Farley, J. A., Student

Cincinnati 45201-45221
Andrews, O. E., Arbitration
Barrows, D. W., Mead Containers
Cochran, S. A., Student
Cravanas, V.A., Government
Crudo, F. C., AFTRA
Donnelly, L. I., Xavier Univ
Eviston, R. J., Kroger Co
Ferree, J. L., NLRB
Fitch, S. J., Proctor & Gamble
Fuller, D. C., Urban League
Gaubeca, M. J., Student
George, T., Bus-Industrial Rels
Hawkins, M. W., Dinsmore & Shore
Hedrick, C. B., Proctor & Gamble
Herman, E. E., Univ of Cincinnati
Homann, A. Y., Cincinnati Cordage Paper
Johnson, L. L., Westin Hotel
Kearney, W. J., Univ of Cincinnati
Keenan, F. A., Arbitrator
Kramer, L. H., Armco Bldg Systems
Leftwich, H. M., Univ of Cincinnati
Loeb, B. L., Bus-Management
Marmo, M. J., Xavier Univ
Roos, J. P., Cincinnati Gas & Electric
Seinsheimer, W. G., Arbitrator
Skinner, G. S., Univ of Cincinnati
Standriff, D. M., Cincinnati Indus Inst
Stokes, D. M., Student
Suarez, H. A., Student
Weber, D. C., Positrol Inc
Weyls, R. C., Student
Williamson, B. G., IBEW

Xenia 45385
Cook, R. F., Student

Dayton 45431-45435
Blake, C. H. Jr., Wright State Univ
Bush, M. L., Academic
Showell, C. H. Jr., Academic
Stuadter, D. V., Arbitrator

Springfield 45501
Goulet, J. C., Wittenberg Univ

Athens 45701
Christenson, C., Ohio Univ
Tracy, L., Ohio Univ
Yost, E. B., Ohio Univ

Marietta 45750
Potash, S., Marietta College

Findlay 45840
Smith, B. E., Cooper Tire & Rubber

OKLAHOMA

Norman 73069-73071
Champlin, F. C. III, Univ of Oklahoma
Fitzgerald, W. R.
Woolf, A. H., Arbitration
Woolf, D. A., Univ of Oklahoma

Oklahoma City 73106-73120
Farwell, C., Government
Firestone, F. N., Oklahoma City Univ

Stillwater 74074-74078
Greer, C. R., Oklahoma State Univ
Pearce, T. G., Oklahoma State Univ
Shearer, J. C., Oklahoma State Univ

Tulsa 74103-74137
Barnes, R. L., Nichols & Wolfe Inc
Birmingham, M. N., Attorney
Krolikowski, R. J., Bus-Industrial Rels
Neas, R. C., Arbitrator
Quinn, F. X., Arbitration
Rittenoure, R. L., Univ of Tulsa

Muskogee 74403
Ginkel, A. O., Bacone College

OREGON

Lake Oswego 97034
Abernathy, J. H., Arbitration
Williams, T., Western Arbitration Assn

Portland 97201-97229
Cabelly, A., Portland State Univ
Fries, H. W., Retired
Haney, M. D., Academic
Lovell, H. G., Academic
Martyn, R. G., Sloan, Silver, Florin & Martyn
Ockert, R. A., IWA
Osa, J. M., Union
Stevens, C. M., Reed College

Tigard 97223
Crumpton, R. G., Oregon Educ Assn

Salem 97301-97309
Flegel, J. R., Student
Hallock, M., SEIU
Herrick, C. T., Arbitration
Snow, C. J., Willamette Univ

Corvallis 97331-97339
Fraundorf, M. N., Oregon State Univ
Harter, L. G. Jr., Oregon State Univ
Keltner, J. W. Consulting Assoc
Rettig, J. L., Oregon State Univ

Eugene 97402-97440
Conant, E. H., Univ of Oregon
Gallagher, J. J., Univ of Oregon
Garcia, D. A., Student
Hundley, G. S., Univ of Oregon
Mayer, S. J., Student
Via, E. F., Univ of Oregon

Ashland 97520
Axon, G. L., Arbitrator

Sisters 97759
Turner, M. S., Retired

Pendleton 97801
Wrathall, L., Union

PENNSYLVANIA

Beaver
15009
Poff, F. M., Student

Belle Vernon 15012
Lenart, S. A., Academic

New Kensington 15068
Chick, M. J., Bus-Management

Allison Park 15101
Uber, A. E. Jr.,Westinghouse Electric Co

Bethel Park 15102
Newman, S. J., United Steelworkers of Amer
Robinson, E. W. Jr., Bell of Pennsylvania

Coraopolis 15108
Corcoran, F., Robert Morris College

West Homestead 15120
Thomas, J. R.

Monroeville 15146
Biondo, J., FMCS
Lewis, J. D., Union
Nickl, C. E., Academic

Wilmerding 15148
Perich, G. H., Westinghouse/Amer Standard

Pittsburgh 15206-15263
Ayoub, E., United Steelworkers of Amer
Blaufeld, S. S., Attorney
Chesler, H. A., Univ of Pittsburgh
Cigich, A. L., Academic
Craft, J. A., Univ of Pittsburgh
Crawford, A. C., Carnegie Mellon Univ
Creedon, G. T., Monongahela Connecting RR
Creo, R. A., Arbitration
Dean, I. J. Jr, Arbitrator/Attorney
Dissen, R. W.
Extejt, M. M., Univ of Pittsburgh
Fischer, B., Carnegie Mellon Univ
Fitzpatrick, R., St. Francis College
Flora, J. A., Union
Greenberg, B., Retired
Hazard, L., Consultant
Heekin, W. C., Charles Mullin Inc
Householder, R. W., FMCS
Joseph, M. L., Carnegie Mellon Univ
Kaminski, D. B., Bus-Management
Katz, A., Univ of Pittsburgh
Knapp, A. S., Univ of Pittsburgh
Kobell, G., NLRB
Labowitz, T. A., Student
Meals, R. L., Bus-Personnel
Mitchell, J. J. IV, Academic
Mullen, C. H., Student
Neumeier, E., Arbitrator
Nicoson, J. P., Bus-Management
O'Connell, E. J., Arbitrator
Orsatti, E. B., Jubelirer, Pass, Intrieri
Peterson, D. A., USS/USWA
Randolph, R. D., Buchanan Ingersoll
Richman, H., Academic
Sabatini, V. B., Eckert, Seamans, et al
Schano, J. F., Amer Arbitration Assn
Schutte, R. M., Government
Shore, H., Arbitration
Sipilker, K. J.,
Thomas, K. W., Univ of Pittsburgh
Trezise, D. L., Westinghouse Electric
Wuslich, G. L., Jones Laughlin Steel Corp

East Washington 15301
Robertson, T. H., Bethlehem Mines Corp

Union Town 15401
Miller, D. E., Columbia Gas Dist Co

California 15419
Zeffiro, J. A., California State College

Bedford 15522
Guth, D. J., Student

Huntington 15642
Karako, J. J., Health & Hosp Care

Stahlston 15687
Garrett, S., Iron Ore Indus Bd of Arb

Indiana 15701-15705
Andreassi, S. J., Student
Martini, B. E., Student
Maza, M. A., Student
McPherson, D. S., Academic
Miller-McMillan, K., Student
Morand, M. J., Indiana Univ of Penna
Ray, S. E., Student
Sedwick, T.
Serra, A. T., Bus-Management
Williard, D. M., Student

Punxsutawney 15767
Huot, J. J., Student

Torrance 15779
Bullard, J. K., Student

Johnstown 15902-15905
Duranko, P. N., ABEX Corp
Jasper, D. A., Professinal Assn

Ebensburg 15931
Croyle, T. J., Penna Mines Corp

Loretto 15940
Nicholson, R. P., Student

Seward 15954
Treasure, M. G., Florence Mining Co

Butler 16001
Kuhr, M. I., Student

Grove City 16127
Markovitch, G. J., Valley Mould Microdot

Meadville 16335
Koop, D. H., Bus-Industrial Rels

Erie 16505
Tann, C. J., Arbitrator

Altoona 16602-16603
Dancha, D. R., Student
Doyle, J. F., Government
Leopold, A. S., Retired

Hollidaysburg 16648
Aboud, Antone, St. Francis College

Patton 16668
Wagner, E. M., Academic

University Park 16802
Filippelli, R. L., Penna State Univ
Hogler, R. L., Penna State Univ
Smith, F. D., Student
Susman, G. I., Penna State Univ

Clearfield 16830
Rougeux, N. I.

Annville 17003
Evans, R. K., Government

Camp Hill 17011
Decoen, E. G., Harsco Corp
Wolf, C. M., Harsco Corp

Carlisle 17013
Bellinger, W. K., Dickinson College
Reinhold, R., United Telephone System

Grantham 17027
Musser, S. J., Messiah College

Hummelstown 17036
Cole, G. S., Penn State Univ

Lebanon 17042
Engle, D. E.
Harrison, C. I., Cleaver Brooks

Mechanicsburg 17055
Ezbiansky, D., Government
McGill, W. R., Government

Middletown 17057
Liggett, M. H., Penna State Univ

Harrisburg 17101-17121
Bausinger, K. E., Penna DOT
Berger, M., ILGWU
Biggica, R. J., State of Penna
Dunlap, C. R., Bureau of Labor Rels
Fox, E. M., AFSCME
Grove, K., Penna Nurses Assn
Harmon, C. M., Penna State Educ Assn
King, S. P., Capitol Products Corp
Kirschke, G. J., Capitol Products
Kornfeld, M. C., Penna State Educ Assn
Kurtz, C. R., APSCUF
Lindsay, R. E., AFSCME
MacNett, K. S., Government
MacNett, S. C., Government
Maffeo, M. R., Dept Auditor General
O'Neill, J. N., AFSCME
Sariano, J. P., Dept of Labor & Ind
Stober, R. P., Penna Nurses Assn
Tama-Troutman, C., Bus-Industrial Rels
Uehlein, J., Penna AFL-CIO
Uehlein, M. L., Journalism
Wagner, M. O., AFSCME
Zamboni, R. A., AFSCME
Zervanos, C. J., Director of Labor Rels

Chambersburg 17201
Holoviak, S. J., Academic

Saltillo 17253
Hasson, E., Academic

Shippensburg 17257

Hanover 17331
Kerr, F. L., Alloy Rods Div/Chemetron

York 17405
Jones, N. W., Teledyne McKay
Salmon, K., Teledyne Readco
Smith, S. E., Teledyne McKay

Millersville 17551
Cauler, S. L., Bus-Industrial Rels

Lancaster 17601
Helfrich, T. G., Bus-Personnel

Sunbury 17801
Kamber, F., Kury-Kamber

Bethlehem 18015-18018
Hyclak, T. J., Lehigh Univ
Stevens, J. E., Lehigh Univ
Suppes, D. E., Bethlehem Steel Corp

Thornton, R. J., Lehigh Univ
Tripp, L. R., Lehigh Univ

Easton 18042
Gendel, E. B., Lafayette College
Handsaker, M. L., Morrison-Handsaker
Handsaker, M., Aribtrator

Mahon, C. J., Consulting

Northampton 18067
Mooney, J. A. Jr., Apollo Metals Inc

Hazelton 18201
Levy, B., Business

Allentown 18103-18104
(Includes Cetronia)
McGowan, W. H., Bus-Industrial Rels
Schneck, D. M., Arbitration
Zirkel, P. A., Health & Hosp Care

Scranton 18505-18510
Kurowski, D. S., Student
Megley, J. E., Univ of Scranton

Exeter 18643
Fleming, L. A., Journalism

Ottsville 18942
Insley, P. J., Union.

Richboro 18954
Kane, E. T. Jr., Bus-Industrial Rels

Rosemont 19010
Beletz, E. E., Bus-Management
Suojanen, W. W., Attorney

Secane 19018
Scott, H. T., Bus-Management

Flourtown 19031
Gershenfeld, G., Phila College of Textile & Science
Gershenfeld, W. J., Temple Univ

Haverford 19041
Northrup, H. R., Academic

Jenkintown 19046
Dash, G. A. Jr., Arbitrator
Halpin, C. A. Jr., LaSalle College
Stein, K. L., Government

Levittown 19054
O'Brien, J. J. Jr., Bus-Industrial Rels

Media 19063
Meli, J. T., Widener Univ

Yardley 19067
Mulcahey, T. S., Mobil Oil

Swarthomore 19081
Estey, M. S., Swarthmore College
Pierson, F. C., Retired

Villanova 19085
Burke, D. R., Villanova Univ

Willow Grove 19090
Hamm, E. V., Attorney

Philadelphia 19101-19174
Abel, T., Philadelphia Electric Co
Bell, J., Kleinbard, Bell & Brecker
Bellace, J. R., Academic
Beres, M. B., Temple Univ
Braff, J. L., Wolf, Block, Shoor et al
Buller, C. R., Montgomery, McCracken et al
Campbell, D. C., Student
Coleman, J. L., Bus-Management
Dawson, W. A., SJ, St. Joseph's Univ
Daymont, T. N., Temple Univ
De Treux, W. H. III, Student
Elson, B. R., Cohen & Shapiro
Fox, M. B., Consulting
Gaffni, M. L., Freedman & Lorry
Galfand, S. H., Galfand, Berger, Senesky et al
Gentile, C., UFCW Local #1357
Gomberg, W., Univ of Pennsylvania
Hancox, R. E., Penn Mutual Life Ins Co
Harrington, C. R., Temple Univ
Havener, R. V.
Herrick, N. Q., Academic
Hochner, A., Academic
Howard, W. E., Univ of Pennsylvania
Ingster, B., Consulting
Jennings, T. W., Attorney
Kapner, A., Government
Ketcham, R., Scott Paper Co
Kisch, V. J., Student
Koziara, K. S., Temple Univ
Krendel, E. S., Univ of Pennsylvania
Latta, G. W., Consulting
Leone, R. D., Temple Univ
Little, A., Sun Refining & Marketing
Loewenberg, J. J., Academic
Lovelace, R. F., The Graduate Hospital
Markle, J. Jr., Drinker, Biddle & Reath
Markovitz, J. L, Attorney
McGrath, M. D., Woodhaven Center
McMullen, J., Government
Melamed, J., Government
Merchant, C. S., FMCS
Morris, J. P., Teamsters Local 115
Morrison, M. H., Univ of Pennsylvania
Mullaly, E. J. SJ, Comey Inst of Ind Rels
Pasek, J. I., Pasek, Jeffrey & Ivan
Pereles, E. A., Arbitrator
Perry, C. R., Univ of Pennsylvania
Perry, M. S., Profession Assn
Portwood, J. D., Temple Univ
Powell, W. H., Arbitrator
Rico, L., Univ of Pennsylvania
Rowan, R. L., Univ of Pennsylvania
Salandria, V. J., Phila School Dist
Samoff, B. L., Univ of Pennsylvania
Schmidt, S. M., Temple Univ
Schmidt, T. J.
Scheon, S. H., Washington Univ
Schulman, R. S., Drexel Univ
Schwartz, S. J., Rider College
Seltzer, L. E., Arbitrator/Attorney
Shea, G. P., Univ of Pennsylvania
Simpkins, J. P., Attorney
Stayt, J., Penn Mfgs Assn
Thurschwell, H., Bell Telephone Co of PA
Wald, M., Schnader, Harrison Segal et al
Watkins, D. W., USB
Wachter, M. L., Univ of Pennsylvania
Weinstein, D., Temple Univ
Wright,J. C. Jr.,Montgomery, McCracken et al
Zappin, B. I., ARA Services Inc
Zeytinoglu, I. F., Student

Paoli 19301
Buckner, J. B., Bus-Labor Rels

Exton 19341
Thomas, P. B., Foote Mineral Co

Malvern 19355
O'Donnell, L. A., Villanova Univ

King of Prussia 19406
Vogel, M. S., The Andre Group Inc

Collegeville 19426
Lentz, B. F., Ursinus College

Pottstown 19464
Thomas, J. C., Bechter Power Corp

Spring House 19477
Muir, N. W., PSEA

Valley Forge 19482
Budd, J. L., Alco Standard Corp

Reading 19601
Brown, M. L., Academic

PUERTO RICO 00658-00926
Gurabo 00658
Rey, M. W., Univ of Puerto Rico

Hato Rey 00918
Hernandez-Benetez, F., Dept of Labor

Rio Piedras 00929
Mullan, B. F., Univ of Puerto Rico
Roldan, P., Student

RHODE ISLAND
East Greenwich 02818
Bockoven, K. B., Arbitration
Shogren, M. A., Bostitch Div of Textron

North Kingston 02852
Gordon, J. G., Brown & Sharpe Mfg Co
Overton, C. E., Academic
Schmidt, C. T. Jr., Univ of Rhode Island

Portsmouth 02871
Wilcox, M. E., Retired

Wakefield 02879
Coates, N., Bus Admin
Kingston 02881
Gersuny, C., Univ of Rhode Island

Warwick 02889
Venditto, J. G., Warwick School Dept

Providence 02901-02908
Brennan, P. J., Federal Products Corp
Carter, C. L., Textron Inc
Casey, E. A. Jr., R. I. Federation of Teachers
Chiaravalli, R. L., Bus-Industrial Rels
Grande, J. A., Providence Teachers Assn
McAuliffe, C. J., Attorney/Arbitrator
McNeil, P. J. Jr., Union
Michaelson, R. C., Arbitrator
Miller, R. B., Student
O'Brien, F. T., Providence College
Pendergast, J. J. III, Hinckley & Allen
Pesaturo, G. S., Bay Water Quality Mgmt
Rodio, O., Attorney
Sullivan, A. R., AFSCMS Local 2871

Cranston 02910
McKenna, A., Nortek Inc

East Providence 02916
McGann, F. M., Fram Corp

Smithfield 02917
Pollard, H. G., Bryant College

SOUTH CAROLINA
Blythewood 29016
Ullman, J. C., Academic

Columbia 29204-29211
Betton, J. H., Student
Clamp, J. C. Jr., Academic
Knight, H. S. Jr., Nelson, Mullins, Grier et al
Lockhart, J. S., Office of the Governor
Nolan, D. R., Univ of South Carolina
Terrill, T. E., Academic
Ullman, J. C., Academic
Wheeler, H. N., Univ of South Carolina

Charleston 29401-29402
Holmes, A. R., Gibbs & Holmes
Wall, R. J., American Paper Institute

Greenville 29613
Roberts, R. C. Jr., Furman Univ

Clemson 29631
Skelton, B. R., Clemson Univ

Rock Hill 28730-29733
Norman, R. C., Celanese Fibers Operation
Perselay, G., Winthrop College
Weikle, R. D., Student

Aiken 29801
Storey, D. R., Arbitrator

TENNESSEE
Fairview 37062
Farabee, B. B., France

Murfeesboro 37132
Hall, G. A., Samsonite Firm

Nashville 37203-37235
Berg, I. E., Vanderbilt
Finegan, T. A., Vanderbilt
Gall, G. J. Tennessee State Univ

Signal Mountain 37377
Cook, A. J. D., Academic

Chattanooga 37412
Hannah, R. L., TVA

Johnson City 37601-37614
Frank, R. M., House of Ronnie
Spritzer, A. D., East Tennessee Univ

Bristol 37620
Noble, A. C., Retired

Oak Ridge 37830
Blair, L. M., Oak Ridge Assn Univ
Chaffins, G. E., Bus-Industrial Rels

Knoxville 37902-37966
Addington, T. H., TVA
Betts, R. J., TVA
Bowlby, R. L., Univ of Tennessee
Gordon, M. E., Univ of Tennessee
Groeniger, L. M., Retired
Hagood, L. R., Arnett, Draper & Hagood
Renner, D. L. W.
Schriver, W. R., Univ of Tennessee
Sedlmeier, E. J., Government
Wortman, M. S. Jr., Univ of Tennessee

Memphis 38101
McClure, D. I., Memphis Light, Gas & Water

Cookeville 38505
Menefee, M. L., Tennessee Technological Univ

TEXAS

Plano 75074
Charney, A. R., Rockwell

Richardson 75081
Berryhill, R. D., Rockwell
Esselman, M. S.

Sherman 75090
Brown, D. H., Arbitration
Simonette, J. E., Bus-Management

Dallas 75201-75275
Baker, J. B., Rockwell Intl
Beaty, J. R. Dresser Ind
Carter, A. V. Arbitrator
Goodstein, B. M., Arbitration
Hack, L., Hack & Derer
Hearne, W. M.
Kirkpatrick, G. J., Mediation
Larson, L. V., Souther Methodist Univ
McIlvain, C. L., City of Farmers Branch
Moore, A., Gifford-Hill Co
Moore, L. L., Southern Union Co
Morris, C. J., Southern Methodist Univ
Smedinghoff, M. L., Bus-Industrial Rels
Walton, E. A., Rockwell Intl
Wolff, H. O., Amer Arbitration Assn
Vygantas, P. V., Sky Chefs

Longview 75604
Sadinsky, M. L., Continental Can Co

Arlington 76011-76019
Bell. J. W., Business
French, J. L., Univ of Texas
Gray, D. A., Univ of Texas
Knezek, L. D., Academic
Wheeler, K. G., Univ of Texas

Ft. Worth 76116-76148
Chown, D. W., Texas Christian Univ
Drost, D. A., Texas Christian Univ
Kurko, N. H., Union
Levy, C. S.
Levy, H. D., Consultant
Tyer, C. W., Academic

Denton 76201-76203
Allen, W. S., Student
Dunn, J. D., North Texas Univ
Krumweide, J., Peterbilt Motor Co
Ledgerwood, D. E., North Texas State Univ
Manning, N. J., Student
McKee, W. L., Academic
Powers, R. S., Bus-Industrial Rels
Sharp, W. H., North Texas State Univ
Stephens, E. C., North Texas State Univ

Sanger 76266
Tedlock, R. M., Arbitration

Houston 77001-77253
Ball, E. L. USA Dist 37
Barger, M., Maxwell House Div
Bertani, C. L, IAM & AW Lodge 15
Bradburn, W. V. Jr., Crown Central Petroleum
Britton, R. L., Attorney
Castelluzzo, R. F., General Foods
Chandler, J. C., FMCS
Coleman, G., Bus-Management
Cook, W. R., ARMCO-NCSD
Daugherty, R. D., Pennzoil Co
Doran, W. W., Mitchell & Doran
Ferraro, J., Bowen Tools Inc
Glenn, J., St. Joseph Hospital
Hale, K. W., McEvoy Oil Field Equip Co
Harvey, W. J., FMC Corp
Hinkson, R. E., Denka Chemical Corp
Huddleston, G., Kroger Co
Hunsucker, J. L., Univ of Houston
Kaiser, E. H., ILA Local 1351
Kajander, J., Pennzoil Co
Kincaid, E. D., FMCS
Kuhn, T., Aldrich, Buttril & Kuhn
Lewis, H. W., Metro Transit Authority
Lindberg, B. N., National Supply Co
Londa, J. C., Butler & Binion
Marlatt, E. E., Arbitrator
McGinnis, J. R., Denka Chemical Corp
Meeks, J. R., B. J. Hughes Machinery Div
Miller, L. A.
Mirsky, J., Beckman Office Supply
Mitchell, J. M., Texas Co Inc
Monroe, C. R., Bus-Personnel
Morris, D., Hydril Company
Padula, C. A., Shell Oil Co
Payne, J. M., Exxon Chemical Americas
Philipps, J. P., AMI
Polk, R. C., Metro Transit Authority
Reynolds, B. L., IBEW Local 716
Rice, W. V. Jr., Univ of Houston
Richardson, D. A., AFL-CIO
Rogers, A., Schlumberger, Well Service
Stranger, C. E., Groth Equipment Co
Talos, E. V.
Tatum, J. E., National Elec Contr Assn
Taylor, C. M., B. J. Hughes Inc
Theiss, J. L., Houston Engineers Inc
Timmons, R. L., AFSCME
Tissue, D., OPEIU Local 129
Towarnicky, J. M., Bus-Industrial Rels
Trevino, R. I., National Supply Co
Tuck, K. W., IAM & AW Lodge 15
Walker, D., Academic
Watson, J. R. Jr., Flynn & Bensik
Weeks, J. R., Baker & Botts
Williams, D. A.
Zuckerman, J. V., Consulting

Pasadena 77502
Sauter, J. B., Carpenters Local 1226

Deer Park 77536
Ross, K. T., Shell Oil
Schliep, R. L., Shell Oil Co

La Porte 77571
Grimes, J. A., Arbitration
Koenig, E. C., Arbitration

Liberty 77575
Seckinger, W., National Pipe & Tube

Seabrook 77586
Brown, C. N., Bus-Labor Rels

Texas City 77590
Kendall-Abbott, R., Union Carbide Corp
Reid, H. O., III, Monsanto Chemicals
Scruggs, T. J., GAF Corp
Whittington, D. B., Union Carbide

Port Arthur 77640-77641
Parigi, S. F., Academic
Young, J. C., U. S. Industrial Chemicals

Beaumont 77704
Durkay, J. J., Attorney

Bryan 77805
Fox, M. P., Academic
Fox, M. J. Jr., Academic

College Station 77840-77843
Ferris, G. R., Texas A & M
Johnson, R. D., Texas A & M
Masters, M. F., Texas A & M
Stavros, D., Texas A & M
Stone, B. D. Jr., Texas A & M
Youngblood, S. A., Texas A & M

Laredo 78041
Ghitelman, S. G., American Consulate

San Antonio 78205-78285
Davis, J. C., Trinity Univ
Kutchins, K. O., PS Etc
McDermott, T. J., Arbitration
Raffaele, G. C., Univ of Texas
Whellan, F., Harte-Hanks Newspapers

Corpus Christi 78412-78469
McCoy, W. D., Corpus Christi State Univ
Pierce, T. J., H. E. B. Grocery Co

Edinburg 78539
Ellard, C. J., Academic

Fredericksburg 78524
Kiss, B. M., Research
Kiss, J. S., Arbitration

Edna 09160
Johnson, H. L.

San Marcos 78666
Morgan, C. A., Southwest Texas State Univ

Austin 78704-79759
Byrd, B. K., Student
Cohen, W. J., Univ of Texas
Ellinger, R., Texas AFL-CIO
Glover, R. W., Univ of Texas
Groesbeck, J. D., Huston-Tillotson College
Helburn, I. B., Univ of Texas
Hubbard, H., Texas AFL-CIO
Kaska, E. W., Attorney
King, C. T., Government
Labig, C. E. Jr., Univ of Texas
Marshall, F. R., Univ of Texas
Rodgers, R. C., Academic
Santos, R., Univ of Texas
Watson, W. H., Retired
Wolitz, L. B., Health & Hosp Care

Post 79356
Earl, L. H., Consulting

Lubbock 79409-79413
Abernethy, B. R., Arbitrator
Macy, B. A., Texas Tech

El Paso 79968
Stephens, D. B., Univ of Texas

UTAH

Midvale 84047
Cooley, M. W., Bus-Industrial Rels

Salt Lake City 84101-84117
Bancroft, K. L., Utah Transit Authority
Dean, E. C., Student
Hallberg, A. C., Union Pacific RR
Mangum, G. L., Univ of Utah
Richardson, R. C., Univ of Utah
Simpson, R. B.
Wann, A. J., Univ of Utah
Wendt, A. C., Academic

Logan 84322
Hansen, G. B., Utah State Univ

Provo 84602
Ritchie, J. B., Brigham Young Univ
Woodworth, W. P., Brigham Young Univ

VERMONT

Burlington 05401-05405
Duffy, W. E., Med Center Hosp of Vermont
Gurdon, M. A., Univ of Vermont
Nadworny, M. J., Academic

VIRGINIA

Annandale 22003
Doranz, J. D., Government
Liess, M. T., Student

Fairfax 22030-22032
Amann, J., Government
Kolb, J., Union
Rush, F. M. Jr., Government

Falls Church 22041-22046
Bates, C. M., Government
Caudhill, R. A., Potomac Uniserv Unit
Flanagan, G. J., Government
Lipton, B. B., Arbitrator/Attorney
Lowenstern, H., USDL
Mullen, M. A., Government
Seidenberg, J., Labor Arbitrator

Reston 22090-22091
Conlan, K. M., Union
Meier, E. L., Government
Oreson, K. A., GTE Bus Communication
Reichenbacher, M. C., Bus-Management
Scott, C. A.

McLean 22101-22102
Bussey, E. M., Arbitration
Greenberg, D. H., Academic
Socknat, J. A., World Bank
Valtin, R., Arbitrator

Manassas 22110
Neal, R. G., PR Williams School Board

Oakton 22124
Gregorio, C. A., Student

Springfield 22150-22152
Bailey, W. R., Government
Eisenhower, R. W., Fairfax Co Public Schools
Fidandis, N. A., Joint-Labor Mgmt Comm-Retail Food
Kassalow, G. M., Government
Panzera, D. P., Government

Vienna 22180
Chretien, B. C., Public Service Research Found
Gilroy, C. L., Government
Newell, R., IAM
Plambeck, D. L., Research
Trumble, R. R., Government

Arlington 22201-22301
Bedell, W. R., Labor/Mgmt Committee
Belous, R. S., Mediation
Bowers, M. H., Government
Burdetsky, B., Academic
Converse, M. H., Mediation
Dean, E. R., Government
Hammerman, H., Government
Henle, P., Academic
Hilz, E. R., Government
Hoska, L. E. Jr., Indus College Armed Forces
Husselmann, P. L., Labor Educ
Maggiolo, W. A., Consulting
Muessig, E., Consulting
Preli, S. A., Government
Slater, C. M., Consulting

Alexandria 22304-22333
Aronin, L., Arbitration
Braun, K., Consultant
Dale, C., US Army Research Inst

Davey, H. L., Arbitration
Diggs, C. Jr., Student
Gustafson, D. M., Union
Leroy, D. R., Government
Marchant, J. D., Government
Marx, H. S., Student, G. Mason Univ
Masters, W. F., Union
Pilenzo, R. C., Amer Soc Pers Admin
Rens, L. G., Attorney
Rosenberg, M., Arbitrator
Rosenblum, M., Government
Ross, R. J., Government

Locust Grove 22508
Heimbach, W. W., Retired

Harrisonburg 22807
Horn, R. N., James Madison Univ
Kohen, A. I., James Madison Univ

Charlottesville 22903-22906
Anderson, R. L., Univ of Virginia
McCulloch, F. W., Univ of Virginia
Snook, J. L. Jr., Univ of Virginia

Midlothian 23113
Liberson, D. H., Bus-Industrial Rels

Williamsburg 23185
Bourdon, C. C., Bus-Industrial Rels
Roadley, C. R., Arbitrator

Richmond 23220-23225
Gray, G. R., Virginia Commonwealth Univ
Underhill, R. S., Consulting

Norfolk 23508-23510
Jones, M. B., Old Dominion Univ
Ryan, J. M., Vandeventer, Black et al

Newport News 23606-23607
Sedgwick, W. S., Retired
Savas, D. T., Newport News Shipbuilding

Yorktown 23690
Clark, P. L., Amoco Oil Co

Blacksburg 24060-24061
Hoover, D. J., Student
Houska, M. D., Academic
Madigan, R. M., Academic
Murrmann, K. F., Academic
Murrmann, S. K., Academic
Robinson, J. F., Virginia Polytech Inst
Taylor, G. S., Student

Christiansburg 24073
Hoover, J. J., Academic

Lynchburg 24502
Revell, J. M., Union

Scottsville 24590
Wilson, A. A., AID

South Boston 24592
Matlack, R. E.,Westinghouse

WASHINGTON

Federal Way 98003
Skratek, S. P., Wash Educ Assn
Slye, J. M., Wash Educ Assn

Kent 98032
Robertson, J. P., Research

Mercer Island 98040
Irwin, D. M., Bus-Labor Rels

Seattle 98040-98195
Aalund, L. A., Sax & MacIver
Croll, R. W., Arbitrator
Dear, J. A., Washington Labor Council
Derr, B. W., SMACNA
Fenn, M. P., Univ of Washington
Fischnaller, J. E., Reaugh & Prescott
French, W. L., Retired
Gillingham, J. B., Retired
Hanselman, K. H., Union
Julnes, T. E., Student
Kang, M. R., NLRB
Kenney, L. C., Wash Labor Council AFL-CIO
Kienast, P. K., Univ of Washington
Lorenz, F. J., F. J. Lorenz & Assoc
Matt, E. C., Municipality of Seattle
McCarger, G. L., NLRB
Mercer, W. J., Attorney
Merker, G. E., Reaugh & Prescott
Napier, N. K., Univ of Washington
Ober, J. H., Law
Patrick, J. R., Municipality of Seattle
Peterson, R. B., Univ of Washington
Saxberg, B. O., Univ of Washington
Semerad, D., Bus-Industrial Rels
Stuteville, W. M., Washington State Nurses

Everett 98206
Lees, T. S., Scott Paper Co

Marysville 98270
Barsotti, F., Hewlett Packard

Bremerton 98312
Turnbull, W. O., Union

Hansville 98340
McCaffree, K. M., Arbitration

Poulsbo 98370
Rennels, M., Wash Educ Assn

Tacoma 98401
Skidmore, R. W., Judge

Wenatchee 98801
Paulson, S., WEA

Cheney 99004
Snyder, R. A., Eastern Wash Univ

Chewelah 99109
Saunders, C. S., Bus-Industrial Rels

Spokane 99201-99220
Cederbloom, M. L., Assoc General Contractors
Dahlke, G. A., Paine, Lowe, Coffin & Hamblen
Hennes, T. M., Union
Nichols, H. W.
Pierce, C. F., Assoc General Contractors
Schwappach, R. A., Kaiser, Aluminum
Wilson, D. M., Duane Wilson & Assn

Kennewick 99336
Cooper, J. P., Bus-Management

Richland 99352
Rutt, F. Jr., Dept of Energy

Walla Walla 99362
Knopf, K. A., Whitman College

WEST VIRGINIA

Pineville 24874
McGlone, P. D., Academic

Belle 25015
Harrah, J. C., Student

Crown Hill 25052
Robinson, L. G., Student

EastBank 25067
Damron, B. J., Student

Glasgow 25086
Ferrell, D. L., Student

Institute 25112
Brookshire, M. L., WV College Grad Study

Kincaid 25119
David, J. P., Academic

Nitro 25143
Mahler, M. E., Monsanto

Charleston 25304-25313
Barkey, F. A., Academic
Kurcina, J. A., Business
Stout, J. S., Consulting
Worden, R. G., WV Manufacturers

Lobata 25677
Runyon, A. H., Rawl Sales & Processing

Huntington 25701
Adkins, R. L., Marshall Univ
Cook, W. G., Marshall Univ
Thomas, W. W., Marshall Univ
White, L. G., Marshall Univ

Beckley 25802
Burns, D. E. Student
Fanok, S., Eastern Assoc Coal Corp

Wheeling 26003
Kirkpatrick, F. H., Academic
Papini, F. E., Union

Weirton 26062
Pietranton, A. F., Federated Investors

Wellsburg 26070
DeBonis, J. R., Eagle Mfgr Co
Thomas, W., Business

Parkersburg 26104
Deel, K. W., Government

New Martsinville 26155
McIntosh, S. S., PPG Industries

Pine Grove 26419
Russell, B. A., Business

Morgantown 26503-26506
Barnes, R. D., Student
Bihun, J. D., Bus-Industrial Rels
Byrne, W. F., Stone, Gallagher & Byrne
Curia, S., Student
Decker, R. L., West Virginia Univ
Elkin, R. D., West Virginia Univ
Humphreys, R. W., West Virginia Univ
Lockhart, S. J., Bus-Management
Miller, R. W., West Virginia Univ
Schaupp, D. L., West Virginia Univ
Smith, W. J., West Virginia Univ
Tapper, O. A., West Virginia Univ
Tuttle, P. A., Student
Veneri, D. A., Student
Yurko, S., Student
Zeller, F. A., West Virginia Univ

WISCONSIN

Brookfield 53005
Donoian, H. A., AIW Health/Welfare

Hartland 53029
Boettcher, J. W. Conley Assoc Inc

Mequon 53092
Epstein, I. S., Arbitration
Olsen-Tjensvold, R., Retired

West Bend 53095
Moberly, R. L., Retired

Burlington 53105
Chybowski, R. M., Union

Kenosha 53140-53141
Applebaum, L., U of Wis-Parkside
Fesko, R. J., American Motors Corp
Lyons, D. E., Snap on Tools
Smith, A. D., Univ of Wis-Parkside

Muskego 53150
Curtis, F.

Waukesha 53186
Grenig, J. E., Academic
Merisalo, C. B., Business-Ind Rels

Whitewater 53190
Domitrz, J. S., Academic
Pulich, M. A., Univ of Wis-Whitewater
Refior, E. L., Retired
Rosenbaum, R. P., Univ of Wisconsin-Whitewater
Saueresigg, R., Univ of Wis-Whitewater

Milwaukee 53201-53233
Asmondy, R. N., IUOE
Barnhill, H. I., Barnhill-Hayes Assoc
Bau, F. J., City Hall
Baumann, C. A., A. O. Smith Corp
Berkoff, M. R., Michael, Best & Friedrich
Bernheim, J. L., Attorney
Bosanac, P. A., Government
Brenner, D. J., Miller Brewing Co
Briggs, S., Marquette Univ
Busacker, A. W., Wis Electric Power Co
Cashmore, P. J., Milwaukee Labor Press
Clark, W. B., Universal Food Corp
Diggelman, R. E., NLRB
Dreiblatt, D. M., Union
Falvey, P. J., Milw Metro Sewerage Dist
Fulrath, T. A., Miller Brewing Co
Gallentine, R. J., Arthur Young & Co
Garnier, K.
Garnier, R. C., Fastback Ltd
Geissner, J. W., City of Milwaukee
Glaser, R., United Steelworkers
Gottschalk, I. E., NLRB
Guernsey, S. K.
Harney, J. R., Union
Hayman, E. J., Lindner, Honzik, Marsack et al
Hesse, D. L., NLRB
Hopkins, A. S., Oster
Housfeld, D. R., Oster
Huffman, J., Government
Huggins, C. D., United Assn
Jirikowic, R. A., Milw County Labor Council
Joy, H. L., Harnischfeger Corp
Kessler, F. P., Silverstein, Halloran, Kessler
Knoblock, R. M., Student
Lerman, D. M., Student
Lindner, D. G., Lindner, Honzik, Marsack et al
Lurie, M., Univ of Wis-Milwaukee
MacDonald, J. A., Allied Ind Workers
MacDonald, R. W., AIW
Martin, R. M., Eaton Corp
McCormick, T. P., Michael, Best & Friedrich
McNamara, B. N., Union

Meier, A. L., Milwaukee Public Schools
Myers, H. N., Shneidman, Myers et al
Notaro, S. A., Marquette Univ
Nystrom, P. C., Univ of Wis-Milwaukee
Owley, C., AFT
Panfil, J. F., IUOE
Pirkey, N. L., Mulcahy & Wherry
Presser, R. A., Intl Assn Machinists & Aerospace Wkrs
Previant, D., Goldberg, Previant, Uelmen
Ropella, M. E., Ropella & Van Horne
Rynecki, S. B., Von Briesen & Redmond
Schmidt, R. F., Medical College of Wis
Schmitt, J. W., Wis State AFL-CIO
Seitz, R. C., Marquette Univ
Shindell, A. B., Attorney
Simon, S. F., Consultant
Skowronski, A. M., Union
Squillacote, G. F., NLRB
Vattendahl, O. J., United Steelworkers
Wiedeman, H. P., Foley & Lardner
Wilberg, W. R., Wis Assn of Mfg & Commerce
Zubrensky, R. J., Consulting

Racine 53401
Hales, E. E., Arbitrator/Mediator

Albany 53502
Lerman, D. M., Student

Beloit 53511
Kreider, L. E., Beloit College
Rothe, H. F., Retired

Cambridge 53523
Stehling, D. J., Student

Middleton 53562
Byers, J. F., Student
Jarley, P. A., Student

Waunakee 53597
Heling, K. J., Student

Madison 53701-53719
Ahrens, D., AFSCME
Aldag, R. J., Univ of Wisconsin
Ansell, S. D., Wis Bd of Voc Tech & Adult Educ
Bauman, S. J., Attorney
Barbash, J., Univ of Wisconsin
Bellman, H. S., State of Wisconsin
Bernfeld, J., AFSCME
Buchen, J. W., Wis Transportation Dept
Cain, G. G., Univ of Wisconsin
Carlson, C. E., Academic
Chisholm, L., AFSCME
Christianson, A. A., Business
Cochran, S. T., Student
Cohn, S. R., Univ of Wisconsin
Davila, R. J., Student
Davis, P. G.
DeClercq, N. G., Univ of Wisconsin
Dennis, B. D., Univ of Wisconsin
Deprey, K. W., Wis Dept Health Soc Svcs
Eaton, A. E., Student
Ewing, D. F., Business
Exo, S., Univ of Wisconsin
Fleischli, G. R., Arbitrator
Gerhart, B. A., Student
Goff, N. A., Student
Goodson, M. J., Student
Griffin, M. L., Student
Hagglund, G. S., Univ of Wisconsin
Hansen, W. L., Univ of Wisconsin
Heneman, H. G. III, Univ of Wisconsin
Herrnstadt, O. E., Student
Haller, A. O., Univ of Wisconsin
Hill, H., Univ of Wisconsin
Houlihan, W. C., Government
Hutchison, K. B., Arbitrator
Johnson, A. C., Univ of Wisconsin
Johnson, D. B., Univ of Wisconsin
Johnson, R. H., Oscar Mayer & Co
Jones, J. E. Jr., Univ of Wisconsin
Kassalow, E. M., Univ of Wisconsin
Kassalow, S. D.
Keenan, J. F. X., Business
Kennedy, K. M., Student
Kent, R. C., Union
Keppler, M. J., Student
Klaas, B. S., Student
Klitzkie, A. G., Government
Krahn, D. E., Wis Educ Assn Council
Krinsky, E. B., Arbitration
Lamb, M. A., National IRRA
Lampman, R. J., Univ of Wisconsin
Leigl, K., Student
Leifer, L. A., L & M Enterprises
Leifer, M. J., National IRRA
Levine, S. B., Univ of Wisconsin
Lieberthal, M., Univ of Wisconsin
Linden, N. A., Attorney
Lipnick, B. N., Student
Lyons, R. W. AFSCME
Malamud, S., Mediation
Maurer, G. C., Empl Assn of Greater Wis Inc
McElroy, K., Government
Mericle, K. S., Academic
Miller, R. U., Univ of Wisconsin
Nay, L. A., Student
Ozanne, R., Univ of Wisconsin
Plantz, F. D., Student
Portz, J. H., Student
Ratner, R. A., Univ of Wisconsin
Rosen, M. I., Univ of Wisconsin
Rothstein, M. F.
Runke, J. M., Student
Russell, G. P., Student
Schell, C. A., Student
Schwab, D. P., Univ of Wisconsin
Sherer, P. D., Student
Simon, S., Univ of Wisconsin
Stern, J. L., Univ of Wisconsin
Stevens, J. B., Student
Thal, R. L., Student
Thompson, M. C., Student
Torosian, H., Government
Ullman, D., Wis Educ Council
Vliet, D. G., Student
Voos, P. B., Univ of Wisconsin
Weisberger, J., Univ of Wisconsin
Wright, K. B., Office of Labor Rels
Young, E., Univ of Wisconsin
Zimmerman, D. R., Mathematica Policy Research
Zwerling, H. L., Student
Zylberstajn, H., Student

Platteville 53818
Karsten, M. F., Univ of Wis-Platteville

New Richmond 54017
Klasen, G. U., Doboy Packaging Mach Inc

Green Bay 54302-54305
Better, M. B., Univ of Wisconsin
Droege, J. D. L., Green Bay Packaging Inc
Jackson, G., James River-Dixie Corp

Wausau 54401
Quarles, M. V., Uniserv Council-West

Plover 54467
George, S. W., Ore-Ida Foods

Rothschild 54474
Lavanway, P. J., Reed Lignin Inc

Stevens Point 54481
Clayton, R. E., First Financial S & S
Haferbecker, G., Academic
Sullivan, M. F., Univ of Wisconsin

LaCrosse 54601
Abbey, A., Univ of Wisconsin
Imes, S. K., Arbitrator

Sparta 54656
Rice, Z. S., Arbitrator

Eau Claire 54701
Bergmann, T. J., Univ of Wisconsin
Vernon, G., Arbitrator

Oshkosh 54901-54903
Feinauer, D. M., Academic
Franz, V. R. W., Univ of Wisconsin
Morton, C. W., Universal Foundry Co
Mounts, P. H., Univ of Wisconsin
Voelker, K. E., Univ of Wisconsin

Winneconne 54986
Bracken, W. G., Wis Assn of School Boards

WYOMING

Laramie 82071
Allen, R. E., Univ of Wyoming
Keaveny, T. J., Univ of Wyoming

CANADA

ALBERTA

Calgary

Ponak, A. M., Univ of Calgary
Serediak, M. S., Mount Royal College
Thomas, J. E., Business

Edmonton

Bemmels, B. G., Univ of Alberta
Fisher, E. G., Univ of Alberta
Frans, K. J., Government
Hameed, S. M. A., Univ of Alberta
Hegedus, D. M., Univ of Alberta
Melnyk, A. M., Attorney
Urquhart, W. G., Alberta Govt Telephones

BRITISH COLUMBIA

Burnaby

Andstein, C., BC Government Employees
Davidson, A., BC Federation of Labour
Dyck, R. G., IBEW #213
Gallagher, G. B., Attorney
Maki, D. R., Simon Fraser Univ
Rogow, R., Simon Fraser Univ
Thomas, P. H., BCIT Staff Society

Coquitlam

Taggart, J. D., Union

Port Moody

Strand, K. T., Simon Fraser Univ

Vancouver

Alley, D. M., BC Packers
Clifford, R. J., R. J. Clifford & Assoc
Doidge, J. L, MacMillan & Bloedel Ltd
Fraser, C. R. P.,
Graham, J. W., Univ of BC
Hickling, M. A., Univ of BC
Knight, T. R., Univ of B. C.
Koerner, S., Union
McAllister, P. J., Health Labor Rels Assn
McKee, C. B., Clive McKee Ltd
McPhillips, D. C., Univ of BC
Morgan, H. J., Labatt Breweries
Nikaido, R. S., Health Labor Rels Assn
Stablein, R. E., Univ of BC
Thompson, M. E., Univ of BC
Verma, A., Univ of BC

Victoria

Koerner, S., Union
Walsh, W. D., Univ of Victoria

MANITOBA

Winnipeg

Chapman, J. M., Simkin Gallagher
Hercus, T. F., Univ of Manitoba
Patterson, R. A., Univ of Manitoba

NEW BRUNSWICK

Fredericton

Giles, A. J., Univ of NB
Jain, H. C., Univ of NB
Kircher, K. K., Univ of NB
Stanley, D. C., NB Ind Rels Council

NORTHWEST TERRITORY

Yellowknife

Halback, D. G., Government

NOVA SCOTIA

Halifax

Duffy, J. F., Academic

ONTARIO

Downsview

Jick, T. D., York Univ
Lucas, R., York Univ
McKechnie, G. H., York Univ
Rubenstein, B., Arbitration

Georgetown

Mitchell, A. L., Student

Hamilton

Adams, R. J., McMaster Univ
Agarwal, N. C., Mcmaster Univ
Jain, H. C., McMaster Univ
Rose, J. B., McMaster Univ

Ilderton

Bergman, P. D., Student

Islington

Nielsen, P. B., Oshawa Group Ltd

Kingston

Downie, B. M., Queens Univ
Godard, J. H., Academic
Goyet, F. R., Queens Univ
Kumar , P., Queens Univ
Lagrott, W. A., Student
Marcotte, M. A., Student
Marlow, N. A., Student
McShane, S. L., Student
Wood, W. D., Queens Univ

London

Peach, D. A., Univ of Western Ontario
Portis, B.
Wettlaufer, J. J., Univ of Western Ontario
Whitehead, J. D., Univ of Western Ontario

Ottawa

Brown, J. H., Public Service Staff Rels
Craig, A. W., Univ of Ottawa
Daniel, M. J., Canada Post Corp
Deschenes, G., LeDroit
Fryer, J. L., Natl Union Provinicial Govt Empls
Haythorne, G. V., Retired
Leonard, L. P., Dept of Labour
Ostry, S., Government
Pyle, D. G., Retired
Quinet, F., Public Serv Staff Rels
Schwartz, S., Academic
Subbarao, A. V., Univ of Ottawa
Vallee, E., United Steelworkers

Toronto

Joyce, R. D., Consulting
Kervin, J. B., Univ of Toronto
Kruger, A. M., Univ of Toronto
Meltz, N. M., Univ of Toronto
Parks, W. J.
Phillips, D., Bell Canada

Reid, F., Univ of Toronto
Sack, J., Sack, Charney et al
Scott, W. S., Bell Canada
Sen, J., Studies in Educ Inst
Vitalis, E. L. Jr., Ryerson Polytech Inst
Wilson, S. F.

Waterloo
Frenzel, K. A., Wilfrid Laurier Univ
Wright, R. L.

Welland
Repar, G., Niagara College

Windsor
Andiappan, P., Univ of Windsor
Cattaneo, R. J., Univ of Windsor
Clarke, J. D., Univ of Windsor
Kovacs, A. E., Univ of Windsor
Singh, V. P., Kendan Mfg Ltd
Solomon, N. A.

PRINCE EDWARD ISLAND
Charlottetown
Revell, J. J., PEI Labour Rels Bd

QUEBEC
Anjou
Lequin, J. A.

Aylmer
Barriere, L. F.

Beauharnois
Allard, M., Chromasco Ltd

Cap Rouge
Boivin, J., Laval Univ

Charlesbourg
Delorme, F.

Dollard des Ormeaux
Dellarocca, L.

Lac Beauport
Saint Laurent, J.

Montreal
Abenhaim, L. L., Student
Altomonte, V., Student
Armenti, C., Student
Bairstow, F., McGill Univ
Beer, R., Student
Bourdon, R., Bell Canada
Brody, B., Univ of Montreal
Cote, P. M., Student
D'Amborosio, N.
Desjardins, N. J., FED CPD
Dolan, S., Univ Montreal
Downer, B. M., Student
Dunberry, F. J., Paperworkers
Gauthier, F., Inst Natl de Productivite
Giroux, M.
Goldenberg, S. B., McGill Univ
Hebert, G., Univ of Montreal
Klamph, B. J., Student
Larouche, V., Univ of Montreal
Ledoux, D., O.I.I.Q.
Lemelin, M., Hautes Etudes Commerciale
LaPage, F., McGill Univ
Mailloux, N., Retired
Mercier, P., Student
Rajan, G. S.
Sen, J., Concordia Univ
Skanes-Taylor, J., Student
Thibodeau, G., Dominion Textile Corp

Quebec
Belanger, J., Univ Laval
Bernier, J., Univ Laval
Deom-Camire, E., Academic
Dion, G., Univ Laval
Laflamme, G., Univ of Laval
Mercier, J., Univ of Laval
Rondeau, C., Univ of Laval
Sexton, J., Univ of Laval

Rimouski
Gosselin, L., Univ Quebec

Sherbrooke
Bouvier, E. E., Academic
Petit, A., Univ of Sherbrooke

St. Foy
Audet, M.,Univ Laval
Lajoie, M., Academic
Leclerc, C., Academic

St. Laurent
Macklan, R., Student

St. Leonard
Giubilaro, P.

Trois Riviers
Fabi, B. C., Univ Quebec

Valleyfield
LePage, L., Produits Chimiques Expro

SASKATCHEWAN
Regina
Muthuchidambaram, S. P., Univ of Regina
Wartman, D. B., Sask Wheat Pool

Saskatoon
Sharma, B. D., Univ of Sask
Walmsley, P. Y., Univ of Sask.
Wetzel, E., Univ of Sask.
Wetzel, K. W., Univ of Sask

OTHER COUNTRIES AND TERRITORIES

ARGENTINA
Buenos Aires
Mantilla, E. S., Business

AUSTRALIA
Callus, R., Univ of Sydney, NSW
Corina, J., Epping, Sydney, NSW
Deery, S. J., Univ of Melbourne, Parkville, Victoria
Dowling, P. J., Univ of Melbourne, Parkville Victoria
Dufty, N. F., West Australia Inst Tech, S. Bentley
Hancock, K. J., The Flinders Univ, Bedford Park
Hotchkiss, W. E., Univ of New South Wales, Kensington
Lansbury, R. D., Macquarie Univ, North Ryde, NSW
McPhee, J. M., David Syme Bus School, East Victoria
Moore, J. C., Council & Arb Comm, Sydney
Niland, J. R., Univ of NSW, Kensington
Oxnam, D. W., Dalkeith, Western Australia
Plowman, D. H., Univ of NSW, Kensington
Smith, R. E., Australian Natl Univ, Canberra
Worland, D., Ivanhoe, Victoria

AUSTRIA
Auer, H., Teacher, Vienna

BELGIUM
Blanpain, R. R., Univ of Leuven

BOLIVIA
Asin, C. G., Business, Cochabamba

BRAZIL
Padilha, T. M., Inst Euvaldo Lodi, Rio de Janeiro
Pastore, J., Sao Paulo

CHILE
Walker, F., Univ of Chile, Santiago

CYPRUS
Phiniotis, S.P., Acropolis, Nicosia

ENGLAND
Bain, G. S., Univ Warwick, Coventry
Bamber, G. J., Durham Univ, Durham
Barrett, B. C., Univ of Bath, Claverton Down
Berry, A. P., Engineering Empl Assn, Coventry
Brewster, C. J., Empl Rels Res Ctr, Cambridge
Donovan, C. E., British Gas Corp, London
Gillies, J. G., J. G. Gillies & Assoc, Oxford
Gospel, H. F., Univ of Kent, Canterbury
Grude, J. K., Student, St. Aldych, London
Halmos, A. M., Sheperds Bush, London
Marsh, A. I., St. Edmund Hall, Oxford
Naylor, P. G., Bestobell Place, Slough, Berkshire
Roberts, B. C., Univ of London
Robinson, D., Univ of Oxford
Speyer, D. B., Student
Willman, P., Imperial College, London

ETHIOPIA
Etukudo, A. J., ILO, Addis Ababa

FIJI ISLANDS
Moore, C. C., ILO, Suva
Young, F. J. L., Permanent Arbitrator, Suva

FINLAND
Luoma, V., Retired, Turku

FRANCE
Benhamou, A., UIMM, Paris
Clarke, O., OECD, Paris
Oechslin, J.J., Council French Employers, Paris
Parguel, N., Bagneux
Piganiol, C., Plaisir
Rellini, G., OECD, Paris
Rojot, J. R., Paris
Weiss, D., Univ de Paris

HONG KONG
Levin, D. A., Univ of Hong Kong

INDIA
Johri, C. K., Shri Ram Centre, New Delhi
Kumar, P., HSC Society
Patrudu, B. V. S., Andhra Univ, Waltair
Rao, M. G., Andhra Univ, Waltair
Srikrishna, B. N., Attorney, Matunga, Bombay

ISRAEL
Abboushi, S., Birzeit Univ, Birzeit
Bialogorsky, R., Tel Aviv Univ, Tel Aviv
Friedman, A., Hebrew Univ, Jerusalme
Gat, N., Koor Foods Industries, Haifa
Halperin, Z., Tambour Askar Paints Ltd, Haifa
Harel, G. H., Technion, Haifa
Macarov, D., School of Social Work, Jerusalem
Miron, Y., Israel Ports Authority, Tel Aviv
Rosenstein, E., Technion, Haifa
Shirom, A., Tel Aviv Univ, Tel Aviv

ITALY
Biagi, M., Univ di Modena, Bologna
Giugni, G., Univ of Roma, Roma
Mazzocchi, G. C., Univ Cattolica, Milano
Sciarra, S., Firenze
Tarantelli, E., ISEI, Roma
Veneziani, B., Univ Professor, Bari

JAPAN
Ballon, R. J., Sophia Univ, Tokyo
Fujiwara, M., Nanzan Univ, Nagoya
Fukami, F., Shizouka Univ, Ohya Shizouka-Shi
Hayashi, H., Kumamoto Univ of Commerce
Kojima, N., Toyama Univ, Gofuku
Maeshima, I., Tokai Univ, Hiratsuka-City
Masakame, Y., Toyama Univ, Toyamo-shi
Mihara, Y., Nagasaki Univ, Nagasaki
Okubayashi, K., Kobe Univ, Kobe
Ono, T., Yokohama
Shimada, H., Keio Univ, Tokyo
Takeshi, I., Hosei Univ, Tokyo
Toshokan, S. D., Sapparo
Tsuda, M., Hitotsubashi Univ, Tokyo
Umetani, S., Urawa Saitama
Yoneda, K., Kokusai-Shoka College, Kawagoe-shi

KOREA
Kim, H. J., Yonsei Univ, Seoul
Kim, S., Korea Development Inst, Seoul

KUWAIT
Madkour, M. T., Kuwait Oil Co, Koc Ahmadi

MALAYSIA
Ghani, T. B., Natl Productivity Center, Petaling Jaya
Smith, W. A., Natl Univ, Bangi Selangor
Thong, G. T. S., Univ of Malaya, Kuala Lumpur

NETHERLANDS
Bolweg, J. F., Hengelstraat, Gilze
Reynaerts, W. H. J., Tilburg Univ, Tilburg

NEW ZEALAND
Geare, A. S., Univ Otago, Dunedin

NIGERIA
Aderinto, A., Univ of Lagos, Lagos
Arewah, P. J. O., Lagos State
Fashoyin, T., Univ of Lagos, Yaba Lagos
Igbo, G. A., Ist Bank of Nigeria, Lagos
Iwuji, E. C., Natl Industrial Court, Lagos
Oni, I. O., Univ of Ibadan, Ibadan
Opara, R. U., Federal Ministry, Bendel State

PERU
Aparicio, L., Analisis, Laboral, Lima

PHILLIPPINES
Pizarro, Z. Q., Intl Rice Inst, Manila

SAUDI ARABIA
Butler, J. C., Saudi Arabian Airlines, Jiddah

SCOTLAND
Beaumont, P. B., Univ of Glasgow, Glasgow
Johnston, T. L., Edinburgh
Leopold, J. W., Univ of Glasgow, Glasgow
Thomson, A. W. J., Glasgow Univ, Glasgow

SINGAPORE
Cheng, L. T. L., Singapore

SOUTH AFRICA
Griffiths, H., Univ of Witwatersrand, Johannesburg
Jones, R. A., Univ of Witwatersrand
Steenkamp, T. I., Gencor, marshalltown
Suchard, H., Univ of Witwatersrand
Wilhelm,C., IPM Southern Africa, Braamfontein

SPAIN
Rey, S., Facultad de Ciencias, Sevilla

SWEDEN
Gonas, L. K., Arbetslivscentrum, Stockholm
Nordlander, A., Verkstadsforening, Stockholm

SWITZERLAND
Gladstone, A., Geneva
Kruglak, G., ILO, Geneva
Poncini, C., ILO, Geneva
Taylor, D. P., ILO, Geneva

THAILAND
Chareon, S., AID, Thonburi
Hongladarom, C., Thammasat Univ. Bankok
Priebjrivat, V., Thammasat Univ, Bangkok

USSR
Koval, V., Academy of Sciences, Moscow Center

VENEZUELA
Parra A, F. I., Caracas
Perez, A. H., Urb Avila Alta Forida, Carcas

WEST GERMANY
Gerlach, K., Hannover
Herding, R. G., Info-Dienst, Frankfurt
Losche, P., Univ of Gottingen, Gottingen
Pagenstecher, U., Nurnberg-Mogeldorf

WEST INDIES
Beckles, L., Trinidad Home Developers, Trinidad
Birch, J., AID, Kingston
Cezair, P. L., Port of Spain
James, A., Trinidad
Johnson, C. L, Caribbean Development Bnk, Barbados
Leslie, A. N. ILO, Barbados
Ramlochan, M., Abel-Clay & Concrete Div, Trinidad
Ramsubeik, G., Trinidad

OCCUPATIONAL LIST OF MEMBERS

Members are classified by the principal business or professional category they designated on the *Directory* questionnaire or from the current IRRA mailing list. Those who do not fit into the major categories, or for whom no occupation was specified, are listed in the "Other" categories. Second and third occupations, when indicated by the member, can be found in the member's biography. In using the Directory, it should be noted that the categories "Arbitration" and "Consulting" exclude many members who do this work but did not indicate it was their primary occupation.

ACADEMIC

UNIVERSITY ADMINISTRATION

Aboud, Antone
Allen, Russell W.
Aller, Curtis C.
Altman, Steve
Alutto, Joseph A.
Auzenne, George R.
Bakken, Gordon M.
Banks, Robert Frederick
Bartosic, Florian
Benjamin, Ernst
Benson, Frances
Bernstein, Paul
Bialogorsky, Raphael
Bienstock, Herbert
Bonifield, William C.
Bouvier, Emile E.
Box, J. Richard
Brown, James Douglas
Bush, Ronald W.
Carlson, Charles E.
Cohen, Malcolm S.
Cushman, Edward L.
Devino, William Stanley
Dillingham, Alan Edward
Dolan-Greene, Colleen
Domitrz, Joseph S.
Dufty, Norman Francis
Edwards, Bruce H.
Einbecker, Richard C.
Exstrom, J. Fredrik
Emmet, Thomas A.
Exo, Susan
Ford, Lucille G.
Fredian, Alan J.
Friedman, Harvey Leonard
Geetter, Joan
Gershenfeld, Walter J.
Ginkel, Alfred Oscar
Gitlow, Abraham L.
Goldberg, Frank
Goldberg, Stephen M.
Gray, Lois Spier
Groty, Charles Keith
Gujarati, Ruth P.
Gutteridge, Thomas George
Haber, William
Hancock, Keith Jackson
Hardbeck, George W.
Herzog, Paul M.
Hudson, Harriet Dufresne
Izutsu, Glenn T.
Jacobs, Arthur Theodore
Johnson, Howard Wesley
Johnson, Ronald D.
Jones, Ethel B.
Kilgour, John Graham
Kimmett, Charles T.
Knezek, LaVerne D.
LaPenta, Thomas M.
Leader, Alan Howard
MacKenzie, John Robert
MacQueen, William J.
Mannix, Thomas M.
Maxey, Charles
Meli, John Thomas
Miller, Alice R.
Mowry, Christine B.
Neale, William S.
Newton, David
Noble, Albert Charles
Notaro, Salvatore A.
O'Donnell, Joseph Patrick
Owen, John Pipkin
Padhila, Tarcisio M.
Palomba, Neil Anthony
Parry, James
Penfield, Robert Verdon
Potter, Richard H.
Powers, Edward W.
Pulhamus, Aaron R.
Ratner, Robert A.
Reeves, T. Zane
Rehmus, Charles Martin
Robinson, James William
Robson, R. Thayne
Rony, Vera
Salerno, George P.
Salten, David G.
Samoff, Bernard L.
Schmidt, Robert F.
Schramm, Leroy H.
Simmelkjaer, Robert
Small, Francis X.
Spritzer, Allan D.
Stover, Walter F.
Strait, Dorcas L.
Thomas, Benjamin F.
Tom, Linda
Van Cleve, Roy R.
Warner, Aaron W.
Weber, Arnold R.
Weissenberg, Peter
White, Donald Joseph
Wittenberg, Carole A.
Young, Edwin

ACADEMIC: BUSINESS ADMINISTRATION

Anderson, Claire J.
Anderson, Donald A.
Andiappan, Palaniappan
Aussieker, Bill
Ayres, Richard C.
Barkey, Fred A.
Barnum, Darold T.
Barocci, Thomas Andrew
Barrett, Brian Colin
Barrett, Eamonn
Baum, Jeffrey
Belcher, David W.
Bella, Salvatore Joseph
Berry, John Elwood
Bies, Robert J.
Bigoness, William J.
Bourne, Richard M.
Brown, Douglas Vincent
Burke, Donald R.
Burstein, George
Byars, Lloyd L.
Calvasina, Gerald E.
Campbell, Archie E.
Champlin, Frederic C., III
Christenson, Christina
Clarke, John D.
Conlon, John Thomas
Cook, Roy A.
Craft, James A.
Crane, Donald Paul
D'Ambrosio, Normand
De Blander, William B.
Decenzo, David Anthony
Eisele, C. Frederick
Evans, Eugene Emerson
Extejt, Marian M.
Fisher, Edward George
Fottler, Myron David
Franke, Arnold
Gadon, Herman
Gallagher, Daniel J.
Gilman, Tamara Ann
Griffiths, Howard
Gurdon, Michael A.
Ha, Chester Chiduk
Harris, Philip
Hartley, William B.
Hershfield, David Charles
Hill, Richard Emmett
Hutter, Dean E.
Johnson, Alton C.
Karim, Ahmad R.
Kearney, William J.
Kessler, Paul
Klein, Janice A.
Kleiner, Morris Michael
Knight, Thomas Rockwell
Kropp, Steven H.
Kuhn, James Wesley
Ledgerwood, Donna E.
Livernash, Edward Robert
Lowenstein, Henry
Mamer, John W.
Mathys, Nicholas J.
McCabe, Douglas M.

McPhee, Joan Melville
McShane, Steven L.
Miles, Raymond Edward
Mills, Daniel Quinn
Mitchell, James L.
Moberly, Russell L.
Mohr, Coenraad Luttig
Mooney, Marta J.
Moore, David G.
Nollen, Stanley D.
Novak, Henry Linton
O'Brien, Fabius Prince
Ornati, Oscar A.
Peach, David Alan
Perselay, Gerald
Peterson, Richard Byron
Pomnichowski, Alex S.
Portis, Bernard
Potash, Sidney
Prenting, Theodore O.
Puff, Harold Frederick
Purcell, Theodore Vincent
Rettig, Jack L.
Richards, Emory H.
Rogow, Robert
Rose, Michael L.
Rosenbaum, Edward
Schaefer, Stephen C.
Schlender, William E.
Shields, Janice Christine
Solomon, Janet Stern
Stepina, Lee P.
Stevens, John E.
Sullivan, Michael Fuller
Thompson, Mark E.
Thong, Gregory Tin Sin
Tomlinson, William H.
Ullman, Joseph C.
Verma, Anil
Villere, Maurice Francois
Walker, J. Malcolm
Walker, Kenneth Frederick
Walmsley, Peter Yates
Wettlaufer, John J.
Wetzel, Eva
Whitehead, J. David
Williams, Douglas A.
Wilson, Steven F.
Wolfmeyer, Pamela V.
Zoller, John Harry

ACADEMIC: ECONOMICS

Abowd, John M.
Abraham, Katharine G.
Adams, John P., Jr.
Adams, Leonard Palmer
Aderinto, Adeyemo
Adkins, Roger L.
Ahlburg, Dennis Allan
Alexander, Joseph
Alexander, Kenneth O.
Allen, Steven G.
Applebaum, Leon
Aronson, Robert L.
Ashenfleter, Orley
Austermiller, Carl J.
Bain, Trevor
Baird,William M.
Ballantine, John Winthrop
Barbash, Jack
Barkin, Solomon
Barlow, Robert F.
Barnes, Scott D.
Behman, Sara
Beinhauer, Myrtle T.
Beller, Andrea H.
Bellinger, William K.
Berkowitz, Monroe
Bers, Melvin K.
Bishop, John Hillman
Blackman, John L., Jr.
Blake, Charles H., Jr.
Blau, Francine D.
Blicksilver, Jack
Bloom, David Elliott
Boardman-Free, Rhona
Borus, Michael Eliot
Bowlby, Roger L.
Briggs, Vernon Mason, Jr.
Brown, Clair
Bumas, Lester O.
Butler, Arthur D.
Cain, Glen G.
Cain, Leonard F.
Callahan, Charles, III
Campbell, John, Jr.
Carey, Philip A.
Cassidy, George Wesley
Cederlund, Albert Merrill
Christian, Virgil L., Jr.
Cohen, Martin A.
Cohen, Sanford
Cohen, Wilbur J.
Conant, John L.
Cook, Robert F.
Cook, William Glenn
Copps, John Alden
Coz, Richard T.
Crisafulli, Virgil C.
Crist, William Dale
Crowell, Elizabeth
Curington, William Peter
Curtis, Frank Judson, Jr.
Cypin, Jack G.
Davis, Joe C.
DeFreitas, Gregory E.
Dickens, William T.
Doeringer, Peter Brantley
Donnelly, Lawrence I.
Drake, Charles Goodloe
Dunlop, John Thomas
Edelman, Milton T.
Edwards, Linda N.
Eisenberg, Harry H.
Elbaum, Bernard Louis
Ellard, Charles J.
Erenburg, Mark E.
Erickson, Herman
Evans, Robert, Jr.
Farber, Henry S.
Fearn, Robert Morcom
Finegan, Thomas Aldrich
Flanagan, Robert Joseph
Fraundorf, Martha Norby
Frenzel, K. Arnold
Gaghen, Harry W.
Gallagher, John Owen
Garnel, Donald
Gendel, Eugene B.
Gerlach, Knut
Ghilarducci, Teresa
Gifford, Adam
Ginsburg, Helen
Ginzberg, Eli
Gitelman, Howard M.
Gitter, Robert J.
Gleason, Alan Harold
Gleason, Sandra E.
Glover, Robert W.
Goldfarb, Robert Stanley
Gordon, Margaret S.
Gouke, Cecil Granville
Goulet, Janet C.
Grayson, Gerald H.
Greenberg, David Hillel
Groesbeck, James D.
Haferbecker, Gordon
Hamermesh, Daniel S.
Haney, Martin D.
Hansen, W. Lee
Harter, Lafayette G., Jr.
Hausman, Leonard Joel
Haworth, Charles T.
Helfgott, Roy B.
Heliker, George B.
Helmreich, Theodore C.
Hendricks, Wallace
Herlihy, H. Murray
Herman, Edward Emil
Herrnstadt, Irwin L.
Hoffman, Emily P.
Holzer, Harry J.
Hongladarom, Chira
Horn, Robert N.
Horowitz, Morris A.
Houchins, Joseph Roosevelt
Houska, Mary Dittmer
Hurd, Richard W.
Hyclak, Thomas J.
Iwuji, Eleasar Chukudike
Jantzen, Robert H.
Johnson, C. L.
Johnson, William G.
Johnston, Thomas Lothian
Johri, Chandra Kumar
Jones, Derek C.
Jones, Lamar Babington
Joseph, Myron L.
Kahn, Lawrence M.
Kahn, Shulamit
Kahne, Hilda
Kasper, Hirschel
Kassalow, Everett M.
Katz, Arnold
Kaufman, Bruce E.
Kelly, Erwin L., Jr.
Killingsworth, Mark R.
Kim, Hwang Joe
King, Clay B.
Klein, Lawrence R.
Knight, Robert Edward Lee
Knopf, Kenyon A.
Koeller, Charles Timothy
Kohen, Andrew I.
Kojima, Noriaki
Kovacs, Aranka Eve
Koval, Vitalina
Kreider, L. Emil
Krislov, Joseph
Kruger, Arthur Martin
Kuptzin, Harold
Kurth, Edmund Anthony
Kyle, James T.
Lampman, Robert J.
Lang, Kevin
Lawson, Luther D.
Lee, Joseph Shing
Lenihan, Patrick M.
Lentz, Bernard F.
Lester, Richard Allen
Levin, Henry M.
Levinson, Harold Myer
Levitan, Sar A.
Lovell, Hugh G.
Lurie, Melvin
Lyman, Jay Rich
Lynch, Lisa M.
Maki, Dennis R.
Mangum, Garth L.
Mangum, Stephen L.
Marshall, F. Ray
Martin, Philip L.
Masters, Stanley H.
Matilla, John P.
Maxwell, Nan L.
Mazzocchi, G. Carlo
McLain, James M.
McLauchlan, J. Michael
McLaughlin, Francis M.

Mead, John Ford
Medoff, James L.
Meltz, Noah Moshe
Mikrut, John Joseph Jr.
Miller, Glenn W.
Mincer, Jacob
Mitchell, Olivia S.
Moore, William J.
Morgan, Celia A.
Moser, Collette H.
Mullenix, Grady Lee
Murphy, John Michael
Naples, Michele I.
Neumann, George R.
Newman, Ted E.
Oaxaca, Ronald L.
O'Donnell, Liguori A.
Oettinger, Martin P.
Olayiwola, Peter Olu
Oppenheimer, Margaret Ann
Orton, Eliot Smith
Osterman, Paul S.
Parigi, Sam F.
Parker, Carl D.
Parnes, Herbert S.
Pearson, Donald W.
Peirce, William Spangar
Perline, Martin Michael
Perry, Herbert Anthony
Pierson, Frank Cook
Podgursky, Michael John
Prosper, Peter Anthony Jr.
Pullen, Robert White
Radar, Jennette S.
Ragan, James
Reed, Jeffrey A.
Refior, Everett Lee
Reid, Frank
Reynolds, Lloyd George
Ridgel, Gus Tolver
Rittenoure, R. Lynn
Roberts, Ray C., Jr.
Robinson, Derek
Rock, Charles P.
Rogers, David E.
Rohrlich, George F.
Rondeau, Claude
Rosenbaum, Rene P.
Rosenberg, Samuel
Rungeling, Brian Scott
Ryan, Edward William
Santos, Richard
Saunders, W. Phillip Jr.
Schaffer, Beverly K.
Scheuch, Richard
Schnell, John F.
Schulman, Rosalind Sadoff
Schumacher, A. Rebecca
Schwartz, Arthur R.
Seeborg, Michael C.
Segur, W. H.
Sharp, Walton Henry
Shearer, John C.
Shimada, Haruo
Skinner, Gordon S.
Smith, Lewis H.
Smith, Ralph Ely
Smith, Robert Stewart
Smith, Russell Edward
Snyder, Russell A.
Sobel, Irvin
Spellman, William E.
Spitz, Herbert
Spitz, Ruth Sachere
Stein, Bruno
Steinberg, Harvey A.
Stephan, Paula Elizabeth
Stevens, Carl Mantle
Stevens, David Walter
Stevenson, Thomas Martin
Stewart, Joann Phelps
Strand, Kenneth T.
Strober, Myra Hoffenberg
Sweeney, John G.
Taira, Koji
Thayer, Ralph Ira
Thomas, Wade L.
Thompson, Allen Rupert
Thornton, Robert J.
Troy, Leo
Turnbull, John G.
Turner, Marjorie S.
Udis, Bernard
Ulman, Lloyd
Umetani, Shunichiro
Voelker, Keith Emery
Wachter, Michael L.
Wagner, Frank E.
Walker, Roger Williams
Wallace, Phyllis A.
Walsh, William David
Weber, Charles T.
Weinstein, Paul A.
Wend, Jared Scudder
Werner, Herbert Dennis
Williams, Donald R.
Winters, B. C.
Witney, Fred
Woodbury, Stephan A.
Wool, Muriel B.
Zaidi, Mahmood A.

ACADEMIC: INDUSTRIAL RELATIONS

Abboushi, Suheil
Adams, Roy Joseph
Allen, Robert Edward
Anderson, Roger L.
Andrisani, Paul James
Aranoff, Arthur M.
Audet, Michel
Azvedo, Ross Eames
Baderschneider, Jean Ann
Bain, George Sayers
Bairstow, Frances
Bakhtiari, Paul
Balanis, Frank A.
Balfour, G. Alan
Bamber, Greg J.
Barrett, Jerome T.
Bazerman, Max H.
Beach, Dale Stuart
Beaumont, Phillip B.
Becker, Brian
Begin, James P.
Belanger, Jacques
Bemmels, Brian G.
Bergmann, Ralph H.
Berkeley, Arthur E.
Bernier, Jean
Bernstein, Irving
Bethke, Arthur Leon
Bickner, Mei Liang
Blanpain, Roger Robert
Block, Richard Norman
Blum, Albert A.
Blunt, Keith Roger
Bognanno, Mario Frank
Bogue, Bonnie Cebulski
Bohlander, George W.
Boivin, Jean
Boss, Andrew C.
Boyer, John William Jr.
Boyle, George V.
Bradley, G. Wayne
Brady, Thomas F.
Brannen, Dalton E.
Braun, Kurt
Brickner, Dale G.
Briggs, Steven
Brody, Bernard
Brooks, George W.
Brookshire, Michael Leo
Brown, Mark L.
Brumm, John M.
Buckley, Louis F.
Bullock, Paul
Burdetsky, Ben
Burton, John F., Jr.
Busman, Gloria Brooks
Cabelly, Alan
Callus, Ron
Cambridge, Charles D.
Campagna, Anthony Frank
Cappelli, Peter H.
Carmel, Alan Stanley
Cassell, Frank H.
Castellano, John J.
Chaison, Gary N.
Chamberlain, Neil W.
Chandler, Margaret K.
Chaubey, Manmohan D.
Chelius, James R.
Chernick, Jack
Chesler, Herbert A.
Chick, Michael John
Chown, David W.
Chu, Paul B. J.
Cohen, Cynthia Fryer
Coleman, Charles J.
Conant, Eaton H.
Cook, Alice H.
Cooke, William N.
Corcoran, Frank
Corina, John G.
Craig, Alton W. J.
Crawford, Angela C.
Crawford, James F.
Cullen, Donald E.
Culley, Jack F.
Curry, Theodore H, II
Cutler, S. Oley
Dale, Leon A.
Daly, James H.
David, John P.
Davidson, Naomi Berger
Dawson, William A.
Dayal, Sahab
Daymont, Thomas N.
Deane, Richard Glen
Decker, Robert L.
Deery, Stephen James
Deitsch, Clarence
Delaney, John T.
Dempsey, Joseph R.
Dennis, Barbara D.
Deom-Camire, Esther
Derber, Milton
Desjardins, Normand J.
Dibble, Richard E.
Dion, Gerard
Dobbelaere, Arthur G., Jr.
Doherty, Robert E.
Donn, Clifford B.
Donnelly, John Thomas
Donovan, Ronald
Douglas, Joel M.
Downie, Bryan McKay
Drotning, John Evan
Dworkin, James Barnet
Ehrenberg, Ronald G.
Elkin, Randy L. D.
Elkiss, Helen
Ellerbrock, Geraldine B.
Engle, Dennis E.
Erb, Charlotte M.
Estey, Marten S.
Fadem, Joel Alan
Fashoyin, Tayo

Ferman, Louis A.
Feuille, Peter
Figler, Robert Albert
Fiorito, Jack T.
Fischer, Ben
Fisher, Edward George
Fitzgerald, Mark J.
Flagler, John J.
Foegen, Joseph Henry
Fogel, Walter
Foltman, Felician F.
Forkosch, Morris D.
Forsythe, Edwin J.
Fossum, John Anthony
Foster, Howard George
Foulkes, Fred Klee
Franke, Walter H.
Friedman, Abraham
Fries, Henry William
Fujiwara, Michio
Fukami, Fumio
Fulmer, William E.
Galin, Amira
Gallagher, Daniel Gerard
Gant, Jocelind
Garbarino, Joseph W.
Gavin, Mortimer Hugh
Geare, Alan James
Geraghty, William V.
Gerhart, Paul F.
Gershenfeld, Gladys
Ghani, Tembon Bin
Giles, Anthony James
Gillingham, J. Benton
Gilmore, Carol Bankart
Giroux, Mario
Gladstone, Alan
Goldberg, Isadore
Goldenberg, Shirley B.
Gomberg, William
Gonas, Lena Kristina
Gordus, Jeanne Prial
Gospel, Howard F.
Graham, Harry Edward
Gramm, Cynthia L.
Grant, Alice B.
Gray, David Allen
Gray, George R.
Greer, Charles R.
Greis, Theresa Diss
Gross, James A.
Hagglund, George S.
Halevy, Irving
Hall, Charles Albert
Halpin, Charles A. J., Jr.
Hameed, Syed M. A.
Hansen, Gary B.
Harel, Gedaliahu H.
Harmon, Cheryl M.
Harpaz, Itzhak
Harrison, Edward L.
Hart, William S.
Hauck, Vern E.
Hawley, Langston T.
Hayford, Stephen L.
Healy, James J.
Hebert, Gerard
Helburn, Isadore B.
Helsby, Robert D.
Heneman, Robert Lloyd
Hercus, Terry F.
Heshizer, Brian P.
Higgins, Thomas James
Hill, Herbert
Hill, Marvin F.
Hills, Stephen Moore
Hobart, Christine L.
Hoffman, Helen G.
Hogler, Raymond Louis
Holley, William H., Jr.
Holoviak, Stephen Julian
Hoover, John J.
Hotchkiss, W. E.
Howard, Wayne E.
Hoyman, Michele Matis
Hubner, Walter Frank
Humphreys, Richard W.
Hundley, Gregory Stephen
Hunsucker, John L.
Hutchinson, John
Ichniowski, Bernard E.
Jacobs, David C.
Jacoby, Sanford Mark
Jain, Harish C.
Jain, Hem C.
Jedel, Michael Jay
Jennings, Kenneth M.
Jensen, Vernon H.
Johnson, David B.
Jones, Dallas Lee
Jones, Max B.
Jones, Robert A.
Judge, Jerome Joseph
Juris, Hervey A.
Kahn, Mark L.
Karper, Mark D.
Karsh, Bernard
Katz, Harry C.
Kaufman, Jacob J.
Kelley, Maryellen R.
Kelly, Eileen Patricia
Kelly, Matthew A.
Kennedy, Thomas Maynard
Kervin, John B.
Kienast, Philip K.
Killingsworth, Charles C.
Kim, Sookon
Kircher, Kraig Kay
Kleingartner, Archie
Knott, Ildiko
Kochan, Thomas Anton
Kopelman, Richard E.
Kowalski, Ronald E.
Koziara, Karen Shallcross
Kozlowski, Rick J.
Krider, Charles E.
Kruger, Daniel H.
Kuechle, David
Kumar, Pradeep
Labig, Chalmer E., Jr.
Laflamme, Gilles
Lajoie, Mario
Lansbury, Russell Duncan
Larouche, Viateur
Lawler, John Joseph
Leahy, William Henry
LeClerc, Claudine
Leftwich, Howard M.
Lemelin, Maurice
Leonard, Jonathan S.
Leone, Richard David
Leopold, John Watt
Lequin, Jacques A.
Levenstein, Aaron
Levine, Marvin Jacob
Levine, Solomon Bernard
Lewin, David
Liggett, Malcolm Hugh
Lillich, John E.
Lipsky, David Bruce
Loewenberg, J. Joseph
Ludlow, Howard T.
Luoma, Vaenoe
MacLeod, Angus G. S.
Maeshima, Iwao
Magenau, John M., III
Magnusen, Karl O.
Malinowski, Arthur A.
Maranto, Cheryl Lynn
Marett, Pamela C.
Markowitz, James R.
Marmo, Michael J.
Marsh, Arthur Ivor
Martin, James E.
Masakame, Yoshizo
Masters, Marick Francis
McBrearty, James Connell
McCollum, James Kenneth
McConnell, John W.
McConnell, Robert C.
McFarland, C. K.
McGrath, Marie Dorothea
McIntire, Warren W., Jr.
McIntosh, Barbara R.
McKechnie, Graeme H.
McKee, William L.
McKelvey, Jean T.
McKersie, Robert B.
McLaughlin, Doris B.
McPherson, Donald S.
McPhillips, David C.
Meer, Claudia Gaillard
Megley, John E.
Mercier, Jacques
Meyers, Frederic
Mihara, Yasuhiro
Miljus, Robert C.
Miller, Christopher S.
Miller, Mona
Miller, Richard Ulric
Mills, Miriam K.
Mire, Joseph
Mitchell, Daniel J. B.
Mitchell, John J., IV
Monat, Jonathon S.
Moore, Gary A.
Morand, Martin J.
Morrison, Malcolm H.
Mullaley, Edward J.
Munchus, George, III
Murphy, Charles J.
Murrmann, Kent F.
Murrmann, Suzanne K.
Muthuchidambaram, S. P.
Myers, Charles Andrew
Nadworny, Milton J.
Najita, Joyce M.
Nelson, Nels E.
Nestor, Oscar W.
Neufeld, Maurice Frank
Niland, John R.
Nitta, Michio
Northrup, Herbert Roof
O'Brien, Francis T.
O'Brien, Rae Ann
Ofong, Chigbo
O'Grady, James P.
Olson, Craig
Oni, I. O.
Ono, Tsuneo
Overton, Craig E.
Owens, Stephen Dennis
Oxnam, Desmond W.
Pagenstecher, Ulrich
Patrudo, B. V. S.
Pearce, Thomas G.
Pegnetter, Richard C.
Perry, Charles R.
Peters, Ronald J.
Petersen, Donald J.
Piganiol, Claude
Pigors, Paul
Plowman, David H.
Poe, Lawrence J.
Pollard, Hinda Greyser
Ponak, Allen M.
Powers, Kathleen Jay
Powers, Robert S.
Pulich, Marcia A.
Raffaele, Gary Charles

Rajan, G. S.
Ramos, Elias T.
Ramsubeik, George
Ranhand, Samuel
Rao, M. Gangadharo
Raza, M. Ali
Redwood, Anthony Leo
Reinerth, Michael W.
Remington, John
Reynaerts, Wim H. J.
Reynolds, Roy R.
Rice,William V., Jr.
Richardson, Reed C.
Rico, Leonard
Roberts, B. C.
Roberts, Higdon C., Jr.
Robinson, Jerald Francis
Rocha, Joseph Ramon Jr.
Roderick, Roger Duane
Rogers, Robert Charles
Rojot, Jacques R.
Roomkin, Myron
Rose, Joseph Barker
Rosen, Stephen J.
Rosenstein, Eliezer
Rothbaum, Melvin
Rowan, Richard Lamar
Rubenfeld, Stephen A.
Sabghir, Irving H.
Sadinsky, Matthew L.
Saint Laurent, Jacques
Salipante, Paul F., Jr.
Saltzman, Gregory Martin
Sandler, Melvin
Sandver, Marcus H.
Scarpello, Vida
Schaupp, Dietrich L.
Schmidt, Charles T., Jr.
Schneider, Betty V. H.
Schumann, Paul L.
Schuster, Michael H.
Schwab, Donald P.
Schwartz, Rosalind M.
Schwartz, Stanley J.
Scoville, James Griffin
Sedwick, Thomas
Seeber, Ronald L.
Seltzer, George O.
Sen, Joya
Serediak, Martin S.
Sexton, Jean
Sharma, Basu D.
Sherman, James Joseph
Shirom, Arie
Shister, Joseph
Shulenburger, David E.
Siegel, Abraham J.
Silverblatt, Ronnie
Sinicropi, Anthony V.
Skelton, B. R.
Sloane, Arthur Allan
Smith, Anna D.
Smith, Wil J.
Snook, John Lloyd Jr.
Sockell, Donna
Solie, Richard John
Solomon, Norman A.
Soltow, Martha Jane
Spirn, Steven
Stallworth, Lamont Edward
Stark, Harry F.
Staudohar, Paul David
Stephens, David B.
Stephens, Elvis Clay
Stern, James L.
Stieber, Jack
Stochaj, John M.
Strauss, George
Sturmthal, Adolf F.
Subbarao, Aremanda V.
Suchard, Hazel
Suntrup, Edward L.
Swiercz, Paul Michael
Swinehart, David P.
Taylor, Marla
Theeke, Herman Arthur
Thomas, James R.
Thomson, A. W. J.
Tomkiewicz, Joseph
Torrence, William David
Tosohkan, Sapporo Daigaku
Tracy, Lane
Tsuda, Masumi
Tyer, Charles William
Voos, Paula Beth
Wagner, Edwin M.
Wagner, Martin
Walker, Francisco
Wasmuth, William J.
Watkins, Thomas L.
Weinberg, William M.
Weiss, Dimitri
Weisz, Morris
Wendt, Ann C.
Wesman, Elizabeth Claire
Wetzel, Kurt Winston
Wheeler, Hoyt Noland
Wheeler, Kenneth Gerald
White, Luther Glenn
White, Rudolph A.
Widick, B. J.
Wiggins, Ronald Luther
Williams, Richard C.
Willman, Paul
Windmuller, John P.
Witteried, George C.
Wolitz, Louise Berman
Wolkinson, Benjamin W.
Wolters, Roger S.
Wood, W. Donald
Woods, Leslie Earle
Woolf, Donald Austin
Worland, David
Wrong, Elaine
Wyman, Earl J.
Yoder, Dale
Yoneda, Kiyotaka
Young, Dallas M.
Zeffiro, Jay A.
Zeller, Frederick Anthony

ACADEMIC: LAW

Aaron, Benjamin
Atleson, James Benjamin
Barron, Paul
Bellace, Janice R.
Berger, Mark
Bernstein, Merton Clay
Biagi, Marco
Bloom, Gordon F.
Blumrosen, Alfred Wm.
Blumrosen, Ruth G.
Bornstein, Tim L.
Chareon, Siribhand
Colosi, Marco L.
Connolly, Walter B., Jr.
Cooper, Christine Godsil
Craver, Charles Bradford
Donald, Carrie G.
Draznin, Anne L.
Drogin, Ira
Edwards, Harry T.
Feller, David E.
Fillion, John A.
Firestone, Frederic N.
Giugni, Gino
Goetz, Raymond
Goldberg, Michael J.
Goldberg, Stephen B.
Goldman, Alvin L.
Gosslein, Louis
Gould, William B.
Gregory, Gordon A.
Grenig, Jay Edward
Hanes, Walter W.
Hayashi, Hiroko
Heinsz, Timothy J.
Hickling, M. Anthony
Jones, Edgar A., Jr.
Jones, James Edward Jr.
Kaden, Lewis B.
King, George Savage
Knapp, Andria S.
Kohler, Thomas C.
Konvitz, Milton R.
Koretz, Robert F.
Krendel, Ezra S.
Lamberti, Thomas M.
Larson, Lennart Vernon
Lee, Barbara A.
Lehman, Hans J.
Leonard Arthur S.
Lowry, David R.
Lynch, William F.
Madden, John V.
Malin, Martin H.
Mann, J. Keith
McDade, Robert Joseph
Meltzer, Bernard D.
Merrifield, Leroy S.
Moberly, Robert B.
Morris, Charles Jacob
Moses, Mary Helen
Murphy, William Patrick
Nolan, Dennis R.
Parra, A. Fernando Ignacio
Pateracki, John A., Jr.
Pincus, S. Richard
Rey, Salvador
Ruben, Alan Miles
Ruffo, Philip J.
Rutherford, William T.
Rutledge, Ivan C.
Saint Antoine, Theodore J.
Schramm, Carl Jude
Sciarra, Silvana
Sharpe, Calvin W.
Shieber, Benjamin M.
Silverstein, Eileen L.
Snow, Carlton J.
Spencer, Janet M.
Vause, William Gary
Veneziani, Bruno
Ver Ploeg, Christine D.
Walton, Lamont M.
Weckstein, Donald T.
Weinstein, David
Weisberger, June
Wolfe, Katie J.
Wollett, Donald H.
Zimarowski, James B.
Zirkel, Perry A.

ACADEMIC: ORGANIZATION BEHAVIOR/PERSONNEL

Abbey, Augustus
Abbott, Jarold Guy
Aldag, Ramon J.
Amba-Rao, Sita C.
Andrews, Fraya Wagner
Angle, Harold L.
Anthony, William Philip
Atchison, Thomas Joseph
Barclay, Lizabeth Ann
Beres, Mary Beth
Berger, Chris J.
Bergmann, Thomas J.
Bolweg, Joep F.
Boudreau, John W.

Boynton, Robert Edward
Brett, Jeanne M.
Brophy, John M.
Bruning, Nealia Sue
Cattaneo, R. Julian
Chacko, Thomas I.
Coates, Norman
Cole, George S.
Cook, Arthur J. D.
Cummings, Larry L.
Curtis, Frances
Dansereau, Alfred E., Jr.
Day, David Robert
Dolan, Shimon
Dowling, Peter John
Drost, Donald A.
Duffy, John F.
Dunn, J. D.
Dyer, Lee Douglas
Fabi, Bruno
Farkash, Alexander
Fay, Charles H.
Feinhauer, Dale M.
Ferris, Gerald R.
Finston, Howard V.
French, John L.
French, Wendell Lowell
Glover, Betty E.
Graham, Jill W.
Greenhalgh, Leonard
Hegedus, David M.
Henderson, Robert D.
Heneman, Herbert G., III
Heneman, Herbert G., Jr.
Hochner, Arthur
Hoyer, Denise Tanguay
Hoyt, Daniel Rexford
Jerdee, Thomas Harlan
Jick, Todd David
Karsten, Margaret F.
Keaveny, Timothy J.
Kolb, Deborah M.
LaVan, Helen
Lawrence, Paul R.
Lerbinger, Otto
Lonergan, Wallace G.
Lucas, Robert
Lundberg, Craig Carl
Macy, Barry A.
Madigan, Robert M.
Massarik, Fred
McInerney, Marjorie L.
Menefee, Michael L.
Miceli, Marcia Parmerlee
Mikan, Kurt W.
Milkovich, George Thomas
Miller, Edwin Leroy
Miner, John Burnham
Moore, Michael Lee
Mounts, Philip Harry
Musser, Steven J.
Napier, Nancy K.
Newman, Jerry M.
Norgren, Paul H.
Novit, Mitchell Sheldon
Nystrom, Paul Clifdon
Okubayashi, Koji
Patten, Thomas Henry Jr.
Patterson, R. A.
Perry, James Lee
Petit, Andre
Portwood, James D.
Radom, Matthew
Raelin, Joseph A.
Ritchie, J. Bonner
Rodgers, Robert Charles
Rosenberg, Howard R.
Rotter, Naomi G.
Saueressig, Robert
Saxberg, Borje Osvald
Schmidt, Stuart Maxwell
Schoen, Sterling H.
Schriesheim, Chester A.
Shea, Gregory P.
Shrout, Ethel H.
Sonnenfeld, Jeffrey A.
Stablein, Ralph E.
Stern, Robert N.
Stoess, Alfred William
Stone, Bryce Douglas Jr.
Susman, Gerald Isaiah
Thomas, Kenneth W.
Vinton, Karen Lynn
Vitalis, Earl L. Jr.
Watson, Wilfred H.
Weiss, Richard Mark
West, Jude P.
Whaley, George L.
White, Harold Clifford
Whyte, William Foote
Woodworth, Warner P.
Wortman, Max S., Jr.
Yost, Edward B.
Youngblood, Stuart A.

ACADEMIC: PSYCHOLOGY

Benson, Philip Gerald
Fitzpatrick, Robert
Gordon, Michael E.
Hammer, Tove Helland
Maccoby, Michael
Mailloux, Noel
Miller, Robert W.
Smith, Frederick D.

ACADEMIC: SOCIOLOGY

Aldrich, Howard Earl
Berg, Ivar Elis
Cohn, Samuel Ross
Edelstein, J. David
Fauman, S. Joseph
Frank, Murray W.
Franz, Verl R. W.
Gersuny, Carl
Godard, John Hamilton
Haller, Archibald O.
Hanlon, Martin Daniel
Jewell, Steven Corbet
King, Charles Douglas
Landsberger, Henry A.
Leopold, Anna S.
Levin, David Allen
Macarov, David
Miller, R. Berkeley
Mullan, Brian Francis
Pomer, Marshall
Radine, Lawrence B.
Roman, Michael R.
Root, Kenneth
Rothstein, William G.
Siegenthaler, Jurg K.
Takeshi, Inagami
Tausky, Curt

ACADEMIC: STUDENT

Adams, Jon S.
Aden, Irma
Akarakcian, Arlene A.
Albritton, James W.
Allen, William S.
Altomonte, Vincenzo
Anderson, Carolyn S.
Andreassi, Scott J.
Andren, Marc David
Atlas, Craig M.
Azar, Elias R.
Baek, Gwang-Gi
Baker, Howe Edward
Barnes, R. David
Bartter, Nancy Ellen
Bauer, Scott C.
Beer, Richard
Bergman, P. D.
Betcherman, Gordon
Betton, John H.
Bhattacherjee, Debashish
Blaser, Anne Catherine
Block, Justin M.
Bloom, Steven
Bluth, Arlene
Bomzer, David J.
Botan, Carl H.
Bottorff, Roger N.
Bourassa, David W.
Brewer, Catherine Helene
Brock, Patrick E.
Broderick, Renae F.
Brodsky, Deborah M.
Brown, Patra Helena
Buccellato, Vito
Bullard, Christopher King
Bullard, Jennie K.
Burns, Dean E.
Byers, James F.
Byrd, Barbara K.
Camp, Sidney Lamar Jr.
Campbell, Duncan Colin
Carlson, Timothy Eric
Carnevale, Carol Marie
Castelli, Ronald J.
Clarke, Pamela Lynn
Cochran, Steven A.
Cochran, Susan Terrell
Colelle, Jennifer M.
Cook, Richard F.
Cooper, Martha R.
Corbitt, Leslie F.
Cote, Pierre-Marcel
Cotler, Miriam P.
Curia, Samuel
Damron, Bobby James
Dancha, Dana Renee
Davidson, Michael Eugene
Davila, Ramon Jose
De Treux, Walter H., III
Dean Earl C.
Deeds, Warren Derrick
Deel, Ken W.
Dellarocca, Luciano
Desouza, Angela C.
Devol, Karen Roberts
Diekhoff, Paul R.
Diggs, Cecil Jr.
Dornbaum, Michael L.
Downer, Beverley Marcia
Dozier, Janelle B.
Drayer, Wendy
Durso, Carole G.
Eaton, Adrienne E.
Eckhardt, Christy A.
Emery, Susan K.
English, Lynn H.
Erdheim, Andrea Ruth
Falkner, Michael J.
Farley, Jeffrey A.
Felhauer, Larry Wayne
Ferrell, David Lee
Fiedler, Susan
Filgut, Paul Ross
Fina, Paul J.
Fisher, Anne
Fitch, David Paul
Fitch, Mary
Fitzgerald, William T.
Flegel, James Richard
Florkowski, Gary Walter
Foissotte, Colette M.

Foley, Mary Cosgrove
Funk, Christine M.
Garcia, David A.
Gatti, Michael R.
Gaubeca, Michael Jess
Gerhart, Barry Alan
Gherson, Diane J.
Gilson, James Edward
Giubilaro, Pina
Gleason, Joyce G.
Goff, Nadine A.
Goldbaum, Karen M.
Goldfield, Michael H.
Goodson, Michael J.
Goodwin, William Joseph
Gore, Charlotte Jean
Goyet, Fernand Rene
Gregorio, Coleen Anne
Griffin, Mary Louise
Grise, Sherry K.
Grude, Jan
Guth, Dennis Joseph
Haberberger, Michael J.
Hagan, Jessica M.
Hames, David Scott
Hanson, Gregory A.
Harrah, Jeffrey C.
Harris, Dawn A.
Harris, Joy T.
Harris, Timothy A.
Hartanto, Frans Mardi
Haven, Charles P.
Havlovic, Stephen J.
Hayworth, Kelly Joe
Heim, John H.
Heling, Kevin J.
Henson, Theresa M.
Hernandez, Michelle Marie
Herrnstadt, Owen Edward
Hershey, Margaret L.
Holt, Katherine E.
Hoover, David J.
Horowitz, Avery M.
Horvath, Alex
Hubbard, Debra Ann
Hubert, Blake L.
Huybregts, Gerardus A. C.
Janacek, Michael J.
Jarley, Paul A.
Johnson, Nancy Brown
Julnes, Theresa Eileen
Kahn, Miriam K.
Kaiser, Stacy S.
Kalwa, Richard W.
Karwoski, Caryn S.
Kaupins, Gundars E.
Kemmerer, Barbara E.
Kennedy, Karen M.
Keppler, Mark J.
Kirsch, Charles John
Kisch, Victor J.
Klass, Brian S.
Klamph, Ben Joseph
Klinedinst, Mark A.
Klinshaw, Robert J.
Knoblock, Rachel Marie
Kolman, John Robert
Koutouzos, Georgia D.
Kramer, Robert E.
Krause, Edward Francis
Krause, Mary A.
Kroul, Russell
Kuhr, M. I.
Kurowski, David Steven
Labovitz, Trudy A.
Lagrott, Wayne A.
Lake, Angela L.
Lane, Peggy Ann B.
Lanigan, John J.
Latino, Michael T.
Lawsky, Paul John
Lawson, Gary Michael
Lee, Michael B.
Lefebvre, Linda H.
Lehman, Mary L.
Leigl, Kathy
Lengnick-Hall, Mark L.
LePage, Francois
Lerman, David Migel
Liess, Michael T.
Love, Shelley B.
Lucchi, Gina Diane
Macklan, Richard
Manning, Nora Jean
Marcotte, Marilee Ann
Marlow, Nancy Aileen
Martini, Barry E.
Maskin, Norman H.
Massaros, Anthony G.
Mayer, Steven J.
Maza, Miguel A.
McWilliams, Shaun W.
Mercier, Pierre
Meyer, Gordon William
Miller, Kathryn S.
Miller, R. Berkeley
Molini, Paul Joseph Jr.
Monet, Steven A.
Montgomery, B. Ruth
Morishima, Motohiro
Motsepe, Oscar W. E.
Na, Boon Chong
Nadler, Charles H.
Nay, Leslie A.
Nelson, Pamela K.
Nenner, Rodney Andrew
Nicholson, Robert Paul
Nicolai, David A.
Nsiah-Yeboah, Richard
Oberholtzer, Dawn M.
O'Neal, Keith Alan
O'Reilly, Anne B.
Osofsky, Debra
Oyaga, Gladys T.
Papini, Frank E.
Parsons, William F., Jr.
Paul, Melinda M.
Petree, Daniel L.
Pettengill, Marian M.
Philippi, Marilynn
Plantz, Frederick David
Poff, Frank M.
Porter, Thomas B.
Portz, John H.
Premack, Steven
Puccini, Nancy Ann
Radle, Janice Ann
Ray, Steven Eric
Rayman, Dale M.
Reardon, Jack E.
Reed, Thomas Francis
Roach, Bonnie L.
Robinson, Donald John
Robinson, Lisa G.
Rohde, Diane M.
Roldan, Pedro
Rosen, Mark I.
Ross, Marcia E.
Roth, Jeremy Alan
Rozek, B. J.
Russell, Gary Peter
Schell, Catherine Ann
Schemanske, Jane Marie
Schwarz, Joshua L.
Schwochau, Susan Gertrude
Segalla, Michael
Seim, Douglas Rocco
Sekas, Maria Helene
Shalley, Christina E.
Shatz, Sanford
Sherer, Pamela Darlene
Sherer, Peter D.
Sherman, Patricia Joan
Shibota, Atsuo
Sienghtai, Sununta
Silvia, Stephen J.
Skanes-Taylor, J.
Smith, Judith Cantrell
Song, Kye-Chung
Sparks, Joan Kee
Speyer, David Blair
Stassen, Marjorie A.
Stehling, Donald J.
Suarez, Herta A.
Sullivan, Francis W., Jr.
Sullivan, Kathleen Ann
Taylor, G. Stephen
Thal, Richard L.
Thomas, Nancy M.
Thompson, Stephen L.
Thorna, Sandra Lee
Troyer, Steven Alan
Tuttle, Pamela Mae
Van Laan, Rick
Vasa-Sideris, Sandra
Veneri, Darren A.
Venick, Charles
Viane, Nicole Kristine
Vorys, Gail Arch
Warters, Richard Adam
Washburn, Lynn Anne
Watts, Bridget E.
Way, Philip Keith
Weikle, Roger Dale
Weil, David
West, Robin Kay
Wever, Kirsten R.
Weyls, Richard C.
Williard, David M.
Wolf, Andrew J.
Wolkoff, Regina Lois
Woodham, Brent A.
Wright, Sue Ellen
Yurko, Susan
Zeytinoglu, Isik F.
Zoladz, Joseph M.
Zwerling, Harris L.
Zylberstajn, Helio

ACADEMIC: OTHER
(Including Unspecified)
Abenhaim, Lucien Lewys
Abers, Jacob H.
Allan, Peter
Akabas, Sheila H.
Anthony, Cher
Aparicio, Luis
Auer, Helga
Ballon, Robert Jean
Barres, Samuel Lawrence
Benson, Frances
Berger, Susan Lynne
Better, Maurice Bernard
Birnbaum, Robert
Blum, Peter R.
Brecher, Charles
Brown, Robert Edward
Comerford, Richard D.
Coombs, W.
Cunningham, J. David
DeClercq, Neill Gerard
Davis, Charles H.
Denker, Joel S.
Dubois, Eileen C.
Dwyer, Richard E.
Elkin, Sol M.
Ewing, David W.
Filippelli, Ronald Lee
Fox, Mary P.

Fox, Milden J., Jr.
Freedman, Marcia
Fried, Morris L.
Fukami, Cynthia G.
Gall, Gilbert J.
Galvin, Miles Eugene
Gastwirth, Joseph L.
Greenberg-Edelstein, Ruth
Guernsey, Sandra K.
Hammon, Diane Lynn
Hardin, Einar
Harper, Shirley F.
Hasson, Edwin
Havener, Ronald V.
Heler, Edward
Herman, Francine April
Hiestand, Dale L.
Hoska, Lukas E., Jr.
Ilyashov, Anatoli
Johansen, Elaine
Johnson, Ralph Arthur
Kaplan, Michele
Kerchner, Charles T.
Kerrison, Irvine L. H.
Klein, Bernard
Kleywegt, C. John
Knauss, Keith D.
Kranz, Harry
Laporte, Philip Anthony
Lee, Edgar
Lenart, Sharon Ann
Leung, Cho Kin
Lewis, Albert L.
Lieberthal, Milferd
Losche, Peter
Lyons, Dee
MacLachlan, Gretchen E.
McAlinden, Sean Paul
McGlone, Patrick Daniel
Mericle, Kenneth S.
Meyer, David Glenn
Miller, James Gormly
Miller, Lynn
Mitchell, Amy Lynn
Moore, Edgar
Murphy, Frank J.
Nelson, Elinor
Nesselroth, Saul H.
Ozanne, Robert
Patton, David B.
Peace, Nancy E.
Pendleton, Edwin Charles
Pigage, Leo C.
Priebjrivat, Vuthiphong
Rey, M.
Reber, Robet Allen
Revitte, John Lawrence
Rhodes, Gary Boyd
Rogers, Joel E.
Romney, Sue I.
Root, Lawrence S.
Rosen, Stanley
Russo, Charline S.
Schmidman, John T.
Schriver, William Ragan
Shaffer, Doris
Showell, Charles H., Jr.
Simon, Sharon
Smith, Clifford Ellsworth
Smith, Wendy Anne
Socknat, James A.
Sorcinelli, Eugenio G.
Spencer, David C.
Springer, Beverly J.
Sproat, Kezia
Stavros, Demo
Sulzner, George T.
Tapper, Owen A.
Terrill, T. E.
Thomas, William Walter
Tomey, E. Allan
Turnbull, William O.
Vande Vord, Neil
Via, Emory F.
Wann, Andrew Jackson
Wilensky, Harold L.
Wolchok, Harold
Wolozin, Harold
Yancy, Dorothy Cowser

ARBITRATION

Abernathy, John H.
Abernethy, Byron Robert
Adelson, Yolande Chambers
Adler, Sara
Ahern, John Thomas
Ahern, Robert William
Alexander, Gabriel N.
Amsler, Terry
Anderson, Arnold O.
Anderson, Ruth
Anderson, Wayne G.
Andrews, Orville E.
Aronin, Louis
Ashe, Julian L.
Axon, Gary L.
Bailer, Lloyd Harding
Barrington, Karen
Barry, Joseph Clement
Beadles, N. A.
Beckman, David L.
Bedikian, Mary
Beitner, Elliot I.
Belcher, A. Lee
Bell, James F.
Berger, Ralph S.
Berkowitz, Norman
Berry, Donn J.
Bloch, Richard I.
Bockoven, Kathrine B.
Bodle, George E.
Boner, Patrick J.
Bordwell, Charlotte
Bowers, Mollie Heath
Brams, Stanley Howard
Brent, Alfred H.
Bressler, Robert
Bridgewater, Barbara
Brisco, C. Chester Jr.
Britton, Raymond L.
Brown, Barry C.
Brown, David Hunter
Brown, Deborah A.
Brown, Gerald Alton
Brown, Susan R.
Bullen, Frederick H.
Bussey, Ellen M.
Buzbee, Ellen W.
Cabe, Carl
Cahn, Sidney L.
Caples, William G.
Carey, Thomas F.
Carson, Robert G., Jr.
Carter, Albert V.
Casey, John F.
Cassady, Paul A.
Castrey, Robert T.
Cezair, Percy Lucien
Chapman, Jack M.
Chiesa, Mario
Clark, Charles E.
Clarke, Jack
Cloke, Kenneth
Cloney, John C.
Cobb, Jay Joseph
Cohen, Nathan
Concepion, David A.
Cooper, Charles A.
Corpora, Angelo J.
Coulson, Robert
Coyle, John B.
Creo, Robert A.
Croll, Richard W.
Cull, Clement Paul
Cushman, Bernard
Dallas, Sherman F.
Dansby, Edgar R.
Dash, G. Allan Jr.
Dawson, J. L.
Dean, Irwin J., Jr.
Denenberg, Tia Schneider
Denson, Fred L.
Derr, Baron W.
Deye, James R.
Dilts, David A.
Dissen, Richard W.
Dobry, Stanley T.
Doering, Barbara W.
Dolin, Ken R.
Dolnick, David
Dornbaum, Charles
Dorr, John Van N., III
Draznin, Julius N.
Dworkin, Jonathan
Dyke, Annmarie K.
Dyke, Theodore
Eischen, Dana E.
Eisenberg, Walter L.
Encinio, Philip A.
Epstein, Ira Stephen
Eskay, Henry H.
Everitt, Alice Lubin
Fallon, William James
Feigenbaum, Charles
Feldacker, Bruce S.
Feldman, Marvin J.
Fellman, Gerry L.
Fish, Hy
Fisher, Patrick J.
Fishman, Harry
Fleischli, George Robert
Florey, Peter
Franklin, Linda Robbins
Freeman, Dave
Friedman, Clara H.
Gandel, Mattye
Gannon, Frank Arthur
Garrett, Sylvester
Geiger, Martha
Geltman, Oscar
Gentile, Joseph
Gentry, John Newton
Gilson, Thomas Quinlevan
Glasser, Joseph
Gold, Charlotte H.
Goldsmith, Steven J.
Goldberg, Milton M.
Golob, Howard M.
Goodman, Donald P.
Goodstein, Barnett M.
Gottlieb, Bertram
Grabowski, Donald J.
Greenbaum, Marcia L.
Grimes, John A.
Gruenberg, Gladys W.
Gwiazda, Suzanne Butler
Hacker, Richard Bruce
Halperin, Susan E.
Hamm, Elmer Vaughan
Hammer, Lawrence I.
Handsaker, Morrison
Harkless, James McConnell
Hawkins, John M.
Hearne, William M.
Heiser, David M.
Hellquist, James K.
Henle, Peter
Hergenhan, Robert J.
Hernandez-Benitez, F.
Herrick, Christine T.
Higgins, George G.
Higgins, John E.
Higgins, Richard G.
Hill, Samuel Ervin
Hoellering, Michael F.
Holtzmann, Howard M.
House, Malcolm G.
Howlett, Robert Glasgow
Hutchison, Kay B.
Ilivicky, Joan
Imes, Sharon K.
Ipavec, Charles Francis
Irsay, Leonard
Jaffe, Ira F.
Johnson, Harry L.
Jones, Harold D., Jr.
Kahn, Ruth E.
Kaiser, Charles M.
Kakazu, Cheryl K.
Kamm, Renee E.
Kanner, Richard L.
Kaplan, David M.
Kapsch, Francis E., Sr.
Katz, Jerome
Kearns, Oliver E.
Keenan, Frank Arthur
Kell, Paul G.
Kelly, Joseph T.
Kennedy, John W.
Kent, Andrew Graham
Kershen, Harry
Kessler, Fredrick P.
Kiss, Joseph S.
Koenig, Edward C.
Koss, J. J.
Kotin, Leo
Krebs, Paul J.
Krinsky, Edward B.
Kugler, Israel
Lamanna, Judith
Lang, Theodore H.
Larkin, John Day
Larney, George Edward
Lawson, Eric W. Jr.
Leach, Donald B.
Ledoux, Deo
Leventhal, Robert Mark
Levin, Edward
Levin, William
Lewis, Dawson James
Lieberman, Irwin Martin
Lipton, Benjamin B.
Luskin, Bert L.
MacDonald, Donald M.
MacGregor, Robert W.
Madden, Stanford C.
Magdon, Maida S.
Maggiolo, Walter A.
Maher, Roger Edward
Malamud, Sherwood
Malin, Susann
Malkin, Julus L.
Maloney, Emily
Marceau, Leroy

Markowitz, Irving R.
Marlatt, Ernest E.
Marx, Herbert L., Jr.
Matthews, Daniel E.
Maxwell, Eugenia
McAllister, Robert W.
McAuliffe, Cornelius J.
McCaffree, Kenneth M.
McCausland, Allan Stuart
McCulloch, Frank W.
McDermott, Thomas Joseph
McDonnell, Frank S., Jr.
McKee, Clive B.
McKone, Frederick W.
McMonigle, Bernard
McMullen, James
McPherson, William Heston
Mead, John P.
Micallef, Charles N.
Michaelson, Rita C.
Mitrani, Robert L.
Mittenthal, Richard
Monitto, Angelo
Moore, John Cochrane
Morgan, Gary R.
Morgan, Howard J.
Muessig, Eckehard
Murphy, Jay W.
Myers, A. Howard
Naimark, Richard
Neas, Russell C.
Neigh, Charlotte
Neumeier, Elizabeth
Nevins, David C.
Nichols, George N.
Nicolau, George
O'Brien, Robert M.
O'Connell, Edward J.
Oliveira, Myra
O'Loughlin, William
O'Reilly, James Michael
Orsatti, Ernest B.
Paprocki, John L.
Parent, Guy M.
Pearce, John J., Jr.
Pelhan, Ralph E.
Pereles, Edward A.
Perley, James Dwight
Perry, Samuel Strode
Peterson, David Arthur
Phelps, James C.
Pincus, David M.
Pinkus, Edward C.
Polley, Ira
Pool, C. Allen
Porter, Arthur R., Jr.
Post, William B.
Powell, Walter H.
Pribble, Edward David
Procopio, Mario A.
Quinn, Francis X.
Rains, Harry H.
Randall, Geraldine M.
Randall, Roger L.
Randles, David C.
Rappaport, Lois A.
Rappaport, Michael D.
Reed, James E.
Reifler, Elizabeth Ann
Reilly, Richard Menton
Rezler, Julius
Rice, Zel S.
Rich, Joseph M.
Richter, David James
Ricker, Edwin R.
Riker, William Ed
Rimer, J. Thomas
Roadley, C. Robert
Roberts, Thomas T.
Robins, Eva
Role, Theodore
Rolle, Laverne
Rosen, Sumner Maurice
Rosenberg, Max
Rosenberg, Reuben
Roth, Thomas R.
Rothstein, Michael F.
Roukis, George S.
Rubenstein, Benjamin
Rubenstein, Jerome S.
Rubin, Milton
Rule, William S.
Runyon, Arch H.
Santer, Mark
Schano, John F.
Schneck, David M.
Scholtz, Edward
Schor, Robert M.
Schroeder, Harold H.
Schultz, L. Lawrence
Scott, Mary Thomas
Seibel, Laurence E.
Seidenberg, Jacob
Seidman, Marshall J.
Seinsheimer, Walter G.
Seitz, Reynolds C.
Seldin, Gilbert J.
Seltzer, Louis E.
Shaw, Paul F.
Shaw, Sue Olinger
Shemke, Raymond A.
Shore, Henry
Silver, Jonas
Silverman, Harry
Simpkins, John Paul
Smith, Kirby J., Jr.
Spalding, Francis O.
Sparrow, Dorothy G.
Spilker, Kathleen Jones
Stark, Arthur
Staudter, Donald V.
Stevens, David W.
Storey, Donald R.
Strasshofer, Roland Jr.
Swenson, Charles E.
Tamoush, Philip P.
Tann, Charles John
Taylor, John R.
Taylor, Richard B.
Tener, Barbara Zausner
Tener, Jeffrey Booth
Thomson, Louis Mills Jr.
Tillem, Jack D.
Tilles, C. Evans
Trachtenberg, Bruce S.
Tripp, L. Reed
Turnquist, Dan E.
Twohey, Jerilou Cossack
Vallone, Peter D.
Valtin, Rolf
Van Alstyne, Cary Brownell
Van Alstyne, Vance B.
Van Helden, Ronald M.
Van Wart, Arthur Thomas
Vana, Robert Joseph
Varga, Paul V.
Vernon, Gil
Walt, Alan
Warns, Marian Kincaid
Washington, John Levi
Waxman, Bruce I
Weinmann, Richard A.
Weisenfeld, Allan
Weizenbaum, Sharon K.
Werther, William B., Jr.
Weston, Joseph A.
Wilcox, Jean
Williams, J. Earl
Williams, Jerry J.
Williams, Tim
Wilson, Andrea
Winkler, Ralph
Winton, Jeffrey B.
Wirpel, Sander W.
Wolff, Helmut O.
Woolf, Anne Holman
Yagoda, Louis
Yarowsky, Sol M.
Young, Frederick John L.
Zack, Arnold Marshall
Zechar, R. Dale
Ziskind, David
Zumas, Nicholas H.

BUSINESS: MANAGEMENT/ADMINISTRATION

Anthony, Cher
Barton, David R.
Beaumont, Richard A.
Beletz, Elaine E.
Bell, Jeffrey Wayne
Bennett, Joseph C., Jr.
Berenblum, Marvin B.
Bernstein, Seymour
Betts, Robert James
Bloomquist, Carl A.
Bogart, Agnes
Bongiovanni, Anthony
Borden, William S.
Bornman, John W.
Boyd, Ilene Rae
Boyer, Gregory P.
Boyle, Edward F.
Bradburn, Walter V., Jr.
Buckner, Jean B.
Burnett, Phyllis O.
Bush, Michael L.
Camerano, Franklin
Cassidy, William James
Cheng, Leonard Tye-Loke
Christ, Peter Eric
Clamp, Jesse Carl Jr.
Clark, C. Howard
Clayton, Suzanne L.
Clinton, Daniel J.
Clinton, J. Hart
Coleman, James L.
Connerty, Richard A.
Cooper, Jerry Philip
Crane, Lili
Crea, Marie
Cunningham, Edward P.
Davids, John R.
Day, Virgil B.
Descheneau, Michael D.
Dewit, Garry Dale
Dillard, Richard B.
Dixon, Thomas J.
Every, Allison
Farrell, Robert A.
Feigenbaum, Armand Vallin
Foy, Mary Christine
Frank, Robert M.
Fremont, Joseph W.
Gardner, Philip M.
Gibson, E. L.
Gillis, Marilyn J.
Glenn, Jim
Green, George W.
Gresock, Nicholas F.
Groeninger, Louis Martin
Hahn, Lloyd E.
Hale, Kenneth Wade
Hansen, George C.
Hannigan, Thomas A.
Harvey, Scott Barrett
Hashimoto, Richard
Hee, Harold S. Y.
Heekin, William C.
Hinkson, Robert E.
Hogue, James C.
Holtgrave, Ralph R.
Insidioso, Richard C.
Jabin, Norman E.
Jackson, Carole Ann
Jenkins, Michael E.
Jones, John D.
Juenger, Robert
Kaminski, Donald Bernard
Kane, E. Leonard
Kenney, Thomas F.
Kessler, Richard
Lavanway, Paul J.
Lawrence, Doreen S.
Ledoux, Deo
Leifer, Richard P.
Levine, Louis L.
Levy, Clara S.
Levy, Robert Alan
Lindemann, A. J.
Lockhart, Sharon J.
Lodato, Michael J.
Loeb, Barry L.
Longenecker, Kathie
Lovelace, Robert F.
Lucas, Freddie H.
Mantilla, Enrique Santago
Martin, Roberta M.
Mascola, Francis X.
Mason, Marianne
Mattern, Thomas R.
McCann, Richard A.
McCutcheon, Aubrey V., Jr.
McGann, F. Michael
McGinnis, James Roberts
McGuire, James J.
McKew, John J.
Merlo, Theodore C., Jr.
Metzger, Norman
Miron, Yeshayahu
Mirsky, Joe
Molner, Ernest
Moore, Gregory Lee
Moore, Lester L.
Morton, Charles William
Moskow, Michael H.
Moskowitz, Leon David
Naylor, Peter Geoffry
Neidorff, Michael F.
Nickl, Carl E.
Nicoson, John Patrick
Norton, Daniel Jay
Noune, Michael Anthony
Nowicki, Henry H.
Nye, David Paul
O'Donnell, Thomas L. P.
O'Grady, John P.
Olson, Julie Eileen
Perna, Nicholas S.
Phiniotis, Stelios P.
Polk, Robert C.
Porter, Robert Gerard
Procelli, Matthew S.
Pryor, Grace T.
Ray, Wendell F.
Reid, Henry O. III
Reisman, Marshall M.
Roeser, John F., Jr.
Sampson, Merle
Sanders, Kenneth M.
Sato, Frances F.
Savas, D. Thomas
Schwartz, Sharron
Scott, Hugh Thomas
Sedgwick, W. Stewart
Serra, Anthony T.
Shapiro, Sumner
Simonetti, Joan E.
Smith, Edward A.
Smith, Nathan
Smith, Sterling E.
Soutar, Patricia L.
Standriff, Donald M.
Steenkamp, Thomas I.
Stein, Robert Gary
Sterling, William P.
Stubbs, Daniel G.
Sullivan, John F.
Tapper, Gordon A.
Tarolli, Mario P.
Taylor, Charles M.
Taylor, Vicky
Thomas, James Edward
Tonti, Don G.
Treaseh, Ronald L.
Uber, Arthur E. Jr.
Venditto, John G.
Verbin, Shelley C.
Vygantas, Peter Vytautas
Walker, Bradley J.
Wallace, Lawrence A.
Wayland, William F.
Weber, David Christian
Wesse, David Joseph
Whellan, Floyd
Wilhelm, Crous
Wilson, Duane M.
Younglove, Peggy C.

BUSINESS: PERSONNEL/INDUSTRIAL RELATIONS

Abel, Theodore
Addington, Thomas H.
Adoma, Osei J.
Ahern, Eileen
Akins, J. Reid Jr.
Alden, John R.
Allard, Michel
Allen, Roger K.
Alley, Douglas M.
Allison, James Michael
Anderson, Joan
Anderson, Samuel L.
Andrews, Joel Francis
Andriani, Robert Nicholas
Andris, Vanessa O.
Antczak, Ken
Armiger, Susan S.
Asher, William S.
Asin, Carlos Guillermo
Austin, Dennis George
Bachman, Al
Badella, Marsha Ellen
Bailey, Bart
Baitsell, John Morton
Baker, Jackie B.
Banas, Paul A.
Bannister, R. Scott
Barger, Michael
Barnes, Ann W.
Barnes, Jerry B.
Barr, Kevin A.
Barr, S. William
Barrows, David Wayne
Barsotti, Frank
Bartareau, Earl
Bates, Charles W.
Baumann, Charles A.
Beaty, John R.
Beckles, Lionel
Begley, Constance L.
Benjamin, Dale L.
Bennett, Donald J.
Berryhill, Ronnie D.
Betts, Robert James
Bier, Joseph V.
Biggica, Russell J.
Bihun, John D.
Billet, Lewis M.
Birch, Juan
Bishow, Howard
Bistline, William J.
Bjerke, Paul
Bjurman, Gerald Ludvig
Blake, William E.
Blalock, M. Lynn
Blandford, Linda
Bloss, Brien H.
Boddy, Donna C.
Bourdon, Clint C.
Bourdon, R.
Bowen, W. S.
Bowman, Gerald J.
Bowman, Yvonne Marie
Boyajian, Haig M.
Braun, Thomas Michael
Breitenbeck, Joseph T.
Brennan, John Paul
Brennan, Paul J.
Brenner, David Jon
Brewster, Chris John
Broas, Leslie C.
Brocci, John Frederick
Brooks, Brenda McChriston
Brown, Andrew B.
Brown, Charles N.
Budd, James L.
Bujan, Ronald James
Burchett, Harold D.
Burns, Robert T.
Burns, Steven R.
Butler, Gerald L.
Butler, James C.
Cannon, Richard S.
Carey, James F.
Carillon, James W.
Carlson, Charles K.
Carlton, James M.
Carrig, Kenneth J.
Carrigan, Bart O.
Carter, J. N.
Carvalho, Dennis M.
Casey, Eileen
Cauler, Sandra L.
Chaffins, Gary Edward
Champi, Paul L.
Charney, Andrew Robert
Cheaney, Nikki N.
Chiappetta, Cynthia
Chiaravalli, Robert Lind
Childers, Kathie Lou
Christianson, Alice Ann
Christianson, Virgil J.
Cigich, Alan L.
Clark, Paul L.
Clark, Robert W.
Clark, Wayne B.
Clarke, Carol L.
Clayton, Robert E.
Clemens, John P.
Clifford, R. James
Coburn, Kitty
Coffin, Dwight C.
Cohane, John J.
Coleman, Glenn
Colinsky, Edgar Garris
Colinsky, Richard W.
Collyer, Robert J.
Colosimo, Frank E.
Comerford, John K.
Conte, Michael R.
Conway, James E.
Cook, William R.
Cooksey, John P.
Cooleen, John P.
Cooley, Maynard Wayne
Corley, Susan
Corradino, Bartholomew P.
Corvino, Anthony J.
Cox, David R.
Creedon, Gerard T.
Cripe, Lawrence Everet
Croyle, Thomas J.
Cullerton, John E.
Cureton, John Porter
Cusack, John J.
Daffara, John C.
Daniel, Mark J.
Daugherty, Ronald D.
Davies, Al
Davis, James D.
De Bonis, John R.
Decoen, Emile G.
Deeds, Ralph E., Jr.
Delaney, Jeffrey M.
De Morris, Randall S.
Dempsey, Michael Lee
Desantis, Nora Stevens
Deschenes, Gilbert
Dess, Susan A.
Diali, Azuka O.
Dilallo, Michael
Dillon, Peter C.
Dillon, William A.
Dodd, Richard A.
Doering, Rick Robert
Doerr, Elaine Kay
Doherty, Thomas G.
Doidge, J. Lloyd
D'Onofrio, Joseph D.
Donovan, Charles Edward
Donovan, Dennis Michael
Doom, George P.
Down, Richard John
Droege, John D. L.
Dubay, Constance M.
Duffe, William C.
Duffy, William E.
Dunn, W. Steven
Dunning, John C., Jr.
Duranko, Peter N.
Dussey, Charles Jevens
Edwardson, Ron W.
Eisenga, Larry C.
Elegreet, Frank J.
Ellenberg, Martin
Ellery, Lawrence Fenn
Ellis, Geraldine
Emanuele, Benedict D.
Englebrecht, Mark Alan
Esselman, Mark S.
Estenson, Jerry D.
Etukudo, Akanimo Jonathan
Eviston, Robert J.
Ewing, David Flagg
Fairchild, Charles
Fanning, Mark Stephen
Fanok, Stephen
Farabee, Barrett B.
Favor, Leda Fuller
Fechter, Alan E.
Ferraro, Jean
Fesko, Robert J.
Fine, Joel Marc
Fischer, Rudolf L.
Fishburn, Drew H.
Fisher, Clarence Robert
Fitch, Stona J.
Flaherty, Bernard
Fleischmann, Fred L.
Florkey, Ellen M.
Flynn, Thomas F.
Folcarelli, John Walsh
Forbes, Patricia C.
Forst, Robin Ilene
Foss, Gary Clare
Foster, Donald
Fromm, Gerard P.
Fromm, Kenneth N.
Fulrath, Thomas A.
Gat, Neri
Gentile, Patricia
George, Danny
George, Scott W.

George, Timothy
Gerber, Caro Janet
Germani, Philip J.
Gewin, Michael E.
Gibberman, Clifford T.
Gibbons, John E.
Giebel, Richard Earl
Gifford, Nancy Paton
Gilles, Donald L., Jr.
Giordano, Donald A.
Goetz, Alan F.
Goldberg, Stanton H.
Gordon, John G.
Graber, Nancy Ruth
Greco, Albert Nicholas
Green, William F.
Greenberg, Ronald
Greene, James P.
Greenhouse, Scott J.
Greenstein, Fred H.
Griesbach, Fern C.
Griffen, Leslie G.
Griffin, Ellen E.
Gronbach, Robert Charles
Grzywacz, Rosemary A.
Gudenberg, Harry R.
Haebig, Robert C.
Hahn, Ana Teresa
Halan, John P.
Hall, Gary A.
Hall, John Wesley
Hall, Marsha Kay
Hallberg, Al Carsten
Halperin, Zvi
Hammerman, Herbert
Hancox, Robert E.
Hankinson, David W.
Hardiman, Kevin P.
Harrington, C. Robert
Harrison, Constance I.
Hartstein, Raymond E.
Harvey, W. J.
Hasenstab, Karen Ann
Hatcher, W. J.
Hauserman, Bob B.
Hedrick, Charles Barnhart
Helfrich, Thomas George
Hercules, Dennis Charles
Herington, Carl David
Hetrick, Jerry Lynn
Heyser, Marlene K.
Higdon, Robert B.
Higgins, Norman G.
Hillary, Timothy B.
Hinds, Julie G.
Hirschey, K. David
Hirsh, Steven J.
Hisatomi, Mindy Midori
Hollister, Sally
Holm, Linda L.
Holton, Gary
Homann, Anne Y.
Hopkins, Arthur S.
Horowitz, Louise M.
Horton, James W., Jr.
Horton, Lemuel Leonard
Housfeld, Daniel R.
Huddleston, Gary
Igbo, Gregory A.
Imri, Ernest P.
Iorio, Timothy William
Irwin, Donald M.
Ito, Carl S.
Jackson, George
James, Antonio
Jethro, Paul G.
Johnson, Laurie L.
Johnson, R. H.
Johnson, William S.
Johnston, Donald Richard
Jones, Nancy W.
Jordan, James Harry
Jourdan, Michele Marie
Juenger, Robert
Juliano, Jan M.
Juneman, Ronald C.
Jung, George T.
Kadau, Gary Scott
Kajander, John
Kane, Edward T., Jr.
Kane, Steven
Kanne, Marvin G.
Kaplan, Alvin I.
Kaufman, Anne T.
Kawakami, Steven S.
Keenan, John Francis X.
Keller, Robert E.
Kellett, Norman M.
Kendall-Abbott, Rosemary
Kenney, Thomas F.
Kerins, Paul T.
Kerr, Frederick L.
Kessing, Stephen L.
Ketcham, Raymond
Kimpan, Jeffrey K.
King, Stanley P.
Kirschke, Gerald J.
Klasen, Gerald U.
Kleckner, Willard R.
Koop, David H.
Korn, Richard Henry
Kramer, Lynda H.
Krebs, Linda
Kresin, George L.
Krolikowski, Richard John
Krumwiede, Jerry
Kulchin, Bernard A.
Kumar, Praveen
Kunnecke, Benton F.
Kurcina, Joyce A.
Kuromoto, Perry K.
Kyrouac, Richard C.
Laedtke, Glenn Marvin
Lakich, Steve
Lamb, Cynthia Ann
Lange, John Patrick
Laperch, William J.
Latimer, Murray Webb
Lawrence, James B.
Leask, William M.
Lees, Thomas Sutton
LePage, Leon
Levensaler, Walter L.
Levy, Bruce
Lewis, H. Nelson Jr.
Lewis, H. Theresa
Lewis, Howard V.
Lewis, Nancy L.
L'Heureux, Wayne D.
Liberson, Dennis H.
Liddle, Walter T.
Lindberg, Bonita
Little, Alfred
Lloyd, William V.
Loney, Timothy John
Long, Lyle Herbert
Loughran, Charles S.
Lowenstein, Deborah J.
Lowrey, Jay
Lunnie, Francis M., Jr.
Lynch, Michael P.
Lyons, Donald E.
Lysaght, Walter J.
MacDonald, J. Randall
Mackin, Marian C.
Madkour, M. Taha
Maher, William J.
Mahler, Merle E.
Manausa, Kathleen R.
Mandrell, Robert Roy
Mankoff, Charles Howard
Manzanores, Andy J.
Marcello, Frank E.
Marcus, Leonard
Margadonna, J. Robert
Markovitch, George John
Martin, Raymond M.
Mason, Kenneth B.
Masondo, James Lincoln S.
Massery, R. David
Mater, Patti R.
Matlack, R. E.
Matthews, Keith B.
Maurer, George C.
McAllister, Peter John
McAuley, Donan B.
McAuliffe, Paul S.
McCarthy, Robert Joseph
McClure, Dwight I.
McCormack, Joseph H.
McGinty, Ian Gregory
McGowan, William H.
McIntosh, Stephen Scott
McKenna, Alex
McMahon, Bernard J.
McNichols, James F.
Meader, Leland V.
Meals, Ruth L.
Meany, Peter Michael
Meck, Judith
Meeks, John R.
Mehl, Deborah Kay
Melis, Patricia A.
Merisalo, Carl B.
Meyer, Richard F.
Miller, Donald E.
Miller, Edward J.
Miller, Waldo G.
Ming, Leo Hezekiah Jr.
Minter, Milton M.
Monaco, Angelo G.
Monroe, Charles Richard
Monty, Gerald A.
Mooney, James A., Jr.
Moore, Alger
Moore, Jim L.
Mooring, Kelly D.
Moran, Michael L.
Morrison, David D.
Morse, Jennifer B.
Mulchahey, Terry S.
Mullady, Sarah F.
Muth, Lawrence William
Naylon, James A.
Nazzaro, Stewart E.
Newman, Lloyd N.
Newman, Theodore
Nicholas, Charles E.
Nicholson, Percival L.
Nielsen, Paul B.
Nikaido, Roy S.
Norman, Richard Calhoun
Novick, David S.
Nygren, James William
Oberstein, Robert F.
O'Brien, James J., Jr.
O'Connor, Frank
Olin, Bruce Kevin
Oliva, Henry
Oliveira, Myra
Orchard, Robert
Oreson, Keith A.
Orr, Andrew
Oscadal, Martin G.
Osika, Thomas
Padula, Cheryl A.
Paneral, Allen J.
Parguel, Norbert
Parsh, Steven Francis
Passmore, Sandra Betty

Patrick, James R.
Patterson, Elaine Feldman
Paul, Kathleen M.
Paulson, Gary D.
Pavlinsky, Nancy Marie
Payne, J. M.
Peckham, James D.
Pedevillano, Mary Theresa
Pelle, Michael A.
Peltier, James W., Jr.
Perez, Arvelo Humberto
Perich, George H.
Peterman, Mary C.
Petersen, Ralph C.
Petrack, Michael J.
Petralia, Jean
Petty, Raymond D., Sr.
Phillipp, Joseph Paul
Phillips, Dace
Phillips, Gary T.
Phillips, Jack J.
Pierce, Daniel
Pierce, Thomas J.
Pietranton, Anthony F.
Pineau, Charles A.
Pizzurro, Robert D.
Poff, Frank M.
Polca, Robert Francis
Pollo, Steve A.
Poore, K. E.
Potts, Anne M.
Prasse, Fred C.
Priggins, George M.
Prior, John J.
Putnam, David Ross
Qualls, John Robert
Queen, Lloyd J.
Quick, D. L.
Quigley, Robert J.
Radtke, Robert C.
Ramlochan, Mootoor
Rappaport, Cyril M.
Reagan, Paul Marion
Reiff, Sidney
Reinhold, Robert
Renton, George G.
Ridenour, Karen Sue
Rideout, Marc P.
Rikard, Dorothy J.
Ritt, Donald D.
Rizzo, James M.
Roberts, John F.
Robertson, Thomas Henry
Robinson, Edward W., Jr.
Rocheleau, Dennis W.
Rogers, Art
Romero, Jose Ramon
Rosen, Sherman D.
Ross, Katy T.
Rosst, Warren A.
Rothe, Harold Frederick
Rothrock, Clifford D.
Ruby, Donald P.
Runcie, John F.
Russell, Beverly Ann
Salmon, Karl
Sanchez, Julian P.
Santos, Scott Stuart
Saunders, Cheryl S.
Savoie, Ernest J.
Sawka, Jacob R.
Scavuzzo, Rosemary T.
Schenone, Ronald Joseph
Schinella, Michael R.
Schliep, R. L.
Schmidt, Thomas J.
Schnipke, Gregory C.
Schramm, Steven Edward
Schwappach, Roy A.
Schwindt, Robert F.
Scott, Curtis Anthony
Scott, William S.
Scruggs, T. J.
Seckinger, William
See, Kim Marie
Seligman, Sidney David
Semrad, David
Senior, Kent Richard
Sens, James F.
Shaffer, Donald T.
Shair, David I.
Shaulis, P. A.
Shaw, Roger D.
Shea, Dennis F.
Shogren, Marshall A.
Simmons, Robert L.
Shupe, Philip M.
Siporin, David
Sisson, Jeffrey D.
Skinner, Edward E.
Smedinghoff, Mary Lynn
Smith, Bruce E.
Smith, James R.
Smith, Maurice R.
Smith, Neal F.
Smith, Robert C.
Smith, Robert Edward Jr.
Smith, William E.
Sniadecki, Alan F.
Snow-Godfrey, Janet
Soetaert, Lynn A.
Solomon, Mark
Soper, David E.
Soutar, Douglas H.
Spargo, Paul
Spence, Mary Otto
Spichtig, John J.
Steadman, Wallace Patrick
Stealy, Patricia
Stenmark, John H.
Stevens, Donald M.
Stevenson, Ann Frances
Steward, Phyllis R.
Stiller, W. A.
Stimmel, Thomas W., III
Stovall, J. R.
Suppes, David E.
Talos, Earl V.
Tama-Troutman, Catherine
Tarczali, Edward R.
Taylor, James C.
Theiss, Jerry L.
Theule, Bernard L.
Thibodeau, Gilles
Thomas, John C.
Thomas, Peter B.
Thomas, William
Tittle, Joseph O.
Tokarz, Joel C.
Toland, Mary M.
Towarnicky, John M.
Treasure, Martin G.
Trevino, Rose I.
Trezise, David L.
Tront, Marie A.
Uhlinger, Charles W.
Umhoefer, Gary
Urquhart, Warren George
Vacarro, Vincent A.
Valenzuela, Dany
Valoris, Bruce W.
Vaughn, William M.
Verrastro, Dominic N.
Vosburgh, Donald F.
Wago, Sharen F.
Waldmann, Paul J.
Wall, Charles
Walton, Edward A.
Warman, David S.
Wartman, David B.
Watkins, David W.
Watson, J. Peter
Webb, Robert L.
Weber, R. S.
Weikel, Frank K.
Weinberg, Paul
Weinstein, Howard Gary
Wenzler, O. Fritz
Wenzler, Richard Arthur
West, David H.
Wheeler, Gary R.
Whittington, D. B.
Wiant, Rex Harlan II
Wilberg, William R.
Willett, Teresa Lynn
Williamson, Thomas
Witham, Dennis
Witt, Ray E.
Wolf, Charles M.
Woodhouse, Robert J.
Wooley, Thomas R.
Wright, Gerald W.
Wuslich, Gary L.
Young, John C.
Zappin, Bruce I.
Zimmerman, Steven Arthur
Zurvalec, David Stanley
Zurvalec, Susan H.

CONSULTING

Austen, H. Mattson
Azzan, Cynthia Conway
Barnhill, Helen I.
Barriere, Lionel F.
Barth, Michael Carl
Basil, Thomas Anthony
Bedell, Willard R.
Bell, Lynn
Bloch, Joseph W.
Bloom, Edwin J., Jr.
Bloom, George R.
Boettcher, Jack W.
Bracken, William George
Brandon, Daniel Joseph
Brody, Doris Pearl
Brown, Montague
Buckingham, Mark H.
Burrows, Seymour J.
Burtt, Everett Johnson Jr.
Butler, John Bruce
Cassetta, Raymond Anthony
Cornford, D. N.
Cotabish, Matthew I.
Counts, J. Curtis
David, Henry
Dennis, Leslie E.
Dodd, Richard A.
Donoian, Harry Avedis
Earl, Lewis Harold
Edwardson, Ron W.
Farber, David J.
Fedrau, Ruth H.
Fein, Mitchell
Fisher, Paul
Fletcher, Louise J.
Fox, Marion B.
Fraser, Christopher R. P.
Friedman, Bruce
Friedman, Bruce L.
Friedman, Jack J.
Frost, Carl F.
Frye, Jack G.
Gallentine, Roger J.
Ganz, Samuel
Garnier, Robert Charles
Gillies, J. G.
Glassberg, Elyse J.
Glidden, Priscilla A.
Goldstein, Harold
Gray, Charles W.
Greenberg, Leon
Griggs, Howard S.
Hale, Judith A.
Harter, Philip J.
Haythorne, George Vickers
Hazard, Leland
Herrick, Neal Q.
Hirshorn, Barbara
Hogan, Curtis J.
Horvitz, Wayne L.
Imberman, E. Woodruff
Ingster, Bernard
Johnson, Roger J.
Jones, Ralph Thomas
Joyce, R. D.
Kamber, Victor
Kaplan, Herbert
Katz, Edward C.
Kellerman, Stephen H.
Keltner, John William
Kennedy, Ralph Wilkes
Kenny, Robert A.
Kerr, Clark
Kirkpatrick, Forrest H.
Kohn, Emanuel Louis
Korn, Amy
Kulash, Marjorie
Kutchins, Kay Overton
Lagerquist, Walter W.
Langbaum, Eric
Lange, Carl B. A., III
Latta, Geoffrey W.
Lawrence, Daniel G.
Levy, Harold David
Lewis, Irving
Lloyd, Kenneth L.
Lorenz, Fred J.
MacKenzie, Malcolm R.
Mahler, Walter Robert
Mahon, Clyde John
Martyn, Robert G.
McCarthy, Paul F.
McCorkle, Lois Pake
McGinnis, Jeanette M.
McGinnis, William John Jr.
McMillan, William R.
Metcalf, Charles E.
Milke, Tom
Miller, John Wade Jr.
Mirengoff, William
Misa, Kenneth F.
Morris, John P.
Murbach, Richard T.
Nathanson, Leslie
Neal, Richard G.
Newman, Jack B.
Odell, William Lucien
Olsen-Tjensvold, Reynolds
Orr, Marsha J.
Palomba, Catherine A.
Parks, Walter J.
Passant, Greg S.
Paul, Robert D.
Perkel, George
Perkins, Charles Wilbur
Peterfreund, Stanley
Polland, Harry
Prins, John Robert
Reesman, Cilla J.
Reichenbach, Robert R.
Reynolds, Calvin
Rosen, Howard
Rosenblatt, Annalee Z.
Rosenblum, Paul
Roth, Herrick S.
Rubinstein, Sidney P.
Ruttenberg, Stanley H.
Salmon, David W.
Salsburg, Sidney W.
Saltzman, Arthur William
Schell, Catherine Ann
Schiemann, William A.
Schimel, Ruth Mara
Schneider, Donald J.
Schneider, Kenneth B.
Schneider, Stephen A.
Scobel, Donald
Selby, Mary E.
Shaw, Kimball
Sheridan, Philip J.
Simon, S. Fanny
Simsarian, Arax
Singh, Vishwanath Prasad
Slater, Courtenay M.
Sloan, Stanley
Smith, Michael K.
Solie, Elsie E.
Staller, Jerome M.
Stein, Barry A.
Stern, Bernard Wolf
Sternstein, Herman
Stocker, Norman James
Stoikov, Judith
Stout, James S.
Sydney, Leonard F.
Thomas, Rita E.
Thorn, Jerry
Truell, George F.
Underhill, Richard Sands
Usery, William J.
Ward, Randall P.
Weinberg, Edgar
Weiner, Herbert
Weisinger, Robert S.
Wolfe, Kenneth B.
Woodbridge, Henry Sewall
Wool, Harold
Wynne, David Jeffrey
Yee, Kenneth
Young, Robert C., Jr.
Zubrensky, Ruth J.
Zuckerman, John V.

GOVERNMENT

Agonia, Robert J.
Ahmuty, Alice Lynne
Akselrod, Leonard Jeffrey
Aldrich, Emmett I.
Allen, Edward William
Allmendinger, Raymond C.
Amann, Joseph
Amar, James C.
Ames, C.
Anderson, Arvid
Anderson, James K.
Ansell, Sherman David
Arewah, Peter Joseph Omo
Bailey, William R.
Baldwin, Stephen E.
Balog, Julius Jr.
Bancroft, Karen Low
Barone, Dale V.
Bates, Christopher M.
Bau, Frederick J.
Bauman, Alvin
Bausinger, Kenneth E.
Beaty, John William
Becker, John P.
Behr, Armin
Belitsky, Abraham Harvey
Bellman, Howard S.
Ben-Asher, Daniel L.
Benca, Theodore John
Benjamin, Jesse
Bensinger, Stephen C.
Bergstrom, Robert B., Sr.
Berman, Michael B.
Berry, Elawrence
Bierlein, Marcilee A.
Bigler, Esta R.
Biondo, Joseph
Blake, Charles A.
Blakey, Madge M.
Blank, Dale L.
Blumengarten, Louis Hiram
Bonebrake, Daniel
Bosanac, Paul A.
Bouknight, Barbara E.
Bowers, Phillip A.
Bradford, W. S.
Brandwein, Seymour
Bress, Joseph M.
Brown, J. H.
Buchan, John F.
Buchen, John W.
Budlong, Carol A.
Burgeson, Glenn F.
Cantfil, August F.
Carter, Richard W.
Castrey, Bonnie P.
Chandler, James C.
Charonis, Virginia
Cheek, Roger Newby
Chester, Robert W.
Christovich, Leslie Jean
Clark, John H.
Clarke, Oliver
Cohany, Harry P.
Coleman, Paul T.
Collins, Ronald Douglas
Connors, Edward Owen
Crannan, Herbert J.
Cravanas, V. Alex
Dadalt, Ann Moriarty
Dale, Charles
Davey, Harold L.
Davis, Peter G.
Dean, Edwin R.
Deel, Ken W.
Deloor, Ruth M.
DeLorme, Francois
Denaco, Parker A.
Dennis, Barbara Hanson
Deprey, Kenneth Wayne
Despol, John A.
Deutermann , Cynthia
Deutermann, William V., Jr.
Diggelman, Robert E.
DiLorenzo, Gloria
Dolin, Ken R.
Dolski, Erwin R.
Doranz, Jeffrey David
Doyle, Jane F.
Drohan, William D.
Duffy, Constance D.
Dunlap, Chris R.
Eakle, William E.
Edmondson, John J.
Ege, Roger Donald
Ehrenhalt, Samuel M.
Eisenberg, Arthur
Eisenhower, R. Warren
Evans, Richard K.
Evans, W. Kenneth
Ezbiansky, Donald
Falvey, Pamela J.
Fanning, John J.
Farber, Evelyn W.
Farwell, Carol
Faschan, Kristine M.
Fechter, Alan E.
Feldman, Lloyd
Fernandez, Manuel
Ferree, James L.
Fibish, Nancy Connolly
Fisher, Stephen Todd
Flanagan, George Jay
Fleischman, William E.
Fleischmann, Ross A.
Franklin, Sam
Frans, Klaas Jan
Friedman, Pamala F.
Furdyna, Michael Adam
Fylypowycz, Taras
Gabel, Sukhreet
Garst, Voltairine W.
Gauthier, Fernand
Gayer, Paul David
Geissner, James W.
Gerard, Irwin
Ghitelman, Steven G.
Gilroy, Curtis Lloyd
Glazer, Mildred
Glinsman, William J.
Goldberg, Joseph P.
Goldstein, Allen P.
Gottschalk, Irving E.
Green, Daniel H.
Hagen, Karen Marie
Halback, Donald Gordon
Hall, R. D.
Halter, Patrick John
Hamlin, Terese A.
Haney, William J.
Hanna, James S.
Hannah, Richard Lloyd
Harper, Harriett J.
Hartfield, Edward F.
Hebein, Peter J.
Heimbach, William Webster
Hendrix, Thomas C.
Hesse, Dana L.
Hilz, Edward Richard
Hodes, Nancy L.
Hoexter, Elsie Goodman
Hoffman, Eileen Barkas
Holiber, Caryl Lois
Holland, Susan S.
Horan, Marcia D.
Horn, Theodore B.
Houlihan, William C.
Householder, Robert W.
Huey, Reginald T.
Huffman, John
Hunter, Stephen Bennett
Husselman, Peter L.
Jackson, Robert Dewitt
Jacob, Nancy
Jacobsen, Maggie
Kaden, Andrea Lynn
Kahl, Anne S.
Kang, Melvin R.
Kapner, Alex
Kaska, Edward W.
Kassalow, Gerald M.
Kaut, James I.
Keir, Jeffrey B.
Keller, Anna D.
Kemp, Homer Robert Jr.
Kendellen, Gary Thomas
Kenney, Karen Rae
Kerner, Benjamin A.
Kiers, Peter C.
Kincaid, Elmer D.
King, Christopher T.
Klinshaw, Robert A.
Klitzkie, Alan George
Kobell, Gerald
Koch, David H.
Kolodrubetz, Walter W.
Koreckis, Paul H.
Kovenetsky, Sam
Kramer, Jay
Kristall, Wayne Paul
Kucherov, Tanya L.
Kujawski, Karl R.
Lafferty, Linda A.
LaMartina, James
Lando, Mordechai E.
Lefkowitz, Jerome
Leifer, Nancy L.
Leonard, Lorne Peter
Leroy, Douglas R.
Littman, Daniel Alan
Lockhart, Janet S.
Lombardo, David D.
Lowenstern, Henry
Ludwig, Larry G.
Lunden, Leon E.
Lyle, Jerolyn R.
MacEachern, J. Angus
MacKenzie, Helen R.
Mackraz, James Augustine
MacNett, Kathryn S.
Maffeo, Mario R.
Mandel, Elliot J.
Marchant, J. Douglas
Marcou, Ross Anthony

Mark, Jerome A.
Marutani, Herbert K.
Mason, Frank A.
Matt, Eugene C.
McCafferty, John K.
McCarger, George L.
McCoy, Walter D.
McElroy, Kathleen
McGill, William R.
McIlvain, Charles L.
McWold, Ronald R.
Meier, Elizabeth L.
Melamed, Jerome
Melas, Nicholas J.
Menez, Joseph Robert
Mercer, Walter James
Merchant, Christin Sickles
Millen, Bruce H.
Miller, Mollie A.
Mixer, Madeline Codding
Moberly, Gary L.
Morgenbesser, Leonard Ira
Morton, Herbert Charles
Moses, Evelyn B.
Mrozak, Jack Lawrence
Mrozek, John S.
Mulkern, Paul Vincent
Mullen, Mary Ann
Mullins, Carol M.
Munns, Victor George
Murphy, Joseph Anthony
Nagatomo, Lawrence M.
Newman, Harold R.
Nichols, Henry W.
Nixon, Kathleen A.
Northrop, James B.
Norwood, Janet L.
Nowakowski, Michael G.
Obermayer, Peter Earle
O'Brien, Francis D.
O'Brien, Thomas H.
O'Brien, Thomas M.
Olbrich, Richard
Onanian, Edward Donald
Opara, Rose Ujunma
Orr, Lois Brands
Ortiz, Katherine
Ostry, Sylvia
Panzera, Donald P.
Papier, William Bernard
Parnell, Edward J.
Pastore, Jose
Piculin, Laurette
Pisegna, Dominick
Poglianich, Antonio
Portner, Davis A.
Posthuma, Richard A.
Power, Donald F.
Power, James F.
Preli, Sorine A.
Proctor, William McKenzie
Prouty, E. Keith
Pyle, Donald G.
Quinet, Felix
Raisian, John
Rallis, John J.
Readdean, Shirley
Reed, Ted
Reichenbacher, Mark C.
Reutlinger, Blossom M.
Revell, Joseph J.
Reynolds, Joy K.
Richman, Hyman
Robinson, Sarah A.
Rose, Leo M.
Rosenblum, Marc J.
Rosofsky, Rose G.
Ross, Richard J.
Roth, William
Roumasset, Charles
Rowland, Clifford V.
Rubin, Harold
Rush, Francis Michael Jr.
Rush, Kevin
Rutt, Fred Jr.
Sack, J. Erica
Sariano, John P.
Schellace, Frank N.
Schrauf, Jeremy P.
Schutte, Robert M.
Schwenk, Albert Ernest
Sedlmeier, Edward John
Sheifer, Victor J.
Shultz, George P.
Siegenthaler, Linda
Sirutis, Donna
Skidmore, Robert W.
Slater, Walter
Sleister, Mickey K.
Smith, Charles L.
Smith, Louis Warren
Snyder, William C.
Soffer, Benson
Soltes, Cynthia Yvonne
Soutar, Patricia L.
Southon, Priscilla Jeanne
Sperka, Shlomo
Sprehe, J. Timothy
Spring, Ellan H.
Spring, H. Charles
Squillacote, George F.
Stein, Josephine C.
Stein, Kenneth L.
Stover, Thomas
Strasser, Arnold
Swanson, Robert
Swerbilow, Sally Parker
Symkowiak, Ronald J.
Taggart, Karin E.
Tanner, Lucretia Dewey
Tanzman, David S.
Thede, Kay Anderson
Thompson, James T.
Tipton, John B.
Torosian, Herman
Townley, Rosemary A.
Triplett, Jack E.
Truesdale, John C.
Trumble, Robert R.
Veysey, Victor V.
Wakin, Thomas
Wallmark, Carlton F.
Warburton, Rex M.
Warnock, John A.
Wauck, Lawrence Andrew
Weinstein, Harriet G.
Westman, Carl R.
Wieting, John Lewis
Wilcox, Mary Elizabeth
Wilson, Andrew A.
Wineriter, Gayle
Worley, G. Thomas
Wright, Kenneth B.
Yager, Paul
Zervanos, Christ J.
Zipp, Glenn Arthur
Zumbolo, Anthony

LEGAL PRACTICE

Aalund, Lee A.
Abrams, Nina Dodge
Alexander, Joan B.
Ames, Claude Dawson
Ames, Martin
Asher, Lester
Axelrod, Jonathan G.
Balk, Madeline
Barbash, Joseph
Barnes, Richard L.
Bassen, Ned H.
Bauman, Susan J.
Bee, Peter A.
Bell, Joseph
Berkelhamer, Lester
Berkoff, Marshall R.
Bernheim, Jacob L.
Berry, James H., Jr.
Birmingham, Mary Neil
Blank, Ira Leonard
Blaufeld, Samuel S.
Blum, Peter R.
Boonin, Robert A.
Braff, Jeffrey Lewis
Brauer, Walter C. III
Bredhoff, Elliot
Brook, Richard
Brossman, Mark Edward
Buford, Thomas G.
Buller, Carter Redvers
Bulsiewicz, Karen A.
Buratto, Raymond Joseph
Burstein, Herbert
Byrne, Jerome Camillus
Byrne, William F.
Carroll, Brian
Cavanaugh, Victor A.
Christensen, Andrea S.
Christensen, Thomas G. S.
Cohen, George H.
Coleman, Francis Thomas
Coleman, Richard William
Conti, Adam J.
Cook, Alan J.
Coppess, James B.
Corbett, Laurence Paul
Crost, Paul
D'Alba, Joel Abbott
Damon, C. F., Jr.
Darcy, William Richard
Daughtery, Ronald D.
Denise, Malcolm L.
Donley, Ray N.
Doran, W. Wiley
Dorf, Gerald L.
Drachman Allan W.
Durkay, John J.
Edwards, Charles A.
Eggemeyer, Gerald A.
Elliott, Clifton L.
Ellison, Myron K.
Ellsburg, Donald B.
Elson, Barry R.
Emer, William Howard
Farber, Henry E.
Ferguson, Tracy H.
Ferris, John E.
Fine, Ned Arnold
Fischnaller, Joseph E.
Flamm, Arthur J.
Forkosch, Morris David
Francis, Edna E. J.
Freilicher, Frederic
Fries, Robert T.
Gaba, Richard M.
Gafni, Miriam L.
Galfand, S. Harry
Gallagher, G. Bud
Garchik, Jerome
Garnholz, Edward W.
Garwood, Thomas C., Jr.
Geraty, John M.
Gibson, Rankin MacDougal
Gordon, Michael David
Gray, Ruth Russell
Green, Ronald M.
Gross, Ernest
Gruenberg, Harold
Gruender, Daniel F.
Hack, Linda
Hagood, Lewis R.
Hales, Edward E.
Harper, John J.
Hathaway, Gerald T.
Hawkins, Michael W.
Hayman, Eugene J.
Heinen, Mark L.
Helfand, Richard
Hildebrandt, Ann
Hodges, Ann C.
Holmes, Allan Riley
Hott, Timothy R.
Hotvedt, Richard C.
Hoyt, Ralph B.
Hurley, John P.
Hyde, Philip Ralph
Israel, Dave
Jascourt, Hugh Donald
Jauvtis, Robert Lloyd
Jennings, John Paul
Jennings, Thomas W.
Johnson, Gary C.
Jolley, William A.
Joy, William Francis
Kamber, Frayda
Kampas, Bradley W.
Kaufman, Adam D.
Kaufman, Fay G.
Kelly, Randall M.
Kidston, Roger G.
Killion Leo V.
Kilroy, W. Terrance
Kleiman, Bernard
Kleiner, A. Robert
Klinger, Allan H.
Knight, Henry S., Jr.
Kuhn, Ted
Lackey, Gerald B.
Lapidus, Lawrence Searle
Leff, Irwin
Leong, Ronald Y. K.
Levin, Noel A.
Levy, Abe F.
Levy, Joe L.
Liddle, Jeffrey L.
Lindau, David S.
Linden, Nicholas A.
Lindner, Dennis G.
Linville, Ronald G.
Livingston, Frederick R.
Londa, Jeffrey C.
Lubin, Stan
Lucas-Wallace, Kathleen
Lyon, Richard Martin
Major, Lee F., III
Markle, John Jr.
Markovitz, Jerome L.
Mather, E. Bruce
McCormick, Thomas Patrick
McManemin, Joseph P.
Melnyk, Anton M.
Menard, Arthur P.
Merker, George E.
Mesch, Craig R.
Millman, Bruce R.
Milmet, Morris
Moore, Ernest C., III
Moore, Maureen N.
Morgan, Charles A.
Motiuk, I. Leo
Myers, Howard N.
Newmark, Melvin L.
Nolan, Terrance J.
Odza, Randall M.
Oliver, Anthony Thomas Jr.
O'Reilly, John F.
Orenstein, Sidney
Pace, Stanley D.
Pasek, Jeffrey Ivan
Pellow, David
Pendergast, John J., III
Perlman, Seymour W.
Perry, James B.
Pinto, E. Nicholas
Pirkey, Nancy L.
Platt, Harry H.
Ploscowe, Stephen A.
Pollard, Dennis R.
Potter, Edward E.
Previant, David
Pritzker, Malcolm L.
Rader, Wilma R. K.
Randolph, Robert D.
Raudabaugh, John N.
Reitman, Sidney
Rens, Laverne Gene
Robbins, Michael Arlen
Rogers, Daniel C.
Roitman, Harold B.
Ronner, Walter Valentin
Ropella, Myron Edward
Rose, Irwin A.
Rostov, Stanley David
Rothenberg, Martin R.
Rowe, Robert H.
Runyan, John Robert Jr.
Ryan, Edward F.
Ryan, John M.
Rynecki, Steven B.
Sabatini, Vicki B.
Sachs, Theodore
Sack, Jeffrey
Salandria, Vincent J.
Salsberg, Richard M.
Saxton, William M.
Scheer, Alan I.
Scher, Martin H.
Schoeberlein, William F.
Schwartz, Allen D.
Schwartz, Marvin
Sears, Kelly D.
Segal, Robert M.
Seham, Martin C.

Sherr, Mitchell Avrum
Shindell, Anne B.
Shuster, Frank Barry
Siegel, Boaz
Siegel, Jay S.
Simon, Kenneth Marshall
Simons, Mark N.
Singletary, Cary Robin
Smith, Joel A.
Smith, Jules
Spellman, David J., III
Srikrishna, Bellur N.
Stanley, Douglas C.
Stapp, Michael
Statham, C. Gordon
Stawnychy, Petro R.
Suojanen, Wayne William
Swift, Maris Stella
Taylor, Douglas
Tepper, Allan Arthur
Theep, Raymond T.
Thurschwell, Hubert
Vaas, Francis J.
Vladeck, Judith P.
Waks, Jay W.
Wald, Martin
Waldron, William Augustus
Watkins, Thomas D.
Watson, James R., Jr.
Wax, Harvey I.
Weisman, Robert D.
Weiss, Michael H.
Wenig, Jerome
Westerkamp, Patrick
Whipple, C. David
Wiedemann, Herbert P.
Wilhelm, Julian Augustus
Winegar, Cynthia
Winograd, Daniel M.
Wisniewski, Stanley C.
Wood, David P.
Wright, John C., Jr.
Zolot, Norman

UNION

Acosta, Robert A.
Ahern, Lawrence James
Ahrens, David
Alicen, Bobbie
Allen, Russell W.
Andstein, Cliff
Angell, H. Thomas
Annunziato, Frank
Armitage, G. Nelson
Asmondy, Robert N.
Ayoub, Edmund
Balanoff, Thomas
Ball, Edgar L.
Bargmann, Jeanne M.
Bargmann, Russell M., Jr.
Bell, Deborah E.
Benedetto, Frederick
Berger, Martin
Berger, Richard B.
Bernfeld, Jack
Berry, Alan Percival
Bertani, Charles L.
Bingman, Michael B.
Blair, Sanford S.
Blank, Doris S.
Bliss, Karen S.
Bliss, Raymond C.
Blitzstein, David S.
Booth, Paul R.
Bova, Daniel
Brandt, Gary
Bransted, Zelda N.
Bremer, Charles E.
Brickman, Elizabeth S.
Brophy, Jacqueline A.
Browne, Dolores
Burbine, Henry W.
Burgess, Bruce Sampson
Burkhardt, Francis Xavier
Burki, Fred A.
Burnell, Stan E.
Burns, May C.
Burns, William L.
Busca, Morris James
Bynum, Theodore R.
Byrnes, Louise
Campion, Diane Lee
Cantor, Arnold Bruce
Carpenter, George E., Jr.
Casey, E. A.
Cashmore, Patsy J.
Caudill, Roy A.
Chester, Harry L.
Chisholm, Les
Chybowski, Robert M.
Clem, C. Stephen
Collins, A. Michael
Confer, Stephen H.
Conlan, Kathleen M.
Converse, Mary H.
Cooke, Jacqueline R.
Copas, William H.
Cordtz, Richard W.
Crowley, John F.
Crudo, Fernanda Cynthia
Crumpton, Robert G.
Cullinan, Martin J.
Culver, Warren D.
Czarnecki, Edgar R.
Czerbinski, Joseph P.
Dabney, Henrietta L.
Daniels, Wilbur
Davia, Albert B.
Davidson, Astrid
Dear, Joseph A.
Demers, W. C.
Devereux, Greg D.
Dittmer, Roger A.
Dodt, Harold
Draves, Edward F.
Dreiblatt, Dean M.
Driscoll, John J.
Dunberry, Fernand J.
Durham, John L.
Dyck, R. Gordon
Edgington, John C.
Edstrom, Thomas J.
Ellinger, Ruth
Faherty, Joseph C.
Fillion, John A.
Firestone, Bernard J.
Fischer, Lydia Helena
Fitton, Patricia A.
Flora, Judith
Forman, Howie
Foster, James D.
Fox, Edward M.
Fryer, John Leslie
Gale, Edward R.
Garcia, Martha A.
Garst, James D.
Gentile, Charles
George, Charlene A.
Gibson, Giles H.
Glaser, Robert
Glazer, Joseph
Golodner, Jack
Gottesfeld, Gary I.
Grande, Joseph A.
Gray, Mark L.
Greenberg, Bernard
Greendorfer, Jeffrey R.
Gretz, Clare Burt
Grosland, David A.
Grove, Richard Lee
Gruenberg, Robert
Gualtiere, James Lawrence
Gustafson, Donna M.
Haener, Al
Hallock, Margaret
Hamai, Albert T.
Hanselman, Kristeen Hunt
Harasim, Chester
Harney, John Robert
Haynes, Glenn M., Jr.
Hendrickson, Steven J.
Hennes, Thomas M.
Himmelmann, William C.
Hofmann, Joseph P.
Hubbard, Harry
Huggins, Charles D.
Insley, Patrice J.
Isenberg, Harold J. T.
Jacobs, James Kevand
Jaffe, Ludwig
Janicki, Norman K., Jr.
Jaquay, Joseph N.
Jensen, Robert R.
Jirikowic, Ralph A.
Johnson, Arthur Brannon
Johnson, Walter L.
Kaiser, Earl H.
Kane, Arthur Francis
Kaplan, David
Kardash, James D.
Kaufmann, Dennis R.
Kaye, James H.
Kearsley, Dora F.
Keefe, Jeffrey H.
Kennedy, Francis Jr.
Kenney, Lawrence C.
Kent, Ronald Charles
Kersten, Edward A.
Kirrane, William
Klass, Irwin E.
Knox, Robert E.
Koerner, Stephen
Kohl, George H.
Kolb, Jean
Kornfeld, Marc C.
Kowalczyk, Robert S.
Krahn, Donald E.
Krashevski, Richard S.
Kruse, Roy
Kuehn, Donald H.
Kuhl, William Owen
Kurtz, Cary R.
LaSalle, Jon G.
LaSalvia, Maria C.
Leal, Ben C.
Lelling, Bernard H.
Levin, Douglas
Levinson, Alan
Lewis, Jeffrey Dean
Leyden, John F.
Leibes, Richard A.
Lilore, Doreen
Lindsay, Richard E.
Lipper, Stuart J.
Locigno, Paul R.
Lubell, Scott K.
Lyons, Robert W.
MacDonald, Jeffrey A.
MacDonald, Raymond Wilbur
Madison, Joseph James
Mahoney, Donald L.
Malmo, Diane M.
Malone, Renee H.
Mapp, Milton Marvin
Marcus, Susan E.
Marsh, Milan
Mason, Robert H.
Massagli, Mark Tully
Masters, W. Frank
Matthews, Marilyn S.
Mauk, Ellen Schuler
Maurer, Ann H.
McCloskey, Margaret M.
McDonald, John Michael
McGivern, Edward J.
McMahon, June
McNamara, Bertram N.
McNeil, Paul J., Jr.
Melnick, Harold H.
Miller, Joyce D.
Miller, Vera
Minamoto, Jennifer N.
Mishel, Lawrence R.
Montross, William
Moon, Gary Lee
Moore, Thomas F.
Morgan, Bill E.
Morris, John P.

Muir, Norman William
Murch, Ken
Murphy, Kevin R.
Musto, J. N.
Nangeroni, Jill E.
Neft, Darrell K.
Neimeiser, Mark M.
Ness, Debra L.
Newell, Reginald
Newman, Stephen J.
Newman, Winn
Nobili, Ronald Bruce
Nordlander, Ake
Novogrodsky, David
Nulty, Leslie E.
Ockert, Roy Anthony
O'Connor, Paula
O'Leary, John
Oliver, Howard Wayne
O'Neill, John N.
Osa, Joseph M.
Oswald, Rudolph Alphonsus
Owley, Candice
Paliwodzinski, Robert L.
Panfil, James F.
Patino, Antonio J.
Paulson, Steven
Peterson, Raymond A.
Phillips, Mark B.
Pinto, Nicholas F.
Porter, Karen E.
Presser, Richard A.
Preston, Valerie Knox
Prosten, Richard M.
Quarles, Mary Virginia
Radcliffe, John H.
Randol, George C.
Reader, Mark M.
Reed, Theodore E.
Rembold, Chris J.
Rennels, Marline
Rennison, Ralph
Revell, John M.
Reynolds, Benny L.
Reynolds, J. C.
Reynolds, J. C.
Richardson, Douglas A.
Richardson, Gerald
Roberts, Markley
Rodgers, Thomas J.
Rosenberg, Emily J.
Roy, Wayne Paul
Russell, Lucas G.
Sammis, Robert Lyle
Sanders, Ellen M.
Sano, Joseph B.
Sapiro, Bernard L.
Sauter, Jerold B.
Schmitt, John W.
Schuster, Richard N.
Schwartz, George William
Scott, Gerold G.
Seidman, Bert
Shea, George R.
Sickler, A. David
Singer, Paula
Skowronski, Audrey M.
Skratek, Sylvia P.
Slye, Joann Mertens
Smedley, Lawrence Thomas
Smith, Brian J.
Smith, Dorothy F.
Solana, Lucille
Spangler, Thomas James
Sparrough, Michael E.
Sperling, Herman J.
Sperry, John C.
Staats, Charles E., Jr.
Stein, Leon
Stober, Richard P.
Stodghill, William
Stokes, Michal Lee
Stout, Larry A.
Straw, Ronnie J.
Stuteville, Walter M.
Sullivan, Anne
Sullivan, Edward T.
Summerlott, Paul Nash
Sweeney, John J.
Taggart, John David
Tam, Richard
Taylor, Merlin L.
Teper, Lazare
Thaker, Harshadray H.
Thomas, Patrick H.
Thompson, Ann R.
Thornton, John A.
Timmons, Richard Lee
Tissue, Dorothy
Trask, Tommy
Tuck, Kenneth W.
Twomey, Timothy
Uehlein, Julius
Ullman, Donna
Unger, William R.
Vattendahl, Obert J.
Velotta, Charles V.
Viani, Alan R.
Vigil, Patrick R.
Wagner, Marlin O.
Walker, Donald P.
Wallace, Paul
Wallick, Franklin
Ward, John T.
Ward, Robert J.
Wasserman, Donald S.
Watroba, David R.
Weinberg, Nat
Weintraub, Norman A.
Welsh, Robert
Whitford, Ann M.
Wick, Margie
Willea, Cliff
Williams, Roy L.
Williamson, B. G.
Witkower, Philip
Wrathall, Leila
Wykert, Timothy R.
Zalusky, John Lucas
Zamboni, Richard A.
Zander, Jack
Zellers, James Anthony

OTHER (INCLUDING UNSPECIFIED)

Abers, Jacob H.
Alers, Benjamin
Anderson, Bernard E.
Annable, James E., Jr.
Arndt, Catherine C.
Bailey, Thomas R.
Bassen, Harold R.
Beaudin, Brian V.
Belous, Richard S.
Benhamou, Annie
Berkley, Gail W.
Blair, Larry M.
Blaustein, Saul J.
Borba, Philip S.
Brandwein, Ethel
Brazier, James Edward
Brody, Matthew
Brunnhuber, Gregory R.
Buskirk, Phyllis R.
Caropreso, Anthony C.
Chase, Thomas C.
Chretien, Barbara C.
Clark, Robert W.
Colosi, Thomas RI
Decristofaro, Maryann
Deeny, Ray
De Frehn, Randy G.
Dennison, Cynthia Ellen
Diemer, Bernard
Dilorio, James D.
Dillon, Catherine M.
Douty, Harry Mortimer
Duzak, Thomas
Emerson, Wayne
Ezratty, Arlene
Fegatilli, Diane
Fidandis, Nicholas Andrew
Fisher, Caricia J.
Fleming,Loretta A.
Frank, Murray W.
Freedman, Audrey
Fuller, Dewey C.
Gallagher, James J.
Gallery, Maureen L.
Garnier, Katherine
Garvey, John Joseph
George, Jack R.
Goldman, Barbara S.
Grove, Kathryn
Hale,Randolph M.
Halmos, Anthony M.
Handsaker, Marjorie L.
Hansen, Jerome F.
Hedges, Janice Neipert
Herding, Richard Gunther
Herling, John
Hirozawa, Betty F.
Hoerr, John P.
Hunt, Allan
Huot, John J.
James, Clinton S., III
Jasper, Debbie Ann
Johnson, Marvin E.
Kales, Robert G.
Karako, Jeffrey J.
Kassalow, Sylvia D.
Kazazean, Susan Jane
Kerachsky, Stuart H.
Kirkpatrick, Gary J.
Kiss, Bertha
Kruglak, Gregory
Lamb, Marjorie Anna
Leifer, Lorenz A.
Leifer, Marion J.
Leslie, Astley Noel
Levin-Epstein, Michael
Mackell, Thomas James Jr.
Maetzold, Thomas O.
Mahoney, Caryl B.
Mann, Seymour Z.
Marx, Harriet S.
Mauro, Martin John
Maynard, Rebecca
McKinney, Edward C.
McLean, Beth A.
McLennan, Kenneth
Meier, Anne L.
Meisler, George
Meloon, James Allen
Miner, Mary Green
Mitchell, J. M.
Moberg, David
Moffett, Kenneth E.
Moore, Charles Coty
Murase, Jerry L.
Murbach, Ilene G.
Mullen, Charlene H.
Mushkin, Phyllis
Oechslin, Jean-Jacques
Peevey, Michael Robert
Perl, Peter
Perry, Michael S.
Phillips, Barbara Ashley
Pierce, Carolyn F.
Pilenzo, Ronald C.
Pizarro, Zosimo Q.
Plambeck, Donald L.
Poncini, Conchita
Raskin, Abraham Henry
Ray, Phillip Everette
Rees, Albert E.
Rellini, Giampiero
Renner, Donna L. Wilson
Repar, George
Robertson, Juan P.
Rohrer, Jennifer
Rosow, Jerome M.
Rougeux, Nanette I.
Ryan, Hubert B.
Ryan, Steve M.
Scalone, John A.
Scannell, Raymond Matthew
Schlesinger, Carl T.
Schwab, Robert M.
Schwartz, Herb A.
Schweinberg, Joseph
Serumgard, John R.
Sharpe, Marjorie Johnston
Simpson, Karl Franklin Jr.
Sinclitico, Joseph A.
Smith, Oscar S.
Socha, John L.
Stark, Dorothy C.
Stayt, John
Stephenson, James R.
Stessin, Lawrence
Stranger, Charles E.
Tarantelli, Ezio
Tatum, James E.
Taylor, David P.
Totten, Jan Laube
Trupiano, John
Uehlein, Mary L.
Vecellio, Denise McDonald
Vogel, Michael S.
Vroman, Wayne
Wada, Mary Matsuko
Walker, Darlene
Wall, Robert John
Wary, Curt
Wasser, Leonard
Waugh, David A.
Weeks, D. A.
Weiss, Harry
Weitz, Peter R.
Wendling, Wayne Roger
West, Michael D.
Westerkamp, Paul R.
White, Lee Francis
Whiting, Basil John Jr.
Wirpel, Estelle M.
Worden, Robert G.
Young, Joseph A.
Zimmerman, David Roy

Geographic Distribution of IRRA Members and Subscribers

AREA	1966	1972	1979	1984[a]	AREA	1966	1972	1979	1984[a]
Alabama	11	19	25	26	Nevada	4	5	11	13
Alaska	1	2	1	5	New Hampshire	8	10	18	17
Arizona	9	18	38	26	New Jersey	91	132	242	195
Arkansas	4	4	8	10	New Mexico	11	13	15	12
California	210	299	476	395	New York	473	474	642	589
Colorado	16	22	49	30	North Carolina	14	22	32	28
Connecticut	41	63	86	75	North Dakota	2	1	3	3
Delaware	6	9	7	12	Ohio	117	165	176	179
Washington DC	233	233	287	192	Oklahoma	14	10	14	16
Florida	17	27	60	72	Oregon	22	31	41	33
Georgia	30	38	63	64	Pennsylvania	150	187	321	273
Hawaii	19	27	24	41	Puerto Rico	[b]	12	4	4
Idaho	4	3	15	6	Rhode Island	6	12	12	26
Illinois	231	253	287	256	South Carolina	5	8	18	21
Indiana	45	58	73	58	South Dakota	0	0	0	0
Iowa	27	35	38	39	Tennessee	33	25	58	29
Kansas	13	35	32	27	Texas	57	96	199	167
Kentucky	12	15	20	30	Utah	5	18	23	15
Louisiana	6	10	19	17	Vermont	1	2	3	4
Maine	8	7	14	4	Virginia	24	70	103	96
Maryland	38	101	113	132	Washington	29	30	58	51
Massachusetts	142	193	201	187	West Virginia	12	22	28	45
Michigan	174	198	318	320	Wisconsin	162	191	212	208
Minnesota	52	44	59	57	Wyoming	0	3	4	3
Mississippi	6	5	9	6	Canada	158	233	261	218
Missouri	43	162	147	111	Other Countries	127	187	256	212
Montana	2	2	3	7					
Nebraska	8	10	11	12	TOTALS	2,933	3,851	5,237	4,680

[a] Member statistics for 1984 do not include several categories that were included in previous years, such as local IRRA chapters, institutions receiving complimentary publications and members who were not current in dues payments.
[b] Indicates that the category was not listed separately in that particular issue of the Directory.

Occupational Classification of IRRA Members[a]

Occupational Category	1966	1972	1979	1984[b]
Academic				
Administration	26	152	130	104
Business Administration	[c]	215	176	116
Economics	587	410	394	298
Industrial Relations	193	367	617	469
Law	28	45	100	89
Org. Behavior/Personnel	[c]	[c]	94	117
Political Science	9	14	13	11
Psychology	20	25	23	8
Sociology	66	52	36	27
Student	168	142	381	299
Other (Including Unspecified)	74	99	86	107
Academic Totals	1,171	1,379	2,046	1645
Arbitration	[c]	107	233	387
Consultation	187	143	209	172
Government	390	487	554	360
Legal	116	171	246	256
Business: Management/Administration	494	625	193	170
Business: Personnel/Indus. Relations	[c]	[c]	624	627
Union	154	214	325	344
Other (Including Unspecified)	124	158	235	163
Members Listed in Occupational Section of Each Directory	2,636	3,426	4,665	4,124

[a] See page 316 for occupational comparisons with the IRRA Local Chapter Membership.
[b] Member statistics for 1984 do not include several categories that were included in previous years, such as local IRRA Chapters, institutions receiving complimentary publications and members who were not current in dues payments.
[c] Indicates that the category was not listed separately in that particular issue of the Directory.

IRRA LOCAL CHAPTERS*

Information is listed on the 55 local chapters currently affiliated with the national Association. Entries include each chapter's official address (by state, and including Canada and Paris), number and schedule of meetings, and name of a chapter member designated as a contact for information. Meeting schedules are included to enable attendance by IRRA members traveling in other areas. Annual updating, as well as program and other details, can be found in IRRA's February Newsletters. Free copies may be obtained from the IRRA national office.

*The chapters numbered 19 in 1966, 32 in 1972, 53 in 1979, and 55 in 1984.

UNITED STATES

ARIZONA
Arizona IRRA-Phoenix
Margie Wick
CWA Local 8519
9224 N 5th St
Phoenix, AZ 85020
602/242-8519
Quarterly Seminars

CALIFORNIA
Calif Central Coast IRRA-San Luis Obispo
William Aussieker
Mgmt Dept, School of Business,
Calif Polytechnic State Univ
San Luis Obispo, CA 93407
805/546-1301

Central Calif IRRA-Fresno
Flora Gaudin, Personnel Manager
R. T. French Co
3366 E Muscat Avenue
Fresno, CA 93725
209/486-1330
Dinner Meeting, 3rd Wednesday

Northern Calif IRA-Sacramento
Wayne Harbolt
3101 Stockton Mall
Sacramento, CA 95820
916/448-3252
Dinner Meeting, 2nd Thursday

Orange County IRRA
Constance L. Begley
PO Box 5781
Huntington Beach, CA 92646
213/587-6171
Six Dinner Meetings

San Diego IRRA-San Diego
Adam Gifford
Director, Inst Labor Economics
San Diego State Univ
San Diego, CA 92182
619/265-5471
Quarterly Dinner Meetings

San Francisco Bay Area IRRA-San Francisco
Magdalena Jacobsen FMCS, 29th Floor
525 Market St
San Francisco, CA 94127
415/974-9864
Luncheon Meetings, September - June

Southern California IRRA-Los Angeles
Jim Santangelo, Teamsters Local 848
1616 W 9th St #223
Los Angeles, CA 90015
213/385-2036
Dinner Meetings, October-June

COLORADO
Rocky Mountain IRRA-Denver
Louise Byrnes
2522A S Worchester Ct
Aurora, CO 80014
303/292-6601
Dinner Meetings, September-April
All Day Seminar in April

CONNECTICUT
Connecticut Valley IRRA-Hartford/Storrs
Morris L. Fried
Labor Education Center
Univ of Connecticut
Storrs, CT 06268
203/486-3417
Quarterly Dinner Meetings

Southwestern Connecticut IRRA
George N. Nichols
Cummings & Lockwood
PO Box 860
Bridgeport, CT 06601
203/366-3438
Dinner Meetings
September, January, Spring

DISTRICT OF COLUMBIA
Washington DC IRRA
Donald S. Wasserman
AFSCME
1625 L St NW
Washington DC 20036
202/429-1219
Luncheon Meetings, Sept-April (not December)
Dinner Meeting, May

FLORIDA
Central Florida IRRA-St. Petersburg
Gary Vause
1401 61st St. S
St. Petersburg, FL 33707
813/343-1214
Quarterly Dinner Meetings
Fall Conference

GEORGIA
Atlanta IRRA-Atlanta
Beverly K. Schaffer
Department of Economics
Emory University
Atlanta, GA 30322
404/329-6361
Luncheon Meetings
Sept-May/June

HAWAII

Hawaii IRRA - Honolulu
Joyce Najita
Industrial Relations Center
University of Hawaii
2425 Campus Rd
Honolulu, HI 96822
808/948-8132
Four Luncheon Meetings
December Conference

ILLINOIS

Central Illinois IRRA-Springfield
Anne Draznin
Center for Legal Studies
Sangamon State University
Springfield, IL 62708
217/786-6343
Quarterly Dinner Meetings

Chicago IRRA-Chicago
Judith Hale
Hale & Associates
200 W Monroe 1607
Oak Park, IL 60606
312/236-3122
Dinner Meetings
October-May

Labor & Industrial Relations Assn-Champaign
Janet Eakman
Assistant to Director
504 E Armory Ave
Champaign, IL 61820
217/333-1482
Monthly Meetings

MARYLAND

Maryland IRRA-Baltimore
James Whattam
Wineberg & Green
100 South Charles St
Baltimore, MD 21201
301/332-8681
Dinner Meeting, 4th Wednesday
September - May

MASSACHUSETTS

Boston IRRA-Boston
Rick Reilly
American Arbitration Association
60 Staniford St
Boston, MA 02114
617/367-6800
Three Dinner Meetings
October, January, May

MICHIGAN

Detroit Area IRRA-Detroit
Mark Kahn
MAIR, Wayne State University
5165 Gullen Hall
Wayne State Univ
Detroit, MI 48202
313/577-4380
Dinner Meeting, IstThursday
October-May

Mid-Michigan IRRA-Lansing
Pam Gignac
Blue Cross & Blue Shield
313 S Washington Square
Lansing, MI 48933
517/372-8700
Dinner Meeting, 2nd Wednesday
September-May

Northeast Michigan IRRA-Saginaw
Thomas Basil
Saginaw Valley State College
University Center, MI 48710
517/793-6462
Dinner Meeting, 3rd Thursday
September-May

Southwest Michigan IRRA-Kalmazoo
R. D. Jackson
Federal Building/B96
410 W Michigan Ave
Kalamazoo, MI 49007
616/345-2409
Dinner Meeting, 1st Monday
September-May

West Michigan IRRA-Grand Rapids
William Proctor
250 Federal Building
110 Michigan St NW
Grand Rapids, MI 49503
616/456-2402
Dinner Meeting, 2nd Tuesday
October-May

MISSOURI

Gateway Chapter-St. Louis
Greg Boyer
Metro Sewer District
2000 Hampton
St. Louis, MO 63139
314/768-6213
All Day Seminar
October, February, May

Greater Kansas City IRRA-Kansas City
Carlton Wallmark
FMCS, 23rd Floor
324 E 11th St
Kansas City, MO 64106
816/374-3027
Dinner Meeting
Fall, Winter, Spring

NEW JERSEY

Central New Jersey IRRA-Trenton
F. Lucidi
Teamsters Local 35
620 Route 130
Trenton, NJ 08691
609/585-4400
Dinner Meeting, 2nd Wednesday
September-May

New Brunswick IRRA-New Brunswick
Betty Derco
Ryders Lane, Box 231
Rutgers University
New Brunswick, NJ 08903
201/932-9022
Dinner Meeting, 1st Monday
September-May

NEW YORK

Central New York IRRA-Syracuse
Joseph Gentile
NYS Mediation Board
335 E Washington St
Syracuse, NY 13202
315/428-4068
Dinner Meeting, September, November,
January, March, May

Long Island IRRA
Robert W. MacGregor
284 Bretton Woods Dr
Coram, NY 11727
516/732-4792
Dinner Meeting, September,
December, February, June

New York Capital IRRA-Albany
B. Taylor
Personnel & Employee Rels
Rensselaer Polytechnic Inst
Troy, NY 12181
518/270-6586
Dinner Meeting
September-May (except December)

New York City IRRA-New York
Phillip Harris
Dept of Mgmt, Baruch College
17 Lexington Ave
New York, NY 10003
201/725-7122
Dinner Meetings, 2nd Thursday
September-May (not December)

Western New York IRRA-Buffalo
Norman J. Stocker, Town-Tonawanda Labor Rels
PO Box 710
Buffalo, NY 14202
716/877-1974
Dinner Meetings
September-May

NEVADA

Southern Nevada IRRA-Las Vegas
George W. Hardbeck
3659 Descanso
Las Vegas, NV 89121
702/739-3362
Meetings 1st Tues, September-June

OHIO

Central Ohio IRRA-Columbus
Mark Sandver
Human Resource Research
Ohio State University
5701 N High St
Worthington, OH 43085
614/888-7309
Luncheon Meeting, 1st Tuesday
October-May (except December)

Greater Cincinnati IRRA-Cincinnati
Donald M. Standriff
Cincinnati Ind Inst
2495 Langdon Farm Rd
Cincinnati, OH 45237
513/731-2211
Dinner Meeting, 3rd Monday
September-May

Northeast Ohio IRRA-Cleveland
Erwin R. Dolski
FMCS, Room 508, Mall Building
118 St. Clair Ave NE
Cleveland, OH 44114
216/522-4806
Dinner Meeting, September, November,
February, April/May

PENNSYLVANIA

Central Pennsylvania IRRA-Harrisburg
D. Fealtman
Pennsylvania Nurses Association
PO Box 8525
Harrisburg, PA 17105
717/234-7935
Dinner Meeting, 3rd Monday

Philadelphia IRRA-Philadelphia
G. T. Sheahan
Teamsters Local 115
2833 Cottman Ave
Philadelphia, PA 19149
215/335-0100
Dinner Meeting, 2nd Tuesday
October-May

Western Pennsylvania IRRA
Pittsburgh/St. Francis College/Indiana University
Antone Aboud
Industrial Relations, St. Francis College
Loretto, PA 15940
814/472-7000
Quarterly Dinner Meetings

RHODE ISLAND

Greater Rhode Island IRRA
Charles T. Schmidt Jr.
Director, Labor Research Center
University of Rhode Island, Kingston, RI 02881
401/792-2239
Quarterly Dinner Meetings

SOUTH CAROLINA

South Atlanta IRRA-Columbia
Hoyt N. Wheeler, College of Business Admin
University of South Carolina
Columbia, SC 29208
803/777-5959
Quarterly Dinner Meetings

TEXAS

Alamo Area IRRA-San Antonio
Gary C. Raffaele
Division of Business
University of Texas
San Antonio, TX 78285
512/691-4311
Quarterly Dinner Meetings

Greater Houston IRRA-Houston
Ernest E. Marlatt
PO Box 13199
Houston, TX 77019
713/961-1594
Quarterly Dinner Meetings

North Texas IRRA-Dallas
Helmut O. Wolff
American Arbitration Association
1607 Main St
Dallas, TX 75201
214/748-4979
Dinner Meeting Every Six Weeks
September - May

South Texas IRRA-Austin
Ruth Ellinger
PO Box 12727
Austin, TX 78711
512/477-6195
Meetings - Fall, Winter and May

UTAH

Utah IRRA-Salt Lake City
Ann Wendt
412 Kendall D Garff Bldg
University of Utah
Salt Lake City, UT 84112
801/581-5572

WASHINGTON

Inland Empire IRRA-Spokane
Carolyn Pierce
Associated General Contractors
PO Box 3266
Spokane, WA 99220
509/535-0391
Lunch and Dinner Meetings
September-May

Northwest IRRA-Seattle
Ben Yotsey
FMCS
2615 4th Ave
Seattle, WA 98121
206/442-4559
Quarterly Lunch Meetings

WEST VIRGINIA
West Virginia IRRA-Morgantown
Vivian Kidd
WV Education Fund
1126 Kanawha Valley Bldg
Charleston, WV 25301
304/342-7850
Spring Conference

WISCONSIN
Wisconsin IRRA-Milwaukee
S. B. Rynecki
Von Briesen & Redmond
757 N Broadway
Milwaukee, WI 53202
414/276-1122
Luncheon Meetings, 2nd Friday
September-May

CANADA

ONTARIO
Hamilton District IRRA-Hamilton
Harish C. Jain
Pers/IR, Bldg KTH, Rm 226
McMaster University
Hamilton, Ontario L8S 4M4 Canada
416/522-4971

BRITISH COLUMBIA
British Columbia IRRA-Vancouver
David McPhillips
University of British Columbia
203-2053 Main Mall
Vancouver, BC V6T 1Y8 Canada
604/228-2191
Dinner Meetings
September-May

FRANCE

Paris IRRA
Oliver Clarke
OECD Ind Rels Div
2 Rue Andre-Pascal
Paris XVIE France

IRRA NATIONAL-LOCAL CHAPTER COMPARISONS

Occupational Classifications in 1966, 1972, 1979 and 1984

	Total Members	Academic	Government	Arb, Legal Consulting	Management	Union	Student	Other/ Not Identified
1966 (19 Chapters)								
National IRRA	2636	1003(38%)	390(15%)	303(11%)	494(19%)	154(6%)	168(6%)	124(5%)
Local Chapters	2359	343(14%)	399(17%)	388(16%)	720(31%)	377(16%)	132(6%)	
1972 (32 Chapters)								
National IRRA	3426	1379(40%)	487(14%)	421(13%)	625(18%)	214(6%)	142(4%)	158(5%)
Local Chapters	4420	533(12%)	490(11%)	754(17%)	1498(33%)	949(22%)	196(5%)	
1979 (49 Chapters)								
National IRRA	4589	1590(35%)	532(11%)	651(14%)	829(18%)	360(8%)	510(11%)	137(3%)
Local Chapters	6619	705(11%)	1000(15%)	1138(17%)	1922(29%)	1562(24%)	292(4%)	
1984 (55 Chapters)								
National IRRA	4124	1239(30%)	360(9%)	815(20%)	971(24%)	344(8%)	299(7%)	270(6%)
Local Chapters	8557	899(11%)	1004(12%)	1631(19%)	2536(30%)	1866(22%)	276(3%)	345(4%)

LIBRARY AND OTHER INSTITUTIONAL SUBSCRIBERS

The library and other institutional subscribers are listed: *1.* In the USA in alphabetical order by state and within each state by zip code, 2. In Canada and other countries in alphabetical order by cities.

UNITED STATES

ALABAMA

Auburn
Auburn University
Serials Department
Ralph Brown Draughon Library 36849

Mobile
University of South Alabama
Library Serials Department
307 University Blvd, 36688

University
University of Alabama
Business Library, 35486

ARIZONA

Tempe
Arizona State University
Library Periodicals, 85287

Tucson
University of Arizona
Library,85721

ARKANSAS

Fayetteville
University of Arkansas
University Library
Serials Section, 72701

State University
Arkansas State University
D. B. Ellis Library, 72467

CALIFORNIA

Berkeley
University of California-Berkeley
Serials Dept, General Library, 94720

University of California-Berkeley
Institute of Industrial Relations Library
2521 Channing Way, Room 110, 94720

Claremont
Claremont Colleges
Honnold Library, 91711

Davis
University of California-Davis
Library Acquisitions Department, 95616

Fresno
University of California-Fresno
Library Acquisitions Department, 93740

Fullerton
California State University-Fullerton
Library-Acquisitions, 92634

Irvine
University of California-Irvine
Library Serials Department, 92664

Los Angeles
California State University/LASO
JFK Memorial Library
5175 State College Drive, 90032

Kindel & Anderson
Law Library
555 S Flower St, 26th FL, 90071

Los Angeles Public Library
361 S Anderson St, 90033

Loyola Law School
Library, 1440 W 9th St, 90015

University of California-Los Angeles
University Research Library, 90024

Western Conference of Teamsters
Research Department
2323 W 8th St, 90057

Whittier College
Law School Library, 90020

Oakland
Kaiser Aluminum Chemical Corp
300 Lakeside Dr, 94643

Pomona
California State Polytechnic University
3801 W Temple Ave, 91768

Riverside
University of California-Riverside
Library Serials Dept, PO Box 5900, 92507

Sacramento
California State University-Sacramento
Library, 2000 Jed Smith Dr, 95810

San Diego
San Diego State University
Malcolm Love Library, 92182

University of Calif-San Diego
Acquisitions Department Library, 92093

San Francisco
California Labor Statistics/Research
Department of Industrial Relations
PO Box 603, 94101

San Francisco State College
Library, 1630 Holloway Ave, 94132

San Jose
San Jose State University
Clark Library
1 Washington Square, 95192

San Luis Obispo
California State Polytechnic University
Dexter Memorial Library, 93407

Santa Barbara
University of California-Santa Barbara
Library Serials Department, 93106

Stanford
Stanford University
Graduate School of Business
Jackson Library, 94305

Stanford University
School of Law-Library, 94305

Stanford University
Libraries Serials Department, 94305

Turlock
California State University-Turlock
Stanislaus Library, 95380

COLORADO

Boulder
University of Colorado
Libraries, 80309

Denver
University of Denver
Libraries, 80210

Fort Collins
Colorado State University
Libraries, 80523

CONNECTICUT

Bridgeport
Cummings & Lockwood, Attorneys-at-Law
PO Box 860, 06601

Hartford
Trinity College
Library, 06106

New Haven
Yale University
Library Acquisitions Dept
1603A Yale St, 06520

Yale University
Law Library, 06520

Yale University
Social Science Library
Box 1958 Yale Station, 06520

DELAWARE

Newark
University of Delaware
Library, 19717

DISTRICT OF COLUMBIA

AFL-CIO Library
815 16th Street NW, Room 102, 20006

AFSCME, Information Center
1625 L Street NW, 20036

American University-Library
Massachusetts & Nebraska Aves NW, 20016

Catholic University of America
Mullen Library, 20064

CWA Information Library
1925 K Street NW, 20006

George Washington University
Gelman Library, 20052

Georgetown University
Library Serials Department
37th & O Streets NW, 20057

Library of Congress
Congressional Research Service, 20540

Mathematica Policy Research
Library, Suite 550
600 Maryland Ave, 20024

National Education Association
Program Development
1201 16th St NW, 20036

National Science Foundation
Library, Room 1242
1800 G Street NW, 20550

UFCW International Union
Research Office, 1775 K St NW, 20006

U. S. Labor Dept
Library Acquisitions Dept, RM N2452
200 Constitution Ave, 20210

U. S. NLRB Library
Room 900, 1717 Pennsylvania Ave NW, 20570

U. S. Office Personnel Management
Librarian Room 5L45
1900 E Street NW, 20415

University of District of Columbia
IRC Bldg 39, Room B-07
4200 Connecticut Avenue, 20008

FLORIDA

Coral Gables
University of Miami
Library Serials Department
PO Box 248214, 33124

Jacksonville
University of North Florida
Library, Box 16761, 32216

Tallahassee
Florida State University
Robert W. Strozier Library, 32306

Tampa
University of South Florida
Library Serials Dept, 33620

GEORGIA

Athens
University of Georgia
Serials Section-Libraries, 30602

Atlanta
Georgia Institute of Technology
Library Director
225 N Avenue NW, 30332

Georgia State University
Pullen Library
100 Decatur St SE, 30303

HAWAII
Honolulu
University of Hawaii
Industrial Relations Center
2425 Campus Dr, 96822

IDAHO
Moscow
University of Idaho
Serials Section-Library, 83843

Pocatello
Idaho State University
Serials Deparment, Library, 83209.

ILLINOIS
Carbondale
Southern Illinois University
Morris Library, 62901

Charleston
Eastern Illinois University
Booth Library, 61920

Chicago
DePaul University
Libraries, 25 East Jackson Blvd, 60604

Illinois Institute of Technology
Kemper Library
3300 S Federal St, 60616

Loyola University
Library, 6525 N Sheridan Rd, 60626

University of Chicago
Business Library
1100 E 57th St, 60637

University of Illinois
Library Serials Section
PO Box 8198, 60680

Decatur
Millikin University
Staley Library, 1184 W Main St, 62522

DeKalb
Northern Illinois University
University Libraries, 60115

Edwardsville
Southern Illinois University
Lovejoy Library, 62026

Evanston
Northwestern University
Library Serials Department, 60201

Lake Forest
Lake Forest College
College Library, 60045

Northbrook
Management Contents
PO Box 3014, 60062

Springfield
Sangamon State University
Library Acquisitions, 62708

Urbana
University of Illinos
Library Serials
1408 W Gregory Dr, 61801

University of Illinois (2)
Serials Dept-Library, 61801

INDIANA
Bloomington
Indiana University
Library Serials Dept, 47405

Indiana University
Midwest Labor Center, 47405

Lafayette
Purdue University
Libraries Serials Unit, 47907

Notre Dame
University of Notre Dame
Law School Library, 46556

South Bend
Indiana University
South Bend Library, PO Box 7111, 46634

IOWA
Ames
Iowa State University
Serials Department-Library, 50011

Des Moines
Drake University
Technical Services Dept-Library, 50311

Iowa City
State University of Iowa
Libraries, 52242

KANSAS
Lawrence
University of Kansas
Serials Department-Library, 66045

University of Kansas
School of Business
101A Summerfield Hall, 66045

Manhatten
Kansas State University
Library Serials Division, 66506

Wichita
Wichita State University
Library Serials Dept, Box 68, 67208

KENTUCKY
Bowling Green
Western Kentucky University
Margie Helm Library, 42101

Lexington
University of Kentucky
MI King Library, 40506

Louisville
University of Louisville
Ekstrom Library, 40292

Richmond
Eastern Kentucky University
Crabbe Library, 40475

LOUISIANA

Baton Rouge
Louisiana State University
Serials Dept-Library, 70803

New Orleans
University of New Orleans
Earl K. Long Library, 70148

Ruston
Louisiana Technical University
Prescott Library, 71272

MARYLAND

Baltimore
Johns Hopkins University
Library Acquisition Dept, 21218

Towson State University
Albert Cook Library, 21204

University of Maryland
Baltimore County Campus Library
5401 Wilkins Ave, 21228

University of Maryland
School of Law Library
20 N Paca Street, 21201

U. S. HEW Social Security Admin
Library, Room 571, Altmeyer Bldg, 21235

College Park
University of Maryland
McKeldin Library, 20742

MASSACHUSETTS

Amherst
University of Massachusetts
Labor Rels & Research Center
125 Draper Hall, 01003

University of Massachusetts
Library Serials Section, 01003

Babson Park
Babson College Library, 02157

Boston
Boston Public Library
Serials-Receipts, PO Box 286, 02117

Harvard Business School
Baker Library, 02163

Northeastern University
Library, 360 Huntington Ave, 02115

Cambridge
Harvard Hilles Library
Fifty-Nine Shepard St, 02138

Harvard Law School
Library-Langdell Hall, 02138

Harvard University
Littauer Library, 02138

Massachusetts Institute of Technology
Industrial Relations Library, 02139

Chestnut Hill
Boston College
School of Management Library, 02167

South Hadley
Mount Holyoke College Library, 01075

Springfield
Western New England College
Library, 1215 Wilbralham Rd, 01119

Waltham
Brandeis University
Library Serials, 02154

Wellesley
Wellesely College
Library, 02181

Westwood
MTS Company LTD
Check-in-Service, 15 Southwest Park, 02090

Nanzan University Library
Check-in-Service, 15 Southwest Park, 02090

Williamstown
Williams College
Serials Dept-Library, 01267

Worcester
Clark University
Goddard Library, 01610

MICHIGAN

Ann Arbor
University of Michigan
Industrial Relations Library
322 School of Business Administration, 48109

Dearborn
University of Michigan
Dearborn Center Library
4901 Evergroon Road, 48128

Detroit
Detroit Public Library
5201 Woodward Avenue, 48202

UAW Research Department
8000 E Jefferson Ave, 48214

UAW Research Library
8000 East Jefferson, 48214

Wayne State University
Purdy Library, 48202

East Lansing
Michigan State University
Library Serials, 48824

Flint
University of Michigan-Flint
Periodicals-Library, 48503

Kalamazoo
Western Michigan University
Dwight B Waldo Library, 49008

MINNESOTA

Minneapolis
Minneapolis Public Library
300 Nicollet Mall, 55401

University Minnesota
Industrial Relations Reference Room
271-19th Ave S, 55455

University of Minnesota
Law Library, 229 19th Ave S, 55455

University of Minnesota
Library Serials Div, 55455

St. Paul
JJ Hill Reference Library
80 W 4th St, 55102

MISSISSIPPI

Mississippi State
Mississippi State University
Mitchell Memorial Library, 39762

University
University of Mississippi
Serials Section-Library, 38677

MISSOURI

Columbia
University of Missouri
Library Serials Dept, 65201

Kansas City
University of Missouri-Kansas City
General Library, 5100 Rock, 64110

Rolla
University of Missouri-Rolla
Library Serials, 65401

St. Louis
Saint Louis University
Pius XII Memorial Library
3655 West Pine, 63108

Washington University
Libraries, Skinker & Lindel Blvds, 63130

NEBRASKA

Lincoln
University of Nebraska
Libraries Acquisition Dept, 68588

University of Nebraska
Bureau of Business Research, 68588

University of Nebraska
College of Law Library, 68583

Omaha
University of Nebraska-Omaha
University Library, 68182

NEVADA

Las Vegas
University of Nevada
Library Serials, 89154

Reno
University of Nevada-Reno
Bureau of Business/Econ Research, 89557

NEW HAMPSHIRE

Contoocook
Yankee Book Peddlar
PO Box 307, 03229

Durham
University of New Hampshire Library, 03824

Hanover
Dartmouth College (2)
Baker Library, Serials Section, 03755

NEW JERSEY

Camden
Rutgers State University-Camden
Camden Library, 300 N Fourth St, 08102

Lawrenceville
Rider College
Franklin F. Moore Library, 08648

New Brunswick
Rutgers State University
Inst of Mgmt & Labor Relations Library, 08903

Newark
Essex County Labor Relations
Hall of Records, Room 511, 07102

New Jersey Institute of Technology
Robert W Van Houten Library, 07102

Newark Public Library
5 Washington Street, 07101

Norwood
Walter J Johnson, Inc
355 Chestnut St, 07648

Princeton
Princeton University
Serials Division-Library, 08544

NEW MEXICO

Albuquerque
University of New Mexico
Zimmerman Library, 87131

Las Cruces
New Mexico State University
University Library, Box 3475, 88003

NEW YORK

Albany
New York State Library
Cultural Education Center
Empire State Plaza, 12230

New York State Teachers
159 Wolf Rd, 12212

SUNY-Albany/Univ Library
1400 Washington Avenue, 12222

Brockport
SUNY-Brockport
Drake Memorial Library, 14420

Bronx
Fordham University Library, 10458

Brooklyn
Brooklyn College
Library Serials Section
Bedford Ave & Ave H, 11210

Brooklyn Public Library
Business Branch, 280 Cadman PZ W, 11201

Brooklyn Public Library
Technical Services Center
109 Montgomery St, 11225

Buffalo
Buffalo & Erie County Public Library
Lafayette Square, 14203

Canisius College
Andrew L. Bouwhuis Library
2001 Main St, 14208

Clinton
Hamilton College
Burke Library, 13323

Garden City, Long Island
Adelphi University-Library, 11530

Hempstead
Hofstra University
Library Acquisitions Dept, 11550

Herkimer
Herkimer County Community College
Library, 13350

Ithaca
Cornell University
NYSSILR-Library, 14853

Jamaica
York College Library, 11451

Mineola
Superior Officer Assn
1490 Franklin Ave, 11501

New Rochelle
Iona College
Ryan Library, 10801

New York
Baruch College CUNY
Library, 156 E 25th St, , 10010

City College
Library Serials
Convent Ave & West 135 St, 10031

Columbia University
Business/Economics Watson Library
Box 130, Uris Hall, 10027

Columbia University
Law Library, 435 W 116th St, 10027

Cornell University/NYSSILR
Metropolitan Distric Library
3 E 43rd St, 10017

Federal Reserve Bank
Research Library, 33 Liberty St, 10045

New York University
Graduate Business Library
19 Rector St, 2nd Floor, 10006

New York Public Library
Mid-Manhatten Business
455 5th Ave, 10016

New York Public Library
Division E, Grand Central Station
PO Box 2221, 10017

New York University
Elmer Holmes Bobst Library
70 Washington Square S, 10012

New York University
School of Law Library
40 Washington Square S, 10012

New York University
Tamiment Library
70 Washington Square, 10012

Organization Resource Couns
Information Center, 15 Floor
1211 Avenue of the Americas, 10036

Oneonta
SUNY-Oneonta
James Milne Library, 13820

Poughkeepsie
Vassar College
Acquisitions Dept-Library, 12601

Rochester
University of Rochester
Library Serials, River Campus Station, 14627

Saratoga Spring
Skidmore College Library, 12866

Syracuse
Syracuse University
Library-Serials Div, 13210

Troy
Rensselaer Polytechnic
Serials Dept-Library, 12181

NORTH CAROLINA

Chapel Hill
University of North Carolina
Wilson Library 024-A, 27514

Charlotte
University of North Carolina
Atkins Library-Serials Dept, 28223

Durham
Duke University
Fuqua Business Library, 27706

Duke University Library, 27706

Greensboro
North Carolina A & T
F. D. Bluford Library, 27411

Hickory
Lenoir Rhyne College
Rudisill Library, 28603

Raleigh
North Carolina State
D. H. Hill Library, PO Box 5007, 27650

Winston-Salem
Wake Forest University
Library, Box 7777, Reynolda Station, 27109

OHIO

Akron
University of Akron
Bierce Library, 44325

Athens
Ohio University Library, 45701

Cincinnati
University of Cincinnati
Serials-Library, 45221

Cleveland
Case Western Reserve
Sears Library, 10900 Euclid Ave, 44106

Cleveland Public Library
325 Superior Ave, 44114

Cleveland State University
Library Order Unit
1860 E 22nd St, 44115

Columbus
Ohio State University
Labor Information Center
1810 College Road, 43210

Ohio State Univ National Center
Research Vocational Education
Labor Information Center
1960 Kenny Road, 43210

Ohio State University
Main Library, 1858 Neil Avenue, 43210

Gambier
Kenyon College
Chalmers Memorial Library, 43022

Kent
Kent State University
Libraries Serial Record Unit, 44242

Oberlin
Oberlin College Library, 44074

University Heights
John Carroll University
Grasselli Library, 44118

Worthington
Ohio State University
Center Human Resource Library
5701 N High St, 43085

Yellow Springs
Antioch College Library, 45387

OKLAHOMA

Stillwater
Oklahoma State University
Edmon Low Library, 74078

OREGON

Corvallis
Oregon State University
Library Serials Department, 97331

Eugene
University of Oregon
Library Serials Section, 97403

Portland
Portland State University
Library, PO Box 1151, 97207

United Metal Trades
906 NE 19th Avenue, 97232

Salem
Oregon State Library
State Library Building, 97310

PENNSYLVANIA

Bethlehem
Lehigh University
Linderman Library, Bldg 30, 18015

Chester
Widener University
Wolfgram Memorial Library, 19013

Doylestown
Delaware Valley College
US Route #202, 18901

Easton
Lafayette College
Skillman Library, 18042

Harrisburg
Pennsylvania State Library
Bureau of Technical Service
Box 1601, Room 46, 17105

Haverford
Haverford College Library, 19041

Loretto
St. Francis College
Pius XII Memorial Library, 15940

Philadelphia
Consolidated Rail Law Library
1138 6 Penn Center Pl, 19104

Drexel University
Library Serials Department
32nd & Chestnut Streets, 19104

St. Joseph's University
Drexel Library
City Ave at 54th Street, 19131

Temple University
Library Serials Dept, 19122

University of Pennsylvania
Lippincott Library/CH, 19104

Pittsburgh
Carnegie-Mellon
Hunt Library, 15213

LaRoche College
John J. Wright Library
9000 Babcock Blvd, 15237

Point Park College Library
201 Wood St, 15222

University of Pittsburgh
Graduate School Business Library
138 Mervis Hall, 15260

University of Pittsburgh
Law Library, 409 Law Building
3900 Forbes Ave, 15260

University Park
Pennsylvania State University
Department of Labor Studies
901 Liberal Arts Building, 16802

Pennsylvania State University
Pattee Library W209, 16802

Villanova
Villanova University
Falvey Memorial Library, 19085

RHODE ISLAND

Providence
Brown University
Library Serials Division, 02912

SOUTH CAROLINA

Clemson
Clemson University
Cooper Library, 29631

Columbia
University of South Carolina
Thomas Cooper Library, 29208

University of South Carolina
Coleman Karesch Law Library, 29208

Rock Hill
Winthrop College
Dacus Library, 29730

TENNESSEE

Johnson City
East Tennessee State University
Library Acquisitions Dept
PO Box 22450A, 37614

Knoxville
University of Tennessee
Library Serials Department, 37996

Murfeesboro
Mid Tennessee State University
Periodicals Department Library, 37132

Nashville
Vanderbilt University
Library, 419 21st Ave S, 37203

Sewanee
University of the South
J. B. DuPont Library, 37375

TEXAS

Arlington
University of Texas/Arlington
Library Serials Dept
PO Box 19497, 76019

Austin
University of Texas
General Libraries, 78712

Beaumont
Lamar State College Tech
Librarian, PO Box 10021, LU Station, 77710

Canyon
West Texas State University
Library, Box 748
West Texas Station, 79016

College Station
Texas A & M University
Library Serials Record, 77843

Dallas
Southern Methodist University
Underwood Law Library, 75275

Denton
North Texas State College Library, 76203

Houston
Rice University
Foundren Library, Box 1892, 77251

University of Houston
Libraries, 4800 Calhoun Rd, 77004

Nacogdoches
Stephen F. Austin State University
Library Serials Records
Box 13055 5FA Station, 75962

San Antonio
Trinity University
Library Periodicals Department
715 Stadium Drive, 78284

Waco
Baylor University Library, 76706

UTAH

Logan
Utah State University
Merrill Library, 84322

Salt Lake City
University Utah
Marriott Library, 84112

University of Utah
Law Library, 84112

VERMONT

Middlebury
Middlebury College Library, 05753

VIRGINIA

Blacksburg
Virginia Polytechnic Inst & State Univ
Carol Newman Library, 24061

Fairfax
George Mason University
Library, 4400 University Dr, 22030

Hampton
Nelson Community College
c/o Robert Walker, PO Box 9407, 23670

Lexington
Washington & Lee University
McCormick Library, Cyrus Hall, 24450

Richmond
University of Richmond
Library, School of Business Admin, 23173

WASHINGTON

Olympia
Washington State Library
Serials Section, 98504

Pullman
Washington State University
Social Science Library, 99164

Seattle
University of Washington
Acquisitions Div Serials Library, 98195

Tacoma
Pacific Lutheran University
Mortvedt Library, 98447

WEST VIRGINIA

Montgomery
West Virginia Inst of Technology
Library, 25136

Morgantown
Regional Research Institute
Benedum Prof, West Virginia Univ, 26506

West Virginia University
Library-Downtown Campus, 26506

WISCONSIN

Appleton
Lawrence University
Library Orders Dept, 54912

Eau Claire
University of Wisconsin-Eau Claire
W. D. McIntyre Library, 54701

Madison
University of Wisconsin-Madison
Memorial Library, 728 State St, 53706

Milwaukee
Milwaukee Public Library
Serials Section, 814 W Wisconsin Ave, 53233

Mulcahy & Wherry S.C., Law Library
Suite 1600, 815 E Mason St, 53202

University of Wisconsin-Milwaukee
Golda Meir Library, PO Box 604, 53201

WYOMING

Laramie
University of Wyoming Library
Box 3334, University Station, 82071

CANADA

Brandon, Manitoba
Brandon University
John E. Robbins Library, R7A 6A9

Burnaby, BC
Burnaby Municipal, Graham Leslie
Labor Relations Department
5050 Kingsway, V5H 2E2

Simon Fraser University
Acquisitions-Serials, Library, V5A 1S6

Calgary, Alberta
University of Calgary Library
2500 University Dr NW, T2N 1N4

Downsville, Ontario
York University
Scott Library, 4700 Keele St, M3J 2R2

Edmonton, Alberta
Alberta Department Labor
Labour Research Library
10808 99th Ave, T5K 0G2

Athabasca University Library
15015 - 123rd Ave, T5V 1J7

University of Alberta
Serials Library, T6G 2J8

Fredericton, NB
University of New Brunswick
Harriet Irving Library, PO Box 7500

Halifax, Nova Scotia
Dalhousie University
Law Library, B3H 4H9

Dalhousie University
Library Serials Dept, B3H 4H8

Hamilton, Ontario
McMaster University Library
1280 Main St W, L8S 4P5

Kingston, Ontario
Queens University
Law Library, K7L 3N6

London, Ontario
University of Western Ontario
D. B. Weldon Library, N6A 3K7

Mississauga, Ontario
Erindale College
Library Serials
3359 Mississauga Rd N, L5L 1C6

Montreal, Quebec
Canadian National Railroad
HQ Library, PO Box 8100, H3C 3N4

Ecole Hautes Etude
Bibliotheque/Commerciales
5255 Decelles, H3T 1V6

Fapuq Inc
2715 Cote Ste Catherine, H3T 1B6

Institut Recherche Appliquee Sur Travail
1290 Rue St-Denis, H2X 3J7

McGill University
University Libraries
3459 McTavish St, H3A 1Y1

Pouliot Mercure & Associates
1155 Dorchester Blvd W, H3B 3S6

Sir George WMS University
Acquisition Department
1455 De Masionneuve Blvd, H3G 1M8

University of Montreal
Bibliotheque, Periodiques
CP 6202 Succursale A, H3C 3T2

University of Montreal
Centre Resl Industrielles, H3C 3J7

Ottawa, Ontario
Canada Labour Congress
Ronald Lang, Dir of Res & Legis
2841 Riverside Dr, K1V 8X7

Carleton University
Library Serials Dept
Colonel By Drive, K1S 5B6

Economic Council of Canada
Library, PO Box 527, K1P 5V6

Government of Canada (2)
Department of Labour, K1A 0J2

Government of Canada
Employment and Immigration, K1A 0J9

Government of Canada
Dept Finance & Treas Board
160 Elgin St, K1A 0G5

Government of Canada
Library, Labor Relations Board
240 Sparks St, K1A 0X8

Government of Canada
Public Service Staff Relations Library
PO Box 1525, Station B, K1P 5V2

Government of Canada
Statistics Canada Library
R. H. Coates Building, K1A 0T6

National Defence Empl
NDE Research Library
330 McLeod St, K2P 2C5

Quebec, PQ
University of Laval
Pavillon/Bibliotheque
Division Des Acquistions, G1K 7P4

Regina, Saskatchewan
Sask Dept Labour Library S4P 4V4

University of Regina
Library Serials Dept, S4S 0A2

Saskatoon, Saskatchewan
University of Saskatchewan
Serials Library, S7N 0W0

St. Johns, Newfoundland
Memorial University Newfoundland
Library-Periodicals, A1B 3Y1

Thunder Bay, Ontario
Lakehead University Library
955 Oliver Rd, P7B 5E1

Toronto, Ontario
Metro Toronto Library
Business Dept
789 Yonge St, M4W 2G8

Ontario Ministry of Labor
Library, 400 University Ave, M7A 1T7

University of Toronto
Centre for Ind Relations
123 St George St, M5S 1A1

University of Toronto (2)
Library Serials Dept, M5S 1A5

Vancouver, BC
Employers Council of British Columbia
800 W Pender St, V6C 2V6

University of British Columbia
Library Processing Centre
2206 East Mall, V6T 1Z8

Vancouver Public Library
750 Burrard Street, V6Z 1X5

Victoria, BC
British Columbia Dept Labour
J Murphy Library
880 Douglas St, V8W 2B7

University of Victoria
McPherson Library/Serials, V8W 3H5

Waterloo, Ontario
University of Waterloo
Library-Serials Department, N2L 3G1

Wilfred Laurier University
Library-Periodicals, N2L 3C5

Windsor, Ontario
Leddy Library-Serials, N9B 3P4

Winnipeg, Manitoba
Manitoba Legis Library
200 Vaughan St, R3C 0P8

University Manitoba
Elizabeth Dafoe Library, R3T 2N2

University of Winnipeg
Library, 515 Portage Ave, R3B 2E9

OTHER COUNTRIES AND TERRITORIES

AUSTRALIA

Adelaide University
Barr Smith Library, Adelaide, S. Australia

Flinders University
N. Stockdale Library
Bedford Park, S. Australia

Latrobe University
The Borchardt Library
Bundoora VIC 3083

Australian National University
Library Chifley
PO Box 4, Canberra ACT 2601

National Library Australia
Preliminary Processing
Canberra ACT 2600

Monash University
Library Periodicals Dept
Clayton 3168, Victoria

Australian Grad School Mgmt Library
Univ of New South Wales
PO Box 1, Kensington, NSW 2033

University of New South Wales
Library Serials Dept
Kensington PO Box 1, NSW 2033

Royal Institute of Technology
Saunders/Management
167 Franklin St
GPO Box 2476V, Melbourne 3001

University Western Australia,
Reid Library
Nedlands, Western Australia 6009

University of Newcastle
Auchmuty Library
Newcastle NSW 2308

University of Melbourne
Baillieu Library Serials
Parkville, Victoria 3052

University of Sydney
Fisher Library, Sydney, NSW 2006

Riverina College, Merrylees Library
PO Box 588, Wagga Wagga, NSW 2650

BRAZIL
Brazilian Ind Rels Library
Esplanada dos Ministerios
Brazilia, Brazil, CEP 70059

CZECHOSOLOVAKIA
500 Institute Management
Information Center
Reznicka 4-115 49 Praha 1

DENMARK
Statsbiblioteket
Tidsskriftsafdelingn
Inst Statskundskab
DK 8000 Aarhus C

ENGLAND
University Library
Librarian Serials Dept
Bailrigg, Lancaster LA1 4YH

University of Birmingham
Main Library
PO Box 363, Edgbaston, Birmingham, B15 2TT

British Library
AccessionsLending Div, Boston Spa-Wetherby
Yorkshire LS23 7BQ

University of Kent
Library, Canterbury

University of Warwick
Coventry, Warwickshire

British Library
London School of Econ/Poli Sci
Houghton St. Aldwych, London WC2A 2AE

Loughborough University
Univ of Technology Library
Loughborough, Leicestershire, LE11 3TU

Manchester Business School
Library, Booth St West, Manchester M15 6PB

Bodelian Library
Dept of Printed Books, Oxford

Institute Econ & Statis
St. Cross Bldg, Manor Road, Oxford

Nuffield College
Library, Oxford OX1 1NF

Oxford University Library
Dept External Studies, Rewley House
Wellington Square, Oxford OX1 2JA

Brunel University
Library Journals Div
Uxbridge UB8 3PH

FINLAND
Abo Akademis
Ekonomiska Sectionens Bibliotek
Henriksgatan 7, 20500 ABO 50

FRANCE
Foundation National des Sciences Politiques
27 St Guillaume 75 341, Paris Cedex 07

Universiti Paris
Bibliotheque IX Dauphine
6E Etage Mele Niel/Dawson
PL Du Mal Lattre Taasigny
F 75116 Paris

HONG KONG
University of Hong Kong Library

INDIA
Tamilnadu Institute
Institute Labour Studies
5 Kamarasar Salai
Madras 600 005

ISRAEL
Jewish National & Univ Library
Periodicals Dept
PO Box 503, Jerusalem 91-004

Institute Productivity
Library, PO Box 33010, Tel Aviv, 61330

Tel Aviv University
Library Periodicals Dept
PO Box 39038, Tel Aviv

ITALY
Univ Degli Studi di Trento
Biblioteca Centrale
Via G Verdi 26, Trento

JAPAN
Kinki University
Rodo Mondai Ken-013
Kowakae Higashi-Osaka, 577 MZ

International Christian University
Library, 3-10 Osawa Mitaka City, Tokyo

Japan Institute of Labour
Labour Reference Library
Chutaikin Bldg, 7-6 Shibakoen, 1-Chome
Minatoku, Tokyo

Keio University
Inst Mgmt and Labor Studies
Mita Minato-Ku, Tokyo

KENYA
University of Nairobi
Librarian-Main Library
PO Box 30197, Nairobi

MALAYSIA
University of Malaya
Library Serials Div
Pantai Vally/Kuala Lumpur 22-11

MEXICO
Institute Banca Finanza
Adacelia Lopez R
APDO Postal 94 BIS
06000 Mexico D F

NETHERLANDS
Rijksuniversiteit
Bibliotheek Tijdschriftenafdeling
Postbus 9501, 2300 RA Leiden

Rijksuniversiteit
Limburg Bibliotheek SE
Postbus 616, 6200 MD, Maastricht

NEW GUINEA
University Papua & New Guinea
PO Box 319, Univ PO Box 4189,Papua

NEW ZEALAND
Victoria University
Librarian, Private Bag, Wellington

NORTH IRELAND
Queens University
Library, Belfast 7.

PUERTO RICO
University of Puerto Rico
General Library, Rio Piedras

SCOTLAND
Aberdeen University
Queen Mother Library, Aberdeen AB9 2UE

The University
The Library, Glasgow W2

SINGAPORE
National University
Central Library, Kent Ridge 0511

NTUC Research Unit
Librarian, Trade Union House, Shenton Way

SWITZERLAND
International Labour Office
Periodicals Section Old
CH 1211 Geneva 22

TRINIDAD, WEST INDIES
Personnel Management Service
Management Consultants, 42B Saddle Rd, Maraval

TUNISIA
University of Tunis
45 Avenue de la Liberte
Cite Bouchoucha, Le Bardo, Tunis

SOUTH AFRICA
NIPR/CSIR
Industrial Rels Group
PO Box 32410, 2017 Braamfontein

University of South Africa
Inst of Labor Rels, Documentation Centre
PO Box 392, Pretoria 0001

WEST GERMANY
Universitatsbiblio
Memmingerstrasse 6/14
8900 Augsburg

FR-Ebert-Stiftung Bibliothek
Zeitschriftenabteilung
Godjesberger Allee 149, D-5300 Bonn 2

Universitats und Stadtbibliothek
Universitatsstrasse 33
5 Cologne-Lindenthal

Fakultatsbibliothek
Wirtschaftswissenschaften
Wunstorfer Str 14, D-3000 Hannover 91

Bayer Staatsbiblthek
Ludwigstrasse 16, 8 Munich 34

Universitaets Bibliothek 003
4790 Paderborn, Postfach 162

Universitatsbiblio
Postfach 409, 84 Regensburg 2

COLLEGE AND UNIVERSITY INDUSTRIAL RELATIONS PROGRAMS

College and university industrial relations programs that have been brought to the attention of the national IRRA office are listed alphabetically by state and by city, followed by Canada and Australia.

UNITED STATES

ALABAMA

Center for Labor Education & Research
University of Alabama
Birmingham, AL 35294

Human Resources Institute
University of Alabama
Box J
University, AL 35486

CALIFORNIA

Industrial Relations Institute
University of California
2521 Channing Way
Berkeley, CA 94720

Industrial Relations Institute
University of California
Los Angeles, CA 90024

Industrial Relations Center 1-90
California Institute of Technology
Pasadena, CA 91125

DISTRICT OF COLUMBIA

Labor Studies Center
University of District of Columbia
724 9th St NW, Suite 500
Washington DC 20001

GEORGIA

Employee Relations Institute
University of Georgia
Athens, GA 30601

Institute of Industrial Relations Center
Georgia State University
Atlanta, GA 30303

HAWAII

Industrial Relations Center
University of Hawaii
2404 Maile Way
Honolulu, HI 96822

IDAHO

School of Business
Boise State University
Boise, ID 83725

ILLINOIS

Institute of Labor and Industrial Relations
University of Illinois
504 East Armory Avenue
Champaign, IL 61820

Institute of Industrial Relations
Loyola University of Chicago
820 North Michigan Ave
Chicago, IL 60611

Industrial Relations Center
University of Chicago
1225 East 60th St
Chicago, IL 60638

INDIANA

Center for Ind Rels/Cont Educ
Indiana Central College
4001 Otterbein Ave
Indianapolis, IN 46227

Industrial Relations Committee
489 Krannert Graduate School of Mgmt
Purdue University
West Lafayette, IN 47907

IOWA

Industrial Relations Center
Iowa State University
80 East Hall
Ames, IA 50011

Industrial Relations Institute
College of Business Administration
University of Iowa
Iowa City, IA 52242

KANSAS

Director of Doctoral Program
307 Summerfield Hall
University of Kansas
Lawrence, KS 66045

KENTUCKY

ILRB Director
Public Admin Dept
Northern Kentucky University
Highland Heights, KY 41076

LOUISIANA

Department of Econ & Finance
University of New Orleans
New Orleans, LA 70122

MARYLAND

M. S. in Pers & Ind Rels
University of Baltimore
1420 N. Charles St,
Baltimore, MD 21201

Program of Ind & Labor Studies
Div of Behavioral & Social Sciences
University of Maryland
College Park, MD 20742

MASSACHUSETTS

Labor Rels & Research Center
University of Massachusetts
125 Draper Hall
Amherst, MA 01002

Institute Empl, Trng, Labor Policy
Boston University
220 Bay State Rd
Boston, MA 02215

Harvard Trade Union Program
Harvard Business School
Harvard University
Soldiers Field
Boston, MA 02163

Sloan School of Management, MIT
50 Memorial Drive, (Rm E52-454)
Cambridge, MA 02139

MICHIGAN

Institute of Labor and Industrial Relations
University of Michigan
Victor Vaughan Bldg, 1111 E Catherine St
Ann Arbor, MI 48109

MA Programs, Ind Relations
Wayne State University
5165 Gullen Mall
Detroit, MI 48202

School of Labor & Ind Rels
Michigan State University
South Kedzie Hall
East Lansing, MI 48824

MINNESOTA

Industrial Relations Center
University of Minnesota
537 Business Administration
271 19th Avenue South
Minneapolis, MN 55455

MISSOURI

Labor Education Program
University of Missouri
1004 Elm Street
Columbia, MO 65201

School of Business and Admin
Saint Louis University
3674 Lindell Blvd
St. Louis, MO 63108

NEW JERSEY

Industrial Relations & Human Resources
Ryders Lane, PO Box 231
Rutgers University
New Brunswick, NJ 08903

Industrial Relations Section
Princeton University, Box 248
Princeton, NJ 08540

NEW YORK

NYSSILR-Cornell University
47 East 43rd Street
New York, NY 10017

School of Ind & Labor Rels
Cornell University
Ives Hall
Ithaca, NY 14853

Baruch College-CUNY
17 Lexington Avenue
PO Box 322
New York, NY 10010

Conservation of Human Resources
Columbia University
116th St & Broadway
New York, NY 10027

Institute of Labor Relations
New York University
8 Washington Place
New York, NY 10003

Industrial Relations Dept
Pace University
41 Park Row
New York, NY 10038

College of Business Admin
Niagara University
Niagara, NY 14109

Center for Labor and Ind Rels
New York Inst of Technology
Old Westbury, NY 11568

Dean of Admissions
North Road
Marist College
Poughkeepsie, NY 12601

Coordinator Labor Management Studies
SUNY-Stony Brook
Stony Brook, NY 11790

Industrial Relations Dept
Lemoyne College
Syracuse, NY 13214

Pers & Ind Rels, School of Mgmt
Syracuse University
Syracuse, NY 13210

NORTH CAROLINA

Research Administration
North Carolina A & T State Univ
Greensboro, NC 27411

OHIO

Coordinator, MAIR Program
Department of Economics
University of Cincinnati
Cincinnati, OH 45221

Department of Mgmt & Labor Rels
Cleveland State University
2121 Euclid Avenue, Room 533
Cleveland, OH 44115

Industrial Relations & Human Resources
Ohio State University
1775 College Road
Columbus, OH 43210

OKLAHOMA

College of Business Admin
University of Oklahoma
Norman, OK 73019

Manpower Research/Trng Center
College of Business Admin
Oklahoma State University
Stillwater, OK 74074

OREGON

Institute of Ind & Labor Rels
University of Oregon
730 Prince Lucien Campbell
Eugene, OR 97403

PENNSYLVANIA

Center for Study of Labor Rels
#1 Lewis House
Indiana Univ of Pennsylvania
Indiana, PA 15701

Graduate School of Ind Rels
Saint Francis College
Loretto, PA 15940

Comey Inst of Ind Rels
St. Joseph's University
5600 City Avenue
Philadelphia, PA 19131

Ind Rels & Org Behavior
Temple University
Philadelphia, PA 19122

Wharton School, 317 Vance Hall
University of Pennsylvania
Philadelphia, PA 19104

Center for Labor Studies
School of Urban & Public Affairs
Carnegie-Mellon Univ
Pittsburgh, PA 15213

Human Resources & Labor Rels
University of Pittsburgh
Pittsburgh, PA 15260

Dept of Mgmt/Marketing
Shippensburg State College
Shippensburg, PA 17257

Dept of Labor Studies
901 Liberal Arts Tower
Pennsylvania State University
University Park, PA 16802

RHODE ISLAND

Industrial Relations, Ballentine Hall
University of Rhode Island
Kingston, RI 02881

SOUTH CAROLINA

Personnel & Ind Rels
School of Business
Winthrop College
Rock Hill, SC 29733

TENNESSEE

Dept of Econ and Finance
Middle Tennessee State University
Murfreesboro, TN 37132

TEXAS

Labor & Ind Rels Institute
North Texas State University
N. T. Box 13644
Denton, TX 76203

College of Business Admin
Texas Tech University
Lubbock, TX 79409

UTAH

College of Bus & Human Resources Admin
Utah State University
Logan, UT 84322

Institute of Ind Rels
College of Business
University of Utah
Salt Lake City, UT 84112

VIRGINIA

Industrial Relations Center
204-A Pamplin Hall
Virginia Tech
Blacksburg, VA 24061

WEST VIRGINIA

Industrial Relations & Labor Studies
West Virginia Inst Technology
Montgomery, WV 25136

Industrial Relations Program
West Virginia University
Morgantown, WV 26506

WISCONSIN

Industrial Relations Research Institute
4226 Social Science Building
University of Wisconsin
Madison, WI 53706

Business and Industrial Relations
Marquette University
Milwaukee, WI 53233

MIR Program, Bolton 530
University of Wisconsin-Milwaukee
PO Box 413
Milwaukee, WI 53201

CANADA

Pers & Ind Rels, Faculty of Business
McMaster University
Hamilton, Ontario L8S 4M4

Industrial Relations Centre
Queen's University
Kingston, Ontario

Industrial Relations Centre
McGill University
1001 Sherbrooke St. W
Montreal, PQ H3A 1G5

Ecole de relations industrielles
Universite de Montreal
C. P. 6128, Montreal, PQ H3C 3J7

Centre for Industrial Relations
University of Toronto
123 St. George St
Toronto, Ontario M5S 1A1

Institute for Industrial Relations
University of British Columbia
Vancouver, BC

AUSTRALIA

Department of Industrial Relations
University of Sydney
Australia, NSW 20006

INTERNATIONAL INDUSTRIAL RELATIONS ASSOCIATION

The International Industrial Relations Association (IIRA) was established at a meeting in London on June 30, 1966. Represented at the founding meeting were the Industrial Relations Research Association, Gerald G. Somers; the British Universities Industrial Relations Association, B. C. Roberts; the Japan Institute of Labour, I. Nakayama; and the International Institute for Labour Studies, Geneva, Robert Cox.

The secretariat is located in Geneva, Switzerland. Membership inquiries and applications may be sent to: International Industrial Relations Association, c/o LEG/REL, c/o International Labour Organisation, CH-1211 GENEVE 22, Switzerland.

IIRA World Congresses are scheduled every three years. Previous congresses have been: Geneva, 1967, 1970, and 1976; London, 1973; Paris, 1979; Tokyo, 1983. The next IRRA World Congress will be in September 1986 in Hamburg.

DIRECTORY HANDBOOK QUESTIONNAIRE

1. Return questionnaire no later than **October 15, 1983** to IRRA, 7226 Social Science Building, University of Wisconsin, Madison, WI 53706. Questionnaires must be returned by October 15 to insure inclusion of complete information in the 1984 **MEMBERSHIP DIRECTORY.** Current membership records will be used if questionnaire is not returned in time for inclusion.
2. If your 1984 dues have not been paid, please enclose a check with your questionnaire.
3. If your address is not correct as it appears on the attached label, please correct it in the space next to it. There is a place for your phone number on the other side of the sheet.

OCCUPATION Please designate your principal business or profession with the figure "1" below. This is the occupation by which you will be classified in the **DIRECTORY.** If you have more than one type of occupation, indicate the others with "2" and "3".

ACADEMIC
___Univ. Administration
___Business Administration
___Economics
___Industrial Relations
___Law
___Org. Behavior/Personnel
___Psychology
___Sociology
___Student
___Other Academic (Specify)
____

NONACADEMIC
___Arbitration
___Business:Management/Administration
___Business: Personnel/Industrial Relations
___Consulting
___Government
___Legal Practice
___Union
___Other Nonacademic (specify)
____

EDUCATION AND DEGREE (omit honorary)

Degree-Abbreviate	Year Granted	Institution

REPRESENTATIVE PUBLICATIONS (three only)

1. Book___Article___ ______________________

2. Book___Article___ ______________________

3. Book___Article___ ______________________

OVER

MAJOR FIELDS OF INTEREST: List no more than three of your major fields of specialization in order of importance to you. List them "1", "2" and "3" in order of importance.

___arbitration/mediation
___collective bargaining
___employment/trng programs
___gov't labor policy
___health & hospital care
___income maintenance
___industrial psychology
___industrial sociology
___int'l comparative labor
___labor education
___labor history
___labor law
___labor market economics
___management/education
___org. behavior
___personnel
___methodology/statistics
___union organization/adm
___other (specify)
____

IRRA CHAPTER MEMBER:

No___Yes___Name of Chapter ______________________

OTHER PROFESSIONAL ASSOCIATIONS: (three only)

1. ______________________

2. ______________________

3. ______________________

PRESENT POSITION AS OF SEPTEMBER, 1983:

Title ______________________ Starting Date ________

Institution/Firm ______________________

Address ______________________ Phone ________

____

CAREER DATA: (list two positions, most recent first)

Position ______________________ Starting Date ________

Institution/Firm ______________________

Position ______________________ Starting Date ________

Institution/Firm ______________________